EUROPE
1450 TO 1789
ENCYCLOPEDIA OF THE EARLY MODERN WORLD

Volume 1
Absolutism to Coligny

Jonathan Dewald, Editor in Chief

CHARLES SCRIBNER'S SONS

THOMSON
™
GALE

New York • Detroit • San Diego • San Francisco • Cleveland • New Haven, Conn. • Waterville, Maine • London • Munich

THOMSON
★
GALE

Europe 1450 to 1789:
Encyclopedia of the Early Modern World

Jonathan Dewald, Editor in Chief

For permission to use material from this product,
submit your request via Web at http://www.gale-
edit.com/permissions, or you may download our
Permissions Request form and submit your request
by fax or mail to:

Permissions Department
The Gale Group, Inc.
27500 Drake Rd.
Farmington Hills, MI 48331-3535

Permissions Hotline:
248-699-8006 or 800-877-4253, ext. 8006
Fax: 248-699-8074 or 800-762-4058

LIBRARY OF CONGRESS CATALOGING-IN-PUBLICATION DATA

Europe 1450 to 1789 : encyclopedia of the early modern world / Jonathan Dewald, editor in chief.
     p. cm.
Includes bibliographical references and index.
    ISBN 0-684-31200-X (set : hardcover) — ISBN 0-684-31201-8 (v. 1) —
ISBN 0-684-31202-6 (v. 2) — ISBN 0-684-31203-4 (v. 3) — ISBN 0-684-31204-2 (v. 4) —
ISBN 0-684-31205-0 (v. 5) — ISBN 0-684-31206-9 (v. 6)
  1. Europe—History—15th century—Encyclopedias. 2. Europe—History—1492–1648—
Encyclopedias. 3. Europe—History—1648–1789—Encyclopedias. 4. Europe—Intellectual
life—Encyclopedias. 5. Europe—Civilization—Encyclopedias. I. Title: Encyclopedia of the
early modern world. II. Dewald, Jonathan.
    D209.E97 2004
    940.2—dc22
                       2003015680

This title is also available as an e-book.
ISBN 0-684-31423-1 (set)
Contact your Gale sales representative for ordering information.
Printed in United States of America
10 9 8 7 6 5 4 3 2 1

EUROPE
1450 TO 1789
ENCYCLOPEDIA OF THE EARLY MODERN WORLD

EDITORIAL BOARD

Dedicated in honor of four teachers

Gene A. Brucker

Natalie Zemon Davis

Robert Forster

Orest Ranum

EDITORIAL AND PRODUCTION STAFF

Project Editor, New York
Mark LaFlaur

Production Editor, Farmington Hills
Carol A. Schwartz

Assistant Production Editor
Georgia S. Maas

Art Editor
Joann Cerrito

Map Editor
Melissa Hill

Associate Editors
Anthony Aiello   Mark Drouillard

Editorial Assistants
Kelly Baiseley
Felix Beltran

Manuscript Collection and Database Consultant
Christopher Verdesi

Manuscript Editors
Jonathan G. Aretakis   Patti Brecht   Sylvia J. Cannizzaro   Melissa A. Dobson
Stephen Robert Frankel   Ted Gilley   Anna N. Grojec
Margery M. Heffron   Archie Hobson   Jean Fortune Kaplan
Georgia S. Maas   Katherine H. Maas   Julia Penelope
Robin L. Perlow   Neil Romanosky   Fronia W. Simpson

Proofreaders
Dorothy Bauhoff   Archie Hobson

Chronology Editor
Anna N. Grojec

Cartography
XNR Productions
Madison, Wisconsin

Caption Writer, Archival Maps
Frederick W. Musto
Sterling Memorial Library, Yale University

Archival Map Research
Nathalie Duval

Indexer
Katharyn Dunham, ParaGraphs

Design
Pamela A. E. Galbreath

Imaging
Mary K. Grimes   Lezlie Light   Michael Logusz   Dan Newell
David G. Oblender   Christine O'Bryan   Robyn Young

Permissions
Margaret A. Chamberlain

Compositor
GGS Information Services
York, Pennsylvania

Manufacturing
Rhonda Williams

Editorial Director
John Fitzpatrick

Publisher
Frank Menchaca

ABOUT THE SCRIBNER COLOPHON

The colophon reproduced on this book's spine and back cover shows a lighted lamp before an open book, crowned by a wreath of laurels. The laurel crown, associated with the Greek god Apollo, has long symbolized excellence in the arts and letters. In a revival of an ancient Roman custom of honoring heroes, the poet Petrarch was crowned poet laureate with a wreath of laurels in Rome in 1341. The book, lamp, and laurel logo has appeared on books published by Charles Scribner's Sons since 1887 in various designs by such renowned artists as Stanford White, Maxfield Parrish, and Rudolph Ruzicka. For the firm's reference books, Charles Scribner, Jr. (1926–1995) added the phrase "Enriching the life of the mind."

Charles Scribner (1821–1871) and a partner established a publishing house in the Brick Church chapel near Wall Street in New York City in 1846. Charles Scribner's Sons joined the Gale Group in 1999.

CONTENTS

VOLUME 2

D

E

VOLUME 3

VOLUME 4

M

VOLUME 5

VOLUME 6

T

CONTENTS

USING THE ENCYCLOPEDIA

Tables of contents. Each volume contains a table of contents for the entire *Encyclopedia*. Volume 1 has a single listing of all volumes' contents. Volumes 2 through 6 contain "Contents of This Volume" followed by "Contents of Other Volumes."

Maps of Europe. The front of each volume contains a set of maps showing Europe's political divisions at six important stages from 1453 to 1795.

Alphabetical arrangement. Entries are arranged in alphabetical order. Biographical articles are generally listed by the subject's last name (with some exceptions, e.g., Leonardo da Vinci).

Royalty and foreign names. In most cases, the names of rulers of French, German, and Spanish rulers have been anglicized. Thus, Francis, not François; Charles, not Carlos. Monarchs of the same name are listed first by their country, and then numerically. Thus, Henry VII and Henry VIII of England precede Henry II of France.

Measurements appear in the English system according to United States usage, though they are often followed by metric equivalents in parentheses. Following are approximate metric equivalents for the most common units:

1 foot = 30 centimeters
1 mile = 1 6 kilometers
1 acre = 0 4 hectares
1 square mile = 2.6 square kilometers
1 pound = 0.45 kilograms
1 gallon = 3.8 liters

Cross-references. At the end of each article is a list of related articles for further study. Readers may also consult the table of contents and the index for titles and keywords of interest.

Bibliography. Each article contains a list of sources for further reading, usually divided into Primary Sources and Secondary Sources.

Systematic outline of contents. After the last article in volume 6 is an outline that provides a general overview of the conceptual scheme of the *Encyclopedia*, listing the title of each entry.

Directory of contributors. Following the systematic outline of contents is a listing, in alphabetical order, of all contributors to the *Encyclopedia,* with affiliation and the titles of his or her article(s).

Index. Volume 6 concludes with a comprehensive, alphabetically arranged index covering all articles, as well as prominent figures, geographical names, events, institutions, publications, works of art, and all major concepts that are discussed in volumes 1 through 6.

PREFACE

Between 1450 and 1789, Europe witnessed some of the most dramatic events of its history. These years included Europeans' first encounter with the Americas, the invention of printing, and the first widespread use of gunpowder in warfare. Ideas about the natural world shifted dramatically, and assumptions about the divine order and the purposes of human life underwent wrenching challenges. The period was marked by political revolutions, and it ended with the great French Revolution of 1789. How people lived and related to one another also changed, more subtly but with momentous consequences. The period included moments of terrible violence, as in the French Wars of Religion and the German Thirty Years' War, but it also must be counted among the most creative in the human record. What Europeans did and thought during those years continues to shape our twenty-first-century world.

Europe 1450 to 1789: Encyclopedia of the Early Modern World offers an accessible account of this complicated, crucial phase of European history. Some 450 biographical articles present such leading figures of the period as Peter the Great, Galileo, Rembrandt, Louis XIV, Shakespeare, and Madame de Pompadour, discussing both their lives and the significance of their achievements; other articles summarize the period's wars, revolutions, and other notable events. But this *Encyclopedia* gives as much attention to broad processes as to specific facts. Major articles explore topics like medicine, monarchy, agriculture, the Enlightenment, and the military, and others provide overviews of individual national histories. We have also sought to examine basic mechanisms of early modern life, with articles explicating the workings of business, family, religious practice, and a variety of related topics.

In addressing these questions, the *Encyclopedia* defines Europe broadly, giving extensive attention to Russia, eastern Europe, and the Ottoman Empire, as well as to western Europe. We have sought to make clear the multiplicity of European cultures and social arrangements in these years, the fact that Europe included Muslims, Jews, and Orthodox Christians, as well as Protestants and Catholics. Despite the geographical distances and cultural animosities that set these groups apart from one another, contacts among them were frequent and fruitful. Early modern men and women moved far more often and over greater distances than historians once believed, and they brought with them products, beliefs, and practices.

Similarly, the *Encyclopedia* places European experiences within a context of world history. No events of the period mattered more than those that changed Europe's relations with other regions of the globe. In 1450, Europeans and Americans had no idea of one another's existence, and only intermittent exchanges linked Europe with Asia and Africa. By the late eighteenth century, European imperial regimes dominated the Americas and parts of Asia and Africa, and intense commercial activity bound much of the world together in the first global economy. In eighteenth-century Europe even the poor regularly bought fabrics and tea from Asia and sugar, coffee, and tobacco from the Americas; and they benefited from the forced labor of African slaves, who produced colonial goods cheaply. Partly because Asia, Africa, and the Americas had acquired such importance for the European economy, eighteenth-century European wars included combat in the Caribbean, India, and North America, as well as in Europe itself. The first global economy was accompanied by the world's first experience of global warfare.

Already in the eighteenth century, Europeans debated among themselves the costs and benefits of this globalization. They knew that as they visited other parts of the globe, they brought with them vicious new forms of colonial exploitation and new diseases; in the Americas they caused what may have been the worst population disaster in human history. But the European impact on the rest of the world was not only destructive. For better and for worse, Europe exported its culture as well as its power and microbes, spreading its military techniques, livestock, and churches, and leaving Europe and the rest of the world inextricably entangled. Europeans imported culture as well—hesitantly in the sixteenth century, enthusiastically in the eighteenth. By this time, the varied social arrangements that they encountered elsewhere in the world had become a standing challenge to their assessment of their own civilization and an encouragement to radical social thought. This *Encyclopedia* explores these complex changes in a series of major articles on relations between Europe and other regions of the world. Unavoidably, a history of Europe during these years is also an examination of the "early modern world."

Only since World War II have historians regularly used the term "early modern" to describe these centuries of European history. They have used this new term in part to replace the more traditional division of the period into Renaissance, Reformation, and Enlightenment, and in part to supplement these older concepts. With these other chronological labels available, it may be asked, why have historians added "early modern" to their vocabulary? One reason is that the term has allowed them to draw attention to unities across these different periods, and to see the slow processes of change that extended from the fifteenth to the eighteenth centuries. More important, however, this change in historians' terminology reflects changes in the subject matter of their researches. Such terms as Renaissance, Reformation, and Enlightenment refer most directly to cultural history, and all three terms imply cultural progress. Both "Renaissance" (meaning literally 'rebirth') and "Enlightenment" were coined during the early modern period itself, to express contemporary intellectuals' belief that they had revived European culture after long periods of darkness. In recent years, however, historians have increasingly asked how ordinary Europeans lived and thought. This interest in ordinary people and ordinary doings has led to the development of entirely new fields of study, such as women's history and the history of popular culture, and it has brought new interpretations to long-established fields of inquiry. Military historians have given new attention to the experiences of ordinary soldiers, thus changing our understanding of how battles were won and lost; intellectual historians have explored the career ambitions that moved the great thinkers of the period, and in some cases understanding these social contexts has changed our interpretations of even its loftiest ideas.

These new topics and new approaches to old topics have not fitted well with inherited chronological categories. European women, some historians have argued, simply did not have a Renaissance, excluded as they were from many of the cultural institutions of the age; and their freedoms actually diminished after 1500. Likewise, European peasants—in most regions, 90 percent of the population—were little touched by either Renaissance or Enlightenment. The religious changes brought on by the Reformations *did* affect these ordinary Europeans, but often in ways that surprised and angered religious leaders like Martin Luther. For these and many similar groups, it has proved helpful to view the period through the wide-angle lens of an early modern period, extending from the crises of the late Middle Ages to the French Revolution of 1789. These groups are mainly bystanders in the narratives of cultural renewal suggested by such terms as "Renaissance," with its focus on intellectuals and artists, but they are central players in a history of the early modern period.

This new terminology, however, also raises its own new and difficult questions. The late John Hale, a distinguished historian of the Renaissance, once complained that the concept of an early modern period is bland and neutral, lacking the interpretive clarity of such terms as Renaissance and Enlightenment. In fact, ambiguity is built into the phrase. It points both to the elements of modernity that can be seen emerging during these years and to the contemporaneous persistence of medieval values and ways of living; to speak of "early modernity" is to suggest the hesitations and complexities of historical progress. Evaluating these two sides of the period, setting its modernities against its forms of backwardness, has been a central theme of research and one that emerges repeatedly in the articles that follow. With regard to some topics, addressing this question involves comparing different regions of Europe. Historians have spoken of the seventeenth-century Netherlands, for instance, as "the first modern economy," whereas parts of rural France during the same years had changed little since the Middle Ages. But ambiguity also reigned within individual minds during the early modern period. The sixteenth-century French politician and philosopher Jean Bodin counts among the founders of modern political and economic theory—but he also wrote a tract on the dangers of witchcraft, urging the authorities to take violent measures to stamp out this satanic threat. Making sense of this interplay between medieval and modern ideas remains a central task of early modern studies and is one of the attractions that the period has had for those who study it. Early modern people seem at once very like us and very different from us.

Early modern Europe has attracted an enormous amount of scholarly attention since World War II, completely transforming our understanding of the period. Much of this abundant research has still not been made accessible to nonspecialists, and bridging the gap between researchers and nonspecialist readers is one of the main tasks that we have set for ourselves in bringing together the *Encyclopedia*. Articles have been written with the assumption that many readers will have no background knowledge about the period, and authors have avoided technical language, obscure allusions, and narrow scholarly debates. A chronology of the period opens the book, allowing readers to situate people, cultural achievements, and events in relation to one another; and a detailed index is designed to make it easy for readers to locate articles on specific topics. Numerous maps offer further guidance, and about five hundred illustrations provide some sense of how the world looked to men and women of the time.

But historical study is as much about interpreting facts as assembling them, and this *Encyclopedia* is meant to be a guide to interpretations as well as a summary of what happened. The articles here supply concise summaries of current scholarly views on the problems they address—appropriately, because many of our authors have played leading roles in creating current scholarly views. Given the importance of interpretation to historical research, readers should not expect bland uniformity of opinion in these articles. Our authors come from many different countries and a variety of academic disciplines. Not surprisingly, they emphasize different aspects of the problems they address, and they bring different interpretations to the same sets of facts. Readers may thus encounter differences of emphasis among the articles here, but they also will receive guidance and encouragement in exploring alternative views through the *Encyclopedia*'s system of cross-references. Articles on monarchy, absolutism, divine right, and state and bureaucracy, for instance, present the views of four different authors on topics that overlap, but each article refers readers to the others.

Here then are our hopes for this book: Readers will find in it reliable information about the most important people and events of an important historical era, and they will also find examples of sophisticated historical interpretation, presented in direct, nontechnical language. They will encounter the thoughts of distinguished scholars writing about basic questions, in some cases disagreeing, but together producing a richer, larger description of the period than any single scholar could offer. Ultimately, they will encounter some of the reality of early modern lives—complex, distant, yet also deeply connected to ourselves.

Early modern intellectuals often described themselves as members of a Republic of Letters, an intellectual community that spread across national and confessional boundaries. That community rested mainly on correspondence and books; many of its members never met face to face, yet they viewed themselves as close friends and allies. Editing this *Encyclopedia* has made me aware how fully alive the Republic of Letters remains in today's world. It has been a particular honor to collaborate with the members of the editorial board, distinguished scholars whose work I have long admired and who have put enormous effort into the project. It has been an equal pleasure to work with the authors who have contributed articles, some of them old friends, many more encountered only through their writings or through the recommendation of other scholars. At Scribners Mark LaFlaur, Frank Menchaca, Georgia Maas, Carol Schwartz, Joann Cerrito, Kelly Baiseley, and John Fitzpatrick made the project possible, and made working on it enjoyable as well; and the project also owes a great deal to the contributions of Stephen Wagley, Timothy DeWerff, and Patricia Marino. The dedication acknowledges the intellectual influence of four leading scholars of the period, whose thinking continues to shape the development of early modern studies both in America and in the world at large, and whose kindness has touched many of us in the field.

JONATHAN DEWALD
BUFFALO, JULY 2003

INTRODUCTION
THE EARLY MODERN PERIOD

Historians' terminology conceals acts of interpretation. When they designate long stretches of human activity as "late antiquity," "feudal society," "the Renaissance," and "the Age of Louis XIV," they implicitly assert the fundamental unity of those periods and emphasize differences between what happened in them and what came before and after. The editors of this encyclopedia are no exception. In titling the work *Europe 1450 to 1789: Encyclopedia of the Early Modern World,* we are suggesting ways of looking at a long and complicated period of history. Our title draws attention to common qualities that linked these centuries together, and it indicates the importance of the mid-fifteenth and late eighteenth centuries as historical turning points, separating this period from the Middle Ages on the one side and the modern era on the other. This introduction explores some important themes within the early modern centuries and explains our attention to them. It suggests reasons for viewing these years as a coherent historical era, and for giving them the label "early modern." (Please see the Preface for a fuller account of this term's origins and use.)

BETWEEN TWO CRISES

Defined as the years from 1450 to 1789, the early modern period falls between two major crises in European history, each a time of terrible suffering for millions of people, but each also a time of intense creativity. To observers in the years around 1450, destruction was more visible than innovation. Over the previous century, Europe had experienced devastating warfare, harvest failures, and the return

of bubonic plague, which had been unknown there during the Middle Ages. Social disruptions in turn fostered political instability: in England, Castile, and France, rivals fought for the crown, and there were popular rebellions as well. Christianity itself seemed shaken in these years. Between 1378 and 1415 rival popes claimed sovereign authority over the Roman Catholic Church, and some contemporaries suggested that only changes in church governance could repair the damage. Threats came from outside Christendom as well: the Ottoman Turks had begun advancing into formerly Christian territories in the eastern Mediterranean, and in 1453 they conquered Constantinople, once the capital of eastern Christianity, now renamed Istanbul.

Yet amid these uncertainties the mid-fifteenth century also included a burst of technological innovation, and this too formed part of the early modern period's opening phase. Printing appeared in the Rhineland in the 1440s, and its importance was immediately recognized; by 1500 there were printing presses in every major European city, and a large mass of printed books had become available. At about the same time a cluster of inventions changed the nature of European seafaring, and the effects of these innovations also were quickly visible. By the 1450s Portuguese sailors were exploring the coast of Africa; by the early sixteenth century, they had gone around Africa to India, and a series of expeditions had reached North and South America. Finally, the technology associated with gunpowder first became a significant military factor late in the Hundred Years' War (1337–1453) between France and England. In 1494 French armies made extensive use of artillery in their march through Italy, and their easy success advertised to all that a new era of European warfare had opened.

The early modern period ended as it began, in crisis. Political upheavals in North America and Holland were followed in 1789 by revolution in France, which soon spread to the rest of Europe. In the ensuing wars, French armies conquered neighboring countries and imposed new institutions on them; other areas found themselves forced to respond to the French threat by ending serfdom, promulgating written constitutions, and liberalizing economic life. Despite the controversy it inspired, this trend toward democracy set the norms for European political life during the nineteenth century, and the movement was especially strong because it coincided with dramatic economic and technological changes. Late-twentieth-century scholarship has made the industrial revolution seem less cataclysmic than it once did, but even revisionist historians view industrialization as bringing extraordinary changes to European life. These began in Britain and had the most immediate impact there, but they quickly spread to continental Europe, with implications for agriculture as well as for manufacturing. Railways and steamships now transported agricultural products from the Americas to Europe, forcing once-isolated European peasants to compete in global markets, and new technologies enhanced agricultural productivity. Some historians have described the changes of the late eighteenth and early nineteenth centuries as the most important experienced by mankind since the invention of agriculture in about 4000 B.C.E. However excessive, this evaluation suggests how completely the early modern period ended; after 1789, European society evolved in fundamentally new ways.

TEXTURES OF EARLY MODERN LIFE

By modern standards Europe was relatively empty during the years between these two great crises. At the beginning of the twenty-first century, England had a population of about 50 million. Its population in 1500 was only about 3.1 million, and in 1801, after several decades of industrial development, the country's first census still showed only 8.7 million inhabitants. Other regions, such as France and northern Italy, were more populous, but still far below the levels they would reach in the nineteenth century. In this more sparsely populated world, distance was an enemy: travelers moved through landscapes that were frightening in their isolation, the haunts of thieves, wild animals, and marauding soldiers. Most people lived in small settlements of a few hundred inhabitants.

Population remained low for a variety of reasons, some of them obvious, some discovered only in the course of research since World War II. Life expectancies were short and subject to a variety of threats. The plague remained endemic in most parts of Europe until the later seventeenth century, with one last, terrible outbreak in Marseille in 1719–1720; other diseases were less destructive but still extremely serious. The very young were especially vulnerable to both disease and malnutrition. About one-fourth of infants died before their first birthday, a number that seems not to have improved much over the period. The inadequacies of European agriculture ensured that hunger remained a constant problem. In France people starved during the terrible winter of 1708–1709, and food shortages continued through the Revolution; elsewhere, famine continued into the nineteenth century. Since the great Dutch historian Johan Huizinga (1872–1945) first took up this theme in 1919, numerous historians have explored the psychological and cultural consequences of these facts. Europeans throughout the early modern era lived with insecurity and anxiety, their lives marked by repeated disruptions. Huizinga believed that these experiences created internal instabilities, making the early moderns prone to violence and emotional extremes. Today historians are less sure because modes of behavior seem to have changed even while conditions of life remained so insecure. Infant mortality, for instance, remained very high in the eighteenth century, but in these years contemporaries began to speak with new warmth of children and family life.

But if there was no revolution in material life during the early modern centuries, everywhere there was some progress, and in a few regions progress was very substantial. Agricultural productivity in England, the Netherlands, and northern Italy advanced greatly: England experienced its last famine in the mid-seventeenth century, and thereafter a variety of technological improvements allowed it to become an exporter of foodstuffs. Still earlier, the Dutch took advantage of their location on the North Sea to develop a specialized commercial agriculture. Because the Netherlands could easily import grain from eastern Europe, Dutch farmers could concentrate on dairy production, developing new techniques and enjoying the efficiencies of specialization. In the seventeenth century, they established a system of canals that made transporting bulky agricultural goods still cheaper. In these regions, the early modern period experienced a circumstance new to European history: the necessities of life were reliably available at low prices.

No such triumph over want occurred in most other regions, but elsewhere incremental advances in farming methods and transportation nonetheless brought significant improvements. As a result, early modern society was not so immobile as historians once believed. Despite the persistence of disease and shortages, there was a trend toward demographic and economic growth over the period, a striking vitality even in the face of crisis and destruction. This increase in prosperity did not occur evenly over time. There was rapid growth in the sixteenth century, as Europe recovered from the crises of the fifteenth century, then stagnation in the mid-seventeenth century, before growth resumed in the mid-eighteenth century. But the economic depression of the 1600s involved only a pause, rather than anything like the collapse that had marked the 1400s. Horrific warfare and the plague's continued virulence (at least 30,000 people died in the Milanese plague of 1630, and about 100,000 in the London plague of 1665–1666) only briefly interrupted a general upward movement in population.

One consequence was a limited but steady trend of urbanization. In 1750, 85 percent of Europeans lived in the countryside, and most worked in agriculture. But urban life became more important in these years, both because cities themselves grew and because their influence over society as a whole intensified. In many ways this process only continued medieval developments. Europe's urban network had already emerged in the twelfth century, and few new cities were created in the early modern period; many long-established cities changed little during these centuries. Urbanization

during these years thus did not mean the expansion of urban life everywhere, but rather the dramatic growth of some cities and the intensified activity of many, a process brilliantly described by the historian Jan de Vries. In 1500, he has shown, only four European cities had as many as 80,000 inhabitants, and none had as many as 160,000; with about 50,000, London typified the capital cities of the age, while Madrid and Berlin scarcely existed. By 1700, however, there were fifteen cities with 80,000 inhabitants and two with more than 300,000. These were cities on a modern scale, and by 1800 London had reached one million inhabitants. Such growth resulted above all from political developments; the great cities of the later seventeenth and eighteenth centuries were political capitals and benefited from the tax revenues and people who streamed into them. Partly because they housed the political classes, these cities offered their residents an expanding array of urban amenities: theaters, taverns, coffeehouses, shops; carefully designed plazas, parks, and boulevards; street lighting and policing. By this point, the cities formed focal points of a much larger consumer revolution that touched villagers as well as city dwellers. In villages as in the cities, a new range of cheap luxury goods was now available, ranging from tobacco and coffee to small books, prints, and mirrors. From the period's abundant probate records, historians have established that ordinary people bought increasing numbers of these goods, even in times of economic difficulties.

EUROPE AND THE WORLD

If Europe's economic life showed more resiliency during the early modern period than during the late Middle Ages, despite the Continent's continuing agricultural backwardness and the continuing threat of epidemic disease, one reason lay in the resources that Europeans now drew from the rest of the world. Europe's encounter with the Americas in 1492 had led quickly to imperial exploitation. Having established plantation economies in the Caribbean during the first decades of the sixteenth century, the Spanish conquered Mexico in 1519 and the Inca empire of Peru in the 1530s; precious metals had from the outset been one objective of these conquests, and in the mid-sixteenth century silver mines were duly discovered, producing a rising flow of silver until the early seventeenth century, when shipments began to ebb. Other colonial economies only became important during the seventeenth century. In 1602 the Dutch established the East India Company, and its system of Asian trading posts produced occasionally spectacular profits; later in the century the British began importing tobacco from the Chesapeake Bay region of North America and cotton fabrics from India. Sugar cultivation based on slave labor had already begun, but it became especially important in the eighteenth century, with Britain, France, Portugal, the Netherlands, and Spain all holding sugar colonies. In the mid-nineteenth century, Karl Marx (1818–1883) argued that profits from these ventures formed the foundation for what became known as Europe's industrial revolution. Few historians still share this view, but most agree that colonial products transformed the character of European economic life in another way, by showing the profits to be made from cheap luxury goods like sugar, tobacco, and cotton textiles. Products like these were among the first to demonstrate the economic potential of mass markets.

Historians also remain divided about the sources of Europe's imperial successes. Some have drawn attention to religious values, which encouraged Europeans to spread Christianity to distant places and gave them the remarkable self-confidence they displayed when they got there. Others have noted the importance of Europe's harshly competitive state system, whose relative balance encouraged individual governments to seek advantages in overseas territories—and whose endless warfare had trained Europeans to be especially savage in dealing with other peoples. As important as these cultural and political sources of European success, though, was European military technology. Their possession of weapons using gunpowder allowed Europeans to conquer the Americas; conversely, Asian states quickly adopted the new weaponry for themselves and successfully held off European invaders.

How to evaluate the peoples and societies they encountered elsewhere became a central problem for European thinkers of the early modern period. Many shared the view of the Spanish King Philip II (ruled 1556–1598) that imperial conquest demonstrated God's favor, and some questioned whether the newly discovered Americans were sufficiently human to deserve Christianization. In the long run, however, the opposing view—first laid out by the French nobleman Michel de Montaigne (1533–1592) in the 1570s—proved far more potent: Montaigne argued that native Americans fully shared the Europeans' humanity, and that native American culture, despite its peculiarities, was the equal of the Europeans' own. In the seventeenth and eighteenth centuries, a surprising collection of writers amplified these views. Jesuit missionaries advocated toleration for the cultural differences they encountered in both Asia and the Americas, while such Enlightenment philosophers as Charles-Louis de Secondat de Montesquieu (1689–1755), Denis Diderot (1713–1784), and Jean-Jacques Rousseau (1712–1778) used other cultures as models in their criticism of western Christendom. To missionaries and philosophers alike, the encounter with other societies fostered the emergence of the idea of cultural relativism.

But relativism did not necessarily imply cultural doubt, and ultimately Europeans' encounter with the rest of the world encouraged self-confidence. They relished the fact that no other peoples had established empires comparable to theirs, and in making this comparison they included the Greeks and Romans, whose geographers had not even imagined the existence of the Americas. Past wisdom, it seemed, could not be much of a guide for life in the present; and even the most tolerant Europeans noted their society's material superiority to that of other civilizations. In 1689 John Locke (1632–1704) argued that a native American king "feeds, lodges, and is clad worse than a day-labourer in England." He viewed the native Americans' failure fully to develop their lands as justification for European conquest. Furthermore, as Montaigne had asked in the sixteenth century, who knew what further worlds were still to be discovered? By the eighteenth century, Europe's intellectuals took for granted a vision of social and intellectual progress that placed Europe at the top of a hierarchy of the world's societies.

MODES OF CULTURAL CHANGE

These lessons from the New World paralleled other cultural developments, which both enhanced European self-confidence and raised doubts about traditional beliefs. Cultural change was probably inevitable in the early modern period because the invention of printing produced an explosion in the quantity of cultural goods available. From the outset, printed books were cheaper than manuscripts had ever been, and costs only dropped thereafter. After 1600 some printers turned to mass marketing and developed offerings specifically oriented to popular audiences: books of prayers, home remedies, proverbs, old-fashioned tales. Education advanced also, in part as a response to the overlapping political and ideological struggles of the age. In the fifteenth and early sixteenth centuries, competing governments established universities as a form of self-advertisement; in the sixteenth and seventeenth centuries, rival religions struggled as both Protestants and Catholics sought to explain their faiths and ensure that believers held the proper doctrines; in the eighteenth century, secular purposes again predominated as governments became convinced that well-schooled populations would supply the foundation for economic development—and therefore for state power. These diverse efforts combined to produce a startling increase in European literacy. By the mid-eighteenth century, half of all French men and 60 percent of English men could read and write; women's literacy was significantly lower, with 27 percent of French women and 40 percent of English women literate. Other new media, such as commercial theaters and engraving, supplemented printing's impact.

The culture that these media brought to the public included multiple elements, which interacted in surprising ways and allowed Europeans to hold views that moderns often find contradictory. Despite growing doubts about the ancients' scientific knowledge, for most intellectuals the foundations of cultural life lay in the close study of the literature and philosophy of Greece and Rome. In the Italian city-states of the fourteenth and early fifteenth centuries, Greek and Roman literature had seemed to offer the best training for wealthy young men destined to participate in public life, providing them with the rhetorical skills and historical examples that they would need in political debate. In the years after 1500, this humanist educational program (as historians have usually termed it) was transplanted to the rest of Europe, where its emphasis on the virtues of public life appealed to the growing number of lawyers and civil servants. There was nothing necessarily secularizing about humanism. Religious colleges like those of the Jesuits made it the basis of their training, and religious leaders like Philipp Melanchthon (1497–1560) and John Calvin (1509–1564) doubled as distinguished Latinists. But in fact, study of the ancient world appears to have loosened religious belief by drawing attention to the virtues and great deeds of a non-Christian culture and by offering pagan ideas as basic reference points for reasoning about the contemporary, Christian world.

A second strand of early modern culture was scientific, for the period abounded in both scientific theorizing and factual discoveries. The medieval universities had sponsored a good deal of scientific reflection, and medieval technology had been abundant in innovations. But the sixteenth century brought much more attention to scientific questions, notably in the areas of medicine, astronomy, and physics. By the early seventeenth century, contemporaries knew that they lived in an era of scientific revolution; old scientific theories were being rendered irrelevant and new objects of study were constantly appearing. In around 1600 the English poet John Donne (1572–1631) famously complained that the new science "throws all in doubt," but a century later, with the popularity of Isaac Newton's (1642–1727) writings, anxiety had been replaced by smug self-confidence. The English poet Alexander Pope (1688–1744) wrote that since Newton, "all was light," and Montesquieu described the achievements of Europe's scientists as a fundamental difference between Europe and the rest of the world; science had become a measure of societal development. By this point it had also become a matter of popular interest, rather than the preserve of trained specialists. The Florentine scientist Galileo Galilei (1564–1642) wrote in Italian rather than the learned Latin, with the aim of reaching a popular audience, and scientific discussion groups emerged in Florence and Rome; northern European imitators appeared in 1662, with the English Royal Society, and 1666, with the French Royal Academy of Sciences. In eighteenth-century cities, entrepreneurs established museums of scientific marvels, and it was expected that these would attract women as well as men.

The causes of this scientific revolution remain difficult to sort out. In a brilliant book, the historian Elizabeth Eisenstein underlined the role of printing as one source of scientific change: unlike any medieval scientists, those of the sixteenth century could find in their libraries all previous learning on the topics they studied because printed materials were more easily available and more reliable than manuscripts. If printing helped theorizing, technology supplied a stream of new problems for theorists to consider. Gunpowder artillery posed new questions about momentum and measurement; new mining and metallurgical techniques eventually turned up in studies of chemistry. Travelers returned with a stream of marvels that scientists needed to consider, and these reports stimulated scientists as well as geographers to dismiss the ancients' learning and insist on the value of innovation. Late in the seventeenth century, in the "quarrel of the ancients and the moderns," French intellectuals generalized this idea of progress; for the first time in European history, some intellectuals argued that *all* modern achievements, in the arts and literature as well as in the sciences, surpassed those that Europe had inherited from the ancient world.

For all the secularizing force of humanism and science, European culture during these years remained deeply religious. The fifteenth century was already a period of intense reflection on the meanings of the Christian religion, among both ordinary people and intellectuals. In 1517, publication of the Ninety-Five Theses of the German theologian Martin Luther (1483–1546) transformed this diffuse religious ferment into sharp differences of doctrine. With dissemination made possible by the printing press, Luther's ideas quickly became the basis for breakaway churches in Germany, Britain, Scandinavia, and Switzerland, often with sufficiently sharp differences over doctrine to create institutional divisions among the Protestants themselves. The Catholic Church responded by clarifying its own doctrines in a series of major councils and by determined efforts to win back Protestant converts. Both sides in this ideological struggle saw violence as a legitimate tool, and religious warfare flared repeatedly from the 1530s until the end of the Thirty Years' War in 1648.

This experience of religious fragmentation helps account for the particular tension that surrounded intellectual life in these years and that probably made the early modern centuries more dangerous for dissenting intellectuals than the Middle Ages had been. With printing presses and rising literacy allowing ideas to spread more quickly and to wider social groups, authorities intensified their efforts to control ideas, for new ideas had demonstrated their capacity to produce institutional revolutions. Secular governments established systems for censoring printed books. The Catholic Church established its Index of Prohibited Books in 1559 and refurbished the Inquisition to examine those suspected of heretical views. Protestants were no more tolerant of religious dissidence. Calvin successfully urged the Genevan authorities to execute the Spanish theologian Michael Servetus (1511–1553) for arguing against the doctrine of the Trinity, and the main Protestant churches were unsparing in their persecution of such breakaway groups as the Anabaptists and Quakers. Such persecutions eased somewhat after about 1660 as intellectuals and political leaders increasingly adopted the doubts that Montaigne had expressed in the later sixteenth century: human intellectual fallibility, Montaigne had argued, simply did not allow the kind of certainty that persecution required. But if persecution became less frequent and less flamboyant, it remained a reality in most parts of Europe. Before the eighteenth century, only the Netherlands and some regions of Eastern Europe allowed their inhabitants an approximation of intellectual freedom.

Given Europeans' readiness to kill over religious differences, it is a paradox of the age that amid their bitter disputes Catholics and Protestants shared so many assumptions and objectives. Catholic and Protestant churches alike sought to create a more educated laity, who could understand and reflect on religious teachings. Both churches functioned as forces for literacy, and leaders on both sides undertook broader campaigns of cultural development, seeking to uproot the popular superstitions they encountered among villagers and the urban poor. As important, Catholics and Protestants both sought to establish forms of piety that met the needs of educated Christians living in the secular world. This effort was central to Luther's conception of "the priesthood of all believers," but the Jesuits taught a similar idea. Their schools became the training ground for Europe's Catholic elites, and Jesuit advisors worked closely with politically powerful figures. In both contexts, the Jesuits sought to attune Christian ethical standards with the real needs of people in power, reconciling spirituality with the demands of worldly life. In keeping with this aim, Jesuit schools taught not only religion but dancing, etiquette, and classical literature. They also taught science, illustrating another paradox of early modern culture, for the Jesuits had played an important role in one of the period's most dramatic moments of intellectual persecution, the Catholic Church's condemnation of Galileo in 1633 for his denial that the earth was the center of the universe. The condemnation frightened intellectuals, and to some extent it inhibited intellectual life in Catholic states. But its intellectual effects were less dramatic than historians once thought, and Catholic regions continued to make fundamental contributions to the development of European science and philosophy. Even religious warfare had not destroyed the fundamental unity of European cultural life, a unity reinforced by the readiness of students, intellectuals, and artists to travel around the Continent and to share ideas with both Catholics and Protestants.

FORMS OF STATE POWER

Something similar may be said of Europe's political evolution during the early modern period: differences among European governments mattered less than their structural similarities. Differences there certainly were, the most important having to do with the functioning of monarchy and with the restraints that monarchs would accept on their powers. At one extreme stood the United Provinces of the Netherlands, Europe's most successful economy in the seventeenth century. From the start of their long and ultimately successful rebellion against Spanish overlordship, the United Provinces functioned without kings. They confided the state's legislative powers to a representative institution, the Estates, in which each province had one vote and an effective veto power. Such executive powers as leading the army and representing the country in foreign affairs fell mainly to the princes of the House of Orange, who inherited the position of stadtholder (lieutenant); but they remained formally agents of the Estates, and during most of the period they accepted that limited role. Following the violent upheavals of the seventeenth century, legislation in England too required Parliament's participation, and there were clear limits on what any king might do against Parliament's wishes. In most other countries, on the other hand, representative institutions tended to decay as the period advanced, leaving kings with few formal restrictions on their actions. During the late Middle Ages, France, the Iberian kingdoms, and much of Germany had active representative institutions; the richest regions of Italy had been city republics, governed by councils of the leading citizens. By 1600, in contrast, representative institutions in most of these regions had lost their functions, and in some regions they ceased meeting altogether.

These divergent paths of constitutional development, toward vigorous parliamentary government in England and the Netherlands, and toward more absolute royal power in most other regions, impressed contemporaries, and some historians have seen the contrast as the most important fact of early modern political history. But scholarship since the 1970s has tended to soften this classic contrast between parliamentary and absolutist states and to draw attention to how much they shared, even in the eighteenth century. Some degree of sharing was inevitable, given the competitive nature of the early modern state system; states tended to evolve in similar directions because they coped with similar challenges. For most of the period, competition took the form of nearly constant warfare, crudely aimed at territorial conquest; only after 1715 did acquiring new territories lose some of its legitimacy as a motive for war. Military techniques evolved dramatically during the early modern period, primarily because of gunpowder. In response to the new technology, armies became larger and more reliant on infantry; fortifications and equipment became more complex and expensive; and both officers and common soldiers needed more training. Historians disagree on the timing and some of the implications of the "military revolution" that these changes brought about, but there is no disagreement about its long-term effects: by 1700 states had to recruit, train, and equip immense armies at immense costs. Competition for colonial possessions added another layer of costs, especially in the form of enormously expensive warships.

Whether absolutist or parliamentary, all governments had to raise the large sums of money that armies required; and they needed a growing number of officials to collect this money and manage its expenditure. Taxation was not unknown in the late Middle Ages, of course, but it was viewed as a temporary expedient rather than a normal practice; kings were expected to cover most government expenses from their domain revenues rather than by imposing on their subjects. In this respect the early modern period represented a fundamental revolution in government. Taxation already represented a significant burden on citizens in the sixteenth century, and in the seventeenth—the most war-filled of the period—it rose dramatically. Under these circumstances, even parliamentary governments like that in England saw a rapid expansion in the number of government officials and in their intrusiveness. In the eighteenth century, England in fact had a higher per capita tax rate than France.

If England and Holland experienced much-expanded and more domineering governments as the period advanced, apparently absolute monarchies like France retained more elements of consultative government than contemporary rhetoric suggested. One reason was practical. Lacking easy methods of communication, early modern central governments could not unilaterally impose their will on distant provinces; they needed local cooperation, and to secure it they needed to respect local needs and traditions. Monarchs thus governed partly through negotiation and patronage, favoring the interests of local elites, listening closely to their concerns, and furthering projects that appealed to them. These practical considerations help explain another paradox of the period, the fact that the princes of very small states came closest to putting absolutist ideals into practice. In larger states, distance made real absolutism impossible.

As states' financial needs grew, another consideration further limited monarchical power. To finance their international ambitions, governments needed to borrow money, and claims to absolute power made this difficult; bankers insisted on usurious interest rates from rulers who viewed themselves as unbound by any contract. Governments were slow to learn this lesson, and during the sixteenth century both French and Spanish monarchs repudiated their debts on several occasions. In the seventeenth century, the French kings more carefully disguised their bankruptcies, arresting creditors on grounds of excessive profiteering, but the practical disadvantages of such tactics were becoming apparent. Much smaller states such as Holland and England could match French military spending because lenders trusted parliamentary governments to treat them fairly. Consultative government had proved a source of power, rather than of weakness, and in the eighteenth century governments retreated from absolutist behavior; just before the Revolution the French monarchy even sought to restore local representative institutions.

THE CHARACTER OF AN AGE: UNITIES OF TIME AND SPACE

Was the early modern period a single historical era? European life changed significantly over the period, this essay has argued, and contemporaries were acutely aware of change. The eighteenth century was far less violent than earlier centuries, and eighteenth-century Europeans enjoyed previously unknown amenities. The bubonic plague disappeared after 1720, and though warfare continued, soldiers inflicted much less misery on civilian populations. Harvest failures became less catastrophic, and new consumer goods appeared even in small-town markets. The pessimism of the fifteenth century had been replaced by extreme self-confidence, as Europeans compared their own achievements favorably to those of earlier generations and of other societies.

European society was thus far from static during the early modern period. Yet it remains possible to speak of this as a unified historical era. In the eighteenth century as in the fifteenth, European society was primarily agricultural and aristocratic, and its technology still changed slowly. Government remained primarily monarchical, and most kings still saw themselves as God's agents on earth. Eighteenth-century Europeans, it can be argued, were still wrestling with the ideas and social forces that had emerged in the late fifteenth and early sixteenth centuries, with their sequence of discoveries, inventions, and religious conflicts. This process was not easy, and the term "early modern" suggests the poignancy of the period's inner contradictions. Even as they prided themselves on the novelty of their accomplishments, the early moderns turned anxiously to the study of ancient cultural and religious authorities. Dissent was harshly repressed in these years, even as it became more frequent and more daring; monarchs vacillated in their self-depictions, sometimes stressing their divine right to authority, at other times stressing their duty to rule in society's interests. The late eighteenth-century age of revolutions, with its explosive mix of political, economic, and technological changes, brought many of these contradictions to an end. Like the late fifteenth century, these years reshaped the framework of European society and set before it a collection of new problems—the problems of modernity that, two centuries later, we have not yet fully resolved.

BIBLIOGRAPHY

Beik, William. *Absolutism and Society in Seventeenth-Century France: State Power and Provincial Aristocracy in Languedoc.* Cambridge, U.K., 1985.

Biagioli, Mario. *Galileo, Courtier: The Practice of Science in the Culture of Absolutism.* Chicago, 1993.

Blanning, T. C. W. *The Culture of Power and the Power of Culture: Old Regime Europe, 1660–1789.* Oxford, 2002.

Bouwsma, William J. *John Calvin: A Sixteenth-Century Portrait.* New York, 1988.

Collins, James. *The State in Early Modern France.* Cambridge, U.K., 1995.

De Vries, Jan. *The Economy of Europe in an Age of Crisis: 1600–1750.* Cambridge, U.K., 1976.

———. *European Urbanization, 1500–1800.* Cambridge, Mass., 1984.

De Vries, Jan, and Ad van der Woude. *The First Modern Economy: Success, Failure, and Perseverance of the Dutch Economy, 1500–1815.* Cambridge, U.K., 1997.

Eisenstein, Elizabeth L. *The Printing Press as an Agent of Change: Communications and Cultural Transformations in Early Modern Europe.* 2 vols. Cambridge, U.K., 1979.

Elliott, J. H. *The Old World and the New, 1492–1650.* Cambridge, U.K., 1970.

Hale, John. *The Civilization of Europe in the Renaissance.* New York, 1994.

Huizinga, Johan. *The Autumn of the Middle Ages.* Translated by Rodney J. Payton and Ulrich Mammitzsch. Chicago, 1996.

Israel, Jonathan. *The Dutch Republic: Its Rise, Greatness, and Fall, 1477–1806.* Oxford, 1995.

Le Roy Ladurie, Emmanuel. *The French Peasantry, 1450–1660.* Translated by Alan Sheridan. Berkeley, 1987.

Oberman, Heiko A. *Luther: Man between God and the Devil.* Translated by Eileen Walliser-Schwarzbart. New Haven, 1989.

Parker, Geoffrey. *The Military Revolution: Military Innovation and the Rise of the West, 1500–1800.* 2nd ed. New York, 1996.

Roche, Daniel. *The People of Paris: An Essay in Popular Culture in the Eighteenth Century.* Translated by Marie Evans with Gwynne Lewis. Berkeley, 1987.

Russell, Conrad. *The Crisis of Parliaments: English History 1509–1660.* London, 1971.

Stone, Lawrence. *The Crisis of the Aristocracy, 1558–1641.* Abridged edition. London, 1967.

JONATHAN DEWALD

MAPS OF EUROPE,
1453 TO 1795

The maps on the pages that follow show political boundaries within Europe at six important stages in the roughly three hundred and fifty years covered by this *Encyclopedia:* 1453, 1520, 1648, 1715, 1763, and 1795.

Europe, 1453

— International border
• City

0 100 200 mi.
0 100 200 km

Norwegian Sea

NORWAY

SWEDEN
•Stockholm

Gulf of Bothnia

Gulf of Finland

RUSSIAN STATES
•Moscow

Baltic Sea

TEUTONIC KNIGHTS

•Danzig

POLAND-LITHUANIA

•Warsaw

North Sea

SCOTLAND
•Edinburgh

IRELAND
ENGLAND
•Dublin

•London

DENMARK
Copenhagen•

Brandenburg

•Cologne

Bohemia
•Prague
Moravia

Silesia

MOLDAVIA

HOLY ROMAN EMPIRE

Vienna•
Austria

Buda•
•Pest

HUNGARY

WALLACHIA

Black Sea

ATLANTIC OCEAN

•Paris
Brittany•

FRANCE

Bay of Biscay

•Milan

Venice•
VENICE

•Genoa

Florence•
PAPAL STATES

BOSNIA

SERBIA
VENICE

Bulgaria

Constantinople•

OTTOMAN EMPIRE

NAVARRE

PORTUGAL

ARAGÓN
•Barcelona

Madrid•

CASTILE

Lisbon•

Corsica (Holy Roman Empire)

•Rome

NAPLES

Adriatic Sea

VENICE

Minorca (Aragón)
Majorca (Aragón)
Iviza (Aragón)

Sardinia (Aragón)

Tyrrhenian Sea

Sicily (Aragón)

Ionian Sea
VENICE

Athens•
VENICE

Crete (Venice)

GRANADA

Mediterranean Sea

1453. In the years around 1450, Europe settled into relative political stability, following the crises of the late Middle Ages. France and England concluded the Hundred Years' War in 1453; the Ottoman Turks conquered Constantinople in the same year and established it as the capital of their empire; and in 1454 the Treaty of Lodi normalized relations among the principal Italian states, establishing a peaceful balance of power among Venice, Florence, the duchy of Milan, the Papal States, and the Kingdom of Naples.

Europe, 1520

— International border

• City

0 100 200 mi.

0 100 200 km

1520. In 1520, the Habsburg prince Charles V was elected Holy Roman emperor, uniting in his person lordship over central Europe, Spain, the Low Countries, parts of Italy, and the newly conquered Spanish territories in the Americas. For the next century, this overwhelming accumulation of territories in the hands of a single dynasty would remain the most important fact in European international politics. But in 1520 Habsburg power already faced one of its most troublesome challenges: Martin Luther's Reformation, first attracting widespread notice in 1517, would repeatedly disrupt Habsburg efforts to unify their territories.

Europe, 1648

— International border
• City

0   100   200 mi.
0   100 200 km

1648. The 1648 Peace of Westphalia ended the Thirty Years' War, one of the most destructive wars in European history. The peace treaty formally acknowledged the independence of the Dutch Republic and the Swiss Confederation, and it established the practical autonomy of the German principalities—including the right to establish their own religious policies. Conversely, the Holy Roman Empire lost much of its direct power; although its institutions continued to play some role in German affairs through the eighteenth century, the emperors' power now rested overwhelmingly on the Habsburg domain lands in Austria, Bohemia, and eastern Europe.

Europe, 1715

— International border
• City

0   100   200 mi.
0 100 200 km

1715. The Peace of Utrecht (1713) ended the War of the Spanish Succession, the last and most destructive of the wars of the French king Louis XIV. The treaty ended Spain's control over present-day Belgium and over parts of Italy, and it marked the end of French hegemony within Europe. In the eighteenth century, France would be only one of five leading powers.

Europe, 1763

— International border
--- Internal border
• City

0 100 200 mi.
0 100 200 km

1763. The 1763 Treaty of Paris ended the Seven Years' War, a war that involved all the major European powers and included significant campaigns in North America and southern Asia, as well as in Europe. The war made clear the arrival of Prussia as a great power, at least the equal of Austria in central and eastern Europe.

Europe, 1795
— International border
---- Internal border
• City

0 100 200 mi.
0 100 200 km

N

Norwegian Sea

DENMARK AND NORWAY

SWEDEN

Finland

Gulf of Bothnia

Helsingfors

Gulf of Finland

•St. Petersburg

•Christiania

•Stockholm

•Moscow

Scotland

•Edinburgh

North Sea

RUSSIA

Ireland
GREAT BRITAIN
Dublin•

England

London•

UNITED NETHERLANDS

Amsterdam•

•Hanover

•Copenhagen

•Königsberg

PRUSSIA

•Berlin

Prussia

•Warsaw

Brussels•
Austrian Netherlands

Saxony

GALICIA

ATLANTIC OCEAN

•Paris

FRANCE

HOLY ROMAN EMPIRE

Bohemia

Munich•
Bavaria

Austria

Vienna•

Buda•
•Pest
HUNGARY

TRANSYLVANIA

SWISS CONFED.

Bay of Biscay

•Milan
Venice•

Genoa•

Florence•
TUSCANY

Black Sea

Adriatic Sea

Constantinople•

Corsica (France)

•Rome

Albania

OTTOMAN EMPIRE

PORTUGAL

Lisbon•

•Madrid

SPAIN

Minorca (Great Britain)

SARDINIA

Naples•
SICILY-NAPLES

Tyrrhenian Sea

Corfu (Venice)

Athens•

Majorca (Spain)

Iviza (Spain)

Ionian Sea

Cephalonia (Venice)

Zante (Venice)

•Algiers

Tunis•

Sicily

Crete (Ottoman Empire)

FEZ

ALGIERS

TUNIS

Mediterranean Sea

1795. By 1795, French armies had repelled an attempted invasion by Prussia, Austria, and England, and France had begun annexing territories in Belgium and western Germany. These military successes ensured the continuation of the French Revolution, but they also meant that European warfare would continue until 1815, when the modern borders of France were largely established. Warfare with France did not prevent the other European powers from conducting business as usual elsewhere: with agreements in 1793 and 1795, Prussia, Austria, and Russia completed their absorption of Poland.

LIST OF MAPS

VOLUME 5

VOLUME 6

COMMON ABBREVIATIONS
USED IN THIS WORK

A.D.   *Anno Domini,* in the year of the Lord

A.H.   *Anno Hegirae,* in the year of the Hegira

b.   born

B.C.   before Christ

B.C.E.   before the common era (= B.C.)

c.   *circa,* about, approximately

C.E.   common era (= A.D.)

ch.   chapter

d.   died

ed.   editor (pl., eds.), edition

e.g.   *exempli gratia,* for example

et al.   *et alii,* and others

etc.   *et cetera,* and so forth

exh. cat.   exhibition catalogue

fl.   *floruit,* flourished

i.e.   *id est,* that is

MS.   manuscript (pl. MSS.)

n.d.   no date

no.   number (pl., nos.)

n.s.   new series

N.S.   new style, according to the Gregorian calendar

O.S.   old style, according to the Julian calendar

p.   page (pl., pp.)

rev.   revised

S.   *san, sanctus, santo,* male saint

SS.   saints

Sta.   *sancta, santa,* female saint

supp.   supplement

vol.   volume

?   uncertain, possibly, perhaps

CHRONOLOGY

The Chronology is arranged year by year from 1450 to 1789 (and a little beyond) and is organized under six major headings to cover the *Encyclopedia*'s scope thematically and over time. Most items listed below are discussed in articles within the *Encyclopedia,* and can be located by referring to the Table of Contents and the Index.

Works first published in Latin, French, German, Italian, or Spanish are given in their original titles; translations are supplied for works first published in less commonly known languages.

Rulers and popes are identified at the beginning of their reign, with inclusive dates of rule. For example, at 1558: "Elizabeth I (England) 1558–1603."

Because the section headings are not always mutually exclusive, certain subjects may be listed under more than one heading. For instance, a philosopher may sometimes be listed under Literature and Scholarship as well as under Religion and Philosophy.

Works and events in mathematics and statistics are listed under Science and Technology.

Abbreviations:
- co. = company (pl., cos.)
- d. = died
- est. = established
- fd. = founded
- ft. = fort
- HRE = Holy Roman Emperor/Empire
- incl. = included, including
- mt. = mount, mountain (pl., mts.)
- publ. = published
- r. = ruled, reigned
- Tr. = treaty

DATE	POLITICS AND SOCIETY	RELIGION AND PHILOSOPHY	SCIENCE AND TECHNOLOGY
1450	Francesco Sforza, duke of Milan, 1450–1466		
1451	Mehmed II (Ottoman Empire), 1451–1481		
1452	Frederick III (HRE), 1452–1493, first Habsburg		
1453	Hundred Years' War ends; Turks capture Constantinople; Millet system est. by Sultan Mehmed II		
1454	Henry IV (Castile), 1454–1474; Peace of Lodi; Thirteen Years' War between Poland and Russia, 1454–1466		
1455	Wars of the Roses (England), 1455–1485; Portuguese fleets reach Senegal River, begin to exchange slaves and manufactured gifts for gold	Pope Callistus, 1455–1458; d. Zygmunt Oleśnicki, cardinal and Polish regent, 1434–1447	
1456	d. János Hunyadi		
1457	Christian I of Denmark reigns as king of Sweden, 1457–1464		
1458	Turks sack the Acropolis; George of Podebrady (Bohemia), 1458–1471; Matthias Corvinus (Hungary), 1458–1490; John II (Spain), 1458–1479; Portuguese occupy Ksar as-Saghir on Moroccan coast	Pope Pius II, 1458–1464	

ART AND ARCHITECTURE	DRAMA AND MUSIC	LITERATURE AND SCHOLARSHIP	DATE
		1450 Vatican Library fd.	*1450*
		Glasgow University fd.	*1451*
Leon Battista Alberti, *De Re Aedificatoria;* Lorenzo Ghiberti completes Gates of Paradise			*1452*
		Johannes Gutenberg prints Bible	*1453*
			1454
d. Fra Angelico; d. Lorenzo Ghiberti; d. Antonio Pisano, il Pisanello		d. Juan de Mena	*1455*
			1456
		d. Lorenzo Valla	*1457*
			1458

DATE	POLITICS AND SOCIETY	RELIGION AND PHILOSOPHY	SCIENCE AND TECHNOLOGY
1459			Fra Mauro creates world map for Portuguese king Afonso V
1460	d. Prince Henry the Navigator (Portugal); James III (Scotland), 1460–1488		
1461	Edward IV (England), 1461–1470; Louis XI (France), 1461–1483		
1462	Ivan III (Muscovy), 1462–1505, first to called himself tsar of all Rus'	First Monte di Pietà est. by Franciscans in Perugia	
1463		d. Catherine of Bologna	
1464	Piero I de' Medici, ruler of Florence, 1464–1469; Charles XIII (Sweden), 1464–1465; Postal service est. in France by Louis XI	d. Nicholas of Cusa; Pope Paul II, 1464–1471	
1465	Christian I of Denmark reigns as king of Sweden, 1465–1467		
1466	Peace of Toruń ends Thirteen Years' War between Poland and Russia; Teutonic Knights return conquered territories to Poland		Leon Battista Alberti invents cypher disk system
1467	Charles the Bold, duke of Burgundy, 1467–1477; Charles VIII (Sweden), 1467–1470		
1468			

ART AND ARCHITECTURE	DRAMA AND MUSIC	LITERATURE AND SCHOLARSHIP	DATE
		d. Gian Francesco Poggio Bracciolini	*1459*
		d. Guarino Guarini	*1460*
			1461
		Platonic Academy est. by Marsilio Ficino	*1462*
		d. François Villon	*1463*
			1464
Antonio del Pollaiulo, *Battle of the Nudes;* Andrea del Verrocchio, *Christ and Doubting Thomas,* 1465–1483			*1465*
d. Donatello			*1466*
			1467
		d. Johannes Gutenberg	*1468*

DATE	POLITICS AND SOCIETY	RELIGION AND PHILOSOPHY	SCIENCE AND TECHNOLOGY
1469	Marriage of Ferdinand of Aragón and Isabella of Castile lays groundwork for unification of Spain; Lorenzo de' Medici, ruler of Florence, 1469–1492		
1470	Henry VI (England), 1470–1471; Portuguese arrive in São Tomé, Ano Bom, and Príncipe		
1471	Vladislav II (Bohemia), 1471–1516; Edward VI (England), 1471–1483; Sten Stur the Elder, regent of Sweden, 1471–1497; Portuguese occupy Arzilla and Tangier; Italian city-states begin striking coins known as "testons"	d. Thomas à Kempis (author of *Imitation of Christ*); Pope Sixtus IV, 1471–1484	
1472	Ivan III of Muscovy marries Sofiia (Zoë) Paleologue	d. Cardinal Bessarion; d. Janus Pannonius	
1473			
1474	Isabella, queen of Castile, 1474–1504; Ferdinand serves as king consort (as Ferdinand V, 1474–1504)		
1475	Cologne recognized as an imperial free city by HRE Frederick III; Crimean Khanate accepts vassalage to Ottoman sultan		
1476			d. Regiomontanus (Johann Müller)

ART AND ARCHITECTURE	DRAMA AND MUSIC	LITERATURE AND SCHOLARSHIP	DATE
d. Filarete (Antonio di Pietro Averlino); d. Fra Filippo Lippi			*1469*
		Sir John Fortescue, *De Laudibus Legum Angliae;* First printing press in Paris est. by Guillaume Fichet and Johann Heynlin	*1470*
		d. Thomas Malory; Lorenzo Valla, *Elegantiae Linguae Latinae Libri Sex*	*1471*
d. Leon Battista Alberti		d. Peter Luder	*1472*
		Printing press est. at Lyon	*1473*
	d. Guillaume Dufay		*1474*
Dormition Cathedral constructed by Aristotele Fioravanti in Moscow Kremlin, 1475–1479			*1475*
Hugo van der Goes, *Adoration of the Magi* altarpiece, 1476–1478 (commissioned by Tomasso Portinari for church of St. Egidio)		William Caxton sets up printing press at Westminster	*1476*

DATE	POLITICS AND SOCIETY	RELIGION AND PHILOSOPHY	SCIENCE AND TECHNOLOGY
1477	Burgundy divided between France and HRE after death of Duke Charles the Bold		
1478	Megli Giray, Crimean khan, 1478–1515; Novgorod conquered by Muscovy; Pazzi conspiracy in Florence	Spanish Inquisition est.	
1479	Ferdinand II becomes king of Aragón, 1479–1516, rules Aragón and Castile jointly with Isabella; Tr. of Alcacovas		
1480	Ivan III confronts Golden Horde, ending Mongol supremacy in Russia; Ludovico Sforza, duke of Milan, 1480–1499		
1481	Bayezid II (Ottoman Empire), 1481–1512; John II (Portugal), 1481–1495; Agreement of Stans guarantees internal autonomy and mutual support of Swiss cantons		
1482	Peace of Arras; Kiev plundered by Mengli Giray; d. Federico da Montefeltro; Fort of São Jorge da Mina (Ghana) est. by Portuguese		
1483	John (Denmark and Norway), 1483–1513; Edward V (England), 1483, followed by Richard III, 1483–1485; Charles VIII (France), 1483–1498		
1484	Portuguese arrive at Congo River	Pope Innocent VIII, 1484–1492	

ART AND ARCHITECTURE	DRAMA AND MUSIC	LITERATURE AND SCHOLARSHIP	DATE
Sandro Botticelli, *La Primavera*	Johannes Tinctoris, *Liber de Arte Contrapuncti*	University of Uppsala fd.	*1477*
			1478
		Copenhagen University fd.; d. John Fortescue	*1479*
		d. Jan Długosz, after completing *Historia Polonica*	*1480*
d. Jean Fouquet			*1481*
d. Luca Della Robbia			*1482*
			1483
Annunciation Cathedral built as Kremlin palace church, 1484–1489; Sandro Botticelli, *Birth of Venus*			*1484*

DATE	POLITICS AND SOCIETY	RELIGION AND PHILOSOPHY	SCIENCE AND TECHNOLOGY
1485	Battle of Bosworth field; Henry VII (England), 1485–1509, first Tudor king; Portuguese reach Angola; Saxony divided by dukes Albert and Ernest		
1486	Maximilian I becomes co-regent with his father, HRE Frederick III; Frederick III "the Wise," elector of Saxony, 1486–1525		
1487			
1488	James IV (Scotland), 1488–1513		
1489			
1490	Vladislas I (Hungary), 1490–1516, king of Bohemia (as Vladislav II) from 1471		
1491	Anne of Brittany becomes queen of France by marriage to Charles VIII, 1491–1498		
1492	Piero II, ruler of Florence, 1492–1494; John I Albert (Poland), 1492–1501; Alexander, grand duke of Lithuania, 1492–1506; Ivan III of Muscovy invades Lithuania, 1492–1494; Capitulation of Granada to Spain; Jews expelled from Spain; first voyage of Christopher Columbus, 1492–1493	Pope Alexander VI, 1492–1503	Martin Behaim's globe (omits America)

ART AND ARCHITECTURE	DRAMA AND MUSIC	LITERATURE AND SCHOLARSHIP	DATE
		Thomas Malory, *Le morte d'Arthur*	*1485*
		Pico della Mirandola, *De Hominis Dignitatis Oratio*	*1486*
Faceted Palace built in Moscow Kremlin, 1487–1491			*1487*
d. Andrea del Verrocchio			*1488*
Michelangelo Buonarroti, *Madonna of the Stairs,* 1489–1492			*1489*
			1490
		d. William Caxton	*1491*
d. Piero della Francesca			*1492*

DATE	POLITICS AND SOCIETY	RELIGION AND PHILOSOPHY	SCIENCE AND TECHNOLOGY
1493	Maximilian I (HRE), 1493–1519; Pope Alexander VI issues bulls *Inter Caetera,* dividing New World between Spain and Portugal; second voyage of Christopher Columbus, 1493–1496		
1494	Habsburg-Valois conflict (Italian Wars), 1494–1559; French invade Italy; Medici exiled from Florence, republican rule 1494–1512; Tr. of Tordesillas		
1495	Charles VIII of France enters Naples; Diet of Worms; Manuel I (Portugal), 1495–1521		
1496	City of Santo Domingo fd. by Christopher Columbus	Isaac Abravanel, *Wellsprings of Salvation*	
1497	Cabot's voyage to Canada; Vasco da Gama begins voyage to India; Muscovite law code *(Sudebnik)* promulgated; Spanish doubloon introduced, becomes common gold coin of international trade; John of Denmark reigns as John II of Sweden, 1497–1501	Oratory of Divine Love fd. in Genoa by Ettore Vernazza	
1498	d. John Cabot; third voyage of Christopher Columbus, 1498–1500; Louis XII (France), 1498–1515; Vasco da Gama reaches Malabar coast (southwest) of India	d. Girolamo Savonarola (burned at the stake for heresy); d. Tomás de Torquemada	

ART AND ARCHITECTURE	DRAMA AND MUSIC	LITERATURE AND SCHOLARSHIP	DATE
		Nuremberg Chronicle printed	*1493*
d. Domenico Ghirlandaio		Sebastian Brant, *Das Narrenschiff*; d. Pico della Mirandola; d. Angelo Poliziano	*1494*
Hieronymus Bosch, *The Garden of Earthly Delights*; Leonardo da Vinci, *The Last Supper*, 1495–1498		Aldus Manutius the Elder's Aldine Press issues first book (*Erotemata* of Constantine Lascaris)	*1495*
		d. Filippo Buonaccorsi (Callimachus)	*1496*
			1497
d. Antonio Pollaiuolo		d. Giulio Pomponio Leto	*1498*

DATE	POLITICS AND SOCIETY	RELIGION AND PHILOSOPHY	SCIENCE AND TECHNOLOGY
1499	Anne of Britanny marries Louis XII, becoming queen of France for the second time, 1499–1514; Amerigo Vespucci voyages to America; Perkin Warbeck executed		
1500	Álvares Pedro Cabral reaches Brazil; Fort of Cabo das Redes est. by Portuguese; d. Bartolomeu Dias; Second Muscovite-Lithuanian War, 1500–1503		
1501	Alexander (Poland), 1501–1506; Sten Stur the Elder, regent of Sweden, 1501–1503		
1502	Last voyage of Christopher Columbus, 1502–1504		
1503	d. Sofiia Paleologue; Seville becomes center of Spanish commerce with the Americas; Spanish rule in Naples begins	Desiderius Erasmus, *Enchiridion Militis Christiani*, Pope Julius II, 1503–1513	
1504	Tr. of Lyon; Joanna I, "the Mad" (Spain), 1504–1555, queen of Castile from 1504 and Aragón from 1516 (until 1506 power exercised by husband Philip I, until 1516 by father Ferdinand II, and thereafter by son Charles I); Spain takes over Kingdom of Naples (until 1713); Svante Nilsson, regent of Sweden, 1504–1512	"Judaizers" condemned and executed in Russia	

ART AND ARCHITECTURE	DRAMA AND MUSIC	LITERATURE AND SCHOLARSHIP	DATE
Michelangelo Buonarroti, *Pietà*		University of Alcalá de Hanares fd. by Cardinal Cisneros; d. Marsilio Ficino; Aldus Manutius prints illustrated edition of Francesco Colonna's *Hypnerotomachia Poliphili*	*1499*
Hieronymus Bosch, *Ship of Fools;* Lucas Cranach the Elder, *Crucifixion*		Aldus Manutius (Venice) introduces octavo format for printed books; University of Valencia fd.	*1500*
Michelangelo Buonarroti, *David*, 1501–1504			*1501*
d. Francesco di Giorgio Martini; Leonardo da Vinci, *Virgin and Child with St. Anne,* c. 1502–1516		Konrad Celtis (Pickel), *Quattuor Libri Amorum;* Estienne Press est.; University of Wittenberg fd.	*1502*
Raphael, *Coronation of the Virgin;* Leonardo da Vinci, *La Gioconda (Mona Lisa)* and *Battle of Anghiari,* c. 1503–1506			*1503*
		Jacopo Sannazaro, *Arcadia;* University of Santiago de Compostela fd.	*1504*

DATE	POLITICS AND SOCIETY	RELIGION AND PHILOSOPHY	SCIENCE AND TECHNOLOGY
1505	Francisco d'Almeida razes Swahili coastal city of Kilwa; Vasilii III (Muscovy), 1505–1533		
1506	d. Christopher Columbus; Sigismund I (Poland), 1506–1548		
1507	d. Cesare Borgia; Portuguese occupy Safi and Azemmur on Moroccan coast, 1507–1513	Tommaso de Vio (Cajetan) writes commentary on *Summa Theologica* of Thomas Aquinas, 1507–1520	Martin Waldseemüller, *Cosmographia Introductio*
1508	League of Cambrai	d. Isaac Abravanel; d. Nil Sorskii	
1509	Henry VIII (England) 1509–1547; Portuguese reach Malacca		
1510	Muscovy annexes Pskov; Portuguese conquer Goa	d. St. Catherine of Genoa	
1511	Portuguese conquer Melaka (Malay peninsula)	King of France and HRE convene council at Pisa to force reforms on Pope Julius II; Johannes Reuchlin, *Augenspiegel*	
1512	HRE adopts official title "Holy Roman Empire of the German Nation"; Third Muscovite-Lithuanian War, 1512–1522; Selim I (Ottoman Empire), 1512–1520; Sten Stur the Younger, regent of Sweden, 1512–1520; d. Amerigo Vespucci	Fifth Lateran Council, 1512–1517	

ART AND ARCHITECTURE	DRAMA AND MUSIC	LITERATURE AND SCHOLARSHIP	DATE
Giorgione, *The Tempest;* Raphael, *The Grand Duke's Madonna*			*1505*
Laocöon discovered; d. Andrea Mantegna		University of Frankfurt an der Oder fd.	*1506*
			1507
Michelangelo paints Sistine Chapel ceiling, 1508–1512; Raphael, frescoes in the Stanza della Segnatura in Vatican papal apartments, incl. *The School of Athens,* 1508–1511		Guillaume Budé, *Annotationes in Pandectas,* d. Konrad Celtis (Pickel)	*1508*
		St. Paul's School fd. in London by John Colet	*1509*
d. Sandro Botticelli; Giorgione, *Sleeping Venus;* d. Giorgione	*Everyman* first performed		*1510*
	d. Johannes Tinctoris	Erasmus, *Moriae Encomium*	*1511*
			1512

DATE	POLITICS AND SOCIETY	RELIGION AND PHILOSOPHY	SCIENCE AND TECHNOLOGY
1513	Christian II (Denmark and Norway), 1513–1523; James V (Scotland), 1513–1542; Vasco Nuñez de Balboa crosses Isthmus of Panama to reach Pacific Ocean; Juan Ponce de León discovers Florida	Pope Leo X, 1513–1521	
1514	d. Anne of Brittany; Peasant uprising in Hungary, led by György Dósza; Muscovites capture Smolensk	Roman Oratory fd.	
1515	d. Alfonso de Albuquerque, first Portuguese governor general of Goa; Francis I (France), 1515–1547; Milan annexed by France; Cardinal Thomas Wolsey, lord chancellor of England, 1515–1529	d. Joseph of Volokolamsk	
1516	Louis II (Bohemia and Hungary), 1516–1526; Charles I (Spain), from 1519 HRE as Charles V, 1516–1556	Concordat of Bologna rescinds 1438 Pragmatic Sanction of Bourges; Gasparo Contarini, *On the Office of Bishop;* Desiderius Erasmus publishes new Latin version of New Testament	
1517		d. Cardinal Francisco Jiménez de Cisneros, Spanish Franciscan reformer; Martin Luther's Ninety-Five Theses	
1518	Mercurio de Gattinara, chancellor to HRE Charles V, 1518–1530	Huldrych Zwingli begins preaching in Zurich	First book on coded messages published; Royal College of Physicians fd.

ART AND ARCHITECTURE	DRAMA AND MUSIC	LITERATURE AND SCHOLARSHIP	DATE
Albrecht Dürer, *Knight, Death, and the Devil, St. Jerome in His Study,* and *Melancolia I*		Niccolò Machiavelli writes *The Prince* and the *Discourses on the First Ten Books of Titus Livy*	*1513*
d. Donato Bramante			*1514*
Château of Blois built in Loire Valley, 1515–1524		Guillaume Budé, *De Asse et Partibus Ejus; Ein kurzveilig Lesen von Till Eulenspiegel;* Lateran Council forbids printing of books without approval of Roman Catholic authorities; d. Aldus Manutius the Elder	*1515*
d. Giovanni Bellini; d. Hieronymus Bosch; Raphael, *Sistine Madonna;* Titian, *The Assumption,* 1516–1518		Ludovico Ariosto, *Orlando Furioso;* Desiderius Erasmus, *Institutio Principis Christiani;* Sir Thomas More, *Utopia;* d. Baptista Spagnoli (Mantuanus)	*1516*
d. Fra Bartolomeo della Porta; Raphael, *The Transfiguration;* Andrea del Sarto, *Madonna of the Harpies*		Maciej of Miechów, *Tractatus de Duabus Sarmatiis*	*1517*
		Desiderius Erasmus, *Colloquia*	*1518*

DATE	POLITICS AND SOCIETY	RELIGION AND PHILOSOPHY	SCIENCE AND TECHNOLOGY
1519	d. Lucrezia Borgia; Charles V (HRE), 1519–1556; Hernán Cortés's expedition to Mexico; Fuggerei, first welfare housing project, fd. by Jakob II Fugger; Ferdinand Magellan sails around the world, through tip of South America (Strait of Magellan), to Philippine Islands, 1519–1521; *Joachimstaler* coins (*talers* or dollars) first produced	d. John Colet	
1520	*Comuneros* Revolt, 1520–1521; Christian II of Denmark rules as king of Sweden, 1520–1521; Field of the Cloth of Gold; Suleiman the Magnificent (Ottoman Empire), 1520–1566	King Henry VIII of England, *Defense of the Seven Sacraments;* Martin Luther, *An den christlichen Adel deutscher Nation* and *Von der Freiheit eines Christenmenschen;* Sigismund I of Poland bans Lutheran books	
1521	Turks capture Belgrade; Diet of Worms; Parma becomes part of Papal States; John III (Portugal), 1521–1557; Hernán Cortés conquers Tenochtitlán; d. Ferdinand Magellan	Pope Leo X excommunicates Martin Luther (*Decet Romanum Pontificem*); Henry VIII named "Defender of the Faith"; Philipp Melanchthon, *Loci Communes*	
1522	Milan taken from France by HRE; Turks capture Rhodes; Francis I introduces bonds *(rentes)* guaranteed by Paris city government and est. bureau to sell state offices	Pope Adrian VI, 1522–1523; Martin Luther publishes German translation of New Testament; Complutensian Polyglot Bible	
1523	Kalmar Union between Denmark, Sweden, and Norway dissolved; Frederick I (Denmark and Norway), 1523–1533; Gustav I Vasa (Sweden), 1523–1560	Pope Clement VII, 1523–1534	Schöner's map (includes both American continents)

ART AND ARCHITECTURE	DRAMA AND MUSIC	LITERATURE AND SCHOLARSHIP	DATE
Château of Chambord built in Loire valley, 1519–1550; d. Leonardo da Vinci		d. John Colet; Maciej of Miechów, *Chronica Polonorum*; Claude de Seyssel, *La grant monarchie de France*	*1519*
d. Raphael Sanzio; Titian, *Bacchus and Ariadne,* 1520–1523		d. Henry Estienne the Elder; Pico della Mirandola, *Examen Vanitatis*	*1520*
d. Piero di Cosimo	d. Josquin des Prez	d. Sebastian Brant; Niccolò Machiavelli, *Arte della guerra*	*1521*
	d. Jean Mouton	Biernat of Lublin, versified Aesop; d. Johann Reuchlin	*1522*
Hans Holbein the Younger, *Erasmus of Rotterdam;* d. Perugino; d. Luca Signorelli		Mikołaj Hussowczyk (Hussovianus), *Carmen de Statura, Feritate, ac Venatione Bisontis;* Hans Sachs, *Der Wittenbergisch Nachtigall;* Juan Luis Vives, *De Ratione Studii Puerilis*	*1523*

DATE	POLITICS AND SOCIETY	RELIGION AND PHILOSOPHY	SCIENCE AND TECHNOLOGY
1524	German Peasants' War, 1524–1525; Council of the Indies est. to govern Spanish colonies in America; d. Vasco da Gama		d. Nicolò Leoniceno, scholar of medicine
1525	Battle of Pavia; Francis I taken prisoner; Albert of Brandenburg, grand master of Teutonic order, converts East Prussia into secular duchy; d. Jakob II Fugger, "the Rich"	d. Thomas Müntzer; William Tyndale publishes English translation of Bible	
1526	Battle of Mohács; d. Louis II (Bohemia and Hungary); Ferdinand I (Bohemia and Hungary), 1526–1564, HRE from 1556; János Zápolya (Szápolyai), 1526–1540, rival to Ferdinand I of Habsburg as king of Hungary; Spanish conquest of Yucatán, 1526–1546	New Testament translated into Swedish by Laurentius and Olaus Petri involved	
1527	Henry VIII seeks annulment of marriage to Catherine of Aragón to marry Anne Boleyn; Sack of Rome by HRE Charles V's troops		
1528	Francis I makes Paris his principal place of residence		
1529	Turks besiege Vienna; First Lithuanian Statute	Colloquy of Marburg	

ART AND ARCHITECTURE	DRAMA AND MUSIC	LITERATURE AND SCHOLARSHIP	DATE
d. Hans Holbein the Elder	Gian Giorgio Trissino, *Sofonisba*	Pietro Aretino, "Aretino's Postures"	*1524*
		Galeazzo Flavio Capella, "On the Excellence and Dignity of Women"	*1525*
Correggio (Antonio Allegri), *Mystic Marriage of St. Catherine;* Jacopo da Pontormo, *Deposition*			*1526*
		Bartolomé de Las Casas begins *Historia apologética,* preface to *Historia de las Indias;* d. Niccolò Machiavelli	*1527*
d. Albrecht Dürer; Galerie François I built at Fontainebleau; d. Matthias Grünewald; d. Jacopo Palma (Vecchio)		Baldassare Castiglione, *Il cortegiano*	*1528*
		Heinrich Cornelius Agrippa, "On the Nobility and Excellence of the Feminine Sex"; Guillaume Budé, *Commentarii Linguae Graecae;* d. Baldassare Castiglione; Collège de France fd.; d. John Skelton	*1529*

DATE	POLITICS AND SOCIETY	RELIGION AND PHILOSOPHY	SCIENCE AND TECHNOLOGY
1530	Imperial Diet at Augsburg; Medici return to Florence; Polish monarchy becomes elective; Francisco Pizarro begins conquest of Peru; d. Cardinal Thomas Wolsey	Augsburg Confession; Ignatius of Loyola, *Spiritual Exercises*	
1531	Schmalkaldic League formed by Lutheran princes; Stock exchange est. at Antwerp; Portuguese est. trading post at Sena on Zambezi River (Mozambique)	Sebastian Franck, *Chronica: Zeitbuch und Geschichtsbibel;* Politian, translation of Epictetus's *Enchiridion* (Handbook); d. Huldrych Zwingli, at Battle of Kappel; Second Religious Peace of Kappel provides for religious coexistence in Switzerland	
1532	Thomas Cromwell becomes principal advisor to Henry VIII, 1532–1540	Solomon Molcho (Diogo Pires) burned at the stake for heresy	Otto Brunfels, *Herbarum Vivae Eicones*
1533	Ivan IV, "the Terrible" (Russia), 1533–1584; Cuzco conquered by Francisco Pizarro		
1534	Affair of the Placards in France; Jacques Cartier sets out to explore Gulf and River of St. Lawrence; Christian III (Denmark and Norway), 1534–1559	Act of Supremacy passed in England; Anabaptist rule in Münster, 1534–1535; Martin Luther publishes German translation of Bible; Pope Paul III, 1534–1549	d. Otto Brunfels
1535	Lima fd. by Francisco Pizarro; Spain absorbs Duchy of Milan after death of Francesco II Sforza	Company of St. Ursula fd. by Angela Merici; Miles Coverdale prints first complete English Bible; d. Jan van Leyden (executed)	
1536	Buenos Aires fd.; Gonzaga family of Mantua acquires Montferrat	John Calvin, *Institutes of the Christian Religion;* First Helvetic Confession; Inquisition est. in Portugal; d. Jacques Lefèvre d'Étaples; d. William Tyndale (executed)	Paracelsus, *Great Surgery Book*

ART AND ARCHITECTURE	DRAMA AND MUSIC	LITERATURE AND SCHOLARSHIP	DATE
Lucas Cranach the Elder, *The Judgment of Paris*		Collegium Trilinguae (or Collège Royale, later Collège de France) fd. by Francis I; d. Jacopo Sannazaro	*1530*
d. Vincenzo Catena		Jan Amos Comenius, *Janua Liguarum Reserata;* Robert Estienne, *Dictionarium Seu Linguae Latinae Thesaurus;* University of Granada fd.	*1531*
		François Rabelais's *Gargantua and Pantagruel* stories appear, 1532–1564	*1532*
d. Veit Stoss		d. Ludovico Ariosto	*1533*
d. Correggio (Antonio Allegri); Titian, *Venus and Adonis,* 1553–1554			*1534*
Hans Holbein the Younger, *Henry VIII*		d. Heinrich Cornelius Agrippa of Nettesheim; Guillaume Budé, *De Transitu Hellenismi ad Christianismum;* d. Sir Thomas More	*1535*
		d. Desiderius Erasmus; Francesco Guicciardini writes *Storia d'Italia,* 1536–1540	*1536*

DATE	POLITICS AND SOCIETY	RELIGION AND PHILOSOPHY	SCIENCE AND TECHNOLOGY
1537	Cosimo I de' Medici, duke of Florence, 1537–1574	*Consilium de Emendanda Ecclesia,* Pope Paul III condemns enslavement of American natives	
1538	Holy League against Ottomans, 1538–1540; Secret treaty of Nagyvárad divides Hungary	King Henry VIII of England excommunicated by Pope Paul III; d. David Reuveni	
1539		Six Articles define Anglican faith	Olaus Magnus produces a map of the world
1540	Thomas Cromwell executed; Milan given to Philip of Spain; Tr. between Venice and Turkey	Edict of Fontainebleau defines heresy as treason against God and king; Philipp Melanchthon, *Variata;* d. Angela Merici	
1541	d. Francisco Pizarro	Gustav Vasa's Bible (complete Swedish version); New Testament translated into Hungarian; Society of Jesus approved by Pope Paul III; d. Juan de Valdés	d. Paracelsus
1542	"Great Debasement" of coinage in England; Mary (Stuart), Queen of Scots, 1542–1567; New Laws stipulate that *encomienda* in Spanish America cannot be a hereditary grant	d. Gasparo Contarini; d. Sebastian Franck; Roman Inquisition (Holy Office) est.	Leonhard Fuchs, *De Historia Stirpium*
1543		d. Gian Matteo Giberti; Petrus Ramus, *Dialecticae Institutiones* and *Aristotelicae Aminadversiones*	Nicolaus Copernicus, *De Revolutionibus Orbium Coelestiam;* d. Copernicus; Andreas Vesalius, *De Humani Corporis Fabrica;* First university botanical gardens fd. at Pisa
1544			Sebastian Münster, *Cosmographia*

ART AND ARCHITECTURE	DRAMA AND MUSIC	LITERATURE AND SCHOLARSHIP	DATE
Sebastiano Serlio, *Trattato di architettura*	d. Gil Vicente	d. Andrzej Krzycki (Cricius)	*1537*
d. Albrecht Altdorfer; Titian, *Venus of Urbino*		Juan Luis Vives, *De Anima et Vita Libri Tres*	*1538*
			1539
Il Bronzino, *Eleonora of Toledo and Her Son Giovanni de' Medici;* d. Jean Clouet; d. Giovanni Battista di Jacopo, il Rosso Fiorentino; d. Parmigianino		d. Guillaume Budé; d. Francesco Guicciardini; d. Juan Luis Vives	*1540*
Hôtel Grand Ferrare built by Sebastiano Serlio, 1541–1548	Giambattista Giraldi, *Orbecche;* d. Fernando de Rojas		*1541*
			1542
d. Hans Holbein the Younger		d. Klemens Janicki (Janicius)	*1543*
		University of Königsberg fd.; d. Clément Marot; printing press brought to Mexico	*1544*

DATE	POLITICS AND SOCIETY	RELIGION AND PHILOSOPHY	SCIENCE AND TECHNOLOGY
1545	Duchy of Parma and Piacenza created by Pope Paul III; Pier Luigi Farnese becomes duke, 1545–1547; Silver deposits discovered at Potosí, Peru	Council of Trent, 1545–1563; Bartolomé de Las Casas, *Confesionario*	Botanical gardens fd. at University of Padua
1546	Schmalkaldic War, 1546–1547	d. Martin Luther; d. Francisco de Vitoria	
1547	d. Francisco de los Cobos; d. Hernán Cortés; Edward VI (England), 1547–1553; Henry II (France), 1547–1559; Ivan IV crowned tsar of Russia; Moscow destroyed by fire; right to plead before royal courts in England restricted to students of the Inns of Court	Catechism of Martynas Mažvydas printed (first printed book in Lithuanian); d. Jacopo Sadoleto; d. Tommaso de Vio Cajetan	
1548	Sigismund II Augustus (Poland), 1548–1572; Gonzalo Pizarro executed; pure-blood statute first imposed in Toledo	HRE Charles V issues *Interim*	
1549		Book of Common Prayer authorized for use in Church of England; Jesuits arrive in Brazil; Francis Xavier arrives in Japan to found Jesuit mission	
1550	New Russian law code (*Sudebnik*) issued	Pope Julius III, 1550–1555	

ART AND ARCHITECTURE	DRAMA AND MUSIC	LITERATURE AND SCHOLARSHIP	DATE
Benvenuto Cellini, *Perseus and Medusa*, 1545–1554	First documented commedia dell'arte troupe of actors for hire formed in Padua	Conrad Gessner, *Biblioteca Universalis*	*1545*
Il Bronzino, *Allegory of Venus*			*1546*
d. Sebastiano del Piombo; Tintoretto, *San Marco Freeing the Slave*		d. Pietro Bembo; d. Vittoria Colonna; Marguerite de Navarre, *Les Marguerites de la Marguerite des princesses;* d. Jacopo Sadoleto	*1547*
Sinan completes Sehzade mosque; Titian, *Charles V on Horseback*		John Bale, *Illustrium Maioris Britanniae Scriptorum;* d. Jan Dantyszek (Dantiscus); first Jesuit school opens in Messina, Sicily	*1548*
		Joachim Du Bellay, *Défense et illustration de langue française;* d. Marguerite de Navarre	*1549*
Andrea Palladio, Villa Rotonda, near Vicenza; Sinan, mosque of Suleiman I in Istanbul, 1550–1557; Giorgio Vasari, *Lives of the Artists;* Villa d'Este built near Tivoli	Hans Sachs, *Der farent Schüler im Paradei*	d. Andrea Alciati; Girolamo Muzio, *Il duello;* Pierre de Ronsard, *Odes;* Gianfrancesco Straparola, *Piacevoli notti;* d. Gian Giorgio Trissino	*1550*

DATE	POLITICS AND SOCIETY	RELIGION AND PHILOSOPHY	SCIENCE AND TECHNOLOGY
1551	Henry II est. first mechanized mint in Paris	d. Martin Bucer; Council of Russian Orthodox Church enacts Hundred Chapters; Luigi Lippomano, *Sanctorum Priscorum Patrum Vitae,* 1551–1560	Conrad Gessner, *Historiae Animalium,* 1551–1587
1552	Kazan' conquered by Moscow	Polish Diet vacates decisions of ecclesiastical courts against heretics and tithe-resisters; d. Francis Xavier	d. Sebastian Münster
1553	Jane (England) (Lady Jane Grey), 1553; Mary I Tudor (England), 1553–1558; English expedition to White Sea, reaches Archangel'sk and est. trade links with Moscow		
1554	Mary I Tudor marries Philip of Spain; Jane Grey executed		
1555	Religious Peace of Augsburg; Philip II of Spain inherits Southern Netherlands; English Muscovy Company est. by Sebastian Cabot and London merchants; Havana sacked by French pirates	Pope Marcellus II, 1555; Pope Paul IV, 1555–1559	

ART AND ARCHITECTURE	DRAMA AND MUSIC	LITERATURE AND SCHOLARSHIP	DATE
Titian, *Philip II*		Collegio Romano fd.; Andrzej Frycz Modrzewski, *Commentarium de Republic Emendenda Libri Quinque;* University of Lima, Peru, est.; d. Joachim Watt (Vadianus)	*1551*
Titian, *Self-Portrait*		Marcin Kromer, *De Origine et Rebus Gestis Polonorum Libri XXX*	*1552*
d. Lucas Cranach the Elder; Titian, *Danaë*		University of Mexico est.; d. François Rabelais	*1553*
Arezzeria Medicea fd. (to produce tapestries); Cathedral of St. Basil the Blessed built in Moscow, 1554–1556; d. Sebastiano Serlio; Giorgio Vasari appointed court architect and painter in Florence		d. Gaspara Stampa	*1554*
Tintoretto, *St. George and the Dragon*		François Billon, *Le fort inexpugnable de l'honneur du sexe femenin;* Johannes Magnus, *Historia de Omnibus Gothorum Sueonumque Regibus;* Olaus Magnus, *Historia de Gentibus Septentrionalibus;* Johannes Sleidanus, *De Statu Religionis et Republicae Carlo Quinto Caesare Commentarii;* d. Johannes Sleidanus	*1555*

DATE	POLITICS AND SOCIETY	RELIGION AND PHILOSOPHY	SCIENCE AND TECHNOLOGY
1556	Ivan IV conquers Astrakhan; Ferdinand I (HRE), 1556–1564; Philip II (Spain) 1556–1598	Thomas Cranmer executed; d. Ignatius of Loyola; Peresopnytsia Gospel (Church Slavonic/ Ukrainian), 1556–1561	
1557	Livonian War, 1557–1583; Sebastian I (Portugal), 1557–1578	New Testament of Geneva Bible; Serbian patriarchate restored at Peć by Ottomans	
1558	Elizabeth I (England), 1558–1603		Giambattista della Porta, *Magiae Naturalis*
1559	Francis II (France), 1559–1560, with Catherine de Médicis as regent, 1559–1589; Tr. of Cateau-Cambrésis ends Habsburg-Valois (Italian) Wars; Frederick II (Denmark and Norway), 1559–1588	Calvinist Genevan Academy fd.; Pope Pius IV, 1559–1565; Index of Prohibited Books issued; Sigismund II Augustus of Poland grants religious liberty to Prussian towns	
1560	d. Andrea Doria; Charles IX (France), 1560–1574; John Sigismund, rival to Habsburgs as king of Hungary, 1540–1570; Eric XIV (Sweden), 1560–1568; Michel de L'Hôpital becomes chancellor of France, 1560–1568	Complete Geneva Bible (English translation); d. Melchio Cano; d. Philipp Melanchthon; Scottish parliament introduces Presbyterian Confession of Faith, inspired by John Knox	
1561	Philip II moves Spanish court to Madrid; Livonian Order secularized and territory granted to Poland	Colloquy of Poissy; d. Menno Simons	

ART AND ARCHITECTURE	DRAMA AND MUSIC	LITERATURE AND SCHOLARSHIP	DATE
d. Lorenzo Lotto		d. Pietro Aretino; Matthias Falcius Illyricius, *Catalogus Testium Veritatis;* d. Tinódi Lantos; John Ponet, *A Short Treatise of Politic Power*	*1556*
Michelangelo Buonarroti works on dome of St. Peter's in Rome, 1557–1561; d. Jacopo da Pontormo		Stationers' Company chartered in England to issue licenses to print; d. Gianfrancesco Straparola	*1557*
		Christopher Goodman, *How Superior Powers Ought to Be Obeyed;* Marguerite de Navarre, *Heptameron,* 1558–1559; Mikołaj Rej, *Proper Likeness of the Life of the Honorable Man;* d. Julius Caesar Scaliger	*1558*
Pieter Bruegel the Elder, *Battle of Carnival and Lent*		Jacques Amyot's translation popularizes Plutarch's *Lives;* d. Robert Estienne; University of Geneva fd.	*1559*
Galleria degli Uffizi built in Florence, 1560–1580		d. Joachim Du Bellay	*1560*
		d. Claude Garamond	*1561*

DATE	POLITICS AND SOCIETY	RELIGION AND PHILOSOPHY	SCIENCE AND TECHNOLOGY
1562	Toleration granted to Huguenots in some areas of in France by edict of Catherine de Médicis; Wars of Religion (France), 1562–1598	Second Helvetic Confession; St. Teresa of Ávila writes her *Life* (1562–1564), founds order of Discalced Carmelites	
1563	François, duke of Guise (leader of Ultra-Catholic party in France) assassinated; Statute of Artificers in England; plague spreads across Europe	John Foxe, *Book of Martyrs;* d. Martynas Mažvydas; Thirty-Nine Articles of Church of England	
1564	Maximilian II (HRE), 1564–1576	d. John Calvin; Théodore de Bèze becomes head of Company of Pastors; Council of Trent ends; Tridentine Index of Prohibited Books issued; Tridentine Profession of Faith proclaimed; Congregation of the Council est.; d. Bartolomé de Las Casas	d. Andreas Vesalius
1565	*Oprichnina*, 1565–1572; Miguel López de Legazpi founds Cebu, Philippines	Jesuits introduced into Poland by Bishop Stanisław Hosius	d. Conrad Gessner
1566	Netherlands revolt against Spanish rule, 1566–1648; d. Diane de Poitiers; Selim II (Ottoman Empire), 1566–1574; Sultan declares Transylvania an autonomous principality under Ottoman suzerainty; Second Lithuanian Statute; unauthorized dueling declared a capital offense in France	Pope Pius V, 1566–1572; Standard catechism issued by Catholic Church	d. Nostradamus

ART AND ARCHITECTURE	DRAMA AND MUSIC	LITERATURE AND SCHOLARSHIP	DATE
Benvenuto Cellini, *Autobiography;* François Clouet, *Diane de Poitiers*		Mikołaj Rej, *Menagerie*	*1562*
Pieter Bruegel the Elder, *Tower of Babel;* Escorial built, 1563–1567; Florentine Accademia di Disegno est.; Germain Pilon designs tomb of Henry II and Catherine de Médicis, 1563–1570		d. Étienne de La Boétie	*1563*
d. Michelangelo Buonarroti; Tuileries constructed, 1564–1572			*1564*
Tintoretto, *Crucifixion, Flight into Egypt*			*1565*
		Jean Bodin, *Methodus ad Facilem Historiarum Cognitionem;* Łukasz Górnicki, *Polish Courtier;* d. Charles Du Moulin; d. Stanisław Orzechowski	*1566*

DATE	POLITICS AND SOCIETY	RELIGION AND PHILOSOPHY	SCIENCE AND TECHNOLOGY
1567	Spanish army under Duke of Alba invades Netherlands and establishes Council of Troubles; James VI (Scotland), 1567–1625, becomes James I of England in 1603		
1568	John III (Sweden), 1568–1592	Uniform Breviary issued by Catholic Church	
1569	Union of Lublin; Philip II suppresses revolt of Moriscos in Spain	Moscow Metropolitan Filipp murdered by Ivan IV, "the Terrible"; Petrus Ramus, *Scholae in Liberales Artes*	
1570	Holy League formed by Spain, Venice, and the papacy against the Turks; Massacre in Novgorod by Ivan IV	Queen Elizabeth of England excommunicated by Pope Pius V; Roman missal issued by Catholic Church; Sandomierz synod unites Lutherans, Calvinists, and Czech Brethren in Poland; Laurentius Surius, *De Probatis Sanctorum Historiis*, 1570–1573	First English translation of Euclid's *Elements* edited by John Dee
1571	Battle of Lepanto; Nicosia and Famagusta (Cyprus) fall to the Turks; Manila fd.; Portuguese crown gives land south of Kwanza River (Angola) to Paulo Dias de Novais	Congregation of the Index est.; Moses ben Israel Isserles, *Mappa*	

ART AND ARCHITECTURE	DRAMA AND MUSIC	LITERATURE AND SCHOLARSHIP	DATE
		François Hotman, *Anti-Tribonian*	*1567*
Giorgio Vasari, *Lives of the Artists* (rev. ed.)		Jan van der Noot, *Theater for Voluptuous Worldlings*	*1568*
Pieter Bruegel the Elder, *The Blind Leading the Blind;* d. Pieter Bruegel the Elder; Sinan, mosque of Selim in Edirne, 1569–1578		Philip Marnix van St. Aldegonde, *The Beehive of the Roman Church;* d. Mikołaj Rej, first literary writer in Polish vernacular	*1569*
d. Philibert Delorme; d. Jacopo Sansovino; Andrea Palladio, *Il quattro libri dell' architettura;* d. Francesco Primaticcio	Académie de Poésie et de Musique fd.	d. Jan Amos Comenius	*1570*
d. Benvenuto Cellini		d. Robert Estienne the Younger; Harrow School chartered	*1571*

DATE	POLITICS AND SOCIETY	RELIGION AND PHILOSOPHY	SCIENCE AND TECHNOLOGY
1572	Henry of Navarre (later Henry IV) marries Marguerite of Valois, daughter of Catherine de Médicis; Admiral Gaspard (II) de Coligny assassinated; St. Bartholomew's Day Massacre; d. Sigismund II Augustus; end of Jagiellon dynasty in Poland; Polish monarchy becomes elective by all nobles	Szymon Budny prints Ruthenian catechism at Nesvizh; Pope Gregory XIII, 1572–1585; d. Moses Isserles; d. John Knox; d. Isaac ben Solomon Luria; d. Petrus Ramus	Leonard Fioravanti, *Dello specchio di scientia universale*
1573	d. Michel de L'Hôpital; Henry Valois elected king of Poland; Henrician Articles; d. Ruy Gómez de Silva, prince of Éboli	Compact of Warsaw confirms official religious toleration in Commonwealth of Poland-Lithuania	
1574	Henry III (France), 1574–1589; Murad III (Ottoman Empire), 1574–1595; Tunis falls to the Turks		Ulisse Aldrovandi, *Antidotarii Bononiensis Epitome*
1575	Stephen Báthory, king of Poland, 1575–1586; First Portuguese settlement in Angola est. at Luanda Bay; Monetary reform in France; silver *franc* and copper *denier* (penny) introduced	Confessio Bohemica; d. Heinrich Bullinger	
1576	Rudolf II (HRE), 1576–1612; Martin Frobisher's voyages to Canada begin; dueling deemed treasonous in France	Ostrih Academy fd. by Kostiantyn Ostrozky	

ART AND ARCHITECTURE	DRAMA AND MUSIC	LITERATURE AND SCHOLARSHIP	DATE
d. François Clouet	Andrea Gabrieli, *Primus Liber Missarum*	Henri Estienne, *Thesaurus Graecae Linguae;* Luís Vaz de Camões, *Os Lusíadas;* d. Andrzej Frycz Modrzewski; Ducal Library at Wolfenbüttel opens	*1572*
Paolo Veronese, *Adoration of the Kings; Feast in the House of Levi*	d. Giambattista Giraldi	François Hotman, *Francogallia*	*1573*
d. Giorgio Vasari		University of Berlin fd.; Théodore de Bèze, *De Jure Magistratum; Le reveille-matin*	*1574*
		d. Anna Bijns; University of Leiden fd.	*1575*
d. Titian (Tiziano Vecelli)	d. Hans Sachs	Jean Bodin, *Six livres de la république; Mémoires de l'estat de France sous Charles neufsième* published, incl. Étienne de La Boétie's *Discours de la servitude volontaire;* Imperial Library in Vienna reorganized; University of Warsaw fd.	*1576*

DATE	POLITICS AND SOCIETY	RELIGION AND PHILOSOPHY	SCIENCE AND TECHNOLOGY
1577	Francis Drake begins voyage around the world		
1578	d. Don Juan de Austria; Alexander Farnese, duke of Parma, becomes governor general of the Netherlands; Henry (Portugal), 1578–1580		
1579	Union of Utrecht formed by seven northern provinces of Netherlands, led by Holland and Zeeland; William of Orange. "the Silent", stadtholder; Walloon provinces and Walloon towns in Flanders form Union of Arras; d. Joseph Nasi, duke of Naxos	Akbar, Mughal ruler of India, requests Jesuits to explain Christian faith; d. Stanisław Hosius	François Viète, *Canon Mathematicus Seu ad Triangula*
1580	d. King Henry of Portugal; Philip II of Spain inherits Portuguese throne; Buenos Aires refd.	Théodore de Bèze, *Histoire ecclésiastique*	
1581	United Provinces of the Netherlands formed, declaring independence from Spain	Church Slavonic Bible published at Ostrih	
1582	d. Fernando Álvarez de Toledo, duke of Alba; Tr. of Iam Zapol'skii; Ermak Timofeevich's Cossack expedition conquers Sibir; beginning of Russian conquest of Siberia; Free and Imperial Cities acquire voting rights in HRE Diet	d. St. Teresa of Ávila	Gregorian calendar promulgated (accepted in Catholic countries that year or within the following few years)

ART AND ARCHITECTURE	DRAMA AND MUSIC	LITERATURE AND SCHOLARSHIP	DATE
Accademia di San Luca fd. in Rome		Raphael Holinshed, *Chronicles of England, Scotlande, and Irelande;* Marcin Kromer, *Polonia, Sive de Situ, Populis, Moribus, Magistratibus et Republica Regni Polonici Libri Duo*	*1577*
	Jan Kochanowski, *The Dismissal of the Grecian Envoys*		*1578*
	John Lyly, *Euphues*	George Buchanan, *De Jure Regni apud Scotos;* Philippe Duplessis-Mornay, *Vindiciae contra Tyrannos;* Frankfurt book fair comes under supervision of imperial censors; Edmund Spenser, *Shepheardes Calendar*	*1579*
Giambologna, *Mercury;* d. Andrea Palladio		d. Raphael Holinshed; Jan Kochanowski, *Laments;* Michel de Montaigne, *Essais;* d. Luís Vaz de Camões	*1580*
		Torquato Tasso, *Gerusalemme Liberata*	*1581*
		George Buchanan, *Rerum Scoticarum Historia;* Crusca Academy fd. in Florence; University of Edinburgh fd.; Richard Hakluyt, *Divers Voyages Touching the Discoverie of America*	*1582*

DATE	POLITICS AND SOCIETY	RELIGION AND PHILOSOPHY	SCIENCE AND TECHNOLOGY
1583		d. Thomas Erastus	
1584	Fedor I (Russia), 1584–1598, last Rurikid ruler of Russia; Holy Catholic League organized by Henry, duke of Guise	d. Carlo Borromeo, cardinal and archbishop of Milan; Justus Lipsius, *De Constantia* (On Constancy)	
1585	Antwerp surrenders to Spanish forces under duke of Parma	Pope Sixtus V, 1585–1590; Latvian catechism printed at Vilnius	
1586	Johan van Oldenbarneveldt becomes Holland's *landsadvocaat*, 1586–1618	Robert Bellarmine, *The Controversies*, 1586–1593	
1587	Mary Stuart executed; Sigismund III Vasa (Poland), 1587–1632; United Provinces vest sovereignty in States General	d. John Foxe; Vatican Press fd.; d. Baltramiejus Vilentas	
1588	Christian IV (Denmark and Norway), 1588–1648; Henri, duke of Guise, and Louis II, cardinal of Guise, assassinated; Spanish armada defeated; d. Álvaro de Bazán, first marquis of Santa Cruz, Spanish admiral; Duke of Medina Sidonia becomes Captain General of the Ocean Sea; Third Lithuanian Statute; first stock exchange in German territory opened in Hamburg	Luis de Molina, *Concordia Liberi Arbitrii cum Gratiae Donia*	d. Bernardino Telesio

ART AND ARCHITECTURE	DRAMA AND MUSIC	LITERATURE AND SCHOLARSHIP	DATE
Giambologna, *Rape of the Sabine Women;* Tintoretto, *Annunciation,* 1583–1587	Queen's Company of Players formed	Elzevier Press est.; Josephus Justus Scaliger, *Opus de emendatione tempore;* Luis de León, *De los nombres de Cristo* (1583–1585); Sir Thomas Smith, *De Republica Anglorum*	*1583*
	Orlando di Lasso, *Psalmi Davidis Poenitentiales*	Escorial library fd. in Spain; d. Jan Kochanowski	*1584*
Bologna Academy of Art fd. by Carraccis		d. Pierre de Ronsard	*1585*
d. Lucas Cranach the Younger	d. Andrea Gabrieli	Dirk Coornhert, *Ethics, That Is, The Art of Living Well;* d. Sir Philip Sidney	*1586*
Vatican Library constructed by Domenico Fontana, 1587–1590	Andrea Gabrieli, *Magnificat* (published posthumously); Christopher Marlowe, *Tamburlaine the Great*	François de La Noue, *Discours politiques et militaires*	*1587*
El Greco, *Burial of the Conde de Orgaz;* d. Sinan; d. Paolo Veronese		University of Jena fd.	*1588*

DATE	POLITICS AND SOCIETY	RELIGION AND PHILOSOPHY	SCIENCE AND TECHNOLOGY
1589	Henry III and Henry of Guise (chief of Catholic party) assassinated; Navarre becomes part of France; Valois dynasty ends; Henry IV, first Bourbon king of France, 1589–1610	Justus Lipsius, *Politicorum Libri Sex;* Lorenzo Scupoli, *Combattimento spirituale;* Metropolitan of Moscow becomes patriarch	
1590	d. Sir Francis Walsingham	Pope Urban VII, 1590; Pope Gregory XIV, 1590–1591	d. Ambroise Paré
1591	d. Tsarevich Dmitrii; Ottoman-Habsburg War, 1591–1606	Giordano Bruno, *Frankfurt Trilogy;* Pope Innocent IX, 1591; Richard Hooker, *Of the Laws of Ecclesiastical Polity;* d. St. John of the Cross	François Viète, *In Artem Analyticem Isagoge*
1592	d. Alexander Farnese, duke of Parma, governor general of the Netherlands; Ranuccio I, duke of Parma and Piacenza, 1592–1622; Sigismund (Sweden), 1592–1599, also king of Poland	New edition of Vulgate Bible issued by Catholic Church; Pope Clement VIII, 1592–1605	Galileo, *Della scienza mechanica*
1593	Henry IV (France) converts to Catholicism	d. Szymon Budny	
1594	Willem Barents sets out to find northeast route through Arctic Ocean to Asia; First Dutch ships leave for East Indies; d. Martin Frobisher		d. Gerardus Mercator
1595	Mehmed III (Ottoman Empire), 1595–1603	Mikalojus Daukša prints Lithuanian translation of Diego de Ledesma's Catholic catechism	Jan Huyghen van Linschoten publishes maps and sailing directions for spice trade in Asia; Gerardus Mercator's atlas published

ART AND ARCHITECTURE	DRAMA AND MUSIC	LITERATURE AND SCHOLARSHIP	DATE
	William Shakespeare, *Henry VI*	d. Christophe Plantin; Jean Boucher, *De Justa Henrici Tertii Abdicatione*	*1589*
d. Germain Pilon	Christopher Marlowe, *Jew of Malta*	d. Dirk Coornhert; d. François Hotman; Edmund Spenser, *Faerie Queen*	*1590*
		John Lyly, *Endymion;* Philip Sidney, *Astrophel and Stella;* Trinity College, Dublin, fd.	*1591*
d. Jacopo Bassano	Thomas Kyd, *Spanish Tragedy;* Christopher Marlowe, *Edward the Second;* William Shakespeare, *Richard III* and *Comedy of Errors*	Juan de Mariana, *Historiae de Rebus Hispaniae;* d. Michel de Montaigne	*1592*
Caravaggio, *Bacchus;* El Greco, *Crucifixion;* d. Giuseppe Arcimboldo	London theaters closed due to plague; Christopher Marlowe, *Doctor Faustus;* d. Christopher Marlowe; William Shakespeare, *Taming of the Shrew*	d. Jacques Amyot	*1593*
d. Tintoretto	d. Thomas Kyd; d. Orlando di Lasso; London theaters reopened; d. Giovanni Pierluigi da Palestrina; William Shakespeare, *Romeo and Juliet*	d. Bálint Balassi	*1594*
	William Shakespeare, *Richard II* and *A Midsummer Night's Dream*	d. Torquato Tasso	*1595*

DATE	POLITICS AND SOCIETY	RELIGION AND PHILOSOPHY	SCIENCE AND TECHNOLOGY
1596	d. Francis Drake	Union of Brest; Clementine Index of Prohibited Books	Galileo invents thermometer; Johannes Kepler publishes defense of heliocentrism
1597	d. Willem Barents; Maximilian I, duke of Bavaria, 1597–1651	Piotr Skarga, *Sermons before the Diet*	
1598	Edict of Nantes; Tr. of Vervins; Philip II bestows Netherlands on Isabel Clara Eugenia and Albert of Habsburg; Philip III (Spain), 1598–1621; Fernando Sandoval Rojas, duke of Lerma, advisor to Philip III of Spain, 1598–1618; Boris Godunov (Russia), 1598–1605; Time of Troubles in Russia, 1598–1613; d. William Cecil		
1599	Charles IX, regent of Sweden, 1599–1604	First Polish translation of Bible by Jakub Wujek	
1600	Sir Edward Coke, *Reports*, 1600–1615; English East India Company fd.; Linköping Bloodbath	Giordano Bruno executed for heresy; d. Richard Hooker; d. Abraham ben-Eliezer ha-Levi Berukim; d. Luis de Molina	William Gilbert, *De Magnete, Magneticisque Corporibus, et de Magno Magnete Tellure*
1601	Poor Law (England); Fedor Nikitich Romanov (later Patriarch Filaret) exiled by Boris Godunov		d. Tycho Brahe
1602	Dutch East India Company fd.; Perot Rocaguinarda, Spanish bandit, first appears	d. Jonas Bretkunas	

ART AND ARCHITECTURE	DRAMA AND MUSIC	LITERATURE AND SCHOLARSHIP	DATE
Caravaggio, *Lute Player*	William Shakespeare, *The Merchant of Venice*	d. Jean Bodin	*1596*
Lodovico Cardi Cigoli, *Martyrdom of St. Stephen*	Giovanni Gabrieli, *Sacrae Symphoniae*	d. Aldus Manutius the Younger; first Piarist school ("Pious School") for working-class boys opened in Rome by José Calasanz	*1597*
Caravaggio, *The Calling of St. Matthew* and *The Martyrdom of St. Matthew* for Contarelli chapel, 1598–1601; Jan Brueghel the Elder, *Adoration of the Magi*	William Shakespeare, *Much Ado about Nothing* and *Henry V*	d. Henry Estienne the Younger; Richard Hakluyt, *Principal Navigations, Voyages, Traffics, and Discoveries of the English Nation;* Juan de Mariana, *De Rege et Regis Institutione*	*1598*
	Globe Theater opened; William Shakespeare, *Julius Caesar* and *As You Like It,* 1599–1600	Jesuit *Ratio Studiorum* issued; d. Edmund Spenser	*1599*
	William Shakespeare, *Hamlet*	Lucrezia Marinella, *The Nobility and Excellence of Women and the Defects and Failings of Men*	*1600*
Caravaggio, *Conversion of St. Paul*	d. Thomas Nashe; William Shakespeare, *Twelfth Night*	John Donne writes the *Holy Sonnets,* 1601–1615; University of Parma and school for noble boys fd.; Mikołaj Sęp Szarzyński, *Rhythms, or Polish Verses*	*1601*
d. Agostino Carracci		Bodleian Library opens at Oxford; Tommaso Campanella, *La città de sole*	*1602*

DATE	POLITICS AND SOCIETY	RELIGION AND PHILOSOPHY	SCIENCE AND TECHNOLOGY
1603	d. Elizabeth I (England); Union of Crowns between England and Scotland; James I (England), 1603–1625; Ahmed I (Ottoman Empire), 1603–1617; Samuel de Champlain explores St. Lawrence River and Great Lakes	Matteo Ricci, *The True Meaning of the Lord of Heaven*	Accademia dei Lincei est.; d. William Gilbert; d. François Viète
1604	French settlement est. in Acadia; Charles IX, king of Sweden, 1604–1611	Justus Lipsius, *Manductionis ad Stoicam Philosophiam* and *Physiologiae Stoicorum*	Johannes Kepler, *Optics*
1605	Gunpowder Plot; Fedor II (Russia); First False Dmitrii rules as tsar in Moscow, 1605–1606; d. Jan Zamoyski	Antitrinitarian confession of faith adopted at Raków; Johann Arndt, *Vier Bücher vom wahren Christentum*, 1605–1609; d. Théodore de Bèze; Pope Paul V, 1605–1621	d. Ulisse Aldrovandi
1606	Guy Fawkes executed; Vasilii Shuiskii (Russia), 1606–1610; first False Dmitrii overthrown; Treaties of Vienna and Zsitvatorok; Zebrzydowski rebellion in Poland, 1606–1607		
1607	English colony est. at Jamestown, Virginia	d. Cardinal Cesare Baronio; Héribert Rosweyde, *Fasti Sanctorum Quorum Vitae in Belgicis Bibliotecis Manuscriptae*	
1608	d. Kostiantyn Ostrozky; Protestant Union fd., led by Frederick V, elector palatine; French fd. Quebec; Mughal Emperor Jahangir grants English East India Company permission to trade at Surat; Amsterdam Exchange est.		d. John Dee

ART AND ARCHITECTURE	DRAMA AND MUSIC	LITERATURE AND SCHOLARSHIP	DATE
		Johannes Althusius, *Politica Methodice Digesta*	*1603*
	Orlando di Lasso, *Magnum Opus Musicum;* William Shakespeare, *Othello*		*1604*
	William Shakespeare, *King Lear* and *Macbeth;* Tomás Luis de Victoria, *Requiem*	Miguel de Cervantes, *Don Quixote;* Guy Coquille, *Coutumes du pays et duché de Nivernais*	*1605*
	Ben Jonson, *Volpone, or the Fox*	Bartholomäus Keckermann, *Systema Disciplinae Politicae;* d. Justus Lipsius	*1606*
Caravaggio, *Seven Works of Mercy* and *Beheading of St. John the Baptist;* d. Domenico Fontana	Claudio Monteverdi, *Orfeo*	Antoine Loisel, *Customary Institutes*	*1607*
d. Giambologna		Charles Loyseau, *Traité des seigneuries*	*1608*

DATE	POLITICS AND SOCIETY	RELIGION AND PHILOSOPHY	SCIENCE AND TECHNOLOGY
1609	Catholic League fd., led by Maximilian I of Bavaria; Twelve Years' Truce partitions Netherlands between Dutch Republic (north) and Spanish Netherlands (south); Spanish fd. Santa Fe; Bank of Amsterdam est.	Moriscos driven out of Valencia, Aragón, and Castile, 1609–1614; François de Sales, *Introduction to a Devout Life*	Johannes Kepler, *The New Astronomy;* Telescope built by Galileo Galilei
1610	Henry IV (France) assassinated; Marie de Médicis becomes regent; Louis XIII (France), 1610–1643; Frederick V, elector palatine, 1610–1623; Polish forces in Moscow after overthrow of Tsar Vasilii Shuiskii, 1610–1612	d. Matteo Ricci; Meletii Smotrytskyi, *Threnody;* Visitation of Holy Mary order of nuns fd. by Jeanne de Chantal and François de Sales	Galileo Galilei, *Siderius Nuncius;* Nicolas-Claude Fabri de Peiresc discovers Orion Nebula
1611	English Parliament dissolved; d. Henry Hudson (?); Gustavus II Adolphus (Sweden), 1611–1632	King James Bible; Oratory of Jesus and Mary fd. by Pierre de Bérulle	Johannes Kepler, *Dioptrics*
1612	d. Robert Cecil; Mathias (HRE), 1612–1619; Axel Oxenstierna, chancellor of Sweden, 1612–1654	d. Piotr Skarga	
1613	Michael Romanov, first Romanov tsar of Russia, 1613–1645	Gallicanism condemned by Pope Paul V; Péter Pázmány, *Guide to Divine Truth*	
1614	Danish East India Company fd.; Estates General called by Marie de Médicis; Hohenzollerns inherit Cleves on Rhine	Christianity outlawed in Japan; *Fama Fraternitatis* inspires Rosicrucian movement; Jews driven out of Frankfurt	John Napier discovers logarithms
1615		Kiev Academy fd.	Galileo faces Inquisition; d. Giambattista della Porta

ART AND ARCHITECTURE	DRAMA AND MUSIC	LITERATURE AND SCHOLARSHIP	DATE
d. Annibale Carracci	Lope de Vega, *El arte nuevo de hacer comedias en este tiempo*	Ambrosiana library opens in Milan; Étienne Pasquier, *Interpretation of the Institutes of Justinian;* Josephus Justus Scaliger, *Thesaurus Temporum;* William Shakespeare, *Sonnets;* d. Josephus Justus Scaliger	*1609*
d. Michelangelo Merisi da Caravaggio	Ben Jonson, *The Alchemist*	Henning Arnisaeus, *De Jure Majestatis;* Paolo Sarpi, *History of the Council of Trent,* 1610–1618	*1610*
Peter Paul Rubens, *Descent from the Cross*	William Shakespeare, *The Tempest;* d. Tomás Luis de Victoria	John Donne, *Anniversaries,* 1611–1612; University of Rome fd.	*1611*
El Greco, *Baptism of Christ*	d. Giovanni Gabrieli; John Webster, *The White Devil*	Francisco Suárez, *De Legibus*	*1612*
Guido Reni, *Aurora,* 1613–1614	Globe Theater burns; John Webster, *The Duchess of Malfi*	Luis de Góngora y Argote, *Soledades*	*1613*
d. El Greco; d. Robert Smythson, English architect	Ben Jonson, *Bartholomew Fayre*	d. Isaac Casaubon; Walter Raleigh, *History of the World;* University of Groningen fd.	*1614*
		d. Étienne Pasquier	*1615*

DATE	POLITICS AND SOCIETY	RELIGION AND PHILOSOPHY	SCIENCE AND TECHNOLOGY
1616	Dutch ship rounds southern tip of South America	Cosmology of Galileo Galilei condemned by papacy; Meletii Smotrytskyi translated Church Slavonic Homiliary Gospel into Ruthenian	Galileo forbidden to pursue scientific work
1617	Jan Pieterszoon Coen, governor general of Dutch East India Co., 1617–1629; Louis XIII assumes personal power, end of regency of Marie de Médicis; Mustafa I (Ottoman Empire), 1617–1618	d. Francisco Suárez	d. John Napier
1618	Defenestration of Prague; Thirty Years' War, 1618–1648; Osman II (Ottoman Empire), 1618–1622; Tr. of Deulino between Russia and Poland; Hohenzollern elector of Brandenburg inherits Duchy of Prussia; Walter Raleigh executed; Dutch West African Company fd.	Synod of Dort (Dordrecht), 1618–1619	Johannes Kepler, *Epitome Astronomiae Copernicae,* 1618–1621
1619	Ferdinand II (HRE), 1619–1637; Estates of Bohemia depose Ferdinand II and elect Frederick V, elector palatine; d. Alonso Pérez de Guzmán, duke of Medina Sidonia; Johan van Oldenbarneveldt executed; Batavia (Jakarta) fd.; first African slaves brought to Virginia; Germany's first merchant bank fd. in Hamburg	d. Antoine Arnauld, "the lawyer"; Patriarch Filaret (Russia), 1619–1633	Johannes Kepler, *Harmonice Mundi*
1620	Battle of the White Mountain; Plymouth Colony fd. in Massachusetts	Orthodox hierarchy restored in Ukraine	

ART AND ARCHITECTURE	DRAMA AND MUSIC	LITERATURE AND SCHOLARSHIP	DATE
	d. Francis Beaumont; d. William Shakespeare	George Chapman's translation of *Odyssey;* d. Miguel de Cervantes; d. Richard Hakluyt; University fd. at Altdorf, near Nuremberg	*1616*
	Gerbrand Bredero, *The Spanish Brabanter*	d. Louis Elzevier	*1617*
d. Antonio Carracci	Farnese Theater est. in Parma	Christoph Besold, *Politicorum Libri Duo*	*1618*
d. Ludovico Carracci; d. Nicholas Hilliard; Inigo Jones, Banqueting House at Whitehall, 1619–1622	d. Richard Burbage	Meletii Smotrytskyi, grammar of Old Church Slavonic	*1619*
Artemisia Gentileschi, *Judith and Holofernes;* Peter Paul Rubens, *Christ on the Cross (Le coup de lance);* d. John Thorpe, English architect		Francis Bacon, *Novum Organum*	*1620*

DATE	POLITICS AND SOCIETY	RELIGION AND PHILOSOPHY	SCIENCE AND TECHNOLOGY
1621	Protestant Union dissolved; Philip IV (Spain), 1621–1665; d. Albert of Habsburg, archduke of Austria; Dutch West India Company est.	d. Robert Bellarmine; Pope Gregory XV, 1621–1623; Piarist order fd.	d. Thomas Harriot
1622	Mustafa I (Ottoman Empire), 1622–1623	Congregation for the Propagation of the Faith fd. by papacy; d. St. François de Sales	
1623	Murad IV (Ottoman Empire) 1623–1640; Gaspar de Guzmán y Pimentel, Count of Olivares, becomes chief minister to Philip IV (1623–1643) after death of Don Baltasar de Zúñiga	Pope Urban VIII, 1623–1644; Council of the Chief Lithuanian Jewish Communities *(vaad)* est.	
1624	Cardinal Richelieu becomes chief minister to Louis XIII	d. Jacob Boehme; Lord Herbert of Cherbury, *De Veritate*	
1625	A. W. E. von Wallenstein appointed head of all HRE forces; Breda surrenders to Spanish troops; Charles I (England), 1625–1649; French colony est. on St. Kitts		
1626	"Union of Arms" among Spanish kingdoms proposed by Count of Olivares; Catalonia refuses; New Amsterdam fd.; d. Roger Davies		
1627	Bohemia receives constitutional charter from HRE; Huguenot rebellion in La Rochelle, led by Duke of Rohan	Last urban Protestant church in Poland destroyed at Lublin	

ART AND ARCHITECTURE	DRAMA AND MUSIC	LITERATURE AND SCHOLARSHIP	DATE
		Robert Burton, *Anatomy of Melancholy*; Étienne Pasquier, *Recherches de la France;* University of Strasbourg fd.	*1621*
Gian Lorenzo Bernini, *Apollo and Daphne,* 1622–1624; d. Francesco Carracci		Marie de Gournay, *Equality of Men and Women;* Kasiian Sakovych, *Verses on the Sorrowful Funeral of the Noble Knight Petro Sahaidachnyi*	*1622*
Gian Lorenzo Bernini, *David*		Francis Bacon, *The Advancement of Learning;* John Donne, *Devotions upon Emergent Occasions;* d. Paolo Sarpi	*1623*
Frans Hals, *Laughing Cavalier;* Nicolas Poussin, *Rape of the Sabine Women*		d. Juan de Mariana; Martin Opitz, *Buch von der deutschen Poeterey*	*1624*
d. Sofonisba Anguissola; d. Jan Brueghel the Elder; d. Paolo Carracci	d. John Fletcher; d. Orlando Gibbons; Joost van der Vondel, *Palamedes;* d. John Webster	Hugo Grotius, *De Jure Belli ac Pacis;* University of Mantua fd.; d. Giambattista Marino	*1625*
		d. Francis Bacon	*1626*
Rembrandt van Rijn, *The Money Changer*	Heinrich Schütz, *Dafne*	Francis Bacon, *New Atlantis;* d. Luis de Góngora y Argote; d. Francisco Suárez	*1627*

DATE	POLITICS AND SOCIETY	RELIGION AND PHILOSOPHY	SCIENCE AND TECHNOLOGY
1628	Siege of La Rochelle, Louis XIII and Cardinal Richelieu defeat Huguenots; War of the Mantuan Succession between France and Spain, after Gonzaga dynasty dies out, 1628–1631; Petition of Right; Sir Edward Coke, *Institutes of the Laws of England*, 1628–1644; Portuguese East India Company, 1628–1633		William Harvey, *On the Movement of the Heart and the Blood*
1629	Edict of Restitution returns secularized property to Catholic Church; Peace of Alais; Code Michau; Peace of Lübeck	d. Pierre de Bérulle	
1630	A. W. E. von Wallenstein forced to resign as commander of HRE troops; Gustavus II Adolphus lands army on Pomeranian coast; Day of Dupes in France; Plague in northern Italy kills quarter of population; Statuta Valachorum; Dutch West India Company occupies northeastern Brazil, 1630–1654		d. Johannes Kepler
1631	Siege and sack of Magdeburg; Battle of Breitenfeld	d. Edmond Richer, chief proponent of Gallicanism	
1632	Battle of Lützen; Gustavus II Adolphus killed; Johann Tserclaes Tilly fatally wounded; Christina (Sweden), 1632–1654; Władysław IV (Poland), 1632–1648; Smolensk War, 1632–1634; d. Michel de Marillac	Arminians and Catholics tolerated in Dutch Republic; Colony of Maryland est. in North America as haven for English Catholics	

ART AND ARCHITECTURE	DRAMA AND MUSIC	LITERATURE AND SCHOLARSHIP	DATE
Frans Hals, *The Merry Toper*		d. Fulke Greville	*1628*
Peter Paul Rubens, *Allegory of Peace and War*		Konstantinas Sirvydas, *Dictionarium Trium Linguarum;* d. Szymon Szymonowicz	*1629*
Inigo Jones designs Covent Garden			*1630*
		d. John Donne	*1631*
Jacques Callot, *Miseries of War;* Anthony Van Dyck arrives in London, appointed court painter to Charles I; Rembrandt van Rijn, *Anatomy Lesson of Dr. Tulp*		d. Giambattista Basile' Cardin Le Bret, *De la souveraineté du Roi;* Jacob Cats, *Mirror of Old and New Times;* University of Dorpat, Sweden, fd.	*1632*

DATE	POLITICS AND SOCIETY	RELIGION AND PHILOSOPHY	SCIENCE AND TECHNOLOGY
1633	d. Isabel Clara Eugenia	Cosmology of Galileo Galilei condemned by papacy; d. Patriarch Filaret; William Laud, archbishop of Canterbury, 1633–1645; Peter Mohyla becomes Orthodox metropolitan of Kiev; d. Meletii Smotrytskyi; Polish king recognizes legality of Orthodox and Uniate hierarchies in Poland	
1634	A. W. E. von Wallenstein assassinated on orders of HRE; Swedes defeated at Nördlingen; Form of Government adopted in Sweden; d. Sir Edward Coke		*Atlas Novus (Theatrum Orbis Terrarum)* published by Willem and Joan Blaeu, 1634–1662
1635	Peace of Prague; Catholic League dissolved; France declares war on Spain; French claim Martinique and Guadeloupe; Construction of Belgorod Line, 1635–1658		Académie Parisienne formed by Marin Mersenne
1636	HRE declares war on France; Anthony van Diemen, governor general of Dutch East India Co., 1636–1645		
1637	Ferdinand III (HRE), 1637–1657; Portuguese fort of Mina taken by Dutch; Ship-money case in England; Tulip bubble bursts	René Descartes, *Discours de la méthode;* d. Péter Pázmány	
1638	Scottish Revolution; Portuguese fort of Arguim taken by Dutch	Antitrinitarian center at Raków destroyed; d. Cornelius Otto Jansen	d. Willem Blaeu

ART AND ARCHITECTURE	DRAMA AND MUSIC	LITERATURE AND SCHOLARSHIP	DATE
Anthony Van Dyck, *Charles I*		Wojciech Dębołęcki, *Genealogy;* d. George Herbert; Herbert's *The Temple: Sacred Poems and Private Ejaculations* publ. posthumously	*1633*
		Giambattista Basile, *Lo cunto de li cunti;* d. George Chapman; University of Utrecht fd.	*1634*
d. Jacques Callot; Claude Lorrain (Gellée), *Liber Veritatis;* Peter Paul Rubens, *Venus and Adonis*	Pedro Calderón de La Barca, *El médico de su honora* and *La vida es sueño;* Tirso de Molina, *El burlador de Sevilla;* d. Lope de Vega	Académie Française fd.; University of Budapest fd.	*1635*
Rembrandt van Rijn, *Danaë*	d. Johannes Messenius	Harvard College fd.	*1636*
	Pierre Corneille, *Le Cid;* d. Ben Jonson	d. Nicolas-Claude Fabri de Peiresc; John Milton, *Lycidas*	*1637*
Francesco Borromini, S. Carlo alle Quattro Fontane, 1638–1641; d. Pieter Breughel the Younger			*1638*

DATE	POLITICS AND SOCIETY	RELIGION AND PHILOSOPHY	SCIENCE AND TECHNOLOGY
1639	Battle of the Downs; First Bishops' War; Japan expels Portuguese	Marie de l'Incarnation founds first Ursuline convent in North America; Pope Urban VIII condemns enslavement of natives in the Americas	
1640	Catalonian revolt against Castilian rule; Portuguese War of Restoration, 1640–1668; John IV (Portugal), 1640–1656; "Long Parliament" in England, 1640–1653; Second Bishops' War; Ibrahim I (Ottoman Empire), 1640–1648; Dutch navy defeats Spain near Recife, Brazil; Frederick William (Brandenburg-Prussia), known as "the Great Elector," 1640–1688	Cornelius Otto Jansen, *Augustinus;* Peter Mohyla composes *Orthodox Confession of the Faith*	John Wilkins, *Discourse concerning a New Planet*
1641	Massacre of Protestant settlers in Ulster; Star Chamber abolished by Long Parliament; Japanese expel all Europeans except Dutch, and confine Dutch to island near Nagasaki	d. St. Jeanne de Chantal; René Descartes, *Meditationes de Prima Philosophia*	
1642	English Civil War, 1642–1649; d. Marie de Médicis; d. Cardinal Richelieu; Cardinal Mazarin becomes chief minister; d. Henri Coeffier-Ruzé d'Effiat, marquis de Cinq-Mars		Sir Thomas Browne, *Religio Medici;* d. Galileo Galilei; Raimondo Montecuccoli, *Sulle battaglie*

ART AND ARCHITECTURE	DRAMA AND MUSIC	LITERATURE AND SCHOLARSHIP	DATE
Peter Paul Rubens, *Judgment of Paris*		d. Tommaso Campanella; d. Martin Opitz	*1639*
Construction of Hôtel Lambert begun by Louis Le Vau; Rembrandt van Rijn, *Self-Portrait* and *The Night Watch;* d. Peter Paul Rubens	Pedro Calderón de la Barca, *El alcalde de Zalamea*	Academy fd. at Åbo, Sweden; Imprimerie Royale fd.; d. Maciej Kazimierz Sarbiewski (Sarbievius)	*1640*
d. Anthony Van Dyck	Claudio Monteverd, *Il ritorno di Ulisse in patria*	Samuel Hartlib, *Macaria;* Anna Maria van Schurmann, *Dissertation on the Aptitude of the Female Understanding for Science and Letters*	*1641*
Château of Maisons built by François Mansart; d. Guido Reni	Claudio Monteverdi, *L'incoronazione di Poppea;* Theaters closed in England	Thomas Hobbes, *De Cive;* Pieter Hooft, *Dutch Histories*	*1642*

DATE	POLITICS AND SOCIETY	RELIGION AND PHILOSOPHY	SCIENCE AND TECHNOLOGY
1643	Louis XIV (France), 1643–1715; Anne of Austria serves as regent (officially until 1651), with Cardinal Mazarin; Solemn League and Covenant between English Parliamentarians and Scots; War between Denmark and Sweden, 1643–1645; Count of Olivares falls from power	Jesuits publish *Acta Sanctorum*, 1643–1794; Antoine Arnauld, *De la fréquente communion*	Barometer invented
1644	Queen Christina of Sweden begins personal rule	Pope Innocent X, 1644–1655; *A Directory for Publique Worship in the Three Kingdoms* issued in Britain	d. Jean Baptiste van Helmont; Marin Mersenne presents research on "Mersenne numbers"
1645	Battle of Jankov; Peace of Brömsebro ends Swedish war against Denmark; Leveller movement arises in England; d. Gaspar de Guzmán y Pimentel, Count of Olivares; Alexis I Mikhailovich (Russia), 1645–1676; War between Venice and Ottoman Empire, 1645–1670	d. William Laud (executed)	
1646	Russian landowners required to enter names of all peasants in government registers; peasants regarded as attached to estates	d. Peter Mohyla	
1647	Levellers issue *An Agreement of the People*; Revolt of Naples, begun under leadership of Masaniello, 1647–1648	Samuel Hartlib, *Considerations Tending to the Happy Accomplishment of England's Reformation in Church and State*	

ART AND ARCHITECTURE	DRAMA AND MUSIC	LITERATURE AND SCHOLARSHIP	DATE
	d. Claudio Monteverdi	Philip Hunton, *A Treatise of Monarchy;* John Milton, *Doctrine and Discipline of Divorce;* William Prynne, *The Soveraigne Power of Parliaments and Kingdomes*	*1643*
d. Bernardo Strozzi		John Milton, *Areopagitica* and *Of Education*	*1644*
Gian Lorenzo Bernini, *The Ecstasy of St. Teresa,* 1645–1652; Georges de La Tour, *St. Joseph and the Carpenter*		d. Hugo Grotius; d. Francisco de Quevedo	*1645*
	Andreas Gryphius, *Leo Armenius*	Richard Overton, *An Arrow against All Tyrants*	*1646*
	Folio edition of *Comedies and Tragedies Written by Francis Beaumont and John Fletcher, Gentlemen;* d. Pieter Hooft		*1647*

DATE	POLITICS AND SOCIETY	RELIGION AND PHILOSOPHY	SCIENCE AND TECHNOLOGY
1648	Peace of Westphalia ends Thirty Years' War; Bohdan Khmelnytsky's Cossack uprising, 1648–1654; Parlement of Paris insists on right to pronounce edicts unconstitutional; Wars of the Fronde, 1648–1653; Frederick III (Denmark and Norway), 1648–1670; Mehmed IV (Ottoman Empire), 1648–1687; John II Casimir (Poland), 1648–1668	d. Edward Herbert, Lord Cherbury; Shabbetai Tzevi proclaims himself messiah	d. Marin Mersenne; John Wilkins, *Mathematical Magic*
1649	King Charles I of England executed; Commonwealth declared in England; Cossack Hetmanate fd.; Russian Law Code *(Ulozhenie);* Time limitations on returning fugitive serfs abolished in Russia		
1650	d. William II, stadtholder of Holland, no new stadtholder elected for twenty-two years; hearsay evidence no longer admissible in English courts; sugar cane brought into West Indies; beginnings of plantation economy	d. René Descartes	
1651	English Royalists routed at Worcester; Charles II leaves England; Navigation Act; end of Anne of Austria's regency in France; Ferdinand, elector of Bavaria, 1651–1679; Bohdan Khmelnytsky formally accepts Ottoman suzerainty over Cossacks		

ART AND ARCHITECTURE	DRAMA AND MUSIC	LITERATURE AND SCHOLARSHIP	DATE
d. Antoine and Louis Le Nain; Nicolas Poussin, *Holy Family on the Steps;* Royal Academy of Painting and Sculpture fd. in France	d. Tirso de Molina		*1648*
Diego Velázquez, *Pope Innocent X;* d. Simon Vouet		d. Richard Crashaw; John Milton, *Tenure of Kings and Magistrates;* Madeleine de Scudéry, *Artamème, ou Le Grand Cyrus,* 1649–1653	*1649*
			1650
		Thomas Hobbes, *Leviathan;* John Milton, *Pro Populo Anglicano Defensio;* Miklós Zríny, *Siege of Sziget*	*1651*

DATE	POLITICS AND SOCIETY	RELIGION AND PHILOSOPHY	SCIENCE AND TECHNOLOGY
1652	First Anglo-Dutch War, 1652–1654; Castilians reconquer Catalonia; Dutch capture Cape of Good Hope from Portuguese, est. post at Cape Town; Polish Sejm broken up by *liberum veto* for the first time	Patriarch Nikon begins reforms of Russian liturgy and ritual, 1652–1666; Old Believer movement arises in response	
1653	Instrument of Government adopted; Oliver Cromwell becomes Lord Protector; Johan de Witt, grand pensionary of Holland, 1653–1672	d. Sir Robert Filmer; Jansenism condemned by Pope Innocent X	
1654	Queen Christina of Sweden converts to Catholicism and abdicates; Charles X Gustav (Sweden), 1654–1660; d. Axel Oxenstierna; Pereiaslav Agreement; Tr. of Westminster ends first Anglo-Dutch War	d. Johann Valentin Andreä	
1655	First Northern War, between Poland and Sweden, 1655–1660	Pope Alexander VII, 1655–1667; d. Pierre Gassendi; St. François de Sales canonized	
1656	Koprülü Mehmed Pasha, grand vizier under Ottoman sultan Mehmed IV, 1656–1661; Afonso VI (Portugal), 1656–1667; Plague in southern Italy, kills quarter of population (half of population of Naples), 1656–1657	d. Roberto de' Nobili, Jesuit missionary in India; Blaise Pascal, *Lettres provinciales,* 1656–1657	
1657	d. John Lilburne, leader of Levellers; Period of "Ruin" in Ukraine, 1657–1686		Accademia del Cimento, Florence; d. William Harvey

ART AND ARCHITECTURE	DRAMA AND MUSIC	LITERATURE AND SCHOLARSHIP	DATE
d. Inigo Jones; d. Jusepe de Ribera; d. Georges de La Tour			*1652*
Rembrandt van Rijn, *Aristotle Contemplating the Bust of Homer*	Pedro Calderón de la Barca, *La hija del aire*	Izaak Walton, *The Compleat Angler*	*1653*
d. Bernardo Cavallino; d. Artemisia Gentileschi; d. Massimo Stanzione	Joost van der Vondel, *Lucifer*	Madeleine de Scudéry, *Clélie*, 1654–1660	*1654*
		Thomas Stanley, *History of Philosophy*, 1655–1662; d. Savinien Cyrano de Bergerac	*1655*
Public square and colonnade of St. Peter's in Rome designed by Gian Lorenzo Bernini; Diego Velázquez, *The Maids of Honor*		James Harrington, *The Commonwealth of Oceana*	*1656*
	Andreas Gryphius, *Carolus Stuardus*		*1657*

DATE	POLITICS AND SOCIETY	RELIGION AND PHILOSOPHY	SCIENCE AND TECHNOLOGY
1658	d. Oliver Cromwell; Richard Cromwell becomes Lord Protector; Hadiach agreement; Leopold I (HRE), 1658–1705	Russian patriarch Nikon retires to monastery	Pierre Gassendi, *Syntagma Philosophicum*
1659	Richard Cromwell resigns; Peace of the Pyrenees ends war between France and Spain (began in 1635)	d. János Apáczai Csere	Christiaan Huygens discovers shape of rings of Saturn
1660	Duchy of Prussia becomes independent of Polish crown; Long Parliament dissolved; Charles II (England), 1660–1685; Charles XI (Sweden), 1660–1697	Henry More, *An Explanation of the Grand Mystery of Godliness;* d. St. Vincent de Paul	Royal Society of London for the Advancement of Natural Knowledge fd.
1661	d. Cardinal Mazarin; Louis XIV assumes power personally; Jean-Baptiste Colbert becomes senior Intendant of Finances; Köprülü Fazil Ahmed Pasha, grand vizier under Mehmed IV, 1661–1676; Cavalier Parliament convenes	d. Jacqueline-Marie-Angélique Arnauld	Marcello Malpighi uses microscope to discover capillaries, confirming William Harvey's findings
1662	Copper revolt in Moscow; Act of Settlement (England), decentralizes administration of Poor Law	Book of Common Prayer revised; d. Blaise Pascal	Boyle's law; John Graunt, *Natural and Political Observations . . . Made upon the Bills of Mortality;* Sir William Petty, *Treatise on Taxes and Contributions*
1663	Perpetual Diet at Regensburg begins; Turkish armies begin to move up the Danube	Société des Mission Étrangères (Society of Foreign Missions) fd. in Paris	Henry Oldenburg becomes secretary of Royal Society
1664	British take New Amsterdam, renamed New York; French East India and West India Companies fd.; Turks accept twenty-year truce		

ART AND ARCHITECTURE	DRAMA AND MUSIC	LITERATURE AND SCHOLARSHIP	DATE
Jan Vermeer, *Girl with a Water Jug*		Georg Stiernhielm, *Hercules*	*1658*
			1659
Art academy fd. in Seville by Bartolomé Esteban Murillo and Francisco de Herrera the Younger; d. Diego Velázquez	Molière, *Les précieuses ridicules*	d. Jacob Cats; Samuel Pepys keeps diary, 1660–1669	*1660*
Jan Vermeer, *View of Delft*; Reconstruction of Versailles, 1661–1710	Académie Royale de Danse fd. in France	French Royal Library reorganized under Jean-Baptiste Colbert	*1661*
Academy of Arts fd. at Nuremberg (first in Germany)	Jean-Baptiste Lully becomes music master to the French royal family	d. Samuel Hartlib; François de La Rochefoucauld, *Mémoires*	*1662*
Royal Academy of Painting and Sculpture (France) reorganized by Jean-Baptiste Colbert	Andreas Gryphius, *Peter Squentz*; Molière, *L'école des femmes*		*1663*
Rembrandt van Rijn, *Jewish Bride*; d. Francisco de Zurbarán	d. Andreas Gryphius; Molière, *Le Tartuffe*; Heinrich Schütz, *Christmas Oratorio*; Joost van der Vondel, *Adam in Exile*	d. Mikós Zrínyi	*1664*

DATE	POLITICS AND SOCIETY	RELIGION AND PHILOSOPHY	SCIENCE AND TECHNOLOGY
1665	Second Anglo-Dutch War, 1665–1667; Great Plague in London, 1665–1666; Charles II (Spain), 1665–1700		d. Pierre de Fermat; Robert Hooke, *Micrographia; Philosophical Transactions* fd. (journal of Royal Society in London)
1666	Great Fire in London	Council of Russian Orthodox Church, 1666–1667; Patriarch Nikon deposed; Old Belief declared schismatic; Avvakum Petrovich excommunicated and exiled	Marcello Malpighi is first to see red blood cells; Royal Academy of Sciences fd. in France
1667	Andrusovo Truce; Tr. of Breda ends second Anglo-Dutch War; War of Devolution, 1667–1668; London Rebuilding Act; Pedro II (Portugal), 1667–1706, deposes brother Afonso VI; Stepan Razin's uprising, 1667–1671	Pope Clement IX, 1667–1669	Paris Observatory est.
1668	Petro Doroshenko, Cossack hetman of Right-Bank Ukraine, allies with Ottomans; Spain recognizes independence of Portugal	Henry More, *Divine Dialogues*	
1669	Michael Wisniowiecki (Poland), 1669–1673		Marcello Malpighi investigates structure and development of the silkworm; Nicolaus Steno, *De Solido intra Solidum Naturaliter Contento Dissertationis Prodromus*

ART AND ARCHITECTURE	DRAMA AND MUSIC	LITERATURE AND SCHOLARSHIP	DATE
Murillo, *Rest on the Flight into Egypt;* d. Nicolas Poussin; Jan Vermeer, *Allegory of Painting*	Molière, *Don Juan*	*Journal des sçavans* fd.; François de La Rochefoucauld, *Maximes*	*1665*
French Academy at Rome fd. by Charles Le Brun; Prix de Rome est.; d. Frans Hals; d. François Mansart	Molière, *Le misanthrope*	John Dryden, *Annus Mirabilis*	*1666*
d. Francesco Borromini; First public display of works by artists of Royal Academy of Painting and Sculpture in Paris; Jan Vermeer, *Girl with a Red Hat*	Jean Racine, *Andromaque;* Joost van der Vondel, *Noah*	Margaret Cavendish, *The Life of the Thrice-Noble Prince William Cavendish;* John Milton, *Paradise Lost;* Samuel Pufendorf, *De Statu Imperii Germanici;* Thomas Sprat, *History of the Royal Society of London*	*1667*
Rembrandt van Rijn, *Self-Portrait,* 1668–1669		John Dryden, *Of Dramatick Poesie, an Essay;* John Dryden becomes English poet laureate, 1668–1688; Jean de La Fontaine, *Fables,* 1668, 1678–1679, 1694; *Giornale dei letterati* fd. (Rome); University of Lund, Sweden, fd.; François de La Mothe le Vayer, *Du peu de certitude qu'il y a dans l'histoire*	*1668*
d. Pierre le Muet, French architect; d. Rembrandt van Rijn; Jan Vermeer, *The Geographer;* Christopher Wren becomes royal surveyor of works	Royal Academy of Music fd. in France	H. J. C. von Grimmelshausen, *Simplicissimus;* d. Lars Wivallius	*1669*

DATE	POLITICS AND SOCIETY	RELIGION AND PHILOSOPHY	SCIENCE AND TECHNOLOGY
1670	Secret Tr. of Dover between Charles II (England) and Louis XIV (France), agreeing that England would aid French against Dutch; Hudson's Bay Company fd.; French Company for the Levant fd.; Christian V (Denmark and Norway), 1670–1699	Pope Clement X, 1670–1676; Blaise Pascal, *Pensées;* Baruch Spinoza, *Tractatus Theologico-Politicus*	Hôtel des Invalides fd. in Paris
1671	Stepan Razin executed	Henry More, *Enchiridion Metaphysicum*	Johan de Witt, *The Worth of Life Annuities Compared to Redemption Bonds*
1672	d. Johan de Witt and Cornelis de Witt, murdered by a Dutch mob; "Dutch War"; Louis XIV attacks Netherlands, occupies three provinces, 1672–1678; French receive Indian coastal town of Pondicherry; British Royal African Company est.; Charles XI (Sweden), 1672–1697	d. Marie de l'Incarnation; Avvakum Petrovich, autobiography, 1672–1673	Robert Hooke describes phenomenon of diffraction; Sir William Petty, *Essays in Political Arithmetic;* d. John Wilkins
1673	Dutch provinces vote to make stadtholderate hereditary in House of Orange; William III becomes stadtholder; Jacques Marquette and Louis Joliet explore interior of North America	Test Act	Christiaan Huygens, *Horologium Oscillatorum*
1674	John III Sobieski (Poland), 1674–1696		d. John Graunt; Antoni van Leeuwenhoek begins to observe bacteria and protozoa under a microscope

ART AND ARCHITECTURE	DRAMA AND MUSIC	LITERATURE AND SCHOLARSHIP	DATE
Christopher Wren, St. Paul's Cathedral, London, 1670–1711; d. Louis Le Vau	Molière, *Le bourgeois gentilhomme*		*1670*
French Royal Academy of Architecture fd.		John Milton, *Paradise Regained* and *Samson Agonistes;* Marie de Sévigné composes most of her letters to her daughter, Mme de Grignan, 1671–1678	*1671*
	Molière, *Les femmes savantes;* d. Heinrich Schütz	Clarendon Press fd. at Oxford; College of censors est. in France; d. François de La Mothe le Vayer; *Mercure galant* fd.; Samuel Pufendorf, *De Jure Naturae et Gentium;* d. Georg Stiernhielm	*1672*
d. Salvatore Rosa	d. Molière	d. Joan Blaeu; François Poulain de la Barre, *On the Equality of the Two Sexes;* d. Margaret Cavendish	*1673*
		Nicolas Boileau-Despréaux, *L'art poétique;* Samuel Columbus, *Odae Sueticae;* d. Robert Herrick; d. Lars Johannson (Lucidor); d. John Milton; Anthony Wood, *Historia et Antiquitates Universitatis Oxoniensis*	*1674*

DATE	POLITICS AND SOCIETY	RELIGION AND PHILOSOPHY	SCIENCE AND TECHNOLOGY
1675	Russian serf owners allowed to sell serfs independently of land; Heneage Finch, earl of Nottingham, lord chancellor of Britain, 1675–1682; Victor Amadeus II, ruler of Savoy, 1675–1730	d. Boiarynia Morozova; Philipp Jakob Spener, *Pia Desideria;* Baruch Spinoza, *Ethica* (completed)	Gottfried Wilhelm Leibniz discovers integral and differential calculus
1676	Fedor III (Russia), 1676–1682	Pope Innocent XI, 1676–1689; d. Shabbetai Tzevi	
1677	François-Michel Le Tellier, marquis de Louvois, secretary of state for war under Louis XIV, 1677–1691; Fort of São João Baptista de Ajudá est. in Dahomey by Portuguese, 1677–1680	d. Francis Glisson; d. Baruch Spinoza	d. Henry Oldenburg
1678	Tr. of Nijmegen; Sieur de La Salle explores interior of North America		Robert Hooke states inverse square law of planetary motion
1679	Affair of the Poisons; Exclusion Bill; Maximilian II, elector of Bavaria, 1679–1726; Plague in Vienna kills one-third of population; Louis Hennepin explores interior of North America	d. Anne Conway	

ART AND ARCHITECTURE	DRAMA AND MUSIC	LITERATURE AND SCHOLARSHIP	DATE
d. Jan Vermeer			*1675*
Dome of the Hôtel des Invalides constructed by Jules Hardouin-Mansart		d. H. J. C. von Grimmelshausen; d. Matthew Hale	*1676*
d. Mathieu Le Nain	Jean Racine, *Phèdre*	Nicolas Boileau-Despréaux and Jean Racine become historiographers to Louis XIV; d. James Harrington	*1677*
d. Jan Brueghel the Younger; d. Cosimo Fanzago		John Bunyan, *The Pilgrim's Progress;* Seigneur du Cange, *Glossarium ad Scriptores Mediae et Infimae Latinitatis;* Marie-Madeleine de La Fayette, *La princesse de Clèves;* d. Andrew Marvell; Elena Lucrezia Cornaro Piscopia receives doctorate of philosophy from Padua; Richard Simon, *Critical History of the Old Testament*	*1678*
d. Jan Steen	d. Joost van der Vondel	d. Thomas Hobbes	*1679*

DATE	POLITICS AND SOCIETY	RELIGION AND PHILOSOPHY	SCIENCE AND TECHNOLOGY
1680		Sir Robert Filmer, *Patriarcha;* d. Joseph Glanvill; d. Athanasius Kircher; Nicolas Malebranche, *Traité de la nature et de la grâce*	d. Jan Swammerdam
1681	Sir Josiah Child becomes governor general of English East India Company; Louis XIV's troops occupy Strasbourg	Colony of Pennsylvania est. in North America as haven for Quakers	Denis Papin invents steam-powered piston device
1682	Peter I, "the Great," tsar of Russia, 1682–1725, co-ruler with Ivan V, 1682–1696; Sofiia Alekseevna, regent, 1682–1689; Louis XIV moves royal court from Paris Louvre to Versailles; Bantam (Indonesia) becomes Dutch East India Company colony	Four Gallican Articles adopted; Louis XIV issues edict condemning belief and practice of magic; d. Avvakum Petrovich, burned at the stake	d. Sir Thomas Browne; Halley's Comet identified by Edmund Halley
1683	d. Jean-Baptiste Colbert; War of the Holy League against the Ottomans, 1683–1699; Turks defeated at Vienna after siege; d. Anthony Ashley Cooper, Earl of Shaftesbury	d. Benjamin Whichcote	First drawing of bacteria (by Antoni van Leeuwenhoek) appears in London Royal Society's *Philosophical Transactions*
1684	War between Venice and Ottoman Empire, 1684–1699; Delegation from Siam arrives in Paris	d. Louis-Isaac Le Maistre de Sacy	
1685	Edict of Nantes revoked by Louis XIV; Code Noir est. basic legal principles of French Caribbean slave society; James II (England), 1685–1688		

ART AND ARCHITECTURE	DRAMA AND MUSIC	LITERATURE AND SCHOLARSHIP	DATE
d. Gian Lorenzo Bernini; d. Sir Peter Lely	Comédie Française formed	d. Samuel Butler; Henry Neville, *Plato Redivivus;* d. Simeon Polotskii; d. François de La Rochefoucauld; Madeleine de Scudéry, *Conversations sur divers sujets*	*1680*
	d. Pedro Calderón de la Barca	John Dryden, *Absalom and Achitophel;* Jean Mabillon, *De Re Diplomatica,* est. science of diplomatics	*1681*
d. Claude Lorrain (Gellée); d. Bartolomé Esteban Murillo			*1682*
	d. Daniel Caspar von Lohenstein	d. Algernon Sidney (executed); d. Isaak Walton	*1683*
	d. Pierre Corneille	*Nouvelles de la république des lettres* est. by Pierre Bayle; d. Elena Lucrezia Cornaro Piscopia	*1684*
		Haquin Spegel, *God's Work and Rest*	*1685*

DATE	POLITICS AND SOCIETY	RELIGION AND PHILOSOPHY	SCIENCE AND TECHNOLOGY
1686	League of Augsburg formed; "Eternal peace" between Poland and Russia; Turks driven out of Hungary; d. Louis II de Bourbon, prince of Condé	Hermann August Francke opens Bible study, Leipzig; Gottfried Wilhelm Leibniz, *Discours de métaphysique*	John Ray, *Historia Plantarum,* 1686–1704
1687	Ivan Mazepa, Cossack hetman, 1687–1709; Suleiman II (Ottoman Empire), 1687–1691	d. Henry More	Isaac Newton, *Philosophiae Naturalis Principia Mathematica;* d. Sir William Petty
1688	Frederick III, elector of Brandenburg (after 1701 as Frederick I, king in Prussia), 1688–1713; "Glorious Revolution" in England; Turks driven out of Belgrade; War of the League of Augsburg, 1688–1697	Christian Thomasius, *Institutiones Jurisprudentiae Divinae* and *Introductio ad Philosophiam Aulicam;* d. Ralph Cudworth	

ART AND ARCHITECTURE	DRAMA AND MUSIC	LITERATURE AND SCHOLARSHIP	DATE
		Bibliothèque universelle et historique est. by Jean Leclerc, 1686–1693; Official censorship of printed materials est. in Sweden	*1686*
	d. Jean-Baptiste Lully	John Dryden, *The Hind and the Panther;* d. Constantijn Huygens; Slavonic-Greek-Latin Academy fd. in Russia by Patriarch Ioakim; d. Edmund Waller	*1687*
		Aphra Behn, *Oroonoko, or the History of the Royal Slave;* Jean de La Bruyère, *Les Caractères de Théophraste traduits du grec avec les caractères ou les moeurs de ce siècle;* d. John Bunyan; Seigneur du Cange, *Glossarium ad Scriptores Mediae et Infimae Graecitatis;* d. Seigneur du Cange; Christian Thomasius issues periodical *Entertaining and Serious, Rational and Unsophisticated Ideas on All Kinds of Agreeable and Useful Books and Subjects*	*1688*

DATE	POLITICS AND SOCIETY	RELIGION AND PHILOSOPHY	SCIENCE AND TECHNOLOGY
1689	William III and Mary II (England), 1689–1702; Bill of Rights, Toleration Act enacted by Parliament; Tr. of Nerchinsk between Russia and China; Peter the Great ousts regent Sofiia Alekseevna to assume personal rule of Russia; Koprülü Fazil Mustafa Pasha, grand vizier, 1689–1691; Ottoman armies under Fazil Mustafa recapture Belgrade and Niş; d. Christina, former queen of Sweden	Pope Alexander VIII, 1689–1691; Pierre-Daniel Huet, *Censura Philosophiae Cartesianae;* John Locke, *Letter on Toleration* and *Essay concerning Human Understanding*	d. Nicolaus Steno
1690	Battle of the Boyne; William III defeats Jacobite army led by former king James II	John Locke, *Two Treatises on Government*	Christiaan Huygens, *Treatise on Light*
1691	Ahmed II (Ottoman Empire), 1691–1695; Irish Jacobites defeated at siege of Limerick	d. Richard Baxter; Balthasar Bekker, *World Bewitched;* d. George Fox, founder of Quakers; d. Lo Wen-tsao (Gregorio López), first Chinese bishop; Pope Innocent XII, 1691–1700	d. Robert Boyle
1692	Massacre of MacDonalds by Campbells at Glencoe, Scotland		
1693	Famine in France, 1693–1694		
1694	Bank of England est.; British national debt created; Frederick Augustus I, elector of Saxony, 1694–1733, King Augustus II of Poland from 1697	d. Antoine Arnauld	d. Marcello Malpighi

ART AND ARCHITECTURE	DRAMA AND MUSIC	LITERATURE AND SCHOLARSHIP	DATE
	Henry Purcell, *Dido and Aeneas;* d. Aphra Behn		*1689*
d. Charles Le Brun		Sir William Temple, *Essay upon Ancient and Modern Learning*	*1690*
		Richard Bentley, *Epistola ad Joannem Millium*	*1691*
	Henry Purcell, *The Fairy Queen* (for *A Midsummer Night's Dream*)	French Royal Library opens to the public	*1692*
		d. Marie-Madeleine de La Fayette; John Locke, *Some Thoughts concerning Education;* d. Jan Andrzej Morsztyn	*1693*
Dreifaltigkeitskirche (Salzburg) by Johann Bernhard Fischer von Erlach, 1694–1702		d. Samuel Pufendorf; William Wotton, *Reflections upon Ancient and Modern Learning*	*1694*

DATE	POLITICS AND SOCIETY	RELIGION AND PHILOSOPHY	SCIENCE AND TECHNOLOGY
1695	Capitation (poll tax) introduced in France; Mustafa II (Ottoman Empire), 1695–1703	Official Swedish hymnbook by Joseph Swedberg	d. Christiaan Huygens
1696	d. Ivan V, co-tsar with Peter the Great; fall of Ottoman fortress of Azov to Russia		
1697	Peter the Great visits western Europe, 1697–1698; Peace of Ryswick ends War of the League of Augsburg; Augustus II, "the Strong" (elector of Saxony), king of Poland, 1697–1704, 1709–1733; Charles XII (Sweden), 1697–1718; Battle of Zenta; Prince Eugene of Savoy drives Turks out of Hungary	François Fénelon, *Explication des maximes des saints sur la vie intérieure;* d. Miguel de Molinos	
1698	Omanis conquer Mombasa and Kilwa from Portuguese		
1699	Peace of Karlowitz; Frederick IV (Denmark and Norway), 1699–1730; Louisiana est. by French		
1700	d. John Cecil; Great Northern War between Russia and Sweden, 1700–1721; Battle of Narva, forces of Charles XII defeat Peter the Great; Philip V (Spain), 1700–1746	d. Patriarch Adrian of Russia; patriarchate left vacant; Pope Clement XI, 1700–1721	Gregorian calendar accepted in Protestant German states; remaining United Provinces accept it 1700–1701

ART AND ARCHITECTURE	DRAMA AND MUSIC	LITERATURE AND SCHOLARSHIP	DATE
Winter palace of Prince Eugene of Savoy built by Johann Bernhard Fischer von Erlach, 1695–1711	d. Henry Purcell	d. Jean de La Fontaine; England and Wales end pre-publication censorship of written materials when Licensing Act lapses; Wespazjan Kochowski, *Polish Psalmody*	*1695*
Kollegienkirche (Salzburg) by Johann Bernhard Fischer von Erlach, 1696–1707		d. Jean de La Bruyère; d. Marie de Sévigné	*1696*
		Mary Astell, *A Serious Proposal to Ladies;* Marie-Catherine d'Aulnoy, *Contes de fées;* Pierre Bayle, *Dictionnaire historique et critique;* Gunno (Eurelius) Dahlstierna, *Hymn to the King;* Charles Perrault, *Contes de ma mère l'oye*	*1697*
		Richard Bentley, *Dissertation upon the Epistles of Phalaris;* Algernon Sidney, *Discourses concerning Government;* Society for the Reformation of Manners fd. in London	*1698*
	d. Jean Racine	François Fénelon, *Les aventures de Télémaque*	*1699*
d. André Le Nôtre, French garden designer	Raoul-Auger Feuillet, *Choréographie*	d. John Dryden; Kit-Kat Club fd. in London by Jacob Tonson	*1700*

DATE	POLITICS AND SOCIETY	RELIGION AND PHILOSOPHY	SCIENCE AND TECHNOLOGY
1701	Act of Settlement stipulates that no Catholic may be king of England; Capitation (poll tax) permanently reintroduced in France; Frederick I (Prussia), 1701–1713 (Frederick III of Brandenburg becomes king in Prussia); War of the Spanish Succession, 1701–1714		Thomas Newcomen builds steam engine, widely employed to pump water from coal pits
1702	Anne (England), 1702–1714; Camisard Revolt, 1702–1705		
1703	Ahmed III (Ottoman Empire), 1703–1730; "Tulip Period" of Ottoman Empire; Rebellion in Hungary led by Prince Ferenc II Rákóczi, 1703–1711; Buda and Pest made royal free cities within HRE		d. Robert Hooke
1704	Battle of Blenheim; Stanisław I Leszczyński, king of Poland, 1704–1709, while Augustus II the Strong deposed	d. John Locke	Isaac Newton, *Optics*
1705	Joseph I (HRE), 1705–1711		Maria Sybilla Merian, *Metamorphosis Insectorum Surinamensium;* d. John Ray
1706	John V (Portugal), 1706–1750; Battle of Turin; Austria replaces Spain as ruler of Lombardy		d. Walter Charleton
1707	United Kingdom of Great Britain est. by union of England and Scotland; Mantua incorporated into Austrian Empire after last Gonzaga duke exiled		

ART AND ARCHITECTURE	DRAMA AND MUSIC	LITERATURE AND SCHOLARSHIP	DATE
		d. Madeleine de Scudéry	*1701*
Petersburg fortress built			*1702*
		d. Charles Perrault; d. Samuel Pepys; First Russian newspaper, *Vedomosti*	*1703*
Blenheim Palace built, 1704–1725; French Royal Academy of Painting and Sculpture exhibitions moved to Grande Galerie of Louvre; Rachel Ruysch, *Flowers*		Antoine Galland, *Les mille et une nuits,* 1704–1717 (French adaptation of the *Thousand and One Nights*); d. Jacques-Bénigne Bossuet	*1704*
d. Luca Giordano			*1705*
	Jean-Philippe Rameau, first book of harpsichord music; d. Johann Pachelbel	d. Pierre Bayle	*1706*
	d. Dieterich Buxtehude; Isaac Watts, *Hymns and Spiritual Songs*		*1707*

DATE	POLITICS AND SOCIETY	RELIGION AND PHILOSOPHY	SCIENCE AND TECHNOLOGY
1708	Hetman Ivan Mazepa and Cossacks join Swedes against Russians; United English East India Company formed by merger of Britain's two rival East India Companies		Herman Boerhaave, *Institutiones Medicae*
1709	Battle of Poltava; d. Ivan Mazepa; Augustus II the Strong regains throne of Poland, 1709–1733		Herman Boerhaave, *Aphorismi de Cognoscendis et Curandi Morbis*
1710	*Dixième* tax on personal income introduced (in effect until 1721); Robert Harley, chancellor of the Exchequer, 1710–1714; Plague in Stockholm kills one-third of population; Turkey enters Great Northern War against Russia, 1710–1711	First Hasidic community fd. by Dov Baer; George Berkeley, *Treatise concerning the Principles of Human Knowledge*; Gottfried Wilhelm Leibniz, *Théodicée*	
1711	Charles VI (HRE), 1711–1740; Peter the Great replaces Boyar Duma with Senate; South Sea Company fd.; Peace of Szatmár ends Hungarian rebellion		
1712	Plague outbreak in Hamburg, 1712–1713; Toleration Act (Great Britain)		

ART AND ARCHITECTURE	DRAMA AND MUSIC	LITERATURE AND SCHOLARSHIP	DATE
		Bernard de Montfaucon, guide to Greek paleography	*1708*
Johann Friedrich Böttger discovers technique for making porcelain		Jacques-Bénigne Bossuet, *Politique tirée des propres paroles de l'écriture sainte;* First Copyright Act in England; *The Tatler* published by Richard Steele, 1709–1711	*1709*
Porcelain manufacturing est. at Meissen			*1710*
d. Hans Georg Asam; Schönbrunn Palace in Vienna completed	Rev. Arthur Bedford, *Great Abuse of Musick*	d. Nicolas Boileau-Despréaux; Alexander Pope, *Essay on Criticism; The Spectator* published by Richard Steele and Joseph Addison, 1711–1712	*1711*
		d. Jan Luyken; Alexander Pope, *The Rape of the Lock,* 1712–1714	*1712*

DATE	POLITICS AND SOCIETY	RELIGION AND PHILOSOPHY	SCIENCE AND TECHNOLOGY
1713	Russo-Ottoman War ends; Pragmatic Sanction est. Habsburg Monarchy's indivisibility and right of female succession; Frederick William I (Prussia), 1713–1740; Treaties of Utrecht (1713) and Rastadt (1714) conclude War of Spanish Succession; by Tr. of Rastadt, Austria annexes Spanish Netherlands, Milan, Naples; Britain receives *asiento* (privilege of providing Spanish America with African slaves); French lose Acadia to British	George Berkeley, *Three Dialogues between Hylas and Philonous; Unigenitus Dei Filius* (Pope Clement XI) denounces Jansenism	
1714	George I (England), 1714–1727, first Hanoverian monarch; Isabel Farnese marries Philip V to become queen of Spain; War between Venice and Ottoman Empire, 1714–1715	Gottfried Wilhelm Leibniz, *Monadologia*	
1715	Louis XV (France), 1715–1774, under regency of Duke of Orléans; Jacobite rebellion in Scotland	d. Archbishop François Salignac de la Mothe-Fénelon; Nicolas Malebranche	Emanuel Swedenborg begins publishing *Daedalus Hyperboreus,* first Swedish scientific journal
1716	John Law est. central bank in France	d. Gottfried Wilhelm Leibniz	

ART AND ARCHITECTURE	DRAMA AND MUSIC	LITERATURE AND SCHOLARSHIP	DATE
		Matthew Hale, *History of the Common Law; Hamburger Vernunftler* fd. (first German weekly); Royal Spanish Academy fd.; d. Thomas Sprat	*1713*
Great Palace built at Peterhof, 1714–1728		Bernard de Mandeville, *Fable of the Bees;* Madame du Tencin opens her salon	*1714*
d. François Girardon			*1715*
Weltenburg Monastery (Asam family), 1716–1735			*1716*

DATE	POLITICS AND SOCIETY	RELIGION AND PHILOSOPHY	SCIENCE AND TECHNOLOGY
1717	Mughal Emperor Farrukhsiyar grants firman to English East India Company, regularizing status, privileges, and trading terms throughout Mughal empire; Casa de Contratación est. in Cádiz to administer Spanish monopoly on trade with Americas; French *Compagnie d'Occident* (Mississippi Company) fd. for trade with Louisiana		d. Maria Sybilla Merian; Smallpox inoculation introduced into England from Turkey by Lady Mary Wortley Montagu
1718	New Orleans est.; Tr. of Passarowitz; Peter the Great has his son Alexis put to death; Ulrika Eleonora (Sweden), 1718–1720; War of the Quadruple Alliance, 1718–1720		
1719		d. Pasquier Quesnel	
1720	Sicily reunited with Naples; South Sea Bubble and Mississippi Bubble break; Frederick I (Sweden), 1720–1751	Feofan Prokopovich draws up *Spiritual Regulation*	
1721	Tr. of Nystad ends Great Northern War; Robert Walpole, British prime minister, 1721–1742; d. Louis Dominique Cartouche, Parisian highway robber	d. Bishop Pierre-Daniel Huet; Russian patriarchate abolished by Peter the Great; replaced by Holy Synod; Pope Innocent XIII, 1721–1724	

ART AND ARCHITECTURE	DRAMA AND MUSIC	LITERATURE AND SCHOLARSHIP	DATE
Antoine Watteau, *Pilgrimage to Cythera*	George Frideric Handel, *Water Music*	First Masonic Grand Lodge est. in London	*1717*
			1718
Balthasar Neumann begins work on Residenz in Würzburg		d. Joseph Addison; Daniel Defoe, *Robinson Crusoe*	*1719*
			1720
Johann Bernhard Fischer von Erlach, *Entwurf einer historischen Architektur;* Esterházy palace built; Antoine Watteau, *The Signboard of Gersaint;* d. Antoine Watteau		Charles-Louis de Secondat de Montesquieu, *Lettres persanes*	*1721*

DATE	POLITICS AND SOCIETY	RELIGION AND PHILOSOPHY	SCIENCE AND TECHNOLOGY
1722	d. John Churchill, duke of Marlborough; office of Cossack hetman abolished; Peter the Great changes law of succession in Russia; tsar may name successor; introduces Table of Ranks; Jacob Roggeveen discovers Easter Island	Last known execution for witchcraft in Europe takes place in Scotland; d. John Toland	
1723	Louis-Henri, prince of Condé, becomes chief minister to Louis XV, 1723–1726	Bishop Pierre Daniel Huet, *Traité de la faiblesse de l'esprit humaine*	d. Antoni van Leeuwenhoek
1724	d. Robert Harley; Paris stock exchange est.	Pope Benedict XIII, 1724–1730	Herman Boerhaave, *Elementa Chemiae*
1725	Catherine I (Russia), 1725–1727		St. Petersburg Academy of Sciences fd.
1726	Charles Albert, elector of Bavaria, 1726–1745, HRE from 1742 (as Charles VII); Cardinal Fleury, chief minister to Louis XV, 1726–1743; José Patiño y Morales becomes leading minister in Spain, 1726–1736		
1727	Autonomy of Cossack hetmanate restored; Peter II (Russia), 1727–1730; George II (England), 1727–1760	Brotherly Agreement of Herrnhut outlines communal ideal of Moravian settlements; d. Hermann August Francke	d. Isaac Newton
1728	Vitus Bering sets out from Russia in search of northeast passage; Spanish Royal Compañia Guipuzcoana fd.	d. Christian Thomasius	

ART AND ARCHITECTURE	DRAMA AND MUSIC	LITERATURE AND SCHOLARSHIP	DATE
	Johann Sebastian Bach, *The Well-Tempered Clavier* 1722–1744; *Critica Musica* published by Johann Mattheson in Hamburg, 1722–1725; Jean-Philippe Rameau, *Traité de l'harmonie*	Daniel Defoe, *Moll Flanders; Spectateur français* fd.	*1722*
d. Johann Bernhard Fischer von Erlach; d. Godfrey Kneller; d. Christopher Wren	Johann Sebastian Bach, *St. John Passion*	Ludovico Antonio Muratori, *Rerum Italiacarum Scriptores*	*1723*
		d. Glueckel of Hameln; Professorships of modern history est. at Oxford and Cambridge	*1724*
Duc d'Antin mounts 10-day painting exhibition in Grand Salon of Louvre	Prague opera house opens	Antoine Manasses de Pas, *Mémoires sur la guerre;* Benito Feijoo, *Teatro crítico de errores communes;* Giovanni Battista Vico, *Scientia nuova*	*1725*
		Imperial Library in Vienna opens to the public; Jonathan Swift, *Gulliver's Travels*	*1726*
	d. Alessandro Scarlatti		*1727*
		Alexander Pope, *Dunciad;* Ephraim Chambers, *Cyclopaedia*	*1728*

DATE	POLITICS AND SOCIETY	RELIGION AND PHILOSOPHY	SCIENCE AND TECHNOLOGY
1729		John Nepomuk canonized	
1730	Anna (Russia), 1730–1740; Christian VI (Denmark and Norway), 1730–1746; Patrona Halil uprising in Istanbul; Ahmed III deposed and replaced by Mahmud I, 1730–1754	d. Jakob Amman; Pope Clement XII, 1730–1740	
1731	Parma incorporated into HRE after Farnese dynasty dies out; Swedish East India Co. est.		
1732			
1733	War of the Polish Succession, 1733–1738; Frederick Augustus II, elector of Saxony and King Augustus III of Poland, 1733–1763		
1734	Kingdom of the Two Sicilies formed; Charles III rules 1734–1759; New law code adopted in Sweden		Emanuel Swedenborg, *Opera Philosophica et Mineralia*

ART AND ARCHITECTURE	DRAMA AND MUSIC	LITERATURE AND SCHOLARSHIP	DATE
Church of St. Johann Nepomuk, Munich, 1729–1745	Johann Sebastian Bach, *St. Matthew Passion* and *Brandenburg Concertos*	d. Richard Steele	*1729*
			1730
		d. Mary Astell; Corps of Cadets fd. in Russia; d. Daniel Defoe; *Gentleman's Magazine* (London); *De Hollandsche Spectator*, 1731–1735; Abbé Prévost, *Manon Lescaut;* Royal Dublin Society fd.	*1731*
William Hogarth begins *Rake's Progress*	Covent Garden opera house opens in London	Laura Bassi teaches at University of Bologna, 1732–1778; Maurice de Saxe, *Reveries on the Art of War; The Swedish Argus* published by Olof von Dalin, 1732–1733	*1732*
		d. Bernard de Mandeville; Alexander Pope, *Essay on Man*	*1733*
		Pietro Giannone, *Il triregno, ossia del regno del cielo, della terro, e del papa;* George Sale translates Koran into English; Charles-Louis de Secondat de Montesquieu, *Considérations sur les causes de la grandeur des Romains et de leur décadence;* Voltaire, *Lettres philosophiques*	*1734*

DATE	POLITICS AND SOCIETY	RELIGION AND PHILOSOPHY	SCIENCE AND TECHNOLOGY
1735	Ottoman war on Russia and Austria, 1735–1739; Preliminary peace of Vienna between France and Austria		Carl Linnaeus, *Systema Naturae*
1736	d. Eugene of Savoy; d. José Patiño y Morales	d. Feofan Prokopovich; Nikolaus Ludwig von Zinzendorf banished from Saxony	
1737	Tuscany incorporated into HRE after Medici dynasty dies out; Philip Yorke, earl of Hardwicke, lord chancellor of Britain, 1737–1756		
1738	Tr. of Vienna ends War of the Polish Succession	Freemasonry condemned by Pope Clement XII (bull *In Eminenti*); John Wesley draws up Rules of the Band Societies	d. Herman Boerhaave
1739	Peace of Belgrade; d. Dick Turpin, English bandit (executed); War of Jenkins' Ear between England and Spain, 1739–1748	David Hume, *A Treatise of Human Nature*	
1740	Maria Theresa, archduchess of Austria and queen of Hungary, 1740–1780; Frederick II the Great (Prussia), 1740–1786; War of the Austrian Succession, 1740–1748; Frederick the Great invades Silesia; Ivan VI (Russia), 1740–1741, under regency of Johann Ernst Biron and then Anna Leopoldovna	"Great Awakening" in American British colonies; Pope Benedict XIV, 1740–1758	Berlin Academy of Sciences fd. by Frederick the Great; Emanuel Swedenborg, *Oeconomia Regni Animalis*
1741	Elizabeth (Russia), 1741–1762		

ART AND ARCHITECTURE	DRAMA AND MUSIC	LITERATURE AND SCHOLARSHIP	DATE
Engravers' Copyright Act (Britain)		Vasilii Trediakovskii, *New and Concise Method for the Composition of Russian Verses*	*1735*
Ursulinenkirche at Straubing (Asam family), 1736–1739			*1736*
Salons initiated in France by Philibert Orry		University of Göttingen fd.	*1737*
Excavations begin at Herculaneum	Johann Sebastian Bach, *Mass in B Minor*		*1738*
d. Cosmas Damian Asam		Louis de Rouvroy Saint-Simon begins his *Memoirs*	*1739*
		Olof von Dalin, *The Tale of the Horse;* Samuel Richardson, *Pamela*	*1740*
	George Frideric Handel, *Messiah;* d. Antorio Vivaldi		*1741*

DATE	POLITICS AND SOCIETY	RELIGION AND PHILOSOPHY	SCIENCE AND TECHNOLOGY
1742	Charles VII (HRE), 1742–1745 (Elector Charles Albert of Bavaria); Charles Theodore, elector palatine, 1742–1799; Joseph-François Dupleix appointed governor-general of all French establishments in India, 1742–1754		
1743	Marqués de la Ensenada becomes prime minister to Spanish king, 1743–1754; d. Cardinal Fleury		Jean-Baptiste Bourguignon d'Anville, *Atlas général*
1744			
1745	Tr. of Dresden; Austria concedes Silesia to Prussia; Francis I (HRE), 1745–1765; Maximilian III, elector of Bavaria, 1745–1777; Jeanne-Antoinette Poisson presented at court and made marquise de Pompadour by Louis XV; Jacobite rebellion: Charles Edward Stuart ("Bonnie Prince Charlie") invades Scotland; d. Robert Walpole		
1746	Ferdinand VI (Spain), 1746–1759; Frederick V (Denmark and Norway), 1746–1766	d. Francis Hutcheson	
1747			Julien Offroy de La Mettrie, *L'homme machine;* School est. for roadbuilding engineers in France

ART AND ARCHITECTURE	DRAMA AND MUSIC	LITERATURE AND SCHOLARSHIP	DATE
		d. Richard Bentley; Henry Fielding, *Joseph Andrews*	*1742*
Balthasar Neumann, church of Vierzehnheiligen at Lichtenfels, 1743–1753		Benjamin Franklin fd. American Philosophical Society	*1743*
Medici art collection given to Florence	d. Aleksandr Sumarokov	d. Antiokh Dmitrievich Kantemir; d. Alexander Pope; d. Giovanni Battista Vico	*1744*
Giovanni Battista Piranesi, *Prisons;* Sans Souci Palace built in Potsdam, 1745–1747		d. Jonathan Swift	*1745*
		Étienne Bonnot de Condillac, *Essai sur l'origine des connaissances humaines*	*1746*
d. Francesco Solimena		Załuski Library opens in Warsaw	*1747*

DATE	POLITICS AND SOCIETY	RELIGION AND PHILOSOPHY	SCIENCE AND TECHNOLOGY
1748	Peace of Aix-la-Chapelle ends War of Austrian Succession	David Hume, *Enquiry concerning Human Understanding*	Leonhard Euler, *Introductio in Analysin Infinitorum*
1749	Bohemia's constitutional charter revoked; Ferdinand VI replaces Castile's historic kingdoms with 24 provinces; Ohio Company est. by British		
1750	José I (Portugal), 1750–1777	Beginnings of Hasidism, fd. by Ba'al Shem Tov (Israel ben Eliezer)	
1751	Adolph Frederick (Sweden), 1751–1771	Freemasonry condemned by Pope Benedict XIV	Ferdinando Galiani, *Della moneta;* d. Julien Offroy de La Mettrie
1752			England accepts Gregorian calendar
1753	Wenzel Anton von Kaunitz, Austrian state chancellor, 1753–1792	d. George Berkeley	Carl Linnaeus, *Species Plantarum*

ART AND ARCHITECTURE	DRAMA AND MUSIC	LITERATURE AND SCHOLARSHIP	DATE
Excavations begin at Pompeii	Jean-Philippe Rameau, *Pygmalion;* d. Isaac Watts	John Cleland, *Fanny Hill, or Memoirs of a Woman of Pleasure;* Marie-Thérèse de Geoffrin opens her salon; d. Pietro Giannone; Montesquieu, *Esprit des lois;* Samuel Richardson, *Clarissa;* Tobias Smollett, *Adventures of Roderick Random*	*1748*
	George Frideric Handel, *Music for the Royal Fireworks*	d. Mátyás Bél; Henry Fielding, *Tom Jones;* Friedrich Gottlieb Klopstock, *The Messiah,* 1749–1770; d. Claudine Aléxandrine du Tencin	*1749*
d. Egid Quirin Asam; Thomas Gainsborough, *Mr. and Mrs. Andrews;* Giovanni Battista Tiepolo, *The Banquet of Antony and Cleopatra;* d. Rachel Ruysch	d. Johann Sebastian Bach	d. Ludovico Muratori; Jean-Jacques Rousseau, *Discours sur les sciences et les arts*	*1750*
Palace at Tsarskoe Selo remodeled, Amber Room built		Denis Diderot and Jean Le Rond d'Alembert, *Encyclopédie,* 1751–1768; École Militaire fd.	*1751*
Johann Joachim Winckelmann, *Gedanken über die Nachahmung der griechischen Werke in der Malerei und Bildhauerkunst*	*Querelle des Bouffons* in Paris, 1752–1754		*1752*
British Museum est.; d. Marc-Antoine Laugier, *Essai sur l'architecture* (Essay on architecture); d. Balthasar Neumann, German rococo architect		British Library est.; Friedrich Melchior von Grimm begins publishing biweekly newsletter on French culture; Academy of Letters fd. in Sweden; "Thought Builders" literary society est. by Swedish poets	*1753*

DATE	POLITICS AND SOCIETY	RELIGION AND PHILOSOPHY	SCIENCE AND TECHNOLOGY
1754	Albany Plan of Union proposed; Joseph-François Dupleix, French governor general in India, recalled to Paris; Osman III (Ottoman Empire), 1754–1757	d. Christian Wolff	Dorothea Erxleben becomes first woman medical doctor in Germany
1755	Robert Clive's first governorship of Bengal, 1755–1760; Earthquake in Lisbon; d. Robert Mandrin, French bandit		
1756	Seven Years' War, 1756–1763; Suraja Dowla expels British from Calcutta		
1757	Mustafa III (Ottoman Empire), 1757–1774; Battle of Plassey		Albrecht von Haller, *Elementa Physiologiae Corporis Humani*, 1757–1766
1758	British take Ft. Duquesne and Louisbourg; Magdalen Hospital fd. in London	Pope Clement XIII, 1758–1769; Emanuel Swedenborg, *On Heaven and Its Wonders and on Hell*	François Quesnay, *Tableau économique*

ART AND ARCHITECTURE	DRAMA AND MUSIC	LITERATURE AND SCHOLARSHIP	DATE
Winter Palace built in St. Petersburg, 1754–1762		Étienne Bonnot de Condillac, *Traité des sensations;* Benedykt Chmielowski, *New Athens, or the Academy Full of Every Sort of Science;* d. Henry Fielding; Antonio Genovese holds first university chair in Mechanical Arts and Commerce (political economy) at Naples; Royal Society for the Encouragement of Arts, Manufactures, and Commerce fd. in Britain; Lancelot Turpin de Crissé, *Essai sur l'art de la guerre*	*1754*
		Samuel Johnson, *Dictionary of the English Language;* d. Montesquieu; Moscow University fd.; Jean-Jacques Rousseau, *Discours sur l'origine et le fondements de l'inégalité parmi les hommes;* d. Louis de Rouvroy Saint-Simon	*1755*
Manufacture Royale de Porcelaine moved from Vincennes to Sèvres; Giovanni Battista Piranesi, *Le antichità romane;* Venetian Academy of Painting and Sculpture fd.		Voltaire, *Essai sur les moeurs*	*1756*
Academy of Arts est. in Russia; d. Rosalba Carriera	d. Domenico Scarlatti	Edmund Burke, *A Philosophical Enquiry into the Origins of Our Ideas of the Sublime and Beautiful*	*1757*
		Mikhail Lomonosov, *Preface on the Use of Church Books in Russian Literature*	*1758*

DATE	POLITICS AND SOCIETY	RELIGION AND PHILOSOPHY	SCIENCE AND TECHNOLOGY
1759	Charles III (Spain), 1759–1788; Battle of Plains of Abraham; Quebec falls to British	Adam Smith, *Theory of Moral Sentiments*	
1760	George III (England), 1760–1820	d. Ba'al Shem Tov (Israel ben Eliezer); d. Nikolaus Ludwig von Zinzendorf	
1761	William Pitt the Elder, prime minister of Britain, 1756–1761		
1762	Peter III (Russia) frees Russian nobility from compulsory service; overthrown by Catherine II the Great (Russia), 1762–1796	Trial of Jean Calas	
1763	Famine in Naples and Sicily, 1763–1764; Peace of Paris between Britain and France; Peace of Hubertusburg between Austria and Prussia	Justinus Febronius, *De Statu Ecclesiae et Legitima Potestae Romani Pontificis*	
1764	Robert Clive's second governorship of Bengal, 1764–1767; Cossack Hetmanate abolished; d. Madame de Pompadour (Jeanne-Antoinette Poisson); Stamp Act; Stanisław II Augustus Poniatowski (Poland), 1764–1795; John Wilkes expelled from House of Commons	Monastic lands confiscated by state in Russia	

ART AND ARCHITECTURE	DRAMA AND MUSIC	LITERATURE AND SCHOLARSHIP	DATE
British Museum opens to the public	d. George Frideric Handel	Claude-Adrien Helvétius, *De l'esprit; Journal des dames* fd.; Voltaire, *Candide*	*1759*
First public exhibition of art at Society of Artists of Great Britain, London		Jean-Jacques Rousseau, *Julie, ou la nouvelle Héloïse*	*1760*
Jean-Baptiste Greuze, *The Village Betrothal*	Carlo Goldoni, *L'amore delle tre melarance*	d. Kelemen Mikes; d. Samuel Richardson	*1761*
Anton Raphael Mengs, *Reflections on Beauty and Taste in Painting*	Christoph Willibald von Gluck, *Orfeo ed Euridice*	Denis Diderot, *Le neveu de Rameau;* d. Lady Mary Wortley Montagu; Jean-Jacques Rousseau, *Du contrat social* and *Émile;* John Wilkes publishes *The North Britons*	*1762*
		Louis René de Caradeuc de la Chalotais, *Essai d'éducation nationale;* d. Olof von Dalin; Samuel Johnson meets James Boswell; d. Hedvig Charlotta Nordenflycht; d. Abbé Prévost; Voltaire, *Traité sur la tolérance*	*1763*
Esterházy palace expanded, 1764–1784; d. William Hogarth; Johann Joachim Winckelmann, *Geschichte der Kunst des Altertums*	d. Jean-Philippe Rameau	Cesare Beccaria, *Dei delitti e dei pene;* Samuel Johnson forms literary club; Mme. Necker and Julie Lespinasse open salons in Paris; Voltaire, *Dictionnaire philosophique*	*1764*

DATE	POLITICS AND SOCIETY	RELIGION AND PHILOSOPHY	SCIENCE AND TECHNOLOGY
1765	Joseph II (HRE), 1765–1790, co-ruler with Maria Theresa of Austrian Habsburg dominions, 1765–1780, sole ruler, 1780–1790; Leopold, grand duke of Tuscany, 1765–1790		Free Economic Society est. in Russia
1766	Louis-Antoine de Bougainville sails around the world, 1766–1769; d. Isabel Farnese, former queen of Spain; Count of Floridablanca becomes chief minister of Spain; Frederick VI (Denmark and Norway), 1766–1808; Stamp Act repealed	Peć patriarchate abolished by Ottomans, replaced by metropolitanate of Sremski Karlovci in Croatia	
1767	Legislative Commission convened by Catherine the Great; Maria Theresa limits peasant labor services; First Mysore War, 1767–1769; Samuel Wallis and Louis Antoine de Bougainville reach Tahiti (separately)	Moses Mendelssohn, *Phädon, oder über die Unsterblichkeit der Seele*	
1768	Confederation of Bar, 1768–1772; James Cook makes first voyage to Pacific; Corsica purchased by France from Genoa; Russo-Turkish War, 1768–1774		François Quesnay, *Physiocratie*
1769	Daniel Boone explores Kentucky; French East India Company dissolved due to bankruptcy; José Ortega reaches San Francisco Bay; John Wilkes fd. Supporters of the Bill of Rights	Pope Clement XIV, 1769–1774; d. Gerrit Tersteegen	Sir Richard Arkwright invents water frame; James Watt invents steam engine

ART AND ARCHITECTURE	DRAMA AND MUSIC	LITERATURE AND SCHOLARSHIP	DATE
Jean-Baptiste Greuze, *The Father's Curse* and *The Prodigal Son*		d. Elżbieta Drużbacka; d. Mikhail Vasilievich Lomonosov; Patriotic Society of Hamburg fd.; Horace Walpole, *The Castle of Otranto*	*1765*
Jean-Honoré Fragonard, *The Swing*		Sir William Blackstone, *Commentaries on the Laws of England*, 1765–1769; Péter Bod, *Hungarian Athenaeum*; Adam Ferguson, *Essay on the History of Civil Society*; Christoph Martin Wieland, *Geschichte des Agathon*	*1766*
	Christoph Willibald von Gluck, *Alceste*; Gotthold Ephraim Lessing, *Minna von Barnhelm*; *Hamburgische Dramaturgie*, 1767–1768; d. Georg Philipp Telemann	Laurence Sterne, *Tristram Shandy*	*1767*
d. Giovanni Antonio Canaletto; Royal Academy fd. in Britain; d. Johann Joachim Winckelmann		Society for the Translation of Foreign Books est. in Russia; d. Laurence Sterne; d. Vasilii Kirillovich Trediakovskii	*1768*
		Catherine the Great est. literary journal *Bits of This and That*; Nikolai Novikov est. journal *The Drone*	*1769*

DATE	POLITICS AND SOCIETY	RELIGION AND PHILOSOPHY	SCIENCE AND TECHNOLOGY
1770	Marie Antoinette married to the future Louis XVI; Lord North, British prime minister, 1770–1782; Johan Friedrich von Struensee, chief minister of Denmark, 1770–1772		
1771	Gustav III (Sweden), 1771–1792; René-Nicolas-Charles-Augustin de Maupeou, chancellor of France, 1771–1774; Parlements stripped of power to block reform, magistrates exiled; Stock exchange est. at Vienna	d. Johann Heinrich Gottlob von Justi; Emanuel Swedenborg, *True Christian Religion*	
1772	First Partition of Poland; James Cook's second voyage (1772–1775) proves that southern continent does not exist	Hasidim excommunicated by Elijah ben Solomon, Gaon of Vilna; d. Emanuel Swedenborg	Jacques de Guibert, *Essai général de tactique;* Joseph Priestley, *Experiments and Observations on Different Kinds of Air*
1773	Boston Tea Party; London Stock Exchange est.; Pugachev's rebellion, 1773–1775; Regulating Act for India; Warren Hastings, governor general of British East India Company possessions in India, 1773–1785	Jesuit order suppressed by Pope Clement XIV	

ART AND ARCHITECTURE	DRAMA AND MUSIC	LITERATURE AND SCHOLARSHIP	DATE
d. François Boucher; Thomas Gainsborough, *The Blue Boy;* d. Giovanni Battista Tiepolo		Baron d'Holbach, *Système de la nature;* Nikolai Novikov est. *The Tatler*	*1770*
Anton Raphael Mengs, *Parnassus* (fresco at Villa Albani, Rome)		*Encyclopaedia Britannica,* first ed.; d. Claude-Adrien Helvétius; Mikhail Matveevich Kheraskov, *Rossiiada,* 1771–1779; Friedrich Gottlieb Klopstock, *Odes;* Tobias Smollett, *Expedition of Humphry Clinker;* d. Tobias Smollett	*1771*
	Gotthold Ephraim Lessing, *Emilia Galotti*	Commission for National Education set up in Poland; Nikolai Novikov est. *The Painter*	*1772*
d. Luigi Vanvitelli		Christoph Martin Wieland est. literary periodical *Der teutsche Merkur;* Commission of National Education est. in Poland	*1773*

DATE	POLITICS AND SOCIETY	RELIGION AND PHILOSOPHY	SCIENCE AND TECHNOLOGY
1774	Abdülhamid I (Ottoman Empire), 1774–1789; Tr. of Kuchuk Kainarji; Grigorii Potemkin becomes lover of Catherine the Great; Louis XVI (France) restores powers and privileges of parlements, 1774–1793; d. François Quesnay; Anne-Robert-Jacques Turgot, finance minister in France, 1774–1776; Britain revokes charter of Massachusetts; d. Robert Clive		
1775	First Maratha War, 1775–1782; Provincial Reform divides Russia into *guberniia*s; Tariff union of Bohemia, Moravia, and Austrian duchies; War of American Independence, 1775–1783	Pope Pius VI, 1775–1799	Johann Kaspar Lavater, *Essays on Physiognomy*, 1775–1778; Franz Anton Mesmer presents theory of "animal magnetism"
1776	James Cook sails on third voyage; North American colonies declare independence from Britain; Turgot introduces Six Edicts, incl. abolition of guilds and *corvée*; Turgot dismissed after failure; Viceroyalty of Río de la Plata carved out of Spain's Viceroyalty of Peru	d. David Hume	
1777	Charles Theodore (elector palatine since 1742), elector of Bavaria, 1777–1799; Bavarian and Palatine Wittelsbachs reunited; Maria I (Portugal), 1777–1816; Jacques Necker, French director of finances, dismissed; replaced by Charles-Alexandre de Calonne; Treaties of San Ildefonso and El Pardo		d. Albrecht von Haller

ART AND ARCHITECTURE	DRAMA AND MUSIC	LITERATURE AND SCHOLARSHIP	DATE
	Christoph Willibald von Gluck, *Iphigénie en Aulide*	Johann Wolfgang von Goethe, *Die Leiden des jungen Werthers;* Maria Theresa mandates grammar schools in every parish of Austrian empire	*1774*
	Pierre-Augustin Caron de Beaumarchais, *Le barbier de Séville*	Ignacy Krasicki, *Mouse-ead*	*1775*
		Edward Gibbon, *Decline and Fall of the Roman Empire*, 1776–1788; Ignacy Krasicki, *Adventures of Nicholas Experience;* Thomas Paine, *Common Sense;* Adam Smith, *Enquiry into the Nature and Causes of the Wealth of Nations*	*1776*
Giovanni Battista Piranesi, prints of Greek temples at Paestum	Richard Brinsley Sheridan, *The School for Scandal*	d. Marie-Thérèse Geoffrin; Nikolai Novikov publishes journal *Morning Light*, 1777–1780	*1777*

DATE	POLITICS AND SOCIETY	RELIGION AND PHILOSOPHY	SCIENCE AND TECHNOLOGY
1778	France allies with American colonists and declares war on Great Britain; James Cook reaches Hawaii; War of the Bavarian Succession, 1778–1779		d. Carl Linnaeus
1779	d. James Cook	David Hume, *Dialogues concerning Natural Religion*	
1780	d. William Blackstone; d. Maria Theresa; Dutch enter American War of Independence on side of Americans, 1780–1784; Second Mysore War, 1780–1784; Movement of county associations est. in England to promote change in electoral system; Wall constructed around Paris to aid in tax collection; Judicial torture abolished in France		
1781	Joseph II abolishes serfdom in Bohemia; Anonymous pamphlet *To the People of the Netherlands* (by Joan Derk van der Capellen tot de Pol) appears; d. Jacques Turgot	Edict of Toleration issued by HRE Joseph II; Immanuel Kant, *Kritik der reinen Vernunft*	
1782	William Pitt the Younger, prime minister in Britain, 1782–1806		

ART AND ARCHITECTURE	DRAMA AND MUSIC	LITERATURE AND SCHOLARSHIP	DATE
d. Giovanni Battista Piranesi		Comte de Buffon, *Les époques de la nature;* Fanny Burney, *Evelina;* Ignacy Krasicki, *Monachomachia;* Nikolai Novikov takes out 10-year lease on Moscow University Press; d. Jean-Jacques Rousseau; d. Voltaire	*1778*
Antonio Canova, *Daedalus and Icarus;* d. Jean Baptiste Siméon Chardin; d. Anton Raphael Mengs	Christoph Willibald von Gluck, *Iphigénie en Tauride;* Gotthold Ephraim Lessing, *Nathan der Weise*		*1779*
Medici Museum at Uffizi modernized by Luigi Lanzi		Gaetano Filangieri, *Science of Legislation,* 1780–1785; Christoph Martin Wieland, *Oberon*	*1780*
	Johann Christoph Friedrich von Schiller, *Die Räuber*	Christian Wilhelm von Dohm, *Über die bürgerliche Verbesserung der Juden;* d. Gotthold Ephraim Lessing; Jean-Jacques Rousseau, *Confessions;* Christoph Martin Wieland, *Geschichte des Abderiten*	*1781*
Étienne-Maurice Falconet, *Bronze Horseman* (St. Petersburg); Elisabeth Vigée-Lebrun, *Self-Portrait in a Straw Hat*	Vittorio Alfieri, *Saul;* d. Farinelli (Carlo Broschi); d. Pietro Metastasio	Aagje Deken and Betje Wolff, *The History of Miss Sara Burgerhart;* Choderlos de Laclos, *Les liaisons dangereuses*	*1782*

DATE	POLITICS AND SOCIETY	RELIGION AND PHILOSOPHY	SCIENCE AND TECHNOLOGY
1783	Tr. of Paris ends American War of Independence; Russia annexes Crimea	Moses Mendelssohn, *Jerusalem oder über die religiöse Macht und Judentum*	d. Leonhard Euler; First hot-air balloon, launched by Joseph and Étienne Montgolfier
1784	India office created in British ministry		Royal commission investigates Franz Anton Mesmer
1785	Affair of the Diamond Necklace; Charter to the Nobility, Charter to the Towns (Russia); Joseph II abolishes personal subordination of peasants to lords in entire Austrian empire; Dutch stadtholder flees The Hague	Immanuel Kant, *Grundlegung zur Metaphysik der Sitten;* William Paley, *The Principles of Moral and Political Philosophy*	Coulomb force described by Charles-Augustin de Coulomb
1786	Frederick William II (Prussia), 1786–1797; Patriot Revolution in Dutch Republic, 1786–1787	Illuminati suppressed in Bavaria; d. Moses Mendelssohn	
1787	Orangist regime restored in Dutch Republic; Assembly of Notables convened in attempt to reform French fiscal system; *Junta de estado* (cabinet) est. in Spain; Constitution of the United States; Russo-Turkish War, 1787–1792		Antoine Lavoisier, *Méthode de nomenclature chimique*

ART AND ARCHITECTURE	DRAMA AND MUSIC	LITERATURE AND SCHOLARSHIP	DATE
	d. Antonio Soler	d. Jean Le Rond d'Alembert; Catherine the Great allows private ownership and operation of printing presses; Russian Academy of Letters fd.; Princess Catherine Dashkova becomes first president; First Hebrew press in Lithuania est. at Shklov	*1783*
Jacques-Louis David, *Oath of the Horatii*	Pierre-Augustin Caron de Beaumarchais, *Le mariage de Figaro*	d. Denis Diderot; Johann Gottfried Herder, *Ideen zur Philosophie der Geschichte der Menschheit*, 1784–1791; d. Samuel Johnson; Immanuel Kant, "Was ist Aufklärung?"	*1784*
Claude-Nicolas Ledoux builds toll houses around Paris, 1785–1789	Franz Joseph Haydn, *Paris Symphonies*, 1785–1786	*Cabinet des fées*, 1785–1789; d. Gustav Philip Creutz	*1785*
	Wolfgang Amadeus Mozart, *Le nozze di Figaro*	Swedish Academy est.	*1786*
	d. Christoph Willibald von Gluck; Wolfgang Amadeus Mozart, *Don Giovanni* and *Eine Kleine Nachtmusik*	Dorothea Schlözer becomes first woman to receive Ph.D. from a German university (Göttingen); Thomas Paine returns to Europe	*1787*

DATE	POLITICS AND SOCIETY	RELIGION AND PHILOSOPHY	SCIENCE AND TECHNOLOGY
1788	Austro-Ottoman War, 1788–1791; Charles IV (Spain), 1788–1808; Four-Year Sejm in Poland, 1788–1792	Immanuel Kant, *Kritik der praktischen Vernunft*; Thomas Reid, *Essays on the Active Powers of Man*	Joseph-Louis Lagrange, *Analytic Mechanics*
1789	French Revolution begins: Estates-General convened, Bastille stormed, privileges abolished, Declaration of Rights of Man and Citizen issued; Alexander Mackenzie crosses Rocky Mts.; Mutiny on the *Bounty;* Selim III (Ottoman Empire), 1789–1807; United Belgian States proclaimed in revolt against HRE Joseph II	Jeremy Bentham, *Introduction to the Principles of Morals and Legislation;* church property confiscated in France	Antoine Lavoisier, *Traité élémentaire de chimie*
1790	Leopold II (HRE), 1790–1792; Third Mysore War, 1790–1792	Civil Constitution of the Clergy (France); Immanuel Kant, *Kritik der Urteilskraft*	d. William Cullen
1791	Louis XVI arrested at Varennes; Declaration of Pillnitz; New constitution of France est. constitutional monarchy; 3 May Constitution in Poland; Bill of Rights added to U.S. Constitution; d. Grigorii Potemkin; Slave revolt in French colony of St. Domingue	French Republic annexes Avignon and Comtat Venaissin from Papal States; d. John Wesley	Luigi Galvani, *De Viribus Electricitatis in Motu Musculari Commentarius*

ART AND ARCHITECTURE	DRAMA AND MUSIC	LITERATURE AND SCHOLARSHIP	DATE
d. Thomas Gainsborough	d. Carl Philipp Emanuel Bach; Wolfgang Amadeus Mozart, *Symphony No. 40 in G Minor* and *Symphony No. 41 in C Major (Jupiter)*	d. Georges Louis Leclerc, comte de Buffon; First (incomplete) version of Louis de Rouvroy Saint-Simon's *Mémoires* published	*1788*
		d. Baron d'Holbach; Abbé Siéyès, *Qu'est-ce que le tiers état?*	*1789*
	Wolfgang Amadeus Mozart, *Così fan tutte*	Carl Michael Bellman, *Fredman's Letters;* Edmund Burke, *Reflections on the Revolution in France;* Hugo Kołłątaj, *Political Rights of the Polish Nation;* Aleksandr Radishchev, *Journey from St. Petersburg to Moscow;* d. Adam Smith	*1790*
	Wolfgang Amadeus Mozart, *Die Zauberflöte;* d. Wolfgang Amadeus Mozart	Carl Michael Bellman, *Fredman's Songs;* James Boswell, *Life of Samuel Johnson;* Olympe de Gouges, *Rights of Woman;* Thomas Paine, *Rights of Man;* Marquis de Sade, *Justine*	*1791*

DATE	POLITICS AND SOCIETY	RELIGION AND PHILOSOPHY	SCIENCE AND TECHNOLOGY
1792	Confederation of Targowica in Poland; Kaunitz resigns as Austrian state chancellor; Francis II, last HRE, 1792–1806; Gustav IV Adolf (Sweden), 1792–1809; Tr. of Jassy ends Russo-Ottoman War; France declares war on Austria and Revolutionary wars begin; French Republic proclaimed; George Vancouver explores northwest coast of North America		
1793	Terror in France, 1793–1794; Louis XVI and Marie Antoinette guillotined; France declares war on British and Dutch; Second Partition of Poland; Slaves of St. Domingue emancipated; George Lord Macartney's mission to China	Immanuel Kant, *Die Religion innerhalb der Grenzen der blossen Vernunft*	
1794	Kościuszko insurrection; Odessa est.; Prussian Civil Code; Slavery declared illegal in all French territories		d. Antoine Lavoisier
1795	Third Partition of Poland; Poland disappears from the map; France annexes Belgium; Directory in France, 1795–1799		
1796	Paul I (Russia), 1796–1801; Princess Catherine Dashkova forced to leave St. Petersburg	d. Thomas Reid	

ART AND ARCHITECTURE	DRAMA AND MUSIC	LITERATURE AND SCHOLARSHIP	DATE
Bank of England building (Sir John Soane), 1792–1793; d. Joshua Reynolds		Nikolai Karamzin, *Letters of a Russian Traveler, 1789–1790*; Nikolai Novikov arrested; Mary Wollstonecraft, *Vindication of the Rights of Woman*	*1792*
Jacques-Louis David, *À Marat*	d. Carlo Goldoni	Marie-Jean Caritat, marquis de Condorcet, *Esquisse d'un tableau historique des progrès de l'esprit humaine;* d. William Robertson	*1793*
Franz Anton Maulbertsch, frescoes at Strahov, Prague		d. Cesare Beccaria; d. Marie-Jean Caritat de Condorcet; d. Camille Desmoulins; d. Edward Gibbon	*1794*
d. Josiah Wedgwood		d. James Boswell; d. Carl Michael Bellman; Johann Wolfgang von Goethe, *Wilhelm Meisters Lehrjahre;* d. Johan Henrik Kellgren	*1795*
d. Franz Anton Maulbertsch		d. Robert Burns	*1796*

DATE	POLITICS AND SOCIETY	RELIGION AND PHILOSOPHY	SCIENCE AND TECHNOLOGY
1797	Tr. of Campo Formio; 1797; Frederick William III (Prussia), 1797–1840; Paul I of Russia decrees succession in male line; d. John Wilkes		
1798	Batavian Republic est.; Irish uprising		
1799	Napoleon Bonaparte's coup; Consulate, 1799–1804; Fourth Mysore War		
1800			
1801	Act of Union est. United Kingdom of Great Britain and Ireland; Paul I (Russia) assassinated in favor of his son Alexander I (r. 1801–1825)		
1802			
1803			
1804			
1805			
1806	Francis II abdicates, HRE abolished		

ART AND ARCHITECTURE	DRAMA AND MUSIC	LITERATURE AND SCHOLARSHIP	DATE
Francisco de Goya, *Caprichos,* 1797–1798	Franz Joseph Haydn, *Die Schöpfung*	d. Edmund Burke; d. Horace Walpole	*1797*
		d. Giovanni Giacomo Casanova	*1798*
		Novalis, *Geistliche Lieder*	*1799*
	Johann Christoph Friedrich von Schiller, *Wallenstein* trilogy, 1800–1801	Novalis, *Hymnen an die Nacht*	*1800*
			1801
			1802
			1803
	Johann Christoph Friedrich von Schiller, *Wilhelm Tell*		*1804*
			1805
			1806

EUROPE
1450 TO 1789
ENCYCLOPEDIA OF THE EARLY MODERN WORLD

ABSOLUTISM. Early modern European princes liked to promulgate the myth that they held "absolute power." For modern observers, both words create confusion. In contemporary English, the word *absolute* defines a dichotomy of this or that: a king would either have "absolute power," or he would not. Early modern Europeans lived in a world of accepted ambiguity: they believed the sovereign prince's power to be both "absolute" and "limited." Nothing could be further in spirit from the sovereign prince's "absolute power" than the modern idea that "absolute" means "unlimited."

ABSOLUTISM, DESPOTISM, TYRANNY

The term *absolutism,* first used in a political sense in various European languages between 1796 (French) and 1830 (English), became popular through the work of late-nineteenth-century historians proselytizing for modern republicanism. The American John Motley's use of it in *The Rise of the Dutch Republic* (1856) offers a perfect illustration: he quotes Cardinal Granville, chief minister of Philip II of Spain (ruled 1556–1598), who wrote to the king that "I shall never be able to fulfill the obligations of slave which I owe to your Majesty." Motley concludes: "[Granville] was a strict absolutist. His deference to arbitrary power was profound and slavish."

Motley's treatment of Philip and his father (Emperor Charles V, ruled 1519–1556) as "despots" enables us to trace the roots of the confusion among several pejorative terms. He juxtaposes *absolutism* and *despotism* in a way that has lasted into the present: modern specialists of the eighteenth-century monarchies of east central Europe speak of *enlightened absolutism,* but outside that field the older term *enlightened despotism* is used instead. Dictionaries follow Motley's lead: a *despot* is a "ruler with absolute power" or a "tyrant." Making despot, tyrant, and absolute monarch synonymous concepts, however, completely misrepresents the political order of early modern Europe.

The myth of absolutism contains a kernel of truth. The prince's prerogatives enabled him to act in an arbitrary, even extralegal manner, but within certain well-defined limits. Few questioned the exclusive right of kings to the regalian powers conceptually inherited from the Roman Empire: to coin money, to act as the supreme judge in the kingdom, to declare war and make peace. Two other such powers, making law and taxing, had an ambiguous status. Medieval Europeans believed that God had made the law; the king merely "discovered" it. They also insisted on the necessity of consent for state taxation, another sharp variance with Imperial Rome. Even in the military sphere, the constant outbreak of civil disturbances illustrates the unwillingness of early modern elites to accept the state's monopoly of organized violence.

Most European states emphasized the contrast between a monarchy, a legitimate form of "commonwealth" (or "republic") in which one man ruled in the interest of all, and its illegitimate mirror image, tyranny, in which one man ruled in his own interest. In the vocabulary of early modern Europe, the state chancery defined a king as a legitimate ruler simply by calling him a "monarch." Political theorists adopted the classic republican comparison of the state to a ship: the citizens were its owners, the king merely its captain. The king/captain had "absolute power" in moments of crisis (battle or storm), but the citizens/owners regained full control once the crisis passed. In the perpetual crisis of the late sixteenth century, some European kings sought to take advantage of the tempests by making "absolute power" permanent. States traditionally had a mixed form of commonwealth, combining legitimate rule by one person (monarchy), by a few people (aristocracy), and by many (timocracy). (The categories came from Aristotle, for whom—as for early modern Europeans—the word *democracy* did not mean legitimate rule by the many, as it does today, but anarchy.) In the late sixteenth century, however, princes sought, in the name of order, to create an unfettered monarchy.

AUTHORITY, POWER, RULERSHIP

The nineteenth-century substitution of "absolutism" for "absolute power" also blurred the distinction between power and authority. From the Middle Ages onward, Europeans spoke of the king's "absolute power" (Latin, *potestas*) but rarely of his "absolute authority" (Latin, *auctoritas*—the supreme source of legitimacy in the polity). For them, God alone had absolute authority: *auctoritas* rested with their sovereign prince only when he acted in accordance with divine law, in a just government. In the late seventeenth century, however, monarchs and their apologists, such as Bishop Jacques-Bénigne Bossuet (1627–1704) in France and Robert Filmer (c. 1588–1653) in England, tried to claim "absolute authority," based on the king's divine right. Far from being a coherent theory of government, the divine right of kings was an incoherent, desperate attempt to salvage royal authority. Works such as Bossuet's *Politique tirée des propres paroles de l'écriture sainte* (1709; Politics drawn from the Holy Scriptures) were riddled with inconsistencies and anachronisms, a fact gleefully seized upon by their opponents.

Yet the central premise of a Bossuet or a Filmer—the connection of God and ruler—permeated even the humblest official publications. The 1768 catechism sent by the Prussian government to local schools summed it up succinctly:

Q: From whence comes the power held by the ruler?
A: This power comes from God. . . .

Q: What does it mean to resist authority?
A: To resist authority is to rebel against the divine order.

The problem for eighteenth-century monarchies was that however much they might push such ideas with ordinary people, elites had rejected them. This division reflected larger cultural currents: while eighteenth-century elites bought secular books, peasants who became literate invariably bought religious ones. The religious cosmology of rural dwellers propagated the sacred element of monarchy at the same moment that the increasingly secular cosmology of urban elites rejected it.

Three different elements of rulership—*potestas* ('power'), *auctoritas* ('supreme legitimizing authority'), and *imperio* ('rulership')—overlapped in early modern political theory. *Auctoritas* could not be divided, because it emanated solely from God. Power and rulership could be divided: tens of thousands of European nobles had their own courts, which tried the cases of tens of millions of peasants. To Europeans, as the Prussian catechism says, the just monarch mediated divine authority, providing legitimacy to the power and rulership carried out by many. The Reformation destroyed this neat arrangement, because a Protestant subject naturally did not accept the idea that a Catholic king mediated God's will, so monarchs had to find new tools to reforge the connection. The 1768 catechism, created for Catholic students living in a Protestant state ruled by a deist king, is evidence more of that earlier failure than of "absolutism."

The French legal philosopher Jean Bodin (1530–1596) created the new political synthesis that undergirded the new monarchies by redefining sovereignty in *Les six livres de la République* (1576; The six books of the commonwealth). Bodin made sovereign power into the perpetual, inalienable, and indivisible supreme lawmaking authority in the state: "The first mark of the sovereign prince is the power to give law to all in general and to each in particular." Subsequent European political theorists, like Samuel Pufendorf (1632–1694) in Germany and Thomas Hobbes (1588–1679) and John Locke (1632–1704) in England, took up Bodin's definition of sovereignty.

Monarchies adopted the idea that sovereignty rested with the lawmaking prince, giving us one measure of the anachronism of Bossuet's claim that the king was chiefly a judge, discovering laws that were "sacred and inviolable." Bossuet's master, Louis XIV (ruled 1643–1715), stripped his chief law courts, the parlements, of their right to the title "sovereign court," precisely because he rejected the idea that his sovereign power to make law could be shared with anyone. A century later Louis XV, speaking to the Parlement of Paris (1766), spelled out the monarchy's underlying premise: "The sovereign power resides in my person only . . . my courts derive . . . their authority from me alone . . . to me alone belongs the legislative power." His subjects disagreed: the Parlement of Paris, in the name of the "nation," sent remonstrances to Louis XV insisting that his arrest of a high royal official, on grounds of "a law of the state," meant that "all orders of birth and distinction, all bodies [corporations], all ranks, all dignities must henceforth fear the imperious force of absolute power." This exchange pointed out the obvious contradiction between defense of the interests of the nation and of the privileges of the few.

LIMITATIONS ON "ABSOLUTE" RULERS
Bodin's original definition of sovereignty had limited the "absolute" sovereign prince in two ways. First, "all the Princes of the Earth are subject to the laws of God and of nature, and to many human laws common to all people." Second, the sovereign had "absolute" power only in the realm of public law; the citizens had control of private law. Theory and practice struggled most at those points, such as taxation and religion, where private and public law intersected. Bodin believed the king had no right to taxation without citizens' consent; Bossuet urged the king to act justly but gave the subjects no right of consent. All European states struggled with the question of whether or not religious choice was a matter of individual conscience, and hence private, or of social concord, thus public. The French case here demonstrates the extraordinary meaning of arbitrary power: Henry IV issued the Edict of Nantes (1598), which defined religion as a matter of conscience and thus permitted Protestants to worship; his grandson Louis XIV revoked it (1685), claiming to defend public order, and thus made Protestantism illegal in most parts of his kingdom. Waves of

persecution and massacres of Protestants, as well as a mass emigration, soon followed.

So-called "absolute" rulers found themselves limited in many ways. They had unlimited right to make public law but no right to touch private law, or "custom." Privilege ("private law") protected virtually every powerful member of every European society. Nobles everywhere had special rights, special courts, and a wide array of inviolable legal rights (according to their view) or privileges (according to the prince). Citizens of towns had many of the same privileges, and clergymen (especially in Catholic regions) had their own laws and courts and exemptions. Provincial customs almost everywhere in Europe, except in England, governed property transfers such as inheritances. "Absolute" rulers like Louis XIV of France and Joseph II of Austria (ruled 1780–1790) had no legitimate authority to change such customs, which governed even weights and measures.

THE DECLINE OF THE COMMONWEALTH AND THE RISE OF ABSOLUTISM
Modern discussions of "absolutism" often forget the direct connection between the breakdown of religious unity and the creation of a new theory of "absolute power" in the 1570s. The old theories, with their direct ties to *auctoritas* and thus to laws promulgated by the prince but authorized by God, were not likely to convince a Protestant subject to obey a Catholic king, or vice versa. Political discourse everywhere in Europe moved away from the time-honored concept of "the public good," embodied in a commonwealth, and toward "the good of the king's service" in a monarchical state.

Most Europeans lived in a commonwealth—a political society based on citizens—between the fourteenth and sixteenth centuries. These citizens, as in an ancient Greek city, formed a small percentage of the adult male population: only nobles and certain wealthy commoners (above all urban elites) participated in governance. Almost all participation in governance happened at the local level, usually in a town; when sixteenth-century townsmen spoke of being "citizens," they invariably meant citizens of their town. These commonwealths usually relied on a mixed constitution (*forma mixta,* an ideal Europeans took from the ancient historian Polybius), in which a prince, the aristocracy, and the broader group of prominent men shared power. In the last third of the sixteenth century, however, a Europe-wide constitutional crisis destroyed most of the commonwealths.

The flirtation of European monarchies with "absolutes" had two stages. In the first, defensive stage during the seventeenth century, monarchs from the tsar of Russia to the king of Spain claimed "absolute power" to remedy the chaos around them. Many of their subjects, hungry for order, went along with them. In the second, offensive stage, states claimed absolute authority to act on behalf of the community. The sixteenth-century commonwealths had collapsed constitutionally because of the conflicts between the ruler and the common good, above all with regard to religion. In restoring civil order, seventeenth-century monarchs sought to consolidate power, and they did so in a long, bloody, socially disruptive process that destroyed the civic order.

In the late seventeenth century, however, the old distinction between power and authority became more fluid. The great monarchies claimed an implied "absolute" authority in the name of public utility. Whereas citizens had once protected the common good through governance, with oversight and assistance from a small state apparatus, now the state became its guardian. In France, urban elites and some nobles shared power through the state apparatus, deliberately shunning the republican mechanisms (representative assemblies, elected judges, elected financial officials) proposed by the provincial nobility in the 1560s and 1570s. By the eighteenth century, secure in the identification of the state and the common good, officials sought to "reform" society, relying on the "absolute" authority of the ruler. Moreover, that authority had become progressively more secular, as cultural currents desacralized the monarchy in the eyes of elites.

ABSOLUTISM IN PRACTICE

In German lands, this transition from the old state of orders, the *Standestaat,* to a state of laws, or *Rechtstaat,* relied on cameralist and Pietist philosophers such as Johann Heinrich Gottlob von Justi (1717–1771) and Christian Wolff (1679–1754). Cameralism and Pietism provided secular and religious rationales for a philosophy of social action, carried out by the only universal social organ: the

state. Everywhere in German lands, rulers sought to create the well-ordered police state, through laws promulgated by an "enlightened" state, under the "absolute" authority of the prince. In Austria, for example, Maria Theresa signed an edict (1774) mandating the creation of grammar schools in every parish in her empire; the edict also created an upper school and a training school for teachers in each provincial capital.

The uneven implementation of the 1774 edict illustrates the reality of "absolutism." Maria Theresa's empire had many nationalities and religions. Some groups viewed the creation of state-run schools as an attack on their ethnic or religious identity, but other ethnic groups used the schools for their own ends. Bohemia implemented the edict so thoroughly that two-thirds of its children enrolled in grammar schools by 1790, while Hungary enrolled virtually no one. Even in Austrian lands, school attendance rates ranged from 30 to 70 percent, in all cases a significant improvement, but evidence of radically different local responses to central action.

Prussia also tried to implement broader schooling. Johann Felbinger, the driving force behind these reforms in both places, voiced the same frustrations as any French or Russian bureaucrat when he wrote of the Prussian reform in 1768: "It is almost beyond comprehension that the express commands of such a powerful monarch, commands which a royal minister and two provincial chambers have sought to execute for the past several years, have had so little effect." Practical realities placed great limits on the real exercise of power. News and royal orders traveled at a horseman's pace, armies even more slowly. It could take months to move troops from one part of France or the Habsburg Empire to another. Early modern monarchies had to mediate the interests of kings and local elites, creating a compromise that preserved their common interests, in order to accomplish anything.

Princes in the post-commonwealth monarchies, having destroyed civic society during the search for order, boldly challenged the traditional limits on their prerogatives in the second, offensive phase of development. Monarchs could carry out grandiose personal projects, like Versailles or the Schönbrunn palace, or even construct a new capital city, as in the case of St. Petersburg. In wartime, rulers could trample on the most precious privileges of the powerful: in 1695 Louis XIV created the *capitation,* a tax on all French people, including otherwise exempt nobles, clergy, and urban elites. He created the tax by his simple will, even in provinces that still had Estates, which were legally subject only to voted taxes. Monarchs did not use this greater authority simply to levy taxes or build fancy palaces, however; European states became more involved in education, health care, poor relief, and transportation and communications. Above all, states created new laws. In France, the process began in earnest with Francis I (ruled 1515–1547), who issued more edicts and ordinances than all his predecessors combined. In German lands after 1680, cameralist ideas led to the promulgation of staggeringly detailed "police ordinances" that regulated every conceivable aspect of daily life. In England, Oliver Cromwell's Puritan Commonwealth (1649–1660), acting just as "absolutely" as any monarchy, even outlawed Christmas.

In the final stage of the assault, monarchs such as Joseph II of Austria attacked the holy of holies, customary property rights. Using the new calculus of utility to revive an idea of the commonwealth days, both Joseph (1781) and the French Revolutionaries (1790) confiscated church property in the name of the "public good" and abolished contemplative monasteries and convents as "useless." Joseph eliminated a third of all abbeys and secularized 40 percent of the monks and nuns in his lands. He also attacked lay property, "abolishing" in 1781 many of the personal restrictions on serfs, allowing them to marry, move freely, and choose their professions, and trying to legislate reductions in the forced labor *(robot)* they performed as rent for their lands. The most notable response to his efforts was a peasant uprising in Transylvania, where Romanian rebels burned noble manors and murdered their oppressive Hungarian lords. Joseph sent troops to butcher the rebels, whose leaders were drawn and quartered, their body parts publicly displayed. Joseph wrote to the governor: "I never imagined that such a terrible thing could happen . . . after the advice which I have given so often and so assiduously to promote the general good and general security."

In the eighteenth century, three developments changed the relationship among the monarch, the state, and society. First, the social and economic system became more capitalistic, abetting profound cultural shifts, such as a greater level of literacy and the creation of a broader and more vocal public opinion. Second, the state apparatus grew exponentially, enabling the state to interfere in everyday life in ways unimaginable in earlier times. Third, European elites demanded greater accountability from their rulers. In England, that meant more power for Parliament; in France, it meant a vigorous intellectual challenge to the established order by writers such as Charles-Louis de Secondat de Montesquieu (1689–1755), Voltaire (1694–1778), and Jean-Jacques Rousseau (1712–1778). In east central Europe monarchs like Joseph II or Frederick II the Great of Prussia (ruled 1740–1786) unilaterally implemented "enlightened" ideas.

Such action attacked the rights of the citizens (almost all of them nobles) in the name of public utility. Only those with privileges, like the Hungarian nobility with its powerful diet, could stand up against this new state offensive. The tumultuous events of 1789 in France bear witness to the strains on the new relationship. One of the Revolutionary leaders, Honoré-Gabriel Riqueti, the count of Mirabeau, aptly remarked (August 1789) that "privileges are essential as a defense against despotism, but [are] an abomination used against the nation." The great conflict between monarchies and citizens at the end of the eighteenth century became a cataclysm, because the states made their assault on the old citizenry at precisely the moment when a new, more inclusive definition of citizen came into being. Thus people like Mirabeau could support the Parlement of Paris in its conflict with the king in 1788, because they viewed the Parlement as the protector of "rights" against a "despot," yet could demand the abolition of that same Parlement a year later, because the French Revolution had placed political power in the hands of the nation, making the Parlement, as a defender of "privileges," an anachronism.

CONCLUSION

Early modern political vocabulary used words like *absolute* or *commonwealth* to mean different things than they do today. Modern dictionaries define a *republic* or *commonwealth* as "a political order whose head of state is not a monarch," yet most sixteenth-century Europeans, like Bodin, viewed monarchy as the best form for a commonwealth. The seventeenth-century linguistic shift, in which *republic* and *monarchy* became antonyms, informs us about fundamental changes in the nature of European monarchies. Sixteenth-century documents often refer to rulers as "sovereign seigneurs," showing the ambiguity of the prince's status. Those petitioning the ruler called themselves "loyal and very faithful servants" of the prince. Seventeenth-century documents speak of the "sovereign" and of "very humble and very obedient subjects." The citizens of the states that preserved the old commonwealths, such as the United Provinces of the Netherlands or Venice or the Polish-Lithuanian Commonwealth, described the "sovereign" princes of their neighbors as "despots," because in their view these rulers had broken the covenant with the citizens.

"Absolutism" exists as a term to define, in largely pejorative ways, a given phase of European monarchies. Nineteenth-century liberal historians, spokesmen for a middle class struggling for political power in a secular state, created it to bludgeon defenders of the old order into submission. Little wonder that it is not an effective description of early modern monarchies. Many European states evolved in three stages from the fifteenth to the eighteenth centuries. In the commonwealth stage, various levels of government shared sovereignty, both theoretically and practically. Starting in the late sixteenth century, political theory defined sovereignty as indivisible, making the old divided sovereignty intellectually obsolete. These sovereign monarchies struggled throughout the seventeenth century to establish the internal order that would enable them to use indivisible sovereignty to expand the central state's power. By the 1690s European states of every kind sought to regulate even private life. Peter I the Great of Russia (ruled 1682–1725) could force his boyars to cut their beards, while the English Society for the Reformation of Manners could convince the government rigorously to prosecute swearing. Given the reality of such state interference in daily life, and the massive extension of the sphere of public law, monarchies in which the prince had no theoretical limits to his right to make public law posed a profound threat to elites.

The theoretical powers of a monarch changed very little from the fifteenth to the eighteenth centuries; the states ruled by those monarchs, however, underwent fundamental transformation. Lying on his deathbed in 1715, Louis XIV remarked, "I am going, but the state will remain." Louis understood that the state had begun to supersede the monarch, which made all the more urgent what Gouverneur Morris, a member of the American Constitutional Convention, rightly identified from Paris in February 1789 as "the great Question, shall [France] hereafter have a Constitution or shall Will continue to be Law." Because of the far greater power of the central state and because of its claims, increasingly derived from secular foundations, to universal authority in society, European elites could no longer allow a political system in which one man's will made the law.

See also **Autocracy; Divine Right Kingship; Enlightened Despotism; Equality and Inequality; Monarchy; Representative Institutions; Sovereignty, Theory of; State and Bureaucracy; Tyranny, Theory of.**

BIBLIOGRAPHY

Beik, William. *Absolutism and Society in Seventeenth-Century France: State Power and Provincial Aristocracy in Languedoc.* Cambridge, U.K., and New York, 1985.

Blanning, T. C. W. *Joseph II.* London and New York, 1994.

Bluche, François. *Louis XIV.* Translated by Mark Greengrass. Oxford, 1990.

Collins, James. *Classes, Estates, and Order in Early Modern Brittany.* Cambridge, U.K., and New York, 1994.

———. *Fiscal Limits of Absolutism: Direct Taxation in Early-Seventeenth-Century France.* Berkeley, 1988.

———. *The State in Early Modern France.* Cambridge, U.K., and New York, 1995.

Kivelson, Valerie L. *Autocracy in the Provinces: The Muscovite Gentry and Political Culture in the Seventeenth Century.* Stanford, 1997.

Lieberman, Victor, ed. *Beyond Binary Histories: Re-imagining Eurasia to c. 1830.* Ann Arbor, Mich., 1999. This collection of essays effectively places European developments in their Eurasian context.

Major, J. Russell. *From Renaissance Monarchy to Absolute Monarchy: French Kings, Nobles, and Estates.* Baltimore, 1994.

Melton, James Van Horn. *Absolutism and the Eighteenth-Century Origins of Compulsory Schooling in Prussia and Austria.* Cambridge, U.K., and New York, 1988.

———. *The Rise of the Public in Enlightenment Europe.* Cambridge, U.K., and New York, 2001.

Moote, A. Lloyd. *Louis XIII, the Just.* Berkeley, 1989.

JAMES B. COLLINS

ACADEMIES, LEARNED.

At the beginning of the 1750s, four French academies—the local academies at Nancy and Pau in 1751, at Montauban in 1753, and the prestigious French Academy in Paris in 1755—advertised competitions for the best essay on different versions of the following question: Had academies advanced learning and the arts and was the multiplication of learned societies a good thing for society? In the decade following Jean-Jacques Rousseau's prize-winning essay (1750) for the Dijon Academy, in which he famously argued against the utility of the arts and sciences in improving the condition of mankind, no one was really sure if academies were a good thing or not. But their ubiquity made them a key feature of the institutional and cultural landscape of early modern Europe.

By the middle of the eighteenth century the number of learned academies and societies in Europe and its overseas colonies was in the hundreds, and many academies had come and gone in the preceding two centuries. Capital cities such as Paris, London, Berlin, Rome, Florence, Madrid, and St. Petersburg boasted multiple academies, often funded by royal patronage as well as private initiative, that organized virtually every imaginable form of knowledge, invention, and artistic endeavor. Smaller cities and towns typically had one or two academies to promote knowledge as both a cultural and utilitarian endeavor; such academies were typically founded by leading citizens who considered the academy a civic necessity. Colonial outposts such as Philadelphia, Boston, Richmond, Rio de Janeiro, Mexico City, and Cap François formed their own academies, whose members were in correspondence with European academicians. Bernard le Bovier de Fontenelle, perpetual secretary to the Paris Academy of Sciences (founded 1666), dubbed the late seventeenth and the eighteenth century the age of academies. He was absolutely right in his assessment that academies had become a crucial means of making knowledge a social endeavor that increasingly promoted the public good.

The eighteenth-century image of the academy as a nucleus of the Republic of Letters was a far cry from the academy's origins as a fifteenth-century reinvention of Plato's famous lyceum in ancient Athens. Prior to 1530, we can identify no more than twelve academies, all of them closely associated with the humanistic revival of ancient knowledge and the arts in Renaissance Italy. The term *academy* first appeared in the mid-fifteenth century as a means of describing associations of learned men who were devoted to revival of the values of Greco-Roman antiquity in one form or another. Most famous was the Platonic Academy, established in 1462 by the philosopher and physician Marsilio Ficino under the patronage of the Florentine ruler Cosimo de' Medici, which celebrated and disseminated the works of Plato and other Greek authors through translations of important manuscripts. During the late fifteenth and early sixteenth centuries there were many informal gatherings of scholars who never made their meetings part of any official organization. By contrast, the desire to give one's group a name, write up statutes that described the scope of its activities, elect a head of the academy, vote on candidates for new membership, appoint a secretary to record minutes, and create publications that celebrated its activities represented a different stage in the evolution of institutions of learning—the establishment of an alternative to the university as a structure dedicated to the promotion of knowledge. The academy, in other words, was a self-conscious scholarly community.

In the second half of the sixteenth century, academies multiplied rapidly, especially in the Italian city-states. On the Italian peninsula, 367 academies were founded before 1600. We can also find a few academies in northern Europe by the late sixteenth century, such as the Palace Academy of Henry III of France (ruled 1547–1559). During this period the key characteristics of the Renaissance academy emerged. These early academies were largely private gatherings of men and occasionally a few women who met to share their mutual interest in culture and conversation, often under the sponsorship of a "prince" who held a position of power within the local community. In such settings, scholars assessed new ideas in relation to more established traditions of learning. Whether attacking Aristotelian learning, debating the merits of Dante over Petrarch, or arguing for (or against) Tuscan as the preferred literary language of the Italian peninsula, Renaissance academicians came together to display their wit and erudition in public. Often such academies were encyclopedic rather than focused in their intellectual goals. The kind of wide-ranging, highly rhetorical learned dialogue described by Baldassare Castiglione in his best-selling *Book of the Courtier* (1528)—a fictionalized reflection of the culture of conversation at the court of Urbino—became the model for how an academician should speak about ideas.

Many Renaissance academies lasted not more than a decade, sometimes even just a few years, because they were not truly institutions but creations of individual patrons who wished to promote learning; they were private rather than public organizations. One key exception to this general rule was the Florentine Academy, which was founded informally by a group of Florentine scholars in 1540 and subsequently enjoyed official sponsorship of Cosimo I de' Medici; its goal was the preservation and dissemination of Tuscan literature and language. In this instance, we can speak of the early state-sponsored academy whose cultural mission was deeply political, since it played an important role in resolving the debate about literary Italian in favor of the Tuscan vernacular. Its successor, the Accademia della Crusca (founded 1582), created a series of important etymological dictionaries in the seventeenth and eighteenth centuries that standardized this language and its usage. The success of Tuscan academies of science, art, and culture inspired other states to think of the academy as more than just a private association of scholars. French scholars explicitly invoked the Medicean model in urging their monarchs and ministers to found royal academies such as the Académie Française (founded 1635), Académie Royale des Inscriptions et Belles-Lettres (founded 1663), and the Académie Royale des Sciences (founded 1666). This last offered paid stipends and living quarters to Europe's most talented astronomers, mathematicians, and natural philosophers, essentially making them employees of the state.

During the seventeenth century a new kind of academy came into existence that had greater longevity than its predecessors and reflected the new intellectual concerns of the period. The Italian and French academies devoted to language and culture gave way to a succession of academies whose members often explicitly declared that they would put aside religious and political differences in order to make common cause in the study of nature. Beginning with the Accademia dei Lincei (1603–1630), founded by a Roman noble, Federico Cesi, and counting the Florentine mathematician and philosopher Galileo Galilei among its members, the idea of the scientific academy promoted the centrality of natural knowledge to early modern society. The Lincei was followed by the Accademia del Cimento (1657–1667), a Florentine academy of followers of Galileo devoted to the pursuit of experimental knowledge, as well as more permanent endeavors such as the Royal Society of London (founded 1660), which included such figures as Robert Boyle, Robert Hooke, John Locke, and Isaac Newton among its early members. The Royal Society engaged in international correspondence with other philosophers, collected natural specimens, perfected instruments such as the air pump and the microscope, and published the results of experiments, reports of intriguing natural phenomena, and book reviews in *Philosophical Transactions* (established 1665), the first periodical published by an academy. Francis Bacon had dreamed about the idea of a scientific society in his posthumously published *New Atlantis* (1627), and this dream was now on the verge of becoming a reality. While lacking the kind of financial support enjoyed by the Académie Royale des Sciences, the Royal Society nonetheless could claim royal patronage and an earlier and more successful publication program that was widely discussed in many countries.

Between 1660 and 1793 approximately seventy scientific academies and societies were founded, invoking either London or Paris as their model. The German philosopher Gottfried Wilhelm Leibniz found himself realizing Bacon's fantasy of advising rulers about how to make science central to the state when he helped to design the academies of science in Berlin for the Electress Sophie Charlotte (founded 1700) and in St. Petersburg for Tsar Peter I the Great (founded 1725). At the beginning of the eighteenth century scientific academies such as the Istituto delle Scienze of Bologna (founded 1711) had an explicitly pedagogical purpose that made their utility more explicit. While King Charles II of England (ruled 1660–1685) never quite figured out whether Boyle's air pump experiments were good for anything, enlightened patrons of academies did not share his confusion about the promise of science. The founder of the Istituto delle Scienze, Luigi Ferdinando Marsigli, created professorships in subjects such as physics, chemistry, astronomy, natural history, cartography, and military science because the university curriculum did not adequately cover these subjects. He had the Istituto's professors offer lessons at hours that did not conflict with the university curriculum in order to ensure that students could take advantage of both courses of study. He created an astronomical observatory in his academy and filled the rooms with specimens and instruments. Visitors thought it was the New Atlantis realized.

Marsigli's idea of the academy as an alternative educational institution reached its fulfillment at mid-century when the majority of new academies and societies were founded on the premise of making knowledge available to a broader public. The academy became associated with the idea of progress and increasingly focused on subjects designed to produce this result. The Patriotic Society of Hamburg (founded 1765) described itself as a "Society for the Promotion of Manufactures, Arts, and Useful Trades," drawing inspiration from French and British models of learned associations that emphasized the role of such organizations in improving society through knowledge. The members of the Patriotic Society envisioned literate farmers and artisans as their potential audience. The Royal Dublin Society (founded 1731)—which published a weekly column in the *Dublin News Letter* in order to ensure a wider circulation of practical knowledge on a wide variety of subjects ("Husbandry, Manufactures, and Other Useful Arts," as the full academy name enumerated)—had a similar target audience, as did Britain's Royal Society for the Encouragement of Arts, Manufactures, and Commerce (founded 1754), on a national level. The concern of such groups was the application of learning to key problems of society, among them the creation of an agricultural science, the development of better machines and instruments, and the appli-

cation of scientific principles to the political, moral, and economic problems of the day. The academy was no longer a closed world of experts talking primarily to each other, but was now a site for enlightened citizenship. These new societies, as they were more often called to distinguish them from earlier academies, no longer favored Latin as the language of learning. Instead they preferred to communicate in the local vernacular, on the premise that their audience was no longer the international Republic of Letters, already well served by the seventeenth-century learned academies, but local citizens who needed to be persuaded that learning might improve their lives.

The more academicians argued for the utility of academies, the more they also wondered how useful they really were. As academies became true institutions, housed in buildings stocked with well-furnished libraries and collections of natural specimens, instruments, and models of machines and bodies to stimulate the curiosity of their members, and as they became sufficiently endowed to sponsor prizes and publications, academies more readily facilitated the global exchange of knowledge within the Republic of Letters. Provincial scholars throughout Europe and the Americas found books, periodicals, and pamphlets in plentiful supply, and academies served to legitimate the idea that a knowing person was a productive, perhaps even patriotic citizen who could collaborate with others in solving society's problems. But did knowing more make one think better of humanity? A young Rousseau, responding to the Dijon Academy's question in 1750, was quite pessimistic about what the age of academies had wrought. Therein lay the paradox of the new system of knowledge that early modern Europeans had created.

See also **Art: Artistic Patronage; Citizenship; Classicism; Communication, Scientific; Enlightenment; Humanists and Humanism; Renaissance; Republic of Letters; Scientific Revolution; Universities.**

BIBLIOGRAPHY

Berry, Henry F. *A History of the Royal Dublin Society.* London and New York, 1915.

Cochrane, Eric W. "The Renaissance Academies in Their Italian and European Setting." In *The Fairest Flower: The Emergence of Linguistic National Consciousness in Renaissance Europe.* Florence, 1985.

———. *Tradition and Enlightenment in the Tuscan Academies, 1690–1800.* Chicago, 1961.

Field, Arthur. *The Origins of the Platonic Academy of Florence.* Princeton, 1988.

Hahn, Roger. *Anatomy of a Scientific Institution: The Paris Academy of Sciences, 1666–1803.* Berkeley, 1971.

Hunter, Michael. *Establishing the New Science: The Experience of the Early Royal Society.* Woodbridge, U.K., and Wolfeboro, N.H., 1989.

Lowood, Henry E. *Patriotism, Profit, and the Promotion of Science in the German Enlightenment: The Economic and Scientific Societies, 1760–1815.* New York, 1991.

Maylender, Michele. *Storia delle Accademie d'Italia.* 5 vols. Bologna, 1926–1930.

McClellan, James E., III. *Science Reorganized: Scientific Societies in the Eighteenth Century.* New York, 1985.

Quondam, Amadeo. "L'Accademia." In *Letteratura italiana.* Vol. 1, *Il letterato e le istituzioni.* Edited by Alberto Asor Rosa. Turin, 1982.

Roche, Daniel. *Le siècle des lumières en province: Académies et academiciens provinciaux, 1680–1789.* 2 vols. Paris, 1978.

Yates, Frances Amelia. *The French Academies of the Sixteenth Century.* London, 1947.

PAULA FINDLEN

ACADEMIES OF ART. Academies of art were either private or official institutions. During the early modern period both kinds were part of the development of academies in general.

PRIVATE ACADEMIES

The first and most numerous art academies were privately organized. Following the example of the many other academies of the time, they were formed as voluntary societies for mutually satisfactory interaction. But artists' academies centered on communal drawing, after sculpture or a live model. The first instance in which drawing appears as the content of an academy occurs in a engraving bearing the date 1531 and an inscription that identifies a gathering of artists working by candlelight as the "Academia" in Rome of the sculptor Baccio Bandinelli (1493?–1560). By the end of the century, the number of academies had increased, as had the range of the recorded activities. Drawing remained the main purpose of these academies, but as the common name *accademia del nudo* ('academy of the nude') indicates, the focus was drawing from a live model. Drawing after sculpture and casts continued, and lectures on geometry, perspective, and anatomy were occasionally mentioned, as were convivial events. The costs of space, lights, and model fees were shared among a group of artists or paid for by a single master or a wealthy patron. A patron sometimes also provided prizes for the winners of drawing competitions. But, however the academies were financed, the core function of instruction remained the same.

Meetings took place outside working hours, participation was voluntary, and members interacted as equals regardless of their status in the outside world. As did academies generally, artists' academies sometimes chose a name and an emblem (*impresa*) to identify themselves, adopted rules to regulate behavior, and chose officers to carry them out. Unfortunately, little of this kind of information has survived. Knowledge of even the best-known of such academies, that founded by the Carracci at Bologna in 1583, is sketchy at best, but because of the range of its activities, this academy has often been assimilated to the much better documented academies of the second kind.

OFFICIAL ACADEMIES

The second type of artists' academy was the result not of private initiative, but of official policy. Rather than providing artists with opportunities for sociability and personal profit, it aimed at promoting and disciplining the profession. Such academies typically restricted membership in some way, and because they were created under authority of law, they had both privileges and responsibilities. The first officially established academy was the Florentine Accademia del Disegno (1563; Academy of Drawing). It was proposed by a group of artists, led by Giorgio Vasari (1511–1574), who sought to remake the artists' Company or Confraternity of St. Luke into an academy along the lines of the already established Accademia Fiorentina. The organization chartered by the duke of Florence, Cosimo I, in 1563 was two-tiered, with authority over the body of the artists—the Compagnia—invested in a "choice of the best," who constituted the Accademia. Although bound to their several traditional guild affiliations, painters, sculptors, and architects were now united in a single institution, which in 1571 was reintegrated into the existing system by being incorporated as a guild. Its hybrid structure and history have generated considerable controversy over the extent to which the academy's goals and practices anticipated those of later academies. Its guild functions and an apparent failure to fully implement its educational program tell against it, whereas its intent to intervene in artistic training and to elevate the status of art and artist by supplementing practice with theory argue in its favor. The mere fact of the academy's existence and its exalted patronage ensured its fame and its importance as a model.

In the Roman Academy of St. Luke something of the same pattern repeated itself. Once again the academy was placed over the minor arts, and once again its statutes charged the members with educating the young, in this case in the interest of religion and the papacy. In Rome, as in Florence, this program was put into practice only sporadically. Following an initial burst of activity in the 1590s under the leadership of Federico Zuccaro (c. 1540–1609), only in the second half of the seventeenth century did the round of lectures, life drawing, and student competitions with prizes take on a regular rhythm, and by this time the Royal Academy of Painting and Sculpture in Paris had emerged as the dominant arts institution in Europe.

The Académie Royale de Peinture et de Sculpture in Paris owed its foundation in 1648 to a number of artists who sought to escape guild rule by placing themselves under royal patronage. After a rocky start, its fortunes rose with the end of the Fronde and the consolidation of royal power in the mid-1650s. From the 1660s, under the direction of the king's minister, Jean-Baptiste Colbert, and his first painter, Charles Le Brun (1619–1690), the Royal Academy set the model for later academies. In the service of the state, the academicians were to train young artists, as well as articulate and maintain a collective set of standards that mediated between artist and patron. Following the example of the academies in Florence and Rome, drawing remained the core of instruction in Paris. From 1665 winners of the competitions were sent to Rome for a period of study at the French Academy there, which with drawing from casts reinforced the value attached to ancient Roman and modern Italian art. Public lectures stimulated theory and criticism and

with the initiation of public exhibitions made the academy answerable for its privileges and work.

Although by the end of the seventeenth century the Royal Academy's program had lost much of its rigor, it remained important for the training and recognition of artists, and, after 1737, when the public exhibitions, or salons, which were restricted to members, became regular events, it regained some of its luster. Moreover, if not the only model, the Royal Academy's marriage of state and artists' interests had an enormous influence on what became an explosive growth of academies and schools of art across Europe. By 1790 over one hundred such royal and national institutions had been established in cities ranging from Madrid to Vienna and from Naples to London, Copenhagen, and St. Petersburg.

See also **Britain, Art in; Carracci Family; Colbert, Jean-Baptiste; Florence, Art in; France, Art in; Rome, Art in; Vasari, Giorgio.**

BIBLIOGRAPHY

Barzman, Karen-edis. *The Florentine Academy and the Early Modern State: The Discipline of "Disegno."* Cambridge, U.K., and New York, 2000.

Boschloo, Anton W. A., et al., eds. *Academies of Art between Renaissance and Romanticism.* The Hague, 1989.

Goldstein, Carl. *Teaching Art: Academies and Schools from Vasari to Albers.* Cambridge, U.K., and New York, 1996.

Pevsner, Nikolaus. *Academies of Art Past and Present.* Reprint, with a new preface by the author. New York, 1973.

GEORGE C. BAUER

ACCOUNTING AND BOOKKEEPING.

Early modern Europe witnessed a gradual diffusion of sophisticated techniques of accounting. The breeding ground for innovation was Italy, where commercially sophisticated states had been involved for centuries in business and long-distance trade. Evidence already exists in the twelfth and thirteenth centuries of systematic calculation of profits, distinct from the primitive forms of tabulation used in medieval manorial accounts.

The most important Italian innovation was double entry bookkeeping. Scholars disagree about

Accounting and Bookkeeping. *The Money Changer* by Quentin Metsys (1466–1530). THE ART ARCHIVE/FINE ART MUSEUM BILBAO/DAGLI ORTI (A)

when and where it began. The first undisputed example is in the accounts of treasury officials of the city of Genoa in 1340. By the late fourteenth and fifteenth centuries double entry had been widely adopted in Italy. The great Florentine international merchant banking house of Francesco Datini (1335–1410) and the Medici bankers of Florence used it, as did their counterparts in Milan, Genoa, Pisa, and Venice.

The great German writer Johann Wolfgang von Goethe (1749–1832) has one of his characters in *Wilhelm Meisters Lehrjahre* (1796) call double entry "among the finest inventions of the human mind." The technique provided a rational way of figuring accounts through careful calculation of assets and liabilities and determination of profits and losses. Each transaction was recorded twice, as both a debit and a credit. The debits and credits were then cross-indexed to corresponding accounts in a ledger and then balanced. The method was well suited to partnerships and permanent commercial associations, which dealt in credit and had numerous customers

in foreign markets. Double entry differed markedly from single entry "charge and discharge" techniques, which recorded the flow of goods but did not measure profit and loss. It made cheating more difficult and facilitated efficient management.

The Venetian form of double entry is perhaps the most famous. Merchants kept their accounts in "bilateral" form *(alla veneziana)*, with debits recorded on the left side of the page across from credits. The extant books of the merchant Andrea Barbarigo (1418–1449) are typical of the style. They point to a highly evolved system, using several books, carefully cross-indexed and coordinated to form a coherent whole. Practices differed, however, from one region to another. Tuscan bankers, for example, drew up regular (often yearly) balance sheets, which gave a snapshot of assets, liabilities, and profits.

It was primarily the Venetian method that was disseminated to the rest of Europe. It radiated out from the city via foreign merchants and through the work of Luca Pacioli (c. 1445–1517), a Franciscan monk, mathematician, and university teacher, who served as tutor to the sons of a rich Venetian merchant. In 1494, Pacioli published *Summa de Arithmetica,* a discursive treatise that contained a short section on Venetian-style double entry. Pacioli described the use of three books: a *memoriale,* a ledger, and a journal. Each transaction was first noted in the *memoriale,* then listed in debit and credit form in the journal, and then posted in the ledger. Pacioli is revered today as "the father of modern accounting." In 1994, the five-hundredth anniversary of the publication of his book, accountants from all over the world gathered at Pacioli's birthplace in the town of San Sepulcro to honor him.

Pacioli's work inspired others. Domenico Manzoni published *Quaderno Doppio* in 1540. It was essentially a restatement of Pacioli, though it clarified some of the earlier writer's points. Dutch merchant Jan Christoffels Ympyn wrote a treatise on double entry, which appeared simultaneously in Flemish and in French in 1543 and four years later in English. A German treatise, fashioned after both Pacioli and Manzoni, was published by the merchant Wolfgang Schweicker in 1549.

Double entry made especially notable headway in southern Germany. It was probably introduced there in the early fifteenth century by merchants from Nuremberg who traded in Venice. Johann Gottlieb's two treatises, *Ein Teutsch Verstendig*, published in 1531, and *Buchhalten Zwey Kunstliche*, published in 1546, helped popularize the method. Matthaus Schwarz, a bookkeeper for the great Fugger bank of Augsburg, introduced the technique to that company after learning it as an apprentice in Italy. The Fugger bank added safeguards and even sent auditors to bank branches to examine accounts and check inventories.

The use of double entry spread elsewhere in the sixteenth and seventeenth centuries. The Spanish banking houses of Ruiz, Miguel, and Garcia of Salamanca kept their accounts in double entry, as did the English draper Thomas Howell. Sebastian Gammersfelder, a schoolmaster in Danzig, helped introduce the method to northern Germany with the publication of a book on the subject in 1570.

But the adoption of the method was generally slow in northern Europe and did not keep pace with the growing complexity and volume of business there. Merchants were just as likely to continue using older, simplistic but more familiar methods. Despite the high volume of their trade, Hanseatic merchants preferred rudimentary tabular accounts. In northern Holland, the records of an anonymous trader show claims and debts recorded in random order. In England, double entry was restricted to a handful of merchants. Government offices used a system of single entry until the nineteenth century. There is no evidence of double entry in Scotland before the seventeenth century. Even in Italy the technique was not universally adopted. The Milanese bankers the del Maino did not use double entry. It was, indeed, possible to keep orderly accounts and undertake rational planning without recourse to double entry. The northern German merchant Johann Pisz eschewed the method but arranged his books using a sophisticated and effective single entry alternative.

Scholars have debated the significance of double entry. To some it constitutes a driving force in the transformation of Europe from a feudal to a capitalistic society. To others, it is merely a business method that helped manage accounts and minimize fraud, with no broader significance. An intriguing recent interpretation has it that double entry reflected not a secular capitalistic ethic, but a Christian one that emphasized a measured approach to the accumulation of wealth.

See also **Banking and Credit; Capitalism; Commerce and Markets; Money and Coinage; Venice.**

BIBLIOGRAPHY

De Roover, Raymond. "The Development of Accounting Prior to Luca Pacioli According to Account Books of Medieval Merchants." In *Business, Banking, and Economic Thought in Late Medieval and Early Modern Europe: Selected Studies of Raymond de Roover*, edited by Julius Kirshner, pp. 119–180. Chicago, 1974.

Edwards, J. R. *A History of Financial Accounting*. London, 1989.

Lee, T. A., Ashton C. Bishop, and R. H. Parker, eds. *Accounting History from the Renaissance to the Present: A Remembrance of Luca Pacioli*. New York and London, 1996.

Nobes, Christopher, ed. *The Development of Double Entry: Selected Essays*. New York and London, 1984.

Parker, R. H., and B. S. Yamey. *Accounting History: Some British Contributions*. Oxford, 1994.

Yamey, B. S. "Scientific Bookkeeping and the Rise of Capitalism." *Economic History Review* 2 (1948–49): 99–113.

WILLIAM CAFERRO

ACOUSTICS. When he first mentioned the "Acoustique Art" in his *Advancement of Learning* (1605), Francis Bacon (1561–1626) was drawing a distinction between the physical acoustics he expanded in the *Sylva Sylvarum* (1627) and the harmonics of the Pythagorean mathematical tradition. The Pythagorean tradition still survived in Bacon's time in the works of such diverse people as Gioseffo Zarlino (1517–1590), René Descartes (1596–1650), and Johannes Kepler (1571–1630). In Bacon's words: "The nature of sounds, in some sort, [hath been with some diligence inquired,] as far as concerneth music. But the nature of sounds in general hath been superficially observed. It is one of the subtilest pieces of nature" (Bacon, p. 390).

Bacon's "Acoustique Art" was therefore concerned with the study of "immusical sounds" and with experiments in the "majoration in sounds" (p. 451), that is, the harnessing of sounds in buildings (architectural acoustics) by their "enclosure" in artificial channels inside the walls or in the environment (hydraulic acoustics). The aim of Baconian acoustics was to catalog, quantify, and shape human space by means of sound. This stemmed from the *echometria,* an early modern tradition of literature on echo, as studied by the mathematicians Giuseppe Biancani (1566–1624), Marin Mersenne (1588–1648), and Daniello Bartoli (1608–1685), in which the model of optics was applied in acoustics to the behavior of sound. It was in a sense a historical antecedent to Isaac Newton's (1642–1727) analogy between colors and musical tones in *Opticks* (1704). Athanasius Kircher's (1601–1680) *Phonurgia Nova* of 1673 was the outcome of this tradition. Attacking British acoustics traditions, Kircher argued that the "origin of the Acoustical Art" (p. 111) lay in his own earlier experiments with sounding tubes at the Collegio Romano in 1649 and sketched the ideology of a Christian baroque science of acoustics designed to dominate the world by exploiting the "boundless powers of sound" (p. 2).

Seventeenth-century empirical observations and mathematical explanations of the simultaneous vibrations of a string at different frequencies were important in the development of modern experimental acoustics. The earliest contribution in this branch of acoustics was made by Mersenne, who derived the mathematical law governing the physics of a vibrating string. Around 1673 Christiaan Huygens (1629–1695) estimated its absolute frequency, and in 1677 John Wallis (1616–1703) published a report of experiments on the overtones of a vibrating string. In 1692 Francis Robartes (1650–1718) followed with similar findings.

These achievements paved the way for the eighteenth-century *acoustique* of Joseph Sauveur (1653–1716) and for the work of Brook Taylor (1685–1731), Leonhard Euler (1707–1783), Jean Le Rond d'Alembert (1717–1783), Daniel Bernoulli (1700–1782), and Giordani Riccati (1709–1790), who all attempted to determine mathematically the fundamental tone and the overtones of a sonorous body. Modern experimental acoustics sought in nature, as a physical law of the sounding body, the perfect harmony that in the Pythagorean tradition sprang from the mind of the "geometrizing God." Experimental epistemology in acoustics also influenced the studies of the anat-

omy and physiology of hearing, especially the work of Joseph-Guichard Duverney (1648–1730) and Antonio Maria Valsalva (1666–1723), that in the nineteenth century gave rise to physiological and psychological acoustics.

See also **Alembert, Jean Le Rond d'; Bacon, Francis; Euler, Leonhard; Huygens Family; Kircher, Athanasius; Mersenne, Marin; Newton, Isaac; Physics; Scientific Revolution.**

BIBLIOGRAPHY

Bacon, Francis. *Sylva sylvarum.* In *The Works of Francis Bacon.* Edited by J. Spedding, R. L. Ellis, and D. D. Heath, vol. 2, pp. 385–436. London, 1858–1859.

Dostrovsky, Sigalia. "Early Vibration Theory: Physics and Music in the Seventeenth Century." *Archive for History of Exact Sciences* 14 (1974–1975): 169–218.

Gouk, Penelope Mary. "Acoustics in the Early Royal Society, 1660–1680." *Notes and Records of the Royal Society of London* 36 (1982): 155–175.

Hunt, Frederick Vinton. *Origins in Acoustics: The Science of Sound from Antiquity to the Age of Newton.* New Haven and London, 1978.

Kircher, Athanasius. *Phonurgia Nova.* Kempten, 1673.

PAOLO GOZZA

ACTIVE POWERS. *See* **Matter, Theories of.**

ADDISON, JOSEPH (1672–1719), English poet, essayist, and critic. Addison helped to elevate the literary status of English prose while holding important political offices for the Whig party. He was born in 1672 at Milston, Wiltshire. His father, the Reverend Launcelot Addison, was the dean of Lichfield, Staffordshire, and Addison attended Lichfield Grammar School and then, in 1686, Charterhouse School in London, where he met Richard Steele. Addison's study of classical poetry and his Latin poems at Queen's College, Oxford, won him a demy (scholarship) in the 1690s to Magdalen College, where he took his M.A. and was a fellow from 1697 to 1711. His classical scholarly knowledge, especially on the Roman idea of citizenship, informs the moral beliefs in his writing.

Addison's passionate interest in and deep knowledge of Roman poetry and history are evident in his early prose works evaluating the best Roman poets, his translations of such poets as Virgil and Ovid (1694 and 1717), and his own highly praised imitations of Latin poets such as Horace. He modeled his own prose style after the formal elegance and familiar diction of Latin poetry, which he praised. After writing a celebratory poem on John Dryden—"To Mr. Dryden"—he wrote an introductory essay on Virgil for Dryden's translation of the *Georgics* in 1697. Addison's own translations provided English readers with an accessible text through adding explanatory commentaries and replacing obscure allusions with familiar ones. Eight of Addison's Latin poems were included in an anthology he edited at Oxford in 1699, *Musarum Anglicarum Analecta* (An assembly of English muses).

One poem, "Pax Gulielmi Auspiciis Europae Reddita" (Peace returned to Europe under William's auspices), compliments William III's ability as a monarch and celebrates the 1697 Treaty of Ryswick, which ended the War of the Grand Alliance. A partisan of Protestantism and the Whigs, Addison in his earliest poetry supported the Protestant succession of William of Orange and Mary. "Poem to his Majesty" was dedicated to John Somers, an important Whig, and "William's Peace" was dedicated to Charles Montagu, Lord Halifax, the Whig treasurer. Montagu became Addison's patron and secured him a pension of £200 to undertake a grand tour on the Continent between 1699 and 1704. Addison toured several countries and studied French neoclassical literary theorists; his itinerary, particularly to places of classical literary interest, is recorded in *Remarks upon Several Parts of Italy,* published in 1705.

Addison's eulogy on John Churchill, duke of Marlborough's victory over the French at Blenheim in his poem "The Campaign" in 1704 secured him a position as excise commissioner of appeals and brought him increasing popularity. His involvement with the Kit-Kat Club, a political and literary society for Whig writers and politicians, renewed his friendship with Steele, and he contributed to Steele's play *The Tender Husband* (1705). Commissioned to write an English opera to counter the trend for Italian opera, he produced the unsuccessful *Rosamond* in 1707. Meanwhile, the status of his politically administrative appointments increased because of

his anti-Jacobite pamphlets such as "The Present State of the War." He became a prominent spokesman for the Whigs, progressing from undersecretary of state to Charles Spencer, earl of Sunderland, in 1706 to chief secretary to the earl of Wharton, Lord Lieutenant of Ireland, in 1709.

Assisting Steele in his editorship of the *London Gazette* in 1708, Addison then wrote forty-nine issues of *The Tatler,* the successful periodical established by Steele, moving between England and Ireland in 1709 and 1710. His essays focus on the classics, character types, and natural religion and oscillate between a witty, humorous tone and a moral seriousness, making reference to classical antecedents. His support of Whig policies continued with his writing five issues of the *Whig Examiner* during the elections of 1710, and becoming member of Parliament for Malmesbury, Wiltshire. Addison's essays in *The Spectator,* which appeared six days a week from March 1711 to December 1712, established his reputation for popularizing literary theory and new philosophies in a carefully poised, accessible, and sustained format. He wrote a series of essays on English tragedy, on the opera, on John Milton's poem *Paradise Lost,* and on the imagination, all designed to enlighten and improve the common reader. Addison later revived *The Spectator* briefly to support George I.

In 1713, his tragedy *Cato* ran for thirty nights at Drury Lane Theatre. A story of the struggle of a Roman republican, the play's political overtones ensured its success. It was praised by Voltaire as the first English "rational tragedy" and translated into French, Spanish, Italian, and Latin. Awaiting the accession of Prince George of Hanover, Addison was appointed secretary of the Regency in 1714. He published the periodical *The Freeholder, or Political Essays* (1715–1716) supporting George I during the Jacobite rebellion. His most prestigious political appointment was secretary of state in 1717. His last play, the comedy *The Drummer,* in 1716, was a failure. The same year he married the Countess of Warwick and lived in Holland House in London. Along with his increasing ill health, Addison quarreled with former friends such as Alexander Pope, over a rival translation of the *Iliad,* and Richard Steele, over the restriction of hereditary peers in the peerage bill. Addison died, estranged from Steele, on 17 June 1719.

See also English Literature and Language; Jacobitism; Pope, Alexander; Steele, Richard.

BIBLIOGRAPHY

Primary Sources

Addison, Joseph. *Cato.* Edited by William Alan Landes. London, 1996.

———. *The Commerce of Everyday Life: Selections from "The Tatler" and "The Spectator."* Edited by Erin Mackie. London, 1997.

———. *The Freeholder.* Edited by James Lehemy. Oxford, 1980.

———. *The Spectator.* Edited by Donald F. Bond. 5 vols. Oxford, 1965.

Secondary Sources

Bloom, Edward A., and Lillian D. Bloom. *Joseph Addison and Richard Steele: The Critical Heritage.* New York, 1995. A useful survey of the history of criticism and influence of Addison and Steele on English prose writers.

Maurer, Shawn Lisa. *Proposing Men: Dialectics of Gender and Class in the Eighteenth Century English Periodical.* Stanford, 1998. Examines the role of periodical publications like *The Spectator, The Tatler,* and others in constructing the domestic realm as an arena of masculine control.

Otten, Robert M. *Joseph Addison.* Boston, 1982. A useful introduction.

Smithers, Peter. *The Life of Joseph Addison.* 2nd ed. Oxford, 1968. The only complete biography of Addison to date.

MAX FINCHER

ADVICE AND ETIQUETTE BOOKS.

Advice and etiquette books have many names: courtesy books, books of conduct, books of manners, and books that teach "civility." They are different from practical "how to" books of advice, the manuals that taught Europeans how to cook, how to duel, and how to conceive a male child. Advice and etiquette books had other goals. They set forth the inherent or acquired qualities which the gentleman or gentlewoman must possess. They described the education, interests, and amusements that formed the ideal gentleman and gentlewoman. They discussed social conduct, what the individual should and should not do in the society of others. And the manuals emphasized moderation: nothing should be done in excess. The golden rule was to follow the mean. Advice and etiquette books also had a moral dimension and a high tone. The authors believed that individuals who followed their advice would grow in moral probity with benefits for all of society.

Advice and etiquette books were written and read throughout Europe. The most popular works were quickly translated from Latin into vernacular languages, or from one vernacular language to another, and widely sold and read. Many were written for both men and women but focused primarily on the behavior of men and boys. A growing number of works intended exclusively for women appeared over time, especially in eighteenth-century England.

The Renaissance was the golden age of advice books. It produced many, including the three most influential works of the period 1500 to 1800. The first was *Il cortegiano* (1528; The book of the courtier) of Baldassare Castiglione (1478–1529). It is far more than a courtesy book. It is a rounded, subtle, evocative, idealized but also equivocal picture of the high-ranking men and women who comprised the court of the small north Italian Renaissance princedom of Urbino between 1506 and 1508. It delves into profound philosophical issues and has some off-color humor, which later editors sometimes expurgated. It is a beautifully written classic of Italian literature.

But later readers viewed it as an advice and etiquette manual describing the qualities that a successful courtier should have in order to get ahead. These included a sound education to be worn lightly, many social accomplishments such as dancing and swordsmanship, and the ability to engage in graceful conversation. Above all, the courtier had to perform with grace and without seeming effort, with what Castiglione called *sprezzatura.* The book's appearance at a propitious moment in the evolution of European politics ensured popular success. The city-state republican government, in which a range of citizens from merchant and professional ranks participated, was giving way to a Europe of princedoms and monarchies, in which winning favor from those higher in politics and society was all-important. Castiglione's book seemed to offer the ideal training for getting ahead in this new world of the courts of princes and kings. Later editors and translators stressed this aspect. By the seventeenth century, *The Book of the Courtier* was increasingly seen as a guide to civilized behavior for Europe's noble classes and those who wanted to join them. The original Italian text and translations into English, French, German, Dutch, Spanish, and Latin reached a total of 150 editions by 1750, and it had many imitations.

In 1530 Desiderius Erasmus (1466?–1536) published a short work called *De Civilitate Morum Puerilium* (On good manners for boys). While addressed to boys, it told parents and tutors what they should strive to achieve in their sons and pupils. The book dealt with proper appearance, posture, table manners, dress, behavior in church and at banquets, ways of meeting people respectfully, appropriate games, and admonitions to pardon the shortcomings of others. It was a manual of external behavior for boys based on the belief that the molded boy would become the polished man. It did not deal with the complex issues found in Castiglione's classic. The third Renaissance manual of deportment with wide influence was *Il Galateo* (published 1558) of Giovanni Della Casa (1503–1556). The subtitle announced that it was a treatise of manners, customs, and the uses of conversation. It dealt with manners in the limited meaning of table manners and external social behavior. It described how one might to get along and rise in a world of superiors and inferiors. An adroit combination of education and social graces would help the individual survive the buffets of fortune. These two works also had many printings, translations, and imitations.

Advice and etiquette books in the next two-and-one-half centuries echoed, refined, and modified the advice found in the earlier works without challenging their basic principles. The new ones summarized or expanded the material and adapted it to social circumstances. Many had a more overt moralizing tone. Some new manuals were specifically directed to those who would serve monarchs and princes.

In France treatises on *l'honnête homme,* the gentleman who was well bred, courteous, honorable, civil, polite, and moderate, and knew how to please at court, began to appear in the middle of the seventeenth century. Sometimes the advice was reduced to pithy epigrams. For example, the Spanish Jesuit priest Baltasar Gracián (1601–1658) published his *Oráculo manual y arte de prudencia* (Oracle manual and the art of prudence) in 1647. It summarized correct behavior in epigrams such as "Avoid victories over your superior. . . . Conceal your purpose. . . . Know how to be all things to all men." While it conveyed much of the same advice as other advice and etiquette books, its tone was darker. It also was translated into English, French, Italian, Latin, and Hungarian and had considerable influence.

Books of advice and etiquette intended for women, especially gentlewomen, were particularly numerous in eighteenth-century England. These books wanted women to have a broad but not deep education, including French, drawing, sewing, and the ability to sing or play a musical instrument. Women should know how to dance. The books emphasized the importance of a polite tongue to be employed in useful and pleasing conversation. Laughter and wit were encouraged, but should not be so loud as to give offense or so sharp as to hurt others. Women should avoid vanity, behave modestly, and guard their chastity. Above all, good character led to good deportment and manners. Good manners reflected an inner good nature, which was a mix of good will and pleasant behavior incorporating refined taste and discrimination. The heroines of the novels of Jane Austen (1775–1817) almost always embodied the ideals of eighteenth-century English courtesy books for women. Fortunately, Austen's heroines displayed far more wit, humor, and perception, along with proper behavior, than did the manuals.

Advice and etiquette books were extraordinarily popular throughout the sixteenth, seventeenth, and eighteenth centuries because they met a need. Men and women wanted advice about how to behave well and how to maintain self-respect while climbing the ladder of success or holding to high rungs. Advice and etiquette books seldom dealt with the unpleasant tradeoffs between success and honor.

See also **Aristocracy and Gentry; Castiglione, Baldassare; Court and Courtiers; Erasmus, Desiderius; Gentleman.**

BIBLIOGRAPHY

Primary Sources

Castiglione, Baldessare. *The Book of the Courtier.* Translated by Charles S. Singleton. Garden City, N.Y., 1959, plus many reprints.

Della Casa, Giovanni. *Galateo.* Translated with introduction and notes by Konrad Eisenbichler and Kenneth R. Bartlett. Toronto, 1986.

Erasmus, Desiderius. *De civilitate morum puerilium.* In *Erasmus: Literary and Educational Writings,* 3. Edited by J. K. Sowards. Translated by Brian McGregor.

——. *Collected Works of Erasmus,* 25. Toronto, Buffalo, and London, 1985. English translation on pp. 269–289.

Secondary Sources
Burke, Peter. *The Fortunes of the Courtier: The European Reception of Castiglione's Cortegiano.* University Park, Pa., 1996.

Fritzer, Penelope Joan. *Jane Austen and Eighteenth-Century Courtesy Books.* Westport, Conn., and London, 1997.

PAUL F. GRENDLER

AESTHETICS. *See* **Art: Art Theory, Criticism, and Historiography.**

AFFAIR OF THE POISONS. *See* **Poisons, Affair of the.**

AFRICA

This entry contains two subentries:
NORTH AFRICA
SUB-SAHARAN AFRICA

NORTH AFRICA

The three dynastic successors to the empire of the Almohads in North Africa (Maghrib)—the Hafsids of Tunis, the Zayyanids of Tlemcen, and the Marinids/Wattasids of Fez—continued to experience internal political and economic fragmentation in the fifteenth century as a result of the decline of their established trade routes and the extension of the *Reconquista* to Muslim North Africa. The Treaty of Alcaçovas of 1479 recognized the exclusive rights of Portugal over the Atlantic coast of Morocco and its hinterland as far as Fez and of Castile over the Mediterranean coastline from Melilla to Tunis. Portuguese and Castilian efforts to dominate the Maghrib and its commerce intensified after the fall of Granada in 1492 and culminated with the establish-

ment of a number of naval bases on the Atlantic and Mediterranean coasts. The "African Crusade" provoked a powerful military response from the rising Ottoman Empire, which further threatened the survival of Maghribi polities already in the midst of profound social transformations.

The eclipse of Almohad power in the late thirteenth century unsettled the traditional solidarities between state and society in Andalusia and the Maghrib and mobilized a religious resurgence that challenged local governing elites. As the Almohad state deteriorated politically and economically, provincial Sufi notables and confraternities assumed essential sociopolitical functions in order to meet the needs of their communities and organize the defense of the collapsing Muslim frontier. The history of the Maghrib from the fifteenth to the eighteenth centuries was thus dominated by the regional confrontations between Europeans, Ottomans, and local Muslim dynasties and impressed by the varying degrees of contest and accommodation between the rulers of the post-Almohad states and fractious Sufi-led forces.

THE SHARIFIAN DYNASTIES OF MOROCCO

The Portuguese offensive concentrated on the Atlantic Straits and coastline of Morocco, and by 1495, six maritime enclaves *(fronteiras)* had been established in the realm of the Wattasids. The attacks aggravated the dire economic condition of the Wattasid regime, and the latter invariably submitted to tributary arrangements with the *fronteiras.* Local Sufi leaders condemned the manner in which the war against the Christians was being waged. They exhorted their followers to transfer their allegiance from the Wattasid sultan to revered descendants of the Prophet (sharifs) who, by virtue of their saintly lineage and moral rectitude, were more certain to conduct a successful war against Portugal. Between 1515 and 1537, the domestic balance of power shifted irreversibly in favor of the Saadi sharifs as their coalition scored a succession of military victories against the Portuguese and the Wattasids. By 1554 the Saadis had captured the Wattasid seat of Fez and reduced the Portuguese presence to the garrisons of el-Ksar as-Saghir, Tangiers, Asila, and Ceuta.

With the Saadis, prophetic descent became a pillar of political legitimacy in Morocco. Hence-

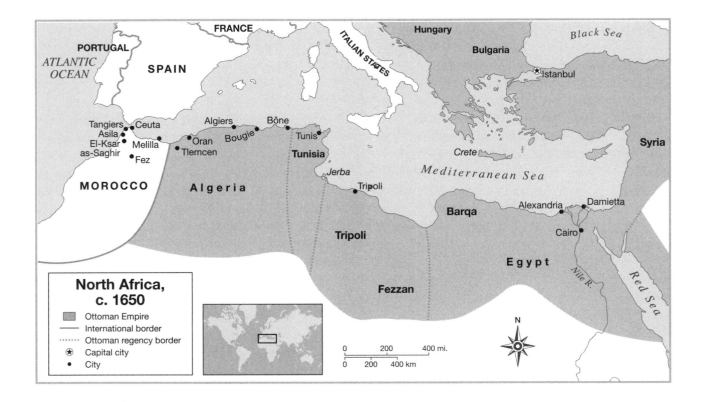

North Africa, c. 1650

- Ottoman Empire
- —— International border
- ········ Ottoman regency border
- ✪ Capital city
- • City

forth, the authority of Moroccan sovereigns was confirmed by investing their political practices with symbols and rituals of divine grace *(baraka)*. The Saadi claim to sharifian descent was contested by the Ottoman Empire. Firmly established in Egypt after 1517, the Ottomans' continuing expansion in the western Mediterranean carried them to the Moroccan border by 1545. The Ottoman threat remained a determining factor in Saadi politics for the rest of the century. Encircled by Ottomans, Spaniards, and Portuguese, Morocco grew isolated from the larger Muslim world, and its rulers survived by playing off their regional rivals, often allying themselves with the Christian powers against the Ottomans. The divisive politics of the Saadis culminated in August 1578, when the Ottomans defeated the Saadi caliph and his Portuguese allies in the Battle of the Three Kings. However, the confrontation also eliminated the Ottoman contender to the Saadi throne, thereby providing al-Mansur, the new sovereign, with respite to consolidate his authority and reduce his dependence on any regional power.

Al-Mansur modernized his army and, in 1591, launched a military expedition targeting the salt and gold mines of Songhay. With the influx of Sudanese gold, al-Mansur promoted commercial and diplomatic ties with Europe, joining briefly with England

in a compact against Spanish interests in the western Mediterranean. Finally, he established alliances of patronage and service with "tribal" confederations in order to extend the reach of his central administration *(al-makhzan)* to the remoter provinces *(al-siba)*. His death in 1603 marked a turning point in the history of Morocco as internecine battles fragmented the country into several contending entities. Still, the political commitment to sacred authority remained steadfast, and in 1631, a realignment of provincial Sufi forces carried another sharifian family to power. The Alawi sharifs reunited Morocco between 1659 and 1677, and under Mawlay Ismail (ruled 1672–1727) further reduced the influence of Portugal and Spain by developing diplomatic and commercial relations with Italy, France, Holland, and England. At the death of Ismail, the generals of his self-perpetuating army of slaves seized power, and much of provincial Morocco broke away from government control anew. The Alawi rulers regained political autonomy from the slave generals by 1757, largely as a result of their sustained efforts to reform the tax system, reestablish commercial contacts with Europe, and conscript "native" elements into the army. The unrelenting opposition of provincial Morocco to the centralizing tendencies of the state after 1727 would provide the main thrust of anticolonial resistances in the nineteenth century and would contribute to the colonial division of Morocco after 1912 into "useful" *makhzan* and "unruly" *siba*.

THE OTTOMAN REGENCY OF ALGIERS

The Habsburgs began their military offensive in the central Maghrib in 1505 with the capture of Mers al-Kabir, followed by Oran, Bougie, and Tripoli (1509–1510). Algiers agreed to pay tribute to the Spaniards, who built a presidio (el Peñón) on the largest of the four islets outlining the city's harbor. In 1516, the notables of Algiers solicited the succor of the privateer brothers Aruj and Khayr al-Din. Khayr al-Din Barbarossa took control of the city in 1519 and swore allegiance to the Ottoman sultan, who named him regent (Beylerbey) of North Africa, and sent him a military contingent of two thousand artillerymen and four thousand janissaries. With the reinforcements, Barbarossa consolidated his hold over the surrounding territories and towns, defeated a Habsburg counteroffensive, razed the Peñón in 1529, and established Algiers as his base for naval operations in the Mediterranean. By the time he was promoted to admiral-in-chief of the Ottoman navy in 1533, Barbarossa had erected the primary institutions that governed the regency until the French conquest of 1830.

Given the paucity of resources in the middle Maghrib, the political and economic viability of the Regency of Algiers depended on the Ottoman capital for the continued renewal of its administrative personnel and military contingent, and on external sources of revenue (namely, maritime trade, piracy, and privateering) for the replenishment of its state coffers. Sociopolitical stability was thus tied to the activities of two military institutions: the corps of janissaries that was committed to the defense of the Sultan's territorial possessions, but was also central to the tax-collecting operations of the local government, and the corporation of the captains of the fleet that protected Algerian commerce and merchant ships, and raided European harbors and vessels in search of captives and spoils. The janissary corps was a highly restricted ethnic military caste that safeguarded its privileges through the executive council *(diwan)*. By 1556, the corps and council constituted the most cohesive political institution in the regency. Yet the overall economic welfare of Algiers hinged upon the continued success of the privateer captains in ensuring the inflow of supplementary revenue and capital. The ability of the regent to remunerate his janissaries and exercise authority depended on the effectiveness of the privateer captains in pouring wealth and plunder into the local economy.

The janissaries exercised direct control over the city and environs of Algiers, and delegated the administration of the provinces to governors (beys) who were instructed to maintain order and collect taxes in their districts *(beyliks)* with the help of local Sufi and tribal notables. The central administration rarely extended beyond the district governorates and was regularly checked at the boundaries by pastoral and seminomadic communities that did not submit to Ottoman sovereignty. By relying heavily on native intermediaries and clients, the provincial administration gradually acquired an "Algerian" character. Beys intermarried locally and founded hereditary Turco-Algerian dynasties. In 1586, Istanbul started appointing its own governors (pashas) to Algiers in an unsuccessful attempt to curtail the growing political autonomy of the *diwan*. In 1659, the janissaries secured the consent of the imperial government in selecting their commanding officer *(agha)* as head of state. With the *aghas,* the political power of the janissaries reached its apogee, but its success coincided with the repeated inability of the state to remunerate its troops due to the growing importance of European navies and mercantile concessions in the Mediterranean.

The subordination of political considerations to the economic predicament of Algiers culminated in 1671 when the janissary corps transferred executive power to the admiral of the fleet and conferred upon him the title of dey. The deys attempted to enforce more balanced policies of fiscal extraction, and attained a modicum of equilibrium between 1710 and 1750 by exploiting Tunisian resources and commerce, and reducing the size of the janissary contingent and the corporation of captains. Still, deteriorating relations with European states and a series of inadequate agricultural harvests and fatal epidemics after 1787 deepened the structural imbalances in the political economy. Unprecedented encroachments by official tax collectors were met in the impoverished provinces with Sufi-led insurgencies that paralyzed their levying operations and forced the dey to develop alternative sources of political support. A fundamental realignment in the urban politics of the regency was effected in 1817 when Dey Ali Khodja broke free from the hold of the janissaries and transferred the public treasury to the citadel (al-qasbah) of Algiers. After the defeat of the janissaries, the reign of Husayn Dey (1818–1830) heralded the emergence of social and political structures that reflected the more equitable distribution of power between Algiers and the provinces. The decade preceding the French conquest in 1830 was thus marked by a gradual "de-Turkification" of the administration, driven by the ascendance of the native-born Turco-Algerians, and by the greater avenues of participation for provincial notables.

HAFSID AND HUSAYNID TUNIS

Unlike Morocco or Algeria, Hafsid Tunis could rely on its productive urban agricultural economy, lucrative commerce with Europe, and competent rulers to weather the political crises of the post-Almohad period. In 1510, Spain began to control Hafsid trade from its enclaves in Bougie and Tripoli. For the next half-century, Tunis remained at the center of the strategic struggle between Habsburgs and Ottomans for hegemony in the western Mediterranean. When the Ottomans finally dislodged the Spaniards from Tunis in 1574, they organized their new possession along the same lines as the regency of Algiers: a central authority in Tunis headed by an appointed pasha, assisted by beys in the provinces, and supported by a corps of janissaries under the command of deys. Senior military officers formed a *diwan* that acted as executive council. Yet the janissary contingent in Tunis did not grow overly dependent on privateering and continued to derive its main income from agricultural surpluses and international trade. Despite its incorporation into the Ottoman realm, Tunisia preserved its traditional institutions, and local notables remained involved in administrative decision making.

In 1590–1591, the janissaries reacted to the "nativization" of the administration and forced the pasha to recognize their dey as chief executive. This, however, did not impede or restrict the access of provincial beys to local resources, and they continued to recruit and employ Tunisian elements in their administration and army. Sufi and mainstream religious establishments also resisted bureaucratic centralization and united with the beys. Gradually, there emerged a Turco-Tunisian dynasty of beys that was widely regarded as "native" to Tunisia. The devolution of power to the provinces was confirmed in 1612 when the Ottoman sultan recognized Murad Bey as pasha, and granted him the right to transmit the title to his descendants. In 1671, the Muradids deposed the dey and transferred their seat to Tunis. They were themselves overthrown in 1702, following a military coup that reinstated temporarily the office of dey. The restored regime soon collapsed in defeat at the hands of invading Algerian troops. In the provinces, resistance to the Algerians was led by a coalition of Sufi elements and the remnants of the Turco-Tunisian notability. Husayn ibn Ali repelled the invaders and invested Tunis in 1705, thereby instating a dynasty that would rule Tunisia until 1957. Political stability under the Husaynids generated economic prosperity, and commercial treaties were concluded with France, England, Spain, Holland, and Austria. After 1784, however, Tunisia was again weakened by military incursions from Algeria and, more importantly, by a considerable deterioration of its terms of trade with Europe, a process that would reorient its economy in the next century toward cash-crop exports and dependence on European markets.

See also **Habsburg Dynasty: Austria; Ottoman Empire; Spain.**

BIBLIOGRAPHY

Abun-Nasr, Jamil. *A History of the Maghrib in the Islamic Period.* Cambridge, U.K., and New York, 1987.

Boyer, Pierre. "Introduction à une histoire intérieure de la Régence d'Alger." *Revue Historique* 235, no. 2, (1966): 297–316.

Devisse, Jean. "Routes de commerce et échanges en Afrique Occidentale en relation avec la Méditerranée." *Revue d'Histoire Économique et Sociale* 50 (1972): 42–73, 357–397.

Julien, Charles-André. *Histoire de l'Afrique du Nord: Des origines à 1830.* Paris, 1994.

Laroui, Abdallah. *The History of the Maghrib: An Interpretive Essay.* Princeton, 1977.

Lévi-Provençal, Évariste. *Les historiens des Chorfa.* Paris, 1922.

Terrasse, Henri. *Histoire du Maroc des origines à l'établissement du protectorat français.* Casablanca, 1975.

Valensi, Lucette. *On the Eve of Colonialism: North Africa before the French Conquest.* New York, 1977. Translation of *Le Maghreb avant la prise d'Alger, 1790–1830,* 1969.

O. W. ABI-MERSHED

SUB-SAHARAN AFRICA

By 1450, sub-Saharan Africa was characterized by kingdoms, federations, and decentralized lineage-based polities loosely linked to different environ-mental, economic, and geographic configurations. In the Sahel region immediately south of the Sahara, the kingdoms of Mali and Songhay thrived off the trans-Saharan trade in gold, slaves, salt, and forest produce. On the fertile Ethiopian highlands, the royal Solomonid dynasty traced its ancestry to the biblical union between King Solomon and the Queen of Sheba. Peoples of the rainforests of central and west Africa, by contrast, organized themselves in decentralized units led by "big men." On the

savannah, south and east of the rainforest, rulers of centralized polities prospered from gold, iron, and copper production; the vast herds of cattle that they managed to amass measured their wealth and status. On the east African littoral, elegant Swahili towns had ties with Persia, south Asia, and China.

Contact between these African polities and Europeans increased dramatically from the fifteenth to the eighteenth centuries. While the Atlantic slave trade is the best-known aspect of the early modern European-African encounter, recent historical research suggests that ties were diverse and complicated. Only in the eighteenth century did exports of slaves begin to dominate trade and define the political, economic, and cultural encounter.

EXTENT AND ITEMS OF TRADE

Prince Henry the Navigator of Portugal (1394–1460) pioneered ties with the Sahel and west Africa to spread Christian rule and to gain access to African gold. Legends of vast quantities of African gold were common since stories of the Malian King Mansa Musa's (ruled 1307–1332) fabulous riches, displayed during his pilgrimage to Mecca (1324–1325), circulated around the Mediterranean world. Portuguese fleets reached the Senegal River in 1445 and began to exchange slaves and manufactured goods for gold with Akan and Guinea Coast gold traders. By 1455 Portugal declared a monopoly over the west African trade routes, a policy that was further elaborated in the papal treaties of Alcaçovas (1479) and Tordesillas (1494).

In 1498 the Portuguese Captain Vasco da Gama (c. 1460–1524) reached India after Swahili navigators instructed him on the use of the Indian Ocean monsoon winds. King Manuel I of Portugal (ruled 1495–1521), who declared himself "Lord of Conquest and Commerce of India and all Adjacent Lands," sent a number of expeditions to establish

trading centers on the east African coast that would help to monopolize trade between India and Europe and would also benefit from existing Indian Ocean trade networks. In 1505 Dom Francisco d'Almeida and his fleet razed the Swahili coastal entrepôt of Kilwa, leading to the surrender of a string of Swahili coastal towns and the establishment of Portuguese naval bases at Sofala, Mozambique, Zanzibar, and Mombasa. Huge and overloaded Portuguese trading vessels participating in the eighteen-month round voyage between Lisbon to Goa, termed the *carreira da India,* frequently shipwrecked off the dangerous southeastern African coast. In 1698 Omanis conquered Mombasa and Kilwa and precipitated the decline of Portuguese authority on the central and northeastern African coast. The Portuguese turned to the slave and ivory trade from the southeastern port of Sofala and the Zambezi base of Tete.

In the late seventeenth and eighteenth centuries, the extent and intensity of the Atlantic slave trade increased with the involvement of English, French, Dutch, and Portuguese trading companies in the lucrative "triangular trade" between Africa, Europe, and the Americas. The trade in slaves typically took place between European ships and African or Euro-African middlemen at coastal entrepôts that received slaves from a chain of trading connections reaching into the African interior. Several West African kingdoms like Benin, Kongo, Oyo, Asante, and Dahomey taxed the trade in slaves, and in some cases were able to limit its deleterious effects on their own subjects. However, rulers who sought to monopolize access to sought-after commodities became increasingly dependent on Atlantic and Indian Ocean trade goods—such as textiles, metals, alcohol, tobacco, gunpowder, and manufactured goods—to secure the economic patronage

TABLE 1

Estimated Slave Exports from Africa

Export Region	1500–1600	%	1600–1700	%	1700–1800	%	Total	%
Red Sea	100,000	9.3	100,000	4.4	200,000	3.0	400,000	3
Trans-Sahara	550,000	51.0	700,000	31.1	700,000	9.5	1,950,000	18
East Africa	100,000	9.3	100,000	4.4	400,000	5.5	600,000	6
Trans-Atlantic	328,000	30.4	1,348,000	60.0	6,090,000	82.0	7,766,000	73
Total	1,078,000	100.0	2,248,000	100.0	7,390,000	100.0	10,716,000	

TABLE 2

Atlantic Slave Trade by National Carrier, 1701–1800

National Carrier	Number of Slaves	%
English	2,468,000	40.5
Portuguese	1,888,000	31.0
French	1,104,000	18.1
Dutch	349,000	5.7
North American	206,000	3.4
Danish	66,000	1.0
Other	10,000	0.2
Total	6,091,000	

networks upon which their political authority rested.

The demographic, political, and economic impact of the export of slaves and import of various European, American, and Asian goods is a subject of lively historical debate. It is estimated that at least thirty million slaves were captured as part of the Atlantic slave trade (although only eleven or twelve million were exported), with many more killed through slave-related raiding and warfare. While imports of foreign commodities at times challenged African productive capacity, African producers were also able to innovate and adapt to the influx of new trade goods.

TREATIES, EMISSARIES, AND SCHOLARS
In the fifteenth century, African emissaries to the royal courts of Europe were more frequent than European emissaries to Africa. The Christian emperors of Ethiopia sent embassies to southern Europe to forge Christian solidarity in the face of Muslim expansion and to hire European artisans.

TABLE 3

Regional Origin of Slaves in Eighteenth-Century Atlantic Trade (Dutch, British, French, and Portuguese)

Region	1700–1800	%
West-Central	2,331,800	38
Benin	1,223,200	21
Biafra	901,100	16
Gold Coast	881,200	14
Upper West	689,000	11
Total	6,089,700	

SOURCE: Paul Lovejoy, *Transformations in Slavery: A History of Slavery in Africa* (47, 48, 51).

Portuguese aid for the Ethiopians against coastal Muslims in the early sixteenth century helped to narrow the rift between the Ethiopian and the Latin Christian churches; but the intransigence of dispatched papal officials toward Ethiopian Christianity led the Ethiopians to renounce papal decrees in the early 1630s.

In the 1480s, Portuguese ships brought a number of African royal emissaries to Lisbon, including those from the Kongo kingdom (1484), the kingdom of Benin (1486), and the Wolof kingdom (1487); a second Kongolese delegation set up a center for African studies where Kongolese learned European culture and religion and European missionaries were instructed in Kongolese culture and language. One outcome of this encounter was the conversion of the Kongolese royalty to Christianity and, over the next century, the spread of Christian ideas and icons throughout the central African kingdom.

A number of African scholars trained and taught at European universities. In 1652 the Ethiopian priest Abba Gregoryos studied with the German scholar Job Ludolf, whom he tutored in Ethiopian languages. Anton Wilhelm Amo, who was born on the Gold Coast, lectured in philosophy at German universities and was a participant in the German Enlightenment before he returned to his childhood home in 1748. Jacobus E. J. Capitein (1717–1747) defended his dissertation at the University of Leiden in 1742; in eloquent Latin he argued that slavery was compatible with Christianity since servitude of the body should not hinder freedom of the soul. By contrast, while not a scholarly tract, the freed slave Olaudau Equiano's autobiography, first published in 1789, was crucial in promoting the abolitionist cause.

PERCEPTIONS OF THE OTHER
By the sixteenth century, southern Europeans had extensive contact with peoples of sub-Saharan Africa—Africans made up an estimated 10 percent of Lisbon and 7.5 percent of Seville's population. Iberian perceptions of Africans were mediated by religious discourses and only gave way to racial understandings of difference in the eighteenth century. The Portuguese termed Africans of Islamic faith "Moors" whether they dwelt in the west African Sudan or on the Swahili coast. The Portuguese and

Dutch used the term *kaffir,* adapted from Arabic, for Africans who did not follow Christianity or Islam.

Africans were less accustomed to Europeans, who were generally confined to the coast and rarely lived among them. Perceptions of white-skinned Europeans seem to have been ambivalent; Africans accused them of being wizards, cannibals, or ancestors returned from the dead; but they often welcomed them, if only to acquire their valued goods. Africans described Europeans with particular words that referred to their oceanic origins, peculiar dress, itinerancy, and cunning trade tactics.

See also **Slavery and the Slave Trade; Triangular Trade Pattern.**

BIBLIOGRAPHY

Capitein, Jacobus Elisa Johannes. *The Agony of Asar: A Thesis on Slavery by the Former Slave, Jacobus Elisa Johannes Capitein, 1717–1747.* Translated with Commentary by Grant Parker. Princeton, 2001.

Cohen, William. B. *The French Encounter with Africans: White Responses to Blacks, 1530–1880.* Bloomington, Ind., 1980.

Debrunner, Hans Werner. *Presence and Prestige: Africans in Europe: A History of Africans in Europe before 1918.* Basel, 1979.

Equiano, Ouladah. *The Interesting Narrative and Other Writings.* Edited by Vincent Carreta. New York, 1995.

Hastings, Adrian. *The Church in Africa, 1450–1950.* Oxford, 1994.

Lovejoy, Paul E. *Transformations in Slavery: A History of Slavery in Africa.* Cambridge, U.K., 1983; 2nd ed., 2000.

Miller, Joseph. *Way of Death: Merchant Capitalism and the Angolan Slave Trade, 1730–1830.* Madison, Wis., 1988.

Northrup, David. *Africa's Discovery of Europe, 1450–1850.* New York and Oxford, 2002.

Thornton, John. *Africa and Africans in the Making of the Atlantic World: 1400–1800.* New York and Cambridge, U.K., 1992; 2nd ed., 1998.

DAVID M. GORDON

AGNOSTICISM. *See* **Atheism.**

AGRICULTURE. In 1500, between two-thirds and three-quarters of European adults worked primarily in agriculture. The number who lived in the countryside and worked occasionally on farms was even higher—over 90 percent of the population in parts of eastern Europe. The numbers were still large in 1750, when agriculture employed half or two-thirds of the working population in many European countries.

Most Europeans had to labor on farms because agricultural technology was, by modern standards, rudimentary and agriculture itself unproductive. The majority of the population therefore toiled in fields and pastures to feed the minority who lived in manors and cities. Food shortages were common, at least for the poor, and bad harvests triggered food riots and sent the hungry roaming across the land in search of something to eat. In times of dearth, government officials diverted food to cities to prevent urban disturbances and sometimes even barred hungry paupers at city gates.

Agriculture was important for other reasons as well. Military leaders worried about feeding armies and providing them with horses, and with reason; otherwise soldiers would ransack homes. Farms were also a major source of income for the rich and powerful, who lived on the income from agricultural properties. The revenue might take the form of rent, of seignorial dues, or, in regions where serfdom still existed, of obligatory labor on noble estates. On top of all this, peasants paid the tithe to the church and taxes to fund the wars waged by early modern states.

Increasing the meager productivity of European agriculture became a great concern in the eighteenth century, when government officials and agricultural reformers argued about what would make farms produce more. Although there was no extraordinary technological revolution in farming until the nineteenth century, certain regions (such as Catalonia and the German North Sea Coast in the sixteenth century, or the Paris Basin and the wine-growing province of Beaujolais in the eighteenth) did experience increases in agricultural productivity in the early modern period. Two countries—England and the Netherlands—managed to forge ahead of the rest. Why farming advanced in England and the Netherlands, while most other European

Agriculture. *Summer* by Francesco Bassano, c. 1570–1580. In this pastoral scene, Bassano presents images of typical activities: shearing of sheep and harvesting of grain. ©ALEXANDER BURKATOWSKI/CORBIS

countries lagged behind, has been debated for over two hundred years, but new answers to this age-old question have begun to emerge from recent scholarship.

WHO OWNED THE LAND, WHO FARMED IT, AND WHO HAD RIGHTS TO IT

In most of early modern Europe, farmland was subject to a variety of rights and claims that made ownership complex. Technically, the land often belonged to aristocratic landlords (nobles, ecclesiastical institutions, or even merchants or officials), but, particularly in western Europe (eastern Europe was quite different), their rights were frequently limited to collecting insignificant fixed rents and relatively small dues and fees due them as seignorial lords. There were certainly exceptions to this rule, and most aristocratic landlords did have some plots—

the demesne on their seignorial estates—that they could rent out for their full value. But it was the farmers themselves who exercised effective ownership of much of the agricultural land in western Europe, and what they did not own they usually rented. They had to pay the seignorial lord his dues and fees, use his mill, oven, or court; and perhaps provide him with a small amount of underpaid or forced labor. Typically, however, they could sell the land they possessed, bequeath it to their heirs, or sublease it. If they were tenants (rather than de facto owners), they would, of course, be unable to dispose of the property, and they would have to pay significant rent, perhaps to the seignorial lord (if, say, he were leasing out part of the demesne), or perhaps to some other landowner. Whatever the situation, how to farm the land was still their decision.

Most often these farmers were peasants. The most substantial ones had to amass large amounts of capital even if they were tenant farmers. They owned sheep, oxen or horses, plows and other implements, seed grain for planting, and money to hire workers or pay rent, and they saved so that their sons and daughters could be prosperous farmers, too. Other farmers had much less and could not even afford to pay cash rent. With no land of their own, they might enter into a sharecropping contract with a landlord, who would provide livestock, implements, and seed for farming in return for a large share of the crop (typically one-half) as rent. Nearly all the farmers (except for the most prosperous ones, who assumed the role of farm managers) worked on their own farms. They employed family labor, too—women milked cows, tended gardens, and cared for poultry, while even children helped bring in the grain harvest—and often hired long-term servants and temporary workers as well.

In eastern Europe, in contrast, the situation was almost reversed: there landlords managed to impose what is sometimes called a "second serfdom" on peasants during the early modern period. Peasants in much of the region (this is true in particular for what is now Poland, eastern Germany, western Hungary, and the Czech Republic) had exercised effective landownership and enjoyed considerable independence well into the fifteenth century. Thereafter, however, they lost their land to seignorial lords who incorporated it into their demesne, and much of their independence vanished, too. The landlords imposed heavy seignorial dues, forced the peasants to spend much of their time working for little or no pay on seignorial demesnes, and used their political and legal powers to keep them from fleeing or moving away. By the early seventeenth century, peasants in parts of eastern Germany had to work three days a week for their seignorial lords, while an average Polish peasant family might have to furnish two workers and oxen for the same amount of time every week.

Throughout Europe, peasant villages also exercised rights over the land. Villages often controlled access to pastures, waste, or unplowed fields that could be used for grazing. They could bar farmers from entering fields and vineyards to protect ripening crops from damage or theft, and they often determined when harvesting began. In eastern Eu-

rope, landlords weakened the villages when they imposed the second serfdom, but in western Europe the communities were strong enough to defend peasants' communal grazing rights against encroaching landlords. In doing so, the western villages often asserted that they were defending poorer villagers, who relied on the communal grazing rights because they had little or no land. Their claims were sometimes hollow, for in some instances the communal grazing land was the preserve of the community's richest peasants, who masked their monopoly in the language of concern for the poor.

AGRICULTURAL PRACTICES AND TECHNOLOGY

Bread was a staple of the European diet, grain was a major crop, and much European farmland was therefore devoted to growing wheat and rye, alongside oats for horses and barley for beer or soup. Even in major grain-producing areas, though, as much as a third of what farmers produced (after they fed the livestock) came from animals—in particular, wool and lamb from the herds of sheep that were sent to graze on fallow fields to fertilize them. In pastoral regions (such as Scandinavia, western parts of France and of Great Britain, and nearly any place where there were mountains), animals were even more important for the value of the products they provided: not only sheep, but herds of cattle, which were a source of beef, hides, and cheese. Nearly all farms, even small ones, had poultry in courtyards and pigs rooting for acorns in forests. Olives and fruit trees were important near the Mediterranean, and vineyards grew on hillsides and rocky soil even in northern climates. Even in areas that moved toward specialization in crops other than grain—parts of Normandy, for instance, which had shifted toward producing livestock—land was still often reserved for growing some wheat, rye, or oats. High transportation costs (particularly when there were no navigable waterways nearby) made it cheaper for most peasants to grow grain for their own consumption rather than specialize completely in stock raising or viticulture and then buying their food.

In much of Europe grains were grown in a three-year crop cycle known as the three-field system. Cultivation began with a year of fallow, when the land was fertilized with the manure of pasturing sheep and then plowed to rid it of weeds and incorporate organic matter into the soil. In the second year, wheat or rye was sowed, followed, in the third year, by barley, oats, or a fodder crop such as vetch or peas. The land thus produced crops two years out of three. If land was abundant, or if the topsoil was thin or infertile, then the fallow, with its fertilizing and plowing, might repeat every second year, yielding crops one year out of two—what was called the two-field system. In some instances, the fallow might last even longer, and weeds and brush that choked the field would be burned before cultivation resumed.

Where the three-field system predominated—as in much of northwestern Europe—fields were often unfenced and open in order to allow animals to pasture. Fencing would have, in any case, been extremely costly because many peasants farmed narrow strips of land scattered through the various fields: several strips in the field sown in wheat, for instance, several more in the oat field, and still others in the fallow. Open fields were common in some regions of two-field agriculture, too, though not in all. On average (there were exceptions to this rule when soil was fertile or agriculture relatively advanced) the fields ended up producing perhaps only four or five times the seed sown, a tenth of the yield today. The meager yields were one reason so many early modern Europeans had to work in agriculture; another was the enormous amount of labor required to bring in the harvest in an era before mechanical reapers. Armies of men, women, and children invaded the fields to cut the grain with sickles, gather it up, and stack it for drying and storage. The demand would drive up wages in summertime and draw workers from cities. Even then the work was not over, for the grain still had to be threshed before it could be ground into flour. Once the harvest was over, many of the hands would be idle, and that was part of the appeal of rural industry, which provided work doing tasks such as spinning.

The practices of early modern farmers were condemned by eighteenth-century agricultural reformers and, more recently, by modern historians. Most of the critics believe that early modern farmers were wasteful or could have produced more. Some have argued, for instance, that early modern farmers could have replaced the two-field system with the three-field one, which would have yielded crops two years out of three instead of just one year in two, or they could have planted fodder crops (such as alfalfa, sainfoin, or clover) on the fallow fields, which were supposed to add nutrients to the soil and support larger herds of animals, thereby increasing the supply of fertilizer for the grain fields. But these criticisms often fail to take costs and technical difficulties into account. Often the fodder crops did not suit the soil or pay for the additional costs they entailed, and the two-field system was usually a reasonable response to soil conditions or a relatively lower price of land. Shifting to a three-field system would actually have been wasteful or have diminished yields. Similarly, critics might ask why peasants reaped wheat with sickles, when scythes, which had long been used to mow grass or harvest oats, could do the task in much less time. However, the scythe required considerable strength, and even in the hands of a man it tended to knock the kernels off the wheat stalks. Only skilled reapers could wield it successfully, and it was cheaper to employ women, children, and unskilled men, who sawed wheat with sickles. Early modern farmers did not have our knowledge or technology, but they were certainly not wasteful.

THE SUCCESS OF AGRICULTURE IN ENGLAND AND THE NETHERLANDS

Although early modern yields were low, agricultural productivity did jump in the seventeenth and eighteenth centuries in two countries—the Netherlands and England. Although the increase, particularly in England, has often been termed an agricultural revolution, it would probably be better to reserve that term for the truly revolutionary changes—such as chemical fertilizers or the mechanical reaper—that transformed farming in the nineteenth century. Still, there is no denying that agricultural productivity did surge in the Netherlands and England. Perhaps the best measure is an index of what the average farmworker produced in each country, in which all farm products, from grain to meat, are lumped together. This index, constructed by the economic historian Robert Allen, shows that in 1750 Dutch and English farmworkers were producing between 59 and 175 percent more than their counterparts in all European countries but one. The one exception was the southern Netherlands—roughly speaking modern-day Belgium—where farmworkers had

Agriculture. *Summer* by Pieter Breughel the Younger. This painting, which depicts workers harvesting grain, was done from a 1568 drawing by Pieter Bruegel the Elder. ©CHRISTIE'S IMAGES/CORBIS

reached the same high level of productivity back in 1400.

Judging the productivity of whole countries has the disadvantage of glossing over great regional variations. France as a whole had lower agricultural productivity than England or the Netherlands, but there were parts of the country, such as the Paris Basin, where farms were just as productive as those anywhere in Europe. Similar statements could be made about the German North Sea Coast, Catalonia on the Iberian Peninsula, and parts of Italy. Still, whether one focuses on regions or whole countries, why agricultural productivity was so much higher in some places than in others must still be explained. The issue has attracted the most historical attention in England, for it was the first country to industrialize. Yet, back in 1600 its agricultural productivity (the Netherlands's too) was no

different from that of most other European countries.

One common explanation traces England's success back to capitalist landlords, who remade the countryside in what were called enclosures. The enclosures involved putting an end to village control of farming practices, creating large farms by consolidating scattered fields, and fencing in open fields so that new crops could be planted on the fallow or arable land converted to pasture. The enclosures, historians have argued, boosted agricultural productivity by changing property rights, enlarging the scale of farming, and putting capitalist landlords who understood agricultural technology in charge. Elsewhere in Europe, agriculture remained in the hands of peasants, whose farms were too small and who resisted new crops and enclosures, either because they were fearful or ignorant or because poorer villagers wanted to protect their communal grazing rights. For one school of historians, it is population growth that kept most European farms too small and in the hands of backward peasants. For another, it was politics and the strength of the landlord class, for population growth was the same in England as in countries such as France, where agriculture lagged behind.

Recent work, however, casts doubt on these arguments. Enclosures did not boost agricultural productivity much in England, or on the rare occasions when they were tried in France. Bigger farms did not matter much either. They may have helped economize on labor, but most of the increase in English agricultural productivity came not from capitalist landlords, but from yeomen, who were really large-scale peasants, operating farms of sixty acres or so. Peasants as a whole were quite receptive to new agricultural techniques and they adopted them when it paid to do so. Similarly, overlapping property rights and village control of agriculture were less of an obstacle than historians thought. There were problems when land had to be drained or irrigated, but drainage and irrigation cannot account for the difference between French and English agriculture.

Excessive rent, taxes, and seignorial dues depressed agricultural productivity in some parts of Europe, but the damage they did was probably not as great as some historians imagined. Particular rental contracts, such as sharecropping, were less a cause of agricultural stagnation than a way for landlords to lend capital to poverty-stricken tenants. If rent, taxes, and seignorial dues together took less than a third of what a farmer produced, then they probably did not harm agricultural productivity either. If, however, they increased above a third, or if they dulled a farmer's incentives, then they could injure farming. That was a likely cause for the dismal agricultural performance in eastern Europe, where the second serfdom discouraged peasants' initiative and effort, and in Spain, where high taxes drove peasants to sell their property to nobles, who had little reason to farm well.

Warfare also did enormous harm to early modern agriculture. Beyond seizing food and horses, troops disrupted trade, and when frightened peasants fled from advancing armies, fields grew over before it was safe to return, necessitating months or even years of plowing and land clearance before fields could be cultivated again.

England (but not the Netherlands) escaped the worst army, at least on its own soil, but both countries had the added advantage of excellent transportation. The Netherlands built a great network of canals, and England constructed both canals and roads. In other countries, a road might be built to move troops, but in England and the Netherlands the infrastructure facilitated trade. Trade, whether by land or water, encouraged great agricultural specialization in the two countries, and, in turn, specialization increased productivity as farmers adapted crops to soil and prices and worked harder to buy new consumer goods available on the market. This specialization goes a long way toward explaining why agriculture in England and the Netherlands was productive and more innovative than in the rest of early modern Europe.

See also **Daily Life; Economic Crises; Enclosure; Feudalism; Food and Drink; Food Riots; Laborers; Landholding; Peasantry; Physiocrats and Physiocracy; Poverty; Serfdom; Serfdom in East Central Europe; Serfdom in Russia; Technology; Transportation; Villages; Women.**

BIBLIOGRAPHY

Abel, Wilhelm. *Geschichte der deutschen Landwirtschaft vom frühen Mittelalter bis zum 19. Jahrhundert.* 3rd rev. ed. Stuttgart, 1978. Wealth of detail about central Europe for readers of German.

Allen, Robert C. "Economic Structure and Agricultural Productivity in Europe, 1300–1800." *European Review of Economic History* 4 (2000): 1–26.

———. *Enclosure and the Yeoman: The Agricultural Development of the South Midlands, 1450–1850.* Oxford and New York, 1992. Best study of England.

Aston, T. H., and C. H. E. Philpin. *The Brenner Debate: Agrarian Class Structure and Economic Development in Pre-Industrial Europe.* Cambridge, U.K., and New York, 1985.

De Vries, Jan. *The Dutch Rural Economy in the Golden Age, 1500–1700.* New Haven, 1974.

———. *The Economy of Europe in an Age of Crisis, 1600–1750.* Cambridge, U.K., and New York, 1976. Important for the role that transportation played.

Duplessis, Robert S. *Transitions to Capitalism in Early Modern Europe.* Cambridge, U.K., and New York, 1997. Good overview of agriculture throughout Europe with excellent bibliographies.

Finberg, H. P. R., and Joan Thirsk, eds. *The Agrarian History of England and Wales.* 8 vols. London, 1967–2000. Volumes 4 through 6 give exhaustive but somewhat dated coverage of the early modern period.

Hoffman, Philip T. *Growth in a Traditional Society: The French Countryside, 1450–1815.* Princeton, 1996.

Le Roy Ladurie, Emmanuel. *The French Peasantry, 1450–1660.* Translated by Alan Sheridan. Berkeley, 1987.

Meuvret, Jean. *Le problème des subsistances à l'époque Louis XIV.* 3 vols. Paris, 1977–1988. In French, but indispensible for understanding early modern agricultural technology.

PHILIP T. HOFFMAN

Fernando Álvarez de Toledo. LIBRARY OF CONGRESS

ALBA, FERNANDO ÁLVAREZ DE TOLEDO, DUKE OF

(also Alva; 1507–1582), Spanish general and statesman. Fernando Álvarez de Toledo was born 29 October 1507 at Piedrahita, one of his family's estates. Three years later his father died fighting the Muslims in North Africa, and he was raised by his grandfather, Fadrique, second Duke of Alba, who gave him a military education. His tutors included Juan Boscán, who translated Castiglione's *The Book of the Courtier* (1528) into Castilian, and the poet Garcilaso de la Vega. At sixteen Fernando fought at the siege of Fuenterrabía against French forces. After inheriting his grandfather's title in 1531, he served the Holy Roman Emperor Charles V (ruled 1519–1558; king of Spain, ruled 1516–1556 as Charles I) in the campaigns of Vienna, Tunis, Provence, and Algiers. With the beginning of the emperor's wars against the Protestant German Schmalkaldic League in 1546, Alba became the emperor's chief military advisor and played a major role in the victory at Mühlberg in 1547.

Alba returned to Spain in 1548 as Prince Philip's chief of household. He used this position to create a court faction based upon his own extended family and a group of royal secretaries associated with the imperial secretary, Francisco de los Cobos. The royal chamberlain, Ruy Gómez de Silva, developed a rival faction based on his wife's Mendoza relatives and the group of royal secretaries loyal to Cardinal Espinosa (the Inquisitor-General).

As chief of household, Alba went to England with Philip II (ruled 1556–1598) in 1554. When Charles V abdicated, Alba served Philip briefly as viceroy of Milan and then of Naples, where, in 1556–1557, he conducted a successful war against Pope Paul IV and the duke of Guise. When the Habsburg-Valois struggle ended in 1559, Alba helped negotiate the Treaty of Cateau-Cambrésis before returning to Spain as a member of the Council of State. There, his sharp tongue and haughty disposition made him unpopular, but Philip relied upon his military expertise and trusted his religious orthodoxy to the point of consulting him on ecclesiastical appointments.

After 1562, Alba's glorified ideas of royal authority and hatred of heresy made him the court's leading opponent of compromise with the Netherlanders, who were growing restive under Spanish rule. Both he and the king regarded the rioting and iconoclasm of 1566 as rebellion. Philip, with the duke's knowledge, devised a strategy that would send Alba to the Netherlands to crush the opposition. Philip would then claim that his captain-general had exceeded his instructions, go to the Netherlands in person, and mollify its inhabitants with a general pardon. The plan was supported by Alba's enemies, who hoped to discredit him while he was out of the country.

In 1567, the duke led an army of Spanish veterans to the Low Countries, where he established a political court, known as the Council of Troubles, to prosecute dissidents. The Council declared the counts of Egmont and Hoorn guilty of high treason, as presumed leaders of the revolt, and executed them. These harsh measures caused William of Orange and other leaders of the Gueux (a sixteenth-century revolutionary party) to flee to foreign countries. When William of Orange then invaded the Netherlands with an army of German mercenaries, Alba easily defeated him, and by 1568 had pacified the entire country. It was time for the king to come, but the death of his heir, Don Carlos, and the revolt of the Moriscos in southern Spain prevented him from doing so.

Alba remained in the Netherlands for four more years in the face of growing resentment. He used his time to complete ecclesiastical reforms that had been halted since 1560 and to install fourteen new bishops. He also promulgated the first uniform criminal code in Netherlandish history, but, when he attempted in 1572 to impose the Tenth Penny, a sales tax based on the Spanish *alcabala,* the towns rose in revolt. Although Alba's campaign against them was at first successful, his policy of reprisals led to prolonged sieges at Haarlem and Alkmaar, and the king finally recalled him to Spain in 1573. Though Alba retained his seat on the Council of State, his position at court was now far weaker than it had been before he was sent to the Netherlands. Philip imprisoned him briefly in 1579, over the unauthorized marriage of his son Fadrique, but released him in the following year to lead Spain's army in the annexation of Portugal. Here his touch was more subtle and successful than it had been in the Netherlands. He died at Tomar in Portugal in 1582.

Contemporaries thought Alba the greatest soldier of his age. His ideas on warfare were popularized by a school of military writers who had served under his command, and they continued to influence Spanish military practice until the Thirty Years' War (1618–1648). He was capable of successful

diplomacy, but as Philip II's governor in the Netherlands he failed. The duke's harshness and insensitivity to local conditions provoked a full-scale insurrection, and he bears much responsibility for Spain's eventual loss of the northern Netherlands.

See also **Cateau-Cambrésis (1559); Charles I (Spain); Charles V (Holy Roman Empire); Dutch Republic; Dutch Revolt (1568–1648); Guise Family; Habsburg-Valois Wars; Inquisition, Spanish; Moriscos; Netherlands, Southern; Philip II (Spain); Schmalkaldic War (1546–1547); William of Orange.**

BIBLIOGRAPHY

Epistolario del III Duque de Alba, 3v., edited by J. M. del P.C.M.S. Fitz James Stuart y Falco, Tenth Duke of Berwick y Alba. Madrid, 1952.

Maltby, William S. *Alba: A Biography of Fernando Álvarez de Toledo, Third Duke of Alba, 1507–1582.* Berkeley, 1983.

WILLIAM S. MALTBY

ALCHEMY. In the early modern period the term "alchemy" did not refer solely to the transmutation of metals. A variety of laboratory procedures, including the separation of metals, sublimations, and distillations, were generally described in alchemical terms, and alchemy had already for a long time been associated with making medicines. In this regard the medieval tradition of separating from substances a fifth essence, or *quinta essentia,* underscored later attempts among Hermeticists and Paracelsians to extract a celestial, life-giving force from plants, animals, and metals that, in turn, could perfect specific bodies. The sulfur-mercury theory, based in Aristotelian natural philosophy and further articulated by Arab scholars, in which all metals were believed to be composed of an original sulfur and mercury in various degrees of purity, also continued to provide a basis for some alchemical discussions. The extent to which Aristotelian principles continued to influence practical alchemical procedures is well illustrated by a text called *Alchemia* written in 1597 by a German physician, chemist, and schoolmaster named Andreas Libau (c. 1550–1616). Libau's book looks very modern, and has been referred to as the first textbook of modern chemistry. It teaches, among many other things, how to analyze minerals, metals, and mineral waters, how to make use of assaying techniques, and how to prepare medicines from metals and minerals. It describes analytical reactions, presents quantitative methods for determining alloys, and gives precise instructions on how to build a variety of laboratory furnaces and vessels. It also describes extracts and essences at the same time that it provides evidence for various sorts of transmutation. All of this falls under the heading of alchemy.

HERMETICISM AND PARACELSUS

At the same time as some alchemists were being led by older theories to create new chemical technologies, others were inspired by more spiritual traditions, especially by the legacy of Neoplatonism and by the discovery in the second half of the fifteenth century of texts reputed to have been written by an ancient sage named Hermes Trismegistus. The tradition that followed, called Renaissance Hermeticism, viewed the celestial bodies, sometimes through the mediation of a cosmic spirit *(spiritus mundi),* as the link between God and terrestrial things. Divine virtues penetrated everything in nature, and the Hermetic alchemist sought to extract such powers and virtues particularly for the purpose of making useful medicines. A very similar idea prompted the thinking of an especially significant figure in the history of early modern alchemy, Paracelsus (1493/94–1541). Paracelsus described the creation of the physical universe and the processes that maintained the life of the body in essentially alchemical terms. All of nature stemmed from an initial separation of light from dark, earth from water, and so on, and the body operated by means of an "inner alchemist," called the *archeus,* which separated that which was pure and helpful to the maintenance of life from that which was not. Regarding transmutation, Paracelsus, like many others, thought in embracive terms. In a work called *De Natura Rerum* (On the nature of things) he notes, "transmutation is when a thing loses its form or shape and is transformed so that it no longer displays at all its initial form and substance. . . . When a metal becomes glass or stone . . . when wood becomes charcoal . . . [or] . . . when cloth becomes paper . . . all of that is the transmutation of natural things." By this definition almost everyone in the early modern period was engaged in alchemy. "Nature," Paracelsus adds, "brings nothing to light which is completed in itself, rather, human beings have to do the completing. This completing is called

alchemy." To complete the work of nature and to delve into her secrets Paracelsus recommended the processes of distillation, calcination (producing a powdery calx, or oxide, usually by heating a metal), and sublimation (heating to a gaseous state and then condensing a vapor into solid form). Through these one could separate the elements and discover the healing and perfecting tinctures, *magisteria* (substances whose external impurities had been removed and which were then said to be exalted or ennobled), and *arcana* (divine secrets) within things, and learn about the generative qualities associated with the first principles of creation, the so-called *tria prima:* salt, sulfur, and mercury.

The art of separation was, for Paracelsus and his followers, the key to knowledge of both natural philosophy and medicine; in this regard Paracelsus distinguished between what he called *alchemia transmutatoria* and *alchemia medica*. Both types of alchemy involved looking for a powerful agent capable of perfecting or healing. That agent had long gone by several names, including elixir, grand magisterium, or philosophers' stone, and in the early modern period different traditions traced this agent to specific material origins. One tradition linked to Paracelsus sought to prepare the elixir or stone from "vitriol." Others, who followed in the tradition of an alchemical writer named Michael Sendivogius (1566–1636), referred to niter. A third tradition, which included the authors Jean d'Espagnet, Alexander von Suchten, Gaston DuClo, and Eireneaus Philalethes (a pseudonym for George Starchy), pursued processes involving vitriol (sometimes called the remedy of the Green Lion) and mercury.

Works by an author using the name Basilius Valentinus directed attention to the use of antimony in alchemical operations, and those writings supplied seventeenth-century chemical physicians with much information about compounding medicines from antimony. Panaceas of various sorts boasted alchemical heritage; one of the most famous was the drinkable gold *(aurum potabile)* described, among others, by Angelo Sala, Francis Anthony, and Johann Rudolf Glauber (1604–1668). Producing medicines by means of chemical synthesis was a direct outgrowth of alchemical and Paracelsian practices. Both came together as a university subject early in the seventeenth century when Johannes Hartmann (1568–1631) was appointed

Alchemy. Woodcut from a c. 1580 edition of Paracelsus's works depicts Azoth, believed by some early alchemists to be the life-generating spirit inherent in the three essential substances: salt, sulfur, and mercury. FORTEAN PICTURE LIBRARY

public professor of *chemiatria* (chemical medicine) at the University of Marburg. Hartmann's patron, the German prince Moritz, landgrave of Hesse-Kassel (ruled 1592–1627), was one of a number of European potentates, including several Medici princes and the Holy Roman emperor Rudolf II (ruled 1576–1612), at whose courts alchemical projects served economic, political, and aesthetic ambitions. In England, traditions of alchemy and Paracelsianism came together in the hands of social critics and educational reformers. Samuel Hartlib (c. 1600–1662), Jan Amos Comenius (1592–1670), and the dramatist John Webster (c. 1580–c. 1625) each acknowledged the practical results of alchemical labors. Webster especially concluded that the traditions of medieval alchemy and Paracelsus should

find a place within the university as an "art that doth help more truly and radically to . . . discover the secret principles and operations of nature." Outside the court and academy, alchemy in various forms continued to be part of the everyday business of popular culture, reflected in vernacular pharmacy books, books of secrets, and a variety of household manuals.

The Bible itself could be read as an alchemical text. One frequent reference was to the book of Exodus, where Moses grinds up the golden calf and gives it (as a kind of *aurum potabile*) to the children of Israel to drink. The knowledge of Moses, received from Egyptian priests, reflected, many thought, a *prisca sapientia,* an ancient pure wisdom that had been corrupted over time, but which, through the comparison of texts with experience, might be discovered again.

ALCHEMY AND MODERN SCIENCE

As an artifact of the early modern period, alchemy continued to exert an influence throughout the scientific revolution. Robert Boyle (1627–1691) and Isaac Newton (1642–1727) both pursued alchemical programs. That Boyle accepted the reality of transmutation and the validity of claims about the powers of the philosophers' stone is clear from an unpublished dialogue on the transmutation of metals. There opponents of transmutation are soundly refuted with the report of an "anti-elixir" that, when projected onto molten gold, transmutes it into base metal. Among Boyle's papers are hundreds of pages of laboratory processes, many related to metallic transmutations and largely written in code. In one instance he wrote a precise account of a transmutation that he had personally witnessed. To Boyle, the corpuscular philosophy, which defined matter as composed of tiny particles, was not at all inconsistent with alchemical ideas. Transmutations took place, he argued, when changes took place in the sizes, shapes, and motions of the particles of an original matter.

Another adherent of alchemy and corpuscularianism was Isaac Newton. The largest particles of every sort of matter, he theorized, were composed of very subtle sulfurous or acid particles surrounded by larger earthy or mercurial particles, the latter piled up like rings or shells around the volatile center. Every substance, he held, was composed of particles analogous to tiny universes. Transmutation resulted when the larger particles of a substance were reduced to smaller particles and then rearranged. Newton was also fond of ancient texts, especially those related to the Egyptian magus Hermes, and he collected bits and pieces of alchemical wisdom in the form of transcriptions, extracts, and collations of ancient, medieval, and contemporary alchemical authorities. He labored over the construction of an *index chemicus,* an inventory of chemical and alchemical writing arranged by topic that, in its final form, comprised a volume of more than a hundred pages, with 879 separate headings. Another text of "Notable Opinions" consisted of quotations from seventy-five printed and handwritten alchemical sources. The alchemist George Starchy described to him the concept of chemical mediation (the means by which two unsociable bodies are made sociable by means of a third) and recounted also for Newton procedures for making philosophical mercury and for preparing an antimonial amalgam called the "star regulus." Accepting the presence of spiritual agents in nature, Newton thought that metals could both grow and decay as part of a cycle of creation in which the return to chaos gave rise to new substances.

See also **Hermeticism; Magic; Matter, Theories of; Paracelsus; Scientific Revolution.**

BIBLIOGRAPHY

Dobbs, Betty Jo Teeter. *The Foundations of Newton's Alchemy.* Cambridge, U.K., 1975.

Kopp, Hermann. *Die Alchemie.* 1886; rept. Hildesheim, 1971.

Martels, Z. R. W. M. von, ed., *Alchemy Revisited.* Leiden, 1990.

Principe, Lawrence M. *The Aspiring Adept.* Princeton, 1998.

Principe, Lawrence M., and William R. Newman. "Some Problems with the Historiography of Alchemy," in *Secrets of Nature: Astrology and Alchemy in Early Modern Europe,* ed. by W. R. Newman and Anthony Grafton. Cambridge, Mass., 2001, pp. 385–431.

BRUCE T. MORAN

ALDROVANDI, ULISSE (1522–1605).

Bolognese naturalist and collector. Known as the "Bolognese Aristotle," Ulisse Aldrovandi belonged to the generation of Renaissance physicians and apothecaries who rediscovered the importance of empirical study of the natural world. The son of a Bolognese notary, Aldrovandi worked as a notary and studied law before discovering the pleasures of science. He studied philosophy and mathematics at the University of Padua (1548–1549) and, after a narrow escape from the Inquisition, wrote a guidebook to ancient statuary in Rome. He received a medical degree at the University of Bologna in 1553.

By the late 1540s, Aldrovandi had discovered natural history. During his trip to Rome, he met the French naturalist Guillaume Rondelet, then researching ichythology. He subsequently developed a close relationship with the Italian naturalist Luca Ghini, who held the first professorship in "medicinal simples" at both Bologna and Pisa and who founded the Pisan botanical garden in 1543. Ghini encouraged medical students to take the study of the natural world seriously, inviting them on summer botanical expeditions, demonstrating plants in gardens, collecting natural specimens, and illustrating them with the help of artists. Aldrovandi's image of natural history was especially influenced by the practices of his mentor Ghini. He succeeded Ghini as professor of natural history at the University of Bologna in 1556, inaugurating its botanical garden in 1568.

Aldrovandi increased the significance and scope of natural history over the next few decades. He gave natural history some degree of autonomy from medicine by arguing that it was also an important part of natural philosophy. This approach to natural history was evident, for example, in Aldrovandi's choice of subjects for his publications. Rather than writing a new *materia medica,* in the tradition of the ancient Greek physician Dioscorides, Aldrovandi chose instead to follow Aristotle and contemporaries such as the Swiss naturalist Conrad Gessner; he wrote about animals because of his intrinsic interest in their anatomy, physiology, and habits rather than their medicinal uses. Similarly, his work on plants and minerals attempted to describe each specimen comprehensively, in keeping with Aldrovandi's vision of natural history as an encyclopedic project.

Aldrovandi published very little of his research in his lifetime. The first volume of his *Natural History,* the *Ornithology* (1599–1603), did not appear until shortly before his death. The technical difficulties of creating a comprehensive textual and visual portrait of each natural object demanded not simply the skills of a single naturalist but the collaboration of an entire community of collectors, transcribers, and artists devoted to the project of reconstructing nature. Aldrovandi's reputation as a great naturalist was based more on the materials he accumulated in his study than on what he published. His collection of animals, plants, minerals, curiosities, and antiquities was one of the most famous collections of curiosities in western Europe. Visitors described the museum as the eighth wonder of the world. Aldrovandi conceived of his collection not only as the raw ingredients for the writing of natural history but as an experimental laboratory in which to anatomize and archive nature. Princes, popes, and scholars all vied with each other to contribute interesting specimens to his collection.

In 1603 Aldrovandi wrote a will donating his collection to the senate of Bologna in return for their agreement to appoint a custodian who would teach natural history using the materials in the Studio Aldrovandi and to continue to publish his unfinished *Natural History* (ten more volumes appeared between 1606 and 1668). In 1742 the collection was disbanded and its ingredients incorporated into the new museum of the Institute for Sciences in Bologna.

See also **Gessner, Conrad; Museums; Natural History; Renaissance; Scientific Revolution.**

BIBLIOGRAPHY

Aldrovandi, Ulisse. *Aldrovandi on Chickens. The Ornithology of Ulisse Aldrovandi* (1600), vol. II, book XIV. Edited and translated by L. R. Lind. Norman, Okla., 1963.

Findlen, Paula. "The Formation of a Scientific Community: Natural History in Sixteenth-Century Italy." In *Natu-*

Ulisse Aldrovandi. Drawing of an elephant from Aldrovandi's *Natural History.* ©ENZO & PAOLO RAGAZZINI/CORBIS

Ulisse Aldrovandi. Drawing of a man leading a camel from Aldrovandi's *Natural History.* ©Enzo & Paolo Ragazzini/Corbis

ral Particulars: Renaissance Natural Philosophy and the Disciplines, edited by Anthony Grafton and Nancy Siraisi, pp. 369–400. Cambridge, Mass., 1999.

———. *Possessing Nature: Museums, Collecting, and Scientific Culture in Early Modern Italy.* Berkeley and Los Angeles, 1994.

Riedl-Dorn, Christa. *Wissenschaft und Fabelwesen: ein kritischer Versuch über Conrad Gessner und Ulisse Aldrovandi.* Vienna, 1989.

Olmi, Giuseppe. *L'inventario del mondo. Catalogazione della nature e luoghi del sapere nella prima età moderna.* Bologna, 1992.

———. *Ulisse Aldrovandi. Scienza e natura nel secondo Cinquecento.* Trent, Italy, 1976.

Simili, Raffaela, ed. *Il teatro della natura di Ulisse Aldrovandi.* Bologna, 2001.

Tugnoli Pattaro, Sandra. *Metodo e sistema delle scienze nel pensiero di Ulisse Aldrovandi.* Bologna, 1981.

Paula Findlen

ALEMBERT, JEAN LE ROND D'

(1717–1783), French mathematician, scientist, philosopher, and writer. Born 17 November 1717,

Jean Le Rond d'Alembert was the illegitimate son of the famous Claudine Alexandrine Guérin, marquise de Tencin, and an artillery officer, Louis-Camus Destouches. Abandoned on the steps of Saint-Jean-Le-Rond in Paris, he was taken to the Foundling Home and named after the church where he was discovered. Through his father's efforts he was placed with a foster mother, Mme. Rousseau, to whom he remained devoted. His father also saw to it that his son received a good education; he attended first a private school, then the Collège des Quatre-Nations. After three years studying law and medicine, it became clear to d'Alembert that mathematics was his true vocation. In 1741 he was named an *adjoint* (adjunct) at the Academy of Sciences, and in 1743 he published his most important mathematical work, the *Traité de dynamique* (Treatise on dynamics). In addition to six other major scientific treatises, his 1752 *Éléments de musique, théorique et pratique, suivant les principes de Rameau* (Elements of practical and theoretical music following Rameau's principles) is noteworthy as a lucid exposition of Rameau's hugely influential harmonic theory.

Jean Le Rond d'Alembert. THE LIBRARY OF CONGRESS

Today d'Alembert is somewhat undervalued, remembered mostly as coeditor of the *Encyclopédie,* although even in that enterprise he was eclipsed by Denis Diderot (1713–1784). In his day d'Alembert was esteemed second only to Voltaire (1694–1778) in leading the philosophe movement, the very core of Enlightenment ideology. Through his role in the French Academy, to which he was elected in 1754, and of which he became permanent secretary in 1772, the discreet and cautious d'Alembert was able to confer legitimacy on many of the philosophes' deepest concerns while remaining immune to the imprisonments and exiles that punctuated the lives of so many of his colleagues.

Largely because of his scientific reputation, but also because he was a popular, brilliant participant in Parisian salons, d'Alembert was asked as early as 1745 to participate in the production of the *Encyclopédie;* in 1747 he was named coeditor with Diderot and was charged primarily with the mathematical and scientific articles. His nonscientific entry, the infamous "Genève," created a controversy with Jean-Jacques Rousseau (1712–1778) and then with

Genevan Protestants, leading d'Alembert to resign from his editorial post in 1758.

The desire to avoid scandal at all costs, which led to his resignation, was consistent with the public comportment d'Alembert adopted for the rest of his career. Although he shared many of the goals of the other philosophes, his correspondence (in particular with Voltaire) consistently shows not only a refusal to jeopardize his career and freedom to remain in Paris but also an unflinching conviction that enlightenment must be a gradual and tactful process of persuasion rather than a series of attacks, whether open or anonymous. He thought he could best serve that end by promoting the philosophe party at large and especially in the Academy, by mediating disputes within the group and by functioning as a de facto public relations manager as a foil to the polemical outpourings from Voltaire at Ferney and from numerous other quarters (most notably the baron Paul Thiry, baron d'Holbach; 1723–1789). Indeed, it had long been Voltaire's wish that when he died, d'Alembert would succeed him as leader of the philosophes. Much of d'Alembert's immense stature in the eighteenth century, then, came not from his writings but from his ceaseless efforts to unite and promote his colleagues and advance their mutual cause.

In 1759 he laid out his philosophical principles and methodology in his *Essai sur les éléments de philosophie: ou sur les principes des connaissances humaines* (Essay on the elements of philosophy, or on the principles of human knowledge). In this work he provides a synthesis of his prior thought in epistemology, metaphysics, language theory, science, and aesthetics. The *Éclaircissements* (Explanations), added in 1767, round out the *Essay,* forming a composite that represents the ambitious scope of d'Alembert's empiricist philosophy.

However, his most important work is without doubt the 1751 *Preliminary Discourse to the Encyclopedia.* In this concise and occasionally flawed but often brilliant document, d'Alembert seeks to justify the encyclopedic enterprise in a Lockean vein, by showing the unity of all thought from its sensorial origins (in "direct" and "reflected" ideas deriving from corporeal impressions). However, he also attempts to provide a rational, scientific method for the mapping of human knowledge as well as a historical account of the evolution of human thought. The result is not merely an apology for the ends as well as the means of the *Encyclopédie*, it is also a superb summation of Enlightenment empirical and sensualist thought, a forceful rejection of Cartesian metaphysics (if not Cartesian method, which d'Alembert admired), and a valorization of the scientific method of Francis Bacon (1561–1626) and (particularly) Isaac Newton (1642–1727). In the *Discourse*, d'Alembert succeeds in showing the intimate connection between the spirit of the *Encyclopédie* and the concerns of the Enlightenment generally, in a way that is not always obvious to the reader of the encyclopedia's articles themselves.

D'Alembert's last important work, the fifth volume of *Mélanges de littérature, d'histoire, et de philosophie*, was published in 1767. From that point on, his health became increasingly fragile. In his last years he wrote little, instead concentrating on his duties as permanent secretary of the French Academy. As the result of his refusal of an operation (without which his doctors informed him he would not survive) for a painful bladder ailment he had had for years, d'Alembert died on 29 October 1783.

See also **Diderot, Denis;** *Encyclopédie;* **Enlightenment; Mathematics; Philosophes; Voltaire.**

BIBLIOGRAPHY

Primary Sources

Alembert, Jean Le Rond d'. *Œuvres de d'Alembert*. 5 vols, reprint of 1821–1822 Paris edition. Geneva, 1967.

———. *Œuvres et correspondances inédites de d'Alembert*. Edited by Charles Henry. Reprint. Geneva, 1967.

———. *Preliminary Discourse to the Encyclopedia of Diderot*. Edited by Walter E. Rex and Richard N. Schwab. Chicago, 1995.

———. *Traité de dynamique*. Sceaux, 1990.

Secondary Sources

Essar, Dennis F. *The Language Theory, Epistemology, and Aesthetics of Jean Lerond d'Alembert*. Oxford, 1976.

Grimsley, Ronald. *Jean d'Alembert (1717–1783)*. Oxford, 1963.

Hankins, Thomas L. *Jean d'Alembert: Science and the Enlightenment*. Oxford, 1970.

Pappas, John N. *Voltaire and D'Alembert*. Bloomington, Ind., 1962.

PATRICK RILEY, JR.

ALEXIS I (RUSSIA) (1629–1676; ruled 1645–1676), tsar of Russia. Alexis Mikhailovich came to the throne at the age of sixteen in 1645. His long and eventful reign saw the beginnings of the rise of Russia's power and the earliest phases of the Europeanization of its culture. At first he ruled under the influence of his former tutor, the boyar Boris Morozov. Morozov tried to pay for the defenses of the southern frontier and other outlays by changing the tax system, introducing a new tax on salt and other burdens in place of the older general sales tax and tavern monopoly. He consolidated his power at court in January 1648, when Alexis married Mariia Miloslavskaia and Morozov her sister Anna. The tax measures led to increasing discontent and ultimately to a revolt in Moscow in June 1648, which led to the temporary eclipse of Morozov. Gentry discontent added to urban unrest, and the outcome was the Assembly of the Land of 1649, which compiled the first systematic Russian law code, printed by order of the tsar. Morozov was able to come back to power, seconded by the boyar Ilia Miloslavskii, Alexis's father-in-law, and other boyar allies. Discontent in towns and border fortresses led to a further series of revolts (Novgorod and Pskov, 1650).

Alexis also brought to power in the church a group of reformist priests led by his chaplain Stefan Vonifat'ev, who argued for a stricter moral code (for instance, that taverns should be closed on Sundays), changes in the liturgy to make the words more accessible, and preaching. The appointment of Nikon in 1652 to the patriarchal throne made possible the adoption of the program and brought a new and powerful figure to court.

Domestic concerns soon gave way to war with Poland. In 1648 the Ukrainian Cossacks in the Polish-Lithuanian Commonwealth, led by Hetman Bohdan Khmelnytsky, rose against the state and nobility, in defense of Orthodoxy against forced union with Rome and for the rights of Cossacks and peasants. They immediately sent an embassy asking for help from Alexis, but Russia was reluctant to exchange its budding friendship with Poland for an alliance with Cossack and peasant rebels. The urban revolts also complicated the situation. By early 1653, however, Khmelnytsky offered to come under the tsar's "high hand," and Alexis agreed to

Alexis I. Eighteenth-century portrait. THE ART ARCHIVE/RUSSIAN HISTORICAL MUSEUM MOSCOW/DAGLI ORTI (A)

fight Poland, calling an Assembly of the Land to ratify the decision. In 1654 Alexis concluded the Pereyaslav treaty with the Cossacks, making them a sort of vassal state to Russia.

The war at first went well for Russia. In 1654–1655 Alexis conquered Smolensk and almost all of the Grand Duchy of Lithuania. At the same time Sweden entered the war, overrunning much of western Poland. In 1656 Alexis made a truce with Poland, apparently afraid that a complete Polish collapse was undesirable, and declared war on Sweden, continuing without success until 1661. Revived Polish fortunes after the 1660 peace with Sweden led to a standoff, draining Russian resources and resulting in the copper revolt of 1662 in Moscow, a response to adulterated currency. Peace negotiations under Afanasii Lavrentevich Ordin-Nashchokin ended in 1667 with the treaty of Andrusovo.

In the treaty Russia returned Lithuania but received Smolensk and its territory, the Cossack Ukraine east of the Dnieper and the city of Kiev, for two years, which Russia retained after the time was up. The treaty signified a fundamental shift of power away from Poland toward Russia and also gave Russia a southern border much closer to the Crimea and the Ottomans. Those powers and the Ukrainian hetmans were the main concerns for Alexis from then on. He relied on Ordin-Nashchokin to conduct foreign affairs, but the latter's failures in Ukraine led to the rise of Artamon Matveev, from 1671 the tsar's principal favorite. The death of Morozov in 1661 and of Ilia Miloslavskii, Tsaritsa Mariia, and Alexis's eldest son (1669) opened the political field but also endangered the succession. Alexis married Nataliia Naryshkina, the daughter of a musketeer colonel, in 1671. The birth of Peter (later Peter the Great) in 1672 ensured the succession and reinforced the importance of Matveev, Nataliia's ally, to the end of Alexis's reign.

Patriarch Nikon pursued reform in the church, correcting the liturgical texts to agree with the Greek versions. These changes brought forth protests from his former allies, chiefly the archpriest Avvakum Petrovich, who claimed they were incorrect and harmful to the faith. Avvakum and his followers were sent into exile in Siberia and the far north. Meanwhile Nikon's relations with the tsar deteriorated, as Nikon also built up patriarchal power in the church. In 1658 a clash over precedence caused Nikon to leave his duties and retire to the nearby Voskresenskii monastery. As he did not abdicate his office, the church had no head for the next eight years. Attempts to solve the dispute failed, and simultaneously opposition to Nikon's liturgical reforms spread. At a church council in 1666–1667 Nikon was formally deposed and the opposition to the liturgical reforms declared schismatic. The church hierarchy returned to normal, but dissent continued to spread and deepen. The selection of Ioakim (1674) brought to the patriarchate a powerful advocate of the new liturgy, the education of the clergy, and patriarchal power, leading to clashes with Alexis in his last years.

The reforms in the church inspired the invitation of Ukrainian clerics to Moscow. The Ukrainians had studied at the Kievan Academy (founded 1633), which taught a European curriculum in Latin on Jesuit models but with Orthodox faith. Epifanii Slavinetskii (died 1675) made new translations of the church fathers and the liturgy and preached sermons in and around the court. In 1664

Simeon Polotskii (1629–1680) was tutor to Alexis's sons and the first Russian court poet as well as preacher. Among the boyar elite knowledge of Polish and some Latin began to spread, as did interest in the religious culture of Kiev, centered on the baroque sermon. The foreign community of Moscow ("the German suburb"), largely composed of German, Dutch, English, and Scottish merchants and mercenary officers, contributed other Western elements. Alexis established the first theater in Russia at his court in 1672, using a Lutheran pastor for his playwright and the boys from the German school as actors. Alexis acquired Western paintings, a telescope, and other new things.

Alexis also began the reform of the Russian army, substituting infantry armed with muskets and drilling in the Western manner for the gentry cavalry and undrilled musketeers of earlier times. This army allowed him to win against Poland, but it was very expensive, and after 1667 formations of the new type were much less numerous. Russia maintained extensive trade with England and Holland through Arkhangel'sk, though Alexis tried to favor Russian merchants. He revoked the English Muscovy Company's privileges in 1649, using the execution of Charles I as a pretext, and decreed mildly protectionist toll rates. At the same time he gave privileges to the Dutch to set up iron and munitions works. During these years Russia's agrarian base expanded enormously, in spite of serfdom, through colonization of the southern steppe and Volga basin. The reign of Alexis saw the further consolidation of the Russian state and society, important cultural and religious changes, and the rise of Russian power. It laid the foundation for the far-reaching changes wrought by his son Peter.

See also Andrusovo, Truce of (1667); Avvakum Petrovich; Cossacks; Khmelnytsky, Bohdan; Khmelnytsky Uprising; Law: Russian; Michael Romanov (Russia); Nikon, patriarch; Old Believers; Peter I (Russia); Russia; Russia, Architecture in; Russia, Art in; Russian Literature and Language; Russo-Polish Wars; Serfdom in Russia; Sofiia Alekseevna; Ukraine.

BIBLIOGRAPHY

Bushkovitch, Paul. Religion and Society in Russia: The Sixteenth and Seventeenth Centuries. New York and Oxford, 1992.

Fuhrmann, Joseph T. Tsar Alexis, His Reign, and His Russia. Gulf Breeze, Fla., 1981.

Longworth, Philip. Alexis Tsar of All the Russias. New York, 1984.

PAUL BUSHKOVITCH

ALLEGRI, ANTONIO. See Correggio (Antonio Allegri).

ÁLVARO DE BAZÁN, FIRST MARQUIS OF SANTA CRUZ. See Santa Cruz, Álvaro de Bazán, first marquis of.

AMERICA. See British Colonies; Dutch Colonies; French Colonies; Portuguese Colonies; Spanish Colonies.

AMERICAN INDEPENDENCE, WAR OF (1775–1783). The War of American Independence began on 19 April 1775 with firefights at Lexington and Concord, Massachusetts. It ended on 28 June 1783, when a British force ceased operations against the French, who were aiding rebels in southern India. Barring Vietnam, it was the longest war in the history of the United States to the twenty-first century. It involved most European powers as either belligerents or watchful observers. In one way or another it touched every part of what had been British America, including not only the thirteen east coast colonies but also Canada and Native American country as well as the West Indies and the open Atlantic. The war destroyed one empire and created another.

The war was not synonymous with the American Revolution. That larger civil, cultural, social, and economic transformation sprawled over a quarter century between the first colonial challenges to British authority in 1764 and the implementation of the U.S. Constitution in 1789. Unlike the later Southern war to preserve slavery and destroy the United States, it does not have a military narrative strong enough to carry the whole story of the American Republic's creation. But the war was central to the Revolution's process and its outcome.

Two myths about the war need dismissal. One, long favored in patriotic annals, is that virtuous citizen-soldiers put down their plows, threw off tyranny, and returned to daily life. The other is that British power was so overwhelming as to render American victory almost inexplicable. Americans did believe they fought in a good cause, but there were many dissenters. The fiercest fighting pitted white colonials, black people, and Natives in a melee that engulfed them all. For patriot whites the war did end in triumph. Loyalist whites emigrated at the war's end in larger percentages than those in which people left revolutionary France. The war shook slavery severely, and thousands of former slaves also departed with the British. Though most Indians had no reason to count themselves among the war's losers, it ended in disaster for virtually all of them.

THREE PHASES

With hindsight the North American story has three phases. In the first, for roughly a year following Lexington, Britain attempted a police action to contain and put down a local rebellion. The goal was to combine a show of force with relative lenience. This phase is associated primarily with General Thomas Gage (1721–1787), who in 1775 was both civil governor of Massachusetts and commander in chief in North America. But the hope of reconciliation carried over to his successors, the brothers Admiral Lord Richard Howe (1726–1799) and General Sir William Howe (1729–1814), whose appointments made them peace commissioners as well as joint commanders.

From the spring of 1776 until the autumn of 1778 both Britons and Americans understood the confrontation in terms of conventional European warfare. Nonetheless there was a difference. The Howes sought control of American cities. They abandoned Boston (17 March 1776) when Americans placed artillery on Dorchester Heights and made the town indefensible. The British regrouped at Halifax, Nova Scotia, marshaled their largest seaborne force prior to the twentieth century, and seized New York City (15 September 1776). It remained in British hands until 1783. Their forces included regiments of hired German "Hessians,"

named for the principality of Hesse that supplied them.

The American commander in chief George Washington (1732–1799) realized after losing New York that his primary task was to keep his army in existence while it acquired strength, skill, and weapons. Washington bolstered American morale with winter victories at Trenton and Princeton, New Jersey (26 December 1776 and 3 January 1777). The major outcome of this phase was the defeat and capture at Saratoga (17 October 1777), in upstate New York, of a British army led by General John Burgoyne (1722–1792). Burgoyne's goal had been to seize the Champlain-Hudson corridor between Montreal and New York City. The American commander at Saratoga, Horatio Gates (c. 1728–1806), was a former British officer who once had served with Burgoyne. Burgoyne had not expected serious help from Sir William Howe, who was moving on Philadelphia, which he captured from Washington's forces (26 September 1777). Howe's successor, Sir Henry Clinton (1738–1795), evacuated the nominal American capital the following spring to concentrate his forces in New York.

Partisan war marked the third phase. In 1777 civil war broke out in what now is western New York, pitting regular soldiers, settlers turned guerrilla fighters, and Indians against one another on both sides. The same configuration appeared after the British invaded Georgia in 1779 and South Carolina in 1780. These conflicts saw the disintegration of both white and Native communities, with the added element in the South of slaves who sought their freedom where they could find it. The Americans tried to put down the Iroquois country conflict with a conventional invasion in 1779, and the British used the same strategy in the South. Neither effort was successful. The war in northern Indian country spread into modern Ohio, Indiana, and Illinois. Though it ended with Iroquois fragmentation and defeat, Shawnees and others farther west remained powerful enough to resist the United States for a decade.

AMERICAN VICTORY, THANKS TO THE FRENCH

The mainland war ended with a set-piece siege at Yorktown, Virginia (9–18 October 1781). Yorktown became possible for many reasons. Initially the

British invasion of South Carolina in 1780 seemed successful. At Charles Town (Charleston after 1783) Clinton's invaders captured the American army of Benjamin Lincoln (1733–1810), more than five thousand troops. Redressing Saratoga, Clinton's army defeated Americans led by Gates at Camden, South Carolina (16 August 1780), bringing the entire province under British control. Clinton returned to New York, leaving Major General Lord Charles Cornwallis (1738–1805) to complete southern pacification on the assumption that most Americans would welcome the invaders.

Cornwallis moved into North Carolina, where a new American army under Nathanael Greene (1742–1786) inflicted major damage on him at Guilford Court House (15 March 1781). Resistance popped up everywhere as soon as Cornwallis's redcoats pushed on, despite ferocious action against the militiamen by British and Loyalist cavalry under Banastre Tarleton (1754–1833). Nonetheless Cornwallis moved his army north again to subdue Virginia. He had no better luck there and finally took up position at Yorktown (1 August 1781) to await seaborne supplies and possible reinforcements.

The relief never came. Instead, a combined Franco-American force besieged and captured Cornwallis's entire force. Yorktown proved the major strategic consequence of the fact that France had entered the war in 1778. Clandestine aid had begun arriving even prior to American independence via the government-sponsored trading firm Hortalez et Cie of Bordeaux. French matériel and monetary assistance were of great importance to the American army's ability to remain in the field, and after 1778 the French could provide soldiers and a fleet. Cooperation was not always good. French supply officers had as much difficulty as their American and British counterparts in obtaining foodstuffs from reluctant farmers and profit-seeking merchants.

Washington's main goal from the alliance was to recapture New York City, which he could not do without French naval support. Nonetheless, when he learned that Cornwallis was in the Chesapeake and that a French fleet was en route there from the Caribbean, he and the French commander, Jean de Vimeur, comte de Rochambeau (1725–1807),

agreed to move south. It was a gamble, because there was no guarantee that the French admiral, François-Joseph-Paul de Grasse, comte de Grasse (1722–1788), could gain control of the Chesapeake entrance. Grasse did stave off a British fleet outside the Virginia capes (10 September 1781), taking control of the great Chesapeake Bay and making it possible to move both a French siege train and the combined American and French forces into position around Cornwallis. Grasse returned to the West Indies, and Washington returned to the Hudson Valley, where he continued to plan New York's recapture. But the loss of Cornwallis's entire army at Yorktown broke Britain's political will to continue the North American struggle. The ministry of Frederick North (Lord North, 1732–1792), in power since 1770, fell, and British offensive operations in North America ended.

THE LARGER WAR

The larger war did not end. As early as 1779 British policymakers began to think that the Americans could not be defeated. Thanks to the involvement of France and of Spain as a French ally, Britain's naval resources were stretched thin. In 1779 there was real danger that a Franco-Spanish fleet and army would invade Britain. Every Caribbean island, including Jamaica, was vulnerable, and there were not enough ships to protect them all. That risk finally ended at the Battle of the Saints, fought between the Leeward Islands of Dominica and Îles des Saintes (12 April 1782), when a British fleet under Admiral Sir George Rodney (1718–1792) captured Grasse himself. But Britain did lose Minorca to Spain and came close to losing Gibraltar.

Despite its enormous might, Britain faced great disadvantages during the American war. In diplomatic terms it was virtually isolated. France became an American ally, Spain was an ally of France, and the Dutch were so pro-American that Britain declared war against the Dutch at the end of 1780. Led by Catherine the Great (ruled 1762–1796), empress of Russia, who entertained visions of mediating the conflict, other European powers formed the League of Armed Neutrality, which stretched from Russia to Sicily. That development favored the American cause indirectly by securing Baltic naval stores for France and Spain. Britain, long dependent on American sources for the wood, tar, and hemp its fleets needed, had the advantage only that more of its ships were copper-bottomed to resist fouling and therefore faster and more maneuverable at sea. Although North's ministry was politically secure until the loss of Yorktown, it could not raise enough troops in Britain and Ireland both to fight overseas and to maintain home defense. That was the main reason for hiring the German Hessian regiments.

Sheer distance proved another problem for British policymakers and generals. The thirty thousand troops who arrived in New York harbor with the Howe brothers in July 1776 were an enormous force. But every soldier, whether British or German, was virtually irreplaceable. Despite short enlistments and great suffering in the Continental army, it seemed there always were more Americans. New England's original pickup army inflicted heavy casualties before losing Bunker Hill (actually Breed's Hill) overlooking Boston (17 June 1775). Britain could not afford more such Pyrrhic victories. That may be why the Howe brothers did not pursue their advantage after they trapped Washington's half-trained and demoralized Continentals on Long Island (27 August 1776), allowing them to fall back first to Manhattan, then into Westchester County north of New York City, and finally to New Jersey. Washington's capture of Hessian regiments at Trenton and Princeton and the capitulation of Burgoyne's entire seven-thousand-man army at Saratoga in October 1777 presented the British with losses that were difficult to fill. The British never succeeded in supplying themselves from the American countryside, despite constant foraging. After 1776 New York City was virtually impregnable against recapture, but virtually every tree and fence on Manhattan Island had to be chopped for firewood, and the city needed constant reprovisioning from across the ocean. The same became true in the other two secure British enclaves, Charles Town and Savannah, Georgia.

British strategy assumed that "good Americans" would rally to "government" given any chance. Many did, particularly on Long Island and Staten Island, New York, which were securely loyal, and in New Jersey and South Carolina, where the Revolution virtually collapsed after redcoats arrived. There was strong Loyalism plus neutral "disaffection" in New York's Hudson and Mohawk Valleys, on Maryland's Eastern Shore (between Chesapeake Bay and the sea), and in much of the country where advancing white settlement met Indian resistance. But except for Long Island and Staten Island, Britain never secured its hold over potentially Loyalist country.

Enough Virginia slaves rallied to the offer of freedom in November 1775 made by the royal governor, John Murray, Lord Dunmore (1732–1809), to form his "Aetheopian Regiment." (Most of them died in the smallpox epidemic that broke out that year and swept across most of the continent by 1782.) Clinton repeated that offer when British strategy turned south, with significant results. But Britain never tried to rouse all the slaves, and north of the Carolinas black men could find freedom by serving in the Continental ranks. North and south alike, many Indians recognized Britain as their best hope. However, two of the six Iroquois nations (as well as others) chose the American side, and Americans forced the Cherokee to abandon the British cause in 1779. Finally, though Britain sent the best generals it could find to America, none was of the first rank. Both William Howe and Burgoyne joined the parliamentary opposition after they returned from their American service.

The initial American expectation was that virtuous militiamen could defeat professionals and mercenaries. Early events seemed to support that belief. These included the heavy losses the British expeditionary force suffered on the way back to Boston from Lexington and Concord; the massive red-coat casualties and light American losses at Bunker Hill; the American capture of Fort Ticonderoga on Lake Champlain (10 May 1775), which yielded the artillery that eventually was emplaced overlooking Boston; and the nearly successful invasion of Canada in the winter of 1775–1776. In fact militiamen and part-time soldiers were important throughout the war. Without them the Americans could not have outnumbered and trapped the British at Saratoga, and they did important duty controlling Loyalists, guarding coastlines, and serving as skirmishers. Irregulars did most of the frontier fighting on both sides.

But when Washington assumed command at Boston (3 July 1775), his goal was to create a dependable, disciplined regular army. He could draw on an American tradition of one-year service, which was more than ad hoc militia duty but less than European-style long-term enlistment. The officer corps that assembled around him began imagining itself as composed of "gentlemen" with privileges common soldiers could not have. The fact that some American officers, including Generals Richard Montgomery (1736–1775), Charles Lee (1731–1782), and Gates, had borne commissions in the class-riven British army added to that sense. So did the advent of aristocratic and pseudo-aristocratic European volunteers, including the Marquis de Lafayette (1757–1834), who became an instant American major general; Thomas Conway (1735–?1800); Count Kazimierz Pulaski (Casimir Pulaski, 1747–1779); and Baron Friedrich Wilhelm Augustin von Steuben (1730–1794), who became the Continental army's drillmaster. Continental officers came to command troops who were serving "for the duration." These mostly were young, single men of the sort that might have enlisted for the long-term service and tough discipline of a European army in the absence of any better choice.

OLD-STYLE WAR, REVOLUTIONARY WAR

For the British this was the last war of the *ancien régime*. But for Americans the war was revolutionary. Virtually every American community saw conflict and disruption. In addition to shaking slavery and drastically weakening Indian power, it changed women's understanding of themselves as they learned to deal with businesses their men previously had monopolized. "Your farm" became "our farm" and eventually "my farm." Though the preservation of the Continental army was central to the outcome, militiamen fighting a "people's war" often made the difference at critical moments. The war created both a national elite and a national economy, and these were the basis for the movement that led to the U.S. Constitution in 1787–1788. For the British the war's course led from excessive optimism to humiliation, but otherwise it left them unchanged. For the Americans the war transformed almost everything.

See also **British Colonies: North America; England; Enlightenment; Liberty; Military; Revolutions, Age of.**

BIBLIOGRAPHY

Calloway, Colin G. *The American Revolution in Indian Country: Crisis and Diversity in Native American Com-*munities. Cambridge, U.K., 1995. The war from Native American points of view.

Fischer, David Hackett. *Paul Revere's Ride.* Oxford and New York, 1994. Thoughtful account of the outbreak of war.

Gruber, Ira D. *The Howe Brothers and the American Revolution.* Chapel Hill, N.C., 1972. Biographies of joint British commanders.

Higginbotham, Don. *The War of American Independence: Military Attitudes, Policies, and Practice, 1763–1789.* Bloomington, Ind., 1977. A thorough account from the American viewpoint.

Hoffman, Ronald, and Peter J. Albert, eds. *Arms and Independence: The Military Character of the American Revolution.* Charlottesville, Va., 1984. Essays by the foremost scholars of the subject.

Mackesy, Piers. *The War for America, 1775–1783.* Introduction by John Shy. Lincoln, Nebr., 1992. Originally published in 1964. Thorough account from the viewpoint of British policymakers.

Martin, James Kirby, and Mark Edward Lender. *A Respectable Army: The Military Origins of the Republic, 1763–1789.* Arlington Heights, Ill., 1982. A brief and well-crafted synthesis.

Royster, Charles. *A Revolutionary People at War: The Continental Army and American Character, 1775–1783.* Chapel Hill, N.C., 1979. Exploration of the war in cultural terms.

Schechter, Barnet. *The Battle for New York.* New York, 2002. Narrative of events bearing on New York City.

Shy, John. *A People Numerous and Armed: Reflections on the Military Struggle for American Independence.* Oxford and New York, 1976. Essays in the "new military history."

EDWARD COUNTRYMAN

AMSTERDAM. With a population of around 11,000 in 1514, Amsterdam ranked among the middling towns of Europe at the close of the Middle Ages. Two hundred years later, the city was the fourth largest in Europe, with an estimated population of 200,000. Most of this growth had occurred between 1585 and 1650. It was all the more remarkable because, among Europe's ten largest cities, Amsterdam was the only one that was not a state capital; its expansion was a commercial phenomenon.

Situated on the confluence of the River Amstel, which gave the city its name, and an arm of the sea called the IJ, Amsterdam's location provided a deep

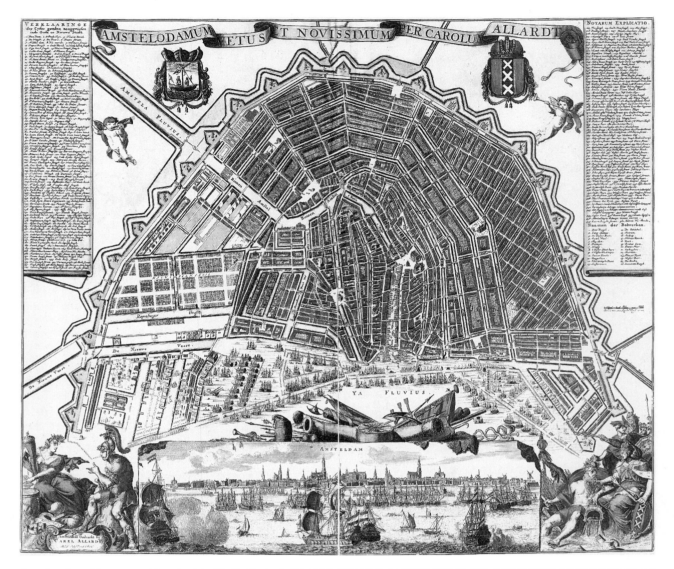

Amsterdam. The many ships depicted in the busy harbor of Amsterdam on Carel Allard's late-seventeenth-century map attest to the importance of the city as a commercial center. After the Spanish capture of Antwerp in 1585, much of the trade formerly concentrated in that city moved to Amsterdam, and by the end of the Dutch Revolt (1568–1648) Amsterdam was the economic and cultural capital of Europe. MAP COLLECTION, STERLING MEMORIAL LIBRARY, YALE UNIVERSITY

and safe natural harbor for international shipping. In the sixteenth century the city was able to capture a substantial share of the expanding trade between Holland and the Baltic, which helped feed the city's waterlogged hinterland. Amsterdam became the most significant of Antwerp's satellite ports in the northern Low Countries.

Amsterdam's position changed dramatically in the course of the Dutch Revolt. Initially loyal to the Spanish king, the city was blockaded for years before it decided to join the rebel side in 1578. Then, in 1585, Antwerp was reconquered by the Spaniards,

and in retaliation the rebels cut off shipping on the River Scheldt. Antwerp's merchant community dispersed, with many eventually settling in Amsterdam. Together with the local merchants they initiated a remarkable boom. Already in the 1590s Amsterdam merchants fitted out ships to explore various routes to the East Indies. Their success led to the establishment of the Dutch East India Company (Vereenigde Oostindische Compagnie, or VOC) in 1602, with Amsterdam merchants providing more than half of the initial capital. When the Dutch West India Company (West-Indische Compagnie, or WIC) was established in 1621, Amsterdam merchants were again the most important providers of capital. During the first half of the seventeenth century Amsterdam developed into the "staple" of western Europe, where every conceivable product available on the world market was sold.

The economic boom attracted large numbers of people to Amsterdam, both from within the Dutch Republic and from other countries. During the seventeenth century roughly one third of Amsterdam's population was of foreign origin, while another third had migrated to the city from within the Dutch borders. To make room for all these newcomers, the city's territory had to be expanded. The most significant additions were made in two stages during the 1610s and the 1660s, when Amsterdam obtained its characteristic shape. The old city center was surrounded by a ring of three main canals, de-

signed especially with the newly rich merchant class in mind. The canals were in turn enveloped by a ring of cheaper housing for artisan and working-class households. These two expansions also thwarted the development of suburbs and ensured that all of Amsterdam's population remained firmly under the control of the city's institutions.

Within the confederate Dutch Republic, Amsterdam enjoyed much autonomy. Its politicians, mostly recruited from the merchant community, were also indirectly involved in determining national priorities, ensuring, for example, that Amsterdam's trade interests in the Baltic remained well protected. Amsterdam's four burgomasters, three of whom were replaced each year, were sometimes considered as the most powerful men in the country. The defense of the town's political indepen-

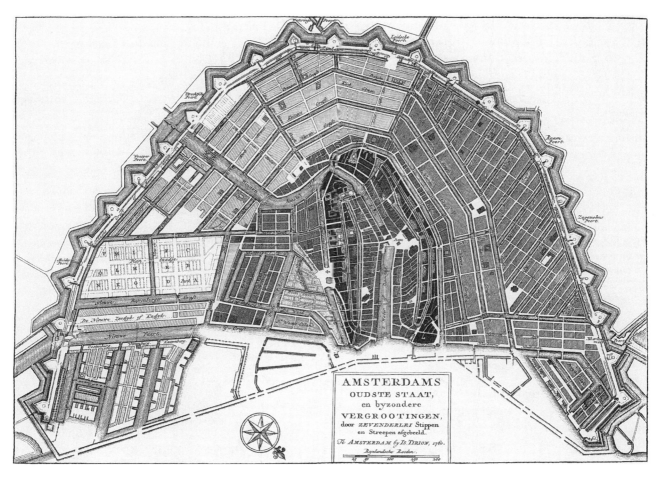

Amsterdam. A plan of Amsterdam by Isaac Tirion from Jan Wagenaar's pictorial history of the city published in 1760. The different types of shading, or hatching, illustrate the planned growth of the city out from its medieval core around a dam on the Amstel River near its confluence with the IJ River. Concentric canals give Amsterdam its characteristic shape and divide the city into small islands linked by bridges. MAP COLLECTION, STERLING MEMORIAL LIBRARY, YALE UNIVERSITY

dence was of great importance to them. The burgomasters ruled Amsterdam itself with the help of a great many corporate institutions. The guilds, for example, were and remained very important in the local economy. During the seventeenth century their number doubled, and they organized as much as a third of the population. Public order was maintained with the help of the civic militias.

The city's culture reflected this emphasis on civic institutions. In 1648 work began on the building of a new town hall, which was to be the largest purely civic building created in seventeenth-century Europe. Its magnificent design in fashionable Dutch classicism, lavishly decorated with monumental sculpture and paintings, was a monument to Amsterdam's achievements. The central hall was significantly known as the Citizens' Hall. Civic virtue was also a central theme in what was to become the most famous painting of Amsterdam's Golden Age, Rembrandt's *Nightwatch* (1642), which depicts the officers of a militia company guarding the town at night. This, and numerous similar collective portraits of militia officers, were created to be displayed in public.

Amsterdam's political independence, and the commercial attitude of its leading citizens, also helped create a tolerant religious climate, most significantly expressed in the treatment of Jewish immigrants. Holland did not have a Jewish community before the end of the sixteenth century, and when the first Jews arrived from Portugal in the 1590s the authorities were very open-minded about their settlement in Amsterdam. Jewish residents could obtain citizenship rights, albeit on restricted conditions. In the course of the seventeenth century two large synagogues were built in Amsterdam. Although a Jewish neighborhood developed in Amsterdam, it was not a ghetto, and Jews were permitted to live throughout the city.

Economic prosperity lasted longer in Amsterdam than in any of the other Dutch towns. However, in the course of the eighteenth century it became clear that Amsterdam's heyday was over. Most tellingly, the growth of its population, already slackening in the second half of the seventeenth century, was really over by 1740. The extra space that had been added by the extension of the 1660s remained partly unoccupied. The merchants, once the most dynamic force of the city, became conservative in their outlook, and many families retired from business altogether. Banking became the most significant element of the city's service sector, but it did little in terms of local employment. Poverty skyrocketed, especially during the 1780s and 1790s, when ultimately one in five families depended on poor relief. By then, the glory days of the Golden Age were still treasured by the small part of the population fortunate—and wealthy—enough to live on one of the main canals. Elsewhere, in the narrow back alleys where whole families were crowded into a single room or cellar, Amsterdam had come to look like any other European city.

See also **Dutch Literature and Language; Dutch Republic; Dutch Revolt (1568–1648); Guilds; Netherlands, Art in the; Rembrandt van Rijn; Trading Companies.**

BIBLIOGRAPHY

Bodian, Miriam. *Hebrews of the Portuguese Nation: Conversos and Community in Early Modern Amsterdam.* Bloomington, Ind., 1997.

Fremantle, Katharine. *The Baroque Town Hall of Amsterdam.* Utrecht, 1957.

Frijhoff, Willem, and Maarten Prak, eds. *Geschiedenis van Amsterdam.* Vols. 2 and 3, *Zeventiende en achttiende eeuw.* Amsterdam, forthcoming.

Gelder, Roelof van, and Renée Kistemaker. *Amsterdam 1275–1795: De ontwikkeling van een handelsmetropool.* Amsterdam, 1983.

Gelderblom, Oscar, "Antwerp Merchants in Amsterdam after the Revolt (1578–1630)." In *International Trade in the Low Countries (14th–16th Centuries): Merchants, Organisation, Infrastructure,* edited by Peter Stabel et al., pp. 234–241. Louvain, 2000.

Haverkamp-Begemann, E. *Rembrandt: The Nightwatch.* Princeton, 1982.

Israel, Jonathan I. *Dutch Primacy in World Trade, 1585–1740.* Oxford and New York, 1989.

Lesger, Clé. *Handel in Amsterdam ten tijde van de Opstand. Kooplieden, commerciële expansie en verandering in de ruimtelijke economie van de Nederlanden ca. 1550–ca. 1630.* Hilversum, 2001.

Lourens, Piet, and Jan Lucassen. "Ambachtsgilden binnen een handelskapitalistische stad: aanzetten voor een analyse van Amsterdam rond 1700." *NEHA-Jaarboek voor economische, bedrijfs- en techniekgeschiedenis* 61 (1998) 121–162.

Nusteling, Hubert. *Welvaart en werkgelegenheid in Amsterdam 1540–1860. Een relaas over demografie, economie en sociale politiek van een wereldstad.* Amsterdam, 1985.

MAARTEN PRAK

ANABAPTISM. Anabaptism is the name for several related branches of continental European lay Protestantism. These groups first began emerging after 1525 and were most prominent in (but not limited to) German- and Dutch-speaking territories. In German and Dutch the terms *Wiedertäufer* and *wederdooper* (rebaptizers) carry old, negative connotations. By contrast, *Täufer* or *dooper* (baptists), *Taufgesinnten* or *doopsgezinden* (the baptism-minded), and Mennonites (strictly speaking a group-specific term that is sometimes applied loosely as an umbrella category for all later Anabaptists except the Hutterites) are used more widely today. In current scholarly English the name Anabaptist ("one who baptizes again") is widely accepted as a neutral term that has lost its older, polemical sense. While the first Anabaptists were often baptized twice, once as infants in the medieval church and again as adults in the early years of the Reformation, the overwhelming majority throughout the early modern era were baptized only once as adults, after first confessing their faith publicly.

There were some features common to most Anabaptist groups throughout the early modern period. Like other Protestants, Anabaptists rejected papal authority in favor of biblical authority. However, while most other Protestants began establishing new professional clerical elites soon after the initial ferment of the Reformation, Anabaptists maintained their reliance on lay leadership much longer, and it was not uncommon among early groups to believe that ordinary men and women could receive direct inspiration from the Holy Spirit. Like other Protestants, Anabaptists emphasized the importance of grace for salvation, but they also placed a great deal of emphasis on the need for true faith to result in the transformation of believers' lives. And like other Protestants, Anabaptists accepted only two sacraments, communion and baptism. Their symbolic, commemorative understanding of communion was similar to that held by Reformed Protestants. But unlike the majority of other major Christian communities, Anabaptists rejected child baptism in favor of believers' baptism as practiced by the earliest Christian communities.

INTERPRETING ANABAPTISM

One of the dominant twentieth-century interpretations of Anabaptist history was outlined by the Mennonite historian Harold Bender in an influential essay from 1944 entitled "The Anabaptist Vision." In it he argued that "Anabaptism proper" had a single point of origin (Zurich) and an unchanging core of ethical features (discipleship, brotherhood, and nonresistance) that defined it. The reason for this narrow definition was to establish a clear distinction between true and false Anabaptists. The latter were those who, although they practiced believers' baptism, also participated in revolutionary politics and/or held mystical, spiritualist beliefs. From the point of view of church historians trying to establish an appropriate pedigree for modern Mennonites, these kinds of "fanatics" were not appropriate forebears.

By contrast, nineteenth- and twentieth-century Marxist historians were among the first sympathetic interpreters to raise the theme of radical politics to prominence in Anabaptist studies. They were interested in Anabaptists as defenders of an ideology of the poor at a crucial stage of the Reformation when mainstream reformers were allying themselves with the interests of capital and the feudal ruling class. Few historians of Anabaptism today are Marxists, but issues the Marxists addressed—the social character of Anabaptist groups and the centrality of revolutionary events like the German Peasants' War of 1525 and the period of Anabaptist rule in Münster from 1534 to 1535—continue to be prominent.

Scholars since the 1960s and 1970s have generally rejected these interpretations. If the older Mennonite scholarship has influence today, it is mainly in the general interest in ethics and beliefs. Scholars since the later twentieth century have continued to investigate these themes, usually without imposing modern denominational assumptions about "Anabaptism proper." In part because of the influence of Marxist research, most acknowledge today that the first Anabaptists held a wide range of views about the use of force, as well as the proper relationship between believers and secular rulers. The newer social and intellectual history has shown that regional diversity was one of the hallmarks of Anabaptism. The way ideas spread among Anabaptist groups plus the important role of women in early Anabaptist groups have also received more attention in recent scholarship.

At the beginning of the twenty-first century it was common to write about Anabaptism as part of the "Radical Reformation." In the 1960s George Williams had defined this term in contrast to the "Magisterial Reformation" and the "Counter-Reformation" and gave it a meaning that emphasized intellectual and theological features. By contrast, in the 1970s the German historian Hans-Jürgen Goertz had proposed defining as "radical" those groups and individuals who broke with the social, political, and ecclesiastical norms of their day. In Goertz's interpretation, anticlericalism and laicism were key impulses shared by the first reforming movements in the early 1520s. By the mid-1520s rifts developed among reformers. Those who founded mainstream Protestant churches moderated their once radical positions when it became possible to establish alliances with secular authorities. Anabaptist groups were among the early campaigners for radical reforms who refused to compromise with authorities and therefore eventually found themselves forced to the margins of society. The early coalitions of radicals included not only Anabaptists, but also spiritualist opponents of child baptism. While leaders at first could campaign for a complete Anabaptist reformation of society, separatism became the main option left open to those proponents of adult baptism who were active a few years after the Peasants' War and the period of Anabaptist rule in Münster. The focus on radical reform is significant, because it integrates Anabaptist history into the main currents of early Reformation studies.

After the first stage of the Reformation, Anabaptist groups underwent a transformation from dynamic early reforming movements to more established communities. The concentration of Anabaptist and Radical Reformation studies on the period until about 1550 has meant that the character of institutionalized Anabaptism of the early modern period remains largely unexplored.

EARLY ANABAPTIST GROUPS

Throughout Europe the first generation of Anabaptists included men and women from a wide range of social backgrounds. University-educated scholars, former priests and monks, and artisans and other commoners were among their first leaders. Even the educated, many of whom quickly fell victim to executioners, tended to hold anti-intellectual prejudices, preferring the simplicity of a life lived according to Christ's example to the intricacies of academic theology. Like medieval dissenters and reformers, most early Anabaptists emphasized active holiness and ascetically disciplined lives as prerequisites for salvation, and they frequently held apocalyptic, prophetic, spiritualistic, mystical, and anti-institutional understandings of their connections with God. Radical reformers like Andreas Bodenstein von Karlstadt, Thomas Müntzer, and Kaspar Schwenckfeld von Ossig were among those who rejected child baptism before 1525. Although they never baptized adults, their influence on Anabaptist groups was strong.

Ever since Klaus Depperman, Werner Packull, and James Stayer published the essay "From Monogenesis to Polygenesis" in 1975, it has been common to make distinctions among three regional forms of Anabaptism: Swiss, southern German and Austrian, and northern German and Dutch. The authors' further research has shown that there were many interactions and exchanges connecting groups, especially in Swiss, southern German, and Austrian territories. Nonetheless, it remains useful to chart differences, as well as interactions, between regional cultures of Anabaptism.

In Swiss, southern German, and Austrian territories there was a strong affinity between the Peasants' War and Anabaptism. In the aftermath of the conflicts of 1525, disillusioned activists sought to give religious expression to the ideals that the peasants and commoners had fought for earlier. The Anabaptist practice of community of goods emerged as a result.

The first adult baptisms began in Swiss territories in early 1525. The Swiss Brethren included many of Huldrych Zwingli's early supporters, who had become dissatisfied with his conservative turn. Key leaders in this branch included Konrad Grebel (1498–1526), Balthasar Hubmaier (1485–1528), Felix Mantz (1498–1527), and Wilhelm Reublin

(c. 1484–after 1559). Their Christianity tended to be legalistic, literal, and scriptural in character. The Schleitheim Articles of 1527 are a famous expression of Swiss Anabaptism in its most radically separatist mode.

Compared to Swiss Anabaptists, southern German and Austrian Anabaptist groups were influenced much more strongly by Thomas Müntzer's brand of spiritualism and mysticism. Apocalyptic expectations among believers were also especially strong into the later 1520s. Key leaders in this branch included Hans Denck (c. 1500–1527), Hans Hut (d. 1527), Pilgram Marpeck (1492–1556), and Melchior Rinck (c. 1493–1553?). After the 1520s these groups became indistinguishable from the Swiss—except for Marpeck's group, which was prominent for publishing ventures in which writings by such diverse figures as Luther and Schwenckfeld were edited to serve Anabaptist doctrinal objectives.

Anabaptists were faced with often severe persecution. From an anti-Anabaptist point of view, the baptism of adults was an anti-Christian rebaptism that threatened to disrupt unity and order in the Christian polity. Thus, sixteenth-century rulers tended to interpret the act of baptizing adults as an act of rebellion and heresy. Although Anabaptists amounted to only a small minority in most territories, the attention paid them by authorities meant that their impact was much greater than their numbers might suggest. At the 1529 Diet of Speyer rebaptism was declared a capital crime in the territories of the Holy Roman Empire. Both Catholic and Protestant governments executed unrepentant Anabaptist men and women.

Anabaptist responses to persecution varied. In the immediate aftermath of the Peasants' War a small minority chose to fight back, though futilely. Some believers recanted when threatened with punishment, while others stayed steadfast in the face of hardship, hoping for rescue upon Christ's imminent return. When confronted with the choice, some preferred martyrdom over the betrayal of their faith; about two thousand died for their faith, about as many as the martyrs drawn from the far more numerous Protestant churches. Another option was Nicodemism, hiding their forbidden faith from cen-

tral authorities while pretending to conform. Many chose exile.

One region where persecution was particularly intense was the Catholic Habsburg Tyrol. Here Anabaptism in the late 1520s was the main form of popular reform. Jakob Hutter (d. 1536) and other leaders arranged the relocation of large numbers of believers from the Tyrol to Moravia, where some members of the local nobility were willing to provide the Anabaptists with land to live in peace. The relative safety of Moravia also attracted many refugees from Switzerland and southern Germany. In the Moravian sanctuaries, competing branches melded into new hybrid forms of Anabaptism.

In Dutch and northern German territories, where the Peasants' War was of little consequence, Anabaptism had a largely (although not entirely) separate history. Melchior Hofmann (c. 1495–1543/1544) began baptizing believers in these territories in 1530. In 1531, after harsh repression, he decided to suspend baptisms until the End Times, which he felt were then soon approaching. The suspension of adult baptism did not halt the movement's spread. A turning point came in February 1534, when an Anabaptist faction won elections in the Westphalian city of Münster. By that time the city had become a New Jerusalem for believers from the surrounding region and the Netherlands after baptisms had resumed. Catholic and Protestant authorities in neighboring territories reacted by laying siege to the city. Under the stresses of the siege, community of goods and polygamy were practiced. The siege armies broke through the city's walls in June 1535. The captured leaders, including Jan van Leyden, the self-styled Anabaptist king, were executed in gruesome fashion.

Dutch and northern German Anabaptists after 1535 had to come to terms with the shock of the Münster years. Melchior Hofmann's distinctive belief in Christ's nature untainted by human corruption remained a characteristic of successor groups for many decades. A number of leaders vied for influence among the Melchiorite remnant after 1535. These included Jan van Battenburg, who led a militant minority; David Joris (1501/1502–1556), whose brand of spiritualism attracted many adherents before 1540; and Menno Simons (1496–1561), a former Catholic priest who advocated the

Anabaptism. *Anabaptist Anneken Hendriks Being Hoisted to the Fire.* This illustration by Jan Luykens appeared in the 1660 *Martyrs Mirror* by Thieleman Janszoon van Braght; the book collects writings concerning Protestants of various sects who were persecuted for their beliefs during the sixteenth and seventeenth centuries. ©BETTMANN/CORBIS

formation of disciplined, separatist communities of nonresistant believers as an alternative to the excesses of Münster. The Mennonites were the most successful faction after about 1540.

LATER DEVELOPMENTS

The character of Anabaptist groups went through some significant transformations over the course of the early modern era. While the first Anabaptists were voluntary converts to the new faith, most Anabaptists after the middle of the sixteenth century were born into established communities of faith. They accepted both adult baptism and political discrimination as part of their inheritance. It was only after the first generation of the Reformation that

nonresistance (which denominational historians emphasized in their interpretations) rose to the central position that it enjoyed throughout most of the rest of the early modern period. Over the course of the sixteenth century the separatist Anabaptists' radical rejection of mainstream society diminished, and secular governments tended to be more accepting of the peaceful, withdrawn dissenters the Anabaptists had become.

In southern territories, persecution forced believers to relocate from cities and towns to the more secluded countryside. Anabaptists in the Swiss highlands were hunted by authorities until the middle of the eighteenth century. The Amish, followers of Jakob Amman (c. 1644–c. 1730), formed in the

1690s, in part to try to establish pure communities of the faithful without any compromises. Many emigrated eventually to North America. Unlike the single-family households the Swiss Brethren preferred, a unique feature of Moravian Anabaptism was that a portion of its members organized themselves in large social, religious, and economic cooperatives that have remained typical of Hutterite communities (named after Jakob Hutter) to the present day. Hutterites thrived in Moravia beside other non-communitarian Anabaptist groups until the beginning of the Thirty Years' War, when they lost noble protection and migrated to new havens in Slovakia, after which they were driven farther east, until in the late nineteenth century they joined the wave of Russian emigration to North America.

Anabaptist groups thrived in the Protestant Netherlands and northern German territories, largely because they had received special privileges from secular authorities after the 1570s. Mennonites, the dominant group of Anabaptists in these regions, had strong communities in the Dutch countryside (as in Friesland) and in urban centers like Amsterdam, and even as far east as Danzig (Gdańsk). Under the stresses of war and persecution, Anabaptists had left the southern Low Countries in the sixteenth century for the relative safety of Protestant-controlled territories to the north. In the sixteenth and seventeenth centuries, new Anabaptist communities formed. These included groups known as Waterlanders, Flemish, Frisians, and High Germans, and later also Lamists and Zonists. Although their ecclesiastical affairs were organized mainly locally and congregationally, conferences or synodal structures did emerge in the seventeenth century to link communities. The Dutch and northern German Mennonites were the first Anabaptists to employ professional, university-trained clergymen.

Most Mennonites were what we might call "conforming nonconformists." They were religious nonconformists in their unique practice of believers' baptism, as well as in their refusal to swear oaths or bear arms. In the seventeenth century, they (like other Protestant groups) commonly expressed their desire to preserve a unique confessional identity by using confessions of faith. In these statements, they also typically emphasized their adherence to the basic doctrines of the Christian creeds, and their politi-

cally conformist view that true Christians were obedient subjects. As communities they paid taxes, even war taxes. In some jurisdictions Mennonites held minor political offices, but in most cases they accepted exclusion from positions of public authority.

Early modern Mennonites were instrumental in creating a sense of pan-Anabaptist identity. They argued that their Anabaptist forebears were not fanatics, heretics, or rebels, as many Catholic and mainstream Protestant polemicists alleged. Rather, they were believers who had been especially faithful to Christ's teachings. A rich martyrological tradition emerged in which Mennonite writers memorialized executed believers from groups all across Europe. Significant numbers of Mennonites prospered economically in the early modern era, and some were able to establish substantial merchant enterprises. They used part of their wealth to support coreligionists suffering hardships in other regions.

In the eighteenth century, Dutch Mennonites tended to be well integrated into their societies, and some even participated in Pietist or Enlightenment circles. In the 1780s a significant proportion were active in the Dutch Patriot Movement during its rebellion against the Orange regime. Some even gave up the principle of nonresistance to bear arms against the government. After the early nineteenth century this radical phase was eagerly forgotten.

See also **Leyden, Jan van; Münster; Patriot Revolution; Peasants' War, German; Pietism; Reformation, Protestant; Zwingli, Huldrych.**

BIBLIOGRAPHY

Driedger, Michael D. *Obedient Heretics: Mennonite Identities in Lutheran Hamburg and Altona during the Confessional Age.* Aldershot, U.K., and Burlington, Vt., 2002.

Dyck, Cornelius J., ed. *An Introduction to Mennonite History: A Popular History of the Anabaptists and the Mennonites.* Scottdale, Pa., 1993.

Goertz, Hans-Jürgen, ed. *Profiles of Radical Reformers: Biographical Sketches from Thomas Müntzer to Paracelsus.* Scottdale, Pa., and Kitchener, Ont., 1982.

The Mennonite Encyclopedia: A Comprehensive Reference Work on the Anabaptist-Mennonite Movement. 5 vols. Hillsboro, Kans., 1955–1990.

Mennonite Quarterly Review. Goshen, Ind., 1927–. One of the key forums for scholarship on Anabaptism. Includes important essays like "The Anabaptist Vision" and "From Monogenesis to Polygenesis."

Packull, Werner O. *Hutterite Beginnings: Communitarian Experiments during the Reformation.* Baltimore, 1995.

Snyder, C. Arnold. *Anabaptist History and Theology.* Kitchener, Ont., 1997.

Snyder, C. Arnold, and Linda A. Hecht. *Profiles of Anabaptist Women: Sixteenth-Century Reforming Pioneers.* Waterloo, Ont., 1996.

Stayer, James M. *Anabaptists and the Sword.* 2nd ed. Lawrence, Kans., 1976.

——. *The German Peasants' War and Anabaptist Community of Goods.* Montreal, 1991.

——. "The Radical Reformation." In *Handbook of European History, 1400–1600: Late Middle Ages, Renaissance, and Reformation.* Vol. 2. Edited by Thomas A. Brady Jr., Heiko A. Oberman, and James D. Tracy. Leiden and New York, 1995.

Stayer, James M., and Werner O. Packull, trans. and eds. *The Anabaptists and Thomas Müntzer.* Dubuque, Iowa, 1980. A collection of influential essays and excerpts from books, many translated from German and Dutch.

Williams, George Huntston. *The Radical Reformation.* 3rd ed. Kirksville, Mo., 1992.

MICHAEL D. DRIEDGER

ANATOMY AND PHYSIOLOGY. The spread of dissection at the end of the thirteenth century—in itself quite unusual and remarkable given religious and anthropological prohibitions—is closely linked to the growing demand for surgical intervention, the increase of postmortem inspections for legal purposes, the epistemological need to provide medical practice with a rational basis founded on ocular demonstrations, and the related use of public anatomies as a means of self-advertisement and of gaining institutional legitimacy against the claims of unlicensed practitioners. Mondino de' Liuzzi's *Anatomy,* written in 1316, indicates that anatomically based inquiries had become part of university medical education. By the fifteenth century, annual anatomies were established as a part of the academic curriculum in the more important universities of Europe. The fifteenth and sixteenth centuries witnessed a shift in the function of dissection from a predominantly educational device providing visual validation for textual knowledge to an independent method of investigation and a source of anatomical and physiological information. It

should be noted that the practice of human dissection was more the business of the physician than of the surgeon. As a consequence of long-established institutional constraints, surgeons were not allowed to practice internal medicine (and therefore to anatomize the so-called three cavities: abdomen, thorax, and head) and their anatomical skill was largely confined to the limbs.

THE DECLINE OF GALENISM

In the Middle Ages, the diffusion of anatomical and physiological knowledge was initially conveyed by the interpretation of authoritative texts rather than by the practice of dissection. Such works as Avicenna's *Canon,* Rhazes's *Almansor,* and Averroes's *Colliget* contained introductory sections on systematic anatomical description. The revival of Galenic texts, first in Bologna, Montpellier, and Paris in the fourteenth century, and then in the rest of the major European universities, contributed to the renewed interest in human dissection. The development of medical humanism (that is, the recovery of the ancients' medical legacy through a critical and philological restoration of their literary achievements) was a key factor in reviving anatomical inquiry. As also in the case of law, greater care for and attention to the ancient legacy generated over time a more critical attitude toward it and so ironically the reconstruction of the Galenic corpus, by bringing to light a series of discrepancies between authoritative text and dissected body, precipitated the decline of Galenism.

It is important to remember that Galen's medical system maintained a certain vitality (and some explanatory flexibility) until the end of the seventeenth century. Eclecticism and syncretism were a more frequent response among early modern practitioners than one might expect, above all because the therapeutic side of medicine continued to be conducted along traditional lines. The decline of Galenic anatomo-physiology among medical humanists and by anatomical investigators such as Andreas Vesalius (1514–1564), Michael Servetus (1511–1553), Realdo Colombo (1516?–1559), and Girolamo Fabrizi d'Aquapendente (c. 1533–1619) was an incremental process and involved the interpretation of specific discoveries.

A crucial watershed in the development of the new anatomy and physiology was William Harvey's

(1578–1657) discovery of the circulation of the blood. In most physiological accounts prior to Harvey's discovery, the functions of pulse, respiration, and nutrition were interwoven into a coherent and self-contained system in which the venous apparatus and the liver constituted a sanguineous and nutritive system and the arterial apparatus and the heart a pneumatic system with the main function of maintaining the body's innate heat and of distributing its effects throughout the body by means of respiration and ventilation. The redefinition of vital functions resulting from Harvey's theory of circulation severed the long-accepted links between the movement of the blood, the nutrition of the parts, and the production of the innate heat. Further anatomical discoveries, such as Gasparo Aselli's lacteals (1622), Jean Pecquet's thoracic duct (1651), and Thomas Bartholin's lymphatics (1653), complemented Harvey's work on the heart and the circulatory system by delineating a separate vascular system in which the chyle was delivered not to the liver but directly to the vena cava and then to the heart. This anatomical research dispossessed several organs (principally the liver and the lungs) of their traditional functions. The discovery of the circulation of the blood, therefore, was only the first of a series of discoveries of various, related "circulations" and their description: the circulation of the nutritive fluid, the circulation of the lymph, and the circulation of the "nervous juice."

With respect to the relationship between anatomy and surgical practice, the status of surgery underwent a dramatic change during the eighteenth century. Surgeons pioneered new techniques and rose in professional standing. In keeping with the Enlightenment emphasis on the benefits of practical knowledge, surgery became a separate science, with a particular emphasis on experimentation. The development of surgery, especially in France, consolidated the association between anatomo-pathology (the view that diseases are anatomically localized), bedside teaching, and the modern hospital. The reunification of surgery with medicine was also facilitated by the fact that during the eighteenth century, for a number of social and institutional reasons, anatomical studies could rely on a more abundant supply of corpses (bodies of criminals, lunatics, and paupers).

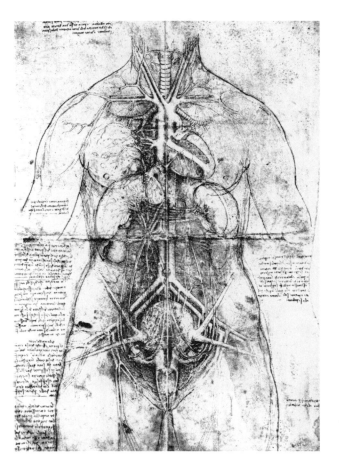

Anatomy and Physiology. An anatomical study of the human torso by Leonardo da Vinci. This is one of the many da Vinci drawings housed in Windsor Castle, Berkshire, England. ©BETTMANN/CORBIS

PHILOSOPHICAL ALTERNATIVES

With the collapse of Aristotelian natural philosophy within the domain of the physical sciences, the philosophical synthesis of Aristotelianism, Hippocratism, and Galenism, which had represented the theoretical framework of the medical sciences for centuries, also began to lose its hegemonic status and was confronted with an array of new philosophical perspectives. Various lines of anatomical and physiological inquiry spread throughout the seventeenth century, founded on different strands of mechanical philosophy, varieties of corpuscularianism, and forms of chemical naturalism. Systems of medical explanation arose with the ambition of accounting for every manifestation of life, from the absorption of food to the circulation of the blood, from the processes of secretion and excretion to muscular activity, and from respiration to sensation. The two prevailing approaches came to be known as iatrochemistry and iatrophysics (being the application, respectively, of chemistry and mechanics to the study of the body). Of course, iatrochemistry and iatrophysics were not entirely discrete systems and it would be difficult to find a purely iatrochemical or iatrophysical account of the body in the seventeenth and eighteenth centuries. Authors as different as Giovanni Alfonso Borelli (1608–1679), René Descartes (1596–1650), and Thomas Willis (1621–1675) made use of chemical explanations to account for the production of the vital energy underlying physiological processes. An example of theoretical versatility was Franciscus de la Boë (called Sylvus; 1614–1672), a determined supporter of Harvey's doctrine who emphasized the importance of the chemical processes of fermentation and effervescence and managed to graft a chemical and circulatory physiology onto an originally Galenic framework.

Respiration was another physiological domain in which the chemical approach proved to be particularly fruitful. The long series of experiments conducted by Robert Boyle (1627–1691), John Mayow (c. 1641–1679), Joseph Black (1728–1799), and Joseph Priestley (1733–1804) led eventually to the final identification of the "vital air" as oxygen by Antoine-Laurent Lavoisier (1743–1794), who also demonstrated that some of the vital air was taken into the blood and had a decisive role in combustion and the maintenance of animal life. Although Georg Ernst Stahl (1660–1734), professor of medicine at the University of Halle, was no anatomist and rejected the findings of microscopic anatomy, he was concerned with the chemical composition of the body, and his chemical views had a certain influence on contemporary physiologists, especially those teaching at Montepellier. He distinguished the immaterial principle of life (the soul) from the body. However, despite obvious similarities to Descartes's dualism, Stahl's identification of the soul with the purposeful activity of nature was characteristic of the medical tradition rather than the Cartesian idea of the mind as a principle of consciousness. Stahl maintained that an organism was a living unit fundamentally different from a mere mechanism and that its material components were instrumental parts controlled by the immaterial soul.

Inspired by the new philosophies of nature advocated by Descartes, Galileo Galilei (1564–1642),

Boyle, and Pierre Gassendi (1592–1655), and in contrast with the iatrochemical emphasis on the vital nature of the inner workings of the body, iatrophysical physiologists held the view that medicine, both in theory and in practice, was based upon purely mechanical principles, namely, matter and motion, particles (whether indivisible atoms or indefinitely divisible corpuscles), action by contact, and movement through pores. The demise of the old belief that anatomical structures and physiological functions were regulated by purposeful tendencies caused a radical change in the explanatory framework of physiology: secretion and excretion were accounted for without resorting to attractive faculties; the function of the lungs became the mixing of the component parts of the blood; digestion was interpreted as a process of grinding and mincing food; and health and disease were considered to depend on the movement, obstruction, or stagnation of the various fluids running throughout the body. With Isaac Newton's (1642–1727) theory of gravitation and Boyle's experiments on air, attention shifted from gross to fine structures, from the paradigm of the clockwork mechanism formulated in rudimentary mechanical terms to a more sophisticated model of hydraulic and pneumatic engineering that came to be understood as an integrated network of vessels regulated by quantitative laws. In addition, with the publication of Newton's *Opticks* (1704), physiologists were encouraged to use the notions of ether and extremely subtle spirituous effluvia in their accounts of physiological operations.

Iatrophysical anatomy was greatly assisted by developments in microscopic observation. Robert Hooke (1635–1703), in his influential *Micrographia* (1665), argued that with the use of the microscope, many so-called "occult properties" might be interpreted as elementary contrivances of nature. Following Galileo's suggestion in *Il saggiatore* (1623; The assayer) that living beings could be seen as assemblages of small machines, Marcello Malpighi (1628–1694) applied the microscope in his anatomical investigations to observe the smallest sections of animal and plant organs. Antoni van Leeuwenhoeck's (1632–1723) expertise in the use of the microscope further confirmed the particulate structure of matter.

The most influential synthesis of iatrophysics was Hermann Boerhaave's (1668–1738) system of medicine. Teaching at the University of Leiden, he explained the physiological operations of the body in mechanical terms. He dismissed the question of the connection between the body and the mind as irrelevant from a physiological point of view. His characterization of the relationship between the body and the soul was reminiscent of Spinoza's philosophy, in which the substantial attributes—thought and matter—were conceived of as two parallel manifestations of one substance; consequently Boerhaave argued that everything that involves extension, impenetrability, or motion had to be referred to the body.

THE EMERGENCE OF MODERN PHYSIOLOGY

Pre-modern physiology was based on a set of fundamental concepts established during centuries of interpretations, translations, and appropriations of Aristotelian and Galenic notions, such as complexion (the specific balance of the primary qualities characterizing each individual), humors (the bodily fluids governing specific functions), faculties (the inherent powers of the different parts of the body), and spirits (the vehicles of natural, vital, and animal operations).

Whereas throughout the Middle Ages anatomy was subordinate to a form of highly theoretical physiology, in the early modern period the relationship was reversed: anatomy became the experimental and observational point of reference on which physiological theorizing was based. This resulted in a steadily growing interest in the investigation of the material basis of life, independently of whether this basis could be explained in mechanical or vital terms. The most remarkable difference from past approaches was that the distinction between living and non-living bodies was viewed less as a result of the activity of the soul than as a function of the internal organization of matter. The so-called vitalist reaction in the eighteenth century was not so much a return to the notion of the soul (although Stahlian "animism" had a certain influence on medical theories at the time) as an affirmation of the specific vital nature of matter. The mechanical approach to the investigation of vital phenomena in the seventeenth century, especially in its Cartesian version, had effaced the concept of life itself by

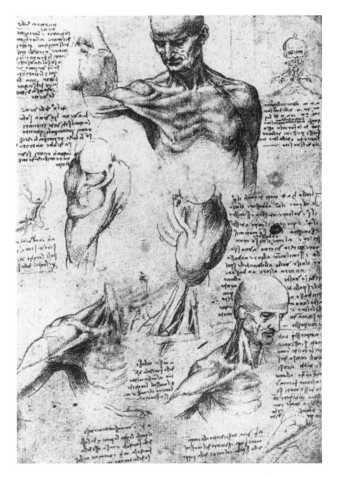

Anatomy and Physiology. Anatomical studies of the muscles of the head and upper torso by Leonardo da Vinci, now housed in Windsor Castle, Berkshire, England. ©BETTMANN/CORBIS

claiming that the manifestations of life were merely the result of various dispositions of inert matter. Eighteenth-century vitalism, therefore, can be seen as the expression of a latent materialism rather than as a form of animism.

Eighteenth-century anatomical investigations into the finer structures of the body placed particular emphasis on study of the nervous system. This, in turn, brought a greater awareness of the interdependence of living organisms and their environment, highlighting the ability of living structures to respond purposefully to their external milieu. It is no accident, then, that the study of the various forms of irritability became a central topic in the eighteenth century. In the second half of the seventeenth century, drawing on Harvey's speculations about the living and sentient nature of the blood, Francis Glisson (1597–1677) elaborated a comprehensive theory of irritability based on the notion of matter as a living and sentient principle. By irritability, Glisson meant the specific properties of the bodily fibers in perceiving and reacting to irritation.

The Swiss physiologist Albrecht von Haller (1708–1777), who taught at the University of Göttingen, adopted Glisson's theory of irritability but attributed the ability to react to external stimuli only to the fibers of the body and not to an allegedly perceptive power inherent in matter. In *Elementa Physiologiae Corporis Humani* (1757–1766; Elements of the physiology of the human body), he characterized the organs of the body as interwoven fibers. Muscles, as any other fibrous part, were deemed to be endowed with a general contractile tendency that he called *vis mortua* (dead power). Active muscular contraction depended on an immanent power that he called irritability. In the famous essay "De Partibus Corporis Humani Sensibilibus et Irritabilibus" (1752), translated into English in 1755 as "On the sensible and irritable parts of animals," he distinguished between irritability (muscular contraction) and sensibility (nerve impulse). He called a part irritable when it contracted upon being touched, sensible when the contact produced an impression in the mind. A great number of physiologists and naturalists working on the irritable properties of living bodies were inspired by Haller's research. William Cullen (1710–1790), professor of medicine at Edinburgh University, defined life as a function of the nervous power and insisted on the importance of the tonic contraction of the muscles. John Brown (1735–1788) maintained, more speculatively, that life was not a spontaneous state but one maintained by continuous stimulation or "excitement"; health was supposed to consist in maintaining the right proportion between them. While never popular in England or France, Brown's system (Brunonianism) was enthusiastically taken up in Italy, Germany, and the United States, where Benjamin Rush (1745–1813) became one of the most vocal supporters of Brown's ideas. Working on gland secretions, Théophile de Bordeu (1722–1776), professor at Montpellier, argued that each organ was naturally endowed with an inherent capacity to respond to external stimuli. A whole series of experiments on generation and regeneration (that is, the capability manifested by plants and some lower animals to grow again after

some parts had been severed) performed by René-Antoine Réaumur (1683–1757), Abraham Trembley (1710–1784), Charles Bonnet (1720–1793), and Lazzaro Spallanzani (1729–1799), among others, provided further evidence for the existence of active vital powers in matter.

At the end of the century, the dominant discourse in physiology was vitalistic. Johann Friedrich Blumenbach's (1752–1840) idea of a "life-force" driving toward regeneration, John Hunter's (1728–1793) belief in a "life-principle" distinguishing living organisms from inanimate matter, and Erasmus Darwin's (1731–1802) notion of an intrinsic motility embedded in the fibers of living beings are only some of the many eighteenth-century conceptions of an original power of life not reducible to the mechanical powers of matter.

See also **Boerhaave, Herman; Boyle, Robert; Cullen, William; Descartes, René; Galileo Galilei; Gassendi, Pierre; Haller, Albrecht von; Harvey, William; Hooke, Robert; Leeuwenhoek, Antoni van; Malpighi, Marcello; Matter, Theories of; Medicine; Priestley, Joseph; Scientific Method; Vesalius, Andreas.**

BIBLIOGRAPHY

Brown, Theodore M. *The Mechanical Philosophy and the "Animal Oeconomy."* New York, 1981.

Carlino, Andrea. *Books of the Body: Anatomical Ritual and Renaissance Learning.* Chicago and London, 1999.

Cunningham, Andrew. *The Anatomical Renaissance: The Resurrection of the Anatomical Projects of the Ancients.* Aldershot, U.K., 1997.

Ferrari, Giovanna. "Public Anatomy Lessons and the Carnival: The Anatomy Theatre of Bologna." *Past and Present* 117 (1987): 50–106.

French, Roger. *Dissection and Vivisection in the European Renaissance.* Aldershot, U.K., 1999.

Hall, Thomas S. *History of General Physiology 600 B.C. to A.D. 1900.* Chicago and London, 1969.

Richardson, Ruth. *Death, Dissection and the Destitute.* London, 1987.

Sawday, Jonathan. *The Body Emblazoned: Dissection and the Human Body in Renaissance Culture.* London and New York, 1995.

Siraisi, Nancy. *Medieval & Early Renaissance Medicine: An Introduction to Knowledge and Practice.* Chicago, 1990.

Temkin, Owsei. *Galenism: Rise and Decline of a Medical Philosophy.* Ithaca, N.Y., and London, 1973.

GUIDO GIGLIONI

ANCIEN RÉGIME. The term *ancien régime* (Old Regime) came into use in the late summer of 1789 as participants in the French Revolution realized how great a rupture they had made from the recent past. *"Ancien régime"* therefore came into existence only after the *ancien régime* was finished. No one was ever very specific about when it began. Sometimes revolutionaries implied that the term referred to the entire past of France at least from medieval times onward. At other times, it meant simply the recent pre-revolutionary past.

The term itself evolved during the Revolution. According to the preamble to the Constitution of 1791, the Revolution had abolished hereditary and feudal nobility, venality of office, the guilds, monastic vows, and all privileges. The text says nothing about the monarchy, the abolition of the tithe, and the ending of the church's corporate existence, and it mentions seigneurialism only by allusion. Undoubtedly, the reason was that when the Constitution was promulgated, these issues were not entirely settled. When the monarchy was abolished and the Republic founded (September 1792), the term took on a much more aggressive meaning; republican politicians portrayed the *ancien régime* as uniformly oppressive and claimed that the Revolution had liberated the countryside from noble domination, clerical superstition, and a cruel monarchy. Early revolutionaries believed that they had reestablished liberty and equality before the law. For the Jacobins, escaping the *ancien régime* was a physical and spiritual emancipation.

Historians like Alexis de Tocqueville in the nineteenth century questioned this assumption that the Revolution was a violent break in national history. Instead, said Tocqueville, it witnessed the culmination of the construction of the centralized state. For modern historians, *ancien régime* is a convenient shorthand. It generally means the period in French history from about 1650 to 1789. It defines a France ruled by divine-right absolute monarchy, accompanied by a society based upon privileges for individuals, groups, corporations, provinces, towns, and so on; and capped by a monopoly of public worship reserved for the Catholic Church. The new regime, by contrast, was a constitutional monarchy based upon the rule of law, religious toleration, and equality of rights.

See also **Divine Right Kingship; France; Monarchy; Revolutions, Age of.**

BIBLIOGRAPHY

Baker, Keith Michael, ed. *The Old Regime and the French Revolution.* Chicago, 1987.

Doyle, William. *The Old European Order, 1660–1800.* 2nd ed. New York and Oxford, 1992.

Tocqueville, Alexis de. *The Old Regime and the French Revolution.* Translated by Stuart Gilbert. Garden City, N.Y., 1955.

DONALD SUTHERLAND

ANCIENT WORLD. During the Renaissance, many Europeans were intensely fascinated with the ancient world, that is, the civilizations of ancient Greece and Rome. This fascination is quite understandable. The physical remains of these civilizations—amphitheaters, theaters, triumphal columns and arches, as well as the ruins of many other structures that had been visible since the fall of the Roman Empire—dotted the entire Mediterranean landscape. An awareness of these civilizations, of course, had persisted throughout the Middle Ages because of these physical remains, popular memory, and the surviving writings of the ancient authors. It was not until the Renaissance, however, that the ancient world was studied with renewed vigor. Spearheaded primarily by humanists, artists, and antiquarians, a broad cultural movement emerged that came to regard the ancient world as the peak of civilization and the medieval world as barbarous. It was these groups that sought to restore much of the splendor of the ancient world.

In the Middle Ages, the ancient world was appreciated mainly because it had provided the stage for the birth of Christ and the early development and spread of Christianity. Much of the ancient world remained a mystery, and the glory of ancient Rome was all but forgotten. The famous Forum in Rome, the economic and political hub of the ancient city, had been reduced to a cow pasture. Some of Rome's grandest buildings had been confused and misidentified in medieval imaginations. The fate of the surviving writings of the ancient authors was little different. Many texts were lost or incomplete. The relationship between the buildings and monuments mentioned in these writings and their ruins was largely a mystery. Moreover, since there was virtually no knowledge of Greek, most of the Greek authors, both pagan and Christian, were unknown, including Homer, the author of the *Iliad* and the *Odyssey*. The renewed interest in the ancient world originated in the Italian peninsula during the thirteenth and fourteenth centuries. Italy was the first region in Europe to recover economically and culturally from the devastation wrought by the disintegration of the Roman Empire in the fifth century C.E. Humanists, artists, and architects began to look back upon the ancient world for inspiration in order to give expression to the pride of the thriving and burgeoning Italian city-states and principalities. Civic pride fueled the race to link the individual regions with the glory of the ancient world, both Christian and pagan. In the Middle Ages, the cities were proud of their saints and of the bones and relics in their churches. In the Renaissance, the Italian cities began again to remember their ancient pagan citizens and inhabitants. Naples, perhaps, had never forgotten its tomb of Virgil (70–19 B.C.E.), since a kind of mythical halo had become attached to the name. When in 1274 the skeleton of a warrior inside a lead coffin was brought to light during excavations in Padua, the remains were thought to be those of Antenor, the Trojan soldier believed to have been the mythical founder of the city, as attested by Virgil in the *Aeneid* (1.242–249). The Paduans claimed to have the remains not only of Antenor but also of the historian Livy. Como claimed both the Plinys for its own, and at the end of the fifteenth century erected statues in their honor upon the facade of the cathedral. In this way the evolving social and political history of the various Italian city-states became anchored within the grand framework of the ongoing mystique of the Roman Empire.

Renaissance humanists played a significant role in the attempt to recover, restore, and revive the culture of classical antiquity. Their most significant contribution was in the field of classical scholarship, that is, the intensive study of the literary and material remains of Greek and Roman civilization. Some of the major scholars in this field were Petrarch, Poggio Bracciolini, Coluccio Salutati, Nicholas of Cusa, and Desiderius Erasmus. Lost works of Latin literature, including Cicero's speeches and letters to Atticus, Quintilian's treatise on rhetoric, twelve new

play by Plautus, and the works of the Roman historian Tacitus, were discovered in monasteries throughout Europe. Unfortunately many of the texts that had survived were filled with scribal errors. The humanists produced critical editions of these texts by comparing the readings found in different manuscripts or by making educated guesses as to what the original text must have been. With the invention of the printing press in the mid-fifteenth century, these texts could be made available to a much wider audience than before—a far cry from the time-consuming process of copying out a manuscript by hand, as practiced throughout the Middle Ages. By the middle of the sixteenth century, most of the surviving literature of classical Greece and Rome, both pagan and Christian, was available in a variety of printed editions at prices, moreover, that most scholars could afford. By means of these texts, the humanists gained a fuller understanding of the classical world and could identify many of the ruins and their abbreviated inscriptions. Classical authors continued to exert an influence on the chief literary figures of the seventeenth and eighteenth centuries, who peppered their works with numerous allusions to classical literature. Many of the important genres of history, drama, biography, the essay, and the novel bear a classical imprint.

The ancient world also inspired artists and architects. Artists drew their inspiration from the Bible, from the literary works of ancient Greek and Roman authors, from the landscape, and from the material remains of the ancient world. Unlike painting, of which few classical examples had survived, many types of sculpture and architecture filled the Mediterranean world. As in literature, lost works of art and sculpture were discovered, such as the famous Laocoön found in Rome in 1506. Sculptors and architects did more than just imitate classical models; they produced a new architectural style to serve the needs of Renaissance society. Renaissance art, sculpture, and architecture served multiple purposes: it provided a public expression of civic pride, it was instructive since it often depicted biblical or classical scenes, and it served to enhance the reputation of the patron.

The fascination with the ancient world declined with the discoveries of the New World and of the scientific revolution. After all, the Roman Empire was relatively small compared with the global empires of the Spanish, French, and English. Furthermore, in terms of science and technology, Europeans had surpassed the ancients. Nevertheless, the presence of the ancient world continued to shape the imaginations of Europeans.

See also **Archaeology; City-State; Erasmus, Desiderius; Humanists and Humanism; Italy; Renaissance; Rome, Architecture in; Rome, Art in.**

BIBLIOGRAPHY

Hope, Charles, and Elizabeth McGrath. "Artists and Humanists." In *The Cambridge Companion to Renaissance Humanism,* edited by Jill Kraye, pp. 161–188. Cambridge, U.K., 1996.

Howard, M. W. *The Influence of Plutarch in the Major European Literatures of the Eighteenth Century.* Chapel Hill, N.C., 1970.

Koortbojian, Michael. "Classical Antiquity." In *Encyclopedia of the Renaissance.* Vol. 1. Edited by Paul F. Grendler, pp. 1–9. New York, 1999.

Kristeller, Paul Oskar. "Renaissance Humanism and Classical Antiquity." In *Renaissance Humanism: Foundations, Forms, and Legacy.* Vol. 1. Edited by Albert Rabil, Jr., pp. 5–16. Philadelphia, 1988.

Reeve, Michael D. "Classical Scholarship." In *The Cambridge Companion to Renaissance Humanism.* Edited by Jill Kraye, pp. 20–46. Cambridge, U.K., 1996.

Weiss, Roberto. *The Renaissance Discovery of Classical Antiquity.* Oxford, 1969.

Zophy, Jonathan W. *A Short History of Renaissance and Reformation Europe: Dances over Fire and Water.* 3rd ed. Upper Saddle River, N.J., 2003.

MILTON KOOISTRA

ANCIENTS AND MODERNS. The quarrel between the ancients and moderns is a recurrent theme in the history of ideas. It was already being argued in the later days of the Roman Empire as an increasing nostalgia for the past developed. The dialogue on oratory attributed to Tacitus is a good example of this burgeoning contest. During the Middle Ages it took a different turn as much of the classical world became obscure, although a keen rivalry developed in Scholasticism between the self-styled *antiqui* and *moderni*, neither of whom was in fact very ancient. It was only with the Renaissance and the deliberate recovery of classical antiquity that the quarrel grew to a head. The authority of the ancients was exalted, and a canon of authors and artists was established that was to reign throughout the early modern period. The only question was how far and to what extent imitation should be carried. (See the famous 1528 "Ciceronianus" dialogue of Desiderius Erasmus, where the issue was formally debated.)

However, modern inventions, such as gunpowder, the compass, and the printing press, soon began to stimulate arguments for the new; and scientists and philosophers like Francis Bacon, Thomas Hobbes, and René Descartes began to affirm their self-conscious modernity. Some efforts were made to tote up the achievements on both sides, as in the works of Alessandro Tassoni (*Pensieri diversi,* 1612), who inclined toward the moderns, and Guido Pancirolli, who defended the ancients in his Latin *History of Many Memorable Things Lost* (1612; English translation 1715). Later in the seventeenth century an explicit rivalry arose between the new science of the Royal Society and the older Aristotelian philosophy that was still installed in the universities. But even Isaac Newton himself continued to believe, against the moderns, in an ancient wisdom reaching back to Moses and Hermes Trismegistus, who had together foreshadowed all that was later to come.

The quarrel was renewed and widened at the end of the century in England and France while all Europe looked on. In England the contest was labeled "The Battle of the Books" by Jonathan Swift, who, with his literary friends Alexander Pope and John Arbuthnot, took the side of the ancients, employing satire as their chief weapon. Swift was defending his patron, Sir William Temple, who had started up the quarrel with a little *Essay upon Ancient and Modern Learning* in 1690. He was answered by William Wotton four years later with a large book that he called *Reflections on Ancient and Modern Learning.* Wotton tried to show that there was a profound difference between those human achievements that depended on imitation and those that had developed by accumulation. Among the first he included the fine and literary arts, including poetry, oratory, and history, as the Renaissance humanists had long proposed. Wotton admitted that the ancients had reached a perfection in those matters that could only be imitated, and perhaps equaled, though not surpassed. Among the moderns he included the whole range of the sciences and philosophy. In all those things the latest were the best since they were able to build upon earlier achievements by collaboration and addition—in a familiar phrase, like dwarfs standing on the shoulders of giants. Here progress was both possible and attainable. Newton's work alone—and despite himself—seemed to prove the point. For the most part this balanced view triumphed during the eighteenth century.

Meanwhile in France a similar quarrel came to a boil almost simultaneously. Charles Perrault recited a poem in 1687 and followed it with some essays in which he extolled the French achievement under Louis XIV and forthrightly challenged the ancients in everything. His work was answered at once by the most celebrated writers in the French academy, among them Nicholas Boileau-Despréaux and Jean Baptiste Racine, who defended the ancients. After the first skirmish, the issue narrowed to the question of the primacy of Homer as the prince of poets. Was he the greatest writer of all time, who could only be imitated but never surpassed? Or was he simply a poet among many who could be improved and modernized (as in the abridged translation by Houdart de la Motte)? Anne Dacier and her husband, André, led the ancients, and their arguments were largely repeated in England by Pope in his translations of the *Iliad* and the *Odyssey*. This contest also ended in a draw, though it had pregnant consequences, for example in Naples, where Giambattista Vico used it as a stimulus for his new science of history.

For a time the neoclassical movement in the visual arts and literature reinforced the claims of the ancients in literature and the visual arts, and it was still possible in 1766 to defend their primacy in philosophy and science, as in Louis Dutens's *An Inquiry into the Origin of the Discoveries attributed to the Moderns: Wherein it is demonstrated, That our most Celebrated Philosophers have, for the most part, taken what they advance from the Works of the Ancients.* Nevertheless, by the end of the eighteenth century, the new sciences, natural and historical, aided by a developing philology and archaeology, were able to undermine further the precedence of antiquity. Philology had been at the nub of the original contest when it was claimed for the moderns by Wotton and his great scholar friend Richard Bentley. It was Bentley's exposure of the *Epistles* of the ancient Greek tyrant Phalaris as a forgery that particularly alarmed the defenders of the ancients, and they ganged up on him in a deliberate attempt to defend the ancient work. For a time they withstood the challenge of modern scholarship, much as the Anglican community was just then trying to withstand the textual criticism of the Bible, but eventually both failed. Scholars showed what Bentley and Vico had suspected all along, that the Homeric poems were composed in an oral tradition long after the events, and they threw doubt on both the authorship of the works and the authenticity of their history. (So too the consistency and integrity of the Bible was simultaneously being challenged.) Meanwhile, the Romantics and their successors rebelled against the whole idea of imitation, and the modernist movement at the end of the nineteenth century may be seen a revolt against the long and restrictive authority of the ancients. New and more radical moderns had replaced the old, while the defense of antiquity receded under the impact of a deeper knowledge of the ancient and pre-ancient worlds, distancing them and estranging them from contemporary use. The classics were largely abandoned in the schools and in public life where they had long reigned. The long quarrel between ancients and moderns was pretty much over.

See also **Boileau-Despréaux, Nicolas; Erasmus, Desiderius; Neoclassicism; Perrault, Charles; Pope, Alexander; Racine, Jean; Swift, Jonathan; Vico, Giovanni Battista.**

BIBLIOGRAPHY

Baron, Hans. "The Querelle of the Ancients and Moderns as a Problem for Renaissance Scholarship." *Journal of the History of Ideas* 20 (1959): 3–22.

Gillot, Hubert. *La querelle des anciens et des modernes en France.* Paris, 1914.

Jones, R. F. *Ancients and Moderns: A Study of the Rise of the Scientific Movement in Seventeenth-Century England.* 2nd ed. St. Louis, 1961.

Levine, Joseph M. "Ancients and Moderns Reconsidered." *Eighteenth-Century Studies* 15 (1981): 72–89.

———. *The Battle of the Books: History and Literature in the Augustan Age.* Ithaca, N.Y., 1991.

———. *Between the Ancients and the Moderns: Baroque Culture in Restoration England.* New Haven, 1999.

Maravall, José. *Antiguos y modernos.* Madrid, 1966.

Rigault, Hippolyte. *Histoire de la querelle des anciens et des modernes.* Paris, 1856.

JOSEPH M. LEVINE

ANDRUSOVO, TRUCE OF (1667).

The treaty between Russia and the Polish-Lithuanian Commonwealth, ending the Thirteen Years' War and, with it, decades of strife over Ukraine was signed at Andrusovo early in 1667. The tsar's representative at the peace negotiations in 1664, Afanasy Lavrentyevich Ordyn-Nashchokin, hoped they would lead to a permanent peace and perhaps even an alliance with the Commonwealth against the Ottomans. Neither of these goals was achieved. But the protocol signed on 30 January 1667 established an armistice for thirteen years, to June 1680, on terms more favorable to Muscovy than to the Commonwealth. Muscovy was required to restore Lithuania, Livonia, and Belarus to the Commonwealth and to recognize Right Bank Ukraine from the Dnieper to the San River as a Commonwealth possession, but the Poles were in turn obliged to cede their claims to Smolensk and Chernigov (lands they had wrested from Muscovy during the Time of Troubles), to surrender part of the Vitebsk Palatinate, and to acknowledge Left Bank Ukraine as a permanent Muscovite protectorate. Moscow was permitted to lease Kiev for two years. Subsequent requests to evacuate Kiev were rebuffed, on the grounds of the Polish crown's inability to protect Right Bank Ukraine from the Turks; the Poles finally relinquished their claim to Kiev in the "eternal peace" signed in 1686.

The Commonwealth and Muscovy remained at peace with each other after 1667, but more from fear of the Turks than from satisfaction with the mutual spheres of influence the armistice had established. The Turks continued to intervene in Ukraine in the 1670s. The permanent division of Ukraine into Left Bank and Right Bank hetmanates was deeply disappointing to the Cossack populations of both banks and led to further war between their hetmans.

See also **Alexis I (Russia); Cossacks; Poland-Lithuania, Commonwealth of, 1569–1795; Time of Troubles (Russia); Ukraine.**

BIBLIOGRAPHY

Kostomarov, Nikolai I. *Ruina: Mazepa, mazepintsy.* Moscow, 1995.

Wójcik, Zbigniew. *Traktat andruszowski 1667 roku i jego geneza.* Warsaw, 1959.

BRIAN DAVIES

ANGLICANISM. *See* **Church of England.**

ANGLO-DUTCH NAVAL WARS.

England and the Dutch Republic fought a series of three wars (in 1652–1654; 1665–1667; 1672–1674) that took place predominantly in the North Sea and the English Channel and its approaches. A fourth conflict (1780–1784) was part of the War of American Independence (1775–1783).

The first three Anglo-Dutch wars involved economic rivalry between two similar states. Because of that theme, their main location, and their close occurrence in time they have been lumped together, but overemphasis on these factors obscures their different causes and contexts. These three wars are unusual in that neither opponent was able to launch a major amphibious or land campaign to complement the naval actions at sea. In naval history the wars mark the beginning of the "Age of Sail," which lasted through 1815 and during which the large oceangoing sailing warship was the predominant vessel as well as the most potent symbol of national power. At the same time the wars mark the early stage in the 150-year period that began the gradual professionalization of the naval officers corps, the creation of the battle fleet and the specialization of warship design for this purpose, the usage of formal line-of-battle tactics, and the growth of bureaucratic control over state navies.

THE FIRST WAR (1652–1654)

By the mid-seventeenth century the Dutch Republic was at its zenith as the predominant maritime economic and naval power in Europe. The English had lost much trade to Dutch competition. The Dutch Republic was in its first "stadtholderless period." At the same time England was in the "commonwealth period." The long-term causes of the First Anglo-Dutch War are the subject of scholarly debate over the relative importance of maritime trade, factional internal politics relating to the character of the opposing governments, and the ideological differences of the two governments in religion and politics.

The immediate events leading up to the war began when Oliver St. John (1598?–1673) and Walter Strickland (d. 1676) arrived at The Hague in March 1651 to demand that the Dutch Republic enter into an alliance and union with England. In October 1651 Parliament passed the Navigation Act to stop Dutch competition in southern European and colonial trade. Despite ongoing negotiations, war preparations began, and incidents occurred, first off Start Point on 22 May 1652 and then when Maarten Tromp (1598–1653) fought the English fleet under Robert Blake (1599–1657) off Dover on 29 May 1652. The Dutch and English both entered the war in June without any clear strategic concept, overestimating their own abilities and underestimating the enemy.

In the major actions Blake attacked Dutch shipping in July, and Sir George Ayscue (d. 1671) fought Michiel de Ruyter (1607–1676) in the English Channel in August. At the Kentish Knock on 8 October, Blake heavily damaged the Dutch under Admiral Witte de With (1600–1658), but on 10 December, Tromp won a major strategic victory over Blake off Dungeness, forcing the English to retreat from the Channel and defend their southern coast. In February 1653 Tromp took a convoy into the Bay of Biscay. On Tromp's return passage, Blake intercepted him in a running battle, 28 February to 2 March. Blake's victory in the Channel fight inflicted heavy damage on the Dutch, forcing them to seek shelter at Calais and leaving England in control of the Channel. Following this battle the English issued tactical instructions that became the initial basis for eighteenth-century tactics. On 12 June 1653 George Monck (1608–1670) defeated Tromp at the Gabbard shoal, the most decisive battle of the war. Monck then blockaded the Dutch coast and immobilized Dutch trade. Challenging the blockade, Tromp was killed off The Texel on 10 August.

Peace negotiations began in March 1653 and were concluded in the Treaty of Westminster a year later. The first war secured Commonwealth England, forced the Dutch to replace some twelve hundred vessels lost in the war, and indirectly caused the end of the Dutch West India Company's Brazil venture.

THE SECOND WAR (1665–1667)

Tensions resurfaced a decade later, following the restoration of the monarchy in England. James, duke of York (later James II; ruled 1685–1688), and other like-minded courtiers and merchants believed that resumption of war would increase English trade and help unite the country. In 1664 Sir Robert Holmes (1622–1692) captured a number of Dutch ships and all but one of the Dutch forts in West Africa, but de Ruyter quickly recovered them. Meanwhile Colonel Richard Nicolls (1624–1672) captured New Amsterdam in August 1664 and renamed it New York, and Sir Thomas Allin (1612–1685) attacked the Dutch Smyrna convoy in December 1664.

War was finally declared in February 1665. The Dutch capture of the English Hamburg convoy in March was offset by the English victory at Lowestoft on 13 June, which the English failed to follow up. As part of an attempt to get Danish and Swedish support, Edward Montagu (1625–1672), earl of Sandwich, made an unsuccessful attack on a Dutch merchant fleet at Bergen, Norway.

In January 1666, after French diplomacy failed to halt the war, Louis XIV (ruled 1643–1715) reluctantly declared war against England under the Franco-Dutch Alliance of 1662, but he awaited the outcome of further naval engagements before committing the French fleet to action. This Four Days' Fight with de Ruyter against Monck (now duke of Albemarle) and Prince Rupert (1619–1682) occurred on 11 through 14 June and was the bloodiest English defeat during the four wars. Five weeks later the English won a victory on Saint James's Day, 3 August, by using line-ahead tactics. A Dutch merchant fleet was destroyed at Terschelling in "Holmes's Bonfire." The Dutch successfully blockaded southeast England, and de Ruyter raided the Medway River on 22 June 1667, capturing the flagship *Royal Charles* and burning others. In the West Indies the English captured several colonies.

In July 1667 the Peace Treaty of Breda gave the advantage to the Dutch. While New York remained English, the Dutch obtained and recovered possessions in West Africa, the West Indies, and the East Indies.

THE THIRD WAR (1672–1674)

Trade was the pretext for a new war that masked a secret agreement between Charles II (ruled 1660–1685) and Louis XIV in the 1670 Treaty of Dover to overwhelm the Dutch Republic. Holmes again led an attack before war was declared, this time on the Dutch Smyrna convoy in the Channel on 23 March 1672. On 27 March, Charles II declared war. In the Dutch Republic the de Witt brothers, Johan (1625–1672) and Cornelis (1623–1672) were losing their effectiveness and were murdered as William III (stadtholder 1672–1702; king of England 1689–1702) reactivated the stadtholdership.

The first phase of the sea war involved bringing the French and English fleets to operate together. Attempting to strike a blow before they could organize, de Ruyter attacked the allied fleet under the duke of York and Jean d'Estrées (1624–1707) in Sole Bay (Southwold Bay) on 7 June 1672. Sandwich died in the action, and only light winds prevented a sweeping Dutch victory. The Dutch withdrew, leaving the allies in control of the North Sea as naval guns and men were needed ashore to defend against the French invasion.

The allies planned a coherent naval strategy for 1673. However, as the English approached de Ruyter in his anchorage at the Schooneveld, de Ruyter attacked them on 7 June and again on 14 June, preventing them from carrying out the blockade and amphibious landing they envisaged. After the allies withdrew, the Dutch attempted to blockade them in the Thames, and Charles II would not authorize further attacks on the Dutch coast. In July a small Dutch squadron under Cornelis Evertsen the youngest (1642–1706) retook New York. Another Dutch victory between Kijkduin and Texel on 21 August proved decisive not by tactics but by the resulting English public opinion criticizing the French performance.

This criticism helped undermine the king's pro-French alliance, and Parliament refused to support operations. In October, Louis XIV declared war on Spain, threatening to draw England into a wider war. On 19 February 1674 Charles II concluded a separate peace with the Dutch and withdrew from

the war. New York reverted to England, but in most other areas Dutch demands were met.

THE FOURTH WAR (1780–1784)

The Dutch Republic initially attempted to remain neutral in the War of American Independence, but merchants and politicians saw advantages in siding with France as British power grew in the Far East and the West Indies. Soon the Dutch showed complicity with the Americans. Just as the republic joined the League of Armed Neutrality in 1780, Britain declared war, confident it could take Dutch overseas territory to offset other losses. Sir George Rodney (1718–1792) captured Saint Eustatius on 3 February 1781. The only fleet engagement, fought off Dogger Bank between convoy escort squadrons under Sir Hyde Parker (1714–1782) and Johan Zoutman (1724–1793) on 3 August 1781, was a tactical draw but a strategic success for Britain. The Dutch were included in the January 1783 cease-fire with the French, Spanish, and Americans, but the war did not formally end until Britain and the Dutch Republic signed the separate Treaty of Paris in May 1784.

See also **American Independence, War of (1775–1783); Dutch Colonies: The Americas; Dutch Colonies: The East Indies; Dutch Republic; Dutch War (1672–1678); Louis XIV (France); William and Mary; Witt, Johan and Cornelis de.**

BIBLIOGRAPHY

Primary Sources

Allin, Thomas. *The Journals of Sir Thomas Allin, 1660–1678.* Edited by R. C. Anderson. London, 1939.

Anderson, R. C., ed. *Journals and Narratives of the Third Dutch War.* London, 1946.

Blake, Robert. *The Letters of Robert Blake.* Edited by J. R. Powell. London, 1937.

Bruijn, J. R., ed. *De Oorlogvoering ter Zee in 1673 in Journalen en Andre Stukken.* Groningen, 1966.

Colendrander, H. T., ed. *Bescheiden uit Vreemde Archieven omtrent de Groote Nederlandsche Zeeoorlogen, 1652–1676.* The Hague, 1919.

Corbett, Julian S., ed. *Fighting Instructions, 1530–1816.* London, 1905.

Gardiner, Samuel Rawson, and Christopher Thomas Atkinson, eds. *Letters and Papers Relating to the First Dutch War, 1652–54.* London, 1899–1930.

Pepys, Samuel. *The Diary of Samuel Pepys.* Edited by Robert Latham and William Matthews. London and Berkeley, 1970–1983.

———. *Samuel Pepys's Naval Minutes.* Edited by J. R. Tanner. London, 1926.

Rupert, Prince. *The Rupert and Monck Letter Book 1666.* Edited by J. R. Powell and E. K. Timings. London, 1969.

Sandwich, Edward Montagu, Earl of. *The Journal of Edward Montagu, first Earl of Sandwich, Admiral and General at Sea, 1659–1665.* Edited by R. C. Anderson. London, 1929.

Weber, R. E. J. *De seinboken voor Nederlandse oorlogsvloten en konvooien tot 1690.* Amsterdam, 1982.

Secondary Sources

Baumber, Michael. *General-at-Sea: Robert Blake and the Seventeenth-Century Revolution in Naval Warfare.* London, 1989.

Capp, Bernard. *Cromwell's Navy: The Fleet and the English Revolution, 1648–1660.* Oxford, 1989.

Carter, Alice Clare. *Neutrality or Commitment: The Evolution of Dutch Foreign Policy 1667–1795.* London, 1975.

Davies, J. D. "A Permanent National Maritime Fighting Force, 1642–1689." In *The Oxford Illustrated History of the Royal Navy,* edited by J. R. Hill, pp. 56–79. Oxford, 1995.

Foreest, H. A. van, and R. E. J. Weber. *De Vierdaagse Zeeslag 11–14 Juni 1666.* Amsterdam, 1984.

Fox, Frank L. *A Distant Storm: The Four Days' Battle of 1666.* Rotherfield, U.K., 1996.

Harding, Richard. *Seapower and Naval Warfare, 1650–1830.* London, 1999.

Israel, Jonathan. *The Dutch Republic: Its Rise, Greatness, and Fall, 1477–1806.* Oxford, 1995.

Jones, J. R. *The Anglo-Dutch Wars of the Seventeenth Century.* London, 1996.

Junge, Hans-Christoph. *Flottenpolitik und Revolution: Die Entstehung der englischen Seemacht während der Herrschaft Cromwells.* Stuttgart, Germany, 1980.

Kitson, Frank. *Prince Rupert: Admiral and General-at-Sea.* London, 1998.

Ollard, Richard. *Man of War: Sir Robert Holmes and the Restoration Navy.* London, 1969.

Powell, J. R. *Robert Blake: General-at-Sea.* London, 1972.

Prud'homme van Reine, Ronald. *Rechterhand van Nederland: Biografie van Michiel Adriaenszoon de Ruyter.* Amsterdam, 1996.

———. *Schittering en schandaal: Biografie van Maerten en Cornelis Tromp.* Amsterdam, 2001.

Rogers, P. G. *The Dutch in the Medway.* London and New York, 1970.

Rowen, Herbert H. *John de Witt, Grand Pensionary of Holland, 1625–1672.* Princeton, 1978.

Shomette, Donald G., and Robert D. Haslach. *Raid on America: The Dutch Naval Campaign of 1672–1674.* Columbia, S.C., 1988.

Tunstall, Brian. *Naval Warfare in the Age of Sail: The Evolution of Fighting Tactics, 1650–1815.* Edited by Nicholas Tracy. London and Annapolis, 1990.

Wilson, Charles. *Profit and Power: A Study of England and the Dutch Wars.* London, 1957; reprint The Hague, 1978.

JOHN B. HATTENDORF

ANGUISSOLA, SOFONISBA

ANGUISSOLA, SOFONISBA (c. 1532–1625), Italian portrait painter. The daughter of Amilcare Anguissola and Bianca Ponzone of Cremona, Sofonisba Anguissola enjoyed international recognition during her lifetime. In the history of art her name has appeared with regularity since Marco Girolamo Vida counted her, at age fifteen, among the most significant painters in *Cremonensium Orationes III Adversus Papienses in Controversia Principatus* (1550), and Giorgio Vasari praised her as "miraculous" in the second edition of *The Lives of the Most Eminent Painters, Sculptors and Architects* (1568). Her known works include small devotional pictures, such as the *Holy Family* (1559, Accademia Carrara, Begamo); numerous portraits, like the life-size *Portrait of Isabel Valoise* (c. 1565, Prado, Madrid); more than a dozen self-portraits, which date principally to her youth; and paintings and finished drawings of her family. Within this corpus, the images depicting her family hold special significance. The intimacy, wit, and captured spontaneity seen in paintings like *The Artist's Sisters Playing Chess* (c. 1555, Muzeum Narodowe, Poznań) and the drawing *Young Girl Teaching an Old Woman the Alphabet* (mid-1550s, Gabinetto Disegni e Stampe degli Uffizi, Florence), were unprecedented, making Anguissola the innovator of what has come to be called "the conversation piece."

Sofonisba Anguissola was the oldest in a family of six daughters and a son. It has been reasonably suggested that her father, who became her most ambitious promoter, decided to provide her and her sisters with a humanist education and artistic training in the hope of alleviating some of the monetary strain of financing six dowries. The rationale, which proved correct, was that the exceptionality of female artists ensured the rarity and desirability of their work. In her early teens, Sofonisba, together with her sister Elena (who died after 1584), was sent to study painting with Bernardino Campi. If the association, which lasted from c. 1546–1549, was not typically that of apprentice to master but resembled more the relationship of paying guest to instructional host, the actual artistic training Anguissola received seems to have followed conventional lines. She was taught the fundamentals of materials and techniques, and instructed to copy the works of her teacher and other masters. Anguissola's small panel painting of the *Pietà* (after 1560, Pinacoteca Brera, Milan), which depends clearly on Campi's *Deposition* (Pinacoteca Brera, Milan), as well as her *Nursing Madonna* (1588, Szepmusveseti Muzeum, Budapest), which replicates the style and composition of works by the Genoese master Luca Cambiaso, indicate that she continued to learn in this way long after her departure from Campi's workshop and even after her subsequent period of study (1549–c. 1552) with Benardino Gatti (1495–1576), called Il Sojaro, had ended.

Throughout this period, Anguissola's father corresponded with an array of influential humanists and potential patrons. Extant letters to Michelangelo Buonarroti reveal Amilcare Anguissola's zeal in seeking the best possible guidance for his artist daughter. In one letter, dated 7 May 1557, he thanks the great master for the "innate courtesy and goodness" that prompted him "in the past to introduce her to art" and requests Michelangelo "to guide her again." Although no image has been securely identified with this correspondence, Anguissola's drawing *Asdrubale Bitten by a Crayfish* (late 1550s, Museo di Campodimonte, Naples), has linked her name to that of Michelangelo since 1562. A considerable number of Anguissola's self-portraits date to this decade. These works, which are very small in scale and somber in tonality, were in all likelihood promotional gifts. Sofonisba presents herself at the keyboard, seated before an easel holding a brush and palette, and even as the subject of a portrait painted by her first teacher, Bernardino Campi. Whether through the efforts of her father, the dissemination of her self-portraits, or both, Anguissola's fame spread within and outside the borders of the Italian peninsula. Her paintings were requested by, and subsequently entered the collec-

Sofonisba Anguissola. *Self-Portrait (1554).* ©Ali Meyer/Corbis

tions of, Pope Julius III and members of the Este, Farnese, Medici, and Borghese families.

In 1559, Anguissola entered the Spanish court as lady-in-waiting and portrait painter to the queen, Isabel of Valois. She remained in Spain until 1573, sharing with Anthonis Mor and Alonso Sánchez Coello the prestige of being a member of the triumvirate of Spanish court painters. While Anguissola executed a few devotional panels during her tenure in Spain, most of her time was devoted to painting portraits of members of the royal court and family. In keeping with the decorum of courtly taste and reflecting the austerity of the religious climate, these portraits, like those by Mor and Coello, are marked by an almost formulaic restraint in composition, color, and light. Despite the reserved formality, poised elegance, and almost petrified stiffness of Anguissola's Spanish subjects, the physiognomies she recorded reveal distinctive personalities. In this respect, Anguissola's roots in the Lombard tradition, specifically the mimetic melding of stark naturalism with a calculated style made popular by Moretto da Brescia and Giovanni Moroni, are clearly evident.

Sometime after August 1569 and through the intervention of King Philip II of Spain, Anguissola married Don Fabrizio de Moncado, the brother of the viceroy of Sicily. Following her return to Italy in 1573, she resided in Palermo. In 1579 or 1580, she remarried, wedding Orazio Lomellino, a Genoese gentleman. By October 1583 she was living in Genoa. An inscribed portrait sketch of Anguissola by Anthony Van Dyck (British Museum, London) confirms that she had returned to Palermo by 1624. Early sources indicate that her late oeuvre consisted primarily of devotional works. Although many of these paintings have yet to be securely identified, those that are known, such as *Holy Family with Saint Anne and the Young John the Baptist* (1592, Lowe Art Museum, Coral Gables), suggest that she responded to the impress of Counter-Reformation sobriety and the influence of Cambiaso's use of modeling and nocturnal luminosity. As is the case with her early works, her later paintings attest to an awareness of current trends in art theory. In accordance with the dictates of Cardinal Gabriele Paleotti's *Discorso intorno alle imagini sacre e profane*, 1582, Anguissola rendered her subjects in a manner that "delights," "teaches," and "moves" the viewer to feelings of contemplative devotion.

See also **Vasari, Giorgio; Women and Art.**

BIBLIOGRAPHY

Primary Source
Vasari, Giorgio. *Lives of the Most Eminent Painters, Sculptors and Architects.* Translated by Gaston Du C. de Vere. Vol. 3, pp. 1646–1649. New York, 1979. Translation of *Le vite de'più eccellenti pittori, scultori ed architettori* (1568).

Secondary Sources
Garrard, Mary. "Here's Looking at Me: Sofonisba Anguissola and the Problem of the Woman Artist." *Renaissance Quarterly* 47 (1994): 556–622.

Jacobs, Fredrika H. *Defining the Renaissance Virtuosa: Women Artists and the Language of Art History and Criticism.* New York, 1997.

Sofonisba Anguissola e le sue sorelle. Exh. cat., Cremona, 1994.

Woods-Marsden, Joanna. *Renaissance Self-Portraiture: The Visual Construction of Identity and the Social Status of the Artist.* New Haven, 1998.

FREDRIKA H. JACOBS

ANIMISM. *See* **Matter, Theories of.**

ANNA (RUSSIA) (1693–1740, ruled 1730–1740), empress of Russia. Anna Ivanovna (or Ioannovna) was the second crowned female ruler of Russia, after Catherine I. The daughter of Peter the Great's half brother and co-tsar for seven years, Ivan V, she spent her adult life residing alternately in St. Petersburg and in the duchy of Courland. Married to the duke of Courland, Friedrich Wilhelm, in 1710, she was soon widowed when he died in the following year. She returned to St. Petersburg for the next six years, after which Peter the Great sent her back to Courland in 1717. Although bereft of any formal authority, Anna maintained a court in Mitau (Jelgava), subsidized by the Russian court and by contributions from local magnates. Her presence provided an anchor for the growing Russian presence in the eastern Baltic, and her retainers doubled as agents of the Russian court.

Anna ascended the Russian throne largely by accident, when the reigning emperor, the fourteen-year-old Peter II, died unexpectedly on 29 January 1730 (18 January O.S.), on the eve of his wedding and less than three years into his rule. Because the law at that time stipulated that the sitting monarch named his or her successor, the unexpected or premature death of a ruler invariably led to a succession crisis, typically resolved by parties at court backed by the powerful guards' regiments. The 1730 succession crisis is particularly noteworthy, because it took place at a time when much of Russia's political elite had assembled in Moscow awaiting Peter II's wedding. His unexpected death left the throne without a designated heir and with relatively few good candidates. Under the guidance of the Supreme Privy Council, a largely aristocratic body established a few years earlier to advise Catherine I, the assembled elite quickly agreed to offer the throne to Anna.

Over the next several weeks, however, a crisis arose over the terms under which she would reign. The Privy Council had prevailed upon her to accept significant restrictions on her authority, in essence obliging her to seek its approval before issuing decrees. These conditions, as they were termed, provoked a storm of protest among the resident nobility at large (the *generalitet* or *shliakhetstvo* as it was officially called), and this larger group prevailed upon the Privy Council to assemble groups to discuss the terms of Anna's rule, as well as to air grievances left over from the Petrine and immediate post-Petrine era. Had the "conditions" remained in place, they would have constituted the first quasi-constitutional limitations on the sovereignty of a Russian ruler. However, competition among the powerful clan networks at court, through which access to position and influence had flowed for generations, quickly overwhelmed the Supreme Privy Council's position. Fearful that the clans represented in the council would gain a permanent advantage, the nobility demanded that there be no conditions, a demand to which Anna readily acceded.

Anna's reign is often seen as unpopular and defined by a vulgarity and arrogance at court, marked by the presence of a large number of Baltic German advisers, most notoriously Count Ernst Johann Bühren (Biron in Russian), after whom the entire experience is named *("bironovshchina")*. Although the unpopularity and tactlessness of this German clique is undeniable, some scholars have argued that Anna's reign was hardly an era of darkness, as the nationalist tradition would have it. She abolished the unpopular Privy Council and severely punished most of its members. More to the point, her closest advisers included several Russians such as Prince Aleksei Mikhailovich Cherkasskii and Gavriil Ivanovich Golovkin. It was during her reign that the Imperial Academy of Sciences established its visibility within Russian society, both through its Russian-language press and through its classes, and within international science through the publication of its scientific monographs. Her reign saw the beginnings of the Corps of Cadets, the elite military academies, as well as the legislation that ultimately led to the establishment of a network of Latin-based religious seminaries. In foreign affairs, Russian interests prevailed over French ones in the war of Polish

Succession in 1733–1735, and Russia made noteworthy, if temporary, gains in Moldova at the expense of Austria and the Ottoman Empire in 1739.

Endeavoring to make her line of the Romanov clan preeminent, and without any offspring of her own, Anna named her infant grand nephew (her deceased sister Catherine's grandson) Ivan Antonovich as heir, with Bühren as regent. The strategy failed, however, as Ivan VI remained on the throne less than two years and was replaced in a coup by Peter the Great's daughter, Elizabeth. Bühren—and the entire German party—fell even sooner, replaced as regent after several months by Ivan's mother, Anna Leopoldovna.

See also **Elizabeth (Russia); Peter I (Russia); Queens and Empresses; Russia.**

BIBLIOGRAPHY

Lipski, Alexander. "A Re-examination of the 'Dark Era' of Anna Ioannovna." *American Slavic and East European Review* 15, no. 4 (December 1956): 477–488.

Meehan-Waters, Brenda. *Autocracy and Aristocracy: The Russian Service Elite of 1730.* New Brunswick, N.J., 1982.

Ransel, David L. "The Constitutional Crisis of 1730." In *Reform in Russia and the USSR.* Edited by Robert O. Crummey. Urbana, Ill., 1989.

"The Succession Crisis of 1730." In *Plans for Political Reform in Imperial Russia, 1730–1915.* Edited by Marc Raeff. Englewood Cliffs, N.J., 1966.

GARY MARKER

ANNE (ENGLAND) (1665–1714; ruled 1702–1714), queen of Great Britain and Ireland. The last Stuart monarch, Anne was the second daughter of James II (ruled 1685–1688) and his first wife, Anne Hyde. Married to the Protestant Prince George (1653–1708) of Denmark in 1683, Anne opposed her by then Catholic father in 1688–1689, when he was overthrown by her brother-in-law William III (ruled 1689–1702) of Orange. This betrayal greatly upset both James and Anne. Anne succeeded to the throne after the death of William, whose coruler, Anne's elder sister Mary (ruled 1689–1694), had died in 1694.

Anne has been reevaluated as an able and independent monarch, less dependent on her courtiers than was previously believed. Leading politicians could not hope for the physical proximity to the monarch that was possible under a king, and the court was less important politically than it had been under earlier monarchs. But that did not mean that Anne lacked weight. She also sought to take a prominent role, modeling herself on Elizabeth I (ruled 1558–1603). However, as she had no domestic program of change, Anne was a relatively uncontroversial figure, and political criticism in her reign was centered on ministers, not monarch. Anne followed William III in sustaining the Grand Alliance created to fight Louis XIV (ruled 1643–1715) of France. In 1701–1714 Britain took a leading and successful role in the War of the Spanish Succession with France, and John Churchill (1650–1722) won great glory as well as promotion in the peerage to the dukedom of Marlborough by triumphing at a series of battles, including Blenheim (1704), Ramillies (1706), Oudenaarde (1708), and Malplaquet (1709). Other British forces captured Gibraltar, Minorca, and Nova Scotia. British conquests abroad under Anne were celebrated in the renaming of the French base in Nova Scotia as Annapolis Royal.

By 1709–1710 Anne realized that a compromise peace would have to be negotiated. Her sense that the war was unpopular and that the vital war goals had already been obtained played a major role in weakening the Whig ministry, which wanted to fight on. Anne had also wearied of her favorite, the increasingly possessive and headstrong Sarah Churchill (1660–1744), duchess of Marlborough, and turned to a new Tory favorite. Without the support of the crown, the Whigs did badly in the 1710 election. Conversely, Anne supported their Tory successors, Robert Harley (1661–1724), earl of Oxford, and Henry St. John (1678–1751), viscount Bolingbroke, in their contentious task of negotiating peace, and was willing to create Tory peers to ensure that the peace preliminaries passed the House of Lords. The Peace of Utrecht of 1713 was seen as a triumph for Britain.

A keen supporter of the Church of England, Anne revived ceremonial and touched for scrofula, the skin complaint known as king's evil, which many believed could be cured by the royal touch. She was personally unhappy in large part because of her failure to have any of her many children live to adulthood. Anne became pregnant eighteen times, but these led to twelve miscarriages, three neonatal deaths, and three children who lived to only seven months, nineteen months, and eleven years respectively. The last, William, duke of Gloucester, died in 1700. As a result, the Act of Settlement of 1701, which had designated the Hanoverian descendants of James I (ruled 1603–1625) as her successors, came into effect when she died. Her last years were affected by severe ill health caused by dropsy, gout, and rheumatism. Ill health led to her heavy dependence on opium in the form of laudanum. She was also much affected by the death of her asthmatic husband in 1708. She had been close to him, and she was left very lonely. Anne would have been happy to be succeeded by her half brother James Edward (James Francis Edward Stuart, 1688–1766), James II's son in his second marriage. But she wanted him to accept Protestantism, and he was unwilling to do so.

See also **Churchill, John, duke of Marlborough; James II (England); Spanish Succession, War of the (1701–1714); Stuart Dynasty (England and Scotland); Utrecht, Peace of (1713); William and Mary.**

BIBLIOGRAPHY

Bucholz, R. O. *The Augustan Court: Queen Anne and the Decline of Court Culture.* Stanford, 1993.

Gregg, Edward. *Queen Anne.* 2nd ed. London and New Haven, 2001.

Harris, Frances. *A Passion for Government: The Life of Sarah, Duchess of Marlborough.* Oxford, 1991.

JEREMY BLACK

ANNE OF AUSTRIA (1601–1666), queen of France. Anne of Austria, the eldest daughter of Philip III of Spain (ruled 1598–1621), married King Louis XIII of France (ruled 1610–1643) in 1615. After Louis's death, she became regent of the realm from 1643 to 1654 under the minority of her son Louis XIV (ruled 1643–1715). Her destiny illustrates how difficult the life of an early modern princess could be. Her wedding to the French king was a political tool used to strengthen the political and religious ties between the Spaniards and the French. The bride and groom were barely fourteen years old, and their characters were close to incompatible. Anne rarely if ever received a nightly visit from her husband for the four years that followed their wedding. But they became closer, and the queen was pregnant in 1622. A miscarriage due to her carelessness—she fell while running through the Louvre with her two closest friends—drew them apart. Louis became suspicious of his wife. As they had to fulfil their political and religious duties, they continued to have a marital life marked by other miscarriages and finally the births of two sons.

Anne, who wanted to play a political role in France, never won the trust of her husband and his principal minister, Cardinal Richelieu (1585–1642). Things went from bad to worse when the duke of Buckingham, a favorite of the English king, fell in love with the queen. Deeply offended, Louis decreed that henceforth no male could visit her quarters unless he was present. Their relationship deteriorated as Louis tried to take control of the queen's entourage. In answer Anne involved herself in political plots. As a Spanish princess, she was especially outraged by the anti-Habsburg policy of Louis and Richelieu. France and Spain were at war, but she developed a secret correspondence with her brother, King Philip IV of Spain (ruled 1621–1665). Although she did not reveal any political secrets, she did write some strong anti-French sentiments. This was close to treason, and Anne narrowly escaped repudiation in 1637. Louis forgave her, and Anne gave birth to their first son on 5 September 1638.

Anne's priorities changed with the birth of the future Louis XIV and, two years later, the birth of her second son Philip. Afraid she could be deprived of their care, she grew closer to the policies adopted by her husband's government. This was too little too late, as the king did not have complete confidence in his wife. As he neared death, Louis XIII tried to limit her grip on power, bequeathing to Anne a regency council whose votes were to be binding. When Louis XIII died, she had his will broken by the Parlement of Paris. For the next ten years she governed France with the help of Cardinal Jules Mazarin (1602–1661), who succeeded Richelieu as principal minister.

Anne inherited a disastrous financial situation. She also had to face a political crisis as many grandees who had fled the authoritarian rule of the previous government came back to France. The

Anne of Austria. Portrait by Peter Paul Rubens. ©ARCHIVO ICONOGRAFICO, S.A./CORBIS

regent had to satisfy their pleas to return to some benefits while satisfying as well the demands of those who had served her late husband. The number of solicitors was simply too large for what the regent had to offer. A movement nicknamed the "cabal of the important" loudly voiced the indignation of its adherents. Anne reacted quickly by arresting its leader, the duke of Beaufort. She thereby demonstrated that she had a strong will and that she intended to keep France on track for Louis XIV.

To the surprise of many, the Spanish regent and her Italian minister continued the financial and political policies of Louis XIII and Richelieu. Although everyone prayed for a peace with Spain, Anne was not ready to sacrifice her son's interests in favor of her Spanish relatives. Despite increased tensions within the realm, she raised old taxes and created new ones to meet the country's military needs. In doing so she was not afraid to attack some of the privileged members of French society. This policy had its dangers, and a period of civil wars known as the Fronde plagued the kingdom from 1648 to 1652. Even though the rebels' principal target was Cardinal Mazarin, Anne was not spared by her enemies. Nevertheless the two managed to put an end to the conflict. The return of peace within the kingdom allowed the queen to educate her son politically, and the war with Spain finally came to an end in 1659. With the help of Mazarin, Anne distilled in Louis's mind the idea of a king's greatness. A shaky marriage to a man who was indifferent toward her, an attachment to her native land, and the difficulties she had faced in the Fronde, during which she never failed France, did not prevent this Spanish princess from passing France's heritage to the Sun King.

See also **France; Fronde; Louis XIII (France); Louis XIV (France); Mazarin, Jules; Richelieu, Armand-Jean Du Plessis, cardinal.**

BIBLIOGRAPHY

Kleinman, Ruth. *Anne of Austria: Queen of France.* Columbus, Ohio, 1985.

Moote, A. Lloyd. *Louis XIII the Just.* Berkeley, 1989.

MICHEL DE WAELE

ANNE OF BRITTANY (1477–1514; ruled 1491–1498, 1499–1514), queen of France. Duchess of Brittany and twice queen of France, Anne was the daughter of Francis II (1435–1488) of Brittany and Marguerite de Foix. She was eleven when a French army defeated her father in the Fools' War in August 1488. Francis died a month after, and Anne inherited the duchy as the elder of his two daughters. Her hand in marriage became a valuable prize. In hopes of preventing the duchy from falling under direct French rule, Archduke Maximilian of Austria (later Holy Roman emperor; ruled 1493–1519), King Henry VII of England, and King Ferdinand of Aragon supported her against the French, and she agreed to marry Maximilian. In 1490 they were married by proxy, but the archduke delayed coming to Brittany. In 1491 French forces entered her capital of Rennes, and she was pressed to marry Charles VIII (ruled 1483–1498) of France. Convinced by her confessor that she was free to marry him, Anne agreed to a marriage contract that stipulated she would have to marry Charles's successor in default of a son from their marriage. The marriage took place at Rennes in December 1491.

Anne's marriage contract with Charles also stipulated that she would remain the ruling duchess of Brittany, and she always took a deep interest in its affairs while living at the French court, although it appears that she could not speak Breton. On several occasions she spent months away from her husband directing the affairs of her duchy. Those absences and that of her husband for sixteen months during the first French invasion of Italy (1494–1495) reduced the opportunities for Anne to become pregnant. She gave birth to a son, Charles Orland, a year after her marriage, but he died of measles at age three. Two more pregnancies resulted in a stillbirth and a son who died after five weeks.

When Charles VIII died suddenly in April 1498, Anne became a widow at age twenty-one. Her obligation to marry his successor, Charles's cousin Louis of Orléans (ruled 1498–1515), was complicated by his marriage to Jeanne of France, the daughter of Louis XI. Louis of Orléans requested an annulment from Pope Alexander VI on the grounds of coercion and nonconsummation. After his son Cesare Borgia was properly rewarded with French titles and treasure, Alexander granted the annulment. In January 1499 Anne and Louis XII were married, making her queen of France for a second time, the only woman for whom that was true. Their marriage contract stipulated that Brittany would continue to be governed separately from France and that it would go to the second son from the marriage or, in default of sons, the second daughter. In the absence of any children, it would go to Anne's closest relative. She was determined to maintain the duchy's autonomy from the French monarchy.

During her marriage to Louis, Anne was a key adviser to her husband, and she served as regent for him during his several Italian expeditions and a serious illness of 1505. The primary duty of the queen, however, was producing a male heir. In that respect Anne was unsuccessful. From at least five pregnancies, two daughters, Claude (born 1499) and Rénée (born 1510) alone survived. Anne strongly supported the betrothal of her young daughter Claude to Charles of Austria in 1503. She was sharply opposed to the proposed marriage between Claude and Francis of Angoulême (ruled 1515–1547), the successor to the French throne in default of any sons from Louis. Anne despised Francis's mother Louise of Savoy (1476–1531) and was eager to maintain Brittany's autonomy, which she perceived would be easier to do with a foreign prince as its duke. Much to her anger, Louis wrote a will in 1505 that repudiated the marriage between Claude and Charles and required their daughter to marry Francis. It was only after Anne's death in 1514 that Claude married Francis. Louis quickly remarried, to Mary Tudor, Henry VIII's sister, but he died in 1515 without having a child with her. Francis, Louis's son-in-law and cousin, became king, and he undid Anne's determined efforts to keep Brittany autonomous by making his heir its duke in 1534, thereby absorbing it into the royal domain.

Anne was a patron of artists and writers. Her most notable commission was for the splendid funeral monument for her father at Nantes.

See also **Brittany; Charles VIII (France).**

BIBLIOGRAPHY

Bridge, John S. C. *A History of France from the Death of Louis XI.* 5 vols. Oxford, 1921–1936. A highly detailed history of France that covers Anne's lifetime.

Matarasso, Pauline. *Queen's Mate: Three Women of Power in France on the Eve of the Renaissance.* Brookfield, Vt., 2001. Study of Anne and two other powerful women of her era, Anne of Beaujeu and Louise of Savoy.

FREDERIC J. BAUMGARTNER

ANTARCTIC. *See* **Arctic and Antarctic.**

ANTICLERICALISM. The idea of "anticlericalism" as such does not belong to early modern Europe. The word describes a range of attitudes and behaviors toward clergy, ranging from mild criticism to loud protest and violence. Anticlericalism was in evidence both in the Middle Ages and the early modern era; it was expressed by laity and clergy alike, whether Catholic or Protestant; and it arose in response to actions, policies, and attitudes perceived as contrary to the ideals and duties of the clerical profession. By the eighteenth century, in France especially, anticlericalism developed into a hostile, self-conscious reaction against the Catholic Church, culminating in the Civil Constitution of the Clergy (1790), which subordinated the church to the French state. In the nineteenth century anticlericalism led liberal movements to abolish the church as a state institution.

Anticlerical criticisms in early modern Europe arose from various sources, including the clergy's insistence on its social superiority, privileges, prerogatives, tax exemptions, immunities from civil jurisdiction, and the payment of tithes and contributions. Other causes included resentment of the demand for blind acceptance of clerical direction and of measures to enforce orthodoxy or punish social, political, and sexual behavior seen as objectionable. Still other causes were clerics' intellectual arrogance, the punitive withholding of the sacraments, widespread clerical ignorance, theological rigidity, or lay hostility toward the papacy. In some cases, anticlericalism arose in response to outright ecclesiastical abuses such as simony, plurality of benefices, absenteeism, concubinage, nepotism, and scandalous or extravagant behavior.

Anticlericalism was not restricted to laypeople, as the clergy themselves often vented anticlerical sentiments toward fellow clergy whom they perceived as acting contrary to their calling. Such forms of anticlericalism ran the gamut from explicit, public denunciations to indirectly censorious and benignly tacit comments. Examples of the latter tactic are St. Francis of Assisi's (1182–1226) admonition to his friars that they not judge others for their luxurious raiment or choice foods and drink, but instead judge themselves (*The Later Rule*, ch. 2), or Ignatius of Loyola's (1491–1556) "Rules for Thinking with the Church," which urged his fellow Jesuits to be more ready to approve and praise the commands, recommendations, and behavior of their superiors than to criticize them.

In the early modern era, as in every other, Scripture proposed a standard of clerical comportment and at the same time drew attention to clerical shortcomings. In the gospel of Matthew, for instance, Jesus stated, "You received without payment; give without payment. Take no gold or silver, or copper in your belts . . ." (Matt. 10:8–9). Many other biblical passages, especially in Luke's Gospel, suggested that Jesus lived poorly and eschewed the haughty attitudes of priestly superiority in his judgments against the Temple priesthood in Jerusalem; these passages were used to reproach ostentatious and inappropriate clerical behavior and displays of pomp, wealth, or exclusivity.

The various medieval antecedents of early modern anticlericalism have roots in the early church, as do ecclesiastical efforts to reform clergy to thwart criticisms and hostilities. Some bishops set forth norms of clerical behavior that were cited throughout the early modern era. The motto of Pope Gregory I (reigned 590–604), "the servant of the servants of God," expressed the attitude that the highest ecclesiastical dignity should be understood as an obligation to serve. Gregory's *Regulae pastoralis liber* (c. 591; Pastoral care) required that clergy value service, humility, and poverty and be single-minded about the things of God. Despite efforts to maintain these ideals, anticlerical attitudes escalated in the High Middle Ages, coinciding with the commercial revolution in Europe and the Crusades. Much anticlericalism was directed at the church's rapaciousness. The Franciscan movement spawned numerous offshoots that made poverty the foundation of Christian life. After the Black Death (1348–1350), deepening hostilities to clerical life and practices arose, which continued unabated into the Reformation era. The fourteenth-century humanist Petrarch (1304–1374) used biblical texts and imagery to lament clerical abuses of wealth and power at papal Avignon. In England the Lollards, followers of John Wycliffe (c. 1330–1384), were fiercely hostile to the institutional church and anticipated the Reformation in their demands.

On the eve of the Reformation, anticlerical sentiments were endemic throughout Europe, mostly from clergymen themselves. François Rabelais's *Pantagruel* (1532) and *Gargantua and Pantagruel* (1532–1564) and many works of Desiderius Erasmus (1466–1536), including *Colloquies, Handbook of the Militant Christian, In Praise of Folly,* and *Julius Exclusus,* are perhaps the best-known anticlerical works. Ulrich von Hutten (1488–1523), Martin Luther (1483–1546), and many other Protestants wrote devastating attacks on the papacy and the Catholic Church, while numerous sympathizers chimed in with books, pamphlets, woodcuts, and poetry castigating the clergy for their ignorance, ineptitude, wealth, dereliction of duty, and dissolute behavior. The Protestant Reformation's criticisms against the clergy were further fueled by Luther's reframing of the very idea of a "clergy" in *An Appeal to the Christian Nobility of the German Nation* (1520), which denied to the clergy their special "indelible character" or status. Luther and other Reformers' writings were enormously assisted by the printing industry, which made anticlerical writings and woodcuts widely available throughout Germany.

Ironically, much of the Reformers' criticism fell in line with criticisms voiced by high-ranking clergy and religious who sincerely wished to reform the behavior of fellow clergy. Such criticisms often led to church synods and councils where corrective action was taken, as at the Council of Trent (1545–1563), which looked into the reformation of doctrine and discipline. In the post-Reformation era, Roman Catholic authorities, aware of the damage incurred through public criticism of the church, intervened to quash it. Ignatius of Loyola's "Rules for Thinking with the Church" reflect these efforts, as do the establishment of the Roman Inquisition (1542) and the Index of Prohibited Books (1559).

Nonetheless, anticlericalism persisted unabated into the Enlightenment. This was especially the case among the educated elites in France, with the relaxation of censorship following the death of Louis XIV (ruled 1643–1715). Criticism of the church increasingly hardened into a secular stance among the philosophes, who polemicized against the dominance of the church in every area of life. Chief among these antagonists were Denis Diderot (1713–1784), Voltaire (François Marie Arouet; 1694–1778), and Jean Jacques Rousseau (1712–1778).

See also **Diderot, Denis; Enlightenment; Erasmus, Desiderius; Ignatius of Loyola; Luther, Martin; Rabelais, François; Reformation, Catholic; Reformation, Protestant; Rousseau, Jean-Jacques; Trent, Council of; Voltaire.**

BIBLIOGRAPHY

Cohn, Henry J. "Anticlericalism in the German Peasants' War 1525." *Past and Present* 83 (1979): 3–31.

Dykema, Peter A., and Heiko A. Oberman, eds. *Anticlericalism in Late Medieval and Early Modern Europe.* Leiden, Netherlands, and New York, 1993.

Haigh, Christopher. "Anti-Clericalism and the English Reformation." *History* 68 (1973): 391–407.

Mellor, Alec. *Histoire de l'anticléricalism français*. Rev. ed. Paris, 1978.

FREDERICK J. McGINNESS

ANTI-SEMITISM. *See* **Jews, Attitudes toward.**

ANTWERP. Few early modern cities experienced such profound changes as Antwerp. The city on the River Scheldt was transformed from a sixteenth-century commercial metropolis to a small town of only regional importance by the seventeenth and eighteenth centuries. In the same period, Antwerp changed from an open cosmopolitan city with strong Protestant influences into a bulwark of the Catholic Reformation.

In the first half of the sixteenth century, the Low Countries were fully integrated into the vast Habsburg empire and the international economy. Antwerp profited greatly from this situation, experiencing unparalleled economic and population growth. Its commercial expansion was based on the convergence of important international trade in English cloth, Portuguese spices, and South German copper and silver. Although this "foreign" under-pinning made the Antwerp world market vulnerable, by the mid-sixteenth century the indigenous Antwerp merchants had gained considerable influence. Commercial expansion stimulated existing industries and attracted new ones. In addition, art production boomed, and many printers, publishers, and booksellers—there were at least 271 in the sixteenth century—traded on the international market. The city also experienced extraordinary demographic growth. The Antwerp population more than doubled within half a century, from around 40,000 in 1496 to 100,000 in 1566. A small mercantile elite owned an overwhelming percentage of the city's wealth, reflecting a social polarization during Antwerp's golden age. Nevertheless, there are strong indications for the existence of a broad urban middle class that profited from the booming economy, socially and culturally. Among other things, this new middle class benefited from Antwerp's well-developed and highly laicized educational system, which included schools for both boys and girls.

The new religious ideas that divided sixteenth-century Europe easily penetrated Antwerp's cosmopolitan community, and the city became a center of Protestantism in the Netherlands. An eclectic evangelical movement in the 1520s and 1530s gave way to Anabaptist and Calvinist communities in the 1550s. For economic reasons, the Antwerp city

Antwerp. *View of Antwerp from the River Schelde* by Jan Wildens (1586–1653). PRIVATE COLLECTION/BRIDGEMAN ART LIBRARY

magistrate (the main political body of the city) cautiously adopted the central heresy placards (legislation to counteract and punish the Protestants), focusing their repression on the poorer Anabaptists. From the 1560s onwards, the fortunes of Protestantism were closely linked with political resistance to central government policy. In 1566, Calvinists and Lutherans were allowed to organize a church; the Calvinist leaders even tried to seize power. The arrival of the duke of Alba in the summer of 1567 ushered in a period of severe repression. The Antwerp city government was put under custody and rebels and heretics were systematically prosecuted. Alba's policy, and the fortunes of war in general, were detrimental to the vulnerable Antwerp metropolis. Anti-Spanish sentiment flourished after the "Spanish Fury," which began on 4 November 1576. Spanish soldiers ransacked the city and killed about 8,000 people. From 1577 onwards, the Antwerp city government supported the politics of William of Orange (William the Silent) and the rebellious States-General. In 1579, the Calvinists gained control of the city administration, two years later proscribing the public exercise of the Catholic religion. Antwerp became a Protestant stronghold of international importance and a backbone of the Dutch Revolt.

The year 1585 was a watershed in Antwerp's history. In August of that year, following a long and brutal siege, the Antwerp city fathers were forced to surrender to Alexander Farnese, duke of Parma, and his Spanish troops. Many people fled the city for religious, political, or economic reasons. In four years, the population halved, falling to only 42,000 inhabitants by 1589. Among the emigrants were merchants, artists, intellectuals, and skilled craftsmen who contributed significantly to the economy and culture of their new homelands, especially the towns in Holland and Zeeland. After 1585, ecclesiastical and civil authorities closely collaborated to build up a new Catholic Church. New religious orders, such as the Jesuits, played a key role in this process of Catholic Reformation, which possessed a clear anti-Protestant stamp.

After a severe crisis in the late 1580s and 1590s, the Antwerp economy experienced an Indian summer. The closure of the Scheldt to navigation after 1585 notwithstanding, the resourceful Antwerp merchants managed to integrate the city into the Iberian trade system. A number of luxury industries recovered, and art production profited highly from the strong demand created by the construction and redecoration of churches. Artists such as Peter Paul Rubens turned Antwerp into an international center of baroque art. Yet, in the second half of the seventeenth and even more in the first half of the eighteenth century, the Antwerp economy declined. The closure of the Scheldt was confirmed by the Peace of Westphalia (1648), and the position of the port was further wounded by the mercantilist measures of the mighty European states. Furthermore, shifts within the economy of the Southern Netherlands were unfavorable for Antwerp and transformed the once thriving city into a provincial town.

See also **Alba, Fernando Álvarez de Toledo, duke of; Dutch Republic; Dutch Revolt (1568–1648); Netherlands, Southern; Parma, Alexander Farnese, duke of; Rubens, Peter Paul; Westphalia, Peace of (1648); William of Orange.**

BIBLIOGRAPHY

Marnef, Guido. *Antwerp in the Age of Reformation: Underground Protestantism in a Commercial Metropolis, 1550–1577.* Translated by J. C. Grayson. Baltimore and London, 1996. Includes lengthy introduction on urban society in sixteenth-century Antwerp.

Soly, Hugo. "Continuity and Change: Attitudes towards Poor Relief and Health in Early Modern Antwerp." In *Health Care and Poor Relief in Protestant Europe 1500–1700,* edited by Ole Peter Grell and Andrew Cunningham, pp. 84–107. London and New York, 1997.

Van der Stock, Jan, ed. *Antwerp: Story of a Metropolis, 16th–17th Century.* Antwerp and Ghent, 1993. Collection of articles written by leading scholars.

GUIDO MARNEF

APOCALYPTICISM. A religious outlook regarding the "last things"—hence a form of eschatology—characterized by a sense of universal crisis and by expectation of a divinely preordained triumph of good over evil, apocalypticism originated among the Jewish prophets around 200 B.C.E. It was a critical aspect of early Christianity, and became an integral though often latent element in the Judeo-Christian tradition. This outlook combines prophetic themes of warning and consolation with the quest for saving knowledge, insight into the divine plan.

The term covers a broad array of beliefs about the imminent end of the world, inevitable conflicts, disasters and tribulations, and a future millennial kingdom, or final age of perfection. Serious contemporary scholarship avoids the assumption that the sociopolitical implications of apocalypticism are inherently violent or revolutionary, noting instead that such thinking has undergirded a wide range of political positions. Yet apocalyptic conceptions were crucial both to the formation of social identities and to the broader transformation of worldviews in the early modern age.

LATE MEDIEVAL AND RENAISSANCE ANXIETY

Medieval ecclesiastical culture generally discouraged apocalyptic expectancy by de-emphasizing historical change and highlighting the fate of individuals at death. Prophetic interests had begun to expand in the high medieval period, but the fourteenth and fifteenth centuries brought a dramatic intensification of such concerns. Upheavals brought on by famine, plague, and war, together with shifting economic conditions and the novelties of urban life, caused heightened anxiety among Europeans and evoked new forms of fear and hope. Social dislocation and suffering became grounds for outbreaks of revolutionary millenarianism, such as that of the Taborites (a group of radical Hussites) in Bohemia. But even millenarian forms of apocalypticism, which foresaw the coming of Christ's temporal rule, could function as conservative political myths by giving established powers a role in preparing for the new age.

The late-medieval apocalyptic ferment drew not only on key biblical texts such as the books of Daniel and Revelation, but also on thinkers such as the Calabrian Cistercian Joachim of Fiore (c. 1135–1202), in whose scheme the ages of the Father (Old Testament) and the Son (New Testament) would be followed by the age of the Holy Spirit, a final period of spiritual fulfillment. Among other influential prophetic sources were ancient textual clusters such as the Sibylline Oracles (collections of ancient Jewish and Christian verses, reputedly by pagan prophetesses), the visions of inspired figures such as Saint Birgitta of Sweden (1303–1373), and classical divinatory methods such as astrology, an art undergoing a powerful revival during the Renaissance.

Together these traditions produced a paradoxical brew of terror and hope.

By the late fifteenth century the printing press was helping to articulate and disseminate a general expectancy, local forms of which included the hair-raising preaching of Girolamo Savonarola in Florence, the prophetically charged journeys of Columbus, and German nightmares of a bloodbath at the hands of the Turks, who were commonly seen as the satanic forces of Gog and Magog (Revelation 20: 8) sent to scourge Christendom before the Last Judgment. Despite the persistence of popular hopes for a final world-reform by a messianic emperor or an angelic pope, fearful dread often predominated. Early in the sixteenth century, for instance, astrologically inspired predictions of a second universal flood to come in 1524 sent waves of panic through central Europe.

MARTIN LUTHER AND REFORMATION EXPECTANCY

This rising expectancy posed severe threats to the established religious culture and formed a central current in the sixteenth-century Reformations, especially among those movements that regarded the papacy as the biblical Antichrist, now unmasked in the last times. Here the prophetic discoveries of Martin Luther were central. Although he by no means escaped late-medieval influences (for example, the assumption of world-historical decline since the Creation), Luther decisively rejected as unbiblical all dreams about messianic emperors, world reform, and a millennial paradise. For him the ultimate reality was a universal struggle between God and the devil that would continue until the Last Judgment. Luther and most of his sixteenth-century heirs saw the recovery of the purified gospel as evidence that the end was imminent. By discrediting many medieval beliefs and ritual practices that had dampened personal anxiety, effectively propagandizing against the newly revealed Roman Antichrist, and directing the religious imagination to scriptural promises of disaster and deliverance, Protestantism focused and intensified the apocalyptic tendencies in European culture.

Millenarian hopes, though marginalized, did not disappear from the early Reformation scene. Many Anabaptists and other radicals held views that were at least quasi-millenarian, and chiliasm, the belief in a literal thousand-year rule of Christ on earth (Revelation 20), gained scattered adherents. But such beliefs tended to be fluid; it is often difficult to pin down the apocalyptic conceptions of radical leaders such as Thomas Müntzer (c. 1488–1525) or Melchior Hoffmann (c. 1500–1543). Again, no necessary link can be found between millenarian hopes and the radicalism of such violent episodes as the German Peasants' War (1524–1525) or the Anabaptist rising at Münster (1534–1535). What distinguished radicals such as Müntzer was mainly their conviction that God's people had an active and immediate role to play in fulfilling the divine plan. This sort of apocalyptic preaching was regarded as threatening to political and ecclesiastical establishments throughout the early modern age.

LATE REFORMATION VARIATIONS

In the late Reformation era (c. 1560–1620), evangelicals in Germany and elsewhere sought to bolster their prophetic faith and sense of confessional identity through strident end-time preaching, searching far and wide for evidence to complement biblical prophecies of the nearing judgment. Apocalyptic expectancy thus propelled inquiry into such realms as historical chronology, natural wonders, and celestial observation. While some evangelical leaders continued to stress the necessary obscurity of all prophetic details, an increasingly eclectic apocalypticism fed rapidly on itself and formed a basic context for the pansophic striving of that era, the quest for universal insight, for a magical key to the secrets of creation.

Early Reformed Protestants proved more hesitant to engage in apocalyptic reckoning, partly because of John Calvin's (1509–1564) pronounced reserve in such matters. Yet Calvinism would prove fertile ground for the revival of millenarianism from the late sixteenth century on. Their confidence in God's promises to the elect led Calvinist thinkers to seize on biblical passages suggesting a final spiritual triumph before the close of time. On the continent, scholars such as Johann Heinrich Alsted (1588–1638) could combine this brand of prophetic confidence with expansive pedagogical ambitions to form visions of a breathtakingly transformed human future. But it was in England that Calvinist millenarianism would have its most pervasive influence. Here, Elizabethan images of England as an elect

nation gained urgency in the political conflicts of the seventeenth century, which seemed in many eyes the final struggle against the Antichrist. The Civil War and Interregnum of the 1640s and 1650s brought to full boil the Puritan dream of a godly society, which exploded into various radical movements, from those of the Quakers, Levellers, and Diggers to Fifth Monarchists, all sharing the sense that a final spiritual outpouring was underway.

Among Catholics, the sacred and social realms remained integrated in ways alien to Protestantism; hence, the impulse to direct fears and hopes toward the historical horizon remained relatively muted. In addition, clerical authorities worked to restrict the spread of popular apocalyptic expectancy. Still, Catholic Europe was affected by the general unease brought on by the rapid changes of the Reformation era. The French Wars of Religion spurred a strain of Catholic apocalyptic preaching against the rise of satanic heresy. Medieval traditions such as hope for a messianic emperor retained currency, as did various forms of Joachimist belief in a final time of earthly perfection. Major religious orders such as the Jesuits and the Franciscans continued to harbor visions of millennial triumph that renewed or reinforced a sense of mission in Catholic Europe, against Protestant heretics, and in the New World.

PROGRESSIVE FAITH AND SKEPTICAL DESPAIR

Especially in northern Europe, tense waverings between hope and terror characterized the early to mid-seventeenth century, when fearfully violent persecution of witches could accompany dreams of the conversion of the Jews and a return to Edenic peace. Yet at the same time, inherited outlooks were evolving in new directions. On one hand, the apocalyptically inspired quest for insight into the patterns of nature and history, seasoned with millennial hope, could spawn highly sanguine visions of human progress. The rise of Baconian science, for example, needs to be regarded in this light, as do early moves to institutionalize the investigation of nature by groups such as the Royal Society in England (founded 1660). Modern notions about the ongoing amelioration of the human condition through the mastery of nature can thus be traced at least partly to Christian faith in a divine plan for collective spiritual fulfillment.

Apocalypticism. *The Four Horsemen of the Apocalypse,* woodcut by Albrecht Dürer, 1498. ©BETTMANN/CORBIS

On the other hand, apocalyptic fears of divine wrath, of human helplessness in the face of inevitable disasters, suffering, and death, were at least one major source for the practical skepticism and agnosticism that grew increasingly evident in the seventeenth century. Among evangelicals, the revelation of the true gospel had from the start meant not only a positive awakening, but also profound disillusionment in regard to humanly invented myths, along with heightened critical awareness and distilled strains of anxiety. With spreading wars, economic dislocations, witch hunts, and general confusion, many Protestants who had felt the nearness of Christ's return, but who were repeatedly and forcefully reminded of their own incapacity to understand or influence God's plan, retreated from the pursuit of apocalyptic insight and turned toward lives of simple practicality. One dramatic mid-seventeenth-century example is offered by the Dutch Collegiants, radical Protestant millenarians whose fervent hopes were consistently disappointed, and who came to accept human reasoning as a necessary if provisional guide during whatever time remained before the divinely wrought transformation of the world.

NATURAL LAW AND PROPHETIC SCIENCE

Apocalyptic hope and despair thus led toward the awkward Enlightenment juxtaposition of progressive faith and skeptical reason. But outwardly at least, the later seventeenth century witnessed a waning of expectancy. Among European elites, the main thrust of intellectual inquiry shifted away from time and history to the seemingly more concrete realm of nature and her timeless patterns, a trend that suited the prevailing desire for order and stability in all aspects of life. Ultimately more significant than the new heliocentric cosmology was the spreading belief in universal, ahistorical laws that were potentially within reason's full grasp. The sort of rational religion proposed by Lord Herbert of Cherbury (c. 1583–1648), which dismissed as superstitious virtually all belief in historical revelation or prophecy, was spreading far and fast by 1700. Moreover, time's terrors seemed to fade in this age of boundless potential wealth and new methods of insurance.

Yet even as apocalyptic expectancy became less visible and its popular expressions came to be de-nounced as "enthusiasm," European thinkers continued to speculate in ways that revealed their deep hopes and fears. Especially among educated Protestants, scripturally based calculations of the closeness of the Last Judgment or the advent of an earthly millennium remained a serious preoccupation. Indeed these reckonings were commonly pursued as a quasi-scientific enterprise—a rational effort to uncover the divinely determined laws of universal history. Isaac Newton (1642–1727) was among those who devoted energies to the careful analysis of biblical prophecy, calculating likely dates for the destruction of Christ's enemies and the realization of the millennium.

EIGHTEENTH-CENTURY MOVEMENTS

Apocalyptic conceptions continued to serve diverse political interests, including those of conservative Anglican bishops, of urbanites who spurned the established churches for "Philadelphian" societies promoting a final worldwide blossoming of love, and of the radical "Camisards" who carried on a guerrilla war against the French monarchy in the years after 1700. In the 1730s a movement of prophetic opposition to the worldliness of the French church was led by the Jansenist "Convulsionaries," who saw themselves as witnesses to the final spiritual outpouring foreseen by the prophet Joel. Yet similar themes would be adopted by the Jansenists' most consistent enemies, the Jesuits, after their suppression by Pope Clement XIV (reigned 1769–1774) in 1773.

If in France millenarian prophecies were often deployed in opposition to established power, in Germany they more commonly cast existing authorities in a positive light, as instruments in God's work to complete the movement of history. German Pietist leaders such as Philipp Jakob Spener (1635–1705) anticipated the fall of the papacy, the conversion of the Jews, and a worldwide reign of peace before the Last Judgment. Pietist thinkers tended more and more toward a progressive outlook verging on nonapocalyptic historical meliorism. Meanwhile, in England the great popular movement of Methodism was driven by widely shared convictions of Christ's imminent advent; the same mood of expectancy leaped the ocean to help fuel a Great Awakening in the New World.

By the second half of the eighteenth century, Christian postmillennialism (expectation of Christ's personal return only after an age of spiritual purity) had become closely intertwined with Enlightenment optimism. In the schemes of learned figures such as Gotthold Ephraim Lessing, historical progress was ongoing and inevitable. But expectations marked by a more pronounced sense of imminence and urgency, while often kept out of public view, remained pervasive. Moreover, with the outbreak of the French Revolution in 1789, the entire storehouse of late medieval and early modern apocalyptic imagery was reopened and thoroughly ransacked in efforts to make sense of a manifestly world-historical upheaval. For revolutionary supporters, these events would mark nothing less than the advent of a new historical dispensation, a millennium of reason and freedom.

Throughout the early modern period, both elites and common folk were influenced by visions of current crisis and future resolution. Such concepts had no consistent sociopolitical implications, but they did function centrally in the formation of various confessional, national, and missionary identities. Apocalyptic outlooks inspired Europeans to intense efforts to understand their experiences in relation to a universal scheme. The modern myth of progress as well as modern skepticism and agnosticism had central roots in apocalyptic perceptions. In no sense a fringe phenomenon, apocalyptic expectancy was a crucial element of early modern European life and thought.

See also **Anabaptism; Calvin, John; Calvinism; Camisard Revolt; Enlightenment; Jansenism; Jesuits; Luther, Martin; Lutheranism; Methodism; Pietism; Reformation, Protestant; Revolutions, Age of; Witchcraft.**

BIBLIOGRAPHY

Primary Sources

The primary sources for early modern apocalypticism are so numerous and varied that any brief listing would be highly arbitrary. For titles by particular authors or on a specific aspect of the theme, the bibliographies of relevant secondary works should be consulted.

Secondary Sources

Cohn, Norman. *The Pursuit of the Millennium: Revolutionary Messianism in Medieval and Reformation Europe and its Bearing on Modern Totalitarian Movements.*

2nd ed. New York, 1961. A classic, still engaging and valuable despite its largely discredited approach.

Fanlo, Jean-Raymond, and André Tournon, eds. *Formes du Millenarisme en Europe à l'aube des temps modernes.* Paris, 2001. Reflects important trends in recent research, but also the regrettable tendency to focus exclusively on millenarian forms of apocalypticism.

Firth, Katharine. *The Apocalyptic Tradition in Reformation Britain 1530–1645.* Oxford and New York, 1979. Among the best overall treatments of the British scene in the sixteenth and seventeenth centuries.

Fix, Andrew C. *Prophecy and Reason: The Dutch Collegiants in the Early Enlightenment.* Princeton, 1991. A pathbreaking study of connections between apocalyptic disillusionment and rationalism.

Historische Kommission zur Erforschung des Pietismus. *Chiliasmus in Deutschland und England im 17. Jahrhundert.* Pietismus und Neuzeit, 14. Edited by Martin Brecht et al. Göttingen, 1988. Includes helpful essays, several in English.

McGinn, Bernard et al., eds. *The Encyclopedia of Apocalypticism.* Vol. 2, *Apocalypticism in Western History and Culture.* New York and London, 1998. Includes excellent bibliographies.

Millenarianism and Messianism in Early Modern European Culture. 4 vols. Dordrecht and London, 2001. Rich collections of scholarly articles.

Oberman, Heiko A. *Luther: Man between God and the Devil.* New Haven and London, 1989. Indispensable on Luther's apocalyptic worldview.

Patrides, C. A., and Joseph Wittreich, eds. *The Apocalypse in English Renaissance Thought and Literature: Patterns, Antecedents, and Repercussions.* Ithaca, N.Y., 1984.

Scholem, Gershom. *Sabbatai Sevi: The Mystical Messiah, 1626–1676.* Translated by R. J. Werblowsky. Princeton, 1973. Exhaustive study of the central episode in early modern Jewish apocalypticism.

Tuveson, Ernest Lee. *Millennium and Utopia: A Study in the Background of the Idea of Progress.* Berkeley, 1949. Somewhat dated, but still useful for its central argument that the modern idea of progress derived from Christian millenarianism.

Webster, Charles. *The Great Instauration: Science, Medicine, and Reform 1626–1660.* New York, 1976. Demonstrates the fundamental importance of millenarianism for the emergence of the new science.

ROBIN B. BARNES

APOTHECARIES. The apothecary struggled throughout early modern times to attain a measure of independence. He first had to free himself from his traditional origins and associations with spicers and grocers. In London it was not until 1617 that the apothecaries of the city were able to break away from the Company of Grocers and establish the Worshipful Society of Apothecaries. In Paris it was 1777 before a royal decree finally separated the apothecaries from the spicers and established the Collège de Pharmacie. Prestigious apothecary corporations had been established even earlier—in Rome, Barcelona, and Nuremberg, for example—but the medical establishment had never conceded independence to the apothecary. The *Collegio medicum,* the prestigious association of the physicians in a particular jurisdiction, which was a fixture of the continental city, usually dominated. In addition, the apothecary was subject to strict controls by civil authority, ubiquitous municipal ordinances, royal decrees, and monopoly-granting court or church *privilegia* (grants, usually hereditary, which gave an apothecary sole right to practice in a given jurisdiction). In England, there was little control; in the provinces, the "surgeon-apothecary" found very little other than the mixed trade guild to which he belonged to impinge upon his practice.

THE APOTHECARY AS PHARMACIST

The work of the apothecary was essentially pharmaceutical. He could identify the drugs, knew how to take care of them, knew how to manipulate the mechanical and chemical apparatus, and became aware of the purported therapeutic qualities of the drug. Given the shortcomings of the medicine of the age, the long tradition of herbal therapeutics to which the apothecary was heir, and the impact of the chemical therapeutics of Paracelsianism with its alchemical basis to which the apothecary was also heir, he became the health provider of the first resort for the general population. Physicians were few in number and expensive. Moreover, the nature of the work of the apothecary inevitably led to diagnosis and prescribing, and the apothecary was often actively encroaching on the prerogatives of the physician. Therein lay the basis for a long and vituperative quarrel between the two.

In France and England the quarrel seemed endless. In a tract war, begun in Paris about 1513, the two groups cast aspersions on each other's abilities and traded insults. The pamphlet war soon spread to England and Germany. Still at odds in 1625,

Parisian doctors put out *Le Médicin charitable,* a do-it-yourself pharmaceutical handbook, and sought to put the apothecary out of business. The apothecary withstood the onslaught, becoming officially, in the late eighteenth century, *pharmacien* rather than *apothicaire,* a change reflecting the lampooning of the *apothicaire* as the administrator of clysters (enemas) in literature and art. In London, the Royal College of Physicians was in conflict with the apothecaries long before the Society of Apothecaries was founded, for there, and in the provinces, the apothecary had unabashedly become the primary medical practitioner. As in Paris, the physicians sought to a destroy the apothecary and chose to do so by establishing, from 1698 to 1725, dispensaries in London where the poor could get their medicines "in penny doses." Again, the apothecaries survived, but in a way unique to England: the House of Lords, in the case of William Rose in 1703, found that prohibiting prescribing by apothecaries was contrary to custom and contrary to public interest, given the small number of physicians. Thereafter, apothecaries in Great Britain became general practitioners of medicine; the "chemist and druggist" took over the practice of pharmacy.

THE APOTHECARY AS SCIENTIST

Toward the end of the fifteenth century, a body of literature directed at, and later written by, the apothecary began to appear. The first of the pharmaceutical handbooks, volumes of formulas, procedures, and expositions, was the *Compendium Aromatariorum of Saladin di Asculi* published in Bologna in 1488. A very popular work, it was soon followed by other such texts, three written by apothecaries in Italy, Spain, and France. In the late seventeenth and throughout the eighteenth century, the *Dispensatory,* a British specialty, became the textbook of pharmacy, but again, it was the work of physicians, not apothecaries.

The apothecary also needed a formulary, or pharmacopoeia, and although the first of these, the Florentine *Nuovo Receptario* that appeared in 1499, was the work of the guild of physicians and apothecaries, apothecaries did not take part in the compiling of a pharmacopoeia until the very end of the eighteenth century. The medical establishment saw the pharmacopoeia as an instrument of control over the apothecary.

Apothecaries. Illustration of an apothecary and a doctor from *Brunschwing Buch der Chirurgy* (Brunschwing's Book of Surgery), c. late fifteenth century. ©BETTMANN/CORBIS

Apothecaries. Woodcut of a pharmacy, sixteenth century. ©CORBIS

Similarly, the interest of the apothecary in botany awaited the pioneering efforts of others. For a knowledge of plants he resorted to the ubiquitous herbals (which by 1483 were illustrated) and to the work of Dioscorides, particularly in the many versions issued by Matteoli. Apothecaries were, of course, involved in the establishment of herb gardens, and, among others, two of them, Basilius Besler in Germany and John Parkinson in England, issued large and copiously illustrated botanical works.

In the eighteenth century several apothecaries made distinctive contributions to botany. The Moravian Georg Joseph Kamel was the first European to describe the flora and fauna of the Philippines; the German Arthur Ernsting's work with pollens paved the way for the discovery of cross-fertiliza-

tion; the Swede Friedrich Erhart made advances in botanic systemization and is noted for his studies of lichen.

While these contributions to botanical science were important, those that the apothecary made to chemistry were more fundamental to the development of the science and were more far-reaching in their influence. The apothecary had always been involved in chemical manipulation. Chemical procedures, learned from the alchemists, were part of the "mystery" of the art of the apothecary.

The ground breaking was again done by others—the seventeenth-century works of Oswald Croll, Jean Beguin, and Jean Baptiste van Helmont, for example. But the apothecary was already gaining recognition as chemist. The first chair in chemistry was held by the apothecary Johannes Hartmann in Marburg in 1609. A series of lectures in chemistry for the public at the Jardin des Plantes in Paris were delivered by a succession of apothecaries, LeFevre, Charas, and Rouelle, among them. Nicaise LeFevre first published his *Traité* (later *Cours*) *de chymie* in 1660. It appeared also in English and German. Nicolas Lémery's *Cours de chymie,* which first appeared in 1675, was reputed to be the most widely used chemistry textbook in Europe for a century. In Germany, the apothecary Caspar Neumann became professor of *Chymiae* practice at the Collegium Medico-Chirurgicum in Berlin in 1724.

The apothecary's contributions to chemistry were seminal. Sixteen of the elements were discovered by five apothecaries between 1750 and 1803. Foremost among them were Carl Wilhelm Scheele, who, in his little shop in Köping, Sweden, discovered seven of the elements (including oxygen, before Priestley's much more publicized achievement), and Martin Heinrich Klaproth of Berlin, considered the founder of modern quantitative analysis, who discovered seven others. Scheele is also credited with the introduction of a long list of organic and inorganic acids into chemistry.

While Scheele's work was basic to the development of the chemical industry, the work of Andreas Marggraf in Germany was the foundation of the beet sugar industry, and it was no coincidence that in Germany, France, and England, it was an apothecary who developed porcelain out of the local clay and who created the porcelain industries in those countries.

The apothecary thus played important roles in early modern history. He was, first of all, the primary provider of health care, and his contributions to science, especially chemistry, were often seminal to the science and significant to the economy and life of the times.

See also **Alchemy; Medicine; Paracelsus; Priestley, Joseph.**

Apothecaries. *The Apothecary's Shop,* by Pietro Longhi, eighteenth century. THE ART ARCHIVE/ACCADEMIA VENICE/HARPER COLLINS PUBLISHERS

BIBLIOGRAPHY

Bouvet, Maurice. *Histoire de la Pharmacie en France des origines à nos jours.* Paris, 1937. Valuable for its detailed attention to various local arrangements.

Burnby, Juanita G. L. *A Study of the English Apothecary from 1660 to 1770.* London, 1983. A comprehensive study with particular attention to the provincial apothecary.

Cowen, David L., and William H. Helfand. *Pharmacy: An Illustrated History.* New York, 1990. Also available in German, Spanish, and Italian. Contains chapters on "The Renaissance" and "The Early Modern Age and the New Science."

Dann, Georg Edmund. *Einführung in die Pharmaziegeschichte.* Stuttgart, 1975. Especially valuable for its chronological lists of pharmaceutical literature and scientific advances.

Helmstädter, Axel, Jutta Hermann, and Evemarie Wolf. *Leitfaden der Pharmaziegeschichte.* Eschborn, 2001. A scholarly overview with considerable attention to science.

Roberts, R. S. "The Personnel and Practice of Medicine in Tudor and Stuart England. Part I. The Provinces. . . . Part II. London." In *Medical History* 6 (1962): 363–382 and 8 (1964): 217–234. The medical activities of the apothecary and his professional difficulties are fully covered.

Schmitz, Rudolf, with the cooperation of Franz-Josef Kuhlen. *Geschichte der Pharmazie Band I von den Anfangen bis zum Ausgang des Mittelalters.* Eschborn, 1998. An authoritative and exhaustive study valuable for the medieval background. A second volume, under the editorship of Christoph Friedrich and Wolf-Dieter Müller-Jahncke, covering 1500–2000, is forthcoming.

Sonnedecker, Glenn. *Kremers and Urdang's History of Pharmacy.* 4th ed. Philadelphia, 1976. Includes individual chapters on Italy, France, Germany, and Britain.

DAVID L. COWEN

APPRENTICESHIP. *See* Youth.

ARCHAEOLOGY. The modern discipline of interpreting the human past by means of material remains is built upon five centuries of antiquarian and scholarly pursuits. Study of the physical remains of the Greco-Roman past complemented the ardent search for classical texts during the Italian Renaissance, since artifacts and monuments provide a visible, tangible, authoritative (and sometimes alternative) past. Early humanists such as Petrarch and Boccaccio studied coins and inscriptions along with their philological inquiries, and Vitruvius's (first century B.C.E.) treatise on architecture stimulated surveys of architectural remains and the topography of Rome by architects such as Leon Battista Alberti (1404–1471), Andrea Palladio (1508–1580), and Pirro Ligorio (1510–1583). Cyriacus of Ancona (1391–c. 1452) recorded ancient inscriptions and buildings during extensive travels in Italy, Greece, Egypt, and the Levant. In Rome, spectacular chance finds of sculpture like the Laocoön (in 1506) and paintings like those in Nero's Domus Aurea (Golden House, 65–68 C.E.) profoundly affected artists, including Michelangelo and Raphael, and augmented papal collections. A lucrative market in antiquities encouraged random digging that sometimes yielded new information, but excavation for the sake of answering historical questions was slow to develop.

During the eighteenth century the grand tour led to Rome as a primary destination, and the enhanced awareness of antiquities and classical topography stimulated further collecting and shaped fashionable tastes. The typical tour was extended to Naples after the discovery of Herculaneum (1709; excavations began 1738) and Pompeii (1748), investigated initially by destructive tunneling in the search for treasures until more systematic efforts began in 1750 under the direction of Karl Weber (1712–1764). Architects visited the temples of Paestum (Giovanni Battista Piranesi) and Sicily and Greece (James Stuart and Nicholas Revett), recording them as antiquities and as models for contemporary practice, while Johann Joachim Winckelmann's publications shifted antiquarianism toward the discipline of art history. The collections of antiquities that bestowed status on wealthy families eventually became central to national collections in the public museums founded in the nineteenth century.

Antiquarians in England (William Camden, John Aubrey, William Stukeley), France (the Comte de Caylus), and Germany and Scandinavia (Olaus Magnus, Ole Worm) focused on regional histories that could be recovered through close observation, walking surveys, and even some deliberate excavation of henges, megaliths, tumuli, barrows, and urn fields. They sought to merge the distinctive local histories attested by such findings with both the Roman past, using appropriate texts, and biblical antecedents, but biblical chronology constrained their efforts. Nonetheless their meticulous drawings and records and their use of hypotheses based on fieldwork set new standards, and they initiated archaeological investigations of cultures predating the Greco-Roman era.

The documentation of Egyptian antiquities during Napoleon's invasion of Egypt (1798) opened the new field of Egyptology and led to further exploration of the Near East. Soon thereafter developments in stratigraphic geology, paleontology, and especially the theory of evolution led to a more scientific and rigorous archaeology. The antiquarians, however, had successfully applied philological methods to the interpretation of inscriptions and physical remains, and their illustrated publications of Greek and Roman antiquities deeply influenced contemporary art and architecture, interior decoration, and consumer items. Their studies contributed a broader understanding of cultural history, creating taxonomies and typologies still in use and important records of material now lost.

See also **Ancient World; Architecture; Classicism; Grand Tour; Neoclassicism; Palladio, Andrea, and Palladianism; Piranesi, Giovanni Battista; Pompeii and Herculaneum; Rome, Architecture in; Winckelmann, Johann Joachim.**

Archaeology. *Laocoön.* Rediscovered in 1506, this Roman sculpture from the Hellenistic period (323–27 B.C.E.) portrays a scene from the *Aeneid* in which the sons of a Trojan priest are crushed by snakes. It was widely viewed as an unparalled depiction of human suffering and influenced the work of a number of Renaissance artists, including Michelangelo. ©ARALDO DE LUCA/CORBIS

BIBLIOGRAPHY

Barkan, Leonard. *Unearthing the Past: Archaeology and Aesthetics in the Making of Renaissance Culture.* New Haven, 1999.

Fagan, Brian M., ed. *The Oxford Companion to Archaeology.* New York, 1996.

Haskell, Francis, and Nicholas Penny. *Taste and the Antique: The Lure of Classical Sculpture, 1500–1900.* New Haven, 1981.

Salmon, Frank. *Building on Ruins: The Rediscovery of Rome and English Architecture.* Aldershot, U.K., and Burlington, Vt., 2000.

Schnapp, Alain. *The Discovery of the Past: The Origins of Archaeology.* London, 1996.

Trigger, Bruce G. *A History of Archaeological Thought.* Cambridge, U.K., and New York, 1989.

Watkin, David. *Athenian Stuart: Pioneer of the Greek Revival.* London and Boston, 1982.

Weiss, Roberto. *The Renaissance Discovery of Classical Antiquity.* 2nd ed. Oxford and New York, 1988.

MARGARET M. MILES

ARCHITECTURE. The monumental inventions of early modern European architecture still mark the modern built environment. Vast boulevards and formal gardens focusing on public buildings denote the capital city everywhere. Domes dominate the skyline in Rome, London, and Washington. Uniform palaces and house facades define the squares of Paris and London, the canals of Amsterdam and St. Petersburg. Churches modeled on imperial Roman baths and basilicas seem to reach outwards, with spectacular baroque facades and multiple columns extending into public space, like the twin columns (inspired by Trajan's Column in Rome) of Vienna's Karlskirche (Fischer von Erlach, 1715–1738), or the colonnades that define the piazza of St. Peter's in Rome (Gian Lorenzo Bernini, 1656–1667). The countryside, too, is transformed by villas and great houses in their landscaped grounds, and in the most famous case, Versailles (Louis Levau and J. H. Mansart, 1668–1689), the out-of-town retreat became the capital of an absolute monarch.

The language of all these buildings is classical, using the columns, arches, cornices, vaults, and triangular pediments still visible in the ruins of ancient Rome, integrating them according to the ancient treatise of Vitruvius, and in some cases directly imitating the few ancient buildings that survived, such as the Pantheon and the Colosseum. But this language was transformed in several ways, going beyond the accomplishments of the Renaissance. In its baroque form, space becomes more complex, and surfaces more agitated and ornate; straight moldings and flat walls curve and break apart, columns spiral, circles turn into ovals, ceilings dissolve into vast trompe l'oeil paintings that seem open to heaven, and solid ornament imitates the movement of angels or the sudden burst of light. Secular buildings undergo the same transformation, especially in their ceremonial staircases and uniform suites of reception rooms that create the impression of infinite power. The best of these designs is orderly and monumental rather than capricious or excessive, yet periodically architects reacted against the baroque, instigating a calmer and more rational classicism. A well-known example is Palladianism, a revival of the late Renaissance architect Andrea Palladio (1508–1580) that came to dominate English country house design in the eighteenth century in reaction to the ornate formality of Versailles and its English baroque rival, John Vanbrugh's Blenheim (1705–1716).

Individual buildings and urban spaces conveyed a powerful message of confidence and control through new forms and crystalline geometry even when they were not very large. Thus Francesco Borromini's (1599–1667) church of San Carlo alle Quattro Fontane in Rome (1634–1667), though only the size of one of the piers of St. Peter's, created a stir among visitors and critics who praised its curved facade and oval dome—or execrated them in equal measure. Sant' Ivo (1642–1660), Borromini's Star of David–shaped chapel for the University of Rome, dazzled with its breathless spiral tower that altered the role of the adjacent Pantheon's dome. Borromini's fastidiousness for building materials and moldings was matched by his French contemporary François Mansart, but the latter's trademark at country houses such as Château Maisons near Paris (1642) and the Orleans wing of the royal palace at Blois (1635) was a limpid and austere classicism. Pietro da Cortona's (1596–1669) facade for Santa Maria della Pace (1656–1659) in Rome applied theatricality to urban design, placing a lavishly columned and curved portico in a small space that caught unprepared visitors by surprise. Paris, Turin, London, and Bath were endowed with geometrical open spaces framed with uniform porticoes and houses, to whose shapes the English word "square" fails to do justice: rather, they were triangular (Place Dauphine), circular (Place des Victoires, Jules Hardouin-Mansart, 1685; the Circus, John Wood, 1754), rectangular (Piazza San Carlo, Carlo di Castellamonte, 1620), hexagonal (Place Vendôme, Mansart, 1698), and elliptical (Royal Crescent, John Wood, Jr., 1767–1777). Countering these residential "squares" were the public spaces of Rome, such as Piazza Navona (Four Rivers fountain by Bernini, 1647–1651), the Spanish Steps (Francesco de Sanctis, 1723–1726), and the Trevi fountain (Nicola Salvi, 1762), each animated by generous displays of statuary, water, terraces, and views. This festive quality of the best early modern urban design was enhanced with additional ornaments, including innumerable triumphal arches, imprinting the city with commemorative meaning.

THE ARCHITECTURAL CITY

The innovations of the Italian Renaissance provided an ample foundation for the developments in architecture of the late sixteenth, the seventeenth, and the first half of the eighteenth centuries. This inheritance was enhanced by the innovations of military defense, altered social and political organizations, and new forms of organized religion. Yet despite significant research in church form and extensive construction of places of worship, the period is marked by a secularization of architecture and urban space.

The seventeenth century was an urban century, whose great cities—defined by the size of the population (according to Giovanni Botero) and the magnificence of their rulers—constituted its new wealth. A large population can be attained through prosperity and security, and the architecture of the early modern era defined the prosperity of the social order and ensured its safety in the face of enemies. Distinguished buildings, significant historical inheritance, artistic collections, and public safety attracted visitors to the great city. Thus consumerism and tourism developed in tandem with the early modern city and its architectural expression.

This was accompanied by the widespread acceptance and application of the revived classical style of architecture in places outside the Italian peninsula—in France, England, the Netherlands, the Germanic states, Sweden, Russia, and the British colonies in the Americas. A specifically Counter-Reformation style of classical architecture, emphasizing massive, ornate spaces and animated forms that propagate the faith by captivating the audience, was disseminated in the colonial towns of Spanish and Portuguese settlers, and in the missionary convents of religious orders in Central and South America, on the western coast of Africa, and on the Indian subcontinent.

In the seventeenth and eighteenth centuries, architecture became an instrument of state control and organization, not only signifying the cultural advantages of its sponsors (as in the fifteenth and sixteenth centuries) but also assuming a defining role in the identity of nascent national states. Thus secularized, classicized, and politicized, architecture transformed the early modern city. The architectural product continued to be defined through three types of design—church, palace, and public square—but each underwent extensive refinement and redefinition. We have cathedrals, parish churches, and monastic churches as before, though now competing for attention through the offer of urban amenities such as colonnades, fountains, and elaborately decorated facades, transformed by the worldly social agenda of the Counter-Reformation. The palace building type came to encompass not only aristocratic town residences (called *hôtels* in France) and the communal homes of religious orders, but also the state agencies of control, management, and reform (such as prisons, almshouses, hospitals, and city halls). The open spaces of the city surrounded by this evolving set of buildings (housing new functions and organized into streets and squares more or less geometrically defined and ordered) became the principal sites of urban meaning. The definition of urban architecture was ultimately achieved through the enclosure of a city within a fortification belt (walls, bastions, outworks, and gateways) that effectively created the separation between town and country and allowed each to develop firm boundaries.

This defining separation was the major contribution of military urbanism. Other military-

Architecture. An aerial view of the Château de Versailles by Pierre Patel. Built by Louis XIV as a royal residence, the chateau later became the seat of the French government and served as the model for palaces across the continent. (See also cover of volume 6.) ©ARCHIVO ICONOGRAFICO, S.A./CORBIS

influenced architectural features were the triumphal arch, the pentagonal citadel, the wide, uniformly framed straight boulevard, and the equestrian statue of the victorious ruler placed at the center of squares used for parades and festivities. The pacification brought about by military architecture encouraged the development of the rural palace or agrarian villa. Palladio's urbane villas (such as the Rotonda outside Vicenza, 1566–1569, and the Villa Barbaro at Maser, 1554–1558) offered a residential type that resonates throughout early modern architecture. Modeled on the French royal château, the palaces at Blenheim, Tsarskoe Selo (Bartolomeo Rastrelli, 1749–1756), and Schönbrunn (Fischer von Erlach, 1696–1711) are among the most prominent examples of the "Versailles syndrome" that swept through eighteenth-century Europe.

This new understanding of architecture, urbane even in its country houses, was promoted through the burgeoning medium of print: illustrated books, single sheets, and specialized studies turned the newly defined city and its buildings into a subject of study, and were collected by all those with pretensions to learning: for the first time in the history of Western civilization, the achievements of architects could be appreciated, studied, and imitated without leaving home. Nonetheless, this graphic documentation stimulated travel in the pursuit of architectural education, making Rome—then Paris, London, and Amsterdam—the destinations for nonreligious pilgrimage.

BAROQUE ROME AND BEYOND

The issues involved in large building operations—budget, conflicting interests of patrons, and variable design talents of architects—can best be illustrated by the seemingly interminable reconstruction of St. Peter's in Rome. Its dome, completed (Michelangelo and Giacomo della Porta, 1590) after nearly a century of indecision and uncertainty, the much desired Renaissance plan of the ideal church as centrally planned—promoted by Bramante (1506) and Michelangelo (c. 1546), the two most acclaimed architects of the sixteenth century—was definitively abandoned. The extension of the church by Carlo Maderno (1607–1612), and the immense facade designed by him, completed the body of the church proper. This signified the coming importance of building elevations in a development that has been labeled facadism—countering the Renaissance's failure to complete the public front of important religious and secular buildings (the facade of San Lorenzo in Florence, for example, whose interior includes Michelangelo's Medicean library and chapel, remains unclad). The elliptical space before St. Peter's, defined by a carefully planted forest of columns, was not completed until the late 1660s by Bernini. The area framed by the facade and colonnade, where pilgrims to Rome were taken to the bosom of the church and whose center was defined by the largest Egyptian obelisk in Rome, represented the epitome of baroque space. The placement of the obelisk under the direction of Domenico Fontana in 1586 marks an important achievement in the history of engineering, considered by architectural historians to be the most influential moment of early modern city planning and a spur to later developments. Facadism then is a crucial element of the concern with the appearance of public space that dominates Western architectural design in the seventeenth century.

Like Florence in the fifteenth century, Rome in the sixteenth and seventeenth centuries was an artistic hub of the highest order. The papal government (with its huge numbers of retainers and accompanying families), the missionary orders that made their headquarters in the city, and the large numbers of pilgrims constituted the elements of a varied and rich patronage system that attracted the best artists to the city. Milan and Naples, Rome's most important rivals in wealth and size of population, were dominated by the Spanish viceroys, whose cultural contributions were more modest; Spanish monarchs beginning with Philip II concentrated their archi-

tectural patronage on the remote palace-monastery El Escorial (Juan de Herrera, 1568–1584). Architects came to work in Rome, but they also came to study, forming "national" groupings lodged among their compatriots in distinct parts of the multicultural city.

By the end of the seventeenth century the Italian tour, though highly recommended, was no longer a requirement for a successful career in architecture. Thus Christopher Wren and Jules Hardouin-Mansart, unlike their predecessors Inigo Jones and Jacques Lemercier, built highly visible religious monuments—St Paul's in London (1675–1711) and the Invalides church in Paris (1679–1691)—modeled on St. Peter's without setting foot in the old city. Inigo Jones put his Italian experience to work designing the queen's house in Greenwich (1616–1635, outside London), a royal villa that later became the centerpiece of Wren's naval hospital (1696–1716), and the Whitehall Banqueting House (1619–1622), which emulated the urban palaces of Palladio in Vicenza. Although his buildings were few, he sowed the seeds of Palladianism, the single most significant classicizing movement in England, whose influence continued through the eighteenth century in the houses designed by John Wood in Bath and Lord Burlington, William Kent, and Robert Adam in the British countryside near London (Chiswick, Syon) and East Anglia (Holkham Hall).

The Dutch version of classicism turned Amsterdam into a Venice of the north and provided the stimulation for the design of St. Petersburg. Russian neoclassicism in the later eighteenth century was leavened by the presence of both Charles Cameron and Giacomo Quarenghi, whose cool white and stripped-down temples and pavilions for the empress Catherine were rooted in the more recent archaeology of the mid-century. Architects at the French Academy in Rome made an inestimable contribution to neoclassicism: they measured and drew antiquities, offering the most accurately reproduced illustrations for those unwilling to travel. By anatomizing antiquities, they acquired a familiarity with the classical forms that led to the transformation of this inheritance, stripping it of baroque accretions.

ARCHITECTURAL ACHIEVEMENTS

Architecture in this period solved problems that had been researched for centuries: how to express the status and ambitions of the patron and how to connect the buildings' public and private functions. Thus the formation of palace facades in Rome, Turin, Venice, Paris, and Vienna can be seen as billboards that explicate the position of their owners. This meant articulating the relation between the exterior (the street or garden facade) and the interior, which in turn must be divided into entry, passage, principal reception room, and private apartments.

While palace and church elevations had been recognized as essential areas of relation between public and interior space (and as carriers of meaning), the formal manipulation of these surfaces was determined by concerns for the appearance of dignity and sobriety. The baroque facade became strongly articulated and richly ornamented with the entire arsenal of architectural vocabulary available to designers. While the liveliness of church facades was meant to stimulate a Counter-Reformation participation, the facades of palaces became essential elements in the highly ritualized definition of power exchanges.

The major architectural innovations—St. Peter's in Rome, Palladio's villas, the Louvre in Paris (1666), and the palace at Versailles—soon acquired the authority earlier associated with ancient Roman and Greek buildings such as the Parthenon, the Pantheon, the Colosseum, and the ancient theater. The new standards were serially emulated, though not always with distinguished results. Thus St. Peter's was the source not only for Mansart's Invalides in Paris and Wren's St. Paul's in London, but also for Jacques-Germain Soufflot's Panthéon (1755–1780) in Paris, stretching as far as the nineteenth-century capitol buildings in Washington and in Providence, Rhode Island. Versailles, itself distantly modeled on the Escorial, spawned numerous imitations in the German principalities and in Vienna, as well as in Sweden and Russia. Palladio's villa designs, capable of absorbing variations in scale, were the basis (through Inigo Jones) for innumerable British country houses, and for Thomas Jefferson's influential Monticello. Bernini's designs for the Louvre, and the realized version by Louis Le Vau and Claude Perrault, drew upon the Farnese palace in Rome, the grandest of Renaissance homes, and propagated countless urban houses, from Guarino Guarini's Carignano palace (1679–1683) in Turin to Viennese town palaces of the eighteenth century.

See also **Baroque; Bernini, Gian Lorenzo; Borromini, Francesco; Britain, Architecture in; City Planning; Estates and Country Houses; France, Architecture in; Gardens and Parks; Mansart, François; Neoclassicism; Palladio, Andrea, and Palladianism; Rome, Architecture in; Wren, Christopher.**

BIBLIOGRAPHY

Ackerman, James S. *The Villa: Form and Ideology of Country Houses.* Princeton, 1990.

Blunt, Anthony. *Art and Architecture of France 1500 to 1700.* New Haven, 1999. First published in 1953.

Botero, Giovanni. *Della grandezza delle città.* 1608.

Millon, Henry, ed. *The Triumph of the Baroque: Architecture in Europe 1600–1750.* Milan, 1999.

Millon, Henry, and Vittorio Lampugnani, eds. *The Renaissance from Brunelleschi to Michelangelo: The Representation of Architecture.* New York, 1994.

Payne, Alina. *The Architectural Treatise in the Italian Renaissance: Architectural Invention, Ornament, and Literary Culture.* Cambridge, U.K., 1999.

Pollak, Martha. *Turin, 1564–1680: Urban Design, Military Culture and the Creation of the Absolutist Capital.* Chicago, 1991.

Rykwert, Joseph. *The First Moderns: The Architects of the Eighteenth Century.* Cambridge, Mass., 1980.

Summerson, John. *The Architecture of the Eighteenth Century.* London, 1986.

———. *The Classical Language of Architecture.* London, 1980.

Waddy, Patricia. *Seventeenth-Century Roman Palaces: Use and Art of the Plan.* New York and Cambridge, Mass., 1990.

Wittkower, Rudolf. *Art and Architecture of Italy, 1600–1750.* New Haven, 2001. First published in 1958.

MARTHA POLLAK

ARCTIC AND ANTARCTIC.
Geographers, explorers, fisherfolk, and entrepreneurs had very different attitudes toward the extreme north and extreme south in the early modern period. Neither pole was seen as inhabitable, although interactions with Inuit and Lapps from the sixteenth century on caused Europeans to modify this view. The northern area was most often seen as

a path to Cathay and the Far East, while the south was completely unknown and only glimpsed by circumnavigators like Ferdinand Magellan (Fernão de Magelhães; c. 1480–1521) and Sir Francis Drake (1540 or 1543–1596).

Theories of the globe changed during the early modern period, affected first by the rediscovery of ancient geographical knowledge and later by exploration reports. From Aristotle and Ptolemy, most Greek and Roman commentators as well as medieval geographers believed that there was simply one continent, or *oikoumene,* that consisted of the known world. For Ptolemy, this *oikoumene* was quite large, from the prime meridian, passing through the Blessed Isles to longitude 180° east; and from 63° north latitude to 16°25′ south lati-

tude. This encompassed the civilized world as Ptolemy knew it and he implied that the world and its map were complete. From 1406, with the rediscovery of Ptolemy's *Geographia,* and with it the longitude and latitude coordinate system, Ptolemaic maps once again appeared. The *oikoumene* remained an important visual depiction of the globe, used for example by Gregor Reisch in *Margarita philosophica* (1504). Throughout the sixteenth century this map was modified, first by the addition of America by Martin Waldseemüller in 1507, but it was not until the world map of Gerhard Mercator, produced in Antwerp in 1569, followed by that of Abraham Oertel (Abraham Ortelius), produced in Antwerp in 1570, that a large northern and southern continent appeared.

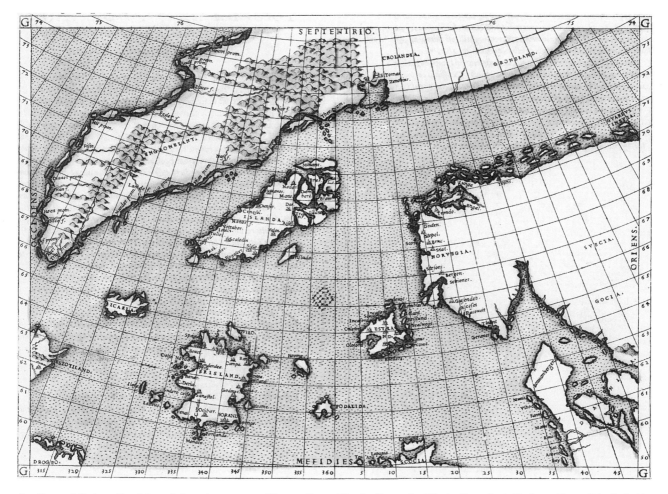

Arctic and Antarctic. A largely imaginary map of the northern Atlantic Ocean by Nicolo Zeno that Girolamo Ruscelli included in his 1561 edition of Ptolemy's *Geography.* Based on the supposed travels of Zeno's ancestors in the North Atlantic circa 1380, the map includes a number of fictitious islands such as Frisland, Icaria, and Estotiland. The map was taken seriously by many at the time of the *Geography*'s publication, and these nonexistent places remained on maps for centuries afterward. MAP COLLECTION, STERLING MEMORIAL LIBRARY, YALE UNIVERSITY

Arctic and Antarctic. Gerhard Mercator's famous 1595 map of the Arctic region, one of the first of that area, represents the late medieval concept of four rivers flowing into a central whirlpool around a large rock at the north pole, but also includes information gathered by polar explorers such as Martin Frobisher, John Davis, and Willem Barentz. The map also reflects the interest in finding a northwest passage between Europe and Asia, which lasted throughout the early modern period. MAP COLLECTION, STERLING MEMORIAL LIBRARY, YALE UNIVERSITY

At the same time, the Greek climatic theory remained important throughout the early modern period. Parmenides had postulated the existence of five climatic zones; the two polar zones were too cold to inhabit, and the torrid zone was likewise uninhabitable, leaving only the two temperate zones for human occupation. During the sixteenth and seventeenth centuries, this theory was modified, since explorers from Christopher Columbus on had demonstrated inhabitants in all regions. Rather, geographers claimed that climate affected temperament and that those living in the Far North were very aggressive, and lacking in culture, government, or laws. Thus, the Europeans from the temperate zone were believed better suited to manage the affairs of those both to the north and the south.

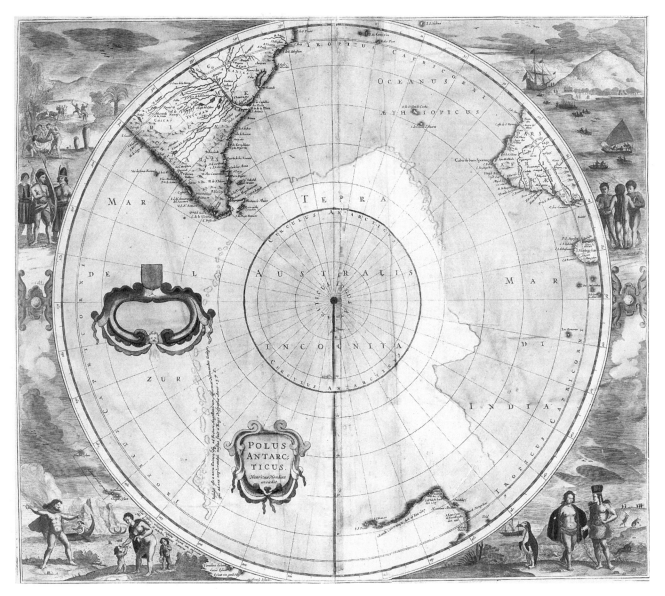

Arctic and Antarctic. On Henricus Hondius's map of the south polar regions, which first appeared in a Dutch atlas by Jan Jansson in 1637, the supposed outline of the unknown southern continent appears faintly around the top and right of the Antarctic Circle. The string of islands to the left of the title cartouche has text indicating their discovery by Magellan. A partial outline of the coast of newly discovered Australia appears at the bottom, with the names of early explorers noted. MAP COLLECTION, STERLING MEMORIAL LIBRARY, YALE UNIVERSITY

Between the fifteenth and seventeenth centuries, Europeans expanded their knowledge of the globe through exploration. They discovered the Americas and, by the end of the period, had sailed to most inhabited regions of the world. Exploration of the Arctic was carried out by northern Europeans, especially Scandinavians, Dutch, French, and English. These northern nations had fishermen who had exploited the northern seas for generations, both in the waters north of Scandinavia and Muscovy, and west to the Grand Banks, where the fish were so plentiful that the catch was well worth the difficult voyage. Building on the success of these fishing expeditions, although usually with other trade and geographical goals in mind, explorers began to search the north for a passage to the most desired trading location of the early modern period: Cathay. They searched for both a northeast and a northwest passage and in the process, set up trading companies and some colonial outposts.

The search for the northeast passage led around Scandinavia to Archangel (Arkhangel'sk), and to the creation of the Dutch and English Muscovy Companies in the 1550s. Although some explorers believed they had discovered unicorn horns, indicating that they were on the right track, the passage to China was never discovered, and trade with Muscovy turned out to be easier across land. The northern waters were left to the whalers.

In the west, English and French explorers were limited to northern exploration by the powerful presence of the Spanish in the more temperate zones. They also sought the wealth that the Spanish and Portuguese were amassing, both through the discovery of gold and silver in Mesoamerica and through trade with China. Through necessity, then, they sailed north, and became convinced that there was a way through the continent in that direction. Some geographers argued that there was a large northern continent surrounding the pole, with a strait below it leading to China. This strait, labeled the Strait of Anián or of the "Three Brothers," appeared on Oertel's map of 1564 and was repeated on other maps well into the seventeenth century. A number of explorers looked for this strait, and occasionally found it. The English mariner Martin Frobisher, for example, was convinced that he was sailing into the strait, on his second voyage of 1577. Explorers such as Frobisher, John Davis, and Henry Hudson all searched for this passage, and while they developed maps of the region, they were ultimately unsuccessful in their quest.

In the south, interest in a polar continent was almost nonexistent until the end of this period. Both Magellan and Drake sailed south around the Americas and in the process saw what they thought might be a southern unknown continent. In 1520 Magellan proceeded through the strait that now bears his name, passing between mainland South America and Tierra del Fuego. He thought that the latter was the tip of a much larger continent, especially because geographers such as Mercator had argued that a southern continent would be necessary to balance the Eurasian landmass in the Northern Hemisphere. Magellan's interest, however, was not with this continent, but rather in the path to the Spice Islands (Moluccas). Drake's later circumnavigation, beginning in 1577, also passed through the Strait of Magellan and again, Drake believed Tierra

del Fuego to be part of a much larger landmass. After clearing the strait, however, Drake's ship was blown farther south, and it began to look as if there was a cape below, like that around Africa. The first search for Terra Australis Incognita was undertaken by the Dutch explorer Abel Janszoon Tasman (1603–1659), who in the 1640s explored the north coast of Australia and discovered Tasmania and New Zealand. The push to discover the great southern continent, however, did not begin until the eighteenth century.

The Arctic and Antarctic were not the primary focus of Europeans in this period, but rather a means to other ends. Voyages there were dangerous and not particularly prosperous. However, theories of the existence of these continents led to colonization and exploration in the eighteenth and nineteenth centuries. By then, the discoveries of the Pacific seemed more appealing than those in the Far North, and the southern continent gained attraction while the northwest passage became a less important quest.

See also **Cartography and Geography; Exploration.**

BIBLIOGRAPHY

Primary Source
Ortelius, Abraham. *Theatrum orbis terrarum.* Antwerp, 1570.

Secondary Sources
Andrews, Kenneth R. *Trade, Plunder, and Settlement: Maritime Enterprise and the Genesis of the British Empire, 1480–1630.* Cambridge, U.K., and New York, 1984.

Parry, J. H. *The Age of Reconnaissance: Discovery, Exploration, and Settlement, 1450 to 1650.* London, 1963.

Whitfield, Peter. *New Found Lands: Maps in the History of Exploration.* New York, 1998.

LESLEY B. CORMACK

ARISTOCRACY AND GENTRY. In most European countries society and politics were dominated during the early modern period by the power and influence that nobles enjoyed, either as individuals or as a social group. Noble hegemony was not always uncontested, but by successfully adapting to political and cultural changes and by integrating competing social elites, nobles managed to maintain their dominant position in most cases until the late eighteenth century. Although noble elites across Europe were defined according to distinct local and national customs and legal criteria, noble men and women from different countries nevertheless tended to recognize each other as members of the same social estate, if not necessarily as equals, united by a specific sense of honor and adherence to common values.

DEFINITIONS OF NOBLE STATUS

Noblemen and noblewomen can most easily be defined as members of a social group that enjoyed a hereditary claim to certain privileges and social status, a claim that was sustained by a specific way of life and social practices that were meant to ensure that non-nobles were excluded from the charmed circles of the elite. However, at the beginning of the early modern period, what distinguished the lower nobility—that is, simple gentlemen—from mere commoners was not necessarily a matter of clear legal distinctions. What made a man and his family noble was rather his or their ability to live according to a specific social code of conduct. In most European countries (the patrician urban elites of the Mediterranean world were, at least at the beginning of our period, a partial exception), noblemen were expected to own landed property, ideally as a fief, held as tenant-in-chief from the crown or a secular or ecclesiastical magnate. They were also expected to lead a life of comparative leisure or at least to refrain from commercial activities that were considered demeaning as, for example, retail trading. In many countries military prowess and the virtues of the warrior were important ideals governing the conduct of noblemen. Ancient lineage, real or sometimes invented, was certainly crucial to lend credibility to the social aspirations of a family. However, if a man bought a fief complete with castle or manor house and the concomitant rights of jurisdiction and lordship, married the right woman or ensured that at least his children married the right partners, and lived in appropriate style, his heirs would stand a fair chance of being accepted as noble by local society in due course. This was certainly true in the earlier sixteenth century in most countries.

Nevertheless, many monarchs and princes gradually tried to control access to noble status more tightly. To some extent this had become necessary

Aristocracy and Gentry. *Eleanora of Toledo with Her Son* by Agnolo Bronzino. This is one of Bronzino's most renowned portraits; his works are characterized in particular by the sense of aristocratic detachment conveyed by their subjects. ©ARCHIVO ICONOGRAFICO, S.A./CORBIS

because the increasing tax burden had made noble status (which often brought freedom from direct taxation) dangerously attractive, all the more so as the feudal obligation to perform personal military service for the crown at times of war had largely become obsolete in an age when battles were no longer fought by the feudal host but by armies of professional soldiers. In France a royal ordinance stated in 1579 that men of non-noble origin who bought noble fiefs should in future remain members of the Third Estate; the silent elevation to the status of nobleman was thereby declared illegal. Admittedly, it took several decades to enforce this legislation. In fact it was not until the reign of Louis XIV, in the 1660s, that systematic investigations were undertaken to weed out false from true nobles. Such nationwide controls of social status were more difficult to implement in other countries. Nevertheless, the tendency to move from a notion of nobility that was based on custom and informal criteria of social prestige to an idea of nobility conceived in terms of written proofs of noble lineage or based on royal letters of ennoblement was visible elsewhere as well. However, outside France it was often not the monarch but noble corporations such as cathedral chapters or the assemblies of Estates (or those sections of these assemblies that represented the nobility) that took the lead in erecting barriers to social newcomers and defining noble status more narrowly. While noble corporations tried to exclude newly ennobled families, titles granted by kings and sovereign princes, especially in moments of political or fiscal crisis, undermined the idea of a natural nobility that did not require a royal or princely grant or confirmation to be valid.

Whereas both the aristocracy and the lower nobility in most European countries were increasingly defined by clear legal criteria, the English gentry formed an exception to this rule. Partly because gentlemen had to pay the same taxes as other royal subjects, the crown had no great interest in restricting access to gentry status and would have lacked the power to do so in any case. Essentially, a man could assume the title "gentleman" or possibly even "esquire" if he felt that he was sufficiently wealthy and powerful to get away with such a claim without exposing himself to ridicule. In the eighteenth century the title "gentleman" became ever more widespread and was used widely by members of the respectable urban middle classes, even sometimes by wealthy shopkeepers.

THE LANDSCAPE OF NOBLE SOCIETY

The contrast between the English gentry and its continental counterparts is only one example of the heterogeneity of noble society in early modern Europe. To start with, the number of noble families per head of population varied greatly. At the European periphery, in Poland, Hungary, and Castile, nobles and their families made up between 5 and 10 percent of the population in the sixteenth and early seventeenth centuries. The percentage sometimes rose to 25 or more in regions such as Asturias in northern Spain or Mazowia in Poland, which had been marked by prolonged periods of warfare in the high or late Middle Ages; in these areas, freeholders who would have been simple peasants elsewhere often became part of the nobility or had special military privileges. In central Europe, in Germany

and France, and also in England (if one includes the gentry), between 1 and 2, or at most 3, percent of all men and women could claim noble status. This was more or less the European norm; regions such as southern Italy, Scandinavia, and Bohemia (where the lower nobility almost disappeared after 1620) had a lower density of noblemen, about 0.5 percent of the population in the eighteenth century.

Areas with numerous nobility were obviously also those that had the greatest number of impoverished noble families in the early modern period. This applies not only to the regions just mentioned but also to parts of France such as Brittany or the southwest, or countries such as Scotland. Partible inheritance did not help either, as it created a great number of noble heirs who stubbornly clung to their status and their inherited privileges, even though the ancient family fortune had long been diminished. Primogeniture, on the other hand, which was valid in England for the peerage and also for gentry families, tended to create an elite of limited size but comparatively solid wealth. Those younger sons who no longer owned enough real estate simply dropped out of the elite and became members of the urban or rural middle classes unless they managed to pursue successful careers as officeholders, lawyers, or soldiers (or sometimes even as merchants), which might give them sufficient wealth and prestige to remain members of the elite.

During the early modern period many noble families tried to defend their economic position against the dangers of mismanagement and waste by introducing forms of inheritance designed to ensure that real estate could neither be sold at will nor divided among several heirs. The strict settlement in England, the *mayorazgo* in Spain, and the *Fideikommiss* ('entail') in Germany and the Habsburg Monarchy stipulated as a rule that younger sons received only stipends and cash payments or, at best, smaller estates not included in the entail. Daughters received dowries; the bulk of the family fortune went to the eldest son, who could not, however, sell the property. Such special forms of inheritance became increasingly popular in the seventeenth century in particular among the high aristocracy. The enormous fortunes of the Spanish *grandes,* the magnates of Austria and Bohemia, and many English peers were protected by such arrangements, although

Aristocracy and Gentry. *Lords John and Bernard Stuart* by Anthony Van Dyck. The official portraitist for Charles I of England, Van Dyck was renowned for his ability to subtly enhance the noble bearing of his subjects. ©NATIONAL GALLERY COLLECTION; BY KIND PERMISSION OF THE TRUSTEES OF THE NATIONAL GALLERY, LONDON/CORBIS

mismanagement by a succession of spendthrift heirs could still spell doom for aristocratic dynasties.

The difference between these magnates and the rank and file of the lower nobility, both in power and in cultural terms, was striking. Although the size of aristocratic households, and in particular the number of male servants, declined somewhat in the seventeenth and eighteenth centuries, some magnates still employed several hundred servants and retainers, whereas many simple country gentlemen could only afford one or two.

In the sixteenth century both magnates and simple gentlemen tended to live in castles or manor houses in the country, outside the towns and cities, in most European countries. Northern and central Italy and large areas of Spain—in particular the south—as well as southern France were, however, an exception to this rule. In fact, in northern Italy the social group that can most easily be classified as noble was the urban patriciate. The economic power base of this group had originally been trade and financial transactions, but later generations often tended to prefer a rentier existence that was unsoiled by visible business activities. In France and to a lesser extent elsewhere as well, a legal career offered special chances of ennoblement. Because most royal offices, including those in the highest courts of law, the parlements, could be bought and inherited, a class of hereditary officeholders was formed in the later sixteenth and the early seventeenth centuries that could lay some claim to noble status, the *noblesse de robe*. Although its members in many French provinces—perhaps less so in the capital—often came from the same families as the rural noblemen belonging to the *noblesse d'epée* (the military nobility), the *robins* had their own ethos and culture, which was distinct from that of the traditional nobility with its concentration on military virtue. The upper echelons of both elites tended to merge in the eighteenth century in social and cultural terms.

In general, the distinction between long-established urban and rural elites became gradually less marked in the course of the seventeenth and in the early eighteenth century. Urban patricians, such as the great families of Milan and Florence and, in the eighteenth century, the regents of Amsterdam, adopted the style of the old feudal nobility. They bought fiefs, manors, and rights of jurisdiction, increasingly spoke and acted like courtiers, and had their sons serve as officers in the army. Meanwhile, the rural nobility, or at least its wealthier members, moved into town, where they built palatial houses in the later seventeenth and early eighteenth centuries. The great capitals such as London, Paris, and Vienna, and also smaller provincial cities, became centers of noble life, in particular during the winter months when life in the country was too dull and uncomfortable. Those rural gentlemen who lacked the means to leave their country houses and adopt the manners and style required by the sophisticated and refined culture of court and city were left isolated and resentful in their villages, cut off from the patronage networks that the noble magnates who were now mostly absent had provided in the past.

PRIVILEGES AND POWER

In most European countries nobles held more or less extensive right of jurisdiction at the local level, ranging from the right to adjudicate small disputes about property or to punish minor misdemeanors to the full authority to impose death sentences for capital crimes. Over time kings and princes tended to restrict noble jurisdiction or subject it to the control of their own courts of appeal. However, particularly in eastern and east central Europe (in Poland or Bohemia and Moravia for example, but also in Germany east of the Elbe River), noble seigneurs ruled their villages—and sometimes small agrarian towns as well—autocratically as late as the mid-eighteenth century and beyond. The peasants were often serfs or were at least subjected to severe restrictions on their personal freedom. They had to provide the lord of the manor with labor services and could not marry or leave their farms without his consent. This strict seignorial regime, which was designed to support the extensive home farms maintained by nobles, had no full equivalent in most parts of western and southern Europe. However, in the Spanish Habsburg Monarchy, the state's fiscal crisis in the late sixteenth and seventeenth centuries led to a large-scale alienation of royal rights of jurisdiction and taxation to noble magnates and rich financiers—who were subsequently often ennobled and integrated into the ancient nobility—that has been described as a process of refeudalization. In kingdoms such as Sicily, Naples, and Castile, the authority of the state was for a time eroded and

Aristocracy and Gentry. *Lady Elizabeth Thumbelby and Dorothy, Viscountess Andover,* portrait by Anthony van Dyck, c. 1637.
©NATIONAL GALLERY COLLECTION; BY KIND PERMISSION OF THE TRUSTEES OF THE NATIONAL GALLERY, LONDON/CORBIS

replaced by that of great noblemen. Elsewhere, for example in France, the agents of a centralizing state, collecting taxes, dispensing justice, and enforcing religious conformity, were more successful in challenging the preeminence of nobles in the localities Historians have often seen this process as the triumph of absolutism over noble power and liberty. However, the relationship between royal authority and noble power was not a zero-sum game, where the gain of one side was necessarily the loss of the other. Monarchs and their officeholders may have undermined the position of noble warlords—the

quintessential overmighty subjects—and taken a dim view of the protection rackets run by petty squires in remote provinces such as the Auvergne in France or Catalonia in Spain, but at least until the eighteenth century, the monarchical state also gave fresh legitimacy to the status, privileges, and honors enjoyed by nobles. In fact, important sections of the nobility took an active part in the state-building process and benefited from it either in the form of offices, pensions, and monopolies or because they were able to siphon off—officially or unofficially—a substantial part of the profits from taxation and other public revenues. Admittedly, there had been times of deep tension and conflicts between monarchs and noblemen in the late sixteenth and early seventeenth centuries in many countries, such as France and the Austrian Habsburg Monarchy. Religious divisions, tensions between competing noble factions at court, royal minorities, dynastic succession crises, and the failure of traditional political institutions such as the assemblies of Estates to integrate potential forces of opposition and to defuse conflicts all contributed to a series of violent confrontations, rebellions, and civil wars. When a new accommodation was achieved after about 1650, the traditional diets and provincial or national Estates, which had as a rule—next to the clergy—been dominated by nobles, were in terminal decline in many countries (they continued to thrive in England, Sweden, and parts of the Habsburg Monarchy as well as in the German ecclesiastical principalities). Nevertheless, a new accommodation between the noble quest for prestige and status and the demands of the state was achieved. Royal patronage managed to defuse the tensions between traditional notions of noble honor and the honors granted by the monarchical state to its servants. Not until the later eighteenth century was this new symbiosis to be challenged both by new non-noble elites and by enlightened nobles themselves.

See also **Absolutism; Class, Status, and Order; Court and Courtiers; Duel; Estates and Country Houses; Honor; Inheritance and Wills; Monarchy; Rentiers.**

BIBLIOGRAPHY

Asch, Ronald G. *Courtiers and Rebels: The Transformation of the European Nobilities, c. 1550–1700.* London, 2003. New survey that looks primarily at Central Europe, France, and Britain, and—to a lesser extent—Spain.

Bush, M. L. *The European Nobility.* Vol. I, *Noble Privilege.* Manchester, 1983. Vol. II, *Rich Noble—Poor Noble.* Manchester, 1988. These two volumes provide essential information, but those who look for lively intellectual debate may well prefer other works.

Clark, Samuel. *State and Status: The Rise of the State and Aristocratic Power in Western Europe.* Cardiff, 1995. Sociological approach, but rich in historical detail; concentrates on England, France, and "Lotharingia," i.e. Savoy, Burgundy, and the Netherlands.

Dewald, Jonathan. *The European Nobility, 1400–1800.* Cambridge, U.K., 1996. Stimulating book, particularly good on cultural developments. Based partly on the author's extensive research on the history of the French nobility.

Heal, Felicity, and Clive Holmes. *The Gentry in England and Wales 1500–1700.* Basingstoke, U.K., 1994. Now the standard account for this period.

Jouanna, Arlette. *Le devoir de révolte. La noblesse française et la gestation de l'état moderne, 1559–1661.* Paris, 1989. Important book by foremost expert on the history of the French nobility in this period. An absolute must for those who want to learn about noble rebellion and noble mentality.

MacHardy, Karen J. *War, Religion and Court Patronage in Habsburg Austria: The Social and Cultural Dimensions of Political Interaction 1521–1622.* Basingstoke, U.K., 2002. Looks at the decades before the outbreak of the Thirty Years' War and the subsequent transformation of the nobility.

Scott, H. M., ed. *The European Nobilities in the Seventeenth and Eighteenth Centuries.* 2 vols., London, 1995. Extremely good collection of essays, though contributions on Italy and England are less informative than others.

Stone, Lawrence. *The Crisis of The Aristocracy, 1558–1641.* Oxford, 1965. Classic statement of a once-influential thesis, that the peerage succumbed to economic problems before 1642. Main argument now widely seen as less than convincing, but book remains a magnificent survey of its subject.

Zmora, Hillay. *Monarchy, Aristocracy and the State in Europe, 1300–1800.* London and New York, 2001. Brief but well-argued survey by scholar who is expert on late medieval and sixteenth-century German nobility.

RONALD G. ASCH

ARISTOTELIANISM. Aristotelianism in the early modern period was the philosophy taught in the schools, typically in the collegiate years preparatory to a bachelor's degree. Thus Aristotelianism and Scholasticism were synonymous at the time, and one cannot talk about Aristotelianism without referring to the important changes in pedagogy that were initiated then. Many colleges and universities reorganized and standardized their curriculum; new teaching orders, such as the Oratory in France (founded 1564; established in France 1613) and the Doctrinaires in France and Italy (founded 1592), were instituted; and the Society of Jesus, which became a very powerful force in education, was established (in 1534), with the aim of using education to counter the effects of the Reformation.

Education during the first half of the seventeenth century became fairly uniform. Students took four or five years of humanities (French, Latin, and Greek language and literature) followed by a year of rhetoric and then the collegiate curriculum, that is, two years of philosophy. The latter was an Aristotelian-based program of logic, ethics, physics, and metaphysics; it was thought necessary as preparation for the higher faculties of medicine, law, and theology. Jesuits covered the same collegiate curriculum in three years with the addition of a course in mathematics. Oratorians followed that pattern and taught a broadly Aristotelian set of philosophy courses. Perhaps because of the propensity of their founder, Pierre de Bérulle, for Platonic thought, the Aristotelianism of the Oratory differed slightly from that of the Jesuits and Doctrinaires. The Jesuits officially leaned toward Thomism, the version of Aristotelian philosophy propounded by St. Thomas Aquinas (1224 or 1225–1274) and his followers, though in practice they mixed their Thomism with other kinds of Scholastic thought, while the Doctrinaires seem to have taught Thomism exclusively.

In the Constitutions of the Society of Jesus, Ignatius of Loyola (1491–1556), founder of the Society, recommended that Jesuits follow the doctrines of Saint Thomas in theology and those of Aristotle in logic, natural philosophy, ethics, and metaphysics. After Loyola, the official position of the Society was further specified; Jesuits were supposed to teach "Aristotle and the true philosophy," interpreted as Thomism. With the succession of Claudio Aquaviva as the fifth general of the Society (1581–1615), these issues took on a new vigor. The Society standardized its curriculum during this time. The Jesuits undertook extraordinary pedagogical discussions, ultimately leading to their *ratio studiorum* (uniform course of studies). The aim of this standardization was to enable Jesuits to propound a single philosophy that would maintain the Catholic faith; as Aquaviva said: "The primary goal in teaching should be to strengthen the faith and to develop piety. Therefore, no one shall teach anything not in conformity with the Church and received traditions, or that can diminish the vigor of the faith or the ardor of a solid piety."

Together with these pedagogical innovations there was an explosion of Scholastic manuals. Among the widely read textbook authors at the time were the Coimbrans and Francisco Toletus. The Coimbrans (the Conimbricenses) were professors at the Jesuit College at Coimbra (Portugal), who issued a series of encyclopedic commentaries on Aristotle's works. Chief among them was Pedro da Fonseca, who wrote his own commentary on Aristotle's *Metaphysics*. Toletus was a professor at the Jesuit Collegio Romano who also published commentaries on Aristotle's works. The Coimbrans wrote volumes by committee, presenting the works of Aristotle that were taught in the curriculum; they followed the model of the great medieval commentaries, each volume treating a specific text (*Physics, On the Soul, On the Heavens,* etc.), but with an elaborate (post-Renaissance) scholarly apparatus, giving both Aristotle's Greek text and its Latin translation, as well as Latin paraphrases and *quaestiones,* the resolution of questions relevant to the text under discussion. Other textbook writers generally followed this pattern, although textbooks like those of Toletus omitted the Greek versions of Aristotle. Ultimately, the Scholastic textbook even omitted Aristotle's text itself. Eustachius a Sancto Paulo, in his *Summa Philosophiae Quadripartita* (Sum of philosophy in four parts, 1609), simply arranged the *quaestiones* in the order in which the curriculum would have presented them, doing so for all the Aristotelian sciences within the frame of the whole philosophy curriculum in a single volume. As their names generally indicated, these works were usually divided into four parts: ethics and logic, physics and metaphysics. However, the *Philosophy* (1644) by the Protestant Pierre du Moulin (whose logic text was also translated into English), was a three-part textbook, metaphysics having been omitted, while the *Philosophy* (1642) of Léonard Marandé added a fifth part: theology.

While the form of Scholastic teaching was fairly stable, its content was not. Aristotle's philosophy dominated the schools in name, but the early modern era also witnessed a growing dissatisfaction with Aristotelian concepts. In fact, the differences among Aristotelians became so widespread that it is difficult to categorize thinkers as Aristotelians based on their doctrines alone. Scholars often regarded themselves as Aristotelians even when they departed from properly Aristotelian thought. One need only consider the case of Théophraste Bouju, whose 1614 textbook was subtitled: "All of it by demonstration and Aristotle's authority, with explanations of his doctrine by Aristotle himself." Despite the subtitle,

Bouju denied in his textbook that there is a sphere of fire and an absolute division between the sublunary and superlunary world. These, most would agree, were essential Aristotelian doctrines; dispensing with them would require one to rework substantially the Aristotelian theory of the four elements, of natural and violent motion, and of the heterogeneity of the sublunary and superlunary world. Many other theses that became canonical with later Aristotelians, such as the doctrine of substantial forms, also found early modern Scholastic critics. There were even textbook writers who proclaimed the compatibility of Aristotelian philosophy and atomism. Certainly, late Scholasticism was not "monolithic," although such pejorative labels have been applied to it from the beginning.

Of course, not everyone thought that the differences among Aristotelians were significant. For example, René Descartes (1596–1650) asserted: "As for scholastic philosophy, I do not hold it as difficult to refute on account of the diversity of the scholastics' opinions, for one can easily upset all the foundations about which they are in agreement among themselves; and that accomplished, all their particular disputes would appear inept." For the Schoolmen, departures from properly Aristotelian doctrines were generally presented as elaborations of Aristotle's intentions; outside the Schools they were often cited as objections to them. The situation naturally lent itself to rhetorical excesses on both sides. By the middle of the seventeenth century, accusations of in-fighting and philosophical inconsistency among the Schoolmen were near routine. Coinciding with this rising criticism, rival systems, such as those of Descartes, Pierre Gassendi (1592–1655), and Thomas Hobbes (1588–1679), were consciously developed as alternatives to traditional interpretations of Aristotelian physics and metaphysics. As a result, there were also thinkers who set out to mitigate the differences between the rival systems and others who self-consciously resolved to be eclectic, that is, to pick out what is best from the new and old philosophies. Naturally, the new philosophies also remained indebted, in varying degrees, to the tradition from which they attempted to break.

See also **Descartes, René; Education; Gassendi, Pierre; Hobbes, Thomas; Jesuits; Philosophy; Scholasticism.**

BIBLIOGRAPHY

Ariew, Roger. *Descartes and the Last Scholastics.* Ithaca, N.Y., 1999.

Brockliss, L. W. B. *French Higher Education in the Seventeenth and Eighteenth Centuries: A Cultural History.* Oxford and New York, 1987.

Dear, Peter. *Mersenne and the Learning of the Schools.* Ithaca, N.Y., 1988.

Des Chene, Dennis. *Physiologia: Natural Philosophy in Late Aristotelian and Cartesian Thought.* Ithaca, N.Y., 1996.

Feingold, Mordechai, ed. *Jesuit Science and the Republic of Letters.* Cambridge, Mass., 2003.

ROGER ARIEW

ARMADA, SPANISH. Often called the "Invincible Armada," the Spanish Armada was the invasion fleet launched against England in 1588 by Philip II of Spain. Its defeat left England Protestant, aided the Dutch Revolt, and compounded the tax burden on Spain's strained economy.

In 1585 worsening relations between Philip II of Spain and Elizabeth I of England erupted into war. Elizabeth signed the Treaty of Nonesuch with the Dutch and permitted Sir Francis Drake to maraud in response to a Spanish embargo. Drake surprised Vigo, Spain, in October, then proceeded to the Caribbean and sacked Santo Domingo and Cartagena.

Philip ordered the marquis of Santa Cruz in Lisbon to form an armada of thirty-four ships to pursue and "punish" Drake. He also asked Santa Cruz and the duke of Parma, his commander in the Netherlands, to submit plans for the "Enterprise of England," that is its invasion, for which he asked blessing and money from Pope Sixtus V. Parma thought that 35,000 men might cross in twelve hours with favorable weather and sufficient secrecy. He eventually collected over two hundred barges and eighty coasters.

Santa Cruz prepared a plan that called for some one hundred fifty fighting galleons and ships, six galleasses, forty galleys, and over three hundred other vessels large and small to transport fifty-five thousand infantry and sixteen hundred cavalry, artillery, and supplies. The troops would land in either Wales or Ireland. Considering the plans, Philip decided on a smaller armada. When English land and sea forces responded to its landing force, Parma would invade Kent, overthrow Elizabeth, and establish a Catholic regime.

Santa Cruz assembled at Lisbon nine Portuguese galleons and another three dozen vessels. From Basque ports Juan Martínez de Recalde and Miguel de Oquendo would bring two dozen armed ships. At Cádiz, Pedro de Valdés assembled fifteen armed Indiamen, while another dozen great ships and four galleasses sailed from Italy with Alonso Martínez de Leyva.

Drake attacked Spain in April–May 1587, destroyed over twenty ships in Cádiz Bay, and disrupted coastal shipping. Too late, Santa Cruz sailed in pursuit. Storms pounded him on his return to Lisbon, where he found plans changed. He was to sail forthwith to the Strait of Dover, cover Parma's invasion of England, and deliver six thousand men. Communication between the armada and Parma, who had to be ready, posed an immediate problem. The Armada had no safe port where it might wait. Communication had so far been through Philip. Despite Philip's demands, Santa Cruz did not sail, prevented by damage, shortages, and weather. Ailing, he died 9 February 1588.

THE ARMADA CAMPAIGN

Philip appointed as successor the duke of Medina Sidonia, experienced in naval administration if not at sea. A council of war would assist him. Though reluctant to take command, the duke had the Armada's 130 vessels, 8,000 seamen, and 19,000 infantry to sea by the end of May. Storm struck off Cape Finisterre, forcing the Armada into La Coruña. On 21 July the repaired Armada sailed, reaching the English Channel on 28 July.

Ordered to join Parma and fight only if compelled, the Spaniards expected to find the English fleet in the Narrows. For battle, they would close, grapple, and board. The Armada's sixty fighting ships were big but bulky, loaded with men and stores; their guns were of mixed sizes and quality, and trained shipboard gunners were scarce. The remaining ships were transports or small craft.

Elizabeth's navy, under Lord Admiral Charles Howard of Effingham, with Drake as vice admiral and Martin Frobisher and John Hawkins commanding squadrons, chose not to wait in the Narrows. Over sixty galleons and great ships, and forty smaller, concentrated at Plymouth, leaving some three dozen under Lord Henry Seymour to watch Parma. Aware of the Spaniards' advantage in ship-

Spanish Armada. *The Defeat of the Spanish Armada, 1583: The Fifth Day,* 1739 engraving. The Spanish ships are shown at center, flanked by British ships. THE GRANGER COLLECTION

board infantry, the English hoped to gain the weather gauge and use their handier ships and superior gunnery to avoid boarding and defeat any invasion attempt. When the Armada reached the Channel, Howard put to sea.

Leyva and Recalde urged Medina Sidonia to assault Plymouth. Prompted by Philip's orders and Diego Flores de Valdés, his chief of staff, Medina Sidonia refused and held course. Using the cover of night, the English by daybreak of 31 July gained the weather gauge. The Armada assumed battle formation, with two wings of twenty strong vessels each, and a main force of another three dozen, behind which sailed the transports. Howard and Drake formed two lines and pounded the Armada, doing little damage. But that evening, collisions and an explosion cost the Armada two big ships. Flores de Valdés persuaded Medina Sidonia to abandon them and hold course, a decision that many argued hurt morale and lost a chance for a boarding action.

The Armada kept course the next three days and sparred with the English, who could not break its formation. Lacking news of Parma, Medina Sidonia sought haven in the lee of the Isle of Wight. In a daylong battle on 4 August, the English kept the Armada from its aim and forced it toward Flanders. Late on 6 August the Armada anchored off Calais, to discover that Parma, who only learned on 2 August that the Armada was in the Channel, required several days to embark his army. Parma needed the Armada's protection against both the English and a Dutch blockade. On the night of 7/8 August, Howard sent eight fire ships blazing on breeze and tide toward the Armada, whose captains cut anchor cables and put out in disarray. A galleass grounded. On 8 August the English fleet, nearly 150 in number but with three dozen doing the fighting, attacked, employing their guns at closer range. It was mid-afternoon before the thirty outgunned ships that did the Armada's fighting recovered formation. One ship sank, two galleons beached, and eight hundred men were killed. With shifting winds the Armada cleared the Flemish banks and reached the North Sea. Its commanders agreed to return to Spain around Scotland and Ireland. Many damaged ships wrecked on the Irish coast; others succumbed to storm at sea. Perhaps sixty-five reached Spanish ports, while a few hired Hanseatic hulks returned home. Over half the crews were lost to battle, ship-wreck, and disease. While the English lost no ships, hundreds of seamen perished of sickness.

Elizabeth and the Dutch hailed God's favor, Philip accepted God's punishment, although Flores de Valdés was court-martialed to placate military critics. The Enterprise had too many flaws, while the English wisely counted on gunnery. In 1596 and in 1597 other armadas sailed against England, to be stopped by storm. Peace came only in 1604, after Philip and Elizabeth were dead.

See also **Elizabeth I (England); Medina Sidonia, Alonso Pérez de Guzmán, 7th duke of; Parma, Alexander Farnese, duke of; Philip II (Spain); Santa Cruz, Álvaro de Bazán, first marquis of.**

BIBLIOGRAPHY

Calvar Gross, Jorge, et al. *La Batalla del Mar Océano: Corpus Documental de las hostilidas entre España e Inglaterra (1568–1604).* 3 vols. Madrid, 1988–1993. Documentary background.

Martin, Colin, and Geoffrey Parker. *The Spanish Armada.* Rev. ed. Manchester, U.K., 1999. Best treatment; benefits from the many books and the 1988 symposia on the armada, when the first, lavishly illustrated, edition appeared; updated bibliography.

Mattingly, Garrett. *The Armada.* Boston, 1959. Marvelously written and atmospheric, fine on diplomacy, outdated on ships and battles.

Parker, Geoffrey. *The Grand Strategy of Philip II.* New Haven, 1998. Masterful.

Rodríguez-Salgado, M. J., ed. *Armada, 1588–1988: An International Exhibition to Commemorate the Spanish Armada.* London, 1988. Splendid catalogue of the exhibition at the National Maritime Museum in Greenwich, England.

Rodríguez-Salgado, M. J., and Simon Adams, eds. *England, Spain and the Gran Armada: Essays from the Anglo-Spanish Conferences, London and Madrid, 1988.* Savage, Md., and Edinburgh, 1991.

PETER PIERSON

ARNAULD FAMILY. Three generations of the Arnauld family played significant roles in the political, religious, philosophical, and literary worlds of the seventeenth century. A parliamentary family, they were well-known figures of the *noblesse de robe* ('nobility of the robe'), a class of hereditary nobles in seventeenth- and eighteenth-century France who acquired their rank by holding high state offices. The Arnaulds were prominently associated with Port-Royal des Champs ('Port-Royal of the Fields'), a convent of Cistercian nuns near Versailles, and members of the Jansenist movement. The Jansenists, under the guidance of Jean Duvergier de Hauranne, abbot of Saint-Cyran, constituted the Augustinian current of the Catholic Counter-Reformation, and read the *Augustinus* (1640) of Jansenius, bishop of Ypres, as a faithful translation of Augustinian doctrine.

The first generation was that of Antoine Arnauld (1560–1619), called the "lawyer," who married Catherine Marion. In July 1594, after an assassination attempt against Henry IV, he represented the University of Paris and pleaded against the Jesuits before the Parlement of Paris. A second assassination attempt by Jean Chastel on Henry IV led to the expulsion of the Jesuits from the jurisdiction of the Parlement of Paris in December of that year. The Arnaulds thus became known as important figures in the Parliamentarian and Gallican (Church of France) worlds, both intensely opposed to the influence of the Jesuits, the main instruments of Vatican policy and doctrine in France.

Antoine Arnauld and Catherine Marion had twenty children, of whom ten survived. The eldest of these was Robert Arnauld d'Andilly (1589–1674). Although his political ambitions were dampened by Cardinal Richelieu, he was a prominent figure at court, and much appreciated by Anne of Austria, Louis XIV's mother. After joining the Solitaires (hermits devoted to study) at Port-Royal, he translated the Church Fathers. Alceste, in Molière's *Le misanthrope*, is probably a caricature of this courtier who "preached solitude in the midst of the court" and led a number of influential ladies (Mme. de Longueville, the Princess de Guémené [Louise de Montbazon], Mme. de Sablé, Mme. de Caumartin, and others) to take an interest in the affairs of Port-Royal.

The second child of Antoine Arnauld and Catherine Marion was Catherine (1590–1651), who married Isaac Le Maistre; their sons were to become famous as Solitaires of Port-Royal. The third child, Jacqueline (1591–1661), was to become a famous abbess of Port-Royal under the name of Mère Angélique. It was she who, in 1609, inspired the return of Port-Royal to the strict observance of mo-

nastic discipline. Her sister Jeanne (1593–1671), fifth child and third daughter, also became abbess of Port-Royal, while three other daughters became nuns there. Their brother Henri (1597–1692) became bishop of Angers and played a prominent role in the opposition of the Port-Royalist movement to the obligation, imposed by the archbishop of Paris and the ecclesiastical hierarchy, to sign the formulary, a formal denunciation of the heresy of Jansenius.

The youngest son and twentieth child of Antoine Arnauld was named Antoine (1612–1694). Known as the "great Arnauld," he was the theologian of Port-Royal, a vigorous enemy of the Jesuits, and the philosophical opponent of Malebranche (1638–1715), the Oratorian philosopher. His defense of the Jansenists led to his exclusion from the Faculty of Theology at the Sorbonne, and, thus, indirectly to the campaign of the *Provincial Letters* written by his friend Blaise Pascal (under the pseudonym Montalte) against Jesuit theological and moral doctrines. In 1668, Antoine Arnauld successfully negotiated the "Peace of the Church," a momentary lull in the persecution of Port-Royal, which allowed him and his colleague Pierre Nicole to devote their energies to anti-Protestant controversy.

The death of Mme. de Longueville in 1679, however, brought an end to her protection of the monastery. When Louis XIV let it be known that he planned to put an end to the Jansenist movement, Arnauld and Nicole fled to the Netherlands. Nicole was to negotiate his return a few years later, but Arnauld refused any compromise. He traveled incognito and pursued his writings: religious polemics against the Jesuits and philosophical treatises against Malebranche. Jurieu's violent tract, *L'esprit de M. Arnauld* (1684; The spirit of Mr. Arnauld), had silenced Arnauld in anti-Protestant controversy, but the harm was done, and the Edict of Nantes was revoked the following year. Arnauld died in exile in 1694, and his heart was brought back to Port-Royal des Champs.

The history of the following generation concerns two families: the children of Robert Arnauld d'Andilly and those of Catherine Arnauld by Isaac Le Maistre. Arnauld d'Andilly had ten children, of whom five daughters were to become nuns at Port-Royal. A sixth was raised at the same monastery.

Arnauld Family. *Mother Catherine Agnès Arnauld (Mother Agnès de Saint-Paul) and Sister Catherine of St. Susan,* painting by Philippe de Champaigne, 1622.

The most famous of his daughters was Angélique de Saint-Jean (1624–1684), who became abbess of Port-Royal. His two eldest sons, Antoine (1616–1698), later known as the Abbot Arnauld, and Simon (1618–1699), marquis de Pomponne, were educated by Martin de Barcos, nephew of Saint-Cyran and, like his uncle, abbot at Saint-Cyran. Their father gave marked preference to Simon, who inherited the family estate of Pomponne and became secretary of state for foreign affairs to Louis XIV. He fulfilled his father's political ambitions, played a prominent role in the life of the literary salons, invited Molière to perform his plays in his home, and maintained the allegiance of the Arnauld family to Port-Royal. His brother, the Abbot Arnauld, recorded his disappointment in his *Memoirs,* often published with those of his father. Their two brothers, Charles-Henry de Luzancy (1623–1684) and Jules-Armand de Villeneuve (1634–1657),

were both brought up in the *petites écoles* of Port-Royal, in the company of Jean Racine, the playwright, Pierre Le Pesant de Boisguilbert, the economist, and Pascal's nephew, Étienne Périer.

The five sons of Catherine Arnauld and Isaac Le Maistre all became Solitaires at Port-Royal. Antoine (1608–1658), a prominent attorney, was guided by Saint-Cyran and retired from public life in 1637. His life provides a striking example of the Port-Royalist conception of a life given to religious values, one incompatible with the social values of *honnêteté* ('politeness'). His example was followed by his brothers, Jean Le Maistre de Saint-Elme (c. 1609–c. 1690), Simon Le Maistre de Séricourt (1612–1650), and Charles Le Maistre de Valmont (c. 1614–1652), all of whom remained laymen. Their brother Louis-Isaac Le Maistre de Saci (1613–1684), who had been guided, with his brother Antoine, by Saint-Cyran, became a priest and confessor of Port-Royal in 1649. He inspired the great Port-Royal translation of the Bible and is also well known for his discussion with Pascal on his conception of apologetics: the *Entretien de Pascal avec M. de Sacy* (Pascal's discussion with Mr. de Sacy), in which Augustine provides the solution to the philosophical opposition between Epictetus the Stoic and Montaigne the skeptic.

More than thirty members of the Arnauld family played a role in the history of Port-Royal, and a number of them figured prominently in the political, theological, philosophical, and literary worlds of the seventeenth century; their lives illustrate the profound influence of Port-Royal Augustinianism on French culture in the classical age.

See also **Cartesianism; Henry IV (France); Jansenism; Jesuits; Louis XIV (France); Nantes, Edict of; Pascal, Blaise; Skepticism.**

BIBLIOGRAPHY

"Antoine Arnauld (1612–1694), philosophe, écrivain, théologien." *Chroniques de Port-Royal, 44* (1995).

Lesaulnier, J., and A. McKenna, dir. *Dictionnaire de Port-Royal.* Paris, 2003.

McKenna, A. "Pascal et Épicure: L'intervention de Pierre Bayle dans la controverse entre Antoine Arnauld et le Père Malebranche." *XVIIe siècle, 137* (1982): 421–428.

Moreau, D. *Deux cartésiens: La polémique Arnauld–Malebranche.* Paris, 1999.

Nadler, S. *Arnauld and the Cartesian Philosophy of Ideas.* Manchester, U.K., 1989.

Solère, J.-L. "Tout plaisir rend-il heureux? Une querelle entre Arnauld, Malebranche, and Bayle." *Chroniques de Port-Royal* 44 (1995): 351–380.

ANTONY MCKENNA

ART

This entry includes five subentries:

ART EXHIBITIONS

Italy and France were the countries that primarily fostered the development of public art exhibitions in early modern Europe.

ITALY

Rome: religious exhibitions. Art exhibitions in Rome were always closely tied to religious celebrations. During the first half of the seventeenth century, paintings began to be specially displayed within some churches on saints' feast days. During the Holy Years of 1650, 1675, and 1700, the lay society of the Congregazione Pontificia dei Virtuosi, composed mainly of artists, mounted juried exhibitions of paintings in the portico of their church, the Pantheon. Concurrently, great private collections of Old Master paintings were brought out of palazzi and displayed in church cloisters.

Florence and Rome: academic exhibitions. Art academies were founded in Florence and Rome in the later sixteenth century. In Florence, the Accademia del Disegno (founded 1562) authorized student exhibitions in its statutes of 1563, to be held in the church of the Compagnia di San Luca. In Rome, the Accademia di San Luca (founded 1577, opened 1593) began to hold student shows on St. Luke's Day starting in 1607; beginning in 1621, the academicians themselves also exhibited on that day for the public.

Venice. As in Rome, exhibitions were tied to religious observances. From the later sixteenth century on, paintings were shown on Ascension Day in the Piazza San Marco and the adjoining Piazzetta. Beginning in the late seventeenth century, the Church and Scuola of San Rocco became a focus of painting exhibitions. On the saint's feast day (and probably for a few days afterward), work by mostly contemporary artists was shown, hung on the exterior of the Scuola and adjacent buildings. By 1699 this was an annual event, recognized as a forum for young artists; it is vividly depicted in Canaletto's *The Doge Visiting the Church and Scuola di San Rocco* (c. 1735, National Gallery, London).

FRANCE

The early academy exhibitions. All developments concerning public art exhibitions in France took place in Paris. There, the Royal Academy of

Painting and Sculpture (founded in 1648) was reorganized in the early 1660s under the leadership of Jean-Baptiste Colbert, King Louis XIV's minister. Beginning in 1664, students' submissions for the Rome prize competition could be viewed annually on 25 August—the feast day of Saint Louis and the king's name day. As had been the case earlier in Florence and Rome, the first public art exhibitions in France were of students' work.

In 1667 the academy held its first public display of the academicians' production—a show of contemporary art, as was to develop later in Venice. The exhibition took place within the premises of the Hôtel de Brion and the courtyard of the Palais Royal, of which the *hôtel* was a part. Later academy displays were held in these locales in 1669, 1671, 1673, 1675, 1681, 1683. In 1699 and 1704 the exhibitions were moved to the Grande Galerie of the Louvre. Unlike the short-lived Italian displays, the academy shows usually lasted one to three weeks. Sponsored by the academy—an extension of the monarchy—the exhibitions were sometimes linked to royal events and presided over by royal and official portraits.

The Place Dauphine exhibitions. The economic distress within France at the end of the Sun King's reign put an end to these exhibitions until 1725, but the artistic void was filled in part by exhibitions held in the Place Dauphine and on the adjoining Pont Neuf. These were an outgrowth of Corpus Christi Day processions, when pictures were hung along the processional route (a practice documented from at least 1644). The Place Dauphine/Pont Neuf exhibits were held on the mornings of Corpus Christi Day and the following Thursday (the Octave); they evolved during the eighteenth century from displays of paintings by Old Masters and established academicians to those featuring young painters and women artists, the latter group having been largely excluded from the academy. After the establishment of the salons in 1737, this outdoor exhibition (now called Exposition de la Jeunesse) continued in diminished form until 1788; a final one was held indoors in 1791.

The Duc d'Antin's initiatives. The annual two-morning Place Dauphine shows were felt to be too brief, and a demand arose for more extended public viewing of contemporary art. The Duc d'Antin (superintendent of the king's buildings since 1708)—perhaps in response to a suggestion made by the academy's director, Louis de Boullongne the Younger—used the occasion of the marriage of King Louis XV to Marie Leszczynska in 1725 to mount a ten-day painting exhibition in the Grand Salon (Salon Carré) of the Louvre. The older academicians abstained from this show in deference to young artists recently admitted to the academy. The success of the exhibition led to the competition of 1727, again initiated by the Duc d'Antin. This event was held among academy history painters (the highest class of artists at the academy), and the paintings were placed on easels (an innovation in exhibition history) in another room at the Louvre, the Gallery of Apollo. The paintings remained on public view for almost two months.

The salons. Despite the public success of the Salon Carré show and the crown's purchase of three entries, academy exhibitions lapsed until the following decade. In 1735 the academy, on the election of its new officers, held a small exhibition of paintings by some of its senior professors in the Louvre space. Although closed to the general public, the display was visited by connoisseurs and art lovers, as reported in the *Mercure de France* (June 1735), which appealed for a public academy exhibition, noting that none had been held for a very long time. The next year an even smaller closed exhibition was held in the academy, and the *Mercure* reported "a considerable crowd of collectors" who again were able to gain access. These shows were proof of a widespread desire among academicians to resume exhibitions, and the publicity generated for these shows by the *Mercure,* as well as the publication's strong appeal for public showings, led in 1737 to the initiation of the salon tradition.

The first salon was the initiative of Philibert Orry, director-general of buildings, controller-general of finances, and vice-protector of the academy. It was mounted in the Salon Carré of the Louvre (previously used for the exhibition of 1725), which gave its name to these shows, always held in that space. The salons occurred annually until 1751 (although there were none in 1744 and 1749), thereafter continuing in odd-numbered years. Only members of the academy could display their works at these exhibitions, which always included sculpture, drawings, and engravings as well as paintings.

Art Exhibitions. *Exhibition in the Salon of the Louvre,* 1787, engraving by Pietro Antonio Martini. ©Foto Marburg/Art Resource, N.Y.

Beginning in 1748, a jury of academicians selected the works to be exhibited by majority vote. The first salon was held from 18 August to 1 September; later ones remained open three to six weeks. Access was available to the general public and free of charge, regardless of class, wealth, profession, or gender; the doors to the salon were open from 9 A.M. to the late afternoon. All evidence indicates that the salons were heavily attended throughout the eighteenth century, providing a cultural event of high entertainment value. They were decisive in promoting the rise of a new art-world phenomenon—the freelance journalist-critic. Gabriel-Jacques de Saint-Aubin's etching *View of the Salon* (1753) shows how the paintings being exhibited were closely hung in stacked registers, but it also conveys the public's animation and excitement when attending the salons.

See also **Academies of Art; Florence, Art in; France, Art in; Rome, Art in; Venice, Art in.**

BIBLIOGRAPHY

Aulanier, Christiane. *Le Salon Carré.* Vol. 2 of *Histoire du Palais et du Musée du Louvre.* Paris, 1950. See pp. 19–39.

Bellier de la Chavignerie, Émile. "Notes pour servir à l'histoire de l'Exposition de la Jeunesse." *Revue universelle des arts* 19 (1864): 38–67.

Berger, Robert W. *Public Access to Art in Paris: A Documentary History from the Middle Ages to 1800.* University Park, Pa., 1999. See chapters 5, 11, and 12.

Clements, Candace. "The Duc d'Antin, the Royal Administration of Pictures, and the Painting Competition of 1727." *Art Bulletin* 78 (1996): 647–662.

Crow, Thomas E. *Painters and Public Life in Eighteenth-Century Paris.* New Haven and London, 1985.

Diderot, Denis. *Diderot on Art. Vol. 1: The Salon of 1765 and Notes on Painting.* Edited and translated by John Goodman. New Haven and London, 1995. Introduction by Thomas E. Crow, with information on the salons, pp. ix–xix.

———. *Salons.* Edited by Jean Seznec and Jean Adhémar. 2nd ed. Vol. 1. Oxford 1975. Discussion of the salons by Seznec and Adhémar on pp. 8–15.

Dorbec, Prosper. "L'exposition de la Jeunesse au XVIIIe siècle." *Gazette des beaux-arts ser.* 3, 33 (1905): 456–470, 34 (1905): 77–86.

Fontaine, André. *Les collections de l'Académie royale de peinture et de sculpture.* Paris, 1910, pp. 43–51.

Guiffrey, Jules. "Notes sur les salons du XVIIIe siècle (1673–1800)." In *Table générale des artistes ayant exposé aux salons du XVIIIe siècle.* Paris, 1873.

Haskell, Francis. "Art Exhibitions in XVII Century Rome." *Studi secenteschi* 1 (1960): 107–121.

———. *Patrons and Painters.* Revised ed. New Haven and London, 1980.

Haskell, Francis, and Michael Levey. "Art Exhibitions in 18th-Century Venice." *Arte veneta* 12 (1958): 179–185.

Koch, Georg Friedrich. *Die Kunstausstellung.* Berlin, 1967. See pp. 127–183.

Loire, Stéphane. "Le salon de 1673." *Bulletin de la société de l'histoire de l'art français* (1992): 31–38.

Marcel, Pierre. "Notes sur les 6 expositions du règne de Louis XIV." *Chronique de l'art et de la curiosité* Nos. 1, 2 (1904): 10–13, 19–20.

Rosenberg, Pierre. "Le concours de peinture de 1727." *Revue de l'art* no. 37 (1977): 29–42.

Wildenstein, Georges. *Le salon de 1725.* Paris, 1924.

Wrigley, Richard. *The Origins of French Art Criticism: From the Ancien Régime to the Restoration.* Oxford and New York, 1993.

ROBERT W. BERGER

THE ART MARKET AND COLLECTING

The art market and art collecting, while distinct phenomena, are closely interlinked in the early modern period. The fourteenth through the eighteenth centuries witnessed the creation of a number of social institutions related to both, including the professionalization of art critics and art dealers, an international art market, large-scale private collections, and the first institutional museums.

THE ART MARKET

The art market, as distinct from art patronage, involves the sale (or resale) and distribution of works of art—including but not limited to antiquities, paintings, sculpture, tapestries, works on paper, ceramics, and metalwork—independent of direct commissions. The nascent early modern art market operated alongside a preexisting patronage system, with the result that many artists produced works both by contract and speculatively, in anticipation of future sales. Similarly, many early modern collections held works acquired by a variety of means, including direct commission, market purchase, inheritance, and as gifts.

The rise of humanism in the late fourteenth century, with its strong emphasis on the revival of classical culture, was a spur to the creation of an art market. Princes, prelates, and scholars avidly collected antique statues, architectural fragments, coins, and other Roman or Greek artifacts. As demand for such objects increased, a class of brokers and dealers arose to facilitate acquisition. The rapid rise in prices for antiquities in the fifteenth century attests to the establishment of effective market mechanisms. Humanism also facilitated the growth of a market for contemporary works of art. Historical and critical literature based on classical models, beginning with Petrarch and Boccaccio, praised artists such as Giotto di Bondone or Simone Martini on stylistic grounds, promoting an interest in individual artistic personalities and a desire to own works by celebrated artists. In turn this led to the practice of signing works or employing signature styles or techniques. More specialized books on art, such as *De pictura* (1435; On painting) by architect Leon Battista Alberti (1404–1472) or *Lives of the Most Eminent Painters, Sculptors, and Architects* (commonly referred to as *Lives of the Artists*; 1550) by painter Giorgio Vasari (1511–1574), addressed the needs and interests of collectors and amateurs at least as much as they did professional artists.

In the north, the fifteenth-century Burgundian court provided a similar impetus for the production, sale, and collection of works of art. The Burgundians, especially under Dukes Philip the Good (1396–1467) and Charles the Bold (1433–1477), set a standard of magnificence and splendor for all of Europe. Courtiers, diplomats, merchants, and bankers who wished to participate effectively at court were obliged to become patrons of its material culture. The high nobility particularly favored tapestries, precious metalwork, illuminated manuscripts, and jewelry. For others, painting was a more affordable option. It is noteworthy that court artist Jan van Eyck appears to have produced paintings only for middle-class clients, with Philip the Good requiring his services for more ephemeral projects.

The Art Market and Collecting. *The Signboard of Gersaint,* by Jean Antoine Watteau, 1720. E. F. Gersaint was a Parisian art dealer and a friend of Watteau; the latter painted this view of the interior of Gersaint's shop for use as a signboard. ©ERICH LESSING/ART RESOURCE, N.Y.

Although the art market often deals in elite objects produced or procured for an elite clientele, it also encompassed more prosaic and functional objects. Antwerp, a major artistic center during the sixteenth century, already had in the late fifteenth century an established site (Our Lady Pand convent) for the sale of ready-made devotional and liturgical paintings and sculpture. Annual fairs, especially the Frankfurt book fair for works on paper, offered another venue for artists to hawk their wares. Paintings, tapestries, and illuminated books formed a substantial component of luxury goods produced in Bruges, Antwerp, Brussels, and Amsterdam for the export market. Such objects were distributed as far away as Turkey, India, and New Spain.

Artists producing works for the market inevitably attempted to secure market niches through specialization, which could take different forms. One approach was to create works to be sold to clients of different means. Thus seventeenth-century Dutch artist Jan van Goyen (1596–1656) developed a technique for quickly producing landscape paintings that could then be sold at comparatively low prices. Countrymen such as Gerrit Dou (1613–1675) or Jan Vermeer (1632–1675) commanded the art market's highest prices for their very finely crafted paintings. Dou is an interesting case in this regard. Through the royal agent Pieter Spiering, Dou was affiliated with the Swedish crown. He continued to produce paintings speculatively, but received an annual stipend from Sweden for the right of first refusal. At the end of the seventeenth century, painter Adriaen van der Werff (1659–1722) stood in a similar relationship to the Düsseldorf court. Another competitive strategy was specialization in subject matter. From the mid-sixteenth century onward, artists throughout Europe developed reputations as practitioners of individual genres. Their areas of specialization could be highly particularized. The painter Pieter Aertsen (1508–1575) for example, was renowned for his paintings of kitchen interiors, while Dutch artist Paulus Potter (1625–1654) concentrated on landscape scenes with cattle.

By the end of the seventeenth century, professional art dealers appeared to cater to the needs of a diverse range of clientele, especially in Paris. There the *marchands-merciers* offered paintings, sculpture, tapestries, and furniture for sale. One dealer, Edmé-François Gersaint (1694–1750), brought the sale of art to a form recognizably similar to the modern market through the publication of sales catalogues and catalogues raisonnés for individual artists. The shop sign that Antoine Watteau (1684–1721) painted in 1720 for Gersaint shows the range of art works and clients to be found in such establishments.

ART COLLECTING

The phenomenon of art collecting had diverse origins. Medieval churches and monasteries accumulated considerable numbers of sculpture, paintings, metalwork, and jewelry. As indicated in the accounts of Abbot Suger (c. 1081–1151), these objects were prized for their aesthetic qualities as well as their functionality. Princely houses in the late medieval period also assembled vast collections of artworks, including tapestries, paintings, metalwork, armor, and jewelry. Until the sixteenth century, most of these artifacts were either in daily use within the household or held in the treasure rooms as items of sumptuous display that could also be converted into ready cash should the need arise. The market for antiquities spurred by humanism, mentioned above, provided another stimulus to the collecting of art.

During the fifteenth and sixteenth centuries, an international court culture promulgated art collecting as an index of political, economic, and cultural status. The sumptuous visual culture of the Burgundian courts set a model for the rest of Europe. The Medici in Florence placed more specific emphasis on the collection of paintings, while Pope Julius II (reigned 1503–1513) commissioned works on a virtually unprecedented scale, from masters such as Bramante, Michelangelo, and Raphael. Humanist culture also promoted an ethos of collecting. The new practices of historical archaeology and philology respectively encouraged gathering classical statuary and coins (valued especially for their inscriptions).

The primary type of collection in the sixteenth and seventeenth centuries was the *Wunderkammer* (cabinet of curiosities) in northern Europe, known as the *studiolo* in Italy. These early collections contained a diverse range of objects, including *natu-*

ralia ('natural objects'), *artificialia* ('things made by human hands'), *technologia* ('mechanical devices'), and *mirabilia* ('wondrous or monstrous things'). They contained objects gathered from the farthest reaches of the globe and aspired to the representation of the world at large. Works of art served a variety of functions within the curiosity cabinet since they could represent the myriad things of the natural and human worlds and could also provide aesthetic pleasure through their supreme craftsmanship. As microcosms, these collections, especially those of princes, were simultaneously displays of wealth and erudition, active research laboratories, sites for constructing familial, institutional, or state histories, and repositories of practical technologies. The curiosity cabinet was thus the ancestor of the modern museums of art, natural history, history, and technology. Both the Habsburg collections in Vienna and the Romanov collections in St. Petersburg were converted in the nineteenth century into modern institutional museum complexes.

See also **Aristocracy and Gentry; Art: Artistic Patronage; Class, Status, and Order; Habsburg Dynasty: Austria; Marvels and Wonders; Museums; Romanov Dynasty (Russia).**

BIBLIOGRAPHY

Alsop, Joseph. *The Rare Art Traditions: The History of Art Collecting and Its Linked Phenomena Wherever These Have Appeared.* New York, 1982.

Campbell, Lorne. "The Art Market in the Southern Netherlands in the 15th Century." *Burlington Magazine* 118 (1976): 188–198.

Impey, Oliver, and Arthur MacGregor, eds. *The Origins of Museums: The Cabinet of Curiosities in Sixteenth- and Seventeenth-Century Europe.* Oxford and New York, 1985.

Montias, John Michael. *Artists and Artisans in Delft: A Socio-Economic Study of the Seventeenth Century.* Princeton, 1982.

North, Michael, and David Ormrod, eds. *Art Markets in Europe, 1400–1800.* Aldershot, U.K., and Brookfield, Vt., 1998.

Pomian, Krzysztof. *Collectors & Curiosities: Paris and Venice, 1500–1800.* Cambridge, U.K., and Cambridge, Mass., 1990.

Smith, Pamela H., and Paula Findlen. *Merchants & Marvels: Commerce, Science, and Art in Early Modern Europe.* New York, 2002.

MARK A. MEADOW

ART THEORY, CRITICISM, AND HISTORIOGRAPHY

Questions that remain relevant and disputed today in art history and theory were first explored at length during the early modern period: What is art? How do images communicate differently from words? What is artistic genius? How does art originate in and reveal an artist's character? How does art change with time and place? How does art reflect society and construct its collective identity? How does one date and attribute paintings?

SOURCES

In 1924 Julius von Schlosser published the bibliographic bible on the literature of art from antiquity to the nineteenth century: *Die Kunstliteratur*. It was not the first free-standing bibliography—that honor goes to Angelo Comolli (1788–1792)—nor was it the oldest published bibliography (Antonio Possevino, 1593). (Full references to source material in this entry can be found in Schlosser.) But it became the definitive one, especially after its updating by Otto Kurz for the third Italian edition in 1964, *La letteratura artistica*. Since then, many early modern manuscripts and pamphlets on art have been discovered and published; many fewer books devoted to art have been rediscovered. However, none have the canonical status of the books listed by Schlosser. Schlosser was more than a diligent bibliographer; his greatest contribution was a judicious analysis of the content of individual works and the historical development of the genre generally.

New approaches require some revision of Schlosser's ideas. Reader-response theory encouraged the study of marginalia, where the reader objects to the text with telegraphic comments, as did the Carracci, Federico Zuccaro, and Sebastiano Resta in their copies of Giorgio Vasari's *Vite* (Perini). Focused reception histories of individual texts have been analyzed (Sohm; Grassman), as has the literary reception of individual paintings (Colantuono). Studies on language have been particularly fruitful: on rhetoric, poetics, and art theory (Lee; Baxandall; Summers; Sohm), and on biography as art criticism (Barolsky). Older histories of ideas (Panofsky) have been revised by important studies on the social contexts of art literature (Crow; Cropper; Goldberg; Wrigley; Ames-Lewis) and the production of theory in the academies (Montagu; Goldstein; Barzman).

Still the most essential category of scholarship is the author-based monograph, and here the advances are particularly impressive even when limited to the English language (Brusati; Cropper; Gibson-Wood; Melion; Muller; Puttfarken; Summerscale; Vries; Warwick).

Schlosser's categories of art literature are: (1) historical and biographical, (2) theoretical and technical, and (3) topographic. Because he established these on the basis of Renaissance art literature, new early modern forms and topics of art writing are often submerged in inappropriate categories, having no other place. The connoisseur's manual, for example, is a mix of the historical, technical, and theoretical. It was first essayed by Giulio Mancini (c. 1617–1621), a physician who autopsied painting surfaces (*craquelure*, varnish, brushwork) much as he did bodies in his medical practice. Although not published until 1956, the manuscript was widely circulated in the seventeenth century as an indispensable guide for art collectors and led eventually to Jonathan Richardson's famous *Connoisseur* (1719). Another new genre was the institutional history of art academies, starting with Romano Alberti's history and lecture synopses from the Accademia di San Luca (1599) and continued by Henri Testelin (1648–1664, Académie Royale de Peinture et Sculpture) and Giampietro Zanotti (1739, Accademia Clementina). The art dictionary originated with Filippo Baldinucci, whose *Vocabolario Toscano dell'arte del disegno* (1681) responded to an expanding, nonprofessional readership of art books. Baldinucci's served as the model for later dictionaries by Roger de Piles (in Charles-Alphonse Dufresnoy, 1667), Jacques Lacombe (1752), A. Pernety (1757), Claude Henri de Watelet (1792), and Francesco Milizia (1797). The biographical dictionary started by Pellegrino Antonio Orlandi in 1704, *Abecedario pittorico* (Pictorial primer), saw many editions and proved in its brevity and alphabetic order to be a format that survives today.

NATIONAL AND CHRONOLOGICAL TRENDS

Using Schlosser's categories and bibliography (but excluding books not devoted entirely or mostly to art), it is interesting to delineate the changing contours of published art literature between 1550, when Vasari first published his *Vite de' pittori*, *scultori ed architetti* (Lives of the painters, sculptors and architects), and 1752, when Johann Joachim Winckelmann's new nonbiographical historiography was published as *Gedanken über die Nachahmung der griechischen Werke* (Reflections on the imitation of Greek works in painting and sculpture).

Italian writers dominated art literature of all kinds and at all times. In terms of artistic practice, Italy's hegemony in Europe began to erode in the mid-seventeenth century; and by the eighteenth century, it was on its way to becoming a cultural backwater, renowned more for its illustrious past than its modern production. In terms of art literature, however, Italy held its ground between 1650 and 1750 because it remained Europe's art center by virtue of its antiquities and Renaissance Old Masters. European artists and amateurs generally made pilgrimages to Italy and even learned Italian.

There was a steady rise in the number of publications between 1550 and 1650, and a sustained explosion thereafter. Art books published outside of Italy before 1650 were, by comparison, few. In France the watershed year, especially in the category of theory, was 1648 when the Académie Royale de Peinture et Sculpture was founded. Germany and England did not become publishing centers until the eighteenth century; Spain produced few art books throughout the early modern period.

Distribution patterns within the categories can also be observed. Whereas the Italians produced roughly the same number of books on theory and history/biography, in France theory overwhelmed history by more than 3:1. This is not simply the result of having fewer historical works of international importance to write about since the ratio in England was 2:1, and for Germany and England it was even less (3:2). Instead, it is a true measure of French interests and achievements in theory (Dufresnoy; Chambray; De Piles). It is not until the eighteenth century that German and English books with a comparable international audience were published. In only one area, not separated by Schlosser as a separate category, were the French, Germans, and English at a par with or even more productive than the Italians: books on artistic techniques, either instructional manuals, drawing pattern books, or historical accounts (Italy: 8; Germany: 7; France: 5; England: 12).

Italy was the greatest exporter of texts by virtue of its famous Renaissance backlist. Leonardo's notebooks appeared in translation in Paris (1651), Nuremberg (1724 and 1747), and Leipzig (1751). Pomponio Gaurico's treatise on sculpture appeared in Antwerp (1609), Leiden (1701), and Strasbourg (1622). Ludovico Dolce's treatise on painting appeared in Amsterdam (1756), Berlin (1757), and London (1770). Books by Benedetto Varchi, Vasari, Giovanni Paolo Lomazzo, Gabriele Paleotti, Resta, and Giovanni Michele Silos each received one or two translations. Just as Italy provided European artists with the "great works" from antiquity to the Renaissance masters, so too did Italian become the lingua franca of the art community. Italian art terminology survives even today in many languages: sfumato, chiaroscuro, fresco, contrapposto. The dominant form of art history (biography and periodized chronology) can also be traced back to Vasari's seminal *Lives*.

By comparison, the Italians were late and seemingly reluctant importers of foreign texts in translation: Dufresnoy (1713 and 1776), Charles Le Brun (1753), André Félibien (1755), De Piles (1769 and 1771), William Hogarth (1771), Sir Joshua Reynolds (1778), and Watelet (1777). The fact that virtually all these translations appeared after 1750 and frequently included seventeenth-century texts as part of a catch-up phase suggests how late it was when Italy reached parity with other European countries in terms of receptivity to international literary culture. A related measure revealing national taste concerns the frequency of reprinted or translated texts compared to original editions. In Italy the ratio was 5:1 (two hundred original texts; forty reprints or translations). In France it was 3:2. The reverse held true for Germany and England where reprints and translations outnumbered original texts by 4:3. Many Italian reprints cluster in the 1730s—Leonardo, 1733; Rafaelle Borghini, 1730; Benvenuto Cellini, 1728 and 1731; Dolce, 1735; Giovanni Baglione, 1733, 1739, and 1743; Giovanni Pietro Bellori, 1728 and 1732—and mark an important moment of historicizing consciousness that also resulted in the reevaluations of Gothic and quattrocento art. The first book of artists' letters was published shortly thereafter by Giovanni Gaetano Bottari (1754) as a source primer for art history.

There is one final epidemiological curiosity: The most frequently translated text was Dufresnoy's *De arte graphica* (The art of painting; 1667, Paris), with translations into French (1673, 1684, 1688, 1751, and 1760), English (1695, 1716, 1728, 1750, and 1754), German (1699 and 1731), Italian (1713 and 1776), and Dutch (1733). No single explanation can account for this. Most art books, when not written by or for theologians, tended to be in the vernacular, and by the late seventeenth century art literature in Latin had become a rarity. Despite its secular content, a powerful mix of literary and artistic theories, *De arte graphica* was written in Latin as part of Dufresnoy's homage to Horace's *Ars poetica* (Art of poetry).

HISTORY AND BIOGRAPHY

Giorgio Vasari, the father of art history, wrote the first universal history of art from Egypt to his own time. It skimmed over the Middle Ages and mentioned non-Italian artists only if they visited Italy, but it remained the definitive work until Baldinucci expanded it (1681–1728) into a pan-European version. By the late sixteenth century when updates to Vasari began to be published (Borghini, 1584; Mancini, c. 1617; Baglione, 1642; Giovanni Battista Passeri, c. 1673), Vasari became a "modern Pliny." He achieved canonical status for art writers in much the same way that his heroes, Michelangelo and Raphael, became the new ancients. Of the Italian Renaissance artists heroized by Vasari, only Correggio was "rediscovered" between 1550 and 1800. Many Italian art writers expressed irritation at Vasari's pro-Florentine stance, part of a Medicean strategy of cultural hegemony; after the next edition of Vasari appeared in print in 1647, many responded by writing alternative regional histories (Carlo Ridolfi, 1648; Marco Boschini, 1660; Carlo Cesare Malvasia, 1678; Raffaele Soprani, 1674). Outside of Italy, biographers like Karel van Mander (1604), Félibien (1666–1688), Joachim von Sandrart (1675), and Aglionby (1685) adapted Vasari's narratives and critical language in discussing the work of their native artists. Like their Italian counterparts, they remained ambivalent toward Vasari, poised between emulation and antagonism. Van Mander became the Vasari of the Netherlands, not just because he translated parts of Vasari into Dutch and used Vasari's template of artists' lives to write about Dutch and Flemish artists, but also because

his *Schilder-Boeck* (1604) became the seminal text for most later art literature in the Netherlands from Philip Angel (1642) to Arnold Houbraken (1718).

Art history originated as biography and dominated its practice for two centuries, a fact traditionally lamented by modernists, but as a historiographic genre, biography helped explain why painters painted the way they did by rendering an account of training, character, and circles of influence. Modernists have also overlooked the powerful developmental model that Vasari included in his three prefaces, each explaining the artistic characteristics and causes of the three ages of modern art (trecento, quattrocento, cinquecento). For Vasari, Mancini, and others, the stages of human life provided the pattern of the "birth, growth and death" of art. Early modern art literature is full of repeated patterns explained by metempsychosis, ontology, and human psychology. Historical recurrence gave history a structure and tied the past and present together in meaningful ways. The Renaissance was a new Antiquity, mannerism a new Gothic, baroque a new mannerism. Similarly, artists were often reborn masters: Michelangelo was a new Parrhasios, Bernini a new Michelangelo, Raphael a new Apelles, Guido Reni a new Raphael, Tiepolo a new Veronese.

Ancient art and its historical development shadowed discussions of early modern art. Just as artists advocated the study of antiquity as a means to achieve artistic excellence, so too did art writers develop their aesthetic, linguistic, and historical ideas from ancient literature, notably Pliny, Vitruvius, Lucian, Cicero, Quintilian, and various other rhetoricians. Vasari appended Giambattista Adriani's history of ancient art to his *Lives* as an orienting preface. All later histories of ancient art made reference to modern art: Felipe de Guevara (late sixteenth century), Franciscus Junius (1637), Carlo Dati (1667), and Winckelmann (1764). Winckelmann's seminal *The History of Ancient Art*, commonly described as the first nonbiographical book on art history, can also be read as a critique of baroque art.

THEORY AND PRACTICE

The Accademia della Crusca, a Florentine literary academy that published the first standard Italian dictionary in 1612, defined theory as "the speculative science that gives rules to practice and restores reason to working." The priority of theory over practice, or, as Leonardo da Vinci had put it, of "mental discourse" over "manual operation," helped artists redefine their activities as a noble endeavor, thus taking art out of the workshop and into the academy, transforming it from a mechanical trade into a liberal art. It is no coincidence that Vasari wrote the first art historical account and at the same time helped found the first art academy (the Accademia del Disegno), both under the sponsorship of Cosimo I de' Medici. Although Leon Battista Alberti (1432) first set the agenda of painting as a liberal art requiring knowledge of geometry, optics, history, and poetry, there was still some resistance to this idea when Vasari tried to institutionalize such a curriculum for artists in 1563. Vincenzio Borghini, a philologist and Cosimo's representative at the Accademia, wanted it to be "an academy of making things not thinking about them." He was on the losing side. Academies were founded in Rome (1577), Paris (1648), Berlin (1697), Bologna (1709), Madrid (1744), Copenhagen (1754), St. Petersburg (1757), and London (1768). Despite the Accademia della Crusca definition, practice did not passively receive its rules from theory. Michelangelo, who was often taken as the embodiment of theory in practice, rejected literary discourse in favor of practice. Theory is contained in practice.

The aspirations and claims of artists to be humanists were not realized in the form of their writing. Theory and other forms of art writing in Italy tended to be the preserve of theologians, physicians, philologists, and other humanists. During the sixteenth century, artists wrote only 30 percent of published books on art. In the seventeenth century this shrank to 24 percent, and in the eighteenth century a mere 11 percent of art books were written by artists. (We have not compiled comparable figures for the rest of Europe.) During the seventeenth century, there arose writers who fit neither category: amateur painters who wrote about art (Malvasia, Baldinucci, De Piles, Resta).

GRAVITATION OF ART THEORY TOWARD TWO COMPLEX ISSUES

(1) What relation should art have to nature? If art should improve upon natural appearance (the view of the majority), should the changes enhance beauty or expression? Should the changes be based on a scientific method, on the imitation of ancient art and the Old Masters, or on a platonic Christian or personal ideal? These questions permeate most discussions on art, but some writers adopted them as their primary subject. Federico Zuccaro (1607), Giovanni Battista Agucchi (c. 1615), Fréart de Chambray (1664), and Bellori (1672) provided influential answers from the idealist point of view during the seventeenth century.

(2) Can great art be taught, or is it impervious to reason and rules? Academic curricula and writers on theory and technique invested themselves in an epistemology that favored objective standards of art production (Armenini; Le Brun). Creativity as a divine or innate spark was never denied, but being uncontrollable and ineffable, it was less subject to verbal scrutiny. De Piles's tenure as director of the French Académie (1699) initiated a phase that was more attentive to problems of sense perception and subjectivity. Jean-Baptiste Du Bos (1710) made an equally compelling argument for sentiment in painting and poetry to the Académie Royale des Inscriptions et Belles Lettres. This can be seen as a turning point away from Le Brun's emphasis as Académie director on art as instruction. Coloring, traditionally devalued as decorative or as a sensual appeal to the ignorant, was elevated almost to an intellectual par with the concepts of design and drawing.

EKPHRASIS

Ekphrasis originated in ancient rhetoric as a form of description, vividly detailing an event in order to persuade an audience of its truth. Philostratus and Lucian adopted the technique to describe paintings. Art books were not illustrated with reproductive prints until the late seventeenth century (Carla Patin, 1691), despite the earlier practice of illustrating instructional manuals (Giacomo Franco; Odoardo Fialetti), archaeological books (Bellori), and art theories in which visual systems of lighting and composition were diagrammed (Félibien; Giovanni Battista Volpato, c. 1685; Gérard de Lairesse, 1707; Baldassare Orsini, 1784). For analyses of existing paintings, however, verbal descriptions were essential. Vasari's *ekphrases* tended to be prosopopoeic, that is, he assumed a transparency of representation so that describing what one sees through a picture frame was much the same as describing a scene through a window frame. In the seventeenth century editorial comments about some artifice (impasto or foreshortening, for example) began to appear more often within the description itself. Bellori experimented with new forms of verbal description whose structure and syntax systematically move the reader through a visual grid. Poussin approved of this method because it resembled the visual strategy that he had proposed to Chantelou for "reading" his *Fall of the Manna*. Also in the seventeenth century, books of *ekphrases* began to appear describing real and sometimes imaginary paintings and statues (Giambattista Marino, 1619; Georges de Scudéry, 1646; Silos, 1673). The ekphrastic book and the systematic descriptions of Bellori and the French academicians led to a new type of art catalogue, the *salon livret*.

ART CRITICISM

Art criticism was an early modern invention that originated within the intricacies of the older genres of biography, theory, and ekphrasis. The self-proclaimed objectivity of theory and the historical perspective of biography yielded in art criticism to the immediate, subjective response of an individual viewer in front of a particular painting. Vasari wanted to separate the "good, better and best," and the impulse to rank into hierarchies was deeply embedded in all critical practices. Is French painting superior to Italian? Is Poussin better than Rubens? Is modern art superior to ancient art? These divisive debates, like most forms of combative behavior, signaled political and personal allegiances as often as coherent philosophical positions.

A belief in objective standards dominated most early modern art criticism to the extent that Roger de Piles and Francesco Algarotti could write up report cards assigning numerical grades to the great masters, using the conventional categories of design, composition, coloring, and expression (Table 1). Other fixed hierarchies can be found in Jean Baptiste de Boyer's comparison of French and Italian painters, in the ranking of pictorial genres, and in the prize systems at the Académie Royale de Peinture et de Sculpture (Paris) and the Accademia di San Luca (Rome). Nevertheless, guardians of artistic beauty during the seventeenth century felt that "each painter introduces precepts according to

TABLE 1

Roger de Piles, "La balance des peintres," in *Cours de peinture par principes,* Paris, 1708.

Names of Painters	Composition	Design and Drawing	Coloring	Expression
Albrecht Dürer	8	10	10	8
Andrea del Sarto	12	16	9	8
Jacopo Bassano	6	8	17	0
Giovanni Bellini	4	6	14	0
Ch. Le Brun	16	16	8	16
The Carracci	15	17	13	13
Correggio	13	13	15	12
Domenichino	15	17	9	17
Giorgione	8	9	18	4
Guercino	18	10	10	4
Guido Reni		13	9	12
Holbein	9	10	16	13
Luca Giordano	13	12	9	6
Cesare d'Arpino	10	10	6	2
Giulio Romano	15	16	4	14
Lanfranco	14	13	10	5
Leonardo	15	16	4	14
Lucas van Leyden	8	6	6	4
Michelangelo	8	17	4	8
Caravaggio	6	6	16	0
Palma Vecchio	5	6	16	0
Parmigianino	10	15	6	6
Paolo Veronese	15	10	16	3
Perino del Vaga	15	16	7	6
Pietro da Cortona	16	14	12	6
Perugino	4	12	10	4
Poussin	15	14	7	10
Raphael	17	18	12	18
Rembrandt	15	6	17	12
Rubens	18	13	17	17
Franc. Salviati	13	15	8	8
Le Sueur	15	15	4	15
Tintoretto	15	14	16	4
Titian	12	15	18	6
Van Dyck	15	10	17	13
Federico Zuccaro	10	13	8	8

his own genius" (Passeri), thereby "infecting painting . . . with many artistic heresies" (Agucchi).

If one wanted to arbitrarily establish a birthdate for art criticism as an independent literary genre, it would be in the lectures given by artists and amateurs at the Académie Royale de Peinture et Sculpture in the mid-seventeenth century. Individual paintings from the royal collection were brought before an assembly of academicians to be critiqued by a lead interpreter and then challenged by the audience; Félibien and Testelin published accounts of the proceedings in 1668 and 1680. Books and pamphlets on a single work or cycle of paintings predate Le Brun's lecture of 1667 on Poussin's *Fall of the Manna:* Francesco Bocchi (1584), Genari (1632), and Malvasia (1652). In its prissy presumption of an individual response—the writer's response—Le Brun's fastidious explanation may seem far removed from Diderot's overtly politicized and moralizing discourse, but they share an academic context (the conferences and salons), a tendency to judge paintings as dramatic performances, and a concentration on individual paintings. As an outgrowth of in camera debates, starting in 1737, the Académie's salons were open to public scrutiny and thus initiated a new literary form: exhibition review pamphlets and articles.

Amateurs helped to advance the description of the emotional pleasures of art by writing in an accessible vernacular and relying on intuition. As public access to the art world broadened, the preserve of art authorities began to erode and with it a certain civility. In 1650 art discourse was relatively discreet, even polite; by 1750, especially in Paris, it had become contentious, vindictive in tone, and given to ad hominem attacks. One salon critic regarded art criticism in the 1750s as nothing other than a venting of "malignities." La Font de Saint-Yenne's review of the 1747 salon garnered greater notoriety than any painting in the salon itself and generated more rebuttals than all preceding salon publications (in total, thirty-three articles and pamphlets). In all these aspects—a demotic language of argot, sexual puns, and sensory evocations as well as opinionated attacks—the anomalous barcarole by Boschini (1660) anticipated such later developments.

See also **Academies of Art; Carracci Family; Diderot, Denis; Vasari, Giorgio; Winckelmann, Johann Joachim.**

BIBLIOGRAPHY

Primary Sources

Baldinucci, Filippo. *The Life of Bernini.* Translated by Catherine Enggass. University Park, Pa., 1966. Translation of *Vita del Cavaliere Gio: Lorenzo Bernino scultore, architetto e pittore* (1682).

Bauer, George ed. *Bernini in Perspective.* Englewood Cliffs, N.J., 1976.

Bellori, Giovanni Pietro. *Lives of Annibale and Agostino Carracci.* Translated by Catherine Enggass. University Park, Pa., 1968. Translation of chapter from *Le vite de' pittori, scultori et architetti moderni* (1672).

Condivi, Ascanio. *The Life of Michelangelo.* Translated by Alice Wohl. London, 1976. Translation of *Vita di Michelangelo Buonarroti* (1553).

Enggass, Robert, and Jonathan Brown, eds. *Italy and Spain, 1600–1750: Sources and Documents.* Englewood Cliffs, N.J., 1970.

Klein, Robert, and Henri Zerner, eds. *Italian Art, 1500–1600: Sources and Documents,* Englewood Cliffs, N.J., 1966.

Van Mander, Karel. *The Lives of the Illustrious Netherlandish and German Painters.* 6 vols. Translated by Hessel Miedema. Doornspijk, The Netherlands, 1994–1999. Translation of the *Schilder-boeck,* 2nd ed. (1616–1618).

Vasari, Giorgio. *Lives of the Most Eminent Painters, Sculptors and Architects.* Translated by G. de Vere. London, 1912 (with reprints in 1927 and 1996). Translation of *Le vite de' più eccellenti pittori, scultori e architettori* (1568).

Veliz, Zahira, ed. and trans. *Artists' Techniques in Golden Age Spain: Six Treatises in Translation.* Cambridge, U.K., and New York, 1986.

Winckelmann, Johann Joachim. *The History of Ancient Art.* Translated by A. Gode. New York, 1968. Translation of *Geschichte der Kunst des Altertums* (1764).

———. *Reflections on the Imitation of Greek Works in Painting and Sculpture.* Translated by Elfriede Heyer and Roger C. Norton. La Salle, Ill., 1987. Translation of *Gedanken über die Nachahmung der griechischen Werke in der Malerei und Bildhauerkunst* (1755).

Secondary Sources

Barolsky, Paul. *Michelangelo's Nose: A Myth and Its Maker.* University Park, Pa., 1990.

———. *Why Mona Lisa Smiles and Other Tales by Vasari.* University Park, Pa., 1991.

Baxandall, Michael. *Giotto and the Orators: Humanist Observers of Painting in Italy and the Discovery of Pictorial Composition, 1350–1450.* Oxford, 1971.

Brusati, Celeste. *Artifice and Illusion: The Art and Writing of Samuel van Hoogstraten.* Chicago, 1995.

Colantuono, Anthony. *Guido Reni's Abduction of Helen: The Politics and Rhetoric of Painting in Seventeenth-Century Europe.* Cambridge, U.K., and New York, 1997.

Cropper, Elizabeth. *The Ideal of Painting: Pietro Testa's Düsseldorf Notebook.* Princeton, 1984.

Crow, Thomas E. *Painters and Public Life in Eighteenth-Century Paris.* New Haven, 1985.

Gibson-Wood, Carol. *Jonathan Richardson: Art Theorist of the English Enlightenment.* New Haven, 2000.

Goldberg, Edward. *After Vasari: History, Art, and Patronage in Late Medici Florence.* Princeton, 1988.

Lichtenstein, Jacqueline. *The Eloquence of Color: Rhetoric and Painting in the French Classical Age.* Translated by Emily McVarish. Berkeley and Los Angeles, 1993.

Melion, Walter. *Shaping the Netherlandish Canon: Karel van Mander's Schilder-Boeck.* Chicago, 1991.

Panofsky, Erwin. *Idea: A Concept in Art Theory.* Translated by J. Peake. New York, 1968. Translation of *Idea: Ein Beitrag zur Begriffsgeschichte der alteren Kunsttheorie* (1924).

Puttfarken, Thomas. *The Discovery of Pictorial Composition: Theories of Visual Order in Painting, 1400–1800.* New Haven, 2000.

———. *Roger de Piles' Theory of Art.* New Haven, 1985.

Rensselaer, Lee. *Ut Pictura Poesis: The Humanistic Theory of Painting.* New York, 1967.

Roskill, Mark. *Dolce's "Aretino" and Venetian Art Theory of the Cinquecento.* New York, 1968.

Rubin, Patricia. *Giorgio Vasari: Art and History.* New Haven, 1995.

Schlosser, Julius von. *Die Kunstliteratur.* Vienna, 1924. Translated into Italian as *La letteratura artistica* by Filippo Rossi. Edited by Otto Kurz. Rome, 1964.

Sohm, Philip L. *Pittoresco: Marco Boschini, His Critics and Their Critiques of Painterly Brushwork in Seventeenth- and Eighteenth-Century Italy.* Cambridge, U.K., and New York, 1991.

———. *Style in the Art Theory of Early Modern Italy.* Cambridge, U.K., and New York, 2001.

Summers, David. *Michelangelo and the Language of Art.* Princeton, 1981.

Summerscale, Anne. *Malvasia's Life of the Carracci: Commentary and Translation.* University Park, Pa., 2000.

Vries, Lyckle de. *Gerard de Lairesse: An Artist between Stage and Studio.* Amsterdam, 1998.

Williams, Robert. *Art, Theory, and Culture in Sixteenth-Century Italy: From Techne to Metatechne.* Cambridge, U.K., and New York, 1997.

Wrigley, Richard. *The Origins of French Art Criticism: From the Ancien Régime to the Restoration.* Oxford, 1993.

PHILIP L. SOHM

ARTISTIC PATRONAGE

The patron served a fundamental function in the development of art in early modern Europe. In addition to being an active consumer of art, he was its initiator, often dictating form and content. Art patronage functioned as proof of wealth, status, and power and could also serve purposes of propaganda and entertainment. Conversely, influential contacts were essential to an artist's well-being.

Patronage was formalized by contracts defining cost, materials, dimensions, artist's participation, content, and time line; a sketch of the project was often demanded. Alternatively, secular and religious princes could retain artists on a monthly allowance, offering them board and provisions as court residents.

In his explanation of cause and effect, Aristotle defined the position of the patron when he distinguished the efficient cause (the artist) and the formal cause (the art object) from the final cause (the patron). The patron offered forms of support that placed him beyond the level of customer, but the balance between patron and artist was never equal and was often a source of tension.

Patronage changed as early modern institutions such as the city, capitalism, and minted coinage developed, leading to an enlarged world of goods, social diffusion of taste, a variety of new forms, namely, to a broad expanse of material culture with a demand for durable goods. For a full understanding of a patron's extravagance, it is necessary to assemble an accounting from his largesse in church construction, desired prestige in palace construction, and temporary decorations for state visits, festivals, dynastic marriages, and political exchanges. Political and social pressures were factors in limiting lavish display. In Venice and Florence, merchants were restrained in their patronage by sumptuary laws, which went so far as to limit the cost and color of clothing and the amount of jewelry worn.

ORIGINS OF ART PATRONAGE

Art patronage in the early modern era had its origins in religious practices as expressed by the fourteenth-century Tuscan merchant Francesco di Marco Datini, who noted that pictures were meant to move a person's spirit to devotion. Thus, the patron who commissioned a painted or carved work of art intended it first and foremost as a devotional object. The portrait placed on an altar or a panel painting or sculpture for a chapel was important primarily as a means of earning grace for the patron in redeeming his soul from the torments of purgatory. In Florence the early patronage of the prominent Medici family took the form of religious projects.

The iconography of a painting, sculpture, church, or palace was often traditional, but circumstances of patronage can be enlightened by iconology. For example, Gentile da Fabriano's *Adoration of the Magi,* of 1423, depicts a story of the Epiphany, a biblical narrative of doctrinal importance as representing Christ's first contact with the Gentiles. Interest in the subject for the painting's wealthy Florentine patron, Palla Strozzi, came from its courtly theme of the reception of ambassadors, and from the fact that Strozzi was a member of the Florentine confraternity of the Magi. The page removing a large gold spur from the foot of the central standing Magus signifies the end of the journey but also alludes to the patron, who was a Knight of the Golden Spur. The unusual subject of Masaccio's Florentine fresco *The Tribute Money* of c. 1427, in which Christ and the Apostles pay a gate tax to enter the city of Capharnaum may have been stimulated by the deliberations of its patron, Felice Brancacci, on the Florentine city council concerning the institution of a new *catasto,* or head tax. In 1472 Andrea del Verrocchio rested his double tomb for Piero I and Giovanni de' Medici on the backs of tortoises as a visual form of the Medici motto, *festina lente,* or "make haste slowly." It has green, white, and porphyry marble representing the Medici colors and family dedication to the theological virtues of faith, hope, and charity. Antonio del Pollaiuolo's bronze *Hercules and Antaeus* of the 1470s rests on a triangular base as a signifier of the Medici triplet identifying its patron.

Patrons are often portrayed in paintings of religious subjects, such as Jan van Eyck's *Madonna of the Canon van der Paele,* where the eponymous donor is depicted graphically at the proper left of the Madonna and Child. Portraiture emerged as an independent genre from such donor portraits. Here patron and work product are one and the same. Initially, donor portraits began as static, profile depictions, likely inspired by images of emperors on Roman coins, but also distancing the donor from the more animated, frontally displayed religious figures, as in Domenico Ghirlandaio's Sassetti Chapel frescoes of 1486, in Santa Maria Novella, Florence, where husband and wife appear in rigid profile surrounded by scenes of Francesco Sassetti's onomastic patron saint. Other donor portraits can include tomb effigies and equestrian monuments.

In the fifteenth century, guilds began to exert corporate patronage in completing the niches of the Florentine grain exchange, Orsanmichele, with statues of their patron saints and assumed responsibility for other commissions such as Lorenzo Ghiberti's doors for the baptistry of the cathedral of Florence. Pope Sixtus IV's commission in 1481 of wall frescoes to decorate his new Vatican chapel with stories from the lives of Moses and Jesus asserted the primacy of the papacy. His nephew would continue the practice after 1508 with Michelangelo's frescoes for the chapel's ceiling and Raphael's frescoes for the Vatican Stanze.

Patronage was often made for propagandistic purposes. Unlike modern approaches to propaganda as a form of advertising or self-promotion, in Renaissance usage, art honoring the ruling family usually increased in intensity and splendor as visitors approached the seat of power. Ambassadors were often received *in camera,* that is, in the private bedchamber of the ruling prince, as in the Ducal Palace at Mantua (see Andrea Mantegna's frescoes of 1465–1474). Other princely examples of patronage include Giulio Romano's designs for the Gonzaga's frescoed Hall of the Giants in the Palazzo del Te, Mantua, 1530–1532, where the presumptuous Titans attempt to scale Mount Olympus only to be beaten back with their world crashing around them—an object lesson, it would seem, to anyone attempting to overthrow legitimate authority.

In Colmar in 1515, the Antonite order commissioned a magnificent altarpiece from the limewood sculptor Nikolaus Hagenauer and the painter Matthias Grünewald with the function of offering hope and consolation to the amputees in their hospital wards suffering from the gangrenous effects of Saint Anthony's fire.

The emergence of print technology in the late fifteenth century, particularly engravings popularized by Mantegna and Albrecht Dürer, made art patronage more democratic, less expensive, and accessible to a broader public. Prints became a popular medium for expanding Renaissance values and Protestant propaganda. An esoteric middle-class audience began to collect small bronzes, prints, and eventually drawings. Works in multiples allowed the artist to substitute mass patronage for the singular patron, allowing volume on a small scale as an alternative to large, expensive commissions, as the European economy burgeoned, material culture grew, and artworks entered the world of durable goods.

In northern Europe, the Protestant Reformation led to civil disorder and the destruction of religious art, such as stained-glass windows, tomb sculpture, and altar panels. A new iconoclasm was founded on the conviction that devotion to such images verged on idolatry. Northern artists lost widespread church patronage, with artists such as Lucas Cranach, Albrecht Altdorfer, and Hans Holbein turning to other genres such as portraiture, landscape, and mythology to satisfy their secular patrons.

In Italy, a different kind of struggle took place between artist and patron as artists began to assert themselves. Humanist interests in central Italy in the writings of Pico della Mirandola on the dignity of man and the Pseudo-Dionysius on the primacy of the self formed the basis for the emergence of artistic personality. Artworks were generally credited to the patrons who commissioned them, as Pope Paul III reminded Benvenuto Cellini that without his patronage the sculptor was nothing. Artists could only counter such an evident claim by noting that their talent and inspiration were of divine origin.

Michelangelo was soon referred to as "Il Divino," as were Raphael, then Federico Barocci later in the sixteenth century. Soon patrons began to request simply "a Michelangelo," "a Raphael," or "something from your hand" as a testament to an artist's original style and talent. But in the sixteenth century patrons also began to reject commissions by artists who were too willful, such as Domenico Beccafumi or Pontormo, particularly with the emergence of mannerism, a style often marked by idiosyncrasy and overintellection, adopting approaches to traditional iconography that seemed to skirt heresy.

In Venice, patrician patronage became the provenance of Titian to the exclusion of his younger rivals, Tintoretto and Jacopo Bassano, who looked to the *Scuole,* or religious confraternities, for patrons. At the end of the century, Veronese developed an opulent style of great appeal to the Serenissima's patrician class. In Florence, the ruling oligarchy consisted of four hundred merchant families who were responsible for all the artworks commissioned there. The most prominent among them included the Medici, Sassetti, Capponi, della Palla,

and Pucci. Although the Medici name stands out for its early association with churches, chapels, and palaces, for mythologies commissioned by Lorenzo de' Pierfrancesco, and for works by Pontormo and Bronzino for Duke Cosimo I, the greatest patron family who continued to request works over several generations from such major artists as Titian, Correggio, Pontormo, Andrea del Sarto, Raphael, Parmigianino, and so forth, and whose history remains to be written, was the Pucci family.

A new type of patron to emerge at the end of the fifteenth century was the female patron, generally in the form of abbesses and widows. Isabella d'Este set the tone in Ferrara in the 1490s with her patronage of Mantegna and her pursuit of works by Giovanni Bellini and Leonardo da Vinci. There was also the confident abbess Gioanna da Piacenza for whom Correggio frescoed an esoteric classical program in about 1519. Widows who came to prominence largely due to dowry inflation in the sixteenth century included Atalanta de Galeotto Baglione, Elena Baiardi, Laura Bagaretto, Elena Orsini, and Maria Bufalini. They commissioned works from the most prominent painters such as Raphael, Andrea del Sarto, Correggio, Titian, Parmigianino, Daniele da Volterra, and Federico Barocci.

PATRONAGE IN AN AGE OF CONSOLIDATION

In the seventeenth century, an age of absolutism as the church and nation states began to consolidate their power, patronage became monopolized. The papacy used Gian Lorenzo Bernini to produce grand statements in his Vatican architecture and sculpture that by their splendor and scale affirmed the truth of the Roman Catholic faith. In Rome the Jesuits and other religious orders engaged Francesco Borromini, Pietro da Cortona, and Giovanni Battista Gaulli for large projects that expressed the confidence and expansive optimism of their patrons.

Patronage took other forms in the Protestant Netherlands as art entered the marketplace, where paintings were literally sold with meat, cheese, fish, and produce. Artists created new genres to solicit patronage from an emerging mercantile class. Popular themes included windmills, seascapes, still lifes, harbor scenes, church interiors, landscapes, and so forth. Jan Vermeer excelled in domestic interiors. Frans Hals produced group portraits, and Rem-

Artistic Patronage. *The Archduke Leopold Wilhelm in His Picture Gallery in Brussels* by David Teniers II, c. 1651. Teniers was the court painter for the archduke as well as curator of his extensive art collection; this is one of several views of the galleries painted by Teniers. ©ARCHIVO ICONOGRAFIO S.A./CORBIS

brandt catered to a sophisticated Amsterdam audience for his biblical subjects, portraits, and etchings.

In Flanders, the magnificent painter and courtier Peter Paul Rubens, like Bernini in Rome, moved with ease in courtly settings, but he also took commissions for church paintings. He served the Gonzagas in Mantua, then painted large cycles of family histories for Marie de Médicis in Paris and Charles I in London.

Patronage in France in the seventeenth century was dominated by Louis XIV, who established the arts to aggrandize the regime, with artists working in concert under the direction of Charles Le Brun and Jean-Baptiste Colbert, the king's minister of culture, with work delegated to specialists. In 1663

Colbert reorganized the Royal Academy of Painting and Sculpture, founded in 1648 under the guidance of its native son, Nicolas Poussin, to educate artists and dictate taste. The king moved the French court to Versailles, where he expanded his father's hunting lodge into a palatial flood plain with the contributions of François Mansart, Louis Le Vau, Jules Hardouin-Mansart, and André Le Nôtre. The Academy exerted its authority over the arts into the nineteenth century. Meanwhile, Poussin spent his career in Rome painting mythologies for a professional upper middle class.

In Spain, Philip IV engaged Diego Velázquez as the official painter of his court, whereas his contemporaries, Francisco de Zurburán and Bartolomé

Esteban Murillo, sought patronage from religious orders.

On the death of Louis XIV in 1715, the court at Versailles dispersed with officials returning to Paris to commission modest hotels filled with entertaining paintings by Jean-Antoine Watteau, François Boucher, and Jean-Honoré Fragonard, while Jean-Siméon Chardin depicted morally uplifting genre scenes for a modest bourgeois patronage. Royal patronage persisted in Bavaria in palace decoration, with Domenico Tiepolo emerging as the major painter in several regal courts in Germany and Spain.

In Rome, as the church finally came to grips with papal nepotism at the end of the seventeenth century, patronage of the great cardinals became more modest. This was inevitable as many major churches and palaces had been constructed in the previous decades, and leading artists of the previous generation, such as Pietro da Cortona and Bernini, had died. Cardinal Pietro Ottoboni, as vice chancellor of the church, dominated patronage in Rome for half a century with his sponsorship of the Academy of the Arcadians, opera performances and oratorios by Alessandro Scarlatti and Arcangelo Corelli, and paintings by his resident artists, Francesco Trevisani and Sebastiano Conca. He dominated taste in Rome, eclipsing six popes beginning with the sixteen-month reign of his great-uncle Alexander VIII in 1689. Ottoboni preferred modest works of the Holy Family expressing tender religious sentiments given focus by strong lighting effects, characterized by the blue and white hues of his livery.

Another type of patronage emerged in Rome with the advent of the grand tour, as French and particularly English travelers to the Holy City commissioned souvenirs of their travels in the form of landscapes, portraits, and views of the great monuments of antiquity. On returning to his native country, each "Milord inglese" would commission portraits from Sir Joshua Reynolds and Thomas Gainsborough, or anecdotal tales from William Hogarth, or, in France, from Jean-Baptiste Greuze. The grand tour alerted visitors to Italy to the remains of Roman antiquity, dictating changes in taste to neoclassicism. This led to the commissioning of works of ancient history and mythology from such artists as Anton Raphael Mengs, Antonio Canova, and Jacques-Louis David. In architecture, patron and artist became one when Lord Burlington designed his Chiswick House in London, and Thomas Jefferson his Monticello in Virginia.

See also **Britain, Art in; Florence, Art in; France, Art in; Medici Family; Netherlands, Art in; Papacy and Papal States; Rome, Art in; Venice, Art in; Versailles; Women and Art.**

BIBLIOGRAPHY

Bauman, Lisa. "Power and Image: Della Rovere Patronage in Late Quattrocento Rome." Ph.D. diss., Northwestern University, 1990.

Goldthwaite, Richard A. *Wealth and the Demand for Art in Italy, 1300–1600.* Baltimore, 1993.

Gombrich, Ernst H. "The Early Medici as Patrons of Art." In *Norm and Form,* pp. 35–57. London, 1966.

Haskell, Francis. *Patrons and Painters: A Study in the Relations between Italian Art and Society in the Age of the Baroque.* New Haven, 1980.

Hollingsworth, Mary. *Patronage in Renaissance Italy: From 1400 to the Early Sixteenth Century.* Baltimore, 1994.

———. *Patronage in Sixteenth Century Italy.* London, 1996.

Kempers, Bram. *Painting, Power and Patronage: The Rise of the Professional Artist in the Italian Renaissance.* London, 1992.

Kent, F. W., and Patricia Simons. *Patronage, Art and Society in Renaissance Italy.* Oxford, 1987.

King, Catherine E. *Renaissance Woman Patrons: Wives and Widows in Italy, c. 1300–c. 1550.* New York, 1998.

Olszewski, Edward J. "The Enlightened Patronage of Cardinal Pietro Ottoboni (1667–1740)." *Artibus et historiae* 23, no. 45 (2002): 139–165.

Wackernagel, Martin. *The World of the Florentine Renaissance Artist, Projects and Patrons, Workshop and Art Market.* Translated by Alison Luchs. Princeton, 1981.

EDWARD J. OLSZEWSKI

THE CONCEPTION AND STATUS OF THE ARTIST

In the Middle Ages all learnable skills—including what we today call "art"—were classified either as liberal (intellectual) or mechanical (manual). The seven liberal arts were divided into the trivium (three approaches) and the quadrivium (four approaches). The trivium comprised grammar, the study of language; rhetoric, the art of persuasion; and dialectics, the pursuit of philosophy, while the quadrivium included the mathematical disciplines

The Conception and Status of the Artist. *Self-Portrait,* 1650, by Nicolas Poussin. By the time this self-portrait was painted, Poussin had become renowned throughout Europe and was arguably the most famous painter of his time. The paintings in the background, with their highly allusive subjects, and his attire clearly suggest the nobility of his vocation, while his facial expression masterfully conveys a sense of world-weariness combined with a sustaining passion for art. THE ART ARCHIVE/MUSÉE DU LOUVRE PARIS/DAGLI ORTI

of arithmetic, geometry, astronomy, and music. The much less prestigious seven mechanical arts (today known as vocational pursuits) consisted of weaving, making armor, navigation, agriculture, hunting, medicine, and the living arts, or sports.

In early Renaissance Italy, an individual's standing in society depended on a number of factors, the most important of which was the rank attached either to birth or occupation. One's occupation was always evaluated on the basis of its proximity to, or distance from, physical labor. Even in antiquity the visual arts had belonged to the category defined as manual and hence in the Middle Ages were placed among the lowly mechanical arts. Poetry's greater intellectual prestige was based on its alliance with rhetoric in the trivium, while music was included in the quadrivium. Indeed, both poetry and music were included in the university curriculum, whereas instruction in the visual arts was confined to craftsmen's workshops until the rise, later, of the acade-

mies. Thus, what we think of today as the creation of art was defined as the fabrication of artifacts, and the artist was characterized as a craftsman with a concomitantly low standing in society. The status of architecture was higher than that of painting and sculpture in that it was self-evidently based on the liberal arts of arithmetic and geometry and also required the greatest supervision of labor, which automatically made it the most socially acceptable. In short, the early history of the "artist" consisted in his struggle to get his manual craft accepted as sufficiently intellectual to be included among the liberal arts and, hence, to obtain a higher social standing. (The artist is here figured as exclusively male.)

Leon Battista Alberti (1404–1472) was the first to articulate in writing the case for the elevation of the visual arts above the level of the mechanical arts in his 1435 treatise *On Painting.* The visual arts needed, he thought, a firm theoretical foundation, by which he meant the mathematical disciplines of the quadrivium. The painter has to be as learned as possible, he said, "but I wish him above all to have a good knowledge of geometry." In order to demonstrate the "scientific" basis of painting, Alberti gave priority to mathematics, geometry, and the theory of proportions, and codified a method of one-point perspective that could be mastered by the practicing craftsman for whom he translated *On Painting* into Italian. Leonardo da Vinci (1452–1519), the most persistent advocate for the elevation of painting to a liberal art in his unpublished writings, also agreed that the "scientific" nature of painting lay in its mastery of the rules of linear perspective based on the laws of geometry.

The two components underlying the creation of a painting or sculpture, conception and execution, were characterized around 1400 by Cennino Cennini (c. 1370–c. 1440) as *fantasia* (imagination) and *operazione di mano* (handiwork), and by Giorgio Vasari (1511–1574) in 1568 as *il mio pensiero* (my considered judgment) and *le mie mani* (my hands). Renaissance society focused on the second component, the *arte* or, in Latin, *ars,* that signified the skill of hand or mastery of illusionism required to execute the work, a skill that could be mastered by practice. The artists themselves, on the other hand, emphasized the *ingegno* or *ingenium,* the inborn talent or creative power needed to conceive the work in the first place, that could not be learned. For Vasari, a key element in the intellectual component of art lay in *disegno* (planning/drawing) which underlay the three "arts of design" (painting, sculpture, architecture). These principles were incorporated into the Florentine Academy of Design (founded 1563) which, although it did not replace the apprenticeship system, did much to elevate the status of artists.

One strategy in the artistic community's campaign to reclassify art as liberal was to deny the role played by manual execution in its creation. "Painting is a mental occupation" *(pittura è una cosa mentale),* wrote Leonardo da Vinci, and Michelangelo Buonarroti (1475–1564) stated equally firmly, "We paint with our brain, not with our hands" *(si dipinge col ciervello et non con le mani).* Leonardo laid down the correct sequence in the creative cycle: the painter must work first in the mind *(mente),* then with the hands *(mani).* Promoting this union of ideation and labor, Vasari maintained that the trained hand mediated the idea born in the intellect, or, as Michelangelo put it in a famous sonnet, "the hand that obeys the intellect" *(la man che ubbidisce all'intelletto),* that is, the hand as an extension of the mind. It was not until the 1590s that one (highly idiosyncratic) artist felt sufficiently self-confident to mention the manual labor involved in artistic creation without first having recourse to its intellectual principles: "We must speak with our hands" *(habbiamo da parlare con le mani),* Annibale Carracci (1560–1609), founder of the Carracci Academy in Bologna, is reputed to have said, equating the artist's hand with the poet's voice for the first time. The writing of treatises was another aspect of the campaign to improve artistic and social status and, in the mid-sixteenth century, artists themselves not only wrote treatises—Paolo Pino (1548), Anton Francesco Doni (1549), Vasari (1550), Benvenuto Cellini (1560s), Pirro Ligorio (1570s), and Giovanni Paolo Lomazzo (1580s)—but some (Michelangelo through Ascanio Condivi in 1553; Cellini, and Vasari) also wrote autobiographies.

The speed of progress of the artistic community's long-term struggle for professional and personal betterment differed from country to country in early modern Europe. In Italy artists had, by the seventeenth century, succeeded dramatically in re-negotiating the standing and value of both artifact and maker. The idea developed that skill should be rewarded, and rates of pay accordingly improved. Many of the artifacts, taking on a heightened aesthetic character and a mystique of greatness, were redefined as "art," and a number of craftsmen succeeded in reinventing themselves as "artists" to be venerated for their godlike powers. The example of Albrecht Dürer (1471–1528) in the North and the "divine" Michelangelo in the South, both of whose works were perceived by contemporaries and successors as belonging to a new realm that transcended ordinary cultural production, were especially important in bringing about this profound shift in the cultural values attached to the visual arts.

See also **Academies of Art; Cellini, Benvenuto; Dürer, Albrecht; Leonardo da Vinci; Michelangelo Buonarroti; Vasari, Giorgio.**

BIBLIOGRAPHY

Barker, Emma, Nick Webb, and Kim Woods, eds. *The Changing Status of the Artist.* New Haven and London, 1999.

Barzman, Karen, ed. *The Florentine Academy and the Early Modern State: The Discipline of Disegno.* Cambridge, U.K., 2000.

Brown, Jonathan. "On the Meaning of Las Meninas." In *Images and Ideas in Seventeenth-Century Spanish Painting,* pp. 87–110. Princeton, 1978.

Pevsner, Nikolaus. *Academies of Art Past and Present.* New York, 1973. Reprint of the 1940 edition.

Rossi, Sergio. *Dalle botteghe alle accademie: Realtà sociale e teorie artistiche a Firenze dal XIV al XVI secolo.* Milan, 1980.

Warnke, Martin. *The Court Artist: On the Ancestry of the Modern Artist.* Translated by David McLintock. Cambridge, U.K., 1993.

Woods-Marsden, Joanna. *Renaissance Self-Portraiture: The Visual Construction of Identity and the Social Status of the Artist.* New Haven and London, 1998.

JOANNA WOODS-MARSDEN

ARTILLERY. *See* **Military: Battle Tactics and Campaign Strategy.**

ARTISANS. What is an artisan? Traditionally, historians answered this question simply, saying that artisans were members of guilds, skilled men who fashioned artifacts with their hands and tools in autonomous workshops without the aid of powered machinery—the classic handicraftsmen. Now, in the light of recent research, our answer is more complex. Historians now broaden the definition and place artisans on a spectrum with apprentices and journeymen working for wages or piece rates at one end, and at the other entrepreneurial masters, almost indistinguishable from merchants, no longer working primarily with their hands, spending most of their time wholesaling products or managing their enterprises. Moreover, the boundaries at each end of the spectrum were porous, with men and, notably, women, sliding into and out of what we think of as artisanal activity. The definition of *artisan* has also become more complex in another way, for traditional institutional and economic frameworks are no longer sufficient to analyze important aspects of the experience of the groups of people—men and women—we label "artisans." Not every such person belonged to a guild (few women did in their own right), nor were tanners (as they would be the first to tell us) simply men or women who happened to cure leather, or shoemakers simply men or women who happened to make footwear. In other words, an adequate definition of *artisan* must also grasp the sense that these men and women had of themselves and that others had of them.

ARTISANS AND THE CRAFT ECONOMY

Historians have long known that the European population stabilized during the first half of the fifteenth century and in the second half entered a sustained period of growth that lasted well into the first half of the seventeenth century and increased Europe's total population by about 20 percent, to about 100 million souls. Population growth was joined by economic growth, although capital tended to concentrate increasingly in the coffers of a wealthy elite of landowners, rentiers, merchants, lawyers, government officials, and some artisans. After 1650 population growth slowed dramatically for a century, and even though the agricultural sector of the economy plunged into recession, a consumer revolution centered on luxury products and on inexpensive manufactured items nonetheless took off, as real wages rose among city dwellers and disposable income increased for many.

Surging demand for an increasingly wide variety of artisanal products triggered significant developments in the community of urban artisans. Artisans everywhere represented a substantial percentage of the stable urban population throughout the early modern centuries, generally ranging from 20 percent (as in Montpellier, France) to 50 percent (as in Cuenca, Spain), although in some places, like Nördlingen in Germany, four out of five taxed inhabitants were craftsmen. Not surprisingly, the numbers of artisans in the construction and luxury trades often registered the greatest increases, and those in textiles the sharpest decreases (as they lost out to accelerating rural production). Behind these percentages, however, a proliferation of various kinds of artisans was taking place, above all in Europe's growing cities (as rural artisans tended to be less specialized). Indeed, the most noteworthy feature of early modern manufacturing is its decentralization. Unlike modern "economies of scale," in which high-volume, standardized, and concentrated production is the rule, the vast majority of early modern urban artisans worked according to the logic of "constant returns to scale," an economic rationale whereby "growth of output required proportional growth of the inputs of labor and raw materials" (de Vries, 91). Increased demand, then, would be accommodated by decentralization, diversification, and specialization, not by concentration or expansion of the physical plant or technological innovation. A look at the division of labor within the early modern urban craft economy amply confirms this.

First, we see everywhere that trades came and went as demand grew and shifted to new products. To take but one example, in the middling French city of Dijon between 1464 and 1750 the number of crafts increased from 81 to 102, but fully 67 new ones had appeared and 45 had vanished. Second, everywhere complex systems of subcontracting became ever more common, so that few items were finished in the shops where their production had begun, and the street resembled an early modern version of an assembly line. As early as 1300 in London, for instance, we find a saddle being produced by a joiner who made the saddle tree, a lorimer who made the leather covering, and painters who did the decoration. The master saddler coordinated the operation, providing the in-

Artisans. *Interior of a Tailor's Shop,* detail, fifteenth-century fresco in the Castle di Issogne, Aosta Valley, Italy. ©ARCHIVO ICONOGRAFICO, S.A./CORBIS

vestment capital and retailing the finished product. In sixteenth-century Augsburg, to take another example of subcontracting, some master furniture makers arranged with lesser masters of their trade to produce component parts of furniture that would then be assembled in the workshop of the contracting master. By the eighteenth century many a European city was like Birmingham or Sheffield, a matrix of small, interconnected, and interdependent workshops. A third response to the vagaries of demand, and consistent with the logic of constant return to scale, master artisans hired and fired workers, retaining only a core of journeymen full-time, and meeting business orders by hiring from a vast and populous periphery of semi-skilled and often transient workers.

Hidden from traditional accounts of European craft folk are female artisans. Until recently historians thought that the early modern family economy and the market economy operated in separate spheres, and because women were central to the former, they were absent from the latter. Recent research has blurred these distinctions, and a consensus is emerging that women participated significantly in the market economy outside the household. Indeed, despite legal exclusion of women from most guilds nearly everywhere in Europe during the early modern centuries, many women practiced artisanal trades in most of Europe's cities. There were female dyers in fourteenth- and fifteenth-century Flemish towns and female glovers, shoemakers, and tailors in sixteenth-century Oxford. There were also female needle and thimble makers in sixteenth-century German cities, and joiners, curriers, and pewterers in York at the same time. Despite this diversity, however, a trend was emerging that would increasingly concentrate women in clothing and textile trades, so that by the eighteenth century a much more rigid gendered division of labor had taken hold.

GUILDS, DISCIPLINE, AND RESISTANCE

During the Middle Ages theologians embraced the idea that labor was a penance imposed on humankind for the original sin. After the Fall, man was commanded to work henceforth "by the sweat of his brow," not to nurture the fruits of nature, but to redeem himself for salvation. The value of labor was not, therefore, its productive capacity, but rather its moral force. During the early modern period this theological notion was elaborated under the spreading influence of the writings of St. Augustine, with their emphasis on obedience and servitude to the commands of God. Work, in the minds of learned men, became a spiritual discipline, and idleness, rank rebellion against God and society. It followed that labor was a bulwark against social disorder, while it protected the soul from the assault of evil. As late medieval and early modern society became increasingly organized across the intersecting axes of hierarchy and subordination, artisans were expected to know their place and stay in it. The sign of this place was labor, and the key institution created to regulate it was the guild. Guilds drafted regulatory statutes that were sanctioned by public authorities. As such, they were fundamentally about disciplining the world of labor.

The triumph of hierarchy in the early modern political world resulted in the growing dominance of an oligarchy within guilds and the progressive exclusion of artisans from the world of municipal governance. Increasingly guilds were dominated by the wealthier craftsmen, the same families tending to run the affairs of their guilds for generations. The composition of the political community varied from one town to the next, with more guildsmen included in some places than in others. During the early modern centuries, however, the trend everywhere was toward control by a patriciate of merchants, legal professionals, and in some places royal officials, and the exclusion of guildsmen. The exclu-

sion occurred first in Renaissance Italy, but by the eighteenth century European artisans rarely possessed the constitutional rights of political participation that they had often enjoyed in the cities and towns of the High Middle Ages. The only political action left to them was the threat or act of rebellion.

Hundreds of artisanal rebellions erupted in Europe's cities from the Late Middle Ages to about 1700. These centered on two interrelated concerns—overtaxation and fiscal maladministration by the municipal elite. From one perspective artisanal rebellions were dismal failures, for none permanently altered the constitutional arrangement of cities or realms, but from another perspective one can see that rebellious artisans were warning the ruling elite that too great a disregard for artisanal interests and concerns would ignite violence. Often the spark for rebellion was fiscal, but the fact that antitax sentiments or concerns about fiscal maladministration leapt to constitutional levels about artisanal participation in politics so quickly suggests that artisans were also deeply concerned about issues that went beyond their pocketbooks and reached the level of the structure and maintenance of the community. How well the government secured the kind of order that artisans needed to maintain the security of their place in the community—their status—was an issue worth fighting over. Medieval and early modern artisanal rebellions, then, were very much about the maintenance of a stratified community and of the artisan's place within it.

STATUS AND HONOR

Artisans from the Late Middle Ages well into the nineteenth century were defined and defined themselves not primarily as producers, as their labels may suggest, but rather as members of an *état*, a rank or "degree," a *Stand*. They designated themselves (and were so designated by the authorities) by occupational labels not just because these described what they did (it often did not), but rather because it was the sign of status. Everywhere late medieval and early modern Europeans divided themselves more and more into a series of graduated ranks. Sometimes this was done formally by institutions authorized by political authorities (for example, guilds), sometimes informally.

As society's elites increasingly distanced themselves from the craftsmen, artisans in turn became

Artisans. Sixteenth-century woodcut of bookbinders in a workshop by Jost Amman. ©CHRISTEL GERSTENBERG/CORBIS

increasingly keen on defining the distance between themselves and their inferiors. The early modern hierarchical system of distinction and difference was animated by a concern for subordination and discipline of inferiors. This preoccupied men at all levels of society, including artisans, be they guild masters, journeymen, or apprentices. From a master's perspective, breach of discipline by journeymen or apprentices reflected not only instability in the labor market, but also, and more dramatically, a perceived threat to hierarchy and to the principle of distinction itself. Masters were deeply sensitive to insubordination by journeymen, and journeymen were keen, in turn, on maintaining the inferiority of apprentices and nonguild wageworkers beneath them.

One's all-important place in this system was signaled by status. At all social levels, this process of dissociation was visualized by cultural markers, and the key badge of status, for artisans no less than anyone else, was honor. This swung on the hinge of respectability, but beyond that it could be expressed in a variety of ways. For the master craftsman it could be economic solvency and heading one's own reputable business and respectable household, while for a journeyman it surely was being subject to no one's discipline, with no restrictions on one's freedom of movement.

ARTISANS AND INDUSTRIALIZATION

The labor historian Christopher Johnson has observed that "a good deal of our work as historians of the industrial transition has concerned the ways in which that vast, amorphous, and ill-defined category of handworkers called 'artisans' experienced the profound legal and economic changes of the

Artisans. Engraving of tailor's workshop, France, 1770, from the *Dictionary of Sciences.* ©HISTORICAL PICTURE ARCHIVE/CORBIS

age" (p. 1047). Scholars have recently discovered that the industrial transition did not immediately destroy small-scale artisanal production as was once thought, but rather for a time (late into the nineteenth century) created a whole new set of possibilities for small commodity producers. Only in the last quarter of the century, even later in some parts of Europe, did mechanized, factory production, in a quantum sense, overwhelm the master's shop. Still, beginning, clearly, in the second half of the eighteenth century, artisans everywhere were affected by the gradual transition to industrial capitalism. Some sank into wage work in the new factories, but many more retained their own shops, working in the interstices of large-scale industry or mass marketing or directing their energies toward neighborhood provisioning. Capitalistic mechanized industries like sawmilling, ironmaking, and eventually steelmaking generated an increase in work for the small workshop of the machinist or toolmaker. Likewise steam-driven sawmills turned out wood that still had to be fashioned in the carpenters' and furnituremakers' shops, while the enormous furnaces of the Black Country in England provided large quantities of material to thousands of local smiths toiling in their own shops. These shops were organized in the traditional manner, with masters taking on or laying off workers and journeymen (labor was abundant due to galloping population growth after 1750) as industrial output and the pace of demand dictated.

Yet beneath the similarities with the Old Regime there lurked a difference, for the seeming independence of artisans was built increasingly on a foundation of dependency. No longer did masters, or shopkeepers for that matter, have much control over access to their materials, now provided by merchant industrialists, factors, and wholesalers. Moreover, masters came to rely on a steady flow of orders, often from only a few middlemen or owners of factories. The same can be said of access to credit and to markets, which was increasingly controlled by merchant operations. Of course, even in the Old Regime masters were not entirely independent, especially in emerging economies of scale and those, like textiles, organized around the putting-out system. But the early modern urban master tailor, shoemaker, cabinetmaker, cutler, butcher, or baker was not as encumbered by these dependencies as his

descendants experiencing the transition to industrialism would be.

The transformation that we call industrialization occurred in production, processing, and retailing, enabled by regularization of demand, which was smoothed by dramatic changes in transport and communication, price elasticity, and capital-intensive and increasingly standardized production. Amid such changes, artisans did not suddenly disappear, but they did become something altogether different, gradually but ineluctably more integrated into production and distribution networks that were controlled by large capital. Intensive subdivision of tasks and subcontracting continued apace, but independence became increasingly a chimera, and artisans gradually evolved into mechanics, shopkeepers, or waged workers.

See also **Capitalism; Commerce and Markets; Guilds; Industrial Revolution; Industry; Laborers; Proto-Industry; Textile Industry; Women; Youth.**

BIBLIOGRAPHY

Crossick, Geoffrey, ed. *The Artisan and the European Town, 1500–1900.* Aldershot, U.K., and Brookfield, Vt., 1997.

de Vries, Jan. *The Economy of Europe in an Age of Crisis, 1600–1750.* Cambridge, U.K., and New York, 1976.

Farr, James R. *Artisans in Europe, 1300–1914.* Cambridge, U.K., 2000.

Howell, Martha C. *Women, Production, and Patriarchy in Late Medieval Cities.* Chicago, 1986.

Johnson, Christopher. "Artisans vs. Fabricants: Urban Protoindustrialization and the Evolution of Work Culture in Lodève and Bedarieux, 1740–1830." *Mélanges de l'école française de Rome: Moyen âge, temps modernes* 99, no. 2 (1987): 1047–1084.

Kaplan, Steven Laurence. *The Bakers of Paris and the Bread Question, 1700–1775.* Durham, N.C., 1996.

Kaplan, Steven Laurence, and Cynthia J. Koepp, eds. *Work in France: Representation, Meaning, Organization, and Practice.* Ithaca, N.Y., 1986.

Mackenney, Richard. *Tradesmen and Traders: The World of the Guilds in Venice and Europe, c. 1250–c. 1650.* London, 1987.

Rule, John. *The Experience of Labour in Eighteenth-Century Industry.* London, 1981.

Sewell, William H., Jr. *Work and Revolution in France: The Language of Labor from the Old Regime to 1848.* Cambridge, U.K., and New York, 1980.

Sonenscher, Michael. *Work and Wages: Natural Law, Politics, and Eighteenth-Century French Trades.* Cambridge, U.K., and New York, 1989.

Walker, Mack. *German Home Towns: Community, State, and General Estate, 1648–1871.* Ithaca, N.Y., 1971.

Wiesner, Merry E. *Working Women in Renaissance Germany.* New Brunswick, N.J., 1986.

Woodward, Donald. *Men at Work: Labourers and Building Craftsmen in the Towns of Northern England, 1450–1750.* Cambridge, U.K., and New York, 1995.

JAMES R. FARR

ASAM FAMILY. The most important members of this family of German architects, painters, sculptors, and stucco workers are Cosmas Damian (1686–1739) and Egid Quirin (1692–1750). Both initially trained with their father, the fresco painter Hans Georg (1649–1711). Cosmas Damian then studied painting at the Accademia di San Luca in Rome, probably 1711–1713; Egid Quirin apprenticed with sculptor Andreas Faistenberger 1711–1716 in Munich, perhaps visiting Rome in 1716.

The brothers worked extensively in fresco and sculpture (primarily Cosmas Damian), and stucco (primarily Egid Quirin), and were involved with a dozen church projects. The interiors, which combine inventive creations of architectural space and light shaped by fresco, sculpture, and stucco in the service of complex religious programs, are their most distinctive and brilliant achievements. They integrated architecture and the arts within settings that were simultaneously emotional and rational, sensual and compassionate, and that pitted victor against vanquished and the marvelous against nature. They also employed contrasts of light and dark as well as stillness and movement. The tensions of encounter and confrontation within these interiors were intended to embrace the churchgoer in a dazzling display of persuasion. The brothers would have seen work produced during the seventeenth century in Rome by such artists as Bernini and Cortona that explored a visual rhetoric for Counter-Reformation purposes, but the scale, brilliance, and sweep of their own creations produced a very different experiential realm.

Immediately upon completing their training, the brothers began work on what would turn out to be two of their greatest projects. In 1716 Cosmas Damian designed the church for the Benedictine monastery at Weltenburg bei Kelheim, located on the Danube west of Regensburg; the following year at nearby Rohr, Egid Quirin produced the Augustinian priory church and its spectacular high altar of the Assumption of Mary.

Weltenburg (1716–1735) was a collaborative work, to which Egid Quirin contributed the stucco and over-life-sized altar sculpture. Within the oval plan, bracketed by a rectangular space for the entrance and organ balcony at one end, and at the opposite end by a similar rectangle (with apse) for the choir, the brothers dramatically transformed the interior by means of chapels, sculpture, paintings, frescoes, contrasts of color and light, a dome that opens to an illusionistic fresco above it, and a choir composed as a proscenium stage. This space, complete with loggia boxes and an architectural stage set, features a St. George astride a spirited horse, lancing the dragon to his right and rescuing the princess to his left, and a fresco on the rearward apse wall ablaze in light. All of these media and effects are orchestrated to bring the history and legends of St. Benedict to life, and celebrate the glory of the church.

At Rohr, Egid Quirin designed a traditional Latin cross basilica, the shape of which was determined in part by existing foundations and sections of wall from the medieval church it replaced. But Egid Quirin also employed this deliberately old-fashioned interior to contrast with the dazzling vision of Mary's ascension that overwhelms the choir and visually determines the interior. Located well behind altar and choir stalls, and staged within a setting of richly colored architecture, complete with sarcophagus and tapestry, the sculptural reenactment of the Assumption employs figures of porcelain white with gilt highlights who witness Mary's ascension into a blaze of golden light and cloud.

Several years later, in 1725, Egid Quirin designed a project for a centralized chapel dedicated to the Holy Spirit that is as audacious as Rohr was conservative; a drawing shows the project in elevation and section. The lively exterior contains an extraordinary, multilevel architecture inside: freestanding stairs curve up to a balcony covered by small half domes, and they in turn support an inter-

Asam Family. The altar of Kloster Weltenburg, built by Cosmas Damian Asam in 1718, with altarpiece of St. George and the dragon by Egid Quirin Asam. ©ADAM WOOLFITT/CORBIS

interior of the existing medieval building. Despite the very different physical conditions and sizes of these buildings, the brothers transformed both interiors through the illusionistic use of stucco and fresco, and the orchestration of light from multiple sources.

See also **Architecture; Baroque.**

BIBLIOGRAPHY

Bushart, Bruno, and Bernhard Rupprecht, eds. *Cosmas Damian Asam, 1686–1739: Leben und Werk.* 3rd rev. ed. Munich, 1986.

Rupprecht, Bernhard. *Die Brüder Asam, Sinn und Sinnlichkeit im bayerischen Barock.* Regensburg, 1980.

Sauermost, Heinz Jürgen. *Die Asams als Architekten.* Munich, 1986.

CHRISTIAN OTTO

nal dome broadly cut away to reveal a fresco above. The extreme animation of the architecture, and the multilevel spatial experience of the airy, openwork forms inside, suggest a revolutionary architecture in which solid elements are honed to thin surfaces and linear elements set within an interior of stunning spatial complexity. Later centralized churches by the brothers, such as that for St. Ursula in Straubing (1736–1741), did not attain the audacity of this project.

The brothers were also involved with several longitudinal but unitary buildings, of which two stand out. One, a monumental version of a house chapel, is in Munich, dedicated to St. Johann Nepomuk and known as the Asam Church since they built it for themselves at their own expense. The other is Freising Cathedral, a remodeling of the

ASIA. Three centuries separate the missions of Vasco da Gama to India in 1498 and George Macartney to China in 1793. Da Gama opened a new sea route to the Orient; Lord Macartney, ambassador of Great Britain, sought to renegotiate the terms of trade with the Qing (Manchu) empire. During the course of the intervening centuries, successive waves of Europeans sailed into Asia—after the Portuguese came the Dutch, English, Spanish, and French. Their experiences taught them that there was more than one Asia. In south and east Asia, there were the powerful and expansive continental empires of the Mughals and the Manchus. In northeast Asia, there were the secluded kingdoms of Korea and Japan. But initially, for the Europeans, there was above all the Asia of the Indian Ocean trading network.

EUROPE ENTERS THE ASIAN TRADE NETWORK

The Indian Ocean network consisted of three interlocking circuits—the Arabian Seas, the Bay of Bengal, and Indonesia–east Asia. It was in this Asia that European merchantmen established small but permanent bases stretching around the entire Indian Ocean littoral, from the port of Mombasa in the west to Nagasaki in the east. From those bases, Europeans pressed for monopoly control over the spices, silks, porcelain, and other products that crossed the Indian Ocean's trading network. Until

1850, European ambitions in Asia raced ahead of their limited resource bases. Before the industrial revolution and the European drive for expansion, European states lacked both the financial means and the military power to effect any grand design in Asia.

As the first to arrive in Asian waters via the sea route around Africa, the Portuguese established a trading empire in the Arabian Seas circuit and maintained partial control over it for most of the sixteenth century. A century later the Dutch constructed the first colonial empire in Asia and revolutionized almost every dimension of the Indian Ocean trading system—from how it was organized to how business was transacted. The English East India Company arrived on the scene contemporaneously with the Dutch but did not become a major force in Asian trade until after the latter went into decline, between 1680 and 1720. Over the course of the remainder of the eighteenth century, the English developed a passion for empire, first in India and then in China. After 1720 they pushed first the Dutch and subsequently the late-arriving French East India Company aside and established themselves as the dominant European trader in Asian waters. Concurrently, they commenced building an empire on the subcontinent of Asia, and in 1793, with the Macartney mission to China, inaugurated a clash between the expanding empires of England and Qing China in the late eighteenth and nineteenth centuries.

Two facets of the early modern history of European empire building in the Indian Ocean deserve to be emphasized. First is the intra-Asian or "country trade," to call it by its eighteenth-century name. From the Asian perspective, the emergence of three great Muslim empires (Ottoman, Safavid, and Mughal) by the sixteenth century and the unprecedented growth of the Kiangnan region in the lower Yangtze valley of the Ming-Qing empire greatly stimulated the expansion of the intra-Asian regional trade, and with it, a nascent consumer culture in Asia. From the European perspective, it was Europe's good fortune to arrive at the moment the Asian system was undergoing a period of unprecedented growth. Once the Europeans learned how the system operated and the role Asian merchants played in it, they sought out partnerships with those merchants. For their part, the European traders

contributed to the further expansion of the system by linking the "country trade" to the long-distance Atlantic trade routes that carried Asian products to Europe's own emergent consumer culture. Thus, over time, these partnerships, such as those between Portuguese and Gujarati merchants or between Dutch and Chinese traders, became one of the central features of the system. The English, too, were attuned to the importance of such partnerships and made a series of them during their eighteenth-century rise to dominance. It is worth repeating that Asian-European partnerships were a key feature of the Indian Ocean trading system and played an important role in its continued growth. From a world-historical perspective, some historians identify this as the "age of partnership" and interpret it as part of the deeper integration and globalization of trade linked to an emergent consumer culture in both East and West.

Alongside the intra-Asian trade, European initiatives came to be central to early modern European empire building in Asia. The collective effect of these initiatives transformed the Asian system of trade. These initiatives came in two chronological waves, the first in the sixteenth century and the second in the seventeenth and early eighteenth centuries. The first wave was primarily Portuguese in origin and included the opening of the Atlantic sea route around Africa to the Orient and the linkage of the intra-Asian regional trade routes to the Atlantic route; the introduction of the large ships called armed merchantmen; and the emergence of cultural intermediaries, the first of whom were Jesuit missionaries. In later centuries, sea voyagers and official embassies from various European countries greatly expanded the fund of European knowledge about Asia.

The Dutch and English sponsored the second wave of initiatives. These initiatives were truly revolutionary in terms of their impact on the Indian Ocean trading networks. Over a two-century period (1600–1800) they fundamentally transformed the Asian trading system. The two most important of these second-wave initiatives were the transplantation of a novel form of business organization (the joint stock company) into Asia and the fusion of private merchant interests and state policy. Ranking close behind these two initiatives in significance were the systematization of the intra-Asian carrying

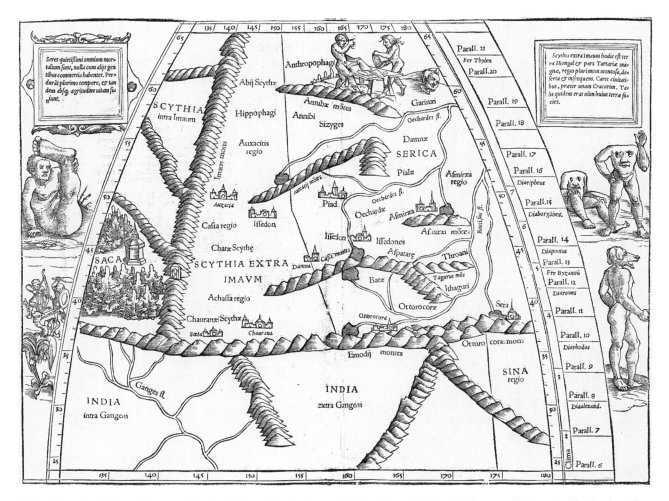

Asia. Sebastian Münster's map of Central Asia and India, from a 1545 edition of Ptolemy's *Geographia,* is noted for its depiction of mythical creatures thought to exist in that part of the world. The creatures were based on reports dating from the early age of European travel to the East prior to Marco Polo's thirteenth-century journeys to Asia. Map Collection, Sterling Memorial Library, Yale University

trade and its transference to European control after 1700; the shift of the center of trade from the west coast of India (the Arabian Seas circuit) to the Bay of Bengal and Indonesian circuits; and the altered composition of the trade, from spices and porcelains to "drug foods" (such as sugar, coffee, tea, and opium) and cotton textiles.

By the mid-eighteenth century, the combined effects of these initiatives were transforming not just Euro-Asian relations but also the world economy. Regarding the former, partnerships more and more resembled patron-client relationships, and Asians west of Guangzhou (Canton) were the clients. Regarding the European initiatives, by about 1750 they had begun to shift the center of gravity of the world economy away from the shores of the Indian Ocean to those of Atlantic Europe. In other words,

the important economic decisions were more often made in Amsterdam and London rather than in Surat or Melaka or Guangzhou. Nonetheless, this shift was incremental. Although still incomplete by the time Lord Macartney undertook his mission to China in 1793, it eventually culminated in an armed confrontation between the expanding British and Qing empires over trade and sovereignty.

THE PORTUGUESE, THE DUTCH, AND THE SPICE TRADE

In 1498, all of this, of course, lay in the future. Neither Vasco da Gama nor his immediate successors, especially Afonso de Albuquerque (1453–1515), the chief architect of the Portuguese empire in Asia, entertained the slightest notion of creating partnerships with Asian merchants. Their intent was to establish trade monopolies and redirect the spice trade away from the Levantine caravan routes, with their links to the Arabian Seas circuit. Between 1500 and 1515, from their base at Goa, the Portuguese used their superior naval forces to effect a significant measure of control over most of this circuit, which included the Malabar Coast of western India, the Persian Gulf, the Red Sea, and the related caravan routes of Persia and the Tigris-Euphrates valley. During that brief period, they identified and then captured control of many of the major choke points of the Indian Ocean, such as strategically located entrepôts of Hormuz at the entrance of the Persian Gulf and Melaka on the Straits of Melaka. The latter controlled the trade of the Far Eastern circuit of the Indian Ocean. However, the Portuguese failed to capture Aden, located at the entrance of the Red Sea. That failure meant that the Levantine trade routes via the Red Sea remained open, and Portugal could not and did not establish a complete monopoly over the spice trade.

The *Estado da India* nonetheless remitted handsome profits from the pepper trade back to Lisbon for most of the sixteenth century. *Estado* officials and private Portuguese traders realized that even greater profits could be made through partnerships with Asian merchants. Together they continued to expand the trade of the Indian Ocean, linked some of its commerce to the new sea route around Africa, and grew wealthy servicing the expanding intra-Asian trade with silver, tin, copper, spices, and horses. By the mid-sixteenth century, the Portuguese had also become involved in the lucrative trade of the Far Eastern circuit. In fact, between about 1550 and 1637, Portuguese merchantmen had linked together all three trading circuits of the Indian Ocean, moving a variety of goods between its major entrepôts.

In 1637, a seemingly minor event in Japan—the decision of the military government to expel the Portuguese for meddling in Japanese politics—set in motion a series of events that undermined the Portuguese in east Asian waters, opened the way for Dutch competitors to displace them, and all but eliminated Japanese participation in intra-Asian trade until the 1860s. In any case, the Portuguese crown had received little if any of the profits from the intra-Asian trade; they primarily flowed into the pockets of corrupt *Estado* officials and private Por-

tuguese merchants and their Asian partners. Thus, within a half-century of the Portuguese seizure of Goa and Melaka, Asians had assimilated most Portuguese into their social world, or, in the case of the Japanese, had expelled them. By about 1600 Asia was looking very much as it had before the Portuguese arrival in 1498.

In Europe, in spite or more likely because of the Wars of Religion, the Dutch seized the opportunity to enter the Asian market. With their powerful market economy, the Dutch were well positioned to enter the arena of long-distance trading. They possessed an astonishingly rich resource base and a working knowledge of Asian waters. Jan Huyghen van Linschoten provided the latter. In 1594, he returned to Holland after serving the Portuguese for ten years, six of them in Goa. Using van Linschoten's maps, sailing directions, and detailed information about the spice trade, separate groups of Dutch merchants posted sixty-five ships to Asian waters between 1595 and 1602. As anticipated, the ships returned with cargoes of fine spices—mace, cloves, and nutmeg—that earned their sponsors handsome profits.

These unplanned ventures came at a cost, a marketplace glutted with spices. In order to remedy this situation, several groups of Dutch merchants agreed to pool their resources to create a unique commercial organization, the United East India Company (*Vereenigde Oost-Indische Compagnie*, or VOC, founded in 1602). Its initial capitalization was an astounding 6.5 million guldens. What made the VOC unique was the separation of investors from the company's professional managers. In the early years of this experiment in business organization, the VOC usually paid between 25 and 30 percent dividends on shares in the company. The Dutch creation would soon be known as a "joint stock" company, a revolutionary business structure that had revolutionary consequences for Asian trade.

THE DUTCH EMPIRE IN INDONESIA

Among the most successful of the first generation of VOC managers were Governors-General Jan Pieterszoon Coen (served 1617–1629) and his able successor Anthony van Diemen (served 1636–1645). Over the course of the seventeenth century, they and their successors fundamentally restructured the Indian Ocean trading network.

When Coen arrived in Asian waters, he discovered that the Spice Islands (the Moluccas) were not only a source of wealth but also stood at the crossroads of trade between India, China, and Japan. He decided that the center of trade had to be moved from the Arabian Seas circuit to the Indonesia–east Asia circuit. This meant abandoning the idea of a trading empire in favor of the establishment of an overseas capital, strategically located in Indonesia. From Indonesia he could deploy superior Dutch naval power, westward toward the Coromandel coast of India and the Bay of Bengal and eastward toward Japan and China. The navy would also be used to maintain control of the Spice Islands themselves.

As a first step, in 1619, Governor-General Coen seized the Javanese port of Jakarta and renamed it

Batavia, the Roman name of Holland; it became the "major naval base, shipbuilding center, and entrepôt for the Dutch East India Company" (Ringrose, p. 158). Coen found local allies in the large Chinese community of Batavia. His two chief Chinese collaborators were Su Minggang, a godfather figure in the Chinese community, and his chief aide Jan Con, whose primary function was to recruit laborers from the southeastern coastal province of Fujian. Su and Jan also advised Coen and van Diemen on market conditions in the two eastern circuits of the Indian Ocean and, on their own initiative, developed the hinterland of Batavia. The Chinese established sugar plantations and harvested the timber resources of Java. In both cases, they used the labor of Fujianese coolies. Coen's collaboration with the Chinese points to an important reality about Batavia, that it was from the outset both a Dutch and a Chinese town. With the passage of time, the Chinese community became more and

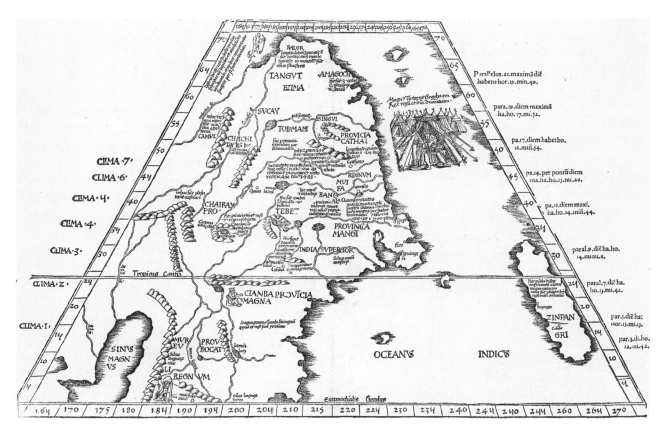

Asia. A woodcut map of China and Japan by Lorenz Fries that was originally published in a 1522 edition of Ptolemy's *Geographia*. Considered the first modern map of the area, it is based on the accounts of Marco Polo's journeys to China. The Great Khan is pictured in the upper right. Japan is shown at the far right, based on information Polo got from the Chinese. The existence of Japan was not confirmed to Europeans until 1542 when the Portuguese landed there. Map COLLECTION, STERLING MEMORIAL LIBRARY, YALE UNIVERSITY

more robust at the expense of the Dutch. Finally, in the mid-eighteenth century, the Dutch turned on the Chinese residents (their former collaborators), massacring ten thousand of them and looting their homes and businesses.

Shocking as this massacre may seem, the Dutch had long before acquired a reputation for cruelty in their empire building. In fact, the systematic use of naval power was a basic tactic in Coen's strategy to create a "ring of force" around the Moluccas and the other Spice Islands (Fernandez-Armesto, p. 326). In pursuit of that goal, the Dutch used maximum force on a number of occasions. For example, in 1621 Dutch forces either killed or deported as slaves the entire population of the island of Banda. When the Ceramese rebelled against Dutch policy and killed 160 Dutch in 1651, the Dutch in retaliation forcibly resettled twelve thousand Ceramese from Ceram Island to Amboina and Manipa.

The Dutch completed their ring of force around the Spice Islands in 1669, when they reduced Makassar (Ujung Pandang), the most powerful of the Indonesian states, to a colony. The defeat of Makassar gave the Dutch a world monopoly over the production of spices. Only Bantam maintained a semblance of independence from the Dutch, but by 1682 it, too, had become a VOC colony. The isolated and fragmented island polities of Indonesia were simply no match for the powerful Dutch navy and the VOC's single-minded drive to control spice production.

Was the spice monopoly worth the price? Most historians would agree that an Asian market for spices remained very active throughout this period, while European spice consumption was declining. Only the growing mid-eighteenth-century popularity of cinnamon from Ceylon increased the total VOC revenue from spices. Still, the question persists, and it may well be that the VOC's spice monopoly was not profitable in the long run. First, it limited the ability of the VOC to maneuver in a changing world market. Although spices were a safe source of profit, they had little potential for growth, at least in Europe. Meanwhile, a consumer culture had emerged in Europe and Asia that was demanding such goods as textiles, tea, and coffee. The VOC seemed incapable of responding to these new demands, because its labyrinthine bureaucratic struc-

ture was tied to the flow of spices. The VOC's chief rival, the English East India Company (EEIC), founded in 1600, had already decided that these new commodities had a much larger potential market than spices. Furthermore, the cost of maintaining a naval force large enough to enforce the VOC's monopoly was enormous. In other words, the cost of empire may ultimately have exceeded its profits. The Dutch were able to reduce the gap between cost and profit only by introducing the cultivation of coffee in the eighteenth century.

Creating a ring of force around the fine spices in Indonesia was but one aspect of the Dutch presence in Asia. Indeed, the largest part of seventeenth-century VOC activity was in the "country trade" of the Indian Ocean. In the 1630s and 1640s the company derived its largest profits from its monopoly over the sale of spices within Asia and its transportation of Japanese silver to China. More importantly, in carving out a major role for the VOC in the "country trade," the Dutch fundamentally altered the intraregional trading system. The revolutionary organizational structure of the VOC allowed the Dutch to systematize the intra-Asian carrying trade in a way never before possible, and, in the process, displace Asian merchants. By 1700, VOC managers through the organizational efficiencies of their company were transforming once-independent Asian merchants into their clients. The decline of the Asian merchants' status continued into the eighteenth century as the Dutch (and later the English) came to control more and more of the country trade through their joint stock companies.

THE RISE OF THE ENGLISH IN ASIA
The decline of the VOC relative to its European competitors, primarily the EEIC, can be placed somewhere between 1680 and 1720. It has been attributed to three factors: excessive dividends; the high cost of maintaining the spice monopoly; and the inflexibility of VOC, which rendered it unable to respond to the demands of new consumer cultures of Europe and Asia. Although the VOC remained a viable economic force in Asia throughout the eighteenth century, the EEIC was also slowly displacing it as the dominant European trader in Asia.

In 1600, no one could have predicted that England would become Europe's most successful empire builder in Asia. The earlier achievements of the Portuguese and Dutch and those of the late-arriving French pale in comparison with English successes of the eighteenth century. In a matter of a half-century, from about 1750 to about 1800, the English had become masters of most of the Indian subcontinent, and in 1793 they were prepared to push farther east and challenge the mighty Qing empire for sovereignty and power in east Asia.

What historical pushes and pulls transformed the English East India Company from its seventeenth-century status as beggar at the court of the great Mughal emperors to that of masters of a British India in the eighteenth century? In 1600, the English did indeed beg the Mughals of India for a *farman,* an imperial directive that would grant England regular trading privileges throughout the Mughal empire and, with it, access to the markets of south Asia. In 1608 Captain William Hawkins (c. 1560–1613), the first of the English East India Company's envoys, received permission for the company to trade at Surat, but the Mughal emperor offered no *farman* encompassing the whole empire. Other envoys followed, Sir Thomas Roe in 1618 and William Hedges in 1682. The latter's mission is particularly revealing of the EEIC's status in late-seventeenth-century Mughal India.

EEIC officials in Bengal and the company's governor in London, Sir Josiah Child, interfered with Hughes's mission, causing Emperor Aurangzeb ('Ālamgir; ruled 1658–1707) to break off the negotiations. Challenged, or, perhaps embarrassed, Child decided on war with the Mughals. "Child's War," 1686–1690, ended in disaster for the English. In 1689 the Mughal fleet commanded by the African Sidi Yakub took Bombay, which had been an English entrepôt since 1668. After a year of resistance, the English surrendered, and in 1690 the company sent envoys to Aurangzeb's camp to plead for a pardon. The company's envoys had to prostrate themselves before the emperor, pay an enormous indemnity, and promise better behavior in the future. The emperor withdrew his troops and the company subsequently reestablished itself in Bombay and set up a new base in Calcutta.

The 1690s were the start of a period of economic expansion for the EEIC in Asia. Only Bombay on the subcontinent's west coast did not share in the general expansion of the company's other major entrepôts, Madras and Calcutta, on the east coast. Bombay's trade suffered because the Marathan admiral Kanhoji Angria targeted its shipping, and until the 1730s, the advantage lay with Kanhoji. Meanwhile, Madras and Calcutta prospered as the volume of trade grew exponentially in such items as cotton textiles, silks, molasses, and saltpeter. Although the tea trade had its origins back in the 1660s, it was not until the turn of the century that it began to take hold as the preferred beverage among English of all social strata; the boom in tea profits had to wait until the eighteenth century. Meanwhile, American silver paid for the bulk of English imports, including tea. London critics denounced the outflow of bullion for Asian goods, but handsome dividends had a way of silencing mercantilist rhetoric.

Beginning in the 1690s and reaching into the 1750s, the EEIC started shedding its beggar status and laying claim to a loftier standing within the Asian trading world. Neither the EEIC nor its ally, the English government, had decided on a course of empire building in Asia. Rather, the convergence of a number of historical developments in the mid-eighteenth century not only made empire building possible but also invited it. First, the EEIC encouraged its servants and free traders to pursue trade aggressively within the intra-Asian trading system. This policy allowed men like the country trader Thomas Pitt, who later became governor of Madras, to earn vast fortunes. A second development was the company's merger with the many private syndicates operating in Asian waters. These syndicates, called "interlopers," had regularly disregarded the EEIC's legal monopoly over Asian trade. The merger resulted in the heavy recapitalization of the EEIC (at about 3.2 million pounds) and its renaming in 1708 as the United East India Company. Third, concurrent with the merger with the "interloper" syndicates was the systematization of the company's bureaucracy. Its streamlined organization gave it a competitive edge over the VOC and Indian-operated shipping. The effects of this combination—heavy English investment and an efficiently functioning bureaucracy—were almost immediately visible. English shipping interests pushed the Dutch aside and greatly reduced Indian participation in the intra-Asian trade of the Indian Ocean. Fourth, the early successes of the EEIC depended upon alliances with Indian merchants, like the house of Jagat Seth. By the mid-eighteenth century, however, the Indian partners had already begun the long slide into dependency on the company. Such dependencies would become a feature of English-Indian relations after 1750, as partnerships gave way to client status for Indian merchants. In this regard, the eighteenth-century English experience in Asia paralleled to a great extent that of the Dutch in Indonesia.

The English East India Company's continued fortunes in south Asia ultimately turned on its ability to obtain an empire-wide *farman* from the now declining Mughal overlords of India. After another English ambassador in 1701 had failed to obtain the elusive guarantee, a new mission to Delhi headed by John Surman threatened to withdraw the company's factors from Surat and its other establishments in Gujarat unless it was granted. Because the company's economic stake in this western region of India generated a significant amount of revenue for the Mughals, the emperor, Farrukhsiyar, relented. He granted a *farman* on 31 December 1716, little realizing the far-reaching consequences of his action. EEIC officials now resembled other imperial officeholders of the Mughal empire. More importantly, under the terms of the directive, the EEIC could take action against anyone infringing on its rights. It was this aspect of the *farman* that opened the way for future intervention in the political affairs of India, and intervention over the course of the eighteenth century eventually led to the incorporation of India into a British empire.

Was English intervention after 1716 a result of an alliance struck between the company and wealthy and powerful Indian merchants, such as the house of Jagat Seth? Was the company drawn into Indian politics in order to safeguard its own growing economic, political, and territorial investments? Was conquest the result of the transplantation of eighteenth-century Anglo-French rivalries into Asian waters, a rivalry that carried over into Indian politics? These are some of the questions historians are presently debating regarding the British conquest of India. The debate continues; the best that can be offered here is a brief account of the stages of the conquest, with an eye toward Macartney's 1793 mission to China.

Eighteenth-century English expansion into India falls into three periods. The first was a period in which the company agents and private traders found their way into "a lively market in commercial, fiscal and military opportunities" (Keay, p. 377). This was the "market opportunities" stage, 1716–1748. "Colonial imperialism" made its appearance in the 1740s. Beginning in that decade, the English and French engaged in a series of wars for empire. In India, the most famous protagonists of these conflicts were Joseph-François Dupleix and Charles de Bussy-Castelnau on the French side and Robert Clive and Charles Watson on the English side. Victory ultimately came to the English in the 1760s because of three factors: the decisive leadership of men like Clive, Watson, and William Pitt, the architect of victory in the Seven Years' War (1756–1763); the superior ability of the English to pay for Indian allies and Indian troops (called sepoys); and finally an appetite for empire, which had begun to emerge during the course of the Seven Years' War in India. Certainly Robert Clive was its first proponent, and almost all of his late-eighteenth-century successors, especially Richard Wellesley, shared Pitt's and Clive's imperial ambitions.

The period between 1764 and the end of the century marked the true beginnings of British dominion in India. The French had been defeated. However, before the English could truly lay claim to the title of *raj*, they had to overcome stiff Indian resistance. In addition to the Four Mysore wars (1767–1804), the three Maratha wars (1780–1803), and the two Sikh wars (c. 1840–1856), there were a host of lesser battles fought and won. The English may not have had a plan of conquest for India, but this succession of wars strongly suggests that their appetite for empire grew with the eating of the Indian pudding. Seen from this perspective, the mission of Macartney to China was but a further extension of England's expanding Asian empire.

Before the Macartney mission, English East Indiamen had been trading on the South China coast since the second decade of the eighteenth century. What had attracted them was tea, a product for which there was an expanding consumer market in the Atlantic world. By the 1780s, Western demand had grown to a point where it was causing balance of payment problems for English merchantmen. As mercantilists they parted reluctantly with their silver, but that was precisely what the Chinese demanded for their tea. Secondly, English traders chafed under Qing empire–imposed restrictions requiring that all commerce must be conducted at the port of Canton (Guangzhou) and through designated Chinese merchants. It was in hopes of ending these trade restrictions and opening markets for English manufactured products as a way to solve the balance of payments problem that the British government dispatched Macartney to China in 1793.

ASIA IN THE EUROPEAN IMAGINATION

By the time Ambassador Macartney sailed for China, Eurocentrically imagined Asians had become familiar figures on the European scene. During the nearly three centuries since Vasco da Gama had made landfall on the Malabar coast, a large body of literature about Asia and Asians had accumulated. Contributors included Jesuit missionaries, land and sea voyagers, official embassies, fictional writers, and "Asianist" scholars of several varieties, none of whom had ever visited any part of Asia, but who still wrote "knowingly" about it. From the fifteenth-century beginnings of Europe's contacts with Asia, Asia became whatever suited the needs of the Western imagination. More importantly, the Western perspective on Asia shifted over time. The shift occurred very late in the early modern period, around the 1770s. Until then an idealized Asia prevailed. At some indeterminate moment in the late seventeenth century China came to represent this idealized Asia. Asia (read China) was a land of wisdom, moral philosophy, and good government by a cultured elite. China was everything Europe should be. The idealization culminated in the eighteenth-century China vogue known as *chinoiserie*. In France, it expressed itself in a cult of Confucius, and in England it influenced everything from art to architecture to garden designs.

Suddenly, in the last quarter of the eighteenth century, this particular Eurocentrically idealized imagine of Asia came crashing down. Those who brought it down were men of the high Enlightenment, the Daniel Defoes, Horace Walpoles, Montesquieus, and Voltaires. Aided by a new "scientific" approach to history, the philosophes discovered that Asia (read China) was backward, despotic, and intellectually stagnant, and that Asians

were physically inferior. From the vantage point of this new perspective, Europeans believed that they had little to learn from Asians, but that Asians had much to learn from progressive, modern Europeans. It was this perspective that Macartney took with him when he met the Qing emperor in 1793. It has been this perspective that has informed much of the writings about Europe's contact with Asia since then. It was only in the last twenty years or so of the twentieth century that a rising generation of historians has sought to revise this Eurocentrically imagined perspective of Asia and reimagine Eurasia in a global setting.

See also **British Colonies: India; Cartography and Geography; Colonialism; Dutch Colonies: The East Indies; Europe and the World; Exploration; French Colonies: India; Gama, Vasco da; Goa; Portuguese Colonies: The Indian Ocean and Asia; Trading Companies.**

BIBLIOGRAPHY

Barendse, R. J. "Trade and State in the Arabian Seas: A Survey from the Fifteenth to the Eighteenth Century." *Journal of World History* 11, no. 2 (2000): 173–225.

Braudel, Fernand. *The Wheels of Commerce.* Translated by Siân Reynolds. New York, 1982.

Chaudhuri, K. N. *Asia before Europe: Economy and Civilisation of the Indian Ocean from the Rise of Islam to 1750.* Cambridge, U.K., and New York, 1990.

———. *Trade and Civilisation in the Indian Ocean: An Economic History from the Rise of Islam to 1750.* Cambridge, U.K., and New York, 1985.

Fernandez-Armesto, Felipe. *Millennium.* New York and London, 1995.

Hevia, James L. *Cherishing Men from Afar: Qing Guest Ritual and the Macartney Embassy of 1793.* Durham, N.C., 1995.

Keay, John. *India: A History.* London, 2000.

Linton, Derek S. "Asia and the West in the New World Economy—The Limited Thalassocracies: The Portuguese and the Dutch in Asia, 1498–1700." In *Asia in Western and World History: A Guide for Teaching.* Edited by Ainslie T. Embree and Carol Gluck. Armonk, N.Y., 1997.

———. "Asia and the West in the New World Order—From Trading Companies to Free Trade Imperialism: The British and their Rivals in Asia, 1700–1850." In *Asia in Western and World History: A Guide for Teaching.* Edited by Ainslie T. Embree and Carol Gluck. Armonk, N.Y., 1997.

Mungello, D. E. *The Great Encounter of China and the West, 1500–1800.* Lanham, Md., 1999.

Parry, J. H. *The Establishment of the European Hegemony: 1415–1715: Trade and Exploration in the Age of the Renaissance.* New York, 1966.

Pomeranz, Kenneth. *The Great Divergence: China, Europe, and the Making of the Modern World Economy.* Princeton, 2000.

Pomeranz, Kenneth, and Steven Topik. *The World That Trade Created: Society, Culture, and the World Economy, 1400 to the Present.* Armonk, N.Y., 1999.

Reid, Anthony. *Charting the Shape of Early Modern Southeast Asia.* Singapore, 2000.

Ringrose, David R. *Expansion and Global Interaction, 1200–1700.* New York, 2000.

Robb, Peter. *A History of India.* Basingstoke, U.K., 2002.

SarDesai, D. R. *Southeast Asia Past and Present.* 4th ed. Boulder, Colo., 1997.

Spence, Jonathan D. *The Chan's Great Continent: China in Western Minds.* New York, 1998.

Thompson, William R. "The Military Superiority Thesis and the Ascendancy of Western Eurasia in the World System." *Journal of World History* 10, no. 1 (1999): 143–178.

CHARLES LILLEY

ASSASSINATION. Assassination, according to Franklin L. Ford, "is the intentional killing of a specified victim or group of victims, perpetrated for a reason related to his (her, their) public prominence and undertaken with a political purpose in view." It is usually an answer to an alleged political crime, the latter being generally defined as an offense by which the criminal betrays his allegiance to principles or persons that bind the political order, or by which the criminal challenges or hinders the political authority.

Early modern societies were predominantly Christian, thus it might seem strange to find so many instances of assassination during that time. After all, murder is prohibited under divine, and humane, law. But there were religious motives behind many of these killings. Assassinations were partly justified by arguments taken from the Old Testament, in which many kings accused of tyranny were killed: Eglon, Absalom, Joram, Holophernes, to name a few. Works of famous Greek philosophers, such as Aristotle, and medieval theologians, such as John of Salisbury or Thomas Aquinas, were also used to vindicate political murders.

It would be an exaggeration to say that every assassination that occurred during 1450–1789 was religiously motivated. For instance, in 1483 in the last stages of the War of the Roses, Richard Duke of Gloucester murdered the twelve-year-old Edward V and his younger brother and was himself crowned Richard III. In 1762, Tsar Peter III was killed, which allowed his wife Catherine to come to power. But more often than not, from 1500 to 1650, when the mortality rate among political leaders was very high, religion played a central role in the events.

During the era of religious wars, many theorists from both sides alleged that a prince who embraced a false religion forfeited his subjects' allegiance. According to the radical George Buchanan, when war was declared between a ruler and his people in such a manner, everybody has the right to kill the enemy. Early in the fifteenth century, the French theologian Jean Petit said that it was "lawful for any subject, without any order or command, according to moral, divine, and natural law, to kill or cause to be killed a traitor and disloyal tyrant." Catholics—one of them a monk—stabbed to death two French kings, Henry III in 1589 and Henry IV in 1610, because they thought the kings were secretly working for the victory of the Protestant cause. In 1634, sectarian hatreds also played a role in the assassination of Albrecht von Wallenstein, a Protestant turned Catholic who had become the supreme commander of the imperial forces during the Thirty Years' War (1618–1648). His reluctance to implement religious measures designed to strengthen the grip of Catholicism in Germany created some suspicions. Convinced of his treason, the emperor Ferdinand II ordered that he be caught dead or alive. On the night of 25 February 1634, von Wallenstein was stabbed to death, along with his closest collaborators.

The early modern political scene was therefore quite violent, especially in comparison to the medieval period, when Christians made every effort to control political violence. Religion was no longer used to forbid assassination. On the contrary, it became an excuse to murder. Popes celebrated the deaths of Protestant princes such as William the Silent, who was killed in 1584 in Holland. Jesuit theologians such as Juan de Mariana and Francisco Suárez wrote texts in which they defended tyrannicide. Protestant leaders like John Calvin and Eliz-

Assassination. A drawing depicts Henry IV of France after his stabbing on 14 May 1610 by the Catholic François Ravaillac. ©STEFANO BIANCHETTI/CORBIS

abeth I also resorted to violence when they wanted to be rid of an enemy. The years 1500–1650 witnessed a great number of civil wars. The end of these wars and the consolidation of states meant that, generally speaking, Damocles' swords were no longer lingering over the princes' head. This quiet came to an end with the revolutionary era of the 1790s.

See also **Crime and Punishment; Monarchy; Revolutions, Age of; Violence; Wallenstein, A. W. E. von.**

BIBLIOGRAPHY

Ford, F. L. *Political Murder: From Tyrannicide to Terrorism.* Cambridge, Mass., 1985.

Minois, G. *Le couteau et le poison: L'assassinat politique en Europe (1400–1800).* Paris, 1997.

Mousnier, R. *The Assassination of Henry IV.* London, 1973.

MICHEL DE WAELE

ASTROLOGY. Defining early modern astrology is a thorny issue. The early modern distinction between "natural" and "judicial" astrology, still widely used among scholars, served to express moral and religious qualifications. Hence, its meaning was highly localized. A more useful starting point is obtained from astrology's status as an academic discipline, which endowed it with more universal pedagogical narratives. Following Hellenistic and Arabic antecedents, Italian professors such as Peter of Abano (1257–c. 1315) distinguished between a "science of motions" and a "science of judgments." While this distinction roughly mirrors that between our "astronomy" and "astrology," a closer look reveals important overlaps. For instance, late medieval astronomical textbooks often included considerations of the distances and size of celestial bodies, astrological aspects, planetary conjunctions, eclipses, and lunar mansions. It is therefore best to approach late medieval astrology as a "science of the stars" that comprised both celestial motions and judgments. Paraphrasing Gervasius Marstaller (1549), we might define our topic as follows: "Astrology aims at predicting and/or studying the power of celestial bodies on earth and measures their positions by means of astronomy."

This definition reflects astrology's position within the disciplinary hierarchies of the late medieval university. The emphasis on prediction reveals the simple fact that astrology was mostly taught as an auxiliary tool for medical prognosis. A practical ability to calculate astronomical data and assess concomitant celestial effects was widely expected from medical graduates. The reference to a more "theoretical" study of celestial effects reflects the pervasive influence of Aristotelian logic, epistemology, and physics, which was institutionalized in the arts faculties. Just like medical physiological textbooks, most introductions to astrology (typically Ptolemy or Alcabitius) sought to express basic parameters like planetary effects, or the nature of zodiacal signs, in terms of Aristotle's four manifest qualities (hot, cold, wet, dry). When this proved unconvincing, astrological effects were counted as "influences," based on "occult qualities": one could perceive their results on earth, but not their manifest action in the celestial bodies. This did not necessarily undermine astrology's academic status. Cardinal Pierre d'Ailly (1350–1420), for instance, promoted a "concordance of astrology and theology" that proved highly successful in several universities.

Many developments in the early modern period can be interpreted as attempts to safeguard astrology's status as it branched out beyond the university. Most academic astrologers were trained to perform a wide range of astrological tasks: they discussed large-scale predictions (mundane astrology), individual fates (natal astrology), or even particular events (horary astrology, subdivided into elections and interrogations). Courts and local town authorities increasingly drew upon political astrological consulting in the late Middle Ages. Beginning in the 1470s, print technology brought these political particulars to a wider, predominantly urban, audience through a new astrological genre: the annual prognostication. The propagandistic value of such initiatives contributed to the formation of close alliances between prognosticators and court culture in Italy, France, Germany, Poland, and the Low Countries in the late fifteenth century.

Such alliances proved to be a liability in times of political or religious crisis. The self-fulfillment of popular prognostications, and their ability to stir unrest, provoked several astrological debates, where both prognosticators and their university learning came under attack. Undoubtedly the most influential example of such criticism was Giovanni Pico's massive *Disputations against Divinatory Astrology* (1494). By the early sixteenth century, humanistic astrologers in both Italy and northern Europe addressed the Piconian challenge through reform proposals. These were often, but not exclusively, directed at the courtly audience that supported the rise of the prognosticators.

In the course of the sixteenth century, astrological reformers accomplished two significant feats. By advocating a return to ancient, mostly Ptolemaic astrology, they inaugurated a departure from the

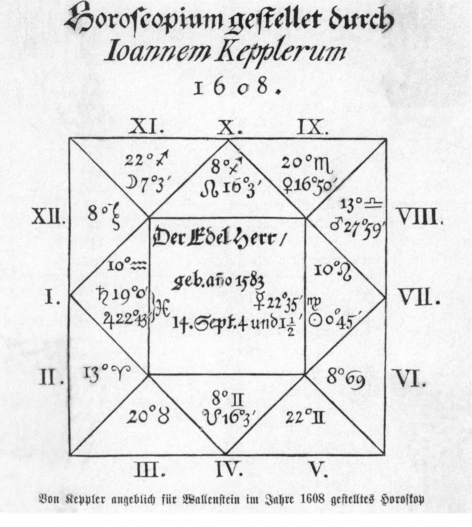

Astrology. A horoscope chart drawn by Johannes Kepler for Albrecht von Wallenstein, 1608.
©BETTMANN/CORBIS

Arabic traditions that dominated the late medieval "science of judgments." And by tackling both astronomical and astrological reform, they legitimized a gradual change in the definition of astronomy. For example, it is now becoming clear that the astronomical innovations of Nicolaus Copernicus, Tycho Brahe, and Johannes Kepler can be interpreted within the framework of Pico's attack. Their reversal of the traditional subordination of mathematics to natural philosophy seems to flow from an attempt to rescue the physical basis of astrology. Likewise, educational reformers like Philipp Melanchthon (1497–1560) strongly emphasized astrology as a part of physics.

This development also provoked a gradual separation of the "science of motions" and "science of judgments." Although Copernican astronomy also presented theological challenges, these were easier to negotiate than the social and religious problems of astrological judgment. As a result, reformers gradually abandoned public astrological predictions: first horary astrology, then natal astrology, and finally weather prediction and some forms of medical astrology. Likewise, "astrological" prediction was gradually ousted from official university curricula. After the 1560s, and well into the second half of the seventeenth century, Catholic and Protestant church authorities issued numerous condemnations of "judicial" or "superstitious" astrology. The "science of motions," on the other hand, was flourishing. It is important to realize that this emerging "astronomy" retained several astrological interests, such as the nature of the heavens, the size and distance of celestial bodies, and the origins of comets.

The pace at which such changes occurred depended on local circumstances. In England, central licensing through the Stationers Company (1603), the absence of strong academic links, and the subsequent explosion of astrological consulting during the Civil War propelled astrological reform projects into the late eighteenth century. Possibly due to local academic structures, Italian medical astrology also seems to have enjoyed a longer lease on life than elsewhere on the Continent. In the seventeenth century, influential astrologers Simon Forman, William Lilly, and Jean-Baptiste Morin remained highly visible, while astrological almanacs even outsold the Bible.

But although extraordinary phenomena like eclipses (1652, 1654) or comets (1664–1665) still provoked general unease, a gradual popularization of astrology occurred in the second half of the seventeenth century. The new royal scientific societies rejected astrology from their research agendas. The upper class no longer found its way to reputed astrological practitioners by the late seventeenth century. After 1650, ecclesiastics and university physicians increasingly left the writing of popular almanacs to surveyors, engineers, or local teachers. Their products became increasingly pseudonymous or anonymous, showed a rapid decline in astrological content, and were mainly distributed in rural areas by peddlers. By the early eighteenth century, the middle class and the nobility were closing ranks in the condemnation of an "irrational" astrology, which, at the same time, became socially innocuous. Paradoxically, this situation may have contributed to the survival of local pockets of astrological beliefs, both "traditional" (such as Ebenezer Sibly) and "modernized" (for example, among British colonial army doctors).

See also **Astronomy; Brahe, Tycho; Copernicus, Nicolaus; Dissemination of Knowledge; Kepler, Johannes; Melanchthon, Philipp; Occult; Philosophy; Popular Culture; Universities.**

BIBLIOGRAPHY

Curry, Patrick. *Prophecy and Power: Astrology in Early Modern England.* Princeton, 1989. Innovative in its systematic focus on the social and political meaning of seventeenth-century astrology, but with a somewhat narrow selection of relevant backgrounds.

Grafton, Anthony. *Cardano's Cosmos: The Worlds and Works of a Renaissance Astrologer.* Cambridge, Mass., 1999. An entertaining introduction to Italian astrology in the Renaissance.

Harrison, Mark. "From Medical Astrology to Medical Astronomy: Sol-lunar and Planetary Theories of Disease in British Medicine, c. 1700–1850." *British Journal for the History of Science* 33 (2000): 25–48.

Smoller, Laura Ackerman. *History, Prophecy, and the Stars: The Christian Astrology of Pierre d'Ailly, 1350–1420.* Princeton, 1994.

Thomas, Keith. *Religion and the Decline of Magic.* New York, 1971.

vanden Broecke, Steven. *The Limits of Influence: Pico, Louvain, and the Crisis of Renaissance Astrology.* Leiden, 2003. Investigates the links between astrological practice in the university, court, and city, and the implications for elite astrology, in the fifteenth and sixteenth centuries.

Westman, Robert S. "Copernicus and the Prognosticators: The Bologna Period, 1496–1500." *Universitas* 5 (1993): 1–5.

STEVEN VANDEN BROECKE

ASTRONOMY. The movement of the stars and planets has fascinated humans for thousands of years. For the vast majority of ancient astronomers, the stars seemed to be equally distant from Earth in what was an Earth-centered (or "geocentric") cosmos. The ancient Greeks observed that the stars revolved westward around the north celestial pole every twenty-three hours and fifty-six minutes, thus constituting a kind of objective clock. Most envisaged these revolving stars to be located on a sphere, composing an incorruptible, celestial orb that could easily be contrasted with the world of change, generation, and corruption on Earth (to which irregular meteorological phenomena such as comets were also understood to belong). Against the backdrop of this outer sphere, the Sun was seen to move along a path termed the ecliptic, while the planets moved within eight degrees of this path. These usually moved eastward, though occasionally they moved in the opposite direction, thus exhibiting retrograde motion. Many Greek astronomers suggested that the Sun could be placed on the equator of an inner sphere that revolved once a year, hence constituting a second sphere in addition to the stellar orb. Following the theories of the fourth-century-B.C.E. scholar Eudoxus, astronomers and natural philosophers became increasingly committed to the idea that the motions of each planet could be accounted for by means of their own specific, homocentric spheres.

DEFENDING AN
EARTH-CENTERED UNIVERSE

The retrograde motion of the planets offended against the apparent simplicity of heavenly motions, as well as the dictum that their orbits were circular. From the third century B.C.E., astronomers began to conceive of planets rotating in small circles (epicycles) around a point that moved on a carrier orbit (or deferent). This accounted for the apparent motions of the planets, including their retrograde motion, although others followed Aristotle in positing the existence of homocentric spheres. After Ptolemy's composition of the *Almagest* in the second century C.E., the movements of the planets could be accurately represented by means of techniques involving the use of epicycles, deferents, eccentrics (whereby planetary motion is conceived as circular with respect to a point displaced from Earth), and equants (a device that posits a constant angular rate of rotation with respect to a point displaced from Earth). These approaches, and arguments over the reality of the celestial orbs, continued to be refined in the following centuries by first Muslim and then Christian astronomers. The geocentric cosmos was readily appropriated by Christians, many of whom believed that God existed outside the stellar sphere and (as evidenced by Dante's fourteenth-century poem *Divine Comedy*) that angels turned the epicycles and spheres in the intervening spaces.

Astronomy had a primarily practical function, and by the thirteenth century it played a central role in determining the dates of religious festivals. Ptolemy's mathematically sophisticated *Almagest*, with various commentaries, formed the basis for advanced astronomy in university curricula from this period onward. In the late fifteenth century, the arrival of the printing press coincided with the transmission to western Europe of a number of important Greek mathematical and astronomical manu-

scripts. These became a new focal point for doing astronomy, as ancient texts could be seen and assessed in their original form (as opposed to being translated into Latin from Syriac or Arabic). Georg von Peuerbach (1423–1461) and his pupil Regiomontanus produced important works that formed the basis of astronomical training for the next century.

Astronomy was equally significant for providing data from which astrological predictions could be made (judicial astrology). The effects that heavenly actions had on earthly events, and the manner in which they were carried out, constituted a problem for most human societies. Astrology was a major part of both daily life and intellectual culture, and was deeply implicated in politics, medicine, and agriculture. However, its use was increasingly questioned by elites in the late sixteenth century; both Catholics and Protestants argued that the notion that the relations between stars and planets influenced or governed human behavior detracted from the primary Christian belief in free will. Nevertheless, this argument was often expressed as a condemnation of *bad* astrology, the implication being that astrology was a credible art or science that could be reformed. However, although it was still taken seriously by Johannes Kepler at the beginning of the seventeenth century, it was almost universally despised by social elites a hundred years later.

In Aristotle's *De Caelo*, heavenly bodies were treated as physical objects and thus as a branch of natural philosophy, or physics. Astronomy thus enjoyed a somewhat bifurcated position within the university system, taught partly in tandem with medicine and astrology, and partly as a higher-level, more technically difficult mathematical enterprise. This mirrored the scholarly distinction between the treatment of the physical reality of the supposedly "crystalline" spheres and such ideas as the epicycles, the actual existence of which was debatable. When Nicolaus Copernicus (1473–1543) published his heliocentric (Sun-centered) *De Revolutionibus Orbium Coelestium* (On the revolutions of the heavenly orbs) of 1543, a number of astronomers believed that his system could be treated as another convenient set of devices for explaining the celestial phenomena without any commitment to the reality of the general cosmology and physics that was prominent in the first part of the book. Indeed, the

Lutheran theologian Andreas Osiander (1498–1552) reassured readers in an anonymous preface to the work that Copernicus had merely devised "hypotheses" that facilitated the calculation of celestial positions.

THE COPERNICAN REVOLUTION

However, Copernicus had indeed upset the standard disciplinary division in universities, and he implied that a mathematical astronomer was entitled to speak about the physical nature of things—the traditional preserve of the more prestigious role of the natural philosopher. Not only did he offer the first modern heliocentric system (although he appealed to the authority of ancient heliocentric systems such as that of Pythagoras), but he asserted that the demonstrations in his work could only be understood by mathematically competent astronomers. He condemned the uncertainty of the calendar, and also of the inability of astronomers to determine the precise motions of the heavenly bodies. He lambasted the inconsistent use of homocentric circles and epicycles, and argued that the systems produced by recent astronomers lacked aesthetic credibility. Instead, with all the different techniques and philosophies in play, they had produced a sort of astronomical "monster."

Although he retained epicycles, Copernicus dispensed with the equant and showed that retrograde motion could be explained by means of a heliocentric system. Indeed, contra Osiander, he could hardly have been more assertive about the truth of his Sun-centered cosmos. He proffered tentative physical explanations of why objects on a revolving earth would not be ejected into the heavens, and argued that the stellar sphere had to be an enormous distance further away than that accepted by traditional astronomers. This meant that his inability to detect stellar parallax (the feature by which the apparent position of a star would vary depending on the time of year, since an observer on Earth would view it from a different position) would not be an argument against his system. Ominously, he also suggested that biblical passages that appeared to support geocentricity were the result of the author "accommodating" his discourse to the capacities of ordinary people. Momentous as it now seems, Copernicus's system had only a handful of adherents in the sixteenth century, although Erasmus Reinhold's

Prutenic Tables of 1551, which were based on methods pioneered by Copernicus, were used to produce the Gregorian calendar (decreed by Pope Gregory XIII) in 1582.

In the last three decades of the sixteenth century, the Danish astronomer Tycho Brahe (1546–1601) was single-handedly responsible for two major initiatives in astronomy. First, he devised a "geoheliocentric" system that, for the half-century before Copernicus's system was broadly accepted, provided the major alternative to a geocentric cosmos. In this, the Sun again revolved around the Earth, with the five planets (not including the Moon) revolving around the Sun; since the Martian and solar orbits intersected, this system could not accommodate the reality of the spheres. Tycho rejected a heliocentric system, partly because he could not abide the massive distances required by Copernicus's system, partly because he could not find stellar parallax, and partly because he was strongly opposed to heliocentrism on scriptural grounds.

Most important, Tycho made a series of naked-eye observations, conducted from 1574 as part of a monumental observation program at his observatory (Uraniborg) on the island of Hven. He designed and made new instruments that were as much as ten times more accurate than those of his predecessors. He also conceived of a means of using each of his devices to cross-check results obtained from other instruments in his collection. His instruments were less cumbersome than previous examples and he introduced new techniques for more precisely dividing them into minutes and seconds of a degree. He turned himself and his workplace—which had its own printing press—into the hub of an extensive network of correspondents, and he used this and personal contacts to train a number of the best astronomers of the next generation. Two of his measurements, linked to exceptional celestial events in the 1570s, demonstrated the precision of his observations. First, he determined the extreme distance from Earth of the terrifying supernova of 1572, and second, he showed for the first time that the comet of 1577 existed beyond the lunar sphere and hence was technically part of the heavens. Independent of any implications of *De Revolutionibus*, both seemed to suggest that the celestial sphere could no longer be considered immutable.

As Tycho's work came to a close, Johannes Kepler (1571–1630) burst on to the stage with his heliocentric *Mysterium Cosmographicum* (The secret of the universe) of 1596. Kepler was trained at Tübingen by the pro-Copernican Michael Mästlin (1550–1631), and throughout his adult life remained committed to a heliocentric system. In the *Mysterium* he famously attempted to show that the distances between the planets could be represented by nested regular solids, although this ultimately failed to fit the astronomical data produced by Tycho and his colleagues. At the end of 1600 Kepler traveled to Prague to work with Tycho, who had only recently been appointed imperial mathematician to Rudolf II. When Tycho died within the year, Kepler gained access to his data concerning the orbit of Mars. Tycho had observed the Martian orbit with astonishing accuracy, finding a discrepancy between the observed orbit and an ideal circular trajectory of eight feet that could not be explained by instrument error, and Kepler sought strenuously over the next few years to provide a harmonious and geometrically satisfying orbit to fit these observations. After many different shapes had been tried, he decided that Mars and the other planets traveled in ellipses, one of whose foci was the Sun, and that each planet swept out equal areas in equal times (considering the area to be drawn out by a line linking the planet to the Sun).

Kepler published his first two laws of planetary motion in his *Astronomia Nova* (New astronomy) of 1609, although they are merely a handful of many mathematical relations that he posed for planetary orbits. In this work he also appealed to the magnetic philosophy devised by the English physicist William Gilbert in his *De Magnete* (On the magnet) of 1600, in order to explain the physical causes of heavenly motion. He suggested that the planets, which all traveled in the same direction and (virtually) in the same plane, were controlled by a motive force emanating from the Sun. His third and final law, first enunciated in his *Harmonice Mundi* (Harmony of the world) of 1619, is more complicated and states that the square of the mean orbital period of a planet is proportional to the cube of its mean distance from the Sun. Kepler combined a Platonic-Pythagorean concern for the reality of harmonies and ratios with a magnetic physics, but from a disciplinary point of view he was explicitly asserting the right of an astronomer such as himself to produce a "celestial physics" that gave the true (non-Aristotelian) causes of heavenly motion. In a work on astrology of 1601, he also attempted to uncover the physical causes underlying the influence that planetary conjunctions had on earthly activities.

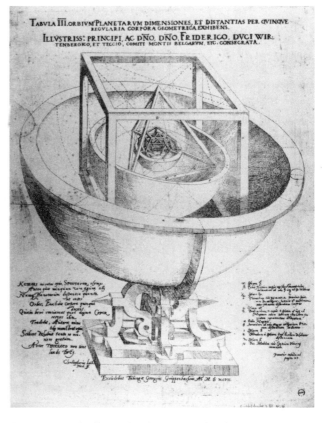

Astronomy. An illustration from Kepler's *Mysterium Cosmographicum*, 1596, in which he suggested that the irregular spacing of the planets could be represented as a series of geometric forms inscribed one within another. NEW YORK PUBLIC LIBRARY PICTURE COLLECTION

THE SCIENTIFIC REVOLUTION

In 1609, the same year that Kepler published his first two laws, Galileo Galilei (1564–1642) used a combination of lenses to look at the heavens, having heard of a similar invention that had been introduced the year before. Within weeks, he had deduced that the Moon had mountains and valleys (and was thus not perfectly smooth), had noted that the Milky Way was actually composed of numerous stars, and proposed that Jupiter possessed four satellites that revolved around it as the Moon revolved around Earth. For his extraordinary discoveries, which appeared in *Sidereus Nuncius* (Starry messenger) of 1610, he was rewarded with the position of court philosopher to his onetime pupil, Cosimo de' Medici (Cosimo II), grand duke of Tuscany. Galileo was now a court intellectual to rival Johannes Kepler, who had succeeded Tycho Brahe as imperial mathematician to Rudolf II. Given the courtly locations of both Kepler and Galileo, twentieth- and twenty-first-century historians have pointed to the prevalence of nonuniversity locations as the most important settings for innovative astronomy. Kepler's friendly stance toward Galileo (he wrote a book praising Galileo's discoveries within months of the work appearing) ensured that there was minimal animosity between them, although this may have been helped by Galileo's apparent complete ignorance of Kepler's own discoveries.

In the next two and a half decades, adherence to the Copernican system met with determined opposition and, notoriously, René Descartes felt obliged to suppress his not sufficiently anti-Copernican *Le monde* (The world) in 1633 soon after Galileo's pro-Copernican *Dialogue* had been condemned by the Roman Inquisition in July. However, the vast majority of astronomers and natural philosophers were avowed Copernicans by the middle of the seventeenth century, and even those, such as the Jesuits, who were slow to accept the Copernican worldview, made substantial contributions to astronomy. Indeed, Galileo's successes can be overstated as contributions to the demise of the notion of a perfect celestial sphere, for previous events and observations had begun to shake confidence in heavenly incorrigibility. Of all his discoveries, only his sightings of the phases of Venus provided overt support for Copernicus's system, although Tycho's system could also account for them. Nevertheless, Galileo's visually striking discoveries—and their implications—were easily understood by a new audience of scholars and gentlemen, and they had a dramatic impact on writers and poets such as John Donne (1572–1631).

It is important to note, as Allan Chapman has properly argued, that the great theoretical advances in cosmology achieved by Kepler, Isaac Newton, and others were facilitated and indeed made possible by improvements in angular astronomical measurement and not by superior visual acuity. Tycho's advances in instrument design and observational accuracy were made possible by the cadre of excellent craftsmen he had at his disposal, and similarly, John Flamsteed, the first British astronomer royal, whose observations were to prove crucial for Newton's enunciation of universal gravitation, had innovative and highly skilled instrument makers working with him. Only with patient astronomy of this sort could precise measurements be made of celestial magnitudes such as distance and size.

In the 1660s telescopic sights were added to quadrants and a zenith sector in the attempt by the French to measure the length of a degree of meridian in France. In Restoration England a number of episodes occurred that acted as a spur to creating an alliance between accurate measurement and theoretical innovation. The Royal Society of London was founded in 1660, followed by the Royal Greenwich Observatory—founded to aid navigation and the determination of longitude by improving astronomy—in 1675. The Observatory was badly stocked with instruments at first, but gradually, with some private support and with the help of occasionally brilliant suggestions from Robert Hooke (1635–1703) for automating observations, Flamsteed was able to build up a stock of the best instruments then available. By the 1690s he had a degree clock that allowed star positions to be measured with extraordinary accuracy, and the ten-to-twelve-seconds error of his mural arc (that is, a large quadrant set on a wall) was a sixfold improvement on the accuracy of Tycho's instruments. Flamsteed used telescopic sights on his instruments but also a filar micrometer, that is, a system of thin wires, minutely movable by means of a carefully graduated screw, that could be placed inside a telescope to finesse its accuracy.

Isaac Newton (1642–1727) developed an early interest in astronomy and became famous initially because of his development of a reflecting telescope in the late 1660s. Flamsteed's data was crucial for Newton in the winter of 1684–1685, when the latter was trying to determine what mutual influence Jupiter and Saturn might have on each other, and again in late 1685, when Newton wanted three items of data (accurate to a minute) on the path of the Great Comet of 1680–1681. This data would constitute crucial evidence for the cosmological system that Newton published in his momentous *Principia Mathematica* (The mathematical principles of natural philosophy) of 1687, for he could now analyze observed deviations from perfect elliptical orbits by means of his concept of universal gravitation. Perhaps of equal significance were the observations Flamsteed put his way in 1694–1695 when Newton had another go at the Moon. This ultimately unprofitable endeavor was part of an effort to solve the (insoluble) three-body problem of the mutual interactions of Sun, Moon, and Earth, all of which Newton later described as the most difficult science he ever did. The pair fell out irreconcilably soon after this, and Newton behaved abominably toward the astronomer royal, practically stealing Flamsteed's laboriously crafted star catalog by claiming it as the property of the state. Not the least of Newton's actions was to downgrade and even efface (in his *Principia*) the contributions made by Flamsteed, who had generously provided the observations that allowed Newton to corroborate and then rework his supreme theory. Whatever his personal dealings with others, Newton's theory provided the basic theory of the heavens that we now take to be true, and his achievements included the recognition that some comets travel in periodic elliptical orbits.

By the early eighteenth century, the London instrument-making trade was widely held to produce the highest quality instruments; Pierre-Louis Moreau de Maupertuis (1698–1759), for example, took a zenith sector and clock constructed by the outstanding London instrument maker George Graham (1673–1751) to Lapland in 1736–1737. It was this expedition that went furthest in determining the shape of Earth, confirming Newton's calculation that it was an oblate spheroid (flattened at the poles). In England, Graham and others made instruments for the astronomers royal who followed Flamsteed, namely Edmond Halley (in 1720) and James Bradley (in 1742). Bradley, who discovered stellar aberration in 1727 and who confirmed Newton's analysis of the extent of the nutation of Earth's axis in the 1740s, combined access to the best instruments of the day with an obsession for accuracy. By the middle of the eighteenth century, measurements were confined to the meridian, and, among other activities, experiments were being undertaken to better ascertain longitude and latitude—an activity seen by the British, the French, and many other naval powers as essential for improving navigation. With massively expensive instrumentation that only large institutions could afford, astronomy had changed beyond all recognition from the medieval period. Religious and other value systems no longer placed barriers on believing in and publishing particular accounts of the cosmos, and all serious intellectuals were heliocentrists.

See also **Aristotelianism; Astrology; Brahe, Tycho; Calendar; Copernicus, Nicolaus; Cosmology; Descartes, René; Galileo Galilei; Kepler, Johannes; Newton, Isaac; Scientific Instruments; Scientific Revolution.**

BIBLIOGRAPHY

Primary Sources

Copernicus, Nicolaus. *On the Revolutions of the Heavenly Spheres.* Translated by A. M. Duncan. Newton Abbott, U.K., and New York, 1976.

Descartes, René. *The World and Other Writings.* Translated and edited by Stephen Gaukroger. Cambridge, U.K., and New York, 1998.

Galilei, Galileo. *Sidereus Nuncius; or, The Sidereal Messenger.* Translated by Albert Van Helden. Chicago and London, 1989.

Kepler, Johannes. *Mysterium Cosmographicum: The Secret of the Universe.* Translated by A. M. Duncan. New York, 1981.

———. *New Astronomy.* Translated by William H. Donahue. Cambridge, U.K., and New York, 1992.

Secondary Sources

Chapman, Allan. *Dividing the Circle: The Development of Critical Angular Measurement in Astronomy, 1500–1850.* 2nd ed. Chichester, U.K., and New York, 1995.

Donahue, William H. *The Dissolution of the Celestial Spheres.* New York, 1981.

Dreyer, J. L. E. *A History of Astronomy from Thales to Kepler.* Rev. ed., with foreword by W. H. Stahl. New York, 1953.

Jardine, Nicholas. *The Birth of History and Philosophy of Science: Kepler's* A Defence of Tycho against Ursus, *with Essays on its Provenance and Significance.* Cambridge, U.K., and New York, 1984.

King, Henry C. *The History of the Telescope.* New York, 1979.

Kuhn, Thomas S. *The Copernican Revolution: Planetary Astronomy in the Development of Western Thought.* Cambridge, Mass., and London, 1957.

Newman, William R., and Anthony Grafton, eds. *Secrets of Nature: Astrology and Alchemy in Early Modern Europe.* Cambridge, Mass., and London, 2001.

Schechner Genuth, Sara. *Comets, Popular Culture, and the Birth of Modern Cosmology.* Princeton, 1997.

Stephenson, Bruce. *Kepler's Physical Astronomy.* Princeton, 1994.

Thoren, Victor E., with contributions by John R. Christianson. *The Lord of Uraniborg: A Biography of Tycho Brahe*. Cambridge, U.K., and New York, 1990.

ROB ILIFFE

ATHEISM. The early modern period in Europe has been called an age of unbelief, with its materialist and mechanistic view of the world in natural philosophy, increased liberalism and toleration in political thought, and advances in the secularization of culture. Early modern atheistic thinkers are supposed to have laid the philosophical groundwork for much of later irreligion.

Early modern Christian writers often failed to distinguish between non-belief in "the true God" and non-belief in a supreme being per se, and atheism usually meant the assertion of the non-existence of the Judeo-Christian God. Strictly speaking, however, atheism is the denial of the existence of a divinity. As such, it is different from agnosticism (a suspension of belief on the question of God's existence) or simple theological heterodoxy. In the sixteenth through eighteenth centuries, however, the term *atheist* was used without great precision, even carelessly. The epithet was applied to religious dissidents, political enemies, and debauched libertines, usually with little concern for a person's real beliefs on the question of God's existence. Thus, when the sixteenth-century French cleric and writer François Rabelais (c. 1494–1553) was accused of being an atheist because of the fun had at religion's expense in his comic novels *Gargantua and Pantagruel,* he lost no time in returning the charge at his sectarian opponents. Agnostics and religious skeptics; rationalists, deists, pantheists, materialists, members of dissenting religious sects, or those belonging to no recognized confessional religion; moral, religious, and political subversives; and general non-conformists as well as true unbelievers were all called atheists. In this respect, the early modern period was no different from earlier historical eras. As Socrates himself had discovered, "atheist" was a convenient label for any person who did not believe what everyone else believed and who showed independent, critical, and iconoclastic tendencies.

It is thus difficult to determine who in this (or any) period was, in fact, an atheist and who was simply unorthodox or annoying. Few individuals actually proclaimed themselves atheists or argued explicitly against the belief in God, and many people caught in the dragnet were undoubtedly innocent of the charge. On the other hand, despite this rhetorical laxity and consequent confusion in the use of the term, the historian Lucien Febvre's claim that before the end of the seventeenth century a true systematic atheism was impossible, and that "atheist" was nothing more than a widely used but nearly meaningless insult, cannot be accepted.

Early modern thinkers distinguished between theoretical or speculative atheism and practical atheism. The theoretical atheist was someone who claimed to believe that there was no God, but for whom this belief had no real pragmatic consequences. It was a philosophical position, not a moral, social, or devotional one, and it had little effect on his behavior. The practical atheist, on the other hand, was someone who, while probably not really denying "in his heart" the existence of God, nevertheless led a dissolute and immoral life and engaged in the overt mockery of religion. While there were undeniably many such libertines in early modern Europe, there was great debate at the time over whether there were, in fact, any sincere theoretical atheists. The idea of a providential God, some asserted, is innate in the human mind. René Descartes (1596–1650) argued as much in his *Meditationes de Prima Philosophia* (1641; Meditations on first philosophy). Although the concept of God may become obscured by the more vivid and compelling material from the senses, ultimately—in dire circumstances or as the end of life approached—all professed atheists were said to acknowledge God.

Another recognized category was the indirect atheist. Although probably not a nonbeliever himself, the indirect atheist was someone whose ideas, if taken to their logical conclusion, led to atheism. Descartes, with his employment of hyperbolic skepticism and, according to his critics, allegedly fallacious demonstrations of God's existence, was often considered a proto-atheist in this sense.

The long list of real and alleged atheists in the early modern period includes, besides Rabelais, the Italian Lucilio Vanini (1585–1619), the English materialist and political philosopher Thomas Hobbes (1588–1679), the Dutch-Jewish philosopher Baruch Spinoza (1632–1677), and numerous French philosophes of the eighteenth century, including Julien Offroy de La Mettrie (1709–1751); Paul Thiry, baron d'Holbach (1723–1789); and the *encyclopédiste* Denis Diderot (1713–1784). While some of these and other figures were indeed atheists in the strict sense of the term, there is nothing that they really have in common other than unorthodox beliefs about God and religion and the fact that they generated a good deal of concern among ecclesiastical and political authorities.

Italy enjoyed perhaps the greatest reputation in the seventeenth century as a congenial home for atheism. This perception was fostered by the presence of thinkers like Vanini, an open and avowed atheist who denied the possibility of an immaterial God creating a material world and communicating with embodied beings. Religion, Vanini insisted, was a fiction, and the only true worship was that of nature. He was burned at the stake for his "blasphemous" beliefs.

Hobbes is often cited by his seventeenth-century contemporaries as one of the period's leading atheists, but his case is a vexed one. His materialism explicitly rules out the possibility of any incorporeal substance (including the human soul and God), and he seems to have had an ambivalent attitude at best toward Christian doctrine. He claims that it is wrong to attribute any human properties to God and thus rules out the personal God of Western religion. But Hobbes nowhere denies God's existence; in fact, he explicitly affirms it, and adds that God should be worshiped. Moreover, he advocated Christianity as the proper civil religion for England. But this did not prevent his critics (including Samuel Clarke) from reading his *Leviathan* (1651) and other works—probably correctly—as expressions of an atheistic philosophy.

Practically all major discussions of atheism in the late seventeenth and eighteenth centuries, however, centered on the ideas and influence of one figure: Spinoza. The excommunicated Jewish thinker was considered to be the most dangerous atheist of his time. The great French philosopher and man of letters Pierre Bayle called him "the greatest atheist who ever lived." However, Bayle also believed Spinoza to be a perfect example of a theoretical atheist: despite his denial of a providential God and his promotion of a view seen as corrupting of others, Spinoza was, Bayle insists, a man of outstanding character and conduct who led an exemplary life.

In his *Tractatus Theologico-Politicus* (1670; Theological-political treatise), Spinoza argued that the Bible is not literally the word of God but simply a collection of human writings. He also believed that while the prophets were men with highly active imaginations, they were not intellectually superior to ordinary human beings and had no privileged access to any kind of divine communication. It is in his *Ethica* (1663, 1677; Ethics), however, that the real nature of Spinoza's atheism appears. Spinoza denies the providential God of Scripture. There is no wise, benevolent, all-knowing, just God governing the world and standing in judgment over us. Such an anthropomorphizing of God, he argues, can lead only to superstition and a life of bondage to the passions of hope and fear. In fact, Spinoza denies that there is a transcendent God at all. Rather, God is nature; or, more accurately, God is equivalent to the most universal, active causal principles in nature, which cover all phenomena. In a famous phrase, Spinoza speaks of "God, or Nature" (*Deus, sive Natura),* and it is clear that his goal is not to deify nature but to completely naturalize God and reduce the divinity to the same laws that govern everything that happens in nature.

Spinoza thus denies the supernatural, and consequently any theology, sectarian religion, or morality that depends upon it. This is not to say that he rejects all religion. Rather, he insists that the true religion consists in the observance of some basic moral principles, above all, love of one's fellow human beings. If what was essential to early modern atheism was the denial of the existence of a transcendent God, a rejection of the creation of the world, and the elimination of any divine foundation for morality, then Spinoza's philosophy, if any, was indeed atheistic. Many thinkers in the late seventeenth and eighteenth centuries were caught up in the controversies around Spinoza, and the term *Spinozist* became synonymous with *atheist* in the period.

In early-eighteenth-century France there was a good deal of "atheism" in the many clandestine manuscripts that circulated in society and especially in the unregulated discussions that took place in the salons and cafés of Paris. Here could be found diverse libertines, radicals, and freethinkers expressing doubts about Christian dogma (including the divinity of Christ) and mocking religious beliefs in general. Many of them (including the declared atheist Nicolas Fréret) were influenced by the writings of Henri de Boulainvilliers (1658–1722), a nobleman who, by the end of his life, was a devout Spinozist. In his *Essai de métaphysique* (c. 1700; Essay on metaphysics), which circulated in manuscript form, Boulainvilliers insisted that the divine creation of the world was impossible, and that nature was governed not by providence but by necessary laws. Above all, he rejected the notion of a transcendent, personal God endowed with the usual moral and psychological characteristics.

An equally great cause of concern for eighteenth-century theists lay in the radical materialism of such thinkers as La Mettrie. In his work *L'homme machine* (1747; Man, a machine), La Mettrie, who was a physician, rejected even the progressive, dualist scientific philosophy of the Cartesians and presented an extreme mechanistic account of the human being, doing away with an incorporeal soul and any non-material causes in nature. Fancying himself a Spinozist, he argued that there was no evidence in nature to support the belief in a transcendent, intelligent, and providential deity. Although La Mettrie has disparaging words to say about atheism—he calls it a "strange opinion"—there can be no question that it is his own position. He undoubtedly agreed with his colleague Holbach, like Vanini one of the few self-proclaimed atheists of the time, who said in his *Système de la nature* (1770; System of nature) that "sacred opinions are the real source of evils among human beings. . . . An atheist . . . is a man who destroys chimerae harmful to the human race, in order to lead men back to nature, to experience, and to reason, which has no need of recourse to ideal powers to explain the operations of nature." Holbach justified atheism not merely on its truth, but also its utility; he insisted that the doctrine was clearly the most conducive to human happiness and tranquility.

The early modern period's attitude toward atheism was complex. On the one hand, the seventeenth and eighteenth centuries were, in important respects, an era of rationalism and enlightenment.

Descartes, Locke, Leibniz, Newton, and others all argued for the separation of philosophy and science from religion, and believed in the general toleration of new or heterodox ideas. But none of these figures was willing to do without the traditional Judeo-Christian conception of God; in fact, all of them devoted a good deal of effort to demonstrating God's existence. (It should be noted, though, that offering a proof for God's existence was not, by itself, sufficient evidence that a thinker was not an atheist. As the case of Spinoza shows, it all depended on what one meant by "God.") The English chemist Robert Boyle sought to counter atheism by appealing to the argument from design, while the French priest and philosopher Pierre Gassendi was concerned to show that the ancient atomism of Epicurus and Democritus could be purified of its atheistic elements and made consistent with Christianity. But as forerunners and leaders of the Enlightenment, they were committed at least in a general way to certain liberal values, including (for the sake of philosophical and scientific progress itself) the free expression of ideas.

And yet there were certain ideas that not even these progressive thinkers were willing to tolerate. Locke, for one, drew the line at atheism. He argued strenuously for the toleration of different religions. But "atheism and epicurism" were not religions, he insisted, and in his *Third Letter for Toleration* (1692) he argued in favor of "the magistrate's power to restrain and suppress them." The intellectual world of early modern Europe had its radical currents, fueled in some cases by atheism, which in turn generated a backlash from its more moderate wing.

See also **Anticlericalism; Deism; Descartes, René; Diderot, Denis; Enlightenment; Hobbes, Thomas; Holbach, Paul Thiry, baron d'; La Mettrie, Julien Offroy de; Rabelais, François; Reason; Scientific Revolution; Skepticism: Academic and Pyrrhonian; Spinoza, Baruch.**

BIBLIOGRAPHY

Buckley, Michael J. *At the Origins of Modern Atheism.* New Haven, 1987.

Fabro, Cornelio. *God in Exile: Modern Atheism; A Study of the Internal Dynamic of Modern Atheism, from Its Roots in the Cartesian* Cogito *to the Present Day.* Translated and edited by Arthur Gibson. Westminster, Md., 1968.

Febvre, Lucien. *The Problem of Unbelief in the Sixteenth Century: The Religion of Rabelais.* Translated by Beatrice Gottlieb. Cambridge, Mass., 1982.

Hunter, Michael, and David Wootton, eds. *Atheism from the Reformation to the Enlightenment.* Oxford and New York, 1992.

Israel, Jonathan I. *Radical Enlightenment: Philosophy and the Making of Modernity, 1650–1750.* Oxford and New York, 2001.

Kors, Alan Charles. *Atheism in France, 1650–1729.* Vol. 1, *The Orthodox Sources of Disbelief.* Princeton, 1990.

Popkin, Richard H., and Arjo Vanderjagt, eds. *Scepticism and Irreligion in the Seventeenth and Eighteenth Centuries.* Leiden, Netherlands, and New York, 1993.

STEVEN NADLER

ATLANTIC OCEAN. The emergence of a new world shaped by contact across and around the Atlantic is one of the single most significant historical developments of the early modern period. Before 1492 the Atlantic Ocean was bookended by two isolated hemispheres, one comprising Europe, Asia, and Africa, and the other, North and South America. Despite Norse settlements in Newfoundland and North America, and myths of Welsh and Irish voyages by Prince Madoc (also Madog ab Owain Gwynedd; 1170) and St. Brendan in 555–573, there was no sustained and meaningful contact across the Atlantic before Christopher Columbus's (1451–1506) momentous voyage in 1492. In that year, a world of vertical connections was transformed into one of horizontal connections: the ensuing circulation of people, pathogens, commodities, and ideas created the Atlantic Ocean and transformed the four continents surrounding it. As a unit of analysis, the Atlantic Ocean transcends the geographic space of those regions literally touched by the sea itself. People who lived far from the ocean were affected by the new transatlantic and circumatlantic interactions of coastal regions. For example, despite location on the Pacific coast, California and Peru were drawn into an Atlantic world, as were African villages hundreds of miles from the coast when inhabitants were ensnared by the slave trade. By the late eighteenth century, the four continents surrounding the ocean were linked by any number of measures: European nations claimed dominion over most parts of the Americas; Europeans and Africans migrated across the Atlantic in the mil-

lions; American commodities transformed the economies of Europe and diets around the world. What happened in one corner of the Atlantic affected people and events elsewhere.

Before the fifteenth century, natural barriers impeded contact within and across the Atlantic. The Canary Current is a north-south flow that separates the Mediterranean from Africa. Its strong movement is mirrored in the winds, which blow in the same direction. As a consequence, while Europeans might sail to West Africa, they could not easily get themselves home again, and the currents and winds provided an impediment to any African voyages north. There were, similarly, strong westerly currents, such as the Equatorial Current from Senegambia to the Caribbean. This current made a western trip across the Atlantic quick, but getting home was a challenge without ships that could sail into the winds. Only with ways to circumvent these natural barriers could sustained contact and exchange develop.

Navigational and technological breakthroughs came first in the eastern Atlantic, as the Portuguese endeavored to develop sea routes to Asia and, closer to home, to west and central Africa. The impulse was trade: gold, salt, ivory, fabrics, and spices—all goods customarily carried by expensive land routes. Improvements in ship construction, most notably the use of triangular sails, enabled ships to tack more adeptly and to sail unconstrained by adverse winds. Navigational instruments, particularly compasses and astrolabes, assisted mariners in determining where they were, how far they had traveled, and how they might return home. These developments enabled mariners to travel off the coast for long distances, and ultimately brought Europeans not only to new places, but also more cheaply and quickly to places that were previously known. The process of European expansion began with the islands of the Atlantic: the Canary Islands (discovered in the 1320s and developed by the Spanish), and the Azores (discovered between 1427 and 1431), Madeira (first visited some time in the fourteenth century, and settled after 1420), and Cape Verde (discovered in the late fifteenth century), all colonized by the Portuguese, were exploited as agricultural colonies, valued particularly for sugar production. In Africa, the Portuguese established São Jorge de Mina (Elmina), off the coast of modern

Ghana, in 1482 as a factory or trading post. This proved to be the model for most European engagement with Africa: Europeans reached the continent as supplicants, able to trade only with the permission of indigenous rulers who distributed monopolies and privileges in return for the benefits (in prestige, wealth, power, and commodities) they might accrue.

Columbus's momentous voyage in 1492 and the three voyages that followed can best be understood within this context of Portuguese maritime and commercial activity, although Columbus actually sailed with Spanish support. The Atlantic was shaped by Europeans' prior experiences elsewhere—in the Mediterranean, in Africa, and in the Atlantic islands—and came to take on its own distinct characteristics. If Europeans were motivated to explore the ocean for reasons of trade—to discover new routes to familiar destinations, to find new treasures, and to identify regions suitable for the cultivation of export crops—trade alone did not dictate the ultimate appearance of the transformed Atlantic. And if it was Europeans who had the initial impulse to explore the ocean and to chart not only its winds and currents but also the material and mineral wealth of the people who lived within and around it, the Atlantic Ocean that emerged was created by the people of four continents—Europeans, Africans, and Americans—and by the many cultural convergences and innovations that accompanied trade and conquest. The Atlantic Ocean was characterized by its discontinuities as well as by its coherence.

EUROPE AND AMERICA: UNDERSTANDING, ASSIMILATING, CLAIMING, COMPETING

Soon after Columbus's voyages, one of the first challenges for Europeans was to assimilate intellectually the new people of the Americas. From a world characterized by a dichotomy between Christian and infidel, Europeans were forced through their interaction with Americans to find new categories and typologies. The American "savage" emerged as a secular version of the Old World's infidel. The struggle to devise appropriate ways of treating these new people occupied the attention of rulers and intellectuals, and was most vividly signaled in the 1550 debate in Valladolid between Bartolomé de Las Casas (1474–1566) and Juan Ginés de Sepúlveda (1490–1572 or 1573) over the status of the people of the Americas. Some Europeans attempted to assimilate these new people through their conversion to Catholicism. Missionaries followed and accompanied voyages of discovery and conquest, and the sixteenth century was a time of particular vigor for the Catholic Church in America, even as it suffered assault in Europe. Indigenous people, for their part, assimilated Christianity in distinctive ways, echoing the process of syncretism that had accompanied the spread of Christianity in Europe. Christian saints acquired the personality traits of indigenous gods, for example, and some Christian holidays received disproportionate emphasis among New World converts because of their close correlation with pre-Columbian belief systems, as was the case for All Souls' Day, or the Day of the Dead, still observed in parts of central America and the southwestern United States.

The assimilation of new people accompanied the gradual process of charting the New World and its many wonders on maps. The Dutch emerged as the great cartographers of the period, but precise delineation of the Atlantic was a protracted affair. Early cartographers filled empty spaces with sea monsters and descriptive text, allowing fanciful fig-

ures to mask ignorance. Cartographic schemes collided during the conquest of America, as illustrated most effectively in the Relaciones Geográficas, the questionnaires and accompanying maps compiled in New Spain for the Spanish crown in the 1570s and 1580s. Indigenous cartographers drafted 65 percent of these maps and employed their own conventions to delineate space, time, and history. They marked these events and places with toponyms, while Spanish clerks added Spanish text. These indigenous and European maps indicate that, for both Europeans and Americans, the process of assimilation and especially of real understanding of the New World was incomplete and hesitant.

Spain and, to a lesser extent, Portugal dominated the Atlantic for the first century of European engagement in the ocean. Bolstered by papal authority, Spain conquered and claimed the major islands of the Caribbean and the great former empires of the mainland, centered in the viceroyalties of New Spain and Peru. The Portuguese claimed Brazil, although they sustained challenges from the French and Dutch. The northern European powers were slower to enter the western Atlantic, hindered in part by the dominance of Spain both in the Americas and in Europe and distracted by internal political and religious crises. Europeans also pursued profit in the Atlantic in ways other than settlement or conquest: fishing in the North Atlantic, for example, was a vital economic activity. When they did elect to settle colonies, they clung near the fringes of Spanish settlement. They sought their own great empires, but no Tenochtitlán or Cuzco awaited them. Instead of cities with buildings plated with silver and full of treasure, the French, Dutch, English, and Swedes who sought to establish colonies in North America and the Caribbean found for the most part semisedentary indigenous people, whose economies were poorly prepared to accommodate newcomers and whose cultures revealed little of apparent wealth that Europeans were able to identify. The perilous location of many of the colonies of Spain's rivals led to their destruction by the Spanish (as in the case of the French settlement at Fort Caroline in Florida in the 1560s) or to their abandonment because of problems of isolated location. Colonies were precarious enterprises, requiring good fortune, a favorable disease environment, generous financial support from the metropole, an ample supply of colonists, and a viable economy, whether based on agricultural production or trade. Easily one-half of all colonies were failures in the first two centuries of European settlement. Some colonies were lost through conquest, others were abandoned, especially because of indigenous resistance, while still others, such as the English settlement at Roanoke, simply disappeared.

By the eighteenth century a variety of colonial styles had emerged in the Atlantic. Trade factories (particularly in regions where indigenous economies provided desirable goods), plantations, and town and urban settlements were scattered around the western part of the Atlantic Ocean. In some of these settlements, Europeans were dependent on amicable relations with indigenous people in order to secure commodities. Europeans had displaced indigenous rulers, and in some regions indigenous people themselves had disappeared, replaced by Europeans and especially by Africans. These mature colonial societies had in most places established their own viable institutional lives, with churches, schools, colleges, social organizations, and institutions of governance in place to allow Creole elites to shape their own colonial world, although still under the regulation (either attentive or neglectful) of metropolitan governments.

THE COLUMBIAN EXCHANGE: PATHOGENS, PLANTS, ANIMALS

With the very first vessels of exploration there traveled pathogens that ultimately transformed the societies of the Atlantic Ocean. European incursions were violent affairs, yet disease explains the diminished populations of the Americas more fully than does the brutality of conquest. The people of the Americas had been isolated for thousands of years not only from the Eurasian land mass, but also from many of the endemic and epidemic diseases familiar to Europeans and generally endured in childhood—smallpox, chicken pox, mumps, measles—all of which were transported by European mariners, soldiers, and merchants. Columbus's second voyage brought an epidemic to the Caribbean; a smallpox epidemic ravaged Tenochtitlán in 1519 and facilitated Hernán Cortés's (1485–1547) conquest of Mexico; an epidemic similarly disorganized the Inca empire before Francisco Pizarro's (c. 1475–1541) assault in the 1530s. Disease also preempted conflict: a smallpox epidemic in southern New England

in 1633–1634 so ravaged the Algonquins of the region that the Massachusetts governor John Winthrop interpreted the disease and its consequence of emptying the land of human habitation as a sign of God's favor for English colonization. When epidemics hit, an infected population might plummet as much as 90 percent. Epidemic diseases dramatically reshaped American societies. They facilitated European conquest, encouraged Americans to convert to Christianity, shattered connections to local traditions and histories, and caused the demise of some tribes and ethnicities altogether and the reformulation of others.

But pathogens were not the only travelers on European ships across the Atlantic. Plants and animals wreaked their own havoc. Pigs, cows, sheep, goats, and horses all damaged native crops that had not previously required protection from large domestic animals. America, in return, offered new food crops to the rest of the world. Maize, tomatoes, peppers, gourds, peanuts, and beans were American crops that transformed diets worldwide. Although American populations plummeted in the wake of contact, the diffusion of American food crops ultimately led to an increase in the world's population. And, finally, insects traveled across the Atlantic, none more destructive than disease-bearers such as the *Aedes aegypti* or the *Anopheles* mosquitoes, both of which flourished in the transformed arable lands of the tropics and among populations of newly arrived Europeans.

COMMODITIES AND TRADE

Europeans did not venture across the Atlantic Ocean in search of the potato: they initially sought routes to the coveted markets of Asia, but once they realized the geographic constraints of their world, they hoped to find in the Americas readily identifiable commodities for sale in Europe. The most precious commodities were minerals: the discovery of silver mines at Potosí in Peru (in present-day Bolivia) and at Zacatecas in Mexico in the 1540s brought unprecedented liquid wealth to the Spanish crown, which in turn catapulted Spain to a position of political dominance in Europe and inspired envy among European rivals. The Spanish fleet system, which saw all the riches of America travel to Spain in a convoy of ships, flaunted this wealth for all to see. The discovery of gold in Brazil at Minas Gerais in the 1690s similarly tantalized people with the promise of quick riches. Other commodities, especially food crops such as sugar, rice, and grains; luxury consumables such as tobacco and chocolate; dye goods such as indigo, madder, and cochineal; naval stores; and pelts, while less immediately lucrative, were in the long run of considerable economic and cultural value. These commodities transformed European tastes, diets, and economies; reoriented indigenous economies; depleted environmental and human resources; and generated enormous labor demands. The vital trades that emerged contributed to new cities in America: Kingston, Bridgetown, Charleston, Newport, Philadelphia, Cartagena, and Havana. In Europe cities grew as a direct result of the wealth and activity of Atlantic trade, as was true for Seville, Glasgow (an important tobacco trading center), Bristol, Liverpool, and Nantes.

Some commodities, such as sugar, created new worlds of their own. Sugar did not require the Atlantic Ocean for familiarity among Europeans, who encountered it as a luxury commodity used as a spice from their first forays to the eastern Mediterranean. But sugar's migration out of the Mediterranean and into areas of the south Atlantic well suited for its cultivation and modified to enhance the environment for production—particularly Brazil and the Caribbean—meant that the crop moved from a luxury to a staple. Sugar, moreover, demanded laborers who could be forced to work around the clock to satisfy sugar's cycle: with sugar came slaves.

For other commodities, such as pelts or dyewood, Europeans initially tried to trade with indigenous people. It is easy to overestimate the power of European traders and the appeal of their commodities. While much that Europeans offered was useful, in semisedentary societies there was a natural limit to the number of goods people wanted to transport with them from one home to another. Moreover, recipients of trade goods altered their function: whereas fabric and knives and axes might be put to familiar use, other commodities were acquired for their social, not utilitarian, value, and have been found by archaeologists in burial sites in North America. Indigenous people did not trade unthinkingly. European weaponry, for example, had limited utility in some conditions of indigenous conflict. A musket would not fire in the rain; at night, a musket flash would reveal the location of a hidden attacker. And weapons required constant maintenance. Thus indigenous people adapted European commodities for their own use. When the barter economy no longer enabled Europeans to extract the commodities and, later, the plantation labor they required, they resorted to slavery, as was the case in Brazil.

The range of commodities identified in the Americas was great, and the extraction of some commodities prompted profound environmental and social transformations. In Peru, Indians were compelled to toil in the silver mines, a debilitating and deadly labor. In North America, the French quest for pelts altered indigenous cultures and economies. Among the Montagnais of North America, for example, women produced 65 percent of daily calories through their farming activities, and held a significant position in society because of the value of the food they produced. The Montagnais, moreover, were matrilocal. But as hunters, men controlled access to furs, and thus controlled trade with Europeans. Through trade, they acquired goods—such as alcohol and metal tools—that conferred social prestige. Christianity, with its insistence on patriarchal family arrangements, likewise elevated the authority of men. Thus European trade and culture could alter indigenous gender conventions and cultural practices. Hunters also pushed farther inland in search of animals, not only encroaching on territory claimed by others—leading to overt conflicts, made more deadly with new European weapons—but also depleting the supply of animals.

While the impact of European trade demands in the Americas could be enormous, historians continue to debate the impact of European trade with Africa. African rulers were able to dictate the terms of trade. Goods were produced specifically for export to European markets. Disease vectors inhibited European incursions inland, and only in Angola and at the Cape were Europeans able to claim any real political control. Yet the trade in Africa was not only for fabrics, salt, ivory, bronze, and gold, but also for people—millions of captives, whose great suffering complicates any discussion of the balance of power in European and African relations.

MIGRATION

The transmission of commodities and pathogens was only one type of circulation in this period. This

TABLE 1

Migrants to the Americas, 1500–1800

Country of Origin/ Region of Departure	Number	Date
Europeans (Country of Origin)		
Spain	437,000	1500–1650
Portugal	100,000	1500–1700
Britain	400,000	1607–1700
Britain [1]	322,000	1700–1780
France	51,000	1608–1760
"Germany" [2]	100,000	1683–1783
Total Europeans	1,410,000	1500–1783
Africans (Region of Departure)		
Senegambia	384,000	1519–1800
Sierra Leone	226,500	1519–1800
Windward Coast	144,000	1519–1800
Gold Coast	974,200	1519–1800
Bight of Benin	1,488,100	1519–1800
Bight of Biafra	1,058,800	1519–1800
West Central Africa	3,261,000	1519–1800
Southeast Africa	78,400	1519–1800
Total Africans	7,615,000	1519–1800

1. Includes between 190,000 and 25,000 Scots and Irish.

2. "Germany" refers to emigrants from southwestern Germany and the German-speaking cantons of Switzerland and Alsace-Lorraine.

SOURCE: For Europeans, this table reproduces Table 1.1 in Ida Altman and James Horn, eds., *To Make America* (Berkeley, Calif., 1991), 3; for Africans, Table 2 in David Eltis, "The Volume and Structure of the Transatlantic Slave Trade: A Reassessment," *William and Mary Quarterly*, 3rd ser., 58 (January 2001): 44.

was literally a world in motion, symbolized by the migration of millions of people across the Atlantic. Most generally cast as a European story, in fact migration was dominated by Africans. Before 1800 an estimated 1.4 million Europeans migrated west across the Atlantic. They were joined by millions of enslaved Africans: an estimated 7.6 million departed Africa before 1800, out of a total through 1867 estimated at 11 million. The numbers of Africans and their American destinations on plantations in the tropics remind us that Atlantic migration was largely a story of Africans, sugar, violence, and coercion, focused on the Caribbean and Brazil.

High mortality in the Americas dictated these high rates of migration, particularly in the sugar plantations on which so many enslaved workers labored. High mortality also determined that some places in the Atlantic remained migrant societies for the entirety of the early modern period, shaped by successive waves of newcomers who always outnumbered the native-born population. Elsewhere, locally born people—called Creoles if they were of European or African descent—predominated.

Most Northern Europeans migrated across the Atlantic in a dependent status. They traveled as bound laborers (indentured servants or engagés) from France and Britain, and as redemptioners from the Holy Roman Empire. Many acquired this status reluctantly: one study of late-seventeenth-century London found that people might wait in the metropolis a full year, first seeking employment in the city, before resigning themselves to failure at home and, in desperation, boarding ships for the colonies as servants. Some were seduced on board ships with promises of opportunity in the New World. Others were tricked and kidnapped—the term "Barbadosed" was coined to describe these illegal methods of procuring servants. Real opportunity was rare except for those servants who ventured to salubrious disease environments and who found good fortune and available land. For many, an early death ended the term of service. Migration was defined by its demographic peculiarities, which joined with early death to hinder the growth of colonial societies: migrants tended to be young and male, as much as 90 percent male for indentured migrants from France and England in the seventeenth and eighteenth centuries.

These aggregates by nation, or by region of departure in Africa, obscure the dominance in any single settlement of particular regions within European nations or of particular ethnic groups among Africans. The story of cultural encounters within the Atlantic is a story of the creation of ethnicity and of nationality: people developed heightened senses of who or what they were when they met those unlike themselves. Historians continue to debate the ability of people to sustain and transmit home cultures from the eastern Atlantic across the ocean to the western Atlantic. In some instances, cultural attributes were muted, in others they disappeared altogether. But in those places where people might settle (by force or by preference) among others from the same region, they were able to continue cultural practices, whether in the form of language, music, worship, diet, dress, construction of homes, or—where political circumstances permitted—the imposition of legal and political forms that shaped emerging colonial societies. At the same time that migrants endeavored to transport familiar cultural practices, residence in the western Atlantic forced and created cultural hybridity. We can see these contrasting trajectories in the development of new languages and the continued dominance of some Old World languages. In parts of eighteenth-century Saint Domingue, for example, the language of Kongo became the lingua franca because of the dominance of slaves from there. Elsewhere, pidgins emerged, as in the case of Gullah and Geechee in the Sea Islands of North America.

Native Americans, too, became migrants in this reconfigured world, although their experience as migrants has largely been overshadowed by their ordeal with the invasion of pathogens and Europeans. Some Americans fled Europe as refugees and exiles, others migrated toward them for purposes of trade and alliances, and still others were forced into labor requirements that took them far from home. These patterns of migration had varied effects on indigenous cultures and economies. In communities where religious beliefs were intimately connected to the physical space of home, religious foundations were fundamentally challenged, facilitating the appeal of elements of Christianity. New communities and ethnicities emerged out of amalgams of newcomers and old-timers in a process that was repeated throughout the Americas. Migration for all people—European, indigenous, and African—induced patterns of cultural adaptability, flexibility, and ultimately hybridity, in the same way that the circulation of commodities, information, and technology transformed all societies that surrounded the Atlantic Ocean.

HYBRIDITY

With the very first appearance of Europeans and Africans in the Americas emerged new social and sexual relations and new mixed-race populations. These relationships generally reflected the power dynamics of conquest and colonial societies, with European men claiming rights to women's sexuality as well as to the material riches of a conquered society. Indigenous and enslaved women occasionally derived benefits from these alliances as well, especially for their children. These unions also furthered political and diplomatic goals. European

traders in Africa sought alliances with prominent families through marriage or informal unions. The first Spanish conquistadors likewise secured their power and legitimacy in conquered territory in America through alliances with noblewomen. Isabel Montezuma, the daughter of Montezuma II, became a useful pawn for Cortés, who arranged for her to marry first her uncle and then a succession of Spaniards. Her marriage alliances established a pervasive pattern. The marriage of John Rolfe (1585–1622) and Pocahontas (c. 1595?–1617) in Virginia in 1614 suggested that the English might follow the same example, but, ultimately, English sexual alliances with indigenous women tended to be informal. Whether officially sanctioned or not, throughout the Americas and in Africa, European men found sexual partners among indigenous women, many of whom, along with their mixed-race children, came to play important roles as cultural mediators. This population of *castas,* or mixed-race people, grew over time. In New Spain in the seventeenth century, 5 percent of the population were classified as *castas;* that percentage grew to 22 percent by the end of the eighteenth century, and a 1792 census in Peru revealed a comparable ratio, with 27 percent described as *castas.* Throughout the Americas, a complex battery of racial classifications developed to describe these different combinations. In most parts of the Americas, moreover, a peculiar logic was at work that suggested that privileges should be available to people in accordance with their percentage of European blood: thus a person who was half-African and half-European had greater legal privileges than an African.

Demographic patterns within migration flows explain some of the varied unions and new populations that emerged in the Americas, but it is important not to disregard the importance of cultural factors. Different nations and empires integrated these unions and their offspring into colonial polities in a variety of ways. In almost every part of the Americas, the children of enslaved women and European or Creole men could be legally and socially recognized by their fathers. Sometimes they were freed; sometimes they were educated. Thus by the eighteenth century the most violent slave societies, including Jamaica, Brazil, and Saint Domingue, contained small but growing populations of free people of color, who participated in colonial society despite a range of legal and social encumbrances that hindered full participation. By the late eighteenth century, the free people of color of Saint Domingue constituted 5.2 percent of the colony's population, held one-quarter of the colony's slaves, and owned one-quarter of the real estate. The single notable exception to acceptance of these interracial unions was British North America, and is best witnessed in the actions of Thomas Jefferson (1743–1826), the Creole revolutionary and later third president of the United States, who, DNA evidence, documentary sources, and oral tradition strongly indicate, had a long-term relationship with his deceased wife's half-sister, the slave Sally Hemings (1773–1835), herself a product of two generations of such unions and, in the terminology of the time, a quadroon. Jefferson's public disavowal of this liaison, and his white descendants' bitter rejection of it, stand in contrast to the conduct of planters in other parts of the British Atlantic world and elsewhere in the Americas.

WAR, REVOLUTION, AND PERIODIZATION

The movement and displacement of people, their connections with each other, the emergence of hybrid cultural forms and of new populations altogether—all point to the ways in which the Atlantic Ocean contained a new kind of culture by 1800, one whose hemispheres were no longer in isolation. One of the most visible symbols of the interconnections within the Atlantic came during times of conflict. War, for example, contributed to migration, as religious refugees and exiles (including Jews, Huguenots, Puritans, and pietists and other Protestants from the Holy Roman Empire) joined defeated (and enslaved) enemies and those displaced by the upheaval of wars in the Americas. Moreover, all European conflicts had their manifestations in the Americas. Thus from the beginning of European dominion in America, Spain's rivals targeted both Spanish settlements, attacked by privateers and more formal armies, and the Spanish fleet, most famously the one seized by Piet Hein (1577–1629) in 1628, an event celebrated to this day in song by football fans in the Netherlands.

Conflict in the western Atlantic also included formal battles. The eighteenth century was a particularly violent period, wracked by several major European wars, all of which had their manifestations in

European holdings around the Atlantic. Particularly affected were those regions where multiple empires claimed territory in close proximity: the Caribbean, with adjacent islands held by rivals, and in some cases single islands shared between powers; the southeastern part of North America, where the French, Spanish, and English held adjacent territories; and the northeastern region of North America, where the French and English shared a volatile border. Often, the diplomatic resolution of wars in Europe left colonial issues unresolved, resulting in lingering resentments and unclear borders, which facilitated subsequent hostilities. Residents of the Americas found themselves at the center of global conflicts, however remote from Europe their settlements might seem. For some, these conflicts could be advantageous. Thus the Spanish governor of Florida enticed slaves from the British colonies to escape to his jurisdiction, promising them freedom and legal privileges should they do so. And indigenous tribes could manipulate these rivalries to their own advantages when Europeans needed to court allies. But international conflicts could also increase the precariousness of existence in border regions. The northern frontier of New England, for example, was the repeated target of French and allied Indian attacks, with regular raids on small frontier settlements. In 1704, French and Abenaki warriors destroyed one-third of the houses in tiny Deerfield, Massachusetts, during Queen Anne's War. The Atlantic world's biggest conflict—the Seven Years' War (1756–1763)—commenced in North America in 1754 in a frontier dispute called the French and Indian War. The Seven Years' War culminated in imperial reforms in all the Atlantic empires, French, Portuguese, Spanish, and British, which illustrated their increased commonalities and their efforts to seek common remedies to European financial, political, diplomatic, and strategic concerns in their American holdings.

Although the histories of early modern Europe and of the Atlantic world are intertwined, the Atlantic requires its own periodization. If early modern Europe's terminus is 1789, that date dissects the Atlantic world's age of revolution at a critical moment. The Atlantic's age of revolution began in the British Atlantic world in the 1770s with the revolution that created the first republic in the Atlantic. It continued through the revolutions in France and

Saint Domingue, the thwarted uprising of the United Irishmen, and into the early nineteenth century with the wars for independence in Latin America. Accompanying these revolutions were a number of resistance movements and aborted slave rebellions and conspiracies that were shaped by the diffusion of revolutionary sentiments and the opportunities for rebellion afforded by colonial conflicts. To separate these different episodes by ending the early modern period in 1789 is to deny the important connections that shaped revolutionary activity. A catechism of the United Irishmen from 1797 conveys this process of transmission and illustrates the ways in which the Atlantic world had become a single zone of exchange by the end of the eighteenth century.

What is that in your hand?
It is a branch.
Of What?
Of the Tree of Liberty.
Where did it first grow?
In America.
Where does it bloom?
In France.
Where did the seeds fall?
In Ireland.
Where are you going to plant it?
In the Crown of Great Britain.
(quoted in Whelan, p. 1)

Thus the standard political terminus for early modern Europe leaves the history of the Atlantic Ocean in the middle of a violent and transformative period, one that witnessed the disintegration of European empires, the creation of new republics (in France, the United States, and Haiti), the dispersal of new political ideas that empowered Creole elites, the creation of circumstances that facilitated the rebellion of slaves, the emergence of a formal and vigorous abolition movement, and the creation of colonies in Africa expressly dedicated to the provision of haven for former slaves. All of these events were connected and in some cases interdependent. By 1800, the Atlantic Ocean was circumscribed by four linked continents in the process of reformulation.

See also **British Colonies; Colonialism; Columbus, Christopher; Europe and the World; Exploration; Portuguese Colonies; Shipbuilding and Navigation; Shipping; Slavery and the Slave Trade; Spanish Colonies; Triangular Trade Pattern.**

BIBLIOGRAPHY

Altman, Ida, and James Horn, eds. '*To Make America*': *European Emigration in the Early Modern Period.* Berkeley, 1991.

Armitage, David, and Michael J. Braddick, eds. *The British Atlantic World, 1500–1800.* New York, 2002.

Bailyn, Bernard. "The Idea of Atlantic History." *Itinerario* 20 (1996): 19–44.

Canny, Nicholas, ed. *Europeans on the Move: Studies on European Migration, 1500–1800.* Oxford, 1994.

Canny, Nicholas, and Anthony Pagden, eds. *Colonial Identity in the Atlantic World, 1500–1800.* Princeton, 1992.

Cook, Noble David. *Born to Die: Disease and New World Conquest, 1492–1650.* Cambridge, U.K., 1998.

Crosby, Alfred W., Jr. *The Columbian Exchange: Biological and Cultural Consequences of 1492.* Westport, Conn., 1972.

Curtin, Philip D. *The Rise and Fall of the Plantation Complex: Essays in Atlantic History.* 2nd ed. Cambridge, U.K., 1998.

Davis, Ralph. *The Rise of the Atlantic Economies.* Ithaca, 1973.

Elliott, John H. *The Old World and the New, 1492–1650.* Cambridge, U.K., 1970.

Eltis, David. *The Rise of African Slavery in the Americas.* Cambridge, U.K., 2000.

Games, Alison. *Migration and the Origins of the English Atlantic World.* Cambridge, Mass., 1999.

Klooster, Wim. "The Rise and Transformation of the Atlantic World." In *The Atlantic World: Essays on Slavery, Migration, and Imagination,* edited by Wim Klooster and Alfred Padula. Upper Saddle River, N.J. Forthcoming.

Kupperman, Karen Ordahl, ed. *America in European Consciousness, 1493–1750.* Chapel Hill, N.C., 1995.

Meinig, Donald W. *The Shaping of America: A Geographical Perspective on Five Hundred Years of History.* Vol. 1, *Atlantic America, 1492–1800.* New Haven, 1986.

Mintz, Sidney W. *Sweetness and Power: The Place of Sugar in Modern History.* New York, 1985.

Mundy, Barbara E. *The Mapping of New Spain: Indigenous Cartography and the Maps of the Relaciones Geográficas.* Chicago, 1996.

Northrup, David. *Africa's Discovery of Europe, 1450–1850.* Oxford, 2002.

"Round Table Conference: The Nature of Atlantic History." *Itinerario* 23 (1999): 48–173.

Schwartz, Stuart B., ed. *Implicit Understanding: Observing, Reporting, and Reflecting on the Encounters between Europeans and Other Peoples in the Early Modern Era.* Cambridge, U.K., 1994.

Thornton, John. *Africa and Africans in the Making of the Atlantic World, 1400–1800*. 2nd ed. Cambridge, U.K., 1998.

Whelan, Kevin. *Fellowship of Freedom: The United Irishmen and 1798*. Cork, 1998.

Wolf, Eric R. *Europe and the People without History*. Berkeley, 1982.

ALISON GAMES

ATOMISM. *See* **Matter, Theories of.**

AUGSBURG. During the late fifteenth and early sixteenth centuries, the free and imperial city of Augsburg entered its golden age as a financial and cultural center. One of the largest of the early modern German cities, Augsburg's population approached thirty thousand in 1500, growing to its highest level of forty thousand around 1618. Augsburg's geographic position between the Lech and Wertach rivers contributed to the development of a strong textile industry after the Lech was diverted into a series of canals running through the city.

Domestic developments and international trade connections enabled Augsburg's guilds *(Zünfte)*, most significantly the merchants *(Kaufleute)*, weavers *(Weber)*, and goldsmiths *(Goldschmiede)*, to grow strong politically and economically. From its establishment following a guild rebellion in 1368 until 1548 (when Emperor Charles V laid siege to the city), Augsburg's "guild constitution" *(Zunftverfassung)* provided that the seventeen craft guilds were to send twelve representatives each to the Great Council and thirty-four guild masters (after 1478) to the Small Council. The guilds thus shared power with the patricians, who retained one of the two positions of mayor and fifteen representatives in the Small Council.

In the late fifteenth century, merchant families, most importantly the Baumgartners, Herwarts, Höchstetters, Fuggers, and Welsers, diversified their regional manufacturing interests into banking and credit. Close associations with trading and banking houses in Venice and Antwerp launched Augsburg merchants into Europe-wide recognition and international trade. The Fugger and the Welser trade routes and business connections extended throughout the Holy Roman Empire, Central Europe, and Italy and through the Netherlands, Spain, and Portugal into Africa, India, the West Indies, and Venezuela. Close financial relationship between the Fuggers and the Habsburg emperors, particularly Maximilian I (ruled 1493–1519), contributed to Augsburg's growing importance in imperial politics, as is evident in the fact that Augsburg hosted twelve of thirty-five imperial diets held between 1500 and 1600. Among the most important of these diets were Martin Luther's meeting with the papal legate Cajetan (1518), the Augsburg Confession (1530), the Augsburg Interim (1547–1548), and the Religious Peace of Augsburg (1555). Jacob Fugger "the Rich" (1459–1525) amassed a fortune, which he used to finance the imperial election of Charles V in 1519 and to found the Fuggerei for poor Catholics, the first welfare housing project in the world, in 1516.

In the early sixteenth century, book production and book collection formed the backbone of intellectual development in Augsburg; individuals such as the humanist Conrad Peutinger (1465–1547), who served on the imperial council and as city council secretary, amassed large personal libraries. Between 1468 and 1555, the Augsburg publishing houses produced around 5,900 works, making Augsburg one of the most significant German printing centers during the Reformation era, second only to Wittenberg in printing Luther's works. Augsburg painters and woodcut engravers—Hans Holbein the Elder (1465?–1524), Jörg Breu (c. 1475–1537), Hans Burgkmair (1473–c. 1531), and Leonhard Beck (c. 1480–1542)—produced numerous early Renaissance paintings and woodcuts that graced books as well as local churches. The foundation of the Latin school at St. Anna in 1531 ensured a continued tradition of humanist education within Augsburg, especially visible in its establishment of the city library in 1537.

A strong ecclesiastical and episcopal presence—including the bishop, cathedral chapter, and seventeen monasteries and convents—dominated late medieval religious life in Augsburg. Christoph von Stadion, the humanist-minded bishop of Augsburg (1478–1543), made an early attempt at ecclesiastical reform with his accession in 1517, but Martin Luther's hearing before the papal legate Cajetan

Augsburg. The Fuggerei. The first low-income housing project, established in 1516 by Jacob Fugger, it comprises 52 houses.
©ADAM WOOLFITT/CORBIS

(1469–1534) in 1518 brought the Reformation directly to Augsburg. Between 1521 and 1534, the Augsburg city council, unwilling to accept the Reformation for economic and political reasons, maintained a policy, designed by Conrad Peutinger, of outward compliance to episcopal and imperial mandates while avoiding direct interference in the growing evangelical movement among the populace and clergy. Ample evidence of the need for this policy can be seen in the July 1524 Schilling Uprising resulting from a city council attempt to banish the evangelical preacher Johannes Schilling. Anabaptist and Zwinglian influences grew in the late 1520s and early 1530s under the leadership of Michael Keller (c. 1500–1548), Hans Denck (c. 1495–1527), and Balthasar Hubmaier (1485–1528), culminating in the "Martyr's Synod," an important gathering of southern German Anabaptist leaders on 24 August 1527. Beginning in 1534, Augsburg's city council introduced a Zwinglian-styled reformation that was favored by the guilds; it was completed in 1537 with the publication of a reformed church order.

During the Augsburg Interim (1547–1548), Emperor Charles V reestablished the rights of Catholics in Augsburg by dissolving the guilds and altering the city constitution to promote a leadership shared between the Catholic and Protestant patricians. After a brief period of shifting power, the Religious Peace of Augsburg (1555) established Augsburg as one of a few fully biconfessional cities. Guild unrest in Augsburg in 1584 known as the *Kalenderstreit*, 'calendar struggle', ostensibly over the imperial acceptance of the Gregorian calendar in 1582, provides evidence that the Catholic and Protestant communities did not always enjoy a harmonious coexistence, either socially or politically. In the late sixteenth and early seventeenth centuries, the Augsburg city council maintained a confessionally neutral policy and sought to diminish social tensions that could lead to guild unrest. The Peace of Westphalia (1648) established *Parität,* 'parity', in

Augsburg, splitting political power proportionally between Catholics and Lutherans. The confessional population distribution shifted from 70 percent Protestant in 1648 to approximately 60 percent Catholic by the mid-eighteenth century.

In the late sixteenth and early seventeenth centuries, Augsburg embarked on an ambitious civic building program, which included the creation of a series of public fountains, such as the Mercury and the Hercules bronzes (1596–1602) designed by Adriaan de Vries (c. 1560–1626), and the redesign of the *Rathaus* (City Hall) with its famous *Goldener Saal* (Golden Hall) as well as numerous public buildings by Elias Holl (1573–1646) during his tenure as the municipal builder between 1601 and 1635. Augsburg's early organization of civic medical and charitable institutions, such as the college of medicine (Collegium Medicum Augustanum, 1582) and city orphanage (1572) served as a model for other German cities.

Augsburg suffered a political and economic downturn in the mid-seventeenth century. The population decreased to a low of 16,422 in 1635 as a result of the effects of plague epidemics (9,000 died in the 1627–1628 outbreak alone) and the Thirty Years' War (5,000 died in the 1634–1635 siege) and recovered to about 20,000 in 1645 and 30,000 around 1770. In the late seventeenth and eighteenth centuries, the Augsburg economy recovered because of its export of decorative silver, the establishment of textile manufacturing, and the city's continuing role in banking and finance. The restoration of modest wealth allowed the continuation of a strong cultural development as seen in such baroque and rococo patrician palaces as the Schaezler Palace (1765–1770) and in the work of Augsburg artists Johann Heinrich Schönfeld (1609–1684) and Johann Ulrich Mayr (1630–1704) in the St. Ulrich, St. Anna, and Holy Cross churches. The Collegium Musicum, which was established in 1713, sponsored works of composers such as the Augsburg native Leopold Mozart (1719–1787). Augsburg attempted to maintain neutrality in the growing military conflicts in Europe, but this did not prevent the siege and occupation of the city in 1703–1704 by French and Bavarian troops in the War of the Spanish Succession nor its loss of independence when Augsburg was integrated into the Kingdom of Bavaria in 1806.

See also **Anabaptism; Augsburg, Religious Peace of (1555); Charles V (Holy Roman Empire); Free and Imperial Cities; Fugger Family; Guilds; Holy Roman Empire; Lutheranism; Reformation, Protestant.**

BIBLIOGRAPHY

Clasen, Claus Peter. *Anabaptism: A Social History, 1525–1618: Switzerland, Austria, Moravia, South and Central Germany.* Ithaca, N.Y., 1972.

Gottlieb, Gunther, et al. *Geschichte der Stadt Augsburg von der Römerzeit bis zur Gegenwart.* Stuttgart, 1984.

Kiessling, Rolf. *Bürgerliche Gesellschaft und Kirche in Augsburg im Spätmittelalter. Ein Beitrag zur Strukturanalyse der oberdeutschen Reichsstadt.* Augsburg, 1971.

Künast, Hans-Jörg. *"Getruckt zu Augspurg": Buchdruck und Buchhandel in Augsburg zwischen 1468 und 1555.* Tübingen, 1997.

Roeck, Bernd. *Eine Stadt in Krieg und Frieden. Studien zur Geschichte der Reichsstadt Augsburg zwischen Kalenderstreit und Parität.* 2 vols. Göttingen, 1989.

Roper, Lyndal. *The Holy Household: Women and Morals in Reformation Augsburg.* Oxford, 1984.

Roth, Friedrich. *Augsburgs Reformationsgeschichte.* 4 vols. Munich, 1901–1911. Reprint, Munich 1974.

Safley, Thomas Max. *Charity and Economy in the Orphanages of Early Modern Augsburg.* Boston, 1997.

Stuart, Kathy. *Defiled Trades and Social Outcasts: Honor and Ritual Pollution in Early Modern Germany.* Cambridge, U.K., and New York, 1999.

Tlusty, B. Ann. *Bacchus and Civic Order: The Culture of Drink in Early Modern Germany.* Charlottesville, Va., 2001.

Zoepfl, Friedrich. *Das Bistum Augsburg und seine Bischöfe im Reformationsjahrhundert.* Munich, 1969.

MARJORIE E. PLUMMER

AUGSBURG, RELIGIOUS PEACE OF (1555).

Enacted by the imperial diet (the general assembly of the Estates of the Holy Roman Empire) at Augsburg in 1555, the Religious Peace was the most significant law created in the Holy Roman Empire between the Golden Bull of 1356 and the Peace of Westphalia of 1648. These three laws formed the empire's constitution until 1803. On 25 September 1555 at Augsburg, the imperial diet approved twenty-four paragraphs to govern the status of the Lutheran Confession of Augsburg and its adherents until such date as the religious schism

might be settled. The Religious Peace, which aimed to neutralize the danger of war that arose from the schism, governed official relations between the Catholic and Protestant imperial Estates until the opening of the Thirty Years' War in 1618. It was renewed with modifications by the Peace of Westphalia in 1648.

The Peace transferred the *ius reformandi* ("right of reformation") from the imperial to the territorial and municipal levels by means of a principle, first proclaimed by the Diet of Speyer in 1526, that until the church could settle the schism, each ruler should act in a way such that he would be responsible to God and the emperor. In 1586 Joachim Stephan (1544–1623), a Greifswald law professor, summarized this principle in a famous phrase, "whose the regime, his the religion" *(cuius regio, eius religio)*. The Estates, the emperor's direct subjects, were to enjoy this right, which allowed them to force dissenting subjects to conform or emigrate, with four exceptions: (1) Calvinists, Anabaptists, and other dissenters were excluded from the Peace's terms and protection; (2) in imperial free cities where both religions were practiced, confessional parity in the regime was to be preserved and the right of each to exercise its religion assured; (3) if converted to the Protestant religion, ecclesiastical princes (bishops, abbots, abbesses) were forbidden to enforce the right of reformation on their temporal subjects, and they had to resign their offices (Ecclesiastical Reservation); (4) Protestant nobles and burghers in the temporal lands of ecclesiastical princes might continue to practice their religion (Ferdinandine Declaration). The Protestant Estates never formally recognized the third exception, which, if enforced, would have prohibited the conversion of episcopal and abbatial sees and lands to their faith. The Catholics did not recognize the fourth exception, which they considered a gross violation of the right of reformation confirmed to them by the Peace. Two other laws of 1555 restored the Empire's supreme court (the Imperial Chamber Court) and reformed the Imperial Circles, regional administrative organs for police, financial, and military affairs.

The Religious Peace was successful within limits. For sixty or more years it withstood pressures from the religious wars that erupted in the 1560s in France and in the Netherlands, as well as from the rising confessional tensions caused by the Calvinist challenge to Lutheranism since the 1560s and the revival of Catholicism since 1580. These tensions caused a cessation of the diet after 1613 and crippled the Chamber Court and the Circles, the chief agencies for enforcing the Religious Peace. A series of violent incidents—Protestant attempts on the sees of Cologne and Strasbourg between 1583 and 1595 and provocations by both sides in the free cities—made clear that the two principal exceptions to the Religious Peace remained unsettled.

The Peace of Westphalia, a pair of treaties that ended the Thirty Years' War in 1648, restored the provisions of the Religious Peace with two important modifications: the Reformed (Calvinist) confession was included as a third licit religion; and princes could no longer force dissenting subjects to emigrate. The reform of the diet into a continuously sitting institution (1663), the suspension of majority rule in religious matters in favor of negotiations between two confessional caucuses of Estates *(itio in partes)*, and the restoration of the Imperial Chamber Court at Wetzlar greatly reduced the religious schism as a source of public contention. The 10,500 Lutherans who in 1730–1731 left the archbishop of Salzburg's lands rather than conform to the Catholic religion, were the Empire's last (illegally expelled) religious exiles.

While an important conclusion to the first phase of the Reformation, the Religious Peace could not be enforced to a degree sufficient to spare the empire a second religious war. Even for its first quarter century, the Peace's importance as a symbol of a liberal irenicism, later destroyed by the Catholic Counter-Reformation, has sometimes been greatly exaggerated. It is more accurate to say that the Peace was exactly what it purported to be, a temporary agreement to last until the achievement of a settlement—which never came—to the religious schism. Only by removing the schism's effects from imperial public life, which happened after 1648, was the Empire's internal peace restored.

See also **Charles V (Holy Roman Empire); Ferdinand I (Holy Roman Empire); Free and Imperial Cities; Holy Roman Empire; Holy Roman Empire Institutions; Reformation, Protestant; Westphalia, Peace of (1648).**

BIBLIOGRAPHY

Brady, Thomas A., Jr. "Settlements: The Holy Roman Empire." In *Handbook of European History, 1400–1600. Late Middle Ages, Renaissance, and Reformation,* edited by Thomas A. Brady, Jr., Heiko A. Oberman, and James D. Tracy, vol. 2, pp. 349–383. Leiden, 1995.

Hermann Tüchle. "The Peace of Augsburg: New Order or Lull in the Fighting?" In *Government in Reformation Europe 1520–1560,* edited by Henry J. Cohn, pp. 145–156. New York, 1971.

Holborn, Hajo. *A History of Modern Germany.* Vol. 1, *The Reformation.* Princeton, 1959.

Lutz, Heinrich. *Christianitas afflicta: Europa, das Reich und die päpstliche Politik im Niedergang der Hegemonie Kaiser Karls V. (1552–1556).* Göttingen, 1964.

THOMAS A. BRADY, JR.

AUGUSTUS II THE STRONG (SAXONY AND POLAND)

AUGUSTUS II THE STRONG (SAXONY AND POLAND) (1670–1733), Elector Frederick Augustus I of Saxony 1694–1733 and King Augustus II of Poland 1697–1704 and 1709–1733. Augustus's father, Elector John George III of Saxony, and his mother, Anna Sophie, daughter of King Frederick III of Denmark, married in 1666 to tie the Danish royal family to the Wettin dynasty of Saxony. At the time of Augustus's birth, his grandfather, John George II, ruled Saxony. Augustus's father, John George III, was only twenty-three and had already sired Augustus's elder brother, John George IV. There seemed little likelihood that Augustus would ever rule Saxony. Therefore, his general disinterest in formal study and an early marked inclination to pursue pleasure and to seek glory hunting, soldiering, and womanizing were tolerated.

After his grandfather died of plague (1680), his father of apoplexy (1691), and his brother of smallpox (April 1694), Augustus became elector. Seeking military glory, he assumed command of an imperial army in the war against the Turks. His campaigns on the Transylvanian front in 1695 and 1696 were failures, though part of the blame must fall on the Imperial War Council, to whom Augustus was ultimately subject.

Augustus spent lavishly and converted to Catholicism to ensure his electoral victory as king of the Commonwealth of Poland-Lithuania in 1697. He levied oppressive taxes upon his Saxon subjects, the majority of whom were Lutheran, to finance the election. The Peace of Westphalia (1648) had contributed to the development of an international system that favored sovereign nation-states over territorial principalities like Saxony whose power was circumscribed by their inclusion in the fragmented empire. Notable German princes, in an effort to elevate themselves, raised armies, entered into European wars, and sought to become monarchs. The elector of Brandenburg had become king of Prussia, and George of Hanover would become king of England. It is against this background that Augustus's ambition must be viewed. While the election was costly, Augustus reasonably expected that Poland would provide lucrative markets for Saxon manufactured goods and was certain that his new title would enhance the status of the Wettin dynasty.

Augustus planned to seize Swedish Livonia to acquire ports for his new kingdom, and, to this end, he formed an anti-Swedish coalition with Denmark and Russia in 1699. Augustus's attack on Riga in February 1700 failed, highlighting his lack of power in Poland. Sweden defeated Russia at Narva, and Denmark sued for peace. Charles XII of Sweden (ruled 1697–1718) turned his mighty army against Augustus. In hindsight, Charles's determination to depose Augustus gave Russia a critical opportunity to rebuild and remold its army and ultimately to emerge victorious over Sweden. Augustus's forces in Poland suffered serious defeats, and he was deposed by the Swedes in January 1704 when a rump Polish parliament elected Charles's client as king. Augustus's Saxon troops continued to fight, suffering a terrible defeat at Fraustadt in February 1706. Swedish troops occupied Saxony for a year. Russia's eventual victory over Sweden enabled her to free Poland from Swedish influence in 1709, and Augustus was restored to the throne. In 1715 Russia thwarted a Polish anti-Saxon coalition opposed to Augustus's rash reforms, and in 1717 the "Dumb Parliament" agreed to Russian conditions that maintained Augustus in power. But Tsar Peter the Great controlled the diplomatic situation, and he took steps to prevent Augustus from turning the Polish monarchy into a hereditary one, and from passing the crown to his sole legitimate heir, Frederick August II of Saxony. Forever scheming, Augustus arranged the 1719 marriage of his heir to the daughter of the Holy Roman emperor, Joseph I, as

on 1 February 1733, of complications from diabetes, in Warsaw.

See also **Baroque; Charles XII (Sweden); Dresden; Frederick I (Prussia); Peter I (Russia); Poland-Lithuania, Commonwealth of, 1569–1795; Saxony; Westphalia, Peace of (1648).**

BIBLIOGRAPHY

Czok, Karl. *August der Starke und seine Zeit: Kurfürst von Sachsen, König in Polen.* Leipzig, 1997.

Held, Wieland. *Der Adel und August der Starke: Konflict und Konfliktaustrag zwischen 1694 und 1707 in Kursachsen.* Cologne, 1999.

Hughes, Lindsey. *Russia in the Age of Peter the Great.* New Haven, 1998. Focuses on the age of Peter the Great and covers Augustus II in some detail.

Pilz, Georg. *August der Starke: Träume und Taten eines deutschen Fürsten.* Berlin, 1986.

Sharp, Tony. *Pleasure and Ambition: The Life, Loves, and Wars of Augustus the Strong.* New York, 2001.

JAMES GOODALE

Augustus II the Strong. Equestrian statue by Ernst Friedrich Rietschel, Dresden. ©JACK FIELDS/CORBIS

part of an unfulfilled plan to transfer the imperial dignity to the House of Wettin.

Augustus was renowned as the most gallant ruler of his time, and his court in Dresden was characterized by fireworks displays, masquerades, tournaments, hunts, and annual celebrations, such as the famed Carnival. Augustus used these feasts, as did all baroque rulers, as occasions for enhancing his status and negotiating with high-ranking guests. Endowed with incredible physical strength, Augustus was rumored to have sired 354 illegitimate children with a series of mistresses, though the actual number was probably closer to ten. Augustus's ultimate failures in statecraft are mitigated, ironically, by the enduring value of the projects upon which he spent so lavishly. He established porcelain manufacturing in Meissen (1710) and initiated projects that transformed Dresden into a magnificent baroque capital—"the Florence of the Elbe." Augustus died

AUSTRIA. A geographic term used to describe the two "archduchies" of Austria above and below the Enns River, "Austria" is also applied to all of the hereditary possessions of the German Habsburgs that were situated along the southeastern flank of the Holy Roman Empire. In addition, it is a political term for the diverse dynastic conglomerate ruled by the "House of Austria," including Bohemia and Hungary.

ORIGINS

This larger conglomeration of states, or *Gesamtstaat*, was formed during the lifetime of Holy Roman Emperor Maximilian I (ruled 1493–1519), who forged a series of fortuitous dynastic alliances with the heiresses of Burgundy (1477), Spain (1496), and Hungary-Bohemia (1515). Maximilian's elder grandson succeeded him as Emperor Charles V (ruled 1519–1556) and ceded the Austrian lands to his brother Ferdinand, who was elected king of Bohemia (1526) and Hungary (1527) following the last Jagellon king's death after the Ottoman victory at Mohács (1526). His eventual election as Holy Roman Emperor Ferdinand I (ruled 1558–1564) completed a division of the Habsburg dominions that left the dynasty's Bur-

**Austrian Habsburg
Territories in the
Eighteenth Century**

Habsburg territories, 1748
Holy Roman Empire, 1763
International border, 1748
Other border, 1748
✕ Battle
• City

lands (with Slovene and Italian spoken in the south), it was a close second to Czech in the Bohemian lands, and, in Magyar-speaking Hungary, prevailed only in the towns. Moreover, the reconquest and resettlement of the Hungarian plain and Transylvania that began in the late seventeenth century added many South Slavs and Romanians. The acquisition of the formerly Spanish Netherlands and Italy (1714) added French, Flemish, and Italian, much as the annexation of Galicia (1772) and Bukovina (1775) contributed large numbers of Poles, Ukrainians, and Yiddish-speaking Jews. Whereas this linguistic kaleidoscope changed little over the centuries, the Reformation brought major changes in religion. By the mid-sixteenth century, Protestants constituted a majority in most areas of Habsburg domination. Catholicism reasserted itself during the Counter-Reformation, however, which left a 10–15 percent Lutheran minority in the Austrian and Bohemian lands, while Hungary split evenly between Catholics and a mix of Calvinist Magyars, Orthodox South Slavs, and German Lutherans.

The Austrian economy struck a balance between the prevailing agriculture (and animal husbandry in the Hungarian plain), substantial mining throughout the Alps and Carpathians, and industrial production in Bohemia, Upper Austria, and later in the Austrian Netherlands and northern Italian lands.

GOVERNMENT

Although the Habsburgs valued the imperial title and always visualized themselves as German princes, their inability to assert full sovereignty within the Holy Roman Empire gradually induced them to focus attention on developing their hereditary German (Austrian and Bohemian) lands, while treating Hungary more like a colony, at least until the eighteenth century. Beginning with Ferdinand I, the Habsburgs gradually coopted imperial institutions such as the Aulic Council (*Reichshofrat*), or shifted functions to competing bodies, including an exchequer (*Hofkammer*), war council (*Hofkriegsrat*), and "Austrian" chancery. They were less innovative in dealing with the Estates. Having acquired the Bohemian and Hungarian lands by inheritance and election, the Habsburgs were at pains to respect their corporate privileges and autonomy. Not to do

gundian, Spanish, Italian, and vast American possessions in the hands of a "Spanish" branch ruled by Charles and his heirs, while a succession of "Austrian" Habsburg emperors ruled the largely contiguous Austro-Hungarian-Bohemian conglomerate.

Contemporaries attributed the dynasty's success to Maximilian's marriage policies, immortalized by the words "Let the strong fight wars. Thou, happy Austria, marry. What Mars bestows on others, Venus gives to thee!" But the key factor behind these alliances lay in the widespread appreciation of the Habsburgs' role as a useful counterpoise to the dual threats posed by the Ottomans in the east and France in the west.

LANDS AND PEOPLES

The monarchy was linguistically and confessionally diverse. Whereas German dominated the Austrian

so risked passive resistance or outright rebellion, which could be assisted by foreign adversaries. As a result, the prevailing political culture favored reaching consensus with the Estates on major issues, a policy that helped sustain the Habsburg dominions' separate cultural, linguistic, and constitutional development.

INDIVIDUAL RULERS

Given the contrived construction of this central European *Gesamtstaat,* its common historical development owed much to the policies of individual rulers. Ferdinand I and his son Maximilian II (ruled 1564–1576) spent much of their reigns resisting the Ottoman seizure of most of Hungary, while attempting to peacefully accommodate the aspirations of the empire's emerging Protestant majority. The Spanish-educated sons of Maximilian II, Rudolf II (ruled 1576–1612) and Matthias (ruled 1612–1619), cautiously embraced the Counter-Reformation, which led to widespread armed resistance, most notably in Bohemia, where the Defenestration of Prague sparked the beginning of the Thirty Years' War (1618–1648). After Ferdinand II (ruled 1620–1637) and his foreign allies had crushed the Bohemian revolt at White Mountain (1620), he purged much of the kingdom's nobility and constitution to enhance royal authority. Systematic Catholicization was carried out there and in the Austrian lands by him and his son, Ferdinand III (ruled 1637–1657), even as they reluctantly accepted religious compromise in the rest of Germany. Leopold I (ruled 1658–1705) completed the process of creating a mutually reliant, trilateral ruling elite of crown, church, and nobility that found artistic expression in the flamboyant Austrian baroque. Catholic religious persecution, principally by Hungary's magnates. led to a major rebellion that was soon assisted by a massive Ottoman invasion and siege of Vienna (1683). The city was delivered by an Austro-German-Polish relief force commanded by Poland's King John III Sobieski (1629–1696), which crushed the Ottomans at the battle of Kahlenberg. Leopold followed up the city's relief by reconquering Hungary at the head of a Holy League (1684–1699). Hungary was also enjoined to revise its constitution in 1687, eliminating the electoral kingship and the nobility's right to resist royal authority *(jus resistendi).* Although Leopold reaffirmed Protestant religious freedom, renewed perse-

cution and heavy wartime taxation inspired the Rákóczi Revolt (1703–1711). Joseph I (ruled 1705–1711) eventually pacified the country militarily while granting generous terms in the 1711 treaty at Szatmár that essentially defined Hungary's status for the next two centuries. The martial exploits of Prince Eugene of Savoy (1663–1736) permitted Joseph to salvage the Italian and Dutch possessions from the dynasty's extinct senior line in the War of the Spanish Succession (1701–1714) and enabled his brother Charles VI (ruled 1711–1740) to round off Hungary's frontiers with the acquisition of the Banat of Temesvár after another Turkish war (1716–1718). With the male line facing extinction, Charles issued the Pragmatic Sanction (1713), which established the monarchy's indivisibility and the right of female succession. His daughter Empress Maria Theresa (ruled 1740–1780) withstood a concerted attempt at partition in the War of the Austrian Succession (1740–1748) but lost the rich Bohemian crownland of Silesia to Prussia. A vain attempt to reconquer it in the Seven Years' War (1756–1763) was sandwiched between two great reform periods that marked the monarchy's transition from the ideology of the Counter-Reformation to a more rational governmental system based on the prevailing German fiscal-administrative science of cameralism and select European Enlightenment ideas. Attempts by Joseph II (ruled 1765–1790) to carry out more sweeping changes without the Estates' consent led to widespread resistance that his brother, Leopold II (ruled 1790–1792), quelled by repealing his most radical reforms. Nonetheless, a generation of political and cultural reform had prepared the Habsburg Monarchy for the ensuing tumult caused by the French Revolution. Indeed, the early modern period had witnessed the emergence and consolidation of both the House of Austria and the territorial conglomerate *(Gesamtstaat)* that it governed as major components of the European world.

See also **Austrian Succession, War of the (1740–1748); Austro-Ottoman Wars; Ferdinand I (Holy Roman Empire); Ferdinand II (Holy Roman Empire); Ferdinand III (Holy Roman Empire); Habsburg Dynasty: Austria; Holy Roman Empire; Hungary; Joseph I (Holy Roman Empire); Joseph II (Holy Roman Empire); Leopold I (Holy Roman Empire); Maria Theresa (Holy Roman Empire); Maximilian I (Holy Roman Empire); Maximilian II (Holy Roman**

Empire); Seven Years' War (1756–1763); Spanish Succession, War of the (1701–1714); Vienna.

BIBLIOGRAPHY

Blanning, T. C. W. *Joseph II*. London and New York, 1994.

Evans, R. J. W. *The Making of the Habsburg Monarchy 1550–1700: An Interpretation*. Oxford and New York, 1979.

Fichtner, Paula. *Emperor Maximilian II*. New Haven, 2001.

———. *Ferdinand I of Austria: The Politics of Dynasticism in the Age of the Reformation*. New York, 1982.

Ingrao, Charles. *The Habsburg Monarchy, 1618–1815*. 2nd ed. Cambridge, U.K., and New York, 2000.

———. *In Quest and Crisis: Emperor Joseph I and the Habsburg Monarchy*. West Lafayette, Ind., 1979.

Macartney, C. A. *Maria Theresa and the House of Austria*. London, 1969.

McKay, Derek. *Prince Eugene of Savoy*. London, 1977.

Spielman, John P. *Leopold I of Austria*. New Brunswick, N.J., 1977.

CHARLES INGRAO

AUSTRIAN SUCCESSION, WAR OF THE (1740–1748). On 20 October 1740 the death of the last male Habsburg, the Holy Roman emperor Charles VI (ruled 1711–1740), precipitated a major European war for the succession both to his territories and to the elected position of emperor. The lands over which Charles had ruled consisted of the Austrian duchies, the kingdom of Bohemia (including Silesia and Moravia), the kingdom of Hungary, the duchy of Milan, and the ten provinces of the southern Netherlands. Over the course of his reign he had sought political guarantees from the territorial princes of the empire and the other great powers that they would uphold the Pragmatic Sanction (an edict he had first promulgated in 1713) and ensure that the succession to the Habsburg lands would pass to his daughter Maria Theresa (b. 1717) in the absence of a son. There were, though, two rival claimants for Charles's inheritance, the daughters of his elder brother, the emperor Joseph I (ruled 1705–1711): Maria Josepha, married in 1719 to Crown Prince Augustus of Saxony, and Maria Amalia, who married Crown Prince Karl Albert of Bavaria in 1722. Despite the renunciations of all claims to the Habsburg inheritance made by the two archduchesses, this did not stop the Saxons and the Bavarians from intriguing

throughout the 1720s and 1730s to secure some or all of the lands upon Charles VI's eventual death. Moreover, the last three years of Charles's reign made a dismemberment of the Habsburg Monarchy all the more likely thanks to a massive increase in the state debt during an unsuccessful and demoralizing war against the Ottoman Empire, which had revealed to the rest of Europe serious deficiencies in the Habsburg military machine.

The War of the Austrian Succession was precipitated in December 1740 by the invasion of Silesia by Frederick II ("the Great") of Brandenburg-Prussia (ruled 1740–1786), who had himself succeeded to his throne only six months earlier on the death of his father, Frederick William I (ruled 1713–1740). Unlike Frederick William, the new Prussian monarch had little respect for imperial law and institutions if they stood in the way of securing his territories; and while Frederick's claims on Silesia had more justification than has sometimes been conceded, nevertheless it was an act that caused alarm across Europe. Following the invasion and Prussia's defeat of the Austrians at Mollwitz in April 1741, Maria Theresa's stubborn refusal to negotiate with Frederick almost cost her the rest of her lands: between May and September 1741 a coalition was assembled consisting of France, Spain, Prussia, Bavaria, and Saxony that intended to seize large parts of the Habsburg Monarchy. Maria Theresa's truce with Frederick II, the Convention of Klein-Schnellendorf in October 1741, came too late to prevent a Franco-Bavarian occupation of Bohemia the following month; and this was followed in January 1742 by the election of Karl Albert (elector of Bavaria since 1726) as the new Holy Roman emperor. However, at the same time that Karl Albert was acclaimed as Charles VII, Maria Theresa's army, consisting in large part of loyal Hungarians, turned the tide, capturing Munich, the new emperor's ducal capital, after liberating Upper Austria from Bavarian control. This was followed in June by the provisional peace of Breslau between Prussia and Maria Theresa, and the final expulsion of the French from Bohemia in December that year.

From then on, the war took on wider European and even global dimensions, as Britain-Hanover and France, ostensibly still neutral, confronted each other in western Germany and at sea. In 1743 the French were almost completely forced out of the

War of the Austrian Succession. Imperial troops under Charles, duke of Lorraine, penetrate Fench-held territories near Strasbourg, 1744. Painting by Zacharias Sonntag. THE ART ARCHIVE/ MUSÉE HISTORIQUE STRASBOURG/DAGLI ORTI

empire, and in March and April 1744 Louis XV (ruled 1715–1774) formalized hostilities by declaring war first on Great Britain and then on Austria. For the previous four years Britain and Spain had already been at war over trade with the Spanish American empire. In Europe, Spain, for its part, had been trying to divest Maria Theresa of Lombardy in northern Italy since 1741, but faced the opposition of Charles Emmanuel III, king of Sardinia and ruler of Piedmont (ruled 1729–1773), and warfare in northern Italy remained indecisive throughout the period up to 1746. In spite of renewed Prussian hostilities toward Austria, when Frederick II signed a full alliance with France in June, the 1744 campaigns in the Low Countries and the empire were also inconclusive.

The death of Charles VII in January 1745 changed the political picture dramatically. Max Joseph, his successor as elector of Bavaria, aware of the impossibility of the Bavarian position, promised to vote for Maria Theresa's husband, Francis Stephen of Lorraine, grand duke of Tuscany, to be the next

emperor, which he accordingly became in October. But the military tide had not by any means turned, for French arms were proving dangerously triumphant in the Netherlands. On 11 May 1745 Maurice de Saxe, marshal of France, defeated the combined Anglo-Austrian-Dutch army at Fontenoy, and went on to capture a string of fortresses in Flanders stretching nearly as far as Antwerp by the end of the year. This was not least because the British contingent under the duke of Cumberland had been withdrawn to deal with the Jacobite rising in Scotland which was threatening to overcome the Hanoverian government of Cumberland's father George II (ruled 1727–1760). They were not to return in force to the continent until well into the following year. Meanwhile, Prussia forced Austria to sign the treaty of Dresden in December 1745, on broadly similar terms to that of Breslau three years earlier.

Nevertheless, Austrian fortunes still showed few signs of improving. Although Charles-Emmanuel largely succeeded in recovering and protecting his

The War of the Austrian Succession, 1740–1748

— Holy Roman Empire
— International border
⋯ State border
░ Habsburg territories
✕ Battle
□ Castle
● City

of Louisbourg on Cape Breton Island, which Louis XV wanted back but could not regain by military and naval means. This was offset by the French capture of Madras from the British in September 1746, the only notable action in India.

The Peace of Aix-La-Chapelle of October–November 1748, which marked the end of the war, preserved most of the inheritance of Charles VI for Maria Theresa: she had formally conceded Silesia to Prussia in the December 1745 treaty of Dresden, and she now had to give up the western third of the duchy of Milan to Sardinia, and the duchies of Parma and Guastalla to Don Philip, half-brother of the Spanish king Ferdinand VI (ruled 1746–1759). But the price France paid for the return of Louisbourg and for Austrian concessions to the Spanish Bourbons was high: Louis XV returned to Austria all his conquests in the Netherlands, to the irritation of French public opnion. Aix-La-Chapelle was more of a truce than a definitive treaty, for even in Italy the creation of stability required another round of agreements in 1752. There was still plenty of unfinished business left over from the years 1739–1740, most notably Maria Theresa's personal refusal to reconcile herself to the loss of Silesia, and the persistent friction between the British on the one hand, and the French and Spanish Bourbons on the other over colonial matters in the Americas and India. Further conflict was both likely and imminent.

See also **Bavaria; Charles VI (Holy Roman Empire); Frederick II (Prussia); Frederick William I (Prussia); Habsburg Dynasty: Austria; Louis XV (France); Maria Theresa (Holy Roman Empire).**

BIBLIOGRAPHY

Anderson, M. S. *The War of the Austrian Succession, 1740–1748.* London, 1995.

Browning, Reed. *The War of the Austrian Succession.* New York, 1993.

McLynn, F. J. *France and the Jacobite Rising of 1745.* Edinburgh, 1981.

Scott, H. M., and Derek McKay. *The Rise of the Great Powers, 1648–1815.* London, 1983. Chaps. 4–6.

GUY ROWLANDS

own territories and those of Maria Theresa in Italy during 1746, the advantages continued to go France's way in the Netherlands: in February, Saxe captured Brussels, while the following year saw him drive along the River Scheldt and into the Dutch Republic, capturing in September 1747 the seemingly impregnable fortress of Berg-op-Zoom. By now, however, a degree of exhaustion was setting in on all sides, symbolized by Saxe's pyrrhic victory over Cumberland at Lawfeld in July 1747. Warfare in the Caribbean had proved largely uneventful, while the British colonial authorities in Massachusetts back in June 1745 had succeeded with the help of the Royal Navy in capturing the French fortress

AUSTRO-OTTOMAN WARS. By the early sixteenth century, there was steady low-level conflict in a border zone roughly defined by the Danube and Sava rivers between the Ottomans and European Christian rulers as a result of the Ottoman conquests of Balkan territory that began in the late fourteenth century. In 1520, a new Ottoman sultan, Suleiman I (also called Suleiman the Magnificent), took the throne. After the Ottomans secured control over Egypt by defeating the Mamluks and established an eastern border by defeating the Safavids of Iran at Chaldiran in 1514, attention turned back to the Balkans. When Louis II, king of Hungary and Bohemia (ruled 1506–1526), rejected Suleiman's demand for tribute, the sultan seized Belgrade and marched north, inflicting a severe defeat on a Hungarian army at Mohács on 28 August 1526. Hungary had been weakened by conflicts between various domestic groups as well as by competition between its ruler and the Holy Roman emperor. The Ottoman army pulled back from the Danube only after conquering Buda in December 1526.

King Louis II drowned as he was fleeing from the advancing Ottomans, which caused a succession crisis between the Habsburg Ferdinand (who later became Emperor Ferdinand I and ruled 1558–1564) and the local Transylvanian ruler, János Szapolyai. Suleiman installed Szapolyai at Buda but conceded the western third of Hungary to Ferdinand. The sultan tried to augment his conquests in Europe over the next few years and first laid siege to Vienna in September–October 1529 but had to retreat because of a snowfall.

THE OTTOMAN-HABSBURG WAR (1593–1606)
By 1568, the Ottomans controlled Transylvania as an autonomous principality, leaving western Hungary to the Habsburgs. For the next two decades, the Austrian-Ottoman border was quiet, but Christian refugees from Ottoman territory were resettled on the Habsburg side of the "military frontier."

Hungary became divided into two parts: Royal Hungary, ruled by the Habsburgs, and Transylvania, ruled by the Ottomans. The Ottoman side of this border witnessed administrative instability and onerous, irregular financial demands made on the peasantry, but with considerable religious tolerance shown to various Christian sects. The Habsburgs maintained a more stable administration but showed little religious tolerance. This frontier experienced a continuous low-level *Kleinkrieg:* a "little war" of incursions and raids by both sides.

Resentment against Habsburg religious intolerance finally exploded into the Fifteen Years' War (1591–1606), into which the Ottoman forces were drawn. Despite Catholic-Protestant animosity, the Ottoman threat to Europe came to be viewed as more serious than Christian sectarian conflicts. In this time of heightened religious tension, several strategic frontier provinces revolted against Ottoman rule. After several encounters in which the Ottomans and the Habsburgs traded fortresses back and forth, a marginal Ottoman victory at Mezö-Keresztes finally halted a major Austrian offensive. When István Bocskay, the ruler of Transylvania, shifted loyalty back to the Ottomans in 1605, Austrian momentum was reduced. In the end, the Habsburgs signed two peace agreements in 1606. The first was the Peace of Vienna, in which the Habsburg emperor, Rudolf II, guaranteed the rights of Hungarian Protestants. The second was the Peace of Zsitvatorok (11 November 1606), in which the existing Austro-Ottoman borders were recognized, although the sultan agreed to forgo Transylvania's tribute payments.

Small border skirmishes then resumed while the Ottomans became embroiled in conflict with Iran, and the Habsburgs focused on European affairs. Competition for control of the Mediterranean between the Ottoman Empire and European powers erupted into a war between Venice and the Ottomans' North African corsairs in 1638. This was the first of many confrontations between the navies of the Ottomans, Venice, and militant religious orders like the Knights of St. John of Malta. Naval skirmishes near Crete and Malta, as well as Dalmatian land battles in the 1640s, set the stage for the Ottoman conquest of Crete in 1669.

THE WAR OF THE HOLY LEAGUE (1683–1699)
With growing fears of Ottoman expansion in the Mediterranean along with reduced tension in Europe after the 1648 Treaty of Westphalia, which ended the Thirty Years' War, Pope Alexander VII formed a Holy League in the 1660s to coordinate a new campaign against the Ottomans. Plans for a showdown between the Ottomans and this European coalition evolved over the next two decades.

Austro-Ottoman Wars. Battle of Mohács, Hungary, 29 August 1526, from a 1588 Ottoman manuscript by Loqman known as the *Book of Accomplishments.* THE ART ARCHIVE/TOPKAPI MUSEUM ISTANBUL/DAGLI ORTI

Sofonisba Anguissola. *The Artist's Sisters Playing Chess,* 1555. Lauded by Giorgio Vasari as "miraculous," Anguissola enjoyed international recognition during her lifetime and was praised in particular for the intimacy and wit of her portraits. ©Ali Meyer/Corbis

RIGHT: Architecture. San Carlo alle Quattro Fontane, 1634–1637, designed by Francesco Borromini. This church is widely regarded as the finest example of baroque architecture and incorporates a great number of Borromini's characteristic innovations, including a gracefully curving facade and a spectacular oval dome. ©Nimatallah/Art Resource

BELOW: Architecture. A view of the Pont Neuf and the Louvre, 1680, by unknown painter of the French School. This view illustrates the dramatic presence of the palace, which was built as a medieval fortress and later greatly expanded by a succession of French monarchs who sought to create a residence that would reflect their power and dignity. The Louvre ceased to be a royal residence in 1682, when Louis XIV moved the court to the magnificent Palace of Versailles. The Art Archive/Musée Carnavalet, Paris/Dagli Orti (A)

Baroque. Detail showing Prudence and Dignity from the *Allegory of Divine Providence* by Pietro da Cortona, frescoes in the Villa Barberini, Rome. Painted on the vaulted ceiling of a two-story reception room of the villa, Cortona's mural exemplifies the baroque in its dynamism and its synthesis of religious and secular iconography. The dizzying upward motion of the fresco as a whole is only slightly suggested in this detail. ©ARALDO DE LUCA/CORBIS

BELOW: Gian Lorenzo Bernini. *Apollo and Daphne.* Bernini was the most renowned and influential Italian artist of his time, and his skill with marble is clearly demonstrated in the exquisite figures of this life-size sculpture, the last of four created for Cardinal Scipione Borghese between 1620 and 1625. THE ART ARCHIVE/GALLERIA BORGHESE ROME/DAGLI ORTI (A)

ABOVE RIGHT: Francesco Borromini. The Church of S. Agnese in Piazza Navona, Rome, completed 1666. This later work by Borromini, completed by others after his death, displays his characteristic concave facade. ©ALINARI/ART RESOURCE

BELOW RIGHT: François Boucher. *Venus Asking Vulcan for Arms for Aeneas,* 1732, in the Louvre Museum. Boucher is regarded as one of the most significant exemplars of rococo style, admired for his versatility as well as his skill. Adept at creating brilliantly colored and sensual paintings such as this, he also created tapestries, sculptures, theatrical sets and costumes, and porcelain pieces. ©ERICH LESSING/ART RESOURCE, N.Y.

OVAL: **Art in Britain.** *Young Man Leaning against Tree among Roses,* portrait miniature by Nicholas Hilliard. Hilliard's portrait miniatures are regarded as the most significant contribution to British visual art of the period, combining realism with outstanding lyrical beauty ©Victoria & Albert Museum, London/Art Resource, N.Y.

LEFT: **Bruegel Family.** *Flowers,* by Jan Brueghel the Elder. Jan was the more successful of Pieter the Elder's two sons and is considered the finest painter of still-lifes of the period. The Art Archive/Musée des Beaux Arts Strasbourg /Dagli Orti

BELOW: **Bruegel Family.** *Wedding Dance in the Open Air,* by Peter Bruegel the Elder. Bruegel is esteemed for his skillful, humorous, and realistic depictions of Flemish peasant life in the sixteenth century. His two sons, Pieter and Jan, also became accomplished painters, but neither is considered to have rivaled the skill of their father. ©Francis G. Mayer/Corbis

BELOW: Caravaggio and Caravaggism. *Death of the Virgin.* This painting demonstrates Caravaggio's innovative use of contemporary settings for biblical and classical subjects, as well as his use of a bright light entering the picture from above to suggest a divine presence. THE ART ARCHIVE/MUSÉE DU LOUVRE PARIS/DAGLI ORTI (A)

ABOVE RIGHT: Ceramics, Porcelain, and Pottery. Meissen Harlequin with jug by J. J. Kaendler, c. 1738. THE ART ARCHIVE/PRIVATE COLLECTION/EILEEN TWEEDY

BELOW RIGHT: Ceramics, Porcelain, and Pottery. Flask with Roman triumph scene, c. 1540–50, Fontana workshop, Urbino Italy. THE ART ARCHIVE/MUSÉE NATIONAL DE CÉRAMIQUES SÈVRES/ DAGLI ORT

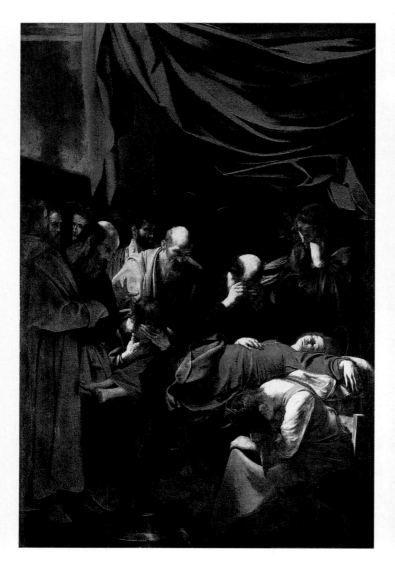

RIGHT: François Clouet. Portrait of the pharmacist Pierre Quthe, 1562, from the Louvre, Paris. Clouet is best known for his portraits of the members of the Valois nobility, painted while he was the official court painter. This portrait of his friend differs from those in its rich draperies and subtle suggestion of depth, presaging the more sensitive works of his later years. ©Scala/Art Resource, N.Y.

BELOW: Claude Lorrain. *Sea Port with Setting Sun,* 1639. This painting is typical of Claude's subject matter of the 1630s, when he experimented with depicting the qualities of sunlight, and illustrates the skills that would make him arguably the most renowned and influential landscape painter of the Western tradition. The Art Archive/Musée du Louvre Paris/Dagli Orti

Two key battles, at St. Gotthard in 1664 and at Chotin in 1673, revealed substantial Ottoman military weaknesses. In the 1670s, an ambitious young Ottoman commander, Kara Mustafa Pasha, developed a plan to achieve fame by seizing Vienna, an objective that had eluded his army for many years.

Because of a new round of conflict within Europe, only the Polish king John Sobieski would commit forces to defend Vienna. The Ottomans advanced to Vienna and placed it under siege on 14 July 1683. As in 1529, they were at a disadvantage because they had failed to bring any heavy artillery—a deficiency that they tried unsuccessfully to overcome by mining Vienna's walls. Vienna's defenders mounted several effective attacks on them and as the siege wore on, Ottoman morale diminished. On 4 September, just as Vienna was finally beginning to weaken under the siege, the Ottomans failed to prevent the arrival of Sobieski's relief force.

The superior armament and tactics of the Polish army forced the besiegers to leave Vienna after only one day. Kara Mustafa Pasha was strangled in Belgrade on the sultan's orders as a result of this retreat as Austrian forces pushed deep into Hungary to take Buda in 1686. The Ottoman army then mutinied and deposed Sultan Mehmed IV, while the Venetians secured territory along the Adriatic and in the Morea (in the Peloponnese of modern Greece).

The new Sultan, Suleiman II, appointed the well-respected Fazil Mustafa as grand vizier in 1689, recapturing Belgrad and Niš. The deaths of both men in 1691 left no effective successors until Sultan Mustafa II took power in 1695. At the same time, other European powers were pressuring Austria to make peace with the Ottomans so that Austrian forces could unite with them against Louis XIV of France. Meanwhile, as many Ottoman areas in Europe fell into anarchy because of administrative and fiscal problems, Mustafa II campaigned to reconquer Hungary in 1697, where his defeat led to the 1699 Treaty of Carlowitz.

THE TREATY OF CARLOWITZ (1699)

In January 1699, the Ottomans, Austrians, and Venetians signed a treaty ending their conflicts based on the idea of *uti possidetis*—whoever controlled a territory at that time would keep it. This marked the first comprehensive peace treaty between the Ottoman Empire and European powers. The Ottomans relinquished Hungary and Transylvania to the Austrians; Dalmatia, the Morea, and some Ionian islands to Venice; and Podolia to Poland. This was the first written Ottoman acknowledgment of military defeat.

THE TREATY OF PASSAROWITZ (1718)

In conjunction with high Ottoman religious officials and the Orthodox patriarch of Constantinople (who had lost revenue from lands in the Morea because of the treaty of Carlowitz), Silahdar Ali Pasha, who had become grand vizier in 1713, started a war against the Venetians in 1715. When it appeared that the Ottomans threatened the Habsburgs in northern Dalmatia, Austria signed an alliance with Venice, which was then on the brink of financial collapse. In 1718, after numerous Austrian victories including Petrovaradin, the Ottomans, Austrians, and Venetians signed a treaty at Passarowitz. It gave the Banat of Temesvar, Lesser Walachia, northern Serbia, and northern Bosnia to Austria, but required Venice to return the Morea and Crete to the Ottomans, although Venice was allowed to keep its Ionian islands and the part of Dalmatia it had received at Carlowitz.

THE OTTOMAN WAR WITH RUSSIA AND AUSTRIA (1736–1739)

The Habsburg emperor Charles VI (ruled 1711–1740) agreed with the tsar in 1734 to cooperate secretly against the Ottomans. This agreement took effect when the Ottomans, encouraged by the French, declared war in May 1736 on both Austria and Russia to protest the placement of a pro-Russian candidate on the Polish throne. The Austrians tried to retake territory that they had given up at Passarowitz and captured Belgrade and Niš. Over the next two years, however, the Ottomans won a series of victories against them, leading them to sign the 1739 Treaty of Belgrade, which restored the border agreed upon at Carlowitz. The Russians, now deprived of the help of their Austrian allies, had to end their own hostilities with the Ottomans and soon signed a treaty that gave Azov back to the Ottomans.

AUSTRIA IN THE RUSSO-OTTOMAN WARS OF 1768–1774 AND 1787–1792

When a major war erupted between Russia and the Ottoman Empire in 1768 after a long period of peace, Austria at first stayed out of it because the

Habsburgs did not want to encourage Russian expansion plans. After Russian success against the Ottomans, however, the Austrians entered the conflict in time to mediate the 1774 treaty of Küçük Kaynarca, but gained little new territory.

Austria was again prodded into action in 1787 by Russia, whose previous success fueled dreams of southward expansion. A series of decisive Russian and Austrian victories left these two powers in possession of much new territory and poised to advance toward Constantinople in the spring of 1790. However, the unfolding French Revolution caused other European powers to put pressure on them to end this war, which the Austrians did at Sistova in August 1791, several months before the Russian-Ottoman peace treaty. With European mediation, Austria agreed to give back its recent conquests in Bosnia and Serbia.

See also **Austria; Habsburg Dynasty: Austria; Habsburg Territories; Holy Leagues; Hungary; Ottoman Empire; Passarowitz, Peace of (1718); Russia; Russo-Ottoman Wars; Suleiman I.**

BIBLIOGRAPHY

Cook, M. A. *A History of the Ottoman Empire.* Cambridge, U.K., and New York, 1976.

Goffman, Daniel. *The Ottoman Empire and Early Modern Europe.* Cambridge, U.K., and New York, 2002.

Shaw, Stanford J. *History of the Ottoman Empire and Modern Turkey.* Cambridge, U.K., and New York, 1976.

ERNEST TUCKER

AUTHORITY, CONCEPT OF.

From the Latin *auctoritas,* the term "authority" was first applied to the Roman emperors, indicating that the emperor not only had political dominion but was also perfect in his person in every respect and deserved obedience and imitation for that reason. In the medieval and early modern eras it had the meaning of identifying men who had predominance in the different areas of human society and were to be esteemed and complied with. In politics it was applied to the Holy Roman emperor; in religion, to the pope; in the family, to the father. All drew on the authority of God over creation. In the areas of culture and learning it referred to those men from the ancient world who were regarded as models in the scholarly disciplines and the arts. Authority was deemed necessary for a well-ordered society, and challenges to authority in any sphere were met with fierce resistance. Authority could be and usually was delegated or transferred.

POLITICAL AUTHORITY

In the Middle Ages the title of emperor (from Latin *imperator*) held the sense of 'possessing universal authority', but whether that meant dominion over the entire world or just over Christendom was much debated. The emperor delegated a portion of his *plenitudo potestatis* ('fullness of power') to kings and princes to help him fulfill his duties of safeguarding the Catholic faith and maintaining peace and stability. When Charlemagne was crowned emperor of the West in 800, he was seen as the direct successor to the authority of the Roman emperors. The Holy Roman Empire thus created eventually became associated with Germany, and by 1500 the term "Holy Roman Empire of the German Nation" indicated the limited extent of the emperor's jurisdiction. With their greater historical awareness, the Italian humanists recognized that the Roman Empire had ceased to exist with the Germanic invasions, and they discarded the Holy Roman emperor's universalist pretensions. The kings of Europe also rejected them, following the lead of the French monarchs, who soon after 1300 were claiming to be "emperor in his own realm." Under Charles V (ruled 1519–1556) with his vast ranges of domains, the emperor's universalist claims were briefly resurrected, but by 1600 it was clear that political authority was held by a broad range of rulers of whom the emperor was only one, ruling lands in Central Europe. Although in parts of Europe, especially France with its Salic law (which restricted royal succession to males), the argument that women should not exercise political authority prevailed, blood right usually trumped gender rules, and early modern Europe had several female rulers who exercised *plenitudo potestatis.*

RELIGIOUS AUTHORITY

The papacy claimed authority in respect to religion. Christ had given the keys to the kingdom of heaven to St. Peter (Matthew 16: 18–19), and the popes, his successors as bishop of Rome, held them absolutely. The pope delegated authority to administer the local churches to the bishops, although he did not necessarily choose them, and he empowered the theologians to interpret doctrine. Whether the pope had supremacy over the emperor or had coequal authority with him was a major point of contention throughout the Middle Ages. The papacy's victory over the emperor in the thirteenth century was undercut both by the rise of the national kingdoms and by the crisis in the papacy itself called the Great Schism (1378–1417). When the rival popes proved incapable of solving the split in the church, it was proposed that the general council was superior to the papacy and had the power to impose a solution. The Council of Constance in 1417 successfully ended the Great Schism, but the restored papacy prevailed over the theory of conciliarism (which held that the council had authority over the church) in the century between Constance and the beginning of the Reformation. Martin Luther (1483–1546) appealed to a free general council presided over by the emperor to settle the issues he had raised, but the papacy succeeded in preventing the meeting of a council that it did not control. The challenge to papal authority posed by Luther and by Protestantism in general, however, went far beyond embracing conciliarism. Only the Bible, *sola scriptura,* could serve as authority in religion. The papacy, the councils, the right to interpret doctrine delegated to the Scholastic theologians, were human traditions that had no basis in Scripture. Every individual human was capable of understanding Scripture if it was read with an open mind and a pure heart. The Catholic Church responded largely through the Council of Trent (1545–1563), which reaffirmed the traditional structure of authority in religion.

FAMILIAL AUTHORITY

The wielders of imperial and papal authority were always males. Their authority was often seen as analogous to or based upon the power of the father in the family. The father or the head of the household had authority over his wife, children, servants, and employees; they were expected to obey, honor, and submit to him. The exact nature of patriarchal authority was vigorously debated, but all agreed that the duty of the father, and secondarily of the mother, was first of all to teach children the true faith, how to be productive, thrifty, and cooperative, and to submit to higher authority. Also debated was whether a widow could serve as the head of the household after her husband died. The argument that such authority was exclusively male was undercut by the practice of allowing widows in most of Europe to manage their households, including their sons until they married and formed their own households.

AUTHORITY IN CULTURE

Authority in the scholarly disciplines and the arts was different from political, religious, and familial authority in that it was not seen as based on divine and natural law. Certain ancients had reached the pinnacle of knowledge and expertise, and all that remained for those who followed was to understand and imitate their achievements. Plato and Aristotle both had that status in philosophy, creating tension between Platonists and Aristotelians. Other examples included Cicero for rhetoric, Virgil for epic poetry, Euclid for geometry, Galen for medicine, Ptolemy for astronomy, and Justinian's *Corpus juris civilis* for law. In art, however, there were rather few examples of ancient art to serve as models, and the names of the artists were largely unknown. The sixteenth century also saw many of these authorities come under attack. Petrus Ramus (1515–1572), for example, sought to displace Aristotle as the philosophical authority, while Nicolaus Copernicus (1473–1543) and Galileo Galilei (1564–1642) more successfully undermined Ptolemy's authority in astronomy, beginning the early modern intellectual revolution.

See also **Divine Right Kingship; Family; Holy Roman Empire; Law; Papacy and Papal States; Reformation, Protestant; Sovereignty, Theory of; Theology.**

BIBLIOGRAPHY

Allan, George. *The Importances of the Past: A Meditation on the Authority of Tradition.* Albany, N.Y., 1986.

Evans, G. R. *Problems of Authority in the Reformation Debates.* Cambridge, U.K., and New York, 1992.

Griffiths, Paul, et al., eds. *The Experience of Authority in Early Modern England.* New York, 1996.

Kristeller, Paul. *Renaissance Thought: The Classic, Scholastic, and Humanistic Strains.* Rev. ed. New York, 1961.

Wilks, Michael. *The Problem of Sovereignty in the Later Middle Ages.* Cambridge, U.K., 1964.

FREDERIC J. BAUMGARTNER

AUTOBIOGRAPHY. *See* **Biography and Autobiography.**

AUTOCRACY. Autocracy is perhaps the concept most widely used to describe the political culture of the Russian state before 1917. Indeed, autocracy, understood as the unlimited rule of the monarch over his subjects, is often taken as the signature characteristic of Russian political culture in general. *Autocracy* is also the term used to describe early modern Russia by many professional historians, especially in the United States, but their understanding is far more nuanced. These historians see the political structure of Russia as essentially oligarchical, with power shared in a mutually beneficial way among various layers of the nobility and the government. This article will present autocracy in the relatively stable political culture from 1450 to 1650 and then will discuss the changes wrought in that culture by massive influences from western Europe under Peter I the Great (ruled 1682–1725) and his immediate predecessors.

Most responsible for the trope of total power of the Russian ruler over his subjects are the accounts of western European visitors to Russia from the fifteenth to the seventeenth centuries. They developed a fairly simple picture of Russian political life, positing a ruler with total power over his subjects, helped in his oppressive rule by his subjects' ignorance, a subservient church, and an ideology that made his orders the equivalent of God's will.

When we turn to evidence that reflects the way Russians themselves thought about politics, however, we find a slightly different picture. Lacking a literary model of abstract political theorizing, Muscovites expressed their political ideas in a wide variety of genres in various media, including saints' lives, chronicles, and other historical texts; icons, mural cycles, and even church building and other types of architecture. This varied body of evidence presents a fairly consistent set of interrelated political ideas. The ruler (grand prince until 1547, tsar thereafter) was understood to derive his political power directly from God. Russians saw their state as a kind of reincarnation of the ancient state of Israel, guided and protected by God so long as the people

kept their faith in God. The Russians' picture of the tsar resembled his picture of God himself: a stern but merciful ruler whose relationship to his subjects was essentially personal.

If the ruler was seen as "chosen by God," was he then free to rule utterly as he saw fit, with no restraints to his power? The answer, not surprising within the context of Christian doctrines of rulership, was "no." Texts, court rituals, and images alike agree that rulers had clear obligations: to be personally pious (and thus open to receive God's will), to preserve the institution and doctrines of the Orthodox Church, and to preserve the social hierarchy while protecting the innocent and vulnerable and punishing wrong-doers.

But what of a ruler who willfully disregarded these obligations? Unlike their counterparts in early modern Europe, Russian thinkers had not worked out an answer to this problem. Even advocates of royal power admitted that subjects had not only the right but the obligation to resist an evil ruler, whom they called a "tormentor" *(muchitel')*, the Slavonic translation of the Greek *tyrannos*. There is considerable evidence that Ivan IV (the Terrible, ruled 1533–1584) was regarded as a tormentor by the end of his reign. Several rulers during the Time of Troubles (a period of civil wars and foreign intervention, 1598–1613) were regarded in the same way. The problem was that since there was no organized mechanism for replacing a God-defying monarch with another, more godly ruler, the declaration that the current ruler was a tormentor could easily lead to the destruction of legitimate government altogether, and thus to chaos.

The monarch's advisers were the main mechanism for preventing this disastrous situation. Advisers were a standard attribute of good rulers in both literary and visual representations of monarchs. They were there to give godly advice to wise rulers or to correct sinful rulers through their counsel. But this theoretical function of providing wise advice remained a personal matter and was never given a legal or constitutional form. It was not firmly attached to the Boyar Duma, a consultative body of representatives of the most prominent aristocratic families and church hierarchs, which met frequently to advise the ruler throughout the early modern period up until the era of Peter the Great.

Although consultative assemblies played a major and necessary role in the seventeenth century, in effect ruling the country on the eve of the election of Michael Romanov as tsar in 1613, the dominance of a personalized, God-dependent theory of governance prevented these assemblies from having a permanent, legitimate role in Muscovite affairs.

Discussion of assemblies brings us into the realm of practical politics. How was real political power distributed in Muscovy? Again, the foreigners' trope of the unlimited power of the monarch has had to be modified. Although there is disagreement among historians, most experts take the view that the successful ruler ruled with and through his boyars and with members of the provincial gentry, and not in opposition to them. Whereas previous historians emphasized the horizontal, corporate divisions in Muscovite society, with power flowing downward from the ruler through a growing bureaucracy, many more recent historians have emphasized a different overlapping structure. Here the great aristocratic families surround the ruler like the protons around the nucleus of an atom, with vertical patronage networks connecting the court with distant corners of the realm. Thus society was bound by the horizontal ties of a hierarchical precedence system (mestnichestvo) and by a growing body of law enforced by a bureaucratic apparatus, as well as by vertical and personal patronage connections across the boundaries of these groupings. Most importantly, the crown and the nobles were more allies than rivals: the crown depended on nobles at all levels to run affairs in the countryside, while the nobles depended on the crown to run national affairs and to protect noble interests in the localities.

Thus, the political culture of Russia on the eve of the eighteenth century had serious vulnerabilities. The legitimacy of any ruler could be challenged (and was challenged, for example, by the Old Believers) on the grounds of failing to carry out God's will, however the latter was interpreted. The ruler was bound by the vaguely defined theoretical obligation to consult with wise advisers and by the very real and growing power of the great aristocratic clans, as well as by a provincial gentry whose power and self-confidence were also growing. Peter tried, with limited success, to resolve these questions.

Borrowing from Western theorists of absolutism and from limited changes in Muscovite political culture at the end of the seventeenth century, Peter and his political assistants substituted reason of state and the common good, as defined by the will of the monarch, for the all-too-vague will of God as the source of legitimate authority in Russia. To be sure, the monarch still claimed to be God's chosen ruler, but to question or even discuss the link between God and the actual ruler became a treasonous act. In spite of the continued use of religious rhetoric, the state changed from an imagined revival of the ancient Israelite theocracy into a self-contained secular system, in which the good order of the state—its military successes and its cultural and social reforms—became the goals of political action.

The relationship of the monarch to the aristocracy was not resolved with similar clarity, perhaps because it did not need resolution. Though he exercised great personal power, used the title "emperor" rather than "tsar" after his victory over the Swedes in 1721, replaced the Boyar Duma with a Senate (1711), and attempted to create an aristocracy of merit through a new Table of Ranks (1722), Peter did not resolve the relationship of the crown to its nobles. Indeed, the power of the aristocracy of birth continued to grow throughout the eighteenth century as it had in the seventeenth. Russian nobles continued to find it advantageous to support the "autocracy" of the ruler at the center, while the ruler gave the nobles ever widening powers in the localities and, in many cases, great informal influence at the center. Thus the contradiction between a rhetoric of "autocratic" rule by one person and an oligarchical political structure, which had misled foreign observers in the pre-Petrine era, continued to characterize the political culture of Russia.

See also **Absolutism; Aristocracy and Gentry; Authority, Concept of; Divine Right Kingship; Duma; Ivan IV, "the Terrible" (Russia); Michael Romanov (Russia); Monarchy; Peter I (Russia); Representative Institutions; Romanov Dynasty (Russia); Russia; Sovereignty, Theory of; State and Bureaucracy; Time of Troubles (Russia); Tyranny, Theory of.**

BIBLIOGRAPHY

Kivelson, Valerie A. *Autocracy in the Provinces: The Muscovite Gentry and Political Culture in the Seventeenth Century.* Stanford, 1996.

Kollmann, Nancy Shields. *Kinship and Politics: The Making of the Muscovite Political System, 1345–1547.* Stanford, 1987.

LeDonne, John P. *Absolutism and Ruling Class: The Formation of the Russian Political Order, 1700–1825.* New York, 1991.

Rowland, Daniel. "Did Muscovite Literary Ideology Place Limits on the Power of the Tsar (1540s–1660s)?" *Russian Review* 49, no. 2 (1990): 125–155.

DANIEL ROWLAND

AVVAKUM PETROVICH (1620–1682), Russian Orthodox archpriest who fought against the liturgical reforms of Patriarch Nikon. Avvakum is usually considered the principal leader of the early Old Believers. The apocalyptic teachings he developed in numerous writings formed the core of Old Believer ideology, and his strong moral convictions provided a heroic example for future generations of Old Believers.

Born into a family of village priests in a hamlet close to Nizhniy Novgorod on the Volga River, Avvakum became a church deacon in 1642 and a parish priest two years later. He quickly became known as a religious zealot for demanding moral discipline and regular church attendance from his parishioners. Avvakum's sermons against drunkenness, gambling, and fornication as well as his attacks on minstrels and dancing bears brought him to the attention of Archpriest Stefan Vonifat'ev, confessor to Tsar Alexis Mikhailovich (ruled 1645–1676). Despite the Kremlin's support (after 1647) for his campaigns, Avvakum suffered brutal assaults, and finally expulsion, at the hands of his angry parishioners. In 1652, the Kremlin rewarded Avvakum for his loyalty by making him archpriest of the unruly Volga town of Iurevets. He again fell victim to popular revolt and had to seek refuge in Moscow.

Avvakum quickly antagonized the newly elected Patriarch Nikon (reigned 1652–1666). Avvakum's vita emphasizes that he opposed Nikon's introduction of the three-finger sign of the cross (replacing the old two-finger sign) and other liturgical reforms, but his only surviving letter from this period (dated 14 September 1653) reveals that he primarily resented the patriarch's secular priorities. On 16 September 1653 Avvakum was sent to Siberia after denouncing Patriarch Nikon as "a great deceiver and the son of a whore" in a public sermon. In the Siberian capitol of Tobol'sk, Avvakum implemented rigorous disciplinary measures and continued to fight ecclesiastical corruption. In 1656, he joined a military expedition sent to convert the natives of Dauria (now the Lake Baikal region) to Russian Orthodoxy. After enduring many hardships, Avvakum returned to Moscow in 1664 as a fervent enemy of the established church, and only then did he begin to polemicize against the liturgical reforms of Patriarch Nikon.

Most of Avvakum's polemical writings are dated after 1667, the year in which he was excommunicated and exiled by a church council to a remote prison colony beyond the Arctic circle. Glorifying the old Russian Orthodox rituals, his letters and treatises (including the *Book of Sermons* and *Book of Commentaries*) condemned the new sign of the cross, the new liturgical books, and many other innovations (such as three hallelujahs instead of two and changes in the wording of the Lord's Prayer) as signs of the approaching apocalypse.

Avvakum was responsible for developing some of the principal ideas of the Old Believer movement. These included a belief that Russian society must be reshaped according to Orthodox moral teachings, and that all secular and foreign influences on the church should be rejected. Avvakum upheld the image of a mythological Russia that was holier than other world cultures. He condemned Patriarch Nikon and his successors as minions of the Antichrist but promised the coming Kingdom of God to those who remained loyal to pre-Nikonian Orthodoxy.

After Avvakum was burned at the stake in April 1682, his writings were carefully preserved and transmitted to later generations of Old Believers in widely copied manuscripts. The authenticity and originality of Avvakum's work has yet to be fully investigated. Many scholars have assumed that Avvakum had a remarkable memory, because he quoted long passages from medieval church texts during his imprisonment without having access to book collections. However, there are significant similarities between Avvakum's writings and those penned by other Old Believers, such as Deacon Fedor Ivanov and Archimandrite Spiridon Potemkin. A handful of scholars have therefore suggested that some of the writings attributed to Avvakum may, in fact, be forgeries. Scholars have also pointed out that Avvakum left almost no trace in documentary records. Other early Old Believers, such as the now largely forgotten Nikita Dobrynin, left significant archival trails, since they were under constant surveillance by the authorities. It is also curious that Avvakum's writings provoked no response in the form of an official church polemic, whereas Dobrynin's *Supplication* generated several book-length rebuttals.

There is little doubt that Avvakum's vita (in its numerous redactions) became one of the most popular Old Believer texts, and no work of early Russian literature has been more frequently translated and published. Nineteenth-century Russian writers such as Fyodor Dostoyevski and Nikolay Leskov further popularized Avvakum's image, and Avvakum has re-mained the dominant focus of Old Believer studies to this day.

See also **Alexis I (Russia); Morozova, Boiarynia; Nikon, patriarch; Old Believers; Orthodoxy, Russian; Russian Literature and Language.**

BIBLIOGRAPHY

Borozdin, A. K. *Protopop Avvakum.* Rostov-na-Donu, 1898.

Demkova, N. S. *Zhitie protopopa Avvakuma: Tvorcheskaia istoriia proizvedeniia.* Edited by V. P. Adrianov-Peretts. Leningrad (St. Petersburg), 1974.

Michels, Georg. "The Place of Nikita Konstantinovich Dobrynin in the History of Early Old Belief." *Revue des Études Slaves* LXIX, no. 1–2 (1997): 21–31.

Pascal, Pierre. *Avvakum et les débuts du raskol: La crise religieuse au XVIIe siècle en Russie.* Paris, 1938.

Scheidegger, Gabriele. *Endzeit: Russland am Ende des 17. Jahrhunderts.* Bern and New York, 1999.

GEORG MICHELS

BACH FAMILY. The Bach family was the most famous musical family of the early modern era. It was, however, only one of many such families that emerged in a specific social and cultural context. The territories of Saxony and Thuringia in central Germany, where the Bachs and other musical dynasties such as the Lämmerhirts and Wilckes emerged, were relatively highly urbanized, with a large number of small and medium-sized and some larger towns. Lutheranism was the official religion of the territories in this area. Music was an important part of the Lutheran liturgy, and there were hundreds of positions as cantor and organist in the region. The numerous towns and (mostly minor) courts provided a further institutional and financial framework, as well as boundless performance and composition opportunities. Saxon and Thuringian towns, courts, boys' schools, and the Universities of Leipzig, Wittenberg, and Jena provided formal and informal training.

The Bachs, who produced over seventy professional musicians, shared many characteristics of other musical families. They emerged in the sixteenth century, when Lutheran, urban, and court liturgical and institutional frameworks were established or overhauled, and declined by the end of the eighteenth, when those institutions also went into a decline. Most of the Bachs were active as instrumentalists rather than as composers. Positions as town or court musician were informally handed down among the various branches of the family, much as artisanal and professional careers were in

Bach Family. Portrait of Johann Sebastian Bach by Elias Gottlob Haussmann, 1746. ©BETTMANN/CORBIS

other families. The Bachs frequently intermarried with other families of musicians. Early musical training in the home made it more likely that talent would develop. Daughters were trained along with sons, often becoming proficient instrumentalists and singers. Most jobs and public performance venues were closed to daughters, however, and after

Bach Family. An undated portrait engraving of Carl Philip Emmanuel Bach. THE ART ARCHIVE/MUSEEN DER STADT WEIN/ DAGLI ORTI (A)

marriage women were expected to devote most of their energies to their families.

Justly the most famous member of the Bach family was Johann Sebastian Bach (1685–1750). Born in Eisenach, Bach moved to the smaller town of Ohrdruf in 1695 to live with his older brother after the death of their parents. From 1703 to 1708, Bach briefly held positions as junior court musician at Weimar and as organist in the towns of Arnstadt and Mühlhausen. From 1708 to 1717 he was the court organist at Weimar; in 1717, he was appointed kapellmeister at the court of Prince Leopold of Anhalt-Cöthen. In 1723 he was appointed cantor of St. Thomas's Church in Leipzig, a position he held until his death. Bach was a multifaceted musician. He was a virtuoso performer on a variety of instruments, most famously the organ. He conducted in church and secular settings, and had a mastery of practical aspects of performance such as tuning instruments and working with the acoustics of a given space. He must also have possessed a great deal of organizational talent: for example, at least

sixty people, mostly students at St. Thomas, worked as copyists for Bach in Leipzig alone.

It is for his compositions, of course, that Bach is best known. These fall into several groups, including the sacred vocal works (especially the more than two hundred cantatas, the motets and oratorios, the *Mass in B Minor,* and the *St. John* and *St. Matthew Passions*); a smaller number of secular vocal works; compositions for the organ; and secular instrumental works for solo instruments (including the partitas for violin, cello, and harpsichord) as well as ensembles (for example, the *Brandenburg Concertos*). Working toward the end of the baroque era, he integrated a variety of approaches drawn from past and contemporary masters into his own style and stretched and gave new meaning to established forms. His style was characterized by an intricate interplay among vocal and instrumental lines, complex but formally clear structures, and underlining of textual meaning by way of melodic, instrumental, and harmonic motifs.

On balance, Bach's works represent a culmination more than they do a pointing to the future. In general, his sacred works, especially the cantatas, are now regarded as pulling together and capping previous traditions. This is true to a degree, and Bach largely stopped writing cantatas after 1729, perhaps partly because he felt that he had explored the possibilities of the genre. Still, the high baroque cantata itself had emerged fully only around 1700, was significantly developed by Bach himself, and was regarded as an innovative and even controversial musical form into the 1720s. "Bach the progressive," by contrast, is often regarded as being represented most clearly in his secular instrumental works. In these pieces, Bach most clearly emphasized his incorporation of new styles drawn from Italy and France. The social context of the performance of these pieces was also modern. The collegium musicum he directed from 1729 provided him with an innovative and highly talented amateur ensemble, mostly made up of university students. He led performances of the collegium in Leipzig coffeehouses, a new type of secular venue.

J. S. Bach married twice—first, in 1707, his cousin Maria Barbara Bach (1684–1720), and in 1721 Anna Magdalena Wilcke (1701–1760). Four of his children with Maria Barbara and six with Anna

Magdalena, in all three daughters and seven sons, survived infancy and early childhood. Little is known about the daughters. Four of the sons achieved renown as composers in the newly emerging styles of the rococo and Sturm und Drang, even pointing the way to early classical style: Wilhelm Friedemann (1710–1784), Carl Philipp Emanuel (1714–1788), Johann Christoph Friedrich (1732–1795), and Johann Christian (1735–1782). They became as well as or better known in their time than their father had in his. The sons were also the last generation of the Bach family to achieve prominence as musicians.

See also **Baroque; Buxtehude, Dieterich; Leipzig; Music; Music Criticism.**

BIBLIOGRAPHY

Bach, C. P. E. *The Letters of C. P. E. Bach.* Translated and edited by Stephen Clark. Oxford and New York, 1997.

Boyd, Malcolm. *Bach: The Brandenburg Concertos.* Cambridge, U.K., and New York, 1993.

Butt, John, ed. *The Cambridge Companion to Bach.* Cambridge, U.K., and New York, 1997.

Geiringer, Karl, with Irene Geiringer. *The Bach Family. Seven Generations of Creative Genius.* New York, 1954.

Kevorkian, Tanya. *Baroque Piety: Religious Practices and Society in Leipzig, 1650–1750.* Forthcoming.

———. "The Reception of the Cantata during Church Services in Leipzig, 1700–1750." *Early Music* 30 (2002): 26–44.

Ottenberg, Hans-Günther. *C. P. E. Bach.* Translated by Philip Whitmore. Oxford and New York, 1987.

Stiller, Günther. *Johann Sebastian Bach and Liturgical Life in Leipzig.* Translated by Herbert J. A. Bouman et al. Edited by Robin A. Leaver. St. Louis, 1984.

Wolff, Christoph, ed. *The World of the Bach Cantatas.* Vol. 1, New York, 1997.

Wolff, Christoph, et al. *The New Grove Bach Family.* New York, 1983.

TANYA KEVORKIAN

BACON, FRANCIS (1561–1626), English natural philosopher, essayist, and statesman. Francis Bacon was the youngest son of Elizabeth I's lord keeper, Sir Nicholas Bacon, and his second wife, Anne Cooke. Nephew by marriage to William Cecil, chief councillor to the queen, young Bacon was well positioned to succeed at court. Educated at Cambridge from the age of twelve, Bacon in 1576 began the study of law at Gray's Inn. He interrupted his legal studies that same year to accompany Sir Amias Paulet on a diplomatic mission to France. His father's sudden death recalled him home after three years' residence abroad. Because Sir Nicholas had not made adequate financial provisions for his youngest son, Francis now had to fend for himself financially. He continued his legal studies, becoming a bencher, or senior member, at Gray's in 1586. In 1584 Bacon became a member of Parliament, but thereafter failed to secure the position of solicitor general despite the assistance of his patron, Robert Devereux, earl of Essex. In 1597 he published the first version of his *Essays*, which he continued to revise and augment in later years. During Elizabeth's reign, Bacon only attained to the post of learned counsel extraordinary and the dubious honor of prosecuting his recalcitrant ex-patron, the earl of Essex, for his treasonous uprising in 1601.

James I's ascension to the English monarchy in 1603 marked a decided turn in Bacon's fortunes. Knighted and appointed to the position of king's counsel, Bacon thereafter became solicitor general (1607), attorney general (1613), member of the privy council (1616), and lord keeper (1617). He married Alice Barnham in 1606. In 1618, he was created Baron Verulam, and became lord chancellor. From 1604 until 1621, when he was impeached for bribery, Bacon advised the king on religious, financial, administrative, parliamentary, judicial, and foreign policy matters, as well as advocating for the political union of England and Scotland. As lord chancellor, he wrote important judicial decisions and sought to reform English law.

During this period, Bacon wrote extensively about ameliorating the human condition through his plans for the advancement of natural philosophy. His *Advancement of Learning* appeared in 1605, his natural philosophic reinterpretation of Greek mythology, *De Sapientia Veterum,* in 1609, the *Novum Organum* in 1620, and the *Historia Ventorum* in 1622. After his impeachment, Bacon devoted his final years to scientific writing and experiments. He died childless in 1626 from pneumonia contracted after a foray into winter snows with a chicken carcass to conduct an experiment in refrigeration.

Francis Bacon. Portrait by Paul van Somer. ©BETTMANN/
CORBIS

Bacon achieved an incisive grasp of the most significant philosophical, social, and political issues of early modernism. In *The Advancement of Learning,* he took the measure of the intellectual ferment that comprised the contemporary intellectual scene. Aristotelian natural philosophy had lost preeminence and now competed with Neoplatonism, empiricism, alchemy, and ancient atomism, among other philosophical theories, in the effort to explicate the natural world. Bacon articulated the weaknesses of each intellectual movement and reincorporated its strengths into his own philosophical program. For Bacon, natural philosophy should begin with empirical observation and the painstaking compilation of natural histories. Inductive inquiry and the noting of particulars would be followed by controlled experiments (under natural and artificial conditions), which would yield first-level axioms or generalizations. These, in turn, would be corrected and refined by further inductive inquiry and experimentation until higher-level axioms, which were capable of producing useful material effects, were attained. To ensure the validity of inductive and experimental findings, Bacon required the natural philosopher to eschew the four "Idols of the Mind," those ways in which the human mind distorted knowledge through the peculiarities of na-

ture, nurture, language, and ungrounded theorizing.

Bacon tried to ensure that his program was politically practical. He designed his new science to fit within the institutional framework of a Jacobean monarchy purportedly interested in mutually beneficial relations with commercial and artisanal sectors. Bacon imagined the scientific enterprise as a grand public works project that would enlist the energies and ideas of broad sectors of society but would remain under the auspices of royal government. Bacon's institution of natural philosophy would be to reconcile private intellectual ambitions with public interests to the benefit of civil society, as his scientific utopia, the *New Atlantis* (1627), envisioned.

Francis Bacon never gained financial or political support for his scientific program during his lifetime. His philosophic influence in England was negligible during the first third of the seventeenth century, although his importance was understood in the 1620s by Continental philosophers such as Pierre Gassendi, Marin Mersenne, René Descartes, Christiaan Huygens, and Isaac Beeckman. By mid-century, however, Bacon's works were highly valued everywhere. In the 1640s, Protestant educational reformists led by Samuel Hartlib saw Bacon as a forerunner. John Wilkins, Seth Ward, and John Webster followed Bacon in attempting to devise an accurate scientific language. But Bacon's greatest influence was on the early members of England's Royal Society (est. 1662), who viewed him as their intellectual progenitor. Bacon's star blazed bright into the eighteenth century, but was clouded in the nineteenth, when biographers charged him with perfidy in prosecuting his treasonous former patron, the earl of Essex. Nonetheless, the upsurge in published studies of Bacon's life and work at the turn of the twenty-first century makes evident his status as a seminal figure in the history of early modern science.

See also **Alchemy; Aristotelianism; Descartes, René; Elizabeth I (England); Empiricism; Gassendi, Pierre; Hartlib, Samuel; Huygens Family; James I and VI (England and Scotland); Mersenne, Marin; Neoplatonism; Wilkins, John.**

BIBLIOGRAPHY

Primary Sources

Bacon, Francis. *The Advancement of Learning.* Edited by Michael Kiernan. Oxford, 2000.

———. *The Essayes or Counsel, Civill and Morall.* Edited by Michael Kiernan. Oxford, 1985.

———. *The New Organon.* Edited by Lisa Jardine and Michael Silverthorne. Cambridge, U.K., and New York, 2000. Translation of *Novum Organum* (1620).

Secondary Sources

Solomon, Julie Robin. *Objectivity in the Making: Francis Bacon and the Politics of Inquiry.* Baltimore, 2003.

Weinberger, Jerry. *Science, Faith, and Politics: Francis Bacon and the Utopian Roots of the Modern Age.* Ithaca, N.Y., 1985.

Whitney, Charles. *Francis Bacon and Modernity.* New Haven, 1986.

JULIE ROBIN SOLOMON

BALKANS. The term "Balkans" stems from the Ottoman Turkish word *balkan,* defined as a pass through wooded and rocky mountains. The designation is quite recent and, in fact, was not universally accepted until the end of the nineteenth century. Earlier European names for the peninsula included Hellenic peninsula, Greek peninsula, Illyrian peninsula, European Turkey, and *Haemus* peninsula. In English, names such as "Balkan Mountains" or "Great Balkans" appear as early as 1835, but the term "Balkan Peninsula" was first used in a book by J. G. C. Minchin on the post-1878 political situation in the region, published in 1886.

GEOGRAPHICAL BOUNDARIES AND TOPOGRAPHICAL FEATURES

The Balkan Peninsula is the easternmost of the three great European peninsulas. (The others are the Iberian and the Apennine Peninsulas.) Three of the peninsula's geographical boundaries are maritime: the Black Sea in the east, the Aegean Sea in the south, and the Adriatic Sea in the west. In the north, from the mouth of the Kupa River into the Sava River, the northern boundary continues up the Sava Valley to the Ljubljana basin in Slovenia to the meeting point of the Dinarid range and the Alps. The westernmost part of the northern boundary is clearly defined by the valley of the River Soca at the border between Slovenia and Italy.

A relief map of the Balkan Peninsula is notable for its three main mountain ranges: the Rhodope massif, the Dinarids, and the Pindus system, between which are the region's main agricultural areas. These geographic features have had a great impact on the area's history. The peninsula can be divided into four geographically defined areas: the Aegean, the east Balkans, the Morava-Vardar basin, and the Pindus-Dinarid areas. The Greek-Aegean coast, the Adriatic coast, parts of Albania, Macedonia, and Herzegovina enjoy a Mediterranean climate; the rest of the peninsula shares its weather with central Europe.

MAJOR CITIES AND HISTORICAL TERRITORIES

Most of the important cities in the Balkans during the early modern era—which coincides with Ottoman predominance on the peninsula—are still among its most important centers. Some of them date back to Roman antiquity, others are the product of early medieval times (Dubrovnik/Ragusa), and a few were founded under the aegis of the Ottomans (Sarajevo, Mostar) or the Habsburgs (Karlovac). The most important historical territories in the Balkan Peninsula are Greece, Bulgaria, Dobrudja, Albania, Serbia, Montenegro, Bosnia, Macedonia, Dalmatia, Croatia, Slavonia, the Croatian and Slavonian military border, Dubrovnik, Istria, and Carinthia.

Today's Greece was a part of the eastern Roman and Byzantine Empire for more than a thousand years (395–1460). During the Middle Ages Bulgaria, Serbia, and Bosnia were the important local powers, kingdoms, and tsardoms. Macedonia, despite its old historical name, never again reached the level of political independence and significance it had enjoyed in the times of Philip of Macedonia and Alexander the Great. However, its vast natural resources and more than perfect geographical position on the crossroads of the major roads and fluvial and maritime communications between Europe and the Near East made it a bone of contention for many polities. After periods of being a part of the Byzantine Empire and the Serbian Kingdom, from the mid-fourteenth century until 1430, it became an Ottoman dominion, and Thessalonica, its capital,

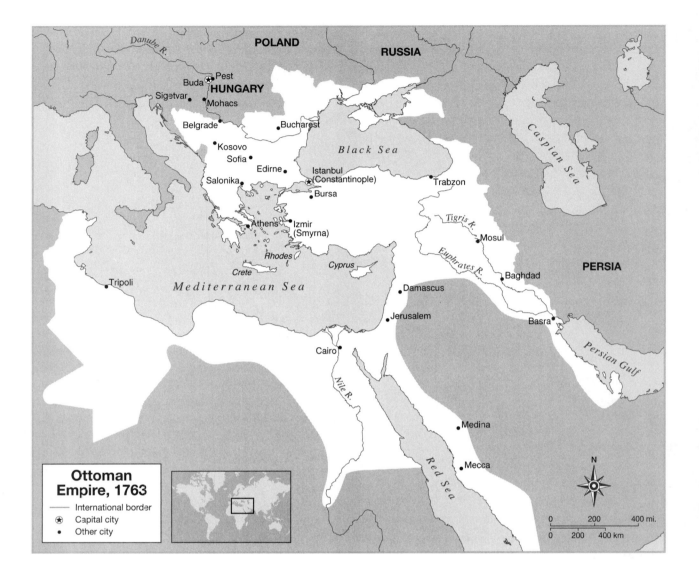

Ottoman Empire, 1763

— International border
⊛ Capital city
• Other city

0   200   400 mi.
0   200   400 km

N

was one of the most important cities of the Ottoman Empire until the expelling of the Ottomans from the Balkans in 1912. Croatia was an independent kingdom that entered fairly early—at the beginning of the twelfth century—into union with the mighty Hungarian kingdom. Dalmatia's overlords in the period between the twelfth and fifteenth centuries were interchangeably Hungary and Venice. Carinthia was an old Slavonic dukedom, but it came quite early under the rule of various Austrian German rulers. Istria was divided between the counts of Gortz and later the Habsburgs on one side and Venice on the other. Parts of Albania were under Byzantine, Angevine, Serbian, and Venetian rule, but some mighty local dynasts enjoyed a high level of actual power during the Middle Ages. The Croatian military border was a creation of the early modern period. The Habsburgs instituted it in 1579 to

halt Ottoman advances into their territories. Dubrovnik (Ragusa) was a tiny aristocratic republic, the importance of which in the economic, social, and diplomatic history of the entire Mediterranean was belied by its minuscule territory and negligible military power.

DEMOGRAPHIC CHARACTERISTICS AND CHANGES, 1450–1789

The main sources for the demographic history of the Balkans in the early modern period are the Ottoman tax registers, but it is sometimes possible to see continuities with the late Middle Ages by using late Byzantine and medieval Venetian registers of various kinds *(praktika, cattastici)*. After the 1560s, in areas with a Catholic population, one can find valuable complementary sources in records of baptisms, marriages, and deaths and in reports by canonical visitors. Estimates of demographic figures in the travel literature of the period are frequently unreliable. The leading authority on Ottoman historic demography, O. L. Barkan, estimated that the Ottoman Balkans in the period 1525–1530 contained some one million taxable households. (Barkan recommends adding at least 20 percent to any counted number to represent the tax-exempt population.)

During the sixteenth century, the major cities of the Balkans showed a dramatic rise in population. Fernand Braudel estimated the population of the Balkans around 1600 to have been around eight million. This number declined by the mid-eighteenth century to perhaps as few as three million. The main reasons for such a sharp decline were the many wars between the Ottomans and the Habsburgs, Venice, and Muscovy (1683–1739) and repeated epidemics of plague and other contagious diseases. In the period 1700–1815 the number of Christians in the Balkans was constantly rising, while the Muslim population was in decline.

The original Ottoman conquests, beginning in the fourteenth century, coincided with substantial demographic changes. Any area the Ottomans planned to conquer was first subjected to repeated seasonal raids accompanied by large-scale enslavement of the local population. These raids caused great waves of migration in the late medieval period. For example, beginning in the fifteenth century, Serbs from Kosovo and eastern Serbia moved to Buda to escape Ottoman seasonal raids, while Catholic Albanians and Slavs crossed the Adriatic Sea and

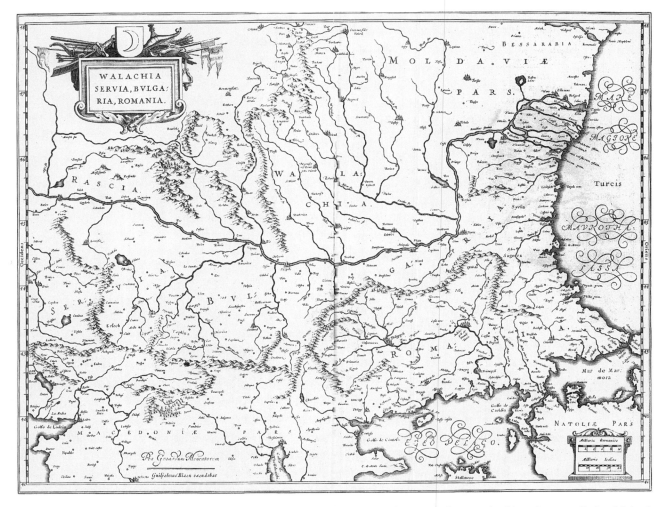

Balkans. Willem Janszoon Blaeu's map of the southeastern Balkans, based on an earlier map by Mercator, was first published in his *Novus Atlas* of 1634. The region was under the control of the Ottoman Turks for most of the fifteenth through eighteenth centuries. However, a short-lived attempt at Romanian unity occurred under Michael the Brave (1593–1601), who defeated the Turks in 1600 and briefly ruled Walachia, Moldavia, and Transylvania. MAP COLLECTION, STERLING MEMORIAL LIBRARY, YALE UNIVERSITY

established colonies in the Papal States and in the kingdom of Naples. After the actual Ottoman conquest, many of the newly acquired areas were frequently subjected either to Turkish ethnic colonization or to population resettlement. The main areas of Turkish ethnic colonization in the Balkans were Bulgaria and Macedonia, with the *Bektashi* and *Halveti sufi* dervish orders playing a significant role.

In addition to the dervishes, the main agents of ethnic colonization were the Turkish tribes (Yürüks), who either resettled on their own, like the Yürüks from southwestern Anatolia in the period 1355–1400, or were expelled from Anatolia, as was the case with certain nomad groups of Mongol origins after 1416. The resettlement, both punitive and voluntary, of Balkan peoples also moved in the direction of old Ottoman centers in the Balkans, as well as Istanbul and even Anatolia. After the conquest of Bosnia, some Bosnian peasants were resettled to the vicinity of Edirne, where remnants of this group still survived in the seventeenth century. After the conquest of Belgrade in 1521, many of its citizens were transferred to Istanbul. They soon lost their language as they melted into the Greek community, but they left their trace in the topography of Istanbul where the area called the Belgrade Forest *(Belgrat ormani)* has been named after them. Serbian expellees from Srijem were resettled to the Gallipoli peninsula in the period between 1521–1528 and survived as a community, preserving their Slavonic tongue until 1912, when they were forced to migrate to Serbia after the Ottoman defeat in the first Balkan war. During the sixteenth century, waves of Sephardic Jews and Marranos of Sephardic origins entered the Ottoman Empire via Mediterranean ports. Soon afterward, they absorbed the old pre-Ottoman communities of Greek-speaking Romaniote Jews. These Sephardic Jews were joined in the mid-seventeenth century by Ashkenazi Jews from Poland and Ukraine, who were fleeing the Khmelnytsky pogroms.

In the eighteenth century, the Cincars, the last remnant of the Roman Balkan population, pushed by the persecution of local Albanian warlords, created a diaspora network of merchants from Moschopolis in today's Epirus to Vienna and Budapest. The Cincars were absorbed quickly into larger Orthodox communities, and some of them became the most fervent advocates of Greek, Serbian, Bulgarian, and Romanian nationalism. In the period 1699–1717, a vast number of Muslim Slavonic speakers from the Ottoman Hungarian territories lost to the Habsburgs were forced to resettle in Bosnia, Serbia, Bulgaria, and Albania. In the same period, the male Balkan Muslim population, seeking work and social prestige, joined the janissary and mercenary regiments deployed throughout the empire, from Belgrade to Cairo. Two of the most famous Ottoman governors and warlords of the Arab provinces were Jezzar Ahmed Pasha of Syria, a Bosniak, and Kavalali Mehmed Ali Pasha of Egypt, an Albanian. Beside the dramatic and massive migrations caused by political and military factors, there were slow movements of population and micromigrations that caused structural changes in Balkan historical demography, and their importance in Balkan history cannot be underestimated.

CONVERSION

Even more important than forceful resettlement and ethnic migration was the Islamization of certain population groups, mainly in Bosnia, Albania, the Rhodope massif, and Crete. The period of Islamization was not the same everywhere. In Bosnia, the process developed predominantly in the period 1463–1600, while in Albania and on Crete the critical years were in the second half of the seventeenth century. In 1468 in Bosnia less than one percent of the population was Muslim; by about 1600 71 percent had been converted.

There are two main perspectives on this phenomenon. One view sees it as a result of a deliberate and forceful action of the Ottoman Islamic state and its Muslim society and citizens; the other stresses the supposed intrinsically tolerant character of the Ottoman state and society and sees conversion as the result of a deliberate choice of the converts themselves. It is undeniable that the inclusive character of Ottoman society and its toleration of subjects who did not subscribe to the belief of the ruler were higher than elsewhere in early modern Europe, with the exception of the United Provinces. Even in those Protestant countries, it was impossible to be a Muslim, while it was quite normal to be Christian, Jewish, and even Hindu in the Ottoman Empire. With the demise of the Bosnian church after the fall of the Bosnian Kingdom in 1463, the majority of its followers gradually converted to Islam, but some

Balkans. A map by Homann Heirs of the central Balkan peninsula, featuring the provinces of Macedonia, Thessaly, and Albania, from a German atlas of 1770. Through most of the early modern period, this area was part of the Ottoman Empire. MAP COLLECTION, STERLING MEMORIAL LIBRARY, YALE UNIVERSITY

Catholics and some Orthodox Christians converted as well.

In Albania, it is clear that the state was interested and directly involved in conversion. This happened especially during the second part of the seventeenth century when the Ottomans tried, through conversion, to suppress the Venetian reconquest of parts of Albania and Greece and to create a Muslim shield from northern Albania to Bosnia in order to halt possible Habsburg intrusions. The Ottoman archival data show how the central and local administration extended gifts in kind, objects, and money to the converts—certainly an incentive to conversion. Chronicles by Ibrahim Peçevi (d. 1649) and travel accounts by Evliya

Çelebi (d. after 1683) preserved reports of sporadic violence, especially in the big cities, which would end with the conversion of individuals or groups of people.

Jews also sometimes converted to Islam. A vivid document from the 1560s describes the troubles of a recently converted Jewish rabbi who was considered a professional threat by the local Muslim intelligentsia. They therefore questioned the sincerity of his conversion in a petition to the Sublime Porte. In addition to converts proper, there were communities of pseudoconverts or half-converts who kept their previous beliefs and customs, while adopting some Islamic ones. Many such communities were still alive in the mountains of northern Albania at the end of the nineteenth century. The Dönmes of Salonika were a special case. They gradually lost their Sephardi Spanish idiom and became linguistically "Turkified," while preserving many rites and customs of Judaism according to their own Sabbetean interpretations.

The story of conversion in the early modern Balkans does not end with the story of its Islamization. Especially in the sixteenth and seventeenth centuries, there were attempts at conversions of Orthodox Christians to Roman Catholicism, and vice versa. Whole zones in the Balkans fluctuated between the two Christian rites. The Habsburgs tried unsuccessfully to bring the Serbian Orthodox population into union with Rome, for example, but they quickly realized that if they wanted to preserve their military border system, they would have to cease proselytizing among their Serbian Orthodox subjects. Venice was even more cautious in that respect. Local missionary work, especially during famines, was more successful than deliberate state action. Some of the most successful conversions of the Orthodox Serbs to Catholicism were achieved by the Franciscans, who gave generous gifts of grain and other food.

OTTOMAN CONQUEST

The Ottoman drive into the Balkans began with the conquest of the insignificant fortress of Tzympe on the Gallipoli peninsula in 1352 and culminated in the seizure of the fortress of Gallipoli itself in 1354, mostly due to an earthquake's destruction of the mighty walls of this key military port. Gallipoli enabled the Ottomans to control traffic between Europe and Asia and between the Aegean and Marmara Seas. In 1361 the Ottomans were already in Adrianople, which by the beginning of the fifteenth century (by then known as Edirne) became the main capital of the empire. The remnants of Byzantine rule in Thrace were almost obliterated by the early 1380s. The Ottomans fought two important battles, at Marica (1371) and Kosovo (1389), with coalitions of Serbian magnates. Bulgaria was subdued by 1394. In 1396 the Ottomans dealt a crushing defeat to the Hungarian and Franco-Burgundian Crusaders in the battle of Nicopolis. Significant parts of the Morea, Epirus, Albania, and Serbia were subdued by 1400.

A halt in these conquests occurred during the Ottoman interregnum between 1402–1422. Salonika, however, came into Ottoman hands in 1430 as one of their most important cities. Serbia was conquered in 1459, Bosnia in 1463, the last remnants of Herzegovina in 1482, Montenegro in 1499, and some important Venetian fortresses in Albania in 1501. The Hungarian banates of Srebrenik and Jajce were liquidated in 1517 and in 1528. The Hungarian defeat at Mohács in 1526 meant the opening of central Europe to the Ottomans. After experimentally installing a vassal kingdom as a buffer against the Habsburgs, the Ottomans took Buda and middle Hungary under their direct control in 1541. Further Ottoman advances in Hungary occurred in the period 1593–1606 and in the 1660s. Venetian territories and dependencies in the Aegean, the Morea, Albania, and Dalmatia diminished significantly, yielding to the Ottomans in the period 1501–1669. In 1669 Crete was finally conquered. The Ottomans twice tried to conquer Vienna without success—in 1529 and in 1683. The "Long War" between the Ottomans and Habsburgs (1593–1606) was exhausting and failed to achieve a breakthrough for either side.

Beginning in 1683, the Ottomans started to lose their territories in central and southeastern Europe. In peace treaties at Karlowitz (1699) and Passarowitz (1717) the Ottoman Empire recognized for the first time in its history significant territorial losses to the Habsburgs and Venetians (Hungary, Serbia, and Dalmatia, with its hinterland, the Morea). The situation was slightly stabilized with the Treaty of Belgrade (1739), when the River Sava was finally determined as the Balkan border between the Ottomans and the Habsburgs. The Treaty of Zistov in 1791 merely confirmed the Treaty of Belgrade, insofar as borders were concerned.

A series of unsuccessful wars with Russia began with disaster in the war of 1768–1774 and concluded with an unfavorable peace treaty for the Ottomans at Küçük Kaynarca. The majority of Russo-Ottoman wars were fought in the nineteenth century. The Napoleonic invasion of Italy in 1796 and the peace treaty between France and Austria signed in Campoformio in 1797 deleted the Republic of Venice from the map. Her territorial legacy was divided between Austria and Napoleonic France. In

1806 the French occupied, and in 1808 formally abolished, the Dubrovnik Republic. In 1804 the Serbs began a series of insurrections that resulted in autonomy, granted to them in 1815; the Greek fight for independence began in 1821. These events marked the end of the *ancien régime* in the Balkans and the beginning of the age of nationalism.

At the beginning of the Ottoman conquests, Thrace had unprecedented importance. It was a cradle of the Ottoman holy warriors who proceeded from it on their raids further west and south. While silver shortages were troubling Europe before the arrival of precious metals from the Americas, the importance of the newly discovered silver mines of Serbia and Bosnia led the Ottomans, always hungry for bullion, to aim their conquests toward these regions. For a long period, between 1459–1541, Serbia and Bosnia were the empire's main Balkan provinces. This played an enormous role in the Ottoman advance toward central Europe. Serbia was on the main military road from Sofia, Edirne, and Constantinople toward Buda and Vienna, and any campaign formations had to pass through it on their way to battle. Bosnia was the repository of the auxiliary troops. Her Muslim population was entrusted with the permanent frontier *Kleinkrieg* ('little war') aimed at exhausting the Habsburgs and Venetians. By the 1480s Bosnian *akincis* (light armored mounted raider volunteers in the Ottoman army) made their raids as far as Friuli in the Venetian Terra Firma and into Carinthia and Styria in today's Slovenia and Austria. In the period 1541–1699, Ottoman Hungary took over much of the border *Kleinkrieg* burden from Bosnia and Serbia. During the eighteenth century, a new Muslim military society came into being in Bosnia, and Albania became a source of irregular auxiliary military troops. Its ports harbored not only pirates but local merchants as well. In Serbia a whole new class of rural Orthodox bourgeoisie came into being in the period after 1739. They amassed wealth by exporting pigs and timber into Habsburg territories and would later be at the forefront of Serbian uprisings and quests for autonomy.

OTTOMAN ADMINISTRATION

From the second part of the fourteenth century until 1541 the Ottoman Balkans were unified in one great province, Rumelia (*Rum eli*—the 'land of Romans', as the Ottomans referred to the Byzantine Greeks), administered by the highest military commander in the European part of the Ottoman Empire, the *beglerbeyi* of Rumelia. Its subprovinces *(sancak)* were administered by *sancakbeyis*. In 1541, when large parts of Hungary came under direct Ottoman rule, some western Balkan *sancaks* were put under the supervision of the *beglerbeyi* of Buda. Finally, Bosnia, too, was elevated to a province, with subprovinces of its own. Generally, subprovinces were divided into judgeships *(kaza, kadilik)*. The Ottoman judges *(kadi)* had, besides their responsibility for the court system, wide administrative duties (tax collecting, military reviews, state inspections, etc.). The smallest administrative units were called regions *(nahiye)*.

By the beginning of the eighteenth century, the *kadi*s were frequently rotated, and many of them saw a good deal of the empire during their careers. In the eighteenth century, many of the more lucrative judgeships were assigned to members of a narrow clique of scholarly aristocratic families in the capital. They preferred to stay in Istanbul and to sublease their appointments to substitutes who would either use them for themselves or resell them in the provinces. The judicial system, after the sixteenth century, started to acquire more organized features. Court registers were coming into use all around the empire by the mid-sixteenth century. Additionally, a specially assigned building for the court and judge *(mahkema)* was a frequent feature of Balkan towns as early as the seventeenth century. However, until the Tanzimat (the reforms of the state and society proclaimed in 1839), judges or deputy judges often adjudicated in the private space of their own homes. Not only Muslims but also non-Muslims, both men and women, made use of the Muslim *sharia* courts. This was especially true in cases of appeal or in the expectation of obtaining a more favorable decision than at their own communal court.

All these institutions were imperial, but the provinces also had institutions of a more local character. Such was the case with the office of "mayor" *(şehir kethüda)*, a local and informal administrative institution. The mayor's main task was to protect the interests of cities and towns when Ottoman governors, their entourages, and the military were passing through. A mayor would make sure that such travelers would not stay too long and become a local burden. Three days of hospitality, accompanied by food, lodging, and gifts, was considered enough. Other important administrative positions were those of guild wardens (*esnaf kethüda*). They took care of the interests of the crafts guilds vis-à-vis the state and individuals outside the guild. The religious composition of guilds varied from place to place and from guild to guild. Guild wardens, however, were predominantly Muslims.

RELIGIOUS ORGANIZATION AND IDENTITY

Islam and its body of religious scholars, teachers, and judges (*ulama*) grew together with the Ottoman Empire, and its religious canon was defined roughly by the 1550s. The religious endowments (*evkaf*; s. *vakif*) supported the provincial network of religious secondary and elementary schools (*medrese, mekteb*), mosques, dervish lodges (*tekke*), libraries, and other institutions. The patrons of these endowments were members of the imperial family, governors, local notables, and wealthy merchants. In poor areas, where there were no available patrons, the imperial administration would establish its own mosques and elementary religious schools. The sale, resale, lease, and sublease of religious posts occurred frequently in the period 1700–1839. Many lower-ranking religious officials had commercial and familial ties to the artisanal classes and the bazaar world, as was generally the case throughout the Ottoman Empire and in Iran at the time.

The main religious authorities among Balkan Muslim communities were jurisconsults (*mufti*), who issued legal opinions pertaining to the Islamic holy law. Any larger town had at least one jurisconsult, usually the most esteemed Islamic scholar in the region. Unlike jurisconsults, religious judges (*molla, kadi, naib*) were predominantly individuals who would not stay long in the places where they were appointed due to rotation rules. Because of their temporary position, they were bound to cooperate closely with local religious authorities, jurisconsults, and professors (*müderris*) of the religious schools. The lowest strata of the Islamic religious hierarchy were the prayer leaders and preachers in mosques (*imam, hatib, vaiz*).

The Ottomans allowed non-Muslim communities to regulate their own internal religious affairs. What the Ottoman state was interested in were the taxes these communities were obliged to pay to the state treasury. The paying of these taxes was regulated in the form of long-term and short-term tax farms, and non-Muslim religious leaders were considered, from the point of view of the Ottoman administration, as tax farmers of the state revenues. A newly appointed Christian or Jewish religious leader was expected to pay an investiture fee for the diploma he was issued by the imperial council and to render yearly taxes to the state treasury in the name of the community. On the other hand, as a member of the ruling Ottoman military class, he could ride a horse, carry weapons publicly, and have personal armored guards, and he was also entitled to collect taxes from his flock for his own needs and those of his office.

The Ottoman authorities assisted these leaders in tax collecting. During the sixteenth and seventeenth centuries, the patriarch of Istanbul, for instance, asked the Imperial Council to assign him a number of Ottoman soldiers to help him while he was touring his dioceses in order to collect taxes. When the Serbian Patriarch Arsenije III Carnojevic was on his pilgrimage to Jerusalem in 1680s, he was accompanied by a guard of four hundred mounted warriors.

The Greek Orthodox patriarchate continued its work immediately after the conquest of Constantinople. In 1557 the Serbian patriarchate, abolished in 1459 after the conquest of the despotate of Serbia, was reestablished. The first Serbian patriarch after its reestablishment was Makarije Sokolovic, a close cousin or, according to some reports, brother of the future grand vizier Sokollu Mehmed Pasha (d. 1579), and the reestablishment of this institution would not have been possible were it not for Mehmed Pasha's intercession.

The Balkan Catholic Church was in a far worse position, given that the Ottomans were much more suspicious toward the real or supposed spy role that Catholic clerics might have been playing. In addition, the popes never abandoned the rhetoric and politics of the Crusades and were staunch supporters of the Ottomans' rivals, the Habsburgs. The Franciscans in the sixteenth and seventeenth centuries monopolized Catholicism in the Ottoman Balkans. By 1463, the Bosnian Franciscans had received privileges from Mehmed II, the Conqueror

(1451–1481), and by the end of the seventeenth century they were in charge of all aspects of the religious lives of Catholics in Bosnia, Croatia, Slavonia, Dalmatia, Hungary, and Bulgaria. Some small oases of the so-called Petrine hierarchy survived in parts of Croatia, Dalmatia, Hungary, and Albania. The Franciscans were extremely jealous of their achieved position, and they strenuously fought attempts by the Jesuits to gain strongholds in Belgrade in the mid-seventeenth century. The situation changed rapidly after 1699, as the Bosnian Franciscans lost control over the territories that the Ottomans were forced to cede to the Habsburgs and Venetians.

As far as Jewish institutions in the Balkans were concerned, in addition to Greece and Salonika (the greatest Jewish center in the empire), small, predominantly Sephardic communities existed in Bosnia (Sarajevo, Travnik), Serbia (Belgrade), Bulgaria (Ruscuk, Sofia, Plovdiv), Macedonia (Skoplje, Bitolj), Dalmatia (Split), Dubrovnik, and Albania (Valona, Skadar). After the Habsburg reconquest of Hungary in the period 1683–1699, many Hungarian Jews resettled in the Ottoman Balkans. The leaders of these communities were rabbis who were not only religious scholars, but also businessmen. Many Jews were physicians, apothecaries, or official translators.

Tensions between lay and religious leaders of non-Muslim communities were especially noticeable among Greeks and Serbs. The conflicts between local church boards, led by lay notables, and patriarchs, archbishops, and bishops took place daily. These conflicts were mostly over the control of the revenues of the church and church taxes, and how they were assessed.

THE MERCHANTS OF THE BALKANS

The Ottoman conquest of the Balkans facilitated a rapid rise in commerce, as it unified a vast territory and submitted it to a fairly unified administrative system. The Ottoman merchant came to be at home on both the Adriatic and the Red Seas. At first, Dubrovnik merchants controlled the empire's Balkan merchant networks, since they possessed the greatest investment capital and shipping capacity. They also controlled a huge network of merchant colonies throughout the Balkans, with Sarajevo, Belgrade, Nish, Skoplje, Sofia, Plovdiv, and Buda as

major centers. By the first half of the sixteenth century, however, archival records show local Balkan merchants beginning to appear at markets on both coasts of the Adriatic and elsewhere. The first among them appear to have been Muslim merchants. Ottoman, Dubrovnik, and Venetian archival records dispel an old myth about the alleged intrinsic Muslim lack of interest in commerce. At first, these merchants were unable to compete with the Dubrovnik merchants, but by the end of the sixteenth century, this was no longer true.

In the seventeenth century, the Dubrovnik and Muslim merchants were joined by Serbian Orthodox, Albanian, and Bosnian Catholic rivals. Bosnian Catholic merchants disappeared around the end of the century as the wars of 1683–1699 dealt a blow to their networks. Having been accused of plotting with the Habsburgs and the pope against the Ottomans, they either resettled to Habsburg territories or lost their wealth and became peasants and miners. On the other hand, the Serbian, Albanian (Muslim and Christian), and Bosnian Muslim commercial networks continued to flourish. While the Bosnian and Albanian Muslim merchants traded predominantly with Venice, Dubrovnik, and other parts of the Ottoman Empire, the Serbian, Bulgarian, Greek, Cincar, and Albanian Orthodox merchants began to migrate into Habsburg territories, a development the Austro-Ottoman Belgrade Treaty of 1739 promoted. These diasporas spread from Vienna to Trieste and Rijeka on one side and to Buda, Sopron, and Pressburg on the other. After the Russian annexation of Crimea in 1783 and the rise of Odessa as a port, these merchants moved into the extremely lucrative shipment of Ukrainian grain. The world of the merchant diasporas was crushed only with the rise of the railroads.

Jews were also present in Balkan commerce, with Salonika, Skoplje, Belgrade, Sarajevo, Dubrovnik, and Valona as their main centers. Jewish merchants were at the peak of their commercial success in the sixteenth and nineteenth centuries. In addition they were engaged in financial operations and moneylending, and in Bosnia and Albania they acquired large farms even before the Tanzimat reforms of 1839, which are usually considered the starting point of free non-Muslim investments in large landed properties.

All these merchant networks were grounded either in family ties or in ties resulting from local solidarity. Specific branches of commerce were monopolized by certain families and local communities. Also significant for Balkan commerce of the period were yearly fairs held all over the Balkans, such as those in Dolkjani in Macedonia and in Uzuncaova in Bulgaria, which were visited by various merchants.

WESTERN EUROPEAN AND RUSSIAN INTEREST IN THE BALKANS

Western Europe never lost its interest in the Balkans. European interest in the Balkans during "Tourkokratia," or Turkish rule, continued after focus shifted from Byzantium after the time of Charlemagne. Russian interest in the Balkans also predates the Ottoman conquest. The first interest in the Ottoman Balkans emerged in the framework of Crusading ideology. Two Crusades took place in the Ottoman Balkans (Nicopolis in 1396 and Varna in 1444), and smaller ones continued into the late sixteenth century. The kingdom of Hungary constructed its ideology around a view of itself as the bulwark of Christendom against the Ottoman peril. This ideology was clearly formulated by Sigismund von Luxemburg (ruled 1386–1437) and espoused by subsequent Hungarian kings, among whom Matthias Corvinus (ruled 1458–1490) was probably the most important. This was also the main ideology behind Habsburg, Venetian, Polish, and Russian engagement in war with the Ottomans in the period 1683–1699, and it would survive into the early eighteenth century.

The Habsburgs stressed that the Muslim population of the reconquered areas should either convert to Christianity or leave for Ottoman territories. Only Joseph II (ruled 1780–1790) proclaimed that in exchange for their loyalty, he would not force the Muslim populations of future conquered areas to convert. Out of the Crusading ideology arose the concept of the so-called Eastern Question, which can be viewed as its secularized variant, whose central goal was the destruction and division of the Ottoman Empire and the reconquest of Constantinople. In the sixteenth and seventeenth centuries the houses of Savoy and Mantua, with papal approval, hired various adventurers who promised they would incite Balkan Christians to rebel. Most of these plans were quite unrealistic, but some of

them, especially in the period 1593–1606, gained some influence over the local Christian populations of Herzegovina, Montenegro, and Albania.

Russian interest in the Balkans appeared slowly and gradually during the sixteenth and seventeenth centuries. In the beginning, the rulers of Muscovy acted as patrons of Orthodox religious institutions in the Balkans; some Balkan Orthodox monasteries got their first gifts from mid-sixteenth century Muscovite rulers. Soon, Balkan Orthodox monks and priests started to go to Muscovy, and later Russia, on long tours in search of alms. By the middle of the seventeenth century, the Russian tsar contacted a member of the Christian *sipahi* (a mounted warrior enjoying the prebend as pay for his service) community in Herzegovina, asking him for help in hiring experienced Balkan miners, as he wanted to improve the state of Russian mining. Peter I the Great (1672–1725) contacted Slavonic navigators living in the Venetian-held Boka Kotorska (Bocca di Catharo) in order to procure skillful commanders and crews for his modern Russian navy. The division of the Ottoman Empire was put on the agenda by Catherine II the Great of Russia and Joseph II of the Holy Roman Empire during the 1770s and 1780s. The Balkans played a significant role in these partition plans, and spheres of interest were clearly defined. The western part of the Balkans was to be under Austrian rule, while the eastern was to go to the Russians. These division plans had a great impact on solutions proposed for the "Eastern Question" during the nineteenth century.

In the final Austro-Ottoman War (1787–1791) the Austrians mustered a significant number of the local Orthodox population in Serbia and Bosnia in special volunteer regiments *(Freikorps)*. Although many of them were pardoned by the Ottomans in the 1790s, a majority of the leaders of the First Serbian Uprising (1804–1815) were actually men who acquired their military expertise while serving in the anti-Ottoman, Austrian-sponsored *Freikorps.*

The interests of Europe in the Balkans in the early modern era cannot be said to have been only military and political. The Ottoman-French alliance existed from 1530 to the French Revolution of 1789. That meant that many French diplomats, adventurers, antiquarians, and would-be missionaries crossed the Balkans heading toward Istanbul. Some of their travelogues are very interesting sources on the Balkans as they appeared to outsiders. The first contact of the Habsburgs with the Ottomans dates to around 1500, even before the imperial family became the rulers of Hungary and Croatia. A plethora of Austrian spy reports, travelogues, and historical works on the Balkans survive as well. Venice was for a long time a place where the most reliable knowledge about the Ottoman Empire and the Ottoman Balkans could be found. The only premodern translation of a pagan Roman classic into any Islamic language, Cicero's *De Senectute,* was commissioned by the Venetian envoy to the High Porte, Marino Cavalli, as a presentation to Suleiman the Magnificent in the late 1550s, and it was translated by a Hungarian convert who worked as an official translator at the imperial council. Around 1600 an Ottoman Balkan chronicler reported that European diplomats were crossing the Balkans and stopping in Srijemska Mitrovica—formerly Sirmium, once one of the most important cities of the Late Roman Empire—to look for the Roman artifacts. This unique report showed how the curiosity of European humanists had been noticed and emulated by a local Muslim scholar.

See also **Habsburg Dynasty: Austria; Islam in the Ottoman Empire; Janissary; Porte; Russo-Ottoman Wars; Suleiman I.**

BIBLIOGRAPHY

Barkan, Ömer Lûtfi. *Osmanli Devleti'nin Sosyal ve Ekonomik Tarihi: Osmanli Devlet Arşivleri uzerinde Tetkikler-Makaleler.* Vols. 1–2. Istanbul, 2000.

Beldiceanu, Nicoară. *Le monde ottoman des Balkans, 1402–1566: Institutions, société, économie.* London, 1976.

Cvijic, Jovan. *La peninsule Balkanique: Geographie humaine.* Paris, 1918.

Inalcik, Halil. *The Middle East and the Balkans under the Ottoman Empire: Essays on Economy and Society.* Bloomington, Ind., 1993.

———. *The Ottoman Empire: Conquest, Organization and Economy.* London, 1978.

———. *The Ottoman Empire: The Classical Age, 1300–1600.* Translated by Norman Itzkowitz and Colin Imber. London, 1973.

———. *Studies in Ottoman Social and Economic History.* London, 1985.

Inalcik, Halil, with Donald Quataert. *An Economic and Social History of the Ottoman Empire, 1300–1914.* Cambridge, U.K., and New York, 1994.

Kissling, Hans Joachim. *Dissertationes Orientales et Balcanicae Collectae.* Vols. 1–3. München, 1986.

Kreutel, Richard, and Otto Spies. *Leben und Abenteuer des Dolmetschers Osman Aga: Eine türkische Autobiographie aus der Zeit der grossen Kriege gegen Österreich.* Bonn, 1954.

McGowan, Bruce. *Economic Life in Ottoman Europe: Taxation, Trade, and the Struggle for Land, 1600–1800.* Cambridge, U.K., and New York, 1981.

Mutafchieva, Vera P. *Agrarian Relations in the Ottoman Empire in the 15th and the 16th Centuries.* Boulder, 1988.

Šabanovic, Hazim. *Bosanski pašaluk.* Sarajevo, 1959.

Stavrianos, Leften Stavros. *The Balkans since 1453.* With a new introduction by Traian Stoianovich. New York, 2000. First published 1958.

Sućeska, Avdo. *Ajani.* Sarajevo, 1965.

Sugar, Peter F. *Southeastern Europe under Ottoman Rule, 1354–1804.* Seattle, 1977.

Zirojević, Olga. *Tursko vojno uredjenje u Srbiji, 1459–1683.* Belgrade, 1984.

NENAD FILIPOVIC

BALLOONS. "Get in a supply of taffeta and of cordage, quickly, and you will see one of the most astonishing sights in the world" (Gillispie, 1983, p, 17). These were the words of Joseph Montgolfier (1740–1810) to his brother Étienne (1745–1799) in 1782, and he was right: the hot-air balloon would soon astonish the world. It rose in public for the first time on 4 June 1783 in Annonay, a small town in southeastern France, and again before the royal family at Versailles on 19 September. Considerably larger than the original at 17.4 meters in height and 12.5 meters in diameter, this second model, equipped with a basket containing a sheep, a rooster, and a duck, reached an altitude of 470 meters and traveled about 3,300 meters. Astronomers armed with quadrants measured the flight, and veterinarians determined that the animals had not suffered ill effects during their ten-minute journey. On 21 November, with a huge crowd present, two "aeronauts" ushered in the era of manned flight. Contemporaries believed that men had acquired a new, visible mastery of the material world and thereby shortened the distance between themselves and the gods.

Joseph Montgolfier hailed from a substantial family of paper manufacturers, and hence it is not surprising that the Annonay balloon was a large bag of sackcloth lined with thin layers of paper. Whereas his brother Étienne was carefully educated in mechanics and mathematics, a sort of industrial architect "steeped in the science" of his craft, Joseph was a largely self-tutored visionary. Still, theirs was a technologically deft and ambitious family, who considered the "vast majority" of their fellow papermakers as "simple workmen" hamstrung by "blind routine." The Montgolfiers, however, experimented restlessly with their art and believed that they would find new technologies to improve their industry; the balloon did not arise from technological innocence. Moreover, the novel science of the day was also within the Montgolfiers' grasp: Joseph was aware that Henry Cavendish had isolated inflammable air (hydrogen) in 1766 and that Joseph Priestley had detected dephlogisticated air (oxygen) eight years later.

Invisible forces, including Isaac Newton's gravity and Benjamin Franklin's electricity, were in the air during the twilight of the Old Regime. But the Montgolfiers soon turned away from relatively expensive hydrogen to boost their device. Instead, their attention focused on heating the air until it was sufficiently rarefied to propel the balloon. (Joseph evidently believed that this process was accompanied by a chemical transformation, rather than simply by the expansive power of heat, which yielded a distinctively light, hence propulsive, gas.) Meanwhile, J.-A.-C. Charles, a popular lecturer in experimental physics, released a hydrogen balloon on the Champ de Mars in Paris on 27 August 1783. Mistakenly assuming that the Montgolfiers had also relied on hydrogen, Charles thought that he was merely replicating the brothers' feat. But rather than a rarefied royal entourage, Charles's device was subsidized by a subscription and its ascent witnessed by a throng of perhaps fifty thousand spectators. The balloon craze had taken off.

"One hundred thousand souls, at least," supposedly wept, cheered, and fainted as a balloon levitated over Nantes in the summer of 1784. Already in December 1783, the chancellor of the Academy of Dijon warned his colleagues that "the public would be astonished that in a town which flourishes in the sciences and the arts, no one has attempted to repeat the wonderful experiments of the Montgolfiers" (Gillespie, p. 259). Emboldened by a provincial zeal to emulate the capital's achievements, the Dijon society sought funds for the construction of a balloon; on 25 April 1784, the chancellor and a companion floated triumphantly to an altitude of 3,200 meters over the city. A wave of barnstorming ensued, as men like J.-F. Blanchard, who raised the funds for his Parisian ascent through newspaper solicitations, capitalized on the craze. Blanchard, in fact, replicated his feat in Rouen, in England, and in North America. Even ballooning's first two casualties, the victims of an attempt to cross the English Channel in 1785, took only some of the air out of the mania. And countless prints turned these men into martyrs, among technology's first, while those aeronauts who returned home were paraded through town like conquering heroes.

They were conquerors. In the frenzy for lightning rods and balloon flight, awe was linked to mastery and uncoupled from fear. Whereas portents and prodigies once signaled the Lord's ungovernable wrath, lightning rods, balloons, and the recent effective harnessing of water vapor as a source of motive power were expressions of growing human dominion over the earth and its forces, and of the power of untrammeled reason. This maturing capacity was celebrated in verse inspired by balloon flight. Meanwhile, the great mathematician Leonhard Euler's last calculation explored the "laws of vertical motion of a globe rising in calm air in consequence of the upward force owing to its lightness" (Gillespie, 1983, p. 32): the earliest recorded mathematical rendering of the flight of aircraft.

Étienne Montgolfier's dream of a commercial fleet of balloons did not materialize during his lifetime. English entrepreneurs largely ignored the device, leaving the field to adventurers and popular entertainment; nor was English science deeply concerned with ballooning. But the Paris Academy of Sciences, the central scientific institution in France, avidly considered principles and practices of aeronautical engineering, pursued effective and inexpensive gas fuels, and considered military applications. For these reasons, and even more the technological awe and optimism it helped to ignite, the Montgolfiers' hot-air balloon deserves to be considered among the macroinventions of the first

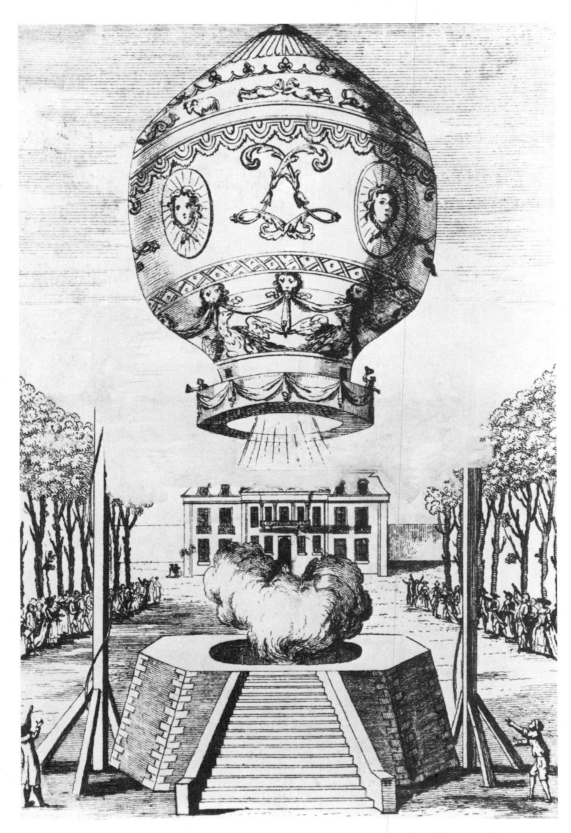

Balloons. *First Ascent of Human Beings in a Balloon,* undated copper engraving. ©BETTMANN/CORBIS

industrial revolution, alongside the steam engine, the Jacquard loom, and gas lighting.

See also **Chemistry; Enlightenment; Technology.**

BIBLIOGRAPHY

Darnton, Robert. *Mesmerism and the End of the Enlightenment in France.* New York, 1968. Excellent discussion of popular science.

Daston, Lorraine, and Katharine Park. *Wonders and the Order of Nature, 1150–1750.* New York, 1998. Encyclopedic account of marvels and their meaning in European history.

Gillespie, Richard. "Ballooning in France and Britain, 1783–1786: Aerostation and Adventurism." *Isis* 75 (1984): 249–268. Clear account of the balloon craze and different national responses to the invention.

Gillispie, Charles. *The Montgolfier Brothers and the Invention of Aviation, 1783–1784.* Princeton, 1983. Authoritative account of the invention and diffusion of the balloon.

———. *Science and Polity in France at the End of the Old Regime.* Princeton, 1980. Exhaustive account of French science and technology during the second half of the eighteenth century.

Mokyr, Joel. *The Lever of Riches: Technological Creativity and Economic Progress.* New York, 1990. Combines valuable narrative with daring analysis.

Rosenband, Leonard. *Papermaking in Eighteenth-Century France: Management, Labor, and Revolution at the Montgolfier Mill, 1761–1805.* Baltimore, 2000. Concise yet evocative account of the Montgolfiers' practice of an earthbound industry.

LEONARD N. ROSENBAND

BALTIC AND NORTH SEAS. Many of the coasts of the North and Baltic Seas are inhospitable and make for hard traveling. It was not easy to travel along the mountainous shores of the Norwegian fjords or the Scottish firths, or to cross the marshes that in places lay close to the German, Dutch, and English coasts. Early modern roads were often unpaved, and in bad weather or in the wrong season might be impassable. In places, however, natural waterways made the hinterlands easily accessible. This was the case, for instance, in the Dutch delta, which contributed to the strong position of the Dutch in trade. To these natural waterways, manmade canals were added, like the system of *trekvaarten* that linked Dutch towns in the coastal provinces from the 1630s or the system of canals that opened up the center of Britain in the second half of the eighteenth century. By the end of the eighteenth century roads had much improved. Nevertheless, for the whole early modern period long-distance transport of people and goods over sea was generally much cheaper than over land. The waters of the North Sea and the Baltic thus acted not only as a natural border between states and a naval battleground for their conflicts, but also as a high road that connected the shores. Fishing, trade, labor migration, travel, pilgrimage, and warfare were among the reasons to cross the waters and to make contact with the inhabitants of other shores.

FISHING AS A CULTURE

Some fishing was a part-time occupation of farmers, but in other cases fishing was a specialized occupation. The coasts of the North and Baltic Seas were dotted with fishing villages. As fishing was governed by other economic laws than farming, fishing villages often lived with their back to the shore, facing the sea. Fishermen were drawn across the waters by fish such as herring, which live in huge shoals and had to be followed by fishing boats to ensure a good catch. Not only the fathers and sons who actually went fishing, but also their wives and sisters who repaired nets, sold fish, and ran the households without the men who were at sea, were attuned to a rhythm of life that differed from that farther ashore. If bad weather drove fishermen to strange shores, they would immediately understand the culture of a "strange" fishing village, and probably find themselves more at home there than in a farming village in their own region.

If fishermen would have recognized each other's way of living, this does not mean that all fished in the same way. Technical innovations that were perfected in the course of the sixteenth century made Dutch salt herring a very competitive product throughout the sixteenth and seventeenth centuries. The large Dutch fishing ships called *buizen* followed the herring out in the open sea, caught large quantities, and treated and salted the catch at sea, which enabled the boats to stay out for weeks on end. In the early sixteenth century, fishermen from all along the coast of the Wadden Sea in northern Germany and Denmark caught herring for the North Sea island of Helgoland. Fishermen met on the fishing grounds, and there was some migration of fishermen from the south to Scandinavia, which may have led to cultural exchanges.

By 1562, when the Danish Sound Toll Registers supply us with information, the Dutch were the main importers of salt herring into the Baltic. In the 1570s and 1580s Norwegian fishermen from the coast of Bohuslen (in present-day Sweden, facing the Skagerrak) took over, only to be ousted from the Baltic market in the 1590s again by the Dutch—the most probable reason being that the fish had moved so far away from the coast that only the larger Dutch vessels could reach them. Dutch export of salt fish into the Baltic grew until the peak of Dutch fishing was reached around 1630. After that, decline set in, more rapidly after the beginning of the eighteenth century. Norwegian, British, and Scottish herring fishing grew in the second half of the seventeenth century. After 1700, Scottish herring drove Dutch herring out of the Baltic. Norwegian herring fishing boomed in 1740–1760.

NORTH SEA AND BALTIC CULTURAL UNITY

In all but the most urbanized coastal regions, by far the largest portion of the population was involved in subsistence farming and usually had cultural or economic contacts only within a quite small and well-circumscribed space, for instance a market town and its hinterland. Exchange between these regions took place through the middlemen who had dealings farther away: local elites who traveled for reasons of education, politics, or warfare, but also traders, sailors, and fishermen, as far as they fished on the open sea.

These smaller regions differed only gradually one from the next. In culture, dialect, and ways of living, one would notice change only gradually when traveling from one place to another. Traders going along the coasts from one of these small regions to another could easily communicate. Most of the languages spoken around the North Sea and southern and eastern Baltic are closely related. According to tradition, Frisians (from the Netherlands province of Friesland and the Frisian Islands in the North Sea) could speak their mother language with the local population in eastern England and in Norway. It is clear that Danish, Dutch, English, and German were considered separate languages long before the early modern period. For official contacts interpreters were needed. But even if people differ-

Baltic Sea, 17th–18th c.

◼ Danish possessions, 1648
▨ Territory lost by Denmark to Sweden, 1658
▢ Swedish possessions, 1658
⬚ Territory lost by Sweden to Russia, 1721
○ Hanseatic port cities

entiated between these languages, it does not follow that their boundaries were clear. Before the establishment of national standard languages and their implantation through state education, a national press, radio, and television in the nineteenth and twentieth centuries, the regional diversity of language was great. The dialects along the North Sea and Baltic coasts changed gradually from the one to the other and did not respect territorial borders, which in some places and times were fluctuating anyway. The same holds true for other cultural practices.

What would develop into national languages in this continuum of dialects depended on political developments. Eventually the dialects of regions that were dominant culturally or otherwise became the national languages. This development could be supported by national policy, for instance through the translation of the Bible. The translation in Dutch offers a good example. For the *Statenvertaling*, the translation of the Bible in Dutch financed by the States General and published in 1637, a committee was formed that represented the leading dialects within the Netherlands. It discussed not only theological context, but also the linguistic choices to be made, and thus contributed to the formation of a standard Dutch language. If the young Dutch Republic had comprised other regions, other choices would have been made and another standard language would have developed. If the Dutch Republic had extended farther along the North Sea, use could have been made of the translation of the New Testament made by the West-Fleming Jan Utenhoven in Emden (in Lower Saxony, Germany) in 1553–1556. He designed a language that could have been understood from Flanders to the Baltic Sea. As Utenhoven's Bible translation shows, the variety of dialects on the eastern shores of the North Sea was bridgeable. There was more distance between English and the languages of the eastern shores of the North Sea than between those languages, but the dialects of English spoken along the North Sea coasts, especially north of King's Lynn, had more in common with other North Sea languages than did standard English, which is a southern dialect. English was harder to grasp for the inhabitants of the eastern North Sea shores than their dialects were mutually, but it was taught and learned. Along the southern shore of the Baltic the lingua franca was Low German, which was much closer to Dutch than is High German.

ECONOMIC IMPORTANCE OF THE NORTH SEA AND BALTIC

During the early modern period the most important centers of world trade bordered on the North Sea: Antwerp during much of the sixteenth century, Amsterdam in the seventeenth and eighteenth, and London in the eighteenth and nineteenth centuries. These cities traded with the whole known world, but in each of the three cases their position was partly based on nearby trade, within the North Sea area. This was especially true for Amsterdam.

The position of Amsterdam was based in the first place on the Baltic grain trade. This was partly paid for with bullion, but the Dutch actively sought return cargo. By 1630 Amsterdam had become the entrepôt for the whole of Europe, not only in grain, but also in wood, tar, and iron. The know-how developed in the bulk trade with the Baltic enabled the Dutch to transport goods cheaply elsewhere. The English resented the large part the Dutch took

in trade with the ports on their eastern shore. By the Acts of Navigation (1651, 1660, 1662, 1663, 1670, 1673) they tried to shield English trade from Dutch competition. By the beginning of the eighteenth century, Britain had become the dominant trading nation along the North Sea, and London had developed into the third consecutive center of world capitalism to be located on the North Sea. In the seventeenth and eighteenth centuries the English turned away increasingly from the Baltic and North Sea markets to new opportunities in the Mediterranean and their colonies, especially across the Atlantic. However, reexports to northwestern Europe remained very important to British trade to the end of the eighteenth century. Throughout the early modern period, much of British and Dutch trade was with faraway markets. Goods like spices, coffee, tea, or calicos introduced new cultural practices in the North Sea area. With the relevant goods, these practices were first introduced in Amsterdam or London, then transported to other ports within the region and ultimately from the coasts inland. By the eighteenth century Hamburg developed into an important competitor of Amsterdam on the European mainland, receiving much British trade.

Not only the great centers but also the smaller towns on the North Sea profited from this trade. The town of Mandal in southern Norway, for instance, around 1700 had regular trade contacts with all North Sea coasts and the southern Baltic. Norway provided wood for shipbuilding and other construction work in England and Holland. Wood was essential to buildings, even buildings in stone. The Norwegian bishop Jens Bircherod is said to have remarked after the London fire of 1666 that many Norwegians had warmed themselves at this fire. In the soggy Dutch soils wooden piles were needed to support buildings made of stone and brick; 13,659 wooden piles were needed, for example, to support the new Amsterdam city hall in 1655. The Dutch poet Joost van den Vondel (1587–1679) wrote that if one turned Amsterdam upside down, one would discover a subterranean Norwegian forest.

Denmark exported grain and cattle to Holland and the north German cities. Denmark and Norway exported fish to the Baltic coasts, as did the Dutch. The fish trade carried the salt trade in its wake, which in its turn was followed by the trade in Mediterranean products. The Scottish lowlands and the

Shetlands depended on imports from England, Holland, and Scandinavia for many primary products. In exchange, the Shetlands exported fish to Bremen and Hamburg. Lowland Scotland exported grain to Norway and Rotterdam, coal (as did northern England) and salt to the whole of northern Europe, and coarse textiles, fish, and cattle. Even contacts between two not very developed areas such as Scotland and Denmark were extensive, although they were relatively unimportant in the system as a whole. The Baltic exported not only grain, but also Swedish iron and naval stores. Tar, pitch, flax (for linen canvas), and hemp (for rope) were essential to wooden sailing ships. The Baltic produced all of these, and access to its trade was therefore of strategic importance to the great maritime powers.

URBANIZATION AND CULTURE

The importance of trade in this system had several consequences. Perhaps the most prominent structural characteristic of the North Sea/Baltic area is urbanization, especially on its southern shores. The Hansa with its civic culture had extended over the North Sea and Baltic coasts. In succession the southern Netherlands, the northern Netherlands and—after 1800—England became the most urbanized areas of Europe.

Reading and writing were strongly stimulated by trade and thus flourished in trading cities. Therefore the North Sea shores saw the early spread of reading and writing. Literacy in Flanders, Holland, and England was already relatively high by 1500, before the printing press or the Reformation could have much influence. The percentage of literate women was also much higher in the northwest than in other parts of Europe.

For the early modern period, these literate town dwellers had a relatively rationalistic and individualistic outlook on life. Holland, with its wet soil, was forced to import bread grain from elsewhere and to specialize in commercial agriculture and other commercial ventures, which were integrated in a world market already before 1500. At this early date, an important number of rural and urban households in Holland were already dependent on wage labor. The provision of bread grain from northern Germany and Poland led to less dependence on local harvests and thus to less insecurity about survival. Trade risks were averted by sharing ships and by developing commercial insurance. This supported a world view that learned to calculate risks. Borrowing against future income became another field that seemed to consist of calculable risks. In some cases financial techniques were borrowed at least to some extent by one North Sea state from the others. In this climate of relatively calculable risks, of increased security and rationality, the belief in witchcraft dwindled. Science prospered.

Protestant culture. Protestantism is an obvious characteristic of the North Sea/Baltic basin, as all coastal areas adopted it. The North Sea and Baltic coasts had already had a religious character of their own in the Middle Ages. In northwest France, on the British Isles, in the Netherlands (with the exception of the southern rim), in northern Germany, and in Scandinavia penance had become a private matter. Public expressions of guilt and penance had grown less important. Carnival had never taken root there. The merchants who carried the center of commercial capitalism from Antwerp to Amsterdam in 1585 were Protestants fleeing religious persecution. Arminian thinking traveled from the Dutch Republic to England. Puritans carried Reformed Pietist thinking in the opposite direction in the 1630s. These religious movements spread along trade routes over England, Scotland, and the Dutch Republic. From the North Sea basin they spread to other areas, both inside and outside Europe, but it is clear that their innovative center lay in English Puritan thought, and to a somewhat lesser extent in Dutch Reformed Pietism.

Migration and cultural exchange. Exchange between the North Sea and Baltic shores was also mediated by migration flows. In the period between 1600 and 1775 the core region of the Dutch Republic, the coastal province of Holland, attracted more than two million immigrants. The majority of these were from the continental coastal regions of the North Sea, especially before 1720. In the case of the Norwegian sailors and servant girls who migrated to the Dutch Republic, we know that they took back home cultural impulses from Holland, to the point of being considered "dutchified." The largest flow of Norwegian youths went to Holland in the years 1680–1725. In peacetime, the Dutch Republic needed some 33,000 men to man its fleets in 1610, and between 44,000 and 50,000 men between 1630 and 1770. From the end of the seventeenth century the English fleets required more men than the Dutch: 55,000 sailors in the last quarter of the seventeenth century, 70,000 by the middle of the eighteenth century, and 95,000 at the end of it. However, England could recruit these from a much larger population, as could other rival maritime powers. On a per capita basis, the Dutch required ten times as many sailors as France, and five times as many as England or Spain. Therefore, the Dutch had to rely on international recruitment to man their fleets. This created the largest international labor market northwest Europe had ever seen.

Diffusion of Dutch navigational knowledge. Crews recruited for the Dutch fleet outside the Dutch Republic in the seventeenth century came mainly from other North Sea and Baltic coasts. This led to a diffusion of nautical knowledge. Dutch teachers and manuals in Dutch were very influential along the German, Scandinavian, and Baltic coasts. Their influence lasted well into the eighteenth, and even into the nineteenth century. Navigation was taught in Dutch in Hamburg from 1749, and in Mecklenburg and Emden from the 1780s. Many a mid-eighteenth century Scandinavian or German sea captain kept his log in Dutch. They certainly brought other Dutch customs home, too. However, by the second half of the eighteenth century Dutch trade had lost its lead, the Dutch fleet was shrinking, and the Dutch labor market had lost its magnetic force.

STRATEGIC CONSIDERATIONS

We already noticed the strategic importance of Baltic naval stores in the age of sail. As long as the Dutch could, they tried to prevent Denmark and Sweden from becoming so powerful that they could close the Sound and hinder Dutch trade with the Baltic. In 1644 and 1645 the Dutch navy escorted Dutch merchantmen through the Sound, preventing the Danish King Christian IV (ruled 1588–1648) from collecting the Sound tolls, and in 1658 it prevented Charles X Gustav of Sweden (ruled 1654–1660) from becoming dominant on both shores of the Sound.

In the seventeenth century the states around the North Sea and the Baltic led the so-called military revolution, with larger professional armies and large permanent, specialized, and therefore expensive fleets. The Dutch Republic, which could raise an army or fleet by borrowing against future tax revenue, is a prime example of a capital-intensive manner of state building. Even if England was slightly more coercive and Denmark and Sweden even more so in their ways of collecting the necessary revenues, none of these states developed a full-blown case of military-bureaucratic absolutism like that of Prussia or France in the eighteenth century. In all four of these countries certain civil rights survived the military revolution. The Dutch bourgeois town regents class and the British Parliament maintained control over taxes and state finances, keeping interest rates low and enabling their respective states to borrow in times of war.

Money was needed for the ever larger armies and fleets that warfare required. England and the Dutch Republic fought three major wars on the North Sea in the seventeenth century and another in the eighteenth. The English claim to sovereignty over these seas lay at the bottom of the conflict. The Acts of Navigation of 1651 helped cause the first of these wars (1652–1654). In it the British employed larger and more heavily armed ships than ever before. These ships, fighting in line, managed to dominate the Dutch fleet, which still consisted partly of armed merchantmen. Already during the war the Dutch States General decided to build bigger and more heavily armed men-of-war. The second Anglo-Dutch War (1665–1667) showed that the Dutch had learned their lesson. Employing the same tactics that had brought the British success in the previous war, the Dutch managed to hold their own in the Four Day Battle in 1666, and successfully attacked the British fleet on the Medway River in 1667. The third war (1672–1674) brought no clear gain to either of the two maritime nations. With hindsight it is easy to see that Britain would have become the dominant trade and naval power even without these wars. Its size and geographical position would have prevailed anyway. But the Anglo-Dutch Wars were important because they fundamentally changed naval warfare, making it much more expensive. One of the first victims of this development was the Dutch Republic, which after 1714 could no longer afford to take part in any major war.

See also **Anglo-Dutch Naval Wars; Baltic Nations; Commerce and Markets; Communication and Transportation; Denmark; Dutch Republic; Dutch War**

(1672–1678); England; Hansa; Mobility, Geographic; Navigation Acts; Poland, Partitions of; Poland to 1569; Poland-Lithuania, Commonwealth of, 1569–1795; Russia; Serfdom in East Central Europe; Shipping; Sweden.

BIBLIOGRAPHY

Kirby, David. *The Baltic World, 1772–1993: Europe's Northern Periphery in an Age of Change.* London and New York, 1995.

———. *Northern Europe in the Early Modern Period: The Baltic World, 1492–1772.* London and New York, 1990.

Kirby, David, and Merja-Liisa Hinkkanen. *The Baltic and the North Seas.* London and New York, 2000.

Macinnes, Allan I., Thomas Riis, and Frederik Pedersen, eds. *Ships, Guns, and Bibles in the North Sea and Baltic States, c. 1350–c. 1700.* East Linton, Scotland, 2000.

North, Michael. *From the North Sea to the Baltic: Essays in Commercial, Monetary, and Agrarian History, 1500–1800.* Aldershot, U.K., 1996.

O'Brien, Patrick, Derek Keene, Marjolein 't Hart, and Herman van der Wee, eds. *Urban Achievement in Early Modern Europe: Golden Ages in Antwerp, Amsterdam and London.* Cambridge, U.K., 2001.

Roding, Juliette, and Lex Heerma van Voss, eds. *The North Sea and Culture (1550–1800).* Hilversum, Netherlands, 1996.

Royen, Paul van, Jaap Bruijn, and Jan Lucassen, eds. *"Those Emblems of Hell"? European Sailors and the Maritime Labour Market, 1570–1870.* St. John's, Newfoundland, 1997.

LEX HEERMA VAN VOSS

BALTIC NATIONS. The Baltic nations (Estonia, Latvia, Lithuania) are now seen as a unit, although they were not so historically. While Latvian, Lithuanian, and Prussian (a language that became extinct around 1700) are counted in the Baltic language group, Estonian belongs to the Finno-Ugrian language family. Estonians and Latvians (with the exception of the Latgallians) became Lutheran after the disintegration of the Knights of the Sword in the sixteenth century; Lithuanians, on the other hand, remained Catholic. In early modern times the history of Lithuania is closely connected with the history of Poland (Union of Lublin, 1569) and will be discussed there.

From the thirteenth century, colonists, mainly from northern Germany, came as knights, merchants, and craftsmen to Livonia and founded the basis of a German-speaking upper class. They settled in or near fortified castles, from which the territories were ruled. During the heyday of the Hansa, a league of towns that connected the merchant towns in northern Germany with the Baltic in the fourteenth and fifteenth centuries, many new places were founded along the Baltic Sea, including Riga, Reval/Tallinn, Dorpat/Tartu, Pernau/Pärnu, Wenden/Cēsis, and Windau/Ventspils. These played important roles in trade with the Belarusan up-country. The merchants from Riga, which is located at the mouth of the Dvina River, ranked first.

The towns were the centers of political life; the guilds, for example, the Brotherhood of the Blackheads, regulated education, production, and social life for their members. Throughout the modern period, the Baltic countries remained mainly an agrarian region with a conservative political structure of a privileged foreign upper class and native peasants without rights (serfdom).

Old Livonia was not a homogeneous state in the beginning of the sixteenth century; it combined six territories: the region of the Livonian knights, the municipal area of Riga, and the territories of the bishops of Riga, Courland, Dorpat, and Ösel-Wiek. Beginning in 1420 the *Landtag* (diet) served as the representative assembly of the country, with great political significance. Military pressure from the Muscovites led to war in the beginning of the sixteenth century.

The Reformation, coming in the 1520s via Prussia to the big Livonian towns, weakened the position of the already outmoded ideals of the crusading Livonian Order and the Catholic bishops. The movement did not encompass the whole population at once, but because of its desire to reach the local population in the vernacular, it helped to develop the native languages. The end of the sixteenth century was characterized by lively German-language chronicles by Balthasar Russow and Salomon Henning. The Lutheran University of Königsberg, founded in 1544 by Duke Albrecht of Hohenzollern, was important for students from the Baltic region as well. The Livonian diet voted for religious freedom of the individual in 1554.

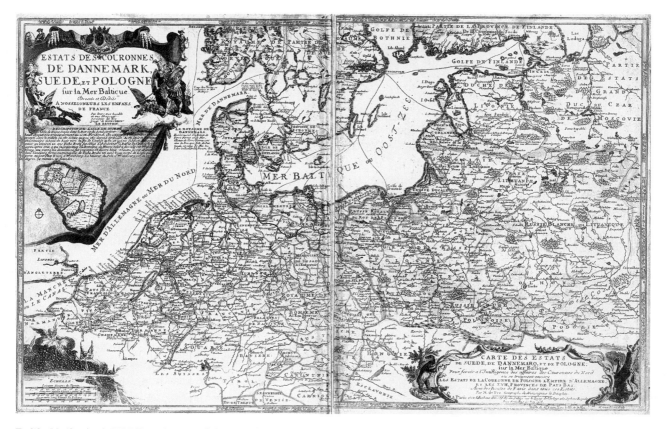

Baltic Nations. A 1705 French map of the area bordering the Baltic and North Seas. Ingria ("Ingrie"), at the top right on the eastern end of the Gulf of Finland, was Swedish territory until captured by Peter the Great in 1702. The map is somewhat unusual in that it includes roads throughout the area, as well as a number of sea routes through the North, Danish, and Baltic Seas connecting the major trade centers of the early 1700s. MAP COLLECTION, STERLING MEMORIAL LIBRARY, YALE UNIVERSITY

The last grand master, Gotthard Kettler (ruled 1561–1587), secularized the order in 1561 and surrendered Livonia to the Polish king Sigismund II Augustus (ruled 1548–1572), retaining the Duchy of Courland and Semigallia, which included the Latvian region south of the Dvina River, for himself as a Polish vassal. In the *Pacta Subiectionis* the Polish king guaranteed the old liberties and the Lutheran confession to the Baltic nobility. The Union of Lublin in 1569, which constructed a real union between Poland and Lithuania, confirmed the situation in the Baltic. In 1558 the First Northern War with Tsar Ivan IV (ruled 1533–1584) started. By the peace of Iam Zapol'skii in 1582, northern Estonia came to Sweden, and Livonia, which included today's southern Estonia and northern Latvia, to Poland. In Livonia the Jesuits started to work in the spirit of Counter-Reformation, but in the short period they stayed there (until the beginning of the seventeenth century) they could not achieve enduring success.

In 1592 the Polish king Sigismund III Vasa (ruled 1587–1632) inherited the Swedish throne, resulting in new struggles between the Catholic Vasa in Poland and the Lutheran Vasa in Sweden that involved Russia as well. The struggle for the *Dominium Maris Baltici* (Control of the Baltic Sea) was mainly fought in Livonia and Prussia. The Polish-Swedish War (1600–1629) ended with the truce of Altmark, by which Livonia fell to the victorious Swedish king Gustavus II Adolphus (ruled 1611–1632). He gained profitable port dues in the Baltic that enabled him to go on with the war in Germany. Poland-Lithuania kept its position on the Baltic only in Polish Livonia (until 1795), today's eastern part of Latvia.

The Thirty Years' War ended in Germany in 1648, but struggles continued as the Second Northern War (1655–1660) in Poland-Lithuania. Cossack uprisings in Ukraine (Bohdan Khmelnytsky's revolt in 1648) weakened the country and helped the Swedes to invade in the mid-1650s, reaching as far as Warsaw. Lithuanian nobles such as Janusz Radziwiłł (1612–1655) planned a union with the Swedes in 1655. Further struggles between Swedes and Russians were mainly fought in the Baltic. The peace treaty of Oliva in 1660 restored the status quo; the imprisoned duke of Courland obtained his duchy again.

The Duchy of Courland, which existed until the Third Polish Partition in 1795, was ruled by the duke and the nobles; policies were made at the assemblies of the *Landtag*. Though the noblemen did not deny the duke's position as a whole, domestic politics were characterized by lasting conflicts between the nobles and the duke. Since the *Formula Regiminis* in 1617, which created a noble oligarchy with a princely head, the noblemen had the right to appeal directly to the Polish king, which facilitated the king's intervention with the inner affairs of the duchy.

The energetic duke Jacob (ruled 1642–1682) was able to gain a strong economic and political position in the Baltic. A supporter of mercantilism, he built ships to bypass the dominant Dutch investors in the Baltic Sea and tried to win colonies (Gambia and Tobago). The heyday of the history of this small duchy ended in the seventeenth century. The last Kettler duke, Ferdinand (ruled 1711–1737), lived abroad in Danzig/Gdańsk. The following dynasty of the Biron was strongly influenced by Russian politics. Nevertheless, they showed some architectural initiative in the construction of castles in Mitau/Jelgava and Ruhental/Rundāle.

From 1629 to 1710, Livonia and Estonia were ruled by Swedish governors-general; the self-government of the nobles remained. The Baltic noblemen were represented over-proportionally in government services and in the Swedish army, where they made up one-third of the higher ranks; frequent ennoblement and distribution of estates followed. In the middle of the seventeenth century, half of the Baltic estates belonged to sixteen Swedish families, including the Oxenstierna, Baner, and De La Gardie. With the Reduction of Land of 1680, that is, the reclamation of royal states alienated illegally, King Charles XI (ruled 1672–1697) again nationalized these estates, weakening the Baltic (and Swedish) nobles. With the Swedish victory in the Baltic, the Lutheran Church also gained. Schools were built, and in 1632 the Lutheran University in Dorpat/Tartu opened. Parts of the Bible were translated into Latvian (1689) and Estonian (1686), and pastors tried to increase education.

At Johann Reinhold von Patkul's (1660–1707) instigation, an anti-Swedish alliance was formed, sparking the Great Northern War (1700–1721) in the Baltic countries. After the defeat of the Swedish king Charles XII (ruled 1697–1718) in the battle of Poltava in 1709, all Swedish possessions in the Baltic countries were occupied by Russia. This situation was officially recognized in the peace treaty of Nystad in 1721. Livonia and Estonia received reasonable conditions from Tsar Peter I (ruled 1689–1725): all old privileges were confirmed, especially the system of justice and the Lutheran confession, states were returned to the nobles, and self-government of the noblemen was restored. Throughout the eighteenth century, the German-Baltic nobility retained its autonomy. Empress Catherine II (ruled 1762–1796), who traveled the Baltic countries in 1764, tried to cut the noblemen's rights during the so-called *Statthalterschaftszeit* (period of governorship), but in 1796 the old constitution was reestablished.

In the second half of the eighteenth century, ideas of Enlightenment came to the Baltic. Johann Gottfried von Herder (1744–1803), who worked in Riga from 1764 to 1769, rediscovered the poetry of the common people and encouraged the small nations to explore their identity. Friedrich Konrad Gadebusch (1719–1788) with the *Livländische Bibliothek* (Livonian library) and August Wilhelm Hupel (1737–1819) with the *Nordische Miscellaneen* (Nordic miscellanea) offered a place of debate for new points of view. People started to think about the situation of the local inhabitants. Garlieb Merkel (1769–1850) insisted in all of his publications on equal rights and liberties for the common natives of the Baltic countries. Pietism and the Herrnhut movement gained influence in Livonia, lending an emotional movement to the peasant community.

In their function as a bridge, the Baltic countries in the eighteenth century played an important part as cultural mediator, promoting the Europeanization of Russia. Baltic nobles played leading roles in the Russian Empire in administration, diplomacy, and the military and contributed significantly to reforms and modernization in Russia. Hermann Karl Keyserlingk (1696–1765), for example, served as ambassador in Berlin, Vienna, and Warsaw, and Jakob Johann von Sievers (1731–1808), governor of Novgorod 1764–1776, worked on many reforms; both Baltic nobles were confidants of Catherine II.

See also **Belarus; Catherine II (Russia); Gustavus II Adolphus; Northern Wars; Peter I (Russia); Poland to 1569; Poland-Lithuania, Commonwealth of, 1569–1795; Reformations in Eastern Europe: Protestant, Catholic, and Orthodox; Thirty Years' War (1618–1648); Vasa Dynasty (Sweden).**

BIBLIOGRAPHY

Primary Sources

Einhorn, Paul. *Historia Lettica. Das ist Beschreibung der lettischen Nation.* (1649). Edited by Theodor Kallmeyer, *Scriptores Rerum Livonicarum*, vol. 2. Riga, 1848.

Henning, Salomon. *Lifflendische Churlendische Chronica: Was sich vom Jahr Christi 1554 bis auf 1590 . . . in Lieffland zugetragen.* (1590). Edited by Theodor Kallmeyer, *Scriptores Rerum Livonicarum*, vol. 2, pp. 195–289. Riga, 1848. Follower of the Kettler dynasty, defender of the political direction toward Poland.

Rüssouw, Balthasar. *Chronica der Prouintz Lyfflandt.* (1578). Edited by Karl Eduard Napiersky, *Scriptores Rerum Livonicarum*, vol. 2, pp. 1–194. Riga, 1848. On the Swedish side, social criticism.

Secondary Sources

Bues, Almut. *Das Herzogtum Kurland und der Norden der Polnisch-Litauischen Adelsrepublik im 16. und 17. Jahrhundert.* Giessen, 2001. The newest interpretation of the history of the Duchy of Courland and the Baltic in early modern times.

Frost, Robert I. *The Northern Wars: War, State, and Society in Northeastern Europe, 1558–1721.* Harlow, U.K., and New York, 2000. A fresh look at the important time of wars in northeastern Europe.

Kiaupa, Zigmantas, et al., eds. *The History of the Baltic Countries.* Tallinn, 1999. The Baltic history textbook project includes scholars from Estonia, Latvia, and Lithuania, with editions in Russian, German, and the Baltic languages.

Kiaupa, Zigmantas, Jūratė Kiaupienė, and Albinas Kuncevičius. *The History of Lithuania before 1795.* Vilnius, 2000. Translation of *Lietuvos istorija iki 1795 metu* (1995). The best English survey of Lithuanian history; unfortunately the translation is not good.

Kirby, D. G. *Northern Europe in the Early Modern Period: The Baltic World, 1492–1772.* London and New York, 1990. The best English-language survey of the Baltic world.

Mühlen, Heinz von zur, ed. *Baltisches Historisches Ortslexikon.* Vol. 1: Estland. Vol. 2: Lettland. Quellen und Studien zur Baltischen Geschichte 8/I, 8/II. Cologne, 1985, 1990. A useful historical dictionary about places in Estonia and Latvia.

ALMUT BUES

BANDITRY. Throughout the early modern period, especially in the seventeenth and eighteenth century, affluent travelers and merchants as well as peasants and farmers were afraid of banditry. The population shared with rulers and governments the general feeling that pilfering beggars and occasional stealers of food and wood among the local poor were something one knew how to deal with. Robber bands, however, as well as vagabonds and gypsies traveling in groups of varying sizes, were both more incalculable and more dangerous. Contemporaries regarded bandits as archenemies of the state and a threat to divine order, denying the state monopoly over the possession of arms and sinning against God's eighth commandment. The penal policy of the early modern state (public executions, large-scale patrols, printed lists of wanted persons) is a proof of this perennial threat.

THE IDEALIZATION OF CRIMINAL ROBBERS
The romanticization of banditry is a phenomenon that started with the popular ballads about prominent ringleaders such as Louis Dominique Cartouche in the eighteenth century. It gained momentum in the nineteenth century, and still persisted in twentieth-century historiography, when historians such as Carsten Küther interpreted preindustrial banditry as a counter-society. The absence of what Eric J. Hobsbawm has named "social banditry" in some territories led to the popular idealization of ordinary robbers, interpreting their deeds as a primitive form of social protest.

There can be no doubt that the discontent of the underprivileged, impoverished, and sometimes marginalized sectors of the population occasionally erupted into popular or mostly local food riots; but it also expressed itself on a smaller scale as "social banditry." It was a form of crime that rose out of political and social crisis, especially in areas over which the government could exercise only very little control, above all mountainous regions and often frontier zones. According to Hobsbawm, the characteristic feature of social bandits is that "they are peasant outlaws who the lord and state regard as criminals, but who remain within peasant society, and are considered by the people as heroes, as champions, avengers, fighters for justice, perhaps even leaders of liberation, and in any case as men to be admired, helped and supported" (p. 17). The late medieval legend of Robin Hood, who robbed the rich, switched clothes with beggars, and helped the poor, was popular not only in England but also in the rest of Europe for hundreds of years. All other bandit-heroes are much more recent, many of them living in the early modern period. There is, for example, Stenka Razin, the insurgent leader of the Russian poor in the seventeenth century. In Italy, the bandits also came from an agrarian background. Marco Sciarra, the famous Neapolitan brigand chief of the 1590s, declared himself a "scourge of God and envoy of God against usurers and the possessors of unproductive wealth" (quoted in Hobsbawm, p. 98). There is evidence that this popular bandit really practiced some kind of redistribution of wealth. For this reason he was highly esteemed by the poor of Naples.

Indeed, the records sometimes confirm the image, insofar as it represents reality and not wishful thinking on the one side and social prejudices on the other. There is ample proof, though hardly needed, that vagrants and social bandits were brothers in hardship and frequently mixed with each other. Impoverished day laborers and domestic servants often joined a gang where young beggars rubbed shoulders with old soldiers, deserters, murderers, expriests, and prostitutes. Social bandits did, in some cases, begin their career with some petty crime or offense that sooner or later brought them in contact with the itinerant underworld.

THE GEOGRAPHICAL DIMENSION

The major haunts of bandits in the early modern period were the Dalmatian highlands between Venice and Turkey, the vast frontier region of Hungary, Catalonia, the Pyrenees near the French border, and some of the low mountain regions in the Holy Roman Empire (e.g., Spessart, Westerwald).

Spanish bandits of this period operated in many parts of the country, especially in Catalonia, Valencia, Murcia, and Castile. One of these bands was known as *los beatos de Cabrilla* (the holy ones of Cabrilla), because its members behaved like "gentlemen," robbing their victims of only half of their goods. The peak of Catalan banditry was during the reign of Philip III (1598–1621). In mountainous areas of early modern Spain, banditry and brigandage remained a continual phenomenon throughout the period under discussion. In the early seventeenth century the most famous Spanish bandit was Perot Rocaguinarda. He started his criminal career in 1602 and even features in Cervantes's *Don Quixote* (1605, 1615). His Italian counterpart was Marco Sciarra, who controlled the countryside around Rome in the 1590s. He was betrayed by a friend and was killed. Other Italian bandits never reached his fame as they lacked popular support. Violence and indiscriminate robberies alienated them from the peasantry.

In early-seventeenth-century France the region of Périgord was infested with bandits. The brigands found their victims mostly among rich merchants traveling through the forest in that part of France. The most famous French bandit of all times was Louis Dominique Cartouche (1693–1721), a celebrated Parisian outlaw, whose name became synonymous with "highway robber" to the French. His adventurous life is the subject of many novels, poems, and even movies. In the 1962 film classic *Cartouche,* Jean-Paul Belmondo plays the role of this infamous eighteenth-century French bandit. In the beginning he is portrayed as an ordinary criminal robbing from everyone in sight. Later Cartouche becomes a kind of Gallic Robin Hood. A beauteous gypsy by the name of Venus (Claudia Cardinale) sacrifices her own life to save Cartouche from harm. He vows to continue his activities in order to avenge her death, but still manages to have a good time doing so. This box-office success, which was later reissued under the completely inappropriate title *Sword of Blood,* is part of the ongoing popularization and romanticization of the premodern underworld. The other French bandit-hero of the eighteenth century, Robert Mandrin (1724–

Banditry. *Armed Attack in a Wood,* detail of painting by Paul Brill (Flemish, 1554–1626). THE ART ARCHIVE/MUSÉE DU LOUVRE PARIS/ DAGLI ORTI

1755) was, as Hobsbawm has shown, a somewhat less suitable candidate for idealization.

In Anglo-American folklore Dick Turpin (1705–1739) is the English counterpart of Cartouche. Turpin's popular image entails many legends. He was born in 1706 in rural Essex, the son of John Turpin, a small farmer. Caught in the act of stealing two oxen, he fled into the depths of the Essex countryside to save himself. After a short time he left his hiding place and tried his hand at smuggling. He eventually settled on robbery. He and his gang invaded isolated farmhouses, terrorizing and torturing the female occupants into giving up their valuables. By 1735, London newspapers regularly reported the exploits of Turpin and his "Essex Gang." In 1739 he was finally brought to court and sentenced to death. Turpin is another fascinating

case of an early modern criminal whom history turned from a ruffian into a glamorous character.

The German equivalent to Dick Turpin is Johann Bückler (1783–1803), alias Schinderhannes (John the Knacker). He is still celebrated in German folklore, being idealized as a "social bandit." Modern research has tried to debunk this myth, but largely to no avail. Other famous bandits of the eighteenth century were Nickel List, who was active around 1700 in North Germany, and Lips Tullian, who committed most of his crimes in the Saxon region of Germany. Tullian and eleven of his associates were ultimately caught and executed.

In Ottoman times, the many wars in the Balkans left poverty and anarchy in their wake—suitable conditions for the work of brigands and bandits. In Serbian, Croatian, and Bosnian collective imaginary, the so-called *haiduks* were men of the people who stood against the hegemony of foreign rulers and the exploitation of the poor by the nobility. However, in some cases it proves difficult to distinguish between ordinary bandits and politically minded heroic outlaws, fighting against the oppressor. In the Balkans, the recorded history of *haiduks* goes back to the fifteenth century, but popular ballads about their lives and deeds did not flourish before the middle of the eighteenth century.

RECRUITMENT

Recent research has revealed that bandits cannot be generally identified with the itinerant population. It was not the traveling life that led some persons to banditry. It was rather the other way round. According to German sources, three-quarters of Christian bandits whose parentage is known to us originated in the sedentary and integrated sectors of society. A particular feature of the German underworld of the eighteenth century is the rather high proportion of Jews among organized robbers. But for them, too, it is clear that the structure of their gangs was decisively shaped by people who had a permanent address. However, in half of the German gangs studied by Uwe Dancker, wayfaring people (among them ex-soldiers, beggars) were overrepresented.

Women played only a minor role in banditry. The women who shared the roving life of bandits normally did not step outside the generally accepted gender role. Despite the popular image, polygyny among bandits was the exception and not the rule. Female gang leaders were out of the question in early modern times, although some of the women associated with organized robbery, such as the famous German archthief named Alte Lisel, could well have commanded a band themselves. In banditry, women usually functioned as supporters and links with the outside world.

See also **Crime and Punishment; Vagrants and Beggars.**

BIBLIOGRAPHY

Barkey, Karen. *Bandits and Bureaucrats: The Ottoman Route to State Centralization.* Ithaca, N.Y., 1994.

Blok, Anton. "The Peasant and the Brigand: Social Banditry Reconsidered." *Comparative Studies in Society and History* 14 (1972): 494–503.

Bracewell, Catherine Wendy. *The Uskoks of Senj: Piracy, Banditry, and Holy War in the Sixteenth-Century Adriatic.* Ithaca, N.Y., and London, 1992.

Comeche, Juan Antonio Martínez, ed. *Le bandit et son image au siécle d'or.* Madrid, 1991.

Danker, Uwe. "Bandits and the State: Robbers and the Authorities in the Holy Roman Empire in the Late Seventeenth Century." In *The German Underworld: Deviants and Outcasts in German History,* edited by Richard J. Evans, pp. 75–107. London and New York, 1988.

Gaunt, William. *Bandits in a Landscape: A Study of Romantic Painting from Caravaggio to Delacroix.* New York, 1937.

Glanz, Rudolf. *Geschichte des niederen jüdischen Volkes in Deutschland: Eine Studie über historisches Gaunertum, Bettelwesen und Vagantentum.* New York, 1968.

Hobsbawm, E. J. *Bandits.* Harmondsworth, U.K., 1972.

Küther, Carsten. *Räuber und Gauner in Deutschland.* Göttingen, 1976.

Lüsebrink, Hans-Jürgen, ed. *Histoires curieuses et véritables de Cartouche et de Mandrin.* Paris, 1984.

Murphy, Agnes Genevieve. *Banditry, Chivalry, and Terror in German Fiction, 1790–1830.* Chicago, 1935.

Ortalli, Gherardo, ed. *Bande armate, banditi, banditismo e repressione di giustizia negli stati europei di antico regime.* Rome, 1986.

Reglà, Joan. *El bandolerisme català.* 2 vols. Barcelona, 1962–1963.

Spraggs, Gillian. *Outlaws and Highwaymen: The Cult of the Robber in England from the Middle Ages to the Nineteenth Century.* London, 2001.

ROBERT JÜTTE

BANKING AND CREDIT. Early modern European banking had its origins in Italy. The profession grew out of the trade boom of the so-called commercial revolution of the High Middle Ages (1000–1350). The first bankers engaged in manual exchange of coins and did not extend credit. By the early modern period, however, banking spread throughout Europe and became complex and increasingly involved in credit transactions.

By the late thirteenth and fourteenth centuries there were three basic types of banks: international merchant banks, local deposit banks, and pawnbroking establishments. The categories were not exclusive: the same businessmen sometimes engaged in two or all three types simultaneously.

INTERNATIONAL MERCHANT BANKS AND BILLS OF EXCHANGE

The international merchant banks were the largest and most sophisticated. They began as a Tuscan phenomenon, established by merchants to facilitate their long-distance trade and the transfer of funds across national boundaries. Several extremely large firms—what modern scholars have called "super companies"—developed in Florence. The second largest of them, the Peruzzi bank, had fifteen branches located throughout Europe and in North Africa. The bank collapsed suddenly in 1345, bringing down with it much of the Florentine banking industry. This demise resulted from a combination of unwise fiscal practices and bad market conditions. The companies organized themselves so that all branches were jointly owned by large extended families. There was no limited liability, and thus investors lost more than what they put into their companies. Whole family fortunes were lost.

The collapse was followed by a new generation of banks. The most famous was the great Medici firm, which lasted from 1397 to 1494. To avoid the calamity of its predecessors, the Medici bank configured itself in the manner of a modern holding company. Members of the family held controlling interest in the branches, but each branch was a separate partnership and thus a distinct legal entity with its own books. When one branch faltered, as the Geneva branch did in 1465, the whole structure did not fall. Investors lost only the amount of money they put into the particular branch.

A major obstacle to making money in the banking business was the church's ban on usury. The basic position was taken from the Gospel of Luke and held that any interest beyond the principal constituted usury. It was therefore illegal for a bank to extend credit to its customers with the expectation of gain. Merchants found ways around the prohibition, the most ingenious of which was the bill of exchange. The bill evolved from letters of payment used at medieval trading fairs. It entailed a merchant lending money in one currency and receiving repayment in another, with the profit disguised in the exchange rate. Repayment could be effected only after the passage of a fixed amount of time, known as usance. This differed from town to town and depended on the amount of time it commonly took to travel between the places. For example, usance between London and Venice was ninety days. Since exchange rates could fluctuate, the precise return on the bill was uncertain. This element of risk helped make the bills more palatable to some Scholastic thinkers, who argued that the uncertainty constituted a justification for profit. The bill often involved two banks. The taker would send it to an affiliate or branch to be repaid, while the drawer would instruct his correspondent to redeem the bill. The bill itself was a small rectangular piece of paper, which usually began with the words "in the name of God."

Apart from its role as a credit instrument, the bill of exchange helped banks remit funds from one place to another and spared merchants the risk of transporting specie. This long remained an Italian phenomenon. Hanseatic merchants on the Baltic, for example, were at first suspicious of the bills and did not use them. But the bills progressively gained wide acceptance, particularly at trade fairs in the fifteenth and sixteenth centuries, and at Antwerp, where the practice of endorsement widely expanded the use of the bills.

The Medici dealt a great deal in bills of exchange, speculating in the international money market. They diversified their business into other areas, notably tax farming and sale of commodities. They used their connections to help market wool cloths and silks produced by their industrial firms. But the Medici bank—and Florentine banking in general—owed its primacy to its connection with the papacy. From early on, the Medici banks served pontiffs in the post of "depositary general," the highest level of the pope's financial hierarchy. Depositary generals performed a wide array of services, including collection of tithes and other sources of revenue. They made money through lucrative tax farms. Papal bankers could also use their access to the pope to gain excommunications against recalcitrant borrowers. The chief drawback to serving the papacy, however, was that it often entailed lending large amounts of money to the popes themselves, who were notoriously bad at repaying loans. One of the counterparts of the Medici, the Spinelli bank, ran into serious fiscal difficulty in 1456 when Pope Calixtus III failed to pay back the principal on a loan for a proposed crusade against the Turks. But loans to popes were, like loans to secular rulers, the price of operating in the market.

The Florentine banking system fell into crisis in the sixteenth century, but Italians remained active in international banking into the seventeenth century. In the meantime, banking on the Italian model grew in southern Germany. The most notable of the firms was the great Fugger company of Augsburg. It derived from the trading activities of a fourteenth-century weaver, Hans Fugger. His son Jacob and grandson Jacob II (d. 1525) parlayed their inheritance into a banking and mercantile empire. Like the Medici, the Fugger banks engaged in a range of activities, including speculation in the money market and trade in commodities. More so than the Medici, however, the Fugger extended enormous amounts of credit to secular rulers. They virtually bankrolled the wars of the German Habsburgs. They lent large sums to Maximilian I (ruled 1493–1519) to sustain his armies and floated immense loans to Charles V (ruled 1519–1556) to help him secure his election as Holy Roman emperor. In return, the Fugger received lucrative tax farms as well as interests in and administration of royal monopolies. They dominated the trade in silver, copper, and mercury. Their operating capital at one point exceeded 2 million gulden, a figure that dwarfed the capital of the Medici in its heyday.

The Fugger bank maintained branches in other cities and also did business with the pope. It oversaw the sale of indulgences in Germany and Scandinavia, including that done by Johann Tetzel in Wittenberg, which moved Martin Luther to issue his famous Ninety-Five Theses (1517) against the practice. The Fugger took from Italian banks the use of double-entry bookkeeping and added the practice of sending auditors out to individual branches to check inventories and accounts. They engaged more forcefully than their predecessors in monopolistic practices. In addition to his control of mines in Tyrol and Hungary, Jacob II Fugger owned the plants that processed the ore. He set up his own merchant fleets and even built housing, the so-called Fuggerei, for his workers. Structurally, the Fugger bank remained a family business. Whereas the Medici brought in outside investors, the Fugger brought in few. The bank survived until the seventeenth century, when its practice of extending large loans finally brought it down.

DEPOSIT BANKS AND FRACTIONAL RESERVE

In addition to international merchant banks, local deposit banks existed in Europe. The first deposit banks arose in Genoa and Venice, where they were known as *giro* firms (from the Italian verb "to rotate"). They serviced merchants, taking in deposits and making transfers from one account to another (hence "rotate"). The transfers were strictly controlled and done in person by verbal order. In Venice and elsewhere, bankers began to invest some of their savings, thus creating "bank money." The fourteenth-century Bruges moneychanger Guillaume Ruyelle kept only 30 percent in cash reserves; the Pisani bank of Venice in the sixteenth century invested savings in galley voyages and lent money for war.

The practice of fractional reserve proved very risky in the volatile business climate of the times. Deposit banks frequently failed. At the turn of the fifteenth century, three out of four such Venetian banks had gone out of business; their counterparts in the Low Countries had also disappeared by then. Similar difficulties were experienced by merchant banks, which were only slightly more stable. By the sixteenth century, only a handful of firms survived in Florence.

To stave off collapse, governments tried to restrict the practice of fractional reserve and transfer of funds. They became directly involved, initiating a species of publicly controlled deposit banks. The first, the so-called Taula de Canvi of Barcelona, appeared in 1401. It acted as fiscal agent for the city of Barcelona and for the kingdom of Catalonia. It accepted deposits from citizens, but could not lend to private individuals. It had to keep sufficient reserves to meet the demands of depositors. The Taula proved remarkably durable, and though it experienced numerous crises, it lasted until the nineteenth century, when it was absorbed by the Bank of Spain. A similar initiative undertaken in Genoa in 1408 was less successful. But public deposit banks gained momentum, particularly in the second half of the sixteenth century. The Spanish introduced several successful ones in southern Italy. The Genoese opened up the Cartulario d'oro in the sixteenth century to handle specie taken by Spain from the New World. This also did well. The most famous of the public banks, however, was the great Wisselbank founded in Amsterdam in 1609. It had a monopoly of transactions involving gold and silver, received deposits in specie, made transfers, but could not lend money to private individuals. It did, however, lend to the government, including to the Dutch East India Company. Similar banks emerged in Middelberg in 1616 and Hamburg in 1619. The Hamburg bank had greater latitude in lending to private individuals.

In England, banking took a different route. It grew from goldsmiths, makers and sellers of plate and jewelry. The profession flourished after King Henry VIII (ruled 1509–1547) dissolved the monasteries in the 1530s, thereby increasing the amount of available gold. By 1640 goldsmiths were taking royal valuables on deposit for safekeeping. The English Civil War (1642–1648) and subsequent troubles broadened business, as members of the gentry placed deposits with the smiths. By 1677 there were forty-four goldsmith banks in London, which functioned essentially as deposit banks. They were known by contemporaries as "keepers of running cashes," because they accepted money for safe custody and gave a receipt in return. They were the precursors of the Bank of England, a public institution that began in 1694.

BANKING, COMMERCIAL FAIRS, AND CREDIT INSTRUMENTS

Despite the restrictions on banks and the precarious nature of their business, the access to credit generally increased for European merchants during the sixteenth and seventeenth centuries. Demographic expansion and the opening of the Atlantic helped quicken the pace of trade. International banking was always closely linked to trade, particularly to commercial fairs. The period saw the growth and development of major fairs in the cities of Lyon, Medina del Campo, Besançon, Frankfurt, and Piacenza. In 1531, the Antwerp bourse emerged as a permanent market that, unlike the seasonal fairs, met all year round. It became a critical exchange point, particularly among English merchants trading in cloth, with German merchants trading in copper and silver and Portuguese merchants trading in spices and sugar. Wars destroyed Antwerp's preeminence in the late sixteenth century, and the mantle was passed to the city of Amsterdam.

Innovations occurred in the context of the fairs and the bourse. The bill of exchange, heretofore used more as a means of transferring capital than as a credit instrument, was transformed by northern merchants into a versatile fiscal device. Endorsement of bills became common, especially at Antwerp, and diffused to other parts of Europe. There are scattered examples of endorsed bills as early as the fourteenth century, but the practice did not become widespread until the seventeenth century. At first, the original drawee remained responsible for the debt, thus limiting the utility of the device. But eventually the beneficiary became responsible for the bill. In the sixteenth century, merchants began discounting bills, that is, selling them to a third party before maturity for a smaller sum. This also became common in the Low Countries after the middle of the century. The Dutch expanded the access to credit even further when authorities passed a decree in 1540 making lending at interest legal. In Catholic France, laws against usury remained in place.

In London, goldsmiths, by the mid-1600s, began issuing convertible cash notes or promissory notes payable to the bearer as receipts for deposits. These receipts were initially used to reclaim the whole deposit, but soon came to be presentable for part payment and, eventually, assignable to others—thus these were the antecedents of the modern banknote. Clients could withdraw money by writing a note requesting a sum to be paid to a third party. In 1661 the Bank of Stockholm issued "letters of credit," which were convertible into copper, an expedient undertaken when the government was at war and needed money. But the bank closed in 1664 when a panic broke out. In France in 1718, the Scottish immigrant John Law founded a bank that issued similar notes. The venture ended in disaster two years later and left in that country a lingering distrust of the banking business. A French central bank was not established until 1800.

PAWNBROKERS AND CONSUMER CREDIT

The system of banking and credit described thus far did not involve the ordinary consumer. When the common man sought credit, he did so not from merchant or deposit banks but from pawnbrokers. They offered short-term loans on pledges of personal property at high interest. The profession developed at the same time as the original moneychangers, or earlier, and was, like that profession, an

Italian phenomenon. The term "Lombard" came to signify a pawnbroker. Jews, who were denied the right to own land in much of Europe, were also involved in the profession, but their numbers were always small in comparison to the number of Christians. Pawnbrokers represented the lower end of the banking profession. They constituted in the minds of the authorities a necessary evil, not unlike gambling and prostitution. Biblical law prevented Jews from charging each other interest, but there was no restriction on Christians. Christians, on the other hand, needed special sanction from local authorities to do the business.

Pawnbrokers could charge high interest, and in Italy there were purportedly rates of 70 percent. Concerns about gouging led Italian authorities to establish public pawnbroking firms, so-called *monti di pieta* (literally 'mountains of piety'). They usually operated under the auspices of a religious house. This movement began in Italy in the fourteenth century and gained momentum throughout Europe in the later sixteenth century. Important public pawnbroking firms opened in the Netherlands and Sweden in the seventeenth century.

See also **Capitalism; Fugger Family; Medici Family; Money and Coinage.**

BIBLIOGRAPHY

Center for Medieval and Renaissance Studies. *The Dawn of Modern Banking*. New Haven, 1979. A still useful collection of essays.

De Roover, Raymond. "New Interpretations of the History of Banking." *The Journal of World History* 2 (1954): 38–76. The most learned brief review of banking prior to the eighteenth century.

———. *The Rise and Decline of the Medici Bank*. Cambridge, Mass., 1963.

Jacks, Philip, and William Caferro. *The Spinelli of Florence: Fortunes of a Renaissance Merchant Family*. University Park, Pa., 2001.

Kerridge, Eric. *Trade and Banking in Early Modern England*. Manchester, U.K., 1988.

Streider, Jacob. *Jakob Fugger the Rich: Merchant and Banker of Augsburg, 1459–1525*. Translated by Mildred L. Hartsough. New York, 1931.

Usher, Abbot P. *The Early History of Deposit Banking in Mediterranean Europe*. Cambridge, Mass., 1943.

Wee, Herman van der. *The Growth of the Antwerp Market and the European Economy: Fourteenth–Sixteenth Centuries*. The Hague, 1963.

WILLIAM CAFERRO

BANKRUPTCY. Bankruptcy is formally understood as the condition in which a debtor, upon voluntary petition or one invoked by his or her creditors, is judged legally insolvent and whose remaining property is administered by those creditors or distributed among them. The condition seems relatively straightforward: bankruptcy is legally recognized insolvency. In early modern Europe, however, it was a far more ambiguous state, freighted with the suspicion of fraud, distinguished from simple indebtedness, and, in some places, limited in its prosecution to certain trades or professions.

BANKRUPTCY AND THE INDIVIDUAL

Some of the earliest criminal codes make these associations and distinctions clear. The Discipline Ordinance, promulgated in Augsburg in 1537, ordered arrest and imprisonment of any individual unable to pay debts in excess of two hundred guldens. Should the defaulter flee—a generally recognized indication of fraudulent intent—his creditors were authorized to seize his property and person by whatever means necessary. The results were often acrimonious and violent free-for-alls, as in the infamous Höchstetter bankruptcy of 1527, in which the bankrupts languished and died in prison. While the creditors scrambled to recover what they could, a few, like the Höchstetters' partners the Fuggers, profited handsomely, but many others were ruined in the process.

Were a more mutually agreeable settlement reached, the bankrupt still faced a humiliating loss of status, a fatal derogation in an economy that functioned largely on the basis of personal relationships and reputation. The ordinance prescribed that he be stripped of his membership in the merchants' corporation, that his stall be removed from the privileged position of honest merchants at the base of Augsburg's watchtower, that he be prohibited from bearing arms in public, and that he be compelled to take his place with the women at the rear of public processions. Even his children could not escape his stigma: those born after the bankruptcy would be forbidden to wear the gold chain that was the emblem of established Augsburger merchants. Bankruptcy ordinances in 1564, 1574, and 1580 retained this emphasis on punishing economic crime.

The presumed connection between bankruptcy and fraud was echoed in other sources and other places. The Imperial Discipline Ordinance of 1548 spoke of "ruined merchants" who engaged in insecure—and, hence, fraudulent—credit transactions and suffered bankruptcy because of carelessness or waste. They were to be treated as common thieves. In England, the Tudor Act Touching Orders for Bankrupts of 1571 limited the term to indicate "traders" or "merchants" who "craftily obtaining into their hands great substance of other men's goods, do suddenly flee to parts unknown, or keep their houses, not minding to pay or restore to any their creditors, their debts and duties, but at their wills and pleasures, consume the substance obtained by credit of other men, for their own pleasure and delicate living, against all reason, equity and good conscience. . . ." Thus, bankruptcy existed in relationship to credit (which was considered a morally ambiguous entity), competence, and crime, all indicators of a crisis in the conduct and conception of business.

The passage of these laws constitutes a first response to the growing frequency of bankruptcies in early modern Europe. Beginning in the early sixteenth century, bankruptcy became a social evil that affected all levels of society and had extraordinary implications for both large and small economies. State profligacy, coupled with the unpredictable nature of economic growth, created conditions in which even the greatest commercial houses were not safe from default and failure. For the less well-connected or well-provided-for, insolvency and bankruptcy were common facts of life, the litigation of which left an unmistakable trail in most European archives. In 1560, the chronicler Paul Hektor Mair would record the names of twenty-six prominent Augsburg merchants who "became bankrupt and because of debts, sought sanctuary, fled the city, or suffered arrest until they settled and were released." Between 1529 and 1580, that number would rise to at least sixty-three and perhaps as many as seventy of the "great and famous commercial houses" of that city. Over the entire early modern period, Augsburg witnessed over 250 bankruptcies and countless insolvencies. Nor was the problem geographically limited. In England, according to one historian, "debt litigation dominated pleading in the courts of King's Bench and Common Pleas" from the mid-sixteenth to the mid-seventeenth century. From the mid-seventeenth to the mid-eighteenth century, no fewer than fifty-eight French merchants engaged in transatlantic trade suffered bankruptcy. Studies of the Parisian credit market for the same period reveal a noteworthy expansion of private borrowing coupled with periodic government defaults and interventions that would have resulted in waves of bankruptcies.

BANKRUPTCY AND GOVERNMENT

The relationship between public and private finance remains dimly understood, but the numbers and patterns of commercial or domestic failures in early modern Europe relate, in part, to a series of spectacular state bankruptcies. In an age when most princes struggled to live within their means, the monarchs of Spain and France, despite rising prices and ambitions, seemed to rule in virtual freedom from such limitations and developed extraordinary debts in pursuit of their policies. France declared bankruptcy in 1559 and defaulted on its short-term debts repeatedly during the reign of Louis XIV, subsisting otherwise on a fiscal system noted particularly for its corruption. Spain suffered bankruptcies in 1557, 1560, 1575, and 1596. The most spectacular, that of 1575, may be taken as emblematic of all. The decision of Philip II to suspend payments to his bankers can be seen as a watershed in his reign (and in Spanish power). The causes are not far to seek: the costs of political and military policies in the Mediterranean and the Netherlands during the 1560s and 1570s outstripped the crown's financial resources. Rather than effect economies, renegotiate terms, or redistribute the burden, Philip and his financial advisers opted to default, forcing a conversion of short-term debt to long-term debt that involved favorable interest rates and the forgiveness of certain obligations. This was a favorite tactic not only of the Spanish crown but also of the French in the early modern period. But in dealing with the bankruptcy of 1575, Spain's bankers (the Genoese above all) did not mildly concede as they did in 1560 (and, later, in 1596) but instead firmly resisted. They suspended all commercial credit to Castile, the fiscal heartland of Spain, and rejected the king's proposed terms. Although the immediate consequences were not fatal, the bankruptcy may be said to mark the beginning of Spanish decline. The suspension of commercial credit within Spain, and especially within Castile, permanently affected trade and, consequently, taxes. The loss also impinged on the effectiveness of Spanish armies in Italy and the Netherlands and led, most immediately, to the sack of Antwerp in 1576, likely rendering any suppression of the Dutch Revolt of 1568–1648 impossible. As important as this bankruptcy may be for the political history of the period, its economic consequences reach far beyond Spain's borders. In the 1577 settlement that ended the bankruptcy and restored Spanish credit, the bankers managed to avoid the worst consequences by recouping or transferring their losses (by calling in other debts). This became apparent in a wave of private failures that mark the interconnections between public and private finance and between larger and smaller commercial enterprises. In Augsburg, for example, 39 of the 63 sixteenth-century bankruptcies cluster around the Spanish defaults: 13 between 1559 and 1561, 14 between 1573 and 1576. Though it is impossible to attribute these and many other failures strictly to the fiscal chicanery of Philip II, their timing cannot be purely coincidental. Bankruptcies marked a shortage of credit—a crisis in money markets—that potentially reached from state treasuries to commercial countinghouses and from powerful bankers to humble artisans.

FINANCIAL RELATIONSHIPS

Of course, bankruptcies illuminate much more than the interconnections of early modern finance; they reveal some aspects of business practice. Early modern merchants, entrepreneurs, and financiers operated in an age of money scarcity and relied, therefore, to a very large extent on credit. Indeed, these men often traded within systems of interlocking credit, owing money to their suppliers or lenders and owed money by their customers and clients. Such systems could be quite fragile; one default could cause others, rippling across the entire network of relationships. In addition, they operated in an economy that lacked legal and fiscal institutions to ensure and enforce credit transactions. As a result, merchants, entrepreneurs, and financiers relied upon personal relationships and personal knowledge to reduce the risk of default. Being a close-knit

community in most places, they often knew who was or was not a good credit source or credit risk. Where personal knowledge would not serve, intermediaries, such as notaries or goldsmiths, often arose, and used their own knowledge of persons (and their means) to mediate and facilitate credit exchange. Questions of reputation and risk, to say nothing of the issue of fraud, were a function of the transmission of information and touch the boundaries between economic and cultural history. They also touch the social history of economic life in early modern Europe. Merchants also depended on a wide range of organizations to reduce risk and reinforce reputations: they formed partnerships among themselves; they entered into collective agreements; they drew upon the resources of their families; they strengthened business agreements with confessional ties (by doing business with people of the same Christian creed). Finally, bankruptcies testify not just to the failures but also to the successes of early modern enterprise, a varying combination of fortune and misfortune, competence and incompetence, honesty and dishonesty. Bankruptcies give us a mirror image of business success; by showing us how merchants and manufacturers assessed risk and managed assets, we learn not only the circumstances of failure but also the conditions of success.

The early modern period supposedly witnessed what scholars have for more than a century generally described as the transition to modern capitalism. Insofar as this is true, bankruptcy reveals some of the continuities and discontinuities in an age of change. Credit played a central role in early modern bankruptcies, and the vitality and ubiquity of early modern money markets is one area in which modern capitalism differs less than expected from its premodern model. The personal nature of credit relations, given the institutional underdevelopment of early modern economies, constitutes a less well understood distinction from modern capitalistic practice. The interpretation of bankruptcy as a criminal act requiring restitution—which remained unaltered until the nineteenth century—raises fundamental questions about business reorganization and capital accumulation on the eve of the Industrial Revolution. The adversarial relationship between private and public finance, revealed strikingly in early modern state bankruptcies, may suggest that their modern symbiotic relationship had not developed. Bankruptcy teaches, finally, that "transition" may be too simple a term for what was a multifaceted, complex, and gradual process.

By the eighteenth century, the bankrupt replaces the monopolist as the quintessential image of ruthless, exploitative capitalism. Bankruptcies were common occurrences against which integrity offered no necessary protection. Yet moralizing tracts and popular periodicals elevated the bankrupt to the level of arch-villain of the local economy. It was a perfect measure of the ways economic principles had and had not caught up with economic practices. Given the importance of bankruptcy not only for the economic history of early modern Europe but also for its political, social, and cultural history, it is surprising that so little scholarship has been devoted to the topic.

See also **Banking and Credit; Capitalism; Commerce and Markets; Economic Crises; Interest; Taxation.**

BIBLIOGRAPHY

Alsop, J. D. "Ethics in the Marketplace: Gerrard Winstanley's London Bankruptcy, 1643." *Journal of British Studies* 28 (1989): 97–119.

Bonney, R. J. "The Failure of the French Revenue Farms, 1600–60." *Economic History Review* 32 (1979): 11–32.

Bosher, J. F. "Success and Failure in Trade to New France, 1660–1760." *French Historical Studies* 15 (1988): 444–461.

Dent, Julian. "An Aspect of the Crisis of the Seventeenth Century: The Collapse of the Financial Administration of the French Monarchy (1653–61)." *The Economic History Review* 20 (1967): 241–256.

Duffy, Ian P. H. "English Bankrupts, 1571–1861." *American Journal of Legal History* 24 (1980): 283–305.

Ehrenberg, Richard. *Das Zeitalter der Fugger: Geldkapital und Creditverkehr im 16. Jahrhundert.* 2 vols. Jena, 1896.

Häberlein, Marc. *Brüder, Freunde und Betrüger: Soziale Beziehungen, Normen und Konflikte in der Augsburger Kaufmannschaft um die Mitte des 16. Jahrhunderts.* Berlin, 1998.

Hoffman, Philip T., Gilles Postel-Vinay, and Jean-Laurent Rosenthal. "Information and Economic History: How the Credit Market in Old-Regime Paris Forces Us to Rethink the Transition to Capitalism." *The American Historical Review* 104 (February 1999): 64–99.

———. "Redistribution and Long-Term Private Debt in Paris, 1660–1726." *The Journal of Economic History* 55, no. 2 (1995): 256–284.

Hoppit, Julian. "Financial Crises in Eighteenth-Century England." *The Economic History Review* 39 (1986): 39–58.

———. *Risk and Failure in English Business, 1700–1800.* Cambridge, U.K., 1987.

Jones, W. J. "The Foundations of English Bankruptcy: Statutes and Commissions in the Early Modern Period." *Transactions of the American Philosophical Society* 69, no. 3 (1979): 1–63.

Kerridge, Eric. *Trade and Banking in Early Modern England.* Manchester, U.K., 1988.

Lamoreaux, Naomi R. *Insider Lending: Banks, Personal Connections, and Economic Development in Industrial New England.* Cambridge, U.K., 1994.

Lovett, A. W. "The Castilian Bankruptcy of 1575." *Historical Journal* 23 (1980): 899–911.

———. "The General Settlement of 1577: An Aspect of Spanish Finance in the Early Modern Period." *Historical Journal* 25 (1982): 1–22.

Marriner, Sheila. "English Bankruptcy Records and Statistics before 1850." *The Economic History Review* 33 (1980): 351–366.

Muldrew, Craig. "Credit and the Courts: Debt Litigation in a Seventeenth-Century Urban Community." *Economic History Review* 46 (1993): 23–38.

Mueller, Reinhold C. *The Venetian Money Market: Banks, Panics, and the Public Debt, 1200–1500.* Baltimore, 1997.

Neal, Larry. *The Rise of Financial Capitalism: International Capital Markets in the Age of Reason.* Cambridge, U.K., 1990.

Safley, Thomas Max. "Bankruptcy: Family and Finance in Early Modern Augsburg." *The Journal of European Economic History* 29 (2000): 53–73.

Tracy, James D. *A Financial Revolution in the Habsburg Netherlands: Renten and Renteniers in the County of Holland, 1515–1565.* Berkeley, 1985.

Van der Wee, Hermann. "Money, Credit, and Banking Systems." In *The Cambridge Economic History of Europe,* vol. 5, edited by E. E. Rich and C. H. Wilson, pp. 290–392. Cambridge, U.K., 1977.

Welbourne, E. "Bankruptcy before the Era of Victorian Reform." *Cambridge Historical Journal* 4 (1932/34): 51–62.

THOMAS MAX SAFLEY

BARCELONA. Barcelona, capital city of Catalonia, is located on the Mediterranean coast in northeastern Spain. The city is nestled on a plain between the Sierra de Collserola and the sea, in the shadow of the promontory of Montjuic, and is bordered to the north and south by the Besós and Llobregat rivers. Key to Barcelona's success as an important port in the fifteenth century was its geographic position within the crown of Aragón. The lack of navigable rivers in Catalonia limited interior trade to overland routes that converged at Barcelona's port. Barcelona served as a major node along the coastal trade route from southern France to Valencia and beyond, and together with the ports of Mallorca and Valencia, controlled the western end of the Mediterranean.

The city originated as a Roman fort constructed on a knoll, which has remained the religious and political center of the city. In the late Middle Ages, the city outgrew this fortification and expanded down to the sea. New perimeter fortifications were constructed, the seaside wall not being completed until 1536. The city's interior was renowned for its numerous religious and civic monuments. As the political seat of Catalonia, Barcelona housed in its center the palaces of the king and the Diputació del General, the principality's treasury. The city was governed from the palace of the Consell de Cent, a council of five executives and a jury of one hundred "honored citizens." The royal shipyard (the *drassanes*) dominated the western end of the port district, and the maritime merchant hall (*Llotja de Mar*) governed the busy port.

Barcelona's medieval prosperity was abruptly cut off by the civil war of 1462; ten years of violence tore apart the political, social, and economic fabric of the city, as well as damaging its international trade. By 1487, the contraction of trade was worsened by a rising of the Catalan peasantry and prosecutions of converted Jews by the Inquisition. By the end of the fifteenth century, Barcelona, with approximately 25,000 inhabitants, was the most densely populated city of Catalonia. Nonetheless, because of repeated waves of bubonic plague, the city's population rose only to about 29,000 by 1516.

The loss of Barcelona's Mediterranean markets was not compensated by the sixteenth-century exploration of the Americas, since this new market was dominated by Castile. Barcelona emerged from an unsuccessful rebellion against the Habsburgs in 1640–1652 with its traditional political privileges intact. It lost those privileges by fighting against Spain's new Bourbon dynasty in the War of the Spanish Succession (1701–1714). Moreover, the city's population, which stood at about 64,000 in 1657, had fallen to 37,000 by 1713. Economically, Barcelona recovered slowly from the war, but by the end of the eighteenth century, the city benefited from a flourishing industry in cotton textiles and the opening of trade to Spanish America.

See also **Catalonia; Catalonia, Revolt of (1640–1652); Spanish Succession, War of the (1701–1714).**

BIBLIOGRAPHY

Carrère, Claude. *Barcelona, 1380–1462: Un centre econòmic en època de crisi*, vol. 2. Barcelona, 1978.

Hughes, Robert. *Barcelona*. New York, 1992.

Kern, Robert, ed. *Historical Dictionary of Modern Spain, 1700–1988*. New York, 1990.

Sobrequés i Callicó, Jaume, ed. *Historia de Barcelona*, 8 vols. Barcelona, 1992.

Treppo, Mario del. *Els mercaders catalans i l'expansió de la corona catalano-aragonesa al segle XV*. Barcelona, 1976.

SHELLEY E. ROFF

BAROMETER. The mercury barometer had its origins in the investigations being made in Italy during the early seventeenth century to discover why it was impossible to build a suction pump to raise water higher than about thirty feet (10 m). Once it was found that the height attainable was related to the density of the liquid, the experimenters exchanged their cumbersome metal tubes filled with water for shorter glass tubes with the heaviest fluid available—mercury—which was mined in Tuscany. The results of numerous experiments undertaken in Rome, Florence, and elsewhere were widely circulated and discussed.

The first apparatus generally accepted as a barometer was that set up in Florence in 1644 by Evangelista Torricelli (1608–1647), a mathematician and physicist. Torricelli filled a glass tube with mercury, sealed it at one end, and inverted it with its open end in a dish of mercury. The level always fell a short way down the tube, then settled at a height of about thirty inches. He concluded correctly that the mercury column was sustained by the weight of the

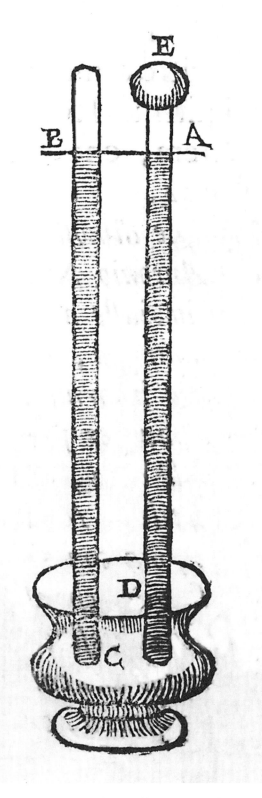

Barometer. Illustration of Torricelli's barometer. LIBRARY OF CONGRESS

air pressing on the open surface of mercury, and further experiments convinced him that the space above the mercury in the tube was a vacuum. He noted that the level rose and fell with changing temperature, but he was unable to use his apparatus to measure variations in the weight of the atmosphere because he had not foreseen that temperature would affect the level of the mercury.

News of this experiment circulated quickly among European scientists, who hastened to replicate the experiment. Torricelli's conclusions were not universally accepted because some disputed whether the air had weight, while both Aristotle and the Catholic Church denied the possibility of a vacuum. In France, the philosopher René Descartes (1596–1650) seems to have been the first person, probably in 1647, to attach a graduated scale to the tube so that he could record any changes attributable to the weather. At around this time Duke Ferdinand II of Tuscany organized the first short-lived meteorological network among scientists in other Italian cities, gathering observations of pressure, temperature, humidity, wind direction, and state of the sky.

Descartes, the Minim friar Marin Mersenne (1588–1648), an important nexus for scientific communications, and physicist Blaise Pascal (1623–1662) also discussed whether the mercury column would be shorter if the experiment was performed at the top of a mountain where, presumably, the atmosphere weighed less. Around 1648 Pascal's brother-in-law Florin Perier (1605–1672) set up a tube at Clermont, where it stood at 26 inches 3½ lines (the French line was one-twelfth of a French inch), and carried another tube to the summit of the Puy de Dôme, where the mercury stood at 23 inches 2 lines.

By 1648, the barometer was serving the three purposes that it continued to serve thereafter: as an apparatus for testing the laws of physics, as an instrument for measuring altitude, and as a weather monitor and, later, prognosticator. The words *baroscope* and *barometer*, meaning 'instrument for measuring weight', first used by Robert Boyle in the early 1660s, were soon adopted into the Latin, French, German, and Italian languages.

THE BAROMETER AS A PHYSICS APPARATUS

Numerous experiments using variations of Torricelli's apparatus were performed by members of the Accademia del Cimento (The Academy of Trial, or Experiment), a group of Florentine virtuosi active from 1657 to 1667, and published in its *Saggi di naturali esperienze fatti nell'Accademia del Cimento* (Examples of experiments in natural philosophy made by the academy) in 1667. They sought to discover if the space above the mercury was filled with vapor or air diffused through the glass, and what effect different shaped tubes would have if the dish of mercury, or the entire apparatus, was covered. Many of these experiments were inconclusive, the academicians being unable to interpret their findings. With Otto Guericke's invention of the air pump, the barometer served as a means of measuring the strength of the vacuum created for a whole series of related experiments.

A DIVERSITY OF SHAPES

By 1650, Pascal had probably devised the siphon barometer, which consisted simply of a sealed tube with its open end curved up at the bottom. In 1663, Robert Hooke, demonstrator to the Royal Society, devised the "wheel" barometer, in which a float on the open surface of mercury in a siphon tube was connected to a cord running over a pulley to a counterweight; a pointer on the pulley axle rotated on a large dial, amplifying the small daily variations in height. Many variations of form, usually to enhance portability or to amplify the scale, were proposed in the following century, often by people with no understanding of the glassblower's abilities or the problems of filling such tubes without admitting some air. Among the more practical forms, some of which still survive, were folded, conical, and angled tubes, and tubes with two liquids. By about 1670, the barometer had found its way into wealthier homes and various types could be bought in London and Paris.

In June 1668, Robert Boyle described and illustrated his "portable" siphon, fastened to a board on which a graduated scale was marked, the idea being to send examples to distant places, but he admitted the difficulty of filling such a tube. Credit for the first truly portable barometer is disputed: the barometer maker John Patrick (1654–1730) may have invented the method, and he opposed the patent of 1695 filed by the clockmaker Daniel Quare (1648/9–1724). The tube was sealed into a boxwood cistern with a leather base; a movable plate driven by a screw pressed up on the bag until the mercury filled the tube, after which the instrument could be safely transported. Quare saw this as a means of making domestic barometers in London for sale to provincial customers, but this eminently practical device enabled the subsequent development of mountain and marine barometers.

MOUNTAIN AND MARINE BAROMETERS

The first such measurement in England was probably that made in 1653 by Henry Power, a physician of Halifax, Yorkshire, who reported that the mercury reached only 26 inches at the summit of his local hill. Robert Boyle recognized that, as the mercury fell, even when ascending a church steeple, so it would rise if the barometer was taken down into a mine. In 1672, this observation was confirmed by George Sinclair, a Scottish mining surveyor.

In the early days, explorers and surveyors carried their glass tube, bowl, leather bag of mercury, and graduated rule, and assembled the barometer for each observation, a practice that extended into the eighteenth century, when French academicians sought to measure altitudes of the high Andean peaks, the highest mountains then known. The mathematical formula for the relationship between the altitude and height of mercury was difficult to establish, and astronomer Edmund Halley's 1685 proposal was only the first step on a complex path.

Although the portable domestic barometer became available in the late seventeenth century, the Genevan scientist Jean-André de Luc (1727–1818) was the first to design, around 1750, a robust apparatus consisting of a siphon tube, with thermometers and a plumb-bob, neatly packed in a wooden case. A scale was laid alongside both levels of mercury to measure the distance between that in the tube and that in the open arm. After taking the reading, the tube was tilted until mercury filled it; then, by closing an ivory tap in the siphon and draining off the surplus liquid, the instrument could be carried safely to the next station. The Genevan scientist Horace-Bénédict de Saussure (1740–1799) carried a de Luc barometer to the summit of Mont Blanc, Europe's highest mountain, in 1787.

De Luc's siphons were soon replaced by straight-tube barometers fitted with a leather bag

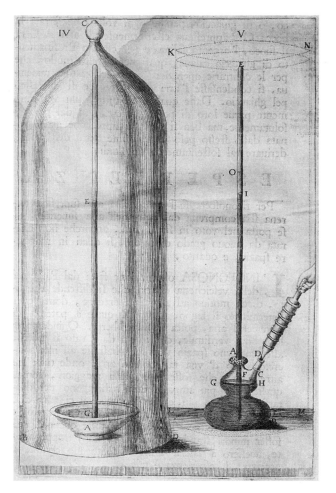

Barometer. An illustration from the 1667 *Saggi di naturali experienze* shows two early experiments in measuring atmospheric pressure. On the left, the mercury tube is sealed in a bell jar; on the right, the tube is immersed in a jar of water. ©DAVID LEES/CORBIS

and portable screw, the whole being contained in a slender cylindrical case. In the higher mountains so much mercury descended from the tube, raising the level in the cistern, that the scale alongside the tube became inaccurate. Because the level in the cistern was invisible, a float was inserted in the cistern; as its protruding tip rose against a small graduated scale, the true distance between the two levels could be calculated from this reading.

In his *Discourse Concerning the Origins and Properties of Wind* (1671), Ralph Bohun (1639–1716) called for the use of a barometer to predict hurricanes, particularly at sea. On board a moving ship, however, the mercury oscillated in the tube and, on occasion, struck the top of the tube and broke the glass. Numerous ineffective designs were proposed in France and England before the London instrument maker Edward Nairne (1725–1806) produced a tube whose central section was constricted to one-twentieth of an inch in diameter. This kept the mercury steady. The barometer, suspended in gimbals, performed satisfactorily on James Cook's second voyage of 1772–1775 and provided the model for marine barometers thereafter.

METEOROLOGY

The height of the mercury column was soon recognized as related to changes in the weather, but the first experimenters were surprised that the mercury fell on rainy days, when they supposed that the water-laden atmosphere was heavier. Soon, however, the correlation between high mercury and fine weather, and between falling or low mercury and rain, encouraged makers to add "Fair," "Changeable," and "Storm" to their scales. Because the mercury expanded and contracted with temperature, small thermometers were put on the frame to correct for this effect.

The barograph, or self-recording barometer, made a late appearance on the architect Sir Christopher Wren's somewhat improbable "Weather Clock." Constructed in 1663, it consisted of several instruments, each of which registered by impressions on a paper chart moved by clockwork. Hooke added a barograph prior to 1681; from the description, he appears to have caused the pulley of a wheel barometer to make similar impressions on the chart. In 1765, the clockmaker Alexander Cumming (1733–1814) constructed a large and elegant continuously recording barograph for King George III (ruled 1760–1820); it was a siphon barometer, the float supporting a light frame carrying a pencil that marked a rotating circular chart. Within a few years similar instruments were being made in France.

See also **Academies, Learned; Boyle, Robert; Clocks and Watches; Descartes, René; Ferdinand II (Holy Roman Empire); Hooke, Robert; Mersenne, Marin; Pascal, Blaise; Physics; Scientific Instruments; Technology; Weather and Climate; Wren, Christopher.**

BIBLIOGRAPHY

Archinard, Margarida. *De Luc et la recherche barometrique.* Geneva, 1980.

Golinski, Jan. "Barometers of Change: Meteorological Instruments as Machines of Enlightenment." In *The Sciences in Enlightened Europe,* edited by William Clark, Jan Golinski, and Simon Schaffer (Chapter 3; pp. 69–93). Chicago, 1999.

McConnell, Anita. "Origins of the Marine Barometer." *Annals of Science.* Forthcoming.

Middleton, W. E. Knowles. *The Experimenters: A Study of the Accademia del Cimento.* Baltimore and London, 1971.

———. *The History of the Barometer.* Baltimore, 1964; reprint, Trowbridge, U.K., 1994.

ANITA MCCONNELL

BAROQUE. The baroque created confusion and dissension among its interpreters following its inception as an artistic term in the mid-eighteenth century. The origins of baroque (often capitalized) as a term are obscure, and once historians in the late nineteenth century began to question the derogatory meaning that had accrued to it, baroque became more contested than other period styles. During the mid-twentieth century, not long after it was used to characterize music, literature, and theater in addition to art history, a consensus developed that is still maintained in the popular press. By this account, baroque designates art and architecture from c. 1580 to c. 1750, and is a proselytizing Catholic art and grandiose power statement adopted by kings, emperors, popes, and other aspiring absolutists. Its multimedia forms were thought to be monumental, exuberant, unstable, theatrical, and metamorphic. Its psychology was self-aware, mystical, manipulative, melodramatic, and playful. Its subjects ranged from the abject to the sublime, from caricatures to idealized portraits, from sexualized ecstasies to bloody dismemberings. Its modes of expression were encomia, catafalques, and epithalamia; its key symbols the mask, the labyrinth, and the telescope and microscope.

This popular view holds much truth for many art forms, but in the second half of the twentieth century, scholars led by Ernst Curtius and Wolfgang Stechow began to question the legitimacy of the baroque as a period of style. They accepted *baroque* as a legitimate stylistic term that may be applied to some late Hellenistic, late Gothic, and other arts, but not *baroque* as a period style for the seventeenth century. The new consensus today asserts that the baroque, like any period style, relies on an essentialist Hegelianism that was discredited along with other totalizing prejudices such as sexism, racism, and nationalism. Furthermore, it was questioned whether an originally pejorative term signifying deformation and mawkish emotionalism could fairly represent a heterogenous phenomenon that included Carlo Dolci's pious quattrocentism, the limpid mist of Vermeer's rooms, and Cassiano Dal Pozzo's artists conscientiously recording, classifying, and reconstructing the ancient past. Like baroque ornaments that entwine buildings, the term *baroque* had spread too far, lately even to economics, and become so variously defined that its utility was lost. As a period style, this may be true, but baroque is currently enjoying a revival as an interpretive key to contemporary art.

ETYMOLOGIES

It seems fitting that for a style known for instability and mutation no secure etymology has been determined. Baroque as a term is shrouded in greater ambiguity than the etymologies of other period styles. Wherever its origins truly lie, one can safely say that *barocco* (Italian and Spanish), *Barock* (German), and *baroque* (French and English) are linguistic mutations and semantic grotesques, much like the style they describe.

The four principal etymologies are presented here, from the most to least frequently accepted definitions:

1. *Barroco,* the Portuguese word for 'deformed pearl' (in Spanish *barueca*), is the etymology preferred by art historians, not for any particular philological reason, but because it signifies a visual form. Just as a spherical unblemished pearl may signify classical perfection, so a baroque pearl signifies its flawed perversion. "Flawed" was a nineteenth-century opinion; in the seventeenth century "baroque" pearls were fashionable.

2. In Italian, a *baroco* was a false scholastic syllogism, a caricature of logic and hence a form of sophistry. Because it originated in rhetoric and language, it became the preferred etymology for literary historians from Benedetto Croce (1929) onward; among art historians, only the textually oriented Erwin Panofsky (1934) ac-

Baroque. *The Garden of Love* by Peter Paul Rubens. ©ALINARI/ART RESOURCE, N.Y.

cepted this as its primary meaning. During the seventeenth century, the French considered *barocco* to be an empty Italian form, identified with academies and devoid of original thought (Michel de Montaigne); Italians understood it more generally as sophistry (Francesco Fulvio Frugoni). *Baroco* was, like rococo, a form of baby talk or parrot chatter, where form is cut loose from its signifiers. Like the baroque pearl, baroque syllogism was not always viewed negatively in the seventeenth century but instead signified a form of wit, "an ingenious quibbling . . . playfully persuasive . . . based on metaphor" (Emanuele Tesauro). Whereas Croce and others regarded baroque syllogism as a "gnostic confusion" and an "empty game," the seventeenth century equated it with an equivocating wit and the associative ambiguities of metaphor that lie at the center of genius and creativity.

3. *Baroccho* from the fourteenth through seven-

teenth centuries signified a type of usury, similar to pawnbroking, and hence by extension something illegitimate.

4. Erich Hubala proposed *baroquer*, used by French cabinet makers to signify turning and curving.

5. Generally unaccepted, but still enticing, proposed terms include *barraqa* (Arabic for 'to open one's eyes') and *bis-roca* (Latin for 'twisted stone').

ORIGINS OF A PERIOD STYLE
Otto Kurz, Bruno Migliorini, and Rossana Bossaglia have traced the earliest applications of *barocco/baroque/Barock* as an art or architectural term to the 1740s. In 1751 Denis Diderot's encyclopedia entry defined *baroché* as "a painter's term used to explain that the paintbrush did not cleanly delineate a contour and that it smeared colors." At the same time, Charles Cochin and Charles de Brosses described baroque forms as twisted, winding, tortu-

ous, and confused. Others likened it to the plague, dropsy, and other diseases, to decadence and lunacy. Francesco Milizia (1768) likened the suicidal and "raving mad" Borromini to the "contagious architectural madness" of his buildings: "He went baroque." De Brosses, picking up on a seventeenth-century epithet of Borromini as "a gothic ignoramus," identified baroque art as neo-Gothic where clear structure is hidden behind "fussy trimmings" and where precious miniature decorations are inappropriately gigantic. Baroque was thus an Asiatic style of sophistry and indiscriminate ornament, and like the Asiatic, it was conceived as foreign. The baroque as Gothic is one example; other critics compared it to Islamic and Chinese decoration (Pompei, 1735; Milizia, 1768).

In these early usages, baroque was not explicitly a period style, not yet Baroque with a capital B, but only a recurring degraded style frequently found in the seventeenth century. Concurrently with the use of baroque as a stylistic quality, early-eighteenth-century critics began to reify the seventeenth century as a cultural unit, a discrete decadent period where the visual and literary arts shared defects of excess, exaggeration, and novelty: "Just as Marino . . . introduced without proper judgment new forms of thought and speech in poetry. . . . so too might be said of Borromini, Bernini, Pozzi and their contemporaries, enriching buildings with new ornaments and deviated from good practice and deforming it" (Pompei, 1735). Others created a baroque canon of the terrible "B's" representing sculpture, architecture, and painting: Bernini, Borromini, and Berretini (that is, Pietro da Cortona). Johann Joachim Winckelmann, who wrote his seminal *The History of Ancient Art* (1764) partly as a critique of the baroque, saw it as a late "superfluous" style, the inevitable end of classicism, much like Late Hellenism and mannerism, all noisy, deformed, exaggerated, and corrupted.

RECOVERIES

The recovery of the baroque as a legitimate independent period style instead of a late bastardized form of the Renaissance began in late-nineteenth-century architectural studies (Wölfflin, 1888; Gurlitt; Riegl). For the architect Cornelius Gurlitt, this historical rehabilitation coincided with his architectural practice in a neo-baroque style. More

than any other scholar, Heinrich Wölfflin came to be associated with the rehabilitation of the baroque, first in *Renaissance and Baroque* (1888; based on his dissertation) and finally in the classic *Principles of Art History* (1915). In the latter, he proposed five paired morphological categories, intended to distinguish Renaissance from baroque but that became for early-twentieth-century art historians universal categories: linear/painter; plain/recession; closed/open form; multiplicity/unity; clearness/unclearness. Although now often dismissed as a "mere" formalist, Wölfflin, in his interest in the psychology of art and perception, influenced a younger generation of art historians (such as Wilhelm Worringer and Henri Focillon).

Many scholars starting in the 1930s resisted the formulation of the baroque as a period style, arguing instead that it should be seen as a perpetually renewing form (Focillon; Panofsky; D'Ors). Much like eighteenth-century critics of seventeenth-century art as a new Gothic (flamboyant Gothic and Spanish Plateresque) or as a new mannerism, they thought of the baroque as much as a recurring type as a chronologically limited period style. Curtius extended this view by showing how the perception of stylistic recurrences is partly a linguistic illusion, one that was created by the fixed rhetorical categories inherited by historians. This, in turn, helped lay the ground for a new historicism (White; Holly).

The German revisionists of the late nineteenth century assumed that the baroque originated in Italy and maintained its purest forms there. By the mid-twentieth century, however, a group of scholars (D'Ors; Francastel; Hatzfeld) proposed Spain and not Italy as its place of origin, partly because of the social control and mystical fervor of the Spanish church, partly because they thought of the baroque as an innately Spanish form of expression that can be traced back to Hispano-Latin writers like Lucan and Prudentius and to the Hispanic absorption of Islamic and North-African ornament. The Spanish origins of the baroque had actually been proposed much earlier, to little effect, by the literary historian Girolamo Tiraboschi (1782). A recent exhibition at the Guggenheim Museum in New York interpreted contemporary Brazilian art as a continuation of baroque traditions (Sullivan).

During the 1950s, a series of seminal studies were published in Italy questioning Croce's syllogistic baroque (*Retorica e Barocco;* Argan). They accepted Croce's baroque as an art of rhetoric, or sophistry as Croce had insisted, but rediscovered its original virtues of persuasion and provocation. Having been sensitized to the linguistic dimension of the baroque, scholars then began a serious exploration of its etymology in the early 1960s (Bossaglia; Kurz; Migliorini). This turn to language was paralleled by contemporary developments in mannerism scholarship.

From the 1970s on, new (but not always convincing) theories of the baroque have been restricted to literature, music, or theater; more promising are those emanating from cultural studies and philosophy (Maravall; Deleuze). Art historians not disenchanted with the viability of period styles have tended to recycle previous ideas.

BAROQUE AND MODERNITY

The rehabilitation of the baroque in the late nineteenth century coincided with the discovery of its modernity. Wölfflin stated this first: "One can hardly fail to recognise the affinity that our own age in particular bears to the Italian Baroque." Impressionism, art nouveau and liberty, symbolism, Richard Wagner's operas, and the philosophical treatises of Wagner's friend Friedrich Nietzsche offered new possibilities for appreciating the baroque. Nietzsche blamed pedants for mistaking the dionysian baroque for merely an irrational delirium. In Carlo Collodi's *Pinocchio* (1883) the metamorphosized *bamboccio* is sent off to an enchanted house of mirrors, the "Casa dei Barocchi," where men are transformed into asses, and it is in this unlikely place that Pinocchio finds his true path.

Not only have ideas on the baroque been reinterpreted in light of modern culture, but the baroque itself is seen as perennially modern. In 1934 Panofsky said the baroque was not the end of the Renaissance but "the beginning of a fourth era, which may be called 'Modern' with a capital 'M.'" More recently Jacques Lacan professed that his riotously polyvalent thought, like a "Borromean knot," was baroque, claiming that modern existence can be best understood through its equivocations. In later-twentieth-century Italian literature, the neo-baroque movement posed linguistic convolutions

to disorient readers. When asked why his literature must be so tortured, Carlo Gadda (one of the neo-*barocchisti*) responded: "I'm not baroque; the world is baroque." Omar Calabrese proposed the baroque as the best conceptual category for late-twentieth-century culture with its transgressions of pop culture into high art, its self-conscious referencing of the past, and its frenetic visual flux and its polymorphic media.

See also **Architecture; Art: Art Theory, Criticism, and Historiography.**

BIBLIOGRAPHY

Primary Sources

Brosses, Charles de. *Lettres familières écrites d'Italie a quelques amis en 1739 et 1740.* Paris, 1799. Letters from his travels in Italy; composed between 1745 and 1755.

Diderot, Denis, and Jean Le Rond d'Alembert. *Encyclopédie, ou dictionnaire raisonné des sciences, des arts et des métiers.* Vol. 2, p. 77. Geneva, 1777–1779.

Milizia, Francesco. *Memorie degli architetti antichi e moderni.* Rome, 1781.

Pompei, Alessandro. *Li cinque ordini dell'architettura civile di Michel Sanmicheli.* Verona, 1735.

Winckelmann, Johann Joachim. *The History of Ancient Art.* Translated by A. Gode. New York, 1968. Translation of *Geschichte der Kunst des Altertums* (1764).

Secondary Sources

Calabrese, Omar. *Neo-Baroque: A Sign of the Times.* Translated by Charles Lambert. Princeton, 1992.

Holly, Michael Ann. "Imagining the Baroque." In *Past Looking: Historical Imagination and the Rhetoric of the Image,* pp. 91–111. Ithaca, N.Y., 1996.

Lacan, Jacques. "On the Baroque." In *Lectures,* edited by J.-A. Miller and translated by B. Fink. New York, 1998. Book XX; originally published in 1975.

Panofsky, Erwin. "What Is Baroque?" In *Three Essays on Style,* edited by Irving Lavin, pp. 19–88. Cambridge, Mass., 1995. Previously unpublished lecture from 1934.

Wölfflin, Heinrich. *Principles of Art History.* Translated by M. D. Hottinger. New York, 1950. Translation of *Kunstgeschichtliche Grundbegriffe* (1915).

———. *Renaissance and Baroque.* Translated by Kathrin Simon. Ithaca, N.Y., 1966. Translation of *Renaissance und Baroque* (1888).

PHILIP L. SOHM

BASQUE COUNTRY.

BASQUE COUNTRY. The lands inhabited by Basque speakers extended between the Adouritz River in southwestern France and the Nervion River in northeastern Spain, comprising most of the western flanks of the Pyrenees Mountains. The Ebro River functioned as a traditional boundary between Basque lands and the kingdom of Castile.

On the Spanish side, Basque provinces included Araba (Alava), Biskaia (Vizcaya), Gipuzkoa (Guipúzcoa), and Nafarroa (Navarre in French, Navarra in Spanish). The provinces under French rule were Lapurdi (Labourd), Soule (Zuberoa), and Benafarroa (Basse-Navarre).

After the final annexation of Navarre to the Spanish crown in the 1510s, the Basque settlements consolidated their loyalty to either Castile or France, with the Bidasoa River as the natural border between the two monarchies. The borders between France and Spain, however, remained particularly blurry in the Basque lands, where jurisdictional disputes arose at the ecclesiastic, provincial, and municipal levels.

Basque common law and political autonomy were traditionally recognized on both sides of the Bidasoa River. In 1452 and 1526 Bizkaian customary laws were recognized in the Fuero Viejo and Fuero Nuevo.

Each town or village had full autonomy and elected its own representatives every year in the churchyard or *anteiglesia*, with wide jurisdiction in economic, political, and military affairs. Rivalries between bordering villages were not unusual, especially regarding access to natural resources (stone, wood, coal, salt, water) and rights of use and exploitation in grazing lands.

The farmstead *(baserri* or *caserío)* was the most important institution in the Basque lands and func-

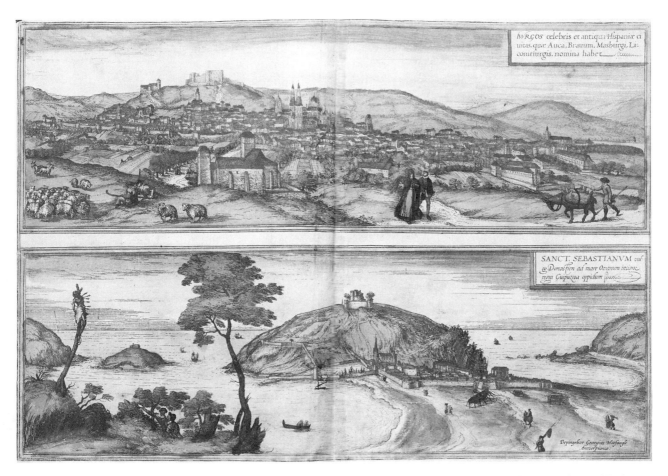

Basque Country. This page from *Civitates Orbis Terrarum,* c. 1572–1618, by Braun and Hogenberg, features views of Burgos (above) and San Sebastian. ©Archivo Iconografico, S.A./Corbis

tioned with economic and political autonomy. Farmsteads *(baserriak)* were small units of land farmed by men and women to produce and harvest corn, apples, fodder, wheat, milk, honey, poultry, and nuts. Outside the *baserri* boundaries, each unit normally raised sheep and goats and had the right to exploit municipal resources. *Baserriak* were deemed indivisible and therefore inherited by only one member of the family the following generation, according to traditional rules that varied across villages and regions.

The most important cities in the Basque area were the ports, given the mercantile and maritime character of Basque enterprises. Shipbuilding and trade with northern Europe and Spanish America were vital economic activities. From the sixteenth century on, Basque merchants traded silver, iron, sugar, and manufactured goods in a transatlantic circuit that extended from Belgium and France to Spanish America and the Philippines. Large-scale fishing, in particular whale and cod, comprised another important activity and required major investments, planning, and management. Bilbo (Bilbao), Donostia (San Sebastián), and Bayonne were the most important towns, and each developed strong local elites based upon a wide range of activities, from shipbuilding to colonial trade and whale fisheries.

Significant emigration to the Americas was a permanent feature in the Basque lands after 1492. Basques were prominent colonial merchants, soldiers, miners, royal officers, ecclesiastical authorities, scribes, lawyers, and doctors. They were also involved in rural enterprises, especially sugar and cacao production.

Basques also played a prominent role in the Spanish monarchy's European affairs, especially in the church, royal bureaucracy, and military. Prominent Basques in the early modern era could be found on all continents, starting with Ignatius of Loyola, founder of the Jesuits in Rome, Saint Francis Xavier, missionary in the Far East, Juan de Oñate and Francisco de Urdinola, colonizers of Northern Mexico and what became the southwestern United States, and Juan de Garay, refounder of Buenos Aires.

See also **Ignatius of Loyola; Jesuits; Spain.**

BIBLIOGRAPHY

Caro Baroja, Julio. *Los vascos.* Madrid, 1973.

Douglass, William A., and Jon Bilbao. *Amerikanuak: Basques in The New World.* Reno, Nev., 1975.

Lefebvre, Thomas. *Les modes de vie dans les Pyrenees atlantiques orientales.* Paris, 1933.

Orella, Jose Luis, ed. *Los vascos a traves de la historia. comportamientos: Mentalidades y vida cotidiana.* Donostia-San Sebastian, 1989.

JUAN JAVIER PESCADOR

BASSI, LAURA (1711–1778), Bolognese physicist, professor, and experimenter. Laura Bassi holds the unusual distinction of having been the first woman to pursue a paid scientific career. A lawyer's daughter, Bassi received her early education from the family physician, Gaetano Tacconi, who subsequently introduced her to the Bolognese scholarly community. With the encouragement of the archbishop of Bologna, Prospero Lambertini (Pope Benedict XIV, 1740–1758), Bassi's patrons proposed her as a candidate for a university degree in philosophy. Following a public defense of forty-nine philosophical theses on 17 April 1732, Bassi received her *laurea* (university degree) on 12 May—the second woman whose graduation we can document from any university. On 29 October 1732, she became professor of philosophy at the University of Bologna. She subsequently taught philosophy, mathematics, and physics there until her death in 1778. By the end of her life, Bassi held two other professorships—an appointment at the Collegio Montalto and, as of 1776, a professorship in experimental physics at the Academy of the Institute for Sciences in Bologna. In collaboration with her husband, the physician Giuseppe Veratti (1707–1793)—whom she married in 1738 and with whom she had eight children—Bassi offered private lessons in physics and performed experiments in her household. She was routinely celebrated throughout her lifetime for these accomplishments, not only by the Venetian philosophe Francesco Algarotti, who sketched a vignette of her in his *Newtonianism for Ladies* (1737), but also by well-known figures in the republic of letters such as the electrical experimenter Abbé Nollet (1700–1770), who visited her, Voltaire, who corresponded with her, and her cousin, the naturalist Lazzaro

Laura Bassi. PHOTO RESEARCHERS, INC.

Spallanzani (1729–1799), who claimed he never would have become an experimenter if he had not studied with her.

See also **Women.**

BIBLIOGRAPHY

Cavazza, Marta. "Laura Bassi e il suo gabinetto di fisica sperimentale: Realtà e mito." *Nuncius* 10 (1995): 715–753.

———. "Laura Bassi 'maestra' di Spallanzani." In *Il cerchio della vita*, edited by Walter Bernardi and Paola Manzini, pp. 185–202. Florence, 1999.

Ceranski, Beate. *Und sie fürchtet sich vor niemandem: Die Physikerin Laura Bassi.* Frankfurt am Main, 1996.

Findlen, Paula. "Science as a Career in Enlightenment Italy: The Strategies of Laura Bassi." *Isis* 84 (1993): 441–469.

———. "The Scientist's Body: The Nature of a Woman Philosopher in Enlightenment Italy." In *The Faces of Nature in Enlightenment Europe*, edited by Gianna Pomata and Lorraine Daston. Berlin, 2003.

Logan, Gabriella Berti. "The Desire to Contribute: An Eighteenth Century Italian Woman of Science." *American Historical Review* 99 (1994): 785–812.

PAULA FINDLEN

BAVARIA. The duchy of Bavaria, which became a prince-electorate in 1623, was one of the larger and more important territories of the Holy Roman Empire. In 1801 it covered about 590 square miles and had about 880,000 inhabitants. Unlike other territories, Bavaria was a nation rather than merely a random territorial unit. The Bavarian people had emerged in a process of ethnogenesis during the reign of the Ostrogoth king Theodoric the Great (c. 453–526; ruled 474/493–526) in the former Roman province of Noricum. From 1180 until it became a republic in 1918, it was ruled by the local Wittelsbach dynasty. After a period of dynastic divisions and succession wars following the reign of the Holy Roman emperor Louis IV "the Bavarian" (ruled 1314–1347), Bavaria became and remained unified at the beginning of the early modern period. This was a result of the law of primogeniture, which was introduced by Duke Albert IV "the Wise" (ruled 1465–1508) in 1506, accepted by the Bavarian Estates, and enshrined in the constitution (*Landesordnung*) of 1516. The Bavarian parliament (*Landschaft*) consisted of prelates, the nobility, and the towns. During the minority rule of William IV (ruled 1508–1550) the Estates in fact governed the country for several years, and afterwards they retained the right of taxation and the administration of finances. However, during the reign of Albert V (1550–1579) the relationship between the Estates and the ruler deteriorated because the higher nobility and parts of the citizenry of major towns like Munich adopted Protestantism and urged the duke to follow their example. However, this was a hopeless idea, since Duke Albert actually became a leader of the Catholic cause during the Council of Trent. When the Estates tried to use tax grants as a weapon in their struggle for religious liberation, it came to a showdown. The duke raided the castles of the most prominent Protestant nobles, Ladislaus von Fraunberg (1505–1566), Pankraz von Freyberg (1508–1565), Wolfdietrich von Maxlrain (1523–1586), and Count Joachim von Ortenburg (1530–1600). Their excellent contacts with Protestant nobles and princes in other parts of the empire, and throughout Europe, were labeled a conspiracy, and political Protestantism in the country was crushed in 1564. According to the Religious Peace of Augsburg of 1555, Protestants were forced to either reconvert or emigrate, and the emigration of Protestant burghers damaged the urban economy substantially.

By assuming leadership of the Counter-Reformation, the Bavarian dukes rose to European importance. In a deliberate program of reeducation, with the University of Ingolstadt as the headquarters of Jesuit influence and with a number of Jesuit high schools, Bavaria managed to shape the ideas of future Catholic elites. Commissioned by the dukes, Jesuits like Petrus Canisius, Gregory of Valencia, and Jacob Gretser molded the religious ideas of the next two generations of Catholic political leaders, including Holy Roman emperor Ferdinand III, and the generation of the Catholic League and of religious warfare in the Thirty Years' War (1618–1648). In 1568 Duke Albert forged an alliance with the house of Lorraine, the political leaders of the French Catholic League. Duke William V "the Pious" (ruled 1579–1597) and his wife Renata of Lorraine led the life of saints and brutally suppressed heresy and witchcraft. They also introduced new and highly popular forms of piety: new forms of prayer, of spirituality, and of religious practices like weekly processions; pilgrimages to Bavarian national shrines such as Mother Mary of Altötting; annual Corpus Christi processions in the capital; and monumental mystery plays. There were new religious brotherhoods such as the Marian Congregation and new religious orders like the female Jesuits of Mary Ward (1585–1645), an English emigrant from Yorkshire who was protected by the Bavarian dynasty even after formal recognition by the Jesuits and the pope had been denied her. Mother Mary was chosen the patroness of Bavaria, with widespread veneration, and Marian columns erected at the central places of all market towns. In 1583 the Bavarian rulers intervened in their first international conflict, sending an army to northwestern Germany to depose the archbishop of Cologne, prince-elector Gebhard Truchsess von Waldburg (ruled 1577–1583), who had converted to Protestantism. The Cologne War secured Catholic domination in the Holy Roman Empire since the Catholic votes (Mainz, Cologne, Trier, and Bohemia) outweighed the Protestant ones (Saxony, Brandenburg, and the Palatinate). Furthermore, it secured the prince-electorate of Cologne for the Bavarian Wittelsbachs (1583–1761), who managed to control a complex of ecclesiastical lands in the north (Cologne, Münster, Hildesheim, Paderborn, Lüttich/Lièges, and the imperial abbacies of Stavelot and Malmédy) well into the mid-eighteenth century.

Bavaria's influence on an international level culminated under the powerful rule of Duke Maximilian I (ruled 1597–1651). Educated by leading Jesuits, married first to a Lorraine princess, and then to a Habsburg princess, he soon gained confidence, and assumed political leadership at the age of twenty-one. When he replaced his father, whose religious zeal had led the state close to bankruptcy, he had already gained the support of the Estates, the councillors, and the Catholic intellectuals. Within a few years of tight personal rule, advised by a group of most able councillors, Bavaria had an efficient government, an intact bureaucracy, healthy finances, and—despite accelerating Catholic reforms—a clearly defined supremacy of state interests, a dominance of the theory of reason of state. Based upon successful internal reforms, a firm Catholic ideology, and excellent political advisers, Maximilian gained the energy for his bold foreign policy. The weakness of Emperors Rudolf II (ruled 1576–1612) and Matthias (ruled 1612–1629) allowed Maximilian to usurp leadership of the Catholic party in the Holy Roman Empire and gather its forces in the Catholic League, using it as an instrument of Bavarian interests. From then Bavaria dominated Franconia and Eastern Swabia, both of which were annexed when the Holy Roman Empire eventually collapsed. Maximilian had already annexed the imperial city of Donauwörth in 1607 and the imperial lordship of Mindelheim in 1616. When the Bohemian Estates elected the Calvinist Elector Palatine Frederick V king of Bohemia in 1619, and Catholic preponderance in the Holy Roman Empire was once again endangered, Maximilian sent an army, defeating the Protestants in the Battle of the White Mountain in 1620. Bohemia remained under Habsburg rule, but Bavarian armies occupied the Palatinate and annexed the Upper Palatinate. Maximilian

Bavaria. Covering what are today parts of Germany, Austria, and the Czech Republic, this map was published in a mid-eighteenth-century history of England. It clearly shows the confusing patchwork of many small temporal and ecclesiastical principalities that was Germany under the Holy Roman Empire. The Duchy (to 1507) and Electorate of Bavaria (1507–1806) was a coveted prize and frequent battleground during the wars of the eighteenth century. MAP COLLECTION, STERLING MEMORIAL LIBRARY, YALE UNIVERSITY

gained the Palatine electoral vote for Bavaria, and the title of prince-elector for himself in 1623.

The Thirty Years' War (1618–1648), which had been triggered by Maximilian I of Bavaria, soon turned into Europe's first world war with the intervention of Spain, France, England, the Netherlands, the pope, and Sweden, but it was as much a catastrophe for Bavaria as for other parts of Central Europe. The country was sacked twice by Swedish troops, and yet "friendly" armies like the Spanish or the imperial armies had an equally devastating effect. Crop failure, famine, epidemics, and two waves

of bubonic plague in 1634 and in 1646 probably caused a population loss of more than 50 percent. A peasant uprising in 1633 showed the level of suffering from the politically induced hardship. The prince-elector now became more cautious, and to the dismay of religious zealots like his Jesuit confessor Adam Contzen (1571–1635), Bavaria supported the Peace of Prague (1635), and invested a lot of energy in forging the Peace of Westphalia (1648), even against the advice of the papacy. Secular interests once more triumphed over religious zeal. In his political testament Bavaria's great prince-elector advised his son to keep the peace, to be a just and pious ruler, and to keep a close eye on finances *(pecunia nervus rerum)*. Prince-elector Ferdinand Maria (ruled 1651–1679) supported baroque Catholic piety, but curbed Jesuit influence, and his wife Henriette Adelaide of Savoy (1635–1676) introduced members of the Italian Theatine order as court confessors. With a successful recovery from the Thirty Years' War, their son Maximilian II Emanuel (ruled 1679–1726) developed the ambition to extend Wittelsbach rule to Spain but was defeated in the War of the Spanish Succession (1701–1714), and Bavaria was occupied by Austrian troops. A national uprising was crushed on Christmas Eve of 1705, the Bavarian peasant army being butchered after their surrender near the village of Sendling, remembered as the *Sendlinger Mordweihnacht* (Sendling Christmas Massacre). Elector Charles Albert (ruled 1726–1745) was another overambitious ruler who managed to get himself elected emperor as Charles VII in 1742, despite strong opposition from the Habsburgs, who again occupied Bavaria.

His successor Maximilian III Joseph (ruled 1745–1777) gave up this sort of ambitious foreign policy in the Peace of Aachen (Aix-la-Chapelle) in 1748, which ended the War of the Austrian Succession, and focused on domestic policy. As an enlightened absolutist monarch he managed to split the clergy and cut down clericalism, to reform education, law, and the sciences, and to introduce road construction and moor draining. Secular intellectuals were encouraged, the Bavarian Academy of Sciences was founded, and journalism and literature were sponsored. Quite deliberately this ruler avoided wars and focused on interior reforms, and his rule was remembered with joy by his subjects. Remaining childless, he was succeeded by one of the Palatine Wittelsbachs, Charles Theodore (ruled 1777–1799), another enlightened prince. His autocratic attitudes made him less appreciated by his subjects, although he opened the "English Garden" in Munich to the public. He was also childless, and his successor Maximilian IV Joseph (ruled 1799–1825), from the Wittelsbach line Zweibrücken-Birkenfeld, became the founder of modern Bavaria. Like Maximilian I he had excellent councillors at his command, in particular Maximilian, count of Montgelas (1759–1838), a former member of the Illuminati, a kind of elitist Freemason secret society that had been suppressed by Charles Theodore. In order to escape this repression, Montgelas had emigrated to Zweibrücken-Birkenfeld, only to return as a prime minister. Still a radical reformer, Montgelas secularized the monasteries and reformed education (creating obligatory state schools) and law (abolishing torture). Maximilian and Montgelas forged a coalition with France and modeled the Bavarian administration after the French pattern as a centralized state, ruthlessly integrating all the newly acquired territories in Franconia and Swabia, several principalities and prince-bishoprics, and scores of counties, imperial cities, imperial abbacies, and lordships, assembling the Bavarian state in its present shape, and raising its status to a kingdom after the collapse of the Holy Roman Empire in 1806.

See also **Austrian Succession, War of the (1740–1748); Holy Roman Empire; Munich; Spanish Succession, War of the (1701–1714); Thirty Years' War (1618–1648); Westphalia, Peace of (1648); Wittelsbach Dynasty (Bavaria).**

BIBLIOGRAPHY

Behringer, Wolfgang. *Witchcraft Persecutions in Bavaria: Popular Magic, Religious Zealotry and Reason of State in Early Modern Europe.* Cambridge, U.K., and New York, 1997.

Prinz, Friedrich. *Die Geschichte Bayerns.* Munich, 1997.

Riezler, Sigmund. *Geschichte Baierns.* 8 vols. Munich, 1878–1914.

Spindler, Max, ed. *Handbuch der bayerischen Geschichte.* 4 vols. Munich, 1967–.

WOLFGANG BEHRINGER

BAXTER, RICHARD

BAXTER, RICHARD (1615–1691), English Protestant clergyman and writer. Richard Baxter was at the heart of seventeenth-century Puritanism despite not having held a significant office. Born near Shrewsbury, in Shropshire, England, Baxter was brought up to fear sin and love the Bible. Such early influences led him to pursue a clerical career, although he did not attend university. In 1638 he was ordained a deacon in the Church of England; it is unlikely that he ever received ordination to the full priesthood. In 1641 Baxter was appointed preacher at Kidderminster in Worcestershire. On the outbreak of the English Civil War

(1642–1649) he fled to Coventry, but he became a chaplain in the parliamentary army in 1645. Later he returned to Kidderminster and engaged in evangelical preaching and personal "conference" with his parishioners. By devoting Monday and Tuesday of each week to this counseling, he was able to erect a voluntary "discipline," but only six hundred of eighteen hundred potential communicants agreed to submit to examination before admission to the sacrament of the Lord's Supper. There was no tradition in the Church of England of giving an account to the minister of one's belief and behavior before being allowed to receive the sacrament, and many resented this Puritan intrusion into their spiritual lives.

In 1652 Baxter formed the Worcestershire Association of Ministers to encourage catechizing and discipline, and ministers in several other counties followed suit. These initiatives brought together clergy of different denominations and were an effective response to the challenge of sects such as the Quakers. In the winter of 1654–1655, Baxter met Archbishop James Ussher and they agreed (allegedly within thirty minutes) on a modified form of episcopacy that ought to be acceptable to both Presbyterians and Episcopalians. Baxter's prominence in moderate Puritan circles guaranteed that his views would be sought at the Restoration. He became a royal chaplain and prepared position papers for the Presbyterians, helping to argue their case at the Savoy Conference (1661) where the Episcopalians and Presbyterians failed to agree on revisions to the Prayer Book. Meanwhile the benefice of Kidderminster had been successfully reclaimed by its previous incumbent and, with the 1662 Act of Uniformity looming, Baxter retired from public preaching. Supported by his pious, resourceful, and wealthy wife Margaret, Baxter spent the 1660s in Acton outside London and attended the parish church while also preaching to his own circle. Under the royal indulgence of 1672, he began to preach publicly in London but suffered mounting persecution until in 1685 he was imprisoned for nearly two years. Old and frail, Baxter spent his last years indefatigably preaching and writing until his death on 8 December 1691.

Baxter's significance stems from three sources: his acknowledged leadership of the moderate wing of dissent; his voluminous and diverse writings, which numbered perhaps 111 publications; and his influence with respect to the way subsequent generations viewed the history and religion of seventeenth-century England. This last was a result of his controversial and practical works and even more importantly of *Reliquiae Baxterianae* (1696), his autobiography edited by Matthew Sylvester, which was in turn comprehensively rewritten by the English clergyman Edmund Calamy as *An Abridgement of Mr. Baxter's History of His Life and Times* (1702). Baxter's extensive correspondence, which has been cataloged, is housed at Dr. Williams's Library, London. Thus we know more about Baxter the man than we do about most individuals of his era. Prickly, awkward, a hypochondriac, and deficient in tact, humor, and a sense of proportion, Baxter could also genuinely claim to have labored for forty-five years in the cause of mutual understanding and the promotion of basic Christian piety. His sincere ecumenism followed from his conviction that "practical" religion and pastoral work were at the heart of the Protestant ministry. His work at Kidderminster and a stream of books such as *The Saints' Everlasting Rest* (1649), *The Reformed Pastor* (1656), and *The Christian Directory* (1673) manifest this belief, as does his repudiation of denominational labels in favor of such badges as "a mere Christian."

Baxter's pastoral focus had theological implications. He feared the antinomianism of the sects and the strict Calvinists on one hand and the superstition of "popery" on the other: his own theology could be described as a Puritan Arminianism. On several occasions he changed his view of the role of bishops and secular rulers in fostering godliness. Although he could accept a "reduced" episcopacy that would not circumscribe the pastoral efforts of the local minister, he soon turned against the lordly prelates who returned with the Church of England in 1662. He suspected that church of aiming at a French-style Catholicism under the authority of the monarchy. Although deeply worried by the proclivities of Charles II and James II, Baxter's faith in "Christian magistracy" as a vehicle for religious reformation was strong under the Protectorate (1653–1659) and once again after the Glorious Revolution (1688–1689) under William III. Baxter exemplifies some of the deepest impulses of seventeenth-century nonsectarian Puritanism.

See also **Church of England; Clergy: Protestant Clergy; Dissenters, English; English Civil War and Interregnum; English Civil War Radicalism; Puritanism.**

BIBLIOGRAPHY

Primary Sources

Baxter, Richard. *The Autobiography of Richard Baxter.* Abridged by J. M. Lloyd Thomas. Edited by N. H. Keeble. London and Totowa, N.J., 1974. Parts of the text of *Reliquiae Baxterianae.*

Keeble, N. H., and Geoffrey F. Nuttall. *Calendar of the Correspondence of Richard Baxter.* Two volumes. Oxford and New York, 1991.

Secondary Sources

Lamont, William. *Puritanism and Historical Controversy.* London, 1996. Sets Baxter against two of his contemporaries in a thought-provoking analysis.

Nuttall, Geoffrey F. *Richard Baxter.* London, 1965. The best biography.

JOHN SPURR

BAYLE, PIERRE (1647–1706), French philosopher and critic. Pierre Bayle counts among the most influential and yet most enigmatic thinkers in history. Richard Popkin has described him as the key intellectual figure at the turn of the eighteenth century, and he has come to be known as the "Arsenal of the Enlightenment," the source of its ideas on toleration, secularism, and a host of other issues. Despite the relative clarity of Bayle's effect on his immediate successors, there is very little agreement on what Bayle himself might actually have believed. He is thus in the curious position of having an influence that he himself might not have fully recognized or intended.

Although he was to become one of the brightest luminaries of French culture, Bayle was born and raised far from its Parisian epicenter, in the foothills of the Pyrenees, and spent almost the whole of his adult life outside France, as a refugee. Conversion to Catholicism under his Jesuit schoolmasters shocked his staunchly Protestant family, but he reconverted upon completion of his studies. Thus regarded by the overwhelming Catholic majority as not just a heretic but a relapsed heretic, Bayle faced a nearly impossible life, and he fled France for Switzerland. Then, after a brief period spent clandestinely in Paris and at the Protestant Academy at Sedan, he fled again, not long before the revocation of the Edict of Nantes, settling permanently in Rotterdam amid the relative freedom of the Netherlands. Through this early period he eked out an existence from menial teaching jobs, which, however necessary, kept him from the scholarly life that was his only interest (he was later to reject otherwise attractive offers of marriage and a university appointment as inconsistent with that life). The commercial success of his publications finally made total devotion to scholarship possible.

Bayle's influence should not be surprising since he was both enormously prolific and widely read. Indeed, his *Historical and Critical Dictionary* was the most popular work of the eighteenth century. Shelf-counts of private libraries from the period show this work appearing far more frequently than anything from distant competitors such as Voltaire, Rousseau, Newton, or Locke. Accounting for its undeniable popularity, or even describing the nature of this work, is not easy. Its only principle of organization is the alphabetical order of its entries. Bayle wrote of people of every sort—philosophers, kings, clowns, some famous, many obscure, often real, of course, but sometimes from myth—and not just people, but rivers, islands, towns, everything under the sun, it would seem. And he did so in a way that furthers the uniqueness of the work. Almost all of his interesting writing occurs not in the actual text of the entries but in the double columns of smaller-print footnotes that occupy most, and sometimes all, of the pages. These notes often contain the utterly unrelated digressions into philosophy, church history, religious polemic, literary criticism, pornography, curious trivia, and other areas that so obviously delighted Bayle. Clearly, this was not a work to be read from cover to cover over its several in-folio volumes but to be dipped into for unconnected episodes of fascinating yet instructive entertainment. No wonder that it had a broad readership from Leibniz, Hume, Voltaire, and Jefferson to many lesser lights.

The *Dictionary* is a very long work that Bayle seemed prepared to expand indefinitely in further editions. But it represents less than half of his total output. The rest of his works are devoted almost entirely to religious polemic in defense of Protestantism's attempted reform of Christianity against Catholicism's Counter-Reformation and in defense of his version of Calvinist Protestantism against his more conservative and more liberal coreligionists. A key to this work is Bayle's advocacy of toleration based on the inviolability of conscience even when objectively it is in error. Bayle discusses an actual case that had taken place in the next town from his birthplace; the wife of Martin Guerre is beyond blame and punishment in yielding to an impostor husband so long as she genuinely believes him to be her husband. What is true of her, moreover, is true *mutatis mutandis* of the religious heretic whose belief, though mistaken, is sincere. In neither case should conscience be forced.

In the history of philosophy, Bayle is typically regarded as a skeptic. But if he was a skeptic, he was not of the Pyrrhonian sort that advocates suspension of belief, for Bayle in his work expressed more beliefs than perhaps anyone in history. In addition, the texts in which he sets out skeptical arguments are very few in number (most notably in the *Dictionary* article on Pyrrho) and his attitude toward them is at best ambiguous. Nor does he seem to have been even a religious skeptic, however much his arguments on a number of topics might point in the direction of atheism. If anything, he practiced academic skepticism, whose defining feature is the virtue of intellectual integrity—of respecting perceived truth not only in one's own voice but also in reporting the views of others. Such a virtue might partially explain why it is that so many different and competing views come across on Bayle's work, which is otherwise so enigmatic.

See also **Philosophes; Skepticism: Academic and Pyrrhonian.**

BIBLIOGRAPHY

Primary Sources

Bayle, Pierre. *The Dictionary Historical and Critical.* New York, 1984. Translated by Pierre Desmaizeaux. London, 1734–1747. 5 vols. A photo-offset edition of a colorful, but complete and accurate, translation of *Dictionnaire historique et critique* (Rotterdam, 2nd ed., 1702; 1st ed, 1697).

———. *Œuvres diverses.* Hildesheim, 1964–1968. A photo-offset edition of the same title (The Hague, 1st ed., 1727–1731; 2nd ed., 1737). Almost the whole of Bayle's work beyond the Dictionary, to which several volumes are being added.

Pierre Bayle. Portrait from the *Dictionnaire historique et critique*, 1765. ©ARCHIVO ICONOGRAFICO, S.A./CORBIS

Secondary Sources

Labrousse, Elizabeth. *Bayle.* Oxford, 1983. An impeccable, accessible introduction and summary.

———. *Pierre Bayle.* Vol.1, *Du pays de Foix á la cité d'Erasme.* Vol.2, *Hétéroxie et rigorisme.* The Hague, 1963–1964. The standard reference work, by the acknowledged doyenne of Bayle scholarship. The first volume is a biography; the second, an analysis of Bayle's thought.

THOMAS M. LENNON

FRANCIS BEAUMONT (1584/5–1616) and **JOHN FLETCHER** (1579–1625), the most famous collaboration in early modern English drama. Both men came from established families with strong writing traditions. Beaumont was born at Grace-Dieu, Leicestershire, the son of Francis Beaumont, a judge, and the brother of the poet John Beaumont. Fletcher was born on 20 December 1579, the son of Richard Fletcher, later bishop of London. Richard's brother, Giles Fletcher, was a poet and diplomat, and father of the "Spenserian" poets Giles, Jr., and Phineas. Both Beaumont and Fletcher attended university: Beaumont entered Broadgates Hall, Oxford, in 1597, before proceeding to the Inner Temple in 1600; Fletcher probably entered Benet College (now Corpus Christi), his father's old college, in 1591.

The collaboration between the two writers is first traced to *The Woman Hater*, written in 1606 for the Children of Paul's (a children's acting troupe). Beaumont had probably already written the erotic narrative poem *Salmacis and Hermaphroditus*, published in 1602. The pair moved from the Children of Paul's to the Children of the Queen's Revels, who first performed *Cupid's Revenge* (1607–1608), *The Coxcomb* (1608–1610), and *The Scornful Lady* (1610). Separately, Beaumont and Fletcher wrote *The Knight of the Burning Pestle* (1607) and *The Faithful Shepherdess* (1608), respectively, for the same company; both plays seem originally to have failed in performance, perhaps because they were too avant-garde for the Blackfriars audience. The success of their collaborative plays, particularly *Cupid's Revenge*, seems to have caught the attention of the King's Men, for whom Beaumont and Fletcher wrote a series of highly successful collaborative plays: *Philaster* (or *Love Lies a'Bleeding*; c. 1609), *The Maid's Tragedy* (c. 1610), and *A King and No King* (1611). Fletcher alone wrote the tragedies *Bonduca* (c. 1609–1614) and *Valentinian* (c. 1610), and the comedy *The Woman's Prize* (or *The Tamer Tamed*; c. 1611), a mock-sequel to Shakespeare's *Taming of the Shrew*.

In 1613 Beaumont married Ursula Isley and seems to have retired from the theater; his last surviving dramatic work is *The Masque of Gray's Inn and the Inner Temple* (Gray's Inn and Inner Temple are two of the four Inns of Court), written for the wedding of James I's daughter Elizabeth in February 1613. It is possible that Beaumont's health was already declining when he retired; he died on 6 March 1616 and was buried in Westminster Abbey. Fletcher, who seems to have preferred writing in collaboration, worked with Shakespeare on three plays for the King's Men in 1612–1613: *Henry VIII*, *The Two Noble Kinsmen*, and the lost *Cardenio*. He also wrote with Nathan Field, firstly for the Lady Elizabeth's Men, for whom Field was a leading actor (*The Honest Man's Fortune* [1613],

Four Plays in One [c. 1614]), and later for the King's Men, for whom Field acted from 1616 (*The Knight of Malta* [1616–1618] and *The Queen of Corinth* [1617]). This period also saw the first performances of Fletcher's *Wit without Money* (1614), *The Chances* (c. 1617), and *Women Pleased* (c. 1618). After Field's death in 1619, Fletcher formed a settled collaboration with Philip Massinger. Their best-known plays include *Sir John Van Olden Barnavelt* (1619), *The Custom of the Country* (c. 1619), and *The Sea Voyage* (1622). He also continued to write plays alone, including *The Humourous Lieutenant* (c. 1619), *The Island Princess* (1621), *The Wild Goose Chase* (1621), and *The Pilgrim* (c. 1621). Fletcher died of plague on 29 August 1625, and was buried at St. Mary Overy, Southwark.

The fame of the Beaumont and Fletcher collaboration is due in part to the publication in 1647 of a lavish folio edition of *Comedies and Tragedies Written by Francis Beaumont and John Fletcher Gentlemen*, in which the plays were accompanied by a series of dedicatory verses written by admirers of the two playwrights, many of which eulogized them as a perfect synthesis. George Lisle, for instance, wrote: "your fancies are so wov'n and knit, / 'Twas Francis Fletcher, or John Beaumont writ." Continuing the tradition, John Aubrey wrote in *Brief Lives*: "They lived together on the Banke side, not far from the Play-house, both batchelors; lay together . . . had one wench in the house between them, which they did so admire; the same clothes and cloake, &c., between them." However, the posthumous union between Beaumont and Fletcher was occasionally contested, and the contribution of Massinger recognized. Aston Cockayne protested that Beaumont would have "frown'd and blush'd" to see his name attached to plays in which he had no claim, and notes that it is Massinger, not Beaumont, who was buried in Fletcher's grave: "So whom on earth nothing did part, beneath / Here (in their Fames) they lie, in spight of death."

The plays of the "Beaumont and Fletcher" canon remained popular throughout the seventeenth century, and Fletcher was regarded as one of the greatest dramatists of the age. While tragicomedies such as *Philaster* and *A King and No King* had a great impact on early seventeenth-century drama, the comedies, particularly those written with Massinger, had a shaping influence on the development of the Restoration theater.

See also **Drama: English; English Literature and Language; Renaissance; Shakespeare, William.**

BIBLIOGRAPHY

Primary Source

Bowers, Fredson, ed. *The Dramatic Works in the Beaumont and Fletcher Canon.* 10 vols. Cambridge, U.K., 1966–1996.

Secondary Sources

Bliss, Lee. *Francis Beaumont.* Boston, 1987.

Clark, Sandra. *The Plays of Beaumont and Fletcher: Sexual Themes and Dramatic Representation.* London, 1994.

Finkelpearl, Philip. *Court and Country Politics in the Plays of Beaumont and Fletcher.* Princeton, 1990.

Kelliher, Hilton. "Francis Beaumont and Nathan Field: New Records of Their Early Years." *English Manuscript Studies 1100–1700,* 8 (2000): 1–42.

McMullan, Gordon. *The Politics of Unease in the Plays of John Fletcher.* Amherst, Mass., 1994.

Squier, C. L. *John Fletcher.* Boston, 1986.

Taunton, Nina. "Biography, a University Education, and Playwrighting: Fletcher and Marlowe." *Research Opportunities in Renaissance Drama* 33 (1994): 63–97.

LUCY MUNRO

BECCARIA, CESARE BONESANA, MARQUIS OF

(1738–1794), Italian economist and proponent of judicial reform. Cesare Beccaria was the author of the most famous Italian work of the Enlightenment, *On Crimes and Punishments* (1764). He was born into a noble family of the state of Milan, which was part of the Austrian Habsburg empire, and was schooled by the Jesuits in Parma. After receiving his law degree from the University of Pavia in 1758, he returned to live in Milan. Beccaria's twenties were the most important decade in his intellectual and emotional life. He was temperamentally inclined to lethargy and anxiety, but when young could also be galvanized by inspiration, and expressed his feelings in the language of Rousseau. He married his first wife in 1761, against strong resistance from his family, and wrote *On Crimes and Punishments* in 1763, when he was twenty-five. His friendships with Pietro Verri (1728–1797) and other ardent young Milanese reformers did not

however, outlast the 1760s, for in their eyes he seemed to lose all of his vitality and to settle into an arid and routine private life, which nevertheless allowed him to hold his melancholy at bay.

Beccaria assumed a prestigious public lectureship in the Scuola Palatine on "cameral sciences" (political economy) in 1768. He mastered the literature of the nascent science of economics, and his teaching was impregnated with the Enlightenment ideal of building a new science of humanity, understanding the evolution of human society, and improving the lives of entire populations. In 1771 Beccaria requested and was granted membership in a government council that dealt with economic affairs. Through a succession of such appointments he rose to become a senior member of the administration of the state of Milan, with responsibilities at various times for agriculture, industry, trade, civil and criminal justice, statistics, and public order.

Beccaria himself dated his discovery of the Enlightenment to 1761, when he began to read the works of the French and Scottish philosophes and discuss them with a circle of young friends led by Pietro Verri. In all the provinces of the Austrian empire, including Milan, absolutist reforms emanating from Vienna continued to encounter entrenched resistance from noble and ecclesiastical corporations and from the juridical culture of the *ancien régime.* Verri, Beccaria, and their cohort wished to modernize and rationalize the economy and the legal system in line with Enlightenment secular morality, and they supported governmental reform. *On Crimes and Punishments* was first published in 1764, with subsequent editions following rapidly. Beccaria prepared the edition now regarded as definitive in 1766. The work became known in France through the translation of André Morellet (1727–1819), who freely altered the Italian text (Beccaria for some reason never protested against this), and then it spread throughout Europe. It was attacked by conservatives everywhere and was defended by adherents of the Enlightenment. Voltaire composed a commentary on it. In October 1766 Verri and Beccaria journeyed to Paris to bask in the admiration of the philosophes there, but Beccaria quickly became despondent and fled back to Milan.

Cesare Beccaria. Undated portrait engraving. ©Bettmann/Corbis

On Crimes and Punishments combines elements from social contract theory with utilitarian positions. It touches on many aspects of law and justice in a rapid, impassioned style, completely abjuring legal technicalities. Criminal law ought to state clearly what is forbidden and what the penalties are and ought to be applied uniformly to all, with no room for discretionary interpretation by jurists or magistrates or gracious pardon from the sovereign. The penalties themselves should be carefully proportioned to the corresponding crimes and calibrated to deliver the minimum of punishment necessary. Beccaria sought in all cases to minimize or abolish the use of violence and the infliction of pain. He argued against the use of torture in the gathering of evidence, highlighting its absurdity, and against the death penalty, emphasizing its failure to deter. The thrust of the work was to guarantee the individual citizen against arbitrariness, delay, secrecy, and useless and excessive violence, in the codification of the law and the application of penal sanctions. Overall the book is a sustained attack on the juridical culture of the *ancien régime* as well as a sketch of the principles on which it ought to be reformed so as to produce "the greatest happiness shared among the greatest number."

Philosophers perhaps foremost among them Jeremy Bentham (1748–1832), statesmen including Thomas Jefferson (1743–1826), and sovereigns including Joseph II (1741–1790; ruled 1765–1790) of Austria and Catherine II of Russia (1729–1796; ruled 1762–1796), were influenced by *On Crimes and Punishments*. Judicial torture and the death penalty were abolished in a number of European states in a climate of public opinion that had been changed forever by Beccaria's book.

See also **Crime and Punishment; Enlightenment; Law.**

BIBLIOGRAPHY

Primary Sources

Beccaria, Cesare. *Edizione nazionale delle Opere di Cesare Beccaria.* Milan, 1984–. Luigi Firpo, founding editor. Vol. 1, *Dei delitti e delle pene* (1984), edited by Gianni Francioni with a detailed study of the early editions by Luigi Firpo, is the edition of reference for all aspects of the text of this work. Other volumes include Beccaria's philosophical and literary works, correspondence, and official government papers.

———. *On Crimes and Punishments and Other Writings.* Edited by Richard Bellamy. Translated by Richard Davies with Virginia Cox and Richard Bellamy. Cambridge, U.K., and New York, 1995. With a valuable introduction by the editor placing Beccaria in the history of political thought and with further bibliography.

Secondary Sources

Venturi, Franco. "Beccaria, Cesare." In *Dizionario Biografico degli Italiani.* Vol. 7, pp. 458–469. Rome, 1965. An article-length monograph by the doyen of modern Beccaria scholars.

———. *Italy and the Enlightenment: Studies in a Cosmopolitan Century.* Edited by Stuart Woolf. Translated by Susan Corsi. London, 1972. See chapter 6, "Cesare Beccaria and Legal Reform."

WILLIAM McCUAIG

BEGGARS. *See* **Vagrants and Beggars.**

BEHN, APHRA (c. 1640–1689), English writer. Aphra Behn was the first female writer to produce a substantial dramatic canon and was also an innovator in prose fiction, and a highly accomplished poet. The details of her early life are unclear. Recent scholarship has concluded that she was probably baptized at Harbledown, near Canterbury, Kent, on 14 December 1640, the daughter of Bartholomew Johnson, a barber, and Elizabeth (née Denham). Her mother seems to have been employed as wet nurse to Sir Thomas Culpepper, who may have provided Behn with an introduction to the nobility and an entry into royalist circles.

Behn indicates in several of her works that she spent time in Surinam during her youth or early adulthood. Although posthumous accounts of her life claim that her father was appointed governor there, it seems more likely that she made her own way, perhaps in service or as a spy or agent. Returning to England around 1664, Behn married a man later described as "a merchant of Dutch extraction." The marriage seems to have been brief, and Behn's shadowy husband may have died in the savage outbreak of plague that took hold of London in 1665–1666.

A clearer picture of her career emerges only in the mid-1660s. In August 1666 Behn was sent to Antwerp on a spying mission, using the code name "Astrea." She seems to have been recommended by Sir Thomas Killigrew, dramatist, theater manager, and sometime politician, perhaps indicating that she already had some involvement in the literary sphere. Whatever its political effects, the trip was financially disabling for Behn, and in 1668 she was forced to appeal directly to Killigrew and Charles II to preserve her from destitution.

On 20 September 1670 her first play, *The Forced Marriage*, was performed by the Duke of York's Company at Lincoln's Inn Fields, London. A total of nineteen plays have been attributed to Behn, the most famous of which include *The Rover; or, the Banished Cavaliers: Parts I and II* (1677, 1680), *The Feigned Courtesans; or, A Night's Intrigue* (1679), *The City Heiress* (1682), *The Lucky Chance; or, An Alderman's Bargain* (1686), and *The Emperor of the Moon* (1687). Although she experimented with tragicomedy and, in *Abdelazer; or the Moor's Revenge* (1676), with tragedy, Behn's characteristic mode was comedic. She frequently claimed an equal status as a writer with her male contemporaries. In a statement appended to *The Lucky Chance* she wrote: "had the Plays I have writ come forth under any Mans Name, and never known to be mine; I appeal to all unbyast Judges of Sense, if they had not said that Person had made as many good Comedies, as any one Man that has writ in our Age; but a Devil on't the Woman damns the Poet." Rather than trying to claim a separate status as a female poet, however, Behn demanded that the "Masculine Part the Poet in me" be taken seriously.

Although she made her living from plays and nondramatic prose, like many writers she seems to have viewed poetry as the more prestigious form. Behn wrote in a variety of genres, many of them generally associated with male poets: erotic poetry, social poetry, and outspoken political verse. She was a staunch royalist, writing in "Pindaric on the Coronation of James II" of the need for her muse to celebrate "the *Royal* HERO . . . Thy *Godlike Patron*, and thy *Godlike King*." Her poems and plays constantly reworked contemporary political issues and the recent past, notably *Sir Patient Fancy* (1678) and *The Roundheads: or, The Good Old Cause* (1681), both staged at times of great political ferment.

Her best-known nondramatic works are *Love-Letters Between a Noble-Man and his Sister* (1684) and *Oroonoko, or the History of the Royal Slave* (1688). The former is a risqué and edgy experiment with the epistolary form, probably based on the affair between Lady Henrietta Berkeley and her brother-in-law Forde, Lord Grey of Werke. The latter is an account of the life and death of the noble African prince Oroonoko, taken to work as a slave in Surinam.

Although her literary output remained prodigious, Behn's health failed in the late 1680s; in an elegy to the poet Edmund Waller she presented herself as one "who by Toils of Sickness, am become / Almost as near as thou art to a Tomb." She died on 16 April 1689, and was buried in Westminster Abbey, a tribute that would probably have pleased her. "I am not content to write for a Third day only," she writes in *The Lucky Chance*, "I value Fame as much as if I had been born a *Hero*."

See also **Drama: English; English Literature and Language.**

BIBLIOGRAPHY

Primary Source

Behn, Aphra. *The Works of Aphra Behn.* Edited by Janet Todd. 7 vols. London, 1992–1996.

Secondary Sources

Duffy, Maureen. *The Passionate Shepherdess: Aphra Behn 1640–1689.* London, 1977.

Goreau, Angeline. *Reconstructing Aphra: A Social Biography of Aphra Behn.* Oxford, 1980.

Todd, Janet. *The Secret Life of Aphra Behn.* London, 1996.

Todd, Janet, ed. *Aphra Behn Studies.* Cambridge, U.K., and New York, 1996.

Wiseman, S. J. *Aphra Behn.* Plymouth, U.K., 1996.

LUCY MUNRO

BELARUS. From the decline of Kievan Rus' to the mid-fourteenth century, the Belarusian principalities were gradually taken over by Lithuanian princes. Initially, the Belarusian elites, who for a long time had shared with their Ukrainian counterparts a common Ruthenian identity, were an influential political and cultural force within the Grand Duchy of Lithuania. Lithuanian princes often converted to Orthodoxy, accepted the Ruthenian language as the official language of their realm, and allowed many norms of the Rus' Law to function in their state. The Union of Lublin (1569) between the Kingdom of Poland and the Grand Duchy of Lithuania, which created a Polish-Lithuanian Commonwealth, left the Belarusian territories within the borders of a semiautonomous Lithuania. It also brought Polish political and cultural influences into the region and opened it to Jewish emigration.

The advent of the Reformation, and especially the struggles over the church union adopted at the Brest Council of 1596 between Roman Catholic and Orthodox Christianity, spearheaded Ruthenian religious and cultural revival in the region. The new intellectual challenges also helped Belarusian elites develop a sense of distinct identity vis-à-vis their Polish and Lithuanian counterparts. The outbreak of the Russian-Polish war in 1654 turned Belarus into a battleground between the Muscovite, Polish-Lithuanian, and Ukrainian Cossack armies. According to the Russian-Polish treaties of 1667 and 1686, the commonwealth maintained its control over all of Belarusian territories except for the Smolensk region, which passed over to Muscovite jurisdiction. In the eighteenth century, growing Polish cultural influences as well as the advance of Roman Catholicism and the Uniate Church helped to widen cultural differences between the inhabitants of Belarus and Russia. The partitions of Poland in 1772–1795 resulted in the incorporation of all Belarusian territories into the Russian Empire.

See also **Andrusovo, Truce of; Lithuania, Grand Duchy of, to 1569; Lithuanian Literature and Language; Poland-Lithuania, Commonwealth of, 1569–1795; Poland to 1569; Ukraine.**

BIBLIOGRAPHY

Gudziak, Borys A. *Crisis and Reform: The Kyivan Metropolitanate, the Patriarchate of Constantinople, and the Genesis of the Union of Brest.* Cambridge, Mass., 1998.

Halecki, Oskar. *From Florence to Brest (1439–1596).* 2nd ed. Hamden, Conn., 1968.

Kaminski, Andrzej Sulima. *Republic vs. Autocracy: Poland-Lithuania and Russia, 1686–1697.* Cambridge, Mass., 1993.

Pelenski, Jaroslaw. *The Contest for the Legacy of Kievan Rus'.* Boulder, Colo., and New York, 1998.

Stone, Daniel. *The Polish-Lithuanian State, 1386–1795.* Seattle, 2001.

Zaprudnik, Jan. *Belarus: At a Crossroads in History.* Boulder, Colo., 1993.

SERHII PLOKHY

BELLARMINE, ROBERT (1542–1621), Jesuit theologian, spiritual writer, cardinal, and archbishop. Robert (Roberto Francesco Romolo) Bellarmine was born on 4 October 1542 in Montepulciano, Tuscany, to Vincenzo Bellarmine and Cintia Cervini. Attending the local Jesuit college, he proved himself to be an excellent student. During his studies, Bellarmine contemplated entering the Society of Jesus. Despite his father's initial opposition, he entered the novitiate at Rome in 1560. Upon the completion of his formation (immersion in the spirituality of the order) and his initial studies in philosophy, Bellarmine was sent in 1563 to the Jesuit colleges of Florence and Mondovì to teach classics. In 1567, he went to Padua to begin his theological studies. Completing his studies in Louvain, Bellarmine was ordained a priest in 1570.

In 1570, the Jesuits opened their own theological college at Louvain, where Bellarmine became its first Jesuit professor. Drawn into the religious controversies of the day, Bellarmine devoted his time to the study of Scripture, church history, and patristics. Utilizing the teachings of the church defined at the Council of Trent, Bellarmine's lectures were devoted to a defense of church doctrine against Luther and Calvin, whose theology he had studied.

Everard Mercurian, superior general of the Society of Jesus, established a professorship in controversial theology in 1576 at the Collegio Romano, to which he appointed Bellarmine. Pope Gregory XIII also requested that Bellarmine teach theology to the English and German missionary students at the college. These lectures became the foundation of his greatest work, *Disputationes de controversiis Christianae fidei huius temporis haereticos* (known as the *Controversies*), a three-volume synthesis of Catholic theology that appeared in 1586, 1588, and 1593. The *Controversies* was the most significant refutation of the theology of the reformers during the Reformation, and long remained Catholicism's most complete response to the issues raised by Protestantism. The *Controversies* avoids a polemical approach, presenting a balanced criticism of reform theology, pointing out both its strengths and its weaknesses.

At the end of 1589, Sixtus V named Bellarmine as theological advisor to Cardinal Enrico Gaetani, the pope's legate examining the conflict in the French church between those who supported the Huguenot king, Henry IV, and those who opposed his reign. This would be the first of several church-state disputes with which he would become involved.

Upon his return to Rome in 1590, Bellarmine resumed his responsibility as spiritual director within the Collegio Romano. In 1592, he was named rector of the college and was appointed to be a member of the commission established to draft a final version of the *Ratio Studiorum,* the outline of the curriculum for Jesuit schools. In 1594, Bellarmine was named provincial of the Jesuit province of Naples. He returned to Rome in 1597 as theological advisor to Pope Clement VIII, and published two catechisms, one designed for children and one designed for teachers.

Robert Bellarmine. LIBRARY OF CONGRESS

Clement VIII entrusted Bellarmine with the important task of revising the official text of the Latin Vulgate Bible begun by Pope Sixtus V. Bellarmine corrected Sixtus V's text, which became known as the Sixto-Clementine Vulgate (1592), and remained the official Latin Bible of the Catholic Church until the twentieth century.

The pope elevated Bellarmine to the rank of cardinal on 3 March 1599, appointing him to various Roman Congregations and commissions. On 21 April 1602 Clement VIII appointed him archbishop of Capua. Leaving Rome to take up residence in his diocese, Bellarmine took his duties as bishop seriously, preaching every Sunday, visiting the parishes, renewing the spiritual life of the religious communities, and providing for the poor.

Bellarmine was called back to Rome by Pope Paul V in 1605 to serve on various congregations. The most important of these was the Holy Office, which would lead to his involvement in the Galileo case in 1615. Both Galileo and Bellarmine agreed that there was no conflict between Scripture and scientific findings. However, Bellarmine insisted on the literal interpretation of biblical passages. In 1616 he was chosen to deliver personally to Galileo the Holy Office's admonition forbidding him from teaching the heliocentric theory (that the earth circles the sun).

During his final years, Bellarmine wrote largely devotional treatises aimed at ordinary Christians that reflected his own personal prayer and piety, as well as the spirituality of the Catholic Reformation. The most popular of his ascetical treatises were *De Ascensione Mentis in Deum* (1614; The mind's ascent to God) and *De Arte Bene Moriendi* (1619; The art of dying well).

Robert Bellarmine died on 17 September 1621 in Rome. His life unfolded in the midst of the church's resolve to reform itself and to combat Protestantism. As the author of *The Controversies* and as a member of the Inquisition, he contributed to the fight against heresy. As a diligent reforming bishop and author of spiritual works, he contributed to the renewal of the church's life. In 1930 he was canonized by Pius XI and in the following year declared a Doctor of the Church, a title given to certain canonized ecclesiastical writers on account of the great advantage the church has gained from their doctrine.

See also **Galileo Galilei; Inquisition, Roman; Jesuits; Reformation, Catholic.**

BIBLIOGRAPHY

Primary Sources

Bellarmine, Robert. *Spiritual Writings.* Translated and edited by John Patrick Donnelly and Roland J. Teske. New York, 1989. Includes *The Mind's Ascent to God by the Ladder of Created Things* and *The Art of Dying Well,* with introductions.

Secondary Sources

Blackwell, Richard J. *Galileo, Bellarmine, and the Bible.* Notre Dame, Ind., 1991. Examines Bellarmine's involvement in the early phases of the Galileo affair, including documents.

Brodrick, James. *The Life and Work of Blessed Robert Francis Cardinal Bellarmine, S.J., 1542–1621.* 2 vols. New York, 1928. The best biography of Bellarmine; reprints Bellarmine's autobiography.

———. *Robert Bellarmine: Saint and Scholar.* London, 1961. Revised and condensed version of the earlier two-volume study.

Godman, Peter. *The Saint as Censor: Robert Bellarmine Between Inquisition and Index.* Leiden and Boston, 2000.

Kuntz, Paul G. "The Hierarchical Vision of St. Roberto Bellarmino." In *Jacob's Ladder and the Tree of Life: Concepts of Hierarchy and the Great Chain of Being.* Edited by Marion Leathers Kuntz and Paul Grimley Kuntz, pp. 111–130. New York, 1987.

Riedl, John O. "Bellarmine and the Dignity of Man." In *Jesuit Thinkers of the Renaissance.* Edited by Gerard Smith, pp. 193–226, 242–254. Milwaukee, 1939.

FRANCESCO C. CESAREO

BENEDICT XIV (POPE) (1675–1758; reigned 1740–1758), Italian pope. Born in Bologna as Prospero Lambertini into a patrician family of modest means on 31 March 1675, he earned a doctorate in theology and a double doctorate in canon and civil law in 1694. Lambertini then became a curial official, rising to important positions in the Congregation of the Council and Congregation of Rites. He was appointed archbishop of Ancona in 1727, made cardinal in 1728, and archbishop of Bologna in 1731. Lambertini was probably the most prolific papal scholar since the Middle Ages. His most enduring work was a four-volume study of the history of canonization (1734–1738), which proposed new procedures followed until the late twentieth century. He also wrote a history of episcopal synods, supporting their use (1748), and works in liturgy and canon law. The complete edition of his works appeared in twelve folio volumes between 1747 and 1751.

When Clement XII died on 6 February 1740, Lambertini was not considered a candidate for pope. But after six months of stalemate and negotiations, he was elected on the 255th ballot on 17 August 1740. Benedict XIV pursued policies of conciliation, moderation, and openness to contemporary intellectual trends. But he had to contend with war and Catholic monarchs determined to rule the church in their lands. Benedict XIV inherited state-church disputes with most of the Catholic monarchies of Europe; they demanded control over church appointments, that church properties be taxed, and that clergymen be subject to civil jurisdiction. Benedict concluded new concordats with Piedmont-Savoy (1741), the Kingdom of Naples (1741), Portugal (1745), Spain (1753), and Austria (1757). Because he was negotiating from weakness, he had to make substantial concessions. In the most extreme case, he gave the Spanish crown the right of appointment to twelve thousand church positions in Spain, leaving the papacy with the right to appoint only fifty-two minor offices. Benedict was forced to concede much in order to retain Spain's support at a time when Austrian armies were ravaging Italy and the papal state during the War of the Austrian Succession (1740–1748). While he conceded rights of patronage, he probably increased the moral authority of papacy and earned goodwill.

Benedict also had to deal with Frederick II, king of Prussia and a nominal Protestant. Frederick annexed Catholic Silesia in 1741 and began to impose civil legislation on Silesia's Catholics in marriage laws, benefices, and jurisdiction. After lengthy negotiations, the pope and Frederick reached an uneasy accommodation in 1748, even though Frederick did not completely keep his word. Still, European public opinion praised Benedict for his willingness to seek accommodation with a Protestant and absolutist ruler. In internal church matters and administration of the papal state, Benedict had greater success. He emphasized the formation of the clergy and the obligation of residence and of regular pastoral visits to his bishops. He prohibited religious excesses by banning trumpets in church services and eliminating public flagellations and some feast days on which work was suspended. In 1742 he resolved a bitter dispute concerning the extent to which missionaries might include other traditions in church rites. Benedict curbed the Jesuit use of Chinese rites but permitted some accommodation to Indian culture ("Malabar rites").

Benedict XIV was open and sympathetic to the activities of some of the leading scholars of the century and enjoyed their company. He supported Ludovico Muratori (1672–1750), Italy's leading historian, some of whose positions on church-state matters displeased the papacy. He added new professorships to the universities of Rome and Bologna, enlarged the Vatican Library collections, and restored some of the monuments of Rome. He provided the money for the completion of the Trevi Fountain in 1742.

In 1745 Voltaire (1694–1778) wrote to Benedict to ask if he would accept the dedication of his play, *Mahomet*. Benedict agreed, and sent Voltaire some gold medals in return, as was the custom.

Pope Benedict XIV. The monument to Benedict XIV in St. Peter's Basilica, Vatican City. ©ALINARI/ART RESOURCE, N.Y.

After Voltaire made the correspondence known, Benedict received criticism for his friendly relations with the notorious anticlerical. He responded that it was important to have some links with a person of such importance in the world of letters. The gesture earned praise from partisans of the Enlightenment across Europe, including Protestant England.

However, the differences between the papacy and the Enlightenment remained strong. Benedict placed Montesquieu's *Esprit des lois* (Spirit of the laws) on the Index of Prohibited Books in 1752, and he renewed the church's condemnation of Freemasonry in 1751. Benedict XIV died on 3 May 1758.

Benedict XIV displayed an openness to Enlightenment thinkers and willingness to embrace change. Perhaps his greatest success was communication with writers and scholars, especially Italians. He negotiated concordats with Catholic rulers but was unable to improve substantially the position of the church. Probably no papal action would have staved off the assaults that began in the 1760s with the suppression of the Jesuits and continued with the seizure of church properties and the suppression of Catholicism during the French Revolution. Benedict XIV stands as a pope who practiced openness and moderation in troubled times with mixed results.

See also **Austrian Succession, War of the (1740–1748); Enlightenment; Frederick II (Prussia); Muratori, Ludovico Antonio; Papacy and Papal States; Voltaire.**

BIBLIOGRAPHY

Haynes, Renée. *Philosopher King. The Humanist Pope Benedict XIV.* London, 1970. Concentrates on his career before becoming pope and scholarship.

Pastor, Ludwig von. *The History of the Popes from the Close of the Middle Ages.* Vol. 25: *Benedict XIV (1740–1758).* Vol. 26: *Benedict XIV (1740–1758). Clement XIII (1758–1769).* Translated by E. F. Peeler. St. Louis, 1949 and 1950. Detailed account of his pontificate.

Rosa, Mario. "Benedetto XIV." *Dizionario biografico degli italiani.* Vol. 8, pp. 393–408. Rome, 1966. Excellent summary of his life with extensive bibliography.

———. *Riformatori e ribelli nel '700 religioso italiano.* Bari, 1969. Pp. 49–85, 264–265 deal with Benedict XIV.

PAUL F. GRENDLER

BERKELEY, GEORGE (1685–1753), bishop of Cloyne, Anglo-Irish philosopher and cleric. Berkeley was born near Kilkenny; little is known of his parents, but they seem to have been minor gentry who claimed some allegiance to the powerful English aristocrats of the same name. In any case Berkeley went to good schools, studying first at Kilkenny College and then Trinity College, Dublin, where he took his B.A. (1704) and M.A. (1707) and became a junior fellow. In his early years at Trinity he wrote *An Essay towards a New Theory of Vision* (1709), in which he argues that our perception of depth is a matter of inference from experience, and the two works in which he expounds his "immaterialism," *A Treatise concerning the Principles of Human Knowledge* (1710) and *Three Dialogues between Hylas and Philonous* (1713), the latter deploying the dialogue form to render his philosophy more attractive and accessible. In the years ahead Berkeley was often absent from Trinity, but he kept his fellowship, eventually becoming Doctor of Divinity (1721).

Berkeley left Ireland for the first time in 1713, spending time in London—where he was quickly drawn into literary circles by his countrymen, satirist Jonathan Swift (1667–1745) and essayist Richard Steele (1672–1729)—before embarking on extensive continental tours as a chaplain and tutor. Serious preferment within the church did not come until 1724, when he was appointed to the deanery of Derry, but by then Berkeley's ambitions lay across the Atlantic. He was proposing to found and preside over a college in Bermuda to educate the sons of settler and indigenous families from throughout the English colonies, partly with an eye to better establishing the English Church in America. Berkeley raised considerable sums by public subscription, but a government grant promised by prime minister Robert Walpole (1676–1745) was not forthcoming.

In 1728, in an attempt to force Walpole's hand, Berkeley sailed for America, where he was to live in Rhode Island for several years. Here he passed his time writing *Alciphron: or, the Minute Philosopher* (1732), an extended defense of Christianity, directed in part against the ethical writings of Anthony Ashley Cooper, 3rd earl of Shaftesbury (1671–1713) and Bernard de Mandeville (1670–1733). The Bermuda college was never built. In 1734, three years after his return to England, Berkeley was nominated to the bishopric of Cloyne, an impoverished see in the south of Ireland, where he spent the remainder of his life. His last major work was *Siris* (1744), an extremely popular medical essay, densely packed with maxims from ancient philosophy, which promoted tar-water as a panacea.

Berkeley is known for the concise and highly original, even idiosyncratic, metaphysical system expounded in the *Principles* and the *Three Dialogues* and usually referred to as "immaterialism." This system is best understood as an intervention in late seventeenth-century doctrines of substance, reacting specifically to the thought of the English epistemologist and political theorist John Locke (1632–1704) and the French Cartesian philosopher Nicholas Malebranche (1638–1715). These philosophers adhered to a dualism that proposed two fundamentally different kinds of substance in the world—matter and spirit. They also accepted that our knowledge of material substances was tenuous at best: we have mind-dependent "ideas" that might somehow represent external objects, but since we have no immediate access to those objects apart from our ideas, we can only surmise their existence. Berkeley proposed a radical simplification: there are only active minds and the passive ideas they entertain; material substances simply do not exist. Berkeley observed that there are ideas we make up ourselves—we can dream of a unicorn or imagine a tree—but there are also the more vivid and orderly ideas of sense experience—the ball we turn in our hands. Since ideas can only be the properties of mind, these potent ideas of sense must come from another, more powerful mind. For Berkeley, the only possible explanation is that our sense experience is a direct communication from the mind of God.

Berkeley vigorously defended immaterialism as vindicated by common sense: our ideas of things are surely sufficient for the business of life, in which we never make reference to the elusive material substances of philosophy. Alarmed by what he saw as the growing skepticism of his generation, he also promoted his theocentric system as an antidote to atheism. But despite all this, Berkeley won no adherents. An age that embraced the philosophy of John Locke and the physics of Isaac Newton (1642–1727) naturally found the elimination of matter difficult to digest. Many refused to take Berkeley seriously—literary critic Samuel Johnson (1709–1784) famously refuted immaterialism by kicking a stone—but English philosophers, notably David Hume (1711–1776) and John Stuart Mill (1806–1873), have studied Berkeley's writings carefully and adapted many of his arguments, even as they refused to admit his conclusions.

See also **Hume, David; Locke, John; Newton, Isaac.**

BIBLIOGRAPHY

Primary Source

Berkeley, George. *The Works of George Berkeley, Bishop of Cloyne.* Edited by A. A. Luce and T. E. Jessop. 9 vols. London, 1948–1957. The definitive edition.

Secondary Sources

Luce, A. A. *The Life of George Berkeley, Bishop of Cloyne.* London, 1949.

Tipton, I. C. *Berkeley: The Philosophy of Immaterialism.* 1974. Reprint: Bristol, 1994. A thorough and accessible study of Berkeley's metaphysics.

PETER WALMSLEY

BERLIN. Berlin rose to prominence through its partnership with the Hohenzollern dynasty to become the center of their Brandenburg-Prussian lands and, later, capital of the Prussian-dominated Second Reich after 1871. The city's development benefited from its situation on the northeast bank of the Spree at the narrowest crossing over the river halfway between the castles of Spandau and Köpenick. Both these castles were eventually incorporated in the city, as was the nearby town of Cölln, on an island in the river that is now the district of Berlin-Mitte.

In the late Middle Ages, Berlin and Cölln felt threatened by mounting disorder in Brandenburg, particularly after the demise of the Ascanian dynasty in 1319. The two towns formed a defensive alliance in 1307 and collaborated with the Hohenzollerns, who became the new rulers of Brandenburg in 1415. Elector Frederick II (ruled 1440–1470) exploited internal divisions between the Berlin council and the guilds to assert his authority in 1442. A revolt known as the Berlin Indignation (1447–1448) failed to stem the growing Hohenzollern presence. The elector built the city palace on confiscated land 1443–1451 as his principal residence.

The Hohenzollerns introduced the Lutheran Reformation in 1539 with the help of the council, but seventy-five years later, most Berliners refused to follow the lead of Elector John Sigismund (ruled 1600–1620) and accept Calvinism (after 1613). The Calvinist minority in Berlin was swelled by the arrival of six thousand Huguenot refugees, welcomed from France by Frederick William, the Great Elector (ruled 1640–1688), after 1677. Jewish refugees also settled after 1670 but enjoyed fewer privileges than the Calvinists who became a thriving commercial community, numbering around a fifth of all Berliners by 1700. From six thousand inhabitants in 1450, Berlin's population had more than doubled by the time the Thirty Years' War came to Brandenburg in 1627. Imperial troops extorted money and supplies until displaced by the Swedes, who demanded the same. The departure of the elector and his family to Königsberg contributed to the economic depression, and the population fell to six thousand by 1648.

Recovery began under the Great Elector, who deliberately promoted Berlin as an economic and political center, particularly through the construction of the Oder-Spree canal in 1662–1669, which improved access to the Baltic. State-sponsored enterprises were established in and around the city, notably the Lagerhaus cloth factory, founded in 1714, which was Germany's largest textile mill, employing 5,000 workers. Other important enterprises included the arms factory in Spandau run by the Splittgerber and Daum consortium (which supplied the Prussian army with small arms), glass and porcelain factories, and the city's first steam engine in 1795; an iron works opened in 1804. The population rose rapidly, already numbering 57,000 by 1710, and reaching 172,000 by 1800, making Berlin one of Germany's largest cities. New suburbs were laid out in Friedrichswerder, Dorotheenstadt, and Friedrichstadt, while Berlin and Cölln were formally merged on 18 January 1709. However, Berliners suffered from price rises and economic fluctuations throughout the eighteenth century. Many enterprises depended heavily on state subsidy and a real industrial takeoff did not start until the 1830s. The fortifications were razed in 1734 and replaced by a 14 km–long "tax wall" two years later to enforce collection of the excise imposed on goods entering and leaving the city. Though the remaining military installations were demolished after 1774, Berlin remained a garrison town. Soldiers and their dependants accounted for a fifth of all inhabitants throughout the eighteenth century, compared with under 3 percent in 1871. Wartime mobilization removed both customers and workers from the city's economy, as well as its defenders: Berlin was temporarily occupied by the Austrians and Russians in 1757 and 1760 during the Seven Years' War.

Elector Frederick III (ruled 1688–1713; king in Prussia as Frederick I, 1701–1713) embarked on an ambitious building program to make Berlin appear a worthy royal capital as part of his bid for a crown. The sculptor Andreas Schlüter (1659–1714) oversaw the construction of some of northern Germany's finest baroque buildings, including the Arsenal (1695) and the Charlottenburg palace (1705), while academies of arts (1696) and sciences (1700) were opened. This program faltered once the elector achieved his ambition in 1700 and stopped altogether under his son and successor, Frederick William I (ruled 1713–1740), who diverted money to expanding the army. War pre-

vented the full implementation of Frederick II's (ruled 1740–1786) ambitious plans to remodel the city after 1740, but an opera house was built (1740–1743), along with St. Hedwig's Cathedral, the Royal Library, and Prince Henry's palace, which was converted into the Humboldt University in 1810. Later public buildings, including the Brandenburg Gate (1788–1791), reflected the influence of Greek neoclassicism and contributed to making Berlin one of Germany's most impressive capitals.

See also Brandenburg; Frederick I (Prussia); Frederick II (Prussia); Frederick William (Brandenburg); Frederick William I (Prussia); Hohenzollern Dynasty; Prussia.

BIBLIOGRAPHY

Badstübner-Gröger, Sybille. Bibliographie zur Kunstgeschichte von Berlin und Potsdam. Berlin, 1968.

Badstübner-Gröger, Sybille, and Jutta von Simson. Berlin und die Mark Brandenburg: Kunstfahren zwischen Havel, Spree und Oder. Munich, 1991.

Neugebauer, Wolfgang. "Staatsverwaltung, Manufaktur und Garnison. Die polyfunktionale Residenzlandschaft von Berlin-Potsdam-Wusterhausen zur Zeit Friedrich Wilhelms I." Forschungen zur Brandenburg und Preussische Geschichte. New series 7 (1997): 233–257.

Ribbe, Wolfgang, ed. Geschichte Berlins. 2 vols. Munich, 1987.

Schultz, Helga. Berlin 1650–1800: Sozialgeschichte einer Residenz. 2nd ed. Berlin, 1992.

Völkel, Markus. "The Hohenzollern Court 1535–1740." In The Princely Courts of Europe: Ritual, Politics, and Culture under the Ancien Régime 1500–1750, edited by John Adamson, pp. 210–229. London, 1999.

PETER H. WILSON

BERNINI, GIAN LORENZO

BERNINI, GIAN LORENZO (1598–1680), Italian sculptor, architect, and painter. Bernini's work in Rome made him the most influential and famous Italian artist of his time. Born in Naples on 7 December 1598, the son of a Florentine sculptor, Bernini was the first artist whose life and its retelling were coordinated to fashion an ideal image. All of the literary motifs that had come to signify identity as an artist are to be found not only in the reports of his contemporaries but also in his practice. As with Giotto (1266/7 or 1276–1337), his genius is apparent at an early age; like Michelangelo (1475–1564), he became the master of painting, sculpture, and architecture; as with Titian (1488/90–1576), his art earned him a knighthood (1621) and exacted the same deference from popes and kings. When Queen Christina of Sweden (1626–1689), reprising the role of Alexander the Great, visited Bernini in his studio, he greeted her in the coarse sculptor's smock he wore when working, and she, far from being affronted by this lèse-majesté, sought to touch it with her own hand.

His father's work at the church of Santa Maria Maggiore brought Bernini to Rome at the age of seven or eight, and with the exception of a five-month trip to Paris in 1665, where he did an unexecuted, but variously imitated, design for the Louvre, he remained in Rome all his life. From his father he acquired the technique that would make marble as yielding as wax; from Hellenistic sculpture, the example of optical surfaces and a way of composing figures on a stagelike plinth with one dominant point of view; and from modern painters like Caravaggio (1573–1610), Annibale Carracci (1560–1609), and Guido Reni (1575–1642), an affective naturalism and psychological immediacy that effaced the boundaries between subject and viewer, art and life. All of these traits are to be seen to such startling effect in the life-size sculptures Bernini executed for Cardinal Scipione Borghese that contemporary reports of his earlier precocity seem entirely plausible. In the *Apollo and Daphne* (1622–1625), the nymph's transformation into root and bark, twig and leaf is no less astonishing to us than to the unsuspecting god; and in the *David* (1623), the grimly determined young hero prepares to loose his missile at a giant Goliath looming over the viewer's shoulder. The inescapable realism and emotional intensity of these works also characterize certain of his portraits, like the bust of Scipione Borghese (1632) or that of the artist's mistress, Costanza Buonarelli (1637–1638), which in its informality and unmeditated spontaneity reconfigures for the viewer Bernini's own lively and passionate response to his sitter.

Beginning in the reign of Pope Urban VIII (reigned 1623–1644) these exercises of personal virtuosity were complemented by equally impressive displays of large-scale organizing in which Bernini engaged the energies and skills of many other artists and craftsmen to realize his ideas. Within a year of the pope's elevation, he was commissioned to erect a gilded bronze canopy, or baldachin, over the tomb of the saint in the then still largely undecorated church of St. Peter's. Commissions from Urban VIII and his successors for the decoration of the crossing and the nave, the tombs of Urban VIII and Alexander VII (reigned 1655–1667), the Sacrament Chapel, and the enormous apparition of Peter's throne in the apse of the church followed. Thus, with his designs for the angels holding the instruments of Christ's Passion on the bridge over the Tiber connecting the Vatican with the city and for the colonnades surmounted by saints fronting the church, visiting St. Peter's became, and remains, an experience largely shaped by Bernini's never surpassed exaltations of Catholic piety and papal authority.

Nevertheless, the originality and religious conviction of Bernini's art is perhaps more readily grasped in the Cornaro Chapel in church of Santa Maria della Vittoria (1647–1652). Here, as elsewhere, he harnesses all the arts to a single, overwhelming effect. The architecture, composed of multicolored marbles, breaks forward over the altar as if forced from within to disclose the white, marmoreal vision of Saint Teresa of Ávila (1515–1582), mysteriously lit from a hidden window above. Swooning in an ecstasy of divine love, which, in keeping with the eroticized imagery of her *Autobiography,* has been provoked by an angel piercing her heart with a flame-tipped spear, Teresa reclines on a bank of clouds, wholly lost in her rapture. Yet the visual metaphor of her wildly cascading drapery belies the quietude of her dangling limbs, parted lips, and half-closed eyes and betrays the depth and violence of her passion. On the floor of the chapel, skeletons in inlaid marble rise toward the light of the Holy Spirit that miraculously bursts through the ceiling and descends in a painted glory of angels. Thus in one apparently transitory image, Bernini merges and illustrates as never before the typically baroque themes of love (physical and spiritual), death (real and mystical), and salvation (Teresa's and the viewer's).

Although many criticized the clothing of the spiritual in the sensual, the persuasive power that resulted made Bernini's works definitive examples for those who sought to move their audience for religious and political ends. At its most aggressive, this desire to compel assent appears in the comedies

Gian Lorenzo Bernini. *The Ecstasy of St. Theresa,* marble, 1645–1652, Cornaro Chapel, Santa Maria della Vittoria, Rome. THE ART ARCHIVE/ALBUM/JOSEPH MARTIN

that from the 1640s the artist staged during the Carnival season before Lent. In these works a rush of strong emotion—astonishment, alarm, fear—bonded the audience to the fiction. In one, a great quantity of water broke through its dike and threatened to soak the spectators; in another, an accidental fire, kindled by the scripted carelessness of an actor, appeared to ignite the theater. Although ephemeral in effect, like his festive decorations and firework displays, a clear continuity exists between these theatrical devices and Bernini's permanent works of architecture, painting, and sculpture. In the *Triton Fountain* (1642–1643) and *Four Rivers Fountain* (1647–1651), the lack of architectural frames and the animation of sculpture and water enable them to take possession of the urban space, and in *San Andrea al Quirinale* (1658–1670) the figurative decorations are coextensive with and inhabit the space of the church. It was this ability to absorb the viewer into a spectacle that seemed to be unfolding before his eyes that made Bernini so influential during the early modern period.

See also **Baroque; Caricature and Cartoon; Rome, Architecture in; Rome, Art in.**

BIBLIOGRAPHY

Avery, Charles. *Bernini: Genius of the Baroque*. London, 1997.

Baldinucci, Filippo. *The Life of Bernini*. Translated by Catherine Enggass. University Park, Pa., and London, 1966. Translation of *La vita del Cavaliere Gio. Lorenzo Bernino* (1682).

Chantelou, Paul Fréart de. *Diary of the Cavaliere Bernini's Visit to France*. Edited and with an introduction by Anthony Blunt, annotated by George C. Bauer, and translated by Margery Corbett. Princeton, 1985. Translation of *Journal du voyage en France du Cavalier Bernin* (1665).

Lavin, Irving. *Bernini and the Unity of the Visual Arts*. New York and London, 1980.

Marder, Tod A. *Bernini and the Art of Architecture*. New York, 1998.

Wittkower, Rudolf. *Bernini: The Sculptor of the Roman Baroque*. 4th ed. London, 1990.

GEORGE C. BAUER

BÉRULLE, PIERRE DE (1575–1629), French ecclesiastic. Founder of the French Oratory, Cardinal Pierre de Bérulle was a leading spiritual writer and a main figure of the Catholic Reformation in his country. It was less by his writings than by his personal relationships, his political actions, and the diffusion of his thought through his disciples that he had such an impact on his contemporaries.

Born in 1575 of a noble family, and educated by the Jesuits and at the Sorbonne, Pierre de Bérulle was ordained in 1599 and became one of Louis XIII's chaplains. For a time, he considered entering the Society of Jesus, to whom he owed most of his education, but he decided against the idea because the Jesuits were still exiled from France at the time. This original link to the Jesuits is essential to understanding his activities as a Catholic reformer because he emulated the many-sided religious activism of the society, involving himself in controversies, education, and missions.

He helped Cardinal Jacques du Perron (1556–1618), a famous preacher and political essayist, in his controversies with the Protestants, but his aim was less to counteract Protestantism than to promote the Catholic Reformation. In particular, Bérulle wanted to remedy the mediocrity of the clergy. For him, the ideal priest should unite spiritual authority, knowledge, and holiness, all qualities too often found lacking among common priests. The Council of Trent promoted the establishment of seminaries to solve that problem, but its decrees, not yet "received" in France, could not be officially put into practice. This is why Bérulle founded the Oratory of Jesus and Mary in 1611—modeled on St. Carlo Borromeo's (1538–1584) Oblates of St. Ambrosius and St. Philip Neri's (1515–1595) Oratorio—whose main activity was the training of priests and the education of young people. The Oratorian communities expanded quickly throughout France (in 1630, seventy-three residences, including seventeen colleges and four seminaries; between 1631 and 1700, eleven colleges and seventeen seminaries were added). Like the Jesuits, their great rivals, the Oratorians ran colleges and organized many missions in the French countryside to instruct and convert the common people and improve the quality of their priests.

Bérulle also worked closely with the laity, particularly with the *dévots* ('devout') who met in his cousin Madame Acarie's (Barbe Avrillot, 1566–1618) salon. There, clerics and the *dévots* explored the works of spiritual masters from the *Devotio moderna* (Modern devotion) to more modern authors and visitors to the salon, such as the Capuchins Benedict of Canfield (author of *La règle de perfection* [The rule of perfection]) and Archange of Pembroke, the Jesuit Peter Coton, and Bishop François de Sales. The aims, means, and practical achievements of the French Catholic Reformation were also intensively discussed by the group. For example, Madame Acarie's group encouraged the restoration of French nunneries and the establishment in Paris of two convents, that of the Spanish Carmel in 1604 and that of the Italian Ursulines in 1610.

Bérulle was also chosen for many diplomatic missions because of his considerable talents as a negotiator. For example, in 1619–1620, he was sent to Marie de Médicis (1573–1642), the fugitive queen mother, in order to make peace with young King Louis XIII (ruled 1610–1643), with whom she was at war (1617–1621). In 1624, Bérulle was chosen to negotiate with Pope Urban VIII the religious terms of the marriage between Henrietta of France, Louis XIII's young sister, and the future king of England, Charles I (ruled 1625–1649). Soon, however, Bérulle and the powerful Cardinal Richelieu clashed over the question of France's political alliances: Bérulle favored the alliance with Catholic Spain, while Richelieu preferred allying with Protestant England against the Habsburgs. As a result, Bérulle was dismissed from favor, but the pope, who held him in great esteem, made him cardinal in 1627, two years before his death.

Busy as he was, Bérulle did not write much: primarily short treatises, lectures, and letters on theology, piety, and mysticism, of which the best known, which deal with the incarnation of Jesus Christ, are *Discours de l'état et des grandeurs de Jésus* ... (Discourse on the state and grandeurs of Jesus Christ [1623]) and *L'élévation à Jésus-Christ sur ses principaux états et mystères* (The elevation to Jesus Christ concerning his principal states and mysteries [1625]). In fact, Bérulle's influence exceeded the fame of his writings. Combining high spiritual experience, contemplation, and action, he gave a variety of people his support: he was in charge of the Carmel, he befriended the royal family, he encouraged René Descartes in his philosophical enterprise, and he taught people as opposed in views as Vincent de Paul and the abbot of Saint-Cyran. Through the Oratory, his thought was spread, and his key ideas were taken over by the founders of the French seminaries and missionary congregations, such as Vincent de Paul (Lazarists or Vincentians), Jean Eudes (Eudists), and Jean-Jacques Olier (Sulpicians).

See also **Borromeo, Carlo; Charles I (England); François de Sales; Jesuits; Louis XIII (France); Marie de Médicis; Reformation, Catholic; Richelieu, Armand-Jean Du Plessis, cardinal; Salons; Trent, Council of; Urban VIII (pope); Vincent de Paul.**

BIBLIOGRAPHY

Brown, Roberta. "Trinitarian mechanisms: From Bérulle to Descartes." *Proceedings of the Annual Meeting of the Western Society for French History* 12 (1985): 40–49.

Cochois, Paul. *Bérulle et l'école française.* Paris, 1963.

Dagens, Jean. *Bérulle et les origines de la restauration catholique (1575–1611).* Bruges, 1952.

Dupuy, Michel. "Bérulle et la grâce: Aspects de la spiritualité en France au XVIIe siècle." *Dix-Septième Siècle* 43 (1991): 39–50.

———. *Bérulle et le sacerdoce: Étude historique et doctrinale.* Paris, 1969.

———. *Bérulle: Une spiritualité de l'adoration.* Paris, 1964.

———. *Le Christ de Bérulle.* Paris, 2001.

Krumenacher, Yves. *L'école française de spiritualité: Des mystiques, des fondateurs, des courants et leurs interprètes.* Paris, 1998.

Morgain, Stéphane-Marie. *Pierre de Bérulle et les carmélites de France: La querelle du gouvernement, 1583–1629.* Paris, 1995.

———. *La théologie politique de Pierre de Bérulle.* Paris, 2001.

Orcibal, Jean. *Le cardinal de Bérulle: Évolution d'une spiritualité.* Paris, 1965.

Thompson, William M. "The Christic Universe of Pierre de Bérulle and the French School." *American Benedictine Review* 29 (1978): 320–347.

Wagley, S. *The Oratory of France, 1629–1672: A Social History.* Ottawa, 1976.

Williams, Charles E. *The French Oratorians and Absolutism, 1611–1641.* New York, 1989.

DOMINIQUE DESLANDRES

BÈZE, THÉODORE (Théodore Beza; 1516–1605), French theologian and poet. Théodore Bèze was born 24 June 1516 in Vézelay,

France; his father, Pierre Bèze, was the king's bailiff and a member of the lesser nobility. Bèze received a humanist education in Orléans, where he excelled in Latin, Greek, and poetry. Under the guidance of Melchior Wolmar, he was exposed to the ideas of the growing Reformed movement in France. Bèze finished his legal studies in 1539 in Orléans, where he first encountered John Calvin (1509–1564), who was briefly studying law there.

In 1539 Bèze moved to Paris to pursue a literary career. There he entered into a clandestine marriage with Claudine Denosse in 1544. Although he had been reading Reformed literature throughout his stay in Paris, an illness in 1548 precipitated a dramatic conversion experience. Abandoning his benefices and birthright, he fled Paris for Geneva and then became a professor at the University of Lausanne in 1549. In 1550 he was condemned as a heretic by the Parlement of Paris and was burned in effigy, so he began his life in exile within the Reformed movement. Calvin's presence in Geneva was the city's primary draw for Bèze. Geneva was also the home of Bèze's friend Jean Crespin (1520–1572), who had witnessed his secret marriage and who ran a publishing house that held the promise of opportunity. Bèze accepted an invitation from Pierre Viret (1511–1571) to teach Greek at the Lausanne academy, but at Calvin's request Bèze returned to Geneva in 1557 to assume the position of professor of Greek at the Genevan academy and to join the clergy. After Calvin's death in 1564, Bèze succeeded him as head of the Company of Pastors, making Bèze leader of the Genevan church and the chief counselor to the Reformed churches in France. He became one of the leading forces in the international spread of Calvinism. Bèze represented French Reformed churches in the important colloquies of Poissy (1561) and Saint-Germain (1562) and attended the synods of La Rochelle (1571) and Nîmes (1572). He also served as an adviser to Huguenot leaders such as Gaspard de Coligny (1519–1572) and Henry IV (Henry of Navarre) (ruled 1589–1610) during the Wars of Religion. Bèze attempted both in writing and in person to mend the increasing rift and hostility between the Lutheran and the Reformed churches, an effort that began in 1586 with the Colloquy of Montbéliard and ended in 1593 with a treatise on the Lord's Supper. Bèze served as head of the Company of

Pastors until 1580; he focused on his position as professor of theology until his retirement in 1599.

Bèze's writings can be divided into three categories: poetic, theological, and polemical-historical. He began his literary career as a poet, producing the collection *Juvenilia* in 1548 while he was still in Paris. Probably his most important poetic work, undertaken at the urging of Calvin in 1560, was the completion of the translation of the Psalms with commentary, begun by Clément Marot (1496?–1544), entitled *Les Psaumes de David* (1561; The Psalms of David) and put into French rhyme. Throughout the collection, the plight of the Huguenots is equated with that of the embattled Israelites, sharing experiences of persecution, displacement, and the role of God's chosen people.

Second only to Calvin in terms of his influence as a theologian of the Calvinist Reform, Bèze devoted most of his work to the defense and expansion of Calvinist doctrine. He is especially known for his exegesis and translations of the Greek editions of the New Testament, which were used to produce later editions of the Geneva Bible.

Bèze's pen was also employed for polemical purposes, producing *De Haereticis a Civili Magistratu Puniendis* (1554; On the heretics who should be punished by a civil magistrate; published in French in 1560) and *Traité de l'authorité du magistrat* (1574; On the right of magistrates). *On the Heretics Who Should Be Punished by a Civil Magistrate,* written in defense of Calvin and the Genevan magistrates for the execution of Michael Servetus (1511–1553), establishes the right of magistrates to defend the "true" religion, laying the groundwork for his later work on resistance theory. *On the Right of Magistrates* provided a legal argument for the armed resistance of the Huguenot faction and created a type of constitutionalist doctrine of the state. Written after the St. Bartholomew's Day Massacre, where the king sanctioned the wholesale killing of Huguenots, it legitimates resistance to a tyrant who has turned from God's word. To the question "Do subjects have any remedy against a legitimate sovereign who has become a notorious tyrant?" Bèze responds with a qualified yes. Subjects may rebel through their magistrates. The defense of the "true" religion is the obligation of the state, and if a king represses this practice, then it is up to the lesser magistrates to defend it, with arms if necessary.

In conjunction with his polemical writings, Bèze edited a valuable *Histoire ecclésiastique* (1580; Ecclesiastical history) and wrote *La vie de Calvin* (1565; The life of Calvin), which paints a highly sympathetic picture of the reformer with intimate knowledge of the man, arguably the best contemporary portrait left to historians. The *Ecclesiastical History* had a different function and purpose. Using Eusebius's (c. 260–c. 339) *Ecclesiastical History* as a model, Bèze assembled a collection of accounts sent to him from Reformed communities and churches and placed them in a larger context, creating a narrative of the development and struggle of the faith. This work includes excerpts from Crespin's *Livre des martyrs* (1554; Book of martyrs) and Regnier de la Planche's *L'histoire d'etat de France* (1576; History of France) along with some of Bèze's own *Life of Calvin* and some autobiographical pieces.

Bèze's role in the religious and political struggles of the Reformation was multilayered. A scholar, a religious leader, and a voice for the Huguenot struggle, he left a lasting legacy in both Geneva and France. Bèze died in Geneva on 7 October 1605 at the age of eighty-four.

See also **Calvin, John; Calvinism; Huguenots; Reformation, Protestant; Wars of Religion, French.**

BIBLIOGRAPHY

Hamon, Léo. *Un siècle et demi d'histoire protestante: Théodore de Bèze et les protestants sujets du roi.* Paris, 1989.

Kelley, Donald R. *The Beginning of Ideology: Consciousness and Society in the French Reformation.* Cambridge, U.K., and New York, 1981.

Kingdon, Robert McCune. *Geneva and the Consolidation of the French Protestant Movement, 1564–1572.* Madison, Wis., 1967.

Manetsch, Scott M. *Theodore Beza and the Quest for Peace in France, 1572–1598.* Boston, 2000.

Maruyama, Tadataka. *The Ecclesiology of Theodore Beza: The Reform of the True Church.* Geneva, 1978.

NIKKI SHEPARDSON

BIBLE

This entry includes two subentries:
INTERPRETATION
TRANSLATIONS AND EDITIONS

INTERPRETATION

The sixty-six "books" which together make the Bible have, more than any others in world history, demanded interpretation. At the start of the early modern period, interpreting the Bible changed radically and permanently. There were two revolutions. The first was firmly within the life and traditions of the church.

The thirty-nine ancient Hebrew books of the Jewish Bible, known to Christians as the Old Testament, have always received active reinterpretation, even as part of their earliest daily religious use. Thus the tradition of *midrashim*, written commentaries on every passage or word, exemplified argumentative, if reverential, discussion down through the centuries. Christians often add fourteen early books found in the Greek version (the Septuagint), not the Hebrew, either printed scattered through the Old Testament or put together between the Testaments as the "Apocrypha."

The twenty-seven books of the New Testament were originally written in everyday *(koine)* Greek. They are dominated by the four Gospels and the thirteen Epistles, or letters, of Paul. The latter, of the greatest importance in the founding of Christian theology, do not set out to lay down a system, but rather to express the unique revelation of God in Christ by means of elaborate rhetoric, extensions of Hebrew expressiveness in image and symbol. Within those original Epistles, active interpretation is assumed by God's help in the light of the rest of Scripture and by that only. As has been said, Christianity was born in hermeneutics (the theory and methods of interpretation).

Humanist investigation, developed from the new philological scholarship in northern Italy (such as that of Lorenzo Valla, c. 1406–1457), worked toward establishing scholarly texts of the Hebrew and Greek originals. Soon printed editions of these were widely available, successfully challenging the Latin Vulgate, which was itself later revised. From these recently printed Hebrew, and then Greek,

Scriptures, printed translations of the whole Bible into the chief European vernaculars were accomplished by the late 1530s—in some countries, of which England was the chief, in the face of ruthless opposition by the church. The church maintained that the Bible, which was only to be known in short passages, was too difficult a book to be understood without the highest learning or a special grace of understanding given to priests. Wide dissemination of manuscripts of the whole Bible in English in the 1380s, under the aegis of the Oxford scholar John Wycliffe, triggered a violent response: the church denounced reading the Bible in the vernacular as a heresy. Such "heretics" were handed over to the civil authorities for the severest punishment, often to the extreme of burning them alive.

TEACHING AND PREACHING

Within the church, interpretation of the Bible was at two levels. Addressing the common people remained, as it had been for over a thousand years, subordinate to the liturgy of the church. The Bible had authority, but alongside traditions and practices, including the "unwritten verities." The aim was—through the people's attentive participation in ceremonies—to enable true penitence, lamentation for sins, and the healing brought by the seven sacraments (baptism, confirmation, the Eucharist, marriage, penance, holy orders, and extreme unction). These would strengthen the bulwark of thorough Christian conduct. To this end, small and digestible selections of the Bible called pericopes, read in Latin in the Catholic Mass, were used as a basis for translation and exposition in the vernacular. Such passages to be interpreted could be a few words, a verse or a short paragraph; they were occasionally longer treatments in cycles based on a particular book. The purpose was always to underpin existing practice. Such sermons reinforced, as aids to pious reflection, the presentation of key Bible events such as the story of Adam and Eve, Noah's ark, and the Crucifixion and Resurrection in paintings on church walls and in stained glass windows, in occasional, and severely local, plays, and, for the wealthy, little books of piety. All these, as well as the readings (in Latin) in the liturgies, contained a great deal that was not in the Bible at all.

University lectures, printed Bible annotations and commentaries, and theological works (always in Latin) also showed considerable movement. At the end of the fifteenth century, John Colet (1466/1467–1519) gave lectures in Oxford (they have not survived) on Paul's Romans and 1 Corinthians. In them a corner had been turned in biblical interpretation, not because Colet dismissed the standard and hallowed method of allegory in Bible interpretation in favor of the literal Greek text (he did not, and in fact knew no Greek), but because he gave lectures on Paul at all and because he associated the apostle with the Christian life. His lectures were not, as could then have been assumed, on one of the basic theological works of the time, based largely on Scholastic method derived from Aristotle's logic, such as the nonbiblical *Sentences* of the twelfth-century Italian theologian Peter Lombard. Though Colet's Paul was on New Testament grounds unrecognizable, being mainly a moralist, he was at least present for himself in Scripture, and that was new. The chasm between medieval Scholasticism and exegesis was beginning to be crossed.

THE GREEK NEW TESTAMENT PRINTED

The great Dutch humanist scholar Desiderius Erasmus (1466?–1536) met and disputed with Colet while lodging in Magdalen College, Oxford. In the summer of 1504, in the Premonstratensian monastery at Louvain, Erasmus read Lorenzo Valla's *Adnotationes in Novum Testamentum* and discovered the possibility of a new humanist exegesis based on scientific philology (he caused that book to be reprinted in 1505). He had already found the commentaries of St. Jerome and the Egyptian Christian Origen's great third-century parallel edition of six versions of the Hebrew Scriptures, his *Hexapla*. Erasmus awoke to his life's work, to nourish moral and spiritual reform by the public renewal of biblical theology, based on scientific understanding of the original texts, linked to his fresh evaluations of the principal church fathers. The most influential result was his 1516 edition of the original Greek New Testament, the first ever printed.

The new philology set out to establish the original texts for study. In Spain Cardinal Francisco Ximénez de Cisneros gathered together the scholars who produced the remarkable four volumes of the Complutensian Polyglott, which printed the New Testament in Greek, and the Old Testament in Hebrew, Greek, and Aramaic alongside the Latin

Vulgate, with elaborate further commentary. The New Testament was ready by 1514, but not printed, lacking the pope's imprimatur, which was not given until 1522.

THE BIBLE AND REFORM

In 1530, the French Bible translation (from the Latin) made by the humanist scholar Jacques Lefèvre d'Étaples (c. 1455–1536) in Paris was part of his larger intention of initiating Catholic reform through Bible preaching. He was attacked by the church authorities for giving the Word of God to "the humble," a criticism compounded by his not being an academic theologian. One of a circle of Catholic reformers, he wrote in favor of the then novel (later accepted) idea that neither the penitent sinner who anointed Christ's feet (Luke 7:37) nor Mary the sister of Martha (Luke 10:38–42) should be identified with Mary Magdalen (Luke 8:2–3, 23:49, 24:10). His generally trenchant views, expressed in prefaces to his 1523 New Testament translation, led, in spite of his royal protection by Marguerite de Navarre, the sister of King Francis I, to his Bible translation later being put on the Index of Prohibited Books. In the Catholic University of Louvain, Frans Titelmans, a lecturer on Scripture, provided in 1533 for Thomas Herentals's *Den Speghel des kersten levens* (The mirror of the Christian life) to be printed with his own *Den Schat des kersten Gheloofs* (The treasure of the Christian faith) with marginal references newly indicating the biblical sources of Catholic teaching and practice. Lefèvre's earlier New Testament in French had been printed in Antwerp in 1525. Though from the Latin, it was condemned on 25 August 1525 by the Paris Faculty of Theology, together with Erasmus's 1516 new Latin translation, his *Novum Instrumentum*. The latter had caused wide offense by its many corrections of the Vulgate text of the New Testament—he dared to open St. John's Gospel ("In the beginning was the Word . . .") with *sermo*, 'everyday speech', for the Word, instead of *verbum*, 'declaration'. At Luke 10:21, Christ thanked the Father for revealing the secrets of the kingdom not to babes but to *stulti*, 'fools'. These and many more caused scandal.

Yet the triumphant fulfilment of Erasmus's aims of reform came increasingly, and then overwhelmingly, outside the church, although that was some-thing he did not wish. He unleashed the second revolution in Bible interpretation by printing in 1516 that New Testament in Greek noted above, setting it alongside his Latin New Testament to justify his many changes. Easily available to scholars throughout Europe, this work became at once the basis for quite fresh translations of the New Testament into all the vernaculars. Within twenty years, ordinary people could read for themselves, or hear read, the whole New Testament.

VERNACULAR BIBLES

In the chief vernaculars, Martin Luther was first in 1522: his large and beautiful German *Septembertestament* (September testament) became a bestseller. A Dutch New Testament followed in 1526, the same year as William Tyndale's very influential English New Testament, which had been printed in Worms and was smuggled into England. Pierre-Robert Olivétan's French Bible of 1535 included a New Testament from Erasmus's Greek. And so it continued.

Revised and always massively reprinted, in the first sixty years of the sixteenth century these and others rapidly widened the scope and shifted the methods and function of Bible interpretation and have never been seriously opposed since. The guiding principle was access to what the text says in the original language, as precisely as possible, rather than the elaborations, often fanciful, permitted by earlier hallowed doctrine or practice.

UNDERSTANDING THE WHOLE BIBLE

Opposing the pope and Catholic tradition as sole authorities, Protestants understood from Scripture itself that it should be exposited to all believers in their own language as a whole text. For Protestants the entire New Testament was paramount, particularly the Epistles of Paul. They declared that the New Testament authorized only two sacraments (the Lord's Supper and baptism), not seven, and that neither purgatory nor the concomitant system of indulgences was biblical. They believed that, following the model of the earliest congregations described in Acts and the Epistles, and newly visible to all readers, the Holy Spirit led the faithful into comprehension of Scripture without an intermediary priest. The words of Jesus were first addressed to the lowly: even plowboys were capable of understanding. The Bible was no longer in a remote language, nor declared to be so difficult that only those lengthily educated (in Latin) could interpret small portions of it for the *parvuli,* the little people attending the liturgies. Preachers could assume in the hearers detailed knowledge of the whole Bible. That knowledge was the new element.

UNIVERSAL READING

The Protestant Reformation was university-led, but biblical theology in its new development was not, as before, consumed only within college walls. Erasmus wanted everyone to read and study the Scriptures—weavers, plowboys, Turks and Saracens, and even women. Erasmus's influential *Paraphrases of the New Testament* in English, published in the 1520s and 1530s and often reprinted, elucidating the Greek text for every New Testament book except the Apocalypse (Revelation), were, after 1549, by royal command to be placed in every English parish church, adjacent to an English Bible.

In Protestant Europe, the new vehicle of interpretation was the whole of Scripture in the vernacular for everyone (massively bought and studied) with prologues, marginal cross-references and commentaries, elaborate concordances, pictures, and maps. Theological teaching now focused on Paul, taken as a whole, with special emphasis on the sinner's justification by his own faith, without intermediary priest, but supported by his local congregation. Martin Luther's Paul in, for example, his Prologue to the Epistle to the Romans in successive New Testaments, or in his influential printed sermons in German, is indeed fully present, almost overwhelmingly, as the touchstone of all Christian faith. Luther's *Preface to Romans* in English was one of the two earliest Protestant documents circulating in England. He found in Paul not only "justification by faith alone" but the imperative to educate the German-speaking people in the new biblical theology, under the banner of *sola gratia, sola fides, sola scriptura* ('grace alone, faith alone, Scripture alone'). His huge output as a theological writer was matched by a similarly large readership.

Sixteenth-century leaders of Bible interpretation—Philipp Melanchthon, Martin Bucer, Huldrych Zwingli, Johannes Oecolampadius, and others—all wrote with the aim of elucidating Scripture. John Calvin (1509–1564) approached the Bible text as a lawyer: not for nothing was a Bible first divided into verses in his Geneva, a convenience for identifying texts in a network of references internal to Scripture. More than Luther, Calvin was a linguist and scholar of ancient languages. The output of Bibles from Geneva in European languages was a response to the desire of Calvin and his colleagues to combine a scrupulous new accuracy of text and the widest popular dissemination.

Under Calvin, Luther's *sola scriptura* reached its full power. Every reader of Geneva Bibles, in French or English, was taught, by means of the marginal annotations and cross-referencing, that Scripture should only be interpreted in the light of Scripture. As Tyndale put it, the kingdom of heaven is the word of God. Calvin's greatest value lay in his insistence that theology, which now meant biblical theology, uniquely revealed not this church practice or that, but the overarching sovereignty of God.

ACCESSIBLE ILLUMINATION OF THE WHOLE

It is important to recognize that fresh interpretation of the Bible in early modern Europe was done, to by far the greatest extent, in the annotations in vernacular Bibles, read in vast numbers (well over a million English Bibles, mostly Geneva versions, were bought before 1640). Individual study, alone or in groups, at home, in the back of the church, or in the field, allowed absorption of marginal interpretation, which was almost entirely direct textual elucidation toward a literal understanding or internal cross-referencing.

See also **Calvin, John; Calvinism; Church of England; Erasmus, Desiderius; Humanists and Humanism; Luther, Martin; Lutheranism; Melanchthon, Philipp; Reformation, Protestant; Zwingli, Huldrych.**

BIBLIOGRAPHY

Cambridge History of the Bible. Vol. 2, *The West, from the Fathers to the Reformation.* Edited by G. W. H. Lampe. Cambridge, U.K., 1969. Vol. 3, *The West, from the Reformation to the Present Day.* Edited by S. L. Greenslade. Cambridge, U.K., 1963.

Daniell, David. *The Bible in English: Its History and Influence.* New Haven and London, 2003.

Moeller, Berndt. "Scripture, Tradition and Sacrament in the Middle Ages and in Luther." In *Holy Book and Holy Tradition,* edited by F. F. Bruce and E. G. Rupp, pp. 113–135. Manchester, U.K., 1968.

Peel, Albert. "The Bible and the People: Protestant Views of the Authority of the Bible." In *The Interpretation of the*

Bible, edited by C. W. Dugmore, pp. 49–73. London, 1946.

Prickett, Stephen. "Introduction." In *Reading the Text: Biblical Criticism and Literary Theory,* edited by Stephen Prickett, pp. 1–11. Oxford and Cambridge, Mass., 1991.

Shuger, Debora Kuller. *The Renaissance Bible: Scholarship, Sacrifice, and Subjectivity.* Berkeley, Los Angeles, and London, 1994.

Wood, James D. *The Interpretation of the Bible: A Historical Introduction.* London, 1958.

Zim, Rivkah. "The Reformation: The Trial of God's Word." In *Reading the Text: Biblical Criticism and Literary Theory,* edited by Stephen Prickett, pp. 64–135. Oxford and Cambridge, Mass., 1991.

DAVID DANIELL

TRANSLATIONS AND EDITIONS

The New Testament was written in Greek. The Hebrew Bible (to Christians, the Old Testament) also reached the earliest known world in Greek, in a translation known as the Septuagint (from the Latin *septuaginta,* 'seventy', because it was traditionally thought to be the work of seventy-two Jewish scholars). The spread of the power of Rome led to the circulation in the Roman Empire of various translations into Latin of the Greek of both Testaments. St. Jerome's fourth-century Latin version (with the Old Testament translated from the original Hebrew) over time became the common one and was eventually christened the Vulgate (from the Latin *vulgata,* 'popular'). That it was not the original Bible text was, over the next thousand years, generally forgotten.

In sixteenth-century Europe, translations of classical texts into the chief European vernaculars, the result of the new humanist scholarship, were printed, and editions of the Greek and Hebrew originals of the Bible became newly available. Soon fresh translations from these were printed, often in large numbers. Cities such as Florence in northern Italy and Worms in Germany were centers of Hebrew scholarship, and Greek was taught in universities throughout Europe. The remarkable Complutensian Polyglott from Alcalá (Latin "Complutum") in Spain, published in 1522 under the aegis of Cardinal Francisco Ximénez de Cisneros of Toledo, printed the Old Testament in Hebrew (with commentary), Greek, and Latin and the New Testament in Greek and Latin.

Desiderius Erasmus (1466?–1536) published the first printed Greek New Testament with his new Latin translation in 1516. As a young monk, he had been inspired by reading Lorenzo Valla's *Adnotationes in Novum Testamentum* (c. 1450), where he found the new humanist philology that clarified the ancient text. Erasmus intended with his translation to correct the many inaccuracies in the Vulgate. His text was based on what Greek manuscripts he could lay his hands on and was, by modern standards, far from good. In places (for example, the last verses of the Apocalypse, also known as Revelation) he found the Greek missing, and made it up from the Latin. Nevertheless, by an accident of nomenclature (by the printer Robert Stephanus in a Geneva edition of 1550), Erasmus's Greek text became the revered *textus receptus* (received text). His translation was seized upon by scholars across Europe, was revised several times during his lifetime, and was unchallengeable for several centuries.

Martin Luther (1483–1546) believed that putting the Bible into the hands of the laity was the key to reform of the church. His *Septembertestament* of 1522, a German translation from the Greek with prologues, marginal notes, and fine woodcuts, had a wide readership that was a factor in unifying the language and thus the nation. Luther's work influenced William Tyndale (c. 1494–1536), an Oxford scholar with fine Greek who was forbidden to translate and print in England. He worked in Germany and in Worms in 1526 printed the first English New Testament translated from the Greek. Smuggled into England, with copies pirated in Antwerp, it was immediately bought in large numbers—and not only banned, but publicly burned, the owners being hunted down and punished. The ban on Bibles in English, set up by the church after the spread of the manuscripts of the English Bible made by followers of the Oxford scholar John Wycliffe in the 1380s, was still in force in the 1530s. The church authorized only the Latin Vulgate, to be expounded only by the learned and by priests. The church maintained that if the common people had access to a whole Bible, they would seriously misunderstand it. Tyndale's text gave to English speakers many common phrases, but above all a Bible language that has remained close to Christian hearts. It was the basis of all the sixteenth-century versions that followed (and indeed, the several thousand translations until

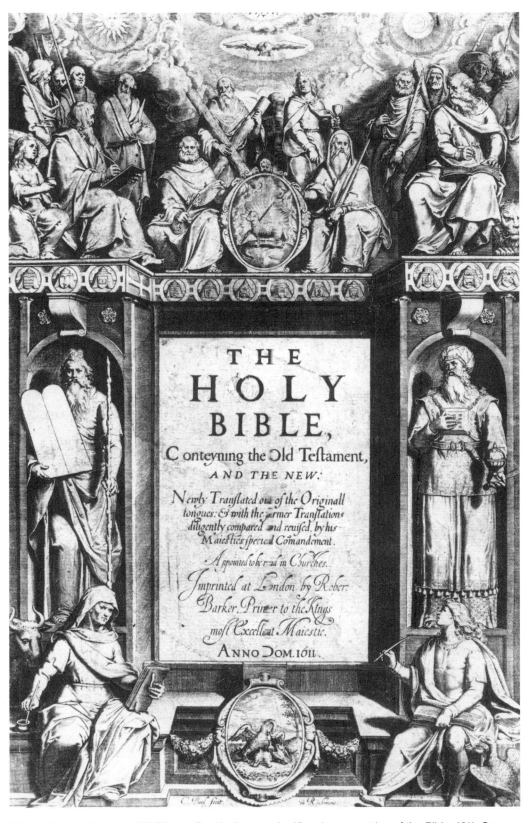

Bible: Translations and Editions. Frontispiece for the King James version of the Bible, 1611. GETTY IMAGES

the twenty-first century), and it provided over 80 percent of the King James Version of 1611.

In Germany, Tyndale learned Hebrew, virtually the first Englishman to do so. His 1530 Pentateuch, from Antwerp, resounded with new phrases: instead of *Fiat lux, et lux erat,* his readers and hearers found "Let there be light: and there was light." Tyndale revised his New Testament in 1534. Another Englishman, Miles Coverdale (1488–1569), who had been in Antwerp at the same time, printed the first complete English Bible, again in Antwerp, in 1535, with notes revealing his pastoral intent. As he made clear, he worked from modern versions, not the originals, relying heavily on Tyndale and also using the Vulgate and Luther's, as well as other, translations. Tyndale was executed as a heretic outside Brussels in October 1536. His work, by then including the Old Testament historical books, was edited and published by John Rogers in Antwerp in 1537, from where it was exported to England. This was the pseudonymous Matthew's Bible, with a license from King Henry VIII (ruled 1509–1547). Coverdale edited his own version, with silent use of Tyndale's work, as the king's gift to the nation (the only Bible ever authorized), the Great Bible of 1539: a copy was to be placed in every one of the nearly nine thousand parish churches in England.

In France, the great French Bible of Pierre-Robert Olivétan (c. 1506–1538), translated from the original languages and published in 1535, became standard. In the Netherlands, Jacob van Liesvelt's first complete Dutch Bible of 1526 was followed in 1528 by Willem Vorsterman's lavish revision and others. A Danish New Testament was first printed in 1524, again followed by others. In Germany, Luther's complete Bible of 1522 was steadily reprinted throughout the sixteenth century, virtually without rivals. It is striking that more Bible translations, of the whole or parts, usually from the original texts, were made in English than in any other European language.

In 1560, the Protestant English scholars who had been exiled to Geneva by the persecutions of Queen Mary Tudor (ruled 1553–1559) produced the first, and remarkable, Geneva English Bible. This finely made volume revised Tyndale and contained elucidatory marginal notes, prologues, commentaries, maps, pictures, concordances, and three versions of the Psalms, all intended to support study. The second half of the Old Testament, consisting of difficult Hebrew poetry, was there translated into English for the first time by a handful of men now almost unknown, although their work was outstanding, and it endured. The Geneva New Testament was revised in 1576, and again in 1599. The Geneva Bible was enormously popular among the populace—at least a million copies were bought.

The official Bishops' Bible of 1568 with few notes, although pressed on the country, translated Hebrew badly and never attained the popularity of the Geneva Bible. The Catholic English version of the New Testament from Reims in 1582, often silently using the "heretic" Tyndale, and rarely reprinted, was followed by the Douay Old Testament in 1609–1610. Under the influence of the third session (1562–1563) of the Council of Trent, the Latin Vulgate began to be revised.

On the accession of James I in 1603, the dominance of Geneva Bibles was halted for political reasons. The so-called King James Version was a revision of the Bishops' Bible made by three panels of fifty-four scholars, and published in 1611. It was largely disliked for having no notes, which crippled understanding of the Hebrew. Influential in the English Civil War, the Geneva versions suffered commercial maneuverings, and were defeated by "King James" by 1660. With the return of the English monarchy in 1660 after the Civil War, the myth was fostered that the King James Version at its appearance in 1611 had been royally authorized. No evidence for such an act has ever been found. As the "Authorized Version," this 1611 English Bible gained exalted status in the late eighteenth century. This version, either as "AV" or as "KJV," has had enormous influence among English speakers throughout the world.

See also **Church of England; Erasmus, Desiderius; Luther, Martin; Printing and Publishing; Reformation, Protestant.**

BIBLIOGRAPHY

Arblaster, Paul, Gergely Juhasz, and Guido Latre, eds. *Tyndale's Testament.* Turnhout, Belgium, 2002. Detailed information on all early modern Bible translations.

Cambridge History of the Bible. Vol. 2, *The West, from the Fathers to the Reformation.* Edited by G. W. H. Lampe. Cambridge, U.K., 1969. Vol. 3, *The West, from the*

Reformation to the Present Day. Edited by S. L. Greenslade. Cambridge, U.K., 1963.

Daniell, David. *The Bible in English: Its History and Influence.* New Haven and London, 2003.

Pelikan, Jaroslav. *The Reformation of the Bible: The Bible of the Reformation.* New Haven and London, 1996.

DAVID DANIELL

BIOGRAPHY AND AUTOBIOGRAPHY.

Though the terms themselves appeared relatively late, "biography" in 1683 (first in English) and "autobiography" in 1789 (in German), writing "lives"—whether one's own or other people's—was practiced throughout the early modern period. A new interest in life narratives stemmed from major cultural changes witnessed by the Renaissance: new notions of the secular individual, an explosion of print culture, an emphasis on experience and on seeking truth in particulars, the development of Christian humanism, and the value attached to individual conscience and consciousness. Biography as a record of a life not merely used to celebrate ideal qualities or to discuss broader philosophical or religious issues but examined for its own sake came into its own in the seventeenth century.

Considered as part of history writing (Francis Bacon defined and encouraged it in *The Advancement of Learning* in 1605), biography was inspired by reading Tacitus, Suetonius, and especially Plutarch, whose *Parallel Lives* were popularized by Jacques Amyot's 1559 translation. Historians such as Pierre de Bourdeille, seigneur de Brantôme (c. 1540–1614) and poets such as Giovanni Boccaccio (1313–1374) recounted lives of rulers, of illustrious men, and of beautiful or gallant women. Religious biographies such as Jean de Bolland's *Acta Sanctorum* (from 1643) were inspired by medieval hagiographies and idealized the saints whose lives they told. Other writers, such as Pierre Bayle in his *Dictionnaire historique et critique* (1697), told the saints' lives from a more critical perspective. Until the eighteenth century, however, such biographies started from similar presuppositions, whether in the form of funeral orations (Jacques-Bénigne Bossuet), religious lives (*The Life of M. Pascal* by his sister Gilberte Périer, 1684), rulers' eulogies (Mme. de Motteville's seventeenth-century *Mémoires pour servir à l'histoire d'Anne d'Autriche*), salon portraits (also found in the baroque novel), or moral "characters" inspired by the ancient Greek philosopher Theophrastus. These biographies explained actions by preexisting virtues or vices and, although sometimes critical, sought to provide a moral lesson through examples, thus resulting in the creation of types rather than actual human beings.

Somewhat more open were short lives and portraits composed by diplomats, such as Ézéchiel Spanheim in his *Relation de la cour de France* (1699), where subtle psychological analysis of court figures grounded political speculation about the future. Realistic psychological analyses based on close observation appear as well in early modern aristocratic memoirs written in French, such as those of Jean-François-Paul de Gondi, cardinal de Retz; Roger de Rabutin, comte de Bussy; Anne-Marie-Louise Orléans, duchesse de Montpensier; and Louis de Rouvroy, duc de Saint-Simon.

Yet the first biographies based on thorough documentary research and an intrinsic interest in a person's singularity were not developed until the eighteenth century: Samuel Johnson's *Life of Savage* (1744) and *Lives of the Poets* (1779–1781), and James Boswell's *Life of Samuel Johnson* (1791) are credited with seeking in their writing a more personal truth. In this respect biography developed alongside the eighteenth-century novel, which often took the form of a full-fledged fictional life and explored themes of interiority, social influence, and historicity. The Romantic sensibility brought about a blossoming of literary and historical life narratives.

Autobiography is considered a subspecies of biography since the life it narrates is the author's own. Before Jean-Jacques Rousseau's *Confessions* (1766–1770), which are considered the first autobiography in the modern sense, writing about the self was to be found in the essay form (Montaigne's enormously influential *Essays* [1580, 1588]), in aristocratic memoirs—often titled "lives" by their authors (Giovanni Jacopo Casanova and the cardinal de Retz) and sometimes even written in the third person (Agrippa d'Aubigné, François de La Rochefoucauld), in journals such as the *Diary* of Samuel Pepys, or in letters. Scarce in the Middle Ages, the genre flourished in the Renaissance, inspired by antiquity (St. Augustine's *Confessions* and Julius Caesar's *Commentaries*) as well as by the humanist ambition of celebrating intelligence (Benvenuto Cellini and Geronimo Cardano) and of painting, through one's individual life, "the entire human condition" (Montaigne). Though early modern men and women could hold the Christian belief that the "self is despicable" (Pascal), they would set out to recount their life moved by spiritual reasons (Teresa of Avila and Mme. Guyon) or the need to illustrate their intellectual trajectory (René Descartes).

In personal memoirs, widely popular among the seventeenth-century French aristocracy, writing about the self stemmed from altogether different motives: the wish to bear witness to history because of the authors' high political rank (Mlle. de Montpensier, La Rochefoucauld, Cardinal de Richelieu), because of their proximity to power (Mme. de Motteville), or, conversely, due to imprisonment or solitude that prompted self-examination (François de Bassompierre and Saint-Simon). While steeped in an aristocratic conviction of personal worth, these writings presented the author as an intrinsically public, political being, and said little about his or her more intimate self: in spite of a distinct personal perspective, they focused on events rather than on the witness and gave priority to actions and words over reflections. They had no literary pretensions and sought mainly to redress history. Some other aspects, however, were more characteristic of autobiography: a wish to relive one's past, to give sense to one's life, a pleasure felt in writing that often comes as a surprise to the author, finally the presence of the genre's defining feature, what Philippe Lejeune calls the "autobiographical pact" made with the reader in which the promise to tell the truth is sealed by the author's name and signature. Other personal writings such as journals by English Puritans or dissenters (John Wesley, George Fox) would in their turn introduce the belief in the inherent dignity of all men as well as the introspective bent acquired through a regular religious practice of self-examination.

Rousseau's *Confessions*—part of his autobiographical writings, which also include the *Reveries of the Solitary Walker* and the *Dialogues* and which were published between 1781 and 1788, mostly posthumously—were the first to combine all these features with two new ideas about the self: its uniqueness, irreducible to any social or religious identity, and its boundless mobility and capacity for transformation. The *Confessions* made the self and its quest for unity the principal object of writing. Together with narrating a unique individual life in its idiosyncrasy, they reflected the features attributed henceforth to the modern self: a tremendously enlarged scope of inner voice, a deeper inwardness, and a radical autonomy. The much-quoted opening lines of the *Confessions* proclaimed Rousseau's awareness of the revolutionary character of his project: "I am resolved on an undertaking that has no model and will have no imitator. I want to show my fellow-men a man in all the truth of nature; and this man is to be myself." Though rightly judging its importance, however, Rousseau was wrong about his posterity: at the close of the eighteenth century, the era of autobiography had only just begun.

See also **Boswell, James; Diaries; Johnson, Samuel; La Rochefoucauld, François de; Montaigne, Michel de; Pepys, Samuel; Rousseau, Jean-Jacques; Saint-Simon, Louis de Rouvroy; Vasari, Giorgio.**

BIBLIOGRAPHY

Coleman, Patrick, Jayne Lewis, and Jill Kowalik, eds. *Representations of the Self from the Renaissance to Romanticism.* Cambridge, U.K., and New York, 2000.

Gusdorf, Georges. *Auto-bio-graphie.* Paris, 1991.

Kendall, Paul Murray. *The Art of Biography.* New York, 1965.

Lejeune, Philippe. *On Autobiography.* Translated by Katherine Leary. Edited by Paul John Eakin. Minneapolis, 1989.

——. *Le pacte autobiographique.* Paris, 1975.

Maschuch, Michael. *Origins of the Individualist Self: Autobiography and Self-Identity in England, 1591–1791.* Stanford, 1996.

May, Georges. "Autobiography and the Eighteenth Century." In *The Author in His Work: Essays on a Problem in Criticism,* edited by Louis L. Martz and Aubrey Williams, pp. 317–333. New Haven, 1978.

——. *L'autobiographie.* Paris, 1979.

Parke, Catherine N. *Biography: Writing Lives.* New York and London, 1996.

Starobinski, Jean. *Jean-Jacques Rousseau: Transparency and Obstruction.* Translated by Arthur Goldhammer. Chicago, 1988.

Weintraub, Karl Joachim. *The Value of the Individual. Self and Circumstance in Autobiography.* Chicago and London, 1978.

MALINA STEFANOVSKA

BIOLOGY. The science of biology as such did not exist in the early modern period; the term *biology* itself came into use only around 1800. Nonetheless, research in subjects now encompassed by biology was avidly pursued, principally by physicians but also by natural philosophers. The philosopher of science Francis Bacon (1561–1626) called for intensified descriptive study of physical forms ("natural history") and the analytical study of their functions, classified as part of "physic." Institutional sites for inquiry included the universities, with those in southern Europe dominant earlier and those in northern Europe later in the period. Private individuals often worked with the support of aristocratic, princely, and ecclesiastical patrons. In the seventeenth century omnibus scientific societies were founded in Rome and Florence. The Royal Society of London (founded 1660) and the Academy of Sciences in Paris (founded 1666) were highly influential. Specialized learned societies came into existence only at the end of the period. Instruments were less important than in physical science, but the microscope proved crucial to advances in knowledge. Much inquiry was tied to the pursuit of fine and technical arts (painting and sculpture, optics, printing and illustrating) and to collecting practices ("cabinets of curiosities"). Public gardens and zoological collections were essential to naturalists from the seventeenth century forward.

NATURAL PHILOSOPHY

At the beginning of the period the natural philosophy taught in the universities was dominated by Aristotelianism as recast by the late Scholastics to harmonize with Roman Catholic orthodoxy. Aristotelian philosophy established the linguistic and conceptual framework for inquiry and conveyed specific doctrines such as the "great chain of being," a posited hierarchy of natural forms ranging from the simplest to the most complex. Aside from Aristotelian influence, medicine was dependent on the legacy of the Greek physician Hippocrates (460–c. 370 B.C.E.), especially the doctrine of the

humors, and of the Hellenistic surgeon and Roman court physician Galen (129/130–199/200 C.E.), whose general teleology and specific teachings in anatomy and physiology undergirded university-based medical training. Competing intellectual traditions derived from Plato (427–348/347 B.C.E.) as well as the occult sciences of the cabala, natural magic, hermeticism, astrology, and alchemy.

The greatest master of the occult sciences in medicine was Philippus Aureolus Theophrastus Bombast von Hohenheim, called Paracelsus (1493–1541). Paracelsus rejected the study of anatomy, basing pathology and therapeutics instead on the doctrine of correspondences between the macrocosm and the microcosm. His "ontological" theory of disease, which held that the "seeds" of all maladies are present in every organism, undermined humor theory and encouraged the search for specific remedies, especially new ones derived from metals. Paracelsianism spread most rapidly in Protestant lands and Protestant enclaves in Catholic Europe. Its diffusion contributed to the decline of Aristotelianism, which was, however, principally undermined by the emergent "mechanical philosophy." Mechanism, which viewed living bodies as sophisticated machines, was dominant from the later seventeenth century until challenged around 1750 by vitalists who posited a distinctive "principle of life" or individuated vital "forces." By the eighteenth century many investigators rejected all "systems" and embraced a scientific ethos based on observation and experimentation.

HISTORICAL CONTEXT

European contact with the New World resulted in a challenge to existing conceptions of creation, the lineage of humankind, and the number and types of living creatures. Other influences included the continuing recovery of the heritage of Greco-Roman antiquity; the emergence of centralizing "new monarchies" and elaborated forms of princely and municipal government; and long-term economic revival from the ravages of the pandemic of plague that first struck Europe in 1348. In connection with these changes, new and fuller editions of the works of ancient philosophers and physicians appeared; the arts and sciences enjoyed expanded prestige and public patronage; and new commodities, both natural and manufactured, came into use. The Protestant Reformation destroyed the religious unity of Europe and encouraged challenges to tradition. The absolutist state emergent in the seventeenth century established new guardians of orthodoxy but also provided new resources for learned inquiry. More powerful government, coupled with economic growth and differentiation, encouraged the spread of literacy and the extension of modes of communication and transportation. These combined forces unsettled social hierarchies based on bloodlines, corporate status, and gender. The self-styled "Enlightenment" of the eighteenth century was marked by a commitment to the methods and values of "science," variously defined, and by a heightened critical spirit. Broader historical developments were linked both as cause and effect to changes in the world of learning that, by the period's end, encouraged the emergence of modern life science.

ANATOMY AND PHYSIOLOGY

Because in Aristotelian-Galenic medicine the heart was considered central, many Renaissance-era inquirers were drawn to the study of this organ. Aristotle viewed the heart as the center of the body, the seat of the "vital heat" that empowered its functions. Galen delineated the structure and functions of the heart and other organs dominant in three body "centers" of head, chest, and abdomen. In his system, blood flowed only as part of an ebb and flow to and from the dominant organ to peripheral structures; arterial blood produced in the right ventricle of the heart seeped into the left ventricle via "pores" in the septum. In his anatomical atlas *De humani corporis fabrica* (1543), the anatomist and professor at Padua Andreas Vesalius (1514–1564) questioned the existence of the septal pores without challenging the overall outlines of Galenic physiology. After Vesalius, other investigators at Padua contributed to the study of the heart. Realdo Colombo (1510–1559) described the "lesser circulation" (the transit of blood from the right to the left side of the heart via the lungs), and Girolamo Fabrici (1533–1619) described the valves in the veins. The Padua tradition was crowned by the achievement of William Harvey (1578–1657), who studied with Fabrici. After taking his medical degree in 1602, Harvey returned to England, where he became a staff physician at St. Bartholomew's Hospi-

tal, Fellow of the College of Physicians, and court physician to the Stuart kings.

A committed Aristotelian, Harvey upheld Aristotle's conception of the heart as the vivifying center of the body and the principle of the perfection of the circle. Yet Harvey was also a powerful innovator methodologically and conceptually. He designed and performed experiments using a wide range of cold- and warm-blooded animals. He drew compelling analogies between the work of the heart and vessels and mechanical actions. Most tellingly, he quantified the amount of blood that passed through the body with each beat of the heart. Judging it too great to be produced by nutritional activity, he was convinced that the blood must move in one great circulatory motion throughout the body. This discovery was incorporated in his *Anatomical Treatise on the Movement of the Heart and Blood* (1628). Although the impact of Harvey's work was delayed because of an entrenched Galenism, in time his findings revolutionized thinking about the heart and blood as well as general physiology. Harvey's work also lent great prestige to the emergent "mechanical philosophy," although Harvey himself was not a mechanist.

The chief intellectual force behind the body-machine analogy was the French philosopher René Descartes (1596–1650). Descartes's cosmology sought to explain all known physical phenomena, including, in his posthumously published treatise *Man* (1664), mechanisms of digestion, respiration, reproduction, and other vital activities. Fruitful applications of mechanist thinking were found in works such as Giovanni Alfonso Borelli's *On the Motions of Animals* (1680–1681), which explored the mechanics of the human muscular and skeletal systems. Mechanist thinking also had a profound impact on inquiry into the cluster of problems called "generation."

THE PROBLEM OF GENERATION

Learned interest in processes of reproduction, including heredity, developed in response both to internal scientific dynamics and to sociocultural pressures for clarity in respect to family lineages, gender roles, and rules for inheritance. Aristotelian teaching posited a union in reproduction of male "form," embodied in semen gathered from throughout the body, with female "matter" (menstrual blood), presenting the male as the "perfect" result while the female was a continuously appearing "monster" of nature. A competing, Galenic account of generation posited two "semens," one male and one female. Inspired by Aristotle, Fabrici and other inquirers at Padua pursued a comparative study of the embryos of horses, sheep, and other animals. Harvey conducted extensive experiments designed to elucidate developmental processes. The most famous was his dissection during and after mating season of does in whom he found no trace of male semen. His *Anatomical Treatise on the Generation of Animals* (1651) declared that "all living beings arise from eggs." This was the beginning of "ovism," which held that the female alone contributed materially to the embryo.

This view was contradicted by Antoni van Leeuwenhoek (1632–1723), who, using a microscope, identified the spermatozoon ("animalcule") in 1677. Ensuing controversy pitted "ovists" against "animalculists," who held that the male contributed all parts of the embryo. In most cases both ovists and animalculists rejected Aristotle's view that the embryo developed in a process of epigenesis, the progressive elaboration of new structures. Both generally favored the "preformationist" view that each individual exists as a preformed miniature in the matter present at conception and develops through mechanical enlargement. The epigenesist-preformationist debate culminated in an exchange between the Swiss physiologist Albrecht von Haller (1708–1777) and the German naturalist Caspar Friedrich Wolff (1733–1794). Initially a preformationist, Haller converted to epigenesis after studying the discovery by Abraham Trembley (1710–1784) of the regenerative capacities of the freshwater polyp. He later settled on ovist preformationism, fearing the irreligious implications of epigenesist theories like that of Georges Louis Leclerc Buffon (1707–1788), who postulated an "interior mold" that shaped development and disregarded the role of the creator. Challenging Haller, Wolff argued for a *vis essentialis,* or essential force, responsible for patterns of differentiation evident in development. Wolff made extensive use of plants to study development and thus effected a juncture with this branch of natural history.

NATURAL HISTORY AND CLASSIFICATION

Early description and ordering of plants and animals was undertaken as an adjunct to both the search for remedies and the humanist effort to identify references in works of the ancients. Herbals based principally on classical, Arabic, and Medieval Latin sources were among the first printed books. Sixteenth-century naturalists such as Conrad Gessner (1516–1565) began organizing local collecting expeditions. Accurate description and representation of distinctive external characteristics of leaf, flower, and fruit were emphasized. The number of species described steadily increased until, in the 1680s, the English naturalist John Ray (1627–1705) described some eighteen thousand species.

Interest in the comparative structure of the parts of plants distinguished the work of Andrea Cesalpino (1519–1603), medical professor first at Pisa and then Rome. Cesalpino sought unifying principles of classification and, after an interval, was followed in that effort by Joachim Junge (1587–1657), also a medical professor. The quest for a "natural" system of classification culminated in the work of Carl Linneaus (1707–1778), the Swedish naturalist whose work formed the basis for modern taxonomy.

Animals were similarly the focus of joint artistic and learned pursuits. Leonardo da Vinci (1452–1519) did his own dissections and compared the structure of body parts in humans, horses, bears, cats, monkeys, and other animals. The humanist lexicographer William Turner (1508–1568) compiled existing accounts of birds and added observations of his own. French naturalists including Pierre Belon (1517–1564) and Guillaume Rondelet (1507–1566) undertook comparative studies of fish. Much seventeenth-century work on the comparative morphology of animals was tied to the investigations into generation discussed above.

The natural history of plants and animals was of keen interest to both trained investigators and the educated public by the late seventeenth century. Religious feeling was central to the popularity of "natural theology." While the mechanical philosophy dispensed with direct intervention in nature by the deity, natural histories such as *Spectacle of Nature* (1732–1750), by Noël-Antoine, the Abbé Pluche, drew attention to the marvels of God's creation. The most influential naturalists of the eighteenth century, Linnaeus and Buffon, focused not on religious but scientific themes, especially the problem of how best to approach classification itself. Buffon's *Natural History,* a general history of the earth and living creatures, was published in many volumes beginning in 1749. Determinedly non-religious, it largely ignored biblical chronology and posited the passage of eons in which natural forms had altered.

HISTORIOGRAPHY

Conventional history of science divided the early modern era into the Renaissance (1400–1550), the scientific revolution (1550–1700), and the Enlightenment (1700–1800), and generally treated life science as peripheral to the revolutionary changes under way in physical science. An alternate scheme divides the era into two phases, roughly 1450–1670 and 1670–1800, more appropriate to biology, with the break marked by a decisive rejection of both Aristotelian thinking and competing occult traditions in favor of inquiry based first on deductive reasoning and, finally, modern inductive science.

Twentieth- and twenty-first-century scholarship has been much affected by the work of the French philosopher Michel Foucault (1926–1984), who overturned traditional labels and periodization. Historians following his lead have questioned presumed continuities with modern science, recovered texts and formulations previously regarded as merely "curious," and investigated the interconnections between learned "discourses" and structures of power. Historical revisionism is also evident in the work of social "constructivists" who emphasize the social creation of knowledge rather than its emergence from autonomous intellectual dynamics.

See also **Anatomy and Physiology; Aristotelianism; Buffon, Georges Louis Leclerc; Gessner, Conrad; Haller, Albrecht von; Harvey, William; Leeuwenhoek, Antoni van; Linnaeus, Carl; Mechanism; Medicine; Museums; Natural History; Paracelsus; Ray, John; Scientific Revolution; Vesalius, Andreas.**

BIBLIOGRAPHY

Ackerknecht, Erwin H. *A Short History of Medicine.* Rev. ed. Baltimore, 1982. A brief account of medical history, with some attention to larger issues in life science.

Butterfield, Herbert. *The Origins of Modern Science: 1300–1800.* Rev. ed. London and New York, 1957.

Clark, William, Jan Golinski, and Simon Schaffer, eds. *The Sciences in Enlightened Europe.* Chicago, 1999. Chapters on biopolitics, monsters, and natural history in the Enlightenment, with emphasis on the social foundations of knowledge.

Crombie, A. C. *Medieval and Early Modern Science.* Vol. 2, *Science in the Later Middle Ages and Early Modern Times: 13th–17th Centuries.* Garden City, New York, 1959. A standard survey of early modern science.

Daston, Lorraine, and Katharine Park. *Wonders and the Order of Nature, 1150–1750.* New York and Cambridge, Mass., 1998. A Foucauldian study focused on the place of marvels in conceptions of natural order.

Foucault, Michel. *The Order of Things: An Archaeology of the Human Sciences.* New York, 1971. An early work of the French philosopher who has revolutionized intellectual and cultural history.

Hall, Thomas S. *History of General Physiology, 600 B.C. to A.D. 1900.* 2 vols. Chicago, 1975. Essential account of the history of physiology.

Impey, Oliver, and Arthur MacGregor, eds. *The Origins of Museums: The Cabinet of Curiosities in Sixteenth and Seventeenth-Century Europe.* Oxford and New York, 1985. A valuable work of institutional history.

Lovejoy, Arthur O. *The Great Chain of Being: A Study of the History of an Idea.* Cambridge, Mass., 1936. Classic study by the master of the "history of ideas."

Magner, Lois N. *A History of the Life Sciences.* 2nd ed. New York, 1994. Places early modern developments within the larger history of biology from the ancients to the era of genetics and molecular biology.

Roger, Jacques. *The Life Sciences in Eighteenth-Century French Thought.* Edited by Keith R. Benson. Translated by Robert Ellrich. Stanford, 1997. Translation of *Les sciences de la vie dans la pensée française au XVIIIe siècle: La génération des animaux de Descartes à l'Encyclopédie.* Magisterial work on the problem of generation, chiefly but not exclusively on French inquirers.

ELIZABETH A. WILLIAMS

BIRTH. *See* **Obstetrics and Gynecology.**

BLACK SEA STEPPE. The land above the northern coast of the Black Sea, bounded by the Prut River in the west and the Kuban River in the east, was of considerable potential economic and geopolitical value in the sixteenth through the eighteenth centuries. Most of it was steppe land well suited to nomadic pastoralism but also offering abundant, rich black soil (chernozem) for agriculture. The Don and Dnieper rivers had the potential to serve important trade routes, as they had in the distant past, linking the ancient trading towns of the Black Sea coast with the interior of eastern Europe. Hegemony over the Black Sea steppe was also seen as key to determining the political fate of Moldavia and Walachia in the west and the Caucasus in the east. But establishing such hegemony required that two great obstacles be surmounted. Turning the steppe over to large-scale agricultural exploitation required heavy plow technology and greater control over peasant tenant mobility; Russians began acquiring these techniques only from the middle of the seventeenth century. Furthermore, steppe colonization carried very heavy protection costs, because the steppe was long fiercely contested by the Crimean Khanate, the Ottoman Empire, Poland-Lithuania, and Russia.

Under Mengli Giray I (ruled 1468–1474 and 1476–1514) the Crimean Khanate, an offshoot of the disintegrating Great Horde, became a major military power claiming sovereignty over most of the Black Sea steppe. The khanate's power was reinforced by Ottoman protection, Mengli Giray I having accepted vassalage to the Ottoman sultan and having recognized Ottoman control over part of Crimea, as an *eyalet* of Kaffa. Some of his successors chafed at the terms of this vassalage and had to be dethroned, but on balance the khanate continued to perform two crucial services to the Ottoman Empire, at least to the end of the seventeenth century. Crimean Tatar cavalry played an important auxiliary role in Ottoman campaigns in Hungary and the Caucasus, while Crimean Tatar attacks on Muscovy and Poland-Lithuania served what Ottoman writers called the Stratagem of Selim I (ruled 1512–1520): that is, they could strike at either power, whichever seemed to be ascendant at the moment, while maintaining that the sultan had no responsibility for the attack. The khanate also was of great economic importance to the Ottomans, for Crimean Tatar slave-raiding into Muscovy and Poland-Lithuania provided the empire with cheap labor on an enormous scale.

Polish-Lithuanian colonization of the Ukrainian steppe made considerable inroads in the fifteenth and sixteenth centuries because it was driven not merely by geopolitical concerns but especially by magnate entrepreneurs responding to demand on the Baltic market for Ukrainian grain and livestock. But the seventeenth century saw the gradual rollback of Polish-Lithuanian power from most of Ukraine. This process began in the 1620s, when the Polish crown's repeated efforts to vassalize or annex Moldavia provoked the first of a series of Ottoman invasions, which eventually led to Ottoman annexation of Podolia and Ottoman attempts to vassalize the rest of western Ukraine. Because Poland's diet was so intent on minimizing royal expenditures and checking the growth of royal absolutism, the Commonwealth's strategy for the defense of Ukraine relied largely on the private armies of march-lord latifundists and on the Ukrainian Cossacks. This strategy broke down altogether in 1648, when the Ukrainian Cossacks rebelled against latifundist exploitation, the Uniate church, and the diet's refusal to reward Cossack service with registration and the king's bounty. By the end of the century the Commonwealth had lost Kiev and Ukraine east of the Dnieper to Muscovy; its control over the greatly depopulated Cossack Hetmanate of western Ukraine was only nominal; and what little remaining power the Polish crown retained under King John III Sobieski (ruled 1674–1696) was squandered on futile attempts to seize Moldavian territory in compensation.

Through most of the sixteenth century Muscovy's southern steppe frontier strategy had focused on protecting central Muscovy against Crimean Tatar invasions. The fortified lines and most of the new garrison towns built in this period were in the forest-steppe zone, not on the steppe, while Muscovite diplomacy aimed at splitting the Nogay tribes from the Crimean khans, maintaining friendly relations with the Ottomans, and offering to restrain Don Cossack raids on Ottoman territory in exchange for the sultans' promises to rein in the Crimean khans. The shift to a more aggressive southern strategy began in the mid-1630s, at the moment Polish-Lithuanian control over Ukraine began to slip, encouraging greater Crimean and Ottoman intervention in Ukraine. The construction of the new Belgorod Line (1635–1658) linking twenty-five southern garrison towns—many of them new and built on the steppe—made it possible to move the field army much farther south and to form large military manpower reserves in Kozlov, Belgorod, and other districts. The 1660s–1690s saw a series of Muscovite military operations down the Don to blockade or capture Azov and other Ottoman fortresses; these operations had the additional purpose of tightening Moscow's control over the Don Cossack host.

From 1654 to 1681 Muscovite armies mobilized from the Belgorod Line fought in Ukraine. In the Thirteen Years' War (1654–1667) they secured Kiev and eastern Ukraine as a Muscovite protectorate; in the ensuing period of Ukraine's "Ruin" (1669–1685) they defeated Ottoman efforts to use the vassal hetmans Petro Doroshenko, Iurii Khmelnytsky, and Gheorghe Duca to consolidate control of western Ukraine and conquer eastern Ukraine. The first significant direct Ottoman-Muscovite military conflict was at Chigirin, where large Ottoman and Muscovite armies fought to a stalemate in 1677 and 1678. The twenty-year Bakhchisaray Armistice (1681) ended this first Russo-Ottoman War on terms generally favorable for Moscow, as it obliged the Tatars and Turks to recognize Kiev and eastern Ukraine as Muscovite possessions. Meanwhile ethnic "herding" raids by Muscovite and eastern Ukrainian forces had so depopulated western Ukraine as to make it impossible for the Turks to consolidate their control of the steppe east of the Bug River. This encouraged the view in Moscow that the Bakhchisaray armistice could be abandoned and the problem of the khanate solved once and for all, especially after Emperor Leopold I (ruled 1658–1705) offered to bring Muscovy into the Holy League, giving it the mission of keeping the Crimean Tatars occupied while he campaigned against the Turks in Hungary and Poland's king John III Sobieski invaded Moldavia. As part of its price for accepting this mission Moscow got the Poles to permanently cede Kiev, eastern Ukraine, and Zaporozhia in the 1686 Treaty of Eternal Peace.

In 1687 and 1689 the Muscovite generalissimus Vasilii Vasilievich Golitsyn led two huge expeditions against the Perekop isthmus, the gateway into Crimea. Neither succeeded in seizing Perekop, but the expeditions did demonstrate the scale of Muscovy's commitment to the League and established Muscovite garrisons on the Samara River to exercise tighter control over the Zaporozhian Host. In 1695 and 1696 Tsar Peter I honored his commitment to the Holy League by conducting two great sieges of the Ottoman fortress of Azov on the lower Don. The fall of Azov in 1696 significantly weakened the Crimean Khanate's power east of the Kalka river, and the Crimean danger to Muscovy was further reduced (although not entirely eliminated) by the treaties of Karlowitz and Constantinople (1699, 1700), which required that the sultan suppress Crimean raiding activity in order to preserve the inviolability of the Porte's new border with Muscovy. Thereafter Russian campaigns (1711, 1735–1739, 1768–1774) focused on the outright conquest of Crimea, the capture of the remaining Ottoman fortresses along the northeastern Black Sea coast, and the rollback of the Ottomans from Moldavia.

See also Cossacks; Imperial Expansion, Russia; Khmelnytsky Uprising; Ottoman Empire; Russo-Ottoman Wars; Ukraine.

BIBLIOGRAPHY

McNeill, William H. *Europe's Steppe Frontier, 1500–1800.* Chicago, 1964.

Rybakov, B. A., ed. *Rossiia, Pol'sha i Prichernomor'e v XV–XVIII vv.* Moscow, 1979.

BRIAN DAVIES

BODIN, JEAN (1529/30–1596), French political philosopher. Jean Bodin came from a comfortable family in Angers and received an excellent humanist education. He studied law and taught briefly at the University of Toulouse but was unable to obtain a permanent academic position. He was employed mostly in the royal administration and for a time was secretary to the Duke d'Alençon. A royalist at heart, Bodin was reformist and liberal in fiscal and social policy. He favored religious toleration as the most *politique* solution to the religious warfare that ravaged France in his time. In 1576, as a deputy of the third at the Estates-General of Blois, he staunchly opposed the grant of new taxation that the crown would have used to prosecute religious war.

Despite his occasional involvement in high politics, Bodin was an indefatigable humanist scholar who sought to encompass and synthesize all the learning of his time. He produced a corpus of extensive treatises on all the main subjects of his day, including the methodology of history, economic theory, comparative public law and politics, witchcraft, comparative religion, natural philosophy, and ethics.

Bodin's *Methodus ad Facilem Historiarum Cognitionem* (1566; Method for the easy comprehension of history) is a guide to the reading of historians that outlined much of his later writing. But his best-known work and the most influential is his *Six livres de la république* (1576; Six books of a commonwealth), which is a massive treatise on comparative public law and policy. The first half of the book is the earliest modern treatise on public law. Its organizing principle is Bodin's pioneering analysis and construction of the concept of sovereignty as the juridical condition for the existence of a state. Bodin also argued, mistakenly, that sovereignty was indivisible, as well as absolute and juridically perpetual. He rejected the possibility of a mixed constitution in which supreme authority was divided between two or more agents, and thus he broke with the received opinion that the constitutions of Rome and other classical republics were mixed. On Bodin's reinterpretation they were either pure democracies or pure aristocracies with respect to the juridical locus of supreme authority, although not necessarily in the day-to-day conduct of affairs.

Most politically significant of all Bodin's revisions of received traditions, however, was his interpretation of the French constitution as a strictly absolute monarchy. He had once admitted and even approved at least some juridical limits on the king. But he was finally driven to absolutism not only by the logic of his position but by his deep-seated fears of anarchy. Bodin had never admitted the right of a people to resist a tyrant and thought, mistakenly, that he could exclude that right juridically by denying the people any authoritative role in government.

Appearances notwithstanding, his reformist views on taxation were technically consistent with his stand on nonresistance. Although he held that all kings, including the French, ordinarily required the consent of the Estates-General for levying new taxation, this was not a limitation that the people had imposed or could legally enforce. It followed directly from the law of nature by which the ruler was responsible to God alone. The need for consent, moreover, did not apply in emergencies, and with Bodin's followers it was reduced to a mere counsel of wise governance.

Perhaps the most interesting of Bodin's works today is his *Colloquium Heptaplomeres de Rerum Sublimium Arcanis Abditis* (Colloquium of the seven about secrets of the sublime), which was written around 1588. Seven interlocutors, meeting in Venice, debated their competing claims as to the true religion and finally agreed to disagree in friendship. So heretical did this seem to Bodin himself and to succeeding generations who knew of it that it was not published until the middle of the nineteenth century. Indeed, the *Colloquium* is remarkable even now. In an arresting anticipation of modern religious pluralism, Bodin argued in effect that worship in any of the major religions was pleasing to God. Underlying all of them was a Neoplatonic natural religion of which all were variations that arose from adaptations to different climates and political circumstances. Each of Bodin's seven interlocutors represented a different religious viewpoint, and the inconclusive debate among them served to show that no positive system could sustain its claims to exclusive truth against the others. At times, however, Bodin seemed to be suggesting that Judaism is the oldest and the best. And it may well be that some form of philosophic Judaism was the ultimate outcome of Bodin's lifelong search for the true religion. The *Paradoxon* (1596), a treatise on ethics that was among Bodin's last endeavors, clearly indicates that Bodin, greatly influenced by the thought of Philo of Alexandria, had turned to a kind of Judaism. Bodin was buried as a Catholic, in accordance with his wishes. But many of his books were placed on the Index of Prohibited Books in a series of steps beginning in 1596.

Yet another contribution to modern thought was Bodin's brilliant 1568 essay, titled *Réponses au paradoxes du sieur de Malestroict*, on the great European price inflation of the time. It was caused, he argued, not by debasement of the coinage, as was widely thought, but by the importation of bullion from America that lowered the value of gold and silver. This was the first application of the quantity theory of money. Another contribution was less enduring. Anticipating Montesquieu, Bodin tried to correlate climate and national character to illumine not only political attitudes but religious tendencies as well.

Perhaps the least known of Bodin's works is his *Theatrum Naturae* (1596; The theater of nature), which is an encyclopedic collection of facts, observations, and principles of nature in the style of late Renaissance science. Its premodern view of nature supports a natural theology purporting to show God's concern for humanity in the natural order.

There are dark spots in Bodin's writing, of which his book on the detection and punishment of witches and warlocks *(La démonomanie des sorciers)*, published in 1580, is a notorious example. But such superstitions of the time apart, his universal synthesis of knowledge, although in large part outdated, was a huge intellectual accomplishment.

See also **Absolutism; Authority, Concept of; Constitutionalism; Natural Law; Neoplatonism; Political Philosophy; Resistance, Theory of.**

BIBLIOGRAPHY

Primary Sources

Bodin, Jean. *Colloquium of the Seven about Secrets of the Sublime.* Translated with an introduction and notes by Marion Leathers Daniels Kuntz. Princeton, 1975. Translation of *Colloquium Heptaplomeres de Rerum Sublimium Arcanis Abditis* (1593).

——. *Method for the Easy Comprehension of History.* Translated by Beatrice Reynolds. New York, 1945. Translation of *Methodus ad Facilem Historiarum Cognitionem* (1566).

——. *On Sovereignty: Four Chapters from the Six Books of the Commonwealth.* Translated and edited by Julian H. Franklin. Cambridge, U.K., and New York, 1992.

——. *The Six Books of a Commonweale.* Edited and translated with an introduction and notes by Kenneth Douglas McRae. Cambridge, Mass., 1962. Translation of *Les six livres de la république* (1576) together with variations from *De Republica Libri Sex* (1586). This is the only complete translation of Bodin's chief work on politics. It is a reproduction of the Richard Knolles translation, which is archaic and difficult to read at times. But McRae's variations and excellent annotations are invaluable.

Secondary Sources

Blair, Ann. *The Theater of Nature: Jean Bodin and Renaissance Science.* Princeton, 1997. An outstanding study of a pre-Baconian and pre-Cartesian philosopher of nature.

Denzer, Horst, ed. *Verhandlungen der internationalen Bodin Tagung in München.* Munich, 1973. Contains eight articles in English on various aspects of Bodin's thought.

Franklin, Julian H. *Jean Bodin and the Rise of Absolutist Theory.* Cambridge, U.K., 1973.

Rose, Paul Lawrence. *Bodin and the Great God of Nature: The Moral and Religious Universe of a Judaiser.* Geneva, 1980.

JULIAN H. FRANKLIN

BOEHME, JACOB (1575–1624), German mystic. Born in Alt Seidenberg, Lusatia, in eastern Germany in 1575, Jacob Boehme (or Böhme) was the fourth child of a successful farmer. The Boehme legend (established by friend and biographer Abraham von Franckenberg) emphasized his humble beginnings and his lack of education. It is clear, though, that his chosen trade of shoemaking was a success, and in Görlitz (where he moved around 1594 after his apprenticeship was finished), the young Jacob absorbed a rich and eclectic, if not particularly formal, education. In 1600, after severe depression over existential issues such as the place of God in an evil and fragmented world, he had a vision triggered by "the glint from a pewter dish." In fifteen minutes, von Franckenberg claims, Boehme learned more about the relationship between God and nature than all the universities could teach. This vision inspired him to write, and in 1612 he produced a partially finished manuscript called *Aurora, oder die Morgenröte im Aufgang* (1656; Aurora: that is, the day-spring or dawning of the day).

The work was passed around among Boehme's friends, and eventually reached the hands of the local Lutheran pastor, Gregor Richter. Incensed at Boehme's seeming unorthodoxy, Richter influenced the town council of Görlitz to silence him. Boehme observed the ruling for six years, although clearly his mystical development continued unabated. He continued his contact with the followers of Paracelsus (1493–1541), Valentin Weigel (1533–1588), and Kaspar Schwenckfeld von Ossig (1489–1561), and by 1618 his enthusiastic friends convinced him to begin writing again. Between 1619 and his death on 15 November 1624 he wrote constantly, producing works that ranged from mystical *(Forty Questions concerning the Soul* [*Vierzig Fragen von der Seele*], *Six Theosophical Points* [*Von sechs*

Punchten]) to alchemical (*Signature Rerum* or *Von der Geburt und Bezeichnung aller Wesen)* to devotional (short writings collected as *The Way to Christ* [*Der Weg zu Christo*]) to theological (*Mysterium Magnum* or *Erklärung über das Erste Buch Mosis)* to polemical (*Apology to Balthasar Tylcken* [*Erst Schutzschrift gegen Balthasar Tilke*]).

DIALECTIC AND WILL

Boehme holds that there is a fundamental dialectic in the emergence of both God and nature. In the *Ungrund*, or primordial chaotic nothingness, forces or wills strive to manifestation. There are two kinds of wills: *Begierde* (craving or desire), an infinite multiplicity of unrealized wills, and *Lust* (free will), which flows through *Begierde* to bring them to order and manifestation. *Begierde* and *Lust* are nothing prior to their dialectical, cooperative emergence.

This emergence takes the form of "Yes and No," an internal dialectical conflict that allows God to be the source and significance of everything natural, but not to be reducible to it. The two original principles, the No (dark, wrathful, or fire world) and Yes (light or love world), are joined by a third principle, that of movement and creation. These three are mutually causing, interpenetrating, and supporting. They emerge through seven "spirits" into what Boehme sometimes calls "eternal nature," and this threefold dialectic exists at every level for him.

The natural world is the flowing through of the emerged God into the multifarious forces of *Begierde*. Here too there is a seven-stage development—the seven forms of nature. All nature partakes of the three worlds, which emerge from God, and to the extent they are manifest, they are good. This process has sometimes been seen as evolutionary, but Boehme was clear that the dialectical emergence from chaos to full manifestation is present at once within everything. Boehme believes that every existing thing made a choice to align itself with one principle. Only humanity still has the choice of which world to live in.

Boehme calls the result of manifestation *Weisheit*, or the Virgin Wisdom, which is within all the processes of life and creation, and is a mirror to God. The entire process of creation is folded into every existing thing, and is available to those who have eyes to see. The dialectical emergence of *Lust* and *Begierde* results in containers, or husks, which both reveal and conceal the will within. Boehme's mysticism explicates the deep spiritual structure of nature, unavailable to the common person using *Vernunft*, or discursive reason. If one has *Verstand* (intuitive reason), one can recognize the common life concealed within the husks, which all of nature shares. "Signatures" are the external evidence of this commonality—they make *Weisheit* visible to the human mind. Boehme uses the image of creation as an instrument, which was broken by the Fall, but repaired by the incarnation of Christ. The instrument is still out of tune, but when one knows how to listen, one will hear sympathetic vibrations through everything. All of nature resonates because it all has the same root. But some of the wills in *Begierde* do not cooperate with *Lust*. They still strive for manifestation and can only achieve this with the destruction of the manifest world. This is Boehme's account of evil—a kind of uncreating.

Some look to Boehme as the inventor of modern dialectic. Some look to him as a theorist of freedom, others as one who introduced the idea of the objectification of the will, others as one who laid the ontological foundations for individuality, and still others as one who solved the problem of evil. Boehme is an heir to diverse intellectual traditions, ranging from Renaissance alchemy, hermeticism, and theosophy (via Paracelsus) to German mysticism (in the Rhineland tradition of writers such as Johannes Eckhart, c. 1260–?1327) to crypto-Calvinism to Lutheran theology. He is sometimes seen as part of a group of eastern German mystics that includes Schwenckfeld, Weigel, and Angelus Silesius (Johannes Scheffler, 1624–1677). But his influence surpassed all of them; Georg Wilhelm Friedrich Hegel (1770–1831) says of Boehme that it was "through him that philosophy first appeared in Germany with a character peculiar to itself."

Boehme's writings were particularly influential in England, where his followers were known as "Behmenists," and in Holland, where many editions of his work were produced. He was also important for seventeenth- and early-eighteenth-century movements such as the Philadelphian Society (Jane Leade, John Pordage), the Quakers (George Fox), Pietism (through Philipp Jacob Spener), and Methodism (through William Law). His influence extended into France (Louis-Claude de Saint-Martin, 1743–1803) and Russia (Vladimir Soloviev, 1853–1900). And he was read closely by later idealists and postidealists (Hegel, Friedrich Wilhelm von Schelling, Paul Johann von Feuerbach), Romantics (Franz von Baader, Novalis, William Blake, Samuel Taylor Coleridge), and existentialists (Martin Buber, Paul Johannes Tillich, Nikolay Berdyayev).

See also **Catholic Spirituality and Mysticism; Methodism; Paracelsus; Pietism; Quakers; Romanticism.**

BIBLIOGRAPHY

Berdyaev, Nicolas. "Ungrund and Freedom." In Boehme, *Six Theosophic Points and Other Writings.* Translated by John Rolleston Earle. Ann Arbor, Mich., 1958.

Stoudt, John. *Sunrise to Eternity: A Study in Jacob Boehme's Life and Thought.* Philadelphia, 1957. Reissued 1995.

Weeks, Andrew. *Boehme: An Intellectual Biography of the Seventeenth-Century Philosopher and Mystic.* Albany, N.Y., 1991.

BRUCE B. JANZ

BOERHAAVE, HERMAN (1668–1738), Dutch professor of medicine, botany, and chemistry. Boerhaave began life as the son of a village minister and ended it as professor at Leiden University and *communis Europae praeceptor* ('teacher to all of Europe'). He lost his mother at five and his father at fifteen, which left his stepmother with nine children to care for. Widow and children moved to Leiden, where student lodgers helped pay the bills and Boerhaave pursued his studies of and love for chemistry.

Though Boerhaave hoped to follow his father's career path, local patronage steered him in a different direction. He graduated from Leiden in 1690 with a philosophy degree and had begun giving private mathematics lessons when he was offered a job cataloging an important book collection for the university library. The university milieu—especially Leiden's library and anatomy theater—fostered a growing interest in medicine, leading Boerhaave to take a medical degree at the University of Hardewijk in 1693. (Hardewijk was famous for the low cost of its degrees.) Patronage brought him back to Leiden University and he began teaching an introductory course for medical students in 1701.

Boerhaave introduced his students, via Hippocrates and Thomas Sydenham (an English physician known as the "Shakespeare of medicine" [1624–1689]), to medicine as a clinical profession. By 1703 he had announced his preference for iatromechanism (the mechanical theory of medicine) and in subsequent publications, such as *Institutiones Medicae* (Institutions of Medicine, 1708), he put his mechanical principles and faith in observation to work. Observation became even more important when Boerhaave became botany professor and director of Leiden's botanical garden in 1709. At his inaugural lecture, he codified his philosophy with the motto *simplex veri sigillum* ('simplicity is the sign of truth'). The more he pursued his work, however, the more of a challenge his creed became. The botanical garden, for example, was planted according to three different systems, and his efforts to bring order to Leiden's botanical collection (see the second volume of his *Index Plantarum* [Index of Plants], 1720), were only partially successful. It was his student, Carl Linnaeus, who first published a consistent botanical system in 1735.

Moving between simplicity of theory and specificity of medical treatment presented a further challenge. In 1714 the increasingly popular Boerhaave began teaching clinical medicine by taking students to visit patients at Leiden's Caecilia Hospital. Here, he and his students directly faced the tensions between theory and practice. On one hand, students learned diagnosis and care. On the other, they learned a systematic way to account for the human body's economy of health and disease. True to his mechanical views and his desire to consider human physiology in a simple manner—that is, apart from metaphysical questions about the relation between physical being and the cause of life—Boerhaave taught students to focus on the circulation of blood and other bodily fluids, along with involuntary functions such as breathing, sweating, heartbeat, and peristaltic motion.

This systematic mediation between theory and practice made Boerhaave's work enormously influential. As his students graduated, they took with them the tools necessary to make medical study and practice both dynamic and authoritative. Once his followers gained official positions, in Austria, for example, alternative forms of medical practice—such as that of Franz Anton Mesmer (1734–1815)—

Herman Boerhaave. The frontispiece to a 1715 collection of Boerhaave's lectures features an engraving of the author in the lecture hall. U.S. NATIONAL LIBRARY OF MEDICINE

simplicity in which theory served to organize increasingly complex laboratory practices (see his *Elementa Chemiae* [Elements of chemistry], 1732). In both medicine and chemistry, Boerhaave's strength lay in connecting theoretical considerations to the demands and challenges of practice. This, rather than any startlingly original discoveries, is what made him a popular and influential educator. He died in 1738.

See also **Botany; Chemistry; Haller, Albrecht von; La Mettrie, Julien Offroy de; Linnaeus, Carl; Mechanism; Medicine; Mesmer, Franz Anton; Scientific Method; Universities.**

BIBLIOGRAPHY

Knoeff, Rina. *Herman Boerhaave (1668–1738): Calvinist, Chemist, and Physician.* Amsterdam, 2002.

Lindeboom, G. A. *Herman Boerhaave: The Man and His Work.* London, 1968.

Luyendijk-Elshout, ed. *Walking with Boerhaave in Leiden: The Trail of the Past.* Leiden, 1994.

LISSA ROBERTS

were driven from court and country. In Edinburgh, Boerhaave's graduates staffed a medical school that eclipsed Leiden's popularity in the second half of the eighteenth century by offering the same kind of inspiring training for a fraction of the price. At the University of Göttingen, Albrecht von Haller (1708–1777) transformed his teacher's mechanical approach into a physiological research program by examining the differences between involuntary and apparently voluntary motion. Refusing to give in to vitalism (the doctrine that life cannot be explained scientifically), Haller argued for the distinction between muscular irritability and nervous sensibility. While Boerhaave and others like him separated theology from medicine out of intellectual modesty regarding divine purpose, and for the sake of clinical and experimental rigor, one former student made a philosophy of this separation. Taking the idea of mechanism to its extreme, Julien Offroy de La Mettrie (1709–1751) argued that humans are nothing but machines.

Boerhaave became Leiden's chemistry professor as well in 1718. His influential lectures presented chemistry's traditional elements (earth, water, air, and fire) as instruments of physical and chemical change. This gave chemistry a level of theoretical

BOHEMIA. The crown lands of early modern Bohemia stretched across a significant portion of central Europe. Though centered on the kingdom of Bohemia proper and oriented administratively around its capital, Prague, they also included Upper and Lower Lusatia, the margravate of Moravia, and the assorted duchies of Silesia. There was little institutional cohesion among these territories; Saxony absorbed Lusatia in 1635, while Prussia seized nearly all of Silesia in 1742. Before the Thirty Years' War (1618–1648), Bohemia boasted a population of three million, more than that of contemporary England. The region was also blessed with an array of natural resources that supported a thriving economy. The Elbe River valley and the southern Moravian plain were fertile agricultural regions while the silver mines of Jihlava (Iglau), Kutná Hora (Kuttenberg) and the German settlement of Joachimsthal (Jáchymov) were known throughout Europe. Also important to the economy were the traditional Bohemian trades of brewing and fish farming combined with a textile industry that had a particularly strong base in Silesia with the commercial center of Breslau (Wrocław) as its most important hub.

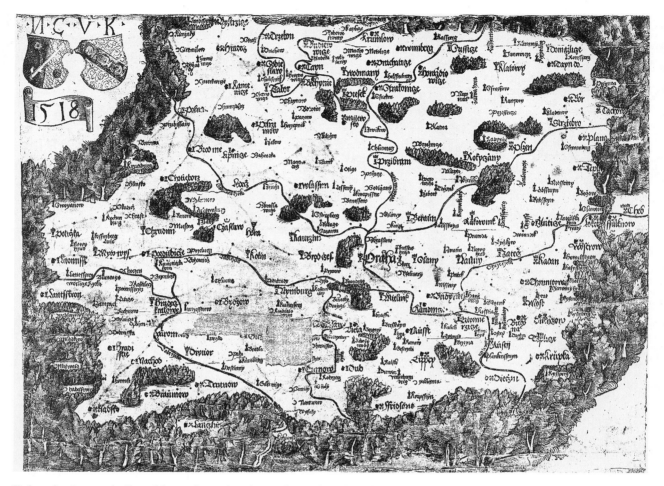

Bohemia. A reproduction of the earliest printed map devoted wholly to Bohemia, drawn by Mikulass Klaudyan in 1518 and printed in Nuremberg. The original map is now in the State Regional Archives in Litomerice, Czech Republic. At the time this map was created Bohemia was ruled by the Jagiellon dynasty (1471 until 1526), but in the latter year Ferdinand I of Austria claimed the throne and established Habsburg rule over the country. MAP COLLECTION, STERLING MEMORIAL LIBRARY, YALE UNIVERSITY

RULERS AND RELIGIOUS REFORM

The crown of St. Wenceslas was elective, and power within the kingdom was divided between the royal court and the three Estates: the lords, the knights, and the burghers. Constitutionally, Bohemia's political status was solidified by Emperor Charles IV (ruled 1355–1378). In 1356 he established the kingdom as one of the empire's seven electoral principalities. Charles founded central Europe's first university in Prague, began an ambitious building program in the city, raised the bishopric to an archbishopric, and initiated a lively cultural exchange with Italy. Both Petrarch and Cola di Rienzo visited Bohemia.

Scholars traditionally date Bohemia's early modern period to the accession of the Habsburgs in 1526. The two most pressing problems the new dynasty faced, however, had their origins in the previous century. Most serious was the issue of religion. Jan Hus (c. 1372/1373–1415) headed a reform movement that accelerated after his execution at the Council of Constance in 1415. Opposition to Rome crystallized around the Four Articles of Prague, which called for a general reform of clerical life and insisted upon the administration of the Eucharist in the form of both bread and wine. The Hussites successfully resisted five crusades and eventually won significant concessions that were negotiated at the Council of Basel in 1437. There were fissures, however, within the original reform movement. The radical contingent of the Hussite revolution would be crushed at the battle of Lipany in 1434. The Utraquists, representing a more conservative ecclesial tradition, would carry on Hus's legacy under the leadership of Jan Rokycana, a former master of the university. The Unity of Czech Brethren, a smaller group with a more biblicist orientation, would emerge as an independent body in the 1450s. The coming of the Reformation in the sixteenth century added further complexity to an already complex religious landscape. Lutheranism gained ground especially in German communities and among the nobility whereas Calvinism had a significant influence on the Czech Brethren. By the time Ferdinand I von Habsburg had ascended the throne, Bohemia had a well-established reputation as a homeland of heresy. The second problem from the Habsburg perspective was political. Their predecessors, the Jagiellonian kings, Władysław II and Ludvík (ruled 1471–1526), were relatively weak rulers. During their tenure the power of the Estates had grown at the expense of the crown.

Ferdinand's approach to these problems was initially gradual and indirect. In terms of politics, he worked around the Estates with his powers of patronage and appointment. He was able to select allies to staff such important positions as grand burgrave and chancellor. This gave him a freer hand at the conclusion of the Schmalkaldic War (1546–1547) to discipline the nobility who had joined the revolt. His response to the towns that had been allied with the rebels was even harsher. He deprived them of many of their traditional liberties and privileges. With regard to religion, Ferdinand, a devout Catholic, had even less room to maneuver. As Bohemia's king, he was constitutionally obligated to uphold the Compactata, those concessions the Utraquists had won at Basel, but he did provide the Catholic Church with an institutional framework upon which they could build. In 1561 he appointed Antonín Brus of Mohelnice as archbishop, a seat that had remained vacant ever since the defection of Konrad von Vechta to the Utraquists in 1421. Even more significantly, he invited the Jesuits to the Bohemian lands. Among their number was the young Edmund Campion (1540–1581), whose confessional rhetoric intensified divisions between the kingdom's various religious communities. The work of the Society of Jesus, especially in education, yielded handsome dividends within a generation.

Ferdinand's successors, Maximilian II (ruled 1564–1576) and Rudolf II (ruled 1576–1612), were more ambiguous confessionally, and Bohemia's non-Catholics made substantial gains during their reigns. In 1575 the Utraquists and Brethren jointly issued a single confession, the Confessio Bohemica, to which Maximilian gave a verbal guarantee of acceptance. More substantial, however, was a written grant of toleration, the Letter of Majesty, that the estates were able to wring out of Rudolf in 1609 as a result of his famous quarrel with his brother and political rival, Matthias. Bohemia's Rudolfine era is far better known for the great flowering of Renaissance culture that developed under the emperor's aegis. Though Ferdinand had commissioned what is arguably Bohemia's most important Renaissance monument, the gracefully arcaded summer palace, Rudolf easily surpassed his predecessors as both patron and collector. The imperial court at Prague attracted artists from across the Continent, including the fascinating Italian Giuseppe Arcimboldo. Both Tycho Brahe and Johannes Kepler enjoyed Rudolf's patronage, while the emperor himself was deeply involved in the hermetic arts. Rudolf even showed an interest in Jewish learning, inviting Prague's most important Cabalist, Rabbi Loew, to an extended interview in the castle. Politically and confessionally, however, tensions were rising to a crisis level by the time Matthias officially ascended the throne.

In his feud with Rudolf, Matthias had supported the Protestants. He disappointed the Czech Estates as king, however, failing to address many of their grievances that had arisen from the growing political power of Bohemia's Catholics. The Estates eventually took matters into their own hands. Although the zealous Catholic, Ferdinand of Styria, had been elected Matthias's successor in 1617, matters quickly changed when, in the following year, leaders of the Estates announced their revolutionary intentions by throwing two imperial officials, along with their servant, from a high window of the Prague castle. Ferdinand II was quickly deposed and replaced by the Calvinist elector palatine, Frederick. As the estates appealed to the broader Protestant world for assistance, the Catholics rallied behind Ferdinand in this dramatic opening chapter of the Thirty Years' War. Bohemia's fate was quickly decided. On 9 November 1620, Catholic forces defeated Frederick's supporters on a chalky upland outside Prague.

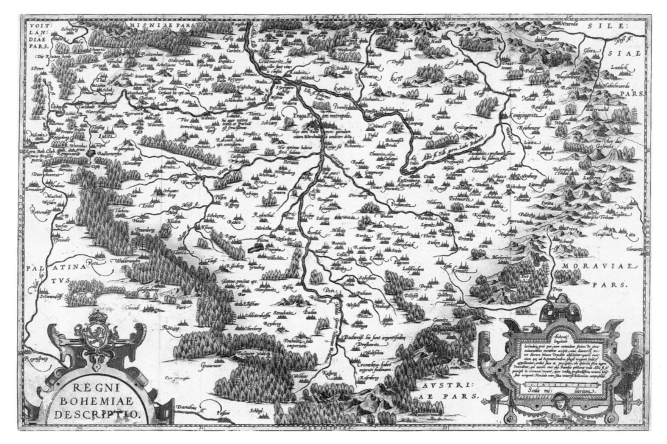

Bohemia. This map of Bohemia, from Abraham Ortelius's *Theatrum Orbis Terrarum,* issued between 1570 and 1641, depicts what is today the western part of the Czech Republic. The Kingdom of Bohemia reached its height in the fourteenth century, but by the late 1500s was in gradual decline under the domination of the Habsburgs. The city of Prague is pictured at the top center of this map, straddling the Moldau River just below its confluence with the Elb. MAP COLLECTION, STERLING MEMORIAL LIBRARY, YALE UNIVERSITY

The imperial victory at White Mountain, a great turning point in Czech history, afforded Emperor Ferdinand II the opportunity to resolve definitively both the political and religious problems of the stubborn kingdom. First, the elective status of the Bohemian crown was abolished in 1624. Then, in 1627 the Renewed Constitution redistributed power and privilege. The Chancellery was moved to Vienna, and the clergy were officially recognized as a new estate. Before 1620 the Catholic community had constituted approximately ten percent of the population. Now, the nobility and townspeople had the option to either convert or leave the kingdom in exile. Nearly a quarter chose the latter. Bohemia also suffered directly from war with a significant population loss and the destruction of its once thriving network of small towns. Before 1618 there were nearly eight hundred towns in the Bohemian kingdom. After the war there were hardly more than two

hundred. Prague itself was occupied in 1631 by the Saxons, while the Swedes overran its left bank in 1648.

Stability slowly returned in the second half of the seventeenth century. The Peace of Westphalia (1648) ensured that Bohemia would remain firmly in the Habsburg orbit, while the suppression of a great peasant revolt in 1680 and the Turkish defeat of 1683 granted Bohemia a degree of security the kingdom had not known for many generations. It was also in this period that Bohemia's traditionally fractious nobility were more thoroughly domesticated. The Czech nobility came to play a substantial role in the governance of the empire. Although Albrecht von Wallenstein was an ambiguous Habsburg ally, there were others who exercised a quieter but important role in the imperial capital. The Lobkowitz, Liechtenstein, Černín, Kinsky, and

Dietrichstein families served the Habsburgs faithfully in a variety of functions. Ironically, it was Kaspar Kaplíř, a grandson of one of the Czech rebels executed by Ferdinand in 1621, who would help lead the defense of Vienna some sixty years later against the Ottomans. Religious issues, too, were more effectively resolved in the two generations after Westphalia. A confessional identity that was thoroughly Catholic but authentically Czech was fashioned in this period. The cults of older but neglected saints were revived while newer ones were established. The old pilgrimage route from Prague to Stará Boleslav, the site of the martyrdom of St. Wenceslas, once more became popular, and newer forms of devotion, such as that to the Infant of Prague, quickly found their place in the religious life of the region. The exuberant art and architecture of the Bohemian baroque reflected the new self-confidence of the secular and clerical elites. This period culminated in 1729 with the canonization of the immensely popular John Nepomuk, who in the fourteenth century had supposedly been thrown into the Moldau for refusing to betray the secrets of the confessional.

THE EIGHTEENTH CENTURY

The death of Emperor Charles VI in 1740 precipitated another crisis in Bohemia as the Bavarian elector, Charles Albert, challenged the claims of Charles's daughter, Maria Theresa. Although he was accepted as king by a narrow majority of the Bohemian nobility, support for the Bavarian was tepid, and after the military victories of the Austrians in Moravia and Bohemia (though not in Silesia), Maria Theresa assumed the reins of government without a major outcry from the nobility. She continued the process of political centralization. The last institutional reminder of an independent Bohemian kingdom was lost when the Bohemian Chancellery was merged with the Austrian in 1749. She also reorganized local government by reducing the Estates' role in its administration. Czechs, however, would continue to exert considerable influence at the imperial court, as best exemplified in the career of the Moravian noble, Prince Kaunitz, who directed Habsburg foreign policy from the 1750s to the 1790s. Economically, the policies of cameralism benefited the kingdom significantly. The Habsburgs focused their efforts on developing important centers of textile production in northern Bohemia and southern Moravia. Financial prosperity would bring its own problems, for Bohemia bore 50 percent of the imperial tax burden, a figure that would increase even more by the 1730s.

Important intellectual and religious reforms came along with these economic changes. After White Mountain, the Jesuits held a virtual monopoly on education. Concerned that doctrinal error might slip back into the region, the Jesuits were cautious and frequently resistant to intellectual innovation. Ironically, reversing the pattern of the seventeenth century, it was the Habsburgs, beginning most notably with Joseph I (ruled 1705–1711), who would push for religious and educational reform within Bohemia. This process of liberalization would culminate with the enlightened policies of Maria Theresa's advisor, Gerhard van Swieten, and Joseph II (co-regent 1765–1780, ruled 1780–1790). Bohemia's first scientific society was founded in the 1770s. A chair of Czech language was established at the university in the 1790s. Most important, however, were the twin edicts of 1781 that abolished serfdom and granted religious toleration. Even the Jews won a series of new privileges. One of the oldest and largest settlements in central Europe, the Jewish community of Prague had experienced a wide range of conditions from Ferdinand I to Maria Theresa. With Joseph II they were allowed to move more freely in Christian society and even attend the university. Although the conservative Francis II (ruled 1792–1835) attempted to rescind many of the reforms of Joseph and his brother Leopold (ruled 1790–1792), the important changes they initiated survived and ultimately transformed Bohemia in the following century.

See also **Habsburg Dynasty: Austria; Hussites; Maria Theresa (Holy Roman Empire); Prague, Defenestration of; Reformations in Eastern Europe: Protestant, Catholic, and Orthodox; Schmalkaldic War (1546–1547); Thirty Years' War (1618–1648).**

BIBLIOGRAPHY

Brock, Peter. *The Political and Social Doctrines of the Unity of Czech Brethren in the Fifteenth and Early Sixteenth Centuries.* The Hague, 1957.

Eberhard, Winfried. *Konfessionsbildung und Stände in Böhmen.* Munich, 1981.

Evans, R. J. W. "The Habsburg Monarchy and Bohemia, 1526–1848." In *Conquest and Coalescence: The Shaping of the State in Early Modern Europe*. Edited by Mark Greengrass. London, 1991. Most concise overview in English on early modern Bohemia (pp. 134–150).

———. *The Making of the Habsburg Monarchy, 1550–1700: An Interpretation*. Oxford, 1979.

Hassenpflug-Elzholz, Eila. *Böhmen und die böhmischen Stände in der Zeit des beginnenden Zentralismus: Eine Strukturanalyse der böhmischen Adelsnation um die Mitte des 18. Jahrhunderts*. Munich, 1982.

Heymann, Frederick. "The Impact of Martin Luther upon Bohemia." *Central European History* 1 (1968): 107–130.

Kaufmann, Thomas DaCosta. *The School of Prague: Painting at the Court of Rudolf II*. Chicago, 1988.

Kerner, Robert Joseph. *Bohemia in the Eighteenth Century: A Study in Political, Economic, and Social History*. New York, 1932.

Macek, Josef. "Bohemia and Moravia." In *The Renaissance in National Context*, edited by R. Porter and M. Teich, pp. 197–220. Cambridge, U.K., 1992.

Muneles, Otto, ed. *The Prague Ghetto in the Renaissance Period*. Prague, 1965.

Polišenský, Josef. *The Thirty Years' War*. London, 1971.

Teich, Mikuláš. "Bohemia: From Darkness into Light." In *The Enlightenment in National Context*, edited by R. Porter and M. Teich, pp. 141–163. Cambridge, U.K., 1981.

Teich, Mikuláš, ed. *Bohemia in History*. Cambridge, U.K., 1998. Chapters 5–8 cover the early modern period.

Zdeněk, David. "The Strange Fate of Czech Utraquism." *Journal of Ecclesiastical History* 46 (1995): 641–668. Important revisionist article on the religious culture of sixteenth-century Bohemia.

HOWARD LOUTHAN

BOHEMIAN BRETHREN. *See* **Moravian Brethren.**

BOILEAU-DESPRÉAUX, NICOLAS

(1636–1711), French satirist, poet and poetic theoretician. Nicolas Boileau-Despréaux was the fifteenth child of a Parisian government scribe and the younger brother of Gilles Boileau (1631–1669), also a poet (the family possession of Despréaux was often added to Nicolas's name to distinguish him from Gilles). Destined for either the law or the church, he found his talent lay in writing verse mocking societal ills and the popular writers of the time. The publication of the *Satires* in 1666 established his literary reputation, and his acceptance in the circle of President Lamoignon, the leader of the Parisian Parlement, gave him proper social status. He recognized early the talents of newer writers, such as Molière (1622–1673), Jean Baptiste Racine (1639–1699), and Jean de La Fontaine (1621–1695), who became his friends. As was typical in his age, he dismissed authors from the Middle Ages and the Renaissance. Wishing not only to follow Horatian poetic theory but to become the French Horace, he turned to writing poetic epistles and a verse *L'art poétique* (Art of poetry), which were published in 1674. In the same volume of collected works were a six-canto, mock-heroic poem "The Lectern" and a prose translation into French of the "Treatise on the Sublime" by the Greek theoretician Longinus (which some claimed was made by his brother Gilles, who had died in 1669). Apart from a few satires and epistles written later in his life, his literary production was limited to the 1660s and 1670s.

In 1677 Boileau and Racine became historiographers to Louis XIV. This was more an honorary title than a writing task, but both accompanied the king on some military campaigns. Elected to the French Academy in 1684, Boileau championed the ancients' cause in opposition to Charles Perrault (1628–1703). In the final decade of his life, having survived most of his fellow classical authors, he refined the exaggerated image of himself, which lasted for two centuries, as the Regent of Parnassus, whose rules defined good literary taste and maintained the aesthetic movement of French classicism.

His most popular and influential satires describe scenes from contemporary life (III, "The Ridiculous Meal" and VI, "The Obstacles of Paris") or literary critiques (II, "To Molière"; VII, "The Satiric Genre"; and IX, "To My Wit") which combine subjects and approaches from Horace (65–8 B.C.E.), Juvenal (c. 60–140 C.E.), and Mathurin Régnier (1573–1613). First read aloud in cabarets and literary gatherings, with different satiric targets substituted to fit the moment, Boileau's satires display oral techniques with a striking opening, rapid narration of events, and variety of verbal techniques to keep the crowd listening and laughing. With a bit

Nicolas Boileau-Despréaux. FRENCH CULTURAL SERVICES

of reported conversation and picturesque detail, the scene comes alive. His subject matter is bourgeois, whether people, places or concepts; he mocks baroque excess, exaggerated gallantry, and precious expression, but not the aristocracy. The epistles, which complement the satires by their moral and didactic intent of praising laudable people and actions, were not nearly as popular. Of interest, however, and concisely expressed, is "Epistle VII, To Racine."

In his masterpiece, *The Art of Poetry*, Boileau distinguishes himself not by the theoretical argument of the content, but by the witty, succinct phrases that summarize concepts examined previously by others. Added to this are several satiric passages that ridicule those authors whose bad taste or poor judgment led them to stray from the ideals of order, simplicity, and reason. In the first of four cantos, general principles of versification and clarity of expression are developed, and the useful service a poet's honest friend and critic can provide are described. The second canto provides the guidelines for the lesser genres, such as ode, elegy, satire, and sonnet. The third canto presents rules for writing the major poetic genres: tragedy, epic, and comedy. The well-known classical principle of the three dramatic unities (time, place, and action) is stated in a memorable couplet. The final canto is general in scope, moving from satire of Perrault to praise for the king, who encourages poetry and civilized discourse.

In one of his last works, "Satire XII, On the Love of God" (1698), Boileau reveals a preference for the simplicity and rigor of Jansenism as he chastises the ambiguities and subtleties cherished by the Jesuits. In both this world and the next, he sought the order and harmony obtained by an adherence to doctrine.

Revered in the eighteenth and nineteenth centuries only to be reviled in the twentieth, Boileau's influence and importance have more recently been placed between these two extremes, in a classical "just middle" that recognizes the technical skill of his poetic ability and the role of the *Art of Poetry* as a commentary on, not a cause of, French classicism.

See also **Academies, Learned; Ancients and Moderns; Classicism; French Literature and Language; La Fontaine, Jean de; Molière; Perrault, Charles; Racine, Jean.**

BIBLIOGRAPHY

Brody, Jules. *Boileau and Longinus.* Geneva, 1958.

Corum, Robert, Jr. *Reading Boileau: An Integrative Study of the Early Satires.* West Lafayette, Ind. 1998.

Pocock, Gordon. *Boileau and the Nature of Neo-Classicism.* Cambridge, U.K., 1980.

White, Julian Eugene, Jr. *Nicolas Boileau.* New York, 1969.

Wood, Allen. *Literary Satire and Theory: A Study of Horace, Boileau and Pope.* New York, 1985.

ALLEN G. WOOD

BOOKKEEPING. *See* **Accounting and Bookkeeping.**

BORDEAUX. Bordeaux, capital of the Guyenne in southwestern France, was part of the dowry of Eleanor of Aquitaine when she married Henry II of England in 1152. Consequently, Bor-

Bordeaux. View from the Château Trompette, 1759, by Claude Vernet. THE ART ARCHIVE/MUSÉE DE LA MARINE, PARIS/DAGLI ORTI

deaux and the Aquitaine were held as fief by the kings of England until 1451, near the end of the Hundred Years' War, when they were conquered by the French army and incorporated into the kingdom of France. Located on the Garonne River, Bordeaux was a port city and a key trading partner of England and Holland, both of which valued its fine wines, made from grapes grown in the premier vineyards of France. Bordeaux's commercial ties with the French West Indies and its role in the lucrative sugar and slave trade enhanced the city's economic and demographic importance in the eighteenth century. Between 1750 and 1790, Bordeaux's population nearly doubled, from 60,000 to around 111,000, making it the third largest city in France. Its wealth underwrote extensive urban renewal, especially under the Marquis of Tourny (in-

tendant of the Guyenne, 1743–1758), and intensified local pride.

Bordeaux was home to one of the twelve prestigious parlements, or sovereign courts of France, and its magistrates, along with the great wholesale merchants, dominated the city's political and cultural life. The political history of the city was turbulent, as its parlement and municipal authorities sought to maintain Bordeaux's traditional privileges and liberties in the face of encroachment by royal authorities. In 1548, the city participated in the uprising against the salt tax (*gabelle*), a revolt that was savagely repressed. Bordeaux also suffered during the Wars of Religion (1561–1593), as the violence and instability interfered with the city's lively commercial activity, but it remained officially loyal to the king. However, Bordeaux was a center of fierce unrest during the Fronde (1648–1652), when members of the Bordelais bourgeoisie formed the Ormée and unsuccessfully demanded reforms.

During the French Revolution, the city of Bordeaux contributed eloquent and influential deputies to the National and Legislative assemblies. Their supporters were called "Girondins" after the *département* in which Bordeaux was now located. Twenty-two of them went to the guillotine during the Reign of Terror. The Revolution and the subsequent Napoleonic Wars were disastrous for Bordeaux's maritime and commercial economy, and the city never fully recovered the economic glory that it had enjoyed in the eighteenth century.

See also **France; Fronde; Wars of Religion, French.**

BIBLIOGRAPHY

Doyle, William. *The Parlement of Bordeaux and the End of the Old Regime, 1771–1790.* New York, 1974.

Forrest, Alan. *Society and Politics in Revolutionary Bordeaux.* London and New York, 1975.

Higounet, Charles, ed. *Histoire de Bordeaux.* Toulouse, 1980.

Jullian, Camille Louis. *Histoire de Bordeaux depuis ses origines jusqu'en 1895.* Bordeaux, 1895.

CHRISTINE ADAMS

BORIS GODUNOV (RUSSIA)

BORIS GODUNOV (RUSSIA) (c. 1551–1605; ruled 1598–1605), tsar of Russia. Boris Fedorovich Godunov rose to prominence at the Russian court in the time of Ivan IV the Terrible's *oprichnina.* He married the daughter of a leading *oprichnik,* and his sister Irina became the wife of Tsar Ivan's son Fedor (ruled 1584–1598). When the latter ascended the throne on Ivan's death, Boris was one of the five-man regency for the weak tsar. By 1587 Boris had exiled many of his rivals and become the de facto ruler of Russia. Tsar Fedor's younger brother Dmitrii was given an appanage in Uglich on the upper Volga, and his mysterious death in 1591 gave rise to rumors of Boris's complicity.

Boris, in Fedor's name, led Russia to victory over Sweden in 1590–1595 and recovered the Russian lands lost in the Livonian War. He laid the foundations for Russian expansion into Siberia and heavily strengthened the southern frontier. He convinced the Orthodox patriarch of Constantinople to raise the metropolitan of Moscow to the rank of patriarch in 1589. Nevertheless, the reign of Fedor was a time of hardship. The wars of his father, Ivan IV, had undermined Russian agriculture and general prosperity, and Boris's government issued the first decrees limiting peasant movement—the beginnings of serfdom. Though trade with the Dutch flourished, Russian towns only slowly rebuilt their trade and crafts.

In 1598 the death of Tsar Fedor brought to an end to the dynasty that had ruled the Moscow principality and Russia since the end of the thirteenth century. An Assembly of the Land representing the boyars, gentry, towns, and the church elected Boris tsar over other aristocrats and lesser relatives of the former dynasty. Even as tsar, Boris did not feel secure. In 1600 he exiled Fedor Nikitich Romanov (later Patriarch Filaret) and other members of his clan, as well as their relatives and allies, such as the princes Cherkasskii. Increasingly isolated from the ruling elite, he tried to raise his prestige through the marriage of his daughter to a prince of Denmark. In 1601–1603 bad harvests led to a famine throughout much of Russia. At the end of 1604 the first "false Dmitrii," probably the monk Grigorii Bogdanovich Otrep'ev, appeared on the southern frontier. Supported by a number of Polish magnates, Otrep'ev claimed to be the tsarevich Dmitrii who had died in 1591, the legitimate heir to the throne, miraculously rescued by God. Boris's army was at first able to contain the threat, but Boris suddenly died in April 1605, leaving the throne to his sixteen-year-old son Fedor. At the news of his death, resistance to the false Dmitrii collapsed. As the pretender moved north, the boyars in Moscow, led by the princes Golitsyn, overthrew and murdered Fedor and his mother.

Boris was at once a successful ruler, especially in foreign affairs, and a spectacular failure. The rivalries at his court rendered the state weak at its center in a time of rising social tension in the countryside and on the southern frontier. The result was the period of state collapse and anarchy known as the Time of Troubles.

See also **False Dmitrii, First; Ivan IV, "the Terrible" (Russia); Oprichnina; Russia; Time of Troubles (Russia).**

BIBLIOGRAPHY

Platonov, S. F. *Boris Godunov, Tsar of Russia*. Translated by L. Rex Pyles. Gulf Breeze, Fla., 1973.

Skrynnikov, Ruslan G. *Boris Godunov*. Translated and edited by Hugh F. Graham. Gulf Breeze, Florida, 1982.

Soloviev, Sergei M. *History of Russia*. Vol. 14, *The Time of Troubles: Boris Godunov and the False Dmitry*. Translated and edited by G. Edward Orchard. Gulf Breeze, Fla., 1988.

PAUL BUSHKOVITCH

BORROMEO, CARLO (1538–1584), cardinal, archbishop of Milan, and leader of the Catholic Reformation. Born on 2 October 1538 at Rocca d'Arona, Carlo Borromeo was the son of Count Giberto Borromeo and Margherita de'Medici. His early education took place in Milan under the tutor Francesco Alciati. In 1552 he went to the University of Pavia, receiving a doctorate in canon and civil law in 1559. On 25 December 1559 his uncle, Cardinal Giovanni Angelo de' Medici, was elected Pope Pius IV. Shortly thereafter, Carlo was called to Rome by the pope, who bestowed upon him various offices and titles, including that of papal secretary of state. On 31 January 1560 he was created a cardinal, thus, as cardinal-nephew embodying the very system that had come under scrutiny and criticism at the Council of Trent, which the pope reconvened in 1560 at Borromeo's urging. Borromeo assisted in formulating the council's agenda, serving as middleman between the papal legates at the council and the pope, defending papal interests against those bishops who sought the reform of the papal institution.

The unexpected death of his older brother Francesco in 1562 marked a turning point in Borromeo's life, shattering the world of patronage and prestige that he had grown accustomed to. Without a male heir, Carlo was urged by his family to marry but decided to pursue the priesthood, taking orders on 17 July 1563. A conversion had taken place that manifested itself in a life of austere piety. He renounced lavish living and collaborated in projects for the completion of the Council of Trent, such as the Roman Seminary and reforms in the missal, breviary, and sacred music, as well as the edition of the writings of the church fathers.

In May 1564, Borromeo was nominated archbishop of Milan. His understanding of the episcopal

Carlo Borromeo. LIBRARY OF CONGRESS

office, in particular the obligation to reside in the diocese, was influenced by Trent. In 1565, he obtained Pius IV's permission to leave Rome and take up residence in Milan, resigning all his curial offices except membership on the new Congregation of the Council. He entered Milan as archbishop on 23 September 1565.

Borromeo had an exalted opinion of episcopal authority. It was his belief that diocesan reform worked through the bishop. Soon after his arrival, he focused on reforming the diocese in accordance with Tridentine norms. During the nineteen years of his episcopacy, Borromeo convoked six provincial councils and eleven synods. The reform program that emerged from these synods was codified in the *Acta Ecclesiae Mediolanensis* (Acts of the church of Milan) in 1582, which treats such areas as preaching, reception of the sacraments, liturgical feasts, the exercise of eucharistic devotion, clerical deportment, and general parochial administration. Other bishops throughout Europe utilized the *Acta* to initiate reform within their dioceses. Besides legislation, Borromeo also undertook an annual systematic pastoral visitation of his diocese.

These various efforts provided Borromeo with the opportunity to renew the life of the church in Milan. However, the key to reform was a better-trained clergy. To accomplish this, Borromeo established a major seminary within the diocese, along with two smaller seminaries—one for preparing rural clergy and the other missionary priests. In 1578 Borromeo founded a new community of priests, the Oblates of St. Ambrose, who were charged with leading clerical reform. In addition, to assist priests in carrying out their preaching obligation, Borromeo issued his *Instructiones Praedicationis Verbi Dei* (Instructions for the preaching of the Word of God).

Borromeo was also concerned with the religious formation of the laity. Schools of Christian Doctrine, staffed by the laity, had been established throughout Milan prior to Borromeo's arrival. In his mind, the teaching of catechism was the prerogative of the clergy. While he eventually brought the schools under clerical direction, he did allow the laity to continue to teach catechism. By the time of his death, there were 740 such schools in Milan.

Borromeo did not focus all of his energies on the implementation of reform, but also showed himself to be a compassionate pastor. During the plague of 1576, he organized the clergy to care for the sick and dying, as well as to provide for the distribution of food. Carlo Borromeo died on 3 November 1584. Heralded as the model of the Tridentine bishop, he embodied and implemented the aspirations of the Council of Trent regarding the episcopacy. While he was a defender of the primacy of the papacy, he also defended the authority of the diocesan bishop. His efforts made Milan a testing ground for the implementation of Trent. Consequently, Borromeo may be considered a champion of the Catholic Reformation. He was canonized a saint on 1 November 1610.

See also **Reformation, Catholic; Trent, Council of.**

BIBLIOGRAPHY

Primary Sources

Borromeo, Charles. *Acta Ecclesiae Mediolanensis a Carlo Borromeo Card. S. Praxedis Archiepiscopo Condita.* Milan, 1599.

————. *"Instructiones Praedicationis Verbi Dei."* In *Acta Ecclesiae Mediolanensi.* Edited by Achille Ratti. Milan, 1890–1897.

————. *Sermoni Familiari di S. Carlo Borromeo.* Padua, 1720.

Secondary Sources

Headley, John M., and John B. Tomaro, eds. *San Carlo Borromeo: Catholic Reform and Ecclesiastical Politics in the Second Half of the Sixteenth Century.* Washington, D.C., and London, 1988. Collection of essays that explore the distinctive features and goals of Borromeo's work in its historical context.

Heuser, Herman J. "Saint Charles Borromeo as a Preacher." *The American Ecclesiastical Review* 7 (1892): 332–340.

Jedin, Hubert. *Carlo Borromeo.* Rome, 1971.

Orsenigo, Cesare. *Life of St. Charles Borromeo.* Translated by Rudolph Kraus. St. Louis and London, 1943. Translation of *Vita di S. Carolo Borromeo.*

Yeo, Margaret Routledge. *Reformer: Saint Charles Borromeo.* Milwaukee, 1938.

FRANCESCO C. CESAREO

BORROMINI, FRANCESCO (Francesco Castelli; 1599–1667), Italian architect, born in Bissone, a fishing village on Lake Lugano, today in Swiss Canton Ticino. With Gian Lorenzo Bernini (1598–1680) and Pietro da Cortona (1596–1669), Borromini epitomizes the Roman baroque style in its most agitated form. Radical design originality characterizes his artistic personality. He went to Milan in 1608, where he gained apprenticeship as a stonecutter on the continuing construction at the huge Gothic cathedral. There Borromini studied the unusual lobed plan and complex geometry of the late antique Basilica of San Lorenzo. These formative experiences served him as he later forged a new design language in Rome, where he arrived in 1619. At first working as a sculptor of architectural details on the nave interior of St. Peter's, Borromini soon assumed duties under Carlo Maderno (1556–1629), architect at the Basilica. During this time he developed his draftsmanship by copying details from the church's tribune designed by Michelangelo, whose anticlassical and sculptural vision of architecture thereafter became Borromini's ideal, and by studying the remains of ancient Roman architecture, particularly those with complicated curvilinear ground plans, swelling mural components, and billowing vault systems, as exemplified by Hadrian's villa near Tivoli. The sinuous architectural forms he fashioned from these sources seemed in the estimation of some later generations to violate the essence of tectonic art, but his place in history is secured by a profound organicism derived from nature and a sculptural conception of design—both subsumed in a disciplined, geometrically based graphic procedure.

Upon Maderno's death in 1629 Borromini was retained to work under Bernini on the giant bronze altar canopy (*baldacchino*) being erected at Urban VIII's behest over the tomb of the apostle at St. Peter's. Borromini provided ornamental details and technical solutions to the daunting problem of scale, but chafed under the dominant figure of Bernini, whom he considered not competent in architecture. Borromini's anger at not receiving the credit due to him for his participation in the design resulted in a break with the powerful papal favorite and colored the remainder of Borromini's professional life. Owing to Bernini's hegemony and, perhaps, Borromini's misanthropic demeanor, the lat-

ter struggled for attention in Rome's competitive design environment. He nevertheless received important commissions from religious institutions and a few private patrons, most notably during the reign of Innocent X (1644–1655), when Bernini's star temporarily waned. All his works were either initiated by someone else, left unfinished, or altered after his death. In some cases he attracted patronage through his Spanish connections, by offering to work without compensation, or by personally guaranteeing structural integrity, but always by producing innovative designs. Despite the vicissitudes of his career, Borromini produced some of the most unusual buildings of the early modern period in Europe.

As a cultural figure of European significance, Borromini is important for his intense dedication to artistic originality and his sense of the supreme value of innovation in the professional practice of architecture. Like Galileo in scientific inquiry and Caravaggio in pictorial investigation, he was a radical naturalist and looked to nature as a validating source for discovery and truth. His synthesis of Gothic

Francesco Borromini. The domed ceiling of the church of San Carlo alle Quattro Fontane. ©ANGELO HORNAK/CORBIS

design principles, imperial Roman buildings, Michelangelesque architectural sculpture, and a determination to transcend rules and norms led him to the extreme boundaries of emotive content and rhetorical expressivity not seen in Western architecture before his time. He brought this persuasive architectural imagery to the service of a re-emergent Catholicism. In the delirium brought on by a fever, he threw himself on a sword and died in agony the next day, but only after having destroyed a large number of his drawings. He may be seen as the baroque prototype of the modern eccentric genius.

Almost all of Borromini's completed work is in Rome. The most important and characteristic examples are the church and monastic complex of San Carlo alle Quattro Fontane, the university chapel of S. Ivo, the Oratorio of the Filippini, the re-constructed nave and side aisles of the Lateran, the facade of the missionary college of the Propaganda Fide (with chapel), the external dome drum and bell tower of S. Andrea della Fratte, and the lower section of the church of S. Agnese. His buildings and published designs—but most of all his free-thinking design spirit—influenced the Theatine priest-architect Guarino Guarini (1624–1683) and two generations of Austrian and German architects, notably Johann Lucas von Hildebrandt, Kilian Ignaz Dientzenhofer, and Johann Balthasar Neumann. During the ascendancy of neoclassicism, critics condemned him as the fountainhead of undisciplined design. Some scholars have seen in his heterodox forms a consistent symbolic language, while recent interpretations have emphasized the importance of cultural context for assessing his imagery. Borromini's heritage has reemerged in the organic naturalism of a group of late-twentieth- and early-twenty-first-century architects, only without his geometrical rigor.

See also **Bernini, Gian Lorenzo; Rome, Architecture in.**

BIBLIOGRAPHY

Primary Sources

Borromini, Francesco. *L'opera.* Edited by Sebastiano Giannini. Rome, 1720. Reprint, London, 1967. Engraved plates of Sapienza project, including S. Ivo and Biblioteca Alessandrina. Some based on lost drawings by the architect.

———. *Opus architectonicum.* Edited by Sebastiano Giannini. Rome, 1725. Reprint, London, 1967. Engraved plates of Roman Oratory project. Based on architect's lost drawings. Insightful text provided by Borromini's Oratorian advocate, Virgilio Spada.

Secondary Sources

Blunt, Anthony. *Borromini.* Cambridge, Mass., 1979. Flawed, but still the standard monograph in English.

Bösel, Richard, and Christoph Luitpold Frommel, eds. *Borromini e l'universo barocco.* Milan, 1999. Collection of essays associated with quadricentennial exhibition held in Rome.

———. *Borromini e l'universo barocco, catalogo.* Milan, 2000. Catalogue of quadricentennial exhibition. Copious and detailed entries.

Connors, Joseph. *Borromini and the Roman Oratory: Style and Society.* New York, 1980. Major reinterpretation of Borromini as architectural designer. Set the standard for many later studies.

———. "Vigilio Spada's Defense of Borromini." *The Burlington Magazine* 131 (1989): 76–90. Fascinating insight into valued qualities Spada saw in Borromini as designer.

Frommel, Christoph Luitpold, and Elisabeth Sladek, eds. *Francesco Borromini: Atti del convegno internazionale.* Milan, 2000. Proceedings of conference. Major interpretive essays, some in English.

Portoghesi, Paolo. *Francesco Borromini.* Milan, 1967. Reprint 1990. Still the major monographic study of the architect in any language. Accompanying interpretive photographs extremely influential.

Steinberg, Leo. *Borromini's San Carlo alle Quattro Fontane: A Study in Multiple Form and Architectural Symbolism.* New York, 1977. First appeared as author's dissertation in 1959. Controversial but seminal early iconographic interpretation.

Studi sul Borromini: Atti del convegno promosso dall'Accademia nazionale di San Luca. 2 vols. Rome, 1967. Proceedings of conference held in Rome on the tricentennial of the architect's death.

JOHN BELDON SCOTT

BOSSUET, JACQUES-BÉNIGNE

(1627–1704), French cleric, preacher, political philosopher, theologian, and writer. Bossuet's father was a magistrate in the parlements of Burgundy and Metz. Born and raised in Dijon, France, Bossuet began his classical studies at the Jesuit College of Godrans in Dijon and completed his education at the College of Navarre in Paris, where St. Vincent de Paul served as his mentor, influencing his education and early career. Once Bossuet completed his

Jacques-Bénigne Bossuet. LIBRARY OF CONGRESS

doctorate and was ordained in 1652, he became a canon in the diocese of Metz.

Although he remained in Metz, Bossuet traveled to Paris often and came to the attention of the royal family. As a result of his growing reputation as an eloquent preacher, he was invited to give the Lenten sermons for the royal family in 1662. In subsequent years, his fame as an orator spread and he provided moving funeral sermons for many members of the royal family including Henrietta Marie, queen of England (in 1669), her daughter Henrietta Anne of England (1670), Maria Theresa, queen of France and King Louis XIV's wife (1683), and the Princess Palatine, Anne de Gonzague (1685). He also gave the funeral sermons for other prominent figures such as Chancellor Michel Le Tellier (1685) and the Great Condé (1686). These sermons were eventually published under the title *Funeral Orations* and remain an important literary legacy.

In 1669 Bossuet became the bishop of Condom, but he resigned soon after his consecration in 1670, when Louis XIV named him tutor to his eldest son, the dauphin. As a result of his duties as the primary educator for the heir to the throne, he eventually published a book on world history, *Discourse on Universal History* (1681), one among many texts he wrote for his student, and was elected to the French Academy. When the marriage of his young charge ended his duties as tutor in 1681, Bossuet became bishop of Meaux. He took an active part as the primary ecclesiastical supervisor for the region, making visits to local parishes and bringing recalcitrant communities, such as the Benedictine Abbey at Jouarre, fully under his authority. He remained in this position until his death.

Bossuet was a great defender of the unity of the Catholic Church and throughout his life worked to this end, both in his dealings with internal Catholic controversies and in his relations with Protestants and Protestant communities. While at his first post in Metz, he sought to convert Protestants using debates, sermons, and writings such as *Refutation of the Catechism of Paul Ferry,* which came out of his debates with Ferry, a local Protestant minister. He also reportedly played a role in the conversion from Protestantism to Catholicism of the celebrated war hero, the duke of Turenne.

From 1679 until 1694, Bossuet corresponded with the philosopher Gottfried Wilhelm Leibniz (1646–1716). Their epistolary debates were part of his effort to reunify Christendom. Leibniz, a Lutheran and under the patronage of the electors of Hanover, also hoped to see an end to infighting among Christian groups and a reunion of all churches, Protestant and Catholic alike. Their exchanges explored possible terms of a reunion between Protestant and Catholic factions, but arrived at no concrete resolutions because Bossuet rejected all compromises that entailed altering existing Catholic doctrine.

Bossuet was also an important mediator between King Louis XIV and papal authority. He defended papal authority and doctrinal unity, but, at the same time, played a major part in the emergence of Gallicanism, policies that allowed the French king more control over some aspects of church institutions in France and increased independence from Rome, especially in regard to secular issues. In the early 1680s Bossuet served as an important negotiator for Louis XIV and Pope Innocent XI when the king sought control over vacant dioceses and their revenues. In the Assembly of Clergy that met in 1682 to discuss the issue, Bossuet gave the opening sermon and also helped to draft the treatise of the four articles published by the assembly as their final ruling on the issue. The four articles contributed to Gallicanism by declaring the king's control over vacant sees and rejecting the pope's authority over secular issues.

The last decades of Bossuet's life, the late 1680s and 1690s, were dominated by the controversy over Quietism, a mystical and spiritual movement led by a French noblewoman, Madame Guyon. At the urging of King Louis XIV, a panel of French theologians that included Bossuet examined Madame Guyon's teachings and found them incompatible with orthodox Catholic doctrine and practice; they officially condemned her methods and writings in 1695. Bossuet's very public feud with fellow French cleric and theologian, François Fénelon (1651–1715), archbishop of Cambrai, followed on the heels of the initial Quietism controversy. Bossuet denounced Fénelon's writings that lauded some aspects of Quietism, such as the notion of "pure love." A papal brief issued in 1699 censured Fénelon's work and finally resolved their bitter public debate, which had been waged in books and pamphlets.

Today, Bossuet is best known for his work, *Politics Drawn from the Holy Scripture* (1709). In this treatise on political philosophy, he articulated the theory of divine-right kingship associated with King Louis XIV's reign, using passages from the Bible to support the theory of an absolute monarch and arguing that the king's political power came directly from God and was, therefore, sacred and indivisible. Under divine-right theory, Bossuet maintained that it was not only unlawful but also a sin to rebel against the king. At the same time, he urged the king to fulfill his duty to protect and care for his subjects in keeping with his godly charge.

See also **Condé Family; Divine Right Kingship; Fénelon, François; Gallicanism; Leibniz, Gottfried Wilhelm; Louis XIV (France); Louvois, François Le Tellier, marquis de; Maria Theresa (Holy Roman Empire); Quietism; Vincent de Paul.**

BIBLIOGRAPHY

Primary Sources

Bossuet, Jacques-Bénigne. *Discourse on Universal History.* Translated by Elborg Forster. Edited by Orest Ranum. Chicago, 1976.

———. *Politics Drawn from the Very Words of Holy Scripture.* Translated and edited by Patrick Riley. Cambridge, U.K., and New York, 1990.

———. *Selections from the Funeral Orations of Bossuet.* Edited by F. M. Warren. Boston, 1907.

Secondary Sources

Meyer, Jean. *Bossuet.* Paris, 1993.

Reynolds, Ernest Edwin. *Bossuet.* Garden City, N.Y., 1963.

SARA CHAPMAN

BOSTON. Founded in 1630 by a group of Puritans led by John Winthrop, Boston was intended to serve as an example to the Protestant world, especially to Anglicans. Boston was the initial settlement and the capital of the Massachusetts Bay Colony, whose towns spread rapidly west into the forests of Massachusetts.

Settled by families rather than soldiers or single men, Boston quickly established schools, churches, and social institutions, including a proto-democratic local government. The Great Migration, which brought more than twenty thousand Puritans to Massachusetts by 1640, contributed to the rapid growth of business, especially shipping and boat building. Like New York and Philadelphia, Boston engaged in extensive shipping and trade with England and the Caribbean. The rich forests of New England contributed wood for boat building, pitch and tar for repairs and export, and a variety of animal products. In addition, Bostonians were deeply involved in the shipping of rum, sugar, and slaves. Business was so successful, in fact, that by the end of the seventeenth century many Puritan leaders grew worried that material gain would weaken religious sentiment among the young.

By the middle of the eighteenth century, the "city on a hill" had indeed moved away from its Puritan roots. Populated by more than sixteen thousand literate, prosperous, politically active citizens of a variety of faiths, Boston became the earliest center of rebellion against Britain. The crown responded with a series of repressive measures, the ultimate effect of which was to radicalize both the local population and other British North American colonies. While Philadelphia gave the Revolution documents, Boston gave men such as John and Samuel Adams, John Hancock, and Paul Revere.

Although Boston's successes were not those envisioned by its founders, it was a remarkable example of orderly colony building in British North America. Free of most disease, growing fast in families and wealth, replete with colleges, churches, artisans, and craftsmen, Boston was unique among early colonies.

See also **British Colonies: North America; New York; Philadelphia; Puritanism.**

BIBLIOGRAPHY

Morgan, Edmund Sears. *The Puritan Dilemma; the Story of John Winthrop,* edited by Oscar Handlin. Boston, 1958.

Nash, Gary B. *The Urban Crucible: The Northern Seaports and the Origins of the American Revolution.* Cambridge, Mass., 1979.

FIONA DEANS HALLORAN

BOSWELL, JAMES (1740–1795), Scottish biographer, lawyer, and man of letters. James Boswell is most famous as the author of the *Life of Samuel Johnson* (1791), perhaps the most celebrated biography in the English language. He was the eldest son of Alexander Boswell, judge and laird of Auchinleck, whose title came from the family estate in Ayrshire, western Scotland. Following his father's advice, Boswell agreed to study law at the universities of Edinburgh and Glasgow, but, lacking enthusiasm, in 1762 he traveled to London seeking a commission in the Foot Guards and, much to his father's disapproval, a more active and glamorous life in the higher echelons of the British army. Boswell's year living in London is recorded in his *London Journal 1762–1763,* a text that details Boswell's daily rounds of socializing, visiting prostitutes, going to the theater, and mixing with London's literary elite, including Samuel Johnson, to whom he was introduced on 16 May 1763 at Thomas Davies' book shop, and with whom he held a lifelong correspondence and friendship. Moving to Holland in 1763 to continue his study of law at Utrecht, Boswell was rewarded for following his father's career advice with a grand tour through Germany, France, and Italy. Visiting Corsica in 1765, and befriending General Paoli, who was fighting for its independence, Boswell turned his experience of traveling to this island into a successful travel book, *An Account of Corsica* (1768), which established his literary reputation in London. In 1769 he married Margaret Montgomerie and, dividing his time between his Edinburgh home and Johnson's house in London, he began to collect material for an intended biography of Johnson, persuading his subject to take a tour of Scotland and the Hebrides with him in 1773, a journey he turned into a travel narrative, *Journal of a Tour to the Hebrides,* which was published in 1785. Elected to Johnson's exclusive Literary Club in 1773, Boswell also contributed essays as "The Hypochondriak" to *The London Magazine* from 1777 to 1783 on subjects ranging from drinking to memory, but perhaps most famously on diary writing, which was a constant and, indeed, obsessive passion of his, causing him to write that "a man should not live more than he can record, as a farmer should not have a larger crop than he can gather in" ("On Diaries," 1783). Following the death of his father in 1782, Boswell spent more time at the family estate in Ayrshire, meeting Johnson for the last time in London in 1784.

After Johnson's death in 1784, Boswell began to work exclusively on the *Life,* assisted by his friend the Shakespearean scholar Edmond Malone in collecting and editing Johnson's voluminous papers and correspondence. The *Life* was finally published in 1791, eclipsing all other biographies of Johnson with its scope and liveliness, and silencing those who thought Boswell was not serious enough to produce a memoir of one of the period's most revered literary figures. In his final years, and despite recurring bouts of ill health, Boswell continued to practice law and to travel the country as "the Great Biographer." Boswell died in London in 1795 and his body was interred in the family vault at Auchinleck. His papers remained in the attic at the estate and were unread until rediscovered by Lord Talbot in 1905. Once uncovered, his papers were shipped to Talbot's estate in Ireland and, after many years of scholarly bidding, were finally collated by Yale University Library in 1949. Yale has since published Boswell's correspondence and journals, and the frankness of these texts reveals intimate details

James Boswell. Engraving after a portrait by Joshua Reynolds. GETTY IMAGES

about his own eventful life and documents fascinating details about literary society in eighteenth-century Britain.

See also **Biography and Autobiography; Diaries; Edinburgh; English Literature and Language; Johnson, Samuel; Scotland; Travel and Travel Literature.**

BIBLIOGRAPHY

Primary Sources

Boswell, James. *The Journal of a Tour to Corsica and Memoirs of Pascal Paoli.* Edited by S. C. Roberts. Cambridge, U.K., 1923. Reprint 1966.

———. *Life of Samuel Johnson: Together with Journal of a Tour to the Hebrides and Johnson's Diary of a Journey into North Wales.* Edited by George Birkbeck Hill. 6 vols. Rev. enl. ed. Oxford, 1934–1964.

———. *Samuel Johnson and James Boswell: A Journey to the Western Islands of Scotland and The Journal of a Tour to the Hebrides.* Edited by Peter Levi. London, 1984.

———. *The Yale Edition of Boswell's Correspondence and Journals.* Edited by Frederick A. Pottle et al. 15 vols. London, 1950–1993.

Secondary Sources

Brown, Anthony E. *Boswellian Studies: A Bibliography.* 3rd rev. ed. Edinburgh, 1991.

Hyde, Mary. *The Impossible Friendship: Boswell and Mrs. Thrale.* Cambridge, Mass., and London, 1972.

Pottle, Frederick A. *Pride and Negligence: The History of the Boswell Papers.* London, 1982.

Rogers, Pat. *Johnson and Boswell: The Transit of Caledonia.* Oxford and New York, 1995.

Sisman, Adam. *Boswell's Presumptuous Task: Writing the Life of Dr. Johnson.* London and New York, 2000.

ALISON STENTON

BOTANY. From antiquity into the late eighteenth century, the medical utility of plants provided the primary motive for studying them. However, from the late fifteenth century on, other reasons for the investigation of plants became increasingly important and gave botany a disciplinary and professional identity distinct from medicine. These included: explicating classical texts; portraying plants accurately in works of art; collecting rarities for natural history cabinets, gardens, and museums; exploiting natural resources; glorifying the wonders of creation; and satisfying the curiosity of natural philosophers. The primary thrust of botany in early modern Europe was plant identification, description, and classification, an effort that culminated in the late seventeenth and eighteenth centuries when systematics assimilated morphology, reproduction, anatomy, and geography.

LATE FIFTEENTH CENTURY TO MID-SIXTEENTH CENTURY

While editing the ancient authorities on medicinal plants—Pliny's *Natural History* and Dioscorides' *De Materia medica* (On the materials of medicine)—in the late fifteenth century, Italian humanists looked at living plants to resolve textual problems. In contrast to medieval doctors' dependence on illiterate herb-gatherers, medical humanists in the early sixteenth century strove to emulate Dioscorides' and Galen's firsthand experience with medicinal plants.

The lack of a shared vocabulary for plant description and nomenclature was circumvented by the addition of accurate, detailed, naturalistic woodcut illustrations to printed herbals—a key innovation introduced by Otto Brunfels's (1488–1534) *Herbarum Vivae Eicones* (Living images of plants, 1530) and Leonhard Fuchs's (1501–1534) *Historia Stirpium* (Notable commentaries on the history of plants, 1542), and imitated by virtually every herbal thereafter. The failure of Leonardo da Vinci's (1452–1519) superb drawings and observations of plant forms—unfinished at his death in 1519—to influence early modern botany underscores the scientific consequences of coupling the technology of printing to skill in depicting plants.

Beginning in the 1530s, medical schools at Padua, Pisa, Basel, and Montpellier established chairs of botany, required lectures, demonstrations, and field trips, and built botanical gardens. Students of Luca Ghini (1500–1556), professor of botany at Bologna and Pisa, spread his technique of preserving pressed, dried specimens throughout Europe.

MID-SIXTEENTH CENTURY TO EARLY SEVENTEENTH CENTURY

The humanist physicians' desire to prescribe the precise plants named by classical authorities spurred Pietro Andrea Mattioli (1501–1578), a Habsburg court physician, to prepare a voluminous illustrated commentary on Dioscorides (first edition, 1544), the best-selling herbal of the period. Its revisions and enlargements helped Renaissance botanists realize that they knew far more plants than their ancient counterparts.

The immense "universal" herbals of the late sixteenth and early seventeenth century—published or projected by major botanists from most European countries, including William Turner (c. 1508–1568), Conrad Gessner (1516–1565), Ulisse Aldrovandi (1522–1605), Jacques Dalechamps (D'Aléchamps, Dalechampius, 1513–1588), Charles de L'Escluse (Clusius, 1526–1609), Matthias de L'Obel (Lobelius, 1538–1616), Rembert Dodoens (Dodonaeus, 1517–1585), Jean Bauhin (1541–1612), Caspar Bauhin (1560–1624), and John Gerard (1564–1637)—represented efforts to describe both long-familiar plants and the flood of new species. Plants entered European gardens and herbaria through the voyages of discovery and conquest and by exploration of local habitats. Informal networks of professional and amateur enthusiasts surmounted religious and political divisions and fostered a rapid international exchange of specimens, books, pictures, and observations.

To organize their entries, most herbals used a pragmatic mixture of systems, grouping some plants by their uses, others by similarities of form or habitats. Some herbals, emblem books, and books on natural magic—reflecting astrology, Paracelsan chemistry, and the search for symbolic significance in nature—stressed plants' hidden, inner properties, manifested by distinctive external "signatures." Appealing to Aristotle and Theophrastus's philosophical emphasis on growth and reproduction as the essential characteristics of the vegetative soul, Andrea Cesalpino (Caesalpinus, 1524–1603) stressed resemblances of seeds and fruits in grouping plants in his influential *De Plantis Libri XVI* (On plants, 1583).

EARLY SEVENTEENTH CENTURY TO LATE EIGHTEENTH CENTURY

Caspar Bauhin (1560–1624), professor of botany and anatomy at Basel, took the first critical step toward a single botanical lexicon of plant names: his *Pinax Theatri Botanici* (Pinax, i.e., Index, for the botanical realm, 1623) summarized the synonyms and literature for some six thousand plants—ten times the number in Dioscorides—and assigned them brief descriptive Latin names that emphasized their affinities. (*Pinax* remains an indispensable guide to identifying plants in earlier works.) An equally important step came from Joachim Jung's (1587–1657) astute analysis of plant parts, which reached John Ray (1627–1705)—English cleric, naturalist, natural philosopher, and fellow of the Royal Society—by 1660 in manuscript. Between 1660 and 1704, Ray linked taxonomy, nomenclature, morphology, and bibliography in a series of strictly botanical books that brought together firsthand accounts of many previously undescribed plants, new technical terminology (such as petal, calyx, cotyledon), close observations of growth and form, and deep reflection on method.

Ray spelled out the combinations of essential morphological features that defined natural classes of plants. While acknowledging natural groupings at least at the genus/species level (categories that went back to Aristotle), the French botanist, J. P. de Tournefort (1656–1708), countered with a convenient and widely adopted artificial system of classification based primarily on the disposition of flower parts.

The chemical composition of plants and the form and function of plant parts, previously regarded as unimportant, came under the scrutiny of botanists trained in iatrochemistry—notably Guy de la Brosse (1586–1641), the founder of the Paris Jardin des Plantes in 1640—and in microscopy. Robert Hooke (1635–1703) and Nehemiah Grew (1641–1712) in England and Marcello Malphighi (1628–1694) in Italy reported to the Royal Society in the late seventeenth century on their experimental investigations of plant cells and tissue structures. Stephen Hales (1677–1761) in the 1720s and Joseph Priestley (1733–1804) and Jan Ingen-Housz (1730–1799) half a century later devised chemical and physical experiments to measure plant nutrition and metabolism.

The demonstration of sexual reproduction in flowering plants—in an obscure 1694 publication, *De Sexu Plantarum Epistola* (On the sex of plants), by Rudolf Jacob Camerer (Camerarius), professor of medicine at Tübingen—both resolved a long-standing question and provided the brilliant Swedish botanist Carl Linnaeus (1707–1778) with the basis of a taxonomic system that overrode all earlier proposals.

Believing that God had created species and genera, Linnaeus embedded their essential characters in his binomial nomenclature—henceforth giving the terms "genus" and "species" distinctive scientific meanings. Although Linnaeus clearly recognized larger natural groupings (plant families were methodically elucidated by the French botanists Antoine-Laurent de Jussieu [1748–1836] and Michel Adanson [1727–1806] in the late eighteenth century), his *Species Plantarum* (Species of plants, 1753) constructed a deliberately artificial system of classification, easily understood by anyone—even "ladies"—who could count the sexual parts of flowers. By imposing a common language and rational organization on the plant kingdom, Linnaeus made botany both a symbol of divine order and the epitome of Enlightenment science.

See also **Aldrovandi, Ulisse; Biology; Boerhaave, Herman; Enlightenment; Gardens and Parks; Gessner, Conrad; Hooke, Robert; Leonardo da Vinci; Linnaeus, Carl; Malpighi, Marcello; Medicine; Museums; Natural History; Natural Philosophy; Nature; Para-** celsus; Priestley, Joseph; Ray, John; Scientific Illustration; Scientific Method.

BIBLIOGRAPHY

Primary Sources

Bauhinus, Casparus. *Pinax Theatri Botanici.* Basel, 1623.

Brunfelsius, Otho. *Herbarum Vivae Eicones.* Strasbourg, 1530.

Camerarius, Rudolphus Jacobus. *De Sexu Plantarum Epistola.* Tübingen, 1694.

Caesalpinus, Andreas. *De Plantis Libri XVI.* Florence, 1583.

Linnaeus, Carl. *Species Plantarum.* London, 1957–1959. A facsimile of the first edition, 1753.

Meyer, Frederick G., Emily Emmart Trueblood, and John L. Heller. *The Great Herbal of Leonhart Fuchs:* Vol. 1, *Commentary;* Vol. 2, *De Historia Stirpium Commentarii Insignes,* 1542: Facsimile. Stanford, 1999.

Secondary Sources

Arber, Agnes. *Herbals, Their Origin and Evolution: A Chapter in the History of Botany, 1470–1670.* 3rd ed. Cambridge, U.K., and New York, 1986. Facsimile reprint of second edition (1938), with an introduction and annotations by William T. Stearn.

Findlen, Paula. *Possessing Nature: Museums, Collecting, and Scientific Culture in Early Modern Italy.* Berkeley, 1994.

Koerner, Lisbet. *Linnaeus: Nature and Nation.* Cambridge, Mass., 1999.

Morton, A. G. *History of Botanical Science: An Account of the Development of Botany from Ancient Times to the Present Day.* London and New York, 1981.

Reeds, Karen Meier. *Botany in Medieval and Renaissance Universities.* New York, 1991.

KAREN REEDS

BOUCHER, FRANÇOIS

BOUCHER, FRANÇOIS (1703–1770), French painter, draftsman, and etcher. Boucher was born and died in Paris, where he lived out his illustrious career as one of the preeminent figures of the European art world during the eighteenth century. His father, Nicolas Bouché, was an artisan-painter with connections to the Académie de Saint Luc—a vestige of the old guild system that was eventually suppressed and superseded by the more prestigious Royal Academy of Painting and Sculpture. Boucher was celebrated for his gallant rococo mythologies and picturesque pastorals. Over the course of his career he would rise to the highest ranks of the academy: five years before his death he was named

François Boucher. *Madame de Pompadour,* lithograph after the painting by Boucher. ©HISTORICAL PICTURE ARCHIVE/ CORBIS

its director and first painter to the King. It is probable that Boucher's father was his first teacher; however, the historical sources being regrettably laconic on the subject, little is known about his beginnings as an artist. In his youth he supported himself by working as an etcher and draftsman. He studied for a short time with the great colorist painter François Lemoyne and made the requisite trip to Italy to study after winning the Prix de Rome in 1723 (though without the official funding usually accorded to prizewinners). During his time in Italy, he seems to have attended most closely to the work of such baroque artists as Luca Giordano and Giovanni Benedetto Castiglione and learned particularly important lessons from the latter in terms of his subject matter and bravura brushwork. On Boucher's return to Paris about 1731, he set about the ambitious task of winning admission to the academy as a history painter, a goal he attained in 1734 with his reception piece *Rinaldo and Armida* (Musée du Louvre, Paris). By that time he had also made a

name for himself as a virtuoso painter of lusciously rendered mythological subjects, such as *Venus Asking Vulcan for Arms for Aeneas* (1732, Louvre), *Cephalus and Aurora* (1733, Musée des Beaux-Arts, Nancy) and *The Rape of Europa* (1732–1734, Wallace Collection, London).

Soon after his admission to the academy, Boucher began to receive official commissions from the crown and enjoyed unwavering support from the court and the academy until the end of his life. Though he had many prominent patrons, his name would become identified with that of the marquise de Pompadour, the longtime favorite of Louis XV, for whom he performed numerous functions, from painter of decorative ensembles, to portraitist, to drawing instructor. It was for the marquise that he produced some of his most spectacular canvases, including *The Rising and Setting of the Sun* (1753, Wallace Collection, London), and portraits such as the 1756 *Portrait of Pompadour,* now in Munich (Alte Pinakothek).

Boucher's association with Pompadour was one factor that fueled the increasingly hostile attitudes toward his work that began to be voiced by salon critics at midcentury, when he was at the height of his artistic powers and setting the example for many young painters of the French school. His connection to the marquise similarly affected the subsequent critical fortunes of this artist who, until recently, has been dismissed as little more than the favorite painter of frivolous and decadent aristocrats—especially of aristocratic women. Among other things, this has meant that Boucher's place in (rather than in opposition to) the culture of the Enlightenment has only recently begun to receive consideration.

The critical reaction against Boucher (and rococo art more generally) acquired its most definitive and eloquent expressions in the salons of the philosophe Denis Diderot (1713–1784), though these texts were not widely disseminated until the nineteenth century. Like earlier critics, Diderot objected to Boucher's unapologetically artificial colors, which were very often likened to women's cosmetics, and his tendency to use brilliant painterly effects and sensual subjects over substantive, edifying narrative. The painter's failure to heed the orthodoxies of aesthetic doctrines such as the hierarchy of genres and *convenance* (agreement) between subject matter and mode of rendering also occasioned critical commentary. The critical reaction against Boucher, the emblematic rococo artist, was not purely an artistic matter, however, but was connected to a broader context of Enlightenment ideologies concerning class and gender.

In addition to his stunning prolixity (Boucher is supposed to have produced some ten thousand drawings), what is striking about this artist is his versatility. Sought-after as much for his talents as a "decorative" painter as for his cabinet pictures, Boucher produced designs for tapestries, sculptures, theatrical sets and costumes, and porcelain. An etcher and book illustrator, he sometimes tried his hand at pastel and fan painting and is even said to have once decorated Easter eggs for Louis XV. As a teacher he was well liked, respected, and influential—his most famous pupil was Jean-Honoré Fragonard (1732–1806).

See also **Academies of Art; Diderot, Denis; Fragonard, Jean-Honoré; France, Art in; Pompadour, Jeanne-Antoinette Poisson; Rococo.**

BIBLIOGRAPHY

Brunel, Georges. *François Boucher*. Paris, 1986.

Desboulmiers, J.-A. "Eloge de M. Boucher, premier peintre du roi et directeur de l'Académie royale de peinture & sculpture, mort le 30 mai 1770." *Mercure de France* (September 1770): 181–189.

Diderot, Denis. *Diderot on Art*. Translated by John Goodman. 2 vols. New Haven and London, 1995.

Hyde, Melissa. "The 'Makeup' of the Marquise. Boucher's Portrait of Pompadour at her Toilette." *Art Bulletin* 82, no. 3 (September 2000): 453–475.

Laing, Alastair, ed. *François Boucher (1703–1770)*. Exh. cat. New York, 1986.

MELISSA HYDE

BOURBON DYNASTY (FRANCE).

The Bourbon dynasty succeeded to the French throne in 1589, following the assassination of the last Valois king, the childless Henry III. Through the French Revolution two centuries later, there were only five Bourbon monarchs: Henry IV (ruled 1589–1610); Louis XIII (ruled 1610–1643); Louis XIV (ruled 1643–1715); Louis XV (ruled 1715–1774); and Louis XVI (ruled 1774–1792). The dynasty returned to the throne in 1814, after the fall of Napoleon, but the last Bourbon king fled the Revolution of 1830, and was replaced by a cousin from the Orléans line.

The first three Bourbon reigns included civil wars in their early years, and the fourth opened with an unstable regency government; in each case, disorder resulted primarily from the dissatisfactions of wealthy aristocrats, some of them related to the dynasty itself. But the dynasty's principal characteristic was its successful affirmation of strong kingship, compounded of military, bureaucratic, and ritual elements. With the exception of Louis XVI, all the Bourbon kings were able individuals, and at least through 1715 they all interested themselves in the details of government. They succeeded in improving government's control over French society, and they temporarily restored French dominance within European power politics. With their encouragement, the apparatus of government expanded dramatically, as did the state's investments in culture; the Bourbons showed themselves keenly aware of the propaganda value of artistic sponsorship, most dramatically in works associated with the palace of Versailles. They also insisted on the sacredness of kingship itself. Public acceptance of this idea diminished in the secular atmosphere of the eighteenth century, but like his predecessors, Louis XVI continued to view himself as a sacred being, rather than as a mere administrator of his country.

See also **Divine Right Kingship; France; Henry IV (France); Louis XIII (France); Louis XIV (France); Louis XV (France); Louis XVI (France); Versailles.**

BIBLIOGRAPHY

Antoine, Michel. *Louis XV*. Paris, 1989.

Bluch, François. *Louis XIV*. Translated by Mark Greengrass. Oxford, 1990.

Buisseret, David. *Henry IV*. London and Boston, 1984.

Moote, A. Lloyd. *Louis XIII the Just*. Berkeley, 1989.

JONATHAN DEWALD

BOURBON DYNASTY (SPAIN).

The House of Bourbon, French in origin, was enthroned in Spain upon the death of Charles II, the last Habsburg monarch, who named as his heir to Spain and its overseas empire the duke of Anjou, second son of Louis, the Grand Dauphin of France, and Maria Ana of Bavaria. As Philip V of Spain (1683–1746; reigned 1700–1724 and 1724–1746), the first Spanish Bourbon married Maria Luisa, daughter of the duke of Savoy (1688–1714), and, after her death, Isabel Farnese of the ducal House of Parma, aiming to reinforce Spain's presence in Italy. His abdication in 1724 made way for the brief reign of his eldest son Luis I (1707–1724; reigned 9 February–31 August 1724). Luis's marriage to the French princess Luisa Isabel of Orleans (1709–1742) had not produced children before the young sovereign's death so Philip V was able to resume his kingship without difficulty, despite the constitutional scruples raised by his return.

The most notable result of his dynastic identity was an alliance with France through the so-called Family Pacts (7 November 1733 and 25 October 1743), which gave Philip the support he needed to enthrone his son Charles in the Kingdom of Naples (1734), and his son Philip in the duchies of Parma, Piacenza, and Guastalla (1748), thereby creating two new dynasties in Europe: the Bourbons of the Two Sicilies and the House of Bourbon-Parma. Philip V was followed on the throne of Spain by his son Ferdinand VI (1713–1759; reigned 1746–1759), who married Barbara of Braganza (1711–1758), daughter of the king of Portugal. The marriage proved childless, and Ferdinand was succeeded by his half-brother Charles, king of Naples (1716–1788; reigned in Naples, 1734–1759 and in Spain, 1759–1788), who ceded his Neapolitan throne to his third son Ferdinand, before leaving Naples to become Charles III of Spain. Abandoning the policy of neutrality regarding France and England that had marked the previous reign, Charles returned Spain to its alliance with France, with the third Family Pact of 15 August 1761. His marriage to Maria Amalia of Saxony (1724–1760), daughter of the prince elector and king of Poland, produced his heir Charles IV (1746–1819; king of Spain, 1788–1808), who married Maria Luisa of Bourbon-Parma (1751–1819) and had to confront the political upheavals occasioned by the French Revolution.

War against the regicide French government under the Convention (1793–1795) was followed by a new Spanish alliance with France, sealed by the Treaty of San Ildefonso (1796), which lasted de-

spite vicissitudes until the Napoleonic invasion of 1808. Prior to that, a palace intrigue had persuaded Charles IV to abdicate in favor of his son Ferdinand VII (1784–1833) on 19 March 1808, a decision he ratified on 5 May in the French city of Bayonne. Ferdinand in turn ceded the throne to Napoleon Bonaparte, who gave it to his brother Joseph and invaded Spain. This confusing episode led to an uprising of the Spanish people against Napoleon's army and a protracted war of independence that received crucial support from English forces under the duke of Wellington. After Napoleon's defeat, the Bourbons were restored in Spain in the person of Ferdinand VII. Surviving republican ousters in 1868–1871 and 1931–1936, and the dictatorship of Francisco Franco from 1939–1975, the Bourbon dynasty—in the person of Juan Carlos I—led Spain's democratic, constitutional monarchy into the twenty-first century.

See also **Charles II (Spain); Charles III (Spain); Farnese, Isabel (Spain); Ferdinand VI (Spain); Philip V (Spain).**

BIBLIOGRAPHY

Bergamini, John D. *The Spanish Bourbons: The History of a Tenacious Dynasty.* New York, 1974.

CARLOS MARTÍNEZ-SHAW
(TRANSLATED FROM THE SPANISH BY CARLA RAHN PHILLIPS)

BOURGEOISIE.

BOURGEOISIE. For much of the twentieth century, historians used the term "bourgeoisie" unselfconsciously to denote that rather vague middle group between the nobility and the masses of peasants and urban workers. The middle classes, the middling sort, the *Bürgertum,* the bourgeoisie; these terms were all used to describe the merchants, the guild members, the pensioners, and the elite non-nobles (professionals, financiers, and officials) who dominated much of the early modern urban landscape. They enter the European scene in the Middle Ages—the tradesmen and other urban figures who did not fit neatly into the idealized tripartite society of Three Orders: those who pray, those who fight, and those who work. These individuals worked, but they did not till the land like peasants. While some definitions of bourgeoisie include the artisan, most exclude those whose work soiled their hands. But these urban merchants and manufacturers were economically useful; they dealt in goods, and they dealt in cash. They would become Max Weber's Protestant capitalist, imbued with an ethic of ascetic capitalism, and Karl Marx's budding bourgeois class, the owners of the means of production. We see hints of this nineteenth-century meaning of bourgeoisie in earlier times; workers referred to their employers as "bourgeois," and peasants used the same term for their urban landlords.

DIFFICULTIES OF DEFINITION

Historians of France have led the way in trying to better understand the character and function of the early modern bourgeoisie. Steeped in a Marxist historiography that termed the French Revolution a "bourgeois revolution" fueled by class conflict between a politically aspiring bourgeoisie and a moribund aristocracy, scholars have closely examined the social class structure of Old Regime France in search of an economic and political bourgeoisie that would seize control of the Revolution's direction. But revisionist historians since the early 1970s have worked to demolish the Marxist framework, the notion of a dynamic precapitalist bourgeoisie leading a world-historical Marxian revolution. The bourgeoisie, if it existed prior to the French Revolution, they argue, was risk-adverse and keener on social mobility than class power. As soon as they earned enough money, individuals wanted to leave the bourgeoisie to become part of the nobility. Members of this group were far more attached to the trappings of status than to the accumulation of capital, the fruits of profit. Furthermore, links between the upper reaches of the bourgeoisie and the nobility—who frequently intermarried, and socialized in the salons and academies—were so close as to render meaningless the notion of "class conflict" between aristocrat and bourgeois. The elite—noble and non-noble—was quite unified, certainly more unified than any amorphous "bourgeoisie."

This suggests the importance of social mobility to any definition of bourgeoisie. Traditionally, historians have differentiated between the upper, the middle, and the petty bourgeoisie. There was always some mobility within this group; an education and a profession, not to mention the accumulation of wealth, could move one from the ranks of the petty into the middle, or from the middle into the upper

bourgeoisie. But there was also movement from the upper reaches of the bourgeoisie into the ranks of the elite. As the numbers and power of old noble families began to decline in the fifteenth and sixteenth centuries in a number of western European countries, many wealthy bourgeois families moved in to take their place through the purchase of land, and eventually, the purchase of venal offices, some of which conferred noble title. Social mobility—up and down—blurs the boundaries between the bourgeoisie and other social groups.

These fuzzy boundaries complicate the picture considerably. Focusing on linguistic and cultural categories, Sarah Maza argues that there was no middle class—no "bourgeoisie" beyond a precise set of legal meanings—in pre-Revolutionary France. According to Maza, until there is an actual discourse about the middle class, until it is named and given a social, political, moral, or historical importance, it does not exist; and thus, it did not exist in early modern France. A similar argument has been made for early modern England and for other European countries. Nineteenth- and twentieth-century sociological definitions of the bourgeoisie fit uncomfortably in early modern society, which would not have recognized the categories we impose.

Furthermore, the bourgeoisie—composed of relatively comfortable urban dwellers—was a small segment of the population in any European country before the nineteenth century, seldom more than 10 percent of the total population, except in the commercial countries of Holland and England, where the total urban population surpassed 50 percent and 25 percent, respectively. About 20 to 30 percent of Londoners were members of the middle classes by the eighteenth century, with some 3 to 5 percent in the upper class. During the same period, about 8 percent of the French population could be considered bourgeois—but only about 2 percent of the population counted in the upper reaches of that group. In other words, the size of the upper bourgeoisie in France was roughly equivalent to that of the nobility. The same was true in the city of Nuremburg in the sixteenth century, where rough numerical parity existed between the rich merchants of the city and the aristocracy.

Moreover, lack of real class solidarity attenuated the political importance of the bourgeoisie. Even in Great Britain, which boasted perhaps the largest and proudest middle class in Europe by 1800, the aristocracy dominated the reins of government well into the nineteenth century. If "the middle classes are always rising," as the old adage goes, their ascent had barely begun.

And yet, despite the admonitions of those who would consign the term "bourgeoisie" to the dustbin of history, historians continue to use it, as did early modern individuals themselves. But the sets of meaning that this term conveys are imprecise. Just as the boundaries between the bourgeoisie and other social classes are vague, the definition of "bourgeoisie" is equally so. Depending on context and assumptions, the historian conjures up sometimes radically different images when using the term. Definitions of "bourgeoisie" generally fall into one of four categories: legal, economic, political, and cultural.

LEGAL DEFINITION

The legal definition of bourgeoisie is both the most precise (although it varied from place to place) and the most restrictive. In the eleventh and twelfth centuries, *burgenses* was the term applied to the inhabitants of any seigneurial territory that was granted a written *coutume* or charter. This charter granted privileges to the inhabitants of that territory, but the specific privileges varied from place to place, and indeed, from country to country. Sometimes those privileges were quite narrow; for example, individuals enjoying the title "Bourgeois de Bordeaux" were allowed to bring their wine into the city free of duty and had the monopoly of retail sale within the city limits. Because the privileges associated with the legal title "bourgeois" could be quite specific and quite lucrative, it was not uncommon for nobles to seek the status of "bourgeois." In general usage, however, the term "bourgeois," from medieval times through the age of the French Revolution, referred to the non-noble inhabitants of towns, citizens who enjoyed the privileges associated with living in a particular place.

ECONOMIC POSITION

The economic definition, which emphasizes the economic activity and financial standing of the bourgeoisie, is both more contentious and more compelling. It denotes the bourgeoisie as the capitalist class, the social group that emerged with towns and trade. A market-centered focus and control of commerce and capital made the bourgeoisie a potent rival to the aristocracy in a number of European countries, most notably England and the Dutch Netherlands. In the German states, the small to midsized towns, especially the trading cities on the coast, were also dominated by the merchant, craftsman, and financier. It was the rising power of the capitalist that foreshadowed the end to a European political and economic system governed by aristocrats barred from trade by the threat of *dérogation*—loss of noble title. The bourgeoisie pioneered the commercial capitalism of the early modern era in the same way that it would spearhead the industrial revolution of the eighteenth and nineteenth centuries.

But not all "bourgeois" individuals were involved in trade and manufacture. The term encompasses lawyers, doctors, and non-noble officials, sometimes counted on the fringes of, or even at the center of, the elite. It also includes the so-called *bourgeois vivant noblement,* the "bourgeois living nobly" from the proceeds of investments and no longer required to labor for an income. While status in the early modern era was not invariably linked to wealth, wealth could go far in blurring the lines between middle class and elite, at least for those who were involved in the professions and not directly connected to the less noble function of trade. In many countries—most notably France and Spain—trade was considered a dishonorable profession, one that any person of fortune would try to leave behind as quickly as possible. It is this desire on the part of the bourgeoisie to move out of trade—the dynamic sector of the economy—and to invest in the more respectable lifestyle of land- or office-holding that calls into question Marx's vision of the rising capitalist bourgeoisie, challenging the aristocracy for economic, political, and cultural supremacy. Some historians have blamed the status-seeking French bourgeoisie for the stagnant nature of the French economy in the eighteenth century as compared to the rapidly industrializing British economy where the middle classes were less eager to disinvest from the productive sectors of the economy.

Bourgeoisie. *The Prevost des Marchands and the Echevins of the City of Paris* by Philippe de Champaigne, 1648. ©ARCHIVO ICONOGRAFICO S.A./CORBIS

POLITICAL INFLUENCE

Still, the economic clout of the bourgeoisie as individuals and as a group could go far in conferring political power along with social status. Economic resources allowed bourgeois individuals to obtain professional expertise for their sons through education, as well as to purchase land from the weakened aristocracy. This phenomenon was particularly pronounced in England at the close of the Wars of the Roses (1455–1471), which had wiped out many of the most powerful baronial families, but it was repeated in other regions as well. The wealthy bourgeoisie, the nouveaux riches, embedded in business and administrative circles, moved into the positions of economic and political influence once held by the aristocracy and eventually supplanted them as the new aristocracy. This regeneration of the old elite with social climbers from the bourgeoisie is a common theme in early modern history. The aristocratic

diarist Saint-Simon railed at the tendency of Louis XIV of France (ruled 1643–1715) to choose bourgeois individuals, vile men "raised from the dust," as his ministers at the expense of his traditional advisors, the nobility. Within a few generations, these "vile men" would hold sway as prestigious members of the court. A similar process took place in the Prussian bureaucracy under Frederick William I (ruled 1713–1740).

This would suggest a tight nexus between the rise of absolutism and the role of the bourgeoisie in early modern states. Kings bent on increasing their authority would turn to members of the bourgeoisie to serve the state and carry out the king's will at the expense of the old feudal nobility, whose wealth and regional power bases made it a constant threat to central authority. Affluent commoners, ready for the peace, rationality, and business benefits a centralizing monarch could introduce into the operations of government, eagerly supported the king against the rapacious nobility, and their educated sons entered into royal service. Recent scholarship that indicates more mutual dependence between monarchs and their nobility throws this line of analysis into question. but certainly the perception of an aggressive bourgeoisie usurping aristocratic privileges and rights was a powerful one, as the writings of Saint-Simon indicate.

But another interpretation of the political role of the early modern bourgeoisie also undermines the notion of complicity between king and merchant. The traditional social interpretation of both the English Civil War of the 1640s and the French Revolution of 1789 painted a bourgeoisie confident in its commercial importance, seeking political power commensurate with its economic power. Jürgen Habermas cites the creation of a "bourgeois public sphere" in the seventeenth and eighteenth centuries in which a nascent public opinion called into question the monopoly of state and clergy over political discussion. This desire for a political voice brought the bourgeoisie into conflict with aristocracy and crown, both jealous and unwilling to sacrifice political control. Accordingly, a powerful, independent, and discontented bourgeoisie was essential in bringing about revolution or parliamentary democracy or both in countries like France and England; and the absence or weakness of that same class (as in Prussia or Russia) was responsible for the prolongation of absolutist dictatorship. In the words of Barrington Moore, Jr., "No bourgeois, no democracy." The growing political awareness of the eighteenth-century bourgeoisie and the intense political partisanship linked to the effects of the French Revolution throughout Europe played a key role in shaping middle-class consciousness.

CULTURAL INTERPRETATIONS

But bourgeois identity also had important cultural roots that went beyond political activism, including a belief in property, virtue, and talent as the bases for social advancement, and attachment to religious values, frugality, a work ethic, public service, and especially material comfort. The bourgeoisie is also associated with an emphasis on the conjugal family and sentimental familial relations, in contrast to the focus on lineage associated with the aristocracy.

This sociocultural interpretation of the bourgeoisie, with its focus on values, attitudes, and rules of conduct, has dominated historical scholarship in recent years. This consciousness of difference, of cultural and moral superiority to the idle aristocracy and the lower-class masses, had appeared among the middle classes by the seventeenth and eighteenth centuries, even if a clear-cut notion of class solidarity did not yet exist.

Still, "bourgeois values" were never uncontested, even in the nineteenth century, often heralded as the golden age of the western European bourgeoisie when its ideology triumphed across class lines. Aristocrats were notoriously contemptuous of the bourgeois values of thrift, acquisitiveness, and morality. They ridiculed the lack of culture and refinement, the crudeness, the avariciousness, the "shopkeeper mentality" of the bourgeoisie. They saved their sharpest barbs for the upwardly mobile, the individual who was trying to buy his way up the social ladder, but whose lack of blood and breeding would forever mark him as bourgeois. Molière's *Le Bourgeois gentilhomme* (1671) underlines aristocratic disdain for the wealthy parvenu. And the lower classes, who might have looked to emulate certain characteristics of their bourgeois betters, saw them as calculating, exploitative, and cruel.

Those who give weight to the sociocultural interpretation of the bourgeoisie often underline gender relations within this social group. The ideology of domesticity, which emerged by the eighteenth century, emphasized the importance of harmonious familial relations, a moral private life, prescribed gender roles, and the celebration of the home as a haven from the rational, but heartless, world of the market. The consolidation of bourgeois class status was marked by the movement of women out of family businesses and into the home. Women were central to maintaining the standing of bourgeois families, in creating a moral center for the family and a suitable home with the necessary material comforts.

CONTRADICTIONS IN THE IMAGE OF THE EARLY MODERN BOURGEOISIE

The early modern bourgeoisie emerge as a contradictory group. They are the dynamic proto-capitalists, trading and running manufacturing enterprises, working as lawyers and doctors in the liberal professions, running town and state as government officials; they are the status-conscious upwardly mobile, looking only to accumulate enough wealth to invest in land and venal offices and to withdraw from productive activity. They are toadies of absolute monarchs, imposing centralized governments throughout Europe; they are bold political actors, demanding an end to monarchical despotism and a role in the political process. They are a group that values thrift, order, religious principles, industriousness, gender-appropriate behavior, and material comforts; they are a small-minded, petty, and greedy group whose base roots can never be camouflaged, even if their wealth propels them into a higher social category. These contradictory images cannot be resolved, but contradictions are normal within a group as large and as loosely defined as the early modern bourgeoisie.

Despite the self-confidence and belief in the values of hard work and honesty that were part of bourgeois identity, anxiety also permeated the self-image of the early modern bourgeoisie. The status of these individuals was hard-won and was not undergirded by the security of noble title. While we focus on the success stories, downward mobility was at least as common a phenomenon as upward mobility. A merchant could lose his fortune; a lawyer could lose his clients; an official could face dismissal by his ruler. No social safety net existed to protect him. Work, frugality, and reputation were all that stood between the bourgeois and the downward slide to social oblivion. That anxiety may explain his attachment to the conservative values we consider "bourgeois," often long after he had left the middle classes behind.

See also **Ancien Régime; Aristocracy; Capitalism; Cities and Urban Life; Class, Status, and Order; Law: Lawyers; Mobility, Social.**

BIBLIOGRAPHY

Adams, Christine. *A Taste for Comfort and Status: A Bourgeois Family in Eighteenth-Century France.* University Park, Pa., 2000.

Barber, Bernard, and Elinor G. Barber, eds. *European Social Class: Stability and Change.* New York, 1965.

Barber, Elinor G. *The Bourgeoisie in Eighteenth-Century France.* Princeton, 1955.

Braudel, Fernand. *Civilization and Capitalism, 15th–18th Century.* 3 vols. Translated by Siân Reynolds. New York, 1982–1984.

Davidoff, Leonore, and Catherine Hall. *Family Fortunes: Men and Women of the English Middle Class, 1780–1850.* Rev. ed. London and New York, 2002.

Earle, Peter. *The Making of the English Middle Class: Business, Society and Family Life in London, 1660–1730.* Berkeley and Los Angeles, 1989.

Garrioch, David. *The Formation of the Parisian Bourgeoisie, 1690–1830.* Cambridge, Mass., and London, 1996.

Habermas, Jürgen. *The Structural Transformation of the Public Sphere: An Inquiry into a Category of Bourgeois Society.* Translated by Thomas Burger and Frederick Lawrence. Cambridge, Mass., 1989.

Hunt, Margaret R. *The Middling Sort: Commerce, Gender, and the Family in England, 1680–1780.* Berkeley and Los Angeles, 1996.

Huppert, George. *Les Bourgeois Gentilshommes: An Essay on the Definition of Elites in Renaissance France.* Chicago, 1977.

Jones, Colin. "Bourgeois Revolution Revivified: 1789 and Social Change." In *Rewriting the French Revolution,* edited by Colin Lucas, pp. 69–118. Oxford, 1991.

Lucas, Colin. "Nobles, Bourgeois, and the Origins of the French Revolution." *Past and Present* 60 (August 1973): 84–126.

Maza, Sarah. "Luxury, Morality, and Social Change: Why There Was No Middle-Class Consciousness in Prerevolutionary France." *Journal of Modern History* 69 (June 1997): 199–229.

Moore, Barrington, Jr. *Social Origins of Dictatorship and Democracy: Lord and Peasant in the Making of the Modern World.* Boston, 1966.

Sperber, Jonathan. "Bürger, Bürgertum, Bürgerlichkeit, Bürgerliche Gesellschaft: Studies of the German (Upper) Middle Class and Its Sociocultural World." *Journal of Modern History* 69 (June 1997): 271–297.

CHRISTINE ADAMS

BOYLE, ROBERT

BOYLE, ROBERT (1627–1691), natural philosopher and lay theologian. Boyle was born in Ireland, the youngest son of Richard Boyle (1566–1643), earl of Cork, and was raised as an aristocrat. After attending Eton, Robert Boyle embarked on a grand tour. When his travels were cut short as a result of the economic upheavals caused by the Irish Rebellion, he made his way back to England, where he found his sister, Katherine Ranelagh, living in London. After a brief stay with her (during which he became acquainted with the Puritan reformers of the Dury Circle), Boyle moved in 1645 to "Stalbridge," the estate in Dorset he had inherited from his father. There he wrote a number of ethical treatises and other moralistic pieces before becoming more interested in experimental philosophy. In 1649 he set up a laboratory at Stalbridge and began systematic studies in chemistry (and alchemy).

In 1655 or 1656 Boyle moved to Oxford, where he became a part of the experimental natural philosophy group. There he published some of his more important works in natural philosophy, including *New Experiments Physico-Mechanical Touching the Spring of Air and Its Effects* (1660), *The Sceptical Chymist* (1661), and *The Origin of Forms and Qualities according to the Corpuscular Philosophy* (1666). In 1668 Boyle moved back to London, where he became one of the founding members of the Royal Society of London. He established a laboratory in his sister's home and lived with her for the remainder of his life. Boyle continued his experiments and publications in natural philosophy and in addition published a number of works that were either primarily theological in nature or works in which it is impossible to separate his theological concerns from his work in natural philosophy. Among these are *The Excellency of Theology Compar'd with Natural Philosophy* (1674), *A Free Enquiry into the Vulgarly Receiv'd Notion of Nature* (1686), *A Discourse of Things above Reason* (1681), *A Disquisition about the Final Causes of Natural Things* (1688), and *The Christian Virtuoso* (1690).

As a natural philosopher, Boyle is best remembered for Boyle's Law, for advocating a corpuscularian matter theory, and for being extremely influential in the development of an empirical and experimental method. He had a marked aversion to speculative metaphysics, and in *Notion of Nature* argued against attributing any ontological status to either the Aristotelian notion of "nature" (as in "Nature abhors a vacuum") or to the "hylarchic principle" (or "plastick nature") of the Cambridge Platonists. Boyle argued that entities such as these are not needed to explain the phenomena and ought not be admitted into a theory of nature on the grounds of Ockham's razor (the principle that entities ought not to be multiplied beyond necessity).

Boyle is still honored in introductory chemistry texts as the "father of modern chemistry," the natural philosopher who successfully separated chemistry from its alchemical antecedents. This claim, however, is based on the fact that the work in which he is supposed to have done this, *The Sceptical Chymist*, was misinterpreted until the late twentieth century. Rather than being an attack on alchemy, the work is instead an attack only on certain practitioners and textbook writers—most specifically those who divorced alchemy from any theoretical underpinning. Indeed Boyle was quite involved in alchemical pursuits throughout his life, both in attempts to transmute base metals into gold and in the investigation of alchemical processes for medicinal purposes.

During his lifetime and after his death Boyle was honored as much for his piety as for his work as an experimental philosopher. Boyle considered the investigation of the world God created as a way of worshiping God, seeing the created world as a temple and the investigator of that world as a priest. He was painfully aware of the growing suspicion that the revival of Epicureanism (in the form of the corpuscular philosophy) might lead to a materialist worldview and an accompanying atheism, and he published work after work in which he attempted to show that the astute natural philosopher would become a more devout Christian rather than being led to question God's existence or providence. He advocated a natural theology that was typical of the time, showing that reason alone could prove God's existence and the immateriality of the soul.

Boyle was quite clear, however, that this natural philosophy was only the first step toward belief and that its main purpose was to serve as a bridge to revelation. As Boyle expressed it, knowing that God exists and having come to admire his workmanship, one naturally wants to learn more about the deity, and fortunately God has provided that knowledge via revelation. Boyle wrote extensively in an attempt to privilege the mysteries of Christianity from rational scrutiny, arguing that just as there are aspects of nature that human beings cannot (yet) understand, so too are there mysteries revealed in Scripture that human beings cannot (yet) understand. Indeed Boyle went so far as to argue that, where revelation is concerned, it is sometimes necessary for human reason to affirm apparently contradictory truths, such as God's prescience and human beings' free will (emphasizing that God, in his infinite wisdom, understands how such apparent contradictions are in fact consistent).

The unity of Boyle's thought is revealed in his voluntarism (his emphasis on God's will and power rather than on God's goodness and reason). In Boyle's view God was free to create any world whatsoever. The only way to discover the nature of God's creation is to investigate it, and (because the world was created commensurate to God's infinite understanding rather than to finite human understanding), there will always be aspects of this world that humans are unable to comprehend. The same thing is true of the mysteries of Christianity. God has reserved a full understanding of both nature and theology for the afterlife, thereby providing an incentive for godly living and belief.

See also **Alchemy; Chemistry; Nature; Scientific Method; Scientific Revolution.**

BIBLIOGRAPHY

Primary Sources

Boyle, Robert. *The Correspondence of Robert Boyle.* 6 vols. Edited by Michael Hunter, Antonio Clericuzio, and Lawrence M. Principe. London, 2001.

———. *The Early Essays and Ethics of Robert Boyle.* Edited by John T. Harwood. Carbondale and Edwardsville, Ill., 1991.

———. *Robert Boyle: By Himself and His Friends: With a Fragment of William Wotton's Lost "Life of Boyle."* Edited by Michael Hunter. London, 1994.

———. *The Works of Robert Boyle.* 14 vols. Edited by Michael Hunter and Edward B. Davis. London and Brookfield, Vt., 1999–2000.

Secondary Sources

Anstey, Peter R. *The Philosophy of Robert Boyle.* London and New York, 2000.

Clericuzio, Antonio. *Elements, Principles, and Corpuscles: A Study of Atomism and Chemistry in the Seventeenth Century.* Dordrecht, 2000.

Hunter, Michael. *Robert Boyle (1627–91): Scrupulosity and Science.* Woodbridge, U.K., 2000.

Hunter, Michael, ed. *Robert Boyle Reconsidered.* Cambridge, U.K., 1994.

Principe, Lawrence M. *The Aspiring Adept: Robert Boyle and His Alchemical Quest.* Princeton, 1998.

"Robert Boyle (1627–91)." Robert Boyle Project, University of London. Directed by Michael Hunter. Available: www.bbk.ac.uk/Boyle/index.html.

Sargent, Rose-Mary. *The Diffident Naturalist: Robert Boyle and the Philosophy of Experiment.* Chicago, 1995.

Shapin, Steven. *A Social History of Truth: Civility and Science in Seventeenth-Century England.* Chicago, 1994.

Shapin, Steven, and Simon Schaffer. *Leviathan and the Air-Pump: Hobbes, Boyle, and the Experimental Life.* Princeton, 1985.

Wojcik, Jan W. *Robert Boyle and the Limits of Reason.* Cambridge, U.K., 1997.

JAN W. WOJCIK

BRAHE, TYCHO (1546–1601), Danish astronomer and alchemist. Scion of the network of noble families that ruled Denmark in the sixteenth century, Tycho Brahe was heir to the lordship of the family seat, Knudstrup (in modern south Sweden). He entered the University of Copenhagen in 1559, but when it came time for him to travel and learn the ways and manners that would shape him into a noble warrior and statesman, he was sent abroad to Germany, where he studied at the universities of Leipzig, Wittenberg, Rostock, Basel (in Switzerland), and Augsburg. Mastering the fundamentals of mathematics and natural sciences, he was struck by the lack of precision in astronomy. While abroad he was also exposed to alchemy and the medical ideas of Paracelsus, the German religious enthusiast and physician whose ideas challenged the reigning academic medical establishment and were winning converts among members of Tycho's generation.

Tycho was recalled to Denmark when his father became mortally ill, in order to come into his inheritance and take his place among the feudal elite. Repelled by the life for which he had been bred, he sold his share of the family manor to his younger brother and moved in with his uncle at Herrevad manor, where he observed the stars and explored the nature of terrestrial matter in a small alchemical laboratory. He was walking to the main building from the laboratory in 1572 when he first spied a "new star" (*nova stella*) shining brightly in the constellation Cassiopeia, observation and consideration of which was to captivate his attention and change the course of his life. (It is now known as Tycho's star.)

According to the prevailing theory of the cosmos, drawn largely from Christian interpretations of the geocentric cosmology of Aristotle (384–322 B.C.E.), bodies in the heavens were per-

Tycho Brahe. LIBRARY OF CONGRESS

manent and incorruptible; whatever transitory objects appeared in the sky, such as comets, lightning, and hail, were regarded as terrestrial phenomena, occurring in the air or in the zone of fire imagined to surround it. Tycho, however, showed that the nova did not exhibit any parallax, the daily change of angular measurement that characterizes objects near the Earth, and must therefore be celestial, creating a problem for traditional cosmology. As a result of the treatise he published on the nova, he was asked to undertake a series of lectures on astrology and astronomy at the University of Copenhagen in 1574, and eventually King Frederick II (ruled 1559–1588) offered him lordship over the island of Hven, where, in the summer of 1576, he laid the foundation stone for his new manor house, which he named Uraniborg—castle of the heavens.

Uraniborg was modest in size, but elaborately designed and expensively crafted. In the basement Tycho created what at the time was one of Europe's most lavish alchemical laboratories, equipped with sixteen kinds of ovens for heating and distilling various plant, animal, and mineral substances in order to concentrate their virtues and obtain their spiritual essences. On the main floor were rooms for his family and guests, a kitchen, and a combination library and study. Each end of the second floor of the building housed an array of instruments located under removable roof sections. Tycho had ordered the first of his permanent instruments for measuring angles between celestial objects while in Augsburg and he added to his collection at Uraniborg, continuing to expand the sizes, designs, and materials of these instruments, building a special workshop nearby and employing trained craftsmen for this purpose. Finding that subtle movements of the instruments caused by the wind or by unsteady supports limited the accuracy of observations, Tycho built Stjærneborg ('castle of the stars'), an observatory comprising a central room surrounded by five pits dug into the ground, each of which was covered by a removable lid and housed a particular instrument that was set upon a stone foundation to reduce vibration. With large instruments of such quality, he attained unprecedented accuracy. Christian IV, however, succeeded Frederick II, assuming the throne in 1596, and began to cut Tycho's funding. In response, Tycho packed up his instruments and left Denmark in 1597, securing a position as imperial astronomer to the Holy Roman emperor Rudolf II, who provided him a castle near Prague in which to reestablish his research facilities, both astronomical and alchemical. At this point Tycho hired Johannes Kepler to assist him with the calculations necessary to establish a new astronomical theory on the basis of his accurate data—a theory that Tycho assumed would take a new form, with the Earth at the center of the movements of the Moon and Sun, but with the movements of the rest of the planets centered on the Sun. When Tycho died suddenly in the fall of 1601, Kepler was free to use the valuable data to create his own system, which laid the foundations for Newton's gravitational astronomy.

See also **Alchemy; Astronomy; Cosmology; Denmark; Kepler, Johannes; Paracelsus; Scientific Instruments.**

BIBLIOGRAPHY

Primary Source

Brahe, Tycho. *Tycho Brahe's Description of his Instruments and Scientific Work as given in* Astronomiæ Instauratæ Mechanica. Translated and edited by Hans Raeder, Elis Strømgren, and Bengt Strømgren. Copenhagen, 1946.

Secondary Sources

Christianson, John Robert. *On Tycho's Island: Tycho Brahe and His Assistants, 1570–1601.* Cambridge, U.K., 2000.

Shackelford, Jole. "Tycho Brahe, Laboratory Design, and the Aim of Science: Reading Plans in Context." *Isis* 84 (1993): 211–230.

Thoren, Victor E. *The Lord of Uraniborg: A Biography of Tycho Brahe.* Cambridge, U.K., 1990.

JOLE SHACKELFORD

BRANDENBURG. Brandenburg's importance stems from its position within the Holy Roman Empire and its association with Prussia and the Hohenzollern dynasty. The area that later became known as Brandenburg was conquered from the Slavs in 928, but was only loosely involved in imperial politics until the ruling Ascanian dynasty died out in 1320. Under imperial law, Brandenburg now reverted to the emperor's control, and it was entrusted first to the Wittelsbachs and then to the Luxembourgs as these families successively held the imperial title. Both used it to support their imperial ambitions, resulting in Brandenburg's elevation to an electorate in 1356, permitting its rulers to participate in the choice of all future emperors. As Luxembourg imperial rule crumbled in 1415, Emperor Sigismund gave Brandenburg to Frederick, burgrave of Nuremberg, who became Frederick I, elector and margrave of Brandenburg, initiating over five centuries of Hohenzollern rule.

Brandenburg covered 14,780 square miles (38,280 square kilometers) in northeastern Germany, and was divided into five "marches," or provinces. The Altmark lay west of the Elbe River and had its administrative center in the town of Stendal. The central Mittelmark stretched east from the Elbe to the Oder River and included the major towns of Berlin-Cölln, Frankurt/Oder and Brandenburg itself. The province of Pregnitz was to the northwest as far as the border with Mecklenburg and was governed from Perleberg. The Uckermark extended eastwards from Prignitz between the Mittelmark and the duchy of Pomerania and had its capital in Prenzlau. The fifth province, Neumark, lay east of the Oder and had few towns apart from the fortress of Küstrin (Kostrzyn).

The entire area was known as the "sandbox of the empire" because of its poor soil, which sustained only 250,000 inhabitants even by the mid-seventeenth century. Thanks to intensified land use and economic development, such as the digging of canals to improve riverine transportation to the Baltic and the North Sea, the population increased considerably in the eighteenth century, reaching 980,000. The people lived in 83 towns and 1,967 villages. One third of the latter were under the direct jurisdiction of the ruler and provided much of his total revenue. While urban magistrates exercised jurisdiction over a few of the other villages, most were controlled by the Brandenburg nobility who also dominated the territory's Estates, or representative assembly. Both the elector and the nobles introduced the manorial economy *(Gutswirtschaft)* from the early sixteenth century onwards, binding their dependent peasants to the land and requiring them to work two or more days a week on large fields of rye to produce cash crops for export to western European cities. While still profitable, this economy was reaching its natural limits by 1626 when it was plunged into deep crisis by Brandenburg's involvement in the Thirty Years' War. Berlin's population fell by 40 percent and that of the countryside by between 20 and 90 percent, depending on the region. Historians used to think that this situation uniformly benefited the nobility, who were able to create larger farms by seizing abandoned land. In fact, the shortage of labor increased the bargaining power of the surviving peasants, who demanded improved conditions, including wages for their obligatory work on their landlords' fields. The nobles were in a weak position when they negotiated with Elector Frederick William I, known as the "Great Elector" (ruled 1640–1688), at the territorial assembly in 1653. The resulting agreement, the Brandenburg Recess, confirmed rather than extended aristocratic power over serf labor in return for significant concessions to the elector, who ruthlessly consolidated his power over the next two decades.

The elector and his successors continued to protect the peasants against lordly exploitation, but their interest was primarily fiscal rather than humanitarian. They wanted a stable economic base of viable taxpayers, and they simply diverted profits from the lords' pockets into their own treasury. The economy remained depressed because of renewed warfare after 1655. It recovered slowly from the 1680s, and the population returned to its pre-1618 level by 1713. The nobles derived only limited benefit from these developments, because the Hohenzollerns imposed a form of limited conscription, known as the canton system, by 1733, taking regular drafts of peasants to maintain their inflated military establishment.

Many nobles were reconciled by court, military, and administrative appointments that provided alternative sources of wealth and prestige. However, others continued to oppose Hohenzollern absolutism, not least because of Brandenburg's experience of the Reformation. Lutheranism arrived relatively late, in 1535, and was not fully accepted until the reign of John George (ruled 1571–1598), who secularized church property and introduced church ordinances modeled on those of Saxony to the south. This reflected Brandenburg's junior status in imperial politics where the elector generally followed the lead of his more prestigious Saxon colleague. Elector John Sigismund (ruled 1608–1619) announced a radical new course by converting to Calvinism on Christmas Day 1613. Having only recently adopted Lutheranism, few Brandenburg nobles were prepared to follow the elector's lead, and Calvinism remained restricted to those most closely associated with the electoral family. Unsure of his position at home, the elector abandoned his support for Calvinists elsewhere in the empire and swung behind Saxony's policy of neutrality during the Thirty Years' War. By the time circumstances forced Brandenburg into the war, the electorate was linked dynastically to Prussia, and its subsequent political history is more appropriately discussed under that heading.

See also **Berlin; Frederick William (Brandenburg); Hohenzollern Dynasty; Holy Roman Empire; Prussia; Saxony; Thirty Years' War (1618–1648).**

BIBLIOGRAPHY

Baumgart, Peter, ed. *Ständetum und Staatsbildung in Brandenburg-Preußen.* Berlin and New York, 1983.

Enders, Lieselott. "Die Landgemeinde in Brandenburg: Grundzüge ihrer Funktion und Wirkungsweise vom 13. bis zum 18. Jahrhundert." *Blätter für Deutsche Landesgeschichte* 129 (1993): 195–256.

Fürbringer, Christoph. *Necessitas und Libertas. Staatsbildung und Landstände im 17. Jahrhundert in Brandenburg.* Frankfurt am Main, 1985.

Göse, Frank, ed. *Im Schatten der Krone: Die Mark Brandenburg um 1700.* Potsdam, 2002.

Hagen, William W. *Ordinary Prussians. Brandenburg Junkers and Villagers 1500–1840.* Cambridge, U.K., and New York, 2002.

———. "Seventeenth-Century Crisis in Brandenburg. The Thirty Years War, the Destabilization of Serfdom, and the Rise of Absolutism." *American Historical Review* 94 (1989): 302–335.

Materna, Ingo, and Wolfgang Ribbe, eds. *Brandenburgische Geschichte.* Berlin, 1995.

Nischan, Bodo. *Prince, People and Confession: The Second Reformation in Brandenburg.* Philadelphia, 1994.

Pröve, Ralf, and Bernd Kölling, eds. *Leben und Arbeiten auf märkischen Sand.* Bielefeld, 1999.

Schultze, Johannes. *Die Mark Brandenburg.* 5 vols. Berlin, 1961–1969.

PETER H. WILSON

BRANT, SEBASTIAN (1457–1521), German author and jurist. Sebastian Brant, the celebrated author of *Das Narrenschiff* (1494; Ship of fools), was born sometime in 1457 to Strasbourg innkeeper Diebold Brant and his wife, Barbara, née Picker. The eldest of three sons, Brant proved a talented pupil and, following his father's death in January 1468, his mother labored to provide him with private tutors. Beginning in 1475, he attended the University of Basel, where he developed a conservative brand of humanism under his mentor, the theologian Johannes Heynlin von Stein (a Lapide). After receiving his baccalaureate in 1477, Brant focused on legal studies, obtaining his licentiate in 1484 and becoming doctor of canon and civil law in 1489. At the same time, he continued his study of Latin authors and began teaching literature at the university around 1486. In 1485, he married Elisabeth Burg, the daughter of a Basel cutler. Together they had seven children.

With his deep piety and firm belief in the letter of the law, Brant applied his classical learning toward the preservation of social mores and political order. This underlying concern unites his diverse production of texts, not only those he wrote himself, but also the far more numerous works edited by him for local printers, as many as one-third of all books printed in Basel at this time. He was furthermore a translator, producing German editions of Latin conduct literature throughout the 1490s. As a jurist, Brant wrote the highly successful *Expositiones* (1490), an introductory legal textbook that frequently appeared in later editions together with his turn-of-the-century redaction of Giovanni Battista di Gazalupis's *De Modo Studendi in Utroque Jure* (1467; On studying both civil and canon law). He also edited the *Decretum Gratiani* (1493), one of the cornerstones of canon law, and the proceedings of the Council of Basel (1499).

Beyond his work on folly, the literary production of Brant's Basel years consisted mainly of Latin verse. A volume of devotional poetry, *In laudem Marie Carmina* (Songs in praise of Mary), appeared in 1494, followed by the *Varia Carmina* (Various poems) of 1498. The latter volume reproduces much of the earlier collection, but additionally contains dedicatory verse created by Brant for editions of his own works or for those of friends and acquaintances. Further preserved are poems on meteors, freakish births, and other natural sensations. Brant regarded such wonders as divine portents with consequences for the Holy Roman Empire, and he sought to influence popular opinion by discussing the same events in German in several illustrated broadsides addressed to Emperor Maximilian I (ruled 1493–1519).

It is difficult to overstate the phenomenal success of Brant's lasting literary achievement, *Das Narrenschiff*. Published during Carnival by Johann Bergman von Olpe on 11 February 1494, the original edition presents in 112 brief chapters a veritable taxonomy of fools, each representing a particular human foible. The work moralizes against sins such as sloth and adultery, but also against indulgent parents, bad marksmen, and those who talk in church. Specific chapters touch upon contemporary issues, admonishing the German princes to support Maximilian (chapter 99), or, in the first literary reference to Columbus's discoveries, criticizing explorers who seek gold (chapter 66). The work went through nine German editions, some pirated, before Brant's former pupil Jacob Locher produced his Latin adaptation, *Stultifera Navis* (1497), which served as the basis for translations into French (1497), Dutch (1500), and English (1509).

Although many scholars find the *Narrenschiff*'s image of humanity still largely medieval, the design of the book belongs wholly to the Renaissance and its new medium, printing. Each chapter is prefaced by a three- to four-line motto and a large woodcut that illustrates or expands upon some aspect of the following text. Brant takes credit for the images in the work's preface, and it is likely that he collaborated with as many as five contributing artists on the illustrations. Based on stylistic analysis, it is nearly certain that Albrecht Dürer created the majority of the work's woodcuts during his period as journeyman in Basel (1492–1493). We know that Brant and Dürer collaborated on illustrations for a planned edition of Terence at this time.

In his later years, Brant returned to Strasbourg, becoming legal councillor to the city on 13 January 1501 and advancing to the position of municipal secretary two years later. He continued to edit a variety of texts, producing editions of Aesop (1501), Boethius (1501), Virgil (1502), and Terence (1503), as well as of the gnomic *Bescheidenheit* (1508; Prudence) by the thirteenth-century vernacular author Freidank. He further helped publish two practical law books, Ulrich Tengler's *Laienspiegel* (1509; Legal handbook for laymen) and the anonymous *Klagspiegel* (1516; Handbook of lawsuits), although his actual contribution to these editions is disputed. In 1512 and 1513, Brant directed performances of his "Hercules at the Crossroads"; the corresponding text, entitled *Tugent Spyl* (Play of virtue), appeared posthumously in 1554. Culminating Brant's multimedial collaborations is the so-called *Freiheitstafel* (c. 1513; Mural of freedom), a cycle of fifty-two poems accompanying a series of paintings in the Dreizehnerstube, the meeting room for the thirteen-member inner circle of Strasbourg's town council. The surviving manuscript contains Brant's instructions for an emblem-like pictorial program, a union of text and image not unlike that of the *Narrenschiff*, but serving explicit political ends much like the author's broadsides of the 1490s.

Brant died in Strasbourg on 10 May 1521.

See also **Dürer, Albrecht; Erasmus, Desiderius; German Literature and Language; Humanists and Humanism; Maximilian I (Holy Roman Empire).**

BIBLIOGRAPHY

Primary Sources

Brant, Sebastian. *Das Narrenschiff.* Edited by Manfred Lemmer. 3rd ed. Tübingen, 1986.

——. *The Ship of Fools.* Translated by Edwin H. Zeydel. New York, 1944.

Secondary Sources

Knape, Joachim. *Dichtung, Recht und Freiheit: Studien zu Leben und Werk Sebastian Brants, 1457–1521.* Saecula Spiritalia, vol. 23. Baden-Baden, 1992.

Knape, Joachim, and Dieter Wuttke. *Sebastian-Brant-Bibliographie: Forschungsliteratur von 1800 bis 1985.* Tübingen, 1990.

Rupp, Michael. *"Narrenschiff" und "Stultifera navis": Deutsche und lateinische Moralsatire von Sebastian Brant und Jakob Locher in Basel, 1494–1498.* Studien und Texte zum Mittelalter und zur frühen Neuzeit, vol. 3. Münster, 2002.

Van Cleve, John. *Sebastian Brant's "The Ship of Fools" in Critical Perspective, 1800–1991.* Columbia, S.C., 1993.

Wilhelmi, Thomas. *Sebastian-Brant-Bibliographie.* Arbeiten zur mittleren deutschen Literatur und Sprache, vol. 18/3. Bern and New York, 1990.

Wilhelmi, Thomas, ed. *Sebastian Brant: Forschungsbeiträge zu seinem Leben, zum "Narrenschiff" und zum übrigen Werk.* Basel, 2002.

Zeydel, Edwin H. *Sebastian Brant.* New York, 1967.

GLENN EHRSTINE

BREAD RIOTS. *See* **Food Riots.**

BRITAIN, ARCHITECTURE IN. The history of architecture in England between 1500 and 1800 can be seen as a series of stages defined by the interests of patrons and, within the forms of the buildings themselves, by the variety of responses possible to the forms of Renaissance architecture in continental Europe. In such a history, England always had problems in its cultural and political relations with other countries, Italy in particular. In addition, there was the Reformation, which, after the early 1500s, led to an immediate decline in ecclesiastical architecture. Throughout this entire period, problems of royal patronage also existed. If in France or Italy new traditions of design had been established by those in authority, in England the parlous state of the finances of the monarchy, even

with two extremely active patrons, King Henry VIII and King Charles I, always severely limited what was built.

England is geographically far from Italy. Some of the early forms of Italian design were known almost immediately, but until the end of the sixteenth century most of what was built in England was still based on the local traditions of Gothic building. It was only later that there were sufficient masons and craftsmen trained in the ways of Renaissance architecture to know how to incorporate it effectively into whatever they built.

Of the architecture constructed for Henry VIII, the most important surviving example is Hampton Court, confiscated from Cardinal Thomas Wolsey in 1529 and then extended; most notable is its Great Hall, where the structure was still essentially Gothic but much of the ornamentation—the *putti,* scrolls, and balusters, as well as other details elsewhere in the palace—hinted at a newer style from Italy. At Nonsuch Palace in Surrey, begun in 1538, there was a clear attempt to rival Chambord, built by King Francis I a decade earlier; though the plan of two great courts there was traditional, for many of the decorative details foreign craftsmen were brought in, some of whom, like Nicholas Bellin, had worked at Fontainebleau in similar ways.

Tudor architecture was still largely Gothic. But the plans of the buildings, seen in historical context, tended now to be symmetrical; the blocks were seen as individual units, rather than being brought together under the form of linear patterning that had been so much a part of the older English style. To make the effect very different from what had been built even fifty years earlier, new forms of decoration also appeared: simple octagonal towers, polychrome brick, niches, plaques, and decorated chimneys. They may be observed at Barrington Court, Somerset (1515–1548), Compton Wyngates, Warwickshire (c. 1520), and Sutton Place, Surrey (1523–1527).

The next great period was that of Elizabethan architecture, as seen in the large manor houses and great courtly houses built from the 1560s onward, often by newly wealthy merchants or courtiers and ministers of state. Some important examples are Wollaton Hall, Nottinghamshire (1580–1588), Longleat Hall, Wiltshire (1572), Burghley House,

Architecture in Britain. An aerial view of Hardwick Hall, an Elizabethan manor house in Derbyshire, built 1590–1597. ©JASON HAWKES/CORBIS

Northamptonshire (1577–1585), and Hardwick Hall, Derbyshire (1590–1597). The style and plans of these houses, in their symmetry and details, were more clearly indebted to Renaissance architecture. If the windows now often took up much of the wall, the decorations around them, taken as much from Flanders as from Italy—the false niches and strapwork, the grotesques and broken columns—had a new visual power and seemed to mirror perfectly, as if in heraldry, the power and new wealth of their owners. It was also at this time that the first two English architects became known by name: Robert Smythson (1535–1614), the designer of Hardwick and Wollaton, and John Thorpe (1568–1620), many of whose drawings have survived. But still the play between native traditions of masonry building and new forms of Italian design took time to be worked out. Notable examples of this mixed style,

often referred to as Artisan Mannerism, can be seen at Hatfield House, Hertfordshire, begun in 1607; a collegiate building like Wadham College, Oxford, built from 1610–1613; and Swakeleys, Middlesex, built in 1638.

All of this was to change quickly with Inigo Jones and the patronage he received from King Charles I. Jones had been to Italy, and his books and notes show how well he learned the principles and practice of the new architecture. If in the end he was able to design only a few completed buildings, such as the Queen's House, Greenwich (1616–1639), and the Banqueting House, Whitehall (1616–1639), the simple classical style he used for them, based on the example of Andrea Palladio, was to transform completely the idea of architectural design in England. He also produced a number of designs, never built, for country houses, and these

Architecture in Britain. The Banqueting House, Whitehall, London, designed by Inigo Jones and completed in 1639. Jones transformed the idea of architecture in Britain with his simple classical style. ©PHILIPPA LEWIS; EDIFICE/CORBIS

are reflected in the plain, astylar (without columns) character of buildings like Thorpe Hall, Huntingdonshire (1653–1656), and Lees Court, Kent (c. 1640). And in the houses designed for the duke of Bedford at Covent Garden (begun in 1631), Jones established a style of urban architecture that was to influence much of what was built in cities in England for the next two centuries.

However, it was the work of Christopher Wren and that of the next generation of architects— Hugh May, Robert Hooke, and others—that finally fully established the style of classical architecture in England. And in Wren's work, whether for colleges at Oxford and Cambridge, or at Greenwich, or again at Hampton Court, and then in numerous city churches and St. Paul's Cathedral, a version of the baroque was brought to England, rich and grand enough to be comparable to what was available in the other countries of Europe.

A battle of styles was to nevertheless continue. After Wren, there was in the work of Nicholas Hawksmoor and Sir John Vanbrugh—as at Blenheim Palace, Oxfordshire (1704–1725), or St. Anne's, Limehouse, London (1714–1724)—a grand classical style, in its effect recalling something of Elizabethan architecture, but against this was now set the Palladianism advocated by Lord Burlington. It effectively brought English architecture back to the classical roots of Palladio and the designs of Jones. Burlington was himself an architect and a powerful and tireless patron of art. At Chiswick House, London (begun in 1725), Wanstead House, Essex (1713–1720), and Holkham Hall, Norfolk (begun in 1734), he was able with the help of Colin Campbell and William Kent to define a tradition of apparently replicable, classicizing architecture that, with new ideas about the natural landscape taken from Rome and even China, gave both architects and new patrons alike firm ideas about

310

designing buildings and gardens that would be socially and intellectually acceptable.

However, all of this was happening at a time when familiar concepts of beauty were beginning to be questioned by philosophers like David Hume and Edmund Burke. And with the political and cultural changes taking place in Europe, classical buildings even beyond those of Italy were now accessible to anyone interested in travel and a fresh view of the history of architecture. In this regard, Greece was to become very important. Despite the fact that with figures like Sir William Chambers and Robert Adam, by the end of the eighteenth century, architects were working more professionally, with full offices and staffs, there were also many more theoretical disputes about the propriety of styles: whether the refined traditions of Italy should remain the model, or the simpler and more primitive styles of Greece were superior. The result, especially as the eighteenth century came to an end, was a mix of styles, with some architects like Chambers still working in an Italianate style, as at Somerset House, London (1776–1780), and others preferring a simpler Greek style, as at Dover House, London (1787), designed by Henry Holland. Other architects, such as Horace Walpole at Strawberry Hill, London (1748 onward), or James Wyatt at Fonthill Abbey, Wiltshire (1795–1807), developed a new version of the native Gothic style that elicited very different responses from those engendered by the purer, more rational classicism of the new Palladianism.

There was no one way to resolve these differences, especially when other stylistic elements were soon to appear, as in the garden buildings at Kew, designed in the 1770s and 1780s, and clearly influenced by the buildings of Moorish Spain, the architecture of India and China, and the Gothic past of England. The last great classical architect in England was Sir John Soane; in buildings like the Bank of England, London (1792–1793), or the library in his home at 12 Lincoln Inns Fields (1792), he suggested an architecture that was at once deeply individual, yet recalled the traditions of a native yet distinctly Roman style that had been used by Vanbrugh and Hawksmoor. This was a moment of stylistic eclecticism, but it was from these possibilities that architecture could develop as it did in the next century, using new materials of glass and iron, and often for structures like bridges, railway stations, and factories, in a classical style, one completely different from what had developed when Renaissance architecture was first brought to England.

See also **Estates and Country Houses; Gardens and Parks; Jones, Inigo; London; Palladio, Andrea, and Palladianism; Wren, Christopher.**

BIBLIOGRAPHY

Brooks, Chris. *The Gothic Revival.* London, 1999.

Mowl, Timothy. *Elizabethan and Jacobean Style.* London, 1993.

Stillman, Damie. *English neo-Classical Architecture.* London and New York, 1988.

Summerson, John. *Architecture in Britain: 1530–1830.* 9th ed., rev. New Haven, 1993 Originally published in 1953.

Worsley, Giles. *Classical Architecture in Britain: The Heroic Age.* New Haven, 1995.

DAVID CAST

BRITAIN, ART IN.

In the period between the sixteenth and eighteenth centuries, the visual arts in Britain underwent a significant change in status, closely connected to Britain's rising mercantile power and prosperity. Although the focus of patronage shifted from the court of the Tudor and Stuart dynasties to the bourgeois market of the eighteenth century, painters in Britain continued to find their main source of income in the field of portraiture. With the first public exhibitions of art in 1760 at the Society of Artists and the founding of the Royal Academy in 1768, artists in Britain achieved the professional organization necessary to foster the training of native-born talent.

Throughout this period, Britain was host to numerous foreign-born painters and craftsmen, many of whom had immigrated there to escape the religious and political turmoil of the Continent and to take advantage of the increasing wealth of Britons. The German Hans Holbein the Younger (1497?–1543) is the artist most closely associated with the reign of Henry VIII (1509–1547). After an initial visit from 1526 to 1528, during which he painted the portraits of Sir Thomas More (Frick Collection, New York) and his family, Holbein returned to

Art in Britain. Queen Elizabeth I, the "Pelican" portrait, c. 1574, by Nicholas Hilliard. The name is derived from the pelican pendant Elizabeth wears; associated in legend with self-sacrifice, the bird symbolizes Elizabeth's devotion to her subjects. ©WALKER ART GALLERY, LIVERPOOL, MERSEYSIDE, U.K./ TRUSTEES OF THE NATIONAL MUSEUMS & GALLERIES ON MERSEYSIDE/ BRIDGEMAN ART LIBRARY

London in 1532. Henry's break with the Catholic Church in Rome in 1533 necessitated the creation of a new royal imagery, and Holbein's life-size portrayal of the king in 1536 emphasized his role as head of both church and state.

Another consequence of the founding of the Church of England was the necessary move away from religious imagery in sculpture. Inventories show that before the break with Rome, households owned more sculptural objects than paintings; however, these were mostly religious in function. From the 1530s onward, the staple of sculptural production was funerary monuments, which were protected by a 1560 proclamation of Elizabeth I.

With the accession of Queen Elizabeth in 1558, following the five-year reign of her Catholic half-sister Mary I, royal portraiture took on a new function: to bolster visually her decision to remain unmarried. Portraits of Elizabeth, dating from the 1570s, employ symbols tying her virtue to her country. For example, in William Seger's portrait (c. 1597; Hatfield House, Hertfordshire) she appears with an ermine, a symbol of chastity, and in the famous "Ditchley" portrait (c. 1592; National Portrait Gallery, London), Elizabeth stands on a map of England.

Although the Ditchley portrait is full-length and life-size, the most significant contribution to the visual arts in Britain at this time was the miniature painting of Nicholas Hilliard (1547–1619). Called limning, miniature painting was related to manuscript illumination and often painted on vellum. The practice had been brought to England by the Flemish artist Lucas Hornebolte (c. 1490/95–1544), who had taught the method to Holbein. Hilliard praised Holbein and advanced his theories in a treatise entitled *A Treatise Concerning the Art of Limning,* advocating that miniature painting be limited to gentlemen and that the technique be kept secret. With images such as *Young Man among Roses,* probably Robert Devereux, second earl of Essex (c. 1587; Victoria and Albert Museum, London), Hilliard painted the visual equivalent of Elizabethan sonnets. Hilliard trained his son, Laurence, as well as his most successful follower, Isaac Oliver.

The succession in 1603 of James I, and with him the Stuart dynasty, saw a move away from the emblematic emphasis of Elizabethan royal portraiture. However, foreign artists such as Paul van Somer of Flanders continued to dominate. Among the artists who came to England from the Netherlands was Daniel Mytens the Elder (c. 1590–1647), who was granted an annual life pension of £50 by James I and appointed by Charles I to the position of "picture-drawer."

The sculpture-lined hallways in Mytens's portraits of Thomas Howard, earl of Arundel, and his wife (c. 1616; Arundel Castle) point to an important aspect of the arts during the reign of James I: the establishment of significant collections by courtiers such as Howard and George Villiers, the first and second dukes of Buckingham. Charles I's decision to accumulate a great collection of Old Masters was formed on his 1623 trip to the court of Philip IV of Spain, where he was impressed by the prestige with which the great works of Titian (born Tiziano Vecelli), Veronese (born Guarino da

Verona), and other Italian masters endowed the Spanish monarch. Charles's most significant purchase was part of the collection of the Gonzaga family of Mantua, whereby he acquired some of the master works of Andrea Mantegna, Titian, Caravaggio (born Michelangelo Merisi), and Raphael (born Raffaello Sanzio), among others.

A second aspect of Charles's accumulation of art was his patronage of contemporary artists. On Peter Paul Rubens's diplomatic trip to England between June 1629 and March 1630, Charles commissioned the Flemish painter to decorate the ceiling of Inigo Jones's Italianate Banqueting Hall, Whitehall. The resulting *Apotheosis of James I* (1630–1634), a visual depiction of the Stuarts' allegiance to the notion of the divine right of kings, is considered the one full-fledged example of baroque painted decoration in England.

Rubens's star pupil, Anthony Van Dyck (1599–1641), made a brief trip to London in the winter of 1620–1621, probably on the recommendation of Arundel, who introduced him to James I. Van Dyck returned there permanently in 1632 and through his portraits gave Charles I and his court an image of natural authority. Charles anticipated the visual impact Van Dyck would have on the image of his reign; upon Van Dyck's return, the king knighted him, appointing him "principalle paynter in ordinary to their Majesties."

In such full-length works as *Charles I on Horseback* (c. 1637; National Gallery, London) and *William Feilding, 1st Earl of Denbigh* (1633–1634; National Gallery, London), Van Dyck takes his subjects out of the confines of the rigid costume pieces that conveyed static permanence and into the lush natural environment. He infuses his sitters with movement, accentuated by the rich coloring he learned from Titian and Rubens. Van Dyck's role in the development of portraiture in Britain continued to endure long after his death in 1641.

Even during the unsettled years of the Civil War, the royal family and royalist officers continued to commission portraits. Between 1642 and 1646, English-born William Dobson (1611–1646) served the court, painting with a naturalism similar to that of Van Dyck, but with a less refined tenor suitable to the martial times.

Art in Britain. Equestrian portrait of Charles I by Anthony Van Dyck, c. 1637. ©NATIONAL GALLERY COLLECTION; BY KIND PERMISSION OF THE TRUSTEES OF THE NATIONAL GALLERY, LONDON/ CORBIS

One of the most significant events in the art world during the commonwealth's interregnum was the sale of Charles I's collection. Charles's vast expenditure on art works from the Catholic Continent had been a source of widespread suspicion and discontent during his reign, seen as symbolic of his authoritarian tendencies. Its dispersal, however, severely set back the development of a royal or central art collection in Britain. The sale began in October 1649. In addition, the collections of Buckingham, Arundel, and Hamilton were contemporaneously sold.

Although the interregnum may seem a bleak period for painting in Britain, it was during this time that Sir Peter Lely (1618–1680) established a prosperous career in London after having received his training in Haarlem. Lely arrived in England in the early 1640s and his earliest known portrait of this period, from 1647, is of Charles I and the duke of York (duke of Northumberland, Syon House).

Nevertheless, Lely quickly adapted to the political climate of the commonwealth. His adaptability is seen once again during the Restoration with his appointment as principal painter.

In the 1660s Anne Hyde, duchess of York, commissioned Lely to create a series of the most beautiful women at court, now called the *Windsor Beauties*. It and his series of "Flagmen" at Greenwich exemplify his facility for different poses. Lely's vast output was facilitated by studio assistants who would paint the backgrounds and draperies of his works, as well as copies of them. Lely dominated this period of British painting and was knighted in 1680.

The crown was also the most significant patron of the virtuoso wood-carver Grinling Gibbons (1648–1721). The best examples of his naturalistic depictions of flora, fauna, and textiles may be found in the Royal Apartments at Windsor Castle, where he worked between 1677 and 1682.

With Lely's death at the end of 1680, Dutch-born Godfrey Kneller (1646–1723) dominated the portrait market. Kneller had trained with Ferdinand Bol in Amsterdam and, before his arrival in London in 1676, had traveled to Rome and Venice. By 1679 he was painting the portrait of Charles II. With the Glorious Revolution and the arrival of William III and Mary II in 1688, Kneller shared the position of principal painter with native-born portraitist John Riley. He was knighted in 1692 and made a baronet in 1715.

Kneller is best known for his series of portraits of the members of the Kit-Cat Club (painted 1700–1720). The format of these portraits, in which the sitter's head, shoulders, and one or both hands were shown, was innovative, and the size was thereafter termed a "Kit-Cat." Kneller's popularity, like Lely's, necessitated a large studio; the sometimes mediocre quality of its work did unfortunately undermine Kneller's posthumous reputation. Kneller was also the first governor of an academy for painting and drawing, which opened in 1711.

Contemporaneous with Kneller's career was the vogue for decorative schemes in the great houses of Europe. Practitioners of this late baroque form came from Italy (for example, Antonio Verrio, Giovanni Antonio Pellegrini, and Sebastiano and Marco Ricci) and France (Louis Laguerre). Verrio's illu-

sionistic, decorative work can be seen at the duke of Devonshire's Chatsworth, where he painted various rooms and ceilings during the 1690s. However, the emergence of a nationalistic impulse can be seen in the competition for the decoration of St. Paul's Cathedral. English-born James Thornhill (1676–1734) vigorously lobbied for this prestigious commission and worked on it from 1715 to 1717.

Thornhill's nationalistic mantel was taken up by his son-in-law William Hogarth (1697–1764). Although Hogarth's style showed a clear knowledge of French painting, he was vociferous in his antagonism toward English patronage of foreign artists, especially in the area of historical painting. His *Sigismunda* (1759; Tate Gallery, London) was an attempt to demonstrate the superiority of English historical painting after a supposed Correggio on the same subject was bought for over £400 at auction; however, his work was met with ridicule.

By then it had become customary for well-born Englishmen to finish their education by undertaking a grand tour of Europe. An important aspect of these travels was the purchase of works of art commemorating their visit. The Venetian view painter Canaletto (born Giovanni Antonio Canal; 1697–1768) was so popular with his English patrons that he came to London in 1746, staying until 1755. Landscape painting in Britain had been characterized by topographical accuracy used to detail the house and grounds of estates. Under the influence of seventeenth-century landscape painters Claude Lorrain (born Claude Gellée), Nicolas Poussin, and Salvator Rosa, Richard Wilson instead gave the English landscape a classical, idealized expression. Nevertheless, Wilson died in poverty, and Thomas Gainsborough famously complained that he could only support a family through the practice of portraiture.

Hogarth was instrumental in popularizing the small-scale group portrait called the conversation piece, a format that had been brought to England by Watteau's follower Philippe Mercier. Hogarth's own innovation of the "modern moral subject" was itself influential on the Continent, and his promotion of the Engravers' Copyright Act of 1734 to protect artists' engravings secured him an important source of income.

Art in Britain. *Life Drawing Class at the Royal Academy,* by Thomas Rowlandson, 1808. ©HISTORICAL PICTURE ARCHIVE/CORBIS

Hogarth's full-length portrait of Captain Thomas Coram (1740, Thomas Coram Foundation for Children, London) epitomizes the shifting sources of patronage in mid-eighteenth-century England. The increasingly prosperous merchant classes adopted the forms of aristocratic portraiture. Moreover, Coram had established the Foundling Hospital. Hogarth and other artists donated works to this charitable institution for orphans, and it became the first venue for the public display of paintings in England.

Although Hogarth had lobbied for a democratically structured academy for training artists, the official academy that was founded in 1768 was given a royal charter and had a strict hierarchy. Sir Joshua Reynolds's centrality in the art world of the eighteenth century was confirmed by his election as its first president. In his renowned fifteen *Discourses on*

Art, presented to the students and members of the academy during his tenure, he articulated his concern for raising the intellectual status of the artist in society. With its schools and annual exhibitions, the Royal Academy dominated the course British art was to follow for the next hundred years.

See also **Academies of Art; Britain, Architecture in; England; Gainsborough, Thomas; Hogarth, William; Holbein, Hans, the Younger; Jones, Inigo; London; Portrait Miniatures; Reynolds, Joshua; Van Dyck, Anthony; Wren, Christopher.**

BIBLIOGRAPHY

Primary Source

Hilliard, Nicholas. *A Treatise Concerning the Art of Limning.* Reprint, transcribed by Arthur F. Kinney. Boston, 1983.

Secondary Sources

Brown, Jonathan. *Kings and Connoisseurs: Collecting Art in Seventeenth-Century Europe.* Princeton, 1995.

Gent, Lucy, ed. *Albion's Classicism: The Visual Arts in Britain, 1550–1660.* New Haven and London, 1995.

Llewellyn, Nigel. *Funerary Monuments in Post-Reformation England.* Cambridge, U.K., 2000.

Solkin, David H. *Painting for Money: The Visual Arts and the Public Sphere in Eighteenth-Century England.* New Haven and London, 1993.

Waterhouse, Ellis. *Painting in Britain, 1530–1790.* 5th ed. New Haven and London, 1994.

Whinney, Margaret. *Sculpture in Britain, 1530–1830.* 2nd ed., revised by John Physick. Harmondsworth, U.K., 1988.

ELIZABETH A. PERGAM

BRITISH COLONIES

This entry includes three subentries:

THE CARIBBEAN

INDIA

NORTH AMERICA

THE CARIBBEAN

The British Empire that ended in the twentieth century began at the very end of the sixteenth century with chartered commercial ventures in the East Indies to secure tropical spices and cotton cloth. Peace then allowed further private ventures into the Caribbean (which was called the West Indies) in the early seventeenth century; these expanded into settlements to grow further high-value tropical crops, initially tobacco, later cotton and indigo and then, from the 1640s, sugar cane. With the spread of the plantation economy in the Caribbean after about 1650, the need for cheap labor helped support a booming slave trade. England's new North American colonies then found a ready market for their lumber and foodstuffs.

BEGINNINGS

The Caribbean islands consist primarily of three major groups: the Bahama Islands, including the Turks and Caicos islands, the Greater Antilles (Cuba, Jamaica, Hispaniola, and Puerto Rico), and, southeast of Puerto Rico, the Lesser Antilles (Leeward Islands, Windward Islands, Barbados, Trinidad, and Tobago). European colonization of the Caribbean islands started after Christopher Columbus landed on several of them in the 1490s and claimed the entire area for Spain. Foreign traders were also excluded. From the mid-sixteenth century, English ships' captains began to participate in the highly profitable smuggling trade that supplied the Spanish-American settlements and continued into the late 1570s. Then, as Europe's Counter-Reformation became increasingly bitter, Caribbean voyages, on which captains threatened local officials with violent attacks before they commenced trading in order to allow the officials to claim overwhelming force, became ventures for both commerce and raiding. These targeted the Spanish plate fleets as they traversed the Caribbean as well as local coasting traffic. English, French, and Dutch all participated. The institution of a grudging peace in the early seventeenth century allowed the resumption of the earlier smuggling trade. England, France, and the Netherlands all began establishing their own colonies in the Caribbean in the 1620s and 1630s.

The first year-round British settlements in the region were in South America; these were established to grow tobacco in the first decade of the seventeenth century in the Amazon delta and later along the coast of Guyana. None lasted long, each one being expelled by Spanish forces. The mixed motives for these early settlements—with planters hoping to grow lucrative tropical crops and ship captains seeking havens for contraband deals with Spanish colonists, as well as courtiers' profit-taking and the conflicting objectives of European policies—would all complicate the region's subsequent development.

The British settlements in the Leeward Islands (Anguilla, Barbuda, Dominica [which became part of the Windward Islands in the nineteenth century], Saint Christopher's, Nevis, Antigua, and Montserrat) and Barbados in the Windward Islands, proved in the 1620s and 1630s more permanent than those earlier footholds on the South American mainland. Colonies were founded in St. Kitts in 1623 and in Barbados in 1627. Settlers from St. Kitts expanded onto Nevis in 1628 and Antigua and Montserrat in 1632. These island colonies got their start in part because they were established when Spain was preoccupied in European wars, although local Spanish forces still staged some successful attacks. Another reason was that these islands were mostly uninhabited, since the indigenous Carib tribes had been enslaved a century before or had fled to the Windward Islands (Dominica, Grenada, Saint Lucia, Saint Vincent, and the Grenadines) where they defended their independence, and the Spanish had neglected the Leewards and set up colonies primarily in the Greater Antilles.

After the English began settling the islands as plantations, West Indian havens offered operation bases for seamen engaged in smuggling or in raiding Spanish towns and ships. In the early 1660s, some of the buccaneers on Tortuga, off Hispaniola, moved their operations to the recently won English colony of Jamaica (taken from the Spanish in 1655), where, besides bringing in sorely needed cash, their ships helped deter Spanish attacks. In the Bahamas, which were first settled by the English in 1646, pirates operated until the 1720s.

Early colonial populations on the islands were shaped by economic downturns and high death rates. Agricultural colonies such as Barbados began growing tobacco as an export crop, but, after the tobacco boom collapsed Barbados's planters, leaving them with only poor-quality tobacco to sell, they turned to experimenting with cotton, then with indigo. However, during the 1640s these commodities became early casualties of Britain's civil war, with the market for imports collapsing. The planters then welcomed Dutch merchants who gave easier credit, had access to shipments of slaves from West Africa, and helped teach them how to process sugar. The resulting "sugar revolution" transformed Barbados's society. Sugar promised a profitable crop, but setting up a sugar estate demanded sizable initial outlays for labor to gather the crop and for machinery to process the canes. Large estates benefited from economies of scale while small plantations could no longer compete. Large-scale planters then found it cheaper to buy out their neighbors than clear virgin land.

Whatever the crop, labor remained a pressing issue. From the first, planters aimed to control their workforces. They restricted their indentured servants' mobility, punished them for time lost to pregnancies or running away, and limited appeals against even the worst masters. These harsh "customs of the country" underlay the slave codes that were developed to deal with a type of property not dis-cussed in English case law. To secure workers, the planters would grab whomever they could find. These included African slaves purchased from passing ships and some enslaved Native Americans. In the first stages of settlement, narrow profit margins left little room for extensive slave purchases. The early planters used white workers. Unemployment in Britain and Ireland during the 1630s produced a succession of English, Irish, and some Scots willing to mortgage their future labor in exchange for a passage to the West Indies and the hope of a new start at the end of their service. During the 1650s, prisoners of war or survivors from failed uprisings provided more field hands. However, during the late seventeenth century, recruitment shrank as Britain's demographic growth slowed, pushing up the price for individual contracts, while the cost of acquiring slaves from Africa fell. African slaves then comprised increasing proportions of the work gangs. These social transformations took place on different islands at different times. Barbados was generally the path-breaker while the Bahamas were spared the introduction of large-scale sugar estates.

New settlements provided new opportunities. Groups of colonists had leap-frogged out from St. Kitts to the other Leeward Islands in the 1630s. After the Surinam settlement was captured by the Dutch, the planters in Barbados helped promote settlement in South Carolina. In 1647 a religious split in the Bahamas pushed a puritan group to establish a settlement there, while in 1651 pro-royalist planters in Barbados established new plantations on the South American mainland along the Surinam River. An expedition sent out from England secured a footing in Jamaica in 1655 and the ousting of Jamaica's last Spanish holdouts in 1661 gave the newly restored king of England an excuse to retain the island. Later, in the 1680s, Jamaican merchants encouraged timber cutters on the coast of Central America (today's Belize). Local initiatives shaped English settlements in the West Indies through to the 1690s.

Natural disasters hampered development across the Caribbean during the late seventeenth century. Hurricanes—a term that English readers did not encounter until the mid-seventeenth century—further harmed the islands' fragile ecosystems, which had already been damaged by various droughts and floods and by erosion due to land clearance. In the 1670s, a blight wiped out Jamaica's cacao plantations. Earthquakes and fires destroyed several towns and plantations. In the 1680s, yellow fever became prevalent, making a region already susceptible to outbreaks of other diseases still more inhospitable. By the 1690s yields were falling in the older settled islands.

Wars compounded the damage. As Britain fought conventional wars in Europe with the Netherlands and France, vicious local campaigns took place where governors allied with Carib warriors or undertook raids to seize slaves and burn plantations. Few major slave uprisings occurred, but all slaveholding societies feared that one such uprising might succeed and spread. The elaborate conspiracies discovered in almost every colony demonstrated how real the threat was. Defenses proved costly: erecting coastal fortifications, building barracks, paying garrisons of European regulars, and requiring frequent militia service from free resident males drained island economies. Some churches were built, but few schools were established. Successful planters who had initially sent their daughters "home" to England for an education now sent their sons back too, and planned to become absentees themselves.

EIGHTEENTH-CENTURY DEVELOPMENTS

The social structures that were hammered out by 1690 shaped the region for the next century. Although punitive labor laws and slave codes received little revision, a number of other changes occurred. Changes in the islands' populations were the result of the higher than average death rates from yellow fever among European groups, the reduced opportunities faced by European immigrants after planters claimed land reserves and, above all, the increased numbers of slaves imported after the inefficient official monopoly on the British slave trade was ended in 1698. Most new slaves simply replaced the dead, as the region's birth rates did not sustain the population well into the nineteenth century. Because women comprised a large proportion of the field gangs, overwork kept slave reproduction rates low. In most colonies, island-born Creole populations remained a minority. Populations of free people of color also remained small and mostly urban, but their reproduction levels were higher than other groups. Among the white settlers, reproduction

rates were very low and population numbers fell. The makeup of this last group altered even more after England's 1707 Act of Union with Scotland, which joined the two kingdoms into the new United Kingdom of Great Britain. This union enabled Scotland to partake of free navigation and trade throughout the entire kingdom, including the British colonies. Thus, Scots from all social levels arrived in the Caribbean during the eighteenth century.

Regional political geographies also changed, as did the priorities of British politicians. Some helped the colonists by removing former local threats. In Jamaica, a 1739 treaty with the groups of free maroons there (fugitive black slaves and their descendants) ended forty years of skirmishing—and constrained slaves' options. In the eastern Caribbean, European colonization began on the Caribs' former island strongholds and grew to dominate each island. Meanwhile, threats from Europe grew. Military expeditions to the West Indies made conquest a real risk. Negotiators sometimes returned captured islands in peace treaties, but islands seized in the West Indies could be traded away for other imperial assets. After the Seven Years' War (1756–1763) Britain still acquired several new territories, securing Dominica, Saint Vincent, and Tobago, besides gaining Grenada in exchange for Saint Lucia. In this treaty Martinique and Guadeloupe were returned to France to end French claims to Canada. Afterward, a sizable proportion of British slave shipments to the West Indies carried slaves to the newly settled islands. Metropolitan schemes then extended further, as proposals to rein in slavery and the slave trade began to gain proponents among some senior colonial bureaucrats.

Whatever was intended, far broader social changes occurred during and after the American War of Independence (1775–1783). Only remarkable good fortune at the naval Battle of the Saints in 1782 allowed Britain to retain its West Indian colonies against the Americans' French and Spanish allies. The 1783 Peace of Paris that ended this war, where the British formally recognized their former American colonists' independence, also allowed the British to regain the eastern Caribbean islands seized by the French, along with the Bahamas, which the Spaniards had captured. Peace changed the British islands in the Caribbean, in part because the subjects of King George III (ruled 1760–1820) were forbidden to do business with their former American trading partners, and Canadian lumber and English and Irish provisions offered poor substitutes. After hurricanes flattened slaves' provision grounds, several islands endured famines. Attempts to introduce new food crops, such as breadfruit in the late eighteenth century, were impressive, but still failed to compensate for the lack of cheap American grain. The process of change continued as North American loyalists resettled across the West Indies after the war. In the Bahamas, they transformed the character of the hitherto sparsely settled archipelago. Several African Americans, free and slave, had, during this migration, encountered the evangelical revivals that had spread across British North America, and the congregations they founded then survived to transform the slaveholding societies.

In 1790 the British West Indies appeared at the height of their prosperity and influence. In the early years of the French Revolutionary Wars (1792–1802), Britain poured half of its total military expenditure into West Indian campaigns. The failure to acquire Saint Domingue (Haiti) and the return of most British gains in the Treaty of Amiens that concluded the French Revolutionary Wars was a watershed in British policy making. The costs of prolonged warfare on the islands' economies and on planters' profit margins further undercut the influence of the West Indies lobby. Retaining slavery no longer appeared a clear asset. At the same time, the spread of humanitarian revulsion toward slavery in Britain increasingly diverged from the West Indian colonists' stridently asserted "English" values. Meanwhile, evangelical missionaries' visits to the islands and the contacts that local evangelicals, black and white, made with their British co-religionists encouraged the circulation of harsher reports of slaveholders' brutality.

The West Indian "sugar islands" would continue to prosper in the early nineteenth century. The West Indian political lobby had sufficient influence to veto proposals that Britain retain Martinique and Guadeloupe after the wars, for fear of the competition that these islands' output would offer to the existing British colonies, although the undeveloped Dutch mainland settlements of Demerara and Esquibo (modern Guyana) were

kept. But, after 1783, the defenders of West Indian slavery had lost the support of the North American planters when they argued their case to an increasingly skeptical British public. In the face of competition from "free sugar" from the East Indies and from sugar beet from continental Europe, West Indian profits declined. The debts remained. Profits from the first British empire helped to generate the capital that funded Britain's industrial revolution. Afterward, the claims offered by the West Indian planters that their brutal slave societies were "English" no longer appeared so persuasive in England. The societies that the seventeenth-century "sugar revolution" had produced still took a very long time to pass away.

See also **American Independence, War of (1775–1783); Colonialism; Dutch Colonies: The Americas; French Colonies: The Caribbean; Mercantilism; Seven Years' War (1756–1763); Shipping; Slavery and the Slave Trade; Spanish Colonies: The Caribbean; Sugar; Tobacco; Trading Companies.**

BIBLIOGRAPHY

Batie, Robert C. "Why Sugar? Economic Cycles and the Changing of Staples in the English and French Antilles, 1624–1654." *Journal of Caribbean History* 8–9 (1976): 1–42.

Beckles, Hilary McD. *A History of Barbados: From Amerindian Settlement to Nation-State.* Cambridge, U.K., 1990.

———. "The 'Hub of the Empire': The Caribbean and Britain in the Seventeenth Century." In *Oxford History of the British Empire*, edited by William Roger Louis. Vol. 1, *The Origins of Empire: British Overseas Enterprise to the Close of the Seventeenth Century*, edited by Nicholas Patrick Canny and Alaine M. Low, pp. 218–240. Oxford, 1998.

———. *Natural Rebels: A Social History of Enslaved Black Women in Barbados.* New Brunswick, N.J., 1989.

———. *White Servitude and Black Slavery in Barbados, 1627–1715.* Knoxville, Tenn., 1989.

Braithwaite, Edward Kamau. *The Development of Creole Society in Jamaica, 1770–1820.* 2nd ed. Oxford, 1978.

Brown, Christopher L. "Empire without Slaves: British Concepts of Emancipation in the Age of the American Revolution." *William & Mary Quarterly* 3rd ser. 56 (1999): 273–306.

Buisseret, David. "The Process of Creolization in Seventeenth-Century Jamaica." In *Historic Jamaica from the Air.* 2nd. rev. ed. Kingston, Jamaica, 1996.

Buisseret, David, and Steven G. Reinhardt, eds. *Creolization in the Americas.* College Station, Tex., 2000.

Cateau, Heather, and S. H. H. Carrington, eds. *Capitalism and Slavery Fifty Years Later: Eric Eustace Williams—A Reassessment of the Man and His Work.* New York, 2000.

Craton, Michael, and Gail Saunders. *Islanders in the Stream: A History of the Bahamian People.* Vol. I, *From Aboriginal Times to the End of Slavery.* Athens, Ga., and London, 1992–1998.

Gaspar, David Barry. "'Rigid and Inclement': Origins of the Jamaican Slave Laws of the Seventeenth Century." In *The Many Legalities of Early America*, edited by Christopher L. Tomlins and Bruce H. Mann, pp. 78–96. Chapel Hill, N.C., and London, 2001.

Geggus, David Patrick. "The Enigma of Jamaica in the 1790s: New Light on the Causes of Slave Rebellions." *William & Mary Quarterly* 3rd ser. 44 (1987): 274–299.

Greene, Jack P. "Changing Identity in the British Caribbean: Barbados as a Case Study." In *Colonial Identity in the Atlantic World, 1500–1800,* edited by Nicholas Canny and Anthony Pagden, pp. 213–266. Princeton, 1987.

Higman, Barry William. *Montpelier, Jamaica: A Plantation Community in Slavery and Freedom, 1739–1912.* Kingston, Jamaica, 1998.

O'Shaughnessy, Andrew Jackson. *An Empire Divided: The American Revolution and the British Caribbean.* Philadelphia, 2000.

Pares, Richard. *Merchants and Planters.* Economic History Review Supplement, no. 4. Cambridge, U.K., 1960.

Pulsipher, Lydia Mihelic. *Seventeenth-Century Montserrat: An Environmental Impact Statement.* Historical Geography Research Series, no. 17. Norwich, U.K., 1986.

Sheridan, Richard B. "The Formation of Caribbean Plantation Society, 1689–1748." In *Oxford History of the British Empire.* Edited by William Roger Louis. Vol. II, *The Eighteenth Century,* edited by P. J. Marshall, pp. 394–414. Oxford, 1998.

———. *Sugar and Slavery: An Economic History of the British West Indies, 1623–1775.* Barbados, 1994.

Watson, Karl. *The Civilised Island: Barbados, A Social History, 1750–1816.* St. George, Barbados, 1979.

Watts, Arthur P. *Une histoire des colonies Anglaises aux Antilles, de 1649 à 1660.* Paris, 1924.

Watts, David. *The West Indies: Patterns of Development, Culture and Environmental Change since 1492.* Reprint. Cambridge, U.K., 1987.

JAMES ROBERTSON

INDIA

The establishment of a colonial relationship between Britain and India through the medium of a trading company had a long gestation period of over a century and a half. The complete formalization of this relationship, with the British crown assuming direct responsibility for the Indian dominions, took yet another century.

It was on the last day of the year 1600 that a charter granted by Queen Elizabeth I incorporated some 219 members under the title of The Governor and Company of Merchants of London Trading into the East Indies. This was the body that came to be known as the East India Company. The trade carried on by the company between Europe and Asia increased rapidly, and by the end of the seventeenth century, the value of this trade almost equaled that carried on by its principal rival, the Dutch East India Company. By about 1740, the English had decisively forged ahead of the Dutch, a lead they retained through the rest of the eighteenth century. It was, however, only in 1765 that the company became the instrument for establishing a colonial relationship between Britain and India.

Like other Europeans, the principal interest of the English in the East, initially at least, was to procure pepper and other spices for the European market. The first two voyages were, therefore, directed at Bantam in Java, where a trading station was established in 1602. But given the strong presence of the Dutch East India Company in the Indonesian archipelago, the English found it prudent to move gradually out of the region and concentrate on India. An imperial edict conferring formal trading rights on the company was obtained from the Mughal emperor and a trading station established at Surat in Gujarat in 1613. A station had earlier been established in Masulipatnam on the southeast coast of India in 1611. The company's trade extended into Bengal in the early 1650s with the establishment of a trading station at Hughli.

The spectacularly growing role of textiles and raw silk in the exports from Asia made India central to the company's trade, accounting for as much as 90 percent of the total exports from Asia at the turn of the eighteenth century. While the company, by and large, concentrated on Euro-Asian trade, its servants, acting in their private capacity together with a limited number of British citizens residing in the company's settlements in India, carried on a

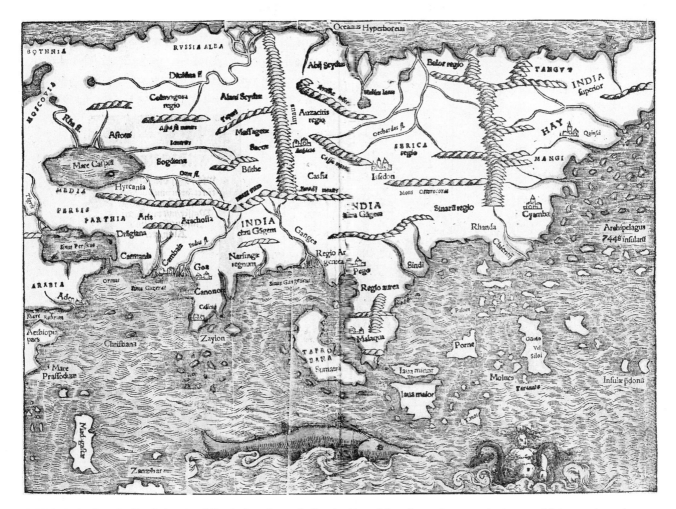

British Colonies: India. Sebastian Münster's rather primitive-looking sixteenth-century woodcut map of Asia was based on recent discoveries by Portuguese navigators. Shown in India are Calicut, where Da Gama landed in 1498, Goa, taken in 1510, and the settlement at Cannanore. The Portuguese trade monopoly did not last long, and by the 1600s had attracted British, Dutch, and French competition. MAP COLLECTION, STERLING MEMORIAL LIBRARY, YALE UNIVERSITY

substantial amount of port-to-port trade within Asia.

The increase in the output of textiles and the other export goods in the subcontinent in response to the rising demand for these goods by the English and other East India companies would seem to have been achieved through a reallocation of resources, a fuller utilization of existing productive capacity and an increase over time in the capacity itself. The English and other European companies' trade would thus have become a vehicle for an expansion in income, output, and employment in the subcontinent. The principal underlying circumstance behind this positive state of affairs was the fact that the relationship between the Indian intermediary merchants and artisans on the one hand and the

European trading companies including the English Company on the other had been entirely free of coercion and determined exclusively by the market forces of supply and demand. The growth of the Europeans' demand for Indian textiles and silk at a rate consistently higher than the rate of growth of their supply had increasingly turned the market into a sellers' market.

This scenario, however, underwent a substantive modification during the second half of the eighteenth century. It began when the English East India Company assumed political leverage in different parts of the subcontinent. The process began in southeastern India where the English and the French became allies of contestants for the succession of the Nawab of Arcot and the Nizam of

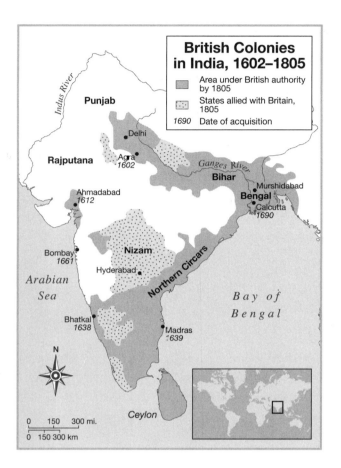

British Colonies in India, 1602–1805

- Area under British authority by 1805
- States allied with Britain, 1805
- *1690* Date of acquisition

Indus River

Punjab

Delhi

Rajputana

Agra
1602

Ganges River

Bihar

Ahmadabad
1612

Murshidabad

Bengal

Calcutta
1690

Bombay
1661

Nizam

Hyderabad

Arabian
Sea

Northern Circars

Bhatkal
1638

Madras
1639

Bay of
Bengal

N

0   150   300 mi.
0 150 300 km

Ceylon

Hyderabad. War ebbed and flowed across southern India with little intermission from 1746 until complete English victory brought the fighting to an end in 1761. British victory meant that the territories of the English-backed Nawab of Arcot became a client state of the English East India Company. Much more fundamental in importance was the incorporation of Bengal as a province under actual British rule. The 1765 Treaty of Allahabad was an outcome of the battle of Plassey in 1757 and that of Buxar in 1764. According to this treaty, the Mughal emperor conferred on the East India Company the *diwani*, or the responsibility for the civil administration of Bengal; at the same time, the wazir of Awadh accepted a British alliance and a British garrison. This settlement gave the British rule over some 20 million people in Bengal, together with access to a revenue of about £3 million, and it brought British influence nearly up to Delhi.

The acquisition of political leverage by the East India Company brought to an end the level playing field that the intermediary merchants and artisans doing business with it had hitherto enjoyed. Through an extensive misuse of its newly acquired political power, the company subjected suppliers and artisans to complete domination, imposing upon them unilaterally determined terms and conditions, which significantly cut into their margin of profit.

Seemingly paradoxically, while the East India Company's exports from India were undergoing a substantial increase during the second half of the eighteenth century, the import of bullion by the company into the subcontinent to pay for the goods purchased was practically coming to an end. The explanation lies in good measure in the substantial quantities of rupee receipts obtained by the company locally against bills of exchange issued to English and other private European traders, payable in London and other European capitals. Another source used for the purpose was the surplus from the provincial revenue of Bengal. Such a diversion of the revenue was obviously unethical, and indeed the Parliamentary Select Committee of 1783 indicted the company for these practices. By 1765, a sizeable territorial dominion had been established and the East India Company had become a regional Indian power of consequence. From this beginning, British power was to engulf the whole of the Indian subcontinent within a hundred years, with the crown assuming direct responsibility for the Indian dominions in 1858, following the Indian mutiny and the liquidation of the East India Company.

See also **Colonialism; Commerce and Markets; Dutch Colonies: The East Indies.**

BIBLIOGRAPHY

Marshall, P. J. "The British in Asia: Trade to Dominion, 1700–1765." *The Oxford History of the British Empire.* Vol. 2, *The Eighteenth Century.* Edited by P. J. Marshall. Oxford, 1998.

———. "The English in Asia to 1700." In *The Oxford History of the British Empire.* Vol. 1, *The Origins of Empire, British Overseas Enterprise to the Close of the Seventeenth Century.* Edited by Nicholas Canny. Oxford, 1998.

Prakash, Om. "The English East India Company and India." In *The Worlds of the East India Company.* Edited by H. V. Bowen, Margarette Lincoln, and Nigel Rigby. Rochester, N.Y., 2002.

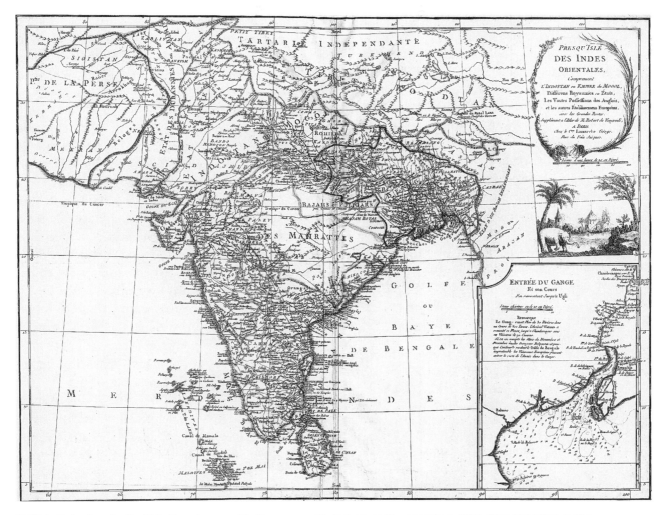

British Colonies: India. This French map of India appeared in Robert de Vaugondy's c. 1790 *Atlas Universal.* In the seventeenth century the British East India was content to dominate trade in the region and maintain peaceful relations with the Mughal empire. But when the empire was weakened in the eighteenth century, Britain and France fought for control of the area. British rule began with the defeat of the Nawab of Bengal in 1757 and by 1818 the British controlled most of India. MAP COLLECTION, STERLING MEMORIAL LIBRARY, YALE UNIVERSITY

―――. *European Commercial Enterprise in Pre-Colonial India.* Vol II.5 of *The New Cambridge History of India.* Cambridge, U.K., 1998.

OM PRAKASH

NORTH AMERICA

English interest in North America began soon after Christopher Columbus's first discoveries when John Cabot (c. 1450–c. 1499), a Venetian sailor, was commissioned by Henry VII in 1497 to find a northwest route to the East. The voyage proved ineffectual and for the next seventy years England remained on the sidelines of westward exploration, largely because of political and religious divisions at home. Interest did not really revive until the fourth quarter of the sixteenth century, when the success of the Spanish and Portuguese empires demonstrated the economic and strategic value of having colonies. Since the North American continent remained largely free of European settlement, the new advocates of colonization, notably English geographer Richard Hakluyt (c. 1552–1616), argued that the settling of these territories would allow the production of valuable tropical products like sugar, silk, olives, spices, hardwoods, and vines. These items had to be purchased from foreign rivals, resulting in a trade deficit and loss of bullion. In addition, Hakluyt argued, the possession of colonies would increase the maritime power of England, making her a force to be reckoned with among the nation-states of Europe.

FIRST SETTLEMENTS

Since the crown lacked the resources for such ventures, it was initially left to individuals like Sir Walter Raleigh (1554–1618) to fulfill these dreams. Unfortunately, Raleigh's attempt to settle Roanoke Island along the North Carolina coast between 1585 and 1587 proved unsuccessful, mainly because he lacked the necessary resources. However, the development of joint stock companies promised to solve this problem by allowing funds to be pooled on a large scale. Not that these new entities found colonization easy, as the attempts of the Plymouth and Virginia companies proved. The former failed to establish its colony of Sagadahoc in 1607 on the coast of present-day Maine, while the latter had to struggle for twenty years to ensure the success of Jamestown, England's first permanent settlement on the mainland of North America. In reality, too little was known about the Chesapeake region when the first settlers arrived in 1607, and the project came close to collapse several times.

Despite these difficulties, other schemes duly followed, though the impulse was increasingly religious rather than commercial. England, like much of Europe, was experiencing religious turmoil, and America seemingly offered a refuge to those suffering persecution at home. Accordingly, in 1620 a group of Pilgrims led by the Separatist church leader William Brewster (1567–1644) set sail in the Mayflower to establish the Plymouth colony, while from 1629 to 1640 twenty thousand Puritans left England to establish the colonies of Massachusetts Bay in 1630, Rhode Island and Connecticut in 1636, and New Haven in 1637. Nor were Protestants alone in this exodus. In 1632 George Calvert, the first baron Baltimore (c. 1580–1632), obtained a charter from Charles I for a colony allowing religious toleration for Roman Catholics, which he called Maryland in honor of the queen.

Baltimore's charter differed from those granted to the Virginia and Massachusetts Bay Companies in that authority was vested in a single proprietor. Otherwise, both types of charter gave the grantees extensive powers, including authority to make local ordinances for the better government of their territories, providing such ordinances were consistent with the laws of England. The crown also retained the right to a fifth of all precious minerals found in their settlements. However, in 1618 the Virginia Company decided to establish a local assembly as a more effective way of involving the inhabitants in the success of the venture. This pattern was soon adopted in other colonies, notably Massachusetts, not least because that colony's charter, based on the joint stock model, required its officers to be elected annually by the shareholders. Even the autocratic second baron Baltimore (Cecilius Calvert, 1605–1675) found it politic to give his settlers an assembly as a means of attracting support. The qualifications for voting varied. In Maryland and Virginia it was generally restricted to freeholders (meaning males with property), but in Massachusetts the Puritan leadership quickly substituted church membership as the criterion for participation in the affairs of the colony.

SECOND WAVE

Although English settlement of North America was interrupted at the outbreak of the English Civil War in 1641, the restoration of Charles II in 1660 allowed a second wave of colonization, beginning in 1664 with the conquest of the Dutch colony of New Netherland in present-day New York. It was seized partly for economic reasons, to secure entry to the northern fur trade; partly to create a patrimony for the duke of York, the king's younger brother; and partly as a strategy: to close a dangerous gap between the New England and Chesapeake Bay settlements. But even before the seizure of the Dutch colony, another scheme was afoot to settle the area south of Virginia. Here, too, the founding of the Carolinas was partly commercial, to tap the possibilities of exotic cash crops in a subtropical climate; partly strategic, to provide a buffer between Virginia and the Spanish in Florida; and partly an attempt to endow the eight proprietors sponsoring the scheme with the privileges of semifeudal palatine princes. Not that religious considerations were entirely forgotten after 1660. In 1682 William Penn (1644–1718) secured a proprietary charter to provide a haven for the Society of Friends, or Quakers, as they were more commonly known. But as was the case with the Carolinas, the colonization of Pennsylvania had a strong economic rationale: to exploit the rich potential of the Delaware River area. It was also intended to enhance the dynastic aspirations of the proprietary family.

For much of the seventeenth century, England's control of its burgeoning empire was necessarily weak, given the distance of the colonies from England and the confused state of the mother country. Compounding the problems was the fact that there was no common system of government in the various settlements. Virginia, the oldest colony, had a governor appointed by the crown, a council appointed by the governor, and an elective assembly representing the propertied classes, and this was to be the model most favored by the crown after 1689 as its best means of maintaining control. However, the New England colonies at this time were largely self-governing commonwealths, while the Carolinas, Pennsylvania, and New York were all under proprietary control.

Even so, the period was not without some tightening of the imperial reins. In 1651 the first Navigation Act was passed to protect England's growing trade with its empire in the West Indies and mainland North America, and this was followed by several similar such laws in the next twenty-five years. Then in 1680 New Hampshire was separated from Massachusetts and made into a royal colony on the Virginia model. More grandiosely, in the mid-1680s James II attempted to merge the northern colonies into one entity, the Dominion of New England, to allow a more effective defense and use of scarce resources. That scheme proved too unpopular and was discarded during England's 1689 Glorious Revolution, which limited sovereign power and ended the concept of the divine right of kings. Nevertheless, some changes were effected. Massachusetts now had to accept a charter on the Virginia model, albeit with the concession that the lower house still helped nominate the governor's council, as had been required under the old charter of 1629. The crown also had a further success in East and West Jersey in the early 1700s, when the proprietors decided to surrender their governmental rights over the territory. Finally, in the 1720s the crown, with Parliament's help, engineered a similar outcome in the Carolinas, after the proprietary government failed to defend those colonies successfully from Spanish and Indian attacks. However, Pennsylvania and Maryland remained proprietary colonies while Connecticut and Rhode Island anomalously retained their corporate charters, which had originally been granted by Parliament during the English Civil War.

DENOMINATIONS AND DIVERSITY

During the seventeenth century the colonies' population was overwhelmingly English in origin, with only a few pockets of non-English stock, most importantly in Pennsylvania, where Penn settled a group of lower Rhineland Pietists at Germantown in 1686, and in New York, where the Dutch remained a distinct group. But already there was a growing number of African slaves, especially in the South, and this trend toward a more diverse population continued during the eighteenth century, aided by the absence of any restrictive immigration laws. In 1707 the Act of Union between England and Scotland officially opened the way to Scottish emigration, while the cessation of the War of the Spanish Succession in Europe in 1714 permitted further German emigration from the Palatinate and Rhineland areas. In addition, large numbers of Scots Irish began to arrive after 1717 following the termination of their leases in Ireland. All these European peoples came seeking a better life where land was plentiful and religious discrimination was minimal. Prior to 1715 the New England region had been uniformly Congregational, the South largely Anglican, with the Dutch Reformed and Society of Friends preeminent in the Hudson and Delaware Valleys. Now, outside New England, there were Presbyterians, Baptists, Moravians, and German Reformed and Lutheran churches, all adding to the multireligious and multicultural nature of the colonies and establishing a trend that has continued ever since.

ECONOMY

The economy of Britain's North American colonies was similarly varied, primarily as the result of differences in the climate and soil. The relatively temperate climate of the New England and Mid-Atlantic colonies allowed their inhabitants to practice European-style farming in cereals, root crops, and animal husbandry. And as in Europe, most northern farms relied on their families to meet their labor requirements. In the South, on the other hand, the longer and warmer growing season permitted the cultivation of more exotic cash crops like tobacco in the Chesapeake Bay area and Albemarle Sound region of North Carolina and rice in the lower part of

North Carolina, South Carolina, and Georgia (after 1733). Since these crops were labor-intensive, their production presented a problem, not least because most Native Americans refused to acculturate to European-style production methods and were in any case too few in number. Initially the labor problem was solved in the Chesapeake region by the system of indentured servitude. However, indentured servants served for only a few years, after which they were free to compete with their former masters. As a result, southern planters began increasingly to use African slave labor, especially when the cost of doing so dropped toward the end of the seventeenth century. The early settlers in South Carolina, in any case, deployed African slaves, being familiar with their use from their previous experience as sugar planters in Barbados.

Another difference between the northern and southern economies was the North's greater diversification. The northern colonies had no high-value commodities to export other than those obtained through the extractive pursuits of fishing and lumbering. Consequently, they had to be more self-sufficient, which led to the development of craft industries and the beginnings of manufacturing in pottery and iron ware. Shipbuilding was also widespread, and commerce generally flourished, which in turn stimulated urban growth. By the mid-eighteenth century, Boston, New York, and Philadelphia all had populations of more than ten thousand, with Philadelphia ranking as the second-largest city in the British Empire. The South, by contrast, had only one town of any consequence: Charleston in South Carolina.

By 1750 the thirteen British mainland colonies had a population around 1.5 million (including 250,000 persons of African descent) who provided a third of all British trade.

THE CAUSES OF REVOLT

Thus, although the British had been late to enter the race for overseas colonies (compared to Spain and Portugal), their settlements now constituted perhaps the most valuable possessions of any European nation. It was this realization that led Britain to attempt a strengthening of the imperial ties after the Seven Years' War (1756–1763). Among the more important initiatives were the Proclamation of 1763, which attempted to limit westward expansion; the Sugar Act of 1764, to raise revenue and strengthen the laws of trade; and the Stamp Act of 1765, to raise additional revenue for the running of the empire. But far from strengthening imperial control, these measures antagonized the colonial population and led to disputes over the sovereignty of Parliament and the rights of the colonists, especially on matters of taxation. It was failure to resolve these issues, among others, that led to the Declaration of Independence in 1776 and creation of the United States, signaling an end to the first British Empire.

See also **American Independence, War of (1775–1783); Boston; Charleston; Colonialism; Commerce and Markets; Divine Right Kingship; Dutch Colonies: The Americas; Exploration; Navigation Acts; New York; Philadelphia; Puritanism; Quakers; Slavery and the Slave Trade; Taxation; Triangular Trade Pattern.**

BIBLIOGRAPHY

Andrews, Charles M. *The Colonial Period of American History.* 4 vols. New Haven, 1934–1938. Reprint, vols. 1–3, 2001.

Bailyn, Bernard. *The Peopling of British North America: An Introduction.* New York, 1986.

Bonwick, Colin. *The American Revolution.* Charlottesville, Va., 1991.

Butler, Jon. *Becoming America: The Revolution before 1776.* Cambridge, Mass., 2000.

Egnal, Marc. *New World Economies: The Growth of the Thirteen Colonies and Early Canada.* New York, 1998.

Kammen, Michael. *Deputyes & Libertyes: The Origins of Representative Government in Colonial America.* New York, 1969.

Meinig, Donald William. *The Shaping of America: A Geographical Perspective on 500 Years of History.* 3 vols. New Haven, 1986–1993. Volume one is *Atlantic America, 1492–1800.*

Middleton, Richard. *Colonial America: A History, 1565–1776.* 3rd ed. Oxford, 2002.

Nash, Gary B. *Red, White, and Black: The Peoples of Early America.* Englewood Cliffs, N.J., 1974.

Vickers, Daniel. *A Companion to Colonial America.* Oxford, 2003.

Wood, Betty. *The Origins of American Slavery: Freedom and Bondage in the English Colonies.* New York, 1997.

RICHARD MIDDLETON

BRITTANY. Jutting into the ocean, far from Paris's central state, Brittany had close economic and cultural ties to its Atlantic neighbors. Until 1550, when larger and more efficient Dutch ships displaced them, Breton fleets swarmed European coastal waters, carrying salt, linen, hemp, hides, grain, and wine to distant ports. They returned with oranges, leather, and silver from Spain, with herring, cheese, and naval stores from Holland, and with cloth from England, Holland, and Flanders. Brittany remained a bustling manufacturing power until 1680: its two million inhabitants gave it a population density matched in Europe only by the urban regions of the Low Countries.

In western Brittany, war between France and England disabled the manufacture of linen, crucial to the region's economy, at the end of the seventeenth century. This region lapsed into an enduring poverty, and became a leading center of emigration to Paris in the nineteenth century. Nantes followed a different path: it prospered mightily in colonial trade, becoming the largest French slaving port, and reexporting West Indian sugar and coffee throughout Europe.

Brittany enjoyed a quasi-independent status until 1491, when the last Breton ruler, Duchess Anne (1477–1513), married Charles VIII of France (ruled 1483–1498). He died childless; she then married Louis XII (ruled 1498–1515). Their eldest daughter, Claude, married Francis I (ruled 1515–1547); Claude's son, Henry II (ruled 1547–1559) inherited the duchy, making it the personal property of subsequent kings of France.

Brittany until 1790 preserved its provincial Estates, which met annually until 1626 and biannually after 1630; a full complement of local courts, headed by the parlement at Rennes; its customary laws; and its tax system, run primarily by the Estates. These local institutions enabled the Breton nobility to maintain unusually tight control over the province: alone among early modern French peasant rebels, the Breton *bonnets rouges* ('red caps') in

Brittany. Seventeenth-century engraving of the island city of St. Malo. The site of a sixth-century monastery, St. Malo later became an important Breton seaport and during the seventeenth and eighteenth centuries served as a base for privateers. The Art Archive/Private Collection Paris/Dagli Orti

1675 targeted noble landlords, rather than royal taxes.

Western Brittany stood out culturally because its inhabitants spoke Breton Gaelic. Many French speakers shared the views expressed by the marquis of Lavardin, lieutenant general of Brittany, in 1675: Celtic Brittany "is a rude and ferocious country, which produces inhabitants that resemble it. They poorly understand French and scarcely better reason." The Catholic Church sent out "missionaries," led by the Jesuit Julien Maunoir, to "convert" the nominally Catholic Bretons, whom it viewed as pagans. One of his hymns set forward the church's view of peasant sociability: "Listen all of you [Bretons]/ The evil of your veillées,/ And your savage dances/ That the mad devil/ Has brought here/ To plunge young people/ Into eternal torments … From these dances/ Come lewd thoughts!" (The *veillées*, evening village gatherings, for storytelling, matchmaking, and general socializing, remained a staple of Breton life into the 1930s.)

Bretons left a visual legacy of their remarkably rich civilization in parish *closes,* ensembles of churches, Calvary scenes, and ossuaries. The wealth produced by linen and livestock enabled the peasant-merchants of a St-Thégonnec or a Pleyben to commission magnificent statuary, often created by the workshop of Jean Dauré (1706?–1736/1747?) of Landerneau. Artists richly decorated the interiors of the rural churches, either with imaginative paintings on ceilings and pillars, or with stunning altars, as at Lampaul-Guimiliau, whose gilded fallen angels are based on a painting by Rubens (1577–1640). These masterpieces show the European dimension of early modern Breton civilization, and offer some of the richest rewards rural France has to entice the twenty-first-century visitor.

See also **Anne of Brittany; Charles VIII (France); France; Louis XII (France); Provincial Government.**

BIBLIOGRAPHY

Collins, J. B. *Classes, Estates, and Order in Early-Modern Brittany.* Cambridge, U.K., and New York, 1994.

Croix, Alain. *L'âge d'or de la Bretagne, 1532–1675.* Rennes, France, 1993.

Tanguy, J. *Histoire de la Bretagne et des pays celtique: La Bretagne province 1532–1789.* Morlaix, 1986.

JAMES B. COLLINS

BROWNE, THOMAS (1605–1682), English physician, naturalist, and essayist. Browne reflected and harmonized in his life and work many of the religious and scientific trends characteristic of the seventeenth century. He was born in London on 19 October 1605 and enjoyed a stable childhood among devout and devoted parents and four sisters, though his father, a cloth merchant, died when Thomas was eight. The elder Browne left a generous inheritance, however, which supported his son in his extensive education in England and abroad. Thomas entered Winchester College in 1616, where he studied classics and rhetoric and absorbed the Anglican and Royalist spirit of the place. He went on to Oxford in 1623, where his classical education was broadened and supplemented by training in the natural sciences. He received his B.A. in 1626 and his M.A. in 1629. Following graduation, having been inspired to become a physician, he departed for the Continent to seek the superior medical training available there. He went first to the University of Montpellier and then to Padua, where, a century before, Andreas Vesalius (1514–1564) had revolutionized the study of anatomy, where, twenty years earlier, Galileo Galilei (1564–1642) had first trained his telescope on the stars, and where William Harvey (1578–1657) had studied prior to his recent discovery of the circulation of the blood. Browne imbibed the unparalleled clinical instruction offered at Padua but soon moved on to Leiden for further study and obtained his M.D. there in 1633. After an apprenticeship in England, he acquired an M.D. from Oxford and in 1637 set up practice in the city of Norwich. He married Dorothy Mileham in 1641, and they had twelve children, only six of whom survived into adulthood.

Browne's era was one of great political and religious unrest and scientific ferment. His first and most famous written work, *Religio Medici* (The religion of a doctor), appeared in 1642 at the onset of the English Civil War, or Puritan Revolution. In this work Browne offers a candid exploration of his elastic Anglican views, shaped by a mixture of traditional and contemporary ideas, regarding such issues as God's relation to nature, the interplay of faith and reason, and the conciliatory effects of Christian charity and humility. Browne envisioned human beings as microcosms of the universe, and *Religio Medici* itself can be seen as an epitome of its author, embodying his religious background, his classical and scientific education, and his humane tolerance acquired from wide experience of diverse national and religious cultures. Aside from its content, the poetic literary quality of the book, which displays a musical sensibility striking resonant chords along a scale between certitude and doubt, has long established Browne as one of the finest prose stylists in the history of English literature.

In addition to becoming a respected physician through decades of practice in Norwich, Browne was a recognized authority on the flora and fauna of East Anglia. He was intent on sorting out truth from error in natural history and general knowledge and in 1646 published his systematic inquiry into contemporary beliefs called *Pseudodoxia Epidemica,* which became commonly known as *Vulgar Errors.* In the spirit of Francis Bacon's *Advancement of Learning,* Browne assayed hundreds of presumed truths about the world, often utilizing the newly ascendant intellectual instruments of empirical observation and experimentation. This book, which was his longest, enjoyed great popularity and, like other works appearing near the dawn of modern science, helped foster critical and constructive modes of thought among its wide audience. Browne conducted diverse scientific investigations, was in contact with many leading scientific figures of his day, and was elected a fellow of the Royal College of Physicians, but he remained on the margins of the scientific community of seventeenth-century England and never became a fellow of the Royal Society.

Browne's other important literary and philosophical works include the companion essays *Hydriotaphia, or Urn Burial* and *The Garden of Cyrus,* which were published together in 1658. The first, which displays his antiquarian interests, is a meditation on death and decay prompted by the unearthing of ancient burial urns near Norwich. The second is an exploration of the "mystical mathematics" of the number five manifested in human designs and botanical life and reveals Browne's abiding Platonic belief that the visible world is but an image of an invisible order. He thought that the quintessence of human identity lies in living a sort of amphibious existence traversing those two worlds, and he tried passionately, in an age of shifting religious and scientific worldviews, to keep the two together.

Browne was knighted by Charles II in 1671 as an honor for Norwich's most distinguished citizen. Fittingly for a man whose favorite sacred symbol was the circle, Browne's life came to a close on the date of his birth in 1682.

See also **English Literature and Language; Mathematics; Philosophy; Scientific Method.**

BIBLIOGRAPHY

Primary Source

Browne, Sir Thomas. *Works.* Edited by Geoffrey L. Keynes. Rev. ed., 4 vols. Chicago, 1964. The standard edition of Browne's writings.

Secondary Sources

Huntley, Frank L. *Sir Thomas Browne, A Biographical and Critical Study.* Ann Arbor, Mich., 1962. Classic scholarly and sympathetic treatment.

Patrides, C. A., ed. *Approaches to Sir Thomas Browne: The Ann Arbor Tercentenary Lectures and Essays.* Columbia, Mo., 1982. Collection of authoritative essays from many perspectives.

Post, Jonathan F. S. *Sir Thomas Browne.* Boston, 1987. Good overview and analysis of Browne's life and works with an annotated bibliography.

GORDON L. MILLER

BRUEGEL FAMILY. The Bruegels were a family of painters active from the mid-sixteenth century through the seventeenth century, primarily in Antwerp. The Bruegel family employed many spelling variants of their name, as was common in the early modern period. The spellings used in this article are those most frequently used by the particular artists concerned.

The origins of the Bruegel family are unclear; the earliest records concerning Pieter Bruegel the Elder date from his immigration to Antwerp. Ludovico Guicciardini, the Italian chronicler, and Karel van Mander, the painter-author of the first comprehensive history of artists from the Netherlands, both state that Bruegel came from or near Breda. He was born c. 1525–1530 and died in 1569.

Pieter Bruegel the Elder moved to Antwerp in the 1540s, perhaps to study with the painter Pieter Coecke van Aelst. He entered the St. Luke's Guild of painters in Antwerp in 1551 and soon afterward left for Italy. He journeyed via the Alps, which he sketched during his travels and later incorporated into many of his compositions. Upon his return to Antwerp in 1555, Bruegel produced drawings for the Antwerp publisher Hieronymus Cock, including allegories in the style of Hieronymus Bosch, landscapes, and genre scenes. Partly on the basis of these early compositions, such as *Big Fish Eat Little Fish* (1556), Bruegel's earliest critical reputation was as a Bosch follower. Among his painted works, Bruegel's affinity with Bosch is seen in *Dulle Griet* (*Mad Meg*, c. 1562) and *The Fall of the Rebel Angels* (1562).

Bruegel's earliest signed works, the *Landscape with Christ on the Sea of Tiberius* (1553) and the *Landscape with the Parable of the Sower* (1557), are within the world-landscape tradition of Joachim Patinir. Starting in 1559–1560, Bruegel turned his attention to the folkloric subjects for which he is best known, with such painted compendia as the *Netherlandish Proverbs* (1559), *Battle of Carnival and Lent* (1559), and *Children's Games* (1560). In

1563 Bruegel married Mayken Cocks, the daughter of Pieter Coecke van Aelst. Mayken then resided in Brussels, to which Bruegel immigrated. Starting in 1562–1563, Bruegel extended his repertoire to include paintings depicting biblical history, often set in dramatic landscapes employing alpine scenery. Among these works are the *Suicide of Saul* (1562), the *Tower of Babel* (1563), *Landscape with Flight into Egypt* (1563), and *The Procession to Calvary* (1564), Bruegel's most complex composition.

In the latter 1560s, Bruegel again turned to vernacular subjects, producing a series of the year's months for Nicholas Jonghelinck, a local patrician. He also depicted peasant festivities in such works as the *Wedding Dance* (1566) and the *Peasant Wedding* (1568). In paintings like *The Cripples* (1568) and *The Parable of the Blind Leading the Blind* (1569), Bruegel returned to his earlier works to select details as the subjects for entire compositions. He died in 1569 at the age of forty-four. Bruegel was long critically regarded as a naïve artist originat-

Bruegel Family. *Peasant Dance* by Pieter Bruegel the Elder, c. 1567. ©FRANCIS G. MAYER/CORBIS

ing from the rural peasantry he portrayed. With the discovery of his close relationship with the geographer and humanist Abraham Ortelius, his reputation shifted to that of an accomplished intellectual. Most recently, scholars situate Bruegel within the culturally dynamic middle class of Antwerp.

Pieter Breughel the Younger (1564–1638), elder son of Pieter I, was only five years old when his father died. He probably received his earliest training from his grandmother Mayken Verhulst, an accomplished miniaturist, followed by an apprenticeship with the landscape artist Gillis van Conincxloo. He enrolled in the Antwerp painter's guild in 1584–1585. Pieter the Younger was a tireless, if uninspired, copyist of his father's works. These include numerous versions of the *Netherlandish Proverbs, The Census at Bethlehem,* and the *Winter Landscape with a Birdtrap.* Pieter the Younger's copies also provide visual access to some of the now lost works of his father, such as the *Crucifixion* (c. 1615) and *The Visit to the Farm* (c. 1620). Pieter the Younger also created works like the humorous *Peasant Lawyer* (1516) and *Egg Dance* (1620) that, although painted in the mode of his father, appear to be his own compositions. Pieter the Younger was also a landscape painter in his own right, as seen in the charming *Peasant Village with Dance around the May Tree* (1634). Pieter the Younger's eldest son, also named Pieter, entered the painter's guild in 1608, but little else is known of his career.

Jan Brueghel the Elder (1568–1625) was a more accomplished and financially successful artist than his brother. He traveled to Italy while still quite young, and his arrival in Naples by 1590 is documented. In 1592–1595 he resided in Rome, under the patronage of Cardinal Colonna, where he produced his earliest work, the *Bay with Warship.* By 1596 Jan had relocated to Milan to work for his lifelong patron, Cardinal Federico Borromeo. He entered the St. Luke's Guild in Antwerp in 1597. Jan's success as an artist is confirmed by his close relationship with the Brussels court, as a result of which he received special privileges from Archduke Albert, although he appears never to have received an official appointment as court painter. Jan died in 1625 during a cholera epidemic, together with three of his children.

Jan Brueghel employed a meticulous technique (earning him the nickname "Velvet Brueghel"), perhaps acquired from his maternal grandmother, the previously mentioned miniaturist Mayken Verhulst. He worked in a variety of genres, including landscapes, mythological scenes, hell scenes, floral still lifes, and allegories. Jan specialized in works on copper, such as his *Adoration of the Three Magi* (1598), utilizing the reflective ground to create images with brilliant color and the effect of light. These works were likely produced for princely collections, which he also thematized in his five *Allegories of the Senses* (now in Madrid). In addition, Jan collaborated with Peter Paul Rubens, Hendrik van Balen, and others to create works in which floral wreaths by Jan surround religious or mythological groups of figures by the other painters.

Jan Brueghel the Younger (1601–1678) was the only child from Jan the Elder's first marriage. Trained by his father, he was sent in 1622 to Italy, under the protection of Cardinal Borromeo. He traveled extensively, returning to Antwerp in 1625, whereupon he entered the painters' guild. He worked in his father's atelier, which he took over after his death. Jan Brueghel the Younger's work is firmly entrenched within his father's tradition, including landscapes and still lifes, with garlands surrounding devotional scenes.

Ambrosius Brueghel (1617–1675) was the son of Jan Brueghel the Elder by his second wife. His training possibly began with his father and continued under van Balen; he entered the St. Luke's Guild in 1647. The few works ascribed to Ambrosius, all oil on panel, are either landscapes loosely following his father's style, or symmetrically balanced floral still lifes.

Jan Peeter Brueghel (1628–1680) was the eldest son of Jan Brueghel the Younger. Registered with the St. Luke's Guild in Antwerp in 1646, he later traveled to Italy, where he remained until his death. His known works are all floral still lifes, either composed in vases or as wreaths surrounding devotional or narrative scenes.

Abraham Bruegel (1631–?1680), the second son of Jan the Younger, had already sold his first work, a small floral painting, by the age of fifteen. Like his brothers, he immigrated to Italy, residing in Rome as a member of the rowdy Schildersbent

Bruegel Family. A vase of flowers, painted by Jan Brueghel the Elder. ©Archivo Iconografico, S.A./Corbis

group of expatriate Netherlandish artists. He produced elaborate still lifes in oil on canvas, such as the *Woman with Fruit Still Life* (1669). A third son of Jan the Younger, Jan Baptist Brueghel (1670–1710), also specialized in still lifes and resided in Rome.

See also **Netherlands, Art in**.

BIBLIOGRAPHY

Brink, Pieter van den, ed. *Brueghel Enterprises*. Maastricht, Brussels, and Ghent, 2001.

Bruegel: Une dynastie des peintres. Brussels, 1980.

Ertz, Klaus, and Christa Nitze-Ertz. *Breughel-Brueghel: Pieter Breughel le Jeune (1564–1637/8), Jan Brueghel l'Ancien (1568–1625): une famille des peintres flamands vers 1600*. Lingen, 1998.

Gibson, Walter. *Bruegel*. London and New York, 1977. Meadow, Mark A. *Pieter Bruegel the Elder's Netherlandish Proverbs and the Practice of Rhetoric*. Zwolle, 2002.

Winkelmann-Rhein, Gertraude. *The Paintings and Drawings of Jan "Flower" Bruegel*. New York, 1968.

MARK A. MEADOW

BRUNO, GIORDANO (1548–1600), Italian philosopher. Born to a military father, in Nola near Naples, in 1548, Bruno was baptized Filippo. He became Giordano in 1565 on entering the Dominican monastery in Naples. He was ordained a priest in 1573, but was soon in trouble for reading forbidden books. Bruno was forced to flee from Naples, and later from Rome, to escape an official enquiry.

Discarding his monk's habit, Bruno traveled north through Genoa and Venice, giving private lessons on cosmology. In 1579, he left Italy for Geneva, where he found work with the printers. Bruno repudiated John Calvin's radical concept of predestination, and was soon obliged to leave Geneva after publishing a libel, no longer extant, criticizing one of the city's most distinguished professors of philosophy. He fared better in France where, after two years teaching philosophy at the University of Toulouse, he arrived in Paris in 1581.

Bruno was soon noticed by the French king, Henry III, for his art of memory which linked the classical art, considered as a part of rhetoric, with the use of memory icons as a part of logic proposed by the thirteenth-century mystic, Ramon Lull. Appointed as one of the royal lecturers, Bruno published in Paris in 1582 his first surviving work, *De Umbris Idearum*, which explains his art of memory. In the same year, Bruno published in Italian the comedy *Candelaio*, which paints a vividly realistic picture of the corrupt activities of plebeian Naples. It is thought by some to have influenced major Elizabethan dramatists such as Shakespeare and Ben Jonson.

In the spring of 1583, Bruno left Paris for London, where he became a gentleman attendant on the French ambassador, Michel de Castelnau, who was secretly supporting the cause of the Catholic Mary, queen of Scots. With the ambassador, he visited the court of Queen Elizabeth I and the University of Oxford, where he later returned to lecture on cosmology. His attempt to propose Copernicus's heliocentric astronomy was a disaster.

Accused of plagiarism and treated with contempt, Bruno returned to London where, between 1584 and 1585, he wrote and published his six Italian dialogues, which argue for a post-Copernican, infinite universe in which each star is a sun, giving rise to an infinite number of solar systems similar to our own.

After returning to Paris in autumn 1585, Bruno wandered through central Europe teaching and publishing his philosophy in Wittenberg, Prague, Helmsted, and Frankfurt. In 1591, he published his Latin masterpiece, known as the *Frankfurt Trilogy,* prefixing his cosmological picture *(De Immenso)* with the first systematic modern treatise proposing an atomistic conception of matter *(De Triplici Minimo).* The second volume of the trilogy *(De Monade)* on Pythagorean number symbolism announces Bruno's final works, left unpublished at his death, which show an increased attention to magical and mystical themes in a Neoplatonic and Hermetic perspective.

Bruno returned to Italy in summer 1591, invited by a Venetian nobleman, Giovanni Mocenigo, to teach him his art of memory. In May 1592, Mocenigo denounced him to the Inquisition for heretical opinions. Bruno was arrested and tried in Venice until February 1593, when he was extradited to Rome. Refusing to recant, Bruno was burnt at the stake in Campo dei Fiori in Rome on 17 February 1600.

At the center of Bruno's philosophy lies his new picture of an infinite, homogeneous, atomistically articulated cosmos, full of infinite life. From this idea derives his concept of God as Monad, or the ineffable One whose seal or shadow is the infinite world; his refusal of the Christian incarnation on the basis that the whole universe, filled with the divine spirit, is an incarnation of God; his search for that God through a logical hunt that follows the traces of divine order observable within the natural universe; his idea of magic as filling the gap that opens up between the infinite whole and the finite mind of the philosopher, entrapped in time and space; his search for new mathematical and mnemonic arts capable of comprehending the infinite, universal whole.

Considered a precursor of major philosophers such as Baruch Spinoza or Friedrich Wilhelm Jo-

Giordano Bruno. Undated woodcut of the statue in the Piazza Navona, Rome. ©BETTMANN/CORBIS

seph von Schelling, Bruno was appreciated in the nineteenth century above all for his contribution to the scientific revolution and in the twentieth for his Hermetic magic and interest in the occult. The agenda for the new century appears oriented toward a more balanced and complete view of him as a thinker who amalgamated apparently conflicting doctrines of knowledge in a complex but rich oeuvre that Bruno himself referred to as "the Nolan philosophy."

See also **Academies, Learned; Cosmology; Magic; Philosophy; Scientific Revolution; Spinoza, Baruch.**

BIBLIOGRAPHY

Primary Sources

Bruno, Giordano. *The Ash Wednesday Supper* (1584), edited and translated by E. A. Gosselin and L. S. Lerner. Hamden, Conn., 1977. Reprint: Toronto, 1995.

——. *The Cabala of Pegasus* (1585). Edited and translated by S. L. Sondergard and M. U. Sowell. New Haven and London, 2002.

——. *Cause, Principle and Unity* (1584) and *Essays on Magic*. Edited and translated by R. J. Blackwell and Robert de Lucca. Introduction by Alfonso Ingegno. Cambridge, U.K., 1998.

——. *The Expulsion of the Triumphant Beast* (1584). Edited and translated by A. D. Imerti. New Brunswick, N.J., 1964.

——. *The Heroic Frenzies* (1585). Edited and translated by P. E. Memmo. Chapel Hill, N.C., 1964.

——. *His Life and Thought, with Annotated Translation of his Work, On the Infinite Universe and Worlds* (1584). Edited and translated by D.W. Singer. New York, 1950.

——. *On the Composition of Images, Signs and Ideas* (1591). Edited and translated by C. Doria and D. Higgins. New York, 1991.

——. *Opera latine conscripta*. Edited by F. Fiorentino et al. 3 vols. in 8 parts. Naples and Florence, 1879–1891. Facsimile reprint, 1962.

Secondary Sources

Aquilecchia, Giovanni. *Schede bruniane (1950–1991)*. Manziana, 1993.

Canone, Eugenio. *Giordano Bruno 1584–1600: Mostra storico documentaria*. Florence, 2000.

Ciliberto, Michele. *Giordano Bruno*. Rome and Bari, 1990.

De Léon Jones, Karen. *Giordano Bruno and the Kaballah*. New Haven and London, 1997.

Firpo, Luigi, and Quaglioni, Diego. *Il processo di Giordano Bruno*. Rome, 1993.

Gatti, Hilary. *Giordano Bruno and Renaissance Science*. Ithaca, N.Y., 1999.

——. *The Renaissance Drama of Knowledge: Giordano Bruno in England*. London, 1989.

Gatti, Hilary, ed. *Giordano Bruno: Philosopher of the Renaissance*. London, 2003.

Hodgart, Amelia Buono. *Giordano Bruno's 'The Candle Bearer': An Enigmatic Renaissance Play*. Lewiston, U.K., 1997.

Mendoza, Ramon. *The Acentric Labyrinth: Giordano Bruno's Prelude to Contemporary Cosmology*. Shaftesbury, U.K., 1995.

Ordine, Nuccio. *Giordano Bruno and the Philosophy of the Ass*. New Haven and London, 1996.

Yates, Frances. *Giordano Bruno and the Hermetic Tradition*. London, 1964.

HILARY GATTI

BUDAPEST. Buda and Pest, which along with the rural borough of Óbuda (Old Buda) united in 1873 to form the modern Hungarian capital Budapest, were Hungary's geographical and economic centers in the early modern era. By the mid-fifteenth century Buda had become an economically and culturally vibrant royal city and seat of government. In 1541 it was conquered by Sultan Suleiman the Magnificent (ruled 1520–1566), and until its reconquest by the allied forces of the Holy League in 1686 it remained the center of the Ottoman Empire's northernmost province. From 1686 until 1703 Buda and Pest were under the jurisdiction of the Viennese Court Chamber (*Hofkammer*). In 1703 they regained their status as royal free cities, opening the way for their spectacular development within the Habsburg Monarchy. Buda, however, never regained its former status as the royal seat, for the Habsburgs ruled Hungary from Vienna, their imperial capital situated over 150 miles to the west.

The population of Buda at the end of the fifteenth century is estimated at twelve thousand, while that of Pest was around ten thousand; under Ottoman rule (1541–1686) Buda and Pest had, respectively, about eight thousand and twelve thousand inhabitants. As a result of Habsburg policy and immigration, the eighteenth century saw a spectacular population surge. By 1820 Pest had become Hungary's largest city, with more than fifty thousand inhabitants as compared to Buda's thirty thousand. In the fifteenth century the majority of Buda's inhabitants were Hungarians, and there were significant German and Jewish minorities. Under the Ottomans, Muslim Turks and Orthodox Slavs made up 50 to 75 percent of the population. By 1714 Germans constituted 52 percent of the population, followed by the Serbs (41 percent) and a tiny minority of Hungarians (5 percent). The relative proportions did not change significantly during the remainder of the century. Although at the beginning of the eighteenth century Hungarians had a plurality in Pest (40 percent), by mid-century Pest, too, had become a German city; in 1746, 67 percent of its population was German, while Serbs and Hungarians made up 17 and 16 percent, respectively.

The administration and economic life of Buda from the 1420s until the Ottoman conquest was regulated by the *Ofner Stadtrecht* (Buda book of statutes). Under King Matthias I Corvinus (ruled 1458–1490) Buda became the center of the Hungarian Renaissance, contributing significantly to education and culture. The king's library, the Bibliotheca Corviniana, housed some three thousand volumes and was one of the richest libraries in Europe, equaled only by that of the Vatican. Under Ottoman rule, Buda and Pest acquired a clear Oriental character, with mosques and Turkish baths, several of which were still in use at the beginning of the twenty-first century. In the eighteenth century Buda and Pest regained their status as the country's political and cultural centers. New churches, monasteries, and schools were built by various religious orders—Jesuits, Franciscans, Poor Clares, Carmelites, Capuchins, and Augustinians. These new edifices, along with the baroque palace erected by Holy Roman Emperor Charles VI (ruled 1711–1740; king of Hungary as Charles III) and Maria Theresa (queen of Hungary, 1740–1780), gave the twin cities their distinct baroque look.

See also **Austro-Ottoman Wars; Habsburg Territories; Hungary.**

BIBLIOGRAPHY

Balázs, Éva H. *Hungary and the Habsburgs, 1765–1800: An Experiment in Enlightened Absolutism.* Translated by Tim Wilkinson. Budapest, 1997.

Fekete, Lajos. *Buda and Pest under Turkish Rule.* Budapest, 1976.

Gerő, András, and János Poór, eds. *Budapest: A History from its Beginnings to 1998.* Translated by Judit Zinner, Cecil D. Eby, and Nóra Arató. Boulder, Colo., 1997.

GÁBOR ÁGOSTON

BUDÉ, GUILLAUME (1468–1540),

French scholar. Budé was born into a prominent Paris bourgeois family with ties to the French crown and a large collection of books and manuscripts. He dropped out of law school but experienced a "conversion" around 1491, turning to a life of humanistic study and advocacy of *bonae literae* (good letters). Calling himself self-taught and late-to-learn, he eventually became known for massive works of great erudition and complexity.

Budé was the preeminent humanist of the early years of the French Renaissance and the foremost European Hellenist of his time, famous for his encyclopedic knowledge of ancient law, monies and measures, and the Greek language. Considered on the level of Desiderius Erasmus, Budé was the very embodiment of a thesis dear to his heart: that leadership in literary culture was passing from Italy to France. Today he is remembered for his historical approach to law, economics, and politics, and for a ponderous prose style full of classical allusions, symbols, and metaphors. His advocacy of humanist learning influenced French cultural policy to some extent, although he cannot be said to have tempered the harsh reaction of the crown to the Reformation.

Budé held prominent political positions, beginning as a royal secretary to Charles VIII (ruled 1483–1498). His service to Francis I (ruled 1515–1547) began in 1517, when he corresponded with Erasmus about forming a French trilingual college. Their letters span a decade, but there was a falling-out after Budé judged Erasmus's lighter works "insignificant" and Erasmus found Budé's overly obscure and flowery. Budé corresponded with many other humanistically inclined persons, sometimes in Greek, occasionally engaging in controversies about humanist reputations.

Budé's active life included duties as *maître des requêtes* (master of requests of the royal household, a position he held for life, requiring considerable travel with the royal court), a term as *prévot des marchands* (provost of Paris merchants, the most important royal officer in the city government), and *maître de la librairie du roi* (master of the king's library, another lifetime post). The humanist was considered an asset to the monarchy, and Budé welcomed such honors and duties as an opportunity for promoting the cause of letters and the foundation of a college of royal readers (later the Collège de France). However, he often complained that public responsibilities, personal affairs, and chronic poor health interfered with his study and writing.

His first major work was a historical study of excerpts from earlier jurists contained in Justinian's

Guillaume Budé. Portrait by Jean Clouet, c. 1535. ©RÉUNION DES MUSÉES NATIONAUX/ART RESOURCE, N.Y.

Corpus iuris civilis. The *Annotationes in Pandectas* (Annotations on the Pandects, 1508) included a scathing attack on traditional "Italian-style" legal scholarship; Budé was the main founder of the *mos gallicus* (French) school of legal humanism. This work is an early example of Budé's philological practice, reading ancient texts mindful of their historical context. He expanded upon this method in later *Annotationes* (1526). The *De philologia* (On philology) and *De studio litterarum recte et commode instituendo* (On the proper institution of the study of letters) of 1532 extended his cultural and educational projects to include more spiritual pursuits.

Budé's *De asse et partibus ejus* (On the pound and its parts), a vast inventory and study of ancient coinage and units of measure, appeared in 1515. Despite its prolix Latin style and rather polemical digressions on political economy and attacks on social and clerical abuses and the vanities of wealth, it was reedited five times during Budé's life and was long the standard work on the subject.

Budé's next works are associated with his career as an official and advisor of Francis I, who did not read Latin. One was a manuscript compendium of translations from ancient sources with advice to the ruler (the *Institution du Prince,* presented to the king in 1519 but published only in 1547), another a French summary of *De asse* prepared for the king in 1522.

His *Comentarii linguae graecae* (Commentaries on the Greek language) of 1529, based on years of research, had a lasting influence on Greek language studies in the West; editions of this lexicographical work appeared the following year in Basel, Cologne, and Venice as well as after Budé's death.

Budé's role in Reformation controversies remains a subject of discussion by scholars. Although he was in a position to influence the king and to disarm hostility to the "good letters" that were increasingly linked to Reformation ideas, there is no evidence that he opposed the persecutions of reform-minded humanists. His final major work, *De Transitu Hellenismi ad Christianismum* (On the transition from Hellenism to Christianity) of 1535 reflects ambivalence and concern over the relationship of humanism to Reformation controversies. It calls for a moral regeneration through the pursuit of higher, Christian wisdom and has been viewed as a serious attempt to transcend the apparent conflict between sacred and profane knowledge. Writing in an atmosphere of hysteria over Protestant subversion, Budé condemned new religious doctrines in *De Transitu.*

Some have wondered about Budé's true religious feelings, for he was buried unceremoniously at night, and his family moved to Protestant Geneva soon after his death. Surely his great love for classical philology was eclipsed by the Reformation crisis, and at the end of his life his enthusiasm for pagan learning waned in favor of more spiritual pursuits. His letters, philosophical works, and political ideas continue to interest students of the period, and his legendary reputation for encyclopedic erudition and philological expertise remains intact.

See also **Erasmus, Desiderius; Francis I (France); Humanists and Humanism; Libraries.**

BIBLIOGRAPHY

Primary Source

Budé, Guillaume. *Opera omnia*. Basel, 1557. Reprinted Farnborough, U.K., 1967.

Secondary Sources

Gadoffre, Gilbert. *La révolution culturelle dans la France des humanistes: Guillaume Budé et François Ier*. Geneva, 1997. Study of cultural politics of sixteenth-century France.

La Garanderie, Marie-Madeleine de. *Christianisme & lettres profanes: Essai sur l'humanisme français (1515–1535) et sur la pensée de Guillaume Budé*. 2nd ed. Paris, 1995. Emphasizes philosophical and spiritual aspects of Budé's thought.

McNeil, David O. *Guillaume Budé and Humanism in the Reign of Francis I*. Geneva, 1975. General treatment of Budé's life and works.

DAVID O. MCNEIL

BUENOS AIRES. The southernmost city in the Spanish colonial empire, Buenos Aires was first founded in 1536 and refounded in 1580. It was located on the edge of a large alluvial plain, the Pampas, where a wide estuary, the Río de la Plata, flows to the South Atlantic. Lacking a sedentary indigenous population or a climate suited for tropical export crops, the city languished on the fringes of empire. Although of moderate strategic importance because of its proximity to Portuguese Brazil, Buenos Aires was forbidden from participating in the official trade linking Spain and America. Consequently, the city survived as a contraband center, supplying slaves to the interior in exchange for silver smuggled from the mines of Alto Peru (now Bolivia).

In 1776 Spain carved the viceroyalty of Río de la Plata out of the viceroyalty of Peru; Buenos Aires became the viceregal capital. Included in its jurisdiction were present-day Bolivia, Paraguay, Uruguay, and Chile. Two years later, the city was allowed to participate in the new "free trade" network created by Spain. These dramatic changes produced rapid growth in the city's administrative and commercial sectors as well as an increase in the city's population.

Late-eighteenth-century warfare on the European continent greatly affected the city's legal trade. Because of Spain's involvement in those wars, the crown was periodically forced to permit trade with neutrals, thus throwing the port of Buenos Aires open to non-Spanish trading partners. The English invaded the city twice (1806 and 1807) during the Napoleonic wars but were defeated by militia units composed of local residents. The new political climate born of the heady victories over the world's most powerful nation raised the city's political consciousness. In May 1810, in a town council meeting called to discuss the region's future, participants voted to depose the viceroy and create a ruling junta. Thus Buenos Aires became the first region successfully to declare itself free from Spanish rule, foreshadowing the revolutionary period that followed.

See also **Colonialism; Spanish Colonies: Peru.**

BIBLIOGRAPHY

Gallo, Klaus. *Great Britain and Argentina: From Invasion to Recognition, 1806–26*. New York, 2001.

Socolow, Susan M. "Buenos Aires at the Time of Independence." In *Buenos Aires: 400 Years,* edited by Stanley R. Ross and Thomas F. McGann, pp. 18–39. Austin, Tex., 1982.

———. "Buenos Aires: Atlantic Port and Hinterland in the Eighteenth Century." In *The American Atlantic World*, edited by Franklin W. Knight and Peggy K. Liss, pp. 240–261. Knoxville, Tenn., 1991.

SUSAN M. SOCOLOW

BUFFON, GEORGES LOUIS LECLERC (1707–1788), natural historian. Born to an aristocratic family in Montbard (Burgundy), where he also received his early education, Buffon was originally directed toward a bureaucratic career common for his class. A chance meeting with a young English nobleman in 1738 led to a continental tour through France, Italy, and England. During this year-long sojourn, Buffon studied natural history and the new philosophical positions of Isaac Newton (1642–1727), the influential English natural philosopher and was exposed to the work of John Ray (1627–1705), England's most important naturalist. When he returned to France, Buffon published translations of one of Newton's works along with a work on botany by Stephen Hales (1677–1761), and his new interest in the sciences was clear.

Georges Buffon. ©LEONARD DE SELVA/CORBIS

Privileged economically by birth, Buffon then turned his attention exclusively to natural philosophy. By 1739 he was made a member of the French Academy of Sciences and then appointed to direct the Jardin du Roi (now Jardin des Plantes) in Paris. As director, Buffon established himself as one of the most influential natural historians of the eighteenth century, one of the most important figures of the French Enlightenment, and one of the most politically and administratively powerful individuals in the French bureaucracy prior to the Revolution.

Buffon's first task at the Jardin was to build its collections and expand its physical size. Once these tasks were well underway, he dedicated himself to a large writing project, his multivolume work *Histoire naturelle, générale, et particulière* (1749–1788, 1789), along with a shorter introductory work describing the natural development of the Earth, *Les époques de la nature* (1778). Buffon's written work established him as the leading contributor to a thoroughly naturalistic interpretation of the formation of the Earth and all its botanical and zoological residents. His literary productions, lavishly illustrated and featuring the engaging and humanistic style common among the philosophes of the Enlightenment, led to the spread of his fame throughout Europe, England, and the United States. By the end of his life, he had been elected as a member to most learned societies throughout the western world.

It is difficult to provide a simple description of Buffon's ideas about the natural world, since they developed over the course of his career. But essentially, Buffon attempted to adopt a Newtonian approach to natural history. That is, he aspired to describe the workings of nature as being under the control of natural forces. Although the exact nature of the forces was unknown, naturalists could observe their action through the effects they produced; that is, through the formation of the multitude of geological forms, botanical specimens, and zoological beings. With these force concepts, Buffon was completely freed from reliance on catastrophic events occurring over a short period of time, or miraculous events within the natural world, or to teleological explanations especially steeped in religious doctrine or divine intervention. His system was completely and unabashedly naturalistic and dynamic.

Central to Buffon's system for plants and animals was the notion of the *moule intérieur*, loosely defined as internal mold or pattern. This was a force concept he borrowed self-consciously from Newton. As such, it controlled the organization and operation of each specific organism. Thus, a horse took on the form and behavior of horses because it was endowed with "horse" *moule intérieur*. Just as gravity always produced the same result when it operated upon the same material, so Buffon's notion created order and regulation for nature's organic production. In practice, however, Buffon's ideas proved to be more problematic. Completely opposed to the fixed system of nature proposed by his Swedish contemporary, Carl Linnaeus (1707–1778), he ultimately was unable to describe systematically how the *moule intérieur* operated. Was this on the level of the individual species or was it on a higher level of organization? In other words, were all horses the same species or did a specific *moule* explain the great variation between the Shetland pony and the Arabian horse?

Georges Buffon. An undated engraving depicts Buffon's reflecting mirror. ©BETTMANN/CORBIS

Despite problems in applying his philosophical system to the collections at the Jardin, Buffon exerted a tremendous influence over natural history in the eighteenth century, an influence that lasted well into the nineteenth century with the work of Charles Darwin (1809–1882). After Buffon, it became impossible for naturalists to refer uncritically to nonnatural explanations for natural phenomena. Basing his philosophical position on the epochal work of Newton, Buffon demonstrated successfully that the natural world was a world controlled by natural forces, from the workings of the tides to the production of species. His arguments, presented in an elegant writing style, elevated Buffon to one of the most prominent positions in eighteenth-century science.

See also **Bacon, Francis; Biology; Botany; Linnaeus, Carl; Natural History; Newton, Isaac; Ray, John; Zoology.**

BIBLIOGRAPHY

Mayr, Ernst. *The Growth of Biological Thought: Diversity, Evolution, and Inheritance.* Cambridge, Mass., 1982.

Roger, Jacques. *Buffon: A Life in Natural History.* Translated by Sarah Lucille Bonnefoi and edited by L. Pearce Williams. Ithaca, N.Y., 1997.

KEITH R. BENSON

BULLINGER, HEINRICH (1504–1575),

Swiss reformer, theologian, and church leader. Born in Bremgarten, the son of a priest, Bullinger was educated at Emmerich, where he came under the lasting influence of the Brethren of the Common Life. His move, at age fifteen, to the university at Cologne exposed him more fully to humanism and the study of the church fathers. He returned to his native land in 1523 to become a teacher at the Cistercian monastery at Kappel, southwest of Zurich. Education and its provision were to be lifelong concerns for Bullinger, and in the 1520s he sought to reform the monastery along humanist lines. During this period he became acquainted with the Swiss theologian and reformer Huldrych Zwingli. From 1529 to 1531, during the height of Zwingli's influence in Zurich, Bullinger was the preacher in his native Bremgarten. A military force from Zurich, accompanied by Zwingli as chaplain, was surprised and defeated at Kappel by an army from the central cantons of the Swiss Confederation, also known as the Five Forest Cantons. Zwingli was killed in the battle (11 October 1531). Following the defeat at Kappel and Zwingli's death, Catholic forces expelled the evangelicals from Bremgarten, and Bullinger arrived in Zurich as a refugee. His teaching, writing, and preaching had already earned him a formidable reputation, and in 1531 he received separate calls to head the churches of Berne, Basle, and Zurich. Out of loyalty to Zurich, he accepted a call from the Council was elected head of the church on 13 December 1531.

After Zwingli's death Bullinger had to reconstruct the institutional basis of the Zurich church. This required him to balance conflicting principles. First, the Zurich magistrates and population were no longer prepared to tolerate an independent clergy who used *sola scriptura* ('Scripture alone', that is, the authority of the Bible as superior to all other authorities), to force political agendas contrary to will of the people—such as Zwingli's war against the Catholics in 1531. Yet Bullinger was not prepared to lead a church in which the clergy were not free to preach God's Word. The compromise, which shaped Bullinger's tenure as leader of the Zurich church, was built around an agreement that the council would give Bullinger a relatively free hand in running the church as long as he controlled the clergy and prevented them from either preaching on political matters or causing scandal through their sermons or in their personal lives. The agreement worked because Bullinger was trusted by the political leaders, with whom he had strong personal contacts, and, with few exceptions, contentious issues were hammered out behind closed doors.

Bullinger was a prodigious theologian, preacher, and historian. He regularly preached two or three times a week, and many of his sermons were printed. As a theologian, his central concern was to demonstrate that the Reformed Church stood in line with the teachings of the early church. In the Zurich tradition, his theology was directed toward pastoral application, emphasized the clarity of Scripture and the role of the Spirit, and drew heavily from the Old Testament. He stressed the practical nature of Christianity and the doing of good works, although he did not accord them a salvific role. Bullinger saw himself primarily as an expositor of Scripture, and most of his major works took the form of sermons or biblical commentaries *(The Decades, Sermons on Revelation)*. On the matter of the Eucharist he remained close to Zwingli, but the influence of Johannes Oecolampadius (1482–1531) and Philipp Melanchthon (1497–1560) is now recognized in his writings. He worked closely with John Calvin (1509–1564) and played a crucial role in the latter's return to Geneva. Their relationship was not especially warm, but they understood the necessity of cooperation, as evidenced by their statement on the Lord's Supper of 1549 *(Consensus Tigurinus)*.

Bullinger was committed to building the wider European community of the Reformed churches. The word "Reformed" was crucial as he had little faith that there would be reconciliation with Luther or Lutheran theology. The seismic split between Luther and Zwingli dominated Bullinger's life as head of the Zurich church. There were sporadic attempts at reconciliation, and Bullinger did have good relations with men such as Melanchthon, but he felt honor bound to defend his predecessor. In contrast, he was an enthusiastic supporter of Reform movements in Eastern Europe, France, Italy, and, most famously, England. His surviving correspondence of around twelve thousand letters bears witness to his work on behalf of the international Reformation—all the more remarkable for a man who almost never ventured outside the walls of Zurich.

As leader of the Zurich church, Bullinger gathered in the city a group of humanists (Konrad Pellikan, Theodor Bibliander, Conrad Gessner) whose work on Scripture, history, education, and natural science made Zurich an intellectual center for Reformed Protestantism. Bullinger's own contribution, not sufficiently recognized, was as a historian. In addition, Bullinger's Zurich was also a center for religious refugees from Italy, France, Netherlands, and England. Bullinger stood at the center of this international communication system and was in his day a leading figure of the European Reformation.

See also **Calvin, John; Luther, Martin; Melanchthon, Philipp; Reformation, Protestant; Zurich; Zwingli, Huldrych.**

BIBLIOGRAPHY

Bächtold, Hans Ulrich. *Heinrich Bullinger vor dem Rat: Zur Gestaltung und Vewaltung des Zürcher Staatswesens in den Jahren 1531 bis 1575.* Berne, 1982.

Baker, Wayne J. *Heinrich Bullinger and the Covenant; The Other Reformed Tradition.* Athens, Ohio, 1980.

Biel, Pamela. *Doorkeepers at the House of Righteousness: Heinrich Bullinger and the Zurich Clergy, 1535–1575.* Berne, 1991.

Gordon, Bruce. "Heinrich Bullinger." In *The Reformation Theologians,* edited by Carter Lindberg, pp. 170–183. Oxford, 2002.

Gordon, Bruce, and Emidio Campi, eds. *Heinrich Bullinger (1504–1575) and the Formation of the Reformed Tradition.* Grand Rapids, Mich., 2004.

BRUCE GORDON

BUNYAN, JOHN

BUNYAN, JOHN (1628–1688), English Nonconformist author. John Bunyan was born in Elstow, Bedfordshire, England, where his father, Thomas Bunyan, was a brazier. Educated at a petty school and perhaps briefly at a grammar school, John Bunyan served during the civil war in the parliamentary garrison at Newport Pagnell, Buckinghamshire, from November 1644 until about September 1646 and reenlisted briefly in 1647. By 1649 he had married, and his wife's dowry consisted of two books by Lewis Bayly and Arthur Dent that influenced Bunyan's religious development.

Following his spiritual awakening in 1650, Bunyan experienced recurring bouts of depression and spiritual doubt that lasted until late 1657 or early 1658, recounted in his spiritual autobiography, *Grace Abounding to the Chief of Sinners* (1666). During this period of crisis he joined the open-membership congregation at Bedford in 1655 and under its auspices began to preach. Among his earliest religious foes were "Ranters," by whom he meant antinomians and deniers of a physical Resur-

rection and external worship. He also challenged the Quakers, engaging in a literary dispute with Edward Burrough in 1656–1657, and he wrote a tract, now lost, against witchcraft. In the late 1650s he was influenced by the millenarian tenets of the Fifth Monarchists.

Refusing to cease preaching at the Restoration, Bunyan was arrested in November 1660. Although he would have been released had he promised to relinquish his preaching, he refused and was incarcerated in the Bedford county jail until the spring of 1672. Some of his time was spent making shoelaces to support his family, including his second wife, Elizabeth, whom he had married in 1659 following the death of his first wife the preceding year. In prison he continued to write, manifesting a discipline that enabled him to produce some sixty books during his career. His most important theological work, *The Doctrine of the Law and Grace Unfolded,* an exposition of covenant thought, had appeared in 1659, and his early prison writings included poetry, an attack on the Book of Common Prayer (*I Will Pray with the Spirit* [1662]), and a millenarian tract, *The Holy City* (1665). Following the completion of *Grace Abounding,* he turned in 1667 to a sermon about the Christian life, *The Heavenly Foot-Man* (1698).

While working on this sermon, Bunyan was inspired to write his famous allegory *The Pilgrim's Progress,* begun about March 1668 and completed three years later, though not published until 1678, partly because some colleagues deemed it insufficiently serious. The allegory was both a guide to the Christian life and a contribution to the debate over liberty of conscience that raged in the late 1660s and the 1670s. Drawing extensively on the Bible, Bunyan was also influenced by the pilgrimage theme in the Christian tradition and his own experience. The allegory denounced persecution and provided a critique of the Church of England, the restored monarchy, and society.

While still in prison, Bunyan entered the debate over church membership and baptism in *A Confession of My Faith* (1672), which sparked attacks from the Baptists Thomas Paul and John Denne. Bunyan defended himself in *Differences in Judgment about Water Baptism* (1673) and *Peaceable Principles* (1674); his position was that of an open-membership Baptist. In the meantime he engaged the debate over justification by attacking Edward Fowler's *The Design of Christianity* (1671) in *A Defence of the Doctrine of Justification, by Faith* (1672), his last imprisonment work. Shortly before Bunyan's release, the Bedford church appointed him a pastor on 21 December 1671. When on 4 March 1675 a new warrant for his arrest was issued, accusing him of teaching at conventicles, he went into hiding. He was apprehended in December 1676 and was confined until June 1677.

As the nation divided over alleged Catholic conspiracy, the anticipated succession of James, duke of York (James II; ruled 1685–1688), allegations of arbitrary rule, and the treatment of dissenters, Bunyan wrote some of his best work. Those contributions include *The Life and Death of Mr. Badman* (1680), a searing critique of Restoration society; *The Holy War* (1682), a complex allegory about soteriology as well as an attack on Charles II (ruled 1660–1685) and the Tory-Anglicans; *Of Antichrist* (1692), a treatise criticizing the Stuarts, Catholicism, and the Church of England; and the second part of *The Pilgrim's Progress* (1684), which focuses on the dissenting pastor Great-heart and Christian's wife Christiana.

After James II introduced his policy of toleration, Bunyan was cautiously cooperative. Seven members of his church were named to the Bedford Corporation, and another was considered for appointment as a justice of the peace. On 31 August 1688 Bunyan died in London, and he was buried several days later in Bunhill Fields. He was survived by his wife, three sons, and two daughters; his blind daughter, Mary, had predeceased him. Transcending its polemical context, *The Pilgrim's Progress* became one of the most widely published works in history, reaching more than 1,300 editions by 1938.

See also **Dissenters, English; England; English Civil War and Interregnum.**

BIBLIOGRAPHY

Primary Sources

Bunyan, John. *The Miscellaneous Works of John Bunyan.* Edited by Roger Sharrock. 13 vols. Oxford, 1976–1994.

———. *The Pilgrim's Progress from This World to That Which Is to Come.* Edited by James Blanton Wharey. 2nd ed. Revised by Roger Sharrock. Oxford, 1960.

Secondary Source

Greaves, Richard L. *Glimpses of Glory: John Bunyan and English Dissent.* Stanford, 2002.

RICHARD L. GREAVES

BURGUNDY. The early modern state of Burgundy was the product of a historical accident. When Charles the Bold (1433–1477), the last Valois duke of Burgundy (1467–1477), was murdered in 1477, his various and sundry lands and estates were divided up between the king of France and the Holy Roman emperor. While the large duchy of Burgundy was soon incorporated into the kingdom of France, the free county of Burgundy just across the Saône River (Franche-Comté) was quickly absorbed into the empire. Moreover, all the territories that made up the Burgundian Netherlands—the counties of Flanders, Holland, Zeeland, Hainaut, and Namur as well as the duchies of Brabant, Limburg, and Luxembourg—also swore allegiance to the emperor. Thus what had once been a politically powerful buffer state that separated France and the empire and stretched from the North Sea to the Franco-Swiss border was now divided between these two European powers. With its twin courts at Brussels and Dijon permanently separated, Burgundy's political influence was no longer as significant as it had once been, when it held the balance of power between England and France in the Hundred Years' War (1337–1453).

These Franco-Habsburg tensions intensified less than two decades after Charles the Bold's death, when the French king Charles VIII (ruled 1483–1498) invaded Italy in a dispute over the emperor's claim to the vacant duchy of Milan, starting the Habsburg-Valois Wars (1494–1559). Charles V (1519–1556), the grandson and heir of Maximilian I (ruled 1493–1519), later tried to reunite the duchy to the rest of the Burgundian state under Habsburg control. Having captured King Francis I of France (1515–1547) on the battlefield at Pavia in Italy in 1525, Charles succeeded in getting him to renounce the duchy of Burgundy as part of the deal to release him. Francis reneged on his promise once he acquired his freedom, however, and the duchy remained in French hands. Moreover the Burgundian political elites of the duchy made it known to all that they were loyal Frenchmen and had no desire to be transferred to the sovereignty of the emperor to reunite with the other former Burgundian territories in the empire. Although neither Francis I nor Charles V managed to gain any permanent territorial advantage in Italy from the Habsburg-Valois Wars, this conflict served as a backdrop to the foreign policies of both states for the rest of the early modern period. Indeed even after the Peace of Cateau-Cambrésis formally ended the wars in 1559, Habsburg-Valois tensions continued to ferment, a situation not helped by the advent of Protestantism in both states.

With the coming of the Reformation in France, the duchy of Burgundy became a bastion for the traditional religion and a bulwark against the new Calvinist faith, which most Burgundians, like most French Catholics, tended to see as heresy. The royal governor of Burgundy from the 1530s to the 1590s was a member of the militantly Catholic Guise family, so the many patronage networks of the Guises worked long and hard in the province to prevent the spread of heresy. Calvinism nevertheless managed to gain a foothold in some of the principal Burgundian towns by 1560, and tensions between the two faiths broke out in violence, as it did in many towns throughout the kingdom in the early 1560s. Most Burgundians had supported the attempts of Kings Henry II (ruled 1547–1559) and Francis II (ruled 1559–1560) to suppress Protestantism, by force if necessary. But they were explicitly hostile to the edict of January 1562, since it gave legal recognition to the French Protestants for the first time. When the French Wars of Religion officially broke out in 1562, Burgundy fought against both the Protestants and the crown's continuous attempts to make peace with them over the next four decades. Burgundy remained a bastion of Catholicism and became a stronghold of the Catholic League after the death of the last Valois heir in 1584 made Henry of Navarre (Henry IV; ruled 1589–1610), the leader of the French Protestants, presumptive heir to the throne.

The battles with the crown over religion in the sixteenth century turned to politics in the seventeenth century. First Henry IV began to intervene in local elections for mayor in several Burgundian towns in 1609, altering a process of independence that had originated under the Valois dukes. Then in the 1630s his son and successor, Louis XIII (ruled 1610–1643), attempted to take away the province's traditional right to assess and collect its own taxes through its provincial Estates. When Louis tried to suppress the Estates and replace them with royal tax officials, many in the province fought back. A band of citizens in Dijon—mainly winegrowers and artisans—actually burned down the houses of several members of Dijon's parlement (sovereign court) who spoke out in favor of the king's plan. Louis went in person to Dijon to punish the culprits as well as to chide the elites for not fully supporting his venture. By the time of the Fronde in 1648, Burgundy's elites had been won over to the crown's wishes on virtually all political matters, as the king continued to reward them handsomely for their cooperation. As a result there was no opposition to the crown in Burgundy when parlements in other regions revolted in 1648. And for the most part Burgundy's elites continued to support French kings right up to the Revolution of 1789.

Louis XIV (ruled 1643–1715) managed to reunite the free county of Burgundy with the duchy in 1674, when his troops occupied Franche-Comté and brought the county under French control. Thus the two Burgundies, as contemporaries were still referring to the duchy and the county, were both under the authority of one prince for the first time since 1477. Like their fellow subjects in the duchy, the elites of Franche-Comté tended for the most part to be willing, loyal subjects of the king of France in return for largesse, rewards, and perquisites. From one-time enemies of France during the Hundred Years' War, Burgundians by the late seventeenth century had become some of the most ardent defenders of the Catholic Church and the French crown.

See also **Charles the Bold (Burgundy); Habsburg-Valois Wars; Holy Roman Empire; Valois Dynasty (France).**

BIBLIOGRAPHY

Drouot, Henri. *Mayenne et la Bourgogne: Étude sur la Ligue, 1587–1596.* 2 vols. Dijon and Paris, 1937.

Farr, James R. *Hands of Honor: Artisans and Their World in Dijon, 1550–1650.* Ithaca, N.Y., 1988.

Holt, Mack P. "Wine, Community and Reformation in Six-teenth-Century Burgundy," *Past and Present* 138 (February 1993): 58–93.

Vaughan, Richard. *Valois Burgundy.* London, 1975.

MACK P. HOLT

BURKE, EDMUND (1729–1797), British statesman and orator. Born in Arran Quay, Dublin, Edmund Burke was educated at Trinity College, Dublin, and studied law briefly at the Inns of Court in London. He published two early books, *A Vindication of Natural Society* (1756) and *A Philosophical Enquiry into the Origin of Our Ideas of the Sublime and Beautiful* (1757; expanded 1759), which caught the eye of David Hume, Samuel Johnson, and other illustrious contemporaries and established him as an author. Burke had shown from the first a strong interest in politics, informed by copious knowledge, and this led to his appointment in 1759 as private secretary to a member of Parliament, William Gerard Hamilton. He found a new position in 1765 as secretary to the marquess of Rockingham, the leader of a group of Whigs then pressing the House of Commons to assert its independence from the king. Given a seat in Parliament as the representative from Wendover, Burke distinguished himself as a strategist for the Rockingham administration of 1765–1766 and substantially assisted in its major achievement, the repeal of the stamp tax on the American colonies.

In the late 1760s an attempt by the king's ministers to prevent John Wilkes from taking his seat in Parliament led Burke and his party to concert a policy against the aggrandizement of the crown. Burke's reading of the constitution at this crisis emerged in his first major political work, *Thoughts on the Cause of the Present Discontents* (1770), a full-scale defense of the idea of a political party. An organized opposition, says Burke, is an indispensable bulwark of liberty, and the reasons for forming such a party are plain: "When bad men combine, the good must associate; else they will fall, one by one, an unpitied sacrifice in a contemptible struggle."

Whatever might change in his stance, Burke would continue to speak for political association against the privilege of court favorites or the unchecked power of the people. He once said that he believed the principles of politics were only the principles of morality enlarged. Accordingly, Burke was skeptical of theories of the social contract that codified the rights of citizens. In the 1770s and 1780s, most of his energy was given to enlarging the liberty of the people by increasing the protections against monarchical abuse of power, and yet he was never a believer in popular government: statesmanship always carried for him a sense of the dignity and ceremony that should accompany great enterprises. Elected in 1774 as a member of Parliament from Bristol, Burke soon pleaded for a sympathetic reception of the American protests against taxation. His speech on conciliation with the American colonies (1775) urged a policy of concession to the point of disclaiming any further intention to tax the colonists. The three-hour speech has been considered from that day to this one of the greatest orations in the language. "An Englishman," Burke told his listeners, "is the unfittest person on earth to argue another Englishman into slavery." The right use of the American colonists, he asserted, was to cherish them as equal partners in trade and as allies in time of war. "Magnanimity in politics is not seldom the truest wisdom; and a great empire and little minds go ill together." He concluded that anything the colonists gave beyond their friendship should be freely given.

During his Bristol years, from 1774 to 1780, Burke stood out as a defender of free trade with Ireland, liberalization of the laws controlling imprisonment for debt, and the repeal of Catholic disabilities—all unpopular positions in a Protestant and mercantile city. When threatened with loss of his constituency in 1780, he gave an unswerving defense of his actions in his speech at Bristol guildhall: "I did not obey your instructions. No. I conformed to the instructions of truth and Nature, and maintained your interest, against your opinions, with a constancy that became me." Before reentering the House of Commons as the representative from Malton, he found the cause that would occupy the rest of his career: exposure of the injustices of the East India Company ("a government in the disguise of a merchant") and impeachment of the governor-general of Bengal, Warren Hastings.

Burke's own practical proposal, ventured in his speech on Fox's East India Bill (1783), was to reorganize the company and place its officers under the direct control of Parliament. Rejection of this plan by the House of Commons precipitated the fall of the Fox-North coalition, with whose prospects Burke's own political fortunes were bound up. Nevertheless, he chose to pursue Hastings as a manager of his impeachment by the House of Commons in proceedings that lasted from 1788 to 1795. The process ended in acquittal. Yet Burke looked on his efforts to reform British India as his major accomplishment, "my monument."

A securer fame in his lifetime would come from his criticism of the French Revolution in a series of pamphlets of the 1790s, above all *Reflections on the Revolution in France* (1790). Burke warned against a great change in the spirit of society, from aristocratic to democratic manners and from the authority of an ancient landed nobility to that of a mobile commercial class. He speaks as a believer in precedent and prescription and a defender of natural feelings such as reverence for an established church and a hereditary nobility. Against the promise of a society based on contract, he offers his vision of a society based on trust—"a partnership not only between those who are living, but between those who are living, those who are dead, and those who are to be born." The onset of democracy, Burke supposed, would destroy that partnership. A democracy would be unable to correct the errors that a crowd in power would commit on a new and terrifying scale.

In 1794 Burke was awarded a pension by William Pitt and George III and retired to his estate in Beaconsfield. His final writings, the *Letters on a Regicide Peace* (1796–1797), were a sustained attempt to persuade England to fight a counterrevolutionary war against France. He died in 1797, ending as he began, in isolation. Burke's greatest political legacy may be the example of a statesman who uses his freedom of conscience to extend the public debate of public matters. In literature his influence has been deeper, though harder to trace. He was a historian and a prophet of the powers of sympathy and imagination by which people can be awakened to generous action.

See also **British Colonies: India; British Colonies: North America; Constitutionalism; Hastings, Warren; Monarchy; Parliament; Political Parties in England; Political Philosophy; Rhetoric; Sublime, Idea of the; Taxation.**

BIBLIOGRAPHY

Primary Sources

Burke, Edmund. *The Works of Edmund Burke.* 9 vols. Boston, 1839.

———. *The Writings and Speeches of Edmund Burke.* 9 vols. Oxford and New York, 1981.

Secondary Sources

Blakemore, Steven. *Burke and the Fall of Language.* Hanover, N.H., 1988.

Cobban, Alfred. *Edmund Burke and the Revolt against the Eighteenth Century: A Study of the Political and Social Thinking of Burke, Wordsworth, Coleridge, and Southey.* London, 1929.

Cone, Carl B. *Burke and the Nature of Politics.* 2 vols. Lexington, Ky., 1957–1964.

Lock, F. P. *Edmund Burke.* Oxford and New York, 1998.

O'Brien, Conor Cruise. *The Great Melody: A Thematic Biography and Commented Anthology of Edmund Burke.* Chicago, 1992.

Parkin, Charles W. *The Moral Basis of Burke's Political Thought, an Essay.* Cambridge, U.K., 1956.

DAVID BROMWICH

BURNEY, FRANCES (Mme. d'Arblay; 1752–1840), celebrated English novelist, diarist, playwright. The daughter of music historian Charles Burney, Frances was born in King's Lynn in Norfolk, but grew up in London, where her father associated with many famous literary figures including Samuel Johnson and his "Club" and members of the Blue Stocking Circle, an informal group of learned women who, during the 1750s, held receptions for important literary figures and met to discuss art and literature.

Burney started writing in 1768 when she began keeping a journal (addressed "to nobody") that she continued to keep for the rest of her life. In 1778, she published her first novel, *Evelina, or a Young Lady's Entrance into the World,* having written it in secret and arranged for it to be published anonymously. The story of a naïve and innocent young woman introduced into fashionable, and often eccentric, aristocratic London society, *Evelina* was an instant success. When the *London Review* reported that "there is much more merit, as well respecting stile, character & Incident, than is usually to be met with in modern Novels," Burney felt confident to confess to her father that she was its author, and she was subsequently introduced into London literary society, with the help of Samuel Johnson's friend Hester Thrale, as an accomplished novelist.

Encouraged by her celebrated arrival on the literary scene, Burney's writing career took off. In 1782 she published her second novel, *Cecilia, or Memoirs of an Heiress.* The story of a young woman with a large fortune in search of a suitable husband, *Cecilia* was immensely successful, being an accurate reflection of the eighteenth-century marriage market. Having begun, and then abandoned, her first play, *The Witlings,* in 1778, Burney was exhausted by the writing of *Cecilia* and did not complete any further novels or plays for six years.

In 1786, following a number of unsuccessful courtships, Burney was offered, and accepted, a position as second keeper of the robes to Queen Charlotte, moving into the queen's lodge in Windsor in June that year. Upholding this position until poor health forced her to retire in 1791, Burney dutifully recorded her years as a member of the royal household in her *Court Journals.* During this time she also wrote more plays, including the tragedy *Edwy and Elgiva,* which was staged at the Theatre Royal, Drury Lane in 1795, though it survived only one performance. Other plays quickly followed: *Hubert de Vere* and *The Siege of Pevensey* in 1790, and the incomplete *Elberta* in 1791.

Having left the royal household, Burney began a secret courtship with a French Catholic General, Alexander d'Arblay, who was living in exile in England. They married in 1793, and continued to live in England, during which time Burney completed and published (1796) her third novel, *Camilla, or a Picture of Youth,* which, like her two earlier novels, told the story of the entrance into society of a beautiful, intelligent, but inexperienced young woman. Two years later she wrote another play, this time a comedy, *Love and Fashion,* which was accepted for Covent Garden Theatre but never performed. In 1800 she wrote two more comic plays, *A Busy Day* and *The Woman-Hater,* neither of which were performed in her lifetime.

In 1802, when General d'Arblay felt it was safe to return home and recover his family estates, he and Burney moved to France, where they lived in Paris for ten years. During this time, Burney's health deteriorated and she realized she was suffering from breast cancer. In 1811 she underwent a mastectomy without anesthetic, and, remarkably, lived to enjoy relative good health and record the details of her operation in a frank and extraordinary letter to her sister.

In 1812 Burney and her husband returned to England. Two years later she published her fourth and final novel, *The Wanderer, or Female Difficulties,* which did not enjoy anything like the success of her earlier works. The remainder of her life was spent in London and Bath; in 1832 she published the *Memoirs of Doctor Burney,* as well as her father's papers, and edited her own journals and letters in preparation for their likely publication after her death. She died in London in 1840, outliving most of her family and, to an extent, her literary reputation. *The Diaries and Letters of Madame D'Arblay* (1778–1840), edited by her niece Charlotte Barrett, was published in seven volumes in London, 1842–1846, confirming her reputation as one of the eighteenth century's most important novelists, and her importance as an inspiration for later woman writers like Jane Austen, who greatly admired her works.

See also **Defoe, Daniel; Diaries; Drama: English; English Literature and Language; Johnson, Samuel; Richardson, Samuel; Smollett, Tobias; Sterne, Laurence.**

BIBLIOGRAPHY

Primary Sources

Burney, Fanny. *Camilla, or A Picture of Youth.* Edited by Edward A. Bloom and Lillian D. Bloom. Oxford and New York, 1983.

———. *Cecilia, or Memoirs of an Heiress.* Edited by Peter Sabor and Margaret Anne Doody. Oxford, 1988.

———. *The Complete Plays of Frances Burney.* Edited by Peter Sabor and Stewart J. Cooke. 2 vols. London, 1995.

———. *The Early Journals and Letters of Fanny Burney.* Edited by Lars E. Troide. Oxford and New York, 1988–.

———. *Evelina, or The History of a Young Lady's Entrance into the World.* Edited by Edward A. Bloom and Lillian D. Bloom. Oxford and New York, 1982.

———. *The Journals and Letters of Fanny Burney (Madame d'Arblay).* Edited by Joyce Hemlow. 12 vols. Oxford, 1972–1984.

———. *The Wanderer, or Female Difficulties.* Edited by Margaret Anne Doody, Robert L. Mack, and Peter Sabor. Oxford and New York, 1991.

Secondary Sources

Cutting-Gray, Joanne. *Woman as "Nobody" and the Novels of Fanny Burney.* Gainesville, Fla., 1992.

Doody, Margaret Anne. *Frances Burney: The Life in the Works.* Cambridge, U.K., 1988.

Epstein, Julia L. *The Iron Pen: Frances Burney and the Politics of Women's Writing.* Madison, Wis., 1989.

Grau, Joseph A. *Fanny Burney: An Annotated Bibliography.* New York, 1981.

Harman, Claire. *Fanny Burney: A Biography.* London and New York, 2000.

Straub, Kristina. *Divided Fictions: Fanny Burney and Feminine Strategy.* Lexington, Ky., 1987.

ALISON STENTON

BUXTEHUDE, DIETERICH

BUXTEHUDE, DIETERICH (also spelled "Dietrich"; c. 1637–1707), considered one of the most important seventeenth-century German composers and organists between the time of Heinrich Schütz (1585–1672) and Johann Sebastian Bach (1685–1750). Buxtehude was also the most highly respected church musician of his generation, and he contributed significantly to the development of middle baroque organ music. The exact place of Buxtehude's birth is unknown; he was probably born in Denmark, either in Helsingör (Elsinore) or Helsingborg (now part of Sweden), or else in Oldesloe, Germany.

At Skt. Olai Kirke in Helsingör, where his father worked (c. 1641–1671), Buxtehude studied organ and gained firsthand knowledge of organ building, and he probably also received formal musical training at the Latin school in Helsingör. By the age of twenty-five he was considered an expert in organ design and structure. It is possible that he continued his education in Copenhagen in the late 1650s. In late 1657 or early 1658 he accepted the position of organist at Skt. Maria Kirke in Helsingborg, where his father had previously worked, and remained there until 1660. From 1660 until 1668 he was employed at Sct. Mariae Kirke in Helsingör, after which he was appointed as organist, *Werkmeister* (church secretary and treasurer), and parish administrator at the Marienkirche in Lübeck, the most prestigious church-organ position in northern Germany and a post he held until his death. Shortly after moving to Lübeck, he married Anna Marga-

the Tunder, the youngest daughter of his predecessor, Franz Tunder. They had seven children, four of whom survived until adulthood.

The city of Lübeck was not as adversely affected by the Thirty Years' War as was the rest of central Europe. It did, however, suffer financially, and the city fathers worked to rebuild the local economy. In spite of this hardship, Lübeck maintained an excellent and well-paid band of musicians in its employ. The city also had a reputation as an important center of string playing, especially viola da gamba (bass viol). Buxtehude wrote two sets of sonatas for violin, viola da gamba, and harpsichord continuo (Op. 1, c. 1694, and Op. 2, 1696). These virtuosic and melodic compositions—the only instrumental works published during his lifetime—reflect the high level of instrumental performance in Lübeck.

Apart from his duties of providing music for church services, Buxtehude oversaw an annual concert series, the *Abendmusiken,* which was held on five Sundays in Trinity and Advent. As the director of the series, he raised money, wrote music, hired musicians, and conducted performances. Under Buxtehude, the *Abendmusik* concerts usually featured oratorios (dramatic sacred operas) that he had written based on biblical texts and lyrical poetry and, occasionally, programs of various choral and solo vocal music, as well as instrumental music. The musical forces that performed at *Abendmusik* concerts were substantial. Buxtehude demonstrated his business acumen in his administration of this series: he kept the concerts free to the public by soliciting funds from local businesses. The series continued until 1810 in Lübeck and served as a model that was imitated throughout Europe.

Buxtehude's reputation as an organist and improviser extended outside of Lübeck. George Frideric Handel (1685–1759) visited him in Lübeck in 1703, and in 1705 J. S. Bach walked from Arnstadt to Lübeck, more than 200 miles, to hear him perform. It is also possible that Bach made the trip to inquire about obtaining Buxtehude's position at the Marienkirche, after learning about the organist's impending retirement. But to be awarded the contractual title of Werkmeister, a prospective applicant was required to marry the master's eldest daughter, a tradition that Buxtehude had followed thirty-seven years earlier but that did not appeal to Bach. When Buxtehude died in 1707, he was succeeded by Johann Christian Schieferdecker (1679–1732). Buxtehude was buried at the Marienkirche, next to his father and four daughters who had predeceased him.

Buxtehude's compositions encapsulate the seventeenth-century German baroque aesthetic. His instrumental works—especially the preludes for organ, with their dramatic rhapsodic passages, changing textures, and improvisational-sounding embellishments—make full use of the appropriately named *stylus phantasticus,* a freely improvisatory style favored by north German organists during that period, which Buxtehude often juxtaposed with short, contrasting sections of imitative counterpoint. His other keyboard works include canzonas, chorale settings, suites, and variation sets.

Although Buxtehude's position in Lübeck did not require him to write vocal music, he composed more works for voice than for keyboard or chamber ensemble. The two principal vocal genres he favored were the sacred concerto and the aria, both of which had been developed earlier in Germany by Michael Praetorius (1571–1621), Schütz, and others. Buxtehude's vocal concertos are set primarily to biblical texts in German and Latin, and the majority of the arias within these works have strophic texts. Many concertos begin with an instrumental movement and conclude with a highly structured "Alleluia" or "Amen." His other vocal works include chorale settings and cantatas, most of which are four-voice settings based on a preexisting Lutheran hymn tune.

With the renewed interest in early music in recent decades, as well as the attention given to his compositions by J. S. Bach, Handel, and other composers, Buxtehude has been assured a permanent place in the organ and vocal repertory.

See also **Bach Family; Baroque; Handel, George Frideric; Hymns; Music; Schütz, Heinrich.**

BIBLIOGRAPHY

Snyder, Kerala J. "Buxtehude, Dieterich." In *The New Grove Dictionary of Music and Musicians.* Edited by Stanley Sadie. 2nd ed. London, 2001.

———. *Dieterich Buxtehude: Organist in Lübeck.* New York, 1987.

Webber, Geoffrey. *North German Church Music in the Age of Buxtehude.* Oxford and New York, 1996.

GREGORY MALDONADO

CABALA. The commonly used term for the mystical, magical, and theosophic teachings of Judaism from the twelfth century onward, the cabala (also cabbala, kabbala, or kabbalah) was considered the esoteric and unwritten portion of the revelation granted to Adam and again to Moses, while the Bible represented the exoteric revelation. (Although the term is often spelled with a 'k' when referring to the Jewish tradition and with a 'c' in the Christian version, it is spelled here with a 'c' for simplicity's sake.) The word means "that which is received" or "tradition," implying that the cabala was a body of knowledge that passed orally from generation to generation. A distinction is generally made between theoretical and practical cabala, the first dealing with theosophical issues, and the second with producing specific practical and eschatological effects (healing the sick, hastening the advent of the Messiah, attaining an ecstatic state) through the use of divine names and Hebrew letters.

The cabala proper developed from diverse esoteric and theosophical currents among Jews in Palestine and Egypt during the first Christian centuries. Early strands of Jewish apocalypticism and Merkabah (throne) and Hekhalot (palaces) mysticism were influenced by Hellenistic, Iranian, and gnostic thought, although scholars disagree about the extent and importance of these external influences. Merkabah and Hekhalot mysticism was devoted to descriptions of the dangerous ascent through various worlds and palaces that culminated in the vision of the divine throne described in Ezekiel. The *Sefer Yezirah* (Book of formation), a major source of later cabalistic speculation, belongs to the same period (second to sixth century). It describes the creative power of the twenty-two letters of the Hebrew alphabet and the ten *sefirot* (numbers or manifestations of God) through whom the world came into being.

During the Middle Ages these traditions of early Jewish mysticism were fused with Christian and Islamic (Sufism) mysticism and Islamic and Christian Neoplatonism to produce the German Hasidic movement (Ashkenazi Hasidism), which peaked between the eleventh and the thirteenth centuries. Its leading figures were Judah he-Hasid (d. 1217) and his pupil Eleazar of Worms (d. 1238), who produced popular works combining elements of Merkabah mysticism and theurgy with mystical speculations about letters and numbers.

The cabala originated simultaneously from these same sources in southern France in the twelfth century. Among its most important proponents were Rabbi Abraham ben David and his son Rabbi Isaac the Blind (d. c. 1235). The *Sefer ha-Bahir,* composed in the late twelfth century, circulated among these cabalists. It elaborated on the idea of the ten *sefirot,* describing them as divine powers emanating from the hidden God *(En Soph).* This became a dominant motif in later cabala. Cabalist centers developed in Burgos, Toledo, and Gerona. Azriel of Gerona applied Neoplatonic philosophy to cabalist concepts. For Gerona cabalists the highest human goal was to attain *Devekut* (communion with God) through prayer and meditation on the *sefirot*. Nachmanides (c. 1194–1270) was the most famous member of this group. Many of the ideas of Ashkenazi Hasidism were absorbed by cabalists in Spain and southern France, who established new schools of cabala in Europe, Italy, and the East. Although there were considerable differences between the teachings of the various mystical and cabalistic groups in the medieval period, a common theme was the idea of the Godhead as a unity of dynamic forces.

A school of prophetic Cabala arose in connection with the teachings of Abraham Abulafia (c. 1240–1292), who devised "the science of combination," a mystical technique of meditating on the divine names and the Hebrew letters in order to draw down the divine spirit and attain ecstatic experiences. The main product of Spanish Cabala, however, was the *Sefer ha-Zohar* (The book of splendor), written largely between 1280 and 1286. More of a library than a book, the *Zohar* consists of some twenty independent works. While it was attributed to the second-century Rabbi Simeon ben Yohai, a renowned sage of the school of Rabbi Akiva, the actual author was the contemporary Spanish cabalist Moses de Leon. The whole thrust of the *Zohar*, and the Cabala in general, is to understand the nature of God and man's relation to him, but the picture that emerges is different from that found elsewhere in Judaism. Instead of the lawgiver and ruler of *halakhah* (Jewish law), the merciful father of *aggadah* (allegorical rabbinic literature), the awesome king of Merkabah and Hekhalot mysticism, or the necessary being of the philosophers, the *Zohar* envisions God as ten *sefirot* joined in a dynamic, organic unity. Each represents a distinct attribute of God, such as "wisdom," "understanding," "power," "beauty," "endurance," and "majesty."

Humanity is accorded tremendous power in the *Zohar*. Because people are made in the image of God and originate from the Godhead, they have the power to influence and act in the divine realm for good and ill. Through devotion in prayer and by fulfilling the commandments, people become active participants in the "mystery of unification" (*sod ha-yihud*), the process through which the divine forces are united, perfected, and return to their source. The notion that man can participate in the restoration, repair, and amendment of this world is stressed throughout the *Zohar* in the notion of *Tikkun*, which literally means 'restoration'.

In the sixteenth century a new form of Cabala appeared, derived from the teachings of Isaac Luria (1534–1572). Where the *Zohar* and earlier cabalistic works concentrated on cosmology, the Lurianic Cabala focused on exile, redemption, and the millennium. Luria reasoned that in order for there to be a place for the world, God had to withdraw from a part of himself. This doctrine of *Tsimsum* (withdrawal) was both profound and ambiguous. It provided a symbol of exile in the deepest sense, within the divinity itself, but it also implied that evil was intrinsic to the creation process and not attributable to man alone. Two other doctrines are crucial to Luria's radical theology, the *Shevirat-ha-Kelim* (breaking of the vessels) and *Tikkun* (restoration). Both explain how the evil that emerged with creation represented a temporary state that would eventually end with the perfection of all things.

According to the complex mythology of the Lurianic cabala, after God withdrew from himself, traces of light were left in the void. These were formed into the image of the primordial man, Adam Kadmon, who was the first manifested configuration of the divine. However, at this point a catastrophe occurred. Further divine lights burst forth from Adam Kadmon, but the "vessels" meant to contain them shattered. With "the breaking of the vessels" evil came into the world as sparks of light (souls) became sunk in matter.

In the Lurianic cabala man is given an even more central role than in the *Zohar*, for it is only through human actions (observing the commandments, studying the Torah, and mystical meditation) that the souls, trapped among the shards of the broken vessels, can be reunited with the divine light. Luria viewed history as an ongoing struggle between the forces of good and evil played out by the same cast of characters, who experience repeated reincarnations *(Gilgul)* until they become perfect. Although the process of *Tikkun* will be long and arduous, restoration will eventually occur as each exiled being moves up the ladder of creation, becoming better and increasingly spiritual until finally freed from the cycle of rebirth. The Lurianic cabala transformed mysticism into an activist historical force, involving individuals in a cosmic millennial drama in which their every action counted. The Lurianic cabala was the first Jewish theology to envision perfection in terms of a future state, not in terms of some forfeited ideal past.

Gershom Scholem believed that the Lurianic cabala became "something like the true theologia mystica of Judaism" from 1630 onward (*Major Trends in Jewish Mysticism,* p. 284). He attributed the emergence of the heretical movement connected with Shabbetai Tzevi (also Sabbatai Sevi; 1626–1676) to the messianic ideas inherent in Lurianic cabala. In Scholem's view, Shabbetai Tzevi's eventual apostasy and conversion to Islam led to a crisis in Judaism that precipitated the *Haskalah,* or secular Enlightenment. The cabala thus played a key role in transforming Jewish history and culture. Not all scholars agree. Idel and others deny that Messianism was a significant element of Lurianic cabala. In their view the Sabbatean movement was an outgrowth of popular apocalyptic Messianism and secularization that was largely the result of increased social and intellectual contact with Christians.

The last stage in the development of Jewish cabala occurred with the emergence of the modern Hasidic movement, founded by Rabbi Israel Baal Shem Tov, in the mid-eighteenth century. This movement created a serious rift within Judaism between Hasids and their rationalist opponents (the *Mitnagedim*), who claimed that Hasidism ignored important aspects of the Jewish law, especially Torah study and prayer, and placed too much emphasis on the redeeming role of the Hasidic rabbi, or *Tsaddik* (holy one).

CHRISTIAN CABALA

Christian interest in the cabala emerged at the end of the fifteenth century in the Platonic Academy at the Medici court in Florence. The cabala was seen as a source for retrieving the *prisca theologia,* or ancient wisdom, but being Jewish and not pagan in origin, cabalistic writings were regarded as the purest source of this divine knowledge. This was the view of Giovanni Pico della Mirandola (1463–1494), who studied the cabala with the assistance of several Jewish teachers, Samuel ben Nissim Abulfaraj, Yoseph Alemano (1435–1504) and the converted Jew Raymond Moncada, also known as Flavius Mithradites (fl. 1470–1483). Pico's cabalis-

tic studies were aimed at converting the Jews by showing them that their own ancient wisdom supported the truth of Christianity. Forty-seven of his famous nine hundred theses were taken directly from the cabala, while another seventy-two were based on his speculations about the cabala. As a result of his study, he concluded that "no science can better convince us of the divinity of Jesus Christ than magic and the cabala," an opinion the Catholic Church condemned. Pico's work influenced the German Christian Hebraist Johannes Reuchlin (1455–1522), who wrote *De Verbo Mirifico* (1494; On the miracle-working name) and *De Arte Cabalistica* (1517; On the science of the cabala). Reuchlin claimed that God revealed himself in three stages: first, to the Patriarchs through the three-letter name *Shaddai* (shin, dalet, yod); then in the Torah as the four-letter Tetragrammaton (yod, he, vav, he); and finally as the five-letter name *Yehoshua* (yod, he, shin, vav, he) or Jesus. Pico's and Reuchlin's work encouraged other Christians to explore the cabala. Cornelius Agrippa included discussions of the practical cabala in *De Occulta Philosophia* (1531), which led to the association of the cabala with magic and witchcraft. Cardinal Egidio da Viterbo (1465–1532) wrote a treatise on the Hebrew letters. The Franciscan Francesco di Giorgio (1460/66–1540) incorporated material from the *Zohar* in his *De Harmonia Mundi* (1525) and *Problemata* (1536). Guillaume Postel (1570–1581) translated the *Sefer Yetzirah* and parts of the *Zohar* into Latin with annotations. A fusion between the cabala and alchemy emerged in the sixteenth and seventeenth centuries, appearing in Heinrich Khunrath's *Amphitheatrum Sapientiae Aeternae* (1609) and the writings of Robert Fludd (1574–1637) and Thomas Vaughan (1622–1666).

During the seventeenth century Jakob Boehme's (1575–1624) work was noted for its affinity to the cabala, and the German Jesuit Athanasius Kircher drew a parallel between Adam Kadmon and Jesus. The most influential Christian cabalist, however, was Christian Knorr von Rosenroth (1636–1689), whose *Kabbala Deundata* (1677, 1684) offered the Latin-reading public the largest collection of cabalistic texts available before the nineteenth century. This collection was especially important because it included selections from the *Zohar* (with annotations and commentaries) and translations and synopses of treatises written by Luria's disciples Hayyim Vital and Israel Sarug. Scholars have recently begun to investigate the way in which this work and the cabala in general influenced such thinkers as Henry More, Gottfried Wilhelm Leibniz, John Locke, and Isaac Newton, contributing to the modern idea of scientific progress and the concept of toleration. The German Pietists led by Friedrich Christoph Oetinger (1702–1782) were also influenced by von Rosenroth's translations, and he in turn influenced Franz von Baader, Martines de Pasqually, Louis-Claude de Saint-Martin, Georg Wilhelm Friedrich Hegel, and Friedrich von Schelling. Georg von Welling published his popular *Opus Mago-Cabbalisticum et Theosophicum* in 1735. The last great work of Christian cabala was Franz Josef Molitor's (1779–1861) *Philosophie der Geschichte oder Ueber die Tradition,* which in spite of its Christological approach received high praise from Scholem, influencing his own view of the cabala. The theosophical systems of eighteenth-century Freemasons, Illuminati, and Rosicrucians also reflect cabalistic concepts and symbolism. This connection unfortunately played into the hands of anti-Semites, who claimed that a Jewish "cabale" of revolutionary Freemasons and cabalists were infiltrating European institutions and destroying them from within. The legacy of the cabala in Europe is thus Janus-faced: on the one hand it contributed to ideas at the heart of the Enlightenment: scientific progress, the ability of man to shape his own destiny, and religious toleration; on the other hand, it fed into the anti-Semitic rhetoric that laid the foundation for genocide.

See also **Catholic Spirituality and Mysticism; Enlightenment; Freemasonry; Haskalah (Jewish Enlightenment); Jews and Judaism; Leibniz, Gottfried Wilhelm; More, Henry; Newton, Isaac; Shabbetai Tzevi; Vaughan, Thomas.**

BIBLIOGRAPHY

Altmann, Alexander. "Lurianic Kabbala in a Platonic Key: Abraham Cohen Herrera's Puerta del Cielo." *Hebrew Union College Annual* 53 (1982): 317–355.

Blau, Joshua. *The Christian Interpretation of the Cabala in the Renaissance.* New York, 1944.

Cohn, Norman. *Warrant for Genocide: The Myth of the Jewish World-Conspiracy and the Protocols of the Elders of Zion.* Chico, Calif., 1981.

Coudert, Allison P. *The Impact of the Kabbalah in the Seventeenth Century: The Life and Thought of Francis Mercury van Helmont, 1614–1698.* Leiden, 1999.

———. *Leibniz and the Kabbalah.* Dordrecht, 1995.

Fine, Lawrence, ed. *Essential Papers on Kabbalah.* New York, 1995.

Goldish, Matt. "Newton on Kabbalah." In *The Books of Nature and Scripture: Recent Essays on Natural Philosophy, Theology, and Biblical Criticism in the Netherlands of Spinoza's Time and the British Isles of Newton's Time,* edited by James E. Force and Richard H. Popkin. Dordrecht, 1994.

Idel, Moshe. *Kabbalah: New Perspectives.* New Haven, 1988.

———. "The Magical and Neoplatonic Interpretations of the Kabbalah in the Renaissance." In *Jewish Thought in the Sixteenth Century,* edited by Bernard Dov Cooperman, pp. 186–242. Cambridge, Mass., 1983.

Journal des Études de la Cabale. Available at http://www.chez.com/jec2/

Katz, Jacob. *Jews and Freemasons in Europe, 1723–1939.* Translated by Leonard Oschry. Cambridge, Mass., 1970.

Krabbenhoft, Kenneth. "Kabbalah and Expulsion: The Case of Abraham Cohen de Herrera." In *The Expulsion of the Jews 1492 and After,* edited by Raymond B. Waddington and Arthur H. Williamson, pp. 127–146. New York, 1994.

Liebes, Yehuda. *Studies in the Zohar.* Translated by Arnold Schwartz, Stephanie Nakache, and Penina Peli. Albany, N.Y., 1993.

Ruderman, David. *Kabbalah, Magic and Science: The Cultural Universe of a Sixteenth Century Jewish Physician.* Cambridge, Mass., 1988.

———. "Science, Medicine, and Jewish Culture in Early Modern Europe." The Spiegel Lecture in European Jewish History. Tel Aviv University, 1987.

Scholem, Gershom. *Kabbalah.* New York, 1974.

———. *Major Trends in Jewish Mysticism.* New York, 1954.

———. *On the Kabbala and Its Symbolism.* Translated by Ralph Manheim. New York, 1965.

———. "Zur Geschichte der Anfänge der christlichen Kabala." In *Essays Presented to Leo Baeck on the Occasion of His Eightieth Birthday,* pp. 158–193. London, 1954.

Secret, François. *Le Zohar chez les Kabbalistes chrétiens de la Renaissance.* Paris, 1958.

Tishby, Isaiah. *The Wisdom of the Zohar: An Anthology of Texts.* Arranged and rendered into Hebrew by Fischel Lachower and Isaiah Tishby; with introductions and explanations by Isaiah Tishby. Translated by David Goldstein. 3 vols. The Littman Library of Jewish Civilization. Oxford and New York, 1991.

Wirszubski, Chaim. *Pico della Mirandola's Encounter with Jewish Mysticism.* Cambridge, Mass., 1989.

ALLISON P. COUDERT

CABINETS OF CURIOSITIES. *See* Marvels and Wonders; Natural History

---

CÁDIZ. The Spanish city Cádiz is located in the southwestern corner of the Iberian Peninsula, close to the Strait of Gibraltar, between the Atlantic Ocean and the Mediterranean Sea. This location explains the historically strategic position of the city in international trade routes that linked Europe, Africa, and America. The commercial activities in the city started with the Phoenicians three thousand years ago, and trade financed the first defensive walls built to protect the city against pirates in the Middle Ages. Commercial specialization was reinforced by the fact that land and water for agricultural purposes were scarce and by the large bay suitable for use by numerous heavy ships.

Between the thirteenth and the fifteenth centuries fishing and trade with North Africa were the main economic activities of the Cádiz inhabitants (1,255 in 1465). Both fishing and trade attracted merchants and fishermen from northern Spain (Biscay) and Italy (Genoa in particular). In the fifteenth century peace on the Iberian Peninsula and Castilian expansion into the Atlantic favored the transformation of a village of fishermen into a larger city. The end of the Granada War against Muslim Spain in 1492 and the Castilian conquest of the Canary Islands and America increased enormously the stra-

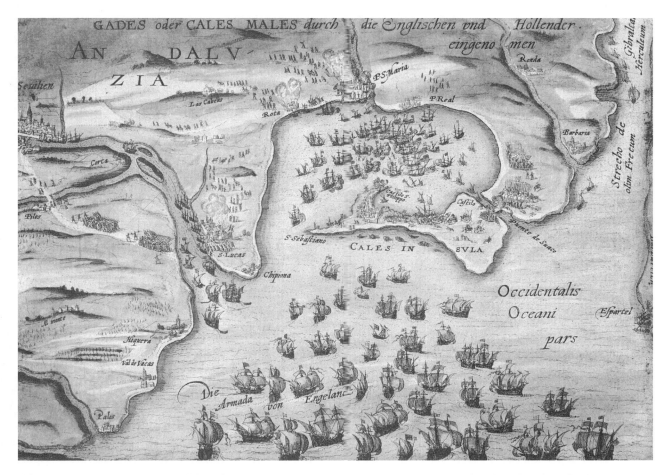

Cádiz. *English and Dutch Taking Cádiz, Spain, June–July 1596,* engraving by Hogenberg. After decades of conflict between England and Spain, in 1596 a combined English and Dutch fleet captured and partially destroyed the city. THE ART ARCHIVE/ UNIVERSITY LIBRARY GENEVA/DAGLI ORTI

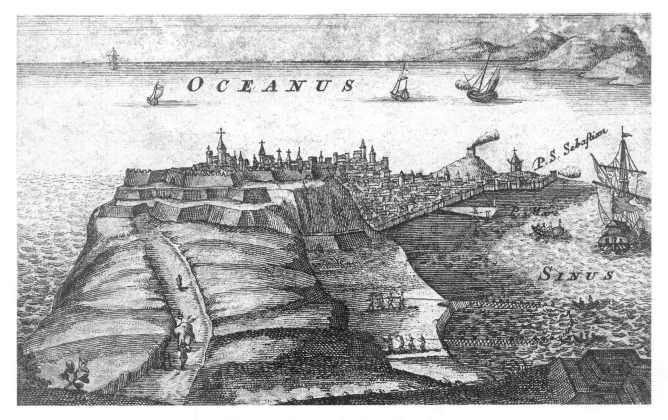

Cádiz. A 1708 engraving. THE ART ARCHIVE/MUSEO DE LA TORRE DEL ORO SEVILLE/DAGLI ORTI

tegic and commercial importance of Cádiz in the crown of Castile.

Growing trade and wealth in the sixteenth century stimulated manufactures, guilds, religious and educational establishments, and cultural life. Commercial prosperity also spawned numerous attacks from Portuguese, North African, and British pirates or corsairs in the second half of the sixteenth century.

During the seventeenth and eighteenth centuries merchants and institutions of Spanish American colonial trade moved from Seville to Cádiz because its geographical and commercial conditions were better adapted to increasing shipping tonnage and the value of commercial exchanges. Cádiz became the only legal center allowed to administer the Spanish monopoly of trade with America from the establishment in 1717 of the Casa de Contratación (House of Trade) and Consulado de Comercio (Mercantile Association). Despite the end of the legal monopoly after 1765 and 1778, Cádiz remained a major center of Spanish colonial trade until the last decade of the eighteenth century and

the first decades of the nineteenth century. Between 1778 and 1788 exports from Cádiz increased 400 percent and came to represent 72 percent of all legal exports sent from Spain to its American colonies. The crown protected colonial revenues by installing the military headquarters of the Capitanía General de Andalucía (a regional department of the Spanish army) in Cádiz in 1768.

The increasingly multicultural mercantile community of the city, composed of hundreds of merchants from the rest of Spain, France, Italy, Ireland, England, Germany, Russia, the Low Countries, Portugal, and the American territories, enjoyed religious and cultural protection from royal officers. Immigration increased the total population of a city characterized by low fertility rates and led to the city's demographic growth from 30,000 inhabitants in 1709 to 77,500 in 1791, with a density of nearly 9,000 inhabitants per square kilometer in 1791. Foreigners represented approximately 15 to 21 percent of the total population on average, most of them involved in colonial trade. Spanish merchants by and large worked as commissioners for foreign merchants, who benefited most from Spanish colonial trade in the city. Nevertheless, research in notarial archives has revealed that important percentages of foreigners did not return to their countries with the profits from colonial trade but stayed in the city, married, and founded families who lived in Andalusia for several generations, thus reinvesting their wealth and maintaining commercial networks in Spain.

See also **Commerce and Markets; Spain.**

BIBLIOGRAPHY

Bustos Rodríguez, Manuel, ed. *Historia de Cádiz: Los siglos decisivos.* Madrid, 1990. A general overview.

Fernández Pérez, Paloma. *El rostro familiar de la metrópoli: Redes de parentesco y lazos mercantiles en Cádiz, 1700–1812.* Madrid, 1997. A study of the mercantile community of Cádiz in the eighteenth century, with a focus on multicultural coexistence, gender, and the creation of networks of family groups in the firms.

García-Baquero González, Antonio. *Cádiz y el Atlántico 1717–1778: El comercio colonial español bajo el monopolio gaditano.* 2 vols. Cádiz, 1976. An economic study of Spanish colonial trade in Cádiz.

Pérez Serrano, Julio. *Cádiz, la ciudad desnuda: Cambio económico y modelo demográfico en la formación de la Andalucía contemporánea.* Cádiz, 1992. A specialized book on the demography of the city in the transition from early modern to late modern times.

PALOMA FERNÁNDEZ PÉREZ

CALDERÓN DE LA BARCA, PEDRO

(1600–1681), Spanish dramatist. Pedro Calderón de la Barca was one of the greatest dramatists of Spain's literary Golden Age. Born into a well-established Castilian family with ties to the court, Calderón received his early education at the Jesuit Imperial College of Madrid and went on to study logic, rhetoric, and mathematics at the University of Alcalá de Henares and canon law at the University of Salamanca. As a young man he lived an adventurous life in Madrid and gained the favor of King Philip IV (ruled 1621–1665), who rewarded him with knighthood in the Order of Santiago in 1636. Calderón also spent time in the military and earned a reputation for gallant service during the Revolt of Catalonia (1640–1652). Shortly thereafter he traded his weapons for a priest's vestments, taking clerical orders in 1651 and eventually serving as chaplain to Philip IV.

Despite this rich and varied career, Calderón is best remembered as a dramatist. He began to write plays at an early age and continued to produce dramatic works of high quality until his death in 1681. As Lope de Vega (1562–1635) receives credit for developing early popular theater in Spain, so Calderón is recognized for bringing it to its artistic height. Whereas Lope's drama was lively and spontaneous, focusing on dynamic action, Calderón's was carefully crafted and intellectual, built on subtle constructions of symbolism and metaphor. During the 1630s and 1640s Calderón's writing consisted principally of *comedias,* secular three-act plays that drew on a wide variety of subject matter, both comic and tragic. Among these, the tragedies frequently dealt with themes such as the tension between free will and fate, the conflicts inspired by the obligations of honor, and the role of the individual in a web of social and political ties. His comedies, nearly always placed in contemporary Spanish settings, were known as cape-and-sword plays for plots that centered on nobles caught up in love, jealousy, intrigue, mistaken identities, and the ensuing complications thereof. Whether light or serious, Calderón's works for the public theater always engaged the salient religious, moral, and philosophical issues of his day.

Calderón's best-known works from this period include *La vida es sueño* (1635; Life is a dream) and *El médico de su honra* (1635; The physician of his honor). *La vida es sueño* deals with a young prince, isolated in a tower, whose father tests his abilities by giving him the chance to rule for a day. Failing the test, the prince is told that the entire experience was a dream. When a rebellion gives him the chance to rule again, he has learned to control himself regardless of the circumstances and demonstrates that he is a worthy successor to the crown. *El médico de su honra* features a husband who suspects his wife of betrayal; though the audience knows she is innocent, he ultimately has her murdered, with the approval of the king. In the first case, Calderón explores questions of illusions and reality, freedom and destiny, and the proper qualities and responsibilities of a ruler. In the second, he pursues the internal logic of honor to its most heartless extremes. Although Calderón had a predilection for

Pedro Calderón de la Barca. GETTY IMAGES

twenty minor theatrical pieces (including the musical *zarzuelas*). These were performed, published, and translated throughout Europe in the seventeenth century. Calderón was the last great writer of the seventeenth century in Spain, and his death in 1681 drew to a close the Golden Age of literature.

See also **Drama: Spanish and Portuguese.**

BIBLIOGRAPHY

Primary Sources

Calderón de la Barca, Pedro. *Eight dramas of Calderón.* Translated by Edward FitzGerald. Urbana, Ill., 2000.

———. *Obras completas.* 3 vols. Edited by A. Valbuena Briones. Madrid, 1960–67.

Secondary Sources

Hesse, Everett W. *Calderón de la Barca.* New York, 1967.

McGaha, Michael D., ed. *Approaches to the Theater of Calderón.* Washington, D.C., 1982.

Parker, Alexander A. *The Mind and Art of Calderón: Essays on the Comedias.* Edited by Deborah Kong. Cambridge, U.K., 1988.

JODI CAMPBELL

challenging themes and contemporary issues, scholars frequently disagree on whether he intended to defend or to criticize the existing social and political order.

After being ordained to the priesthood in 1651, Calderón was appointed official dramatist of the Spanish court. Whereas his earlier work was written for the wide audience of the public theaters, his later plays were often commissioned to celebrate birthdays and other festive occasions for a more limited audience in the royal theaters. Calderón's court drama dealt predominantly with allegorical themes from Greek mythology, such as the stories of Echo and Narcissus, Venus and Adonis, and Andromeda and Perseus. These plays were also more visually striking, taking advantage of the greater resources of court stages and scenery to produce elaborate effects and fantastical illusions. During this second stage in his career, Calderón also wrote *autos sacramentales,* short religious plays that were performed yearly for Madrid's Corpus Christi celebrations.

By the end of his life Calderón had produced over one hundred *comedias,* eighty *autos,* and

CALENDAR. It was widely recognized in the early sixteenth century that the calendar was inaccurate, but the question of how it should be reformed and who had the authority to do so raised fundamental issues. It was some two hundred and fifty years before all of Europe had changed.

The Christian Church had adopted the Julian calendar from the Roman Empire at the Council of Nicaea in 325 C.E.: the first general council of the church, its authority acknowledged thereafter by East and West, Protestants and Catholics. A slight error in the original Roman calculations had by 1500 accumulated to ten days, leaving the real spring equinox on 11 March instead of 21 March. What really bothered the Roman Catholic Church (though not, apparently, the Orthodox Church) was the error this produced in the date of Easter. This was supposed to fall on the Sunday on or after the full moon after 21 March, but it now often fell a month late relative to the real equinox. Nicolaus Copernicus's *De Revolutionibus Orbium Caelestium* (1543; On the revolutions of the celestial orbs) had originally been commissioned as a basis upon which to reform the calendar, but the intervening Reformation and Copernicus's heretical views about the solar system overlaid the issue.

One of the last acts of the Counter-Reformation Council of Trent was to order a reform of the calendar, which it was hoped would provide a basic measure of agreement between Protestants and Catholics on at least one fundamental issue. The observations and calculations were undertaken by the Jesuit astronomer Christoph Clavius (1537–1612), and the results embodied in Pope Gregory XIII's bull of 1582. Ten days were to be removed from October 1582 to bring the calendar back in line with the seasons, and the system of leap years was modified to keep it on track; from then on there was to be a leap year only at the end of every fourth century, and not of every century as before. The old formula for calculating the date of Easter was modified but retained. The Gregorian reform was fundamentally religious rather than astronomical, and the Roman Catholic Church continued to reject Copernicus.

Only a handful of countries (Spain, Portugal, Poland, and parts of Italy) adopted the new Gregorian calendar on time, not least because the bull was promulgated so late. By 1585 most Roman Catholic countries had followed. Most Protestant states—including large parts of Switzerland, Germany, the Protestant Low Countries, Great Britain, and Scandinavia—retained the Julian calendar for another century or more, creating a patchwork of calendrical practice throughout Europe, particularly complex in the Holy Roman Empire. The key issue was not astronomical accuracy but papal authority. By accepting a papal bull, states would appear to be recognizing the authority of the pope not only to interfere in civil affairs but also to alter decisions of the early church; indeed, most Roman Catholic countries took care to adopt the new calendar by their own civil acts. In England, the mathematician and astrologer John Dee (1527–1608) argued that the time of Christ, rather than that of the early church, was the appropriate "radix of time" for Protestants, and proposed his own Elizabethan imperial calendar one day ahead of Rome, but his views were unwelcome to the authorities and in the end England did nothing.

In 1700, with the gap between the two calendars set to widen to eleven days, most Protestant states followed a resolution of the imperial Diet of Regensburg and adopted a modified version of the Gregorian calendar. They did so using their own calculations, following the German astronomer Johannes Kepler (1571–1630), and substituting an astronomical Easter for the traditional version, to the same practical effect. In Britain, where antipopery remained strong, the new calendar was not adopted until September 1752, when eleven days were omitted and a third Easter calculation adopted, also to identical effect. Sweden pursued its own course, coming fully into line in 1753. The churches of the East remained unmoved, standing fast by the decisions of early Christendom; the fast-secularizing states of eastern Europe generally went Gregorian for civil purposes around the time of World War I.

PRACTICAL PROBLEMS

Did the calendar change create practical, as opposed to political, problems? Undoubtedly it did, especially in international communications and where Protestant and Catholic jurisdictions were interspersed, as in much of central Europe and the Low Countries. The modest disruption of the familiar relationship between the feasts of the church and the seasons was quite quickly overcome, but the actual details varied according to how the reform was implemented. In Britain in 1752, for example, the eleven days September 3–13 inclusive were omitted from the calendar, bringing human events eleven days forward in the natural year. Fairs however were left at the same place in the natural year, putting their calendar dates back by eleven days (although many fairs in practice moved forward). Financial payments too kept their full natural term, leaving the financial year ending on 5 April rather than the traditional 25 March. At the same time, the start of the legal year was altered from 25 March to 1 January. The arrival of the new Christmas Day eleven days early took many by surprise in a society that still reckoned by feasts and fairs as much as by dates and diaries. There was widespread resistance and resentment, although the tale that people rioted for their eleven lost days is a myth. In Bohemia and in Augsburg, though, there were several years of strife between Catholics and Protestants over the issue in the 1580s, known as the "Kalenderstreit."

In navigating between old-style and new-style calendars, it is necessary to remember that in general Roman Catholic states were ten days ahead of Protestant and Orthodox states from 1583 until 1700. Care must be taken in the 1580s, and with Britain, Sweden, the Netherlands, and Switzerland. Catholic minorities in Protestant states may have adopted either calendar for religious purposes. For clarity, historians often note "O.S." or "N.S." after Julian and Gregorian dates respectively.

The issue of the calendar is a reminder that the reference points for the calculation of time express the most basic assumptions of society. The disputes it engendered were symptomatic of religious and political divisions in a world where nothing could be taken for granted.

See also **Copernicus, Nicolaus; Dee, John; Kepler, Johannes; Time, Measurement of; Trent, Council of.**

BIBLIOGRAPHY

Cheney, C. R. *A Handbook of Dates for Students of British History.* Rev. ed. London, 2000.

Coyne, G. V., M. A. Hoskin, and O. Pedersen, eds. *Gregorian Reform of the Calendar: Proceedings of the Vatican Conference to Commemorate its Four Hundredth Anniversary, 1582–1982.* Vatican City, 1983.

Poole, Robert. *Time's Alteration: Calendar Reform in Early Modern England.* London, 1998.

Richards, E. G. *Mapping Time: The Calendar and Its History.* Oxford and New York, 1998.

Whitrow, G. J. *Time in History: The Evolution of Our General Awareness of Time and Temporal Perspective.* Oxford, 1988.

ROBERT POOLE

CALLOT, JACQUES (1592–1635), French (Lorrainese) draftsman and printmaker. Born in Nancy, son of a herald-at-arms to Charles III, duke of Lorraine, Callot studied with a little-known court painter, Claude II Henriet, and a goldsmith, Demange Crocq. He departed for Italy in 1608, and continued his studies in Rome with the well-known printmaker Philippe Thomassin. In 1614 Callot moved to Florence, where he became an artist at the Medici court under Grand Duke Cosimo II, and he remained there for seven years. While in Florence, he honed his skill at using methods of perspective, probably during his studies with Giulio Parigi, the

court architect, engineer, and impresario. Callot established a reputation as an engraver through his many prints recording events at the ducal court (*Catafalque of Emperor Matthias,* 1619, and *Soliman,* 1620), and became known especially for his ability to represent vast scenes without sacrificing detail as in his *Fair at Impruneta,* 1620, which features more than a thousand active figures.

Callot returned to his native country in 1621, and in 1623 was appointed an artist to the court of Henri II, duke of Lorraine at the ducal capital of Nancy. Callot's later production included prints depicting genre scenes, religion (*The Temptation of St. Anthony,* 1635), and events at court (*Combat at the Barrier,* 1625, and the *Parterre de Nancy,* 1625). He also depicted the brutality of war in a series of etchings recording the horrors he witnessed during the Thirty Years' War (*The Miseries of War,* 1633), and in three vast multi-plate depictions of military sieges at Breda, The Netherlands, 1627, and at La Rochelle and nearby Saint-Martin-de-Ré, both 1630. However, despite his skill in seamlessly blending topographic precision with the more conventional genre of the battle scene, it is particularly noteworthy—and perhaps a reflection of his patriotism—that he politely but defiantly declined Louis XIII's commission to depict the Siege of Nancy in 1633.

Callot was one of the most prolific, creative, and influential draftsmen and printmakers of the seventeenth century. He made more than 1,400 prints and developed technical innovations, such as hard-ground etching, that became standard procedure for all Western printmakers. During his time in Lorraine, Callot visited Paris often and established a relationship with printmaker and publisher Israël Henriet (c. 1590–1661), who was also the son of his first teacher. The younger Henriet obtained hundreds of Callot's copper plates through both inheritance and purchase. To satisfy the unceasing demand for Callot's work, Henriet continued publishing them for years after his friend's death. Callot was also renowned for his drawings, about two thousand of which have survived. These were often studies for his many prints, and they reveal his enormous power of invention, his love of detail and the grotesque, his brilliant contrasts of tone, and the confident, fluid, swelling, and tapering late-man-

Jacques Callot. Engraving of the hanging of hostages during the Thirty Years' War, from *The Miseries of War.* ©Bettmann/ Corbis

nerist line that made them, and his more widely proliferated etchings, internationally famous.

See also **Commedia dell'Arte; Mannerism; Prints and Popular Imagery; Thirty Years' War (1618–1648).**

BIBLIOGRAPHY

Lieure, Jules. *Jacques Callot.* 5 vols. Paris, 1924–27.

Meaume, Édouard. *Recherches sur la vie et les ouvrages de Jacques Callot, suite au peintre-graveur de M. Robert-Dumesnil.* 2 vols. Paris, 1860; Würzburg, 1924.

Musée historique lorrain. *Jacques Calllot, 1592–1635.* Exh. cat., Paulette Choné and Daniel Ternois, eds. Nancy, 1992.

National Gallery of Art. *Jacques Callot: Prints and Related Drawings.* Exh. cat. Texts by H. Diane Russell, Jeffrey Blanchard, and John Krill. Washington, D.C., 1975.

Ternois, Daniel. *Jacques Callot: Catalogue complet de son oeuvre dessiné.* Paris, 1962.

———. *Jacques Callot: Catalogue de son oeuvre dessiné, supplément (1962–1998).* Paris, 1999.

Ternois, Daniel, ed. *Jacques Callot (1592–1635): Actes du colloque, 1992.* Paris and Nancy, 1993.

ALVIN L. CLARK, JR.

CALVIN, JOHN (Jean Cauvin; 1509–1564),

French theologian and reformer. Calvin was the leading second-generation Protestant reformer, yielding only to Martin Luther in influence. He was born in Noyon, Picardy, a town under the rule of the prince-bishop but one that also retained a medieval communal tradition. His father, despite his lack of formal advanced education, held several lay legal positions for local church bodies. His mother was from the family of a wealthy hotelkeeper. Calvin's early education was at a local school, and perhaps also in the company of the youth of the local high noble family that controlled the office of prince-bishop and several other ecclesiastical positions.

He received his university education in Paris, supported in part by church benefices his father had secured for him. Following his father's wishes, he initially aspired to a career in the church but then turned to Roman law, in which he received a degree after studying at Orléans and Bourges. In his university studies and the law studies he pursued at Orléans under the jurist Pierre de l'Estoile, Scholasticism was preponderant. However, he also acquired a strong grounding in humanism through his tutelage by the renowned pedagogue Mathurin Cordier and his attendance at lectures by leading lights of the newly formed Collège Royale in Paris and at those of the jurist Andrea Alciato at Bourges, as well as through more informal studies. Indeed his first major work, a commentary on the Stoic philosopher Seneca's *De clementia* (On clemency), shows him as a highly capable humanist scholar-commentator. It also reveals a young man filled with the desire to make a name for himself as a humanist literary figure, but ambivalent about this goal and uncomfortable with the cultivation of elite patrons, then so necessary for the attainment of legal or literary success.

Until 1533, there is little to suggest that Calvin was more than a follower of the moderate religious reform exemplified by Desiderius Erasmus and Jacques Lefèvre d'Étaples. On 1 November 1533 his friend Nicolas Cop, who had been elected rector of the University of Paris, gave an inaugural address containing a mixture of Lutheran and Erasmian ideas. But the monarchy of Francis I had turned against even moderate reform, and Cop had to flee Paris, as did Calvin himself. By early 1534 Calvin had turned from a spectator into an active reformer. By this time it had also become clear that the reception for his Seneca commentary did not fulfill his hopes. Protected for a few months at Nérac by Marguerite de Navarre (Marguerite d'Angoulême), the sister of Francis I, he soon gave up his minor benefices and moved to Basel and then to Geneva.

Central to Calvin's influence was his ability to define comprehensively the doctrine and liturgy of Christianity in the face of several alternative forms of Christianity. He confronted not only the Catholic Church but also conflicts among such reformers as Luther and Huldrych Zwingli, the recent German Peasants' movement with its more socially revolutionary understanding of Christianity, and the mostly pacifist but separatist movements known collectively as Anabaptism. Indeed, at about the time of his conversion, the most bizarre and uncharacteristically violent expression of Anabaptism was unfolding in Münster.

Calvin's first theological work, the *Psychopannychia* (written 1534), attacked a doctrine concerning the soul after bodily death, popular among some Anabaptists. By 1536, with the appearance of his most important work, the *Christianae Religionis Institutio* (Institutes of the Christian religion), Calvin had set out most of the fundamental tenets identified with his name. With Luther and Zwingli, he strongly advocated justification by faith alone and denied any role for one's own works in salvation (his insistence on predestination was a logical consequence of this doctrine). Like them, he retained only two of the Catholic Church's seven sacraments, baptism and Communion. He was more innovative in espousing a doctrine of the Eucharist that, in contradistinction to both

Luther and the Catholic Church, denied any physical presence of Christ in the Communion elements, yet, in opposition to Zwingli, accepted a spiritual but nevertheless very real presence of Christ. His rejection of a role for Christ's physical body was part of a larger mistrust of any role in worship for that which took physical form or was apprehended primarily through visualization. Thus he espoused a categorical opposition to religious images, including images of Christ, again in contrast to the German reformer. His view undermined the patronage of religious art, whether by groups or individuals, by clerics, nobles, or craftspeople.

By 1539 Calvin had formulated his doctrine of the calling, in which he counterposed godly productive work to work motivated by the pursuit of honor and usually involving flattery of highly placed or well-connected individuals. In practice those "called" were approved and regulated primarily by fellow members of the craft or profession in question, as evidenced by the appointment of ministers and by Calvin's doctrine of the lesser magistrate. Moreover, he associated godly work in one's calling with steady, persevering, disciplined emotions, while he linked the pursuit of fame and status to unsteady and turbulent emotions. This way of distinguishing sacred from profane experience harks back to his early interest in Stoicism (which also rejected the pursuit of fame). The emotional qualities he depicted as marks of the sacred also have a strong affinity with those accompanying disciplined scholarly reading, teaching, and writing, activities that predated his activity as a religious reformer.

Calvin also stands out in his attitude to secular authorities. While he asserted that individuals could not take up arms against even a tyrannical ruler, he also forbade those who found themselves in Catholic-dominated areas from participating in Catholic forms of worship; they could neither participate in the Catholic Eucharist nor show honor to religious images. He insisted that such practices were offensive to God, and he argued that such participation communicated to others affirmation of these practices, regardless of one's own private intent. Thus individuals caught in this predicament risked drawing the attention of the authorities but could not resist persecution with force. Their only alternatives were escape or the risk of martyrdom. However, Calvin allowed for resistance to evil rulers by other recognized political authorities, the doctrine of the "lesser magistrate" (his examples included, from antiquity, the Spartan ephors, Roman tribunes, and Athenian demarchs, and, from his own day, the assemblies of the three Estates). In this way he provided an opening for active resistance to persecution—an opening that was elaborated by his followers during the religious wars of the later sixteenth century in France and elsewhere. The sources and impact of Calvin's views on this and other subsequent religious and political conflicts continue to be lively areas of research.

Calvin distinguished the invisible church, which encompassed all those, living and dead, who had been elected to salvation, from the visible church. The visible church could and did include people who were not among the elect and only feigned Christian faith. The true visible church he distinguished from false churches by their preaching of correct doctrine and proper administration of the sacraments, and not by the moral perfection of their officers or members. Since the elect could be known only to God, all but people whose religious profession or moral behavior obviously denied Christ were included in the visible church. Thus an established, visible church could be coterminous with any existing political jurisdiction, as in Geneva. Yet in keeping with his doctrine of the calling, Calvin insisted upon the independence of the church from secular authorities in matters of doctrine and liturgy. In Geneva the church had four offices: pastors and teachers (their functions overlapped as both were involved in ascertaining and teaching doctrine, although teachers also had primary responsibility for education); elders, who were concerned with overseeing religious orthodoxy and moral discipline among Geneva's citizens; and deacons, who were charged with care of the poor and sick. Calvin continually pressed for the independence of church leaders from the Genevan government, including the control of excommunication. He was initially rebuffed and expelled from Geneva and spent three years ministering in Strasbourg. But the Genevan rulers, concerned to end religious discord, called him back in 1541. Aided by the influx of French Protestants fleeing persecution in their homeland as well as by considerable local support, Calvin was able to defeat opposition from several powerful, interlinked Genevan families. By 1555 he had won for

John Calvin. Sixteenth-century portrait engraving. ©Archivo Iconografico, S.A./Corbis

the consistory, the church body charged with surveillance of religious doctrine and morality, the right of excommunication, a powerful symbol of the church's independence from secular authorities, although in Geneva civil authorities continued to hold key church functions. The factors involved in this dispute are an important area of current scholarship. With most of his contemporaries Calvin did not favor religious toleration; the most notorious example is his support for the execution of Michael Servetus for heterodox views on the Trinity in 1553. However, he favored noncapital penalties for those of less extreme heterodox views.

Although favoring a church embracing the entire community rather than the elect, Calvin, like the Anabaptists, sought to bring all members of the community into at least outward conformity with the religious beliefs and moral behavior he considered appropriate to Christians. Through the surveillance of the consistory, in which he was preeminent, he had considerable success in imposing a restrictive moral regime on Geneva's inhabitants, excluding not only heterodox religious practices, but dancing and card playing as well as more commonly recognized vices. Yet the consistory did not merely chastise moral failings; it frequently brought about reconciliation of the parties to familial and community conflicts.

Calvin's views regarding women are an important topic of current scholarship. The reformer allowed a role for women in public preaching only when suitably trained men were not available. It is a matter of current debate whether he excluded women because he believed that they were inherently less capable or because he thought it inappropriate to his own time. The consistory, over which Calvin presided, probably did not take women's heretical statements as seriously as those of men, but suspected women more often than men of Catholic practices. Like most other Protestants, Calvin allowed divorce; he limited it to grounds of adultery or desertion. During his tenure, the consistory applied the same criteria to rich and poor, women and men, in divorce cases before it. However, since separation was now deemed illicit, and cruelty was excluded as grounds for divorce, women were generally required to remain with abusive husbands. The death penalty was applied for particularly egregious cases of adultery, but Calvin probably did not take the lead in pressing for it. The ongoing publication and translation of the Genevan consistory records has shed much new light on this and many other aspects of the social history of Geneva, and no doubt will continue to do so.

In addition to his other activities, Calvin found the time to comment on almost all of the New Testament, on the Pentateuch, the Prophets, and several other books of the Hebrew Bible. In his commentaries he seeks to square the entirety of scripture with his doctrines. His commentaries on the Hebrew Bible reveal a tension that sometimes approaches the breaking point: Calvin displays a historical understanding of the Hebrews' beliefs and practices unsurpassed by other commentators of his time, an understanding derived from humanism; but he also displays a strong tendency to impute to the whole of Scripture, including the Hebrews, his particular understanding of Christian doctrine and practice, an ability rooted in the synthesizing, generalizing tendency of the medieval Roman law tradition in which he had been educated. The role of humanist and Scholastic assumptions in Calvin's in-

terpretive and teaching practices continues to be an important area of research.

Finally, using Geneva as a base, Calvin and his fellow members of the Genevan Company of Pastors advanced the cause of reform on an international scale, continually advising their confreres in France and elsewhere. By his death he had helped to organize a corps of highly educated and effective preachers who had succeeded in establishing a network of French churches and were making inroads elsewhere in Europe as well.

See also **Anabaptism; Calvinism; Geneva; Huguenots; Luther, Martin; Lutheranism; Münster; Reformation, Protestant; Women; Zwingli, Huldrych.**

BIBLIOGRAPHY

Bergier, Jean-François, et al., eds. *Registres de la compagnie des pasteurs de Genève au temps de Calvin.* 2 vols. Geneva, 1962–1964.

Bouwsma, William J. *John Calvin: A Sixteenth Century Portrait.* Oxford and New York, 1988.

Breen, Quirinus. *John Calvin: A Study in French Humanism.* 2nd ed. Hamden, Conn., 1968.

Cottret, Bernard. *Calvin: A Biography.* Translated by M. Wallace McDonald. Grand Rapids, Mich., 2000.

Crouzet, Denis. *Jean Calvin: Vies parallèles.* Paris, 2000.

Douglass, Jane Dempsey. *Women, Freedom, and Calvin: The 1983 Annie Kinkead Warfield Lectures.* Philadelphia, 1985.

Kingdon, Robert M. *Adultery and Divorce in Calvin's Geneva.* Cambridge, Mass., 1995.

———. *Geneva and the Coming of the Wars of Religion in France, 1555–1563.* Geneva, 1956.

Kingdon, Robert M., Thomas A. Lambert, Isabella M. Watt, and Jeffrey R. Watt, eds. *Registres du consistoire de Genève au temps de Calvin.* 2 vols. to date. Geneva, 1996–. Translation in Kingdon, Robert M., Thomas A. Lambert, Isabella M. Watt, and Jeffrey R. Watt, eds., M. Wallace McDonald, trans. *Registers of the Consistory of Geneva in the time of Calvin.* One vol. to date. Grand Rapids, Mich. 2000–.

Millet, Olivier. *Calvin et la dynamique de la parole: Étude de rhétorique réformée.* Paris and Geneva, 1992.

Monheit, Michael L. "'The Ambition for an Illustrious Name': Humanism, Patronage, and Calvin's Doctrine of the Calling." *The Sixteenth Century Journal* 23, no. 2 (Summer 1992): 267–287.

———. "Young Calvin, Textual Interpretation and Roman Law." *Bibliothèque d'Humanisme et Renaissance* 59, no. 2 (1997): 263–282.

Monter, E. William. *Calvin's Geneva.* New York, 1967.

Muller, Richard. *The Unaccommodated Calvin: Studies in the Foundation of a Theological Tradition.* Oxford and New York, 2000.

Naphy, William G. *Calvin and the Consolidation of the Genevan Reformation.* Manchester, U.K., and New York, 1994.

Watt, Jeffrey R. "Women and the Consistory in Calvin's Geneva." *The Sixteenth Century Journal* 24, no. 2 (Summer 1993): 429–439.

Wendel, François. *Calvin: The Origins and Development of His Religious Thought.* Translated by Philip Mairet. London and New York, 1963.

Wengler, Elisabeth. *Women, Religion, and Reform in Sixteenth-Century Geneva.* Ph.D. diss., Boston College, 1999.

MICHAEL L. MONHEIT

CALVINISM. Traditionally placed after Lutheranism as the second major part of magisterial Protestantism, "Calvinism" is now used by experts as a somewhat old-fashioned shorthand for something they prefer to call the Reformed theological tradition, which spawned a cluster of different but doctrinally related churches scattered across several disconnected parts of Europe and its colonies; it included many other Protestant theologians from several European countries, including places where this type of church never flourished. The Reformed tradition preceded John Calvin (1509–1564), who was simply its single most influential exponent; indeed, "Calvinist" was an insult coined in 1553 to describe Protestants who were willing to burn other non-Catholic Christians as heretics. Therefore, this entry will describe some of Calvin's achievements in his adopted city of Geneva, which certainly deserves its nickname of the "Calvinist Rome," and examine the various fates of Calvinism not only where it became the established religion (as in Scotland, New England, and the Netherlands), but also where it enjoyed only limited success, as in Calvin's native France, the German Empire, and England. Calvinism's enduring reputation as an unusually austere and highly disciplinarian form of Protestantism, notorious for an obsession with the problem of double predestination, seems at least partly justified.

Experts often prefer to begin the history of Calvinism not with Calvin himself, but with Huldrych Zwingli (1484–1531) and the early Reformed tradition in Switzerland. By the time Calvin became a Protestant theologian and reached Geneva, the Protestant movement begun in Zurich by Zwingli and continued by Heinrich Bullinger (1504–1575) after Zwingli's early death at the battle of Kappel in 1531 had deeply colored the theological and political backgrounds where Calvin worked. Bullinger's forty-four years in Zurich overlapped Calvin's ministry in Geneva (1536–1564) on both ends; fortunately for the Reformed church, his relations with Calvin were entirely amicable. Bullinger's influence on Calvin is difficult to assess: Bullinger's writings saw about three-fourths as many sixteenth-century editions as Calvin's; and Bullinger was a prodigious letter writer, with a corpus of about fifteen thousand extant letters (roughly three times as many as Calvin), so extensive that no scholar has yet managed to read all of them.

Although Calvin is most famous for his *Institutes of the Christian Religion,* which he reworked and expanded several times between 1536 and 1560, it was only one of his many published works. They were widely distributed across Europe, going through almost five hundred different editions in nine different languages between 1532 and 1600. Almost two hundred titles by Calvin were printed in his native French and over one hundred fifty more in Latin, the best vehicle for reaching educated people anywhere in Europe. Another sixty-six editions of Calvin's works appeared in English before 1600, and twenty-eight editions in German. However, the number of sixteenth-century vernacular editions of Calvin's works does not necessarily match the degree of success his ideas enjoyed; for example, there were only fifteen editions in Dutch, although Calvinism became the official state church of the Dutch Republic, barely exceeding his eleven editions in Italian, when Italy had no Calvinist churches whatsoever.

Calvin's emphasis on predestination bothered Bullinger and other fellow Protestant theologians, who agreed with most of the theory but thought it was imprudent to preach in public. However, this doctrine did not necessarily frighten Calvin's local audience. One of them, Michel Roset (1534–1613), a Genevan chronicler, claimed that "great and small spoke of the subject" and called it "a singular grace and counsel of God, who by this means made this subject of predestination (previously obscure and almost inaccessible for the most part) most familiar in this church for the consolation and assurance of its children, who know that their salvation is founded on his eternal and unchangeable judgement" (quoted in Benedict, p. 303). To an optimist, it provided a source of comfort, rather than anxiety, in troubled times.

DISCIPLINE AND THE CONSISTORY

The most famous institution associated with Calvin, the Genevan consistory, was undoubtedly central to his purpose of reforming Geneva's inhabitants into correctly educated Christians who behaved as such. Bullinger, his indispensable ally in Zurich, expressed uneasiness about its "excessive sharpness" and its independence from the magistracy. Nevertheless, Calvin's consistory was widely admired and copied because early Reformed churches needed some way to maintain discipline over their members so that the Lord's Supper—their only important ceremony, usually celebrated only four times a year—could be properly administered. The elders, who staffed and implemented proper Christian discipline, comprised the third of Calvin's four orders of a Reformed ministry, ranking behind the rather ill-defined teaching ministry and ahead of the deacons who were responsible primarily for social welfare. (The four orders are preachers, teachers, elders, and deacons.)

Geneva's new consistory began work in February 1542, shortly after Geneva's government had approved Calvin's set of ecclesiastical ordinances. Lay elders always presided, but Calvin personally attended its meetings whenever he could; in the 1540s, he was frequently the only pastor present. Although its first ten cases concerned marriage promises and it soon handled a few divorce cases, such matters were never its principal concerns. Within a month, the consistory required people summoned before it to demonstrate a satisfactory knowledge of the Lord's Prayer and a short version of the Apostles' Creed in their spoken language, not "papist" Latin. By year's end, although most people were summoned for faulty doctrine or failure to attend sermons, others were accused of quarreling in public, fornication, blasphemy, gambling, singing parodies of hymns, using superstitious cures, or even being disobedient to their parents. Although the consistory occasionally investigated doctrinal is-

sues, such behavioral problems preoccupied it by the mid-1540s and remained predominant until Voltaire's day.

Only after a hard struggle in the mid-1550s was Calvin able to impose the consistory's autonomous power to excommunicate obstinate sinners. Its activities multiplied prodigiously. At its statistical peak in the late 1560s, Geneva's consistory summoned almost one adult in eight every year for reprimands. Nearby rural parishes, which were far slower to become "Calvinist," saw many people excommunicated for superstition, dancing, singing lewd songs, or fornication. Urban misbehavior was different, mainly involving quarrels with family or neighbors and a huge range of "scandals," including such trivial offenses as a woman urinating in a cooking pot or a man urinating in the street without turning his back. No other place in Europe, Protestant or Catholic, even remotely approached these levels of official moral surveillance.

Such extreme measures apparently got results. For example, some bits of statistical evidence support the claim of John Knox (c. 1510–1572) that Calvin's Geneva became "the most perfect school of Christ seen on earth since the days of the apostles." One indication comes from baptisms of illegitimate children, which were recorded throughout Europe in this era. At Geneva, they reached the lowest levels yet found by demographic historians: barely one illegitimate child per thousand live births, a ratio that seems unimaginably low anywhere in the world today. Another indication gains value because it comes from an extremely hostile source, an Italian Jesuit who visited Geneva in 1580. "What caused me some surprise," he noted, "was that during the three days I was in Geneva, I never heard any blasphemy, swearing, or indecent language, which," he hastened to add, "I attributed to diabolic cunning to deceive the simpleminded by having the appearance of a reformed life" (quoted in Benedict, p. 103).

THE MARKS OF CALVINISM

Calvinism and the Reformed tradition expanded rapidly after the mid-sixteenth century. From their original base in modern Switzerland (its early French-speaking strongholds, including Geneva, did not become Swiss cantons until the nineteenth century), they reached into most parts of European

Christendom, except Scandinavia, which remained entirely Lutheran, and Mediterranean Catholic countries with national Inquisitions (Spain, Portugal, and Italy), where its nascent movements were successfully repressed. Everywhere else—from southern France to Scotland in western Europe, through the Netherlands and scattered bits of the Holy Roman Empire, as far east as Poland and Hungary—networks of Reformed churches were established, decreeing professions of faith and organizing synods. Most of them also included disciplinary organizations modeled to some degree on Calvin's consistory.

Although no early "Calvinist" churches adopted exactly the same confession of faith, they shared many common features. One easy and simple way to distinguish them from other Protestants is by considering what sixteenth-century theologians called *notae,* or marks of the true church. Luther—and every other Protestant leader—insisted that preaching the Word of God correctly was the very first requirement. Nearly all of them added a second mark: the correct administration of the sacraments (Protestants agreed that there were only two, baptism and the Eucharist, but disagreed vehemently from the outset about how to perform them). Beyond these two, Luther occasionally mentioned other signs of a true church, including proper discipline; some of his more radical rivals added even more (the founder of the Mennonites had six, while other Anabaptists went up to a dozen). In general, churches within Calvin's Reformed tradition acknowledged only three *notae,* placing a correct form of church discipline immediately after correct preaching and administration of both sacraments. Interestingly, Calvin himself, despite the care he lavished on creating and maintaining Geneva's consistory, never insisted that discipline was a necessary mark of the true church. But many early official confessions of Reformed churches, including those made during Calvin's lifetime between 1560 and 1562 in Scotland, Belgium, and Hungary, made discipline their third and final mark. It was clearly a fundamental aspect of mainstream Calvinism and remained so.

THE SPREAD OF CALVINISM

In the Holy Roman Empire, the year 1555 saw the Religious Peace of Augsburg with its famous formula *cuius regio, eius religio*—the religion of the prince determines the religion of his people. This was precisely the moment when Calvinism began spreading extremely rapidly across many parts of Europe, and its relative degree of success usually depended heavily on the ruler's attitudes toward the Reformed faith. For example, in France, Calvin's native land and Europe's largest kingdom, steadfast royal opposition prevented its triumph. In the Holy Roman Empire, only one important ruler adopted it: an electoral prince established Calvinism after 1563 much as a Saxon elector had established Lutheranism a generation earlier. Elsewhere, unusual circumstances did enable it to triumph twice despite a sovereign's opposition. In Scotland, an incompetent sovereign enabled Calvinism to become the official faith, while in England, a Protestant (but not Calvinist) sovereign struggled to tame it. In the Netherlands, a powerful but distant and unpopular sovereign ultimately failed to prevent Calvinism from triumphing in half of his lands—although not in the regions where it had originated.

In France, the Reformed faith grew with amazing rapidity in the late 1550s, establishing clandestine churches in towns throughout the kingdom and converting many noblemen, including some from princely houses. Starting in the 1560s, both France and the Netherlands experienced extremely long and bitter cycles of civil wars, which historians conventionally call the "Wars of Religion." Much ink has been shed over how far the Reformed churches went, in both France and the Netherlands, in provoking revolts against legitimate rulers; it seems clear that they provided some of the logistical infrastructure as well as most of the propaganda for these risings, and they reaped the benefits of whatever successes the rebels enjoyed. Although French Huguenots lost both battles and members during the wars, the French crown repeatedly granted them some freedom of worship in order to stop the fighting. In the Netherlands, the rebels also lost most of the battles. However, after they gained a foothold in defensible northern positions after 1572, the greatest civilian mass migration in sixteenth-century Europe eventually brought dozens of thousands of Calvinists into the region. Although the rebels soon established the Reformed faith in Dutch provinces, historians have pointed out how few full members these "official" churches actually had even in the mid-seventeenth century.

In the British Isles, the rapid success of Calvinism in Scotland, destined to become one of its major strongholds, was unexpected. But despite the popularity of both Calvin's works and the Geneva Bible in England, it never dominated the doctrines of the established Protestant church there. In a way, both results connect to a notorious 1558 pamphlet against the "monstrous" rule of women by John Knox, the most famous English-speaking sixteenth-century Calvinist. Knox wrote a history of the Reformation in Scotland, recounting how he outmaneuvered and bullied Queen Mary Stuart until she lost her throne in 1567; however, Elizabeth I, who became England's Protestant ruler in 1558, never trusted Knox or his followers afterward.

The conversion of an unusually studious German prince, the elector palatine Frederick III (ruled 1559–1576), provides our clearest example of a major Calvinist church established solely by the ruler's will. In 1563, he issued a new church order that followed the Reformed manner of celebrating Communion and accompanied it with a relatively brief catechism that quickly provoked Lutheran wrath for upholding the "damnable sect" of Zwingli and Calvin. When other Protestant rulers had Frederick summoned in person to the 1566 imperial diet and questioned him about his religious beliefs, he solemnly swore before the emperor that he had read some of Luther's writings but nothing by Calvin, and pointed out that he had signed the Augsburg Confession. This sufficed. The Palatinate, home of Germany's oldest university at Heidelberg, became Germany's first major Reformed state. It was also the only important one. On the eve of the Thirty Years' War (1618–1648), the German empire counted about a dozen Reformed state churches (scattered among more than two hundred lay and ecclesiastical principalities) and four civic churches (among eighty free cities), plus two confessionally mixed regions in the far northwest. Overall, Reformed Protestants comprised only 6 percent of Germany's population and controlled four of its twenty-six universities, including Heidelberg.

Isolation apparently increased Palatine aggressiveness. Frederick III intervened militarily to help French Huguenots; by grasping for the Bohemian crown in 1618, his successors ultimately devastated their possessions, although the Reformed church they built proved sufficiently sturdy to survive subsequent persecutions. In theological terms, they provided the Reformed faith with one of its major confessional documents, the Heidelberg Catechism; it was adopted by the synod of Emden, on the Dutch border, in 1571, and soon afterward by the Reformed churches of Hungary and Poland. In ecclesiological terms, the Palatinate created the largest network of consistorial discipline in central Europe; but it also produced the doctrine of Erastianism, the most extreme Protestant version of the subordination of church to state.

In eastern Europe, state power was far weaker, and the Reformed church acquired a different configuration. The widespread use of Latin among the nobility and literate minority enabled Calvin and Bullinger to get their message across in Polish- or Magyar-speaking lands. Calvin sent numerous letters to Poland's king and leading noblemen in 1555, and local Protestant churches invited him to come and advise them. Before the tide began turning against them after 1580 and exposed the shallowness of their roots, over 250 Reformed churches had been established in Poland and another 225 in the Lithuanian parts of the kingdom; at that moment, Calvinists formed the largest single religious group in the Polish Senate. Meanwhile, Calvinism sank much deeper roots in the kingdom of Hungary, shattered by a Turkish victory that left Budapest under Ottoman occupation for 150 years. By 1600, the Reformed church claimed almost half of Hungary's population, and they even proselytized among the Orthodox Romanians. Many of Hungary's Reformed churches, like those in the Palatinate, managed to survive despite political persecutions in the seventeenth century.

SEVENTEENTH-CENTURY CALVINISM

The history of Calvinism changed dramatically in the seventeenth century. In Europe, it stopped growing through armed struggle with Catholic governments, and instead it lost ground in many places. In Poland-Lithuania, it disappeared entirely through a peaceful Catholic reconquest. Its only new foundations, destined to become important in subsequent centuries, were in overseas colonies like New England or South Africa. Occasionally, Calvinism still seemed bellicose after 1600. Historians still debate the extent to which an international Calvinist conspiracy provoked the Thirty Years' War in 1618 by encouraging the ill-fated adventure of the elector palatine Frederick V, who became Bohemia's "Winter King." It was a last gasp, like the final Huguenot rebellion in France, which broke out in 1621 and ended with Cardinal Richelieu's capture of the greatest Huguenot stronghold, La Rochelle, in 1628. Ironically, the only successful military rising by seventeenth-century Calvinists came against a Protestant ruler, Charles I of England, in 1639. In places where it had become established, like the Netherlands or Scotland, Reformed church membership continued to increase, and Calvinism sank much deeper roots among the population. But elsewhere, it often receded into insignificance. Even in Calvin's native France, where the Reformed church seemed safely protected by the Edict of Nantes after 1598, its seventeenth-century membership eroded slowly before it was formally abolished by Louis XIV in 1685.

Most historians consider the seventeenth century the apogee of a "confessionalized" Europe, and Calvinism fits this pattern perfectly. From the beginning, all Reformed churches had demanded a properly trained clergy; at Calvin's insistence, Geneva had created a famous academy in 1559, and Dutch rebels founded a university at Leiden in 1575. By the time Harvard College was founded in Massachusetts in 1636, Reformed churches had created at least two dozen institutions of higher learning. After 1600, at least 95 percent of all Reformed pastors in the Netherlands or the Palatinate boasted university training in theology; most did even in the remotest Scottish isles. In such places as Scotland, Zweibrücken in Germany, or New England, a typical seventeenth-century Calvinist pastor owned over a hundred books, or about four times as many as their Catholic counterparts in northern Italy (Benedict, p. 450). Under such conditions, theology and ecclesiology, rather than politics, came to dominate its seventeenth-century history. Two major theological "summit conferences" were held, where issues about predestination dominated discussions, with questions about the proper organization of

church discipline close behind. Protestantism has always displayed a penchant for spinning off new branches. Even in places where it was established, seventeenth-century Calvinism splintered: Remonstrants opposed Counter-Remonstrants in the Netherlands; Presbyterians and Episcopalians quarreled violently in Scotland. New variants, most notably Congregationalism, emerged elsewhere.

The Synod of Dort (Dordrecht) in the Netherlands, summoned in order to resolve the conflict between Remonstrants and Counter-Remonstrants, offers the closest approximation to the Council of Trent within the Calvinist or Reformed tradition. It held no fewer than 154 official sessions between November 1618 and May 1619, and included nineteen voting colleges representing four national churches (the French Reformed church also tried to send delegates, but King Louis XIII forbade them to leave the country). A majority of the voting colleges represented the host nation: nine provincial synods, plus the Walloon churches and the theological faculties of Dutch universities, while the other eight colleges represented British, Swiss, and German churches. The Synod of Dort succeeded in its original purpose by marginalizing the Remonstrants (who included the world-famous jurist Hugo Grotius, already imprisoned before the synod met). Two details suggest its importance in the English-speaking world. John Robinson (c. 1575–1625), the theological leader behind the 1620 Plymouth Pilgrims, greatly admired it; King James I (ruled 1603–1625), who famously vowed to "harry [Puritans like Robinson] out of the land," forbade any public criticism of its resolutions.

The Synod of Dort canonized what subsequently became known as the five cardinal points of official Calvinism, which English-speaking followers memorized through the acronym TULIP: total depravity, unconditional election, limited atonement, irresistible grace, and the perseverance of the saints. Considering the importance—and now, the relative obscurity—of these doctrines, they deserve a bit of elaboration. "T" (also known through the famous rhyme in the *New England Primer,* "in Adam's fall/ we sinned all") means that ever since Adam and Eve were expelled from Eden, all of humanity has been in a state of corruption and helpless to obtain salvation. "U" asserts that election is founded on God's purpose "even before the beginning of the world."

"L" claims that Christ's atonement applies only to the elect but not to the rest of corrupt humankind. "I" claims that the soul's inner regeneration is entirely the "mysterious and ineffable" work of God. And "P" asserts that God will somehow preserve the elect from falling from grace, despite their occasional and inevitable lapses into sin.

A second and much longer lasting institution met during the Puritan revolution and eventually reshaped English-speaking Calvinism into its best-known forms. From July 1643 until February 1649, an Assembly of Divines held 1,163 sessions in Westminster Abbey. Of its 151 members, all but 30 were "learned, godly and judicious divines" hand-picked by the Long Parliament (three, who had settled in Massachusetts, declined the invitation); the remainder were themselves members of Parliament. The assembly prepared a book of discipline for the English church, providing a presbyterian form of discipline similar in essential aspects to arrangements among French and Dutch Calvinists. It then prepared a confession of faith, which essentially repeated the "LIP" parts of the Dort formula while avoiding the most abstract aspects of predestination. In 1647, it produced both shorter and longer versions of what we now call the Westminster Catechism.

Although created in England, the presbyterian system was essentially stillborn in its native land long before the Church of England was restored in 1660. Even in London, its greatest center of support, presbyteries were founded in only 64 of the city's 108 parishes (Benedict, p. 402). However, its arrangements were enthusiastically adopted in Scotland, where they had a durable impact. Following a long episcopalian parenthesis after 1661, they were grudgingly reimposed in 1690 after a Dutch prince, William III, who believed in predestination and spoke about achieving consensus on terms "wherein all the Reformed churches do agree" (Benedict, p. 415), occupied the Scottish as well as the English throne.

In New England, a local "summit conference," the Cambridge synod, which lasted from 1646 until 1648, also adopted the Westminster Assembly's theological decrees. The preamble to its resolutions, which retained nominal authority in New England until about 1760, boasted of their doctrinal agreement with "all the reformed churches of Christ in Europe." But in Massachusetts, Westminster's "presbyterian" decrees about polity and discipline were replaced by an entirely different system, stressing the complete autonomy of every parish. The Cambridge synod thus created a new branch of Calvinism, the one we now call Congregationalism, which became a de facto established church throughout most of New England.

New Englanders were the most famous Calvinists to settle in America before 1700, but they were certainly not the only ones. The Dutch settlers of New Amsterdam, later New York, had established their Reformed church by 1640 (by 1665, the Dutch had also established it in South Africa, which still remains a bastion of the Dutch Reformed church). After 1685, some two thousand Huguenots, fleeing France after Louis XIV revoked the Edict of Nantes, reestablished their Reformed churches after settling in places as far apart as Boston and South Carolina. Soon afterward, thousands of Scots-Irish colonists from Ulster (Northern Ireland) fled in order to escape Protestant persecution; they settled mostly in the middle colonies and formed their first presbytery at Philadelphia by 1706. Methodism, the largest neo-Calvinist Protestant church in America, arrived there by the mid-eighteenth century. As the history of Calvinist emigration to America testifies, such seventeenth-century intra-Protestant confessional quarrels were often high-stakes issues for laymen. They were even more so for clerics because public authorities quickly removed ministers from theologically incorrect factions. After 1619, Remonstrants were deprived throughout the Netherlands; in Scotland, many Episcopalians were deprived after 1639, and Presbyterians were deprived in about one-fourth of its thousand parishes after 1661. The situation was worst in Stuart England, which exceeded its previous pastoral purges under the Tudors in 1553 and 1559. During the Puritan Revolution, over two thousand of England's nine thousand parishes lost Royalist pastors for being insufficiently Calvinist. After the Restoration of 1660 gave the Church of England a head (Charles II) who had once remarked that "Presbyterianism is not a religion for gentlemen," two thousand more were removed as insufficiently Episcopalian. After the Glorious Revolution of 1688, another four hundred British clergy were deposed for refusing to swear allegiance to William and Mary.

CALVINIST AUSTERITY

The most important features linking the practices of Europe's various "confessionalized" Reformed churches—and simultaneously separating them from other Protestant as well as Catholic traditions—revolved around their methods of disciplining church members for various forms of misbehavior. Wherever the Reformed faith became an official church, as in Scotland, the Netherlands, or the Palatinate, its organizations for ecclesiastical discipline operated hand in glove with public authorities. Records from such institutions in various parts of Europe enable us to form some general impressions about how Calvinist discipline actually worked in the heyday of confessionalism. The first thing to notice is that no established Reformed church even remotely approached the levels of investigation or punishments found in Calvin's Geneva. Consistories in Scotland or French Switzerland summoned between one adult in thirty and one in sixty each year, while those in Holland or France excommunicated no more than one adult in one hundred fifty each year; both ratios were roughly six times higher in Calvin's Geneva.

Another distinctive feature of Reformed Protestantism was its remarkably small number of official holidays. Calvin himself saw no need and no scriptural basis for any holiday other than Sunday, and Reformed Protestants usually celebrated extremely few of them. Their most austere churches, Geneva and Scotland (or seventeenth-century New England), observed none at all—not until Geneva's magistrates overruled their pastors and finally declared Christmas an official holiday in 1694. Such situations were, however, exceptional. The mainstream of established Calvinism, the Reformed churches of Zurich, Bern, France, the Netherlands, and the Palatinate, celebrated four holidays besides Sundays: Christmas, Easter, Ascension Day, and Pentecost; the Dutch and the Palatinate also added New Year's Day. Keeping only a handful of holy days marked an enormous departure from Catholic practices, which in most places celebrated anywhere from forty to sixty holidays each year. Other mainstream Protestants were far less radical than Calvinists: Lutherans kept a large number of holy days,

while the Church of England became a target for Puritan scorn by observing a total of twenty-seven holidays. Early Massachusetts went further and took the most extreme Calvinist position about the Christian calendar: not only did the colony ban all holidays, but its General Court briefly reformed the "pagan" names of the months as well, dating by "first month," "second month," and so forth.

Many Calvinists compensated for this paucity or absence of other holidays with a strict observance of Sunday, almost in an exact correlation. Scotland became Europe's most notorious example in 1579, when serious punishments were first threatened for Sabbath-breakers; by 1649, they had forbidden such practices as fishing on Sunday. Scotland's extremely rigid taboos about Sabbath observance lasted far into modern times; it has been suggested that "Thou Shalt Not" made the best title for a history of Scotland, with its longest chapter called "Never on Sunday." Another specifically Calvinist ritual was the special day of community fasting, proposed by pastors and decreed by secular authorities, usually intended to divert God's wrath at times of extraordinary danger. We find fast days observed as early as the 1560s by the beleaguered churches of the Low Countries or France, and later in seventeenth-century New England; they remained a feature of Genevan life until the nineteenth century.

CONCLUSION

Calvinism's distinctive cultural contributions to the modern world seem more problematic than they did fifty years ago, when historians confidently assumed that Reformed churches had consistently opposed tyranny and fostered individualism. They seem vastly more problematic than they did a century ago, when the German sociologist Max Weber asserted a causal connection between Calvinist self-discipline, which he called "other-worldly asceticism," and economic success. The best way to approach such major issues today is by noting that although Calvinism's various European branches were mostly stable or defensive after 1650, they remained dynamic in Europe's overseas colonies and former colonies until the twentieth century. The consequences seem peculiarly paradoxical in America, where advanced education has become entirely secular, while a crypto-Calvinist "salvationist" evangelical Protestantism maintains an enduring hold over much of the population.

Few readers today will swallow the assertion that New England's Calvinist Puritanism "produced a type of human being that no just and informed mind can think of without admiration" (McNeill, pp. 340–341). Nevertheless, Calvinism, argues its most prominent recent historian, "still merits a prominent role in certain metanarratives of Western modernization" (Benedict, p. 542). By shrinking beliefs about holy days and seasons to a minimum, it affected a more thorough, although incomplete, "disenchantment of the world" than its rivals, and its strict codes of individual conduct powerfully reinforced individual consciences.

See also **Calvin, John; Dort, Synod of; Dutch Republic; Geneva; Grotius, Hugo; Huguenots; Knox, John; La Rochelle; Luther, Martin; Lutheranism; Methodism; Palatinate; Puritanism; Reformation, Protestant; Reformations in Eastern Europe: Protestant, Catholic, and Orthodox; Zwingli, Huldrych.**

BIBLIOGRAPHY

The outstanding recent synthesis by Philip Benedict, *Christ's Churches Truly Reformed* (New Haven, 2002), includes an extremely rich and up-to-date bibliographical survey about various topics connected with "Calvinism." It almost entirely replaces the older account by John T. McNeill, *The History and Character of Calvinism* (Oxford, 1954).

Its fragmented history has often made Calvinism a topic for collective research in multinational contexts during the past generation. A slightly older example of this genre is Menna Prestwich, ed., *International Calvinism, 1541–1715* (Oxford, 1985). Three useful and relatively recent collections of documents and essays should also be mentioned: Alastair Duke, Gillian Lewis, and Andrew Pettegree, eds., *Calvinism in Europe, 1540–1610: A Collection of Documents* (Manchester, U.K., 1992); Andrew Pettegree, Alastair Duke and Gillian Lewis, eds., *Calvinism in Europe, 1540–1620* (Cambridge, U.K., 1994); and Raymond A. Mentzer, ed., *Sin and the Calvinists: Morals Control and the Consistory in the Reformed Tradition* (Sixteenth Century Essays & Studies, XXXII; Kirksville, Mo., 1994). Those who read French can enjoy a handsome coffee-table book: Pierre Chaunu, ed., *L'aventure de la Réforme: Le monde de Jean Calvin* (Paris, 1986); even those who cannot might enjoy its illustrations. There are some valuable essays in Karen Maag, ed., *The Reformation in Eastern and Central Europe* (Aldershot, U.K., 1997).

WILLIAM MONTER

CAMBRAI, LEAGUE OF (1508).

The League of Cambrai was an alliance of European powers against the Venetian Republic signed on 10 December 1508. Named for the town in the Netherlands where the treaty was signed, the alliance against Venice included France, Spain, England, Germany, and the papacy, as well as the Italian states of Savoy, Ferrara, and Mantua. All swore to avenge the injuries, violations, and damages caused by the state of Venice.

The Venetian Republic offended the other European powers when it began to extend its empire on the Italian mainland. In the fifteenth century, the changing nature of the Venetian economy required such an expansion of territory. The Ottoman conquest of Constantinople in 1453 severely damaged Venice's sea trade in the Mediterranean. In addition, Venetian trade in the Far East was threatened by Portuguese ships sailing around the newly discovered Cape of Good Hope. Thus, the Venetians had begun to transform themselves from a sea to a land power. Recent conquests in the Veneto, including the cities of Padua, Verona, and Friuli, raised alarm among the other European powers.

The League of Cambrai was orchestrated by Pope Julius II (reigned 1503–1513), who wanted to strengthen and extend the Papal States at the expense of Venice. But all of the members of the league had something to gain from the alliance, for the territories of Venice were to be divided between them. Desperately, Venice tried to pay the emperor Maximilian 200,000 Rhenish florins for his alliance, but to no avail. The onslaught arrived on 10 May 1509 at the battle of Agnadello, where the French army surrounded the Venetian forces with cavalry and Swiss pikemen. The Venetian forces were routed, and the defeat destroyed the morale of the troops, who were mainly mercenary soldiers with little loyalty to Venice. Within two months, Venice lost all of her territory on the mainland and was in fear of losing the islands themselves.

Fortunately for Venice, in the summer of 1509 several cities were beginning to rally to the side of their former lords, including Padua, Vicenza, and Verona. Diplomatically, the Venetians were able to ameliorate their situation as well. They reconciled with the papacy on 24 February 1510, and the League of Cambrai against Venice became the Holy

League, an alliance against France. Through the Holy League, Pope Julius II intended to force the "barbarians" out of Italy. The pope's martial behavior was criticized by many pacifist humanists including Erasmus of Rotterdam, who penned the dialogue *Julius Excluded from Heaven* in 1513.

For Venice, the results of the League of Cambrai were devastating. Although the republic had survived and eventually managed to regain many of its territories on the mainland, it destroyed the dream of an empire on the Italian peninsula, or terra firma. The republic never regained the prestige, wealth, and military importance of earlier times. After the League of Cambrai, Venice relied on diplomatic maneuvering between the European powers rather than on military force for its survival in the early modern era.

See also **Julius II (pope); Venice.**

BIBLIOGRAPHY

Gilbert, Felix. *The Pope, His Banker, and Venice.* Cambridge, Mass., 1980.

Hale, J. R, ed. *Renaissance Venice.* London, 1973.

Oman, Charles. *A History of the Art of War in the Sixteenth Century.* London and Mechanicsburg, Pa., 1999.

REBECCA BOONE

CAMBRIDGE PLATONISTS.

The Cambridge Platonists are so called because they were all educated at the University of Cambridge and were all indebted to Platonist philosophy. The senior member of the group was Benjamin Whichcote (1609–1683), and its most important philosophers were Henry More (1614–1687) and Ralph Cudworth (1617–1688). The group also included Peter Sterry (1613–1672), John Smith (1618–1652), Nathaniel Culverwel (1619–1651), and John Worthington (1618–1671). Their younger followers included George Rust (d. 1670), Anne Conway (1631–1679), and John Norris (1675–1711).

Cambridge Platonism may be defined not so much by a strict set of doctrines as by a loose framework of values and philosophical preferences. This Platonism was of the syncretic model familiar since the Renaissance, which was open to other strands of thought, including, in this case, new developments in science and philosophy, in particular Cartesianism and the experimentalism of the Royal Society. While the Cambridge Platonists' individual writings exhibit marked differences of emphasis and style, the major premise of their thinking is the compatibility of reason and faith and the view that the human mind is equipped with the principles of knowledge and morality. Their tolerant Protestantism, underpinned by a liberal theology of grace, is matched by an optimistic view of human nature, according to which human beings are capable of self-improvement through the exercise of reason and free will. These views set them in opposition to the dogmatic Calvinism of their day, as well as to the philosophical determinism of Thomas Hobbes and Baruch Spinoza. The main themes of their writings were the defense of the existence of God and of the immortality of the soul and the formulation of a practical ethics for Christian conduct. They propounded a philosophy of spirit, according to which mind or soul is antecedent to matter, the truths of the mind are superior to sense-knowledge, and spirit is the main principle of causal agency. The most distinctive accounts of the latter are More's hypothesis of the spirit of nature and Cudworth's analogous hypothesis of plastic nature. The fullest and most systematic exposition of their philosophy of spirit is set out in More's *Of the Immortality of the Soul* (1659) and *Enchiridion Metaphysicum* (1671; Manual of metaphysics). Cudworth never completed his main work, *The True Intellectual System of the Universe* (1678). Nonetheless this substantial volume is a compendious philosophy of religion, which surveys ancient philosophy as a *philosophia perennis* ('perennial philosophy'). It broaches a number of themes more fully treated in Cudworth's unpublished writings "On Liberty and Necessity" and his posthumously published *Treatise concerning Eternal and Immutable Morality* (1731). The *Treatise* is the most comprehensive statement of innate-idea epistemology by any seventeenth-century philosopher. The most accessible summary of the ethos and assumptions of Cambridge Platonism is John Smith's posthumously published *Select Discourses* (1660). More also took care to communicate his philosophy in more popular works like his *Philosophical Poems* (1647) and *Divine Dialogues* (1668). Nathaniel Ingelo's romance *Bentivolio and Urania*

(1660) contains an outline of their views for popular consumption.

Despite difficulties occasioned by the upheaval of contemporary political events, the legacy of the Cambridge Platonists was far-reaching. On the religious front, they inspired the Latitudinarians who adopted a nonrestrictive approach to matters of doctrine within the Church of England. In philosophy, More and Cudworth were read by Gottfried Wilhelm Leibniz, while their British adherents included Lord Shaftesbury, Richard Price, and Thomas Reid. The works of More, Cudworth, and Whichcote continued to be printed well into the eighteenth century.

See also Cartesianism; Church of England; Descartes, René; Hobbes, Thomas; More, Henry; Leibniz, Gottfried Wilhelm; Spinoza, Baruch.

BIBLIOGRAPHY

Primary Sources

Conway, Anne. *The Principles of the Most Ancient and Modern Philosophy.* Translated by Taylor Corse and Allison P. Coudert. Cambridge, U.K., 1996.

Cragg, Gerald R., ed. *The Cambridge Platonists.* New York, 1968.

Cudworth, Ralph. *A Treatise concerning Eternal and Immutable Morality.* Edited by Sarah Hutton. Cambridge, U.K., 1996.

——. *The True Intellectual System of the Universe.* London, 1678.

Culverwel, Nathaniel. *An Elegant and Learned Discourse of the Light of Nature.* Edited by Robert A. Greene and Hugh MacCallum. Toronto, 1971.

Ingelo, Nathaniel. *Bentivolio and Urania.* London, 1660.

More, Henry. *A Collection of Several Philosophical Writings.* London, 1662.

——. *A Collection of Several Philosophical Writings of Dr. Henry More.* Cambridge, U.K., 1662. Reprinted 1978.

——. *H. Mori Cantabrigiensis Opera Omnia.* London, 1675–1679. Latin translation of all More's theological and philosophical works.

Patrides, C. A., ed. *The Cambridge Platonists.* London, 1969.

Smith, John. *Select Discourses.* New York, 1978.

Secondary Sources

Darwall, Stephen L. *The British Moralists and the Internal Ought, 1640–1740.* Cambridge, U.K., and New York, 1992.

Hutton, Sarah. "Lord Herbert and the Cambridge Platonists." In *British Philosophy and the Age of Enlightenment,* edited by Stuart Brown. Vol. 5 of *Routledge History of Philosophy.* London and New York, 1995.

Hutton, Sarah, ed. *Henry More (1614–1687): Tercentenary Studies.* Dordrecht, Netherlands, 1990.

Passmore, John Arthur. *Ralph Cudworth.* Cambridge, U.K., 1951.

Rogers, G. A. J., J.-M. Vienne, and Y.-C. Zarka, eds. *The Cambridge Platonists in Philosophical Context: Politics, Metaphysics, and Religion.* Dordrecht, Netherlands, 1997.

Scott, Dominic. *Recollection and Experience: Plato's Theory of Learning and Its Successors.* Cambridge, U.K., 1990.

SARAH HUTTON

CAMERA OBSCURA. The camera obscura is an optical instrument that was the forerunner of the modern photographic camera. It can range in size from a small tabletop device to a room-size chamber. The term is Latin for 'dark room', which describes the simplest form of the camera obscura, a darkened room into which light is admitted through a tiny opening in one of the walls or windows. An inverted image from the outside world appears against the wall or screen opposite the opening. The principle of the camera obscura has been known since ancient times, and the device was used for viewing astronomical phenomena such as solar eclipses from at least the thirteenth century. During the eighteenth century the camera obscura enjoyed widespread popularity, and large camera obscuras were constructed for use as public entertainments.

In the early modern period the camera obscura was used as a model of the structure and function of the eye and as a demonstration of theories of vision. Leonardo da Vinci (1452–1519) discussed the camera obscura in the context of the eye, but Giambattista della Porta (1535?–1615) was the first to suggest that the camera obscura could be used as a tool for artists. In his *Magiae naturalis* of 1558, della Porta suggested that artists and others could use the camera obscura for making drawings by projecting the image onto a sheet of paper and tracing it. Della Porta also suggested placing a lens in the opening, or aperture, of the camera obscura to improve the quality of the projected image, and this innovation contributed to the wider use of the device. Although many sixteenth- and seventeenth-

Camera Obscura. This is the simplest form, in which a room is darkened and light allowed in through one small hole. LIBRARY OF CONGRESS

century writers noted that the camera obscura could serve as a useful tool for drawing, the question of whether and to what extent the instrument was utilized by early modern artists has long been a subject of debate among art historians. Very few written accounts describing the actual use of the camera obscura by artists exist prior to the eighteenth century, and therefore arguments about the use of the camera obscura by artists in earlier centuries have been based on internal evidence gleaned from paintings and drawings. The work of the famous Delft painter Jan Vermeer (1632–1675) has been the focus of much of this research, as many scholars believe that the extreme contrasts of perspective and thickly painted highlights present in the construction and composition in many of Vermeer's paintings are evidence of the use of an optical device. While the question of Vermeer's and other early modern artists' use of the camera obscura as a compositional aid has not been resolved, most scholars agree that many early modern artists were interested in optical devices and may

have been inspired by the visual effects produced by instruments such as the camera obscura. Other scholars have approached the camera obscura as a means of theorizing the nature of vision in the early modern period, interpreting the instrument as a metaphor for early modern—as opposed to modern or postmodern—modes of looking.

See also **Optics; Scientific Instruments.**

BIBLIOGRAPHY

Primary Source

Della Porta, Giambattista. *Magiae naturalis.* Naples, 1558.

Secondary Sources

Alpers, Svetlana. *The Art of Describing: Dutch Art in the Seventeenth Century.* Chicago, 1983.

Crary, Johnathan. *Techniques of the Observer: On Vision and Modernity in the Nineteenth Century.* Cambridge, Mass., 1990.

Gernsheim, Helmut. *The Origins of Photography.* New York, 1982.

Lindberg, David C. *Theories of Vision from Al-Kindi to Kepler.* Chicago, 1976.

Seymour, Charles, Jr. "Dark Chamber and Light-Filled Room: Vermeer and the Camera Obscura." *Art Bulletin* 46 (1964): 323–331.

Wheelock, Arthur K., Jr. *Vermeer and the Art of Painting.* New Haven and London, 1995.

JANICE L. NERI

CAMISARD REVOLT. The Camisard Revolt (1702–1704) began in the remote Cévennes mountains of southern France and spread from there to the plains bordering the cities of Montpellier, Nîmes, and Alès (formerly Alais). It resulted from efforts by the monarchy of Louis XIV to destroy orthodox Calvinism following the revocation in 1685 of the Edict of Nantes (1598), which had granted French Protestants limited tolerance. The monarchy proved successful in expelling or executing pastors and elders and dismantling the French Reformed Church, but its success inadvertently opened the way to less orthodox methods of religious expression in the mountains of the Cévennes. Episodes of popular prophetism resulted, and men, children, and especially women began to receive revelations directly from the Holy Spirit. For women, prophetism represented a new and powerful avenue by which they might exercise authority in their faith, and they formed the backbone of support and supply for the rebellion. A male prophet, Abraham Mazel, organized the first of several rebel bands in 1702 with explicit orders from the Holy Spirit to destroy the Catholic Church. Called "Camisards" after the *camisa,* or white smocks they wore, the rebels attacked and burned churches, killed priests and accused persecutors, and battled royal armies, winning several small victories.

The Camisards fought a strikingly modern guerrilla war, depending on the support of their native villages and intimate knowledge of familiar terrain to ambush royal detachments and disrupt communications. The commanders sent to crush the revolt were used to fighting a very different kind of war and proved incapable of finding and defeating the bands, which seemed to appear and disappear without trace. Convinced that the only way to stop the rebellion was to cut off its supplies, royal officials finally resorted to burning some five hundred villages in the mountains and conducting murderous military pogroms aimed principally at the civilian population.

Still fired by apocalyptic prophetism, but losing popular support and lacking supplies, the rebellion began to fade when a new commander, the pragmatic Maréchal de Villars, employed amnesties to negotiate its end. Jean Cavalier, the most powerful and successful rebel chief, was the first to surrender. The death soon after of the rebellion's most charismatic leader, Roland Laporte, effectively finished the conflict. While some tiny groups of rebels persisted in the mountains for a few years, there were no more religious wars in France.

The Camisard rebellion demonstrated the classic conflict of faith and reason. The rebel prophets never understood the extent to which the church they hoped to destroy had merged with the monarchy to which they repeatedly declared their loyalty. Likewise, royal officials and generals, standing on the cusp of the Enlightenment, never grasped the apocalyptic and mystical nature of the prophetism that fired and motivated the rebellion. Despite its failure, the revolt did ensure that Protestantism would never be entirely rooted out of this region of France, and it laid the groundwork for the reestablishment of a more orthodox French Reformed Church in the years that followed.

See also **Nantes, Edict of; Popular Protest and Rebellions; Reformation, Protestant.**

BIBLIOGRAPHY

Primary Source

Misson, Maximilien, ed. *Le théatre sacré des Cévennes.* Paris, 1996. Eyewitness accounts of prophetism and Camisard memoirs of the conflict originally published in 1707.

Secondary Sources

Bosc, Henri. *La guerre des Cévennes, 1702–1710.* 6 vols. Montpellier, France, 1985–1993.

Joutard, Philippe. *La légende des Camisards. Une sensibilité au passé.* Paris, 1977.

W. GREGORY MONAHAN

CAMÕES, LUÍS VAZ DE (c. 1525–1580), Portuguese poet. Luís Vaz de Camões, Portugal's first great poet, was probably born in Lisbon, and he died in that city on 10 June 1580. The author of his country's national epic, *Os Lusíadas* (1572; The Lusiads), Camões was also a playwright—*Anfitriões* (The Amphytrions), *El-Rei Seleuco* (King Seleucus), and *Filodemo*—and a prolific lyric poet. His work in all the lyric genres of his age—odes, elegies, eclogues, songs, and sonnets—was collected and published posthumously in *Rhytmos* (1595; Rhythms).

Facts in Camões's biography are sparse, shadowy, and often indeterminate. It is thought that he came from a noble family from the north of Portugal, probably Galicia (now part of Spain). Because of specific geographical references in his writings as well as his obvious erudition, he was probably university trained, although tradition also has it that he left the University of Coimbra before completing his studies. As a nobleman he was received at court, and as a poet he was invited to aristocratic salons.

In 1546 Camões was banished from Lisbon, putatively because of his forbidden love for Catarina de Ataíde, a lady of the court (celebrated in poetry by Elizabeth Barrett Browning), or, even less likely, because of an indiscreet allusion to the king in his play *El-Rei Seleuco*. For two years, beginning in 1547, Camões was in military service in Ceuta, the Moroccan setting for the first Portuguese overseas victory in 1415. While there Camões suffered the loss of his right eye in a skirmish or fight. In 1553, back in Lisbon, King John III (ruled 1521–1557) pardoned him for wounding a royal officer in a street fight. At this time Camões was sent to India in the king's service. He spent the next seventeen years exiled from Lisbon, serving in Goa and in Macau (China), where tradition has it that he began to write *Os Lusíadas*. Evidence culled from his poetry seems to indicate that, during his time in the East, Camões participated in naval expeditions, fought in battles, suffered imprisonment, and survived shipwreck. His shipwreck survival in the Mekong Delta is enhanced by the legendary detail that he succeeded in swimming ashore while holding aloft the manuscript of his still-unfinished epic.

In 1570 Camões finally made it back to Lisbon, where two years later he published *Os Lusíadas*. In recompense for his poem or perhaps for services in the Far East, he was granted a small royal pension by the young and ill-fated King Sebastian (ruled 1557–1578). Tradition has it that, his pension notwithstanding, Camões died improvident in a Lisbon

Luís Vaz de Camões. GETTY IMAGES

poorhouse—a fate the American writer Herman Melville memorialized in poetry three centuries later.

Os Lusíadas, which was soon translated into several European languages, is considered Camões's masterwork. The first of many translations into English, Richard Fanshaw's *The Lusiad, or Portugals Historicall Poem*, appeared in 1655. The most truly national epic of the early modern era, *Os Lusíadas* has also been regarded as the first notable poetic apology for worldwide European mercantilism and empire. Born a generation after Vasco da Gama (c. 1460–1524) became the first Portuguese sailor to reach India by rounding the Cape of Good Hope (1497–1498), Camões constructed his poem celebrating the drama and glories of Portuguese history around the stages of Gama's voyage. Among Camões's most effective creations in this historical poem is Adamastor, the monstrous Spirit of the Cape who awaits the Portuguese mariners. The figure of Adamastor has suffered varied interpretations and adaptations. He has been transformed, particularly in southern Africa, into the sinister symbol of

Europe's own perfidy, betrayal, and violence in Africa.

Posthumously Camões's position as a lyric poet has been characterized by numerous attempts to enlarge the canon. The 65 poems attributed to Camões in 1595 were joined by 287 others by 1860. The vogue for Camões's lyrics reached its apogee with the spread of literary Romanticism throughout Europe. In the English-speaking world, Lord Strangford's loose and permissive translations in 1803 set the tone and laid the lines for the appreciation of the Portuguese poet for the rest of the century. Among Camões's most famous lyrics are the sonnet "Alma minha gentil" (Oh gentle spirit), his most frequently translated poem, and "Sobolos rios que vão" (By the rivers of Babylon), a magnificent personal meditation. The latter, which Lope de Vega once called "the Pearl of all poetry," starts with a paraphrase of Psalm 137 of the Old Testament.

See also **Gama, Vasco da; Portugal; Portuguese Literature and Language.**

BIBLIOGRAPHY

Primary Source

The Lusiads. Translated by Leonard Bacon. New York, 1950. Annotated translation.

Secondary Sources

Bell, Aubrey F. G. *Luís de Camões.* London, 1923. Biocriticism.

Hart, Henry Hersch. *Luís de Camoëns and the Epic of the Lusiads.* Norman, Okla., 1962.

Monteiro, George. *The Presence of Camões.* Lexington, Ky., 1996. Influence on English-language writers.

GEORGE MONTEIRO

CANALS. *See* **Communication and Transportation.**

CANON LAW. *See* **Law: Canon Law.**

CANOVA, ANTONIO (1757–1822), Italian sculptor. The leading proponent of neoclassi-

cism and Italy's last internationally famous artist, the sculptor Antonio Canova, born in the village of Possagno in 1757, rose to celebrity from humble origins. The son and grandson of provincial stonecarvers in the rural Veneto, he was brought up and trained by his paternal grandfather, Pasino Canova, after his father Pietro's death in 1761 and the almost immediate remarriage of his mother, Angela Zardo. He attracted the attention of members of the patrician Falier family and, with their help, moved to Venice, where he studied sculpture in the studio of Giuseppe Bernardi (c. 1696–1774). There he learned to work in a rococo naturalistic idiom that he quickly abandoned after his permanent move to Rome in 1780.

In Rome, the center of artistic innovation and birthplace of neoclassicism, Canova was supported by a pension from the Venetian senate and lodged with the Serene Republic's ambassador to the Holy See, Girolamo Zulian. It was a commission from Zulian, *Theseus and the Dead Minotaur* (1781–1783), that initially established Canova's reputation as a neoclassical sculptor of great promise. The success of the Zulian statue earned him the commission for the tomb of Pope Clement XIV Ganganelli (1783–1787) for the Roman basilica of the Holy Apostles and a second funerary monument to the Venetian Pope Clement XIII Rezzonico for Saint Peter's (1787–1792). Papal tombs, the most prestigious commissions possible for sculptors, were erected in public spaces and listed in guidebooks, facts that helped to promote Canova's reputation far beyond Rome.

The French invasion of the Papal States in 1796 and the collapse of the pontifical government of Pius VI in 1798 sent Canova home to the Austrian-ruled Veneto, where he lived in exile as an opponent of the French puppet Roman Republic (1798–1799). From Possagno, he journeyed to Vienna to help gain support for the deposed pope and received the commission for his most important tomb, the moving *Monument to the Archduchess Maria Christina of Austria,* erected in the church of the Augustinians in Vienna in 1805. His Austrian contacts led to additional commissions, including *Theseus Struggling with the Centaur* (1804–1819).

Despite wars and political upheaval, Canova was able to maintain a flourishing professional practice

Antonio Canova. *Theseus Struggling with the Centaur.* ©MASSIMO LISTRI/CORBIS

after 1800 because he refused to allow politics to determine his patrons. During the hegemony of Napoleon from 1800 to 1814, he often worked for members of the Bonaparte family, executing statues for Napoleon himself (*Napoleon as Mars the Peacemaker,* 1803–1806), for Bonaparte's mother Letizia (*Madame Mère as Agrippina,* 1804–1807), and for the emperor's sister Pauline (*Pauline Borghese as Venus Victrix,* 1804–1808), among others. As a conservative Catholic and Venetian patriot (the French had destroyed the political independence of Venice), Canova was essentially francophobic. The question of cynicism in working for the Bonapartes is still a matter of scholarly debate.

The sculptor's admiration for Napoleon's first wife, Joséphine, and his delight in working for her, however, are beyond dispute. She was an Old Regime aristocrat who wished only to have the best specimens of Canova's chisel for her gallery at the château de Malmaison. Canova found her highly sympathetic and executed several works for her such as *Hebe* (1800–1805), *Dancer* (1805–1812), *Paris* (1807–1812), and *The Three Graces* (1812–1816). The Malmaison gallery briefly formed the finest private collection of Canova's sculpture in existence and featured the graceful, elegant mythological figures that were the artist's specialty. These statues passed into the Russian imperial collections after

Joséphine's death in 1814 and are still exhibited in the Hermitage in St. Petersburg.

Elegant, graceful, coyly erotic, and smooth-surfaced marble statues of mythological and literary figures were also extremely popular among Canova's British patrons, who formed the majority of the sculptor's clients, especially after 1814. He executed *Psyche* (1789–1792) for Henry Blundell, a second version of *The Three Graces* (1815–1817) for John Russell, sixth duke of Bedford, and *Mars and Venus* (1816–1821) for the Prince Regent George, who also commissioned *Monument to the Last Stuarts* (1817–1819) for Saint Peter's. While in London in 1815, Canova testified before the parliamentary committee in favor of the acquisition of the Elgin Marbles from the Parthenon in Athens. British assistance to Canova while he was in Paris in 1815 to oversee the repatriation from the former Musée Napoléon of stolen works of art was crucial to Italy's recovery of a highly significant part of its cultural patrimony.

Canova's last years were spent in executing commissions for various British patrons and in the construction and decoration of a parish church in Possagno, which still stands as a monument to his Catholic piety, fame, and neoclassical aesthetic. He died in Venice in 1822.

See also **Neoclassicism; Sculpture; Venice, Art in.**

BIBLIOGRAPHY

Johns, Christopher M. S. *Antonio Canova and the Politics of Patronage in Revolutionary and Napoleonic Europe.* Berkeley, 1998.

Licht, Fred. *Canova.* New York, 1983.

Pavanello, Giuseppe, and Giandomenico Romanelli, eds. *Canova.* Venice, 1992.

CHRISTOPHER M. S. JOHNS

CAPITALISM. Europe went through remarkable economic transformations between 1500 and 1800, including agricultural change, urbanization, industrial development, commercial expansion, and growing financial sophistication. Capital was accumulated and productively invested; it helped to create (and became increasingly essential to) the new forms of social organization used to exploit economic opportunities. Labor became more of a commodity to be bought and sold. Occupational diversification proceeded alongside a growing polarization of wealth, creating a large group of wage-dependent laborers and an emerging, but increasingly assertive, middle class that embraced the productive ideal.

These changes were once thought to be associated with a fundamental transition from one type of economic, social, and political form (feudalism) to another (capitalism). However, economic change in early modern Europe is better conceived as a changing balance between sectors and regions, some of which moved rapidly, others only slowly. Overlapping (if sometimes contradictory) forces helped Europe to become more capitalist over time, but noncapitalist forms existed alongside this trend and shaped the path it took.

Different degrees of capitalism coexisted in constantly changing alignments from the Middle Ages to the nineteenth century, and all regions of Europe had some dynamism at some periods. The richest "core" parts of Europe in 1500 were the lands ruled by the Habsburgs in Spain, northern Italy, southern Germany, and the Low Countries. Northern Europe was, by comparison, economically peripheral. By 1650 the economic hub of Europe had shifted irrevocably to the northwest seaboard, leaving the Mediterranean as the "periphery."

COMMERCIAL CAPITALISM
At the end of the Middle Ages, Europe's largely subsistence economies were small, fragmented, and lacking dynamism. Demand was slack, and what trade existed was in foodstuffs and a few luxuries. Goods needed an expanding market, which extralocal commerce seemed to provide by short-circuiting some of the inherent constraints on economic growth. Thus began greater intra-European trade and, crucially, the voyages of discovery, which—for better or worse—brought Europeans into direct contact with the wider world. Supplies of new goods were brought to Europe, and new demands were created: for commodities like sugar, tea, and tobacco, and for semidurables like crockery or cotton and silk clothes. European manufactures found new markets abroad.

It was once thought that the profits so earned were concentrated in the hands of capitalists, who helped to fund further economic development. Direct and indirect benefits accrued. Production for exchange rather than use became the norm, and with it a specialization of function, or "division of labor." Successful merchants could diversify into industry. Transportation and transaction costs would be reduced by innovations in carrying. Ships had to be built, outfitted, and victualed, further stimulating production and technological innovation. Long-term credit, changes in the law on multiple ownership, which made possible "joint-stock companies," and increasingly sophisticated exchange facilities (including banknotes) fostered the rational and systematic maximization of net returns, which is a keynote of capitalism.

Historians conventionally believed that international trade, especially with the New World, was the prime force behind the primitive accumulation of capital, leading eventually to the industrial and commercial revolutions of the nineteenth century. Certain significant mercantile groups in the towns of northwest Europe benefited, but the overall stimulus to early capitalism should not be exaggerated. Overseas commerce was a risky business involving no more than one percent of European production. Dynamic and glamorous as international trade may seem, more mundane aspects of early modern economic life need to be considered. In order of numbers employed, commerce came a long way behind agriculture and industry. Once thought less dynamic than trade, the agricultural world in particular had considerable potential for economic change because of the nature of social class relations in some areas of rural Europe.

AGRARIAN CAPITALISM
Social status and wealth in rural Europe were determined by the legal rights people had to the land they worked and consequently by their share of the surplus they extracted. Some parts of Europe had many peasant proprietors, but mostly the land was owned by a few rich people and worked by "tenant" farmers and landless or land-poor laborers. In France the political needs of the late-medieval French crown led it to foster peasant proprietorship. This created a substantial body of semi-independent peasantry, but they were generally poor, and the rural economy was relatively immobile. Scandinavia was similar. In contrast, the English peasantry was politically weaker, and independent freeholders

were gradually turned into tenant farmers. This facilitated subsequent social change (expropriation) and economic improvements (based ultimately on consolidation of holdings) required for capitalism. Ownership of the means of production became concentrated in fewer hands, landholding units became larger, and specialized techniques were introduced to raise yields. Thus, fluid social relations of production were adapted to capitalism, and other, increasingly capitalistic, means of raising net profitability were introduced.

This is true of parts of northwest Europe, notably England. Yet a simple imbalance of power relationships in favor of the owners of the means of production did not necessarily promote capitalist development. Powerful landowners east of the River Elbe reacted to growing western demands for grain during the sixteenth-century population expansion by exploiting more intensively their feudal privileges over serf labor. For example, the rights of Russian lords over their peasants were consolidated and extended by comprehensive laws passed in 1649. Serfdom in the east was characterized by restricted personal freedom and the exploitation of the peasantry by legal and political rather than purely economic means. Labor power had not been turned into a simple commodity for, in addition, the relation between capital and labor retained a personal dimension, and workers had means of support other than selling their labor. The experience of eastern Europe is a reminder that a commercialized economy is not the same as a capitalist economy. It also shows that economic change did not always bring with it more capitalistic forms of social organization and that a polarized society is not necessarily a capitalist one.

INDUSTRIAL CAPITALISM
Commercial explanations of capitalist development, which focus on extrinsic forces, may underestimate the internal dynamism of European agriculture, industry, and towns. Some regions of Europe had been net importers of food and exporters of finished products since the Middle Ages. The economically dynamic northern Italian city-states are an example in the late Middle Ages. During the sixteenth century, the Dutch imported as much as a third of their grain needs from the Baltic, allowing specialization within pastoral agriculture alongside a level of urbanization and industrial employment that would

have been unthinkable if their economy had been closed.

Just as some regions depended on trade, so too did most European families. Far from being merely self-sufficient, production for exchange was common. It is unlikely that most households made items such as clothes for their own use, because the manufacturing process from raw material to finished garment was far too complicated and time-consuming. Even in the more isolated economies there was a considerable degree of specialization and therefore exchange. Incomes fluctuated, but in good times there were surpluses to spend on marketplace purchases. Thus, there were opportunities for growth and change even within "traditional" economies.

Factories and capitalism are conventionally linked, but most early modern industrial production was located in the home and in the countryside: it is commonly known as "cottage industry." Across northwest Europe between a sixth and a third of all men living in the countryside were primarily employed in nonagricultural jobs such as textile manufacture. These rural domestic producers were both independent artisans producing for local markets and dependent employees whose work might reach extralocal markets. The latter form is known as "putting-out," and its advantage to capitalists was that it was cheap and flexible. Breaking free of guild restrictions on quality, price, and employment, urban merchant entrepreneurs were able to find plenty of eager workers among the underemployed poor of rural Europe. In the major cloth-producing areas such as Picardy in northeast France or the English West Country, these entrepreneurs bought raw wool or flax to be prepared and spun into yarn. They then gave the yarn to specialist weavers and bought back the cloth, which was taken for finishing and finally for selling, often in national or international markets. Urban specialists added more value to the product by dyeing cloth and tailoring it, but the majority of ordinary woolen and linen fabric was made in the countryside.

Putting-out thus embodied important capitalistic elements. Capital was controlled not by individual workers, but by entrepreneurs; the production process involved a clear division of labor; workers were paid wages, for, while some might own their own looms, the only commodity they were selling was their labor; and goods were sold in nonlocal markets. Capitalism is ultimately defined, as Karl Marx (1818–1883) argued, not by the performance of an economy, but by its specific relations of production between capital and labor. However, small-scale production organized by master weavers rather than merchants continued to characterize the woolen-cloth industry of the seventeenth-century Low Countries. Even within a single English county like Yorkshire, putting-out and independent artisan cloth production coexisted. And rather than a linear progression from independence to dependence, workers sometimes moved back and forth between them.

URBAN CAPITALISM

It is understandable that historians searching for early modern capitalism focused on agrarian change and on the agricultural origins of industry. Most Europeans lived on the land and it provided not only their subsistence, but also most of the raw materials for industry (wood, leather, and fibers for making cloth); apart from wind and water, energy came mainly from organic rather than mineral sources. Some 8 percent of all Europeans lived in towns of 10,000 or more in 1600 and 10 percent in 1800. Most of this growth can be accounted for by a trebling in England's proportion from under 6 percent to over 20 percent. London alone grew from 200,000 inhabitants to nearly 600,000 during the seventeenth century and to one million by 1800. As early as 1700 nearly a third of the Dutch lived in towns, but there and elsewhere in continental Europe the percentage did not grow any further. In eastern Europe the urban component remained minimal—as little as 3 percent in 1800.

Despite their often small size and low proportion of national population, towns were the motors of economic change. They functioned as centers of production (especially finishing and luxury goods), transportation and exchange; they provided legal, financial, and educational services; they served as bases for secular and ecclesiastical bureaucracies; they acted as communications nodes, providing verbal, written, and printed information; they offered increasingly sophisticated leisure facilities. Their impact was felt in all economic sectors. While productivity in French agriculture was generally low, the area around Paris had yields comparable with England; Dutch farming was highly advanced because of the large urban markets.

Towns and capitalism were not always connected. Towns helped to modernize the economies of northwestern Europe, but they had little effect on Russian agriculture, trade, and industry because they were simply military or administrative outposts in a sea of feudalism. Southern Italy had many towns, but they were essentially dormitories for farmers and did not offer the range of industrial, commercial, and service occupations found elsewhere in Europe. Some have even questioned whether the urban elites of seventeenth- and eighteenth-century France were "bourgeois" in any meaningful sense. Most aspired to belong to the nobility and, when able, tried to ape their social norms and economic behavior—including a disdain for trade and a preference for conspicuous consumption. Yet throughout the period there was a strong association between urbanization and the development of different stages of capitalism—in northern Italy, then the Netherlands, then England.

IDEOLOGIES OF CAPITALISM

Towns were hothouses of capitalist development, but other factors also nourished the acquisitive and productive ideal. From the mid-sixteenth century Calvinism appealed to those who believed that wealth was a sign of God's favor and that glorifying God could be done through acquisition. Yet some Calvinists believed it was wrong to exploit other people, and different faiths have also been credited with fostering capitalism: for example, Jews had traditionally been untroubled by Christian reservations about charging interest. Nor was Catholicism an enemy of financial sophistication, for north Italian bankers dominated the commercial and public finances of the fifteenth-century Mediterranean world. Literacy and numeracy had also been high in this region, especially in the cities, during the Renaissance, but it was in the northwest of Europe that literacy developed most rapidly and extensively in the seventeenth and eighteenth centuries.

In the eighteenth century secular intelligentsia took up the banner of capitalism. Enlightenment thinkers analyzed, celebrated, and promoted getting and spending, arguing that commercial intercourse was one way of promoting the social interaction that was the basis of personal and societal improvement. Changes in attitude not only affected the owners of capital. An "industrious revolution," marked by a growing propensity to work in order to consume, fueled the demand side of growth. For many people, incomes and consumption rose. Marx thought that workers would labor more just to stand still, but the capitalism that developed in early modern Europe was fed by a desire not for subsistence, but for betterment, not for "needs," but for "wants." The consolidation and glorification of private property that occurred in the West was an important precondition of an "industrious revolution." In eastern Europe, by contrast, the idea of individual ownership of goods was subordinated to that of family or community interest.

While Enlightenment writers eventually functioned as the ideologues of nineteenth-century laissez-faire capitalism, they did not come from such an environment. A body of laws and assumptions about economic regulation, which were designed to promote social stability over individual gain, restricted the free market. At best, attitudes toward capitalism remained ambivalent. It was "virtuous" to engage in commerce, but only if market relations were equalized, competition was fair, and exchange therefore equitable. Throughout the early modern period, capitalism remained a contested terrain. Just as Calvinism had provided only contingent support for capitalism in the seventeenth century, Enlightenment thinkers saw property and gain entailing moral and civil obligations—both against a backdrop of enduring political support for intervention in support of a "moral economy."

The increasingly centralized territorial states might facilitate, protect, and exploit economic expansion and consolidation, but when there were competing interests, political priorities almost invariably outweighed capitalist ones. Countries like Spain ruined themselves on imperial commitments, although warfare did help indirectly to promote certain aspects of the development of capitalism. Nor were economic and political advantage the only policy considerations. Alongside sometimes rampant economic individualism there existed a greater or lesser commitment to social collectivism. Government policy recognized and encouraged capitalism, but it also tried so to structure its development as to limit its most destructive effects. For its victims there were poor-relief schemes revised and augmented from their medieval origins to cope with the many new vulnerabilities that capitalism brought.

CONCLUSION

Growth, decline, and stagnation coexisted in different sectors and regions of early modern Europe. The preconditions of and paths to progress differed, but the regions that did foster capitalism had shared characteristics. High levels of literacy and urbanization, sophisticated judicial systems, dense and long-established networks for exchanging goods and people, and technological advances unified the North Sea region and enabled it to progress at a faster rate. At the other end of the spectrum were southern and eastern Europe, where high production costs, inadequate transportation, extreme polarization of wealth, illiteracy, a small and undynamic urban sector, and heavy-handed political intervention inhibited economic change.

Change could also have very different implications. Involvement in European or world commerce was a social solvent in England and the Netherlands but involved a hardening of traditional relationships east of the Elbe. At every turn, existing social forms, cultural priorities, and political structures influenced the extent of economic change. Its effects were also contingent. Domestic arrangements and the cultural preferences that underlay them shaped the course of economic development at least as much as capitalism affected the family.

Incomplete as it was even in 1800, the development of a capitalist economy had progressed—albeit hesitantly—especially in and around the North Sea Basin. A proletariat, a class that had no means of subsistence other than wages, was emerging in town and country. From being a conglomeration of parceled regional economies, continent-wide exchanges of grain and of certain raw materials and manufactures helped to create a more unified entity. A rudimentary "world economy" was being founded. New products and new markets were outdating the mercantilist assumption of a "fixed cake." Ideas of intervention and stasis were being replaced by laissez-faire and dynamic growth as the balance of attitudes shifted in favor of capitalism. Capital was being accumulated and used in an increasingly sophisticated and productive way. Technological change had not yet broken down the barriers within traditional economies, making possible the exponential growth of the nineteenth and twentieth centuries, but labor productivity was rising. A fully capitalist European economy was in the making.

See also **Agriculture; Banking and Credit; Commerce and Markets; Communication and Transportation; Economic Crises; Enlightenment; Feudalism; Industrial Revolution; Industry; Inflation; Laborers; Liberalism, Economic; Money and Coinage; Proto-Industry; Serfdom; Shipping; Stock Exchanges; Textile Industry.**

BIBLIOGRAPHY

Aston, Trevor H., and C. H. E. Philpin, eds. *The Brenner Debate: Agrarian Class Structure and Economic Development in Pre-Industrial Europe.* Cambridge, U.K., and New York, 1985.

Braudel, Fernand. *Civilization and Capitalism, 15th–18th Century.* Translated by Siân Reynolds. 3 vols. London, 1981–1984.

De Vries, Jan. *The Economy of Europe in an Age of Crisis, 1600–1750.* Cambridge, U.K., 1976.

Duplessis, Robert S. *Transitions to Capitalism in Early Modern Europe.* New York, 1997.

Kriedte, Peter, Hans Medick, and Jürgen Schlumbohm. *Industrialization before Industrialization: Rural Industry in the Genesis of Capitalism.* Translated by Beate Schemp. Cambridge, U.K., 1981.

Macfarlane, Alan. *The Origins of English Individualism: The Family, Property, and Social Transition.* Oxford, 1978.

Prak, Maarten, ed. *Early Modern Capitalism: Economic and Social Change in Europe, 1400–1800.* New York, 2001.

Tilly, Charles. *Coercion, Capital, and European States, A.D. 990–1990.* Oxford, 1990.

Wallerstein, Immanuel. *The Modern World-System.* 3 vols. New York, 1974, 1980, 1989.

Wrightson, Keith. *Earthly Necessities: Economic Lives in Early Modern Britain.* New Haven, 2000.

R. A. HOUSTON

CARAVAGGIO AND CARAVAGGISM.

Michelangelo Merisi da Caravaggio (born 1571, Milan or Caravaggio; died 18 July 1610, Porto Ercole), called Caravaggio, was the most radical painter in post-Tridentine Italy. In his religious and mythological compositions, he mocked Roman classical tradition by depicting his models—"people in the street" rather than antique marbles—in an unidealized, naturalistic style. He staged his scenes in the costumes and settings of contemporary society, not those of the ancient past. Even the Carracci, who in the 1580s had revolutionized Italian painting at their academy in Bologna, had not attacked tradition (the artificiality and precious classicism of late mannerism) so violently. Symptomatic of this same mentality was Caravaggio's elevation of still life painting (the lowest category of subject matter in the hierarchy of genres) to the level of history painting (the prime example is the *Still Life with a Basket of Fruit*, c. 1600–1601, Ambrosiana, Milan). Caravaggio had the audacity to announce to the Roman art world, for whom drawing the human figure with the beauty of Raphael and the antique was the sine qua non of great art, that "it was as difficult for him to make a good painting of flowers as one of figures." For Caravaggio, the imitation of nature—not idealized nature—was the goal of art.

Caravaggio's most important innovation was the creation of a new vocabulary for depicting moments of divine revelation, conversion, or ecstasy by cloaking his scenes in a bold chiaroscuro (transparent shading) penetrated by a wave of bright light entering the composition from a high, unseen source. The drama of light and dark, always carefully integrated with the poignant gestures, postures, and facial expressions of his actors, gives Caravaggio's images a heightened realism and psychological depth unique to late Renaissance art. It also doubled as a powerful metaphor of divine agency. Caravaggio represents major themes of the Catholic Reformation—poverty and charity, death and redemption, doubt and faith—in a language that is at once populist, poetic, and spiritual.

EARLY COMMISSIONS AND CARAVAGGIO'S ROMAN PERIOD

The first child of Fermo Merisi (d. 1577) and his second wife Lucia Aratori (d. 1590), Caravaggio grew up under the protection of Francesco Sforza, Marchese di Caravaggio (d. 1583), for whom Fermo served as architect and majordomo. Sforza's widow, Costanza Colonna (d. 1622), provided the artist with introductions and protection throughout his life.

Caravaggio's earliest period, when he was apprenticed in Milan (c. 1584–1588) to the Bergamesque painter Simone Peterzano, a pupil of Titian, is still a mystery. No securely attributed works made before Caravaggio moved to Rome have been discovered. But judging from the earliest known pictures, it is clear that he had studied numerous Lombard and Venetian masters: Savoldo, Moretto, and Moroni as well as Titian, Giorgione, Lotto, and Palma Vecchio. Caravaggio's debt to Leonardo, whose naturalism and sfumato (modeling through delicate shading) had transformed Lombard painting in the early sixteenth century, was significant. An early biographer (Bellori, 1672) states that in Milan Caravaggio earned a living making portraits. The strong visual and psychological bond Caravaggio's compositions create between protagonist and spectator no doubt springs in part from this early interest in portraiture. His practice, when executing narrative scenes, of painting directly from the model rather than working from drawings (the norm in Rome) may also stem from the same experiences.

By 1592, or 1593 at the latest, Caravaggio made his way to Rome. He took on menial work until being employed by the Cavalier d'Arpino (Giuseppe Cesari), the most sought-after fresco painter in the city. A practitioner of late *maniera* style, d'Arpino seems nonetheless to have appreciated Caravaggio's naturalistic gifts and hired him to paint flowers and fruits (whether these were independent still lifes by Caravaggio or details added to d'Arpino's larger compositions is unknown). Caravaggio's earliest pictures, such as the *Boy with a Basket of Fruit* or the *Bacchino Malato* (Sick Little Bacchus) of c. 1592–1593 (both Galleria Borghese, Rome) are dazzling displays of still life painting. Their half-length treatment of eroticized boys in off-the-shoulder, togalike costumes also attracted attention. Two collectors in particular, Cardinal Francesco Maria del Monte and his friend Marchese Vincenzo Giustiniani, both connoisseurs of music and painting, purchased or commissioned numerous works by Caravaggio in this mode. Del Monte, who hosted the artist in his palace in c. 1596–1600, owned at least ten paintings by him, including the *Concert of Youths* (c. 1595, Metropolitan Museum, New York). Giustiniani owned at least thirteen, including the *Lute Player* (c. 1596, Hermitage, St. Petersburg). The androgynous protagonists and their solicitous gazes have been interpreted in a homoerotic key by several scholars, who note Del Monte's reputation as a pederast. Many questions remain, however, about Caravaggio's own sexuality

Caravaggio. *The Calling of St. Matthew,* in the Contarelli Chapel, San Luigi dei Francesi, Rome. ©ARALDO DE LUCA/CORBIS

(or bisexuality), since there is ample evidence that he had relationships with women. Moreover, it is important to note that with few exceptions, such pictures cease once Caravaggio became known as a serious religious painter. In these provocative paintings, Caravaggio has taken a Venetian tradition of half-length, portraitlike images of sexy females posing as mythological goddesses and flipped the gender. A good example of this practice is the *Drunken Bacchus* of c. 1596 (Uffizi, Florence). The

fine line Caravaggio walks here between realism and parody is what makes his art so modern.

In 1599, Caravaggio's career took a major turn when he received his first commission for a public work. Left incomplete by d'Arpino, the task of decorating the Contarelli Chapel of the French national church, San Luigi dei Francesi, gave the young artist his first opportunity to paint site-specific works. His paintings (laterals) for the side walls, *The Calling of St. Matthew* and *The Martyrdom of St. Matthew,* are exceptional in their clever compositional structure, skewing perspective axes so as to draw the spectator into the scene. His bridging of the space of the image and the space of the spectator—sometimes called "coextensive" space—would become a central feature of seventeenth-century painting. His treatment of light sources is also part of the integration of the work into its environment. Especially in the case of the *Calling,* we are to understand the light streaking across the wall behind Christ and Matthew as somehow connected with the natural source of illumination in the chapel—the window directly above the altar. He developed these ideas in his next public commission, in the Cerasi Chapel at S.M. del Popolo, where, in competition with Annibale Carracci's robust, classicizing altarpiece, he painted laterals of the *Crucifixion of St. Peter* and the *Conversion of St. Paul* (c. 1600–1601). In the latter, Paul, set diagonally to the picture plane, seems nearly to fall out of the frame toward the viewer.

His first version of the altarpiece for the Contarelli Chapel, *The Inspiration of St. Matthew* (the date is disputed, 1599–1602; formerly Berlin, destroyed), was rejected, but, significantly, it was purchased by Giustiniani. Caravaggio was given another chance, and his second version, painted in 1602–1603, remains in situ. Much has been made of Caravaggio's bad luck with religious patrons in Rome. Indeed, several other pictures were rejected (one or both of the Cerasi laterals) or removed from their original location (the *Madonna dei Palafrenieri,* Galleria Borghese, Rome). But only the *Death of the Virgin* (c. 1603, Louvre, Paris), an altarpiece for the Discalced Carmelites of S.M. della Scala, represents a clear-cut case of Caravaggio's decorum-breaching, earthbound interpretations of divine mysteries meeting with the disapproval of ecclesiastical authorities. It has been suggested that Caravaggio's violent behavior—his numerous run-ins with authorities for brawling, shouting insults, carrying a sword without a license—had so badly damaged his reputation that patrons no longer wanted his works in their churches. But this is a myth built loosely on the basis of negative remarks from biased critics. One biographer, his fellow painter Giovanni Baglione, sued Caravaggio for libel in 1603. Another, Giovanni Pietro Bellori, writing half a century after Caravaggio's death, was a partisan of the classicizing trend begun by the Carracci and developed by Domenichino, Poussin, and others.

FLIGHT FROM ROME AND LATE WORKS

Caravaggio's Roman period came to an abrupt end when he murdered his former friend Ranuccio Tomassoni in a gang fight on 28 May 1606. He fled the Eternal City, never to return. The artist probably received shelter from the Colonna family in Paliano or nearby towns during the summer months before making his way to Naples—safely outside the jurisdiction of the papal authorities—by September 1606. In the nine months or so that he lived in the Spanish-controlled city, Caravaggio produced some of his most remarkable and influential altarpieces. Chief among these is *The Seven Works of Mercy,* completed by January 1607, for the charitable confraternity of the Pio Monte della Misericordia (in situ). Caravaggio's palette, which had become significantly darker in the last works in Rome (such as the *Madonna of Loreto* altarpiece in Sant'Agostino of c. 1605–1606), now restricts itself almost exclusively to a simple, nearly monochromatic array of dark earth tones and silvery whites. The occasional flash of red or yellow nearly jumps off the canvas. Caravaggio's brushwork is now noticeably looser and his models—poor, rough types culled from the Neapolitan streets—more realistically described than ever before.

By 12 July 1607 Caravaggio had made his way to the island of Malta, where he sought a knighthood from the Grandmaster of the Knights of St. John, Alof de Wignacourt (reigned 1601–1622). The artist painted a flattering full-length portrait of the Frenchman with one of his pages (Louvre, Paris). For the Oratory of San Giovanni Decollato annexed to the Church of St. John in Valletta, the Knights' conventual church, Caravaggio painted what many regard as his supreme masterpiece, *The Beheading of St. John the Baptist* (in situ), in which the artist signed his name in the "blood" oozing from the saint's severed neck. This is the only work, so far as we know, that he signed in his career. Though the artist fulfilled his one-year novitiate and received his title, he committed a crime and was imprisoned. He fled Malta in late September or early October 1608 and made his way to Syracuse.

He was defrocked in absentia by the Knights on 1 December 1608.

Caravaggio's brief Sicilian period, during which he moved from Syracuse to Messina and then to Palermo before returning to Naples in September or October of 1609, yielded some of his most moving altarpieces. His revolutionary compositional method developed in Malta, in which a concentrated group of figures is set into a cavernous space of which the top half is left almost completely unarticulated, is made even more expressive by the austerity and compactness of his Sicilian designs. In the *Burial of St. Lucy* for S. Lucia al Sepolcro, Syracuse (before December 1608), or the *Adoration of the Shepherds* of 1609 (Museo Regionale, Messina), Caravaggio compresses his figures into a single mass of humanity absorbed in a single action. Individuality has been reduced. Gestures are nearly eliminated. So thinly painted that large areas of the dark red ground are left exposed, these canvases begin a new trend that Caravaggio would not live to develop. The absorptive quality of his dark chiaroscuro in concert with the introspective glances of his actors generate a pathos unequaled in Italian painting.

Caravaggio's second Naples sojourn is not well documented other than a report of a near fatal slashing of his face by a group of armed men. Under the impression that one of his patrons had set the stage for him to receive a papal pardon, he set sail for Rome in the summer of 1610. However, upon arriving at Porto Ercole he was the victim of mistaken identity—his goods were seized and he was put in prison. Released two days later, he contracted a fever and died soon afterward, on 18 July.

CARAVAGGISM

Much to the dismay of classic-idealist theorists (such as Bellori), Caravaggio's incisive naturalism, genrelike treatment of history scenes, and ardent colorism and tenebrism (in which a painting's dark atmosphere is pierced by a beam of light) became more than a passing fad. Caravaggism, a modern term used to describe the international artistic movement generated by Caravaggio's style, had a considerable life until the early 1630s. It died out first in Rome, in the early 1620s, when the Bolognese Pope Gregory XV (reigned 1621–1623) made the Eternal City a mecca for the Carracci's

pupils and followers such as Domenichino, Lanfranco, and Guercino. Many of the Caravaggisti changed styles or left town (some did both). Caravaggism endured longest in Naples and Sicily, where the style, in its most humble, pietistic, and graphically violent form (for example, in the works of G. B. Caracciolo and especially Jusepe de Ribera), seems to have struck a particular chord in these Spanish-controlled populations. Even in Naples, however, the Bolognese eventually made major inroads. Caravaggio and his followers generally did not practice fresco painting. But many of the great commissions of the mature baroque era called for illusionistic ceiling and mural painting. Both in Rome and Naples, as the Counter-Reformation turned to a more "triumphalist" mode of thought and expression, Caravaggism increasingly must have seemed old-fashioned and dour. The church no longer wanted its saints to be shown as lower-class types with dirty feet, ragged clothes, and sunburned faces crouched on the floors of humble dwellings. Instead they promoted the billowing draperies, levitating bodies, and angel-filled light-and-cloud shows of Lanfranco and Cortona.

In most cases, Caravaggism is not really a style unto itself so much as the grafting of popular elements of Caravaggio's art (boys with plumed hats, hidden candles or lanterns in a murky room, lowclass types impersonating mythological deities) on to other, sometimes even contradictory, styles. There were very few artists who imitated his homoeroticism or attempted to replicate the tension between faith and empirical knowledge that permeates all of Caravaggio's religious works.

Though there is scant evidence that Caravaggio maintained a genuine workshop in which he trained painters, there is no lack of proof of his early popularity. In Rome, Caravaggio's style caught on almost immediately. During his own lifetime, he was imitated by Orazio Gentileschi (c. 1562–c. 1647), Guido Reni (1575–1642), and Giovanni Baglione (c. 1573–1644). Each of these painters had a fully developed style of his own before experimenting with Caravaggism. Gentileschi's conversion, which began in earnest once Caravaggio had left Rome (June 1606), was the most profound and the most lasting (Reni's, by comparison, endured only about a year). In the second decade of the century, Orazio imparted his poetic brand of Caravaggism to his

Caravaggio and Caravaggism. *The Fortune Teller* by Georges de la Tour. The Metropolitan Museum of Art, New York. ©FRANCIS G. MAYER/CORBIS

gifted daughter Artemisia Gentileschi (c. 1597–after 1651), who would develop the style in a unique direction, first in Rome and then in Florence and Naples. She is especially famous for her pictures of violent subjects and female heroines, such as *Judith and Holofernes* (c. 1618, Uffizi, Florence), a theme explored in an exemplary picture of c. 1599 by Caravaggio himself (National Gallery, Rome). All of these artists specialized in history paintings, but there was one Italian Caravaggist, Bartolomeo Manfredi, who, a full decade after Caravaggio had left Rome, seized on the market for genre paintings in the mode of Caravaggio's exceedingly popular *Card Sharps* (c. 1594, Kimbell Art Museum, Fort Worth) and *Gypsy Fortune-Teller* (c. 1598, Louvre, Paris). Manfredi's concepts and techniques were

more easily imitated than Caravaggio's own; foreign artists (especially those from France and the Low Countries) working in Rome in c. 1615–1621 flocked to his studio and imitated what the seventeenth-century painter/biographer Joachim Sandrart called the "Manfredi manner." In pictures such as the *Concert* (c. 1615–1621, Pitti, Florence), Manfredi takes motifs from Caravaggio's early works and represents them in the dark colors and looser brushwork of Caravaggio's post-Roman style. He also made numerous religious and mythological pictures, mining Caravaggio's compositions for ideas.

The attraction of Caravaggism for northern Europeans was no doubt due to the fact that so much of their tradition—the naturalist ideal of Van Eyck,

Dürer, and Bruegel—was reflected and reborn in Caravaggio's art. A trio of Dutch painters from Utrecht, Dirck van Baburen, Gerrit van Honthorst, and Hendrick ter Brugghen, were active in Rome during the second and the beginning of the third decade. Their works are unsurpassed in their bold color and chiaroscuro, exotic costuming, and truly moving representations, whether of everyday life or religious subject matter. The return of these masters to Holland is an important link between Roman Caravaggism and the pictorial language of the young Rembrandt and Hals.

A number of French artists in Rome were also attracted to Manfredi's style, especially Simon Vouet, Nicolas Tournier, and Valentin de Boulogne. It used to be thought that the Caravaggists (especially the foreigners) worked mainly on the fringes of the art market. However, when one considers that Baburen, Honthorst, and Vouet all produced major works for Roman churches (as did Orazio Gentileschi and another Italian Caravaggist, Carlo Saraceni, who painted a replacement for the infamous *Death of the Virgin* commission), this old idea needs modification.

Caravaggism had practitioners in places like Siena (Rutilio Manetti) and Bologna (Leonello Spada), where the artist himself had never traveled and where his works were little known. Perhaps the most exceptional case is that of the Lorraine artist, Georges de la Tour. Poorly documented, La Tour may have visited Rome in 1640. He almost certainly knew Caravaggio's style in Lorraine through the works of the Utrecht school, especially Ter Brugghen. In pictures such as the *Penitent Magdalen* (c. 1639–1640, National Gallery, Washington, D.C.), La Tour transformed standard Caravaggesque tropes such as a candle flickering in a dark room into sublime meditations on Catholic faith and human frailty.

The phenomenal spread of Caravaggism was equaled by few movements in the history of art of the early modern period. However, unlike the baroque classicism of the Bolognese school (Reni and Guercino had a steady following straight through the eighteenth century), Caravaggism had virtually no "survivals" and only one or two strange revivals in the eighteenth century, in a handful of works by Jacques-Louis David and Joseph Wright of Derby.

See also **Carracci Family; David, Jacques-Louis; Gentileschi, Artemisia; Netherlands, Art in; Painting; Rome, Art in.**

BIBLIOGRAPHY

Bellori, Giovanni Pietro. *Le vite de' pittori, scultori e architetti moderni.* Edited by Evelina Borea. Turin, 1976. Originally published in 1672.

Calvesi, Maurizio. *Le realtà del Caravaggio.* Turin, 1990. Detailed account of Caravaggio's patrons and his religious iconography.

Christiansen, Keith. "Caravaggio and 'L'esempio davanti del naturale.'" *Art Bulletin* 68, no. 3 (Sept. 1986): 421–445. Important technical study of Caravaggio's painting procedures.

Cinotti, Mia. *Michelangelo Merisi detto Il Caravaggio: tutte le opere.* Reprinted from *I pittori bergamaschi, il seicento, vol. 1.* Bergamo, 1983. Essential for bibliography. Contains exhaustive entries on known works.

Friedlaender, Walter. *Caravaggio Studies.* Princeton, 1955. Pioneering study with translations of key texts and documents, including Caravaggio's criminal record.

Gash, John. *Caravaggio.* London, 1980.

Gregori, Mina. *Caravaggio.* Milan, 1994.

Hibbard, Howard. *Caravaggio.* New York, 1983. The best, most synthetic study on the artist, though increasingly out of date.

Langdon, Helen. *Caravaggio: A Life.* New York, 1998. Important discussion of Caravaggio's social milieu.

Longhi, Roberto. *Caravaggio.* Rev. ed., Rome, 1982. Groundbreaking study by the art historian most responsible for the rediscovery of Caravaggio.

Marini, Maurizio. *Caravaggio: pictor praestantissimus: l'iter artistico completo di uno dei massimi rivoluzionari dell'arte di tutti i tempi.* 3rd ed. Rome, 2001.

Moir, Alfred. *The Italian Followers of Caravaggio.* 2 vols. Cambridge, Mass., 1967.

Nicolson, Benedict. *Caravaggism in Europe.* 3 vols. 2nd ed., rev. and enlarged by Luisa Vertova. Turin, 1989.

Posner, Donald. "Caravaggio's Homo-Erotic Early Works." *Art Quarterly* 34 (1971): 301–324.

Puglisi, Catherine. *Caravaggio.* London, 1998. Updates Hibbard; excellent illustrations.

Spike, John T. *Caravaggio.* New York and London, 2001. Useful chronology and extensive bibliography.

Stone, David M. "*In Figura Diaboli*: Self and Myth in Caravaggio's *David and Goliath.*" In *From Rome to Eternity: Catholicism and the Arts in Italy, ca. 1550–1650,* edited by P. M. Jones and T. Worcester, pp. 19–42. Leiden, 2002.

DAVID M. STONE

CARICATURE AND CARTOON.

Exaggerated imitation in the form of grotesques, mimicry, and satire has a long history, but graphic caricature in the modern sense as the distortion of specific persons for amusement and ridicule appears only in the late sixteenth century. It emerges as the ideas of civility and sociability, codified in the work of Baldassare Castiglione (1478–1529), Giovanni della Casa (1503–1556), and Stefano Guazzo (1530–1593), spread to include the relations among artists. As a visual form of wit, a then highly prized social skill, caricature became at once an expression of and a means of fostering mutually agreeable interactions among members of a group. Thus the Florentine painter Luigi Baccio del Bianco (1604–1657) is said to have dined out on his ability to render the company "as ridiculous as one could imagine," and Gian Lorenzo Bernini's (1598–1680) delight in caricaturing is said to have derived from the enjoyment it gave his noble victims. The highly abbreviated and comically distorted likenesses drawn by Bernini and others in the seventeenth century differed from earlier grotesque figures and faces by representing individuals rather than types, and from earlier satires of individuals by ridiculing persons rather than their corporate status. And in contrast to later social and political caricature, which acquired a wide and varied public, they were typically made and consumed in face-to-face encounters within a closed circle. That caricaturing originated among artists is confirmed by the earliest name for caricatures, *ritratti caricati,* that is, "loaded" or "charged portraits" (from the Italian *caricare,* 'to weight, load, charge': cf. the later French *portrait chargé*). This form follows that of *colori caricati,* the studio term for intense, deeply saturated colors. *Caricatura* first appears in print and in a letter by Bernini in the 1640s and, via the French *caricature,* gives us the English word.

The traditional view that caricature began in the Carracci workshop in the 1580s—though no examples are now certainly identified—is supported by its popularity among their followers, and it was naturalized in Rome by Bernini, for whom it became a typical expression of his artistic personality. With a few rapid strokes of his pen, the artist shrewdly threw into comic relief the distinctive features of such familiar faces as that of his patron, Cardinal Scipione Borghese (before 1633, Biblioteca Vaticana, Rome). By the early eighteenth century, caricature had become fashionable in Rome and was spreading elsewhere. Pier Leone Ghezzi (1674–1755), a Roman painter and portraitist, documented in more than two thousand amusing, gently mocking drawings the comings and goings of artists, opera singers and musicians, churchmen, and nobles of both sexes, all of whom readily consented to seeing themselves caricatured.

Caricature, evidently unknown in Paris when Bernini visited in 1665, was later occasionally practiced by Jean-Antoine Watteau (1684–1721) and others, and etchings after Ghezzi's work became popular in Germany. But it was in England that the art was to have the greatest resonance. Enthusiastically embraced by amateurs of the aristocracy and the wealthy classes, who pursued it in the sociable spirit of its origins, caricaturing acquaintances became so fashionable that in 1762 a book appeared offering "young gentlemen and ladies" instruction in how to draw caricatures. It was, however, the more formidable resources of print and party that were responsible for the later explosion of English political and social caricature. In the 1750s George Townshend began to turn his talent for caricature to practical ends by printing ridiculing images of his political adversaries. Although widely decried, the factional use of portrait caricature was not to be denied and indeed was greatly strengthened by William Hogarth's (1697–1764) reworking of the seventeenth-century northern tradition of satirical broadsides. In appealing to the high-art traditions of history painting, Hogarth's engravings of such "modern moral subjects" as *A Harlot's Progress* (1731) and *A Rake's Progress* (1733–1734), *Marriage à la Mode* (1743), and *Industry and Idleness* (1747) provided later artists with not only brilliant examples of social criticism but models for the way in which composition, gesture, and symbol could be used to create vivid pictorial narratives. Thus, drawing on Hogarth's inventions, later political prints are both inescapably personal and remarkably convincing, so that the mockery was all the more effective.

Any public person, the royal family not excepted, might be savaged in a scurrilous or libelous attack, often bought and paid for by an opponent, and an eager audience devoured the result. Such license was peculiarly English, and indeed caricature adopted a decidedly nationalist cast with the French Revolution and the advent of the Napoleonic wars. James Gillray (1757–1815), who began making political cartoons in 1778, produced ferocious indictments of republicanism (*Un petit souper à la parisienne:—or—A Family of Sans Culottes Refreshing after the Fatigues of the Day* [1792], directed against the slaughter of the Swiss guards at the Tuileries), and later of Napoleon, his "Little Boney" making an appearance in forty-odd works. The French leader was also targeted by Isaac (1789–1856) and George (1792–1878) Cruikshank, but populist patriotism did not exempt the government and its policies from criticism. In Gillray's *The Plum-pudding in Danger* (1805), William Pitt, the prime minister, happily joins Napoleon at table to slice up the globe, and when John Bull appears in print as the personification of the British people, he is as likely as not being victimized by those in charge.

Political satirists also turned their hand to social satire, on occasion even the rage for caricaturing, but typically the many fashions and foibles of a society coming to terms with its own luxury. Although sometimes aspiring to the moral seriousness of Hogarth and not without sharp edges, they tend to be altogether more tolerant of human nature. In his many drawings mixing exaggeration and likeness Thomas Rowlandson (1756–1827) does not so much castigate vice as expose the humorous aspects of urban and country life. For social criticism to equal the harshness of English political satire, one must turn to the work of Francisco de Goya e Lucientes (1746–1828) in Spain. In his *Caprichos* (1797–1798), Goya depicted such a darkly comic, frequently misogynist, view of human ignorance, superstition, and folly that there seems small hope it can be remedied under the lash of his satire.

See also **Bernini, Gian Lorenzo; Carracci Family; Castiglione, Baldassare; Goya y Lucientes, Francisco de; Hogarth, William; Watteau, Antoine.**

BIBLIOGRAPHY

Bauer, George C., and Linda Bauer. "Artists in Association: Sociability and the Early History of Caricature." In *Music Observed: Essays in Memory of William C. Holmes*, edited by Colleen Reardon and Susan Parisi. Warren, Mich., forthcoming.

Donald, Diana. *The Age of Caricature: Satirical Prints in the Reign of George III.* New Haven and London, 1996.

Gombrich, E. H. "The Cartoonist's Armoury." In *Meditations on a Hobby Horse, and Other Essays on the Theory of Art,* pp. 127–142. London, 1963.

Gombrich, E. H., and Ernst Kris. "The Principles of Caricature" (1938). Reprinted in Ernst Kris, *Psychoanalytic Explorations in Art,* pp. 189–203. New York and London, 1952.

Lavin, Irving. "Bernini and the Art of Social Satire." In *Drawings by Gianlorenzo Bernini from the Museum der bildenden Künste, Leipzig, German Democratic Republic.* Exh. cat., edited by Irving Lavin, pp. 25–54. Princeton, 1981.

GEORGE C. BAUER

CARNIVAL. Celebrated widely across Europe in the early modern period during the days preceding Lent, Carnival perpetuated pre-Christian rites of farmers and herders promoting the springtime renewal of life. The occurrence of such rites in ancient Greece and Rome is formally documented; and their widespread use by various Indo-European groups has been deduced from the many analogous practices surviving into historic times throughout the continent. The name "carnival," which dates to medieval times, was probably based on the Latin *carnem levare* or the Italian *carnelevare,* 'removal of flesh', with "flesh" understood in both its alimentary and erotic meanings. It was also popularly interpreted to mean 'carne vale' or 'flesh rules'.

Carnival included a range of activities that occurred singly or in combination and that varied with local customs and conditions. The struggle between the diminished sun of the old year and the returning sun of the new year was symbolized in a battle for a prize (a castle, a wife, a football) that resulted in the death of one contender, who sometimes miraculously revived. In many locales the battles involved teams and could take the form of a dance, while in others they were replaced by contests such as races. In other traditions the old year or winter was figured as an old woman.

Winter's darkness and death, symbolized by ghostly, demonic, or deformed figures that stalked the community under the leadership of the king or queen of the dead, were frightened away by loud noise, bright colors, and fire in the form of bonfires or torches. The vitality of such activities also en-

Carnival. *The Battle Between Carnival and Lent* by Pieter Bruegel the Elder, 1559. ©Francis G. Mayer/Corbis

couraged the return of the sun and of life-sustaining plants and animals, evoked through the Wild Man and various representations of forest and domestic animals and vegetation. A wedding or sexual activity such as dancing that was actually or symbolically promiscuous expressed the connection between human and agricultural fertility.

Renewal of human society, based on the equality of all community members, took the form of criticism of injustice and behavioral transgressions, mock trials, and rites of misrule or inversion. Low-ranking members of society assumed positions of authority and what had been excluded or despised was temporarily exalted. These rites, which often involved tension-easing comedy and the truth-telling fool, were particularly practiced in sedentary and stratified societies, such as cities and monastic communities, in which superiors and inferiors lived close together.

Masks, which may have originally mimicked the casting off of the old plant's seedhull by the germinating bud of the new plant, were utilized in rituals of release. With personal identity obscured, community members, especially women, violated taboos without fear of sanction, acting in sexually provocative ways and intruding into areas usually prohibited to them. Such freedoms also contributed to an amalgamation of the community, as did the questing or procession throughout the communal space that often accompanied masking.

Food consumption received increasing emphasis with the passage of time and the contrasting of Carnival with the fasting and abstinence of Lent, itself perhaps originating in a pagan practice fostering germination. A community feast was organized in the teeth of late-winter shortages, often through a house-to-house search for ingredients, featuring the meat, eggs, butter, and milk that would soon be prohibited. Special attention was paid to feeding the vulnerable, especially children and the poor. As the name indicates, the eating of meat, especially pork, became central to the festivities. In some locales festivities were concluded by the funeral of Carnival, conducted by the clergy or near the church.

A particularly vital period for Carnival was the late fifteenth and early sixteenth centuries. The revival of humanistic learning and especially of classical theater, which in turn stimulated existing vernacular theater; the increase in population, which threatened the relative prosperity resulting from the great wave of plague and created a variety of social tensions; the discovery of new commercial routes and colonial territories, which benefited Atlantic states and harmed Mediterranean ones; and the revival of evangelical Christianity, which valued the poor and lowly—all contributed to an innovative use of Carnival and the carnivalesque that had begun with the rise of banking and manufacturing in Italy in the thirteenth and fourteenth centuries. Theater, with its human presence and verbosity, offered many opportunities for lower-class characters to either criticize social authorities or to support them, as well as for them to propose inclusive social models and for upper-class characters to assert their control of the situation. The result was a flourishing theatrical scene, many of whose texts were disseminated and preserved through the new device of printing.

The celebration of Carnival was deeply affected by the religious reforms of the sixteenth century and later. With its emphasis on pageantry and the senses, Carnival slowly disappeared from Protestant areas, although it often left some vestigial food celebration. Even in Catholic areas, Carnival was chastened and Christianized in the late sixteenth and seventeenth centuries. Brought more under the purview of authorities, it tended to focus on magnificent ephemera such as elaborate floats. With the growing social openness of the eighteenth century, secular Carnival again flourished, producing some of its greatest theatrical achievements. A further development was its transplantation to the New World colonies, where, in a particularly apt turn of events, the French settlement in Louisiana was established on the eve of Mardi Gras, 2 March 1699. Many of the official European celebrations of Carnival ended with the end of the *ancien régime*.

Scholars have debated at length whether Carnival undermined or affirmed existing social authority. According to the first view, ritualized inversions and battles challenged social authority and proposed a new model incorporating those who had been excluded. In the second view, social authorities permitted Carnival as a safety valve that, through limited criticism, released enough tension to calm dissent and produce a return to the preexisting order. As the debate evolved, it became clear that the terms of Carnival are ambivalent and that the function of Carnival varied with social circumstances.

Particularly important was the strength of the social fabric: if it was too weak to contain dissent, a full-fledged revolt could develop. The function of Carnival also changed with time. The work of Victor Turner indicates that as the abundance of wealth produced by banking and manufacturing dismantled the agricultural cycle and the fixed social stratification upon which Carnival was based, the carnivalesque became suffused throughout society and the year and was more integrated into official values.

See also **Catholicism; Festivals; Folk Tales and Fairy Tales; Food and Drink; Games and Play.**

BIBLIOGRAPHY

Bakhtin, M. M. (Mikhail Mikhailovich). *Rabelais and His World.* Translated by Hélène Iswolsky. Reprint. Bloomington, Ind., 1984. Translation of *Tvorchestvo Fransua Rable i narodnaia kul'tura srednevekov'ia i Renessansa* (1965). Influential study of the elements of popular culture, subversive potential, and ambivalence of Carnival.

Bristol, Michael D. *Carnival and Theater: Plebeian Culture and the Structure of Authority in Renaissance England.* New York, 1985. Influential study of the uses of Carnival in England.

Burke, Peter. *Popular Culture in Early Modern Europe.* Revised reprint. Brookfield, Vt., 1994. Influential study emphasizing ambivalence of Carnival.

Carroll, Linda L. *Angelo Beolco (Il Ruzante).* Boston, 1990. Study of Renaissance playwright who wrote for Carnival.

Davis, Natalie Zemon. *Society and Culture in Early Modern France.* Stanford, 1975. Influential group of essays on the role of Carnival and the Carnivalesque.

Humphrey, Chris. *The Politics of Carnival: Festive Misrule in Medieval England.* Manchester, U.K., and New York, 2001. Emphasizes multiple uses of Carnival in medieval England.

Kinser, Samuel. *Rabelais's Carnival.* Berkeley, 1990.

Le Roy Ladurie, Emmanuel. *Carnival in Romans.* Translated by Mary Feeney. New York, 1979. Translation of *Le Carnaval de Romans* (1979). Influential study of a bloody sixteenth-century Carnival in France.

Meyer, Robert Eugene. *Festivals Europe.* New York, 1954. Describes Carnival traditions in European countries.

Turner, Victor. *From Ritual to Theatre: The Human Seriousness of Play.* New York, 1982. Influential group of studies analyzing the functions of Carnival and theater over time.

LINDA L. CARROLL

CARRACCI FAMILY (Annibale, 1560–1609; Agostino, 1557–1602; Ludovico, 1555–1619), Italian painters. The careers of the Carracci family of painters from Bologna—the brothers Annibale and Agostino, and their elder cousin Ludovico, straddled the sixteenth and seventeenth centuries both chronologically and stylistically. Among the first generation of artists to come of age after Giorgio Vasari had published his history of Italian art, the Carracci were intensely conscious of their own positions within the stylistic progressions, local traditions, and pantheon of great painters set forth by Vasari. Collectively the Carracci are best known for reforming the tenets of painting, rejecting the frigid artificiality of late mannerism prevalent in Bologna, and introducing into their art emotional warmth and freedom of handling, a dynamic and nuanced treatment of light and color, as well as a commitment to direct observation of nature. They are credited with joining the previously immiscible qualities of light and color characteristic of northern Italian painting with the firmness of design and precision of drawing found in central Italian art.

The earliest years of the Carracci are poorly documented. Their biographers, the Bolognese Carlo Cesare Malvasia and the Roman Giovanni Pietro Bellori, are rich, but not unbiased, sources. In the early 1580s all three Carracci traveled to Parma and Venice, and Ludovico also visited Florence. By 1583 the Carracci had set up a workshop headed by Ludovico. Remarkably, they also established an academy in their quarters, first called the Accademia dei Desiderosi ('desirous of learning and achievement'), and later the Accademia degli Incamminati ('those who were on the way'). Although it was a private family academy, and operated rather informally, it was constituted with a serious pedagogical program and a commitment to the theory as well as practice of art. An emphasis on drawing from life was complemented by the study of optics, perspective, and anatomy. Incubated in the academy were new conceptions of genre painting, exemplified by Annibale's broadly painted, caught-in-midaction *Bean Eater* (Rome, Colonna Gallery), and landscape painting, the latter fueled by drawings done on the spot, out-of-doors. Caricature is purported to have been invented by Annibale, and practiced in the academy, but the best surviving examples are by Agostino. While Agostino had first specialized as an engraver, and his production as a printmaker is important and extensive, he subsequently joined his family in their collective enterprise.

The young Carracci collaborated on numerous projects in Bologna, most notably the frescoed friezes of the story of Jason in the Palazzo Fava, about 1593, and the founding of Rome in the Palazzo Magnani, about 1590. When asked who had done each scene, the Carracci, having freely traded ideas and sketches, and having worked elbow to elbow, are claimed to have responded, "Ella e dei Carracci; L'abbiam fatto tutti noi" (It is by the Carracci, we did it together). Such intimate collaboration, in which the individual style was sublimated in favor of a seamless, lively, and highly illusionistic effect, is characteristic of the Carraccis' early period. During this time each of the Carracci also painted several major altarpieces that opened the way for the baroque style of painting in northern Italy, among them Annibale's *Baptism of Christ* (Parma), Agostino's *Last Communion of St. Jerome* (Pinacoteca Nazionale, Bologna), and Ludovico's *Vision of St. Hyacinth* (Louvre).

In 1595 Annibale moved to Rome, answering a request from Cardinal Odoardo Farnese for the Carracci to decorate his immense family palace. Agostino later joined his brother in the execution of Annibale's greatest project, the frescoed vault of the Farnese Gallery. Annibale's vivid evocation of a picture gallery on the theme of the loves of the gods is populated with nudes and classical statues come to life, and its architectural illusionism is irresistible. If its patron, Cardinal Farnese, failed to appreciate it fully, the ceiling nevertheless became one of the most highly esteemed works of art in Italy. Annibale

Carracci Family. *The Triumph of Bacchus and Ariadne,* part of the fresco cycle *Loves of the Gods* at the Palazzo Farnese, created c. 1597–1602 by Annibale Carracci. ©Massimo Listri/Corbis

had developed an unsurpassed ability to draw the human figure, a skill enhanced in the Farnese by a new monumentality derived from his study of Raphael, Michelangelo, and the antique statuary newly available to him in Rome. Blossoming about 1600, Annibale's new synthesis proved the most compelling and enduring model for the entire century of Italian painting to follow. In his last years Annibale's mental state deteriorated, hindering his productivity, but he continued to create powerful works in an austere and tragic key, often assisted by his devoted pupils Francesco Albani, Domenichino, and Sisto Badalocchio. Agostino, whose talents also included music and poetry, and who, unlike Annibale, enjoyed court society, spent his last years on the fresco decoration of Duke Ranuccio Farnese's Palazzo del Giardino in Parma. His natural

son Antonio Carracci (1583?–1618) became a successful painter in Rome.

Ludovico, who remained in Bologna, was devoted to his teaching and to fostering a school of painting that would be the glory of Bologna. It was not by chance that his most important project, the painted cloister of San Michele in Bosco (ruined) was a showcase for the collaborative achievements of the family academy. Guido Reni, Domenichino, Francesco Albani, and Alessandro Algardi were among the major artists who passed through the academy, ensuring its place as the cradle of Italian baroque painting. Noted for his compositional and iconographic inventiveness, Ludovico's commitment to the naturalism of the early academy waned, and he had little use for Annibale's Roman classicist-idealist idiom. Ludovico exploited the expressive effects of anatomical distortion and created images of intense and often irrational emotionalism. The sweet, diminutive figures of his earliest work gave way to an aggressive plasticity of forms deployed in dynamic compositions. His work grew ever more dramatic as he experimented with broken patterns of light and dark, and with what has been called his meteorological chiaroscuro. Ludovico's mature altarpieces filled the churches of Bologna and the surrounding region, eventually carrying the Carracci innovations throughout Italy.

See also **Vasari, Giorgio.**

BIBLIOGRAPHY

Bellori, Giovanni Pietro. *Le vite de' pittori, scultori et architetti moderni.* Rome, 1672.

Benati, Daniele, et al. *The Drawings of Annibale Carracci.* Exh. cat. Washington, D.C., 1999.

DeGrazia, Diane. *Prints and Related Drawings by the Carracci Family: A Catalogue Raisonné.* Washington, D.C., 1979.

Malvasia, Carlo Cesare, Conte. *Malvasia's Life of the Carracci.* Translated by Anne Summerscale. University Park, Pa., 2000. Translation of *Di Lodovico, Agostino, et Annibale Carracci. Ludovico Carracci.* Edited by Andrea Emiliani. Milan, New York, and Fort Worth, 1994.

Posner, Donald. *Annibale Carracci: A Study in the Reform of Italian Painting around 1590.* London and New York, 1971.

GAIL FEIGENBAUM

CARRIERA, ROSALBA

CARRIERA, ROSALBA (1675–1757), Italian painter, known for miniatures on ivory. The eighteenth-century Venetian painter Rosalba Carriera was the first woman painter in history to be credited by many with the initiation of a new style in art, even called by her contemporaries the *goût moderne.* Later negatively dubbed the rococo by Maurice Quaï, a follower of the neoclassicist Jacques-Louis David, this style emphasized pastel colors; a free, spontaneous—almost impressionistic—brushstroke; and an elegance and charm that were highly praised by early-eighteenth-century patrons. Carriera also encouraged new approaches in media, which included miniature works in tempera on ivory and pastel on paper. For the rest of the century, elegant and sophisticated works in these media, inspired by Carriera, were popular with artists and collectors alike.

Rosalba Carriera was born in Chiogga 7 October 1675, the daughter of Andrea Carriera, a government clerk, and the lacemaker Alba Foresti. Her first works were designs for lace patterns, but sometime before 1700 she was encouraged by the French painter Jean Steve to execute miniatures on ivory to decorate the lids of snuffboxes. The light and lively style of these works gained her much notoriety, leading to her acceptance at the prestigious Academy of St. Luke in Rome. For her *morceau de réception* (piece presented on her reception into the academy), she submitted *Young Girl with a Dove* (1705, Academy of St. Luke, Rome), a tempera on ivory miniature. Carriera continued to paint small-scale works until her failing eyesight made such work impossible.

Carriera is best known for popularizing finished works in pastel. She was introduced to this medium by Gian Antonio Lazzarini and Padre don Felice Ramelli. Other artists credited with teaching Carriera are Giuseppe Diamantini and Antonio Balestra. Ramelli and Balestra continued to play an important role in Carriera's life, as is indicated by her correspondence. These letters, as well as her will, a diary she kept in Paris, and brief autobiographical notes, are conserved in the Ashmoleon Collection of the Laurentian Library, Florence.

The earliest known pastel portrait painted by Carriera depicts the connoisseur and collector Anton Maria Zanetti (1700, National Museum, Stockholm). Zanetti collected many works by Carriera and promoted their value to other collectors in his travels throughout Europe. He became friendly with the important Swedish collector Count Carl Gustaf Tessin, to whom he gave this early portrait.

The English consul in Venice, Joseph Smith, was another devoted patron. He amassed a sizable collection of Carriera's works, which were purchased in 1762 by King George III. This collection included one of many self-portraits executed by the artist (1744–1746, Windsor Castle). Carriera's best-known self-portrait, however, is the one she contributed to the Medici collection of self-portraits at the Uffizi. Characteristic of her self-portraits, this work (1709, Uffizi Gallery, Florence) does not idealize her plain features, which include round dark

Rosalba Carriera. *Self-Portrait with a Portrait of Her Sister,* 1715. ©ARTE & IMMAGINI SRL/CORBIS

eyes, a rather bulbous nose, thin lips, and a deep dimple in her chin. Although Carriera achieved fame by glamorizing her sitters, she is brutally honest in representing herself. The emphasis in this work is on her role as a portrait painter, since she appears holding a portrait of her sister Giovanna, who served as Rosalba's assistant. These two unmarried sisters lived with their widowed mother in a sizable residence and studio on the Grand Canal. Here the artist was visited by many international patrons, including Augustus III of Saxony and Poland, who counted over 150 of Carriera's works in his collection (many of these were destroyed during the bombing of Dresden in World War II).

Augustus III first became acquainted with Carriera in 1713 when he visited Venice as a young prince on grand tour. The following year he commissioned a portrait of himself in oil (1714, Kunsthistoriches Museum, Vienna) and, subsequently, many other portraits and allegorical works that Carriera referred to as her "fancy pieces." These included a number of serial works, such as *The Four Seasons, The Four Elements,* and *The Four Continents,* which were once housed in his "Rosalba Room." These allegories were usually represented by scantily clad beauties holding symbols that reference their meaning. In *The Four Seasons,* for example, *America* (1730, National Museum of Women in the Arts, Washington, D.C.) is represented as a dark-skinned, bare-breasted female wearing a feathered headdress and holding an arrow. These sexually alluring allegorical figures capture the spirit of moral freedom, elegance, and charm associated with the early Enlightenment.

Another visitor to Carriera's Venetian studio was the French banker Pierre Crozat, who convinced Carriera to stay with him in Paris from April 1720 until March 1721. While there, she was named a member of the French Royal Academy (1720) even though it had earlier banned (1706) female membership. Her Paris diary records visits with many artists, including Nicolas de Largillière, Antoine Coypel, Jean-François de Troy, and Hyacinthe Rigaud. She particularly admired the work of Antoine Watteau, whose portrait she executed twice (1720, Studdesches Institut, Frankfurt, and 1720–1721, Museo Civico, Treviso). She also executed two portraits of the ten-year-old King Louis XV, one a miniature on ivory, the other in pastel (1720, one version at the Museum of Fine Arts, Boston). The positive reception afforded these works encouraged many requests for autographed copies and a number of French artists to work in pastel—most notably, Maurice Quentin de la Tour.

Although Carriera's style and media influenced many artists, she had only three known students. These were her sisters Giovanna and Angela (who married the painter Giovanni Pellegrini), and Felicita Sartori, who became court painter to Augustus III when Carriera declined the position. Sartori is believed to have posed for Carriera's *Allegory of Painting* (n.d., National Gallery, Washington, D.C.), although there is some question as to whether this work was in fact created by Carriera. It may be a self-portrait of Sartori, whose style was very similar to that of her teacher.

Carriera's fame and prestige made her a source of inspiration to many other women painters. The Scottish-born artist Catherine Read, called the "English Rosalba" by Horace Walpole, wrote to Carriera three times in the years just before her death. In that correspondence Read calls Carriera an artist without equal and praises the honor that she brings to her sex. Read mentions a letter that she received from Carriera, but it was probably written by her then widowed sister Angela, since Rosalba was blind for the last ten years of her life and Giovanna died in 1737.

By the time of Carriera's death on 15 April 1757, the light, spontaneous rococo style that she helped popularize was fast going out of fashion. Nevertheless, the legend of the Great Rosalba would continue to inspire artists—particularly women artists—for the next two centuries.

See also **Portrait Miniatures; Rococo; Venice, Art in; Watteau, Antoine; Women and Art.**

BIBLIOGRAPHY

Primary Sources

Carriera, Rosalba. *Lettere, diari, framente.* Edited by Bernardina Sani. 2 vols. Florence, 1985.

Dobson, Austin. *Rosalba's Journal and Other Papers.* Oxford, 1926.

Secondary Sources

Bjustrom, P., and C. Cavalli-Bjorkmann. "A Newly Acquired Portrait of Anton Maria Zanetti by Rosalba Carriera." *Nationalmuseum Bulletin* 1 (Stockholm, 1977): 31–44.

Cailleux, Jean. "Un portrait de Watteau de Rosalba Carriera." *Miscellanea, I. Q. van Regteren Altena* (Amsterdam, 1969): 174–177.

Cheney, Liana de Girolami, Alicia Craig Faxon, and Kathleen Lucey Russo. *Self-Portraits by Women Painters.* Aldershot, U.K., and Brookfield, Vt., 2000.

Malamani, Vittorio. *Rosalba Carriera.* Bergamo, 1910.

Sani, Bernardina. *Rosalba Carriera.* Turin, 1988.

Wilhelm, J. "Le portrait de Watteau par Rosalba Carriera." *Gazette des Beaux Arts* 164 (1953): 235–246.

KATHLEEN RUSSO

CARTESIANISM. Cartesianism was a set of philosophical theses, a scientific program, and a broad intellectual movement that dominated the European scene in the seventeenth century. The foremost philosophical paradigm of the period, it was the subject of passionate debate and strong opposition both within the universities and in society at large.

The philosophical theses of Cartesianism have their origins in the thought of René Descartes (1596–1650), who first sought in a systematic manner to replace the dominant Aristotelian philosophy of the Schools with a new philosophy, one wedded not to conformity with some ancient or medieval thinkers or a particular religious tradition but to a rationally justified confidence in our own natural cognitive faculties. The new philosophy would liberate society from unreflective obedience to authority, prejudice, and philosophical (and maybe even theological) dogma and contribute to scientific and social progress—not to mention material well-being—by advancing our understanding of nature and the universe

The most prominent and perhaps defining thesis of the Cartesian philosophy is what has come to be called "mind-body dualism." Descartes insisted on the real distinction between mind and matter. Mind (or soul) and matter (or body) are, according to Descartes, two essentially and radically different kinds of substance. Mind is unextended, indivisible, simple thinking. Its modes or properties are particular ideas or thoughts including beliefs, volitions, sensations, and emotions. Matter, on the other hand, is nothing but extension or dimensional space and is therefore divisible, its modes being shape, size, and mobility. There is nothing materialistic about the mind and nothing mental or spiritual about the body.

This doctrine is of great importance not only for understanding the nature of the human being, who is a composite—or, to use Descartes's phrase, a "substantial union"—of these two substances, but also for science. According to Descartes, the physical world is nothing but passive matter or extension, divisible ad infinitum into parts. This was, he believed, a great advance over the Aristotelian world picture. The spiritlike forms and qualities that were used by the Scholastics to explain the behaviors of physical bodies have been banished from nature. All natural phenomena, no matter how complex and regardless of whether they are terrestrial or celestial, are henceforth to be explained solely in terms of matter and the motion, rest, and impact of its parts. Descartes's separation of mind and matter was a crucial step in the scientific revolution of the seventeenth century, and laid the metaphysical foundations for the mechanical philosophy that dominated the period until Newton. (Descartes also believed, at least as a matter of public record, that dualism offered the strongest possible foundation for the doctrine of the immortality of the soul, since the mind as a simple, thinking substance was not subject to the process of decay and destruction that brought about the demise of complex and divisible bodies.)

Descartes's philosophy bequeathed to his many devoted followers a host of difficult philosophical (and theological) problems. If mind and body are so radically different in nature, how do they causally engage one another and interact in the way they seem to do in a human being? If matter is nothing but inert, passive extension, what explains the motion, interaction, and dynamic behavior of bodies? Moreover, Descartes believed that, since matter is pure extension, body is not distinct from space, and a truly empty space (or vacuum) is therefore impossible in nature; the universe is a material plenum. How, then, does there arise a multiplicity of individual bodies, and how is their motion possible? Most distressing to religious authorities—and one of the issues that led to Descartes's works being placed by the Catholic Church on the Index of Prohibited Books in 1663—were the apparent consequences of Descartes's metaphysics for the Catholic dogma of the Eucharist. If any particular body (such as a piece of bread) is just a specific parcel of extension and there are no "real qualities" that are distinct and separable from an underlying substance, how can the Cartesian philosophy account for the miracle of transubstantiation? According to the traditional Aristotelian account adopted by the Church, at the moment of consecration the sensible qualities of the bread remain while its substance is replaced by the substance of Christ's body. Descartes has done away with such qualities, and a body is now just its extension; if the substance of Christ's body takes on the extended dimensions of bread, then, according to Descartes's metaphysics of body, it is just bread.

The first generation of Cartesians included men like Henricus Regius (1598–1679), Johannes de Raey (1672–1702), and Adriaan Heereboord (1614–1661). These Dutch academics' introduction of Cartesian principles into their university courses in medicine, physics, and even theology incited a bitter backlash from the authorities. The new philosophy was perceived as a threat to the established (Aristotelian) order. The Reformed the-

ologian and rector of the University of Utrecht, Gibertus Voetius (1589–1676), was only the most outspoken and determined of Descartes's numerous foes, and his institution was the first among many to issue condemnations of Cartesian philosophy and to prohibit its teaching. The controversy over Cartesianism in the Netherlands raged not only in the academy, but in the broader intellectual culture as well. It spilled over into the social and political realm and became enmeshed in the battles that deeply divided factions of the Reformed Church and opposing political camps of the Republic.

In France, the Saumur physician Louis de la Forge (1632–1666), one of Descartes's early and most faithful followers, produced an illustrated and annotated edition of Descartes's *Treatise on Man,* a work on the physiology of the human body, and supplemented it with his own *Treatise on Man's Soul* (1666), in which he explains, on strict Cartesian principles, the workings of the human mind and its relationship to the body. La Forge recognized some of the metaphysical problems inherent in Cartesian dualism and the physics of extended bodies and was among the first to defend a limited version of the doctrine called "occasionalism." According to La Forge, the motion of extended bodies, which are intrinsically passive, is explained by the causal activity of God. The moving force of a body in motion is nothing but the divine will, which moves the body by recreating it in a different relative place from one moment to the next. Another occasionalist Cartesian, somewhat less orthodox in his fealty to Descartes than La Forge, was the Parisian lawyer Géraud de Cordemoy (1626–1684), who insisted—contrary to Descartes, for whom any parcel of extension, no matter how small, was in principle divisible—that there were atoms, or ultimately indivisible parts, in nature. The Dominican friar Robert Desgabets (1610–1678) pursued his own Cartesian program in the realm of theology and offered suggestions as to how to reconcile Descartes's metaphysics with the Eucharistic doctrine of "real presence." The physicists Jacques Rohault (1620–1672) and Pierre-Sylvain Régis (1632–1707) sought the mechanistic explanations of natural phenomena, experimentally verified, in an attempt to complete those particular and more detailed aspects of physics that Descartes left open.

While united by their adherence to a broad philosophical program, these Cartesians did not constitute an organized group but worked independently to further what they saw as the right and progressive philosophy. By far the most important Cartesian of the seventeenth century, however, was a French Oratorian named Nicolas Malebranche (1638–1715). A bolder and more systematic thinker than the others, Malebranche was not afraid to modify and even depart from Descartes's ideas in highly unorthodox ways. His occasionalism was thoroughgoing: God is the only real causal agent in the universe. All finite things are created and sustained in being by God, and all events, whether mental or physical, are brought about by the divine will. Creatures and their states are only secondary causes, or "occasions," for God to exercise genuine power. Malebranche also argued that the clear and distinct ideas that serve as the objects of human intellectual understanding are not modes or properties of the human mind but rather ideal archetypes in the divine understanding. With his theory of the Vision in God Malebranche sought to make human beings as dependent upon God for their knowledge as all creatures are dependent upon God for their being and activity. His doctrines were attacked by other Cartesians, most notably the Jansenist firebrand Antoine Arnauld (1612–1694), who thought Malebranche's ideas represented not only an unacceptable departure from the true principles of Descartes's philosophy, but also a serious threat to Christian faith.

By the third quarter of the century, Cartesianism, while vigorously condemned by leading religious and political authorities (in 1667 the French court prohibited a public funeral oration from being delivered at the ceremony for the reburial of his remains in Paris), enjoyed immense success. Nonetheless, it suffered from serious internal weaknesses and obvious explanatory failures. The advent of Newtonianism at the end of the century, with its alternative conception of scientific understanding, powerful mathematical presentation, and explicit critique of Cartesianism, brought about the final downfall of this formidable scientific paradigm.

See also **Aristotelianism; Descartes, René; Scholasticism.**

BIBLIOGRAPHY

Des Chene, Dennis. *Physiologia: Natural Philosophy in Late Aristotelian and Cartesian Thought.* Ithaca, N.Y., 1996.

Garber, Daniel. *Descartes's Metaphysical Physics.* Chicago, 1992.

Nadler, Steven M., ed. *The Cambridge Companion to Malebranche.* Cambridge, U.K., and New York, 2000.

Schmaltz, Tad M. *Radical Cartesianism: The French Reception of Descartes.* Cambridge, U.K., and New York, 2002.

Watson, Richard A. *The Breakdown of Cartesian Metaphysics.* Atlantic Highlands, N.J., 1987.

STEVEN NADLER

CARTOGRAPHY AND GEOGRAPHY.

The recovery and diffusion of ancient literary and mathematical writings on geography in fifteenth-century Europe gradually transformed cartographic practices in the later fifteenth century. Earlier models of ordering space lacked uniform standards of denoting terrestrial continuity in mathematically consistent terms—nautical portolan charts noted distance and direction on magnetic compass lines for sea travel, itineraries measured paths of land travel, zonal maps divided the globe, while symbolic *mappae mundi* situated Asia, Africa, and Europe in a circle centered, for theological reasons, at Jerusalem. Renaissance geographic maps, by contrast, plotted the inhabited world as an interrelated network of secular space, translating the spherical globe onto a measured and ordered two-dimensional surface of fixed directions and proportions, as devised by the second-century Greek geographer Ptolemy, to frame a geometrically continuous representation of space.

Ptolemy's system of terrestrial coordinates, which appeared in fifteenth-century world maps, continued to be used to denote position and directions even after inaccuracies in Ptolemy's own projections were corrected. Maps made for manuscripts of Ptolemy's *Guide to Geography* in the century after its translation in 1406 challenged the existence of unnavigable "torrid zones" as well as Aristotelian concentric spheres of elements (water, air, fire), positing instead a network of global relations by transferring the earth's surface to a graticule that divided the surface of the earth according to metric indices. The large circular world map that the Venetian monk Fra Mauro designed for King Afonso V of Portugal in 1459 had combined fifteenth-century navigators' accounts of the coast of Africa and the Indian Ocean with Marco Polo's (1254–1324) ethnographic accounts without using metric indices, pictorially illustrating the wealth of the Far East and showing its potentates and exotic fauna. Fifteenth-century geographic maps defined space within a directional grid, and their depiction of a terraqueous globe with east-west parallels of latitude and north-south meridians of longitude may have led Christopher Columbus to contest the Aristotelian model of the earth before Spanish royal cosmographers, natural philosophers who specialized in the relation of cosmic and terrestrial spheres and based their claims on celestial observations, in 1483–1484. The fact that Ptolemy reduced the earth's circumference probably encouraged Columbus's plans to "sail the parallel" to cross the Atlantic in 1492.

Map projections situated place-names in an abstract grid, creating a record of space that could be easily modified in the face of new discoveries. Printed maps emphasized a geometric organization of the world's surface from 1477 to later maps that included national boundaries (1482), and to the modernized Ptolemaic projections (beginning in 1513) showing the Americas as an independent landmass. Geographic knowledge expanded as Europeans became more familiar with routes beyond the Mediterranean world. Maps were seen as increasingly authoritative and thus could serve to clarify questions of territorial jurisdiction as European powers began to expand overseas. For instance, a Portuguese planisphere showing the African coasts and the Indian Ocean (1502) marked the meridian—960 nautical miles west of Ptolemy's prime meridian at the Canary Islands—by which the Spanish and Portuguese divided the New World at the 1494 Treaty of Tordesillas. (In Ptolemaic maps the Indian Ocean had been depicted as landlocked.) Spanish cosmographers helped resolve the disputes that arose over Ferdinand Magellan's 1519–1521 voyage, due to the limited accuracy of determining position by compass bearings.

Maps also reflected political agendas and cultural attitudes. For example, the French royal mathematician Oronce Fine devised a cordiform (heart-shaped) projection on a central meridian around 1536 in order to foreground France's proximity to the New World. His projection inspired Gerardus Mercator to map the post-Ptolemaic world on parallel meridians "properly adapted for use in navigation" in 1569, allowing sailors to plot nautical direction along fixed latitudes. While not immediately adopted by navigators—Pedro Nuñes's Defense of the Sea chart (1537) counseled the use of hydrographic charts instead—Mercator's projection increased the apparent size of Europe and placed it at the center of a global network, thus symbolically expressing European preeminence in the world. Matteo Ricci, the Italian Jesuit missionary to China, had to confront the Mercator map's bias when he redesigned it in 1584–1602 for a Chinese audience; to please his hosts, he moved China to the map's center.

The use of projections to correlate terrestrial positions served as a framework to mediate new understandings of geography and encouraged the exchange of geographic information. While navigational charts long struggled to map the earth's spherical form onto a two-dimensional surface, new techniques of projection encouraged the growth of descriptive geography. The mathematician Gemma Frisius explained the construction of surveying techniques by means of triangulation in 1533, facilitating the integration of regional maps into continuous projections by means of land surveying. The expanding use of triangulated surveys—which served to define boundaries, lines of property, and military fortifications—together with terrestrial projections encouraged the development of techniques of descriptive geography. Detailed qualitative maps of cities and regions, known as chorographic maps, were gathered in over forty-three editions of Sebastian Münster's *Cosmographia* (1544). Although the rise of triangulation is usually interpreted as the origin of objective and nonpictorial cartography, maps continued to depict topography, costumes, and other cultural features. In the 1570s printers in Amsterdam and Antwerp compiled atlases of considerable elegance, assembling world, regional, and city maps of both the Old and New Worlds.

Despite their claims of detachment from social contexts, maps of the New World reflected political, economic, and ideological interests. J. B. Harley has called attention to how maps serve different rheto-

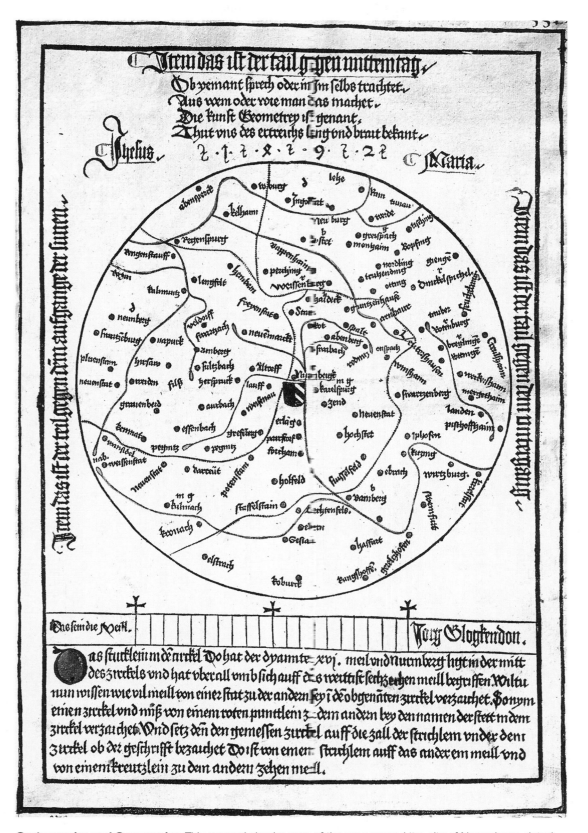

Cartography and Geography. This unusual circular map of the area around the city of Nuremberg, dated 1492, is from a copy of Hartmann Schedel's *Liber Cronicarum*, a pictorial history of the world. The text accompanying the map indicates that it covers a radius of sixteen miles from the center at Nuremberg and that it can be used as a distance indicator to the various surrounding towns by the use of the scale at the bottom. MAP COLLECTION, STERLING MEMORIAL LIBRARY, YALE UNIVERSITY

rical ends, by encoding relations of power, concealing information for political or economic reasons, and using allegorical decoration to further hidden agendas. For example, blank spaces in early maps of the Americas presented those territories as open to European conquest. Harley's arguments have stimulated scholarly work on the use of maps to assert claims of national identity in England and the Netherlands and to stake imperial claims in the New World. As Spain's overseas empire expanded, for example, a variety of maps served to demarcate boundaries of colonial jurisdiction and inscribe the relations of colonizer and colonized. Chorographies played a prominent role in images of frontiers, administrative maps, and military charts in both the Mediterranean and New World. The *Relaciones Geográficas* were commissioned by Philip II to map communities in the New World. The descriptive geographies of the Americas by Münster, Theodore de Bry (1590), and Jean de Léry (1578) glorified European conquest and helped foster a sense of European dominance, which was appealing to Europe's ruling classes.

From the late sixteenth century, mathematical geography included nautical charting. Geography became institutionalized as a tool for navigation and trade at the same time that the mastery of sea routes became a basis for staking national claims. This convergence of technological and political developments demonstrated the pragmatic uses of mapping the globe and thus encouraged wide interest in geography, while also promoting the acceptance of the Mercator projection despite its limited adoption by sailors. Martin Frobisher's search for the Northwest Passage in 1576–1578, Richard Hakluyt's *Principal Navigations, Voyages, and Discoveries of the English Nation* (1589; revised 1598–1600), and Edward Wright's (1561–1615) correction for magnetic variations in the North Sea all synthesized geography with navigation to promote England's imperial aspirations. Sir Walter Raleigh's use of explicitly commercial arguments in his 1596 protocol on the colonization of Guyana cemented the ties between geography and commerce. In response to competition from the Portuguese and the Spanish, state-owned concerns such as the Dutch East India Company (from 1602), the Dutch West India Company (founded 1621), and the Hudson Bay Company (1670) protected their maps as economic and state secrets.

Yet since most maps were confined to coastal areas, and until 1700 considerable interest was directed to mapping navigational routes, much inland territory of the world remained unmapped. There was continued reliance on nautical charting and neglect of inland areas in much of North and South America, driven largely by interest in locating El Dorado or the Northwest Passage. Around 1560–1580, long after Magellan sailed through the tip of South America, the limits of nautical cartography in the Pacific led cartographers to posit a southern "Terra Australis," in order to balance landmasses on the globe; this cartographical fiction only disappeared from maps around 1775, with the voyages of Captain Cook. Inaccuracies in mapping the size of the Pacific continued into the mid-eighteenth century, although global standards of longitude were widely accepted by 1650. Although world maps had described Africa from ancient times, Abraham Ortelius's 1573 map showing the mythical kingdom of Prester John continued to be reprinted for two centuries, and the interior of Africa was not mapped until the late eighteenth century. Similarly, classical constructions like the ends of the earth, or Antipodes, remained in the early modern geographical imagination even as more and more of the world's surface was mapped. The expansion of ethnographic geography, meanwhile, was stimulated by the travels of Jesuit missionaries among the American Indians (1637–1673) as well as collections of missionaries' maps of China in *Description de l'Empire de Chine* (1735) and *Histoire générale du Chine* (1777–1785; translated 1788).

The rise of geography as a mode of assembling facts stimulated increased scrutiny of the sources of geographical knowledge and of the expressive use of cartographic conventions, which helped to redefine cartography as an exact science. The emphasis on the accurate determination of longitude in large-scale eighteenth-century maps exemplified geography's increasingly descriptive function of measuring the earth according to fixed standards. The Bolognese astronomer Gian Domenico Cassini was summoned to Paris to found the observatory in 1669 for Louis XIV by Jean-Baptiste Colbert; there he determined the Paris meridian as a basis for the first large-scale general map of the

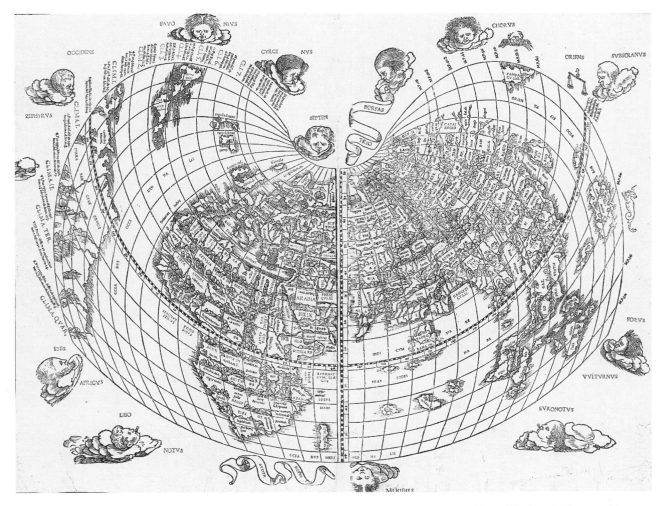

Cartography and Geography. Bernardus Sylvanus included two world maps in his 1511 edition of Ptolemy's *Geographia,* one of them this unusual cordiform or heart-shaped map in which he tried to incorporate knowledge from the new discoveries of the late fifteenth and early sixteenth centuries. It shows the Caribbean islands of Cuba and Hispaniola as well as the coast of South America and, in the North Atlantic, an island labeled "Terra Laboratorus," possibly Newfoundland. MAP COLLECTION, STERLING MEMORIAL LIBRARY, YALE UNIVERSITY

nation. His successors provided similar large-scale topographic maps for political, military, and practical purposes. Official French maps inspired Peter the Great to plan the first map of the Russian empire in 1715, and in 1726 he commissioned French surveyors to map the country. In 1714 the British government, seeking a new tool to bolster its control of the seas, established a prize for the accurate determination of longitude at sea. The problem was finally solved in 1773.

Maps and atlases illustrated and organized power relations both in the home country and in its overseas imperial possessions while reflecting the increased precision of instruments. Atlases commissioned by gentry and nobility in eighteenth-century England defined rigid hierarchies of land ownership up to the 1791 completion of the Ordnance Survey, the first comprehensive synthesis of the nation undertaken for military ends. London became a "clearinghouse" for maps of Britain's imperial system. The first extensive survey of Bengal on a graticule of meridians and parallels by the surveyor-general James Rennell in 1765–1771 stressed political geography, reflecting the competition between French and British interests vying to control the lands of the Mughal empire; his map of India of 1788 illustrated the limits of British dominion and defined the subcontinent as a coherent geographic entity for the first time. In the course of the French invasion of 1798, Napoleon Bonaparte undertook a survey of Egypt based on the Paris meridian, in his

Cartography and Geography. Sebastian Münsters's map of Europe, oriented with south at the top, is one of twenty-one "modern" maps he included in his 1540 edition of Ptolemy's *Geographia*. MAP COLLECTION, STERLING MEMORIAL LIBRARY, YALE UNIVERSITY

desire to gain territorial compensation for France's loss of overseas colonies.

Given the authority invested in maps, cartographic conventions and iconography provided states with the means to stake territorial claims and visually express national identity. The prestige of geography as a natural science led Charles-Louis de Secondat de Montesquieu (1689–1755) to classify Europe, Asia, and Africa as *continents*—a term foreign to ancient geographic writing—in order to explain their cultural differences. The discrepancies in cartographic standards, however, remained striking, given the increased accuracy and detail in maps and atlases that disseminated geographical knowledge to ever wider audiences. Whether geographic maps functioned to register spatial locations or to depict objects of prestige, by 1800 they offered important tools for organizing and transmitting information within European empires and nation-states.

See also **Colonialism; Europe and the World; Exploration; Islands; Shipbuilding and Navigation; Travel and Travel Literature.**

BIBLIOGRAPHY

Campbell, Mary B. *The Witness and the Other World: Exotic European Travel Writing, 400–1600.* Ithaca, N.Y., 1988.

Cormack, Lesley B. *Charting an Empire: Geography at the English Universities, 1580–1620.* Chicago, 1997.

Cosgrove, Denis, ed. *Mappings.* London, 1999.

Edgerton, Samuel Y., Jr. *The Heritage of Giotto's Geometry: Art and Science on the Eve of the Scientific Revolution.* Ithaca, N.Y., 1991.

Harley, J. B. *The New Nature of Maps: Essays in the History of Cartography.* Edited by Paul Laxton. Baltimore, 2001.

Marshall, P. J., and Glyndwr Williams. *The Great Map of Mankind: Perceptions of the World in the Age of Enlightenment.* London, 1982.

Mignolo, Walter D. *The Darker Side of the Renaissance: Literacy, Territoriality, and Colonization.* Ann Arbor, Mich., 1995.

Mundy, Barbara E. *Mapping New Spain: Indigenous Cartography and the Map of the* Relaciones Geográficas. Chicago, 1992.

Nebenzahl, Kenneth. *Atlas of Columbus and the Great Discoveries.* Chicago, 1990.

Randles, W. G. L. *Geography, Cartography, and Nautical Science in the Renaissance: The Impact of the Great Discoveries.* Aldershot, U.K, and Burlington, Vt., 2000.

Sobel, Dava. *Longitude: The True Story of a Lone Genius Who Solved the Greatest Scientific Problem of His Time.* New York, 1995.

Woodward, David, and J. B. Harley, eds. *The History of Cartography.* Vol. 1, *Cartography in Prehistoric, Ancient, and Medieval Europe and the Mediterranean.* Chicago, 1987.

DANIEL BROWNSTEIN

Casanova. GETTY IMAGES

CASANOVA, GIACOMO GIRO-LAMO

(Jean-Jacques, Chevalier de Seingalt; 1725–1798), Italian adventurer, bon vivant, and author. Giacomo Girolamo Casanova, sometimes known as Giovanni Giacomo Casanova, was born in Venice to an actress mother. There is some question as to whether his father was her actor husband or her protector, a member of the patrician Grimani family. After being sent to Padua at an early age to prepare for legal studies, Casanova embarked on the adventurer's life. He was funded by wealthy patrons and questionable endeavors, particularly gambling, for which he showed a marked talent. Espousing a libertine philosophy, he pursued amorous encounters of every variety that eventually broke even the strictest taboos. He traveled widely in the Mediterranean, the Italian peninsula, and the Continent, often finding high-ranking patrons and employers. While in Switzerland he joined the Freemasons.

For a number of years Casanova succeeded in avoiding punishment for his transgressions. However, his use of occult practices to gain the favor and funds of Venetian patricians resulted in his arrest on suspicion of heresy by the Venetian Inquisition. In 1755 he was imprisoned in the dreaded Leads, cells so named for their location under the lead roof of the Ducal Palace. Despite their virtually impregnable location, he effected a harrowing escape in 1756 by studying the structure of the building and ruthlessly manipulating his jailer and cellmate to obtain their assistance. As he recognized, the confinement made him less sure of himself; it also made him more tyrannical and more cruel.

Fleeing the reprisal of the Venetian state, he traveled to the capitals of Europe and endeavored to have himself introduced to the ruling class. Instrumental in these efforts were the title Chevalier de Seingalt, which he conferred upon himself, and his familiarity with occult practices. As he made clear in his autobiography, he did not believe in such practices, but he found many aristocrats who sought his assistance in projects such as being reborn. In spite of some successes in aristocratic circles, he was expelled from host countries as a result of both true and false accusations of shady practices.

Eager to return to his homeland, Casanova wrote a defense of the Venetian system of governance that helped him achieve this goal in 1774. Hired as a spy for the Venetian Inquisition, he also cultivated the literary career to which he had long aspired. When a member of the Grimani family failed to support him in a dispute over money in 1782, he was unable to curb his pen. He wrote a fable (*Nè amori nè donne ovvero la stala ripulita* [Neither love affairs nor women, or the cleansing of the stable]) satirizing the vanity and weakness of the patriciate in general and the Grimani in particular; this resulted in his definitive exile.

Casanova passed his final years as the librarian to Count von Waldstein in Bohemia. His works include treatises on such matters as the troubles of the Polish state; poems; and a translation of the *Iliad* (1775). Some hold that he collaborated with Lorenzo da Ponte (1749–1838) on the libretto for Mozart's *Don Giovanni* (1787), or that he served as an inspiration for the Don. His twelve-volume autobiography, *Histoire de ma vie,* provides a densely detailed account of life in the Old Regime, including the privileges of powerful aristocrats, which he supported and appropriated as his entitlement, the expediencies by which many survived, the unpredictable disruptions wrought by disease and death, and the impulsive grasping of consolatory pleasures. Fascination with his life has given rise to Casanova Societies in many countries. Casanova's love affairs and adventures inspired numerous films, perhaps the most famous of which is Fellini's *Casanova* (1976). His surname has become a byword for the man who practices amorous license.

See also **Aristocracy and Gentry.**

BIBLIOGRAPHY

Primary Sources

Casanova, Giacomo. *History of My Life.* 12 vols. Translated by Willard R. Trask. Baltimore, Md., 1997. Translation of *Mémoires* (1797).

———. *Saggi, libelli e satire.* Edited by Pietro Chiara. Milan, 1968.

Secondary Sources

Childs, J. Rives. *Casanova: A New Perspective.* New York, 1988.

Pollio, Joseph. *Bibliographie anecdotique et critique des oeuvres de Jacques Casanova.* Paris, 1926.

LINDA L. CARROLL

CASTIGLIONE, BALDASSARE (1478–1529),

Italian writer and diplomat. The fame of Baldassare Castiglione rests with his dialogue-treatise *Il cortegiano (The Book of the Courtier),* first published in 1528 and immediately acclaimed in Italy and throughout Europe. For centuries it served as the model "courtesy" book, a guide, both ethical and aesthetic, for the social relations of gentlemen and ladies.

Castiglione was born in Casatico, near Mantua, on 6 November 1478, the son of Cristoforo, a professional soldier in the service of the Marquis of Mantua, and Aloisa Gonzaga, who was related to the ruling family. In 1490 he was sent to Milan to pursue humanistic studies. When his father died in 1499 he returned to Mantua and began a military and diplomatic career, first in the service of Gianfrancesco Gonzaga, then in 1504 with Guidobaldo Della Rovere, later with Francesco Della Rovere, dukes of Urbino. In 1516, he married a Bolognese noblewoman, Ippolita Torelli, who died in 1520 in childbirth. He had by then returned to the service of the duke of Mantua and in 1521 he took minor orders. In 1524 Clement VII named him papal nuncio to the court of Charles V in Spain, where he was received in 1525 and where he spent the rest of his life. The pope blamed him for not preventing the sack of Rome at the hands of imperial troops in 1527, but contemporaries tended to blame the vacillating Clement, who was unable to ally himself firmly with either the French or the Spanish. Castiglione died of plague fevers in Toledo on 8 February 1529.

Besides *The Courtier* (1528), Castiglione wrote a dramatic eclogue, the *Tirsi* (1506), for Carnival at Urbino in 1506 in which he also performed, a Latin letter in praise of his patron, the *De vita et gestis Guidubaldi Urbini Ducis* (The life and deeds of Guidobaldo, duke of Urbino; 1508), and the prologue, now lost, to the *Calandria* (1513), a comedy written by Bibbiena (Bernardo Dovizi), whose first performance he organized in Urbino. Castiglione also wrote conventional poetry in the Petrarchist mode and humanistic verse in Latin. He left a large and important correspondence.

Castiglione had begun writing *The Courtier* by 1513–1514, and it occupied him for most of the rest of his life. The book is a dialogue that follows the classical models of Plato and Cicero, both in its proposal of an ideal type to be imitated, the perfect courtier, and in its choice of dialogic form, for which it is especially indebted to the Ciceronian model. Like Cicero, Castiglione chooses as interlocutors contemporary historical figures, known for the attitudes and actions they represent, who take different sides in the discussion of subjects of contemporary debate, thus lending verisimilitude to the dialogue and giving the conversations a lively, dramatic quality. The book is also autobiographical. The conversations it depicts are set at the court of Urbino in 1506, and the interlocutors are courtiers and ladies many of whom Castiglione met during the years he spent there. He remembers them and those days with nostalgia.

In Book 1 the assembled courtiers and ladies propose games for their entertainment and decide upon one in which they will have to "form in words a perfect courtier." The courtier they envision must be a nobleman, whose principal profession is arms and who engages and excels in physical activities, always maintaining his dignity. He is a connoisseur and a practitioner of the arts and letters, who exhibits moderation in all he does, avoids affectation, and performs with grace *(grazia)* and seemingly without effort (with *sprezzatura*). Outward appearance is of the utmost importance. Book 1 includes digressions on the current debates regarding the vernacular language, on the relative importance of arms and of letters for the courtier, and on the question of the preeminence of painting or sculpture. Book 2 treats the ways and circumstances in which the ideal courtier might demonstrate his qualities and argues the importance of decorum and of conversational skills, especially his ability to entertain with humorous language. Examples are given that constitute a collection of witty stories and practical jokes. Book 3 imagines a suitable female companion for the courtier, who has many of his same qualities and talents, though physical beauty is more important for her, as is her good reputation. The virtue of women is both discussed and demonstrated through examples, ancient and modern,

Baldassare Castiglione. LIBRARY OF CONGRESS

which provide another collection of entertaining stories. In Book 4 we come to the courtier's raison d'être, his service to his prince, and after long discussion the topic of conversation turns to love, a theme introduced in Book 3, and centers on how the courtier, no longer young, should love. The theory of Neoplatonic love is proposed, following closely Marsilio Ficino's Christianizing commentary on Plato's *Symposium*.

Modern critical debate on *The Courtier* has centered on the ethics of its excessive concern with outward appearance, the author's unwillingness to dwell on politics, and on some issues of coherence. However, no one disputes the status of *The Courtier* as a masterpiece, a brilliant original that was never surpassed by any of its many imitators, and a "portrait" of the culture of Italian Renaissance court society in the early sixteenth century.

See also **Advice and Etiquette Books; Court and Courtiers; Gentleman.**

BIBLIOGRAPHY

Primary Sources

Castiglione, Baldassare. *The Book of the Courtier*. Translated by Charles S. Singleton. New York, 1959. Reprinted in the Norton Critical Edition. Edited by Daniel Javitch. New York, 2002.

————. *The Book of the Courtier.* Translated by George Bull. London, 1967. Reprint 1976.

————. *Il libro del cortegiano con una scelta delle Opere minori.* Edited by Bruno Maier. 2nd ed. Turin, 1964.

————. *Lettere.* Vol. 1. Edited by Guido La Rocca. Milan, 1978.

Secondary Sources

Burke, Peter. *The Fortunes of the Courtier: The European Reception of Castiglione's Cortegiano.* Cambridge, U.K., 1995.

Hanning, Robert W., and David Rosand, eds. *Castiglione: The Ideal and the Real in Renaissance Culture.* New Haven and London, 1983.

Quondam, Amedeo. *"Questo povero Cortegiano": Castiglione, il libro, la storia.* Rome, 2000.

Rebhorn, W. A. *Courtly Performances: Masking and Festivity in Castiglione's* Book of the Courtier. Detroit, 1978.

Woodhouse, J. R. *Baldesar Castiglione: A Reassessment of "The Courtier."* Edinburgh, 1978.

ELISSA B. WEAVER

CATALONIA. Catalonia is a land of mountains and seashores in the northeastern corner of Spain. The northern Pyrenees and the western Sierra de Cadi create the mountainous profile visible from the eastern stretch of the Mediterranean coast. The foothills of these mountains extend throughout the region, flattening only at the coastline. Rivers cut through the valleys, making their way to the Mediterranean and connecting the mercantile and industrial cities of the coast with the agricultural interior. To the south, only the flat, marshy delta of the Ebro River resists the Sierran uplift.

A province of approximately 300,000 people by the end of the fifteenth century, Catalonia was the political and economic force of the Crown of Aragón, wielding this power through its capital city, Barcelona. Catalonia was governed by the Corts, the parliament representing the province in dealings with the king, and by the Diputació del General, the treasury and tax-collecting agency of the Corts. The union of Isabella of Castile and Ferdinand of Aragón in 1469 brought the two crowns under one monarchy. Despite this union, Catalonia continued to govern itself, reflecting Ferdinand's vision of a united Spain ruling over coexisting autonomous regions.

Catalonia did not share in Castile's "Golden Age" in the sixteenth century, which was fueled in large part by exploitation of Castile's American territories. Although Ferdinand repeatedly affirmed the Crown of Aragón's right to participate in transatlantic trade, several factors inhibited this. Seville was the official port for Spain's American empire and the most convenient port for the trade, which disadvantaged Mediterranean merchants. Moreover, Catalonia suffered from a lack of capital following a civil war (1462–1472) in addition to a contraction in population caused by repeated waves of plague from the fourteenth century onward. The population of mid-sixteenth century Catalonia (331,000) never reached one-twentieth that of Castile (6,300,000).

During the reign of Philip IV, as Spain faced economic depression and extraordinary expenses in the Thirty Years' War, the crown looked to Catalonia and other parts of its monarchy for increased tax revenues. The Catalans feared the loss of their traditional liberties and resisted the efforts of Philip IV's chief minister, the count-duke of Olivares, to raise their contributions to the Habsburgs' war efforts. Intransigence on both sides led to the Catalan rebellion of 1640–1652, which ended with a royal victory and a wise decision by the crown not to punish the rebels too harshly. Catalonia remained loyal to the Habsburgs when a Bourbon prince inherited the throne of Spain. When the Bourbons retained the throne after the hard-fought War of the Spanish Succession (1701–1714), they determined to bring Catalonia under closer central control. Nonetheless, Bourbon economic policies channeled resources into Catalan industry and commerce in the eighteenth century. Thanks to a boom in industries such as cotton manufacturing, and the opening of the American trade to all Spanish ports after 1765, Catalonia was arguably the most dynamic part of Spain at the end of the eighteenth century, with a population approaching one million. Efforts of French revolutionaries to incite another revolt in Catalonia against the Bourbon monarchy were not effective, and Catalonia shared the fate of the rest of Spain during the Napoleonic invasion and the subsequent war of independence against the French.

See also Barcelona; Catalonia, Revolt of (1640–1652); Charles III (Spain); Ferdinand of Aragón; Isabella of Castile; Spanish Succession, War of the (1701–1714); Thirty Years' War (1618–1648).

BIBLIOGRAPHY

Read, Jan. *The Catalans*. London, 1978.

Vicens Vives, Jaime. *An Economic History of Spain*. Princeton, 1969.

Vilar, Pierre. *La catalogne dans l'Espagne moderne*. Paris, 1986.

SHELLEY E. ROFF

CATALONIA, REVOLT OF (1640–1652).

The Revolt of Catalonia, in which much of what is today eastern Spain revolted against the crown of Philip IV of Spain, was motivated by fiscal, political, and long-standing historical issues. Since the Middle Ages, Catalonia had been part of the former Crown of Aragon, which essentially was joined to the Crown of Castile in 1517 with the reign of Charles V, whose parents, Ferdinand and Isabella, were, respectively, monarchs of the two kingdoms. But though they were joined, with royal viceroys from Castile overseeing the territories, the two realms retained separate representative assemblies, and Catalonia did not pay taxes for the Spanish monarchy's imperial adventures. Castile and Catalonia also spoke different languages and had different political traditions; in particular, Catalan land tenure was closer to French feudalism than to the system that emerged from the Castilian Reconquest.

In the 1620s and 1630s, Philip IV and his chief minister, Gaspar de Guzmán, the Count-Duke of Olivares (1587–1645), gradually found themselves engaged in three European wars: the Thirty Years' War (1618–1648), a renewed fight with the Dutch (beginning in 1621), and in 1635, war with France. Olivares, determined to modernize the army and state finance, insisted that all of Spain, including Catalonia, pay its fair share and be subject to the same laws. In 1625 he proposed the Union of Arms, a military levy that would have drawn conscripts from throughout Spain and its possessions in Italy. The Catalonian representative assembly, the Corts, refused to comply.

After war broke out with France, Olivares tried again to squeeze men and money out of the Catalans, who felt more affinity with the French than with the increasingly demanding Castilians. Though men were conscripted from around the peninsula, the Catalans continued to resist, and Olivares, his threats having failed, decided to convert Catalonia itself into a theater of war. He launched attacks on France from Catalonia, impressing Catalan men and billeting Castilian troops, thus (he thought) ensuring the Catalans' loyalty.

France in 1639 captured the fort of Salses (Roussillon), and a long and bloody siege ensued, which the Catalans were told to finance as well as suffer. Spain finally won the siege on 6 January 1640, but lost Catalonia in the process. Horror at the behavior of the billeted troops, grief over the loss of thousands of men, and outrage as their traditional political rights were trampled made it easy work for patriots, many of them priests, to stir the population. Chief among these patriots was Pau Claris (1586–1641), the canon of Urgell, who became president of the Catalan government, the Generalitat, in 1638. In March 1640, the Spanish viceroy, the count of Santa Coloma, ordered the arrest of one of Claris's government colleagues. In response, armed rebels, many of them peasants, essentially took over the countryside, staging a series of attacks, including the 22 May 1640 release of the imprisoned deputy. Olivares saw that his heavy-handed approach had backfired and tried to mollify the Catalans, but it was too late. On 7 June Santa Coloma was beaten to death by a mob, and the Guerra dels Segadors, or the Reapers War, began.

The Revolt of the Catalans was really two wars at once: a social revolution pitting rich against poor and a political revolt pitting Catalans against Castilians. As the Catalan poor turned against the Catalan rich, the elites turned to France rather than seek common cause with their neighbors, Valencia and Aragon, with whom they shared a language and many traditions. In allying with France, however, Catalonia exchanged one master for another.

In January 1641 the combined military forces of France and Catalonia defeated the Castilian army of the marquis of los Vélez in the Battle of Montjuich (Barcelona). Claris died soon after, and no similarly charismatic leader stepped forward to unite the Catalans. The aristocracy was no fonder of the French than of the Castilians, as the French Bourbon monarchy seemed even less interested in Catalan rights than the Spanish Habsburg Monarchy.

The count-duke fell from power in January 1643 and was replaced by his nephew Don Luis de Haro. In July 1644 the king swore to observe the Catalan Constitution. The following few years produced a military stalemate, but in 1648, when the Dutch Revolt ended (after eighty years) with the signing of the Treaty of Münster, and the Thirty Years' War ended with the Peace of Westphalia, Philip finally was free to devote his full attention to the home front.

Also in 1648, the Fronde broke out, forcing the French to withdraw from Catalonia, leaving the rebels to fight alone. By then, many of the leading Catalan aristocrats had reconciled with the Spanish crown, vastly preferring their Castilian peers to the Catalan rabble. Philip's illegitimate son, Don Juan of Austria, in 1651 initiated a siege of Barcelona; the city was starved into surrender on 13 October 1652.

Philip wisely decided not to humiliate the rebels. Instead, he issued an amnesty, and the Catalan laws and Corts were spared; they survived until yet another unsuccessful war against Madrid, the War of the Spanish Succession (1701–1714), when Catalonia chose to fight with the Habsburgs and against the Bourbons, instead of the other way around. The new Spanish Bourbon king, Philip V, took long-lasting revenge after 1714, eradicating many of Catalonia's laws and liberties.

The Revolt of the Catalans was one of a series of convulsions (including the Fronde, the Thirty Years' War, the English Civil War, and revolts in Italy, Portugal, and Holland) that historians have regarded as indicative of a wider seventeenth-century crisis. These events have also been seen as parts of larger phenomena such as the final transition to capitalism, the collapse of the old aristocracy, the emergence of modern states, and the triumphant authority of centralizing monarchies.

The revolt weakened the Spanish monarchy when it was under attack on multiple fronts, and it inspired the Portuguese to stage an ultimately successful revolt in December 1640. Remarkably, though the monarchy lost wealth, territory, and power, it survived, demonstrating that its resources and perhaps its very structure were more forgiving of crisis than has been thought. The revolt was one of the last tests of the flexibilities and peculiarities of the Spanish Habsburg Monarchy, a whole of many parts which, despite Olivares's intentions, was predicated upon considerable local autonomy and negotiation. The anthem of Catalonia to this day is "Els Segadors."

See also **Dutch Revolt (1568–1648); English Civil War and Interregnum; Juan de Austria, Don; Olivares, Gaspar de Guzmán y Pimentel, count of; Philip IV (Spain); Restoration, Portuguese War of (1640–1648); Thirty Years' War (1618–1648).**

BIBLIOGRAPHY

Elliott, J. H. *The Count-Duke of Olivares.* New Haven, 1986.

———. *The Revolt of the Catalans: A Study in the Decline of Spain 1598–1640.* Cambridge, U.K., 1963.

Lynch, John. *The Hispanic World in Crisis and Change 1598–1700.* Oxford, 1992.

Merriman, Roger B. *Six Contemporaneous Revolutions.* Oxford, 1938.

Parker, Geoffrey. *Europe in Crisis, 1598–1648.* London, 1979.

Stradling, R. A. *Spain's Struggle for Europe, 1598–1668.* London, 1994.

RUTH MACKAY

CATEAU-CAMBRÉSIS (1559). Cateau-Cambrésis is a town in northern France where a treaty was signed ending the last English foothold on the Continent. On 2 April 1559, Henry II of France (ruled 1547–1559) accepted terms that brought the Habsburg-Valois Wars to a close. After a truce in 1556, war had resumed in 1557 and subsequent successes helped determine the nature of the peace. The Spanish forces that invaded France from the Low Countries in 1557 won an important victory at Saint-Quentin (10 August 1557), when a relieving army for the besieged fortress was heavily defeated. In the battle, the Spaniards made effective use of their cavalry, especially of pistoleers, in which they outnumbered the French. Philip II of Spain (ruled 1556–1598) organized the campaign that led to this victory and followed it up by leading the successful storming of Arras.

The following January, however, French forces bombarded Calais, England's last foothold on mainland France, into surrender in a campaign characterized by bold French generalship: Mary Tudor, queen of England (ruled 1553–1558), was the wife of Philip II, and she had declared war on France in June 1557. The French pressed on to try to take Dunkirk by surprise attack, but they were defeated at Gravelines on 13 July 1558. The Spanish pistoleers again outnumbered their French counterparts; they both won the cavalry fight and hit the French pike, who were also affected by Spanish harquebus power.

Aside from being defeated in battle, Henry II was also bankrupted by the heavy cost of the war and alarmed by the spread of Protestantism in France. The ability of the Spaniards to advance into France meant that Henry could not finance his army by ravaging the Spanish Netherlands. The Religious Peace of Augsburg of 1555, in which Henry's German allies had settled their differences with the Habsburgs, had also weakened Henry's position. As a result, he accepted a treaty that left France bereft of what her monarchs had fought for since 1494. Spain was left in control of Milan, Naples, and Sicily, the key positions that established Spanish power in Italy, and that at a time when Italy was the center of the Christian world.

In addition, the French had to yield their positions in Tuscany, which was now securely dominated by the Medici rulers of Florence, allies of Spain, while Savoy and Piedmont, which France had seized in 1536, were returned to Duke Emanuel Philibert of Savoy, a Spanish client. The French, however, kept Calais, and this marked the end of the pursuit by English monarchs of territorial gains in France.

French failure ensured that there was no reversal in the Peace of Cateau-Cambrésis of the removal (by treaties in 1525 and 1529) of Artois and Flanders from the suzerainty of the French crown. This was the first major retreat of the French crown from the frontier originally designated in 843 when Charlemagne's inheritance was lastingly divided. The frontier between the Valois and Habsburg territories in the Low Countries had become that between France and the empire.

This settlement was not to be seriously challenged until the 1640s, in large part because of the weakness of the French monarchy after the death of Henry II following a jousting accident in 1559. This, indeed, ensures that Cateau-Cambrésis is well known, whereas earlier peaces between Philip II's father, Charles V, and French monarchs, such as the Treaty of Madrid (14 January 1526), the Treaty of Cambrai (3 August 1529), and the Peace of Crépy (18 September 1544), are largely forgotten. However, had Henry lived, or been succeeded by another vigorous monarch, France would have tried to contest the settlement. Indeed, in 1572, Gaspar de Coligny, the Huguenot leader, sought to unite France behind a plan for intervening against the Spaniards in the Netherlands. This was preempted when Charles IX turned against the Huguenots, but the policy was to be resumed by Henry IV (ruled 1589–1610). Cateau-Cambrésis should therefore be seen as a stage, not a definitive settlement.

See also **Habsburg-Valois Wars; Henry II (France); Mary I (England); Philip II (Spain).**

BIBLIOGRAPHY

Black, Jeremy, ed. *European Warfare, 1494–1660.* New York, 2002.

JEREMY BLACK

CATHERINE II (RUSSIA)

CATHERINE II (RUSSIA) (1729–1796; ruled 1762–1796), empress of Russia. Catherine II, known as Catherine the Great, was born Princess Sophie in Stettin, Anhalt-Zerbst, a remote and poor German principality on the Baltic Sea. She was betrothed to the heir to the Russian throne, the future Peter III, in 1744. Upon her arrival in St. Petersburg, she converted to Russian Orthodoxy and was given the Russian name of Catherine Alekseevna, after Catherine I, Russia's first female crowned head and the mother of the reigning empress Elizabeth, Peter's aunt. Catherine remained in Russia for the rest of her life, and her stay can be divided into three unequal periods: as wife of the heir apparent (1745–1761), as consort to the emperor (six months in 1762), and as monarch (1762–1796).

WIFE AND CONSORT

By all available accounts—a mixture of personal court gossip, self-serving memoirs, and diplomatic reports—Catherine's marriage to Peter was an emotional disaster, and perhaps unconsummated. Catherine's own narrative of these years (her vaunted memoirs, which remained unpublished until the mid-nineteenth century) described Peter as childish, tempestuous, unloving, and enamored of only three things: his mistress, his toy soldiers, and Prussia. Catherine spent these years relatively excluded from court, but she nevertheless gathered around herself a coterie of admirers and her early lovers, as well as significant figures in the guards' regiments, many of whom found Peter's behavior and his Prussophilia disturbing.

By the time Peter ascended the throne in 1762, he and Catherine were estranged, and by some accounts she was already preparing to replace him as monarch. Her moment came barely six months into his reign, in late June 1762, when several officers of the elite regiments swore allegiance to her, followed immediately by thousands of "cheering" troops. Confronted by this fait accompli, Peter is said to have surrendered meekly, requesting merely that he be allowed to keep his dog (agreed), his toys (agreed), and his mistress (denied). Whether by design or inadvertently, Peter was assassinated within days, thus bringing his bride to the throne as an unacknowledged regicide.

IDEOLOGY AND ENLIGHTENMENT

Once on the throne, Catherine aggressively represented herself as the quintessence of enlightened monarchy, the true heir of Peter the Great. This affinity was reproduced in countless ceremonies and visual images, most famously in Étienne-Maurice Falconet's statue the Bronze Horseman, unveiled in 1782 with the inscription "Petro Primo—Catherina Secunda" ('To Peter the First from Catherine the Second'). Her highly public correspondences with Friedrich Melchior Grimm, Voltaire, Denis Diderot, and other leading *lumières* conveyed the message that Catherine and, through her, Russian statecraft, embodied the highest virtues of reason and order. Perhaps the clearest expression of these views came in her legislative writings, both the major laws and the famous Instruction *(Nakaz)* to the Legislative Commission, written in 1767. This latter text combined an explicit reconfirmation of absolutism with a categorical Europeanness (in the declaration that "Russia is a European state")

and displayed a preoccupation with laws, citizenship, and human happiness that strongly suggested a desire to make Russia into a more orderly, law-driven polity. Historians remain divided whether quasi-liberal sentiments motivated these expressions or, conversely, whether they constituted an interventionist instinct for "a well-ordered police state."

The Legislative Commission was a remarkable semipublic forum that brought representatives of all legally constituted social groups—save the serfs, who were deemed to be represented by landlords—and several ethnic minorities. Although it produced precious little actual legislation and never came close to generating a draft for a new fundamental law, the so-called Great Commission did enable a wide-ranging series of discussions on fundamental issues such as serfdom, social identity, trade, and education. Local deputies came to the sessions armed with instructions from their constituents, and recent research has shown that considerable consultation took place in drafting those instructions. Equally noteworthy, but less frequently acknowledged, is the Commission's afterlife, which extended until the end of Catherine's reign in the form of "particular" or private commissions that continued to discuss issues, albeit more privately and on a less grandiose level. Although these private commissions fell well short of an embryonic civil society, they did allow for an officially sanctioned and ongoing deliberation of law and policy outside of the narrow confines of state institutions.

DOMESTIC POLICY AND LEGISLATION

In the wake of the dangerous Pugachev revolt of 1773–1775 Catherine initiated a decade-long blizzard of important new legislation (sometimes dubbed "legislomania"), collectively designed to strengthen civil and moral order. The first of these statutes, the Provincial Reform of 1775, significantly increased the size of formal provincial government by creating thirty-five provinces with civil administrations that were considerably larger than previously and with a much broader set of responsibilities. The provincial reform gave local nobility every opportunity to take control of these new bodies, while making certain that the key figures, the governor and military governor, would be centrally appointed and chosen from among loyal and high-ranking individuals.

Catherine II. Portrait by Fyodor Rokotov, 1770. ©Archivo Iconografico, S.A./Corbis

Major statutes on urban welfare and police (1782), public education (1782), private publishing (1783), and the Charters to the Nobility and to the Towns (both in 1785) soon ensued. These last two documents sought to codify the corporate status of the empress's subjects (something under ten percent of the total population) who were neither peasants nor legally inscribed ethnic minorities. A similar charter was drafted for the peasants but never enacted. In addition, the state began a major initiative to populate the area north of the Black Sea known as New Russia (Novorossiia) and to develop the agricultural potential of this black-earth temperate zone. This policy encouraged immigration, both from other regions of the empire and from abroad, especially from impoverished German states. These policies enabled Russia to expand its already substantial export of raw materials, including grain, furs, and, by some accounts, large quantities of silver. The Russian economy grew correspondingly, equaling some of the highest rates of expansion in preindustrial Europe.

FOREIGN AFFAIRS
Bracketed by the end of the Seven Years' War at the beginning and the French Revolutionary wars at the end, Catherine's foreign policy was dominated by more immediate neighbors, the Ottoman Empire and the Commonwealth of Poland-Lithuania. The victory over the Ottomans that ended the protracted war of 1768–1774 led to the Treaty of Kuchuk Kainarji, which afforded Russia considerable access to the Black Sea, Crimea, and the Danubian provinces of Moldavia and Walachia. It also strengthened Russia's protectorate over Orthodox Christians in Ottoman territory. Russia's merchant fleet could now sail unimpeded through the Bosporus into the open waters of the Mediterranean. As a result, Russia's Black Sea trade burgeoned, leading to the establishment of the port city of Odessa in 1794. As before, however, its warships were denied access to the Bosporus, notwithstanding the rapid growth of Russia's Black Sea fleet.

With the Polish-Lithuanian Commonwealth the issues were different. Having achieved access to the Baltic and the North Sea earlier in the eighteenth century, Russia, along with Prussia and the Habsburg Monarchy, had been deeply involved in Polish politics, having bought off numerous Polish magnates and placed more than one king on the Polish throne. By the early 1770s the Commonwealth's parliament, or Sejm, had lost any semblance of independence, and its principle of *liberum veto*, originally intended to protect the interests of poorer or remote regions, instead paralyzed the Sejm. The three neighboring states therefore partially partitioned Poland in 1772. The integration of the eastern lands of the Commonwealth (mainly modern Ukraine and Belarus) into the Russian empire proved to be a mixed blessing. Substantive political reform in Poland, leading to the Constitution of 3 May 1791, prompted the second partition by Prussia and Russia in 1793, and Tadeusz Kościuszko's nationalist rebellion of 1794 was crushed by a brutal assault from the Russian army. Soon followed the third partition (1795), by which the three powers eliminated the Polish-Lithuanian state altogether. Henceforth Polish identity defined itself largely in contradistinction to Russian. The partition of Poland also brought a large Jewish population into the Russian empire.

A NOTE ON CATHERINE'S SEXUALITY
Long consigned to prurient anecdotes, Catherine's sexual reputation and the contemporary responses to it have recently attracted serious scholarly attention. As far as is known, she had perhaps twelve lovers between 1752 and her death. One of the earliest, Sergei Saltykov, was almost certainly the biological father of her son, the future Paul I, and two others (Grigorii Orlov and Stanisław August Poniatowski) fathered two additional children, a boy and a girl, never publicly acknowledged. Although most of these men came from distinguished families and had noteworthy political careers (Poniatowski, for example, was elected king of Poland in 1764), none appears to have used his status to affect state policy, with the single and very noteworthy exception of Grigorii Potemkin, with whom Catherine was deeply in love in the mid-1770s and whom, an increasing number of specialists believe, she secretly wed in 1774. Whether true or not, the massive correspondence between the two overflows with affection and mutual respect, even after Potemkin ceased to be the empress's paramour.

Although private liaisons were commonplace for Europe's crowned heads, Catherine's experiences hold particular interest for what they reveal about the implicit strictures of female rule in Russia. Like her predecessors, Catherine was obliged to rule unmarried, to be officially chaste irrespective of the realities of her private life. She could maintain open liaisons, even give birth if need be, but unlike male rulers, she could not remarry or be allowed a consort for fear, one assumes, of polluting the imaginary male line. Such tacit limitations meant that the sexuality of a female ruler would be unavoidably political in ways that a male ruler's would likely never be.

See also **Black Sea Steppe; Elizabeth (Russia); Enlightened Despotism; Enlightenment; Imperial Expansion, Russia; Paul I (Russia); Poland, Partitions of; Poland-Lithuania, Commonwealth of, 1569–1795; Pugachev Revolt (1773–1775); Queens and Empresses; Russia; Russian Literature and Language; Russo-Ottoman Wars.**

BIBLIOGRAPHY

Primary Sources

Anthony, Katherine, trans. *The Memoirs of Catherine the Great.* New York and London, 1927.

Griffiths, David, and George E. Munro, eds. and trans. *Catherine II's Charters of 1785 to the Nobility and the Towns.* Bakersfield, Calif., 1990.

Secondary Sources

Alexander, John T. *Catherine the Great: Life and Legend.* New York, 1989.

de Madariaga, Isabel. *Russia in the Age of Catherine the Great.* London, 1981.

Dixon, Simon. *Catherine the Great.* Harlow, U.K., and New York, 2001.

Griffiths, David M. "The Rise and Fall of the Northern System: Court Politics and Foreign Policy in the First Part of Catherine II's Reign." *Canadian Slavic Studies* 4, no. 3 (1970): 547–569.

LeDonne, John P. *Ruling Russia: Politics and Administration in the Age of Absolutism, 1762–1796.* Princeton, 1984.

Ransel, David L. *The Politics of Catherinian Russia: The Panin Party.* New Haven, 1975.

GARY MARKER

CATHERINE DE MÉDICIS (1519–1589),

queen of France. Wife of King Henry II, mother of Kings Francis II, Charles IX, and Henry III, Catherine de Médicis, the power behind the throne in France for three decades, has generated passionate opinions among contemporaries and historians alike. She was born in 1519 into one of the greatest Italian princely families: her father, Lorenzo de' Medici, was duke of Urbino, and her uncle was Pope Clement VII. Her mother, Madeleine de La Tour, was daughter of Jean, comte d'Auvergne, and Jeanne de Bourbon-Vendôme, both related to the French royal family.

Her marriage in 1533 to Henry, the younger son of Francis I, was a product of French dynastic ambitions in Italy. But the death of the second Medici pope, Clement VII, a year later, negated the political advantage of the match, and Catherine's isolation at court was increased by her husband's devotion to his mistress, Diane de Poitiers. When Henry acceded to the throne on his father's death in 1547, it was Diane who ruled as queen in all but name. Catherine's political role was limited to the production of children: four sons and a daughter survived into adulthood. Her husband's accidental death in 1559 did not at first usher her into the front rank of politics, but the weak Guise-dominated regime of her eldest son, Francis II, increasingly involved her in policy making in order to widen its base of support. Her real political career began at the age of forty-one with the death of Francis II on 5 December 1560 and her elevation as regent on the accession of the ten-year-old Charles IX.

Catherine faced the problem of combating Protestantism while monarchical authority was weak. She appointed Anthony of Bourbon, king of Navarre, as lieutenant-general of the kingdom and promoted a group of moderates to the royal council who were led by the chancellor, Michel de L'Hôpital. Under her aegis, they embarked on a policy of compromise, toning down the repression of heresy and promoting the cause of doctrinal reconciliation between the faiths, most notably at the Colloquy of Poissy (August 1561). When it was clear that doctrinal compromise was impossible, she hoped to foster stability and peace by establishing limited legal toleration of Protestantism, enshrined in the edict of January 1562. Her policies were anathema to many Catholics and as early as Easter 1561 a group of magnates, led by the duke of Guise and the constable of Montmorency, formed the Triumvirate to resist change. The king of Navarre's

Catherine de Médicis. Portrait by François Clouet.
©Archivo Iconografico S.A./Corbis

defection to the Triumvirate following the Edict of Toleration and the outbreak of civil war were a serious blow to Catherine's policy and left her at the mercy of the factions. The assassination of the duke of Guise by a Huguenot in March 1563 allowed her to broker peace anew and recommence the policy of compromise. During the four years of peace that followed, Catherine dominated government and worked hard to rebuild royal authority. To this end she embarked on a tour of France (1564–1566) with her son Charles. Yet during this period Catherine's commitment to toleration was put into question by her growing reliance on a group of Ultra-Catholic Italian advisors. Protestant suspicions of her motives at a meeting in 1566 with the Spanish envoy, the duke of Alba, were partly responsible for the recommencement of civil war in 1567.

Catherine was once again instrumental in negotiating peace in 1570, and to ensure its durability she arranged the marriage of her daughter, Marguerite, to the leader of the Protestants, Henri de Navarre. Her policy began to unravel when French Protestant intervention in the Low Countries threatened to reignite civil war. Her role in the St. Bartholomew's Day Massacre is contentious, but it seems likely that while she sanctioned the murder of the Protestant leader, Gaspard de Coligny, her responsibility for the popular massacre that followed is less certain. She now lost all credit with the Protestants and though her hold on power at court was as great as ever, the fortunes of the monarchy sank to ever lower depths. Until her death in 1589, Catherine continued to enjoy influence during the reign of her favorite son, Henry III, who came to the throne in 1574, most notably brokering a peace with the Protestants in 1578–1579 and attempting to reconcile her son with the rebel duke of Guise in 1585 and 1588. Catherine realized that civil war undermined royal authority, and she worked to reconcile factions, but her methods and motives were not always trusted, leaving her with the mostly unfair reputation of a Machiavellian plotter and conspirator.

See also **Coligny Family; France; Guise Family; Poissy, Colloquy of; St. Bartholomew's Day Massacre; Valois Dynasty; Wars of Religion, French.**

BIBLIOGRAPHY

Diefendorf, Barbara. *Beneath the Cross: Catholics and Huguenots in Sixteenth-Century Paris.* New York and Oxford 1991. Chapter 6 is the most reliable account in English of the Massacre of Saint Bartholomew.

Knecht, Robert. *Catherine de' Medici.* London, 1998.

Nugent, Donald. *Ecumenism in the Age of Reformation: The Colloquy of Poissy.* Cambridge, Mass., 1974.

Soman, Alfred, ed. *The Massacre of Saint Bartholomew: Reappraisals and Documents.* The Hague, 1974.

Sutherland, N. M. *Catherine de Medici and the Ancien Régime.* London 1966.

———. *The French Secretaries of State in the Age of Catherine de Medici.* London, 1962.

———. "The Legend of the Wicked Queen." In *Princes, Politics and Religion, 1547–1589.* London, 1984.

———. *The Massacre of Saint Bartholomew and the European Conflict, 1559–1572.* London. 1973.

STUART CARROLL

CATHOLIC LEAGUE (FRANCE). The Catholic League originated in France in the 1560s, when communities formed local defense organizations to protect themselves against armed Protestants and oppose the implementation of royal policies that gave legal recognition to Protestantism. In 1576, in the wake of the most tolerant royal edict so far, a union of Catholics was formed under the aegis of the nobility in a number of regions, most notably in Picardy, which swore to uphold the faith and protect provincial liberties. King Henry III was able to outmaneuver the nascent league and suppress it. However, in 1584 the death of Henry's younger brother left a Protestant, Henry of Navarre, as heir to the throne. The league was now revived, and its power derived from an alliance between the powerful Spanish-funded Guise family and a radical popular Catholic power base, notably in Paris. In 1588 the league mounted a putsch, seized Paris, and expelled Henry III. When Henry later had the Guise brothers assassinated, large parts of France revolted, dethroned him, and established a regime based on representative institutions and an elective monarchy. Failure to establish a viable administration was due to the financial realities of war against the supporters of Henry of Navarre, undermining the league's appeal as an antitax party. In 1593, internal divisions over the choice of a suitable Catholic king were exploited by Navarre's conversion, removing the major obstacle to his accession. After the loss of Paris the following year, the league slowly crumbled as its leadership was defeated by Navarre; its last strongholds succumbed in 1598.

See also **Guise Family; Henry III (France); Henry IV (France).**

BIBLIOGRAPHY

Baumgartner, Frederic J. *Radical Reactionaries: The Political Thought of the French Catholic League.* Geneva, 1975.

Carroll, Stuart. "The Revolt of Paris, 1588: Aristocratic Insurgency and the Mobilisation of Popular Support" *French Historical Studies* 23 (2000): 301–337.

Diefendorf, Barbara B. "The Catholic League: Social Crisis or Apocalypse Now?" *French Historical Studies* 15 (Fall 1987): 332–344.

Harding, Robert. "Revolution and Reform in the Holy League: Angers, Rennes, Nantes." *Journal of Modern History* 53, no. 3 (1981): 379–416.

Holt, Mack P. *The French Wars of Religion, 1562–1629.* Cambridge, U.K., and New York, 1996.

Ramsey, Ann. *Liturgy, Politics and Salvation: The Catholic League in Paris and the Nature of Catholic Reform, 1540–1630.* Rochester, N.Y., 1999.

Salmon, J. H. M. *Society in Crisis: France in the Sixteenth-Century.* London, 1975.

Salmon, John. "The Paris Sixteen, 1584–1594: The Social Analysis of a Revolutionary Movement." *Journal of Modern History* 44 (1972): 540–576.

STUART CARROLL

CATHOLIC REFORMATION. *See* Reformation, Catholic.

CATHOLIC SPIRITUALITY AND MYSTICISM. Early modern spirituality was practical in orientation as it moved away from contemplation toward a more active apostolate. This resulted in an active spirituality among religious orders, as well as a lay-oriented spirituality that translated into charitable activities. The compulsion toward an active life of good works as a means toward personal sanctification, along with the revival of the sacramental life, the emergence of new forms of meditative prayer, and Eucharistic devotions, came to characterize the basic elements of Catholic spirituality during this period.

CENTERS OF SPIRITUALITY

Numerous men and women renowned for their sanctity, and new religious institutes dedicated either to the reform of the church or to charitable works, emerged in Italy. Oratories, lay or clerical confraternities whose purpose was the personal sanctification of its members, fostered an intense piety that translated into the care of orphans, the education of the poor, and the institution of hospitals. Notable among those who fostered this spirit were St. Catherine of Genoa (1447–1510), a laywoman whose work led to the founding of the Oratory of Divine Love; St. Philip Neri (1515–1595), founder of the Oratorians; St. Angela Merici (1474–1540), founder of the Ursulines; St. Anthony Zaccaria (1502–1539), founder of the Barnabites; and St. Camillus of Lellis (1550–1614), founder of the Ministers of the Sick, also called the Fathers of a Good Death.

Each of these figures sought an inner renewal that would foster reform on a social, institutional, and personal level. Most influential in developing this aspect of Italian spirituality was *The Spiritual Combat* by Lorenzo Scupoli (1530–1610). Emerging from the context of ecclesiastical renewal and reform, this spiritual literature aimed first and foremost at conversion from sin and the cultivation of the interior life. For the Italian mystics of this period this interior perfection was lived out through a mission of social and religious reform.

A different emphasis was apparent in Spain, where spirituality was more scientific and academic. This is evident in the methods of prayer and meditation that came to be known as "spiritual exercises." This new approach, with its systematic meditative form of mental prayer, was first seen as a vehicle for the reform of religious life. However, it was quickly adapted to meet the needs and situations of the laity. This method of prayer became one of the foundations of the new spirituality that spread throughout the church during this period. Highly individualistic in contrast to more communal or liturgical forms of prayer, this approach reflected the individualism of the age.

Sixteenth-century Spain gave birth to a wealth of spiritual literature and saints, most prominently Ignatius of Loyola, Teresa of Ávila, and John of the Cross. Ignatius of Loyola (1491–1556) presented in *The Spiritual Exercises* (1540) a systematic approach to prayer for the purpose of bringing about a personal renewal. For Ignatius, this form of prayer was not exclusive to those in religious life or those who have attained advanced stages of prayer but was open to all persons regardless of where they were spiritually.

St. Teresa of Ávila (1515–1582) occupies a prominent place because of her theology of prayer. In *The Interior Castle* (1588) she described prayer as a loving dialogue between friends and said that one's progress in prayer was an indication of one's progress in the spiritual life. Teresa's view of prayer was not exclusively mystical, despite the predominance of mysticism in her doctrine. Nor did she view the entire spiritual life as flowing from prayer alone. She saw the reception of Communion, the cultivation of humility, fraternal charity, spiritual direction, spiritual friendships, and the apostolate as playing an equally important part in the spiritual life.

Complementing Teresa is St. John of the Cross (1542–1591). The fundamental principle of his theology was that God was everything and the creature was nothing. If, then, one desired to attain perfect union with God, one was required to undergo a purgation of the body and the soul. John of the Cross developed this theology of purification in *The Ascent of Mount Carmel* and *The Dark Night of the Soul*. For St. John, the soul must be completely purified in all of its faculties and powers before it can be fully illuminated by the light of divine union. In the writings of both Teresa and John of the Cross there is less specific guidance on methods of prayer than on the Christian way of life in general.

France was also an important center of spirituality, particularly in the person of François de Sales (1567–1622). François brought the piety of the cloister into the world as he sought to show Christians that, whatever their place in society, their lives must be imbued with the religion they profess. In *The Introduction to the Devout Life*, he developed a complete program for the spiritual advancement of the laity that sought to provide a spirituality for those who remained in the world pursuing their professions and providing for their families.

DEVOTIONAL LIFE

The spirituality of the Catholic Reformation restored the Eucharist to a more central place in Christian life. Frequent Communion was encouraged and became a more common practice among devout laity, which reflected the changes that were taking place in Eucharistic piety. The worship of the Host in such devotions as Benediction of the Blessed Sacrament and Forty Hours exposition was a development of the Catholic Reformation.

Forty Hours devotion became a normative practice during this period. The uninterrupted exposition of the Blessed Sacrament for forty hours throughout a diocese, representing the number of hours that Christ's body lay in the tomb, began in Milan between 1527 and 1537. This practice had been established in Rome by St. Philip Neri prior to 1550. In 1560, Pius IV issued a papal bull of approbation and in 1592, Clement VIII issued a constitution that established the Forty Hours devotion in Rome, granting a plenary indulgence to those who participated.

The time of prayer spent before the Blessed Sacrament during the Forty Hours devotion was oriented to the reform of the church and the Christian life. A spirit of reparation and penitence formed the context of the devotion that flowed out of a meditation on the passion and death of Christ. Through an examination of conscience the supplicant sought a disposition of heart that would lead to contrition, purification, and conversion.

Devotion to the Blessed Sacrament strongly influenced the cult of the Sacred Heart. The introduction of the feast of Corpus Christi in the thirteenth century underscored the close link between the Eucharist and the heart of Jesus, giving the devotion a Eucharistic dimension. The Eucharist was seen as a gift and an abiding presence of the loving heart of Jesus. From the thirteenth to the sixteenth century devotion to the Sacred Heart took on the character of a private, individual devotion rather than a popular devotion. In the sixteenth century, a noticeable shift began to take place as the devotion to the Sacred Heart moved from an exclusively private practice to one that assumed a public and official character within the whole church, especially due to the influence of St. John Eudes (1601–1680) and St. Marguerite-Marie Alacoque (1647–1690).

CONCLUSION

The period of the Reformation and Counter-Reformation marked a turning point in the history of spirituality. In general, a deeper interiority was emphasized. The spirituality of this period was highly sacramental, biblically oriented, and focused on the life and passion of Jesus. Both Protestants and Roman Catholics insisted that a deeply lived spiritual life was possible outside of the cloister, thereby fostering a spirituality oriented toward the laity, which represented a direction hitherto unseen.

See also **Ignatius of Loyola; Reformation, Catholic; Theology; Teresa of Ávila.**

BIBLIOGRAPHY

Primary Sources

The Collected Works of Teresa of Avila. 3 vols. Translated by Kieran Kavanaugh and Otilio Rodríguez. Washington, D.C., 1976–1985.

The Complete Works of Saint John of the Cross, Doctor of the Church. 3 vols. Edited by E. Allison Peers. London, 1943.

DeSales, Francis. *Introduction to the Devout Life.* Translated and edited by Allan Ross. Westminster, Md., 1948. Translation of *Introduction a la vie devote* (1609).

Saint Ignatius of Loyola. *Personal Writings.* Translated by Joseph A. Munitiz and Philip Endean. London and New York, 1996.

Secondary Sources

Aumann, Jordan. *Christian Spirituality in the Catholic Tradition.* San Francisco and London, 1985.

Brenan, Gerald. *St. John of the Cross: His Life and Poetry.* Cambridge, U.K., 1973.

Evennett, H. O. *The Spirit of the Counter Reformation: The Birkbeck Lectures in Ecclesiastical History Given in the University of Cambridge in May 1951.* Cambridge, U.K., and London, 1968.

Leclercq, Jean, François Vandenbroucke, and Louis Bouyer. *The Spirituality of the Middle Ages.* Translated by the Benedictines of Holme Eden Abbey, Carlisle. London, 1968.

Raitt, Jill ed. *Christian Spirituality: High Middle Ages and the Reformation.* New York, 1987.

Rubin, Miri. *Corpus Christi: The Eucharist in Late Medieval Culture.* Cambridge, U.K., and New York, 1991.

Stierli, Josef. *Heart of the Saviour: A Symposium on Devotion to the Sacred Heart.* Translated by Paul Andrews. Freiburg, 1957.

Williams, Rowan. *Teresa of Avila.* Harrisburg, Pa., 1991.

FRANCESCO C. CESAREO

CATHOLICISM. In 1520, Martin Luther (1483–1546) explained—in his famous open letter to Pope Leo X (reigned 1513–1521)—that he considered the Roman Curia "more corrupt than any Babylon or Sodom ever was," and that it was "characterized by a completely depraved, hopeless and notorious godlessness." For hundreds of years thereafter, Luther's remarks were construed as an indictment not just of the Curia, but of the entire Catholic Church. With this picture of corruption and depravity, he established one side of a polemical divide over ways to describe Catholicism in early modern Europe that has endured to this very day. The argument over whether or not Luther's picture of the church was realistic has been engaged by historians for generations, from Cesare Baronio (1518–1607) and Paolo Sarpi (1562–1623) in the late sixteenth century to Massimo Firpo and John W. O'Malley in the late twentieth century. The debate has been clouded by ahistorical commitments—at first simply religious, then political and cultural as well—that serve as an obstacle to a true comprehension of the past. Since roughly 1945, the argument has turned on whether the terms "Counter-Reformation" or "Catholic Reform," or any of a host of other related terms, can describe the period, or if something more innocuous, like "early modern Catholicism," might be better. No matter where one stands on this battle over historical terminology, all agree that Catholicism in this era was variegated, fascinating in its complexity, and riddled with internal and external conflicts that make simple categorization of this institution quite impossible.

Catholicism between 1500 and 1789 has commonly been defined through the conflict between Protestant reformers and Christians who remained loyal to Rome. Luther, like John Calvin (1509–1564) and many Anglican and Anabaptist thinkers who followed, was not so different from medieval reformers who called for change in Christian practices. He may have insisted initially on reconsideration of the best way to explain the necessity of penitence, not just penance, in the process of salvation. The challenge to common church teaching expressed in his Ninety-Five Theses (1517), however, increasingly came to be understood as a threat to papal authority. This perception, which was reinforced by Luther's own words in the three great Reformation treatises of 1520–1521 and by the rallying of other critical voices at his side, encouraged members of the Catholic hierarchy to see him as the latest in a long line of medieval reformers. They could then treat him, as they did his predecessors, as one who would eventually go away without leaving any substantial impact upon the structure of ecclesiastical authority.

THE PAPACY AND THE COUNCIL OF TRENT

The common definition of Catholicism in early modern Europe as hinging on the challenge of Luther and other Protestant reformers, and on Roman reaction to that challenge, has obscured the complexity and multiform nature of the institution. First, consider the complexity of the papacy itself. Popes from Alexander VI (1492–1503) through Pius VI (1775–1799) exhibited many characteristics, but consistency and uniformity were not among them. At the beginning of this era, the papacy was an institution competing for the loyalty of the European people against secular powers attempting to extend the reach of their authority.

Fifteenth-century papal claims to absolute power, both spiritual and temporal, were defined in practice during the pontificates of Julius II (1503–1513) and Leo X as an effort to secure the integrity and independence of the Papal State. They used both diplomatic and military resources to do so. By the end of the early modern era, however, the papacy had become quite ineffective in political terms, having been pushed to the periphery of contemporary political society. For example, Clement XIII (1758–1769) and Clement XIV (1769–1774) were unable to save one of the largest religious orders in the church, the Society of Jesus, from its European enemies. Early modern popes attempted to consolidate their religious and governmental authority in a rapidly changing world, but they did so with inconsistent policies and performance. The popular imagination of today often views early modern popes as warriors against heresy. This may have been true of popes like Paul IV (1555–1559) and Pius V (1566–1572), who personally presided over inquisitorial meetings. But later popes, like Innocent XI (1676–1689), saw devotional and theological developments like Jansenism and Quietism as dangerous and still disapproved of the use of force to deal with them. An even later pope, Benedict XIV (1740–1758), had no trouble reconciling the apparent contradiction between support for clerical education and scientific investigation on the one hand, while at the same time continuing prohibitions on reading with a new Index of Prohibited Books. Similar levels of inconsistency exist when examining the actions of popes in artistic patronage, in promotion of church reform, in support for scholarship, and in creation of public services for the Papal State.

Pope Paul III (1534–1549), an individual whose actions were filled with inconsistencies, might be seen as one who epitomized the early modern papacy. He is considered by many to be the first pope of the Catholic Reformation (or the Counter-Reformation). He not only appointed cardinals who presented him with a stinging indictment of the evils in the contemporary church, known as the *Consilium de Emendanda Ecclesia* (1537), but he also convened the Council of Trent in 1545. In addition, he procured the legitimization of three of the four children he fathered before becoming a priest and bestowed enormous ecclesiastical incomes and properties upon one son and upon the two grandsons he appointed as cardinals. This unreformed approach to the enrichment of his family was contradicted by his generous artistic patronage and by his promotion of reform-minded clerics. Among the latter was a Spaniard, Ignatius of Loyola (1491–1556), whose new religious order, the Society of Jesus, Paul formally approved in 1540. Paul revived the Roman Inquisition in 1542, but designed it to operate with a lenience and moderation that some of his successors rejected. He was a pope like many others in this period: a "reformer" who could never fully break away from the traditions of corruption. They were richly human, defying simple categorization.

The Council of Trent (1545–1563), whose decrees—not to mention the drumbeat of anathema within them—epitomized Catholic reaction against Protestant thought, was a richly complicated event riddled with conflict. According to the standard interpretation, popes controlled the assembly through the papal legates who set the agenda for each session, and through Jesuit theologians who, over those eighteen years, ensured that doctrinal and disciplinary decrees were secured that were acceptable to the popes. From the very beginning, however, legates like Marcello Cervini (1501–1555), Giovan Maria de' Ciocchi del Monte (1487–1555), and Carlo Borromeo (1538–1584) struggled to persuade prelates to attend, to remain once they had arrived, and to get along, sometimes in ways that were much more practical than dogmatic. When they were not breaking up shoving matches among the bishops, legates mediated, rather than dictated, among members of the papal, imperial, and French factions that emerged at Trent, while attempting to promote papal plans. Popes themselves varied widely in their commitment to the gathering as a means to solve the problem facing the church. Paul III convened the council, but he clearly feared the conciliarist leanings of some of the prospective council members. Julius III (1550–1555) and Pius IV (1559–1565) moved the Tridentine assembly vigorously toward completion. In between those two, however, Paul IV insisted categorically that the meeting remain in suspension, convinced that he could carry out the reform on his own through the Roman Inquisition, over whose meetings he presided, and through his personal Index of Prohibited Books. In the end, the decrees were formulated by conciliar bishops, who put themselves in charge of bringing the documents from Trent to life in Catholic practice.

IMPLEMENTING TRENT

Implementation of the decrees of the Council of Trent—a series of clarifications of doctrine, disciplinary decrees, and directives on such matters as clerical education—should have brought a uniform church into existence in short order, but local realities made this impossible. Papal authority was not strong enough to effect any change as broadranging as that outlined at Trent. In France, implementing the decrees was especially slow, as royal control restricted even the publication of the decrees. Bringing clerical behavior there into something resembling conformity with the decrees took centuries, not decades. Recent scholarship on the Netherlands reveals that seventeenth-century bishops faced opposition to their reform plans not just from local constituents, but from Rome as well. They engaged in especially complex negotiations to try to secure claustration of nuns, that Tridentine rule most often cited as evidence of effective, centralized, disciplining control, in local convents. In the end, Netherlandish nuns determined the characteristics of their own common life, apparently at least as much as bishops. In Italy, prelates had the example of Carlo Borromeo (1538–1584), archbishop of Milan, not to mention precedents like Gian Matteo Giberti (1495–1543) in Verona, Bartolomeo de Martyribus (1514–1590) in Braga, and Marcello Cervini in Gubbio, to follow. Borromeo became the model Tridentine bishop, holding diocesan synods, enhancing catechetical instruction, and conducting pastoral visits. But even in Italy the process was relatively slow, as bishops elsewhere butted up against the many cathedral chapters, and monastic institutions that asserted their independence from episcopal control and appealed to Rome any challenge to that independence.

Effective implementation of the decrees was a complicated matter. The process hinged not just on the ability of bishops to operate freely over those at least theoretically under their control, but also upon the determination of some rulers to control their national churches. The papal prerogative of simply naming bishops, let alone controlling their activity, was decidedly limited, especially in Spain, France, and England. The tradition of royal leadership in religious matters in Spain continued throughout the early modern period and was already well established in 1478, when Ferdinand (ruled 1474–1516) and Isabella (ruled 1474–1504) convinced Rome of the need for a Spanish Inquisition controlled by the monarchs. Spanish monarchs retained the right to appoint bishops in the Netherlands, as well as across the so-called New World. Such an arrangement within France was created in the Concordat of Bologna (1516) between Leo X and King Francis I (ruled 1515–1547). Behind these and similar practices—such as monarchical control of appointments to ecclesiastical benefices in England—was a concern over the distribution of revenues that was more financial than religious. When viewed in the context of Tridentine decrees insisting on the appointment only of properly trained clerics who would take seriously the *cura animarum*, 'care of souls', these facts illustrate that Roman determination to control the reform process, as well as the practical ability to do so, varied considerably.

Some of those who drafted the Tridentine decree on seminaries may have desired a highly centralized clergy obedient to Roman doctrine and leadership, but recent research suggests implementation of this directive was desperately slow, and that any such desire went largely unfilled. In places like Milan, seminary training after Trent was anything but uniform. Many candidates studied in multiple institutions, and only some of those were under the control of the archbishop. Diocesan seminaries there were part of a larger system that included schools run by some of the new Catholic religious orders. In Fiesole, the first attempt to found a seminary did not occur until nearly a generation after the assembly at Trent completed its work. Formal seminary instruction in Fiesole did not commence until 1635. Even if trained, the reshaping of local priests into a professional class through episcopal visitations and instructions may have been the intention of early modern bishops, but they apparently made little progress in this era. In Milan, during the archiepiscopal administrations of Carlo and Federico Borromeo (1564–1631), the majority of priests resembled the superstitious, worldly, sinful laity they served far more than the confessional interrogators the archbishops had in mind.

RELIGIOUS REVIVAL

The intention of all Catholic reformers was to revive religious life generally, but locally support for revival and opposition to it were both common. Hence, real change was limited. Seminary education and pastoral visits were supposed to create a consistently well-educated and attentive clergy. Local records suggest that the members of the laity supported such an intention, but in practice, some established members of the clergy challenged the change. Giambattista Casale, a carpenter and late-sixteenth-century diarist in Milan, enthusiastically praised the reform work of Carlo Borromeo. Casale related popular support both for the attention Borromeo devoted to his personal pastoral responsibilities, and for his initiatives to improve the quality of local priests. Clerics there, however, were not so favorably impressed. In 1569 and 1570 they assaulted the archbishop, first verbally and then physically, as his reforming ideals were threatening their clerical positions and income. One can find many examples of ecclesiastical and civic leaders developing new institutions and enhancing the power of old ones, designed to enforce religious orthodoxy, proper notions of political sovereignty, and moral purity. At the same time, crime statistics, court records—including the recently opened central archive of the Roman Inquisition—and other forms of documentation all reveal that the goal of conformity was far from achieved. Archbishops and parishioners in the Netherlands in this era did not completely agree on what constituted a good pastor, but one thing was sure: neither were satisfied with those they observed. The well-noted crackdown on questionable belief and behavior among upper-ranking clerics did not preclude behavior by one—Reginald Pole (1500–1558, the cardinal archbishop of Canterbury and papal legate to the early sessions at Trent)—that led his most recent biographer to assert that he was, for all practical purposes, married to his longtime companion, the Venetian noble and cleric Alvise Priuli (d. 1560).

Where Catholic religious practice was effectively reformed in early modern Europe, it often came through leadership from members of a variety of religious orders. The members of long established orders, like the Franciscans, Benedictines, and Augustinians, initiated reforms to improve adherence to the religious rule each followed, but the reform movements frequently resulted in division and the creation of new branches of these orders. This operation followed a well-established pattern in the Franciscan order, for example. The new Capuchin group founded by Matteo di Bassi (1495–1552) was not unlike the so-called spirituals from an earlier age in its call for stricter observance of the rule of Saint Francis. Their emphasis on preaching and identification with common people, especially in towns, contributed to the spread of reformed Catholicism. Angela Merici of Brescia (1474–1540) and Ignatius of Loyola founded brand new orders, the Ursulines and the Society of Jesus, respectively, whose inspiration turned as much on the goal of serving the needs of others as on the pursuit of perfection among its own members. The Ursulines became educators, especially in catechism, as well as servants of orphans and women in need of shelter. The Jesuits engaged in a wide variety of ministries, but like the Ursulines, their principal influence on the European community came through work in education. They were central to the development of secondary schools that prepared young men for university study, and to the beginnings of seminary education. These were just a few of the many new and newly reformed orders of the early modern period.

Members of the secular (that is, diocesan) clergy on the one hand, and members of religious orders (both clerics in religious orders and nuns) on the other, engaged in disputes that further complicate the picture of Catholicism in this age. In general terms, members of religious orders tended to assert their independence from episcopal control based upon their foundations and authorizations that came directly from the papacy. This was a traditional position for religious orders to take. But when they did so in the early modern period, especially after the Council of Trent, they butted up against bishops armed with the decrees of Trent. Many of these bishops intended to exercise their authority to examine clerics and grant permissions to preach and to hear confessions in their dioceses, whether they were secular or regular clergy. Members of religious orders could often, through appeals to the papacy, gain exemption from such episcopal authority. There was not, however, any general position of the papacy in favor of the independence of regular clergy. Paul IV, to take a notable example,

was decidedly suspicious of the devotional innovations designed by Ignatius of Loyola and the Jesuits to facilitate their pastoral activities. For a time, he even insisted that they recite the divine office in unison, in violation of the Jesuit constitutions established under preceding popes. We ought not to think of this distrust of religious orders as a position taken up exclusively by belligerent popes like Paul IV. When questions were raised concerning the propriety of the independence of the Ursulines and their activities outside the convent, the push to cloister them came not just from authorities in Rome, but also from parents of the sisters and other family members.

European members of both branches of the Catholic clergy increasingly engaged in preaching, a fact that undermines one of the most common stereotypes about Catholicism in this era. A common assumption is that, to the Catholic clergy of this period, preaching was either completely marginal or used only for unjust fundraising operations such as the sale of indulgences. But the historical record of preaching in the early modern period is much more complicated. At the beginning of the period, members of religious orders, like Franciscan and Dominican friars, were exceedingly popular preachers. They delivered well-attended sermons on a daily basis during Lent and Advent. In fact, civic leaders vied to secure the best known preachers among them. The popularity of these preachers was based, at least in part, on the lack of preaching by members of the secular clergy, who were largely absent from their pastoral duties. After the Council of Trent, short homilies within the Eucharistic celebration became increasingly common. There was a veritable explosion of publications related to preaching in the early modern period. The explosion included simple instructions by bishops, handbooks of forms for the composition of sermons, and collections of the work of celebrated preachers, in addition to formal treatises on the topic. This literature reveals that theorists recommended explicitly the utilization of humanist rhetorical ideals and clear explication of basic doctrine in sermons. Court preachers speaking before popes and heads of state retained the prominent characteristic of their medieval predecessors. Preaching held a central place in the religious culture of all early modern Europe, not just Protestant lands.

POPULAR PIETY

Preachers touched local Catholic communities whose common experience of the religion varied considerably. During the late sixteenth and early seventeenth centuries, Milan was a very different place compared to a city in a Protestant territory, like Amsterdam. In the former, priests were on the lookout for both clerics and members of the laity who deviated from the newly defined norms of Trent. They spent the bulk of their time trying to form Catholic identity around those norms, often with minimal success. In the latter, and in many other towns and cities in the British Isles, the Holy Roman Empire, and the Dutch Republic, Catholics created religious spaces in places where such were officially proscribed, but in practice they were tolerated by neighbors and officials who knew well of their existence. At the turn of the eighteenth century, Catholics controlled twenty such semi-secret churches *(schuilkerk)* in Amsterdam. One was a narrow row house whose third-floor church could hold some 150 persons in pews and galleries. Catholics in early modern Spain probably experienced religion in a manner that was closer to that of the Milanese. They surely were the subjects of a plan for orthodox indoctrination. For some, especially in rural areas, their practice may have become outwardly Christian, even approaching Catholic, but it was mixed with appeals to the supernatural through spells and potions that illustrate the difficulty with which "pagan" superstitions died in this era. Moreover, the divide between Christians and Jews in European communities was often anything but complete. Paul IV set up an enclosed ghetto in Rome that is still widely seen as a precursor of Nazi versions in Eastern Europe. But emphasis on this episode encourages ignorance of the more tolerant policy that both preceded and followed his administration. It also hides the fact that, as recent scholarship has shown, Jews and members of the Catholic laity in Rome shared a good deal in common, and that the ghetto had few negative effects on the religious and cultural identity of Jews in Rome.

Believers, especially in urban areas, organized themselves into confraternities, a vast array of diverse organizations that belied the image of contemporary Catholicism as uniform. Confraternities had existed as devotional organizations promoting piety and social service, mainly in the towns of the medieval period. In the early modern period, when centralizing tendencies in the organization of Catholicism allegedly held sway, such organizations and their independence from hierarchical control should, logically, have disappeared. They did not. Instead, they tended to become stronger. Whether their increased strength was based upon enhanced devotion to more clearly defined dogmas, on the Eucharist, or upon an increasing charitable need in contemporary cities is unclear. Some of these institutions seemed on the surface to cooperate with growing states and their centralization of charity. In some places, however, like Bologna, confraternities that took on a more political role allowed patricians to maintain secure hold on certain elements of administration in the Papal State (specifically over the prison system) against centralization under the papacy.

Individual Catholic believers, and not just those in confraternities, seem to have experienced religion much more through their devotional practices than through any conscious adherence to dogma, whether orthodox or heterodox. Popular religious practice varied widely despite the hope of some Catholic leaders to regularize devotional life. Throughout the sixteenth century, there is little evidence to suggest that instruction in dogma went far beyond practice in the memorization of basic prayers and foundational formulas like the Nicene Creed. Later, increasing expansion of the Confraternities of Christian Doctrine and the publication of the *Catechism of the Council of Trent* in 1566 surely facilitated the spread of the doctrines defined at Trent. But real work on that document did not begin at least until late in 1562, if not 1563. Once it was completed under Pius V in 1566, priests had to learn and translate the contents of the massive Latin edition before the process of explaining the ideas in terms accessible to common people could begin. Popular cults honoring the mostly unofficial but locally recognized patron saints continued. Pilgrimage sites that had developed in the Middle Ages, such as Loreto, location of the house in which Mary allegedly grew up—miraculously transported from Palestine to the Adriatic coast—maintained their popularity, along with the sacramentals that attended their use. Popular piety found expression throughout Europe, but frequently outside the confines of standard religious instruction, outside of new Tridentine liturgical parameters, and outside of the sacraments. Processions were often more boisterous than devout, the majority of Catholics received Communion infrequently, and clerical reform rarely touched rural areas in large portions of Europe before 1650. Popular piety could be found in other forms, however, as in the well-attended theatrical productions presented in towns, especially the university towns, of northern Europe. Jesuit colleges were famous for presentations that dramatized the spiritual life with scenes of both angels and hell, and these remained popular, especially in southern Germany, through the middle of the eighteenth century. Some earlier religious dramas produced in the Low Countries during the reign of Emperor Charles V (ruled 1519–1556) included presentation of varying religious positions from contemporary theological debates.

MISSIONARY ACTIVITY

Efforts to spread the faith through missionary activity in Europe and beyond have received scant attention, but consideration of this activity exposes still more variations in the Catholic experience. The revival of Catholicism represented by reform initiatives that predate Luther, as well as those initiatives designed to counteract his work and that of other Protestant reformers, spurred action to spread Catholicism throughout Europe, not to mention the New World. The Jesuits led an attempt to recover believers in the German-speaking territory who were "lost" to the Protestant movement. They were active in cities like Cologne and Vienna in the Holy Roman Empire in the 1550s, where their schools enrolled large numbers and where they attempted to prepare better trained clergy who might help in the recovery process. They tried to do the same in Slavic-speaking lands at approximately the same time, but with much less success. The English crown attempted to thwart Jesuit efforts to spread Catholicism in Britain after the Reformation. Jesuit missionary work there was complicated by the political and theological controversy over the divine right of kings during the age of King James I (ruled 1603–1625). Catholic clerics from a number of religious orders took part in efforts to spread the faith in Spanish and Portuguese holdings in Asia, Africa, the Americas, and the Pacific islands. The standard image of these missionaries arriving on the heels of the conquistadors and forcing adherence to

the new religion, armed with an ideology that permitted coercion, is only partly true. While mass conversions were frequently carried out, missionaries often faced a hostile initial response from local populations, especially in Asia. When they did, some—like Francis Xavier (1506–1552), for example—simply moved on to other towns and regions where they hoped for better luck. Our image of the character of Catholic proselytism in this era must be able to explain not just the mass conversions, but also the retention of Roman doctrine over the long term. It must explain not just those instances where the value of native culture was discounted, but also Catholic missionary work that accommodated local practices. The latter was so extensive in China, for instance, that Jesuits there like Matteo Ricci (1552–1610) were considered promoters of paganism by some Roman authorities.

ART, SCIENCE, AND RELIGION

Perhaps the most enduring image of early modern Catholicism is that of an institution that systematically shut down emergent local culture and freedom of thought. Exploration of the activity of Catholics in art, literature, music, and science demonstrates the inadequacy of that image: the reality was far more complex. In the arts—including sculpture, painting, poetry, drama, prose, oratory, and music—there is no doubt that anti-Protestant ideology contributed to new Catholic production. The Protestant attack on art, not to mention the development of new notions of Christian heroism, certainly influenced the way biographers, preachers, painters, sculptors, and composers expressed themselves. But they looked for effective techniques and for attention-grabbing flourishes to impress audiences and to demand an active response. There is no doubt that rules for propriety in various forms of art, notably oratory and painting, reflect an attempt by church leaders to control. The Tridentine decree on sacred images from the twenty-fifth session (1563) and the discourse on sacred and profane images published in 1582 by Cardinal Gabriele Paleotti (1522–1597) are the texts most frequently cited to suggest that ecclesiastical repression in the world of art was effective. However, the assertion that the attempt was successful ignores a vast body of evidence. Evidence lies in the humanistic oratory of post-Tridentine preachers and funeral eulogists. It can be found in the intense painting and sculpture created by artists like Agostino (1557–1602), Annibale (1560–1609), and Ludovico Carracci (1555–1619), as well as Gian Lorenzo Bernini (1598–1680) and Giambologna (1529–1608). The era was one of bold creativity that followed from humanistic innovations that were only partly subordinated to the goals of religious leaders. The works produced by popular Italian vernacular authors also serve as evidence. They offered everything from legal to occult texts, in addition to the orthodox religious publications associated with the post-Tridentine printing industry. Yet another example can be found in northern Europe. In Germany, Catholics, and even Jesuits, were behind an artistic revitalization that contributed to the survival of Catholicism there, but also to the emergence of the German baroque movement.

Early modern Catholicism allegedly had a stultifying effect on intellectual life, and especially on the development of science, but recent scholarship suggests that this view needs considerable revision. Intellectual historians have insisted that humanism remained a vital, dynamic intellectual movement in the seventeenth century throughout Europe, despite attempts by church authorities to refocus scholarship to support new confessional ideologies. Spanish intellectual life apparently was much more complex than historians in previous generations had thought. In Spain, humanism mixed with more traditional scholastic thought, and writers moved with considerable flexibility between methods: even Spanish inquisitorial records illustrate this reality. Something similar was largely true in Italy, especially in the age of Athanasius Kircher (1602–1680). Jesuits at the Roman College—some from Germany like Kircher, and others from elsewhere—showed considerable favor for the cosmology of Tycho Brahe (1546–1601), even though it stood in sharp contrast to the Aristotelian status quo. The "church," both as an institution and literally as a structure, provided a great deal more support for the development of science, especially astronomy, than most would imagine, given the pervasive image of the struggle Galileo Galilei (1564–1642) had with the bureaucrats of the Roman Inquisition. Observations and calculations carried out in some of the principal cathedral churches of Europe, with the financial support of high-ranking prelates, paved the way for improvements in observational astronomy. They also belie the image of the Catholic Church as an effective, let alone pervasive, barrier to the expansion of learning. However, extreme Catholic opposition to the Enlightenment movement also reared up toward the end of this period. Still, had counter-cultural efforts like these been effective on any significant level, historians would have considerably greater difficulty explaining the emergence of the jarring political revolutions of the late eighteenth century.

If, as the famous American lawmaker Tip O'Neill once said, "All politics is local," then perhaps all history is local, too. The history of early modern Catholicism surely could stand as an example to defend such a thesis. Historians studying more distant ages in the past sometimes face a paucity of sources and data that makes generalization necessary. The early modern period was no such era. It was, on the contrary, the very age in which the passion for record keeping that we take for granted today first emerged. Such records, in their display of local circumstances and realities, illustrate a human complexity that defies categorization. When Martin Luther wrote his letter to Leo X, he set the pattern for consideration of early modern Catholicism, either demon or hero, that is only now being revised and seen with a human face. Further historical investigation will reveal even more wrinkles and complexities. Early modern Catholicism will take a good deal longer to describe, but the description will be closer to the human reality of that fascinating era.

See also **Calvin, John; Clergy: Roman Catholic; Index of Prohibited Books; Inquisition; Jesuits; Luther, Martin; Missions and Missionaries; Papacy and Papal States; Reformation, Catholic; Reformation, Protestant; Religious Orders; Trent, Council of.**

BIBLIOGRAPHY

Biagioli, Mario. *Galileo, Courtier: The Practice of Science in the Culture of Absolutism.* Chicago, 1993.

Bireley, Robert. *The Refashioning of Catholicism, 1450–1700.* Washington, D.C., 1999.

Carlebach, Elisheva. *Divided Souls: Converts from Judaism in Germany, 1500–1750.* New Haven, 2001.

Cochrane, Eric. *Italy, 1530–1630.* Edited by Julius Kirshner. London, 1988.

Comerford, Kathleen M. *Ordaining the Catholic Reformation: Priests and Seminary Pedagogy in Fiesole, 1575–1675.* Florence, 2001.

Delumeau, Jean. *Catholicism between Luther and Voltaire: A New View of the Counter-Reformation.* Translated by Jeremy Moiser. London, 1977.

DeMolen, Richard, ed. *Religious Orders of the Catholic Reformation.* New York, 1994.

Firpo, Massimo. *Inquisizione romana e controriforma.* Bologna, 1992.

Forster, Marc. *The Counter-Reformation in the Villages: Religion and Reform in the Bishopric of Speyer, 1560–1720.* Ithaca, N.Y., 1992.

Gibbons, Mary. *Giambologna: Narrator of the Catholic Reformation.* Berkeley, 1995.

Grafton, Anthony. *Bring Out Your Dead: The Past as Revelation.* Cambridge, Mass., 2001.

Grendler, Paul F. *The Roman Inquisition and the Venetian Press, 1540–1605.* Princeton, 1977.

Heilbron, J. L. *The Sun in the Church: Cathedrals as Solar Observatories.* Cambridge, Mass., 1999.

Homza, Lu Ann. *Religious Authority in the Spanish Renaissance.* Baltimore, 2000.

Hudon, William V. "Religion and Society in Early Modern Italy: Old Questions, New Insights." *American Historical Review* 101, no. 3 (June 1996): 783–804.

Kaplan, Benjamin. "Fictions of Privacy: House Chapels and the Spatial Accommodation of Religious Dissent in Early Modern Europe." *American Historical Review* 107, no. 4 (October 2002): 1031–1064.

Lattis, James M. *Between Copernicus and Galileo: Christoph Clavius and the Collapse of Ptolemaic Cosmology.* Chicago, 1994.

Mayer, Thomas F. *Reginald Pole: Prince and Prophet.* Cambridge, U.K., 2000.

McGinness, Frederick. *Right Thinking and Sacred Oratory in Counter-Reformation Rome.* Princeton, 1995.

McMahon, Darrin M. *Enemies of the Enlightenment: The French Counter-Enlightenment and the Making of Modernity.* New York, 2001.

Nalle, Sara T. *God in La Mancha: Religious Reform and the People of Cuenca, 1500–1650.* Baltimore, 1992.

O'Malley, John W. *The First Jesuits.* Cambridge, Mass., 1993.

———. *Trent and All That: Renaming Catholicism in the Early Modern Era.* Cambridge, Mass., 2000.

Prodi, Paolo, and Giuseppe Olmi. "Art, Science and Nature in Bologna, since 1600." In *The Age of Coreggio and the Carracci: Emilian Painting of the Sixteenth and Seventeenth Centuries.* Washington, D.C., 1986.

Schutte, Anne Jacobson. *Aspiring Saints: Pretense of Holiness, Inquisition, and Gender in the Republic of Venice, 1618–1750.* Baltimore, 2001.

Smith, Jeffrey Chipps. *Sensuous Worship: Jesuits and the Art of the Early Catholic Reformation in Germany.* Princeton, 2002.

Stow, Kenneth. *Theater of Acculturation: The Roman Ghetto in the Sixteenth Century.* Seattle, 2001.

Terpstra, Nicholas. *Lay Confraternities and Civic Religion in Renaissance Bologna.* Cambridge, U.K., 1995.

WILLIAM V. HUDON

CAVALRY. *See* **Military: Battle Tactics and Campaign Strategy.**

CAVENDISH, MARGARET (1623–1673), duchess of Newcastle, English poet, playwright, natural philosopher, biographer, feminist utopianist, and eccentric. Margaret Cavendish was born Margaret Lucas, the youngest child of Thomas Lucas and Elizabeth Leighton Lucas of Colchester, Essex. The death of Thomas in 1625 left the Lucas estate in the hands of Elizabeth Leighton, who had a penchant for land management and advancing her children's fortunes beyond the confines of the local county. Educated at home, Margaret spent much time in philosophical contemplation and daydreaming. Alienated socially from the Essex gentry, the Lucases were High Church royalists whose Essex manor was looted during an antiroyalist riot of 22 August 1642. In late 1642 Margaret was sent from home to serve as maid of honor at Queen Henrietta Maria's temporary court at Oxford. Shy and conversationally ill at ease, Margaret asked, but was refused, permission to return home. With the defeat of the royalist forces in the English Civil War, the queen and her court went into exile in Paris. In 1645, maternal foresight paid off when Margaret caught the eye of fifty-one-year-old William Cavendish, marquis of Newcastle. A womanizing aristocrat and royalist military commander, Cavendish came to Paris to repair his relations with the queen after his disastrous military defeat by parliamentary forces at Marston Moor. With savvy, Margaret managed a short courtship, marrying William Cavendish in December 1645.

Plagued by financial insecurity, ill health, and the failure of royalist aspirations during an extended exile in Paris and then Antwerp, Margaret sought

Margaret Cavendish. A frontispiece for *Philosophical and Physical Opinions* features a portrait of the author. MARY EVANS PICTURE LIBRARY

solace in writing. Inspired by the scientific interests of her brother-in-law, Sir Charles Cavendish, and encouraged by her husband, she published verse on natural philosophical atomism in *Poems and Fancies* (1653). A second collection of poetry, *Philosophicall Fancies* (1653), a philosophical treatise, *Philosophical and Physical Opinions* (1655), and two prose miscellanies, *The World's Olio* (1655) and *Nature's Pictures* (1656), followed shortly thereafter. With the restoration of Charles II in 1660, the Cavendishes returned to England. William was granted the title of duke, and Margaret, thereafter duchess of Newcastle, tried her hand at a variety of literary forms, including drama, poetry, romance, epistles, orations, biography, and autobiography, as well as natural philosophic reflection. The utopian scientific narrative *Description of a New World, called the*

Blazing World (1666) is her best-known literary work.

Clearly conscious of the limitations that marriage and social conventions placed on women, Margaret Cavendish sought a name for herself by playing the eccentric in public—dressing androgynously and behaving outlandishly. But she also sought fame in intellectual circles by debating the ideas of prominent male philosophers like Thomas Hobbes, René Descartes, and Robert Hooke in print. Strongly influenced by Hobbes's materialism, she rejected atomism in 1655 because it represented the world as intrinsically disordered—a viewpoint that conflicted with her political conservatism. Instead, she drew upon Neoplatonic and materialist ideas to construct a philosophical monism or vitalism that conceived all matter to be endowed with elements of reason and spirit. An epistemological skeptic at heart, Cavendish criticized the Royal Society's reliance on empirical experimentalism, its misplaced faith in the accuracy of our fallible senses. Instead, she believed that natural philosophic inquiry could best proceed through rational and imaginative conjecture. She explained some of her antiexperimental ideas in *Observations upon Experimental Philosophy* (1666), in which she also took aim at Robert Hooke's *Micrographia* for its misguided enthusiasm for optical instruments. Cavendish's eccentricity, intellectual eclecticism, and gender led many of her contemporaries to discount her philosophical thought, although twentieth-century feminist scholars have revived interest in her work.

See also **Charles II (England); Descartes, René; English Civil War and Interregnum; Hobbes, Thomas; Hooke, Robert; Neoplatonism.**

BIBLIOGRAPHY

Primary Sources

Cavendish, Margaret. *The Blazing World & Other Writings* (1666). Harmondsworth, U.K., 1992.

———. *The Life of the Thrice Noble, High and Puissant Prince William Cavendishe* (1668). Edited by C. H. Firth. London, 1886.

———. *Poems and Fancies* (1653). Menston, U.K., 1972.

———. *Sociable Letters* (1664). Menston, U.K., 1969.

Secondary Source

Batigelli, Anna. *Margaret Cavendish and the Exiles of the Mind.* Lexington, Ky., 1998.

JULIE ROBIN SOLOMON

CAXTON, WILLIAM

CAXTON, WILLIAM (c. 1422–1491), English printer and publisher. William Caxton, the first English printer, began his career as a London trader, becoming, after an apprenticeship, a freeman of the powerful Mercers Company. For about thirty years, from the mid-1440s until 1476, he lived for the most part in Flanders, as a merchant adventurer trading from Bruges. From 1462 to 1470 he was the governor of the English merchant adventurers, whose dominant members belonged to the Mercers Company. His responsibilities involved him at times in English diplomacy on matters of trade.

In 1470 Caxton resigned or was forced from the governorship. He moved to Cologne, where he lived in 1471–1472. Here he first encountered the new phenomenon of printing shops, although he may well, while in Bruges, have seen some early printed books imported from Mainz and Cologne. Direct contact with Cologne's expanding printed-book trade seems to have awakened new ambitions, for Caxton soon took financial control of one of the Cologne shops, and produced there three printed books, all in Latin. The first was the massive natural history encyclopedia of Bartholomaeus Anglicus, *De Proprietatibus Rerum* (1472; On the properties of things).

In 1473 Caxton returned to Bruges and set up a new printing shop. The first of some half-dozen books he produced was his own translation from the French of the chivalric romance *Recuyell of the Histories of Troy*, completed in late 1473 or early 1474. He dedicated it to Margaret, duchess of Burgundy and sister of King Edward IV. This was the first of a number of royal or noble dedications he made. Four of Caxton's Bruges books were in French and among the earliest to be printed in that language, making him a pioneer in both English and French vernacular printing.

In 1476 Caxton returned to England and set up his third printing shop, near the royal courts and Parliament, within the precincts of Westminster Abbey. He produced some hundred editions, ranging in size from single-leaf printed indulgences to his most substantial translation, Jacobus de Voragine's late thirteenth-century collection of saints' lives, the *Golden Legend* (1484), a large folio of almost nine hundred pages. Caxton's publishing program ranged widely, including school books, law books, and prayer books, but the central emphasis was on vernacular literature, chronicles, and works of popular edification. The discursive prologues and epilogues he contributed to many of the books give them a lively actuality that remains attractive and accessible. No other early printer, in any language, addressed himself so directly, personally, and often amusingly to his intended audience.

In Caxton's lifetime and for generations after, the major Latin works of learning and literature, such as were studied in Oxford and Cambridge, were imported to England from continental shops.

For readers of English, however, Caxton was the dominant figure in respect of both number and quality of publication. He produced the first editions of Chaucer's *Canterbury Tales* (1477; reprinted 1483 with woodcuts), of works by John Lydgate and John Gower, and of Sir Thomas Malory's *Morte d'Arthur* (1485). Among his many translations are *The Game and Play of Chess* (1474; reprinted 1483 with woodcuts), *Aesop's Fables* (1484, with woodcuts), *The History of Charlemagne* (1485), and *Reynard the Fox* (1481; reprinted 1489).

In 1478 and after, other printing shops were begun in London, Oxford, and Saint Albans; they all ceased operation around 1486, and their combined output amounted to little more than half of what Caxton produced.

From Caxton's death in 1491 to the end of the 1520s, as the quantity of English printing considerably expanded, two printing shops dominated: those of Wynkyn de Worde, Caxton's former workman, who succeeded to his master's shop and equipment; and of Richard Pynson, who once referred to Caxton as "my worshipful master," but whose direct connection with Caxton is less clear. Between them, until Pynson's death in 1529, they produced about three-quarters of all printing in England: about 1,350 out of some 1,800 editions. About two hundred more editions were printed in Paris, Antwerp, and other continental cities for export to the English market.

Although they overlapped, it appears that, by and large, de Worde and Pynson divided rather than competed for single control of the bookbuying market. De Worde specialized in cheap pamphlets of popular reading, often illustrated from his large stock of woodcuts, partly inherited from Caxton. He was also active in printing Latin schoolbooks. Pynson's publishing program was in general aimed at a more learned audience, with a particular specialty in books of English common law.

Apart from Caxton himself, almost all the personnel of the English printing shops came from the continent: de Worde was a native of Holland, and may well already have worked for Caxton in Bruges; Pynson was a native of Normandy. An Act of 1484, under Richard III, had specifically exempted "merchant strangers" from any restrictions on either printing in England, or bringing in books from abroad. But the presence of foreigners was always unpopular in the turbulent London of this age, leading to many threats, personal attacks, and even riots. In 1534, under Henry VIII, a new act was passed, placing restrictions on the sale of foreign books and on printing within England by foreigners. A part of Henry's motivation was to exert tighter controls on books and printing at a time when Protestant pamphlet literature was spreading widely and clandestinely. The effects of the act, however, were also agreeable to London merchants in general, who were eager to see that it was enforced. The act of 1534 coincided closely with the death of Wynkyn de Worde. Within a few years, the printed-book trade of England was transformed from a primarily foreign occupation to one that was almost entirely native English.

See also **English Literature and Language; Printing and Publishing.**

BIBLIOGRAPHY

The Cambridge History of the Book in Britain. Vol. 3, *1400–1557*. Edited by Lotte Hellinga and J. B. Trapp. Cambridge, U.K., 2000.

Duff, E. Gordon. *The English Provincial Printers, Stationers and Bookbinders to 1557*. Cambridge, U.K., 1912.

———. *The Printers, Stationers and Bookbinders of Westminster and London from 1476 to 1535*. Cambridge, U.K., 1906.

Hellinga, Lotte. *Caxton in Focus: The Beginning of Printing in England*. London, 1982.

Needham, Paul. *The Printer & the Pardoner: An Unrecorded Indulgence Printed by William Caxton for the Hospital of St. Mary Rounceval, Charing Cross*. Washington, D.C., 1986.

Painter, George D. *William Caxton: A Quincentenary Biography of England's First Printer*. London and New York, 1976.

PAUL NEEDHAM

CECIL FAMILY. William Cecil (1520–1598) was born on 13 September 1520. After being educated at St. John's College, Cambridge, he trained as a lawyer. In 1542 he became an M.P. (member of Parliament), and soon afterward he began a long career in royal government. In 1547 he entered the service of Edward Seymour (c. 1500–1552), duke of Somerset and protector of the young king Edward VI (ruled 1547–1553). In the duke's service Cecil identified himself with the protector's policy of uniting England and Scotland through a marriage between Edward and Mary, Queen of Scots (ruled 1542–1587), and with Protestant reform in England. Surviving his patron's fall from grace in 1550, Cecil ingratiated himself with John Dudley (1502–1553), earl of Warwick, and became secretary of state in 1550. Because he had supported Lady Jane Grey (1537–1554) in 1553, William, on the accession of Mary I (ruled 1553–1558), lost his place on the council. He continued, however, in public life, serving on embassies and as an M.P.

On the accession of Elizabeth I (ruled 1558–1603) in November 1558, Cecil was again appointed secretary of state and a member of the privy council. In 1571 he was created first baron Burghley, and the following year he became lord treasurer. Throughout his ascendancy Cecil struggled with the question of the succession. He used Parliament in an attempt to pressure Elizabeth into marrying or naming a successor, and he supported foreign suitors. In religion, although his own sympathies were probably with the more radical Protestants, he supported the queen's middle way between Puritanism and Catholicism. Cecil was unable, however, to follow a path of moderation as a succession of plots against Elizabeth led to harsh anti-Catholic laws and the execution of the queen's greatest dynastic rival, Mary, Queen of Scots, in 1587. His policy of keeping out of foreign wars also failed in 1585, when England went to war with Spain in support of the Dutch rebels. Toward the end of his life Cecil's preeminence was threatened by Robert Devereux (1566–1601), second earl of Essex, but with his son Robert Cecil, William Cecil was able to maintain his family's position as the leading royal servants. William Cecil died in London on 4 August 1598.

Robert Cecil (1563–1612) was William Cecil's eldest son from his second marriage, to Mildred Cooke. Like his father, Robert served his political apprenticeship in Parliament and on diplomatic missions to France and the Netherlands in the 1580s. In 1589 he began to assume his father's responsibilities as principal secretary and was appointed formally on William Cecil's death. This was achieved despite fierce opposition from Devereux, earl of

Cecil Family. William Cecil, Baron Burghley, from the *Memoirs of the Court of Queen Elizabeth* by Sarah, Countess of Essex. ©STAPLETON COLLECTION/CORBIS

Essex, with whom Robert Cecil had clashed in 1594 over the appointment of the attorney general. When Essex returned from Ireland in 1600, Cecil was among those appointed to try the disgraced peer. Essex's rebellion and subsequent execution in 1601 left Cecil's ascendancy unchallenged, and he was instrumental in securing the peaceful accession of James VI of Scotland (ruled Scotland 1567–1625; ruled Great Britain as James I, 1603–1625) to the English throne in 1603.

Cecil proved himself an able servant, and rewards and titles soon followed. In 1603 he was created baron Cecil, the following year viscount Cranbourne, and in 1607 the earl of Salisbury. In 1608 he began to turn his attentions to financial matters, and two years later, in an attempt to solve the crown's mounting debt problem, presented the so-called Great Contract to Parliament, whereby James would forego his feudal prerogatives in return for an annual income tax. This radical solution to the crown's fiscal plight collapsed, however, amid mutual suspicion. Like his father, Robert Cecil was

Cecil Family. Robert Cecil, First Earl of Salisbury, engraving by Renold Elstrack c. 1605–1608. ©HISTORICAL PICTURE ARCHIVE/ CORBIS

most tangible evidence of Robert Cecil's great wealth.

See also **Elizabeth I (England); James I and VI (England and Scotland); Mary I (England).**

BIBLIOGRAPHY

Alford, Stephen. *The Early Elizabethan Polity: William Cecil and the British Succession Crisis, 1558–1569.* Cambridge, U.K., 1998.

Croft, Pauline. *Robert Cecil.* Profiles in Power series. London, forthcoming.

Croft, Pauline, ed. *Patronage, Culture, and Power: The Early Cecils.* New Haven, 2002.

Graves, Michael A. R. *Burghley: William Cecil, Lord Burghley.* London, 1998.

Guy, John, ed. *The Reign of Elizabeth I: Court and Culture in the Last Decade.* Cambridge, U.K., 1995.

Haynes, Alan. *Robert Cecil, Earl of Salisbury, 1563–1612: Servant of Two Sovereigns.* London, 1989.

Read, Conyers. *Lord Burghley and Queen Elizabeth.* London, 1960.

———. *Mr. Secretary Cecil and Queen Elizabeth.* London, 1955.

DAVID GRUMMITT

eager to avoid expensive foreign wars, and in 1604 he ended the war with Spain. Nevertheless he failed to secure a marriage between Henry, Prince of Wales, and the sister of King Philip III (ruled 1598–1621) of Spain in 1611, and he linked England to the Protestant cause in Europe in 1612 by the marriage of Princess Elizabeth to Frederick, the elector palatine. Cecil's health deteriorated rapidly in 1612, probably as a result of scurvy rather than syphilis, and he died in Marlborough on 24 May that year.

Both Cecils amassed huge profits through royal service. William's most lucrative office was master of the wards, granted in 1562, which enabled him to accept bribes from suitors eager to escape the full weight of the crown's feudal prerogatives. Robert's avarice was even more marked; his underestimation of his taxable wealth was legendary. His physical deformity (Elizabeth called him "my little elf," while posthumously he was known as the "crookbacked earl") became a metaphor for his corruption and moral deficiency. The great mansion at Hatfield, built between 1607 and 1612, was the

CELLINI, BENVENUTO (1500–1571), Italian goldsmith, sculptor, and writer. Cellini was the son of Giovanni Cellini, a Florentine court musician, inventor, and minor engineer. A restless, competitive young man, he trained and worked as a goldsmith in Siena and Bologna (1516), Pisa (1517), Rome (1519–1521, 1523–1527), and Mantua (1527–1528), returning to Florence for brief or long stays after each of these periods. From June 1529 to January 1534, Cellini served as *incisore* at the papal mint; throughout the 1530s, he was known for his fine medals and coins. The artist was in Naples in 1534; in Padua, Ferrara, and Lyon in 1537; and back in Rome thereafter. After serving time in prison there for embezzlement, he traveled in 1540 to France, where he spent the next five years, working among the numerous Italian artists at the court of King Francis I (ruled 1515–1547). In 1545, Cellini returned to his native Florence, where he spent most of the remainder of his life, and where he carried out all of his late works.

Benvenuto Cellini. *Perseus and Medusa.* ©Vanni Archive/ Corbis

Beginning in the 1550s, Cellini became active as a writer, first composing poetry (some of it in reply to encomiastic verses that had been written to his bronze *Perseus*), then an autobiography, then a pair of treatises on goldsmithery and sculpture (his only long works to be published in his lifetime), and a series of other discourses on the arts. Though the autobiography in particular is now admired especially for its low style and colorful language, all of the writings reveal Cellini's close association with academic movements in Florence, including the Accademia Fiorentina, to which Cellini briefly belonged in the late 1540s and which he probably aspired to rejoin in the 1560s, and the Accademia del Disegno, which Cellini tried to help shape after its founding in 1563. Cellini was a close friend of the painter and poet Agnolo Bronzino, the philosopher and historian Benedetto Varchi, and the court

physician Guido Guidi; he was a rival to the goldsmith Leone Leoni, the sculptor Baccio Bandinelli, and the painter and biographer Giorgio Vasari (1511–1574).

It was initially on account of his writings, rather than his art, that Cellini, who had been largely forgotten after his death, came to interest later authors. The *Autobiography,* which was first printed in Italian in 1728 (with a dedication to Richard Boyle), in English in 1771 (in a translation by Thomas Nugent), and in German in 1796 (in a translation by Goethe), went through countless editions in the nineteenth century. Cellini's dramatic accounts of chivalric quests, murders, a prison escape, and activities as a soldier made him seem, to Romantic writers, the paradigmatic Renaissance adventurer; he was the subject of a Berlioz opera and an Alexandre Dumas novel. As an artist, Cellini was also celebrated as an icon of Renaissance "universality." Major studies of Cellini as an artist by Eugène Plon (1883) and Friedrich Kriegbaum (1941), establishing the basis for what most people today regard as his oeuvre, clarified, without exactly overturning, this impression. While Cellini could no longer be connected with the enormous range of precious objects attributed to him in the nineteenth century, he could, by the mid-twentieth century, be appreciated as a marble sculptor, no less than as a metalworker. More recently, interest in mannerist art and in early art theory has lent Cellini a different sort of importance, as few artists who practiced his range of arts wrote as voluminously and as informatively about them as he did.

Cellini's major sculptural works include the *Saltcellar,* commissioned by Ippolito D'Este in Rome, completed for Francis at Fontainebleau, and now in Vienna; the decorations, including the surviving *Nymph* of Fontainebleau, intended to complement Francesco Primaticcio's frescoes for the Porte Dorée at Fontainebleau; the *Perseus and Medusa,* still in its original position in the Loggia de' Lanzi in Florence (though the original base has been moved to the Bargello, and replaced with a copy); a series of marble sculptures of classical subjects, most of them now in the Bargello; and the marble *Crucifix,* originally meant for his tomb, and now at the Escorial in Spain. As an artist, Cellini is probably most significant for having rejuvenated the production of monumental public bronze statuary in central Italy. A number of the important sculptors in the generation after Cellini, including Pier Paolo Romano, Willem de Tetrode, Francesco Tadda, and Stoldo Lorenzi all spent time in Cellini's shop.

See also **Coins and Medals; Florence, Art in; Sculpture.**

BIBLIOGRAPHY

Primary Sources

Ashbee, C. R., trans. *The Treatises of Benvenuto Cellini on Goldsmithing and Sculpture.* New York, 1967. Reprint of 1888 edition.

Cellini, Benvenuto. *The Autobiography of Benvenuto Cellini.* Translated by J. Addington Symonds. 2 vols. New York, 1910.

Ferrero, Giuseppe Guido, ed. *Opere di Benvenuto Cellini.* Turin, 1971.

Secondary Sources

Calamandrei, Piero. *Scritti e inediti celliniani.* Edited by Carlo Cordié. Florence, 1971.

Cole, Michael W. *Cellini and the Principles of Sculpture.* Cambridge, U.K., 2002.

Pope-Hennessy, John. *Cellini.* New York, 1985.

MICHAEL COLE

CENSORSHIP. Censorship began in the sixteenth century as the effort to prohibit religious ideas that were deemed heretical. From the beginning religious censorship was only possible when civil governments agreed that it was needed and provided the police authority for enforcement. In the following two centuries the state gradually took complete control, with little or no participation by clergymen. The effectiveness of censorship waxed and waned according to the perceived threat of alleged heretical, seditious, or immoral books as well as local circumstances. Censorship was strongest during the sixteenth century when Catholic and Protestant states sought to enforce religious uniformity, and weakest during the antireligious and politically liberal Enlightenment era of the eighteenth century. Nevertheless, censorship of books, speech, and theater never completely disappeared because almost all state and church authorities felt that it was a legitimate and necessary means of protecting the populace from destructive ideas.

THE PROTESTANT REFORMATION

Little censorship existed before the outbreak of the Protestant Reformation. Civil governments did not permit overt political criticism within the state, but they could do little about denunciations from beyond their borders. Because there was widespread agreement about the fundamental doctrines of Christianity, little censorship of religious and philosophical ideas existed.

The outbreak of the Protestant Reformation stimulated the beginning of religious censorship. Since Protestants promulgated their views through the printing press, and Catholics replied via the same medium, it was inevitable that both sides would try to control the press. But they waited until all hope of reconciliation ended in the middle of the sixteenth century before establishing censorship machinery. Then both sides developed similar policies.

Press censorship needed three components to be effective. First, an individual or a group had to determine which books, authors, and ideas were dangerous—a commission of experts had to prepare a list of objectionable previously published books. Second, prepublication censorship was needed to ensure that new books propagating heretical, seditious, or immoral ideas would not be published. Governments had to establish committees of readers, composed of clergymen and civil officials, to review manuscripts before issuing permissions to print. Prepublication censorship would become the most widespread and effective kind of censorship. Third, the civil authority used its police powers to keep banned books from entering the state and, if possible, to remove them from bookstores and libraries. This part of censorship was never very effective.

The papacy fulfilled the first requirement by promulgating a series of *Indexes of Prohibited Books,* the most important of which were the Tridentine Index of 1564, so called because the Council of Trent authorized it, and its successor, the Clementine Index of 1596, promulgated by Pope Clement VIII. Additional indexes followed in the seventeenth and eighteenth centuries at widely scattered intervals. Indexes listed authors and titles that could not be printed, read, or held, plus rules to guide those carrying out prepublication censorship and expurgation (elimination of objectionable passages in books otherwise acceptable). Catholic state and church authorities cooperated relatively effectively in censorship actions despite numerous disagreements and jurisdictional conflicts. For example, France never accepted the papal indexes but still banned Protestant books and ideas.

Protestant censorship followed the same paths except that no supranational Protestant church existed to direct and coordinate censorship. Since Protestant religious leaders invested the state with substantial authority over the church, the state assumed the leading role in censorship. Each Protestant state had to decide which books to ban and how to censor. Protestant states banned the publication, importation, and ownership of Catholic works, and sometimes the works of other Protestants. They also condemned books considered immoral and critical of the government. Although Protestant censorship has been little studied, it is likely that England and the Calvinist canton of Geneva had the most effective Protestant censorship in the sixteenth century.

Both Catholic and Protestant churches and states regulated what was preached in the pulpit and taught in universities. Prepublication censors sometimes dictated that scholars accept unwelcome changes in their works. Authors exercised some degree of self-censorship. A few scholars in both Catholic and Protestant worlds lost university positions, or suffered worse, because of their religious views. Political censorship also intensified in the late sixteenth century as governments attempted to stem a flood of vitriolic anonymous political pamphlets criticizing rulers and supporting rebellion, especially in France.

STATE CENSORSHIP

Although censorship began as a result of the religious division of Europe, civil governments quickly took complete control of censorship of books and theater. France is a good example. Beginning in the 1530s the monarchy issued a series of decrees that sought to ban Protestant literature. By the early seventeenth century a multiplicity of censors existed. Hence, in 1672 the monarchy established a college of censors, a group of scholars appointed to read manuscripts intended for publication and to grant the publisher the right to print the book, called a *privilège*. By the eighteenth century the number of French censors ranged from 150 to 200. The college exercised prepublication censorship and awarded exclusive publication rights to one publisher, thus protecting him from piracy by others.

English censorship of printed works began when Henry VIII (ruled 1509–1547) sought to protect the national church from other doctrines and his monarchy from attacks. Succeeding monarchs used censorship to enforce different religious establishments. Edward VI (ruled 1547–1553) allowed Protestant works, while Mary Tudor (ruled 1553–1558) banned them. Elizabeth I (ruled 1558–1603) passed numerous laws censoring the press and the theater to ensure that they respected her version of the English Church, did not publish Catholic views, and did not criticize the monarchy. In 1557 the crown created the Stationers' Company to issue licenses to print. The requirement that every book had to be licensed helped control the press. English monarchs continued a policy of state censorship over the next two centuries, although the purpose of censorship increasingly became that of shielding the monarchy from any criticism. Nevertheless, the shifting policies of the crown toward the national church, Puritanism, and Catholicism produced considerable variation from regime to regime in the seventeenth century, resulting in less effective censorship. Publishers of obscene, seditious, and blasphemous matter simply published without permission. So in 1695 England and Wales ended prepublication censorship of written materials. The practice of locating and destroying books and prosecuting publishers had always been difficult, and that also waned, but censorship of the stage remained.

Every other large and small political unit had similar censorship systems, sometimes including representatives of the local church. But the local nature of censorship, limited to the boundaries of the state or city, was its weakness. Authors and printers wishing to publish political or religious criticism only needed to go to the next state to publish their works. Then the international commercial network of the book trade, including book fairs at Frankfurt and elsewhere, distributed the books throughout Europe. Finally, newspapers in the late seventeenth century created a new publication that was difficult to censor. Because newspapers were local and ephemeral, any censorship had to be quick and local. The censorship machinery of the sixteenth century was organized to censor learned works of religion, philosophy, and politics and could not adapt easily to newspapers, plus broadsides and other ephemeral matter, which were printed overnight on cheap paper, often without the names of author and printer, and were quickly distributed.

THE ENLIGHTENMENT

The Enlightenment of the eighteenth century, especially in the years from 1750 to 1789, significantly weakened but did not eliminate censorship. Many Enlightenment philosophes deplored it, especially religious censorship, partly because they wrote many antireligious works. Rulers such as Frederick the Great of Prussia (ruled 1740–1786), Empress Maria Theresa (ruled 1740–1780) and Joseph II (Holy Roman emperor, 1765–1790; king of Austria, 1780–1790), Empress Catherine II of Russia (ruled 1762–1796), and King Charles III of Spain (ruled 1759–1788), who were influenced by the ideas of the Enlightenment, permitted more religious and literary freedom of expression. However, when writers began to publish works criticizing absolutist government and demanding expanded political rights for citizens, the rulers again tightened censorship. But they did not, and could not, return censorship to its earlier state.

In France, Enlightenment pressures seriously weakened the *privilège* system, as censors permitted the publication of ideas that had previously been banned. Numerous publishers in smaller states just beyond the borders of France published many works without *privilèges*, then sent them into France. The loosening of censorship permitted an avalanche of political pamphlets critical of the monarchy and the church, which helped bring on the French Revolution.

See also **Enlightenment; Index of Prohibited Books; Journalism, Newspapers, and Newssheets; Printing and Publishing; Reformation, Protestant.**

BIBLIOGRAPHY

Primary Source

Index des livres interdits. Edited by J. M. DeBujanda et al. 10 vols. Sherbrooke, Quebec, and Geneva, Switzerland, 1985–1996. Texts and history of the drafting and promulgation of all sixteenth-century indexes of prohibited books.

Secondary Sources

Clegg, Cyndia Susan. *Press Censorship in Elizabethan England.* Cambridge, U.K., 1997.

Eisenhardt, Ulrich. *Die kaiserliche Aufsicht über Buchdruck, Buchhandel, und Presse im Heiligen Römischen Reich Deutscher Nation (1496–1806).* Karlsruhe, 1970. Censorship in the Holy Roman Empire.

Grendler, Paul F. *The Roman Inquisition and the Venetian Press, 1540–1605.* Princeton, 1977. Book censorship in the major Italian publishing center.

Jones, Derek, ed. *Censorship: A World Encyclopedia.* 4 vols. London and Chicago, 2001. Fundamental; see articles on censorship in different countries, Enlightenment, and other topics.

Santschi, Catherine. *La censure à Genève au XVIIe siècle.* Geneva, 1978.

PAUL F. GRENDLER

CENSUS. The word *census* is a Latin term, and efforts during the early modern period to conduct population surveys were historically descended from the Roman census process, which was based on sworn declarations of the age, number of family members, and property of individual households. Early modern political writers were impressed by the Roman state's ability to enumerate and assess its subject population. Because the equation of a commonwealth's population with its strength had by the later sixteenth century become a commonplace, enthusiastic recommendations of the census were made by a host of thinkers, including Jean Bodin (1576), Giovanni Botero (1588), Justus Lipsius (1589), and other political thinkers. Yet, if the historical memory of the Roman census had survived the collapse of the Roman Empire, the administrative ability to actually conduct one did not. As a result, full territorial enumerations were only sporadically carried out in most of Europe until the end of the eighteenth century.

The most significant exception to this generalization was Italy itself, where true censuses (as opposed to household listings and tax surveys) were already being carried out by the end of the Middle Ages. The Italian city-states were especially (and unsurprisingly) advanced in this regard, and censuses had already been carried out in Florence (1380), Treviso (1384), Padua (1411), Verona (1473), Reggio (1473), Palermo (1479), Brescia (1493),

Parma (1508), Venice (1509), and Rome (1526). Enumerations were also conducted in Italian territorial principalities, including the duchies of Ferrara (1431) and Mantua (1451), and in Sicily (1501). The mature administration of these censuses reflects the much greater sophistication of public administration in Italy than elsewhere in Europe, and early modern Italian censuses were much more than simple head counts. The Sicilian censuses, of which there were fourteen between 1501 and 1747, listed every individual by name and relationship to the head of the household, and separated out those males of arms-bearing age. By the sixteenth century, Italian censuses often recorded detailed information on the age structure of the population, and the exact age of every inhabitant was recorded at Pozzuoli (1489), Sorrento (1561), and Carpi (1591). By comparison, the English and American censuses did not list every individual by name until 1841 and 1850, respectively. It is also worth noting that the registration of births began in Siena in 1381, in Florence in 1450, and in Bologna in 1459, whereas parish registers do not survive before the mid- to late-sixteenth century in Protestant Europe, and before the seventeenth century in most of Catholic northern Europe.

Italian precocity did not mean, however, that the rest of Europe had ceased to carry out population surveys altogether, and the early modern period generated a mass of such material. Thus, population surveys begin to appear on monastic estates in France and Germany as early as the ninth century, and by the later Middle Ages full population counts were taken in several German cities, for example in Nuremberg (1449), Nördlingen (1459), and Strasbourg (1473), although these were not followed up on a regular basis.

Especially at the level of the local territory or community, a huge variety of other surveys were conducted with ever greater frequency during the early modern period. Muster rolls listing all men eligible for military service were drawn up on an irregular basis in various European communities. There was also a variety of specialized censuses, such as the Norwich Census of the Poor (1570) and the Castilian educational census of 1764, which was designed to determine the number of students who were attending various education institutions. In the Holy Roman Empire a number of territorial

authorities (for example, the Bishop of Speyer in 1530, and the monastery of Ottobeuren in 1548, 1556, 1564, and 1586) compiled *Leibeigenbücher*, 'serf registers', which recorded the free (or servile) status of every man, woman, and child in the territory. During the sixteenth century both Catholic and Protestant episcopal authorities began conducting parish-by-parish counts of the number of communicants (all persons over twelve to fourteen years of age), and these surveys became ever more detailed and systematic during the seventeenth and eighteenth centuries.

Still more detailed was the *liber status animarum*, or listing of each parish resident, which the papacy, in 1614, ordered every parish priest to maintain. These listings were less commonly compiled than the more familiar baptismal, marriage, and burial registers, but many seventeenth- and eighteenth-century parish listings have survived from Catholic Europe, and in a few areas (Malta after 1687, for example) complete listings have survived for every single parish. Similar records were maintained in many Protestant areas. In England, listings have survived from scattered locations from the later sixteenth century, although it is a rare parish where more than one such survey has survived. More systematic efforts were undertaken on the Continent, especially in Sweden, where parish registration had begun in 1686. In 1749, the Lutheran parish clergy in Sweden and Finland (then a Swedish possession) were further required to maintain a continuously updated list of parish residents and submit quinquennial tabulations to the *Tabellverket* (Tabulation Office) of population numbers broken down by sex, age, marital status, occupation, and social status, in addition to annual statistics of births, marriages, deaths, and (in the nineteenth century) migration.

By far the most common type of early modern enumeration, however, was a survey of hearths or heads of households, made almost always for fiscal reasons. As with the census itself, the earliest such territorial hearth tax surveys were carried out in Italy, as at Pavia (1250), Pistoia (1255), Perugia (1278), Padua (c. 1281), Reggio Emilia (1315), Florence (1351), Sicily (1374), and Venice (1379). The Florentine *catasto* (tax survey) of 1427 went so far as to record not only the name, age, marital status, and profession of the household head, but also the number of other individuals in the family, the type of residence (owned or rented), the number and value of livestock, the value of private and public investments, and the capitalized value of real property.

Beyond Italy, England stands out as a kingdom of very early tax surveys. Because of its unusually centralized monarchy, national tax surveys began in England as early as 1086 (William I's famous Domesday Book), and were repeated with varying degrees of completeness in 1279–1280 (the Hundred Rolls), 1377 (Edward III's Poll Tax), 1524–1525 (Henry VIII's Lay Subsidy), and 1662–1674 (Charles II's Hearth Taxes). Elsewhere in Europe full territorial tax surveys were conducted in France (1328), the German lands of the Holy Roman Empire (1495), Portugal (1527), Bohemia (1653–1655), Moravia (1655–1657), Ireland (1659), and Austria (1749–1750). Before the eighteenth century these large-scale surveys were only infrequently attempted; thus in Portugal there was only a single national survey between 1527 and 1736, and this one (in 1636) was seriously inaccurate. Outside of Italy, perhaps the most regular set of national household surveys were conducted in Castile between 1528 and 1536, 1541, 1552, 1561, 1571, 1587, 1591, and 1596, and were supplemented by the so-called *relaciones topográficas* of 1575–1578, a set of questions about local customs, economic conditions, and institutional characteristics administered in each locality in the kingdom. Even then, the frequency of survey fell off in the following century.

Local hearth and household tax surveys were much more common than their national counterparts and grew in frequency over the course of the early modern period. Nevertheless, there were significant regional differences in detail. Thus, in northern France, local taille (direct property tax) rolls recorded little more than the payment made by each household (and even they are rare before 1650). By contrast, German tax surveys often itemized and valued each item of a household's property, and the level of its debts, as early as the beginning of the seventeenth century.

The close connection between census taking and taxation was, of course, recognized both by administrators and those they surveyed, and fears of excessive taxation would move the British Parliament to reject a census bill as late as 1753. Nevertheless, by the end of the eighteenth century the census was recognized as an essential tool of government, and regular population surveys were initiated (or at least attempted) in Norway (1769), France (1774, 1790), Denmark (1787), Belgium (1797), England (1801), Bavaria (1818), Saxony (1834), and Austria (1850).

See also **Property; State and Bureaucracy; Taxation.**

BIBLIOGRAPHY

Beloch, Julius. *Bevölkerungsgeschichte Italiens.* 3 vols. Berlin, 1937–1961.

Blaschke, Karlheinz. *Bevölkerungsgeschichte von Sachsen bis zur industriellen Revolution.* Weimar, 1967.

Herlihy, David, and Christiane Klapisch-Zuber. *Tuscans and Their Families: A Study of the Florentine Catasto of 1427.* New Haven, 1985.

Hollingsworth, Thomas Henry. *Historical Demography.* Ithaca, N.Y., 1969.

Mols, Roger. *Introduction à la démographie historique des villes d'Europe du XIVe au XVIIIe siècle.* 3 vols. Gembloux, 1954–1956.

GOVIND P. SREENIVASAN

CENTRAL EUROPE, ART IN.

The fluctuating nature of the cultural and political geography of Europe, together with the actual extent of the physical surface of the continent from the Urals to the Atlantic, has meant that the notion of a European center has been diversely interpreted. In physical terms, since the continent is conventionally regarded as stretching from 10° west to 60° east longitude and 70° to 35° north latitude, its center is somewhere near the Polish city of Lublin. The site of the conception of the Polish-Lithuanian Commonwealth in 1569—the political alliance largely responsible for the political face of central European culture during the early modern era—the Lublin region ushered in the new age with the building of a model town according to an "ideal" plan by Chancellor Jan Zamoyski. At the center of major medieval north-south and east-west trading routes, this was Zamosc, designed by Bernardo Morando of Padua (late 1570s; built 1579–1640s). Within an octagon of walls and moats, Morando's interpretation of the Renaissance architectural theories of Serlio and Vignola saw the urban space divided into regularized commercial and residential quarters whose axes were marked by the Zamoyski palace, collegiate church, academy, synagogue, town hall, and two marketplaces. The universalist vision of geometric harmony, which coincided with Zamoyski's inception of the Polish Republic of Nobles, also encompassed the building of Armenian, Jesuit, Greek, and Russian Orthodox churches.

Despite its location and integrative modern concept, Zamosc lies on the northeastern side of the hub of central European visual culture in the early modern period. This core is conventionally considered to comprise the territories around Moravia, the centers for developments in the visual arts being the court metropolises of Prague in the west, Vienna and Pressburg (Bratislava) in the south, and Cracow in the east. Beyond this ring, however, were other major centers of diverse size and artistic direction. Their spread ranged at least from Gdańsk, Königsberg (Kaliningrad), and Vilnius in the Baltic north, through a central belt that stretched from Augsburg and Dresden in the west to Buda and Lwów (Lviv) in the east and included Breslau (Wrocław) and Warsaw, to Agram (Zagreb), Laibach (Ljubljana), Venice, Dar al-Djihad (Belgrade), Sarajevo, and Ragusa (Dubrovnik) in the Adriatic south. Despite the prominence of these cities in the production of visual art during the early modern period, due to the terrain and feudal organization of society across the entire region, much art was produced outside of the major cities in smaller provincial centers and country estates.

In 1500 the cultural map of the area definable as central Europe was divided between three main powers: the Habsburgs, the Ottomans, and the Jagiellonians. Governance from Istanbul covered the provinces of Rumeli (the "Roman" Balkans, including Eflak [Wallachia] and Bosnia), and Macaristan and Bugdan (Hungary and Moldova). The Habsburg dominions included Austria, Styria, and considerable German territories. Jagiellonian power extended from Cracow, west into Bohemia, and east through the Kingdom of Poland to the Grand Duchy of Lithuania. Other powers were Venice, which controlled much of the Dalmatian coast, and the Germanic states, notably Saxony and Brandenburg.

By 1800 the Polish territories had switched from temporary control by the Swedish Vasa and were dominated by Russia, Prussia, and Austria. Hungary, Transylvania, and the Banat, following many years of Turkish rule, became Austrian. The political transitions of the turbulent period, often extremely bloody, were counterparts to religious and social upheaval. The intricate involvement of central Europe in the Protestant Reformation, Catholic Counter-Reformation, Catholic-Orthodox rivalry, Judaic discrimination and Islamicization, and the inherent strength of pagan traditions, meant that all these left indelible marks on the visual arts of the period.

Other principal influences on the development and appearance of the arts included the introduction of new or adapted technologies such as printing and faience; the establishment of major collections, such as the Czartoryski in Poland; and the development of secular education, literature, music, and theater. A further influence was the presence of multiple ethnic groups, many widely dispersed and nonindigenous yet with their own clearly marked traditions and identities, among them Jews, Armenians, and Germans.

THE VISUAL ARTS UNDER THE OTTOMANS

The appearance of Ottoman art in central Europe is dominated by architecture and the applied arts. In architecture, mosques (djami, cami), baths (hamam and ilidje), inns (caravansary and han), charitable foundations (külliye), schools (medrese), mausolea (türbe), markets (bedesten), bridges, tents, and manors (kule) were the principal buildings, while the principal applied arts were textiles (kilim, kaftan, ferace), leatherwork, ceramics, and metalware. Garden and fountain art also was cultivated, as in Sarajevo on the right bank of the Miljacka River and the Feredjusha fountain (destroyed). The most luxurious townhouses (konak) were built for high officials. Their walls were often adorned with floral motifs and painted or tiled Arabic inscriptions whose exquisite calligraphic qualities made them one of the highest forms of visual art. Serbian examples survive in Djakovica, Vranje, Pristina, and Pec.

In Eflak the most remarkable bridge was constructed over the Neretva River at Mostar (1566, Mimar Hayreddin, destroyed 1993), during the reign of Suleiman I. Its emblematic narrow, pointed vault linked the city's Moslem, Croatian, and Serbian quarters. The pile bridge over the Drava River near Osijek (1526) was designed by Suleiman's chief architect, Mimar Sinan, who also transformed Esztergom Cathedral into a mosque, adding a minaret.

The Svrzo House (sixteenth century) in Sarajevo, replete with its stalactite-vaulted entrance, is a fine example of Ottoman-style residential building *(kuca)*. The essential rule of the Ottoman dwelling was that it not convey a sense of wealth or magnificence, either externally or internally. Furniture was sparse and included neither tables nor chairs; the only ornamentation was a few inscriptions *(yafte)* on the walls; household utensils were minimal. Post-and-pane construction was characteristic, with space organized according to gender divisions.

Turkish baths included the Ferizbei (Sarajevo, 1509), Kaplu (Király) and Veli bei (Császár) (both Buda, 1560s–1570s). The Buda thermal baths were built (and later beautified) by Pasha Mustafa Sokoly. Their impressive octagonal bathing rooms *(harara)* are surmounted by a dome supported by squat pillars. One of the finest caravansaries in central Europe was the Kursumli Han in Skopje, Macedonia, probably built by Ragusa merchants in the sixteenth century.

Mosques included the Gazi Husrev-begova (Sarajevo, 1530–1540), Gazi Kassim (Pécs, 1550s–1560s), Tombul (Shumla or Shumen, 1744), Ferhad Pasha (Banja Luka, 1576–1579, destroyed 1993), Aladza (Foca, 1550–1588, destroyed early 1990s), Yakovali Hassan (Pécs, sixteenth century), and Sinan Pasha (Prizren, 1615). According to the seventeenth-century Turkish traveller Evliya Çelebi, the beauty of the latter was unparalleled: "such impressiveness has not been achieved by any previous architect on the planet Earth." The Gazi Husrev-begova, named after its founder, the enlightened and philanthropic governor of Bosnia, has a typical flattened dome on an octagonal drum surrounded by smaller half-domes. The large Ferhad mosque included in its inner court a *shadirvan* (fountain) surrounded by *türbe* of the founder and followers. A popular plan for the mosques, as witnessed, for example, in the Gazi Kassim at Pécs, was square with a central saucer dome on pendentives, conjoined with three lower smaller domes and minaret

that formed an antechamber. The northernmost Ottoman mosque was at Eger, Hungary (minaret extant, sixteenth century). The mid-eighteenth-century Tombul mosque complex built by Pasha Halil Sherif in Shumla is, as evinced through the internal decoration of its walls with polychromatic floral and geometric motifs and Islamic inscriptions, a fine example of a late flourishing in central Europe of Istanbul's "tulip" style.

Lodges *(tekke)* for the Sufi dervish orders could also be significant architectural monuments, such as that of Sersem Ali Baba at Tetova (Kalkandelen, Macedonia, eighteenth century), the Dollma *tekke* at Krujë, Albania, and the Sinan Pasha *tekke* in Sarajevo (1640). A fine example of a domed *medrese* with centralized arcaded courtyard and fountain is the Gazi Husrev-begova Kursunlu *medrese* in Sarajevo (1557). Shortly before the building of the *medrese*, Sarajevo gained one of Central Europe's best examples of a covered bazaar, the hexa-domed Brusa *bezistan* (1557). The Turks also built clock towers, including the Sahat-kula (seventeenth century) in Sarajevo.

Ottoman influence is also evident in the art of the nations connected with the Ottoman territories. Thus, from the seventeenth century colored floral and geometricized Turkish textile design, as well as Turkish fabrics, were incorporated into Polish liturgical vestments and carpets. Embroidered Turkish silk caparisons *(shabrack)* were frequently adopted by the Poles and sometimes converted into altar frontals. Other embroidered work of the Turks was remade into chasubles. Similar transferences were found in Polish and Transylvanian leatherwork (for example, embossed saddles and flasks). Furthermore, the east Serbian town of Pirot became renowned for its kilim production. Following capture as booty in the seventeenth century, the red silk Turkish tent, decorated with gold, silver, green, and light red floral arabesques, became a feature in Polish art, not least in its use during important ceremonial state occasions, official meetings, and garden parties. One of the most important manufactories for Turkish-style canvas tents and woolen carpets was the Koniecpolskis at Brody. Fine ceramicware, including faience jugs, cups, and plates was imported from the Turkish Iznik and Kütahya workshops. This influenced the designs of Anabaptist Habaner majolica produced in Slovakian lands in the late seventeenth century, with its range of stylized floral and architectural motifs, use of cobalt blue, and particular preference for the tulip.

In addition, Ottoman rule allowed for a certain multiculturalism. A synagogue and Orthodox cathedral (both extant) were built in Sarajevo in the sixteenth century. In Karadag (Montenegro) the Orthodox monastery of Moraca became a center for icon painting in the seventeenth century. Georgije Mitrofanović, a monk from Hilandar Monastery on Mount Athos who worked in a post-Byzantine style, led this movement. Further, baroque flourishes are to be seen in the eighteenth-century art of a group of painters from Kotor on the Adriatic coast, notably that of the church decorator Tripo Kokolja and the portrait painter Antun Mazarović. Following the restoration of the Serbian patriarchate at Peć in 1557, post-Byzantine fresco and icon painting revived, the greatest painters being Longin (Decani, Lomnica, and Piva monasteries, late sixteenth century) and Djordje Mitrofanovic (Moraca monastery, 1616–1617).

THE VISUAL ARTS UNDER THE JAGIELLONIANS AND THEIR SUCCESSORS: SIXTEENTH AND SEVENTEENTH CENTURIES

The Jagiellonian dynasty, descendants of the Lithuanian grand duke Jogaila (Władyłsaw) and Jadwiga of Anjou, ruled the vast central European Polish and Lithuanian territories from 1386 through 1572 and were monarchs of Hungary and Bohemia from the late fifteenth century to 1526. Through marriage they were also connected to the subsequent rulers of Poland, the Transylvanian Stephen Báthory, and the Swedish Vasa house. Under their most prominent sixteenth-century kings, Sigismund I and Sigismund II Augustus (ruled 1506–1548 and 1548–1572, respectively) and Queen Anna (1575–1586), the arts flourished, and nowhere more so than in the heart of their kingdom, Wawel Castle in Cracow. Its rebuilding by the Florentine architect known as Francesco Fiorentino meant the creation of an inner arcaded courtyard (1507–1536) with steeply pitched "northern" tiled roof, two levels of round arches, and a high loggia marked by doubled classical columns. In the early 1530s an original form of decoration was applied to the coffered ceiling of the Ambassadors' Hall, where 194 grotesquely expressive wooden heads, carved by the team of Sebastian Tauerbach of Breslau, represented the mix of Polish

society. The humanist range of the heads coincided with that revealed in the vision of Cracowian life presented in the illuminations of Balthazar Behem's *Codex* (1505).

Nobles' castles that followed the Jagiellonian Italianate style included the Piast family stronghold at Brieg (Brzeg, Silesia, c. 1550), the Leszczynski's Baranów Sandomierski (Santi Gucci, 1591–1606), and the Krasicki's Krasiczyn (Galeazzo Appiano, 1597–1630). Another arcaded structure (also castellated) is the town hall in Poznan (Giovanni Battista Quadro, 1550–1560), the scale and decoration of which emphasized the rapid rise of the city's civic status and values.

Italian Renaissance convention was further introduced in the Sigismund Chapel (Kaplica Zygmuntowska, 1517–1533) of Wawel Cathedral by another Florentine, Bartolommeo Berrecci. This has a centralized plan with square base, octagonal drum, and dome. The interior glorification of the monarch and the Virgin Mary through a rich interplay of numerous symbols of harmonic authority is set by walls divided according to the principle of the Roman triumphal arch. All three monarchs are entombed here, their sarcophagi in Esztergom red marble (the latter two by Santi Gucci) featuring recumbent chivalric figures whose peaceful vitality creates a counterpoint to the grotesque wall ornamentation. The pentaptych, or five-panel altarpiece, was executed by Nuremberg artists (1531–1538). A miniature visual counterpart to the chapel was provided by Stanislaw Samostrzelnik, illuminator of prayer books of Sigismund I and his wife Queen Bona Sforza (for example, the latter's *Book of Hours*, 1528, Bodleian Library, Oxford). Simultaneously, Cracowian and other anonymous Polish religious painters began to paint in the style of Cranach, who was active in neighboring Saxony from 1505, after which he also worked for the Polish court.

The fashion for the Renaissance mausoleum grew, culminating in the Boim Chapel, Lwów (1609–1615, Andreas Bemer). Likewise, sepulchral sculpture in similar Renaissance style was to be created by Giovanni Maria Mosca (Il Padovano), as witnessed in the Tarnów Cathedral sarcophagi for the Tarnowski hetmans, and by Jan Michalowicz (for example, Bishop Padniewski's tomb, Wawel Cathedral, c. 1575). Subsequently, a new dynamic monumentalism was introduced and became common for Polish ecclesiastical architecture (such as SS. Peter and Paul, Cracow, 1596–1635, Giovanni Trevano).

A distinctive feature of the "Polish Renaissance" was the "Polish attic," a rhythmical decorative crown that hid the roof and gave a rich accent to the upper levels of a variety of examples of urban architecture: the Cracow Cloth Hall (1557–1558), the town houses of Zamosc and Kazimierz Dolny (early seventeenth century), and Gdańsk Upper (Wyzynna) Gate (1586–1589), arsenal (1602–1605) and town hall (1587–1608). The latter acquired Netherlandish qualities as a result of the arrival of architects and decorators such as Anthonis van Opbergen and Willem, Abraham, and Isaak van den Blocke from the strife-torn Low Countries. While a sublimely tapering Bruges-style clock tower capped the town hall, its internal decoration was also highly ornate, the whole being conceived as part of a lavish civic and Calvinist iconographic program. At the same time in Lwów a new sophisticated blend of Byzantine and Renaissance language was attained in the Orthodox Wallachian Church of the Assumption (1591–1629, Paolo Dominici) and its Korniakta Tower (1572–1578, Pietro di Barbona), built for the Stauropegia Brotherhood.

The new regard for the individual and the societal witnessed in the Wawel and Zamosc was furthered by the development of portrait painting from the mid-sixteenth century. This included the formal, royal, and noble portraits attributed to the Silesian Marcin Kober, who created authoritative character images with figures set against neutral backgrounds, such as *King Stefan Batory* (1583, Wawel Collection, Cracow). The success of these led to his appointment in Prague as painter to Rudolf II. With the decentralization of culture ushered in by Lublin, after the turn of the seventeenth century the vogue for palaces with portrait galleries dedicated to noble family lineage became widespread. French château inspiration is revealed in the hetman's castle at Podhorce, near Brody (1635–1640, Andrea dell'Agua, Guillaume de Beauplan), where Count Stanislaw Koniecpolski also established a major weaving manufactory, producing textiles in adapted Flemish and oriental styles.

Particularly fashionable among the Radziwills, Czartoryskis, Potockis, Lubomirskis, and their peers was an eastward-looking trend known as "Sarmatism." In this the gentry articulated their deemed superiority by regarding themselves as the descendants of the ancient, conquering Sarmatians. They did so by orientalizing their costume and applied arts, from the addition of fur-lined *kontusz* overcoats with sashes to armor such as the *karabela* saber, and the luxurious interior decoration of their new houses. The *ktitor* (noble patron) portrait became especially popular. The apogee of the style was reached in elected King Jan III Sobieski's Sarmatist court taste, as witnessed in its blending with the baroque at his main residence, Wilanow Palace, Warsaw (Augustine Locci, 1677–1696). The prime early exponent of the Sarmatist fashion for Sobieski's predecessors, the Vasas, was Tommaso Dolabella, whose painting (portraits, historical, and religious cycles) had simultaneously introduced Italian baroque conventions. His Gdańsk contemporary Daniel Schultz revealed the osmotic relationship of the trends by painting a *Family Portrait* (1664, Hermitage, St. Petersburg) in the style of Rembrandt. In the eighteenth century Dolabella's place was taken by the versatile Szymon Czechowicz.

EIGHTEENTH CENTURY

The election of the Saxon Wettin dukes, Augustus II the Strong (ruled 1697–1733) and his son Augustus III (ruled 1733–1763), to the Polish throne essentially meant rule from Dresden and a period of cultural provincialization for the Polish lands. However, some outstanding monuments and artists did appear, particularly those connected with the church. The "Saxon era" saw the building of St. George's Cathedral as the seat of the Greek Catholic Uniate metropoly in Lwów (Bernard Meretini, 1744–1761), with a rococo plasticity that coincided with the dynamic, expressive sculptural work of Johann Georg Pinsel, one of its decorators. Prominent architects included the Fontanas, Jakub, Józef, and Pawel, who prefered twin-towered western facades and octagonal naves for their numerous churches, and built the Radzyn Podlaski house of the Potocki family in the French rococo style (1750–1758). Similar aristocratic taste was expressed in the ornate rebuilding and decoration of Choroszcz, the Bialystok palace of the Branickis by the Saxon Sigismund Deybel (1728–1752). The painter best identified with the period was Rome-trained Tadeusz Kuntze, who excelled in a theatrical frivolity and sensuality.

In the same period the arts in Dresden flourished. The Wettin court, which had already seen the creation of the Palais im Grossen Garten (1679–1683, Johann Georg Starcke) in a hybrid Roman-Louis XIV style, became a center of festivities. Orchestrated by the elector-kings, a key venue for these was the extravagant baroque Zwinger palace (from 1709, Matthäus Pöppelmann; sculpture by Balthasar Permoser). The monumental Roman Catholic Hofkirche (1737–1755, Gaetano Chiaveri) and Protestant Frauenkirche (1726–1743, Georg Bähr, destroyed), with their neo-Roman and neo-Greek plans, added an alternative vocabulary to the architectural and cultural dialogue. It was here that the antique sensibilities of the aesthete Johann Joachim Winckelmann and painter Anton Raphael Mengs were nurtured. Further, Wettin oriental taste brought about the manufacture of porcelain at Meissen from 1710. This coincided with a new era of art collecting that saw the creation of Augustus's Green Vaults decorative arts selection and the Stallhof gallery of Old Masters (1720s).

The reign of Poland's last king, Stanisław II Augustus Poniatowski (ruled 1764–1795), saw the introduction of neoclassicism in the visual arts, exemplified in architecture and gardening by the royal Lazienki palace and park complex in Warsaw (1775–1792, Domenico Merlini, Jan Christian Kamsetzer), and, on the magnates' estates, at the Potocki's Palladianist Tulczyn (1775–1785, Joseph Lacroix) and Czartoryski's Pulawy (1780s, Chrystian Piotr Aigner). It was to the latter that Jean-Pierre Norblin, the versatile and topical founder of the Polish national school of painting, emigrated from France. Norblin was also to work for Princess Helena Radziwill in the decoration of her ideal rustic paradise Arkadia (by Lowicz), where Simon Gottlieb Zug introduced a new romantic ambience by blending the neoclassical and neo-Gothic in the landscape architecture (1780–1798). Prior to Norblin, Marcello Bacciarelli, head of Stanisław's art studio in Warsaw Castle, brought new intimacy and elegance to Polish painting, while Bernardo Bellotto (Canaletto) introduced the city *vedute* during his extended stay.

THE VISUAL ARTS UNDER THE HABSBURGS: SIXTEENTH AND SEVENTEENTH CENTURIES

The visual arts in the Habsburg's central European lands developed most significantly after the accession of Ferdinand I, through his Jagiellonian marriage, to the Bohemian and Hungarian thrones in 1526. While small east Bohemian towns such as Pardubice, Nové Mesto nad Metuji, and Telc were rebuilt with regularized Renaissance plans and arcaded squares, Ferdinand's residence at Prague Castle (Hradcany) also acquired a new appearance. First the colonnaded Belvedere Palace (1534–1563, Paolo della Stella, Bonifaz Wohlmut) was created as a modern Italianate garden villa with a "singing" fountain and a hundred sandstone reliefs aggrandizing the Habsburgs. Then other structures by Wohlmut, such as the organ loft in St. Veit's Cathedral (1556–1561) and Ball Court (1567–1569) showed similar awareness of new Italian architectural theory.

Simultaneously, Bohemian and Moravian castles acquired regular plans, arcaded courtyards with superpositioned orders and lavish French Renaissance-style interior decoration, as at Moravsky Krumlov (1557–1562, Leone Garove da Bissone) and Bucovice (c. 1570–1580s), residences of the lord high marshal and steward of the kingdom, respectively. Assembly buildings and town halls followed suit, as at Graz, Brunn (Brno), and Pressburg. Sgraffito and gables of exaggerated forms characterized the exteriors of many of the new buildings across the region. Designer of court festivities and ceilings for Maximilian II and Rudolf II was Giuseppe Arcimboldo (c. 1530–1593), widely known for his painting of allegories in the form of composite heads crafted from animals and still-life objects.

With the establishment of Prague as the imperial capital by Rudolf II (ruled 1576–1612) came a dynamic new era for the visual arts. Chief city planner and architect was Giovanni Maria Filippi, the probable designer of the city's first baroque church, the Lutheran Church of the Holy Trinity (1609–1613). Artists of Netherlandish and German origins and Venetian or Tuscan training were attracted to the city, the Prague court circle that they formed eloquently working in a wide variety of media, genres, and styles. Alongside a new propensity for classical and biblical allegory, genres extended to

Habsburg-Ottoman battle paintings, the erotic, low-life, still-life, and landscape. Painters included Bartholomäus Spranger, Hans von Aachen, Joseph Heintz, and Roelandt Savery. Sculptors included Adriaen de Vries, who went on, in the post-1620 Counter-Reformation period, to decorate Count Albrecht Wallenstein's monumental new palace (1621–1623, Andrea Spezza). Rudolf also built up one of central Europe's most important art collections, the Prague Kunstkammer.

The period after the Thirty Years' War (1618–1648), and particularly the reign of Leopold I (ruled 1655–1705), is most clearly identified with the central European early baroque. Palace architecture, in the wake of the Leopoldine Tract (1660–1666 and, later, Filiberto Lucchese) in the Viennese imperial residence, the Hofburg, became increasingly grandiose. The rise of the Jesuits had led during the second quarter of the century to the construction of new, frequently large-scale, Italianate twin-towered churches and colleges (as Palatine count Miklós Esterházy's Church of St. John, Tyrnau [Trnava], Upper Hungary, 1629–1637, Pietro Spezza; and the Clementium, Prague, 1644–1658, Carlo Lugaro), and militant Catholic *Mariensäule,* 'Mary columns', erected in thanksgiving to the Virgin Mary for deliverance from the threat of the Protestant Swedish forces (for example, 1646, Vienna). The latter anticipated the raising of a series of prominent Habsburg *Pestsäule,* 'plague columns', across the territories, such as the *Dreifaltigkeitssäule,* 'Trinity Column', in Vienna (1679–1694, Matthias Rauchmiller, Paul Strudel, Lodovico Ottavio Burnacini), erected after the 1683 defeat of the Turks at Vienna. The return to Bohemia from Italian exile of Karel Skreta, a painter capable of expressing intense, lyrical feeling in both portraits and votive images, helped lay the foundations of the Bohemian school of painting. His sensitive, Netherlands-trained, religious counterpart was Michael Willmann, an East Prussian who in 1660 established a highly influential painting workshop at the Cistercian monastery of Leubus, Silesia.

EIGHTEENTH CENTURY

The Habsburg imperial style *(Reichsstil)* was established around the turn of the eighteenth century, following the expulsion of the Turks from the northwestern central European territories. It coincided with the establishment of the region's first art academy, initially as the Kaiserliche Akademie (1692–1714) in the house of the court painter Peter Strudel, and then, in 1725, as the Akademie der Maler, Bildhauer, und Baukünstler, under the Flemish portrait painter Jacob van Schuppen. The latter organized it according to the model of the Parisian Académie Royale. Early students included the architect Franz Hillebrandt, who subsequently became chief architect of the Hungarian Treasury, and the portrait painter Daniel Schmidely. Members included the fresco painters Paul Troger, his pupil Franz Anton Maulbertsch, and Michael Angelo Unterberger, all of whom emerged as influential teachers and the baroque image makers of "holy Austria."

The imperial style's leading architectural exponent was Johann Bernhard Fischer von Erlach, who initially participated in the creation of the Trinity Column and designed triumphal arches for Vienna celebrating victories over the Turks and the French and then built the Schönbrunn palace (1696–1711). During the reign of Charles VI, Fischer and his son also built the Viennese Hofbibliothek (Imperial Library, 1722–1735), the interior of which was painted by Daniel Gran according to the Habsburg programmatic conception of the triumph of enlightened civilization. In addition, Fischer designed the imperial Karlskirche (Charles Church, 1716–1737) in a composite style as a Christian, pagan, and masonic embodiment of universal harmony, hence its ovoid space, centralized plan, Roman and Hellenistic idioms, fresco painting by Johann Michael Rottmayr, and flanking by minaret-evocative victory columns. Concurrently, the Belvedere Palace (1714–1716 and 1721–1723, Vienna, Johann Lucas von Hildebrandt) was built for Prince Eugene of Savoy as a monumental, glorifying emblem of his successes against the Turks, replete with trophies and a Neapolitan-style ceiling painting of his apotheosis by Martino Altomonte.

The Austrian, Bohemian, and Hungarian realms saw the raising of numerous abbeys, churches, palaces, and new institutions with similar signification and articulation during the early eighteenth century. Primary examples included Melk Abbey (1702–1714, Jakob Prandtauer); the Ursuline Church of the Holy Trinity in Laibach (Ljubljana, 1718–1726, Carlo Martinuzzi); the Jesuit Church of St. Ignatius in Ragusa (Dubrovnik, 1699–1725, Andrea Pozzo); and the Esterházy commissions in Hungary-Croatia, for example, the Franciscan Church (Frauenkirche, 1695–1702, Francesco Martinelli) and Lanschütz Palace (Cseklész, Bernolákovo, 1714–1733, Anton Erhard Martinelli).

Lanschütz, the residence of the Hungarian chancellor Ferenc Esterházy, was redesigned in the 1770s to include oriental features such as a Japanese pagoda and Chinese teahouse. The changes coincided with the reign of Maria Theresa (ruled 1740–1780), when the nearby city of Pressburg (Poszony, Bratislava) became the Hungarian capital and, as such, site and disseminator of a late baroque boom. This was led by the projects of Hillebrandt, which included the reconstruction or completion of royal and noble palaces in Pozsony and Buda, and which was informed by the infusion of the baroque with a restrained neoclassical spirit as witnessed in the Roman Catholic Cathedral and Episcopal Palace at Grosswardein (Nagyvárad, Oradea) in the Banat; and the university at Tyrnau. Home of the Austrian vice-regents, Marie-Christine and Albert, son of Augustus III Wettin, Pozsony was also the site of the original Albertina art collection. The Primate's palace (1777–1781), built by Melchior Manyhért Hefele, professor of architecture at the Vienna Academy, for Archbishop Count József Batthyány, epitomized the classicizing tendencies of the new era. Adorned with a tetrastyle portico and pedimented cornice featuring an array of allegorical figures by the most expressive sculptor of the age, Franz Xaver Messerschmidt, the palace was complemented by the oval space of the St. Ladislaus chapel, with its painted ceiling dedicated to the glory and sanctification of the holy, chivalric Magyar king who had repelled the oriental Cumans in the eleventh century. It was the work of Maulbertsch, the "Austrian Tiepolo," the outstanding product of the Vienna Academy and central Europe's most sublime monumental painter in the late eighteenth century.

The rococo tendencies and emotional tension evinced by much of Maulbertsch's work brought him into conflict with the Vienna Academy, which, during the centralizing reign of Joseph II and thereafter, promulgated a more severe neoclassicism, as advocated by the director, Friedrich Heinrich Füger, a follower of Winckelmann and Mengs.

See also Architecture; Baroque; Cracow; Dresden; Gdańsk; Habsburg Territories; Jagiellon Dynasty (Poland-Lithuania); Maulbertsch, Franz Anton; Mengs, Anton Raphael; National Identity; Neoclassicism; Poland, Partitions of; Polish Succession, War of the (1733–1738); Prague; Rococo; Sarmatism; Vienna; Winckelmann, Johann Joachim.

BIBLIOGRAPHY

Fučiková, Eliška, ed. *Rudolf II and Prague: The Court and the City.* London, 1997.

Gerö, Gyözö. *Turkish Monuments in Hungary.* Budapest, 1976.

Hempel, Eberhard. *Baroque Art and Architecture in Central Europe.* Harmondsworth, U.K., 1965.

Kaufmann, Thomas DaCosta. *Court, Cloister and City: The Art and Culture of Central Europe, 1450–1800.* London, 1995.

Mojzer, Miklós, ed. *Baroque Art in Central Europe: Crossroads.* Budapest, 1993.

———. *The Metamorphosis of Themes: Secular Subjects in the Art of the Baroque in Central Europe.* Budapest, 1993.

Ostrowski, Jan L., et al. *Art in Poland, 1572–1764: Land of the Winged Horsemen.* Alexandria, Va., 1999.

Pratt, Michael. *The Great Country Houses of Central Europe.* New York, 1991.

Wiebenson, Dora, and József Sisa, eds. *The Architecture of Historic Hungary.* Cambridge, Mass., 1998.

Winters, Laurie, et al. *Leonardo da Vinci and the Splendor of Poland: A History of Collecting and Patronage.* Milwaukee, Wis., 2002.

JEREMY HOWARD

CERAMICS, POTTERY, AND PORCELAIN.

Pottery is made from clays taken from the ground and baked, or fired, in a kiln to a temperature of several hundred degrees. Pottery can take many forms but is best known for items thrown on a spinning wheel, where the potter uses centrifugal force to create a perfectly symmetrical round object. However, round pots and other items can also be made by coiling strips of clay together or by pressing clay into molds. Alternatively, it is, of course, possible to create an item entirely by hand modeling.

If a pot is fired and then covered in a layer of glass, or glaze, and fired again, it becomes nonporous and capable of holding liquids. Such low-fired pottery is called earthenware and can take many

Ceramics, Pottery, and Porcelain. Lead-glazed oval dish with serpent and lizards, school of Bernard Palissy. THE ART ARCHIVE/MUSÉE NATIONAL DE CÉRAMIQUES SÈVRES

forms. Pottery made in medieval Europe was in general of low status, considered inferior to items of metal, and used for storage or basic cookery. However, elaborate inlaid clay floor tiles are found in churches and royal palaces.

By the tenth century in Arab countries, tin oxide was being added to a lead-oxide glaze on earthenware, which turned the glaze white in the kiln to produce a pot with the appearance of porcelain. This could be painted in metallic oxides to produce a metallic layer, or luster, or alternatively in colored oxides to create a pictorial effect. In sixteenth-century Italy, painters of tin-glazed earthenware, or maiolica, such as Nicola da Urbino (d. 1537/1538) and Francesco Xanto Avelli (1487?–1542?) became extremely skillful in adapting prints after Renais-

sance artists such as Raphael (1483–1520) and Michelangelo (1475–1564) to produce ceramics that became independent works of art. More elaborate types, including ewers, basins, and vases, were made in the workshops of the Fontana family in Urbino. Meanwhile, in France the potter Bernard Palissy (c. 1510–1590) was making grottoes (artificial, ornamental caves) and large dishes decorated in colored lead glazes that exactly reproduced the forms of wildlife in imitation of the natural world.

A tougher form of earthenware called stoneware, which was fired to 1200° C, was made in Germany in the sixteenth century and glazed with the addition of salt thrown into the kiln during the firing (salt-glazed stoneware). Large tankards or beer mugs and jugs, suitable for tavern use, with stamped or applied decoration were made at Cologne, Siegburg, Raeren, and the Westerwald, and exported across the whole of the Western world. German stonewares were copied by John Dwight (c. 1635–1703) at Fulham in London and by other potters elsewhere.

Porcelain is a fusion of two special clays, china clay (kaolin) and china stone, at temperatures in excess of 1300° C. Unlike most pottery, it is vitrified (glasslike) and translucent. It was first made in China in about the eighth century C.E. and was known in Europe by the fifteenth century. In the seventeenth century Chinese porcelain began to be imported in large quantities. It was generally decorated in underglaze blue, where gray-black cobalt oxide painted on the once-fired piece before glazing turns blue in the second firing process. Chinese porcelain was copied by tin-glazed earthenware makers at Delft in the Netherlands (Delftware), as well as in Frankfurt in Germany, and in London, Bristol, and Liverpool in England, Glasgow in Scotland, and Dublin in Ireland. Whole rooms were decorated with Chinese and Japanese porcelain from the floor to the ceiling (china rooms).

An artificial, or soft-paste, porcelain, made from the ingredients of ground-up glass, was developed in the Medici workshops in Florence in the sixteenth century, and later in France. Meanwhile the secret of making true hard-paste porcelain like the Chinese had been discovered at Meissen near Dresden in Germany by the alchemist Johann Friedrich Böttger (1682–1719) in 1708. The factory produced vases, figures, and teawares, often decorated with European versions of Chinese scenes (chinoiseries) painted in overglaze enamel colors by the painter Johann Gregor Höroldt (1696–1775), and beautifully modeled figures of animals and humans, notably actors from the Italian commedia dell'arte, by the sculptor Johann Joachim Kändler (1706–1775). The latter were used to decorate the dining table during the dessert course.

Ceramics, Pottery, and Porcelain. Teapot, creamware with green stripes, Wedgwood, c. 1765. THE ART ARCHIVE/ STAFFORDSHIRE UNIVERSITY/SCHOOL OF ART, STAFFORDSHIRE UNIVERSITY

A porcelain factory soon became a status symbol for kings across Europe, and porcelain factories spread to Vienna in 1717 and to sites in Germany (Frankenthal, Nymphenburg, Berlin, Fürstenberg, Höchst). Their wares are visually very similar, though note must be taken of the great rococo modeler Franz Anton Bustelli (1723–1763) at Nymphenburg. There were also many other lesser factories, both in Germany and in Sweden, Denmark, the Netherlands, Switzerland, and Italy. Meanwhile, good-quality tin-glazed earthenware (faience) that copied porcelain shapes and styles of decoration continued to be made in France and Germany.

French soft-paste factories continued to thrive under aristocratic and royal patronage. The wares made at Chantilly in the first half of the eighteenth century imitated the spare colors and white background of Japanese Kakiemon porcelain from the collection of the duc de Bourbon. The factory supported by Louis XV at Sèvres produced some of the most elaborate porcelain ever made, with rich gilding and ground or with background colors framing gold-bordered central panels that could be quite different in style from the rest of the painting (reserves). In England there were private soft-paste porcelain factories at Chelsea, Bow, Liverpool, and other locations; they imitated Meissen or Sèvres or Chinese porcelain, depending on the wealth of their clientele. The factory at Worcester developed decoration with pulls from copper-engraved plates, or transfer printing, which at Caughley became the basis of the Chinese-style willow pattern.

The county of Staffordshire in central England became a major producer of pottery in the eighteenth century, mostly with mass-produced slip cast wares (made by pouring clay into a mold and allowing it to set into a specific shape) for the middle market such as stoneware teapots, or wares in colored glazes based on fruit and vegetables. A more sophisticated taste developed with the work of the great potter Josiah Wedgwood (1730–1795), who used the neoclassical style of the later eighteenth century to sell pottery to the upper classes across Europe. He refined stoneware to create a tinted version in imitation of classical cameos called Jasperware and refined earthenware to produce the pale creamware for everyday use. His products, as well as those of other factories in Staffordshire and Yorkshire, were to put many of the faience makers of Europe out of business by the end of the century.

The Napoleonic Wars of the late eighteenth and early nineteenth centuries created financial problems for many porcelain factories in Europe, and by 1815 the main surviving state-sponsored factories were at Sèvres, Berlin, Meissen, Vienna, and St. Petersburg. They all made wares in the strict neoclassical style. Meanwhile, Staffordshire continued to produce a vast quantity of wares in a huge variety of styles, both in toughened pottery (ironstone) and the new bone china, in which bone ash is added to hard-paste porcelain clays.

See also **Decorative Arts.**

BIBLIOGRAPHY

Ayers, John, et al. *World Ceramics: An Illustrated History.* Edited by Robert J. Charleston. London and New York, 1968.

Coutts, Howard. *The Art of Ceramics: European Ceramic Design, 1500–1830.* New Haven, 2001.

Hannover, Emil. *Pottery and Porcelain: A Handbook for Collectors.* Edited with notes and appendices by Bernard Rackham. London, 1925.

Honey, William Bowyer. *European Ceramic Art from the End of the Middle Ages to about 1815.* London and New York, 1949.

HOWARD COUTTS

CEREMONIAL. *See* **Ritual, Civic and Royal; Ritual, Religious.**

CERVANTES, MIGUEL DE (Miguel de Cervantes Saavedra; 1547–1616), Spanish novelist, dramatist, and poet. Cervantes is known especially for his novel *Don Quixote* (1605; 1615). Read largely as a funny book in Cervantes's time, the Romantics and their later brethren were to focus on Don Quixote's pathos and his quest for impossible dreams. The madman who tilted at windmills and read the world in accordance with the conventions of books of chivalry was to become a symbol of spiritual values and, in the case of Spain, the embodiment of a national ethos (Close, p. 246). Don Quixote has been called "the classic and purest model of the novel as genre" (Bakhtin, p. 325), encompassing a diversity of voices, social speech types, and even languages (Bakhtin, pp. 262–269). Its antiauthoritarian bent has been a source of inspiration to scores of well-known writers, among them the Mexican novelist Carlos Fuentes, who has written eloquently on Cervantes's critique of reading, and the Czech Milan Kundera, who reminds us that with Don Quixote the world ceases to be a given and becomes a problem.

Today, as cultural studies are increasingly marked by identity politics (race, gender, ethnicity), and issues of "alterity" and "hybridity" are brought to the fore, Cervantes's writing has become a field of contention between critics who adhere to traditional humanist and/or historicist readings and those whose work is largely informed by avantgarde, poststructuralist theory. Overall, these battles (fought especially within the North American academy) have enriched the discussion surrounding Cervantes's novelistic project and have had the effect of renewing interest in his *Los trabajos de Persiles y Sigismunda* (1617; Trials of Persiles and Sigismunda), a Byzantine prose fiction narrative that used to be read largely as Christian allegory but is now seen by some as a kind of counternarrative of colonization (Wilson) and as a critique of utopias and religious orthodoxy.

In reading Cervantes's novels and novellas one is treated to extraordinary storytelling skills and devices (multiple authors, narrators, and narratees), which contribute to the larger project of decentering traditional loci of authority. His writing shows a high degree of self-reflexivity and constant testing of classical concepts of poetic discourse that run up against a narrative practice that resists adherence to rules. His experimental fiction incorporates virtually every written and oral genre known in his time: books of chivalry, pastoral romances, picaresque "lives," Italianate novellas, epic narratives, ballads, folk tales, carnavalesque stories and situations, proverbs, masquerades, inquisitorial discourse, devotional and legal writing, and so on. Cervantes was also a poet and a playwright. As a lyric poet he wrote in the vein of Petrarch and Garcilaso de la Vega; as a playwright he was out of sync with Lope de Vega's new theater ("new comedy") which, by the early 1600s, had monopolized the public stage by playing up to the taste of an undiscriminating mass-receiver who internalized the

Miguel de Cervantes. Undated portrait.

myths propagated by this important vehicle of official culture. Perhaps for this reason Cervantes's late plays, together with his comic *entremeses* ('interludes'), are redirected to the private sphere of reading, inscribing within the written text a performance that is only realizable on stage in a distant future. Of his earlier plays one might make special mention of *Los tratos de Argel* (1582; Life in Algiers), a drama of captivity and discovery of self and other in the city of exchange between Islam and Christendom, and *La numancia* (1583; Numancia), a tragedy involving the collective suicide of a city in 133 B.C.E. in defiance of Scipio's legions and Roman rule.

Cervantes's writing drew from a wide range of cross-cultural experiences that went beyond the mediation of reading. He spent time in Italy (especially Rome and Naples) and resided in several Spanish cities, among them Madrid, Valladolid, and Seville, the quintessential city of trade and commerce. He fought in the victorious battle of Lepanto against the Turks (1571), where he lost the use of his left hand, and experienced the despair of captivity in

Algiers (1575–1580) followed by rejection and disillusionment upon his return to Spain, where the hero who had hoped for glory and rewards for the services rendered to his country now found himself a mere survivor. Unable to secure a bureaucratic position in the Indies (1590), he worked as a procurer of wheat for the Invincible Armada (1588); became a tax collector (1595); and landed temporarily in jail in Seville on charges of embezzlement (1597). Just a few years later he was to write (1602) and publish (1605) the first part of what is regarded by some as the greatest novel of all time: *Don Quixote de la Mancha*. Despite the commercial success of *Don Quixote* and the generosity of the 7th count of Lemos, his major patron, Cervantes and his family did not escape poverty.

It was largely during the last decade or so of his life that Cervantes was to give a totalizing artistic expression to his exceptional wealth of experiences. The chronology of his publications is telling: after the appearance of his pastoral prose fiction *La galatea* (1585), and a brief engagement as a practicing playwright toward the end of the sixteenth century, he was heard from again in 1605 when *Don Quixote* was published in Madrid. All of his other works appeared in print between 1613 and 1617: *Novelas ejemplares* (1613, Exemplary novellas); *Viaje del parnaso* (1614; Journey to Parnassus); *Don Quixote II* (1615); *Ocho comedias y ocho entremeses* (1615; Eight plays and eight interludes); and *Los trabajos de Persiles y Sigismunda* (1617; The Trials of Persiles and Sigismunda).

While the international success of *Don Quixote* is undeniable, this extraordinary novel belongs to a more complex project that encompasses Cervantes's entire discursive production, one that is marked by a continuous transgression of the limits of traditional genres, a transgression that constitutes a central point in his epistemological project. In the end, neither novel nor poetry nor theater can "double" the world, so that the metaphor of the mirror that is implied in the traditional theory of *imitatio* has to be substituted for that of the modern shattering glass (Spadaccini and Talens). Cervantes's influence on the development of the novel is substantial, and the universality of *Don Quixote* and Sancho is undeniable. Yet, equally significant is the manner in which his narratives incorporate the multiple and contradictory voices of his own age.

See also **Spanish Literature and Language.**

BIBLIOGRAPHY

Primary Sources

Cervantes Saavedra, Miguel de. *Don Quijote.* Translated by Burton Raffell and edited by Diana de Armas Wilson. New York, 1999.

———. *Don Quijote de la Mancha.* 2 vols. Edited by Francisco Rico with the collaboration of Joaquin Forradellas. Barcelona, 1998.

Secondary Sources

Bakhtin, M. M. "Discourses in the Novel." In *The Dialogic Imagination: Four Essays,* edited by Michael Holquist. Translated by Caryl Emerson and Michael Holquist. Austin, Tex., 1981.

Canavaggio, Jean. *Cervantes.* Translated by J. R. Jones. New York, 1990.

Close, Anthony. *The Romantic Approach to* Don Quijote: *A Critical History of the Romantic Tradition in Quixote Criticism.* Cambridge, U.K., 1978.

Cruz, Anne J., and Carroll B. Johnson, eds. *Cervantes and his Postmodern Constituencies.* New York and London, 1999.

Forcione, Alban K. *Cervantes' Christian Romance: A Study of* Persiles y Sigismunda. Princeton, 1972.

Fuentes, Carlos. *Don Quixote, or the Critique of Reading.* Austin, Tex., 1976.

Kundera. Milan. "Epilogue." In *The Book of Laughter and Forgetting.* Translated by Michael Henry Heim. New York, 1981.

Riley, E. C. *Cervantes's Theory of the Novel.* Oxford, 1962.

Spadaccini, Nicholas, and Jenaro Talens. *Through the Shattering Glass: Cervantes and the Self-Made World.* Minneapolis, 1993.

Wilson, Diana De Armas. *Cervantes, the Novel, and the New World.* New York, 2000.

NICHOLAS SPADACCINI

CHARDIN, JEAN-BAPTISTE-SIMÉON (1699–1779), French painter.

During the first half of the eighteenth century, authors, artists, and intellectuals defined themselves by staking out a position on the central aesthetic question of the period: Should they model their cultural production on the ancients or strike out in new directions as moderns? On the controversy between ancients and moderns, Jean-Baptiste-Siméon Chardin was a modern. In *The Monkey as Antiquarian* (c. 1740, Chartres) he parodies the enthusiast of antiquity by representing him as a foolish monkey scrutinizing an ancient coin through a magnifying glass, a type of image popularized by other moderns like David Teniers the Younger (Flemish, 1610–1690) and Jean-Antoine Watteau (1684–1721).

Chardin was born in Paris. His father was a master artisan who constructed billiard tables, and his mother's father crafted game racquets. His brother became a *marchand mercier* (a person who combined the functions of an antiques dealer and an interior decorator). Although he was trained in painting by Pierre Jacques Cazes (1676–1754) and Noël Nicolas Coypel (1690–1734), both members of the Royal Academy of Painting and Sculpture, Chardin joined the Parisian guild, the Académie de Saint-Luc, before applying for admission to the academy. His association with the guild suggests that, like his family, he originally intended to work within the orbit of the Parisian luxury trades.

In 1728, however, he deserted the guild for the Royal Academy of Painting and Sculpture, which received him as an artist with a specialty in "animals and fruits" on the basis of *The Ray* (c. 1725, Musée du Louvre, Paris) and *The Buffet* (1728, Louvre). At this time, the classifying system of the academy did not include a category for a modern life subject like *The Game of Billiards* (c. 1723; Musée Carnavalet, Paris), a painting in which Chardin represented a congenial group of elite, urbane men watching a billiard match. Paintings of hunting trophies and fruits or flowers, by contrast, had been recognized as legitimate subjects by the Royal Academy since its foundation.

Chardin painted a variety of subjects in an array of formats and manners. *Young Student Drawing* (c. 1734, Nationalmuseum, Stockholm) is a small wooden panel approximately seven inches square that can be held in the hand, but *A Lady Sealing a Letter* (1733, Schloss Charlottenburg, Berlin) is a large composition on canvas over five feet high designed for the wall. In *Rabbit, Copper Pot, Quince, and Two Chestnuts* (c. 1739, Stockholm) his handling of form is broad and rough, whereas in *The Butler's Table* (1756, Carcassonne) it is meticulous and detailed. He created portraits in oil like *Portrait of Charles Godefroy* (c. 1734, Louvre) and in pastel, such as *Self-Portrait Wearing Spectacles* (1771, Louvre). In 1732 he exhibited a trompe-

Jean-Baptiste-Siméon Chardin. *Grace at Table,* 1740. ©Francis G. Mayer/Corbis

l'oeil painting of a bronze relief after a work by the Flemish artist François Duquesnoy (1597–1643), *Eight Children Playing with a Goat,* a motif also seen in the lower half of *The Attributes of the Arts* (1731, Musée Jacquemart-André, Paris). Although the relief looks classical, it is actually not antique but the work of a modern, for Duquesnoy lived in the seventeenth century. Duquesnoy's relief was reproduced by other modern painters, particularly Gerard Dou (Dutch, 1613–1675), with whom Chardin was compared by contemporaries.

Chardin's long and successful career unfolded within the bounds of the Royal Academy of Painting and Sculpture. He became an officer *(conseiller)* of the academy in 1743, pensioned by the crown in 1752, elected treasurer of the academy in 1755, and awarded a studio and lodging at the king's expense in the Louvre in 1757. In 1755 he was also entrusted with hanging the pictures and displaying the statues in the academy's public exhibition known as the salon, a position he retained until 1774. From the first regularly established salon, held in 1737, and for fourteen years thereafter, Chardin exhibited only figure paintings, mainly of modern life subjects like *The Governess* (1738, National Gallery of Canada, Ottawa). These compositions, and the engraved prints made after them, brought Chardin international fame. *Domestic Pleasures* (1746, Nationalmuseum, Stockholm) was commissioned by the crown princess of Sweden. The print made after the image was dedicated to a Swedish countess, and one of them hung, framed and under glass, in the Parisian residence of the marquise de Pompadour. Then Chardin reversed this exhibition pattern in 1753; excepting the late pastels, from 1753 to 1779 his offerings to the salon shifted to still-life subjects and an occasional re-exhibition or repetition of one of his then well-known figure paintings from the 1730s or 1740s.

Chardin confounds nineteenth-century notions of exceptionality by his frequent practice of repeating compositions and motifs. For example, three extant canvases of *The Return from Market* by Chardin's hand are signed and dated, making it impossible to ascertain which is the original (National Gallery of Canada, Ottawa, 1738; Schloss Charlottenburg, Berlin, 1738; Louvre, 1739).

See also **Art: Art Exhibitions; France, Art in.**

BIBLIOGRAPHY

Conisbee, Philip. *Chardin*. Lewisburg, Pa., 1986.

Roland Michel, Marianne. *Chardin*. London and New York, 1996.

Rosenberg, Pierre. *Chardin 1699–1779*. Exh. cat. Paris, 1979.

Scott, Katie. "Chardin Multiplied." In *Chardin*, Exh. cat., pp. 60–75. New York, 2000.

PAULA REA RADISICH

CHARITY AND POOR RELIEF. The practice of charity *(caritas)* was fundamentally transformed in early modern Europe. What had been largely a voluntary good work open to all and available to anyone in need became to a much greater extent institutional, regulatory, and coercive. The poor were examined, identified, categorized, assisted, and regulated. In some places this process was limited to the members of one's own community, one's neighbors, or one's coreligionists. In other places it was limited to certain kinds of poor persons, the orphaned, the sick, or the elderly.

In all places it sought greater efficiency in the administration of its resources and greater accuracy in the selection of its recipients. Poor relief materialized as a result.

By the late fifteenth century poverty had become a more visible and insistent presence in people's lives. The causes were complex. Social and economic change had rendered larger segments of the population vulnerable to poverty. The capitalization of agriculture reduced many peasants to dependency: freeholders became tenants; tenants became laborers. The industrialization of manufacturing had a similar impact on craftspeople: masters and journeymen lost control of production processes; they were reduced to wage labor under the direction of merchant entrepreneurs. Though the economy of the period was expanding, wages never managed to keep pace with prices. A larger proportion of the population lived on the margin, unable consistently to feed, clothe, and shelter themselves or their dependents. They were vulnerable to natural and human disasters. Crop failure or market inelasticity might drive them into poverty and onto the road. No less important than the material changes were cultural changes. As the poor washed over the land and flowed into cities in increasing numbers, attitudes toward them—toward their plight and its causes—seem to have changed, too. Contemporaries perceived that the poor, in their search for sustenance, were less humble and deferential. They seemed increasingly importunate, aggressive, and violent, a threat to personal safety and public order. Moreover, their need was not always genuine. As a result, the poor became not only more visible and insistent but also more ambiguous and dangerous. Their numbers and attitude posed a challenge to the voluntary, pious character and the existing, haphazard structure of charity. Quite apart from the individual handout, an array of institutions, offering a variety of alms or assistance, had come into being by the end of the fifteenth century. The wealthy created pious foundations for the support of the poor. Guilds established confraternities to assist needy members. Monastic orders occasionally fed and housed the hungry and homeless within their walls. Churches and cathedrals maintained tables from which food and money were distributed on Sundays. Towns assumed control of hospitals and founded other institutions to meet a variety of

Charity and Poor Relief. *Charitable Works of the Misericordia,* atelier of David Teniers II, seventeenth century. THE ART ARCHIVE/MUSÉE BARON MARTIN GRAY FRANCE/DAGLI ORTI

needs. Orphanages and sanitariums, foundling homes and pawnshops sprang up. Every town and city offered a variety of such institutions and services, a bazaarlike array of charities that competed for resources and shared responsibilities. The poor could pick and choose, shopping for charity within the same community. Yet as the numbers of poor people increased toward the end of the fifteenth century, they were increasingly turned away. Existing resources were not adequate to feed, clothe, or shelter all those in need. Cutbacks were required. What is more, the impious face of poverty, captured in the image of the sturdy beggar, who begged not out of need but for less legitimate reasons, seemed unworthy of assistance under the circumstances. Some form of discrimination became essential.

Distinguishing the deserving from the undeserving poor was not new in early modern Europe. Canon lawyers and Scholastic theologians had argued the fundamental difference between those who should and those who should not receive assistance since the twelfth century. Early modern authorities, whether intellectual or political, took up these distinctions among the forms and degrees of poverty and made them the basis of administering poor relief. Those whose inability to support themselves might be considered innocent and permanent—the disabled, the elderly, the parentless—were the most easily recognized and least controversial. All agreed that widows, orphans, and cripples should receive assistance, as should the shamefaced poor, those whose poverty was legitimate but whose honor kept them from seeking aid. Those whose need was a matter of circumstance—the unemployed or the underemployed—were no less deserving but more complex because their situation might change and because they were fundamentally able. Most of the poor fell into this group, and the form and duration of their care was subject to vigorous debate and dramatic change.

The problem from the late fifteenth century onward was how to relieve the deserving and exclude the undeserving. Those whose poverty was feigned or voluntary—the sturdy poor—posed a

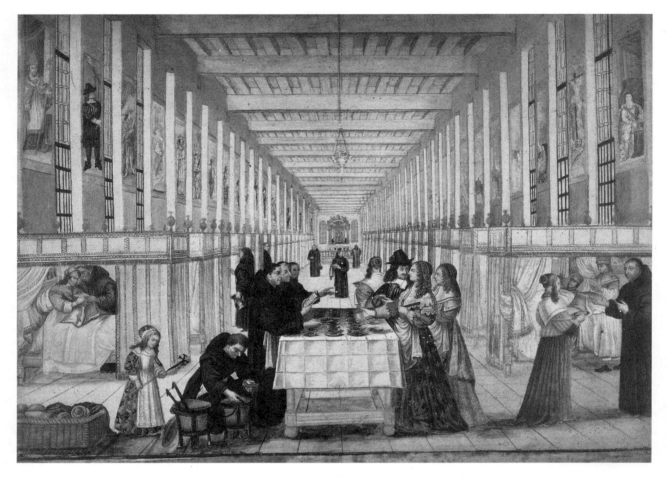

Charity and Poor Relief. *Anne of Austria and the Dauphin Visiting the Charity Hospital,* seventeenth-century engraving by Abraham Bosse. ©ARCHIVO ICONOGRAFICO, S.A./CORBIS

threat to communities and their charities. Their relief was no longer affordable, given the greater numbers of people in need. What was more, their relief was no longer tolerable, given the illegitimacy of their need and the impiety of their manner. Changes in the structure and function of poor relief in the early modern period can be seen as an effort to address these issues: What was affordable? What was tolerable?

Though often associated with the Reformation, the reform of poor relief actually began earlier and was not limited to Protestant cities and states. In Italy, Spain, and some parts of France, inspired by humanist tracts and political concerns, authorities extended administrative oversight to established charitable institutions in an effort to control the disbursement of resources and improve the efficiency of services. Where Protestantism was eventually adopted, the reforms were often part of a broader

effort to introduce evangelical religion. In reforming Christian worship, secular governments not only altered religious practice but also gained new jurisdiction. The relief of poverty became their responsibility as a Christian magistracy. In principle the changes were intended to be dramatic. In the earliest Protestant poor laws, such as those passed in Nuremberg (1522) and Ypres (Ieper) (1525), charitable institutions were placed under a single administrative authority, financial resources were disbursed from a "common chest," specialization of services was introduced to avoid duplication, the poor were closely examined to determine their exact need and appropriate relief, and begging was prohibited as a public nuisance. In practice, however, continuity was the rule. Sweeping reform ordinances notwithstanding, individual institutions continued to exercise extensive administrative independence. The existence of a common fund for the relief of poverty did not prevent these institutions from maintaining their own individual endowments. Omnicompetence—the provision of different kinds of relief for different kinds of poverty in a single institution—continued to be common. Certainly the poor were more closely examined, whether by state officials, as happened in most Protestant lands, or by institutional or ecclesiastical figures, as happened in Catholic lands, where the state's role was consultative rather than administrative. And begging continued despite prohibition or regulation. Confessional differences in poor relief have been somewhat exaggerated.

In the matter of begging, however, Protestants and Catholics parted company. Under the influence of the Reformation, all begging became suspect. Theologians rejected it as a fundamental misunderstanding of justification; no human works, including begging for or giving charity, could affect spiritual salvation. Nor did mendicancy in any way reflect the soul's relationship to God. Thus shorn of its religious signification, begging became a matter for the state to regulate. Protestant governments prohibited it. The poor were to be set to work, whether in the open air or in enclosed institutions. Made productive, they would to some extent compensate for their support and acquire the fixed habit of labor. Catholic authorities likewise opposed begging. They accepted readily the notion that the poor should be rendered self-supporting and disciplined to produce. Yet their policies remained ambiguous. Finally, for Catholics, begging remained a pious act, deeply imbedded in their religious tradition and practice. Some Catholic theologians, notably Domingo de Soto (1494–1560), argued that all persons, regardless of circumstance, should be allowed to beg as a devout undertaking. It could not be prohibited, but it could be controlled. Accordingly specifically defined groups—orphans or patients, for example—were permitted to beg at specific times and in specific places. Others were required to wear a sign that they had been examined and found authentically and honorably poor. Yet different approaches should not obscure similar results: regardless of intention, neither Protestant nor Catholic authorities possessed the means or the will to eradicate begging completely.

Whether indeed they sought to eliminate begging or merely to restrict it, the point was largely

Charity and Poor Relief. *Aiding the Poor,* from *The Venetians,* a series of eighteenth-century engravings by Grevenbroeck. THE ART ARCHIVE/MUSEO CORRER VENICE/DAGLI ORTI

the same. Poor relief might be rendered more efficient by directing charity where it would do the greatest good. This involved directing resources to those most in need and excluding all others, an end that unregulated begging prevented. Early modern poor relief ceased to be voluntary, therefore, and came to rely on principles of discrimination and exclusion. Authorities sought to discriminate according to the nature of a poor person's poverty. They examined the poor to determine the legitimacy of their need and the means to their relief, thus aiding the deserving and excluding the undeserving. Authorities also sought to discriminate according to membership in a community. Protestants restricted aid to needy residents in a government's jurisdiction or a church's parish. In either case poor relief turned on established membership in a narrowly defined secular or ecclesiastical community. All others—transients and foreigners—were refused. At best these unfortunates might expect a free meal and escort to the border. Catholics, too, insisted on membership in a community. Receipt of aid from charitable institutions required proof of local residency, thus fixing the poor where they might be known, monitored, and supervised. Finally, authorities sought to discriminate according to the morality of a poor person's behavior. Assistance became tied to standards of comportment in Catholic and Protestant communities alike. The poor were required to submit obediently to local political authority, to conform piously to local religious practice, and to labor industriously in their own support. The immoral poor—the rebellious, the impious, and the indolent—were excluded from poor relief or subjected to social discipline. Catholic apologists claimed that, by requiring authenticity, residency, and legitimacy, Protestant restrictions drastically reduced the numbers of deserving poor. In fact, allowing once again for local and institutional variation, there was little difference in practice between the confessions. All imposed restrictions to discriminate among the poor and exclude some from relief.

It is this increasingly involuntary process of discrimination and exclusion that separated early modern poor relief from medieval charity. What had been an open ritual binding Christians became a compulsory function imposed on prescribed groups. Scholars have attended to this change and interpreted it variously. Since the beginning of the twentieth century and the writing of Max Weber (1864–1920), scholars generally have understood the establishment of poor relief as a turn from the personal and moral toward the bureaucratic and rational. His great work *Wirtschaft und Gesellschaft* (1922; Economy and society) is the point of departure for any discussion of this historical process and its confluence of sacred and secular impulses. Weber envisioned an absolute distinction between what he called the "postulate of brotherly love" and "the loveless realities of the economic domain." In the course of the early modern period and under the influence of Protestantism, "charity became a rationalized enterprise and its religious significance was eliminated or even transformed into the opposite significance" (Weber, p. 589). His argument has passed more or less intact into the modern historiography on early modern poor relief. Scholars following Otto Winckelmann (1914/15) located the beginning of the reorganization of poor relief in the Holy Roman Empire with the reform ordinances of 1522, presuming a clear association with the Refor-

mation, and identified a series of common features. Regardless of locale, relief was placed in the hands of political authorities, begging was prohibited by law, financial resources were centralized, and assistance was awarded according to individual circumstances. Robert Jütte (1984) separated the reorganization of poor relief from the Reformation, seeing the abandonment of charity as a consequence of a larger social, economic, and religious crisis of the late fifteenth century and the sixteenth century. Yet that reorganization proceeded true to form regardless of time, place, or confession: relief was centralized in civic hands; finances were centralized likewise; the poor were registered; work was required. Allowing for variations of degree and depending on local circumstances, rationalization and bureaucratization ran their course. Similar patterns of development—similar antitheses between traditional charity and modern rationality—were identified in the Netherlands by Catharina Lis and Hugo Soly (1979), in France by Natalie Davis (1975) and Jean-Pierre Gutton (1971), in Spain by Linda Martz (1983), and in Italy by Brian Pullan (1971). The rationalizing trend persisted, albeit with local variations and without confessional dependencies.

Other scholars have focused attention less on the reorganization of poor relief than on its purposes. Self-sufficiency—much less charity—ceased to be the goal. Rather than ameliorate poverty or demonstrate piety, poor relief rendered the lower strata of society docile and dependent by shaping their activities to the economic interests of the elite. According to this scholarship, much influenced by the theories of Karl Marx (1818–1883) and Michel Foucault (1926–1984), poverty is a consequence of the social relations of production. Capitalist enterprise requires state-sponsored support in order to police a reserve of labor and maintain its availability at the lowest possible price. Thus elites wish to preserve and control the poor for their own purposes. David Rothman (1971), Michael Ignatieff (1978), Margaret DeLacy (1986), and Sherrill Cohen (1992) have argued variously that charity, in the form of workhouses, prisons, hospitals, and orphanages, placed the poor in closely regulated regimes that attempted to promote industry, regularity, authority, and obedience in order to encourage economic dependence and social deference. Discrimination and exclusion may have served to make poor relief more efficient, but they also served the more sinister ends of making poverty permanent. Historians of culture and religion, such as Lee Palmer Wandel (1990) and Ole Peter Grell (1997), have questioned these models and their linear trajectories from past to present, arguing instead for the enduring influence of religious and humanitarian ideals in caring for the needy. Allowing for some degree of local variation in accordance with local circumstances, the development of early modern poor relief displays a common pattern of development. State or lay engagement in the provision of poor relief expanded. Resources were regularized and centralized. Functions were standardized, made more efficient, in short, rationalized. None of this had much to do with the Reformation, however. The processes began far earlier. The reasons for change and the forms that change took were determined by local circumstance. Economic efficiency and social discipline were frequently mentioned, but so, too, were Christian charity and "brotherly love." There is no reason to doubt the word of magistrates or laypeople, who claimed repeatedly that they were moved by all four. As a result scholars are coming to appreciate the variety of forms and the complexity of motives in early modern poor relief.

See also **Humanists and Humanism; Laborers; Poverty; Reformation, Protestant.**

BIBLIOGRAPHY

Chrisman, Miriam Usher. "Urban Poor in the Sixteenth Century: The Case of Strasbourg." In *Social Groups and Religious Ideas in the Sixteenth Century,* edited by Miriam Usher Chrisman and Otto Gründler, pp. 59–67. Kalamazoo, Mich., 1978.

Cohen, Sherrill. *The Evolution of Women's Asylums since 1500: From Refuges for Ex-Prostitutes to Shelters for Battered Women.* New York, 1992.

Davis, Natalie Zemon. "Poor Relief, Humanism, and Heresy." In *Society and Culture in Early Modern France,* pp. 17–64. Stanford, 1975.

DeLacy, Margaret. *Prison Reform in Lancashire, 1700–1850: A Study in Local Administration.* Stanford, 1986.

Fehler, Timothy G. *Poor Relief and Protestantism: The Evolution of Social Welfare in Sixteenth-Century Emden.* Brookfield, Vt., 1999.

Flynn, Maureen. *Sacred Charity: Confraternities and Social Welfare in Spain, 1400–1700.* Basingstoke, U.K., 1989.

Gavitt, Philip. *Charity and Children in Renaissance Florence: The Ospedale degli Innocenti, 1410–1536.* Ann Arbor, Mich., 1990.

Grell, Ole Peter, and Andrew Cunningham, eds. *Health Care and Poor Relief in Protestant Europe, 1500–1700.* London and New York, 1997.

Hufton, Olwen H. *The Poor of Eighteenth-Century France, 1750–1789.* Oxford, 1974.

Ignatieff, Michael. *A Just Measure of Pain: The Penitentiary in the Industrial Revolution, 1750–1850.* New York, 1978.

Jones, Colin. *The Charitable Imperative: Hospitals and Nursing in Ancien Régime and Revolutionary France.* London and New York, 1989.

———. *Charity and Bienfaisance: The Treatment of the Poor in the Montpellier Region, 1740–1815.* Cambridge, U.K., and New York, 1982.

Jütte, Robert. "Poor Relief and Social Discipline in Sixteenth-Century Europe." *European Studies Review* 11 (1981): 25–52.

———. *Obrigkeitliche Armenfürsorge in deutschen Reichsstädten der frühen Neuzeit: Städtisches Armenwesen in Frankfurt am Main und Köln.* Cologne, 1984.

Lindberg, Carter. "There Should Be No Beggars among Christians: Karlstadt, Luther, and the Origins of Protestant Poor Relief." *Church History* 46 (1977): 313–334.

Lis, Catharina, and Hugo Soly. *Poverty and Capitalism in Pre-Industrial Europe.* Atlantic Highlands, N.J., 1979.

Martz, Linda. *Poverty and Welfare in Habsburg Spain: The Example of Toledo.* Cambridge, U.K., and New York, 1983.

McKee, Elsie Anne. *John Calvin on the Diaconate and Liturgical Almsgiving.* Geneva, Switzerland, 1984.

Mollat, Michel. *The Poor in the Middle Ages: An Essay in Social History.* Translated by Arthur Goldhammer. New Haven, 1986.

Parker, Charles H. *The Reformation of Community: Social Welfare and Calvinist Charity in Holland, 1572–1620.* Cambridge, U.K., and New York, 1998.

Pullan, Brian. *Rich and Poor in Renaissance Venice: The Social Institutions of a Catholic State to 1620.* Cambridge, Mass., 1971.

Riis, Thomas, ed. *Aspects of Poverty in Early Modern Europe.* 3 vols. Alphen aan den Rijn, Netherlands, and Odense, Denmark, 1981–1990.

Rothman, David. *The Discovery of the Asylum: Social Order and Disorder in the New Republic.* Boston, 1971.

Safley, Thomas Max. *Charity and Economy in the Orphanages of Early Modern Augsburg.* Atlantic Highlands, N.J., 1997.

Wandel, Lee Palmer. *Always among Us: Images of the Poor in Zwingli's Zurich*. Cambridge, U.K., and New York, 1990.

Weber, Max. *Economy and Society: An Outline of Interpretative Sociology*. Berkeley, 1978.

Winckelmann, Otto, "Über die ältesten Armenordnungen der Reformationszeit," *Historisches Vierteljahresschrift* 17 (1914/15): 187–228, 361–400.

Wrightson, Keith, and David Levine. *Poverty and Piety in an English Village: Terling, 1525–1700*. New York, 1979.

THOMAS MAX SAFLEY

CHARIVARI. *See* Popular Culture.

CHARLES I (ENGLAND)

CHARLES I (ENGLAND) (1600–1649; ruled 1625–1649), king of Great Britain and Ireland. Charles I was born in Dumfirmline Castle on 19 November 1600, the second son of James VI of Scotland (ruled 1567–1625; James I of England, ruled 1603–1625) and Anne of Denmark (1574–1619). Charles's childhood and adolescence were unhappy. He suffered from rickets and a severe stammer that bedeviled him almost until his death. His parents had little to do with him, while his elder brother, Prince Henry, the charismatic heir, teased him mercilessly.

On 6 November 1612, however, Henry died unexpectedly from typhoid fever. The new heir took the bereavement badly, and he was almost as upset when his elder sister Elizabeth married and left England to live in Germany. The death of Charles's mother in March 1619 and the fact that his father, James I, found his son a prudish irritation, much preferring the company of his homosexual lovers, did nothing to enhance the adolescent's self-confidence.

Ironically it was one of those lovers, George Villiers (1592–1628), later duke of Buckingham, who liberated the heir from his insecure youth. Villiers befriended Charles, who responded avidly, accepting him as a substitute elder brother. In the spring of 1623 the pair secretly went to Spain to woo Infanta Donna Maria, the sister of Philip IV (ruled 1621–1665). After the Spanish humiliatingly spurned his terms—notwithstanding major concessions on his part—Charles angrily returned home. The trip to Spain not only exposed Charles to the work of artists such as Titian, Michelangelo, and Raphael but augmented both Villier's influence and the authoritarian side of Charles's character. A year later Charles told William Laud (1573–1645), the future archbishop of Canterbury, "I cannot defend the bad, nor yield in a good cause."

RELATIONSHIP WITH PARLIAMENT

For three years after Charles succeeded to the throne on 27 March 1625, Villiers dominated English politics. He and Charles were involved in a number of military expeditions, first against Spain and then France. All were humiliating and expensive failures. To pay for his expeditions, Charles asked Parliament to vote taxes, which that body refused to do unless Charles dismissed Villiers. To protect his friend, Charles dismissed Parliament and collected taxes anyway. In July 1628 the constitutional crisis reached a climax, when Parliament passed the Petition of Right, a statement of their major grievances. Charles assented to the petition with such ill grace that relations between the king and the Commons continued to deteriorate.

A month later John Felton, a deranged army officer, assassinated Villiers. Charles was devastated; his subjects were jubilant. On 2 March 1629 the House of Commons, defying the king's orders to adjourn, passed three resolutions condemning those who supported Catholicism and all who had paid illegal taxes such as the Forced Loan. Outraged by this open defiance of his authority, Charles determined to rule on his own and dissolved Parliament.

CHARLES'S PERSONAL RULE

For the next eleven years, from 1629 to 1640, Charles retreated from the world of politics to that of his court. He came under the malign influence of his wife, Henrietta Maria (1609–1669), a French Catholic who wanted to restore England to Rome. Charles also created one of the finest art collections ever assembled by a British monarch. He purchased the collection of the Gonzaga dukes of Mantua, who were desperate for money. The collection included some of best works by Raphael, Titian, Corregio (Antonio Allegri), and Andrea Mantegna. By the time of Charles's death, the royal collection totaled 1,760 paintings and nearly as many sculptures.

Charles I. Portrait depicting Charles at the hunt by Anthony Van Dyck. THE ART ARCHIVE/MUSÉE DU LOUVRE, PARIS

Charles's artistic taste and judgment were superb. At the age of twenty he knew enough to return a painting to Rubens because it was largely the work of an apprentice. He could also drive a hard bargain, reducing the price of a Van Dyck portrait by half. Nonetheless Charles's art did not come cheap. Parliament sold his collection in 1649 for £59,903. Its modern worth would be staggering.

Charles's art collection not only revealed his connoisseurship but shed light on his personality and policies. An example is the massive set of three paintings Rubens (1577–1640) did on the ceiling of the Banqueting Hall at Whitehall. Designed by Inigo Jones (1573–1652) in the Palladian style, Whitehall was the most significant building erected in England during the first half of the seventeenth century. Intended for the most important state occasions, such as the reception of ambassadors, its main themes were order and harmony. The interior's clean straight lines climaxed where the king sat on his throne. The central ceiling panel, *The Apotheosis of James I,* shows the old king as a divine right ruler ascending directly into heaven. The second panel praises James for uniting the crowns of England and Scotland, while the third acclaims him as a peacemaker and by implication supports Charles's refusal to get involved with the Thirty Years' War (1618–1648), which was ravaging the Continent.

Perhaps the most important portrait the king commissioned was Van Dyck's (1599–1641) *Charles I on Horseback,* which hangs in the National Gallery in London. The masterpiece shows the king not just as a divine right monarch but as an absolutist who brooks no limits on his power. He is the knight-errant, whose sword could be unsheathed at any time to right wrongs, punish the evil, and bring law and order. Fully in control of his powerful stallion, this happy warrior is also a philosopher king—the confident master of all he surveys.

THE CIVIL WAR

By 1639 Charles's policies were coming apart in Scotland. While the taxes, such as ship money, which the king had raised without parliamentary approval, were far from popular, they were not oppressive enough to make his subjects rebel, but his religious policies were.

Apart from their king, the English and the Scots had little in common. The former were Episcopalians, the latter were Calvinists. When Charles introduced a new prayer book into Scotland in 1637, the results were explosive. Congregations rioted. In 1638 hundred of thousands of Scots signed a covenant—some with their own blood—vowing to fight to keep their old religion and to resist the imposition of bishops. Convinced that they in fact were determined not merely to abolish bishops but the monarchy itself, Charles vowed, "I will rather die than yield to their impertinent and damnable demands."

Charles fought two wars against the Scots. Although politically inconclusive, the First Bishops' War of 1639 forced the king to call the Short Parliament in April 1640. After impulsively dismissing this Parliament on 5 May, Charles fought the Second Bishops' War, which he lost. He thus had to call the Long Parliament that opened on 3 November 1640. For over a year the king and the Commons tried to compromise. Parliament wanted to control the crown; the king would accept no real limits on his powers. On 5 January 1642 Charles led a company of armed soldiers to the House of Commons to arrest the five ringleaders of parliamentary opposition, but just before he entered the house they escaped. The breach between the king and Parliament was irreparable. Both the king and Parliament collected arms and courted public opinion in a struggle to control the army raised to put down the revolt in Ireland that had broken out the previous October.

Soon after declaring war against his rebellious subjects on 22 August 1642, Charles raised an army that fought the parliamentary forces at Edgehill on 23 October. The two sides continued to spar during 1643. On 21 August 1643 Charles failed to lift the Siege of Gloucester, but he beat the parliamentarians at the First Battle of Newbury on 20 September. In 1644 the royalists were routed at Marston Moor (2 July), while the Roundheads (the Puritans) surrendered at Lostwithiel on 31 August. The year 1645 was decisive, for on 14 June, at the Battle of Naseby, the New Model Army of Oliver Cromwell (1599–1658) decisively beat the king's forces.

The fighting dragged on for over a year, but on 6 May 1646 Charles surrendered to the Scots army, who on 30 January 1647 handed him over to Parliament. On 3 June 1647 the army seized the king, who on 11 November escaped to Carisbrooke Castle on the Isle of Wight. For the next two years Charles, hoping to divide and thus rule, bargained in bad faith with the Scots, the army, and Parliament. Instead of ruling he produced a second civil war, which was far more brutal than the first. As a result, on 19 December 1648 the army arrested the king and took him to London, where he was tried for treason. The result was inevitable. Charles was executed outside the Whitehall Banqueting Hall on 30 January 1649.

In a way the site was sublimely appropriate. The Banqueting Hall's magnificent ceiling painted by Rubens symbolized Charles's exquisite artistic tastes, which in turn were an excellent guide to his personality. The product of an oppressive childhood, Charles I was too much an authoritarian to deal with his subjects in good faith and too insecure to take decisive action. As Archbishop Laud bitterly concluded, he was "a mild and gracious prince, who knew not how to be, or be made great." For Charles, character was indeed fate.

See also **Charles II (England); Church of England; Cromwell, Oliver; English Civil War and Interregnum; James I and VI (England and Scotland); Laud, William; Scotland; Stuart Dynasty (England and Scotland).**

BIBLIOGRAPHY

Carlton, Charles. *Charles I: The Personal Monarch.* 2nd ed. London, 1995. Originally published in 1983.

Cogswell, Thomas. *The Blessed Revolution: English Politics and the Coming of War, 1621–1624.* Cambridge, U.K., 1989.

Reeve, L. J. *Charles I and the Road to Personal Rule.* Cambridge, U.K., and New York, 1989.

Sharpe, Kevin. *The Personal Rule of Charles I.* New Haven and London, 1992.

Young, Michael B. *Charles I.* Basingstoke, U.K., 1997.

CHARLES CARLTON

CHARLES II (ENGLAND)

CHARLES II (ENGLAND) (1630–1685; ruled 1660–1685), king of England, Scotland, and Ireland. Charles II was the dominant royal figure in England, Scotland, and Ireland for most of the late seventeenth century. Born on 29 May 1630,

Charles II. Portrait by Marcellus Laroon the Younger. THE ART ARCHIVE/CHRIST'S HOSPITAL/EILEEN TWEEDY

Charles succeeded to the throne on 30 January 1649. He could hardly have become king in worse circumstances, for his father, Charles I, had been beheaded by English revolutionaries who then abolished the monarchy. Young Charles had fled to the Continent three years before, and heard the news in exile in Holland. Although his reign legally dates from the moment that his father died, he was left to wander in poverty around western Europe for the first eleven years of it, as the guest successively of the Dutch, the French, the Germans, and the Spanish. In England the republicans who had killed his father continued to provide the real government of the country, most powerfully in the person of Oliver Cromwell, who ruled as Lord Protector between 1654 and 1658. Charles plotted incessantly to regain his thrones by invasion or rebellion, and came closest in 1650–1651, when the Scots crowned him as their king and he invaded England with an army of them. That army, however, was destroyed at Worcester, leaving the English republicans to conquer Scotland and Charles to escape back to continental Europe by hiding in an oak tree and in various country houses owned by royal supporters. When he was invited back to his three thrones in 1660, it was because the republican government had collapsed as a result of internal fighting among its members following the death of Cromwell (3 September 1658). Charles formally acceded to power in his three kingdoms on his thirtieth birthday, 29 May 1660, when he entered London to the cheers of huge crowds. He remarked dryly that he could not understand, in view of all this rejoicing, why none of the people applauding had done anything to help him until that point. The cynicism and suspicion of the remark is significant: always after his return, Charles never fully trusted the British nor felt secure among them.

On returning to his realms, he found many problems left in all three by two decades of war and revolution, but also great enthusiasm for the restoration of the monarchy. He must, therefore, take some blame for the fact that within three years he had become unpopular in England and was quarreling with its Parliament. This was partly due to his financial extravagance and adulterous habits; he married a Portuguese princess, Catherine of Braganza, in 1662 and then paraded his current mistress before her and the court. It was also because he tried to increase his own power over national religion by playing off against each other the newly restored national church and the Protestant dissenters who worshipped outside it. He only succeeded in disappointing both. Charles's response to this situation was to try to regain popularity with a reckless foreign adventure, an unprovoked attack on the Dutch that he thought would win riches and military glory. The resulting war ended in defeat in 1667, however, leaving him humiliated and heavily in debt. He tried to find his way out of these problems by a still more risky adventure, a secret agreement with France to launch another attack on the Dutch state that he believed would avenge his earlier defeat and leave him rich and powerful enough to disregard his critics in Parliament. The result, by 1674, was another defeat and the complete discrediting of his government.

He then hired a brilliant politician, the earl of Danby, to repair his finances and restore his reputation, and for four years this seemed to work. Danby managed Parliament carefully and projected an image of the king as a responsible and patriotic ruler and defender of the Church of England. Charles, however, could not resist another secret deal to take money from the Catholic French as an insurance policy. When this was revealed to the public in 1678, Danby's government fell and for three years Charles repeatedly called and dissolved new Parliaments, finding himself unable to manage a working relationship with any. He steered his way out of the crisis very shrewdly, offering measured concessions to his critics, hiring new and talented ministers, and behaving responsibly. By the time of his sudden death on 6 February 1685, his government was stable and strong again at home, although he was still unable to work with a Parliament and thus could not wage war.

Two very different views of Charles appear in modern literature. One, found mostly in scholarly histories, emphasizes his weaknesses as a monarch: his dislike of paperwork and administration, his duplicity, his vindictive cruelty, his determination to keep his ministers feeling insecure and to set them against each other, and his taste for reckless gambling, in both foreign and domestic affairs. Popular biographies and works of creative literature (and cinema) emphasize his charm, accessibility, affability, wit, and love of novelty, which undoubtedly encouraged the growth of science, architecture, and theater in England. He introduced the ruling classes to yachting, croquet, and champagne, and fathered at least twelve illegitimate children by seven different mistresses. Both portraits are just, but in the last analysis a king is expected to rule, and his shortcomings as a political leader contributed significantly to the instability of the British Isles during his reign. He has enjoyed a popularity in the twentieth century that he never knew in the seventeenth.

See also **Anglo-Dutch Naval Wars; Charles I (England); Cromwell, Oliver; English Civil War and Interregnum; English Civil War Radicalism.**

BIBLIOGRAPHY

Bryant, Sir Arthur. *King Charles II*. London, 1931. A typical admiring popular biography.

Fraser, Antonia. *King Charles II*. London, 1979. A more recent popular biography.

Hutton, Ronald. *Charles II: King of England, Ireland, and Scotland*. Oxford and New York, 1989. The first full-length scholarly study.

Miller, John. *After the Civil Wars: English Politics and Government in the Reign of Charles II*. London, 2000. An evaluation of the nature and impact of policy making during Charles's regime.

———. *Charles II*. London, 1991. Another complete study by a scholar.

Spurr, John. *England in the 1670s: This Masquerading Age*. Oxford, 2000. An analysis of one decade in Charles's reign, especially valuable for its analysis of popular attitudes toward the government.

RONALD HUTTON

CHARLES VIII (FRANCE)

CHARLES VIII (FRANCE) (1470–1498, ruled 1483–1498), king of France. Charles VIII was the last king of France in the direct line of the Valois dynasty. The only son of Louis XI (ruled 1461–1483) of France and Charlotte of Savoy, he was born on 30 June 1470. Because of his frailty as a child, Charles was not allowed to participate in vigorous activity, whether mental or physical. As a result he grew up with a limited education and little training in the arts of war and hunting. He became king at his father's death in 1483. Since he was ten months shy of being fourteen years old, he needed a regent to govern for him. A contentious struggle erupted over the regency between his older sister Anne of Beaujeu (1461–1522) and his cousin Louis of Orléans (ruled 1498–1515). It led to the convocation of the Estates-General in January 1484, which had the widest representation and most significant results of any meeting before 1789, most notably a powerful request for a reduction in taxes. The Estates-General, however, failed to designate a regent, and Charles turned fourteen without having one. Louis XI had designated Anne and her husband as his son's guardians, and they dominated the government for the next decade. Upset by the failure of his schemes, Louis of Orléans with his ally Duke Francis of Brittany (1435–1488) led a revolt known as the Fools' War. After their defeat in 1488, Louis was imprisoned and Francis died soon after. Francis's daughter, Anne (1477–1514), the new duchess of Brittany, had little choice but to agree to marry Charles. The marriage took place in December 1491, after Charles had repudiated his betrothal to Margaret of Austria, the daughter of Holy Roman Emperor Maximilian I.

By then Charles had freed himself from the tutelage of his sister and had begun to rule in his own right. He began planning the expedition to

Charles VIII (France). ©ARCHIVO ICONOGRAFICO, S.A./CORBIS

seize control of southern Italy, known as the First French Invasion of Italy (1494–1495). The Valois claim to the kingdom of Naples dated to 1265, when the pope invested Charles of Anjou with the realm as a papal fief. In the decades after 1265 the French lost control of Naples to the royal family of Aragon. Charles VIII was eager to assert his right to Naples and use it as a base for a crusade against the Ottoman Turks, who had conquered Constantinople in 1453. Encouraged by Ludovico Sforza of Milan, who had his own dispute with King Alfonso of Naples, Charles led the French army into Italy in the spring of 1494. The army consisted of the royal companies of *gens d'armes,* the armored lancers still regarded as the best fighting men in Europe; infantry companies, including six thousand Swiss pikemen, the best foot soldiers of the era; and an artillery train of seventy large bronze cannon, also the best available. The quick reduction of several North Italian forts by the French cannons convinced the Italians that further resistance was futile, and the French marched down Italy to Naples as if on parade. The Neapolitan king fled, and Charles entered Naples in triumph in March 1495.

The steps Charles had taken to secure the neutrality of France's neighbors broke down in light of his success, and Ferdinand of Aragón, determined to vindicate his family, organized a league of the major states of Europe and Italy against Charles. Recognizing that the league threatened to trap him in southern Italy, Charles retreated toward France with half of his army, leaving the rest to occupy Naples. His enemies forced him to give battle at Fornovo, south of the Po River, on 6 July 1495. The bloodiest battle of the expedition was a stalemate, but Charles gained an open route back to France, where he arrived in October 1495. His short time in Italy stimulated Charles's interest in Renaissance art and architecture. His most noteworthy project was the reconstruction of the château of Amboise using Italian artists and artisans, including the noted Fra Giacondo.

Charles and Anne had three children, but only one son survived the first month of life. His death at age three from measles was a devastating blow to the king. It convinced him to give up frivolous pleasures and reduce the tax burden on his people, as the Estates-General of 1484 had requested. Before he could begin to implement his new policies, he died at Amboise on 7 April 1498 after striking his head on a low doorframe. Whether he died from the blow or from aggravating a prior condition is unknown. He was succeeded by Louis of Orléans, who became Louis XII.

See also **Anne of Brittany; France; Italian Wars (1494–1559); Louis XII (France); Naples, Kingdom of; Valois Dynasty (France).**

BIBLIOGRAPHY

Bridge, John S. C. *A History of France from the Death of Louis XI.* 5 vols. Oxford, 1921–1936. A highly detailed history of France that includes the time of Charles VIII's reign. Especially strong on the invasions of Italy.

Labande-Mailfert, Yvonne. *Charles VIII et son milieu, 1470–1498.* Paris, 1975. The best biography of Charles.

FREDERIC J. BAUMGARTNER

CHARLES V (HOLY ROMAN EMPIRE) (1500–1558; Holy Roman emperor,

1519–1556; king of Spain as Charles I, 1516–1556). Charles was born 24 February 1500 at Ghent, the son of Archduke Philip of Habsburg and Joanna I, daughter of Ferdinand of Aragón and Isabella of Castile. Philip's death in 1506 made Charles ruler of the Netherlands under the regency of his aunt, Margaret of Austria. Shortly thereafter, his mother succumbed to mental illness, making him king of Castile under another regency, which lasted until 1516. In that year his grandfather Ferdinand died, leaving him the kingdom of Aragon and its Italian possessions. By this time he had assumed rulership of the Netherlands in his own right. In 1519 the death of his paternal grandfather, the Emperor Maximilian I, brought him the Habsburg possessions in Austria and southwest Germany and made him a prime candidate for election as Holy Roman emperor. By year's end, Charles was unanimously elected emperor after a campaign involving large payments to the electors and veiled threats of force. In the next two decades, his Spanish subjects conquered Mexico and Peru, adding much of the New World to his already enormous inheritance.

The beneficiary of these deaths and conquests was a pale, unprepossessing youth who developed slowly into a conscientious ruler. His tutors, including Adrian of Utrecht (the future Pope Adrian VI), instilled in him a deep, if conventional, piety and a solid understanding of politics. His interests nevertheless remained practical rather than speculative, and though imperial propagandists at one point tried to develop a rationale for universal monarchy, Charles's goals were simpler. Throughout the reign his chief purpose was to preserve his family's patrimony and to protect the Catholic Church.

Even these modest goals faced three obstacles: the intractable hostility of Francis I of France (ruled 1515–1547), Ottoman expansion up the Danube valley and in the Mediterranean, and an ongoing crisis in Germany, which linked the religious Reformation begun by Martin Luther to the growth of princely autonomy. The causes of these problems differed, and each followed a different historical course, but the emperor and his advisors could rarely decide upon a policy in one area without considering its possible impact on the others. Moreover, his adversaries in each case were sometimes able to combine forces against him. Charles therefore spent most of his reign at war.

Charles achieved his greatest successes against Francis I, who disputed his claims in Italy and supported his enemies in the Netherlands. In the course of seven wars with France the emperor made good his claims to Naples, Sicily, and Milan, and consolidated his possessions in the Netherlands. But the French wars crippled his finances and distracted him from other causes that were closer to his heart. Among these was the war against the Turks. The expansion of the Ottoman Empire in the Danube valley brought Muslim armies to the gates of Vienna by 1529. In the Mediterranean, Muslim fleets sailing from the ports of North Africa raided his Spanish and Italian kingdoms, causing widespread suffering and loss. The crusading ideal appealed to Charles, but he had only partial success in turning back the Muslim threat. The Turks retreated from Vienna after Charles relieved the siege of 1532 largely because they had reached the limits of their logistics. In the Mediterranean, Charles captured Tunis in 1535, but failed in 1541 to seize Algiers. The raids continued, because the Christians could not in the long run control all of the North African towns or the hinterland that supported them.

The German problem proved even more difficult to resolve. As a devout Catholic, Charles believed that his duty as emperor compelled him to oppose the spread of Protestantism and to devise a program of imperial reform that would strengthen the empire's institutions, if necessary at the expense of princely independence. His condemnation of Martin Luther at the Diet of Worms in 1521 accomplished nothing. In 1530 at Augsburg and again in 1540 at Regensburg he attempted to achieve peaceful solutions to the religious issue, but in each case negotiations broke down. He defeated the Protestant Schmalkaldic League in 1546–1547, but their cause revived in 1552 with French assistance. In 1555 Charles reluctantly agreed to the Religious Peace of Augsburg, which recognized the right of German princes to determine the religion of their own territories and ensured that the empire would remain as it had always been, a loose federation dominated by the princes rather than by the emperor.

The legacy of Charles V was shaped largely within the context of these struggles. As the reign progressed, he became more dependent upon Spanish wealth and the Spanish army that formed the

Charles V. Portrait by Titian. ©GIANNI DAGLI ORTI/CORBIS

core of his military system. The cost of never-ending warfare forced him to raise taxes, especially in Spain and the Netherlands, and to borrow heavily in the international money markets against his projected Spanish revenues. His son and successor as king of Spain, Philip II (ruled 1556–1598), was forced to restructure this debt in ways that increased borrowing costs in the future, thereby setting a disastrous precedent. Otherwise, Charles made serious efforts to improve administration in each of his realms. Basing his efforts wherever possible on existing institutions, he developed an improved conciliar system of government in Spain and its possessions that lasted until the eighteenth century. In America he supported Spain's leading advocate for the Indians, Bartolomé de Las Casas, and made a sincere if only partially successful effort to protect the native population from exploitation by the colonists. In Naples and Sicily his viceroys maintained order with minimal offense to local sensibilities while Charles personally created a system of patronage that co-opted most of the princes and cities of the north, ensuring relative peace, if not prosperity, for years to come. Everywhere, he insisted on improved record keeping and the establishment of archives.

His impact on the Netherlands is more difficult to assess because the seventeen provinces rose in revolt under his successor. In the course of his reign Charles added Frisia, Utrecht, Gelderland, and a few smaller estates to his existing inheritance. His fiscal demands, perhaps ironically, led to a strengthening of provincial government that contributed to Dutch success in the eventual revolt. The provinces created an elaborate system of funded debt based primarily on new excise taxes, but those taxes caused widespread resentment. His religious policies, too, provoked widespread passive resistance. The emperor's determination to root out heresy at all costs led him to promulgate edicts or placards that, among other things, demanded the death penalty for Protestants. Local magistrates, who shared the more tolerant religious attitudes of their countrymen, often found ways to evade their provisions. Charles did not, however, provoke the Revolt of the Netherlands. When he died, heresy appeared to be under control and the monarchy retained the support of the Netherlandish elites, whose rights he had always been careful to protect. It was left to Philip II to squander whatever goodwill remained through policies that appeared to threaten the interests of nobles and townspeople alike. The resulting war of independence lasted more than eighty years (1568–1648) and resulted in the establishment of the Dutch Republic, though Spain recovered the ten southern provinces by 1585.

By 1550 the emperor's health began to fail, and he succumbed increasingly to paralyzing bouts of depression. He decided to abdicate his offices and retire, reopening the question of his succession. In 1531 he had secured the election of his younger brother Ferdinand as king of the Romans in return for his help in managing German affairs. Ferdinand could therefore expect to succeed his brother as emperor. Charles, who had always planned to leave his Spanish and Italian possessions to his son Philip, began to worry that without Spanish arms Ferdinand could not protect the Netherlands against France or maintain order in Germany. Already in 1548 he had separated the Netherlands from the empire with the intention of leaving them to Philip. Now he proposed that Philip should have the empire as well. After a protracted and bitter family quarrel, it was decided that Philip should have Spain and the Netherlands, but that Ferdinand would become emperor as planned. It had become obvious in any case that Philip could not be elected.

This division of Charles's inheritance had profound consequences. Tying the Netherlands to Spain led to the revolt that exhausted Spanish finances and resulted in the establishment of the Dutch Republic. Ferdinand and his heirs devoted their best efforts to the creation of a Habsburg empire in eastern Europe that lasted until 1918. The Habsburgs preserved and expanded their inheritance, but Charles failed in his efforts to reform the empire or slow the spread of Protestantism, largely because, vast though his resources may have been, they were insufficient to meet his goals. Instead he created a world empire based on Spain that Spain, in the end, could not preserve. Depressed and exhausted, the emperor abdicated his offices in 1555–1556, and in 1557 retired to a small villa built for him on the grounds of the remote Spanish monastery of Yuste. He died in the following year from a fever of unknown origins.

See also **Augsburg, Religious Peace of (1555); Dutch Republic; Dutch Revolt (1568–1648); Ferdinand of Aragón; Habsburg Dynasty: Spain; Holy Roman Empire; Isabella of Castile; Joanna I, "the Mad" (Spain); Netherlands, Southern; Philip II (Spain); Schmalkaldic War (1546–1547); Spain.**

BIBLIOGRAPHY

Brandi, Karl. *The Emperor Charles V: The Growth and Destiny of a Man and of a World-Empire.* Translated by C. V. Wedgwood. London, 1939.

Fernández Alvarez, Manuel. *Charles V: Elected Emperor and Hereditary Ruler.* Translated by J. A. Lalaguna. London, 1975.

Maltby, William S. *The Reign of Charles V.* Basingstoke, U.K., 2001.

Soly, Hugo, et al., eds. *Charles V, 1500–1558, and His Time.* Antwerp, 1999.

Tracy, James D. *Emperor Charles V, Impresario of War: Campaign Strategy, International Finance, and Domestic Politics.* Cambridge, U.K., 2002.

WILLIAM S. MALTBY

CHARLES VI (HOLY ROMAN EMPIRE)

(1685–1740; ruled 1711–1740), Holy Roman emperor and ruler of the Habsburg Monarchy. Charles VI's greatest claim to historical fame is his role as father to Maria Theresa (ruled 1740–1780), one of the great rulers of the eighteenth century. Historians often point to the Pragmatic Sanction of 1713, a document that guaranteed the succession of his daughter to the traditionally male Habsburg inheritance, as the issue that dominated his reign. This document had its roots in 1703 when Leopold I (ruled 1658–1705), Charles's father, wished to regulate the order of succession if his two sons, Charles and Joseph (ruled 1705–1711 as Joseph I), should have no male issue. In the early agreements, Joseph's female heirs were to succeed to Habsburg authority, but in 1713 Charles changed that to provide for the succession of his own daughters. By 1720 Charles had embarked on an extensive campaign to secure recognition for his daughter's succession first from his own crownlands and then from the European powers generally. He achieved that recognition, but upon his death Prussia, Bavaria, and France renounced their commitment to it. This renunciation was followed by the War of the Austrian Succession, which would, after considerable suffering, enhance the Europe-wide fame of and respect for Maria Theresa.

In his younger years, Charles had his own wars to fight. When the Spanish King Charles II died in 1700, Louis XIV of France laid claim to the Spanish throne, a prospect that frightened other great powers, already experienced in struggles against the ambitions of the Sun King. In the ensuing War of the Spanish Succession (1701–1714), the allied powers opposed to Louis (Britain, Austria, Holland, Prussia) adopted Charles as their candidate for the Spanish throne. Charles achieved some success in Catalonia, but, when his brother died in 1711, and he became ruler of the Habsburg possessions, the British and Dutch insisted that he abandon his claim to Spain, and he did so. He oversaw the Austrian role in bringing the War of the Spanish Succession to a close.

Politically Charles fits into the group of late-seventeenth- and early-eighteenth-century monarchs who understood that success of the state depended upon administrative centralization and economic advancement. He was not a thoroughgoing reformer in the stamp of Louis XIV or Peter the Great of Russia, but he did introduce changes that he believed would enhance the development of his state. In Silesia and Bohemia cloth production increased, and he aided the city of Linz in reviving its woolen mills. In 1717 the first cotton plant opened in the town of Schwechat, near Vienna, and in 1718 Charles approved the establishment of a porcelain factory modeled on the Meissen plant that had opened in Dresden just a few years earlier.

To assist these and other establishments, Charles built new roads connecting some of the Habsburg cities, including those from Vienna to Prague and Vienna to Brno. Probably the most famous was the road over the Semmering Pass, which connected the Austrian heartland to Italy. In addition, he declared as free ports Fiume and Trieste, the principal Habsburg cities on the Adriatic Sea, in hopes that they could compete successfully with Venice for Adriatic and eventually Mediterranean trade. His most famous venture was the incorporation of the Ostend Company in his Belgian lands, which was designed to compete with the British and the Dutch for trade in East Africa and in the East and West Indies. This company enjoyed a few years of success until, under considerable pressure from the British and the Dutch, it was changed into a bank in the 1730s.

Charles was less aggressive in war and diplomacy, with the notable exception of his pursuit of recognition of the Pragmatic Sanction. Still, in 1716–1718 his armies, under the brilliant leadership of Europe's foremost military commander, Prince Eugene of Savoy, crushed the armies of the Ottoman Empire and in 1718 imposed upon the Turks the Peace of Passarowitz (Pozerevac), which ceded to the monarchy the mighty fortress of Belgrade at the confluence of the Sava and Danube rivers and its surrounding countryside. This acquisition left Austria poised to advance far into the Balkans, but the backwardness of the area gave Charles and his advisers pause. From 1717 to 1737 the government invested considerable resources to develop Belgrade and the area north of the fortress, called the Banat, but the yields were disappointing, as were additional Habsburg efforts in the Banat in the 1760s and 1770s.

Charles's reign ended in disappointment. Austria entered another war against the Turks in 1737, this time not to win territory for itself but to curb the Balkan ambitions of its ally, Russia. Although the Ottomans were not formidable opponents, poor leadership, logistical problems, and missed opportunities led to the Austrian cession of Belgrade and the lands south of the Danube to the Ottomans. Charles hoped, however, that his success in securing recognition of the Pragmatic Sanction would atone for this defeat by guaranteeing the peaceful accession of his daughter. That accession, however, was far from peaceful.

See also **Austrian Succession, War of the (1740–1748); Habsburg Dynasty: Austria; Holy Roman Empire; Maria Theresa (Holy Roman Empire); Passarowitz, Peace of (1718); Polish Succession, War of the (1733–1738); Spanish Succession, War of the (1701–1714).**

BIBLIOGRAPHY

Henderson, Nicholas. *Prince Eugen of Savoy.* New York, 1964. Reprint, New York and London, 2002.

Ingrao, Charles. *The Habsburg Monarchy, 1618–1815.* 2nd ed. Cambridge, U.K., and New York, 2002.

Wangermann, Ernst. *The Austrian Achievement, 1700–1800.* New York, 1973.

KARL A. ROIDER

CHARLES I (SPAIN). *See* **Charles V (Holy Roman Empire).**

CHARLES II (SPAIN) (1661–1700), king of Spain, Naples, and Sicily (1665–1700), son of Philip IV, and the last Habsburg ruler of Spain. From the reign of Ferdinand and Isabella in the fifteenth century through that of Philip IV in the mid-seventeenth century, Spain was the major power in western Europe, possessing a rich colonial empire and respected for its military prowess as well as its literary and artistic accomplishments. The reign of Charles II is perhaps best known for the decline of this empire. Plagued by poor leadership, monetary inflation, bankruptcy, and a series of military defeats, Spain in the later seventeenth century surrendered its primacy on the European stage to France.

Charles as an individual was sadly symbolic of this decline, as he was known more for his physical infirmity and absence from government than for his accomplishments. The product of generations of inbreeding between the Spanish and Austrian branches of the Habsburg family, he was sickly, frail, and possibly epileptic. Given Charles's weak physical condition, it was generally assumed that he was lacking in intelligence as well, and little was required of him in the way of educational training. He was never able to read and write well, and did not master other basic courtly skills such as horsemanship and fencing. Even in adulthood he did not often attend the meetings of important government councils or countersign their deliberations; official documents generally bear a facsimile of his signature rather than the original. In the last years of his life he was rumored to be bewitched and underwent an exorcism to expel his demons.

Charles's reign was characterized by factionalism in which various figures in the court competed for control in the power vacuum left by the absence of a strong king. Charles inherited his throne in 1665 at the age of four. His mother, Mariana of Austria, acted as regent and relied on a series of favorites (including her confessor, Juan Everard Nithard, and Fernando de Valenzuela, the husband of one of her servants) to assist her in the tasks of government. When Charles came of age in 1676, he too depended on the assistance of others in the court. As a result, there was constant competition to gain access to the king, and factions developed around the individuals most likely to be able to control him. In addition to Mariana of Austria, the most significant of these were Charles's half-brother Don Juan José of Austria (an illegitimate son of Philip IV), a charismatic and popular figure in the court and a constant focus of opposition to the queen mother, and Charles's second wife, Mariana of Neuburg, whom he married in 1689. During the 1680s and 1690s, the king also relied on the assistance of a series of ministers. This practice increased

Charles II (Spain). LIBRARY OF CONGRESS

much administrative and fiscal reform that has been attributed to the reign of the Bourbon kings in the eighteenth century may well have had its roots in the last decades of the seventeenth in the regions outside Castile. Even artistic production, which had declined in Castile because of a lack of court patronage, flourished in provincial cities such as Seville. Although Charles II is a king more often regretted than celebrated in the annals of Spanish history, the negative impact of his personal failings on Spain has been much exaggerated.

See also **Habsburg Dynasty; Spain; Spanish Succession, War of the.**

BIBLIOGRAPHY

Darby, Graham. *Spain in the Seventeenth Century*. London, 1994.

Kamen, Henry. *Spain in the Later Seventeenth Century, 1665–1700*. London, 1980.

Maura, Gabriel Maura y Gamazo, duque de. *Vida y reinado de Carlos II*. Revised edition. Madrid, 1990. Originally published in 1942; somewhat outdated but still the most thorough and detailed account of Charles and his reign.

JODI CAMPBELL

the influence of the aristocracy in the court, but because of factional conflicts, no single minister was able to accomplish much or to remain in power for more than a few years. Charles's final failure was his inability to leave an heir. Anticipating this, the other European powers, particularly France and Austria, spent much of his reign designing plans to partition Spain, and his death in 1700 resulted in the twelve-year War of the Spanish Succession.

Historians of Spain have paid little attention to the late seventeenth century, and those who have described Spain during the reign of Charles II reserve their harshest criticism for the king, associating his personal weaknesses with Spain's decline. Recent studies of the "decline of Spain" argument, however, have questioned whether Charles's reign was truly as disastrous as it appears. While the court in Madrid was preoccupied with its internal power struggles, other regions of Spain experienced a gradual recovery. Although military dominance in Europe clearly passed to the French, recent research indicates that within Spain, population growth, agricultural output, and textile manufacture all began to recover under the reign of Charles II. In fact,

CHARLES III (SPAIN) (1716–1788; ruled 1759–1788), king of Spain. Born in Madrid on 20 January 1716, Charles III died in the same city on 14 December 1788. The son of Philip V of Spain (ruled 1700–1724, 1724–1746) and Isabella Farnese of Parma (1692–1766), he was duke of Parma (1731–1735) and king of Naples (1734–1759) before becoming king of Spain (1759–1788). Following family tradition, Charles III spent his first seven years under women's care (Isabel Ramírez, María Antonia de Salcedo) and afterward under the supervision of court noblemen appointed by his parents. During childhood he received training in geography, history, military strategy, mathematics, and foreign languages (French, Italian dialects). More than studying, he enjoyed hunting, shooting, and making small objects from wood and ivory. His relationship with his parents was close despite frequent absences and separations, according to their own testimonies in private letters that started when Charles was four years old and continued for almost forty years. The letters also reveal the enormous

Charles III (Spain). Engraving after the eighteenth-century painting by Andres de la Calleja. LIBRARY OF CONGRESS

influence and inspiration of his parents on his religiosity, political priorities, and selection of a spouse (Amalia of Saxony). A prudent and sober reformist spirit inspired his government rather than revolution and change, as was also the case with other European kings and queens of the eighteenth century.

Charles III relied on his own judgment much more than did previous Spanish kings, who had relied on powerful ministers. Foreign policy was the greatest priority of his government because of his mother's influence, but above all because Spain was a world colonial power. Alliances with France, however, brought wars with Great Britain, and Spain lost territories (including Florida) and imperial strength during Charles's reign.

Charles III appointed pragmatic ministers whose missions were to reinforce the crown, improve the economy, and maintain a peaceful social order to achieve a strong and stable country from which they would obtain political strength and

wealth. In the first seven years of Charles's government, Italians served as the ministers of war, state, and finance, with Leopoldo di Gregorio, marquis of Squillace, and the marquis of Grimaldi as the outstanding figures above the ministers Charles inherited from his half brother Ferdinand VI (ruled 1746–1759). Fiscal reforms, the rise in prices following the introduction of free trade in grain, proposals to disentail properties of privileged sectors of society, and the law forbidding men to wear traditional broad hats and long capes aroused opposition against the Italian ministers. Sectors of the nobility, the clergy, and thousands of people from Madrid and other Spanish cities initiated riots in 1766 and generated fear of social upheaval and disorder. To restore internal stability and peace, Charles III dismissed his Italian ministers, expelled the Jesuits from Spain and the colonies (1767), and sought a new team of ministers from a group of university-trained Spanish lawyers, among them Pedro Rodríguez Campomanes y Perez (1723–1802), José Moñino y Redondo, count of Floridablanca (1728–1808), and José de Gálvez (1729–1787), who functioned as a team. With his new ministers, Charles III undertook reforms in administration, ecclesiastical policy, and some aspects of commercial and agrarian policies.

First, traditional royal councils were replaced with ministers who regularly met in a council of state, independent councillors were introduced into municipal governments of towns and villages, and the French system of intendants was implemented in the colonies to reinforce the crown's direct control. The final aim of administrative reforms was to impose the power of the crown at all administrative levels in Spain and its colonies and reduce to some extent the autonomy of high aristocrats, municipal councils, and viceroys.

The subordination of the church to the Bourbon monarchy was a second major goal of Charles III. Consequently he required royal authorization for the introduction of papal documents, expelled the Jesuits from all Spanish territories in 1767, and reduced the power of the Inquisition.

Economic reforms were less successful than administrative and religious reforms. The reduction of institutional obstacles to free trade in grain in the peninsula and to free trade between cities of the

Spanish Empire (1765–1778) did little to change structural limits to sustained economic growth. Mercantilist policies and privileges were the rule in Spain as in most other European countries, and they imposed similar limits to the growth of domestic and international trade. On the other hand, hunger, bad crops, and privileged ownership and distribution of land remained the norm in rural Spain. The entailed land of the nobility, the clergy, the municipal councils, and the crown, *mayorazgos, manos muertas, comunes,* and *realengos* respectively, a fundamental obstacle to increased agricultural productivity, was never seriously questioned or reformed.

Charles III and his ministers reinforced the power of the crown and rationalized imperial administration as no other ruler had before in Spain. However, they left the traditional social order intact.

See also **Farnese, Isabel (Queen of Spain); Ferdinand VI (Spain); Philip V (Spain); Spain.**

BIBLIOGRAPHY

Carlos III y la Ilustración. 2 vols. Madrid, 1988–1990.

Domínguez Ortiz, Antonio. *Carlos III y la España de la Ilustración.* Madrid, 1988.

Herr, Richard. *The Eighteenth-Century Revolution in Spain.* Princeton, 1958.

Hull, Anthony H. *Charles III and the Revival of Spain.* Washington, D.C., 1980.

Lynch, John. *Bourbon Spain, 1700–1808.* Oxford, 1989.

PALOMA FERNÁNDEZ PÉREZ

Charles X Gustav. Portrait by Abraham Wuchters. THE ART ARCHIVE/GRIPSHOLM CASTLE SWEDEN/DAGLI ORTI (A)

CHARLES X GUSTAV (SWEDEN)

(1622–1660; ruled 1654–1660), king of Sweden; son of John Casimir of Pfalz-Zweibrücken and Katherine, the half-sister of Gustavus II Adolphus. Charles X Gustav was born and grew up in Sweden. Tutored in history, politics, law, modern languages, and warfare, he spent nearly three years on a grand tour of the Continent. In 1642, he joined Swedish forces in Germany, where he gained military and diplomatic experience and took part in the campaign against Denmark in 1643–1645 (Torstensson's War), which resulted in Sweden's gaining Jämtland and Härjedalen in Norway, Halland on the west coast, and Gotland. Throughout his life he showed a remarkable capacity to work

hard at whatever challenge faced him. He was also prone to bouts of depression and excessively fond of food, drink, and women.

Charles figured importantly in the complex issue of succession. The male line of the Vasa dynasty ended with Gustavus II Adolphus. His daughter Christina, who was only six at his death, was his only legitimate heir. The council nobility took advantage of this situation to enhance its constitutional position, and the monarchy was in danger of becoming little more than symbolic. Christina opposed this trend, especially after reaching her majority in 1644, and viewed assuring the succession as vital. Marriage was the most obvious solution, and her cousin Charles was the most likely candidate. Christina encouraged this idea until sometime in 1645, when she made it clear she could not marry. Rejecting Charles as a possible husband did not mean rejecting him as her successor. He was welcome at court; she made him commander of the Swedish forces in Germany in 1648 and won the parliament's approval of his succession a year later. Following

Christina's coronation in 1650, Charles spent most of his time on his estates on Öland.

Charles X Gustav was crowned king on 6 June 1654, the same day that Christina stepped down and prepared to leave Sweden. He was the founder of the Pfalz/Wittelsbach dynasty, which also included Charles XI, Charles XII, and Ulrika Eleonora (1654–1720). Three themes dominated his short reign: war, state finances, and the constitutional balance between crown and nobility.

Charles X was primarily a warrior king. His foreign policy centered on maintaining the empire, which he viewed as essential to Sweden's security. Although Swedish power reached its peak during his reign, the country faced almost constant threats from Poland, Russia, the Habsburgs, Brandenburg, and Denmark. England, France, and the Netherlands also figured importantly in the complex diplomacy of the region. In 1655, he attacked Poland in what became a costly and largely fruitless conflict. Taking advantage of the situation, the Danes declared war on Sweden in 1657. Charles's campaign against them turned into one of the most daring (or luckiest) in Sweden's history. He easily occupied Jutland and then, due to an abnormally cold winter, was able to march his forces across the frozen Belts; take Fyn, Langeland, and Lolland; and cross to Sjaelland to attack Copenhagen. The Treaty of Roskilde (1658) cost Denmark all of its territories in southern Sweden (Skåne and Blekinge), plus Bohuslän on the Norwegian border, the island of Bornholm, and Trondheimslän in Norway. A second campaign against Denmark was launched in late summer 1658, with the intention of destroying the country and absorbing it into the empire. This time, however, Copenhagen's heroic resistance, new problems in the eastern Baltic, and international concerns about the balance of power in northern Europe worked against Charles. Fate also intervened, as the king died in early 1660. Peace was reached in 1660, and Sweden was lucky to lose only Bornholm and Trondheimslän. The zenith of empire had passed.

Charles X Gustav was a monarchist in the ongoing constitutional battle in Sweden. He supported Christina against the council nobles in the 1640s, and he used the economic troubles arising from the costs of empire and the social discontent resulting from increasing tax burdens to attack the supporters of aristocratic constitutionalism and the vast gains some of the nobility had made in terms of land donations (alienation) from the crown's domain. Crucial in this struggle was the acceptance by the council and the parliament of a complex program to recover some of the lands alienated to the nobility since 1632, called the "quarter reduction," in 1655. War and the king's death prevented the program's full implementation. Twenty years later, a far-reaching reduction and the destruction of the council aristocracy's powers was completed by his son, Charles XI.

See also **Christina (Sweden); Gustavus II Adolphus (Sweden); Oxenstierna, Axel; Sweden; Vasa Dynasty (Sweden).**

BIBLIOGRAPHY

Dahlgren, Stellan. *Karl X och reduktion.* Uppsala, 1964.

Kirby, D. G. *Northern Europe in the Early Modern Period: The Baltic World 1492–1772.* London, 1990.

Roberts, Michael. "Charles X and His Council: 'Dualism' or Cooperation" and "Charles X and the Great Parenthesis: A Reconsideration." In *From Oxenstierna to Charles XII. Four Studies.* Cambridge, U.K., and New York, 1991.

BYRON J. NORDSTROM

CHARLES XII (SWEDEN)

CHARLES XII (SWEDEN) (1682–1718; ruled 1697–1718), king of Sweden. The son of Charles XI of Sweden and Ulrika Eleonora of Denmark, Charles was raised in the context of Sweden's transition to absolutism. From a distinguished group of tutors he learned Latin, modern languages, history, mathematics, religion, military techniques, and Swedish politics and law. He was deeply religious, intense, tireless, self-assured, uncompromising, secretive, and fully committed to the ideas of Sweden's imperial greatness and divine right absolutism. Not yet fifteen when he his father died, he was recognized as ruling king by the parliament a few months later and wasted no time making it clear that Charles XI's absolutist system would continue. Throughout his reign he was in charge, aided by a handful of favorites including Carl Piper, Thomas Polus, and Georg H. von Görtz.

The first few years of Charles's reign were remarkable for their levity. The teenaged king enjoyed culture, parties, food, drink, and hunting—and often mixed all of these in flights of decadence. The fun ended abruptly in 1700, when Frederick IV of Denmark, Augustus II the Strong of Poland-Saxony, and Peter the Great of Russia attacked Sweden's Baltic holdings from three directions. The Great Northern War (1700–1721) consumed the rest of Charles XII's life. It became his obsession, and it was in his conduct of this war that Charles's place in history was forged.

The coalition Sweden faced appeared insurmountable, but the nature of early modern alliances and warfare worked in Charles's favor. He did not have to defeat the combined forces of his enemies. He could deal with them individually. From 1700 to 1708, he was successful, and it was then that he earned a reputation for daring, command skills, and near invincibility. The Danes were forced out of the war in August 1700 (Treaty of Traventhal). The Russians lost the Battle of Narva in November 1700, but were not pursued or truly defeated. Charles's attention turned to Poland, then led by Augustus II the Strong of Saxony, where a series of campaigns and political intrigues spanning six years finally led to peace, concluded at Altranstädt in 1706.

In 1707, Charles launched a campaign against Russia. His plans to strike at Moscow were undone by the Russians' harassing tactics, failure of reinforcements to reach him, dwindling supplies, and the severe winter of 1708–1709. Charles was forced to turn south into the Ukraine. On 28 June 1709, he attacked the Russians at Poltava. The odds were against him. The Russians were well prepared, and the Swedes were outnumbered in every way. Charles, who had been wounded a few days earlier, could not direct the battle effectively, and he underestimated his enemy. Suffering horrible losses, the Swedes were forced to retreat. Two days later what was left of the army and its hangers-on surrendered at Perevolotjna, while Charles and a small body of supporters fled into the Ottoman Empire.

For over five years the war and affairs of state were conducted from exile, first at Bender in Bessarabia and then from Demotika west of Constantinople. Charles was a guest and then a prisoner of the Turks. He was allowed to leave in late 1714, going first to Stralsund and returning to Sweden a

Charles XII (Sweden). Detail of a portrait by David von Krafft, 1719. THE ART ARCHIVE/MUSÉE DU CHÂTEAU DE VERSAILLES/ DAGLI ORTI

year later. During his absence, the coalition reformed and was joined by Brandenburg and Hanover. The Baltic provinces fell; Finland and the German territories were occupied. Charles refused to sue for peace and ordered new armies and new campaigns. The human and material costs to Sweden were enormous. A 1716 campaign against Norway failed. A new campaign began in 1718, when Fredriksten (Fredrikshald) fortress on the Norwegian-Swedish border was besieged and central Norway attacked. On the night of 30 November 1718, while inspecting the works, Charles was shot in the head and died instantly. Who killed him has remained a question ever since. The Norwegian forces were firing from the fortress and could have hit the king. Many have preferred the murder option and argued that he was shot by someone in his own party. Simple war-weariness could have been the motive, or it could have been part of a conspiracy to assure the succession of his sister, Ulrika Eleonora, and her husband Fredrik. In this ongoing debate serious historical research and folk legends have often merged. Whatever the truth, Sweden's age of empire died with Charles. A set of peace treaties ended the war and stripped Sweden of most of its empire. A peaceful change of constitution ended absolutism.

See also **Augustus II the Strong (Saxony and Poland); Denmark; Northern Wars (1655–1660, 1700–1721); Sweden.**

BIBLIOGRAPHY

Berg, Olof Patrik. *Carl XII och enväldet*. Göteborg, 2002.

Englund, Peter. *Poltava. Berättelsen om en armés undergång*. Stockholm, 1988.

Ericsson, Peter. *Stora nordiska kriget förklarat: Karl XII och det ideologiska tilltalet*. Uppsala, 2002. Contains a brief summary in English.

Hatton R. M. *Charles XII of Sweden*. New York, 1969.

Liljegren, Bengt. *Karl XII: en biografi*. Lund, 2000.

Roberts, Michael. "The Dubious Hand: The History of a Controversy." In *From Oxenstierna to Charles XII: Four Studies*. Cambridge, U.K., and New York, 1991.

Voltaire. *The History of Charles XII, King of Sweden*. Translated by Antonia White. London, 1976.

BYRON J. NORDSTROM

CHARLES THE BOLD (BURGUNDY)

(1433–1477), duke of Burgundy. Charles was the last of the Valois dukes of Burgundy. The son of Duke Philip the Good and Isabella of Portugal, he was born in 1433. As a youngster he had a reputation for unbounded energy, a fierce temper, and a determination to win glory in battle. His impetuous nature in politics and battle led to his designation as Charles le Téméraire, "the Bold" but equally "the Rash." Because Charles was more absorbed in war than his father, Charles's court was less important as a center of art, but he had a fondness for music that helped create the Flemish School of Music. Two years before his father's death in 1467 he took control of the vast territories of the House of Burgundy—the duchy of Burgundy, Flanders, and Artois, lands in the kingdom of France; and the county of Burgundy (the Franche-Comté), Brabant, Friesland, Hainaut, Holland, Luxembourg, and Zeeland, units of the Holy Roman Empire. The two Burgundies were separated from his provinces in the Netherlands by Alsace and Lorraine, and one of his goals was uniting his lands by gaining control of the last two territories. Another was gaining the title of king so he would be the equal of his rival, Louis XI of France.

As one of the peers of France, Charles involved himself in plots against Louis. He and his French allies in the League of the Public Weal were victorious over Louis in the Battle of Montlhéry in July 1465, but as they failed in a subsequent attack on Paris, little came of their victory. Charles began negotiations with Holy Roman Emperor Frederick III (ruled 1440–1493) to marry Mary, Charles's daughter with his first wife Isabelle de Bourbon, to Frederick's son Maximilian and to gain from him the title of king. In 1473 negotiations with Frederick over Charles's coronation broke down at the last minute, and Charles decided to win by arms what he could not by bargaining.

After arranging for Edward IV of England to invade France, Charles began a campaign to conquer Alsace and the Rhine Valley in 1474. The Swiss, frightened by Charles's pretensions of reestablishing the old kingdom of Burgundy that included much of western Switzerland, allied with Louis XI. The French paid the Swiss Confederation a substantial sum to wage war on Charles. Involved in Alsace, he was forced to leave the Swiss unpunished after they ravaged the county of Burgundy in 1474. When in 1475 Edward agreed to a truce with Louis instead of undertaking the joint campaign to divide up France with Charles, the latter turned his attention to the Swiss. Assembling the heavy lancers of Burgundy, regarded as the best cavalry in Europe; the cream of Europe's foot soldiers, who included Italian crossbowmen, English archers, and pikemen from the Low Countries; and the best artillery train yet seen, Charles led his forces into Switzerland in February 1476. A brief siege took the town of Grandson, and Charles hanged every defender as an example to the Swiss. As his army moved eastward, it ran into the Swiss forces that, as was their practice, were marching in battle order. Charles had little time to form his lines before the Swiss phalanxes were on top of his men. Desperately trying to rally them, the duke had to be dragged from the battlefield.

Undaunted by this defeat, Charles rebuilt his army with his usual energy. By June he was back in the field. While laying siege to Morat, Charles came under attack from the Swiss, who had rapidly reas-

Charles the Bold. Contemporary portrait painting.
©ARCHIVO ICONOGRAFICO, S.A./CORBIS

sembled. The ability of the Swiss to move quickly across a field of artillery fire allowed them to reach the Burgundian lines and rout them. While Charles got away, most of his men were slaughtered. Yet he once again assembled an army, although smaller than his previous ones. His wrath was especially directed at the duke of Lorraine, who had joined the Swiss at Morat. In late 1476 he moved into Lorraine and laid siege to Nancy. The Swiss arrived in early January and as usual moved immediately into battle. Badly outnumbering the Burgundians, the Swiss routed them on 5 January 1477 and killed Charles. His frozen body with its head cleaved "from crown to chin" by a halberd was found two days later.

Charles's lands passed to Mary, his only child. Louis XI, who took advantage of Charles's death to recover the duchy of Burgundy and Artois for the French crown, pressed her to marry his young son Charles. Being a Burgundian, however, she refused with disdain and married Maximilian of Austria (Holy Roman emperor; ruled 1493–1519). This was the first in the series of marriages that passed

much of Europe to Charles's great-grandson Charles V (ruled 1519–1556), who was named for him.

See also **Burgundy; France; Switzerland; Valois Dynasty (France).**

BIBLIOGRAPHY

Kendall, Paul Murray. *Louis XI, the Universal Spider.* New York, 1970. Detailed political biography of Charles's bitter antagonist.

Vaughan, Richard. *Charles the Bold: The Last Valois Duke of Burgundy.* London, 1973. Fine biography of the duke and the only one in English.

FREDERIC J. BAUMGARTNER

CHARLESTON. Founded by Englishmen from Barbados, Charleston was a port, a center of religious toleration, and a slave society, all from the very beginning. A part of the English colony of "Carolina," which included what is today South Carolina, North Carolina, and Georgia, Charleston was first established (in 1670) on a swampy site several miles from its current location. In 1690 residents relocated to the current city, which is located on a peninsula between two rivers.

Charleston's inhabitants were slave-owning planters intent on cultivating a staple crop. Although rates of disease were high and the land was initially difficult to cultivate, Charlestonians relied on the expertise of African slaves, whose labor built substantial trade in meat, rice, and (later) the dye-producing plant, indigo.

Included in John Locke's 1669 charter for the colony was freedom of worship, noticeably absent in Boston and Virginia. Charleston had a small population of Jews, and in 1685, after the revocation of the Edict of Nantes, numerous Huguenot families migrated to Charleston. In the eighteenth century, Scottish immigrants added to the diversity of the city and surrounding counties.

By 1742, Charleston was the fourth largest city in British North America. Although somewhat distant from other centers of colonial resistance, it furnished numerous Revolutionary leaders, including the president of the first Continental Congress and several signers of the Declaration of Independence. With a population of 12,000 in 1775,

Charleston was an appealing target for the British Navy during the War of American Independence. While an attack on Fort Moultrie failed in June of 1776, the city succumbed to a siege in May of 1780 and remained occupied until hostilities ended in 1782.

Charlestonians were ardent supporters of the Revolutionary ideals of liberty and equality, but their economic and cultural differences from the other new states, especially slavery, strained the unity forged in war. As the eighteenth century ended, sectional tensions emerged, foreshadowing the divide that would separate Charleston from other major cities in the nineteenth century.

See also **American Independence, War of (1775–1783); Boston; British Colonies: North America; Huguenots; New York; Philadelphia; Slavery and the Slave Trade.**

BIBLIOGRAPHY

Edgar, Walter. *South Carolina: A History.* Columbia, S.C., 1998.

Wood, Peter H. *Black Majority: Negroes in Colonial South Carolina from 1670 through the Stono Rebellion.* New York, 1975.

FIONA DEANS HALLORAN

CHARLETON, WALTER (1620–1707),

English physician and natural philosopher. Charleton was born in Shepton Mallet, Somerset, England, in 1619/20 and died in London in 1707. His tutor at Oxford, where Charleton earned a "doctor of physick" in 1643, was John Wilkins. His close relationship with the circle around William Harvey (1578–1657) influenced his thinking. He was appointed physician-in-ordinary to King Charles I, who was then at Oxford. He settled in London in 1650, remaining a loyal Royalist during the Interregnum, and was appointed physician to Charles II in 1660. During 1651 and 1652, he became acquainted with the new French natural philosophy of Pierre Gassendi (1592–1655) and René Descartes (1596–1650). Charleton was one of the original members of the Royal Society. Because of professional jealousy, he was not admitted to the College of Physicians until 1676, although he served as its president from 1689 to 1691. He served as senior censor in the College of Physicians

from 1698 to 1706 and delivered Harveian orations in 1702 and 1706. His medical practice eventually declined as his Royalist patients died off. Charleton died impoverished in London in 1707. His extensive writings included translations and paraphrases of some of J. B. van Helmont's (1579–1644) medical books and of Gassendi's Christianized Epicureanism, some original medical treatises, an explanation of Stonehenge, a biography of William Cavendish, duke of Newcastle, and an oration on the restoration of Charles II.

Charleton's first published work, the *Spiritus Gorgonicus* (1650), is an account of the formation of stones in the body, based on Paracelsian and Helmontian sources. The *Ternary of Paradoxes* (1650) includes a translation of van Helmont's *Magnetic Cure of Wounds,* a work describing the action of the weapon salve by which Paracelsian physicians claimed to be able to cure wounds across considerable distances, by treating the sword that inflicted the wound or other materials containing blood from the wound. The influence of Helmontian ideas remains evident in many of his later medical writings. During the 1650s, Charleton wrote several works, paraphrasing Gassendi's attempt to Christianize Epicureanism. Like Gassendi, Charleton tried to incorporate it into providential Christianity so that it could serve as a theologically acceptable replacement for Aristotelianism. Charleton's books were among the first and most important vehicles by which Epicurean thought came to Britain in the mid-seventeenth century.

The Darknes of Atheism, Dispelled by the Light of Nature (1652) is a self-proclaimed work on natural theology, closely following Gassendi's arguments. Charleton gave an account of the natural world in *Physiologia Epicuro-Gassendo-Charltoniana: or A Fabrick of Science Natural, Upon the Hypothesis of Atoms, Founded by Epicurus, Repaired by Petrus Gassendus, Augmented by Walter Charleton* (1654), a paraphrase of Gassendi's *Syntagma Philosophiae Epicuri* (1649). Like Gassendi, Charleton rejected the materialism of Epicurean atomism. The mechanization of the world was limited by the existence of noncorporeal entities: God, angels, and the human soul. Accordingly, Charleton published a dialogue entitled *The Immortality of the Human Soul, Demonstrated by the Light of Nature* (1657). Charleton presented a modified version of Epicurean ethics in his Introduction to *Epicurus' Morals* (1656). Although he accepted the basic tenets of a hedonistic ethics, Charleton objected to three of Epicurus' assertions: the mortality of the soul; the denial of providence and consequently the lack of obligation "to honour, revere, and worship God"; and the endorsement of suicide as "an Act of Heroick Fortitude in case of intollerable or otherwise inevitable Calamity." Charleton's Epicurean works were well known in the seventeenth century and were one source by which Robert Boyle, John Locke, and Isaac Newton became acquainted with Epicurean philosophy.

See also **Boyle, Robert; Catholic Spirituality and Mysticism; Descartes, René; Gassendi, Pierre; Harvey, William; Helmont, Jean Baptiste van; Locke, John; Medicine; Newton, Isaac; Wilkins, John.**

BIBLIOGRAPHY

Kargon, Robert. "Walter Charleton, Robert Boyle, and the Acceptance of Epicurean Atomism in England." *Isis* 55 (1964): 184–192.

Osler, Margaret J. "Descartes and Charleton on Nature and God." *Journal of the History of Ideas* 40 (1979): 445–456.

Webster, Charles. "The College of Physicians: 'Solomon's House' in Commonwealth England." *Bulletin of the History of Medicine* 41 (1967): 393–412.

MARGARET J. OSLER

CHEMISTRY.

The history of early modern chemistry, understood as a body of ideas and practices related to compounding and decomposing material substances, takes us to alchemy and apothecary laboratories, artisans' workshops, metallurgists and manufacturers, scientific societies, arsenals, royal courts, and public squares. It should not be understood in terms of the victory of scientific theory over arcane beliefs, but of the changing employment of its various technologies and the contexts in and by which they were legitimized.

MATERIAL AND BODILY TECHNOLOGY

Chemistry's material technology—that is, its instruments and laboratory equipment—remained stable throughout most of the period, but was augmented by precision-oriented apparatus in the second half of the eighteenth century as the study of heat and gases, along with early industrial innovations, redir-

ected chemical investigations. Increasingly accurate measuring devices helped bring about standardization in manufacturing ventures (e.g. Josiah Wedgwood's pottery works) while feeding debates over how to organize chemistry as an investigative enterprise. Should the heterogeneous chemical world be disciplined by analyzing qualitative or quantitative data?

The way chemical operators and investigators used their own bodies was part of this historical development and debate. As long as chemical determination rested on examining colors, smells, tastes and textures, the human senses served as crucial chemical instruments. As experimental claims increasingly relied on precise measurements by the late eighteenth century (a hallmark of the chemical revolution), sense evidence became "subjective" and, hence, a questionable foundation for proof. Chemists continued to rely on their senses, but proof became increasingly a matter of quantitative determination.

THEORY AND PRACTICE

The question of what constituted a primary chemical element was not a part of practical chemists' daily routine. Neither, prior to the late eighteenth century, was there a direct correlation between one's theoretical views and how one actually carried out chemical procedures, which can be seen by examining the impact of the mechanical philosophy on chemistry. Textbook writers such as Nicolas Lémery (1645–1715) attributed a substance's qualities to the shape of particles that composed it. But authors left such explanations behind when dealing with actual chemical operations. Robert Boyle (1627–1691), often labeled a mechanical philosopher, made a bigger impact on chemistry through his interests in practical knowledge and alchemy. Even Isaac Newton's (1642–1727) mechanism, which married particles to short-range forces, hardly touched chemical practice—although theorists such as Georges-Louis Leclerc de Buffon (1707–1788) hoped chemical attraction (affinities) could be explained mathematically with Newtonian forces. Working chemists continued to learn their trade through apprenticeship and to be guided by practical recipes. Acquiring tacit knowledge and practical skills, then, were certainly as important for the historical development of chemistry as theoretical knowledge.

It is, however, historically important that matter theory became linked to chemical research in an increasingly instrumental way by the eighteenth century. Paracelsus (1493–1541), who argued for the chemical foundation of medicine (iatrochemistry), claimed that Aristotle's four elements appeared in bodies as mercury, sulfur, and salt. Mercury was the principle of volatility and fusibility, sulfur of inflammability, and salt of incombustibility. Therefore, chemists might recognize a compound not only as heavy or wet, but also as liable to specific chemical processes.

Johann Joachim Becher (1635–1682) substituted three categories of earth for Paracelsus's principles and explained material change largely in terms of their combination with and release from compounds through processes such as combustion. His student George Ernst Stahl (1660–1734) further codified Becher's work, giving the name "phlogiston" (from the Greek verb "to inflame") to Becher's *terra pinguis* (the sulfur of inflammability) and teaching that phlogiston's presence was responsible for characteristics including metallicity, color, and inflammability. In France, the influential chemistry lecturer Guillaume François Rouelle (1703–1770) popularized the idea of phlogiston, associating it with fire. Others such as Joseph Priestley (1733–1804) identified it variously with electricity and hydrogen. Phlogiston was used to explain phenomena including combustion, calcination, and the quality of air, thereby organizing a number of research activities under a set of interconnecting theories and emphasizing the potential reversibility of chemical processes.

Others began considering the Aristotelian elements as material instruments. Stephen Hales (1677–1761) focused on the expansion of air and the way in which it could become "fixed" in bodies. Herman Boerhaave (1668–1738) went further, organizing his chemistry lectures largely around the investigative consequences of considering earth, water, air, and fire as instruments that afforded specific chemical processes. A Newtonian by public pronouncement, Boerhaave actually did much more to stimulate chemical research by focusing on the reactive effects of these elemental instruments. He

related fire (the substance of heat) to the primary processes of expansion and repulsion. He presented air and water as providing containers in which other particles were suspended. It wasn't long before these "instruments" themselves were subjected to chemical analysis, as investigators sought to understand whether their "instrumental" presence was chemically passive or active. Research in the second half of the eighteenth century was marked by investigations of newly discovered gases (qualitatively distinct "airs"), the role of heat, and, in the 1780s, the composition of water.

LITERARY TECHNOLOGY

Chemical theory and instrumental research practices were also linked in the way chemical knowledge came to be organized nomenclaturally and in analytical tables (chemistry's literary technology). Related to the heritage of alchemy and the various contexts in which chemical substances were discovered and used, chemical nomenclature was traditionally a colorfully unsystematic affair. Growing interest in chemical research in the second half of the eighteenth century, especially the investigation of a number of new "airs," led chemists to consider nomenclatural reform. Standard conventions for naming new substances would allow researchers from various communities to communicate. In 1787 Antoine Laurent Lavoisier (1743–1794), Louis Bernard Guyton de Morveau (1737–1816), Antoine François Fourcroy (1755–1809), and Claude Simon Berthollet (1748–1822) revamped chemistry's nomenclature totally, enunciating in their *Méthode de nomenclature chimique* a revolutionary way to structure chemistry's investigative knowledge and practices.

Oxygen's discovery and naming provides a good example. Recognized in the 1770s as a distinct "air" responsible for combustion, supporting respiration, and the process of calcination, it was variously named the "purest part of air," "fire air," "eminently respirable air," and "dephlogisticated air." Lavoisier focused on what he considered its most far-reaching characteristic and argued that it should be called "oxygen," the "generator" of acids. Not only did he use oxygen's causal properties to argue against the existence of phlogiston, he named the substance in a way that simultaneously reflected how the relation between these properties ought to be understood and how chemists ought to pursue future research.

Traditionally, the secretive nature of many alchemical and artisanal practices had combined with chemistry's lack of institutional and disciplinary unity to work against the development of a public, systematic means of recording compositional data. This began changing when Étienne François Geoffroy (1672–1731) presented his "Table of the different relationships observed between different substances" to the French Academy of Sciences in 1718. Recording and publishing these relationships, often called affinities, provided a handy way for chemists to share and expand empirical knowledge without having to agree on their theoretical explanation. As the century progressed, affinity and solvent tables became more sophisticated (recording, for example, how relations were observed), leading chemists to hope that their field might thereby gain the certainty of a scientific discipline. As was true with nomenclatural reform, this was largely achieved by Lavoisier and his colleagues, with revolutionary results. Lavoisier's 1789 textbook *Traité élémentaire de chimie* included tables whose structures redirected research along the same lines as chemistry's new nomenclature.

Lavoisier began his textbook by arguing that humans live in a Condillacian world; chemists should therefore build their discipline on a foundation of sensible facts. Chemistry's nomenclature should express only what chemists actively observed; its basic elements should be defined by laboratory procedures. In fact, Lavoisier began his "table of simple substances" with five elements that could never be isolated, but which he made responsible for fundamental chemical processes. Oxygen "generates" acidity, hydrogen "generates" water. Caloric, the substance of heat, interacts with chemical affinities to regulate composition and decomposition. In place of affinity and solvent tables, Lavoisier filled his textbook with tables that simultaneously recorded and predicted the combinatorial powers of elements such as oxygen. Together they formed an integrated research program intended to discipline chemistry.

CHEMISTRY'S INSTRUMENTALIZATION

Lavoisier's laboratory practices reflected what appeared on the pages of his book, the last third of which treated laboratory instruments. If primary elements couldn't be isolated, Lavoisier argued that their active presence could be quantitatively traced. Unmeasurable phlogiston was out, precision balances were in, as seen in his proof that water is compounded of hydrogen and oxygen. Affinities could not yet be quantified, but the effect of caloric on composition and decomposition could be quantitatively inferred by the melting of ice in an ice calorimeter—an instrument designed by Lavoisier. In general, nomenclature, instrumental theory, and measurement provided a research program for future chemists, in terms of both questions and methods for resolving them.

This culmination of chemistry's instrumentalization was, arguably, the essence of the chemical revolution. Whether others adopted Lavoisier's theories or followed the specifics of his research proposals, the modern discipline of chemistry was permanently marked by the instrumental bounds he prescribed.

See also **Alchemy; Apothecaries; Boerhaave, Herman; Boyle, Robert; Lavoisier, Antoine; Paracelsus; Priestley, Joseph.**

BIBLIOGRAPHY

Bensaude-Vincent, Bernadette. *Lavoisier. Memoires d'une révolution.* Paris, 1993.

Golinski, Jan. *Science as Public Culture: Chemistry and Enlightenment in Britain 1760–1820.* Cambridge, U.K., 1992.

Hannaway, Owen. *The Chemist and the Word: The Didactic Origins of Chemistry.* Baltimore, 1985.

Holmes, Frederick Lawrence. *Eighteenth-Century Chemistry as an Investigative Enterprise.* Berkeley, 1989.

Roberts, Lissa. "The Death of the Sensuous Chemist: the 'New' Chemistry and the Transformation of Sensuous Technology." *Studies in History and Philosophy of Science* 26 (1995): 503–529.

———. "Setting the Table: The Disciplinary Development of Eighteenth-Century Chemistry as Read through the Changing Structure of its Tables." In *The Literary Structure of Scientific Argument,* edited by Peter Dear, pp. 99–132. Philadelphia, 1991.

LISSA ROBERTS

CHILDHOOD AND CHILDREARING.

Children under sixteen constituted at least

one-third and as much as half of the population of early modern Europe at any given time. Despite that prominence, their thoughts and experiences only began to receive attention from historians in the late twentieth century. Early modern publications dealing with ideals of childhood and childrearing advice, by contrast, have long been much more accessible and therefore more fully scrutinized. After a brief summary of the relevant historiography, this article discusses both prescriptive and descriptive evidence on the experience of childhood and childrearing in the early modern era.

THE HISTORY OF CHILDHOOD

Until the second half of the twentieth century, historians of Europe generally neglected the history of childhood, assuming that such an endeavor was either impossible (because of source limitations) or pointless (because of the constancy of childish experience). The major turning point came in 1960 with the publication of Philippe Ariès's *Centuries of Childhood,* which famously made the provocative assertion that "in medieval society the idea of childhood did not exist" (Ariès, 1996). The worlds of adults and children, in other words, were not nearly as distinct as in modern times, and parents did not invest the amount of sentimental affection in their offspring that is typical of modern families. Since then a number of scholarly works have definitively established that this bold generalization is false, though to be fair to Ariès, the English translation of "idea" does not fully convey the sense of the original French "*sentiment.*"

More important, Ariès's controversial work triggered a flood of publications over the next four decades that took on the history of childhood as a subject worthy of scholarly scrutiny. Initially historians accepted Ariès's thesis with minor modifications, focusing on the causes of what were generally considered progressive changes. By the end of the 1980s, though, scholarly consensus had shifted toward continuity from medieval to modern times, much of it biologically predetermined. During the last decade or so of the twentieth century emphasis shifted back toward the importance of different cultural contexts in the ideals and experiences of childhood. Consequently the current points of contention among early modern historians involve which aspects of either the concept or experience of European childhood did in fact change by the beginning of the nineteenth century as well as where, when, and why.

CHILDHOOD PRESCRIBED: IDEALS AND CHILDREARING ADVICE

All debates about childhood during the early modern period revolved around two issues, namely the inherent nature of the child and the subsequent malleability of that nature. Roughly speaking, three approaches emerged in the prescriptive literature. One considered all children evil by nature and therefore in need of strong discipline; a second viewed children as essentially good but still in need of guidance; and a third conceived of children as largely blank slates, neither inherently good nor inherently evil and thus likewise requiring instruction. At the beginning of the early modern era, the first view dominated, but by the eighteenth century it had been mostly supplanted, at least among intellectuals and government leaders, by the second and third ways of thinking. A fourth, more radical, approach argued that education itself was the problem, but this theory had more of an immediate literary and philosophical than practical effect on childrearing.

The common emphasis of all but the most radical approach on the value and necessity of education was in fact a hallmark of the early modern period. Medieval authors, like their classical predecessors, tended to see an individual's childhood merely as indicative of his or her particular character and potential as an adult. This character was for the most part inherited and fixed, usually by social status. Talented individuals could further develop their talents through education, but no amount of training could overcome baseness of birth.

Christianity added an egalitarian aspect to the questions of universal human nature and the power of education, but the implications for childhood were ambivalent. On the one hand, Christian leaders since the time of Jesus had recognized the privileged place of childlike faith and innocence, evident in such Gospel passages as Mark 10:14–15: "Whosoever shall not receive the kingdom of God as a little child, he shall not enter therein." Some ancient authors believed that children had their own guardian angels, and in 374 the Christian emperors Valentinian, Valens, and Gratian made the common

Childhood and Childrearing. *The Children of Habert de Montfort* (councillor in the Paris parlement), painting by Philippe de Champaigne, 1649. THE ART ARCHIVE/MUSÉE SAINT DENIS REIMS/DAGLI ORTI

Roman practice of infanticide a capital offense. On the other hand, many of the church fathers, particularly in the West, stressed the immediate effects of original sin in all children. Saint Augustine (354–430) in particular refuted all notions of childish innocence, arguing that even the newborn infant possessed all of the selfish and lustful appetites that resulted from Adam and Eve's Fall. Augustine's influence was considerable, subsequently giving support to both theological arguments about limbo (a special part of hell reserved for unbaptized infants) and the case for infant baptism itself, a common practice by the early Middle Ages.

By the beginning of the early modern era, the tensions within this dualistic concept of childhood had led to two distinct ways of thinking about childrearing and therefore education. The Augustinian emphasis on the effects of original sin lay at the heart of the salvation process described by Martin Luther (1483–1546) and most other sixteenth-century Protestants. Luther often spoke affectionately about his own children and was devastated at two deaths

among them, yet he also acknowledged their inherently sinful nature, a universal theme in evangelical and Reformed publications. One German Protestant tract of the 1520s argued at length that all infant hearts craved "adultery, fornication, impure desires, lewdness, idol worship, belief in magic, hostility, quarrelling, passion, anger, strife, dissension, factiousness, hatred, murder, drunkenness, gluttony," and so on. Many Catholics shared this dark view of childhood. A century later the superior of the Oration Order in France agreed that "childhood is the vilest and most abject of human nature, after that of death."

Because all children were naturally inclined toward sin, such authors favored strict and constant discipline, usually including corporal punishment when necessary. Most of this training was to take place within the household, but clerical leaders often feared that fathers and mothers had not the time, inclination, or ability for proper religious instruction. In fact religious reformers frequently accused parents of spoiling and indulging their children rather than breaking their stubborn and selfish wills. Universal education consequently became a high priority for Protestant and Catholic leaders alike. Following Luther's example in 1529, each of the major denominations issued its own catechism for the instruction of the young and others in matters of faith. Many secular authorities made catechism classes or Sunday school mandatory; some governments attempted the same for basic grammar school.

The results were mixed. On the one hand, the number of both Latin and vernacular schools went up dramatically during the sixteenth and seventeenth centuries. In Lutheran Electoral Saxony, for instance, only 50 percent of parishes had schools for boys in 1580, and 10 percent had schools for girls. By 1675 the figures had risen to 94 percent and 40 percent respectively. Among Catholics, religious orders with special teaching missions, such as the Jesuits and the Ursulines, thrived, founding hundreds of secondary schools and colleges across Europe. At the same time attendance at such schools was uneven and in many instances almost nonexistent, especially at harvesttime, when the labor of the children was needed most. Visitation reports on various parishes also call into question just how much was learned at such schools, suggesting that initial attempts at both religious indoctrination and teaching literacy failed more than they succeeded. Even when numerous free elementary schools for the poor began to open in the late-seventeenth century, school attendance before the age of thirteen remained spotty until made compulsory almost two centuries later.

A second impetus for education of children outside the home came from a group of individuals with quite different ideas about human nature and childhood. From the fourteenth century on, Italian, and later northern, humanists conducted a literary campaign to promote education as a moral as well as a civic virtue. Human nature, they argued, was both essentially good and malleable. Fluency in the *ars humanitatis,* or humanities, provided the citizens of a republic such as Florence or Venice with the clarity of thinking and eloquence of expression that were essential in all political debates and decisions. The practical skills taught by humanist tutors, moreover, gave young students a leg up on many highly coveted government positions. Finally, a humanist education, admittedly available to a privileged few, had a civilizing effect on young children, allowing them to fulfill the individual potential for good that its advocates saw in all individuals, regardless of birth.

Outside of Italy the humanist education of children took on a much greater moral significance. The Christian humanist Desiderius Erasmus (1466?–1536) elegantly encapsulated his childrearing philosophy in the series of books and pamphlets he published during the 1520s: "[A child] ought to imbibe, as it were, with the milk that he suckles, the nectar of education, [for] he will most certainly turn out to be an unproductive brute unless at once and without delay he is subjected to a process of intensive instruction." Unlike Luther and other pessimists about human nature, Erasmus believed a child's nature was largely unformed, affected by original sin but not incapacitated by it. His method therefore comprised a mixture of play and learning as well as a noticeable absence of corporal punishment. Education—meaning manners as well as literacy and religious instruction—was the indispensable shaper of the adult to be. For Erasmus parental neglect of a child's education was a worse crime than infanticide, since it sentenced the unwitting offspring to a life of ignorance, depravity, and overall bestiality.

During the sixteenth and seventeenth centuries countless pamphlets, tracts, and books appeared on childhood and childrearing. Most took either a Lutheran or an Erasmian line on the subject of a child's nature and education. Among the most innovative publications were those written by English Puritan authors, who combined elements of both approaches. Though inherently inclined toward sin, they argued, the child's will could effectively be channeled rather than broken. Again the household was the ideal setting for this type of formation, and both parents shared a responsibility in childrearing as a whole—a task that predecessors consistently assigned primarily to the father. Puritan authors also displayed the most attention to the particular circumstances of childhood and the most successful methods of education.

By the time of the Enlightenment the negative view of childhood was in clear decline among the learned elites of Europe, though it never died out.

Two authors played especially important roles in this transformation. In *Some Thoughts concerning Education* (1693), the English philosopher John Locke (1632–1704) compared the mind of a child to a blank piece of paper or unformed piece of wax, possessing no innate tendencies toward good or evil. Rather, Locke argued, the responsibility for the child's future character lay with the parents, who could see that the child was well-educated in morality and letters or neglect it to malignant influences. Like Erasmus, Locke considered reason and play much more effective tools than the rod but deplored mothers who weakened their children by coddling them. A self-acknowledged disciple of Locke, Jean-Jacques Rousseau (1712–1778) went to the farthest extreme in his denial of the child's fallen nature, arguing in *Émile* (1762) that the very nature of the child was good and that society, including formalized education, corrupted that goodness. Rousseau's notion of a "natural" upbringing lent support to the contemporary maternal breast-feeding movement in Europe and likewise coincided with many social reformers' complaints about schools and other child institutions. Not until the nineteenth century, though, did his pedagogical philosophy have a significant impact on formal education.

CHILDHOOD EXPERIENCED: *INFANTIA* (BIRTH TO AGE TWO)

The first two years of a child's life, known as *infantia* in most early modern descriptions, were probably the most dangerous in terms of survival. In addition to a high rate of miscarriages and stillbirths, early modern Europe was characterized by an extremely high mortality rate for infants, at least by modern standards. Only seven or eight out of ten newborn babies would live to the age of one, and an additional two out of ten would die before reaching the age of ten. Many factors contributed to this predicament, including swaddling and other poor hygiene conditions, fatal childhood diseases (particularly smallpox, measles, and tuberculosis), and inadequate nourishment. Most of these causes were beyond any parent's control. Physicians could offer no effective cures for any of the deadly diseases and beyond that were unavailable to the great majority of the population, who instead relied on various home remedies, potions, ointments, regimens, and charms. Even a potentially harmful practice that was deliberate, such as swaddling, had a basis in some practical concerns, such as keeping the infant warm and restrained while left unattended for long periods of time. The same good intentions were true of sharing a bed with an infant, which sometimes resulted in overlaying, or accidental suffocation of the baby. Consequently there was no discernible difference in infant mortality by social class until the eighteenth century and no significant improvement overall until the late nineteenth century.

Then as now, the subject of nourishment and breast-feeding in particular could be quite controversial. Whether by choice or necessity, most women apparently nursed their own children at home. This practice was endorsed by physicians as well as folk healers, who recognized mother's milk as the healthiest option, especially given the absence of pasteurized milk until the late nineteenth century. The age of weaning could be anytime between six months and two years, depending on various factors, such as the economic status of the parents, health of the mother, sex and size of the infant, local customs, and so forth. At the same time the practice of wet-nursing, or sending a child to another woman in the country, was also a common practice, particularly in large cities, such as Paris and Milan. An infant's chances of survival were three to four times greater if nursed by its own mother rather than a stranger, but not until the eighteenth century did wealthy women heed the advice of physicians on this question. Many poor working women, on the other hand, had no alternative to wet-nursing for their children and thus continued to send their infants to "baby farms," with their shockingly high rates of infant mortality, well into the nineteenth century.

Infant abandonment was also a fairly common phenomenon in early modern Europe. During the sixteenth and seventeenth centuries the typical foundling (*enfant trouvé,* French; *expósito,* Spanish; *gettello,* Italian; *Findelkind,* German) was the product of an illicit union, abandoned by a single mother who feared the consequences to her reputation. Since, outside of Italy, the numbers were relatively small, and 80 to 90 percent of foundlings under the age of two died within a short period, various foundling homes, orphanages, and hospitals were generally able to cope with those infants who survived into childhood. The eighteenth century, however, witnessed a sharp increase in the number of abandoned children in Europe, particularly in large cities. In Paris, for instance, the annual abandonment rate more than tripled between 1700 and 1789, going from 1,700 to about 6,000 foundlings per year. By the end of the century, one in four babies was abandoned in the cities of Toulouse and Milan, a rate that continued to climb everywhere in Europe until the mid-nineteenth century. Most of the babies continued to be illegitimate, but married couples also increasingly abandoned their children, sometimes as a temporary child-care measure. Many local studies have established a close correlation between rising food prices (often due to famine) and increased abandonment.

The most extreme fate for an unwanted child was death by infanticide. Here too the majority of the perpetrators convicted during the early modern period were single mothers, usually domestic maids, who feared the reputational and economic consequences of giving birth to a bastard child. A number of new ordinances and legal codes during the sixteenth century, most notably the Holy Roman Empire's *Carolina* (1532), brought new attention to infanticide and prescribed precise measures for preventing, detecting, and punishing the crime. There is no basis for believing that such laws corresponded to an actual increase in infanticides. Their social impact, however, was undeniable. By the eighteenth century, infanticide had become the most common cause of female executions in Europe. Only a number of tracts by Enlightenment authors eventually roused pity for the situations of most of these women and led to the abolishment of capital punishment for infanticide.

Historians in the Ariès school have cited the unbearably high possibility of an infant's death as an argument that parents would invest few emotional or material resources in a child until at least the age of two. Here the historical evidence can offer no satisfactory resolution. Despite the obvious logic of withholding one's affections until it was safer as well as the frequent reuse of the names of dead babies, many parents clearly grieved greatly at the loss of an infant. At the same time abandonments that were fairly certain to end in the child's death continued to grow in number throughout the early modern period. No historical evidence is likely to resolve this paradox.

CHILDHOOD EXPERIENCED: *PUERITIA* (AGE TWO TO TWELVE)

Having survived infancy, an early modern child was freed to explore the world outside its crib. Toddlers and small children of the era probably experienced much less adult oversight than modern children—a fact clearly evident by the high number of accidental deaths recorded. In any event they spent the majority of their time with female relatives—mothers, sisters, aunts, grandmothers, nurses, or governesses. Of the major achievements of toddlerhood, walking upright was clearly valued the greatest, prompting parents to employ a variety of strings and props or— among middle- and upper-class families— backboards and iron collars for girls to speed the process. Toilet training, by contrast, often occurred late or haphazardly.

Above all, children under seven enjoyed relative immunity from the world of work. With the exception of a few small tasks requiring little strength or skill (for example, collecting firewood or feeding livestock), their time was devoted completely to play. Some of this entertainment might be provided by adults in the form of nursery rhymes, lullabies, riddles, counting games, and so on. The stories later known as fairy tales were likewise passed down from generation to generation, each invoking its own mixture of fantasy, humor, and monsters ranging from trolls and bogeymen to Turks and—during the Thirty Years' War—Swedes. Some common toys, such as dolls, marbles, and spinning tops, were manufactured, but most playthings were improvised until the proto-industrialization of the eighteenth century brought specialized toy shops selling jigsaw puzzles, board games, and miniature soldiers.

The age of seven marked a key transition in many respects. Until that point, for instance, children were usually dressed in unisex tunics or gowns. Afterward they began to wear clothing more appropriate to their genders, boys putting on breeches and possibly carrying a knife (or a sword among the nobility), girls wearing dresses and skirts. This symbolic joining of adult society usually corresponded to new life experiences for the child. The Catholic Church had long taught that seven was the age of reason (and therefore conscience); popular wisdom held that this was when children became teachable. On farms this meant full participation in the adult work as divided by gender. Occasionally a boy was sent to an apprenticeship at this age, although that usually came more around the age of twelve to fourteen, as did domestic servitude for girls. If a family could afford it, a boy (and sometimes a girl) might be sent to a Latin grammar school, a vernacular school, or one of the unregulated and independent "corner schools." Poor families in cities might send a child to beg in the streets at this age, when she or he was young enough to evoke pity and old enough to make the most of it. Finally, during the seventeenth and eighteenth centuries more and more children were employed in weaving and other forms of cottage industry, in some cases earning up to one-quarter of the household's income. In general child labor was considered quite normal until the excesses of nineteenth-century industrialization.

The new gender specificity in work was also evident in recreation and leisure, with boys and girls gradually playing less with one another and instead separating into "gangs" of boys and smaller groups of girls. Games and pastimes included various forms of chasing, hunting, racing, daring, guessing, and pretending, with sports preferred among the older boys. Occasionally youth groups, especially boys, would engage in rough street games, petty thefts, pranks, and vandalism. In cities these gangs might also engage in violent confrontations with groups from other parishes or neighborhoods, each carving out its own "turf" against rivals. Secular authorities throughout Europe repeatedly complained of rowdy and unruly children in the streets, apparently to little effect.

There was no indisputable age when childhood ended, just as there was no universal age of reaching adulthood. Both transitions, rather, tended to be determined by relative degrees of independence from one's parents and immediate family. By the age of sixteen, for instance, at least one-half of children had left their family homes to work as servants or apprentices, sometimes for relatives but normally for strangers. Usually this involved a written contract specifying the respective expectations of master and servant, including money paid by the child's parent (for an apprenticeship) or by the employer (for a domestic servant). Ostensibly the main purpose of the arrangement, typically lasting three to seven years, was for a boy to learn certain marketable skills and for a girl to earn the money for her dowry. The sojourn away from home, however, also

had the effect of reducing a household's expenditures while the child was away. Those teenagers who remained at home usually worked to contribute to the family's income. For this reason education beyond the age of twelve or thirteen continued to be a rarity in early modern society. Even among nobles service as a page in another aristocratic household was considered essential to proper socialization and thus the norm until the eighteenth century, at which point formal education became more important. Proto-industrialization and industrialization also contributed to the decline of apprenticeships and servant placements among artisanal and lower-class families, since a youth's labor was now an asset needed at home.

CONCLUSION

Within a relatively short span of forty years, the history of childhood has become a burgeoning field of research. Still, the knowledge of the ideals of childrearing far surpasses the understanding of the everyday experiences of early modern children. Like their adult counterparts, children were culturally diverse yet commonly bound by their era's biological and technological "limits of the possible." Apart from their great susceptibility to premature death or the relative primitiveness of their living conditions, they apparently shared more with modern children than not, at least until the age of seven. Even then a key social transformation was well under way by the close of the eighteenth century, with ever more children starting school rather than work. The abolition of child labor in Europe remained far off, but the foundations for modern childhood had been laid.

See also **Education; Family; Gender; Motherhood and Childbearing; Orphans and Foundlings; Youth.**

BIBLIOGRAPHY

Primary Sources

Locke, John. *Some Thoughts concerning Education.* Edited by John W. Yolton and Jean S. Yolton. Oxford, 1989. First published in 1693.

Rousseau, Jean-Jacques. *Émile.* Translated by Allan Bloom. New York, 1979. First published in 1762.

Secondary Sources

Ariès, Philippe. *Centuries of Childhood.* Translated by Robert Baldick. London, 1996. Originally published in 1960.

Cunningham, Hugh. *Children and Childhood in Western Society since 1500.* London, 1995.

Haas, Louis. *The Renaissance Man and His Children: Childbirth and Early Childhood in Florence, 1300–1600*. London, 1998.

McClure, Ruth K. *Coram's Children: The London Foundling Hospital in the Eighteenth Century*. New Haven and London, 1981.

Ozment, Steven. *When Fathers Ruled: Family Life in Reformation Europe*. Cambridge, Mass., 1983.

Ozment, Steven, ed. *Three Behaim Boys: Growing Up in Early Modern Germany: A Chronicle of Their Lives*. New Haven, 1990.

Pollock, Linda A. *Forgotten Children: Parent-Child Relations from 1500 to 1900*. Cambridge, U.K., 1983.

Strauss, Gerald. *Luther's House of Learning: Indoctrination of the Young in the German Reformation*. Baltimore, 1978.

Sussman, George D. *Selling Mother's Milk: The Wet-Nursing Business in France, 1715–1914*. Urbana, Ill., Chicago, and London, 1982.

JOEL F. HARRINGTON

CHRISTIANITY. *See* **Anabaptism; Calvinism; Catholicism; Church of England; Clergy; Huguenots; Lutheranism; Methodism; Orthodoxy, Greek; Orthodoxy, Russian; Papacy and Papal States; Puritanism.**

CHRISTINA (SWEDEN) (1626–1689; ruled 1632–1654), queen of Sweden. The daughter of Gustavus II Adolphus of Sweden and Maria Eleonora of Brandenburg, Christina was one of the most remarkable people in Sweden's early modern history. She was intellectually gifted, well educated, intensely interested in the ideas and culture of her period, clever, passionate, self-centered, and deeply troubled. Her life falls into three periods: childhood, when she was heir to the throne of Sweden and for twelve years under the control of a regency (1632–1644); her time as a governing queen (1644–1654); and the thirty-five years she lived as a former queen and cultural dilettante in Rome (1654–1689).

It is usually said that Christina's birth was a disappointment. Gustavus II Adolphus and Maria Eleonora had lost one infant daughter, and a second child was stillborn. Everyone hoped for a male heir, and when Christina was born, she was at first thought to be a boy. The truth was quickly apparent. As the only surviving child of the royal couple, however, she was raised as heir to the throne. Following her father's death at the Battle of Lützen in 1632, her upbringing became the responsibility of a regency. She was soon separated from her mother, whose melancholy reached dangerous extremes, and raised in the family of her aunt, Katarina. She was educated as a male, learning to ride, fence, and shoot; early on she was exposed to the business of state. Her formal education was in modern and classical languages, the classics, theology, and history. Her passions were philosophy, art, and literature. Her tutor was Johannes Matthiae Gothus, and her mentor in politics was the chancellor, Axel Oxenstierna.

Her life as queen began in 1644 when she reached eighteen, the age of majority. Her ideas and desires put her in conflict with the chancellor and his colleagues in the Council of State. The conflict was both personal and political. The constitutional balance of power in Sweden, which involved the crown, council, nobility, and commons, had shifted with Gustavus II Adolphus's accession in 1611. Sweden seemed to be moving toward becoming an aristocracy, in which real power was in the hands of a few powerful nobles. Axel Oxenstierna was the main architect of these developments, and Christina rejected them.

Christina engaged in several Machiavellian political struggles, which included offsetting the power of the old council nobles, securing peace in Germany, and guaranteeing the survival of hereditary monarchy. She won them all. At court she used favorites, whom she rewarded with important offices, titles, and crown properties. The council swelled from twenty-five to nearly fifty members, and the nobility more than doubled in size. Her excessive donations of the crown properties (the assets of a domain state) shifted the property-owning balance, sapped the state's financial resources, and triggered serious social unrest among the commons.

In the matter of the Thirty Years' War, her wishes for peace were opposed by the chancellor and his supporters, who wanted the war to continue. Sweden was becoming a "warfare state," the costs of security were being paid by allies and ene-

Christina (Sweden). Portrait by Sebastien Bourdon. THE ART ARCHIVE/MUSEO DEL PRADO MADRID/ALBUM/JOSEPH MARTIN

mies, and the nobility benefited. The Peace of Westphalia in 1648 was a victory for Christina.

The succession issue was more complex, involving personal identity, religion, and politics. By 1650 Christina had made it clear she could not marry. This decision arose from her own identity struggles, which may have been complicated by psychological and physiological factors. She also became more discontented with what she thought of as the stifling Lutheran orthodoxy in Sweden, and she was increasingly attracted to Catholicism. Her sense of duty drove her to arrange the succession of her cousin Charles X Gustav of Pfalz-Zweibrücken and his heirs. To do so, she exploited the social and economic concerns of the commons, the tension between the lower nobility and the council aristocracy, and her personal favorites at court. Her abdication, departure from Sweden in 1654, and subsequent conversion to Catholicism followed naturally from these successes.

The longest period of her life, 1654–1689, was spent mostly in Rome. Sensationalizers gossiped about her as a meddler in international affairs, a murderer, and the lover of a cardinal during this period. In fact, she was a minor player in European politics, most notably when she tried to secure the crown of Naples via an arrangement with France in 1656. The murder accusation arises from her prosecution and execution in 1657 of the Marquis Gian Rinaldo Monaldesco, who betrayed those negotiations to Spain. Her relationship with Cardinal Decio Azzolino was platonic.

Christina was intensely intellectual and wanted to bring mainstream European culture to Sweden. She collected works of art and books, and staged plays and ballets at court. She invited European scholars to Sweden. René Descartes died there while her guest. She also founded the first Swedish "academy." When she left Sweden, this spirit and her collections went with her. Sweden became a poorer place as a result, while Rome benefited from her lifelong commitment to the arts and culture.

See also **Charles X Gustav (Sweden); Gustavus II Adolphus (Sweden); Oxenstierna, Axel; Sweden; Thirty Years' War (1618–1649); Vasa Dynasty (Sweden).**

BIBLIOGRAPHY

Lewis, Paul. *Queen of Caprice: A Biography of Kristina of Sweden.* London and New York, 1962.

Mackenzie, Faith Compton. *The Sibyl of the North: The Tale of Christina, Queen of Sweden.* Boston, 1931.

Masson, Georgina. *Queen Christina.* New York, 1968.

Stolpe, Sven. *Drottning Kristina.* Stockholm, 1966.

Weibull, Curt. *Christina of Sweden.* Stockholm, 1966.

BYRON J. NORDSTROM

CHRONOMETER.

CHRONOMETER. The design, construction, and successful replication of marine chronometers, or precision timekeepers, was one of the great scientific triumphs of the early modern period. This scientific instrument was crucial to the accurate determination of longitude (or east-west direction from a given meridian on the globe) to vessels at sea. Hence the development of marine chronometers was a pivotal factor in early modern European navigation, transport, trade, cartography, and colonial enterprise.

THE MAGNITUDE OF THE PROBLEM

Determining longitude remained the most persistent problem facing oceangoing vessels in the early modern world. With the discovery of the New World, the expansion of trade, and the conquest of new territories, there soon followed an increased movement of men, precious metals, manufactured goods, and raw commodities. Hence, more and more was at stake for European ships traveling on the oceans. While scientists and mathematicians had proposed several methods to determine longitude at sea, none of these methods had yet proved practical. The best trained navigators relied on dead reckoning, a crude estimate of the speed and distance traveled, to learn their ship's longitude. In practicality, they could only hope for propitious winds and currents to get them to their ports or destinations safely. In 1707 four British warships under the command of Admiral Clowdisley Shovell crashed into the jagged rocks of the Scilly Isles off the southwest tip of England. As the warships sank, almost 2,000 men perished because of the navigational error. Less dramatic results of erroneous readings of longitude often resulted in protracted voyages, a not inconsiderable danger when scurvy and other disease could break out after ninety days of vitamin C deprivation. Sagging shipboard morale, exhausted food supplies, and even mutiny resulted from unexpected delays at sea.

THE SCIENTIFIC BACKGROUND

While a ship's latitude could be easily established at sea by measuring the height of the sun (or stars, particularly the North Star, above the horizon) with the aid of a good sextant, determining longitude proved a more stubborn problem. The best scientific minds of Europe wrestled with the problem. In 1530 the Flemish astronomer and mathematician Gemma Frisius (1508–1555) published a solution. He predicated that since the Earth rotates 360 degrees in 24 hours, or 15 degrees of longitude per hour, the mechanical clock might be the answer to the longitude problem. He suggested that if an accurate timekeeper were to record the local time of the ship's departure port, and if this were compared to the local time of the ship at noon, (determined by measuring the highest point of the sun in the sky), the difference could indicate longitude. Obviously the difference in hours would be multiplied by 15 degrees, with further refinements for minutes and seconds of time to get correct readings for minutes and seconds of arc. Frisius's solution would ultimately prove the basis of the solution, but innumer-

able practical problems intervened. How to build a clock that would keep accurate time in a rough sea or a pitching and rolling ship? Since ordinary clocks often became erroneous over time, the challenge of accuracy was paramount. Constructing a clock that would be unaffected by changes in humidity, gravity, and temperature presented further obstacles.

Although the clock method would ultimately prove the winner, the logic of this was not at all apparent to many talented scientific and mathematical minds of the early modern era. Rival theories abounded. Among those offered were Galileo Galilei's (1564–1642) proposal of measuring and using the motions of Jupiter's four moons as celestial clocks, and comparing the times when these moons eclipsed one another with the same astronomical event at his local time. While Galileo's method was theoretically correct, and proved useful for finding longitude on land once accurate predictive tables of the positions of Jupiter moons could be drawn up, it was ultimately useless at sea. While some astronomers, including the Danish Ole Roemer (1644–1710) and the Frenchman Jean Dominque Cassini (1625–1712) continued to refine Galileo's method after his death, other astronomers proposed alternate solutions. John Flamsteed (1646–1719) toiled in Greenwich to construct star tables to aid in the determination of longitude. Christiaan Huygens (1629–1695), an accomplished astronomer, worked on both the mechanical and astronomical methods simultaneously. However, not all solutions offered were high-minded. One, proposed by Humphry Ditton in 1713, suggested a series of anchored boats spaced 600 miles apart that would fire cannons to alert nearby vessels of their proximity to known positions of the great guns.

FAME AND MONEY PROVIDE INCENTIVE

In 1598 King Philip III of Spain (ruled 1598–1621) offered a considerable life pension to the discoverer of longitude. Louis XIV (ruled 1643–1715) of France spent considerable money and energy on the problem by erecting the Royal Observatory at Paris and attracting (and paying handsomely) the best minds of Europe to work there. In 1714 the English parliament offered a reward of 20,000 pounds for a solution that would prove no more than one-half degree of error after a six-week voyage at sea. The prize offered in 1714 did exactly what its authors had hoped—it induced a wide array of talented men to labor doggedly at a new solution. The Longitude Act of 1714 established a committee to judge submissions and authorized the award of partial funds to stimulate further investigation of promising proposals. Members of the committee included the most outstanding astronomers and mathematicians of the time, including Edmund Halley, James Bradley, and Neville Maskelyne.

JOHN HARRISON'S CLOCKS

The production of the precision marine mechanical timekeeper was the accomplishment of a self-educated English clockmaker of modest origins, John Harrison (1693–1776). Starting his career by working on wooden clocks, in about 1720 Harrison designed and built a tower clock in Brocklesby Park. As early as 1722 he hit upon three solutions that he would incorporate in his later clocks. He used lignum vitae, a tropical wood that required no oiling since the hardwood naturally secreted its own grease. Eliminating lubricants eliminated the friction and errors introduced by changing viscosity. He also invented the gridiron pendulum, which used strips of two metals—steel and brass—to compensate for the shrinkage in metals caused by temperature changes in the atmosphere. He subsequently designed a new escapement to eliminate friction and wear on the teeth connecting the wheels and the oscillator and referred to his design as a "grasshopper escapement." In his efforts to produce a winning precision scientific instrument, Harrison worked for thirty years and produced four prototypes, known to scientists as H-1, H-2, H-3, and H-4. Each model contained significant technical improvements. Each model earned him the grudging and slow respect of a series of influential friends, if not the commissioners of the Board of Longitude, who alone could award the prize money. Ever his own harshest critic, Harrison continued to scrutinize the defects of his own solutions and to correct them. He completed his final masterpiece, H-4, in 1759: His final solution was a large pocket watch, five inches in diameter, and weighing only three pounds.

TESTING THE CHRONOMETERS ON REAL VOYAGES

The acid test for the Board of Longitude was the accuracy of a timekeeper at sea over time. Harrison's son and assistant, William Harrison, set forth in November 1761, with H-4, aboard the H.M.S. *Deptford* from the English port of Plymouth for Jamaica. William was expected to guard the watch, to wind it daily, and with astronomer John Robison to keep careful records and make astronomical observations of the longitude in Jamaica. During the three-month journey, the ship's captain several times chose to value Harrison's estimation of longitude over the ship's official navigator. Despite rough seas on the return voyage, the watch had lost just under two minutes outbound and homebound combined. Having met the margin of error specified in 1714, Harrison fully deserved the prize. However, machinations of opponents favoring the lunar distance method delayed his receiving the reward. Nathaniel Bliss, the presiding astronomer royal of 1763, declared that the accuracy of H-4 was a chance occurrence and demanded a second trial voyage. In 1764 William Harrison set forth on yet another trial voyage, this time to Barbados. Again the H-4 proved successful: Since it had an error of only 54 seconds over a period of 156 days, it had far exceeded the standards demanded. Delays, favoritism of the lunar distance method, and constant amending of the rules help explain why Harrison was so slow to be recognized the rightful winner of the prize. Required in 1765 to dismantle his watch piece by piece and to explain the function of each part, the board next asked Harrison to reassemble the watch, to surrender H-4 to the judges, and to build two replicas of the H-4 without using the original as a model. Finally awarded one half of the prize money, Harrison had precious little leverage to get the whole prize out of the committee.

REPLICATING AND IMPROVING THE CLOCK

In 1767, the Board, still reluctant to award John Harrison the full prize, hired the respected watchmaker Larcum Kendall to replicate H-4. The attempt to replicate the intricate timekeeper consumed two-and-a-half years of work from Kendall, who named his model K-1. By 1770, the aging Harrison had not yet finished building the first of the two watches the Board had ordered him to make (subsequently called H-5.) Eager for yet another opportunity to test the precious instrument on a long sea voyage, the Board entrusted Captain James Cook to take the K-1 with him on his voyage to Tahiti to observe the transit of Venus. Cook also took with him three other timekeepers made by clockmaker John Arnold. By the time Cook returned to England in July 1775, the famous sea captain was full of praise for Kendall's replica of Harrison's H-4. Cook set an example for other ship captains when he prominently chose to carry the K-1 on his third expedition. Soon other watchmakers were producing accurate imitations of Harrison's H-4 and even improving on the design. John Arnold, Thomas Mudge, and an increasing number of nautical instrument makers were soon offering marine chronometers for sale. Increased precision in mapmaking, navigation, and ocean crossings resulted. Despite the widespread use today of satellite-informed Global Positioning Systems to give ships instant knowledge of their positions at sea, ships still carry chronometers as backup systems. They have proved reliable, simple, and astonishingly accurate.

See also **Cartography and Geography; Clocks and Watches; Communication and Transportation; Exploration; Scientific Instruments; Shipbuilding and Navigation; Shipping.**

BIBLIOGRAPHY

Andrewes, William J. H., ed. *The Quest for Longitude.* Cambridge, Mass., 1996.

Bedini, Silvio A. *The Pulse of Time: Galileo Galilei, the Determination of Longitude, and the Pendulum Clock.* Florence, 1991.

Gould, Rupert T. *John Harrison and His Timekeepers.* London, 1978.

Howse, Derek. *Greenwich Time and the Discovery of Longitude.* London, 1997.

Landes, David. *Revolution in Time: Clocks and the Making of the Modern World.* Cambridge, Mass., 1983.

Quill, Humphrey. *John Harrison, the Man Who Found Longitude.* London, 1966.

Sobel, Dava. *Longitude: The True Story of a Lone Genius Who Solved the Greatest Scientific Problem of His Time.* New York, 1995.

Sobel, Dava, and William J. H. Andrewes. *The Illustrated Longitude.* New York, 1998.

Taylor, E. G. R. *The Haven-Finding Art: A History of Navigation from Odysseus to Captain Cook.* London, 1971.

MARTHA BALDWIN

CHURCH AND STATE RELATIONS.

The relationship between governmental institutions and Christian denominations changed dramatically and varied widely in Europe during the early modern period (1450–1789). The variations in this relationship hinged largely on the characteristics of local government, or the "state," and of local ecclesiastical institutions, or the "church." Those variations depended also on the intentions and abilities of each to exert its will and have its way. Such variations, by definition, were local. The relationship between church and state in any local configuration in Europe was also affected by broader, long-term factors in the political, religious, and cultural development of Western civilization. Those factors included the tradition of caesaropapism, the early modern growth of both national states and monarchical power, the religious changes generally understood under the heading "Reformation," and the cultural and political changes associated with the Enlightenment.

CAESAROPAPISM

Caesaropapism, the approach to government in which both royal and priestly powers are held, in their fullness, by one ruler, was a theory that stood behind attempts by leaders of church and state to exert sovereign control over territories in Europe. This traditional theory had a very long lineage. The term is typically applied to the sort of government created in the Byzantine Empire, with church subordinated to the state. As such, it has been viewed mainly as a relic of the past after the fall of Byzantium to the Ottoman Turks in the mid-fifteenth century. The concept, however, can arguably be found in descriptions of kingship from the earliest Western historical sources, including the *Epic of Gilgamesh,* a literary masterpiece from ancient Mesopotamia. The notion motivated much later efforts to establish complete control over European territories, and not just by secular rulers hoping to subordinate ecclesiastical persons and institutions. Some Christian leaders in early modern Europe had sought to create ecclesiastical control over governmental authorities.

Any explanation of the relationship between church and state in this era must be broad enough to account not just for caesaropapist political leaders in Italian communes and in Germany, Spain, France, England, and Germany, who had long claimed control over religion, but also for individuals like Martin Luther (1483–1546). He could insist that princely power was superior to ecclesiastical authority and, apparently, sense no implicit contradiction between that position and his view of individual religious conscience as being above the authority of either bishops or princes. In practical terms, he and other contemporary religious leaders, both Catholic and Protestant, often wrote like determined theocrats who felt comfortable defining truth. Luther rejected papal supremacy while asserting what should or should not be considered the Word of God. In Geneva, John Calvin (1509–1564) headed an aristocratic political system in which capital punishment, and other forms of restraint, could be meted out for holding anti-Trinitarian views. Divine right monarchy more in line with the standard definition of caesaropapism could be found in England under early Stuart rulers like James I (ruled 1603–1625) and Charles I (ruled 1625–1649), who argued that their power came directly from God. They demonstrated their commitment by making religious and political changes without recourse to Parliament or archbishops.

Caesaropapism remained a goal throughout the early modern period, but it was an increasingly unattainable goal, as the history of the papacy illustrates. Even today, one imagines the pope of this earlier period as possessing extraordinary political and religious power, and a determination to exert his against all opponents. This image remains despite the deep personal inconsistencies of prince-popes like Paul III. Although he reestablished the Roman Inquisition in 1542 and convened the Council of Trent in 1545, during his reign this tribunal demonstrated moderation toward those charged with heresy, and toward the control of suspicious religious texts. The legates Paul sent to Trent, moreover, exercised but limited control of the council's agenda. Popes like Pius V (reigned 1566–1572) and Paul V (reigned 1605–1621) were famous for their centralizing politics in the Papal States, and for their thunderous proclamations of religious and political right in controversies like the Gunpowder Plot in England (1605). Their plans did not have the effect of creating anything close to theocracy, however. Paul V attempted to centralize political control in Bologna during his reign, using client relationship with Bolognese nobles to do so. He was only partly successful, however, as family interests, both social and economic, were more important to those nobles than participation in papal-controlled government. Paul was no more successful in bringing the Venetian Republic to heel through his interdict in 1606 and 1607 than he was in convincing Catholics in England to reject the demand there for an oath of loyalty to the crown. By the third quarter of the seventeenth century, indirect challenges to papal authority fueled by Enlightenment thought culminated in political pressures that forced Clement XIV (reigned 1769–1774) to suppress the Jesuit religious order—the group popularly remembered as unchallenged enforcers of the papal Counter-Reformation—in 1773. The head of the Jesuit order, Lorenzo Ricci, died in the prison of Castel Sant'Angelo in 1775, and both Clement and his successor, Pius VI (reigned 1775–1799), were carried off to France as prisoners.

EARLY MODERN POLITICAL CHANGES

The expanding national states and growing monarchical powers came to dominate the relationship between church and state. The progressive extension of ecclesiastical jurisdiction in France, up until about the fourteenth century, was overcome at the beginning of the sixteenth with the 1516 Concordat of Bologna, which delivered to French monarchs control over episcopal appointments. In this, French kings like Francis I (ruled 1515–1547) exhibited the increasing tendency among such heads of state to assume responsibility for establishing and defending their local definition of "true" religion. In England, Henry VIII (ruled 1509–1547) reinforced plans to create full control over the church with the old medieval assertion that kings had to answer for the exercise of their authority to God alone. In doing so, he anticipated the full-fledged "divine right" argument elaborated by his Stuart successors, James I and Charles II. In other territories, especially within the Holy Roman Empire, princes and magistrates without monarchical claims sought to control religious behavior to a greater or lesser extent, and often for very practical reasons. Some found that toleration leading to relative religious pluralism was both financially profitable and politically necessary. More often, local rulers sought to advance state power into matters of human behavior—like marriage—earlier controlled by church courts. Some magistrates had begun to insist on the right to such control as early as the later fourteenth century, but the action is probably best seen as consistent with government growth by extension of competence and by restriction of previous held immunities from secular law. Such extension characterized monarchical and magisterial governments in the early modern period. For some historians, this growth added up to "social disciplining" that was widespread and effective. While there certainly are some examples where the combination of church and state authority resulted in genuine behavioral change—as in the low rate of illegitimate births in Geneva between 1560 and 1580—whether or not the highly developed plans for social control were efficacious on any broad scale is yet to be determined. Instead, it might be better to view growing secular governments and their increasing control over church institutions as part of an established pattern going back to German kings who dominated the papacy in the tenth century. The increasingly successful attempts to exercise secular control over ecclesiastical institutions in the sixteenth, seventeenth, and eighteenth centuries targeted more than just the Roman Catholic denomination, of course, but the goal was strikingly similar to that of heads of state in earlier actions.

REFORMATION

The religious changes usually categorized under the term *Reformation* also had a profound but local effect on the relationship between church and state in the early modern period. Efforts to improve religious life and devotion across European society, plus the rejection of papal leadership as decisive in creating any such improvement, constituted the beginning—but only the beginning—of the dissolution of the idea that a Christian state had to be a religious and political unity. Writers from the age of Constantine (ruled 306–337 C.E.) all the way through Martin Luther and the age of Reformation took for granted that essential unity. During this early modern era, however, relative religious pluralism—most often in the form of varying Christian denominations—became a fact of life. That pluralism emerged due to increasing examples of the expression of religious dissent, with Luther's Ninety-five Theses (1517) serving as the crucial instance of the amplification of such dissent. But dissent of this nature, delivered as it was in a context of presumed religious and political unity, was initially unacceptable to both authoritative institutions, church and state. Surely the critique of priestly authority implied in much Reformation religious dissent served to enhance secular authorities who could claim moral superiority, at least to the Roman Church, but free expression of religious dissent required a consent from secular authorities that was not always forthcoming. Reformation-era religious dissidents were as likely to be charged with "insurrection" by secular governments as they were to be charged with "heresy" by religious tribunals.

The result was a decidedly limited sort of religious liberty and toleration, a toleration both created and restricted by the same ecclesiastical and secular leaders and institutions. The Religious Peace of Augsburg (1555), for example, delivered some religious liberty in German states, but only to rulers. It gave Lutheran princes all the jurisdiction in their own territories that had once been exercised by bishops. The subjects in these lands remained religious subjects: their religion was to be determined by their prince. Very few European governments allowed all Christian denominations without restrictions, and some that did were in unlikely places: Poland, for instance, after the Warsaw Confederation of 1573. Where papal authoritative structures were repudiated, freedom was not the result. Instead, structures designed to establish religious control were recreated in basically one of three ways: through consistories (local church councils) appointed by the secular government, through democratic bodies replacing church courts, or through royal institutions assuming traditional powers. Early on, Luther himself recognized the need of religious reformers for the assistance of secular governments, and not just for his own personal protection. In accusing Thomas Müntzer (c. 1491–1525) of heresy in 1525, Luther connected theological irregularities and civic disobedience. He increasingly called on secular authorities to intervene in ecclesiastical matters, and, of course, he recommended the slaying of German peasants who cited his ideas in order to secure relief from feudal restrictions. John Calvin, it must be remembered, presided over the repression of anti-Trinitarian thought utilizing various punishments—including capital punishment—carried out by civic authority. Overall, those who were initially vigorous in defending the right to express religious dissent and who expressed such dissent themselves were just as likely to recommend and carry out the persecution of it as were those who initially rejected out of hand any such "right."

THE ENLIGHTENMENT

During the eighteenth century, the intellectual, political, and cultural changes associated with the Enlightenment contributed to the continuing dissolution of the notion of a unified church and state, and had a long-term effect on the relationship between the two. As the leaders of an intellectual movement that encouraged the application of the scientific method to all aspects of human life and behavior, the philosophes who publicized and promoted Enlightenment thought conceived of the entire universe, including political institutions, as regulated by laws comprehensible through reason. They acknowledged a supreme being whose action in establishing these laws could be observed by finding order in nature. The philosophes, and in particular individuals like Voltaire (1694–1778), also aimed their criticism at what they considered unreasonable human behavior. Near the top of their list of targets were ecclesiastical institutions, and religious ways of thinking, that in their view promoted bigotry, intolerance, and violence—all unreasonable responses to the behavior of others. In Europe, Enlightenment thinkers—at least by implication—criticized all religious sects as prone, through their dogma, to intolerance and violence. In practice, European Christian denominations came under heaviest attack, and in particular, the Roman Catholic Church. Clerical misbehavior was identified and lampooned. Enlightenment authors also satirized dogma for creating meaningless distinctions that distracted the faithful. Such authors believed basic ethical standards to be the only worthwhile portion of religious thought—precisely because that portion was not especially religious—and insisted that it was common to all sects in Christianity, Judaism, and Islam. Protestant sectarianism that had contributed to political and religious violence, like Calvinism during the French version of the so-called Wars of Religion (1562–1598), or sectarianism that threatened to lead to further violence, at least for the philosophes, came under similar attack. Enlightenment thinkers idealized religious toleration, and even separation between the institutions of church and state, but these were not even consistently applied ideas, let

alone achievements in fact. Catholics, most frequently, were not included in Enlightenment definitions of religious and political toleration.

CONCLUSION

Some might suggest that it was the relationship between the Roman Catholic Church and the states of Europe that changed most at the end of eighteenth century. Such a position may be a serious oversimplification, and certainly does not take the institutions and events in the history of earlier eras into sufficient account. Throughout Western history, the relationship has been contentious, and characterized by claims for the supremacy of one or the other institution. Those claims have been largely unrealizable, as both institutions have relied, at least in part, on the buttress to their own authority provided by the political, moral, and religious influence of the other. In most instances throughout that history, secular political authorities have, in the main, been the dominant authorities. Locally, and in short-term instances, dominant authority has been in the hands of ecclesiastical institutions, both Roman Catholic and Protestant. In the early modern period, some halting steps toward genuine separation of church and state were taken by both lay and clerical leaders. But those steps often had more to do with attitudes toward the way political and ecclesiastical power ought to be held and exercised than with the actual holding and exercising. And these steps were not boldly creative, for they had precedents in medieval controversies like the eleventh-century investiture crisis and the fifteenth-century development of conciliarist thought. In the early modern period, both political and ecclesiastical institutions attempted to assert themselves, the one over the other. In the attempt, they utilized justifications for their authority that appealed ultimately to the existence of God, and to their own representation of the true will of God.

See also **Augsburg, Religious Peace of (1555); Calvin, John; Calvinism; Divine Right Kingship; Henry VIII (England); Luther, Martin; Lutheranism; Papacy and Papal States; Reformation, Protestant; Trent, Council of.**

BIBLIOGRAPHY

Aston, Nigel. *Religion and Revolution in France, 1780–1804.* Washington, D.C., 2000.

Bedini, Silvio A. *The Pope's Elephant.* Manchester, U.K., 1997.

Carleton, Kenneth. *Bishops and Reform in the English Church, 1520–1559.* Rochester, N.Y., 2001.

Chadwick, Owen. *The Popes and European Revolution.* Oxford and New York, 1981.

Collins, James B. *The State in Early Modern France.* Cambridge, U.K., and New York, 1995.

Duffy, Eamon. *The Voices of Morebath: Reformation and Rebellion in an English Village.* New Haven, 2001.

Fichtner, Paula Sutter. *Emperor Maximilian II.* New Haven, 2001.

Forster, Marc R. *Catholic Revival in the Age of the Baroque: Religious Identity in Southwest Germany, 1550–1750.* New York, 2001.

———. *The Counter-Reformation in the Villages: Religion and Reform in the Bishopric of Speyer, 1560–1720.* Ithaca, N.Y., 1992.

Fragnito, Gigliola, ed. *Church, Censorship and Culture in Early Modern Italy.* Cambridge, U.K., and New York, 2001.

Freedman, Jeffrey. *A Poisoned Chalice.* Princeton, 2002.

Gavin, Frank. *Seven Centuries of the Problem of Church and State.* Princeton, 1938. Reprint 1971.

Kaufman, Peter Iver. *Redeeming Politics.* Princeton, 1990.

Knecht, R. J. *The Rise and Fall of Renaissance France: 1483–1610.* Malden, Mass., 2001.

Kooi, Christine. *Liberty and Religion: Church and State in Leiden's Reformation.* Leiden and Boston, 2000.

Reinhardt, Nicole. *Macht und Ohnmacht der Verflechtung: Rom und Bologna unter Paul V. Studien zur frühneuzeitlichen Mikropolitik im Kirchenstaat.* Tübingen, 2000.

Seidel Menchi, Silvana, and Diego Quaglioni, eds. *Coniugi nemici: La separazione in Italia dal xii al xviii secolo.* Bologna, 2000.

WILLIAM V. HUDON

CHURCH OF ENGLAND.

During the early modern period, the English church experienced major disruption and change. After long debates and a series of reformations, it emerged at the end of the sixteenth century as a national Protestant church with its own distinctive theology and liturgy. During the seventeenth century, differences of view about the nature of the church were a cause of the English Civil War (1642–1649) that resulted in the unpopular Puritan revolution of the 1640s and 1650s. Although a monopolistic church was reintroduced soon after the restoration of the monarchy in 1660, it could not command the loyalty and obedience of all Protestants. Following the 1688 "Glorious Revolution" a Toleration Act was passed that granted freedom of worship to those Protestants whose consciences prevented them from attending Anglican services in parish churches.

THE LATE MEDIEVAL CHURCH: 1450–1530

The central theological beliefs of the late medieval Church were salvation through faith and works, the efficacy of grace transmitted through the sacraments, and transubstantiation.

The Catholic Church taught that while faith in Christ was essential for eternal life, individuals also had to do good works and regularly receive the sacrament of penance. Even then their souls did not usually go directly to heaven, but had to spend time in purgatory, where they would suffer punishment for sins committed on earth that had not been fully expiated through contrition and by penance. People who died without having done penance for mortal sin were damned to hell.

Besides penance there were six other Catholic sacraments: baptism, confirmation, ordination, marriage, extreme unction (the last rites), and the Eucharist, or Lord's Supper. The church taught that, at the celebration of the Eucharist in the Mass, the "substance" of the unleavened bread and wine was transformed into the body and blood of Christ at the moment of consecration by the priest. This miracle—the literal reenactment of Christ's sacrifice—was called transubstantiation and came about through the sacerdotal power of the priest. The ceremony was the most powerful form of intercession that could be offered to God as well as a channel of grace necessary for individual salvation. Lay people usually received the Eucharist annually, when they were offered "Communion in one kind" (the wafer but not the wine). Priests, however, regularly celebrated the Mass and consumed both the consecrated wafer and wine. The ceremony took place behind a rood screen in the chancel, while most of the congregation remained in the nave of the church. Nonetheless, the laity was expected to attend carefully and participate in the service.

The late medieval English Church was part of an international body with its center at Rome and the pope at its head. During the fifteenth century, papal power in England was eroded as the monarch gained greater control over taxation and nominations to benefices. Nonetheless, the pope still taxed the English Church, heard judicial appeals, and retained his spiritual authority over the clergy and laity. The archbishoprics of Canterbury and York were separate provinces of the Roman Catholic Church, each with its own administrative structure and jurisdictions. Since the middle of the fourteenth century, Canterbury had taken precedence over York, and even today its archbishop is the primate of England. The archbishoprics were divided into the twenty-three dioceses of England and Wales, and each diocese was divided into archdeaconries, which were in turn divided into roughly nine thousand parishes. Bishops were responsible for conducting visitations throughout their diocese and supervising the church courts, which administered canon law and dealt with cases concerning moral and church discipline. The consistory courts of the diocese heard appeals from archdiaconal courts, which handled the bulk of cases and were administered by archdeacons.

The priest who served the parish was sometimes the rector, who was entitled to receive the tithe (a tenth of income or produce) from parishioners. But the rectors of over one-third of English parishes in 1500 were the heads of monastic houses and thus absentee. In these cases a vicar was appointed to perform the liturgy and fulfill pastoral obligations. Other parishes too had nonresident rectors, since about one-quarter of English livings were pluralist, meaning that one priest held two or more offices at the same time; here a curate received a small salary to do the work. The appointment of all these clerics rested primarily with the patron—lay or clerical—who had the right to appoint his candidate to the living (a right that was known as an advowson). Lay churchwardens, whose duties were to care for the building and ornaments of the church and to report deficiencies or clerical negligence to the ecclesiastical authorities, also served the parish community.

Historians now tend to agree that the late medieval church in England generally functioned well, and that the accusations of corruption made by later Protestant critics were greatly exaggerated. There is also a scholarly consensus that the number of heretics in England was small and that the vast majority of laypeople were deeply attached to the teachings

and liturgy of the Catholic Church. Historians, however, are less united in their views about the subject of "anticlericalism" on the eve of the Reformation. Some deny its existence while others maintain that a significant number of individuals, as well as interest groups (such as the common lawyers), were critical of clerical privileges and hostile to clerical immunities and jurisdiction.

THE ENGLISH REFORMATION

During the period known as the Reformation, the English Church broke with Rome and underwent major changes in doctrine and liturgy. This began as a top-down process that divided the country and created political instability.

Henry VIII's (ruled 1509–1547) attack on the papacy began when Pope Clement VII (reigned 1523–1534) refused to grant an annulment of the king's first marriage to Catherine of Aragon. Henry had always claimed rights of supremacy over the English church, but not at the expense of Rome. In the 1530s, however, Henry asserted that English kings were answerable to no earthly superior. In 1532, he forced his senior clergy to concede that convocation (the provincial assembly) could not make ecclesiastical law without royal assent. Over the next two years, a succession of parliamentary statutes whittled away papal power in England while recognizing the king's right to reform the church, supervise canon law, and correct errors in doctrine. In 1534 the Act of Supremacy pronounced Henry's status as the supreme head of the Church of England. The English church remained Catholic, but the pope was no longer its head—he was now simply the bishop of Rome.

As supreme head of the church, Henry introduced some notable changes. In 1536 and 1539 the English monasteries were dissolved by acts of Parliament, and a small portion of their revenues was diverted toward educational endowments and the creation of six new dioceses. With their demise, monastic advowsons and appropriation of tithes fell into lay hands. Henry also began an assault on the cult of saints and "superstitious" images, which led to the destruction of shrines and resulted in damage to some cathedrals. He commissioned a new English Bible that was supposed to be placed in each parish church. In 1544 an Exhortation and Litany to be said during processions was published in English; the following year, Henry authorized an English primer (a late medieval devotional book containing various prayers and psalms) that reduced the number of saints' and holy days in the calendar and omitted many traditional prayers.

Despite these innovations, Henry's "reformation" did not seriously challenge Catholic doctrine. With the exception of the denial of papal supremacy and expressions of skepticism about the existence of purgatory, Henry upheld all the central pillars of the Roman Catholic faith. In 1521 he had written an attack on Martin Luther; twenty years later he still considered Lutheran teachings on justification by faith alone, the sacraments, the priesthood, and the Mass to be dangerous and erroneous. For this reason Henry was able to carry with him the majority of his bishops, who continued to see the king as a bulwark against heresy. Others of his Catholic subjects, however, were less compliant. In late 1536 and early 1537, revolts, known as the Pilgrimage of Grace, erupted in Lincolnshire and northern England to demonstrate hostility to governmental policies such as the royal supremacy, the dissolutions of the monasteries, and the royal injunctions of 1536.

During the minority of Edward VI (ruled 1547–1553), England officially became Protestant. In 1547 the lord protector, Edward Seymour, duke of Somerset, prohibited processions and launched a nationwide campaign to destroy all religious images. The Parliament of 1547, meanwhile, repealed the heresy laws, permitted Communion in both kinds, and dissolved the chantries (chapels endowed for saying masses). In 1548 the government banned many traditional religious ceremonies, and the 1549 Parliament permitted clerics to marry. The same Parliament endorsed an English Book of Common Prayer, the work of Thomas Cranmer, archbishop of Canterbury (1489–1556). Its liturgy simplified the traditional Sarum rite dating from thirteenth-century Salisbury and rejected many Catholic doctrines, although some ambiguity did remain.

A second revised prayer book was authorized by the Parliament of 1552. In producing it Archbishop Cranmer took advice from prominent Continental Protestant theologians, all of whom were influenced by the Zwinglian and Calvinist churches of southern Germany and Switzerland. The 1552 Book of Common Prayer was consequently far more radical than

its predecessor in its liturgy and underlying theology. The word "mass" disappeared entirely from the Communion service, clerical vestments were simplified, and ordinary bread replaced the wafer at the Eucharist. The wording of the administration of Communion no longer referred to the body and blood of Christ but emphasized instead the commemorative significance of the sacrament. The new prayer book also included a Communion instruction, later known as the "black rubric," which said that kneeling to receive Communion did not imply Christ's physical presence. In 1553 Cranmer presented the Edwardian church with a statement of faith, the Forty-Two Articles. These articles were uncompromisingly Protestant in their theology and condemned the Roman Catholic doctrines of transubstantiation, purgatory, intercession, and good works. On the main issues in dispute between the Lutheran and Swiss Reformed Churches, namely predestination and the Eucharist, they were closer to Calvinism than to anything else. During the last years of Edward's reign, parish churches and cathedrals were denuded of their altars, plate, bells, vestments, and stained glass.

Under Mary I (ruled 1553–1558), virtually all the changes introduced after 1529 were reversed. Although few monasteries and chantries were endowed and the worship of saints failed to regain popularity, Mary's reign did witness a spontaneous revival of many of the Catholic seasonal ceremonies banned under Edward VI as well as a restoration of altars and images to parish churches. Soon after Elizabeth I's accession in November 1558, all changed again. Despite strong opposition from bishops appointed by Mary, the Acts of Supremacy and Uniformity passed through Parliament in April 1559. The former act gave Elizabeth a new title, "Supreme Governor" of the Church of England; the latter authorized the use of a Book of Common Prayer that was largely modeled on that of 1552. The main change came in the Communion service, which incorporated some of the wording from Edward VI's 1549 Book of Common Prayer and omitted the 1552 black rubric (although it was replaced—with some alterations—in 1662). The royal injunctions of 1559, moreover, enjoined that undecorated wafers should be used at communion rather than bread. The effect was a theological ambiguity about the presence of Christ: was he present physically, spiritually, or not at all? The Thirty-Nine Articles of Faith of 1563 and 1571 attempted to clarify the theology when they asserted that Christ's body was taken in the Lord's Supper "after an heavenly and spiritual manner."

The Thirty-Nine Articles were less clear on predestination. Although they incorporated the Calvinist doctrine of election, no statement was made on assurance or the fate of the reprobate (a sinner condemned by God to eternal punishment). The 1559 prayer book, meanwhile, described the baptized child as "a member of Christ, the child of God, and an inheritor of the kingdom," a form of words that seemed to discount the possibility that the infant might have been born reprobate. Despite this imprecision, the official doctrines taught by the church after 1570 were predominantly predestinarian. In 1595, moreover, the archbishop of Canterbury, John Whitgift, endorsed the nine Lambeth Articles, an unequivocal assertion of the Calvinist position on grace and salvation. The evidence suggests, however, that despite access to a Calvinist catechism, many (possibly most) ordinary laypeople failed to absorb the doctrine of predestination and continued to believe that good deeds played some part in salvation.

Although the Elizabethan church was essentially Calvinist in its theology, some of its practices were traditional. Ministers were required to wear the surplice when officiating at morning and evening prayer and the more elaborate vestments of the alb and the cope for Communion. Although roods (the large crucifix dominating the nave), stone altars, and images were removed from churches, royal proclamations were issued to protect fonts and funeral monuments. Members of congregations were told to uncover their heads and bow at the uttering of the name of Jesus in church, and to use the sign of the cross in baptism, the ring in marriage, and other "popish remnants." At the same time, the diocesan and parochial structure of the church remained untouched, and no measures were put in place to reform the church courts, the tithe, advowsons, or canon law.

PURITANS AND ARMINIANS

Although most committed Protestants were disappointed with the 1559 settlement, they initially accepted it as an interim measure, expecting that further changes would soon be introduced. During the mid-1560s, however, Elizabeth insisted that all clerics conform to the prayer book ceremonies and ornaments (including vestments) and ordered her bishops to suspend Nonconformists from their livings. Furthermore, Elizabeth scotched her bishops' reform initiatives in the 1563 Canterbury Convocation and the 1566 Parliament. For the most zealous Protestants this was a betrayal, and out of their frustration the Elizabethan Puritan movement was born.

Those who were labeled "Puritans" by their enemies preferred to call themselves "the godly." Contemporaries usually identified them by the intensity of their spirituality, for Puritans attended sermons during the week and devoted the Sabbath entirely to God. Puritans were also at the fore of the campaign for reform: they demanded frequent, high-quality preaching, insisted on significant changes in the 1559 Book of Common Prayer, and were critical of the church courts. Nonetheless, Puritans remained part of the Church of England, for they were reasonably satisfied with its Calvinist teachings on predestination and the Eucharist as well as its hostility to images. Largely because of their influence, Elizabeth was unable to eradicate a wide diversity of ceremonial practice in the church. James I (ruled 1603–1625) permitted this diversity to continue provided that Puritans rejected Presbyterianism (church government by presbyters or elders). In practice, therefore, many ministers continued to take Communion standing or sitting, rather than kneeling, and to use bread rather than wafers. Some ministers omitted those parts of the prayer book that they disliked and shortened the liturgy to leave more time for the sermon. While James I's reign brought no major changes in liturgical policy, it did see the publication of a new Authorised ("King James") Version of the Bible in 1611.

A strong defense of the Church of England against its Puritan critics was written in the 1590s by the theologian Richard Hooker (1554–1600), who justified its conservative governmental system and unique ceremonial style as a middle way between Roman Catholicism and Genevan Presbyterianism. Hooker's work, which also modified some contemporary predestinarian assumptions, became a source of inspiration for a number of early-seventeenth-century conservative clerics who were suspicious of preaching and placed great stress on set prayer and the sacraments as sources of grace. These men also rejected the asceticism of Calvinist worship and favored what was called the "beauty of holiness." Another influence on their thinking was the Dutch theologian Jacob Arminius (1560–1609), who argued against the rigidities of predestination. For this reason, these English divines have been misleadingly called "Arminians." Some historians prefer to call them "Anti-Calvinists," others "Laudians" after the Archbishop of Canterbury William Laud (1573–1645).

After Charles I's accession in 1625, Arminians gained dominance in the English Church and implemented important changes. Predestinarian beliefs came under attack, and Laud, who was appointed bishop of London in 1628 and archbishop of Canterbury in 1633, initiated a new "altar policy." Laud and other like-minded bishops pressured their parish clergy to acquire elaborate wooden tables, or preferably stone altars, and to position them permanently at the east end of the chancel, in a north-south, or "altarwise," alignment. The bishops further insisted that chancels should be cordoned off by rails, and that Communion should be received kneeling, though not necessarily at the rails. Other parts of the Elizabethan prayer book that had been allowed to lapse in some communities were now rigorously enforced. Historians disagree about the extent of opposition to this theological and liturgical program. A few scholars claim that only a Puritan minority was outraged by the reforms, but the prevailing view is that the altar policy, at least, was widely resisted. There is also evidence that many mainstream Protestants abhorred the changes as the reintroduction of popery, and feared—albeit mistakenly—that Charles intended to return England to Rome. Few historians would dispute that the religious innovations under Charles I helped bring about the Civil War (1642–1649).

The parliamentary victory in the Civil War resulted in the triumph of Puritanism. In 1645 the prayer book was banned and replaced by a new *Directory of Worship* that contained instructions for the conduct of services and removed rites that Puritans had so long found offensive. The church courts ceased to function in the early 1640s, and in 1646 episcopacy was abolished. Godly observance of the Sabbath was imposed and all feast days, including Christmas, Easter, and Whitsun (or Pentecost), were banned. The Puritans, however, failed to gain popular support, and throughout the late 1640s and 1650s large numbers of clergymen continued to conduct services according to the old prayer book liturgy. At the same time, freedom of worship was granted to Protestant sects, including Baptists and Congregationalists.

THE ANGLICAN CHURCH: 1660–1714

At the restoration of Charles II in 1660, the state church was fully reimposed with the return of episcopacy and the church courts. Its liturgy was based on the Elizabethan Book of Common Prayer of 1559 but included a number of Laudian practices. Altars were returned to many churches voluntarily; after 1680 they began to be imposed and by 1700 they were prevalent. The Act of Uniformity of 1662 demanded that the clergy accept every one of the Thirty-Nine Articles and every aspect of the new prayer book. Everyone was required to attend the Church of England, while the so-called Clarendon Code of the mid-1660s outlawed community worship by Protestant sects in chapels and meeting houses. In 1672 dissenters (Protestant Nonconformists) were also barred from holding civil office. Before the 1688 Revolution, many Dissenters practiced occasional conformity, but thousands of others—especially the Quakers—were subjected to harassment and imprisonment.

Both Charles II (ruled 1660–1685) and James II (ruled 1685–1688) proved unsuccessful in their attempts to broaden the Church of England and allow a measure of toleration for Protestant dissenters and for Roman Catholics. After Mary and William III became joint monarchs in 1689, however, a Toleration Act (1689) was passed that gave all Trinitarian Protestant dissenters the right to worship in their own chapels or meeting houses and permitted nonattendance at church. Thus began the split between church and chapel that marked the eighteenth century. Nonetheless, civil disabilities continued to affect those dissenters who refused to take Communion at least once annually. The Toleration Act, moreover, did not apply to Roman Catholics, who had to wait until the nineteenth century before securing freedom of worship.

Under William III (ruled 1689–1702) and Queen Anne (ruled 1702–1714) a group of churchmen, usually known as Latitudinarians or low churchmen, became prominent in the Church of England. They sought to reduce religious controversy by arguing that the core Christian doctrines were few and that the most contentious issues of the Reformation were "adiaphora" (not essential to salvation) and could be left to the individual conscience. They were therefore willing to embrace all those who conformed to the church no matter how occasionally they attended or took Communion. High churchmen criticized their approach as defeatist and demanded full enforcement of the 1673 Test Act, which required all officeholders to take the oaths of supremacy and allegiance to the king, to receive the sacraments of the Church of England, and to reject the doctrine of transubstantiation; they even tried (unsuccessfully) to extend civil disabilities to occasional conformists who might only take Anglican Communion annually. Despite clashes between low and high churchmen at the beginning of the eighteenth century, the Church of England settled down to operate as a strong, flourishing, and successful institution.

See also **Bible; Dissenters, English; Edward VI (England); Elizabeth I (England); Henry VIII (England); Hooker, Richard; Laud, William; Mary I (England); Puritanism; Reformation, Protestant; Ritual, Religious; Toleration; William and Mary.**

BIBLIOGRAPHY

Bernard, George. "The Church of England, c. 1579–c. 1642." *History* 75 (1990): 183–206.

Collinson, Patrick. *The Religion of Protestants: The Church in English Society.* Oxford, 1982.

Davies, Julian. *The Caroline Captivity of the Church: Charles I and the Remoulding of Anglicanism, 1625–1641.* Oxford, 1992.

Doran, Susan, and Christopher Durston. *Princes, Pastors and People: The Church and Religion in England, 1500–1700.* 2nd ed. London, 2002.

Durston, Christopher, and Jacqueline Eales, eds. *The Culture of English Puritanism, 1560–1700.* Basingstoke, U.K., 1996.

Fincham, Kenneth. "The Restoration of Altars in the 1630s." *Historical Journal* 44 (2001): 919–940.

Fincham, Kenneth, ed. *The Early Stuart Church.* Basingstoke, U.K., 1993.

Green, I. M. *The Re-establishment of the Church of England, 1660–1663.* Oxford, 1978.

Haigh, Christopher. *English Reformations: Religion, Politics and Society under the Tudors.* Oxford, 1993.

Heal, Felicity. *Reformation in Britain and Ireland.* Oxford, 2003.

MacCulloch, Diarmaid. *Thomas Cranmer: A Life.* New Haven and London, 1996.

———. *Tudor Church Militant: Edward VI and the Protestant Reformation.* London, 1999.

Sharpe, Kevin. *The Personal Rule of Charles I.* London, 1992.

Spurr, John. "'Latitudinarianism' and the Restoration Church." *Historical Journal* 31 (1988): 61–82.

———. *The Restoration Church of England, 1646–1689.* London, 1991.

Tyacke, Nicholas. *Anti-Calvinists: The Rise of English Arminianism, c. 1590–1640.* Oxford 1987.

———. *Aspects of English Protestantism, c. 1530–1700.* Manchester, U.K., 2001.

White, Peter. *Predestination, Policy and Polemic: Conflict and Consensus in the English Church from the Reformation to the Civil War.* Cambridge, U.K., 1992.

SUSAN DORAN

CHURCHILL, JOHN, DUKE OF MARLBOROUGH

(1650–1722), soldier and diplomat. Frequently described as early modern Britain's greatest general, John Churchill was born on 26 May 1650, the son of Elizabeth Churchill and Sir Winston Churchill, an impoverished squire and member of Parliament. He attended Saint Paul's School and then in 1665, due to his father's influence, became page to the duke of York, later James II (ruled 1685–1688). On 14 September 1667 Churchill was commissioned into the army as an ensign in the Foot Guards. He served in Tangier from 1668 to 1670, saw duty with the allied fleet during the Third Dutch War (1672–1674), and was promoted to captain. In 1673 he accompanied the English contingent dispatched to assist Louis XIV (ruled 1643–1715) of France in Flanders and distinguished himself in military action at Maastricht (Maestricht, June 1673), his first major land battle. The following year he was appointed colonel of the English regiment operating abroad and performed gallantly at the battle of Sinzheim (1674).

In 1677 Churchill married Sarah Jennings (1660–1744), lady-in-waiting to Princess Anne, later Queen Anne (ruled 1702–1714). Churchill advanced rapidly. He was created Baron Churchill of Aymouth (Scotland) on 21 December 1682, elevated to the peerage as Baron Sandridge in 1685 and, upon the accession of James II (1685), promoted to major general (3 July 1685) and subsequently lieutenant general (7 November 1688).

With the Glorious Revolution (1688), Churchill promptly changed his allegiance to the new Protestant sovereign William III (ruled 1689–1702), who in 1689 rewarded him with the earldom of Marlborough (after which point he is commonly known as Marlborough) and appointed him a privy councillor. Marlborough was also granted a succession of commands between 1689 and 1691 in Flanders and Ireland, in which he was uniformly successful. He also served for a while as governor of the Hudson's Bay Company. Increasingly opposed to William's excessive preferment of his Dutch associates, Marlborough suddenly fell out of favor. In 1692 he was dismissed from his posts and briefly was imprisoned in the Tower of London on suspicion of communicating with Jacobite agents in a plot to restore James II with the support of French military intervention. As these allegations proved groundless, Marlborough was released and, upon reconciling with William, was restored to favor in 1698. He was appointed governor to the duke of Gloucester, was readmitted to the Privy Council, and was returned to his former military rank (18 June 1698). In the face of growing tensions over the Spanish succession, Marlborough was named commander in chief of the Anglo-Dutch forces in Holland (June 1701) and participated in the negotiations held at The Hague to devise a compromise settlement that would satisfy the various claimants and prevent European war.

Following the death of William III on 8 March 1702 and the subsequent accession of Queen Anne, Marlborough reached the peak of his influence. He was appointed captain general of the forces and master general of the ordnance, while his closest ally, Sidney Godolphin, first earl of Godolphin (1645–1712), became lord treasurer. Other Tory supporters took the remaining great offices of state.

Once The Hague deliberations broke down and France's aggressive actions made conflict inevitable, the English, the Austrians, the Dutch, and minor German allies concluded the Grand Alliance (15

May 1702) with a combined army under Marlborough's supreme command. In his first campaign during the War of the Spanish Succession (June 1702) Marlborough relieved pressure on the Dutch by securing a base of operation against French-held fortresses to the south. Overcoming intra-alliance dissension, he successfully pressed on to take the great fortress of Liège (October 1702). For this service he was created duke with a pension of £5,000 a year. He then advanced on the Moselle River. Deceiving the enemy by a feint against Alsace, he swiftly moved to open a crossing of the Danube River at Donauwörth, thus impeding a possible junction of French forces and their Bavarian allies. On 13 August 1704 Marlborough and his confidant, the Austrian commander Prince Eugène (1663–1736), defeated the main French army at Blenheim—a spectacular victory. This was the first major military setback of Louis XIV's reign, and it forced France onto the defensive and saved Austria from near certain invasion. On 23 March 1706 Marlborough won another crushing victory at Ramillies, which led to the expulsion of enemy troops from Italy and the Southern Netherlands. Marlborough and Prince Eugène repulsed a French counteroffensive at Oudenaarde (July 1708) and cleared the road for a direct advance against France. These exploits earned Marlborough a military reputation matched in the eighteenth century only by Frederick the Great (ruled 1740–1786) of Prussia and later by Napoléon I (1769–1821). In recognition Marlborough was made a prince of the empire, and by royal command the magnificent palace of Blenheim was built for him.

Domestically, however, Marlborough's position weakened due to relentless party politics and the growing estrangement between his wife Sarah and Queen Anne, whose former friendship had provided a critical link tying the operational direction of the war to the source of executive power at court. Using a variety of pressure tactics, Marlborough and his ally Lord Treasurer Godolphin managed for a time to coerce the pro-Tory queen into (reluctantly) appointing those congenial Whig ministers who supported their policies. But Sarah became supplanted in Anne's favor by Abigail Masham (d. 1734), an influential Tory sympathizer, and in politics the queen turned for advice to the able Tory leader Robert Harley (1661–1724). Support for the war rapidly declined. Moreover costs steadily mounted, as did war weariness on the allied side. Marlborough, increasingly isolated, was accused of continuing hostilities for personal profit and glory.

The parliamentary elections of 1710 brought in a new and powerful Tory ministry headed by Harley, which enabled Anne to dispense with the personally uncongenial Whig leaders and led to secret negotiations with France. Marlborough remained commander in chief until December 1711, when he was dismissed, falsely charged with corruption and forced into exile on the Continent. Although restored to favor with the accession of George I (ruled 1714–1727), Marlborough, prematurely aged by the strains of war, took no further part in public affairs. He lived in rural retirement until his death, following a paralytic stroke, on 16 June 1722. He was buried with great splendor at Westminster, though his body was later transferred to the chapel at Blenheim, where it was commemorated by an ornate mausoleum.

Bold, energetic, a superb tactician, and a gifted leader, Marlborough advocated swift, offensive action over elaborate maneuvers as the key to decisive victory. In this sense he transcended the military spirit of his age and foreshadowed the more innovative, energetic approach to war typical of the French revolutionary period. His urbanity and tact, discretion and diplomacy were further assets in defusing the inevitable tensions associated with coalition warfare and so made possible the unity essential for cooperation and victory.

See also **Anne (England); Harley, Robert; Spanish Succession, War of the (1701–1714); William and Mary.**

BIBLIOGRAPHY

Primary Source

Great Britain, Historical Manuscripts Commission. *The Manuscripts of His Grace the Duke of Marlborough*. London, 1881.

Secondary Sources

Burton, Ivor F. *The Captain-General: The Career of John Churchill, Duke of Marlborough, from 1702–1711*. London, 1968.

Chandler, David. *The Art of Warfare in the Age of Marlborough*. New York, 1976.

———. *Marlborough as Military Commander*. London, 1979.

Churchill, Winston S. *Marlborough: His Life and Times*. 6 vols. New York, 1933–1938.

Green, David Brontë. *Sarah, Duchess of Marlborough*. London, 1967.

Thomson, George Malcolm. *The First Churchill: The Life of John, 1st Duke of Marlborough*. London, 1979.

KARL W. SCHWEIZER

CISNEROS, CARDINAL FRANCISCO JIMÉNEZ DE (1436–1517), cardinal and archbishop of Toledo, Franciscan friar, and principal adviser and confessor to Queen Isabella of Castille. Frustrated by circumstances, temperament, and worldly abilities, Cisneros sought a monastic life, but labored tirelessly in the secular world. Cisneros viewed rulers as indispensable in guiding their people toward salvation. He gravitated toward power and power gravitated toward him. A man of strong opinions, Cisneros was blunt and assertive and adamant in his will.

Little is known of Cisneros's family background. Born into an impoverished family of the lower nobility, he was sent to school at Acalá de Henares, completed studies for the priesthood at the University of Salamanca, then went to Rome and returned with a papal bull appointing him to the first vacant benefice in Toledo. He claimed Uceda rather than cede it to the appointee, a relative of Toledo's archbishop, Alonso Carrillo. Cisneros was interred at an archiepiscopal prison—until Carrillo relented. In Sigüenza he became vicar to its largely absentee bishop, the royal first minister and cardinal, Pedro González de Mendoza. In 1484 he joined the Franciscan Observance and for eight years lived an ascetic life. Nonetheless, during that time he gained a great reputation for preaching and rose to become guardian of the convent of La Salceda.

When Hernando de Talavera became the first archbishop of Granada in 1492, Cisneros succeeded him as Queen Isabella's confessor at the suggestion of Cardinal Mendoza and, following Mendoza's death in 1495, Cisneros succeeded him as archbishop of Toledo, primate of Spain, and thereafter as first minister to the queen. As Isabella's health declined, she relied more heavily on Cisneros for both spiritual and political guidance. Both queen

Francisco Jiménez de Cisneros.

and minister sought to reform the people of Spain, beginning with the clergy. Cisneros moved Franciscan houses, despite resistance, from the looser Conventual to the more severe Observant rule, and laid plans to reform the secular clergy and to found a university at Alcalá de Hénares (1499), where the study of law, given primary place at the University of Salamanca, would rank below theology.

Then, in 1499, Cisneros went to Granada to speed the conversion of its Muslims to Christianity, and thereby remove a possible subversive element within Spain. Overriding Talavera's preference for persuasive indoctrination, Cisneros enforced conversion through mass baptism, threatened and jailed the recalcitrant, and provoked three years of guerrilla warfare throughout the former Muslim kingdom of Granada. At its end, a royal decree ordered all Muslims in Castile to convert or leave.

From Granada and in the wake of Columbus's discoveries in the New World, Cisneros took charge of evangelizing Native Americans, dispatching to Santo Domingo (now the Dominican Republic) six fellow Franciscans, men of proven ability who re-

ported to him on both religious and political matters. In the following years he chose, instructed, and sent to America more Franciscans, among them veterans of his Granadan evangelization. He influenced the Dominicans, who arrived in 1510, and as regent of Spain in 1516, he sent the Hieronymites to investigate the mistreatment of native peoples. While Isabella set formative Spanish policy in America, Cisneros greatly influenced these policies. Isabella's claim that the Indians were royal subjects who must be instructed in religion and "civilized ways" for the benefit of their souls reflected his own viewpoint.

After Isabella's death in 1504, Cisneros had a hand in brokering the concord with Ferdinand that left Philip of Austria to rule Spain for his ailing wife, Joanna. Cisneros advised Philip, and he became virtual regent after Philip's death in 1506. He was instrumental in resisting a strong party favoring the Habsburg Maximilian and in securing the return to power of Ferdinand, who had been forced to renounce his title of king of Castile upon Isabella's death. By then a cardinal, Cisneros sought to extend the Christian Spanish reconquest into North Africa, reputedly once held by the Visigoths, in 1509, personally leading an expedition that besieged and took Oran. Soon at odds with Ferdinand, Cisneros devoted himself to constructing the University of Alcalá de Hénares (1499) and to directing a group of scholars in producing the Complutensian Polyglot Bible, which restored what he considered the pristine Hebrew of the Old Testament and the Greek and Aramaic of the New Testament, together with the Latin of the Vulgate Bible in parallel columns. The Complutensian Bible was a monumental endeavor of critical scholarship.

Cisneros assumed the regency in 1516, appointed by Ferdinand during the absence of his heir and grandson, Charles of Ghent. At eighty, Cisneros raised an army, put down scattered urban revolts and a widespread uprising by dissident nobles, and forced their recognition of Charles as king. Prior to Charles's arrival in Spain in September of 1517, Cisneros, though in failing health, readied to meet and advise the new king, but died on his way to meet him. Cisneros was instrumental in ensuring that Spain entered the modern era with renewed commitment to conjoined religious and political ends.

See also **Bible; Ferdinand of Aragón; Isabella of Castile.**

BIBLIOGRAPHY

Bleiberg, Germán, ed. *Diccionario de Historia de España.* Madrid, 1979. Vol. 1, pp. 835–836.

García Oro, José. *El Cardenal Cisneros. Vida y empresas.* 2 vols. Madrid, 1992–1993.

Liss, Peggy K. *Isabel the Queen: Life and Times.* New York, 1992.

PEGGY LISS

CITIES AND URBAN LIFE. The names that come immediately to mind when one thinks of early modern cities are for the most part capitals or court cities or major colonial ports. They were grand places, of which much remains and, although smaller than they are today in both area and population, more populous than any city Catholic Europe had known in the Middle Ages (Orthodox Constantinople and Muslim Cordoba may have exceeded half a million inhabitants). However, only a small fraction of the urban population of Europe—itself a fraction of the total—lived in any of them. So we shall first examine a more common type of town, which can tell us what life was like for townspeople and rural visitors alike.

Scattered over the map of Europe were literally thousands of these ordinary towns, ranging from fewer than 1,000 inhabitants to perhaps 20,000, anything larger being reckoned a fairly big city. How many we cannot really say. A legal definition of a town or city depends on the grant at some time of a charter. A functional definition implies a minimum population, an organized periodic market, or a range of occupations besides farming, forestry, or fishing. Even with better and more comprehensive data than we have, different places would qualify as towns according to the criterion chosen. In fact, students of Europe's urban system and its evolution over three centuries have adopted thresholds of at least 5,000 inhabitants. To the extent that large cities fared better than small ones in our period, leaving out the latter exaggerates the growth of the urban share.

How large a share of Europe's population was urban? This varied between regions, and so does the precision of our estimates in this prestatistical era. Most scholars agree that barely one in ten Europeans lived in a sizable (>5,000) town in 1500—as many as one in four in Flanders and in northern Italy, far fewer in most of northern and eastern Europe. Still, adding the smaller towns and those people who spent some time in a town, perhaps one in five persons experienced urban life as more than a visitor. Growth in the urban share was concentrated in regions that were underurbanized in 1500, while those with a high initial share actually became less urban. England stands out from the rest of Europe in the later eighteenth century because the mass urbanization associated with the industrial revolution was under way by 1760 or so. However, the European urban proportion changed little for the period as a whole, with any increase almost within the bounds of uncertainties in measurement.

THE SMALL CITY

What was the "typical" small town like? It was enclosed by a wall, and since building a wall was no small task, a growing town would put up with a lot of crowding before expanding the enclosed area. Conversely, losing population freed up space on which to graze animals or bleach cloth. The town plan could take many forms, a rough circle with four gates and two main roads crossing in the center being common, a neat design, such as a rectangular grid, less so. The plan, the style of the houses, and many other aspects of life had not changed much since the Middle Ages, when the town was founded, nor would highly visible changes take place until well into the industrial age, if then. The churches, the market—a hall or an open place—and a guildhall or town hall were the dominant structures while a few larger dwellings such as a monastery, a noble house, or a ruined castle stood out from the rest in terms of size and style.

The population included officials of the municipality and the territorial authority, either lord or king. Local gentry might also reside in town all or part of the year. Clergy were numerous, especially in Catholic countries, and bishops could still rule cities. Most characteristically urban were craft occupations, often combined with retail trade. Master and journeyman now represented a fairly permanent status, more like modern-day employer and employee. Given the difficulties of travel to a larger city, the town might house a few professionals, such as an apothecary, a notary, and a barber surgeon. The largest category of working people,

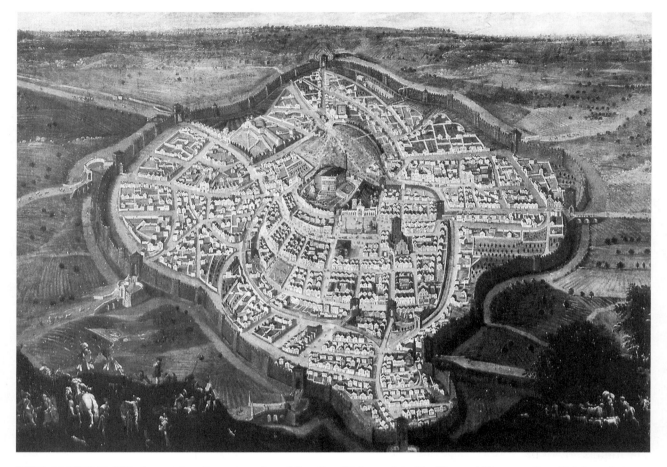

Cities and Urban Life. A seventeenth-century view of the city of Udine, painted by Giovanni Giuseppe Cosattini. A market town in the northern Italian region of Friuli since the thirteenth century, Udine grew rapidly after becoming subject to Venice in 1420. The fortifications date from the period 1220–1440. In the early sixteenth century, following an earthquake, town planners undertook a program of development and modernization that included the erection of a new castle and plaza. ©ELIO CIOL/CORBIS

however, was made up of servants, day laborers, and apprentices—enough servants, in fact, that many larger towns had a female majority. House-keeping was labor-intensive, as were transport and construction, though they employed mostly men.

Women, many of the unskilled, and those who were not native to the town were denied citizenship. The status of citizen or burgher was valued even though self-government was often limited to an elite of merchants, nobles, and officials. Wealth or important skills could procure citizenship, most easily during recovery from some demographic catastrophe. The other outsiders, tolerated and indeed indispensable for many rough tasks, were, like the undocumented aliens in many Western cities today, hard to keep track of. They were less likely to marry and more likely to die at an early age than were citizens. They also had less claim on assistance and

protection, mostly dispensed by the church, than the native-born paupers, orphans, and infirm of the town.

Trades still clustered on particular streets although people might also live in neighborhoods defined by extended families, clans, or loyalty to a powerful man. The center of town was considered desirable (in bigger cities the wealthy were laying out whole districts for their elegant new houses), while the suburbs, outside the walls, lacked status. The countryside, on the other hand, furnished a whole string of necessities, from laborers and wet nurses to food, wood, straw, raw materials, and carting services. In turn, farmers found in town a market, credit, and a range of consumer goods to buy. Burghers earned income from rural property and mortgages, and rich ones often acquired a country estate as a means of entry into the aristocracy (an alternative was to purchase a suitable royal appointment).

Day to day, the town's inhabitants dealt with one another, with the inhabitants of the surrounding countryside, and with those who passed through—peddlers and merchants, pilgrims and gypsies, soldiers and entertainers. But the larger world also impinged, more and more as time went on. A wider range of goods became common, including both colonial products and manufactures. Protoindustrial production could pit town against country, or merchants could enlist both to make and sell goods such as watches, textiles, or cutlery.

The spread of markets presaged the modern or capitalistic economy. But the wider world also affected our prototype town in the distant person of the sovereign, who regulated markets and demanded loyalty, service, and taxes. Since the king might farm out tax collection, and noble privileges and dues persisted, while the church also demanded payment of tithes, etc., the fiscal situation was almost always complicated and contested. Still, a hierarchy of administrative centers developed, with the royal capital at the apex and our little town a basic element. To sum up, towns played a critical role in the structuring of early modern society through both states and markets, coercion and commerce.

PERIODS OF GROWTH AND STAGNATION

Small towns grew in the sixteenth century when Europe finally regained (and surpassed) the population reached before the fourteenth-century crisis marked by the Black Death. Ports flourished along with market centers as the Atlantic Ocean joined the inland seas (Mediterranean, North, Baltic) and Europe's rivers as highways for trade. While regional and royal capitals changed relatively rarely, major ports competed strongly for leadership in commerce and finance. In the north, Bruges gave way to Antwerp and later to Amsterdam and London, while in the south, Genoa and Venice battled for supremacy, with Barcelona and Marseille also contesting for their share. Overall, however, the once-dominant Mediterranean was losing out to the Atlantic–North Sea region. Cities such as Bristol and Glasgow, Bordeaux and Nantes, Hamburg and Lübeck, Lisbon and Seville benefited from trade with the New World, whereas most Mediterranean ports stagnated after 1600.

Patterns of Urbanization in 1700

Population
- Greater than 100,000
- 40,000–100,000
- 20,000–40,000

By 1580, the urban renaissance showed signs of a slowdown. Small towns and free cities, such as Frankfurt and Cologne in Germany, saw their prosperity diminish. The turmoil of the next seventy years, centering on wars of religion, would concentrate growth in a relatively few large royal capitals (successful ports did not multiply their inhabitants to the same degree). Paris and London would at least double in population and surpass the half-million mark. Naples, despite weak trade, kept on growing. Newer capitals grew even faster in this period and the half century following. Madrid barely existed before it became the capital in 1567; by 1750 it had 123,000 souls. Berlin tripled its population after welcoming Huguenots expelled from France in 1685; and in 1703 Peter the Great began to drain a swamp for the Russian capital named after his patron saint. Similar stories can be told about Vienna, Stockholm, The Hague, court cities in Germany, and some subcapitals of empire, such as Brussels and Milan. On the periphery, colonial gateways such as Dublin, Charleston, and Lima combined trade with control by the home government.

The cycle turned again in the middle decades of the eighteenth century. With population growing, agriculture intensifying, and the first new industrial towns springing up, smaller places regained their share of urban growth. Even this reversal, however, did not stop many very small market centers from losing urban functions to nearby larger ones.

THE CAPITAL CITIES

How did a city grow so large merely because the monarch established her or his capital and court there, and what was life like in such a city? In this era of strong monarchy, the capital drew the many who served the sovereign directly. To rule is first of all to tax; hence there was a considerable fiscal apparatus. Senior judiciary and military officials also remained close to the seat of power. Elite military units— "household troops/regiments"—protected the monarch against riots and insurrection, which flourished in big cities, culminating in the Paris revolution of 1789.

Absolute monarchy meant a court, and many nobles added a house in the capital to their country residence. Of course, this additional source of expense added to the financial pressure on the nobility. Louis XIV of France consolidated his power by handing out a variety of pensions and profitable positions and requiring the candidates to stay at court. The more time they spent in Paris (where many nobles actually lived) or Versailles, the more need there was for royal patronage, and the more vital it was to stay around.

The system relied on pomp, ceremony, and festivities, so a court city needed a big working population "backstage." From pastry cooks to fencing masters, carriage makers to performers, lawyers, seamstresses, and chaise bearers, conspicuous consumption provided lots of employment. Along with individual craftsmen working to order, workshops near the demanding clientele produced an increasing range of manufactured luxury goods. Aristocrats and those who aspired to the aristocracy from all over soon looked to Paris or London for their furniture, clocks, ceramics, and bronzes. Monarchs also sponsored royal manufactures for porcelain, tapestries, and carpets or for military goods, where scale of production was important.

So much for the skilled trades. An army of servants, porters, and laborers helped craftsmen do their work and helped the rich get through their festive rounds. Of course, even the most lavish court did not fully dominate a city of several hundred thousand. The same groups we encountered in our small town formed a community of burghers that mostly stood apart from the goings-on of the aristocracy. They merely had less voice, whether in governing the city or in determining its outward appearance. Finally, big cities attracted a substantial underside of society: shady characters who offered forbidden pleasures or peddled banned literature, stealthy or violent criminals, beggars and paupers.

The menials had a big job keeping dirt and congestion from overwhelming the city completely. Huge amounts of food and fuel had to be brought in, and considerable tonnages of waste removed. Potable water was in perennially short supply although water itself might be too abundant. Disease and fire were ever-present dangers. London experienced both in the 1660s but rose again, bigger and busier than ever. However, grandiose plans to rebuild with straight and wide avenues after the Great Fire were shelved. Like most cities, London retained its narrow, winding, sewerless streets. Crowding was the rule, with rickety stories piled on top of leaning houses.

The blunt truth is that investment in urban amenities and infrastructure, particularly in the splendid baroque capitals, badly failed to cope with the numbers who flocked in. In fact, a constant stream of migrants was required, not only to fuel growth but to make up for a substantial natural deficit. Many urban dwellers, clerics and servants for example, remained unmarried, and death rates, for infants and adults alike, were always high and subject to sharp peaks during epidemics. Did this flow stimulate the surrounding countryside or rob it of vital forces? Historians can't agree or at least find examples of both.

The occasional monumental construction, broad boulevard, or elegant new neighborhood of "hotels" or "city-palaces" (often at the western, or windward edge of the older districts), should not deceive us. Mud, dirt, darkness, and pollution were the lot of most people, not just the very poor, and so were crowding, violence, and disease. Yet many came and stayed, preferring the stimulating dangers of the big city to the calm and relative safety of the smaller town or the farming village.

The urban share of the population may not have risen much, but European arts and letters—from the Italian Renaissance, to Dutch painting and Italian music, to the salons of Paris and the coffeehouses of London in the Enlightenment—became resolutely urban pursuits. Even the great country houses were designed and furnished in a fully urban style, and when the early Romantics looked to nature, it was very much from the point of view of city people. Yet unlike politics and culture, the big economic change on the horizon would not originate in the metropolitan cities, though it would eventually transform them. Even before 1800, the industrial revolution was actually being hatched in the countryside. However, cities would continue to dominate commerce and finance, as well as science and education, and in the nineteenth century industry would vastly expand existing towns and create sprawling agglomerations unlike any city before.

Finally, a word about technology. Early modern advances in production or transportation did little to change urban life. The horse remained supreme on land; building techniques did not change; and medicine remained largely powerless. However, two sets of inventions did make a difference to cities. The diffusion of printing and paper put books, newspapers, broadsides, and pamphlets in easy reach of town dwellers and facilitated literacy and schooling. Clocks and watches changed attitudes toward time and quickened the pace of social life and business.

See also **Amsterdam; Antwerp; Barcelona; Berlin; City Planning; Cologne; Hamburg; London; Lübeck; Madrid; Naples; Nuremberg; Paris; St. Petersburg; Seville; Versailles.**

BIBLIOGRAPHY

Abrams, Philip, and E. A. Wrigley, eds. *Towns in Societies: Essays in Economic History and Historical Sociology.* Cambridge, U.K., and New York, 1978.

Braudel, Fernand. *Civilization and Capitalism, 15th–18th Century.* 3 vols. New York, 1982–1984.

Clark, Peter, ed. *Small Towns in Early Modern Europe.* Cambridge, U.K., and New York, 1995.

Clark, Peter, and Bernard Lepetit. *Capital Cities and Their Hinterlands in Early Modern Europe.* Aldershot, U.K., 1996.

De Vries, Jan. *European Urbanization, 1500–1800.* Cambridge, Mass., 1984.

Epstein, S. R., ed. *Town and Country in Europe, 1300–1800.* Cambridge, U.K., and New York, 2001.

Hohenberg, Paul M., and Lynn Hollen Lees. *The Making of Urban Europe, 1000–1994.* Cambridge, Mass., 1995.

Langton, Jack, and Göran Hoppe. *Town and Country in the Development of Early Modern Western Europe.* Norwich, U.K., 1983.

O'Brien, Patrick, ed. *Urban Achievement in Early Modern Europe: Golden Ages in Antwerp, Amsterdam, and London.* Cambridge, U.K., and New York, 2001.

Tilly, Charles, and Wim P. Blockmans, eds. *Cities and the Rise of States in Europe,* A.D. *1000 to 1800.* Boulder, Colo., 1994.

PAUL M. HOHENBERG

CITIZENSHIP. In the modern world, citizenship is a legal status that bestows uniform rights and duties upon all members of a state. Modern citizenship is associated with equality before the law, freedom from arbitrary rule, and a basic sense of human dignity bound up with the idea of human rights. It is a powerful term that evokes not only the rights that citizens may claim, but also the duties to which they are called, including dying for one's country. In early modern Europe, the status of citizen was far feebler and more varied in nature. At the dawn of this period, there were no centralized national states, and the vast majority of the population were servile peasants who lived under the rule of a local lord. The idea of citizenship, that is, a body of free people bound by a common law, was restricted to those who enjoyed full rights of membership in privileged towns, the burghers or bourgeois. There was no concept of universal rights of citizens. Rights took the form of privileges that were legitimated by tradition and distributed inequitably according to place, rank, and membership in other corporate bodies—guilds, parliaments, universities, and the like. Urban citizenship was thus just one form of juridical status that coexisted alongside a wide array of corporate groups entitling members to rights and privileges.

RIGHTS AND RESPONSIBILITIES

In general, the citizenship of towns offered several kinds of benefits. Only citizens could hold municipal office and perhaps engage in lucrative urban trades. They enjoyed the privilege of being tried in a local court by their peers and were usually entitled to reduced taxes. Citizenship was commonly restricted to the propertied elite. Jean-Jacques Rousseau's Geneva, for example, was divided into an inner core of "citizens" and "bourgeois" who exercised full urban rights, and a wider tier of "inhabitants" and "natives," who had the right to live in the city but not to participate in the most profitable professions or hold municipal office.

The actual type and worth of rights conferred by urban citizenship varied by town. In Zurich and London citizenship was not prerequisite for access to the guilds. In fact, guild membership could be a way to acquire citizenship. In sixteenth-century Antwerp, it was not uncommon for members of the city council to register for citizenship just before taking office. In some cases, acquisition of citizenship was turned into a routine commercial transaction. In theory, the laws of sixteenth-century Bologna made it difficult for naturalized citizens to hold municipal office. In reality, citizens selected for office frequently designated a substitute to fill the post, a practice that amounted to a form of office selling. Nonetheless, urban citizenship might offer important advantages to its members. Citizens of Antwerp (poorters), for example, could not be arrested without cause and were exempt from torture. This was of little concern until the 1540s when the number of registrations for citizenship in Antwerp suddenly jumped. At that time, the town council began to use Antwerp's citizenship rights to protect persecuted Protestants.

Citizenship entailed responsibilities as well as rights. Citizens might be required to serve in the urban militia and to pay local taxes supporting the cost of communal self-government and fortifications. The status of citizen was usually inherited, but it could also be acquired by foreigners. Usually, naturalization required establishing a residence within the city for an extended period of time, paying specified taxes, and taking on other obligations of urban membership. Frequently, citizenship was associated with social and moral qualities. Many central European cities refused citizenship to adulterers and bastards.

Citizenship first became the object of more systematic theoretical reflection in self-governing Italian city-states during the early Renaissance. The recovery of Aristotle and other classical authors, combined with the struggle of Italian city-states to assert their independence from emperors and foreign invaders, stimulated thinkers to clarify the basis of political community. One important strand drew on the work of Bartolus of Sassoferato and his pupil, Baldus de Ubaldis, the most influential jurists working in the Roman law tradition. They provided the first philosophical foundation for viewing the city-state as a fully independent, self-governing corporation of citizens.

A second important tradition drew on Florentine civic humanism. Humanists argued that the best form of government was elective, not monarchical, since elected rulers would best work to achieve the goals of the republic: to attain glory, sustain liberty, and preserve the common good. The civic humanist tradition culminated in the *Discourses* of Niccolò Machiavelli, who wrote in a period of tumult following the French invasion of Italy in 1494. Looking back to the tradition of the Roman Republic, Machiavelli urged his fellow citizens to prevent decline by practicing *virtù*. For Machiavelli, *virtù* meant the patriotic love of the republic that led citizens to place the welfare of the political community above individual interests. Good laws and institutions were also necessary to sustain *virtù*. Among the latter, the most important were civil religion to foster a spirit of unity and a citizen militia to encourage a spirit of self-sacrifice and bravery.

NATIVES AND FOREIGNERS

Given its classical, urban, and corporate roots, citizenship was not easily transferred to monarchical realms, where the king reputedly embodied the state and where vast aristocratic patron-client systems created webs of political obligation. A rudimentary idea of citizenship did distinguish native-born subjects of kingdoms (known as denizens in England, *regnicoles* in France, and *naturales* in Spain) from foreigners, who suffered various kinds of disabilities. In Spain, only *naturales* of the five kingdoms of Aragón could hold offices in their respective kingdoms, engage in transatlantic commerce, or emigrate to the New World. In England, aliens could not vote in parliamentary elections, hold real property, own a British ship, or engage in the profitable colonial trade. In France, foreigners or *aubains* (a term originally applied to outsiders moving into the jurisdiction of a feudal lord) paid special taxes, and the king could seize their property upon death. Naturalization removed these disabilities. Naturalization might require proof of assimilation into the national culture, as was the case in Spain, or merely be a routine bureaucratic procedure. In France, one had to do little more than offer evidence of Catholicity and French residence and pay the necessary fees. In England, aliens could apply to Parliament for a private naturalization act, a route that was generally closed to Jews, Catholics, and Dissenters. A lesser status of "free denizen," which bestowed the right to participate in the colonial trade, could be purchased by those groups, but it did not grant exemption from steep alien custom duties.

In most cases, the status of a woman, whether at the municipal or national level, followed that of her husband. At times, however, foreign women married to foreign men seeking naturalization were required to be naturalized independently of their husbands. Because women generally could not hold office or practice lucrative trades, naturalization was of less worth to them than to men. Citizenship for women tended to remain a passive status that granted basic judicial protections, but did not authorize vital rights of political participation. Later, during the French Revolution, the secondary status of women was reconfirmed by the overt creation of "active" and "passive" categories of citizenship.

Throughout the early modern period, the quest for religious freedom and the evolution of citizenship remained closely tied. In the medieval world, the political community was also a closed community of Christian believers. Jews were outsiders, frequently banished, and allowed residence in certain countries only if they lived in specified locales, wore distinctive dress, paid special taxes, and the like. With the Reformation, Christian unity was shattered and states were "confessionalized," so that the enjoyment of civil and political rights became tied to membership in the established church of the realm. Religious dissenters might be prohibited from holding office, bequeathing property, joining guilds, obtaining an education, marrying, bringing up their own children, and receiving a Christian burial. In certain cases, toleration was granted as a concession from the ruler or in limited form, such as

the right to private worship. Freedom of religion as a universal right of citizenship, however, was only conceptualized after natural law theory offered a nondoctrinal way of legitimating membership in the state.

FROM ABSOLUTE MONARCHY TO ENLIGHTENMENT

The period of religious revolt in the later sixteenth and seventeenth centuries was critical to the rise of absolutist citizenship. Rebellious subjects invoked rights of the "ancient constitution" against absolute monarchs, or cited resistance theories that vested sovereignty in the ambiguous notion of "the people." The bloodshed of the period led royal theorists to define the citizen as a subject who owed unquestioned obedience to the sovereign in return for protection. In his *Six Books of the Commonwealth*, Jean Bodin stated that the citizen was "a free subject who is dependent on the sovereignty of another" (p. 19). Approximately a century later, in *De Cive, or, The Citizen* (1642), Thomas Hobbes presented a contractual theory of political society in which men voluntarily gave up the natural rights that they enjoyed in the bellicose state of nature to a ruler or ruling body in order to gain security: ". . . each citizen is called the subject of him who hath the chief command" (p. 68).

Despite Hobbes's theorizing, subjects showed themselves determined to hold onto historic rights. After James II was ousted from the English throne during the Glorious Revolution of 1688, a Bill of Rights declared that hierarchically ordered "estates" would be maintained in their "ancient rights and liberties." At the same time, John Locke's *Second Treatise on Government* pointed the way toward a far more radical interpretation of rights as abstract, natural, and universal in scope. For Locke, rights were "inalienable," derived from a free and egalitarian state of nature. Governments were not products of dynastic inheritance or divine will: they were artificial creations grounded in popular consent whose central purpose was to secure citizens' rights. Popularized through tracts such as Cato's *Letters,* a Lockean conception of rights ultimately became one of the major foundations of the American Declaration of Independence.

By the eighteenth century, then, the usage of the word "citizen" had begun to shed its absolutist association with "subject" and break free from the idea of graded ranks and historically conditioned privileges. This transformation was part of a wider linguistic shift. Words connoting a vertical ordering of society organized by notions of deference and command were abandoned or took on new meaning. The word "king" became uncoupled from "nation," which he had previously embodied. The word "society" no longer meant a business partnership, but a universal field of human relations. Social gradations still existed, but they were often described as classes, which implied productivity and individual effort, rather than as estates, orders, or corps, which suggested a preexisting, divinely sanctioned hierarchy. In the article "Citizen" in his *Encyclopedia,* Denis Diderot defined the citizen not in terms of participation in the privileges of a city, but as "a member of a free society . . . who partakes of the rights of that society and enjoys its privileges."

Two moral qualities were particularly associated with the citizen: utility and virtue. Political economists spread the idea that the most powerful state was the one that counted the greatest number of "industrious" men. The pursuit of plenty, according to these thinkers, was not something to be scorned for its corruption of civic spirit, but to be praised for its ability to unleash national productive power. Utility did not necessarily negate hierarchy, but it did shift the justification for social ranks from innate qualities, like noble birth, to functional attributes available to any hardworking person.

Virtue continued to be defined by reference to classical republican qualities. In his *Spirit of the Laws,* Montesquieu spoke of virtue in terms of "the love of our country, of the thirst of true glory, of self-denial, of the sacrifice of our dearest interests, and of all those heroic virtues which we admire in the ancients" (Vol. I, Bk. III.5, p. 23). Yet virtue also acquired enlightened overtones of sociability and humanitarianism. Rousseau spoke of virtue not only in terms of patriotic self-sacrifice, but also of sensibility and pity revealed through the inner voice of the conscience. For Rousseau and others, virtue was a humanitarian sentiment most easily found among the common people. By imparting moral worth to ordinary people, virtue legitimated their quest to gain a political voice.

Many rejected the ideals of classical republicanism as a model for citizenship altogether. The direct democracy suitable to small, face-to-face societies like the ancient republics would not work in large, culturally diffuse states. Furthermore, too much popular participation had opened up ancient republics to constant factionalism. Rather than relying on direct democracy, men like Jean Louis de Lolme argued, it would be better to set up a passive system of representation and create institutional checks and balances to channel the interests of the people toward the common good. Ancient republics, furthermore, had practiced slavery, denigrated women and domestic life, spurned commercial development, and even permitted infanticide. Republican citizenship would have to be made compatible with the technological progress, commercial prosperity, and humane virtues that most enlightened elites endorsed.

THE SOCIAL CONTRACT

By the end of the eighteenth century, then, two visions of republican citizenship had emerged. One, often labeled "liberal," was derived from a natural law tradition and emphasized the rights of individuals, representation, and material progress. It was concerned with checking arbitrary power and securing the conditions that would allow men and women to enjoy the fruits of their labor in peace. A second, more activist and communal strand inspired by classical republicanism appealed to civic virtues of self-sacrifice, public-spiritedness, and the constant vigilance of citizens against enemies of freedom.

Jean-Jacques Rousseau brought elements of both traditions together in *The Social Contract,* a treatise meant to serve as an ideal, not an actual blueprint, for society. According to Rousseau, men in their natural state were free and equal, but they were also amoral and governed by instinct. Men reached their full human potential only through the exercise of citizenship. In the social contract, each individual gave up his powers from the state of nature to everyone else in order to form a state. The essence of citizenship, then, was participation in the social contract, which created a state of morality, civil freedom, equality, and democratic participation. Citizens were bound by law, but remained free, because they imposed laws on themselves. Citizens were equal before the law, because everyone came into the social contract under the same terms. The public interest or "general will" served as the ultimate source of law, because all individuals had sacrificed their private interests to become part of the state. For Rousseau, citizenship was a legal status, but not a passive one, as it implied moral duties and active participation.

The actual transition to a new form of citizenship stemmed from the practical need to make states more competitive in war. In France the monarchy contributed to a more egalitarian definition of society by attempting to tax privileged members of society. Royal reforming ministers and their allies argued that payment of taxes defined citizenship, because all members of society, even the privileged, owed the state taxes in return for protection. As the Physiocrat writer LeTrosne declared in his work on tax reform, ecclesiastical tax exemptions put the clergy "outside the class of citizens" and stripped them "of all right to civil protection" (p. 501). In reply, the most powerful corporate bodies in France, the sovereign courts known as parlements, stretched corporate politics to the breaking point and went beyond their traditional defense of "fundamental laws." Claiming to speak for "the Nation," the parlements stated that the nation had a right to consent to taxes and thereby made themselves virtual co-sovereigns with the king.

The bankruptcy of the French government in 1788 proved that a new organization of the state was necessary. Drawing on political economy and social contract theory, the Abbé Sieyès in *What Is the Third Estate?* laid out the terms of modern citizenship as a national, egalitarian, and utilitarian status. Citizens were members of the nation, that is, "a body of associates living under common laws" (p. 55). Since privileges were exemptions from the common law, all those who enjoyed privileges, notably the nobility, were noncitizens. Eventually, this logic was used to justify the execution of the king, since an absolute monarch stood outside the common law formed by the social contract and thus could be judged, as Saint Just argued in 1792, "not as a citizen, but as a rebel" (p. 123). Enshrined in "The Declaration of the Rights of Man and of the Citizen" of 1789, citizenship became synonymous with both the enjoyment of fundamental rights and a new vision of national sovereignty. Rather than being one legal status among many in a corporate society, citizenship had become the primary status mediating all other juridical relationships in the state and the primary marker of human worth.

See also **Bodin, Jean; Cities and Urban Life; Class, Status, and Order; Democracy; Diderot, Denis; Enlightened Despotism; Hobbes, Thomas; Locke, John; Machiavelli, Niccolò; Monarchy; Montesquieu, Charles-Louis de Secondat de; Parlements; Political Philosophy; Political Secularization; Revolutions, Age of; Rousseau, Jean-Jacques.**

BIBLIOGRAPHY

Primary Sources

Bodin, Jean. *Six Books of the Commonwealth.* Edited and translated by M. J. Tooley. Oxford, 1955 (First published in 1573).

Hobbes, Thomas. *De Cive, or, The Citizen.* Edited by Sterling P. Lamprecht. Westport, Conn., 1982.

Diderot, Denis. *Political Writings.* Edited and translated by John Hope Mason and Robert Wokler. Cambridge, U.K., 1992. Includes translation of Diderot's article on "Citizen" from his *Encyclopedia.*

Le Trosne, Guillaume François. *De l'administration provinciale et de la réforme de l'impôt.* Basel, 1779.

Locke, John. *Two Treatises of Government.* Edited by Peter Laslett. Cambridge, U.K., 1988.

Machiavelli, Niccolò. *The Discourses.* Translated by Leslie J. Walker, S. J. Edited by Bernard Crick. Harmondsworth, U.K., 1970. Translation of *I discorsi.*

Montesquieu, Charles-Louis de Secondat de. *The Spirit of the Laws.* 2 vols. in one. Translated by Thomas Nugent. New York, 1959. Translation of *L'esprit des lois* (1748).

Rousseau, Jean-Jacques. *The Social Contract.* Translated by Maurice Cranston. London, 1968. Translation of *Du contrat social* (1762).

Saint-Just, Louis Antoine Léon de. "Speech at the Trial of the King, November 13, 1792." In *Regicide and Revolution: Speeches at the Trial of Louis XVI.* Translated by Marian Rothstein. Edited by Michael Walzer. Pp. 120–127. New York, 1974.

Sieyès, Emmanuel Joseph. *What is the Third Estate?* Translated by M. Blondel. New York, 1963. Translation of *Qu'est que le tiers état?* (1789).

Secondary Sources

Baker, Keith Michael. "Transformations of Classical Republicanism in Eighteenth-Century France." *Journal of Modern History* 73 (March 2001): 32–53.

Boone, Marc, Simona Cerutti, Robert Descimon, and Maarten Prak. "Introduction: Citizenship Between Individual and Community, 14th–18th Centuries." In *Statuts individuels, statuts corporatifs et statuts judiciaires dans les villes européenes (moyen âges et temps modernes*), edited by Marc Boone and Maarten Prak. Leuven, 1996.

Brubaker, Roger. *Citizenship and Nationhood in France and Germany.* Cambridge, Mass., 1992.

Canning, Joseph. "A Fourteenth-Century Contribution to the Theory of Citizenship: Political Man and the Problem of Created Citizenship in the Thought of Baldus de Ubaldis." In *Authority and Power: Studies in Medieval Law and Government Presented to Walter Ulmann on His Seventieth Birthday,* edited by Brian Tierney and Peter Linehan. Cambridge, U.K., 1980.

Howell, Martha. "Citizenship and Gender: Women's Political Status in Northern Medieval Cities." In *Women and Power in the Middle Ages,* edited by Mary Erler and Maryanne Kowaleski, pp. 37–60. Athens, Ga., 1988.

Kirshner, Jules, and Laurent Mayali, eds. *Privileges and Rights of Citizenship.* Berkeley, 2002.

Marshall, T. H. *Class, Citizenship and Social Development: Essays by T. H. Marshall.* Westport, Conn., 1973.

Oldfield, Adrien. *Citizenship and Community: Civic Republicanism and the Modern World.* London, 1990.

Pocock, J. G. A. "The Ideal of Citizenship since Classical Times." In *The Citizenship Debates,* edited by Gershon Shafir, pp. 31–42. Minneapolis, 1998.

Prak, Martin. "Citizen Radicalism and Democracy in the Dutch Republic: The Patriot Movement of the 1780s." *Theory and Society* 20 (1991): 73–102.

Rahe, Paul. "Antiquity Surpassed: The Repudiation of Classical Republicanism." In *Republicanism, Liberty, and Commercial Society, 1649–1776,* edited by David Wootton. Stanford, 1994.

Reinhard, Wolfgang. "Reformation, Counter-Reformation and the Early Modern State: A Reassessment." *Catholic Historical Review* 85 (July 1989): 383–404.

Riesenberg, Peter. *Citizenship in the Western Tradition: Plato to Rousseau.* Chapel Hill, N.C., 1992.

Sahlins, Peter. *Unnaturally French: Foreign Citizens in the Old Regime and After.* Ithaca, N.Y., 2003.

Schilling, Heinz, "Civic Republicanism in Late Medieval and Early Modern German Cities." In *Religion, Political Culture and the Emergence of Early Modern Society: Essays in German and Dutch History,* pp. 3–60. Leiden, 1992.

Sewell, William H. "Le Citoyen/la citoyenne: Activity, Passivity, and the Revolutionary Concept of Citizenship." In *The French Revolution and the Creation of Modern Political Culture, Vol. II,* edited by Colin Lucas, pp. 105–123. Oxford, 1988.

Viroli, Maurizio. *For Love of Country: An Essay on Patriotism and Nationalism.* Oxford, 1995.

Wells, Charlotte C. *Law and Citizenship in Early Modern France.* Baltimore, 1995.

Zuckert, Michael P. *Natural Rights and the New Republicanism.* Princeton, 1994.

GAIL BOSSENGA

CITY PLANNING. In early modern Europe city planning was not a profession, as it is today, but a function of public administration and the emerging profession of architecture. Plans for new cities, extensions, and redevelopment were made by monarchs, bureaucrats, municipal authorities, architects, military engineers, and amateurs. From the mid-fifteenth through the eighteenth centuries, the broad trend in the theory of city planning was increased understanding of cities as complex systems of interrelated elements having to do with public utility and beautification.

Planning was informed by practices established in the Middle Ages and memories of ancient Rome. The medieval legacy included municipal building regulations and a repertoire of urban design techniques and features, among which were plans based on grids, such as the *bastides* of France and Spain, and symbolically charged public spaces, such as the Piazza del Campo in Siena. Popes, such as Alexander VII (reigned 1655–1667); kings, such as Louis XIV (ruled 1643–1715); and even the governments of the French Revolution regarded imperial Rome as the supreme model for public administration and urban grandeur and vied to meet the standard of magnificence suggested by ancient ruins and descriptions in Roman literature.

Medieval rulers and artisans involved in planning cities drew on a variety of texts, including the treatise on architecture by the ancient Roman architect Vitruvius (first century B.C.E.), but they did not write systematically on the subject. This task was taken up in the fifteenth century by Italian authors, who, reinterpreting Vitruvius, addressed urban design within comprehensive treatises on architecture. Influential in this respect were Leon Battista Alberti (1404–1472), Filarete (Antonio di Pietro Averlino, c. 1400–c.1469), and Francesco di Giorgio Martini (1439–1502). They posited ideal cities shaped by theories of fortification, social order, and geometry. In their view, urban design was to follow the same compositional principles of hierarchy, symmetry, and regularity that governed architecture. Diagrammatically, the ideal city was contained within walls forming a regular polygon. The street pattern was regular and could be a grid or a radial system. A public square with buildings housing secular and religious authority occupied the center. For over two hundred years, this model served for the planning of military garrison towns such as Palmanova, Italy (1593), and Neuf-Brisach, France (1698). In a few instances, such as Charleville (1608) in France and Zamość (c. 1579) in Poland, local princes adopted the model as an expression of prestige and cultural attainment.

The theoretical treatment of city planning in the sixteenth and seventeenth centuries generally followed themes established earlier, but thinking about planning was hardly stagnant. Developments can be seen best in building regulations. Among the more notable legislative achievements were the Spanish Laws of the Indies, promulgated in 1573, which included many provisions addressing city planning in the New World; the Rebuilding Acts of 1667 and 1670 for the reconstruction of London after the Great Fire (1666); and the regulations governing the construction of St. Petersburg, issued from 1714 to 1737. The London ordinances, for example, addressed building materials and construction techniques, street widths, and standardized house types.

Beginning in the mid-eighteenth century, several new attitudes transformed city planning theory. Military engineering was increasingly regarded as a discrete profession, and the links between fortifications and urban design loosened. Authors such as the French architect Pierre Patte (1723–1814) promoted the creation of master plans that addressed traffic circulation, sewage, and street lighting among other functional and aesthetic concerns. In some settings, questions regarding city planning became matters of public debate. In Paris in 1748, the decision to create a square honoring Louis XV (now the Place de la Concorde) prompted an informal competition attracting amateurs as well as professionals. Other indications of increased public interest are books and pamphlets advocating the adoption of specific plans, such as John Gwynn's (1713–1786) proposal for London, published in 1766.

Urban populations increased significantly in early modern Europe, but most of the growth was in existing cities. New cities were founded as instruments of specific state policies. In addition to garrison cities, specialized types included seaports (Livorno, Italy, 1576), cities supporting princely palaces (Versailles, France, 1660s–1680s), and manufacturing centers (Perm, Russia, 1723). In the second half of the eighteenth century, some designers, among them the French architect Claude-Nicolas Ledoux (1736–1806), regarded such foundations as opportunities for social as well as physical planning. New cities typically were modest in scope. An exception was St. Petersburg (fortress begun 1703), which Peter the Great (ruled 1682–1725) envisioned as a full-fledged capital rivaling Amsterdam, London, and Paris.

City planning throughout early modern Europe primarily addressed the extension, redevelopment, and reconstruction of existing cities. The primary compositional elements of urban design were grid-iron and radial street patterns, public squares, and broad, straight streets aligned with architectural monuments and framed, ideally, by buildings with uniform facades. These elements were refined in Italy during the sixteenth and seventeenth centuries, noted by travelers, and depicted in engravings and paintings. In Rome, influential examples included the improved streets linking major Christian monuments and the public squares designed by Michelangelo on the Capitoline Hill (begun 1538) and Gian Lorenzo Bernini at St. Peter's (1656). Among other celebrated works were Piazza San Marco in Venice (improvements begun 1537) and the extensions of Turin realized throughout the seventeenth century.

The crowded centers of medieval cities were enticing targets for redevelopment, but the high cost of land acquisition limited the scale of most projects. Disasters offered extraordinary opportunities for transformation, as was the case in Lisbon following the earthquake of 1755. In many instances, however, major changes to the street plan could not be implemented. Ambitious new plans by Christopher Wren (1632–1723) and others for London after the Great Fire were put aside in order to simplify reconstruction. Extensions offered the most frequent opportunity for planning. Their scope varied from piecemeal additions (eighteenth-century Berlin) to single plans more than doubling a city's land area (Nancy, France, 1588), and various combinations of speculative and governmental interests drove them. Among the most spectacular examples are the extensions to London and Bath, England, realized by developers throughout the eighteenth century. A distinctive feature of their work was the use of squares, often containing a private park, framed by row houses embellished to a greater or lesser extent by classical details in accordance with the wealth of the intended occupants.

See also **Architecture; Bernini, Gian Lorenzo; Britain, Architecture in; Cities and Urban Life; Classicism; France, Architecture in; Ledoux, Claude-Nicolas; London; Paris; Peter I (Russia); Rome, Architecture in; Russia, Architecture in; St. Petersburg; Venice, Architecture in; Versailles; Wren, Christopher.**

BIBLIOGRAPHY

Primary Sources

Alberti, Leon Battista. *On the Art of Building in Ten Books.* Translated by Joseph Rykwert, Neil Leach, and Robert Tavernor. Cambridge, Mass., 1988. Translation of *De Re Aedificatoria,* c. 1450.

Filarete (Antonio di Pietro Averlino). *Treatise on Architecture.* Translated by John R. Spencer. 2 vols. New Haven, 1965. Original, untitled manuscript dates from c. 1461.

Gwynn, John. *London and Westminster Improved.* Farnborough, U.K., 1969. Originally published in 1766.

Martini, Francesco di Giorgio. *Trattato di architettura, ingegneria ed arte militare.* Edited by Corrado Maltese. 2 vols. Milan, 1967. Original manuscripts date from 1475–1476 and c. 1482–1492.

Patte, Pierre. *Mémoires sur les objets les plus importants de l'architecture.* Paris, 1769.

———. *Monuments érigés en France à la gloire de Louis XV.* Paris, 1765.

Vitruvius Pollio. *Vitruvius: Ten Books on Architecture.* Translated and edited by Ingrid D. Rowland and Thomas Noble Howe. Cambridge, U.K., and New York, 1999. Translation of *De architectura.*

Secondary Sources

Girouard, Mark. *Cities and People: A Social and Architectural History.* New Haven, 1985.

Harouel, Jean-Louis. *L'embellissement des villes: L'urbanisme français au XVIIIe siècle.* Paris, 1993.

Hohenberg, Paul M., and Lynn Hollen Lees. *The Making of Urban Europe, 1000–1950.* Cambridge, Mass., 1985.

Kostof, Spiro. *The City Assembled: The Elements of Urban Form through History.* London, 1992.

———. *The City Shaped: Urban Patterns and Meanings through History.* London, 1991.

Morris, A. E. J. *History of Urban Form: Before the Industrial Revolutions.* 2nd ed. New York, 1994.

RICHARD CLEARY

CITY-STATE. City-states were autonomous, self-governing states led by a city. They controlled land outside the walls, from a few square miles, for many of the imperial free cities of Germany, to the huge land-and-sea empire of the Republic of Venice. All city-states had collective governments, usually a narrow or broad oligarchy. With the exception of the largely rural Swiss city-states, their economies were based on trade and manufacturing. A vital part of European politics, economy, and culture in 1500, city-states declined in importance in the next three centuries.

City-states rose in the Middle Ages in areas of Europe lacking strong territorial monarchies. North Italian towns won their independence from the Holy Roman Empire in the late twelfth and early thirteenth centuries. Geographical remoteness and mountains protected the Swiss city-states from outside rule. In Germany many towns had achieved the status of imperial free city by the end of the Middle Ages. They governed themselves but were expected to follow the lead of the Holy Roman Empire in foreign policy and to provide financial support when necessary.

ITALIAN CITY-STATES

Venice, Genoa, Florence, Siena, and Lucca were the best known, largest, and most important Italian city-states. Venice and Genoa were the leading trading powers of the Mediterranean Sea in the fifteenth and sixteenth centuries, and Venice remained important through the seventeenth century. Trade led to manufacturing and banking. Venice was a printing and glass manufacturing center, while Genoese bankers lent money to monarchs, especially Spain. Florence was a commercial and banking center and a renowned wool manufacturer. Siena was an influential commercial city in central Italy, and Lucca had an important silk industry.

All five Italian city-states had republican forms of government. They viewed themselves and their institutions as the heirs of the city-states of ancient Rome and Greece, despite some considerable differences. A series of interlocking councils made major decisions in the Italian city-states. Leading adult male citizens, except for clergymen, were elected or chosen through lot to fill seats on executive and legislative councils. Terms of office ranged from two months to one year. The franchise and the right to hold office was broad but did not extend to all the inhabitants of the town. The Republic of Venice had a unique form of government. Only adult male nobles whose legitimate ancestry could be traced back to 1297 were eligible to hold office. But this still included about 2,000–2,500 men in a total population of about 175,000 in the late sixteenth century. The gerontocratic nature of Venetian politics further encouraged consensus. A young noble began the climb to high political office in his early twenties under the watchful eyes of his elders and, if found able, reached the most important councils in his mid-fifties. In Genoa a number of prominent families shared governmental responsibility. Both Venice and Genoa elected doges to be ceremonial heads of government with limited authority. Florence was more democratic. In the years between 1498 and 1512, about 3,000 adult males were eligible for public office in a population of about 70,000. The smaller Siena and Lucca were ruled by relatively broad oligarchies drawn from the leading citizens. However, none of the Italian republican city-states offered significant political rights to the inhabitants of their subject territories outside the capital city.

GERMAN CITY-STATES

Some sixty-five cities in what is now called Germany enjoyed the title and privileges of free imperial cities. Not ruled by prince or bishop, they were self-governing states who recognized only the remote overlordship of the Holy Roman emperor. Along with princes, prince-bishops, and knights, the free imperial cities had their own representation in the imperial diet, the consultative body which met periodically to discuss imperial affairs and to grant financial support to the emperor. The most important free cities were located in southwestern Germany. Augsburg had 50,000 people in the early sixteenth century and considerable importance as a commercial center, although its territory was small. Nuremberg had about 20,000 inhabitants inside the city walls and another 20,000 in over 400 villages in the fields and forests ruled by Nuremberg. Other important free cities included Magdeburg, Cologne, Frankfurt am Main, and Strasbourg. Ulm, much smaller in population than Augsburg, controlled some 500 square miles of territory outside its walls. Hamburg, with 20,000 inhabitants in 1550, which rose to about 60,000 in the late seventeenth century, was the most important city-state in northern Germany and a center for shipping, publishing, textile production, and banking. The Hanseatic League cities of Lübeck, Bremen, and Gdańsk (Danzig) were also imperial free cities in northern Germany and Poland.

Oligarchical city councils dominated by leading merchants and professional men from wealthy established families governed the free cities. Although some cities had limited-franchise elections, seats in the city council were often hereditary: When a council member died, his son or nephew succeeded him. By the sixteenth century artisan guilds had almost no formal role in government. Nevertheless, artisans made their views known, and city council members took them into account, because they feared civil unrest. Because both wealthy merchants and modest artisans saw their personal well-being dependent on that of the city, German free cities had a strong communal identity.

SWISS CITY-STATES

The thirteen independent cantons of the Swiss Confederation made up the third group. The Swiss Confederation grew from the three original forest cantons of Uri, Schwys, and Unterwalden, then added Lucerne (1332), Zurich (1351), Glarus (1352), Zug (1352), and Bern (1353). Solothurn and Fribourg were added in 1481, then Basel and Schaffhausen in 1501, and Appenzell in 1513. Geneva won its independence from the House of Savoy in the sixteenth century but did not become a member of the Swiss Confederation until the end of the eighteenth century. Swiss cities and towns were small in population: Geneva had 13,000 people, Basel had 10,000, and Zürich had 7,000 in the early sixteenth century. But compared with the German free cities, they controlled considerable surrounding territory. The cantons of Glarus, Grisons, Schwyz, Unterwalden, Uri, and Zug were rural, mountainous, and forested, with tiny, isolated populations.

Some cantons ruled additional lands outside their borders, while the Swiss Confederation as a whole also held land. However, the Confederation was only a loose association organized to pursue common interests, such as defense against invaders, rather than a central government. It could not prevent wars between cantons. By 1500 the Swiss cantons enjoyed de facto independence from the Holy Roman Empire, a condition recognized in 1648. Councils composed of prominent citizens, either elected or semi-hereditary, ruled individual cantons. The independent city-state of Geneva elected its officials.

RELIGION AND THE CITY-STATES

City-states approached religious matters collectively. Leaders and people believed that the entire city-state was responsible to God for the actions of its inhabitants. Plague, flood, and military defeat were seen as God's punishment on the city as a whole for its sins. Consequently, leaders and people sought agreement on religious issues.

This also meant that city-states approached the local church and its clergymen in a possessive way. They believed that the local church should be responsible to them more than to the papacy. In Italian city-states the leaders of the local church came from prominent local families. In Venice the Senate chose the Venetian patriarch, the leader of the local church. Occasionally the Senate chose a prominent member of the government, who, upon being designated patriarch, became a clergyman. Once in office, the patriarch was expected to follow the lead of the civil government in disputes with the papacy and matters affecting the civil government.

German and Swiss city-states had similar attitudes in different circumstances. Before the Protestant Reformation the bishop was often a nonresident outsider, rather than a member of the ruling group of the city. This produced disputes, anticlericalism, and a receptive audience for the first Protestant preachers. When townspeople began to support the preachers, city councils had to make decisions about the religious direction of the city-states. Since they wished to affirm the unity of the city-state before God and to keep the peace, they often moved the city-state into the Protestant camp. They moved cautiously, usually orchestrating a step-by-step, orderly, and reasonably peaceful transition to Protestantism. German and Swiss city-states were among the first states to embrace the Protestant Reformation. Zurich and Nuremberg are much-studied examples. Geneva won its independence from the House of Savoy and its bishop in the mid-1520s, then became Protestant between 1532 and 1536.

However, as religious differences generated warfare between Protestant and Catholic states, the German free imperial cities were vulnerable. Religious and political warfare was a three-way struggle between empire, princes, and cities. The cities that became Protestant were obliged to form alliances with German Protestant princes, who ruled stronger states and commanded larger armies. These alliances also incurred the vengeance of the emperor, who retaliated against Protestant cities. The free cities that remained Catholic also became weaker, because they had to rely on the emperor for protection and were bled white to support him. After the sixty-year truce following the Religious Peace of Augsburg of 1555, the free cities again suffered during the Thirty Years' War (1618–1648). An imperial army brutally sacked the free city of Magdeburg and murdered twenty thousand of its inhabitants in 1631. Münster and Erfurt, not imperial free cities even though their bishops exercised no control, lost their independence to nearby princes, and Strasbourg came under French domination in the later seventeenth century. The Swiss city-states retained their independence because they were difficult to invade.

DECLINE

Some city-states were already losing their independence in the sixteenth century. In 1532 the Florentine Republic became the Duchy of Tuscany, ruled by the Medici family. Spain conquered Siena in 1555 and then sold the city to Florence in 1557. Genoa became a subservient ally of Spain in 1528, a move that enabled it to survive until 1798. By the eighteenth century the remaining independent city-states were fewer in number and weaker in every way compared with their condition in 1500. When the Holy Roman Empire was formally abolished in 1806, the free German city-states hardly existed except in law. Venice, the largest and most important city-state, lost Cyprus in 1571 and Crete and the rest of its eastern Mediterranean Empire in a series of wars with the Turks between 1645 and 1718. But it remained independent and the ruler of a sizeable part of northeastern Italy. Although its commerce waned, Venice remained a major European cultural, intellectual, artistic, and musical center through the eighteenth century. Then in 1797 the twenty-eight-year-old Napoleon Bonaparte, no respecter of age, conquered the 1,000-year-old Most Serene Republic of Venice. The much smaller Lucca emerged from the Napoleonic period still an independent city-state in 1817, but it was ruled by members of the Bourbon family, until it voted to join the Kingdom of Italy in 1860. The Swiss city-states maintained their independence.

In 1500 the city-states played essential roles in European politics, economy, and culture. But they could not afford the money and manpower to defend themselves against aggressive territorial monarchies and princedoms. They could not compete against national economies. And with the exception of Venice, their artistic and intellectual greatness faded. The city-states were major losers in the centuries between the Renaissance and the French Revolution.

See also Cities and Urban Life; Florence; Frankfurt am Main; Free and Imperial Cities; Gdańsk; Geneva; Hamburg; Hansa; Holy Roman Empire; Lübeck; Nuremberg; Reformation, Protestant; Representative Institutions; State and Bureaucracy; Strasbourg; Switzerland; Thirty Years' War (1618–1648); Venice; Zurich.

BIBLIOGRAPHY

Berengo, Marino. *Nobili e mercanti nella Lucca del Cinquecento.* Turin, 1965. Classic study of the city-state of Lucca.

Friedrichs, Christopher R. *The Early Modern City, 1450–1750.* London and New York, 1995.

Grendi, Edoardo. *La repubblica aristocratica dei genovesi.* Bologna, 1987. Politics, trade, and poor relief in Genoa, 1500–1700.

Lane, Frederic C. *Venice: A Maritime Republic.* Baltimore and London, 1973. The best one-volume history of Venice.

Mackenney, Richard. *The City State, 1500–1700: Republican Liberty in an Age of Princely Power.* Atlantic Highlands, N.J., 1989. A brief account.

Moeller, Bernd. *Imperial Cities and the Reformation.* Edited and translated by H. C. Erik Midelfort and Mark U. Edwards, Jr. Durham, N.C., 1982. First published in 1972. See pp. 41–115 for the title essay. Argues for the importance of free imperial cities in the Reformation.

Monter, E. William. *Calvin's Geneva.* New York, 1967. Excellent short account of Geneva in the sixteenth century.

Strauss, Gerald. *Nuremberg in the Sixteenth Century.* New York, 1966. Good history of all aspects of Nuremberg.

Walker, Mack. *German Home Towns: Community, State, and General Estate, 1648–1871.* Ithaca, N.Y., 1971. Classic, pioneering study.

PAUL F. GRENDLER

CIVIC RITUAL. *See* Ritual, Civic and Royal.

CIVIL ENGINEERING. *See* Engineering, Civil.

CIVIL WAR, ENGLISH. *See* English Civil War and Interregnum.

CLASS, STATUS, AND ORDER. All human societies require systems of classification. These systems straddle the imagined boundary between the ideal and the real, creating a standard by which society can assess, judge, and, if necessary, punish. Early modern Europeans inherited from their medieval ancestors a system of classification called the society of orders, yet they lived in a world increasingly structured by economic status, which modern societies have termed a society of classes. Historians long accepted three simple propositions about European social classification: The Middle Ages had a society of orders; the nineteenth and twentieth centuries had a society of classes; and early modern times had neither, forming a sort of battlefield in which "classes" overcame "orders."

These primitive constructs, the first relying heavily on a sociolegal definition, and the second on often artificial economic categories, provide deceptive simplifications of the most complex human activity: social differentiation. Medieval writers described a society of three orders: prayers, fighters, and workers. This description had real political meaning, because the three orders of so many European medieval representative bodies, like the Estates-General of the Low Countries, were the clergy, the nobility, and the towns.

This simplified general version of the society of orders, however, masked a far more complex system of classification, above all within the "workers," those who were neither members of the clergy nor of noble status. The three-orders model suggested that a wealthy merchant or powerful judge belonged to the same social classification as a rural day laborer. Viewed from the perspective of a rich urban merchant, only an aristocratic snob could take seriously such a view, yet a noble rightly, and legally, could insist that one was either noble or commoner, that the distinction of social order mattered.

NOBILITY AND STATUS

The legal nobility of any European society typically included 1 or 2 percent of the population, but in kingdoms such as Castile or the Polish-Lithuanian Commonwealth, 10 percent of the population held legal nobility. In western Europe, this group owned half or more of the land; in east central Europe, the nobility owned a far greater percentage. Within the nobility, four distinct categories stood out. Three-fourths of the nobility had little wealth. In east central Europe, such a noble might own a single village, or even part of a village; in western Europe, they would own neither a fief nor a château. In France, at the end of the seventeenth century, 80 percent of the nobility fell into this category. In Poland or Hungary, wealthy peasants sometimes enjoyed a much higher standard of living than poor nobles. The impoverished petty nobles of Castile, the *hidalgos*, provided many of the *conquistadores* for the Spanish Empire and even foot soldiers for the king's army.

Next up the ladder came the local lords, who held rights of *Herrschaft* in German lands or of high justice in most of the rest of continental Europe. These people provided the state function in much of rural Europe. Politically, they often demanded "republican" institutions such as provincial estates and an elected local judiciary. They had enough wealth to live comfortably in the countryside; their courts, and their social prestige, made them the dominant social group in much of rural Europe. By

the seventeenth century, many of these people held state offices, such as royal judgeships, through which they controlled local society.

Although European political and social theorists and governments tried to maintain the fiction that this group of nobility provided a permanent, ordered social and political elite, in fact, in much of Europe this group had a steady influx of newcomers. Wealthy urban merchants and lawyers bought rural estates and gradually insinuated themselves into the nobility by means of marriage, social behavior, and political participation. Such permeability mattered little in a place like Poland, where nobles formed 10 percent of the population, so social mobility took place primarily within the nobility, not into it. In England or France, however, a constant flow of commoners became noble (France) or joined the gentry (England). In Lancashire, between 1600 and 1642, more than one third of the 750 gentry families disappeared and were replaced by a like number of newcomers. The carnage of the Hundred Years' War (1337–1453) or of the sixteenth-century religious wars created massive shortages of nobles in England, France, the Holy Roman Empire, and the Low Countries. Each society had need of nobles in order to function; the new families replaced the ones who died out, casualties either of war or of demographic forces. Noble families also intermarried with wealthy commoners; above all, noble men married wealthy non-noble women.

The regional nobility, what some historians call the "second nobility," provided the crucial link between the base of village lords and the great aristocrats. These second nobles served as clients of the great nobles, yet they provided patronage to those at the local level. Their families often held minor bishoprics or headed middling abbeys or convents; the men served in princely armies and commanded fortresses or local noble militias.

The great aristocratic families above them— families like the Esterházy in Hungary, the Schwartzenberg in Bohemia, the Furstemburg in the Holy Roman Empire, the Radziwill in Lithuania, the Corsini in Florence, the Mendoza in Castile, the Rohan in Brittany, the d'Arenberg in the Spanish Netherlands, and the dukes of Bedford in England—had fabulous resources. Even here, new families could join the highest ranks of the aristocracy: Montmorency and Guise families rose to unprecedented heights in sixteenth-century France. Guise and Montmorency started the process of inflation of noble titles in France: They were the first people outside the royal family to obtain the title duke. Even so, France had only eleven duke-peers in 1589, as against forty-eight in 1715. This same inflation of titles happened everywhere in the West, whether in the proliferation of English "baronets" (a title invented by James I in 1611) or the tripling of titled nobles in Austrian lands between 1606 and 1657. The kingdom of Naples had ninety-nine titled nobles in 1528, but 649 in 1750; Spain had fifty-five titled nobles in 1520, but 528 in 1700.

These new titles undermined the status system, while simultaneously reinforcing it. Giving noble titles to prominent and successful commoners kept them from creating an alternative hierarchical system that would challenge the traditional one of the nobility. In those societies, like Holland, in which wealthy urban merchants did not seek to join the nobility, the merchants did, in fact, create a new social and political hierarchy, in which the nobles had virtually no role. In the Estates of Holland, the towns held twenty-four votes, while the collective nobility of the province had only one.

The aristocrats lived in stunning luxury. The Esterházy had their own private orchestra; Franz Joseph Haydn, in service to Prince Paul Anton Esterházy, wrote his *Farewell Symphony* to convince the prince not to leave the musicians behind when the family went on a summer visit to its great palace at Esterháza. Where a middling noble might own several lordships, the duke of Infantado (Mendoza family) held lordship over nearly eight hundred villages. In the kingdom of Naples, 95 percent of the communities lived under the legal jurisdiction of a feudal lord, a situation common in many other parts of Europe.

Income levels within the nobility varied sharply. A well-to-do provincial French noble in the sixteenth century might have an income of 2,000 French pounds; the greatest aristocrats, like the Guise, Bourbon, and Montmorency families, took in 150,000–200,000 pounds a year (the cardinal of Lorraine, a Guise, reached 300,000). Comfortable nobles in England might possess 100 acres, while the Russell family, dukes of Bedford, owned more

than 100,000. They got even wealthier in the eighteenth century, with the development of Russell Square in London, which survives as a lovely example of Georgian architecture. In Spain, the great aristocrats—Mendoza, Guzmán, Toledo—had landed revenues of 50,000–60,000 ducats a year; as in France or England, Spanish aristocrats, or those in the kingdom of Naples, had 100 times more income than a well-to-do country gentleman. Even these figures pale in comparison to the wealth of the magnates of the East; families like the Radziwill owned tens of thousands of villages. The humblest Spanish *hidalgo* held the same noble status as a Furstemburg or a Zamoyski, but the status conferred by wealth and political power made them effectively part of two different social groups.

COMMONERS AND SYSTEMS OF STATUS

The three-orders model common in French-speaking areas did not necessarily apply elsewhere. In England or the Polish-Lithuanian Commonwealth, the representative bodies had only two estates: Lords and Commons in England; Senate and Diet (nobility) in Poland-Lithuania. The English House of Commons or the lower house of the Polish Sejm or Hungarian Diet represented the same group of people, those whom the English termed the landed gentry. In continental Europe, unlike in England, these people held legal noble status. Other states, such as Sweden, had a Fourth Estate for the peasants.

The evolving representative bodies of the fourteenth through seventeenth centuries provide clear evidence as to the changing system of social differentiation. In the fourteenth century, in most parts of Europe the third order was simply the towns. No one really "represented" the peasants because they were not citizens, and only citizens could be represented. In the Holy Roman Empire, in parts of east central Europe, and in parts of France, these peasants were not free people: they were serfs, and thus could not possibly be citizens.

In the fifteenth and sixteenth centuries, however, the third order often came to be called the Third Estate, and it explicitly included peasants. Flanders already had village assemblies in the fourteenth century. By the late sixteenth century, meetings of the French Estates-General gave rise to village assemblies, which elected deputies to bailiwick assemblies, and which drew up lists of grievances for the king. The bailiwick assemblies elected deputies to the Estates-General and created regional grievance lists. Nobles or urban elites would certainly not have accepted the proposition that peasants were citizens, but peasant participation in the political process—the defining mark of citizenship—created uncomfortable ambiguity.

Moreover, peasant rebels, as in the German Peasants' Revolt of 1525, demanded freedom (abolition of serfdom) and a wide range of rights, such as the ability to elect their own pastors. The tie between "freedom" and citizenship was so strong that in England most towns referred to citizenship as "the freedom." In Worcester and countless other English towns, no one could carry on any trade unless he held citizenship. Whether in England or in the towns of western Germany, urban citizenship could range as high as half the adult male population (York), or it could drop to 20 percent or less (Bristol). In early-sixteenth-century Italy, the great Humanists Niccolò Machiavelli (1469–1527) and Francesco Guicciardini (1483–1540) debated the proper proportion of citizens, with Machiavelli suggesting a more "democratic" system and Guicciardini opting for an aristocratic republic, such as that of Venice. Throughout Europe in the sixteenth century, towns took Guicciardini's advice; they became progressively more oligarchic, whether it was the *vroedschappen* of the Dutch cities or the consulates of the Italian ones.

Noble pretensions to the contrary notwithstanding, the status gap between a peasant and a member of the patriciate of Amsterdam, Augsburg, or any other major city mirrored that between a great aristocrat and a poor country noble. Peasants might have status within their village communities; outside them, they did not. Church authorities, drawn from the nobility and the urban elites, viewed the peasants as little better than pagans, sending out "missionaries" to convert these nominal Christians to the official brand of religion. Burghers, in contrast, had real political and economic clout; within their towns, they also had exalted social status. In the state, their social status remained contested; order-based conflict between nobles and commoners remained a norm of European life. That conflict should not obscure, however, the many other fault lines of European society. Status depended every-

where and at all times on one's relationship to others, and it thus took into account a wide array of factors. Because it depended on such relationships, status was also public: it had to be displayed in order to exist.

SOCIAL DIFFERENTIATION

European societies attempted to legislate social distinction. Virtually every town and every state had its sumptuary laws, which carefully defined who could wear different sorts of clothing. In most places, only nobles could wear silk; only members of royal families could have gold or silver thread woven into their clothes; only princes could have certain precious furs line their collars. Sumptuary laws also defined socially appropriate colors, following the model of the famous imperial purple of the Byzantines. Naturally, everyone sought to wear the clothing restricted to the social group above them: Nobles tried to sneak gold thread into their clothes; merchants tried to wear silk.

Sumptuary laws sometimes defined what people had to wear, as well as what they could not. The authorities particularly singled out groups who were in one way or another outside of mainstream society. The group could be a religious minority like Jews, who often had to wear a Star of David or a yellow hat. It could be those who broke certain moral rules, like prostitutes, who sometimes had to display a sign of their profession and status. It could be lawbreakers: Criminals could wear their marks of distinction on their skin—a "V" for thief *(voleur)* in French-speaking lands, or the infamous scarlet "A" for an adulteress in England. A woman's or man's clothes invariably situated her or him within the known social order and thus provided the social transparency so beloved of the authorities. Almost all European states outlawed disguises and nicknames for that reason. Those who sought to subvert the social order could do so simply by putting on a costume, as at Carnival, or by using a sobriquet, a nearly universal practice among craft journeymen. Women, too, used these second, public names, clear evidence of their participation in the marketplace.

Everyone had to display his or her status publicly, especially on certain festive occasions. The public nature of status meant that elites *had* to engage in what we would call conspicuous consumption in order to express, and thus make manifest, their status. A duke or a prince had to live in a great château, had to wear fine silk clothing, had to act as a generous benefactor to his loyal followers. A local lord had to maintain social distance with his neighbors, yet he had to bestow marks of his esteem on chosen servants: Lords and ladies often acted as godparents to children of wealthy peasant tenants. In Flemish or Italian or German towns, a rich merchant or wealth lawyer longed to be asked to do municipal service, just as a member of the English landed gentry obliged willingly when asked to sit as an unpaid judge at the Quarter Sessions.

Society sought differentiation through other means, such as food or language. In some cases, laws created restrictions on food, especially game: Deer in England or wild boar in France were "royal game," which could be eaten only by royals or by royal permission. Throughout Europe, the right to hunt marked off a nobleman. Social differentiation by food, however, tended more often to rely on price. The most expensive bread in many European towns bore the name of "chapter bread," so called because initially only the bakery of the rich cathedral chapter had the right to make it. Town governments spoke of bread fit for consumption "only by the country people," whose coarseness was proverbial. Governments sought to limit access to imported spices. Increasingly, town dwellers differentiated themselves from rural people by the type of food they ate: Urban consumers ate more meat, especially "butcher's meat" (beef and mutton) and wheat bread; peasants ate little meat (and then small game) and rye bread. Outside of wine-producing regions, urban consumers drank far more wine than rural ones, a distinction less evident in those regions where people drank beer or cider (apple or pear). Church authorities, too, interfered in diet: Butcher shops in Catholic areas had to close during Lent, when religious sanctions prevented meat consumption, and Jews everywhere in Europe faced strict dietary laws supervised by their rabbis.

The groups seeking to climb the social scale often tried to emulate their social "betters," who, in turn, sought new ways to differentiate themselves. This process accelerated exponentially in the eighteenth century. "Proper" members of society adopted new manners, such as eating with forks, using porcelain plates, and creating individual "places" at a dinner table. When common people began to use forks, too, the elite began a progressive differentiation of plates, utensils, and glassware, creating elaborate dinner settings that could not be duplicated by the middling and poor. Soon manuals of etiquette appeared in one language after another. Elites consumed new foods, such as vegetables and fruits introduced from the Americas or from Asia, or fancier wines, such as Champagne (France) or Tokai (Hungary). The world market provided elites with tea and coffee, and soon the coffee house/café sprang up in major European cities. Some of these houses, like the famous Demel in Vienna, still exist, selling fancy pastries to clients who linger to read the newspapers provided for the clients. These newspapers, another eighteenth-century innovation, also changed the rules of status, because they provided a new forum for public opinion.

Language offered another everyday, ubiquitous means of social differentiation. The first sentence out of one's mouth invariably established social relationship: Landlords used the familiar second person (*du/tu/*thou) when speaking to peasants; the latter replied using the polite, plural form (*Sie/usted/vous/*you). In workshops, the master said "thou," the journeyman or apprentice said "you." Nobles insisted that they alone had a right to *madame/signora/pani* or their male equivalents; urban elites salivated at the prospect of hearing someone call them *madame* or *pan*.

In early modern societies, status affected an individual every time she or he appeared in public. Status determined how others spoke to you (and you to them), what you wore, where you sat, where (and even if) you marched in parades, where you stood in church—even where you were buried. The middling and lower status people of a village had to settle for the cemetery; the village elite were interred under the church floor. One's status fluctuated at all times: Status depended on the status of those with whom you interacted, even at the highest levels of society. Spanish court etiquette was legendarily rigid, but Spanish practice spread to Austria and France. Commoners greatly resented the public manifestations of their lower status: The grievances prepared by the Third Estate's regional assemblies for the French Estates-General of 1789 universally demanded that their deputies not suffer demeaning treatment. At the opening ceremonies, the stubborn sartorial resistance of some deputies of the

Third Estate, who violated court etiquette by donning their hats in the presence of the king, a privilege reserved for nobles, galvanized the Third Estate's collective resistance to the old order and provided a public display of commoner unity that helped set in motion the French Revolution.

Ordinary people had many opportunities to express their status, perhaps none so dramatic as parades or festivals. Two surviving festivals provide fascinating glimpses of the old ways. The Procession of the Holy Blood, at Bruges (Ascension Day), began in the thirteenth century. The parade presents a series of stories from the Christian Bible, beginning with the Old Testament, continuing through the life of Jesus, and ending with scenes from Flemish life. Just before the reliquary of the Holy Blood, the parade offers tables covered with the many goods one could buy in Bruges, from local cloth to Asian spices. In early modern times, the great guilds, like the weavers or the grain merchants, major monasteries, and the chief foreign communities (Italians and English) all had their own banners, which preceded floats; the minor guilds, like the shoemakers, had to settle for a place in a phalanx of a score or more such banners. Parades such as this one took place all over Europe, and every guild, every religious house, every quarter of the city fought valiantly to preserve its place in the order of march or its role in the festivals. Court records are filled with violent confrontations about group status, which often led to fatalities. Those same records tell a similar tale of personal status: Innumerable cases of violence began with verbal assaults on the status or honor of a neighbor.

European society contained many dichotomies: noble-commoner; ecclesiastical-laic; free-unfree; urban-rural; rich-poor; intellectual labor-manual labor; worthy-unworthy; female-male; educated-unlettered. Status in early modern Europe revolved around all of these distinctions, which frequently overlapped: Serfs usually lived in the countryside, worked with their hands, were commoners and mostly laic. Peasant farmers of a certain standing invariably viewed themselves as among the worthy people, yet those above them on the social scale rarely did so. That same dynamic operated in towns: Artisans' masters were certain they were among the worthy people (*gens de bien; los buenos)*, but merchants and the professionals (lawyers and the like) were just as certain that the artisans were not. The distinction between the worthy and the unworthy had profound practical consequences. Everywhere in Europe courts privileged the testimony of the worthy people, described in the records as witnesses "worthy of faith," and discredited the testimony of those "without attestation," that is, for whom no substantial member of the community could vouch.

Status played a much different role in early modern societies than it does today because they were self-policing. Local citizens had to make arrests and bring the accused to a local judge. Status thus came to play a critical role in the maintenance of local order. In almost all cases, local authorities had to rely on a combination of personal status and the implied threat of future force to make society work. Such status could come from a variety of sources. As in the Middle Ages, nobility could confer such status; royal office could confer status; wealth could confer status; family connections could confer status; personal ability could confer status; education could confer status. This last category is easily overlooked, but the power of the fully literate swimming in an ocean of illiterates was simply staggering in its practical and social implications.

Modern scholarship has often ignored the individual dimensions of status. Historians have debated the importance of "merit" in noble self-image, to cite but one example. The records of the time speak eloquently about the role of merit, of personal worth, as judged by the community. In early seventeenth-century Brittany, the duke of Brissac, lieutenant general of the king, marshal of France, held the universal esteem of his contemporaries. Brissac was a man of considerable abilities, and the documents reflect the status his achievements brought him. His son, duke of Brissac and lieutenant general of the king in his own time, although theoretically holding the same status, received none of the respect accorded his father. Contemporaries made disparaging (and accurate) remarks about his lack of ability; he did not succeed his father as marshal of France. Where the father had been a major power broker, the son had little influence.

Similar examples existed everywhere in early modern Europe, not simply among the aristocracy but among all levels of society. Within the framework established by order, class, occupation, religion, education, gender, age, and many other factors, an individual, female or male, had considerable room to establish an individual status of her or his own. Merit, combined with money, could even enable a family, rarely an individual, to achieve considerable social mobility. The man who made a fortune could reasonably expect his children to rise to a new social level. In France, the great-great-grandson of a draper could become minister of war and the leader of the aristocratic faction at court. In Poland, the grandson of a petty local noble could even be elected king, as in the case of John III Sobieski (also Jan Sobieski, 1629–1696; ruled 1674–1696). Throughout Europe, the supposedly frozen world of the guilds, which historians long thought became progressively more restrictive in membership, in fact allowed constant mobility. In town after town, half or more of the artisan masters were immigrants, making for a staggering turnover in masterships over the course of several decades.

Neither classes nor orders offer a compelling analytical category for examining status in early modern society. Among other factors, status involved wealth, birth, gender, occupation, and education; moreover, any given person's status reflected a mixture of his or her personal standing and the standing of the family, and sometimes occupational group, of which he or she was a member. Status was thus individual and collective, which allowed many European societies to maintain the fiction of immobility—the group remained the "same"—while simultaneously permitting the social mobility, by individuals, necessary for any functioning human society.

See also **Advice and Etiquette Books; Aristocracy and Gentry; Citizenship; Equality and Inequality; Mobility, Social; Sumptuary Laws.**

BIBLIOGRAPHY

Primary Sources

Castiglione, B. *The Book of the Courtier.* Translated by G. Bull. Harmondsworth, U.K., and Baltimore, Md., 1976. The manual of early modern noble behavior, written in the early sixteenth century by an Italian nobleman.

Gluckel of Hameln. *The Memoirs of Gluckel of Hameln.* Translated by M. Lowenthal. New York, 1977. Memoirs of a late 17th-century female Jewish merchant.

Ménétra, J. *Journal of My Life.* Translated by A. Goldhammer. New York, 1986. Memoirs of an 18th-century Parisian glass maker.

Pasek, J. C. *Memoirs of the Polish Baroque.* Translated by C. Leach. Berkeley, 1976. Memoirs of a mid-17th-century Polish nobleman.

Secondary Sources

Amussen, S. *An Ordered Society: Gender and Class in Early Modern England.* Oxford and New York, 1988).

Astarita, T. *The Continuity of Feudal Power: The Caracciolo de Brienza in Spanish Naples.* Cambridge, U.K. 1992.

Bourdieu, P. *Distinction: A Social Critique of the Judgment of Taste.* Translated by R. Nice. Cambridge, Mass., 1984.

Collins, J. *Classes, Estates and Order in Early Modern Brittany.* Cambridge, U.K., 1994.

———. *From Tribes to Nation: The Making of France, 500–1799.* Toronto, 2002.

Dewald, J. *The European Nobility, 1400–1800.* Cambridge, U.K., 1996.

Elias, N. *The Civilising Process.* Translated by E Jephcott. Oxford, 2000.

Farr, J. *Artisans in Europe, 1300–1914.* Cambridge, U.K., 2000.

Foucault, M. *Discipline and Punish: The Birth of the Prison.* Translated by A. Sheridan. New York, 1979.

Garrioch, D. *Neighbourhood and Community in Paris, 1740–1790.* Cambridge, U.K., 1986.

Habermas, J. *The Structural Transformation of the Public Sphere.* Translated by T. Burger. Cambridge, Mass., 1989.

Hundert, G. *The Jews in a Polish Private Town: The Case of Opatòw in the Eighteenth Century.* Baltimore, Md., 1992.

Rappaport, S. *Worlds within Worlds: Structures of Life in Sixteenth-Century London.* Cambridge, U.K., 1989.

Reher, D. *Town and Country in Pre-Industrial Spain, Cuenca, 1550–1870.* Cambridge, U.K., 1990.

Sabean, D. *Power in the Blood: Popular Culture and Village Discourse in Early Modern Germany.* Cambridge, U.K. 1984.

Stone, L. *The Crisis of the Aristocracy, 1558–1641.* Oxford, 1965.

Walker, M. *The German Home Towns.* Ithaca, N.Y., 1971.

Wrightson, K. *English Society, 1580–1680.* New Brunswick, N.J., 1982.

JAMES B. COLLINS

CLASSICISM. In general, *classicism* can be defined as a style in literature, visual art, music, or architecture that draws on the styles of ancient Greece and Rome, especially fifth- and fourth-century B.C.E. Athens and late Republican Augustan Rome. The term can be confusing, because it has taken on many other meanings. It can refer to a general aesthetic characterized by clarity, elegance, and symmetry, or to a style that is generally thought of as exemplifying greatness or perfection. For instance, most people would identify the Boston Pops as performers of "classical music" or John Steinbeck's *Grapes of Wrath* as a "classic" of American literature, even though they have little to do with antiquity. Variations on the term, like *neoclassicism,* can furthermore refer to a specific school or style in a particular time period. Despite this confusion, the term is still useful in describing particular styles and impulses in literature and the arts from the Middle Ages to the eighteenth century.

The Middle Ages experienced two noteworthy revivals of the literature of antiquity that were inspired by and helped to promote classicism. The first is known as the Carolingian Renaissance, so called to recognize the flowering of learning under the reign of Charlemagne (ruled 768–814). The most famous figure of this period was the monk Alcuin (c. 732–804), who amassed a remarkable manuscript collection of classical works in the library of York. At the invitation of the emperor Alcuin developed an educational curriculum at the Palace School in Aachen that included readings of classical authors. He also developed the Carolingian miniscule, a clear script based on classical principles, and promoted the copying and distribution of classical texts. The achievements of the Carolingian age set the stage for the next classical revival, known as the *Renaissance of the Twelfth Century,* a term coined by Charles Homer Haskins (1870–1937) to describe the flowering of classical learning during this period. It was more far-reaching than the earlier revival and had implications beyond the field of literature, most importantly in architecture, the visual arts, and the revival of Roman law.

From the twelfth century on, classicism was the domain mainly of lawyers and churchmen, most notably in the papal curia (the circle of theologians and secretaries who carried on papal business),

where learned men could come together to share their interests in classical letters and style. It was in this environment at Avignon that Petrarch (1304–1374), the father of Italian humanism, first learned about and promoted classical learning. But it was in Florence, particularly among the patrician class, that Petrarch's classicism was most strongly received, most notably through his friend and disciple Giovanni Boccaccio (1313–1375). Up to this point classicism had been mainly a literary pursuit that influenced the art of letter writing, poetry, and rhetoric. In the following generation, the Florentine chancellor Colucio Salutati (1331–1406) helped turn classicism from a literary movement into a powerful tool for shaping politics and society on the Italian peninsula. It was in the works of the humanist historian Leonardo Bruni (c. 1370–1444) that classicism laid the foundation for a republican ideology.

The study of ancient Greek was virtually unknown in western Europe from the fifth century C.E. onward. Greek had been a fundamental part of the Roman educational system; any educated Roman would have known it and been able to quote from its most famous authors and orators, such as Demosthenes, Aristophanes, or Lucian. As humanists in Petrarch's circle read more and more ancient authors they discovered that a full appreciation of their literature required a thorough background in the literature and culture of ancient Greece. Salutati invited the most celebrated Byzantine scholar of the times, Manuel Chrysoloras (c. 1353–1415), to teach in Florence. The revival of Greek learning was aided by growing contact between the Greek and Latin churches at the Council of Ferrara-Florence in 1438–1445 and also by the fall of Constantinople to the Turks in 1453, after which Greek émigrés fleeing the city took up residence in Italy and made a living by teaching Greek to Italian pupils. They also brought with them many Greek texts that had been virtually unknown and unread in western Europe since the fall of Rome. Cardinal Bessarion (1403–1472), a priest who converted from the Greek to the Latin church and was a tireless promoter of ancient Greek studies, bequeathed thousands of Greek manuscripts to the people of his adopted home of Venice, where they formed the nucleus of St. Mark's Library. The works of Plato were especially influential, and a circle of Neoplatonic scholars led by Marsilio Ficino (1433–1499) sought to fuse Christian thought with Platonic philosophy.

Classicism was also the foundation of the educational revolution of the Renaissance, which sought to revive the *studia humanitatis,* the educational system of ancient Rome as set out in the writings of classical authors like Cicero and Quintilian. The schoolmasters Gasparino da Barzizza (1360?–1430) and Guarino da Verona (1370/1374–1460) attracted wealthy students to study ancient literature and culture in their schools, and along with Bruni they wrote educational treatises that outlined their pedagogical method. Their disciples carried on their teachings—both in classrooms and in educational treatises and editions of classical works—and spread them throughout Italy and across the Alps into northern Europe. The introduction of printing in the latter part of the fifteenth century greatly propelled humanist learning, providing stable editions of classical texts to a far wider audience than could have been imagined in the earlier classical revivals of the Carolingian period or the twelfth century. The advent of printing is likely responsible for the permanent establishment of classicism as an integral part of Western civilization from the fourteenth century to the present day.

Classicism was embraced in many ways during the Renaissance in Italy, and it manifested itself in various pursuits. For example, Julius Pomponius Laetus (1428–1497) founded the Roman Academy, whose members took an active role in antiquarianism and the study of the ancient ruins of the city of Rome. They also embraced non-Christian ideas and revived ancient pagan ceremonies, which brought them under the scrutiny of church authorities. The collection and preservation of inscriptions, coins, and buildings by antiquarians were important in the historical reconstruction of the history of Rome, and these activities represented the early development of modern archaeology. Meanwhile, Lorenzo Valla (1407–1457) explored the linguistic aspects of ancient writers and gave the study of the Latin language a more scientific grounding. His most famous work, *Elegances of the Latin Language* (published 1471), was a practical style guide for writing and speaking the most elegant Latin, which he identified with the Latin of the "golden age" of Roman letters. By periodizing Latin style, Valla invented a philological method for the scientific study

of texts that was further developed by Christian humanists like Desiderius Erasmus of Rotterdam (1466?–1536), who used it to challenge the authenticity of the Vulgate Bible. This philological method also laid the foundation for modern textual criticism.

While the classicism of the Renaissance started as a literary pursuit, its most striking and accessible flourishing occurred in the visual arts and architecture at the beginning of the fifteenth century. The sculptor Filippo Brunelleschi (1377–1446) turned his talents to architecture and designed (or redesigned) many churches and palaces in a style that reflected his study of ancient buildings. He was particularly interested in the mathematical proportions behind the design of ancient Roman buildings and in developing engineering processes to build them. His slightly younger contemporary Donatello (c. 1386–1466) used the same principles to create statues that imitated the style of classical sculpture. Along with the painter Masaccio (1401–1428), who included classical elements in the content of his paintings and used newly developed techniques of perspective, these visual artists reflected what is known as the early Renaissance style. Its techniques were recorded and explained in treatises written in the vernacular by Leon Battista Alberti (1404–1472), who made the principles of perspective drawing and painting accessible to a wide variety of artists who wanted to learn this fashionable approach. The new style of art was funded by wealthy patrons, including businessmen, aristocrats, and the popes. Classical styles and themes continued to dominate the period of the High Renaissance in the work of the early-sixteenth-century masters Leonardo da Vinci (1452–1519), Michelangelo Buonarroti (1475–1564), and Raphael Sanzio (1483–1520).

If Italians played the lead role in the revival of antiquity in the fourteenth and fifteenth centuries, in the sixteenth century that role was assumed by northern Europe, where classicism particularly flourished among scholars in France, Germany, Switzerland, and England. While classicism had played a small role in medieval universities like Oxford and Paris, its influence had not been widespread. With the new availability of relatively inexpensive printed books and Italian-trained native teachers, however, the study of classical literature became more accessible, and by the middle of the century it was the norm in most educational curricula.

The study of theology in the sixteenth century was completely overhauled as humanist scholars like Erasmus insisted that a thorough grounding in the three biblical languages (Hebrew, Greek, and Latin) was necessary to understand the Bible. Scholasticism, the prevailing school of theology that had its origins in the twelfth-century Paris schools, did not have any particular animosity toward classicism; indeed, a number of Scholastic theologians of the Middle Ages, such as Jean de Gerson (1363–1429), displayed interest in the classics. But Scholastic theologians did object strongly to the application of the philological method to the text of the Bible and to language study as the foundation of theological training. Humanists like Erasmus and Protestant reformers like Philipp Melanchthon (1497–1560), himself a scholar of ancient Greek, argued that the theologians were hostile to their biblical studies because they disliked and were ignorant of classical literature, thus turning a debate over authority in theology into a debate over classical learning. By mid-century, classical literature was the foundation of the educational program both in Catholic countries, where the Jesuit order promoted classical learning, and in Protestant countries.

Another controversy that arose among classical scholars themselves was over the status and influence of the Roman orator Cicero. Most prominent in Rome, the Ciceronian faction promoted Cicero as the highest standard of Latin usage, and some, like the papal secretary Pietro Bembo (1470–1547), vowed never to use a word that did not appear in Cicero's writings. Erasmus wrote a famous dialogue mocking what he saw as the Ciceronians' slavish following of Cicero, and he argued for a broader-based standard for Latin usage. This debate continued into the seventeenth century as some scholars sought to dethrone Cicero. At the end of the sixteenth century the Dutch humanist and scholar Justus Lipsius (1547–1606) promoted the revival of the Stoic philosophy. Strongly influenced by the Roman philosopher Seneca, Lipsius promoted Stoicism as an alternative to Neoplatonism, which had been so influential in the earlier part of the century. A little later in France, the astronomer and mathematician Pierre Gassendi (1592–1655)

championed the revival of Epicureanism, a more materialist ancient philosophy that was more in tune with the rationalism that was gaining ground at the time.

The dramatic growth of vernacular literature in the sixteenth century hastened the abandonment of classical form in literature, though many of its stylistic attributes were adopted as conventions of vernacular style and content. This is visible in works of the group of sixteenth-century French poets known as La Pléïade, and it continues right through to the plays of William Shakespeare (1564–1616) at the beginning of the seventeenth century. In art classical themes and motifs remained the norm throughout the sixteenth century, but they were challenged late in the century by the emergence of baroque and rococo styles in art, architecture, and music. This movement away from classicism corresponded to a general shift away from the authority of the ancients and toward a greater emphasis on human reason and sense perception, as articulated most strongly in the *Discours de la méthode* (1637; Discourse on method) by René Descartes (1596–1650). In the arts this shift was reflected by a tendency to focus on human emotions and movement, while retaining the grandiose style and form more characteristic of Renaissance art. The Italian painter, sculptor, and architect Gian Lorenzo Bernini (1598–1680) exemplifies the baroque style by infusing classical style with intense emotion, as in his *Ecstasy of St. Theresa* (1645–1652). Likewise baroque music, exemplified by the compositions of Johann Sebastian Bach (1685–1750), retained the classical notion of music expressing the order of the universe but was at the same time lively and tuneful. "Neoclassical" is the name given to the style of art and architecture that prevailed from the middle of the eighteenth century through the nineteenth. In music, Franz Joseph Haydn (1732–1809) and Wolfgang Amadeus Mozart (1756–1791) represent the tenets of classicism, emphasizing balance and proportion. But for Mozart, and even more so for Ludwig van Beethoven (1770–1827), classical elements were mixed with Romantic ones.

Classicism created a standard of civilization against which contemporary society could be judged, a standard that was prevalent in the early modern period. What began as an elitist literary hobby bloomed from the time of Petrarch and was applied to all facets of life—from education and politics to music, visual art, and architecture. The classical ideal was something to strive for, and in striving for it adherents developed new methods to attain the ideal. Along the way they made advances in mathematics, engineering, linguistics, and design that in turn led to advances in other areas. Moreover, classicism was extremely flexible. It could temper the ascetic desires of a Carmelite monk like Baptista Spagnoli (Mantuanus; 1447–1516), known in his own time as the Christian Virgil, just as easily as it could feed the vanity of an artist like Benvenuto Cellini (1500–1571), who in his autobiography boasted of his own talents. The same style of architecture that the Americans used for their new capital in Washington, D.C., in order to present their sense of achievement in gaining independence from the British, had previously been used as a symbol of the opulence of the French nobility and crown at Versailles, and it also enshrined the gods of reason in the Pantheon in Paris. Because the classical world contained a spectrum of thought and style, classicism offered an almost endless variety of models and ideas. Though it continued to be strong in some quarters in the nineteenth and twentieth centuries, classicism never again became as widespread as it had been in the previous five centuries. To a great extent, the discoveries of modern science began to show just how much the ancients had not known, as had been foreshadowed by the European discovery of the "New World" and by Galileo's telescope. As a standard, at least, the ancients were eventually surpassed.

See also **Academies, Learned; Ancient World; Ancients and Moderns; Archaeology; Architecture; Aristotelianism; Art: Art Theory, Criticism, and Historiography; Baroque; Bible; Enlightenment; Humanists and Humanism; Music; Neoclassicism; Neoplatonism; Reason; Renaissance; Republicanism; Rococo; Romanticism; Stoicism; Theology.**

BIBLIOGRAPHY

Benson, Robert L., and Giles Constable, eds. *Renaissance and Renewal in the Twelfth Century.* Cambridge, Mass., 1982.

Berger, Robert W. *A Royal Passion: Louis XIV as Patron of Architecture.* Cambridge, U.K., and New York, 1994.

Duro, Paul. *The Academy and the Limits of Painting in Seventeenth-Century France.* New York, 1997.

Grafton, Anthony. *Commerce with the Classics: Ancient Books and Renaissance Readers.* Ann Arbor, Mich., 1997.

Grafton, Anthony, and Lisa Jardine. *From Humanism to the Humanities: Education and the Liberal Arts in Fifteenth- and Sixteenth-Century Europe.* London, 1986.

Kristeller, Paul Oskar. *Renaissance Thought: The Classic, Scholastic, and Humanist Strains.* New York, 1961.

Nauert, Charles G., Jr. *Humanism and the Culture of Renaissance Europe.* Cambridge, U.K., and New York, 1995.

Rosen, Charles. *The Classical Style: Haydn, Mozart, Beethoven.* Expanded ed. New York, 1997.

Rowland, Ingrid D. *The Place of the Antique in Early Modern Europe.* Chicago, 1999.

Shankman, Steven. *In Search of the Classic: Reconsidering the Greco-Roman Tradition, Homer to Valéry and Beyond.* University Park, Pa., 1994.

Weiss, Roberto. *The Renaissance Discovery of Classical Antiquity.* 2nd ed. Oxford and New York, 1988.

MARK CRANE

CLAUDE LORRAIN (GELLÉE)

(1600/05–1682), French painter, draftsman, and printmaker, active in Italy; recognized as one of the greatest landscape painters of the Western tradition. Claude Gellée—called le Lorrain, Claudio Lorenese, Claude Lorrain, or simply Claude— infused the early sixteenth-century Venetian pastoral with his direct studies from nature, resulting in depictions of an ideal world where man and nature are integrated into a perfected balance harmonized by subtle effects of light. His contribution was critical to the development of Western landscape. He was so successful during his lifetime that he became one of the most expensive and highly sought-after painters in Rome, with innumerable commissions from members of the papal court, the city's international community of diplomats and expatriate aristocrats, wealthy travelers to Italy, and royal courts across Europe.

After Claude's parents died in 1612, he may have been sent from what was then the independent duchy of Lorraine to Freiburg-im-Breisgau to live with an older brother, who was probably his first teacher. It is more certain that he traveled to Italy with an older relative, arriving in Rome as early as 1617. Claude studied with German landscape painter Goffredo Wals (c. 1590/95–1638/40) in

Claude Lorrain. *Landscape with Rest on the Flight into Egypt.* THE CLEVELAND MUSEUM OF ART, LEONARD C. HANNA, JR. FUND, 62.151

Naples for two years sometime between 1618 and 1622, after which he returned to Rome and completed his training with Italian landscape painter and decorative artist Agostino Tassi (c. 1580–1644). Except for a brief return to Lorraine (1625–1627)—where he worked with the court painter Claude Déruet (c. 1588–1660) in the ducal palace at the capital of Nancy—and probable trips to other parts of Italy, he remained in Rome for the rest of his life. He became a member of the Accademia di San Luca in 1633, was offered (but declined) the post of "first rector" in 1654, and accepted the request to be in charge of all resident foreign members in 1669.

One of the key elements of Claude's success with landscape was undeniably linked to his brilliance as a draftsman, which is revealed in more than a thousand extant drawings. During the 1630s and early 1640s, he often intentionally left his studio in order to go into the countryside and draw directly after nature, one of the first landscape artists known to have done so. In the keenly observed studies he made during these outings, he recorded animals, individual elements of foliage, rock formations, and the effects of light and shade in rapidly sketched bucolic scenes (as in *Pine Forest,* late 1630s, Teylers Museum, Haarlem). They clearly provided the raw material for more fully developed compositions done later in his atelier.

An ever-increasing number of forgeries of Claude's work as early as the 1630s attest to his rapidly growing reputation. His response to this threat was to record the composition of each painting he made for the rest of his life in a highly finished drawing that he placed into what he referred to as his *Liber veritatis* (Book of truth), his own very personalized form of copyright. Inscriptions on the versos of these sheets often indicated the client for whom the work was made and, for the later works, the date. This group of drawings, often considered the pinnacle of Claude's draftsmanship, remained nearly intact and protected from light until the middle of the last century. Because of their rare state of preservation, combined with the artist's natural talent, these are regarded as among the most extraordinary European drawings of the seventeenth century that have been handed down to us. Claude's *Pastoral Landscape* of 1644 (L.V. 85, British Museum, London), a record of a painting made

for an unknown Roman client (now in the Prado, Madrid), reveals aspects of the essence of Claude's classicism: open, fluid designs with low horizon lines and architectural groupings or a variety of vegetation to mark one's visual progress through the expanse of the juxtaposed diagonal planes of land or small winding rivers that gently recede into the distance.

Claude explored the potential of printmaking in two distinct periods of his career: 1626–1641 and 1651–1663. Not surprisingly, he chose the painter's medium of etching, for, unlike the arduous manner of engraving that was often left to specialists, etching enabled him to draw on the copperplate in a manner akin to using a pen on paper. More than forty prints, such as his *Goatherd,* 1663 (Mannocci 44, second state, British Museum, London), where every stroke of the etching needle contributed to the atmospheric whole, provide eloquent testimony to Claude's high level of success. These replicable records of his work also ensured that his new ideal and classicizing visual language spread swiftly to artists, amateurs, and collectors across Europe throughout his career.

Fortunately, more than 250 of Claude's paintings have survived. One of his most elegant and important late canvases, painted in 1675 for Prince Lorenzo Onofrio Colonna, his principal patron during his later years, is *View of Carthage with Dido and Aeneas* (Hamburger Kunsthalle), which demonstrates Claude's pivotal role in the history of seascapes and coastal scenes. It is also an excellent illustration of how his marvelous use of light both unifies a composition and imbues it with emotion. This painting also reveals how Claude increasingly varied his most common theme of shepherds tending their flocks with scenes from mythology, history, and religion in order to elevate the significance of the genre of landscape and to broaden the appeal of his work.

Claude's distinguished contribution to humanity's ongoing visual interpretation of its place in the natural world made him the most influential landscape painter in Western art. It is impossible to imagine the work of such later landscapists as Claude-Joseph Vernet (1714–1789), Thomas Gainsborough (1727–1788), John Constable (1776–1837), J. M. W. Turner (1775–1851),

Jean-Baptiste Camille Corot (1796–1875), or Caspar David Friedrich (1774–1840) without the precedent of his paintings, drawings, and prints, which conveyed the ideal beauty and grandeur of nature suffused with the infinite mysteries of light. It remains a legacy that artists continue to confront today.

See also **Gainsborough, Thomas; Lorraine, Duchy of; Painting; Prints and Popular Imagery; Rome, Art in.**

BIBLIOGRAPHY

Askew, Pamela, ed. *Claude Lorrain, 1600–1682: A Symposium.* Center for the Advanced Study of the Visual Arts Symposium Series III, National Gallery of Art Studies in the History of Art, vol. 14. Washington, D.C., 1982.

Bjurström, Per. *Claude Lorrain: Sketchbook Owned by the Nationalmuseum, Stockholm.* Stockholm, 1984.

Haus der Kunst. *Im Licht von Claude Lorrain.* Exhibition catalogue by Marcel Roethlisberger. Munich, 1983.

Kitson, Michael. *Claude Lorrain: Liber Veritatis.* London, 1978.

Lagerlöf, Margaretha Rossholm. *Ideal Landscape: Annibale Carracci, Nicolas Poussin, and Claude Lorrain.* Translated by Nancy Adler. New Haven and London, 1990.

Mannocci, Lino. *The Etchings of Claude Lorrain.* New Haven and London, 1988.

Musée des Beaux-Arts, Nancy. *Turner et le Lorrain.* Exhibition catalogue by Ian Warrell. Nancy and Paris, 2002.

Musée des Beaux-Arts, Nancy, and French Academy in Rome. *Claude Gellée et les peintres lorrains en Italie au XVIIe siècle.* Exhibition catalogue. Jacques Thuillier and Pierre Arizzoli-Clémentel, eds. Nancy and Rome, 1982.

National Gallery. *Claude: The Poetic Landscape.* Exhibition catalogue by Humphrey Wine. London, 1994.

National Gallery of Art and Galeries nationale du Grand Palais. *Claude Lorrain, 1600–1682.* Exhibition catalogue by H. Diane Russell. Washington, D.C., and Paris, 1982.

Roethlisberger, Marcel. *Claude Lorrain: The Drawings.* 2 vols. Berkeley and Los Angeles, 1968.

——. *Claude Lorrain: The Paintings.* 2 vols. New Haven and London, 1961; reprinted New York, 1981.

ALVIN L. CLARK, JR.

CLERGY

This entry includes three subentries:
PROTESTANT CLERGY
ROMAN CATHOLIC CLERGY
RUSSIAN ORTHODOX CLERGY

PROTESTANT CLERGY

The Reformation did not produce a new style of clergy full-grown on its first emergence. It only gradually became clear that a radically new concept of the church and its ministry, distinct and separate from the Roman Catholic obedience, would come into being. The first leaders of the Reformation were in most cases already ordained to the Catholic priesthood. Rare but important exceptions were Philipp Melanchthon, a lifelong layman, and John Calvin, who resigned his Catholic benefices before taking priestly orders. Both exerted immense influence as theologians and church leaders despite never being formally ordained.

THE CLERGY BEFORE THE REFORMATION
Those who had already become priests were trained through the traditional procedures of the pre-Reformation medieval church. Parish priests gave informal practical instruction to trainees who might be in minor orders, as acolytes or altar assistants. Toward the end of the Middle Ages, increasing numbers of schools were founded to train an elite of prospective priests, including some of the English schools like Winchester or Eton and the schools annexed to the houses of the Brethren of the Common Life in the Netherlands. Theological instruction, if received at all, was found in the universities or the *studia* of the orders of mendicants. Dominican friars held many of the most prominent positions in the theology faculties of the major universities of Europe except in Italy, where the universities taught little theology.

Diocesan bishops were expected to examine ordinands for their competence, morals, and conformity to canon law before conferring holy orders. In practice the absence of many bishops and the reliance on suffragans made this examination sometimes perfunctory. The provision requiring prospective priests already to have a title to a benefice was often by-passed, so large numbers of relatively indigent priests were ordained and eked out a meager living as chaplains and mass-priests. Nevertheless, many bishops on the eve of the Reformation strove to improve the selection and quality of the priests in their dioceses. Surviving addresses to clergy, like those preached by William Melton, chancellor of York, in 1510 or by Bishop Christoph von Stadion of Augsburg in 1517, attest the ideal standards of the later medieval church.

CHANGES IN THE CONCEPT OF THE MINISTRY IN THE REFORMATION

Radical changes in the culture and theology of the post-Reformation church required, by their own inner logic, a different kind of clergy from those of the past. First of all, Martin Luther stripped away the theological rationale for the ritual and legal separateness of the clergy. Spiritual people, he argued in 1520, were not a separate class of mortals, ritually set apart by their orders; indeed, ordination was not a sacrament. Priestly celibacy was unnecessary, ungodly, and unrealistic. The legal immunities that protected the clergy from secular law and taxation were unjustified and should be removed. A priest was simply the representative of the community appointed and chosen to lead its spiritual life.

Secondly, the core theology of the Reformation shifted the emphasis in church ministry away from the sacraments and ritual ministrations toward preaching, teaching, and moral discipline. The abolition of private masses, celebrated in vast profusion in the churches, colleges, and chantries of the later Middle Ages, drastically reduced the number of clergy needed to conduct worship. A whole class of clerical proletariat effectively disappeared. In most Protestant countries, the clerical elite, including monks and friars as well as secular collegiate priests and canons of chapters, was either completely abolished or at least much reduced in size (for instance in England). The Reformation church required a less numerous, well-trained cadre of preaching ministers in the parishes. They were to be supervised by a small class of superintendents, whether committees or individuals, and whether called bishops or not. They were to be educated by their intellectual leaders in the universities and academies.

ADMINISTRATION, PATRONAGE, AND FUNDING

This new vision of a better-educated and more specialized ministry required money and challenged the complex and disorderly endowment and patronage systems inherited from the past. Luther initially appeared to favor congregational election, but rapidly retreated from that stance and upheld the traditional systems of patronage at local level. Theory and political reality sometimes clashed. Protestant theologians often hankered after a church run autonomously by its members in their capacity as Christians, rather than as magistrates. In practice the secular power, whether urban, princely, or royal, normally assumed ultimate control over the endowments and resources used to pay the clergy. In Lutheran states a "consistory" functioned effectively as the prince's department for religious affairs. In Zwinglian Zurich the clergy were managed by, and worked in close concert with, the city magistrates. Even in Geneva, despite Calvin's strongly expressed aspirations for an independent self-governing church, the *Ecclesiastical Ordinances* of 1541 reserved ultimate authority over the church in the hands of the city council.

Funding the new style of clergy was a constant problem in the early years of the Reformation. In most countries the state or the municipality amalgamated the wealth of monastic foundations and of all sorts of charitable establishments into "common chests" or the ruler's treasury. At least some of this wealth was to be used to enhance the livings of parish clergy. However, problems arose even in quite fully reformed countries. In Scotland, where the adoption of the Reformation was relatively sudden and bloodless, the vested interests of the old possessors of church benefices were largely protected. In 1561–1562 they were allowed to keep two-thirds of their income, and only one-third was assigned to the state to support new ministers. In England, uniquely among reformed countries, the entire medieval structure (apart from monasteries) stayed more or less intact. Many livings could not support preaching clergy; new anomalies were created when laymen bought tithe rights and church patronage along with monastic lands. In the century after the Reformation, reform-minded laypeople sometimes tried to use this flexibility to endow a better preaching ministry. They diverted revenue formerly assigned to monastic foundations to enrich vicarages, or set up additional "lectureships" for preaching sermons outside the structures of parochial ministry.

In some countries reformed clergy, especially in the reformed or "Calvinist" tradition and among all the non-established sects, were entirely unable to acquire any of the resources of the old church for their support. They might depend on the voluntary contributions of their congregations or (in France or parts of Eastern Europe) on the patronage of favorably disposed members of the nobility. Such support was, needless to say, precarious and fickle.

SOCIAL BACKGROUNDS AND ETHOS

Several detailed studies of the Protestant clergy in the early Reformation have agreed that ministers were usually drawn from the ranks of the mostly urban lower-middle classes. Aristocrats aspired to better careers or to none; most peasants could not attain the education required. Reformed parish clergy were publicly, legally, and almost without exception married. Their families, their education, their need for books, all ensured that they became the most cultivated and among the most wealthy inhabitants of many rural parishes. To sustain an acceptable standard of living, many had to exploit their parish lands or "glebe" to enhance their incomes. Sometimes clergy combined the role of minister with that of schoolmaster, though customs varied.

After a generation or two, however, there was a marked tendency for the ministry to propagate itself. Amongst the most learned and prestigious, whole dynasties of clergy might establish themselves. Examples include: in Lutheranism, the Osiander family, descended from the early reformer Andreas Osiander (1498–1552) of Nuremberg and Koenigsberg; in Calvinism, the Turrettini family, theologians in Geneva through the era of orthodoxy (roughly 1560–1720). Cases have been found in England of not only parish ministers but even bishops being related through descent and by intermarriage as well as invisible lines of clientage. This increased cultural homogeneity must, to some extent, have made the reformed clergy a profession and a class apart. They became like each other and culturally different from the society around them to a degree not seen in the economically and intellectually diverse medieval priesthood.

EDUCATION AND FORMATION

A new approach to ministerial education greatly enhanced this cultural distinctiveness. Protestant min-

isters had to know their Scriptures and theology. While change came gradually, the trend in the early modern period was toward an all-graduate, or at least uniformly trained, body of ministers. In the first generation, the question was not how to train new recruits but how to remedy the often deplorable ignorance of those already in some form of parish ministry. Luther gained his first horrified insights into conditions on the visitation of the Saxon churches in 1527–1528. His response was to issue in 1529 two *Catechisms,* a shorter and a longer version, from which clergy and laity alike could learn. In Zwingli's Zürich from 1525 regular meetings, known as the *Prophezei,* were held in both the main city churches, in which Old and New Testament texts were expounded by the most learned town clergy for the edification of the remainder. In Calvin's Geneva the "congregations" of clergy served a similar purpose, alongside many other available forms of instruction and exhortation. In Elizabethan England zealous clergy, laypeople, and some bishops held "lectures by combination," "exercises," and "prophesyings" to serve as continuous rolling seminars to teach Protestant theology and exegesis. These drew the ire of Queen Elizabeth, who ordered their suppression in 1577. Archbishop Edmund Grindal of Canterbury refused to cooperate and was suspended from his functions.

In Lutheran states of Germany and Scandinavia, the existing structures of schools and universities were reformed and re-shaped to serve the needs of the new churches. The duchy of Württemberg offers an interesting example. The ducal university at Tübingen was reformed, along with the rest of the duchy, when it embraced Protestantism after 1534. Monasteries were closed down; their buildings and endowments were used to create what became the "cloister schools," boarding schools for future ministers. After at least ten years of study, pupils entered the ducal university with not only a strong grasp of Latin and religion but also a powerful cohesive group mentality.

Where a medieval university continued to function in a reformed country, its teaching had to be restructured to meet new demands. The reform of school and university curricula constituted one of the most vital and least recognized aspects of the Reformation. Philipp Melanchthon earned the informal title of "Preceptor of Germany" for his tireless and polymathic work in generating new textbooks for higher education. He personally wrote new textbooks on logic, rhetoric, natural philosophy, and history as well as the definitive text of Lutheran theology, the *Loci Communes* (Common places). He gave his full support to a wide range of academic subjects, including a reformed Aristotelianism, against some anti-intellectual spirits who wished to have nothing taught but the Bible and theology.

In Britain the medieval universities were similarly reformed. In England, however, the process was more gradual. Old collegiate foundations persisted under their old charters. In Oxford and Cambridge colleges, even clerical celibacy survived until the nineteenth century, with the curious effect that many fellows of colleges served only a short term before moving out into parish ministry. Individual donors shaped the ideological cast of their foundations. Sidney Sussex and especially Emmanuel College in Cambridge, under its charismatic head Laurence Chaderton (c. 1536/1546–1640; head of Emmanuel 1584–1622), had a distinctly "puritan" character. Scotland's three medieval universities were reformed in the late sixteenth century (St. Andrews, founded 1413; Glasgow, 1451; and Aberdeen, 1495), and a fourth, at Edinburgh, was added (1582).

In a number of countries it proved impossible to take over the medieval academic establishment. In Geneva and Zurich there was no university to reform. Here specialized academies for the training of future clergy were set up, though with varying degrees of success. One of the earliest and most influential was the academy or *Gymnasium* founded in 1538 at Strasbourg under the guiding hand of Johann Sturm (1489–1553), the educational theorist and reformer. Sturm inaugurated many educational practices (a hierarchical curriculum, tests to be passed at the end of each grade before progressing to the next) that later became normal practice. In the 1530s Zurich organized its ministerial training in what became known as the college or *Lectorium*. The famous academy of Geneva was inaugurated in 1559, partly as a result of the expulsion of teachers from nearby Lausanne (whose academy dated from 1537) following a dispute with the overlord, the city of Berne. It comprised a more junior Latin school or "private school" and the senior,

more famous "public school" to train ministers. Under Théodore de Bèze, its first rector and Calvin's theological heir, it acquired immense prestige as the theological school of reformed Europe. However, it was controversial in the city itself: the magistrates wished it to become a quasi-university teaching the higher disciplines such as law and medicine, while Calvin wished it to focus on vocational training in theology. The academy did not award degrees, and attendance in the early years was often informal and brief, with students and ministers sometimes returning later to refresh their knowledge. Under Geneva's influence, many of the towns of reformed France created academies to train their own reformed clergy, at Nîmes (1561), Orthez (1566), Montpellier, Montauban, and Saumur (all c. 1600).

Protestant clergy education tended to be inclusive and varied. Many future ministers studied at more than one university or academy. Except in strict confessional Lutheranism, churches rarely ensured that students only attended doctrinally homogeneous institutions. Calvinist students attended Lutheran universities without difficulty; Lutherans of one cast attended institutions of another. In the century after the Reformation, student travel became a common feature of Protestant Europe, contributing to the diversity and cosmopolitan culture that many of the reformed clergy acquired.

DISCIPLINE AND CONTROL

Once installed in ministry, Protestant clergy were subject to the oversight of their peers and superiors as to their orthodoxy and good conduct. Like contemporary Catholics, Protestant leaders wished to see more effective discipline than in the past. Usually some form of consistory or standing council was set up to perform this oversight. Whether independent of the state like the Company of Pastors of Geneva, or with lay participation and state control like the Zurich synod or the Wittenberg consistory, these bodies consisted chiefly of senior ministers and dealt with complaints as they arose.

Much recent research suggests that once the older generation that had been ordained as Catholics died off, the second generation of reformed ministers was generally dedicated and competent. Repeated disciplinary failings were rare: between 1532 and 1580 Zurich deposed only eleven ministers, though a much larger number were more gently disciplined. In England, clergy discipline was more contentious, because more political. Under Archbishop John Whitgift (1583–1604) those over-zealous Protestant clergy who refused to use the Book of Common Prayer, or who repudiated the hierarchy or discipline of their church, were investigated and in many cases deprived of their places.

ANABAPTIST CHURCHES

All that has been said so far applies to the main established churches produced by the so-called "magisterial" Reformation. The reformers had no difficulty, theological or political, with the idea that a minister should be a highly trained expert individual distinguished by linguistic and intellectual gifts. In the early modern "radical" movements that believed the Holy Spirit guided the church directly, these assumptions did not hold. Leadership in the various Anabaptist churches was diverse and at times disputed. There was a suspicion of book learning, and sometimes outright hostility to the reformed educational establishment. Nevertheless, most Anabaptist communities had some identified spiritual leader or leaders. A few, like Georg Blaurock, Balthasar Hubmaier, or Menno Simons, were already ordained Catholic priests before their conversion. Among the highly communitarian Hutterites in Moravia, the "shepherd" or "servant of God's Word" was chosen by a vote of the whole community, as was the "overseer" Leonhard Lanzenstiel, who served continuously from c. 1542 to 1565. There was also a "servant for temporal affairs" who managed community goods and property. However, the absence of a fixed hierarchy meant that schism and separation of the various groups of Anabaptists, especially the Dutch Mennonites, was a constant threat.

CONCLUSION

The clergy of Protestant Europe rapidly acquired a distinct cultural, social, and economic character. Ministers were marked off from the rest of society by their dress, their book learning, and their family and social contacts. While instances of all these kinds of distinctness had existed before, the rise of the Protestant clergy generated a clear trend toward the rise of a professional middle class. While many important details (celibacy, for instance) were quite different in Roman Catholicism, some of the same broad lines of evolution occurred in that church also.

See also **Anabaptism; Bèze, Théodore de; Bible; Calvin, John; Calvinism; Church of England; Geneva; Luther, Martin; Lutheranism; Melanchthon, Philipp; Reformation, Protestant; Universities; Zurich; Zwingli, Huldrych.**

BIBLIOGRAPHY

Collinson, Patrick. *The Religion of Protestants: The Church in English Society, 1559–1625.* Oxford, 1982.

Dixon, C. Scott. *The Reformation and Rural Society: The Parishes of Brandenburg-Ansbach-Kulmbach, 1528–1603.* Cambridge, U.K., 1996.

Gordon, Bruce. *Clerical Discipline and the Rural Reformation: The Synod in Zürich, 1532–1580.* Zürcher Beiträge zur Reformationsgeschichte, Bd. 16. Bern and New York, 1992.

Karant-Nunn, Susan C. *Luther's Pastors: The Reformation in the Ernestine Countryside.* Transactions of the American Philosophical Society, vol. 69 pt. 8. Philadelphia: American Philosophical Society, 1979.

Maag, Karin. *Seminary or University?: The Genevan Academy and Reformed Higher Education, 1560–1620.* St. Andrews Studies in Reformation History. Aldershot, U.K., 1995.

O'Day, Rosemary. *The English Clergy: The Emergence and Consolidation of a Profession, 1558–1642.* Leicester, 1979.

Pettegree, Andrew, ed. *The Reformation of the Parishes: The Ministry and the Reformation in Town and Country.* Manchester, U.K., 1993.

Scribner, R. W. "Practice and Principle in the German Towns: Preachers and People." In *Reformation Principle and Practice: Essays in Honour of Arthur Geoffrey Dickens,* edited by Peter Newman Brooks, pp. 95–117. London, 1980.

Strauss, Gerald. "The Mental World of a Saxon Pastor." In *Reformation Principle and Practice: Essays in Honour of Arthur Geoffrey Dickens,* edited by Peter Newman Brooks, pp. 157–170. London, 1980.

Tolley, Bruce. *Pastors and Parishioners in Württemberg during the Late Reformation, 1581–1621.* Stanford, 1995.

Vogler, Bernard. *Le clergé protestant rhénan au siècle de la Réforme, 1555–1619.* Paris, 1976.

EUAN K. CAMERON

ROMAN CATHOLIC CLERGY

Roman Catholic clergy are those men who were assigned by the church's hierarchy to supervise the faithful and to administer the sacraments. The term "clergy" has its roots in the Greek word *kleros,* which expresses the idea of "lot" or "portion." In the first centuries of the church's existence, persons who administered liturgical functions became known as clerics, in contrast to the *laikos* or laity—the common people. Within clerical status there existed various ranks or "orders." During the first centuries of the Christian Church, three orders developed, those of the deacon, priest, and bishop. By the high Middle Ages these orders had developed into seven specific offices with specific liturgical functions. The minor orders included the offices of porter (sacristan), lector, exorcist, and janitor. Major orders included subdeacon, deacon, and priest. Theologians debated as to whether the episcopacy, the office of bishop, was a separate order or the fullness of the presbyterial (priestly) state. Hence sources refer either to the ordination of a bishop or to his consecration.

The ecclesiastical use of the word *order* has its foundation in classical Roman civil vocabulary. In classical Rome those with orders, or rank, were distinct from the plebs, or common Roman citizens. Patristic authors used the term *ordo* to designate those with official duties who were set apart from the rest of the Christian population. Emperor Theodosius II (ruled 408–450) identified this separation when he spoke of the order of ecclesiastics in his code that became effective on 1 January 439. Two aspects of clerical life that evolved during the patristic period became consequential points of debate during the age of reforms: the separate nature of the cleric from that of the general body of believers and the role of the cleric, particularly one in a major order, as the sole dispenser of the Sacraments.

Some summary points must be made concerning the status of clerics by the beginning of the early modern period. Only men were clerics. In most cases clerics were immune from the jurisdiction of the civil courts and the obligation to pay taxes. Men attained clerical status by ordination (the instilling of an order) by a bishop. Those with minor orders could be married, but the promise of celibacy was required of those with major orders. The church established benefices to provide support for those within orders. A benefice, from the Latin for "good work," was the income generated by property or goods assigned to a specific cleric. Frequently a benefice was assigned to a youth to support his education with the expectation that he would continue his career in the church as a priest. John Calvin (1509–1564) was the recipient of such a benefice.

SECULARS AND REGULARS

Clerics (clergy) were referred to as either secular or regular. Secular clergy were directly under the jurisdiction of a bishop and did not profess the evangelical vows of poverty, chastity, and obedience. Seculars (those in major orders) took promises of celibacy and a promise of obedience to their bishop. Regulars, frequently referred to as "religious," were members of religious orders who lived according to a specific way of life or rule and were governed by a religious superior. The term *regular* comes from the Latin *regula*, 'rule', which refers to a specific rule established by a founder of a religious community. Examples of such rules and their dates of official church approval are the Rule of Saint Benedict (c. 530–540), the Rule of Saint Dominic (1221), and Saint Ignatius's rule for the Jesuits, the *Constitutions* (1558). Although all regulars lived under a rule, not all regulars were clerics. Some were members of an order who took the evangelical vows but were not ordained. These persons were frequently referred to as brothers. Since regulars took the vow of poverty, they were referred to as mendicants, from the Latin *mendicare*, 'to beg.' Franciscans and Dominicans were known particularly as *mendicates,* since they did not take a promise of stability to one specific house, as did the Benedictines. Since their areas of activity frequently overlapped, disputes occurred concerning the proper jurisdictions of the mendicants and the seculars. For example, could one go to a *mendicate* to fulfill the obligation of the annual confession, or did one have to confess to his or her parish priest? From whom did a dying person receive the correct final blessing?

Prior to the Council of Trent (1545–1563), the spiritual and academic formation of the clergy within religious orders was superior to that of the secular clergy. Although several prior church councils and synods had recognized the need for a moral and educated secular clergy, the general breakdown of church discipline caused by the Avignon papacy (c. 1308–c. 1378), the demographic collapse of the Black Death (1348), and the western schism (1378–1417) had an adverse effect on establishing norms for forming the clergy. By the end of the fifteenth century there were three possible programs for formal education: monastic schools, episcopal schools, and universities. No specific regulation concerning the education of the secular clergy existed before the Council of Trent.

However, by the end of the late Middle Ages a growing number of clergy received their education at a major university. Ignatius of Loyola (1491–1556) and the first members of the Jesuit order demonstrate this point; they received their degrees from the University of Paris and with these credentials were ordained. University-educated priests set a high standard and perhaps created a sharp contrast with those clerics of limited education (the basic ability to read and write). Although many clerics at the beginning of the Reformation were more educated than ever, they stood in contrast to those with poor or nonexistent preparations for the clerical state. Both these situations created opportunities for abuse. Persons with basic skills and little or no theological training were usually assigned to the care of souls in a parish or recited masses, supported by a benefice. Benefices varied in amounts but provided enough incentive for some to take on clerical office with little regard for its spiritual and temporal duties. University-trained clerics received benefices for their education and usually multiple benefices upon arrival at their new positions. The consequence of this was pluralism, the practice of holding more than one benefice at a time. This created the problem of absenteeism, accepting a benefice without fulfilling the obligation of spiritual and temporal care of souls attached to the benefice. Before the English Reformation almost 25 percent of English parishes were served by an "absentee." Celibacy was disregarded by many clerics as well.

REFORM OF THE CLERGY

Protestant and Catholic Reformers identified the lack of a well-trained clergy, sexual license, absenteeism, and simony (the selling of an office for profit) as the greatest scandals within clerical life. Desiderius Erasmus (1466?–1536) was particularly vehement in his castigation of both seculars and religious. Erasmus, however, was not alone in his desire for reform. A committee formed by Pope Paul III (reigned 1534–1549) in 1536 to identify the problems that beset the church acknowledged in its 1537 publication the ill-trained and immoral lives of religious and secular clerics, echoing many

of the concerns raised on both sides of the confessional divide.

During the first half of the sixteenth century, Catholic and evangelical reformers debated the nature and role of the cleric. No one during the age of reforms disputed that the life, death, and Resurrection of Jesus were fundamentally necessary for salvation; arguments instead centered on how the faithful acquired access to salvation. Catholic theologians, particularly in the Council of Trent, identified the priest, under the jurisdiction of a bishop, as the intermediary through whom the faithful experienced the saving grace of the Sacraments. Hence the priest, as the administrator of the Sacraments, was essential for salvation, and priestly reform was a necessary step in the reform of the entire church. The participants at Trent envisioned a bishop in residence supervising an educated and celibate clergy, each cleric in turn supervising and providing the Sacraments (the means of salvation) to the faithful registered in a parish. The council specifically noted that "it is of the highest import for the salvation of souls that parishes be governed by worthy and qualified men" (Trent, Session 24 canon 18, cited in Tanner, p. 770).

Even before the Council of Trent, Catholic Reformers identified problems within the clerical state and recommended means of reform. Ignatius of Loyola, following the recommendations of the committee appointed by Pope Paul III in 1536, established the first seminary, the German College (1552), as a residential training program for secular clerics, particularly Germans, to prepare them to "support the tottering and in some places collapsed church in Germany" (Ignatius of Loyola, 1959, p. 259). Other Reformers led the way toward a better-trained clergy. Cardinal Francisco Jiménez de Cisneros (1436–1517) of Spain, Cardinal Reginald Pole (1500–1558) of England, and Bishop Gian Matteo Giberti (1495–1543) of Vernona argued for a better-trained clergy as the principal means of reform. Bartholomew Fernández (1514–1590), bishop of Braga, Portugal, advanced clerical reform in his dioceses and was instrumental in the reforms of the clerical state crafted in the twenty-third session (1563) of the Council of Trent. Legislation in that session condemned absenteeism, the giving of benefices to those under the age of fourteen, and simony. One of the most consequential pieces of legislation for clerical formation was the recommendation of separate training for those interested in the priesthood. The council legislated that large dioceses were obliged to provide training for youths in preparation for the priesthood. These "seedbeds" or seminaries were to be strictly supervised by local bishops.

Seminary training, though legislated at Trent, was more the exception than the norm, however. Even one hundred years after the Council of Trent, most priests did not receive a seminary education. The diocese of Lyon, France, did not have a seminary until 1654, and until 1657 its bishop did not require a seminary education for its priests, which even then entailed only a ten- to fifteen-day retreat. A one-year seminary education was not required for those in major orders until the Lyon diocesan statutes of 1707 and 1715 (Hoffman, 1984, p. 77). In Fiesole, Italy, during the seventeenth century only 26 percent of the clergy were educated in a seminary. A seminary education did not lead to better church offices, as all the prestigious positions (bishop, notary, master of the chapel, and so forth) went to nonseminarians. Paris, with its a population of 400,000 persons and 472 parishes in the late seventeenth century, did not have a seminary until 1696.

There were important exceptions to this lack of seminary education. In 1564, the year after the Council of Trent adjourned, three seminaries were established. Cardinal Marcantonio Amulio (d. 1572) of Rieti, Italy, began the first Tridentine seminary in Italy. Cardinal Carlo Borromeo (1538–1584) opened a seminary in Milan with fourteen Jesuit faculty, thirty-four seminarians, and one hundred nonseminarians. Eight years later the number of seminarians increased to sixty. The first seminary in Germany began the same year in Eichstätt (Eichstadt), Bavaria. A year later Pope Paul IV (reigned 1555–1559) established the Roman Seminary and placed it under the jurisdiction of the Jesuits. In 1568 William Allen (1532–1594) established a seminary for English Catholic exiles in Douai, France. Bishops throughout Europe looked to the work of Borromeo, who called provincial councils and diocesan synods, created seminaries, and initiated extensive visitation of parishes, as an example for implementing clerical reform.

Although the church hierarchy of France did not accept Tridentine legislation until 1615, the country eventually became a model for the training of clerics and the implementation of Borromeo's ideals. Earlier in the century requirements for a curé, the head of a parish, were meager: the ability to read and write and ownership of a Bible, a *Lives of the Saints,* the catechism of the Council of Trent, and the legislation of provincial synods. The young bishop of Luçon, France, Armand-Jean du Plessis (1585–1642), the future Cardinal Richelieu, created the first seminary in France in his diocese in 1612 and placed it under the supervision of the Oratorians. The advancement of a deeper spiritual life was the special object of attention of Pierre de Bérulle (1575–1629), founder of the French Oratory, an organization of priests modeled on the oratory of Philip Neri (1515–1595) in Rome.

Adrien Bourdoise (1584–1665) may be considered the principal initiator of clerical reform in France. Vincent de Paul (1581–1660) advanced the character of clerical life in France with conferences for priests and the establishment of seminaries. François de Sales (1567–1622), as bishop of Geneva, conducted conferences for existing priests and carefully screened those who applied for ordination. Jean Eudes (1601–1680) established a congregation of secular priests in 1643 to form educated and virtuous priests. His society of secular priests established seminaries in six French cities from 1644 to 1670.

Because so few clerics received their training in seminaries, other means developed to assure the training of priests as effective implementers of Tridentine Catholicism. The Jesuits established congregations for priests that aimed to develop the spiritual and academic lives of the secular priesthood. During weekly meetings, the Jesuits discussed "cases of conscience," the application of church law to individual situations. So important were these meetings that the Roman diocese in 1721 ordered all priests living within the diocese to attend these or other such meetings. Similar groups met in different cities, especially where Jesuit colleges were located.

NUMBERS OF CLERGY
Enumerating the quantity of clergy, as David Gentilcore (1992) has demonstrated with his stud-

ies of southern Italy, is a difficult task. The Terra d'Otranto in southern Italy had 7,684 clerics for 41,980 hearths. But just less than half of these clerics were actually ordained priests. The kingdom of Naples in the mid-seventeenth century had a total of 58,597 clerics. Lecce at this same time had 404 clerics to its 154 priests, and Gallipoli had 203 clerics to its 139 priests and deacons (Gentilcore, 1992, p. 50). Since the designation of cleric included all those with any type of order (and its consequent benefice), discerning active priests among the total population of clerics necessitates a study of individual diocesan records—a daunting task. In pre-Reformation Europe it was not uncommon for clerics to make up 4 percent of the male population. Early sixteenth-century England maintained twenty to twenty-five thousand priests. Luçon, France, with a population of 100,000 in 1600, had 428 priests. Areas where Catholics were persecuted or were under restrictions have been better studied and hence have generated more statistics. During the reign of Elizabeth I (ruled 1558–1603) the number of priests in Wales was reduced from sixteen to four. In 1623 Scotland had thirteen secular priests. Ireland in 1731 had 1,445 parish priests and curates with an additional 700 religious priests for a Catholic population of 2,293,680.

See also **Jesuits; Reformation, Catholic; Religious Orders; Trent, Council of.**

BIBLIOGRAPHY

Primary Sources

Ignatius of Loyola. *Letters of St. Ignatius of Loyola.* Selected and translated by William J. Young. Chicago, 1959.

Tanner, Norman P., ed. *Decrees of the Ecumenical Councils.* 2 vols. London and Washington, D.C., 1990.

Secondary Sources

Andrieu, M. "Les ordres mineurs dans l'ancien rite romain." *Revue des sciences religieuses* 5 (1925): 232–274.

Blet, Pierre. *Le clergé de France et la monarchie: Étude sur les assemblées générales du clergé de 1615 à 1666.* Rome, 1959.

Bowker, Margaret. *The Secular Clergy in the Diocese of Lincoln, 1495–1520.* London, 1968.

Burke, William P. *Irish Priests in the Penal Times, 1660–1760.* London, 1914.

Comerford, Kathleen M. *Ordaining the Catholic Reformation: Priests and Seminary Pedagogy in Fiesole, 1575–1675.* Florence, 2001.

Congar, Y. M. J. "Aspects ecclésiologiques de la querelle entre mendiants et séculiers dans la second moitié du XIIe siècle et au dèbut du XIVe." *Archives d'histoire doctrinale et littéraire du moyen âge* 28 (1961–1962).

Delumeau, Jean. *Catholicism between Luther and Voltaire.* Translated by Jeremy Moiser. London, 1977. An important study that argues that a thorough "Christianization" of France began only in the second half of the seventeenth century.

Ellis, John Tracy. "A Short History of Seminary Education: The Apostolic Age to Trent." In *Seminary Education in a Time of Change,* edited by James Michael Lee and Louis J. Putz, pp. 1–29. Notre Dame, Ind., 1965.

———. "A Short History of Seminary Education: Trent to Today." In *Seminary Education in a Time of Change,* edited by James Michael Lee and Louis J. Putz, pp. 30–81. Notre Dame, Ind., 1965.

García Oro, José. *Cisneros y la reforma del clero español en tiempo de los Reyes Católicos.* Madrid, 1971.

Gentilcore, David. *From Bishop to Witch: The System of the Sacred in Early Modern Terra d'Otranto.* Manchester, U.K., and New York, 1992.

Heath, Peter M. A. *The English Parish Clergy on the Eve of the Reformation.* London, 1969.

Hoffman, Philip T. *Church and Community in the Diocese of Lyon, 1500–1789.* New Haven and London, 1984.

Logan, Oliver. *The Venetian Upper Clergy in the 16th and Early 17th Centuries: A Study in Religious Culture.* Lewiston, N.Y., 1996.

Maher, Michael W. "Jesuits and Ritual in Early Modern Europe." In *Medieval and Early Modern Ritual: Formalized Behavior in Europe, China, and Japan,* edited by Joëlle Rollo-Koster, pp. 193–218. Leiden, 2002. Discusses the important role of ritual in Catholic reform and the part played by Jesuits in teaching ritual and forming priests.

Marshall, Peter. *The Catholic Priesthood and the English Reformation.* Oxford, 1994.

Olin, John C. *Catholic Reform from Cardinal Ximenes to the Council of Trent, 1495–1563.* New York, 1990. This collection of translated documents contains the report given to Pope Paul III in 1537.

Prosperi, Adriano. *Tra evangelisom e controriforma: G. M. Giberti (1495–1543).* Rome, 1969.

Reynolds, Roger E. *Clerical Orders in the Early Middle Ages.* Brookfield, Vt., 1999.

MICHAEL W. MAHER

RUSSIAN ORTHODOX CLERGY

Clergy in this article is defined as priests, those churchmen ordained to conduct the liturgy (Mass) and administer the sacraments (deacons could administer some sacraments but were not authorized to celebrate the liturgy). In Russian Orthodoxy priests are subdivided into "white" and "black" categories. Monk-priests, or hieromonks, called the black clergy because of the color of their robes, are ordained to conduct the liturgy in male or female monastic communities, and also in parish churches, as necessary (although that practice was discouraged in Muscovite Russia). While hieromonks are pledged to celibacy, the white clergy—parish, or secular priests (because they serve laymen)—are expected to be married. The focus of this article is on the parish clergy.

EDUCATION AND TRAINING

In Muscovite Russia (the principality of Moscow) in the fifteenth and sixteenth centuries, there was no systematic educational system, either ecclesiastic or secular. Schooling typically took place in the home of any priest or deacon willing to take in pupils for a fee. Priests' sons commonly studied under their fathers, if not becoming truly literate, at least memorizing enough services in Church Slavonic, the archaic language of the church dating from the tenth century, to perform portions of the liturgy and other services. In the 1490s the learned Novgorod Archbishop Gennadii petitioned the Moscow metropolitan (head of the Muscovite Orthodox Church) and the Moscow grand prince to set up a school system, but nothing came of it. In the *Stoglav* ('Hundred Chapters'), protocols of the Moscow Church Council of 1551, various remedies were decreed to rectify the situation: schools should be established in the homes of qualified priests, deacons, and readers; bishops should carefully examine candidates to the priesthood before ordaining them or appointing them to a parish; archpriests and priest supervisors should ensure that serving priests were qualified; and so forth. Despite *Stoglav* pronouncements, no discernable improvement in priests' education and training is evident in contemporary sources. It was not until the reign of Peter I the Great (ruled 1682–1725) that bishops were required to introduce ecclesiastical schools and directed to fund them by taxing parish churches and monasteries. Only in the 1780s in the reign of Catherine II the Great (ruled 1762–1796) were seminaries actually functioning in every eparchy (the church was divided territorially into twenty-six eparchies, or dioceses, at that time).

Despite poor and unsystematic education, the parish priest was frequently the only literate or semi-literate person in a village and was frequently called upon to draft or copy various documents like wills, property transactions, and the like.

MARITAL STATUS

The question of whether parish priests should be married, single, or celibate is an old and controversial one in the history of Christianity. Byzantine canons stated that a priest could marry, but that he did not have to; in any case, he could marry only before his ordination. Still following Byzantine canons, if a priest's wife died and the priest married for a second time, he could not serve in a church in any capacity whatsoever.

A preference for married secular clergy developed in Kievan times (tenth to thirteenth centuries). In Muscovy (fifteenth to seventeenth centuries) it was canonically ruled that secular priests had to be married, that they could marry only once, and that, in order for them to continue serving as parish priests, their wives had to be living. Whatever the rationale behind this requirement (one early sixteenth-century source explains that widower priests could not be trusted not to commit adultery), the Muscovite Church developed the policy that secular priests had to retire if their wives died. Various complementary rulings were issued: for example, that a widower priest could either take the tonsure and serve in a monastery as a hieromonk or remain in the secular world and serve in a church choir or as a reader.

Incentives for widower priests to avoid forced retirement must have been strong, and indeed there is evidence that many widower priests were able to continue serving or to take up service elsewhere. Church councils in 1503 and 1551 (the *Stoglav* Council) discussed and condemned various practices of widower priests to avoid forced retirement: for example, taking up with another woman, going to another eparchy, and pretending that the woman was his first wife; becoming ordained as a hieromonk and then taking up a regular appointment in a parish church; remarrying, hoping that the bishop's agents would not detect the uncanonical second marriage, or that, if they did, their silence could be purchased. There are no quantifiable data on the number of hieromonks or twice-married priests who were able to serve uncanonically in secular churches, but, judging by church councils' complaints and foreigners' accounts, the practice was common.

SELECTION, ORDINATION, APPOINTMENT, AND SUPERVISION

Secular priests were appointed to a parish either by a bishop or by the parishioners. Byzantine canons dictated that only a bishop could appoint a parish priest, but popular selection was tolerated in both Byzantine and Muscovite times. Popular election of parish clergy in the Muscovite church was facilitated by the fact that bishops lacked the administrative machinery and personnel to locate, train, and select qualified candidates, or to check thoroughly the qualifications of candidates proposed by parishioners. Nor were all bishops qualified to judge priest candidates. Not all bishops' assistants were above taking bribes. In addition to bishops' officials, who were typically laymen, priests were overseen by archpriests and senior priests although there is little evidence that the system worked, particularly outside cities.

The standard practice for a candidate for the priesthood was apparently the following: first he had to find a willing parish, and then he sought ordination and appointment by the local bishop. His arrangement with the parishioners might be concluded by a written contract, in which he promised to perform his duties over a stated period and parishioners promised to protect and support him; conditions were sometimes stated under which the priest could be dismissed by the parishioners. From his bishop the candidate purchased (or, canonically speaking, received in exchange for a donation) a charter of ordination and a charter of appointment. To the extent that parishioners exercised control over the process, the status of the priest might be no better than that of a parish employee who could be dismissed.

Bishops and their officials retained greater authority over priest appointments at those churches that were subsidized by the grand prince or, less often, by the church hierarchy. Such appointments could be a plum, and some bishops' officials were caught seeking kickbacks from appointees to subsidized churches.

Priests without appointments were effectively without income. Since the church made no provision for maintaining jobless clergymen, their only course was to search for a position, meanwhile begging or serving temporarily at any church or monastery that would accept them. In principle an unemployed priest could obtain (purchase) a charter of transfer or transience from a bishop. From the priest's point of view, the major consideration about charters of ordination, appointment, transfer, and transience was that all these documents cost him money. The legitimacy of allowing any fees at all, particularly for ordination, had long been debated, first in the Byzantine and then the Muscovite Church. By the time of the *Stoglav* Council in 1551, Muscovite practice was to allow fees but to admonish bishops that they should collect equal fees from all candidates and priests.

MEANS OF SUPPORT

The church did not pay priests—rather, it took money from them. Nor was a uniform policy established of how much parishioners were supposed to pay priests. In practice, priests had to exploit a number of sources of income and support, including the following: a plot of arable land set aside by the parish for the personal use of the priest and his family; income from teaching; donations and offerings in money and in kind from parishioners in return for special services like baptisms and memorial services; marriage fees (although, legally, marriage fees were supposed to be remitted in full to the bishop); fees for consecrating a church (more often beneficial to the clergy of large urban churches than of village parishes); whatever trade privileges and income-producing properties the parish church possessed (here, too, this applied more often to large urban churches or cathedrals than to village churches); and, finally, an annual stipend or subsidy from the grand prince's treasury, or, less often, from a bishop or from parishioners.

Although the potential income sources appear numerous, the fact remained that the secular clergy had little income security. In practice the village priest derived most of his support by farming the plot of land allotted to him by the parish; he was, typically, a barefoot peasant farmer, just like his parishioners (some parish contracts stipulate that the priest wear shoes in church when conducting the divine liturgy). Most productive church landholdings belonged to monasteries, some to prelates, almost none to parish churches.

The apparent narrow margin between income and expenses prompted many secular priests to seek an annual stipend or subsidy from the grand prince's treasury (bishops were resistant to making such grants, and village parishes rarely had the means). Funds or goods granted as subsidy might be paid to the parish to defray expenses, or directly to the priest as a salary. One calculation for Novgorod in the sixteenth century numbers seven village churches and approximately fifty urban churches receiving an annual subsidy from the Moscow grand prince. An early seventeenth-century estimate indicates that some 1,500 churches throughout Russia were receiving subsidies. Annual subsidies from the grand prince were so desirable (though their continuance was not guaranteed) that large churches would set up secondary altars, appoint a priest to each, and then request a subsidy from the grand prince. In the seventeenth century, for which statistics become more available, urban churches typically had two or three secondary altars; the Moscow Kremlin Cathedral of the Archangel Michael had twelve altars.

THE SEVENTEENTH CENTURY

Some improvement in clerical education was achieved in seventeenth-century Muscovy when ecclesiastical schools were established in Moscow and Novgorod. Several members of the Zealots of Piety movement, who sought to reform the church and return it to authentic traditions, were educated secular clergy. In the Church Schism of the seventeenth century, when Old Believers rejected changes introduced by the official church, some Old Believer communities even went without priests because they could not accept priests ordained by the official church. To the extent that the church began publishing service books with some scholarly foundation, priests gained access to texts more standardized than those in previous hand-copied books.

THE EIGHTEENTH CENTURY

The secular clergy experienced profound changes in the eighteenth century. As government policies, beginning with Peter I the Great (ruled 1682–1725), placed the church increasingly under government control, the secular clergy became virtual

state employees, more under the authority of bishops and less dependent on parishes for appointments. For the first time in Russia, also beginning with Peter the Great, an ecclesiastical schooling system was begun throughout the country. One unfortunate aspect of the educational system, however, was the extent to which the curriculum was latinized (because of Ukrainian Orthodox influence) and unrelated to the Russian Church. On the plus side, secular priests received more systematic and formal training than ever before; on the negative side, the Latin-oriented educational system did not effectively train them to conduct services in Church Slavonic. Nevertheless, the secular clergy became something of a hereditary professional estate in the eighteenth century, and seminary education, even if one did not pursue an ecclesiastical career, was the best schooling available.

See also **Old Believers; Orthodoxy, Russian; Reformations in Eastern Europe: Protestant, Catholic, and Orthodox; Russia.**

BIBLIOGRAPHY

Freeze, Gregory L. *The Russian Levites: Parish Clergy in the Eighteenth Century.* Cambridge, Mass., and London, 1977.

Kollmann, Jack E., Jr. "The *Stoglav* Council and Parish Priests." *Russian History/Histoire Russe* 7, parts 1–2, (1980): 65–91.

Pospielovsky, Dimitry. *The Orthodox Church in the History of Russia.* Crestwood, N.Y., 1998.

JACK KOLLMANN

CLIENTAGE. *See* **Patronage.**

CLIMATE. *See* **Weather and Climate.**

CLOCKS AND WATCHES. Historians have long pondered why the European world has so highly valued consciousness of time. Economic historian David Landes argues that time consciousness was a major "stimulus to the individualism that was an ever more salient aspect of Western civilization." His argument fits well with Max Weber's contention that in Protestant lands a new work ethic developed that contributed significantly to the rise of a new economic order. Unquestionably, the new work ethic included a heightened sense of the importance of time; this is likely the origin of the familiar saying "time is money." Lewis Mumford put forth the more daring claim that in the modern industrial world, the clock made a more fundamental change than the steam engine. Indeed, the profusion of clocks and watches in the early modern world helped to reinforce a growing social consciousness of time, a consciousness we today take for granted. Clocks and watches prod us to use our time efficiently and are clearly instruments of organization and social control. They tell us when to get out of bed and when to go to work. It was in the urban early modern world that mechanical timekeepers came to replace the sun, the timekeeper of the rural, medieval world. Also in the early modern period, punctuality, along with regularity, temperance, reliability, restraint, and industriousness, was considered a great virtue and an emblem of a disciplined life. Hence, it is not surprising that many of the most talented men of early modern Europe worked to design and perfect clocks and watches.

Mechanical timekeepers were not an invention of the early modern European world, but the era did witness considerable advances in their design, accuracy, and diffusion of ownership. In this period craftsmen, jewelers, carpenters, mathematicians, metalsmiths, artists, and scientists all contributed to the refinement of these devices that dated from the crude tower clocks of the Middle Ages, which were probably invented in England around 1300. In the early modern era more elaborate, more beautiful, more accurate, sturdier, and miniaturized versions of clocks appeared. Far more than our timepieces today, early modern clocks and watches were items of luxury and affirmed the power and prestige of their owners. Gradually in this period clocks moved beyond ownership of prosperous towns and powerful princes to become domestic items available to a wider range of middle-class merchants and gentry. The advantages of mechanical timekeepers over sundials and water clocks were so great that the latter form almost vanished from Europe. Sundials, however, remained in use in Europe long after the clock had been improved—well into the eighteenth century.

TECHNOLOGICAL DEVELOPMENTS

Early tower clocks were subject to vagaries of cold and rainy weather. They were generally made of iron and hence were so big and heavy they could not be put in a house. As the clocksmiths began to use lighter metals—including brass, silver, and steel—smaller scaled clocks became possible. Two technological designs, the spring coil and the fusee, made even smaller scales possible. Thus the watch developed: a timepiece to be worn on the human body, intended to serve as both timekeeper and ornament. Although spring coils (developed around 1400) allowed for a lighter weight clock, the impetus they relayed to the gears and wheels decreased as the clock gradually unwound. Two other devices, the fusee wheel (an intermediary between the mainspring and the wheel train, conical in shape) and the stackfreed helped to equalize the force on the mechanism of the coiled spring as it was unwinding.

Before 1650, most clocks and watches were notoriously inaccurate, but by the mid-seventeenth century, scientists began to apply their talents to making the instruments more precise. Astronomers such as Galileo Galilei (1564–1642) and Ismael Bouillaud (1605–1694), the microscopist Robert Hooke (1635–1703), and the mathematician Christiaan Huygens (1629–1695) made theoretical breakthroughs on the design of clocks. A major development was the pendulum clock, which operated by a pendulum controlled by gravity. Like the coiled spring, the back-and-forth motion of the pendulum is performed in theoretically equal periods of time. The invention of the pendulum and its application to clocks has a curious history, not all of it known. Leonardo da Vinci (1452–1519) and Galileo were both intrigued by the pendulum. Galileo's son Vicenzio made a drawing of a mechanism to maintain a pendulum in motion and may have built a model in 1649. But the oldest surviving pendulum clock was made in 1657 at The Hague by Salomon Coster, in response to the design of a fellow Dutchman, Christiaan Huygens, who published a definitive work on the theory of the pendulum. Within two years clock makers in Paris and London had read the Huygens treatise and were producing their own pendulum clocks. Soon afterward a flurry of technological designs improved the accuracy of the pendulum clock. Pinwheel escapements, anchor escapements, regulation of the length of the pendulum, the balance spring, and dead-beat escapements followed quickly.

A second challenge for the greater precision of timekeeping instruments came from a desire to discover an accurate measurement of longitude at sea. When the British Parliament announced an irresistibly large cash prize, skilled clock makers, as well as mathematicians and scientists, invested considerable effort and energy to finding a solution. The prize would ultimately go to a clock maker, John Harrison.

THE MECHANICAL CLOCK AS METAPHOR

Despite its shortcomings, the mechanical clock in the early modern era was regarded as a triumph of human genius and invention. Clock makers had arranged its parts in a strict spatial and logical order. Causal connections linked the components and careful design had preceded each complex or simple operation. Hence for many Europeans living in a world of political, religious, and economic instability, the clock exemplified order, harmony, and rationality in the cosmos. Many came to regard the relationship between God and creation as analogous to that between the clock maker and the clock; others applied the analogy of the clock to the state where an absolute monarch presided and directed the parts of the machinery with order, rationality, and predictability. Hence, clocks frequently surfaced in figures of speech and metaphors in political, scientific, and religious writings. The astronomer Johannes Kepler (1571–1630), the chemist Robert Boyle (1627–1691), the poet John Donne (1572–1631), the political philosopher Thomas Hobbes (1588–1679), and absolutist King Frederick II of Prussia (ruled 1740–1786) all invoked the clockwork metaphor. Hence the diffusion of clocks helped thinkers of the early modern period to conceptualize and shape the social value of harmonious political and religious obedience.

GEOGRAPHICAL CENTERS OF CLOCK MAKING

Between 1550 and 1650 the unquestioned center of clock and watch manufacture was in Germany, specifically in the towns of Augsburg and Nuremburg. Long known for their self-governing craft guilds and high standards of metalwork, German towns enjoyed princely patronage and general prosperity. With the economic decline consequent to the outbreak of the Thirty Years' War (1618–1648), leadership in clock making moved to France and England, notably to Paris and London, where scientists joined the efforts to improve accuracy and to promote technological improvements. By the eighteenth century, Geneva had enjoyed an influx of Huguenot craftsmen and became an important center of watch production.

THE PHYSICAL APPEARANCE OF CLOCKS AND WATCHES

Before 1650 many clocks were designed to illustrate astronomical information in addition to time. One historian of science, Derek de Solla Price, has argued that the mechanical clock originated from artistic attempts to imitate with mechanical devices the motions of the heavenly bodies, which also tell time. One such famous clock, the original 1574 astronomical clock of the Strasbourg cathedral was fitted with a celestial globe, an astrolabe, and other clock-driven mechanisms to represent the heavenly motions. Other clocks served as impressive works of art and craftsmanship. Some German princes owned elaborate automaton clocks that played music and presented sculptured figures such as soldiers or religious disciples who appeared from behind screens as the clock struck the hour. Goldsmiths and artisans of the highest quality produced such marvels.

The appearance of the pendulum clock strongly changed both the design and appearance of clocks. In general, the function of the clock became more exclusively that of timekeeping. Clock dials became more readable and less cluttered with extraneous information and sculpture. The 29-inch pendulum promoted by Hooke influenced the long case design (popularly referred to today as the grandfather clock design), although pendulum clocks were built as shelf or table clocks as well. The wooden case was originally designed to protect the movement and weights of the timekeeper from extraneous jolts or disturbances. But this also allowed the cabinetmaker to design a case as elaborate and as ornamented as any piece of furniture. Polished mahogany, brass finials, and painted figures of rocking ships or floral motifs abounded in the eighteenth century. In France decorative clocks produced during the reign of Louis XV (ruled 1715–1774) were elaborate and often rivaled contemporary furniture in craftsmanship. Clocks commonly outlasted furniture since they were more prized as domestic ornaments.

A series of technical improvements, notably the freestanding going barrel developed by the French watchmaker Jean Antoine Lepine, allowed watches to be made considerably thinner. Further improvements introduced by Abraham Louis Breguet toward the end of the eighteenth century heightened the accuracy of the timekeeping and even allowed the owner to observe the state of winding and the temperature. Watches remained primarily pocket watches (with ladies' models worn at the neck or more rarely on the fingers in rings as ornaments) and did not move to the wrist until after the early modern era.

DIFFUSION OF OWNERSHIP

Early clocks were heavy and expensive and were owned either by wealthy monasteries or cathedrals, such as the earliest surviving one at Salisbury Cathedral in England. Many indicated time not by dials, but by striking bells. (The Modern English word "clock" comes from the Middle English *clokke*, 'bell'). In the fourteenth and fifteenth centuries clocks were often made for public use and became important symbols of the towns that had commissioned them as public amenities. They regulated the opening and close of markets and had many economic and social functions in the municipality. As it became technologically feasible to build smaller clocks, princely courts became the major centers of patronage of clock makers. For example, Emperor Charles V (ruled 1519–1558) and all later Habsburgs employed the services of clock makers at their courts. The most well-known of these was Jost Burgi (1552–1632), who made uncommonly complicated and precise clocks at the courts of Landgrave Wilhelm IV at Kassel (1787–1867) and at the court of Rudolf II at Prague. Burgi produced clocks of remarkable regularity, introduced technical innovations, including the cross-beat escapement and *remontoire,* and he corresponded extensively with scientists and mathematicians of his day.

Clocks commonly appear in the portraits of German princes and often refer to the authoritarian order, a virtue shared by a well-governed state, a wise prince, and a well-crafted clock. In a society founded on princely patronage, early modern monarchs often presented clocks as gifts intended to impress the recipient with the scientific expertise and mechanical ingenuity of the princely donor. In 1616 the Jesuit missionary Nicholas Trigault took mechanical clocks as well as scientific instruments to China to aid the Jesuit mission in earning the good will of Chinese dignitaries. Similarly, the Habsburgs repeatedly presented mechanical clocks, as well as gold, jewels, and precious textiles, to the Ottoman Porte in Constantinople as part of the annual tribute exacted of them for keeping Hungary. Thus, the presentation of clocks solidified political alliances and symbolized great esteem on the part of the donor or patron.

As clocks became more common, more portable, and less expensive, ownership expanded outside the princely court or the flourishing city. Gradually, well-to-do private citizens could buy clocks and watches; in *Tristam Shandy,* novelist Laurence Sterne has a large house clock appear as part of the domestic furniture of a country merchant whose regular monthly offices as a dutiful head of household included winding the clock and having sexual relations with his wife. By the eighteenth century the clockwork metaphor could be mocked as well as taken seriously. In any event, it was a metaphor with which a wide readership had become quite familiar.

See also **Chronometer; Galileo Galilei; Huygens Family; Scientific Instruments; Time, Measurement of.**

BIBLIOGRAPHY

Bedini, Silvio. *The Pulse of Time: Galileo Galilei, the Determination of Longitude, and the Pendulum Clock.* Florence, 1991.

Edwardes, Ernest L. *The Story of the Pendulum Clock.* Altrincham, 1977.

Landes, David. *Revolution in Time: Clocks and the Making of the Modern World.* Cambridge, Mass., 1983.

Maurice, Klaus, and Otto Mayr, eds. *The Clockwork Universe, German Clocks and Automata, 1550–1650.* New York, 1980.

Milham, Willis. *Time and Timekeepers.* New York, 1923.

Mumford, Lewis. *Technics and Civilization.* New York, 1934.

Price, Derek de Solla. "Clockwork before the Clock and Timekeepers before Timekeeping." *Bulletin of the National Association of Watch and Clock Collectors* 18 (1976): 399–416.

MARTHA BALDWIN

CLOTHING.

Clothing and fashion underwent several transformations in the early modern world, reflecting the changing social, political, religious, and economic forces of which they were a part and an expression. Though major shifts in patterns of production and consumption and the emergence of more varied fabrics and textiles had already taken place in the late Middle Ages, the fifteenth through seventeenth centuries represented a culmination of these trends as well as a distinct and dynamic period in which clothing became an innovative and rapidly changing style form in its own right. Reflecting a heightened clothes-consciousness, men and women constructed their identity by wearing garments that reshaped their bodies and created around them a fluid circulation of meanings. In this sense, clothing, as one writer put it, constituted a "worn world: a world of social relations put upon the wearer's body." At the same time, just as clothing served as a form of personal (if heavily restricted) self-inscription, larger historical developments of the time—changing warfare, the Protestant Reformation, even the emergence of national identity—influenced the choice of a slashed sleeve or a ballooning doublet.

THE EARLY MODERN CULTURE INDUSTRY: PRODUCTION, CONSUMPTION, AND SUMPTUARY LAWS

Though textile centers had existed throughout Europe since the Middle Ages, the birth of the fashion industry originated in the city-states of Italy, where international trade, commercial innovation, and economic growth had coalesced since the twelfth century. The Crusades had opened the way for contact with Asia and, with it, the importation of more varied and luxurious fabrics. In northern Italian states such as Venice and Florence, import-export businesses coexisted with centers of fabric production that created huge fortunes and an accompanying consumer class eager for personal, status-enhancing display. Beginning in the fifteenth century especially, the hedonistic desire to spend on the part of those with more disposable wealth combined with a business strategy of "planned obsolescence" to produce clothes of a distinct cut, piecing, and fit that could be adopted and discarded as "fashion" by wealthy elites who suddenly did not wish to be seen in garments that could be considered out-of-date and behind the style curve of their rivals.

Constraints were placed on the circulation of clothing, however. Though they extended back to the Bible, early modern sumptuary laws had been formulated in the late Middle Ages to regulate consumption of luxury items and to reinforce existing social, economic, and occupational divisions by narrowly delineating items such as clothing or jewelry that an individual could wear. Intended to counter extravagance—which could be loosely defined, though silk, velvet, and brocades were strictly off-limits to the lower classes—laws also served the purpose of encouraging domestic production and protecting the manufacturing sector of a given country while upholding self-proclaimed standards of morality and decency. As a method of social control, sumptuary legislation also upheld hierarchies in a world where class distinctions, at least at the higher levels, could become blurred at times. Wealthy mercantilists, for example, gained economic strength during the early modern period, and proceeded to express themselves in the outer trappings of wealth. The result was a kind of egalitarianism of extravagance, as expressed by the wife of Phillipe Le Bel, who is said to have exclaimed, "I thought I was the Queen, but I see there are hundreds." In Tudor England, on the other hand, finer social distinctions were reinforced by injunctions, for example, that "None shall wear cloth of gold or silver, or silk of purpose color except Earls, all above that rank, and Knights of the King (and then only in their mantles)." Those on the margins—especially those on the margins—were also targeted for sartorial restriction: thus were Jews compelled to don either a star-shaped yellow badge or a yellow hat known as a *bareta,* while in Venice common prostitutes were required to proclaim their station through patches as well as bells, hats, or striped hoods. Sumptuary laws could be subverted or evaded, however, among those of the lower orders. To bypass the law that limited commoners to one color, some individuals as well as noblemen began to slash their garments—doublets, sleeves, hose—to expose the contrasting colors of the interior linings. Courtesans also could sometimes overcome such restrictions and, in fact, mimic the altogether more cloistered noblewomen with their own lavish stylings, down to the extreme shoes known as *chopines,* whose platforms could extend the length of three feet, elevating the woman to towering proportions and requiring her to support her stride with two sturdy male handlers.

FASHION HIGH AND LOW

Sumptuary laws ensured that clothes reflected the age's social stratifications, with more variation occurring in the top ranks of society. Men as well as women were especially aware of the manipulative potentialities in dress and public image, and adorned themselves accordingly, but few did so with such notoriety and effect as Elizabeth I of England. Her astonishing wardrobe was a political expression in its own right, and a useful expedient: because much of her power came from projection—which was especially necessary when she witnessed no small number of threats to her throne, as well as limited funds in her treasury—her gowns were designed to impress with jewels and luxurious fabric, and could even be adapted to international fashion styles, depending on whose court—the French, an Italian city-state—she considered diplomatically useful at any one time. Elizabeth's dress in turn trickled down, at least to ladies of the more elevated class, with its status-enhancing ruffles, complicated bell-shaped sleeves, daunting underpinnings, heavily embroidered gowns, V-shaped waistlines, cinched, tight-fitting bodices, and choices of colors that ranged, in contemporary language, from Bristol Red to Puke and Popinjay Green. Men were equally influenced by Elizabeth's sartorial statements, adopting more elaborate embroidery motifs (including the Tudor rose) as well as rich fabrics and, of course, the ruff, which could extend to a foot outward. But male ornamentation—fanciful boots, rich materials, plentiful decoration—had preceded Elizabeth and been expressed most fully with her father, Henry VIII, whose own puffed styles borrowed from the Continent, most notably from the courts of Burgundy and France.

Among elites, shifts in styles occurred frequently over the course of the sixteenth century, moving from the relatively soft linearity of late Gothic and early Italian Renaissance clothing, when dress tended toward greater simplicity and consisted of a relatively restrained albeit beautifully tailored gown topped by huge sleeves, trailing skirts, and a square or rounded neckline. Headdresses completed the picture, and consisted of a sort of net or caul that seems to have contained the hair. Later on,

the farthingale, a bell-shaped hoop skirt, dominated women's fashion, contributing to an increasingly stiff female posture. As Aphra Behn wrote in *The Lady's Looking Glass*, "I have seen a Woman . . . [who] has screw'd her Body in so fine a Form, that she dares no more stir a Hand, lift up an Arm, or turn her Head aside, than if, for the Sin of such a Disorder, she were to be turn'd into a Pillar of Salt; the less stiff and fix'd Statue of the two." With the introduction in the century of the aforementioned ruff, which enshrouded the neck in starch and lace, the effect was to render women as well as men all the more remote and unapproachable in appearance.

From the mid-sixteenth century on, such aesthetic cues were increasingly appropriated from Spain, where clothes forsook the body's natural contours and instead subjected it to even more geometric silhouettes. Dark silks and velvets were especially valued among those who preferred the classical baroque style, for it allowed them to showcase more effectively the precious stones and jewelry with which they adorned themselves, and which were frequently sewn into the fabric itself. The Spanish style was especially evident among men, who could, nevertheless, vary their adornment in the quest to project masculinity, wealth, status, and sexual allure. The shirt undergarment worn by an early modern man tended to be fitted closer to the body than that worn by a peasant, in order to accommodate the nearly always white linen doublet; nether hose, or pants, were a significant shift from the more gowned medieval world, with men opting for knee-length Venetian breeches or what were known as slops, or paned breeches, which puffed at the thigh and were sometimes adorned with a codpiece. Doublets were jacketlike ensembles that were fastened down the front, tended to come with a high neckline, and were topped by a straight-collared, richly ornamented cloak, almost always worn by noblemen. Despite the encroachments of new fabrics, cuts, and silhouettes for the male body, however, gowns were not entirely obsolete, especially in the early period of the age, when they continued to distinguish their wearers as clergy, scholars, or old and respected gentlemen.

Among the lower orders, the standard apparel for women began with a linen undergarment known as a chemise, or shift, a rectangular smock with long sleeves, a low square neck, and a hem that extended to the calf. Over this women wore one or two linen or wool skirts—cotton would not be mass-produced Europe until the eighteenth century—and supported the body and the garment with a snugly fitting (but not oppressively tight) vestlike bodice. Variations existed: for the Flemish market woman, for example, a linen undergarment was overlaid with a sleeveless kirtle—an open-fronted gown laced in the front—and a partlet, an item of clothing worn over the upper torso.

Surprisingly, more affordable dyestuffs ensured that colors could vary among the lower classes, ranging from pink, fawn, russet, peach, blue, green, and occasionally even bright red, though the latter was frequently associated solely with the upper classes. For a peasant man, on the other hand, the undergarment comprised a linen shirt similarly rectangular in cut—to prevent the linen from unraveling—with long cuffed sleeves and an optional collar. These were usually matched by knee-length breeches often finished with a loose, unstructured, and hip-length vest known as a jerkin, covered in the winter by a wool or linen cloak.

HISTORICAL DEVELOPMENTS AND FASHION
Fashion among the elite tended to be international in scope, to the point where Thomas Dekker compared the "English-mans suit" to a traitor's body: "the collar of his doublet and the belly in France; the wing and narrow sleeue in Italy; the shorte waist hangs over a Dutch botchers stall in Utrich; his huge sloppes speakes Spanish; Polonia [Poland] gives him his bootes; the blocke for his head alters faster than the feltmaker can fit him." The emergence of firmer national boundaries and identities in the early modern period, however, also reflected itself in clothing and in shifting cultural centers, from the Italian city-states to Spain and on to France. During the reign of Louis XIV, and especially from 1660 on, France played an increasingly important role in setting fashion, with gaudiness prevailing in men's dress and exemplified by tiny, open doublets and extremely baggy, knee-length trousers known as rhinegraves. Eventually rhinegraves fell out of fashion, though clothing continued to be decorated with such flourishes as ribbon bows.

Female fashion under Louis XIV was perhaps even more in flux, especially from the 1630s through the 1660s, evolving from high-waisted to long-waisted gowns, low, wide, and horizontal or oval-shaped necklines trimmed in lace, and sleeves set low on the shoulder, opening into a full ruff that ended below the elbow. For all its flourishes, however, women's dress in Louis's France tended to be more subdued and elegant than that of the beribboned male, accentuating in its silhouette the beauty of the female form.

With the emergence of more permanent armies among states, standardized military uniforms began to resurface for the first time since the Roman era. Whereas previously soldiers had either served different armies or were expected to provide their own fighting gear, uniforms now were fashioned to adorn the fighter in times of peace as well as war. Large textile factories in France became increasingly capable of churning out mass quantities of uniformly colored fabric that was cut and decorated by buttons, braiding, and cords in an unvarying manner. Military uniforms also influenced male civilian dress, making the coat or jacket more tight-fitting, with tailored contours, and taming the sleeves into the tubular and simple proportions known today. The soldier's broad-brimmed hat, or tricorn, became fashionable after the Thirty Years' War ended in 1648, as did rows of buttons and broad collars. Because men after the 1650s began to wear their hair much longer, large lace collars were made smaller and then replaced by strips of fabric that were transformed into knotted cravats or silk ribbon bows in the 1670s and 1680s. Jackets were then finished off with a waistcoat called *la veste,* as well as a knee-length suit jacket called a *justaucorps* and breeches less voluminous than had existed before. Despite the substitution of uniformed infantry fighting for armored cavalry attacks, metal sheathings continued to flourish at court, taking on more elaborate engravings. During the mid-sixteenth century especially, armor design was increasingly based on the forms and ornament found in classical art. This renaissance of pseudo-antique armor is most invariably associated with the celebrated name of Filippo Negroli, who was to become the most innovative and celebrated of the renowned armorers of Milan. Though Leonardo da Vinci had earlier sketched his fantastic armor and Verrocchio represented armor in sculpture, Negroli and his Milanese family produced unsurpassed embossed and damascened parade armors that entered into the collections (or perhaps even sheathed the bodies) of the dukes of Urbino as well as the Medici, who proclaimed a Negroli helmet "the greatest marvel."

The Protestant Reformation also played an enormous role in shifting fashion, and while it was not uniquely Protestant to condemn the excesses of dress—sumptuary laws were reinforced earlier on the grounds of morality—groups such as Calvinists or Puritans were especially vehement on the subject. According to James Durham, "men's minds are often infected with lascivious thoughts, and lustful inclinations, even by the use and sight of gaudy clothing; and light, loose, conceited minds discover themselves in nothing sooner than in their apparel, and fashions, and conceitedness in them." Because God "commendeth modesty," sobriety must prevail over clothes that "emasculateth or unmanneth" men and the "dressing of hair, powderings, washings, rings [and] jewels reproved in the daughters of Zion."

The "hethen garments, & Romish rags" of Catholic clergy were also viewed as betraying the precepts—if not the fashion sense—of Jesus and the early apostles. Renaissance popes and cardinals such as Cardinal Francesco Gonzaga (1444–1483) had in fact been profligate, if not unsavory, in their spending habits and choice of dress, with their green or crimson damask gowns and silk slippers earning the ire of Girolamo Savonarola's outraged sensibilities. In comparison to the popes, reformers such as Martin Luther or Thomas Cranmer appeared almost homely in their dark cassocks and simple girdles, while Calvinists or English Puritans took the "plain style" to its extremes, adopting a basic and austere black more appropriate to their religion. The issue of a priest's vestments had in fact been a pressing question in the sixteenth-century clothing controversy in England, when clergy opposed wearing the cap and gown in daily life and the surplice in church; the issue was not a shallow one, as garments were thought to both influence identity and to even align the outer self with one's inner faith.

Theatrical productions, albeit in more altered forms, continued to be accepted (and created) by Protestants, though the more radical among them could inveigh against frivolous masques and entertainments. Clothing certainly contributed to the shaping of theater, and particularly English theater, which spent the greatest amount of its budget on costume. Sumptuous display ensured good box office; at the same time, the presence and circulation of clothes played a central role not only as dramatic devices within plays such as Thomas Middleton's *Your Five Gallants,* but also situated the identity of central and supportive characters alike. Shakespeare's *Twelfth Night,* with its sartorial transformations of Viola into Cesario, is perhaps the best-known example that utilizes the gender- and identity-shaping potentialities of clothing. Shakespeare, however, was borrowing from a rich theatrical tradition of transvestism, in which the so-called "woman beneath" or "man beneath" (or "boy beneath") was hidden by the cover of clothes, voice, and gesture. Masques were also forums for such transgressions, and in the sequins and gilded costumes and elaborately patterned and stitched velvet masks, participants found a liberating refuge of subversion, akin to the costumed inversions that existed among the lower orders at Carnival time.

Contemporary clothing practices, of course, mutually influenced early modern attitudes toward the body, including ideals—sometimes blurred ideals—of beauty, ugliness, femininity, and masculinity. Emphasis on women's full figures had prevailed in the earlier era, though the introduction of increasingly restrictive and breast-compressing whalebone bodices reflected or inspired a slimmer ideal, at least in the waist. Men were equally constrained by their own fashions, including the leg-emphasizing hose, the form-fitting doublet, or even the frequently exaggerated codpiece. In another sense, clothing also served the early modern religious consciousness as a reminder, in Martin Luther's phrase, of the "wretched Fall"; though the nakedness of Adam and Eve was replaced by fig clothing and God-provided animal skins—the "robe[s] of righteousness," according to John Milton—clothes nevertheless served for theologians as a constant evocation, a memory, of one's sin, shame, and death.

See also **Bible: Interpretation; Calvinism; Class, Status, and Order; Elizabeth I (England); Gender; Louis XIV (France); Puritanism; Sexuality and Sexual Behavior; Sumptuary Laws; Textile Industry; Women.**

BIBLIOGRAPHY

Arnold, Janet. *Queen Elizabeth's Wardrobe Unlock'd.* Leeds, U.K., 1988.

Ashelford, Jane. *A Visual History of Costume: The Sixteenth Century.* London and New York, 1983.

Jones, Ann Rosalind, and Peter Stallybrass. *Renaissance Clothing and the Materials of Memory.* Cambridge, U.K., and New York, 2000.

Weiditz, Christoph. *Authentic Everyday Dress of the Renaissance.* New York, 1994.

SARAH COVINGTON

CLOUET, FRANÇOIS (c. 1515/20–1572),

French portraitist, painter to the king. François Clouet was the most important French portraitist of the sixteenth century. He is best known for numerous drawings of the members of the late Valois court executed in a technique adopted from his father, Jean Clouet (c. 1485, Brussels?–1540, Paris). Of a fairly consistent uniformity of composition in which the sitter, sketched in black subtly enlivened with rusty red, is almost invariably depicted bust-length in three-quarter profile from the left, nearly all the drawings measure about 12 in. × 8 ½ in. Although the black medium is frequently referred to as chalk in English (more correctly in French, *crayon,* 'pencil'), it was in fact derived from powdered slate (Zvereva, pp. 19–21). The red was made from clay. A sparing use of blue, yellow, and white pencil occasionally enhances the image. A few portraits were further elaborated with watercolor or white gouache. Although several of François Clouet's drawings are preliminary studies for paintings, the vast majority were created as portraits in and of themselves. The most significant group, numbering in the hundreds, was commissioned or owned by Catherine de Médicis. One of the most remarkable documentary records of historical figures before the invention of photography, they make Renaissance France come to life while simultaneously constituting a final expression of chivalric art.

Jean Clouet (nicknamed Janet in his own time) was not the first French artist to use these media for portraits. Jean Fouquet used them too, and Jean Perréal is believed to have practiced a similar type of portraiture, possibly influenced by, or influencing, Leonardo da Vinci. Perréal or Leonardo may, in

François Clouet. Portrait of Elisabeth of Austria, wife of Charles IX, King of France, painted by Clouet c. 1570. ©BETTMANN/CORBIS

turn, have inspired Jean Clouet to create the delicate black-and-red portrait drawings that are overwhelmingly associated with the name Clouet, which then likely influenced Hans Holbein. Several artists were active in the workshops of the Clouets. Numerous versions or copies of some compositions are known, and the attributions of many drawings are still actively debated.

In 1540 or 1541, upon the death of Jean Clouet, François received his father's appointment as court painter to King Francis I. Little is known of his career before that time. In 1541 he was described as having "well imitated" his father. In 1547, when the king died, Clouet modeled the death mask that was used in the funerary ceremonies around the wax effigy of the deceased ruler. Clouet then entered the service of Henry II, whose wife, Catherine de Médicis, developed an interest in portrait-drawings that quickly surpassed that of her father-in-law. At first she commissioned them from

Germain Le Mannier (active 1537–1559). In 1559, around the time of her daughter Elisabeth's marriage to Philip II of Spain, Catherine commissioned portraits of all the royal children from Clouet. During the celebrations of this union, Henry II was mortally wounded in a jousting accident, and Clouet fabricated his death mask. The documents pertaining to this commission have continually been associated with a terra-cotta of the king's suffering face (Louvre), but this tortured fragment is not a death mask. It is more likely Germain Pilon's preparatory study for the king's tomb in the basilica of St. Denis. Conversely, a series of large bronze portrait medallions (many in the Cabinet des Médailles, Bibliothèque Nationale de France), often erroneously attributed to Pilon, are instead virtual copies of Clouet's portraits.

At the end of 1559, Clouet became responsible for establishing the imagery of French coins. His only known dated work of art (1562) is a painting of his friend, the apothecary Pierre Quthe (Louvre). In its rich draperies and subtle suggestion of depth, it departs strikingly from the formula of the portrait-drawings. This suggests that by then Clouet may have become familiar with portraits by Titian (born Tiziano Vecelli) and Il Bronzino (born Agnold di Cosimo), perhaps during a trip to Italy. *The Lady in the Bath* (National Gallery of Art, Washington, D.C.) also bears Clouet's name, as does a standing portrait of Charles IX (Kunsthistorisches Museum, Vienna). A bust-length painting of the young king's wife, Elisabeth of Austria (Louvre), probably created around the time of their marriage in 1570, is usually attributed to Clouet. Beautifully nuanced in tonality and lavishly decorative with a multitude of regal embellishments, this is one of the loveliest portraits of the French Renaissance. *The Bath of Diana* (c. 1550–59?, Musée des Beaux Arts, Rouen) is also generally ascribed to Clouet. Around 1571, during negotiations to arrange the marriage of her favorite son, the future Henry III, to England's Queen Elizabeth, Catherine de Médicis sent his portrait by Clouet to the British monarch, commenting that the artist "had time only to do the face."

See also **Catherine de Médicis; France, Art in.**

BIBLIOGRAPHY

Adhémar, Jean. *Les Clouets et la cour des rois de France de François Ier à Henri IV.* Exh. cat., Bibliothèque Nationale, Paris, 1970.

Blunt, Anthony. *Art and Architecture in France 1500–1700.* Harmondsworth, U.K., and New York, 1977.

Malzeva, Nataliya Lvovna. *French Pencil Portraits of the Sixteenth Century.* Moscow, 1978.

Zvereva, Alexandra. *Les Clouets de Catherine de Médicis: Chefs d'oeuvre graphiques du Musée Condé.* Paris and Chantilly, 2002.

MARY L. LEVKOFF

COBOS, FRANCISCO DE LOS

(c. 1477–1547), Holy Roman Emperor Charles V's most influential secretary. Born in Ubeda, Spain, descended from poor but noble stock, Cobos rose from humble bookkeeper to a position of remarkable wealth and preeminent power through his penchant for hard work, savvy clientage, and the unfailing trust of Charles V (ruled 1519–1556). In 1522 he married María de Mendoza, a member of the titled aristocracy, with whom he had two children, Diego and María.

In 1493 Cobos left Ubeda to assist an uncle who worked as an accountant for Queen Isabella (Castile, ruled 1474–1504). By 1503 he had entered the service of Hernando de Zafra, a secretary to the queen and chief accountant of Granada. At Zafra's death in 1507 Cobos inherited the Granada post and attached himself to the rising star of Lope Conchillos, secretary of the Indies. Conchillos's disgrace in 1518 again made Cobos heir to his patron's position. He would remain deeply involved in all issues pertaining to the Americas due to his one-percent share of the smelting of precious metals there. In 1510 Cobos took charge of all requests for royal grants, offices, and rewards, thus facilitating his creation of a network of loyal clients throughout the bureaucracy. He joined Charles's court in 1516 in Flanders, and by 1520 had been entrusted with the management of Castilian administration.

Cobos's influence permeated Charles's governmental reorganization (1523–1526), which shaped the Spanish bureaucracy in the early modern era. Cobos helped delimit the authority of many of the new governing councils as a personal secretary of the monarch and as secretary of the Council of

Finance and the Council of the Indies. Prior to these reforms, the responsibilities of the Royal Council were divided between domestic affairs, primarily judicial, and a "private" council for advice on foreign affairs. The former now became the Council of Castile and the latter became the Council of State. Though Charles appointed the Italian Mercurino de Gattinara as grand chancellor, he refused Gattinara's demands that Cobos report to him about Castilian administration.

Initially, the secretary of the Council of State, the Burgundian Jean Lallemand, served directly under Chancellor Gattinara. A rift quickly developed between the two as Lallemand favored leniency with France and Gattinara pushed an anti-French policy centered on establishing Charles's hegemony over Italy. Cobos supported the Burgundian's faction, but Charles's favor enabled him to survive the dismissal of Lallemand, whom he succeeded as secretary of state in 1529. With Gattinara's death the next year, Charles abolished the position of grand chancellor and divided the responsibilities of the Council of State between Cobos, who managed the relations of Spain and Italy, and Nicholas Perrenot, lord of Granvelle, who did the same for the Low Countries and Germany. Both Cobos and Granvelle reported directly to Charles and accompanied the peripatetic emperor on his endless journeys. Cobos never subscribed fully to Charles's grand policies, which meant committing Spanish resources to protect the emperor's German and Italian territories. He preferred more limited, Castilian-centered objectives: a firm peace with France and the pacification of North Africa. Cobos's influence in foreign affairs peaked with his personal involvement in the negotiation of the 1538 Peace of Nice with France.

After 1539 Cobos remained in Castile, perhaps frustrated that he could not alter Charles's commitment to central Europe. He served in the regency governments of Prince Philip, but was most occupied with the difficult task of funding Charles's continued conflicts with the Turks, France, and the Lutheran princes in Germany. Cobos negotiated and renegotiated loans with the great banking houses of Europe, hawked government bonds, sold off lands of the military orders of Castile, and, when the king's share of American treasure proved insufficient, sequestered the gold and silver of transatlantic merchants. These Herculean efforts enabled Charles to achieve his last glorious victory (over the Schmalkaldic League) at the Battle of Mühlberg in April 1547. By then Cobos had returned to Ubeda, where he died the following month. His greatest accomplishment may have been his restructuring of unprecedented budget deficits to avoid state bankruptcy.

Cobos's biographer concludes that he instilled an esprit de corps in the Spanish bureaucracy based primarily on personal loyalty to their workaholic master. One must also add that loyalty to Cobos provided his servants with ample opportunities for self-enrichment at public expense. Only at the end of Cobos's life, when he insisted that Spanish resources had run dry, did he begin to lose favor with Charles. Though a long-overdue investigation would substantially reduce the Cobos fortune after his death, the magnificent Chapel of San Salvador in Ubeda still stands as a testimony to the poor local boy who made good.

See also **Charles V (Holy Roman Empire); Gattinara, Mercurino; Schmalkaldic War (1546–1547); Spain.**

BIBLIOGRAPHY

Carande, Ramón. *Carlos V y sus banqueros.* 3 vols. Barcelona, 1987. Classic study of Charles V's financial affairs.

Escudero, José Antonio. *Los secretarios de estado y del despacho, 1474–1724.* 4 vols. Madrid, 1969. Includes a good analysis of the origins of the Council of State and Cobos's impact on it.

Keniston, Hayward. *Francisco de los Cobos: Secretary of the Emperor Charles V.* Pittsburgh, 1960. A thorough biography of Cobos.

Martínez Millán, José, ed. *La corte de Carlos V.* 5 vols. Madrid, 2000. Detailed study of Charles V's court, councils, and councillors.

DANIEL A. CREWS

COINAGE. *See* **Money and Coinage.**

COINS AND MEDALS. The coinage of the early modern period differs profoundly from that of the Middle Ages in fabric, artistic style, and technology of production. An innovation of this period unknown to the medieval or ancient world was medals having a purely commemorative purpose, portraying princes, artists, and other celebrities. Here we will examine each of these four developments in turn.

FABRIC

For most of the Middle Ages the feudal economy of Europe was served by a monometallic system of silver coins based on the penny, usually weighing less than 1.5 grams. With the increase in trade and urban life in the thirteenth century, the silver coins were supplemented by a new gold coinage, including the florin of Florence and the Venetian ducat, weighing 3.5 grams. These circulated throughout Europe as an international currency, inspiring many local imitations like the English noble, the French écu, and the gulden of various German states.

Beginning with Venice in 1471, the Italian city-states began striking heavier silver coins of 6 to 8 grams, known as testons, from the Italian *testone* 'big head', because they commonly bore the profile portrait of the reigning prince. King Louis XII introduced this coin to the French in 1514, and in England it was first struck by King Henry VII in 1504, where it came to be known as the shilling, worth 12 pence. An important factor leading to the emergence of large silver coins was a shortage of gold in Italy and northern Europe due to Portuguese expeditions along the west coast of Africa. The Iberian *caravels* diverted to Lisbon the gold of Guinea that had previously reached Italy overland through the Sahara and North Africa. At the same time, new sources of silver were discovered by the miners of Tyrol and Saxony, which made possible a large silver denomination capable of taking the place of florins and guldens. In 1519 Count Stephan of Schlick in Bohemia began to produce great quantities of coins of 30 grams from the newly discovered silver deposits of St. Joachimstal. These large *Joachimstaler* (which became known as *talers* or *dollars*) circulated throughout Europe and were widely imitated. The English dollar or crown, the Spanish peso or piece of eight (so called because it was worth eight of the old silver reals), and the French franc, first struck by King Henry III in 1575, were among the important large silver coins introduced to the markets of Europe in the sixteenth century.

A further innovation was the use of copper for fractional or "subsidiary" coinage, replacing the old billon (debased silver) pennies, halfpennies, and farthings. In 1472 the Kingdom of Naples became the first state to strike a pure copper coin, and in 1575 King Henry III of France introduced the copper denier or penny, part of an overall reform of the monetary system that included the new silver franc. In England copper farthings (fourth-pennies) made their first appearance in 1613, followed by halfpennies in 1672, although the penny remained silver until 1797, when Matthew Boulton was commissioned to make copper pennies with his new steam-driven coin press. Thanks to new sources of gold from Guinea, and later from Mexico and Peru, the old florins, ducats, and gulden were replaced by larger pieces such as the gold sovereign or guinea of England. The Spanish doubloon, first minted at Seville in 1497 and worth two ducats, carried the facing portraits of King Ferdinand and Queen Isabella. This became the common gold coin of international trade from the sixteenth to the eighteenth century, thanks in part to the retention of the double portrait long after the death of the two monarchs, making it attractive to conservative bankers and merchants around the world.

STYLE

The Renaissance revival of classicism included the collecting and study of ancient Greek and Roman coins, beginning with Petrarch and other pioneer humanists of the fourteenth century. Under the influence of the antiquarians, the old medieval imagery of heraldic devices and symbolic effigies of rulers gave way to a new iconography of naturalistic portraits and allegorical scenes inspired by classical models. A very early example of this revivalism was the gold *augustales* of the Emperor Frederick II in 1231, which showed his profile bust in the manner of the ancient Roman Caesars, and on the reverse an imperial eagle. Most mint masters were too conservative to make radical changes in the appearance of their coins, however, until the coming of the new large silver pieces of the fifteenth and sixteenth centuries. The Venetian teston of 1471 displayed the profile portrait of Doge Nicholas Tron, and the Roman silver piece was known as the *giulio* because of its fine portrait of Pope Julius II (reigned 1503–1513), who was the first to strike these coins. At the same time, medieval Gothic inscriptions were replaced by Roman letters.

During the sixteenth and seventeenth centuries, a number of important artists produced dies for coins whose beauty and grace have never been surpassed. Benvenuto Cellini served as mint master for Pope Clement VII, and his rival Leone Leoni worked for Emperor Charles V. Leoni's classically inspired teston for Charles shows the emperor wearing a laurel wreath and on the reverse the figure of the goddess Pietas copied from a *sestertius* of Caligula. The silver crowns of King Charles II of England, designed by Thomas Simon, and the gold pieces of King Louis XIII, designed by Jean Varin, with their flowing hair and elegant drapery, are splendid examples of baroque portraiture.

TECHNOLOGY

The ancient and medieval technique of striking coins manually, using a hammer and handheld dies, resulted in coins with irregular edges, and their weight and thickness could vary considerably from the official norm. With the increased production of coins of all metals in the sixteenth century, especially the heavier pieces in gold and silver, mint masters recognized the necessity of maintaining uniformity of size and weight. This was achieved by the invention of the rolling mill for squeezing bullion into standardized sheets, the cutting press for punching out identical round blanks from the sheets, and the screw press for stamping the blanks. The first mechanized mint of this sort was established in Paris by King Henry II in 1551 in a water mill along the Seine. Henry's testons or *monnaies du moulin* were perfectly round and elegantly designed, demonstrating the superiority of the new methods. Due to resistance by conservative mint workers, however, the new technology was slow to catch on, but before the end of the seventeenth century most of the European states had adopted the mechanical production of coins, as well as machines for marking or "milling" their edges with grooves and other designs to prevent clipping.

THE ART OF THE MEDAL

The invention of the commemorative medal—a coinlike object created as a work of art to honor some special person or event—is traditionally attributed to Antonio Pisanello, an Italian painter working at the courts of Mantua and Verona in the 1430s and 1440s. Recent scholarship, however, has uncovered medieval precedents for Pisanello's medals,

including the large gold medallions with portraits of the emperors Constantine and Heraclius produced at the court of Jean de France, Duc de Berry, around 1400, although their intended purpose remains a mystery. Be that as it may, Pisanello established the prototype for the genre in his large (100 millimeters in diameter) bronze portrait medal of the Byzantine emperor John VIII Palaeologus, who came to Italy in 1438 to negotiate a reconciliation between the eastern and western churches. Pisanello's later medals of princes and warlords like Leonello d'Este and Sigismondo Malatesta helped spread the new technique throughout Italy. These early Renaissance medals established the standard format, namely a profile portrait on the obverse, and on the reverse an allegorical scene proclaiming the virtues or accomplishments of the subject.

In the sixteenth century the medal spread beyond Italy, and masters like Benvenuto Cellini, Leone Leoni, Giovanni Cavino, and Jacopo da Trezzo applied the classicism and elegance of the High Renaissance to the new art. Medals were produced in great quantities by sixteenth-century princes and by the admirers of poets, scholars, and artists such as Pietro Aretino and Michelangelo, and were often employed to convey propaganda during the religious and dynastic wars of the day. Leoni's medal of the Emperor Charles V represents him as Hercules overcoming his enemies, whereas da Trezzo's medal of Queen Mary Tudor shows her as the goddess Pax burning the arms of war and bringing peace to England. Because of their size, the early Renaissance medals were cast in molds rather than struck, but the screw press of the sixteenth century made it possible to produce large medallions from engraved dies, allowing more detail and complexity in the portraits and reverse scenes.

During the baroque period of the seventeenth century, the art of the medal reached a zenith of exuberant style and technical perfection. Guillaume Dupré, who worked for King Henry IV of France and Marie de Médicis, and Jean Varin, mint master of King Louis XIII and King Louis XIV, were the leaders of the genre. Varin's 1665 medal of Louis XIV, commemorating the building of the Louvre, portrays the Sun King with long flowing hair and an imperious expression. In Italy, Massimiliano Soldani-Benzi designed medals with scenes of athletic and vigorous gods and goddesses reminiscent of the paintings and sculpture of Rubens and Bernini. An important innovation of this period was the striking of sets of medals summarizing the significant events of a ruler's career—so-called medallic histories—the first being a series of three hundred medals proclaiming the achievements and victories of Louis XIV, issued in 1702. This became the precedent for numerous medallic histories of monarchs, governments, and institutions, often bound together in booklike volumes with accompanying text, produced during the eighteenth and nineteenth centuries.

See also **Cellini, Benvenuto; Money and Coinage.**

BIBLIOGRAPHY

Carson, Robert Andrew Glindinning. *Coins: Ancient, Mediaeval, & Modern.* London, 1962.

Cunnally, John. *Images of the Illustrious: The Numismatic Presence in the Renaissance.* Princeton, 1999.

Doty, Richard G. *The Macmillan Encyclopedic Dictionary of Numismatics.* New York, 1982.

Grierson, Philip. *Numismatics.* Oxford and New York, 1975.

Jones, Mark. *The Art of the Medal.* London, 1979.

Porteous, John. *Coins in History.* New York, 1964.

Scher, Stephen K., ed. *The Currency of Fame: Portrait Medals of the Renaissance.* New York, 1994.

JOHN CUNNALLY

COLBERT, JEAN-BAPTISTE (1619–1683), French statesman.

Colbert, the leading minister during the initial decades of Louis XIV's (ruled 1643–1715) personal reign, was born at Reims, the son of a drapery merchant, on 29 August 1619. Exploiting familial ties with Michel le Tellier, Colbert obtained a royal appointment at a relatively young age in 1643. During the chaos of the Fronde (1648–1653), he served as agent for Jules Mazarin's (1602–1661) affairs while the cardinal was exiled from Paris (1651). Colbert's diligence and business acumen resulted in hefty rewards upon Mazarin's return. On his deathbed (1661), the cardinal recommended Colbert to Louis XIV. To secure his position with Louis, Colbert played a notable role in the denouement of Nicolas Fouquet (1615–1680), the powerful albeit corrupt superintendent of finance.

Colbert was a leading proponent of mercantilism. Among other things, this theory postulated a finite amount of wealth determined by the amount of bullion a country controlled; a positive flow of gold and silver could in turn be facilitated by a favorable balance of trade, especially in manufactured goods and overseas products, with the state heavily involved in both directing and encouraging such activities. From 1661 to 1665 Colbert utilized a *chambre de justice* to correct abuses in the French fiscal system and the collection of royal payments. Several thousand subjects were condemned by this tribunal, and these transgressors were relieved of their ill-gotten windfalls. Colbert also improved the level of crown debt by repudiating some obligations outright and paying off others at a discounted rate. At the same time he sought to increase the king's revenues by revising provisions of the main direct tax, the taille, while increasing indirect taxes. To assist the internal economy, Colbert granted subsidies to select industries. He also oversaw impressive infrastructure improvements involving roads and canals. To help French manufacturers compete against English and Dutch products, Colbert erected protectionist tariffs, particularly in 1667. He sought, generally without success, to abolish the onerous medieval system of internal tolls and tariffs that undermined the competitiveness of French manufactured goods. The so-called Five Great Farms constituted a marginal victory in this campaign. Thanks to these reforms, Louis XIV's revenues probably doubled between 1661 and 1672.

Colbert's mercantilist theories attached pivotal importance to securing a powerful position in European colonial competition in the New World and the Indian Ocean basin. To that end, as secretary of state for the navy (1665), he rebuilt the moribund French fleet from a force of less than a dozen ships to a powerful weapon of about 120 royal ships with thriving shipyards and arsenals at Brest, Toulon, and Rochefort. To accomplish this, he increased yearly expenditures on the navy from about 300,000 livres to nearly 13 million livres. To exploit overseas trade, Colbert also founded a series of state-backed monopoly joint-stock companies, including the East India Company (1664), the West India Company (1664), and the Company for the Levant (1670). Despite problems and competition with the Portuguese, Dutch, and English, these companies man-

Jean-Baptiste Colbert. Portrait by Claude Lefebvre.
©ARCHIVO ICONOGRAFICO, S.A./CORBIS

aged to entrench a French presence overseas, particularly in North America.

Colbert believed the arts and sciences existed in large part to pay homage to the "Grand Monarchy." He formed the nucleus of the Academy of Royal Architecture (1667) by bringing together Louis Le Vau, Claude Perrault, François Mansart, and François Blondel. In painting he established a French academy in Rome and reorganized the academy of painting and sculpture of Cardinal Richelieu. Colbert also helped establish the Academy of Inscriptions and Medals (1663), the Academy of Sciences (1666), and the Academy of Music (1669). As superintendent for public buildings, he oversaw significant additions to the Louvre as well as the expansion of the palace complex at Versailles.

In these impressive achievements, Colbert demonstrated remarkable energy and industry. He was in fact the perfect bureaucrat for the growing Bourbon state. In public life his personality was indeed cold and dour, conforming to the dictum of Madame de Sévigné, who described him as "the North Star." In private life, however, he revealed a more human side of his character. Colbert's accomplish-

ments were undermined beginning with the Dutch War of 1672, a war he supported since it was directed against his arch commercial and imperial rival, the Dutch. Unfortunately, a glorious start in this war soon gave way to diplomatic and military setbacks. These problems forced Colbert to forsake many of his earlier reforms. Politically the shift to a bellicose foreign policy also witnessed the rise of his rival, the marquis de Louvois (François-Michel Le Tellier; 1639–1691). Created marquis de Seignelay, Colbert died in 1683 an extremely rich man with vast estates, leaving a significant legacy for Louis's reign and France.

See also **Academies, Learned; Academies of Art; Architecture; Louis XIV (France); Louvois, François Le Tellier, marquis de; Mazarin, Jules; Mercantilism; Trading Companies; Versailles.**

BIBLIOGRAPHY

Primary Source

Colbert, Jean-Baptiste. *Lettres, instructions et mémoires de Colbert.* Edited by Pierre Clément. 7 vols. Paris, 1861–1882.

Secondary Sources

Ames, Glenn J. *Colbert, Mercantilism, and the French Quest for Asian Trade.* DeKalb, Ill., 1996.

Cole, Charles Woosley. *Colbert and a Century of French Mercantilism.* 2 vols. New York, 1939.

GLENN J. AMES

COLIGNY FAMILY. The Coligny brothers were the among the most zealous and consistent aristocratic supporters of Protestantism in sixteenth-century France. Descended from a Burgundian lineage, they had an important landed base in Brittany and its marches. Gaspard de Coligny (1470–1522), seigneur of Châtillon, fought with distinction in the Italian Wars under kings Charles VIII, Louis XII, and Francis I, becoming marshal of France in 1516. He married Louise de Montmorency, sister of the constable of France; this union produced three sons: Odet de Coligny (1517–1571), count-bishop of Beauvais and cardinal of Châtillon; Gaspard II de Coligny (1519–1572), seigneur of Châtillon and admiral of France; and François de Coligny (1521–1569), seigneur of Andelot and colonel-general of the Royal Infantry.

The Colignys rose to prominence in the 1550s as a result of the patronage of their uncle, the constable Anne de Montmorency, who was the favorite of king Henry II. It was also during this period that the brothers converted to Protestantism. Their mother, Louise, had died in the Reformed faith in 1547. François, seigneur d'Andelot, had been exposed to Reformed ideas from his youth and was encouraged by John Calvin to profess the faith openly in 1556. This infuriated the conservative Henry II, and Andelot was briefly imprisoned in 1558. Gaspard converted during his captivity (1557–1559) following the defeat of the constable's army at Saint-Quentin by the Imperialists. His wife, Charlotte de Laval, played an important role in promoting the faith while he was away, and on his return to France in October 1559, they began to profess openly and frequented illegal Protestant meetings. Odet, cardinal of Châtillon, only adhered to the Reform party after 1561, and even then he refused to give up his benefices; he was destituted by the pope in 1563, and a year later he married Isabeau de Hauteville. He fled to England in 1568.

Gaspard de Coligny first became known as a leading member of the Reform party in 1560 when he submitted a petition to the king from the Protestants of Normandy demanding toleration. During the First War of Religion (1562–1563), he emerged as the most effective Protestant commander, while his brother Odet, cardinal of Châtillon, acted as the Protestant envoy to England. The assassination of François, duke of Guise, the leader of the Ultra-Catholic party, in 1563 sparked a vendetta with the Coligny that was to dominate politics for the next decade. The Guise blamed Admiral Coligny for the murder, and both sides mobilized their kinsmen in a dispute (1563–1566) that cut across the religious divide: Coligny was assured of the support of his Catholic Montmorency cousins; the Guise wooed Louis de Bourbon, prince of Condé, who was Coligny's rival as chief of the Protestant party. A royal declaration of Coligny's innocence in 1566 abated the feud, and allegiances once more coalesced along confessional lines.

Growing suspicion of the policies of King Charles IX's mother, Catherine de Médicis, and Spanish intervention in the Dutch Revolt caused the Protestant leaders to attempt to seize the king at Meaux in September 1567. The subsequent rec-

ommencement of the civil war once more placed the Coligny brothers at the forefront of political and military developments. Condé's death at the battle of Jarnac in 1569 left Gaspard in sole command of the Protestant forces, and despite being defeated at Moncontour (October 1569), his more mobile cavalry army was able to elude the larger royal forces. The war ended in stalemate. On the resumption of peace in 1570, Gaspard's Guise enemies were excluded from court, and he increasingly enjoyed influence with Charles IX. However, his demand that royal policy support the Protestant cause in the Low Countries was resisted by the royal council, and it was probably Gaspard's determination to send an expeditionary force to aid his coreligionists that led Catherine de Médicis to sanction the failed Guise assassination attempt on his life (22 August 1572). Charles IX initially offered Gaspard his protection and agreed to conduct an investigation, but he was forced by his mother, Catherine, and his council to order his murder on 24 August, an act that sparked the St. Bartholomew's Day Massacre.

Coligny Family. Undated portrait of Gaspard de Coligny. THE ART ARCHIVE/UNIVERSITY LIBRARY GENEVA/DAGLI ORTI

The descendants of the Coligny brothers continued to play an important role in the Protestant cause: Gaspard's daughter Louise (1555–1620) married William of Orange in 1583; and his son, François (1557–1591), was a notable captain during the later Wars of Religion and was counselor to Henry of Navarre (Henry IV). During the seventeenth century, the various members of the family gradually reconverted to Catholicism; Gaspard III de Coligny (1584–1646) enjoyed royal favor as marshal of France (1622) before abjuring Protestantism in 1643 in return for the elevation of the marquisate of Châtillon to a duchy.

See also Catherine de Médicis; Condé Family; Dutch Revolt (1568–1648); France; Guise Family; Henry II (France); Henry IV (France); Huguenots; St. Bartholomew's Day Massacre; Wars of Religion, French.

BIBLIOGRAPHY

Shimizu, Junko. *Conflict of Loyalties: Politics and Religion in the Career of Gaspard de Coligny, Admiral of France, 1519–1572.* Geneva, 1970.

Sutherland, N. M. "The Assassination of François duc de Guise, February 1563" and "The Role of Coligny in the French Wars of Religion" In *Princes, Politics and Religion 1547–1589.* London, 1984.

———. *The Huguenot Struggle for Recognition.* New Haven, 1980.

STUART CARROLL

COLLEGES. *See* Education; Universities.